The Irwin Business and Investment Almanac 1994

The IRWIN
Business and Investment Almanac 1994

Edited by

Sumner N. Levine
Professor Emeritus
State University of New York
at Stony Brook
and Editor
Financial Analyst's Handbook
and
The Investment Manager's Handbook

and

Caroline Levine

Professional Publishing
Burr Ridge, Illinois
New York, New York

IRWIN

Concerned About Our Environment

In recognition of the fact that our company is a large end-user of fragile yet replenishable resources, we at IRWIN can assure you that every effort is made to meet or exceed Environmental Protection Agency (EPA) recommendations and requirements for a "greener" workplace.

To preserve these natural assets, a number of environmental policies, both companywide and department-specific, have been implemented. From the use of 50% recycled paper in our textbooks to the printing of promotional materials with recycled stock and soy inks to our office paper recycling program, we are committed to reducing waste and replacing environmentally unsafe products with safer alternatives.

Senior sponsoring editor: Amy Hollands Gaber
Project editor: Karen J. Nelson
Production manager: Ann Cassady
Compositor: Arcata Graphics/Kingsport
Typeface: 8/9 Caledonia
Printer: Arcata Graphics/Kingsport

ISSN 1072-6136

ISBN 1-55623-926-2 ISBN 1-55623-927-0 (Paperback edition)

Printed in the United States of America

1 2 3 4 5 6 7 8 9 0 AGK 0 9 8 7 6 5 4 3

Preface

The 18th edition of the *Business and Investment Almanac* continues to emphasize domestic business and investment information. However, because of the rapid globalization of business and investments we are pleased to announce a companion volume, the *International Almanac: Business and Investments.* As the title implies, the latter provides an extensive collection of information and data which could not be included in this volume without greatly expanding its size and cost. Alas, like "Topsy," information just grows and grows. Together, these *Almanacs* are intended to provide the users with a convenient and comprehensive source of business information.

We appreciate your suggestions.

The Editors

References to companies, securities, and other investment information do not constitute a recommendation or endorsement.

Foreword

The *Irwin Business and Investment Almanac* is one book I would take to a desert island if I had to start a new economy. Why? A virtual library in one book, this almanac is a very effective business tool kit, providing summaries, graphs, and statistics from a variety of respected business sources. You didn't save the Fortune 500? No problem. You don't know where to find the Lipper Gauge in Barron's? Don't worry. You don't know how to read a financial statement. No sweat. It's all here in this attractive, extensively indexed annual compendium.

The Editors, Sumner and Caroline Levine, have created a text that should delight the student, the investor, business people, and the information professional. The book is easy to use, with a detailed table of contents, bibliography, and index.

How does one use the *Irwin Business and Investment Almanac*? There are so many uses for the data that it really depends on you, your project, and where you've already looked. This book is a great place to start, and often you will find that it has sufficiently answered your question. If you need to go into more detail, the authors have clearly sourced and footnoted each chart and provided a bibliography for more searching.

Here are a few more examples and the chapters where you can find information.

Starting your own business?

- Small Business Investment Companies

Getting up to speed?

- How to Read Mutual Fund Quotations
- How to Understand Options and Futures

Investing in the stock market?

- Quarterly Dow Jones Averages
- Industry Surveys
- General Business & Economic Indicators

Doing business in another state?

- State Information Guide
- State Business Assistance Publications
- State Information Offices

Creating a new woman-owned business?

- Women in Business

Where else can I look?

- Business Information Directory
- General Reference Sources
- Selected Bibliography

Whether you are a professional researcher or a consumer, it's a value-added asset to have all the work done for you and to know that the Editors have used the most reliable publications found in business libraries.

Colin McQuillan, Manager
GE Investments Library

Contents

Business in Review

October 1992–September 1993

October 1992

1 ITT is taking a $582 million charge because of losses at its ITT Hartford insurance unit, in a move that could encourage other insurers to recognize losses in their property and casualty operations. The charge largely relates to asbestos and pollution claims and comes on top of ITT Hartford's estimate of hurricane losses.

The racial disparity in mortgage lending doesn't appear to have diminished in 1991, bank figures indicate. Some lenders blamed the recession. Banks also said they learned of the situation too late last year to remedy it.

Italy's lira tumbled against the mark, and the Spanish peseta came under heavy pressure despite efforts by Britain, France and Germany to squelch talk of a "two-speed" Europe. Meanwhile, the dollar stabilized.

Europe's central banks lost $4 billion to $6 billion in their mostly futile attempt to prop up weak currencies last month, traders estimate.

2 The Manufacturing sector shrank in September, posting its worst performance since January, a survey of purchasing managers found. New orders fell for the first time in more than a year, the survey found. Separately, construction spending declined 1.1% in August after inflation.

Stocks slumped on the economic news but bonds rallied on hopes of further U.S. interest rate cuts. The dollar was mixed. The Dow Jones industrials dropped 17.29 points to 3254.37. Treasury bond prices increased ¾ point.

The pound and the lira lost ground and Spanish stocks tumbled as turmoil continued in European markets. In London, speculation mounted that the prime minister would be forced to dismiss his chancellor of the exchequer.

5 Payrolls shrank last month, indicating stagnation in the overall economy and a contraction in the manufacturing sector. The unemployment rate fell slightly to 7.5% due to a drop in the number of people looking for work.

Stocks tumbled on the jobs report and the Fed's failure to respond by cutting interest rates. The dollar also lost ground while bonds were mixed. The Dow Jones industrials dropped 53.76 points, or 1.7%, to 3200.61.

Brazilian stocks plunged after the country's acting president named two little-known figures to economic posts in his cabinet, though the new appointees pledged to continue privatization and trade liberalization.

6 Stocks tumbled around the world amid increasing concerns about the U.S. and European economies. The Dow Jones industrials closed at 3179.00, down 21.61 points for the day, after plunging 104 points in the first two hours of trading. Share prices plummeted 4.3% in Paris, 4.1% in London and 3.6% in Frankfurt.

General Motors' U.S. staffing levels put it at a $4 billion-a-year disadvantage to Ford, a study found. To close the $795-per-car gap, GM would have to slash more than 70,000 blue-collar jobs, the study concluded.

Sales of U.S.-made cars improved slightly in late September from the depressed level of the previous 30 days. The results are considered weak given the heavy discounts offered during the period, which ended the model year.

7 Sears's Allstate unit raised its estimate of damage claims from Hurricane Andrew to $1.73 billion from $1.05 billion. The loss is the biggest ever recorded by an insurer from one event.

Bond prices tumbled on the Fed's failure to cut interest rates. Stock prices and the dollar were mixed. The price of the Treasury's benchmark 30-year bond lost more than ¾ point.

8 Stock and bond prices slid and the dollar soared against the mark as the Fed again refrained from pushing interest rates lower. The Dow Jones industrials declined 25.94 points to 3152.25 in sluggish trading. The price of the Treasury's benchmark 30-year bond declined nearly ⅞ point, sending the issue's yield up to 7.48%.

A growing number of economists say the Fed needs to cut interest rates because they aren't that low compared with the current inflation rate of 3%. But most economists contend a rate cut won't help the economy much.

9 Big retailers posted better-than-expected September sales, helped by Labor Day traffic and strong sales of fall fashions. Analysts estimated the industry's overall sales rose between 5.5% and 7% from a year earlier.

Ford said it plans to sell $1 billion in preferred stock and warned it expects to report a third-quarter loss. The auto maker said its losses could extend into the fourth quarter.

12 The Fed decided last week against any immediate move to lower interest rates, but Greenspan on Saturday denied the central bank has put monetary policy on hold until after the election to avoid appearing vulnerable to political pressure. The Fed chief said such a move would be irresponsible. Describing the economy as still very sluggish, he said the agency is monitoring the situation day to day and hasn't ruled out any action.

Stock and bond prices tumbled and the dollar climbed on the lack of an interest rate cut by the Fed. The Dow Jones industrials dropped 39.45 points to 3136.58, a low for the year, down more than 8% from its high set June 1. The price of the Treasury's benchmark 30-year bond declined ⅞ point.

China agreed to reduce barriers to U.S. exports ranging from cigarettes to refrigerators, averting a costly trade war in which the U.S. was threatening to impose 100% tariffs on $3.9 billion of Chinese goods. The pact could give a political lift to Bush, who has been faulted for his China policy.

Ford stock slid $2.625, or 7%, to $35 after the car maker said it could post a fourth-quarter loss due to troubles in its European operations. Separately, L. Lindsey Halstead is retiring as Ford's top official in Europe. He will be succeeded by Jacques Nasser, head of Ford's Australian auto business.

Some home builders reported unexpectedly strong September sales, and many have grown more optimistic about sales growth next year. The companies cited low interest rates, but for some big builders the increases also reflected gains in market share at the expense of smaller competitors.

13 A London futures market is negotiating to join Globex, an after-hours trading system begun by Chicago's big futures exchanges and Reuters.

The EC and the U.S. adjourned high-level talks on a world trade agreement without resolving a dispute over reducing agricultural subsidies. But both sides held out the possibility of further top-level discussions.

14 New England has lost more than 476,000 jobs since the recession began in July 1990, accounting for 30% of the nation's job losses during the period.

British Coal plans to close 60% of its mines and lay off 30,000 miners. Some union leaders promised strikes against the state-run company.

15 Japan's trade surplus jumped 25% last month from a year earlier, setting a record for one month and marking the 21st consecutive such increase. Exports rose 14%. Imports gained 8.6%.

Retail sales rose 0.3% last month, as did producer prices. But the data don't change the view of a sluggish economy with inflation under control. August's retail sales were revised upward to show no change. September's producer prices, excluding energy and food, increased 0.2%.

Sales of U.S.-made cars tumbled in early October from September's level, starting the 1993 model year on a weak note. But light-truck sales were brisk. Honda and Toyota reported especially weak results for the 10-day period.

16 IBM posted meager third-quarter results that were much worse than expected, and blamed the poor showing on a slowdown in European sales. IBM's stock price tumbled $5.125 to $72.875. The computer giant, meanwhile, cleared the way for its executives to seek the company's first layoffs in more than four decades.

The Dow Jones industrials slid 20.80 to 3174.68 on IBM's sharp drop and a similar earnings-related decline in shares of Philip Morris. But broader stock indexes edged up. Bond prices slipped while the dollar lost ground.

General Motors and the UAW are negotiating a deal to offer thousands of GM blue-collar workers special incentives to leave the company. Such a program could let GM reach its staff-cutting target sooner than planned.

Consumer prices edged up 0.2% last month, indicating the economy is still too weak to sustain big price gains. Based on the latest data, Social Security benefits will go up 3% next year, the smallest rise in six years.

19 Industrial production fell 0.2% in September, the third drop in four months. Separately, the U.S. trade deficit surged in August as exports tumbled 6.1% and imports slid 1.3%. Meanwhile, an index of consumer sentiment fell again early this month.

Iran raised its oil output to four million barrels a day last week, the highest level since the country's 1979 revolution. The nation's oil minister said output will reach 4.5 million barrels by March. But he said Iran would curb production if prices softened.

Companies announced 426 stock buybacks valued at $28.7 billion in the first nine months of this year, easily outpacing last year's buy-back rate. Some analysts contend the volume of repurchases suggests stocks aren't as overvalued as many investors say.

20 The SEC is moving away from forcing companies to let shareholders vote on "social policy concerns," such as whether a company discriminates against homosexuals. The SEC's apparent policy shift would reserve proxies for matters closely linked to corporate performance.

Stocks and the dollar climbed and bond prices slumped as Clinton's big lead in the polls appeared to be helping the stock market but hurting the bond market. The Dow Jones industrials advanced 14.04 points to 3188.45. Treasury bond prices lost about ½ point.

The British government backed away from plans to close two-thirds of the nation's coal industry, in a retreat caused by public outrage and a Tory revolt against Prime Minister Major.

Natural gas prices soared on concern that unusually cold weather forecast for the Northeast and Midwest will cause demand to outstrip supply, which is running below normal.

Compaq slashed prices on its personal computers by up to 32%, and retailers predicted the move would set off another round of a PC price war. Separately, IBM is expected to unveil today its own low-priced PC line.

China said it will set up a central stock-market regulatory agency this year and will introduce a national securities law early next year to help bring the country's stock markets closer to international standards.

21 Bond prices fell sharply again on a growing belief that Clinton will win the election and step up spending to aid the economy. The price of the benchmark 30-year Treasury bond lost ⅞ point, lifting its yield to 7.64%. The rising rates squelched an early stock rally, leaving share prices mixed.

Germany's central bank indicated it is poised to lower interest rates, in a move that could ease the conditions that led to Europe's currency crisis.

European stocks and the dollar surged on the Bundesbank announcement. Stocks gained 2.1% in London, 2.2% in Frankfurt and 3.1% in Paris.

The federal deficit for the current fiscal year is expected to be about $290 billion, much less than previously projected, partly because of a surprising volume of estimated tax payments.

22 EC and U.S. negotiators broke off talks on farm subsidies, dashing hopes for a breakthrough in the effort to reach a new world trade agreement. U.S. officials said their EC counterparts backed away from proposals that they had appeared to view favorably.

23 One-fourth of U.S. companies plan to cut their payrolls during the year that ends next June, a survey found. The 25% level is the highest in the six years the survey has been conducted.

Salomon's profit plunged 93% in the third period as its main Wall Street rivals thrived. The firm's stock sank $4.50, or 12%, to $33.50 on the results, which partly reflected oil-trading losses and slim bond-trading profits.

26 General Motors announced it will shrink its North American car-making operations from six divisions to four, in the operation's second major reorganization in six months. About 10,000 white-collar jobs will be cut, on top of 10,000 salaried workers who have left GM since January. The expected forced departure of Chairman Robert Stempel, meanwhile, may be accompanied by a purge of some other senior company executives.

Sales of U.S.-made cars remained sluggish in mid-October but sales of light trucks, including minivans, jumped 48.8% from a year earlier.

27 Robert Stempel quit as chief executive and chairman of General Motors under pressure from the car maker's board. The resignation came at the start of GM's second corporate retrenchment in seven months, leaving the company in chaos and many of its employees demoralized. Longtime GM director John Smale is likely to take over as

chairman, with the chief executive post expected to go to GM President John F. Smith Jr.

American Express posted a $205 million third-quarter loss after taking a $342 million charge to pay the cost of cutting 4,800 jobs in its flagship card business, mostly through layoffs.

The banking industry's improving condition makes it highly unlikely that taxpayers will have to bail out bank depositors in a repeat of the savings-and-loan crisis, a Fed official said.

28 The economy grew at a 2.7% annual rate in the third quarter, pushing output above the high point reached before the recession began in 1990. But the recovery has been the slowest since the Depression. Other indicators, including consumer confidence, which declined this month, point to continued slow growth.

Bond prices rallied on the third-quarter economic data, which showed low inflation. Gold prices slid, while stocks and the dollar were mixed.

The weak economy may have undercut efforts by lenders to narrow the racial gap in mortgage lending, as banks tightened standards for all applicants, a new Fed study indicates.

General Motors stock slid $1.625 to $32.50 a share as the car maker's directors prepared to install new leaders, and investors focused on the difficulties the company will still face. Some analysts warned GM may have to cut its dividend and take another charge.

29 Orders for durable goods slipped 0.4% in September, matching August's drop, as defense orders sank. Personal income and spending each climbed 0.7%, mostly reflecting a rebound from the effects of Hurricane Andrew. The data appear consistent with a picture of slow and uneven economic growth.

The federal deficit totaled a record $290.2 billion in the fiscal year that ended September 30, compared with a gap of $269.5 billion the year before. The deficit is projected to widen this year.

30 General Motors' outside directors are seeking former GM Chairman Roger Smith's resignation as a director and plan to oust another GM executive from the board. The changes would leave just one management representative on the board. Meanwhile, the company posted a third-quarter loss of $752.9 million.

November 1992

2 Profits climbed 30% in the third quarter from a year earlier, according to a *Wall Street Journal* survey of 621 major companies. Banks and securities firms reported solid gains, while airlines continued to post big losses. Auto makers had mixed results. Forecasters expect profits to continue to rise, though moderately.

Bank lending to small and medium-sized businesses rose slightly in September from the month before, ending a string of 10 consecutive declines. But the amount was still 4.1% less than a year earlier. The increase suggests the reluctance of bankers to lend and businesses to borrow may be easing.

General Motors suppliers are balking at the auto maker's demand that they slash prices by 20%. GM's stance could result in some delays in parts deliveries, suppliers say. Separately, the plans of GM's outside directors to install a new management team are expected to win board approval today.

3 General Motors directors installed former Procter & Gamble Chairman John Smale as chairman of the car maker and put GM President John F. Smith Jr. in the chief executive's spot. The auto giant also gave its top management a younger look by elevating several finance executives.

The manufacturing sector grew last month while inventories and prices declined, according to a survey of corporate purchasing managers. The current low level of inventories means even a modest pickup in the recovery's pace could trigger a significant rise in industrial production.

4 Construction contracts dropped 3% in September, stalling a tenuous recovery in the building industry. Contracting for highways and single-family homes, however, turned up.

The index of leading indicators fell 0.3% in September, matching August's decline and reinforcing the view that the nation is still in economic limbo. The index is up 2.4% so far this year.

5 The U.S. said it plans to act on its threat to impose tariffs on as much as $1 billion in imports from the EC, after talks failed to end a dispute over farm subsidies. The EC expects to respond with its own sanctions. Analysts say a fierce trade war could erupt, dooming efforts to open markets world-wide.

Economic activity is continuing to increase slowly and unevenly across the nation, according to a Fed survey. Several areas reported an encouraging rise in commercial loan volume. Separately, factory orders rose 1.1% in September, but durable-goods orders fell for the third month in a row.

Sales of U.S.-made cars rose in late October from the sluggish level of the preceding 30 days, but remained far less than robust. Sales slumped for Toyota and Honda. At General Motors, business slipped as sales at the company's Oldsmobile division sank 24%.

Stocks slumped in active trading, while bond prices slipped and the dollar advanced. The Dow Jones industrials dropped 29.44 points to 3223.04.

OPEC oil output is rising faster than previously estimated, an organization of oil-consuming nations said. The report sent crude prices sinking. The group repeated its projection of a slight rise in oil demand this year.

6 The U.S. said it will levy 200% tariffs next month on $300 million in imports from the EC of white wine, canola oil and wheat gluten, unless the two sides resolve a dispute over EC subsidies for oilseeds. The U.S. said it is also assembling a list of additional EC products for possible tariffs. The EC warned it would retaliate.

Buyers and shippers scrambled to import as much of the affected goods as possible before levies are imposed.

9 General Motors is warning 21,200 laid-off blue-collar employees that their income-security benefits may expire in January. GM is working on a deal to offer many of the affected workers early retirement and is making similar offers to white-collar workers as young as 50 years old. The moves are a fresh sign the company is intent on accelerating its staff cuts.

The unemployment rate slipped to 7.4% in October from 7.5% in September. But the drop was caused mostly by a decline in the number of people looking for work and doesn't signal a real improvement in the labor market. Separately, consumer credit rose 2.7% in September, the first gain in 1992.

EC officials called for new talks in a dispute over farm subsidies after the U.S. said it will impose 200% duties on European wine and other goods. The EC is unlikely to take immediate retaliatory measures at a meeting today. A senior American official said the U.S. is willing to resume negotiations.

Tobacco-liability lawyers are continuing to pursue suits filed against cigarette makers despite the withdrawal of the best-known such case. These lawyers said their expenses aren't nearly as high as those of the lawyer who dropped the landmark Cipollone smoking case last week.

10 EC foreign ministers rejected a French demand that they draft retaliatory trade sanctions against the U.S. in response to U.S. plans for 200% duties on about $300 million in European products, including white wine. The EC's internal divisions may be the biggest obstacle to settling the dispute.

Saudi Arabia apparently joined some other OPEC members in endorsing new output restraints to support higher oil prices. The kingdom denied it has been producing as much as has been reported. Crude prices rallied.

Fina said it is close to an accord that would give a Saudi group a 50% stake in Fina's U.S. petroleum refining and marketing operation, and would give the unit of Belgium's Petrofina a secure supply of crude oil.

Tokyo stocks sank 2.7% after Japan's opposition parties said they will delay a vote on a spending plan intended to stimulate the economy. The Nikkei fell 452.76 points to 16417.05.

11 European officials signaled they are prepared to compromise in their farm-subsidy dispute with the U.S. The EC's agriculture minister rejoined its negotiating team after dropping out last week, and Germany's foreign minister predicted France will soften its hard-line stance.

Producer prices inched up 0.1% last month, indicating that the weak economy is still holding inflation in check. Excluding the volatile food and energy sectors, wholesale prices fell 0.1%. A consumer price report due Friday is also expected to show little increase.

Bond prices rallied on the price report while blue-chip stocks and the dollar fell. The Dow Jones industrials slid 15.40 to 3225.47 in heavy trading. But over-the-counter issues surged. Treasury bonds rose more than ¾ point.

12 General Motors was warned by S&P that the auto maker's preferred stock rating could fall to junk bond levels if the company continues to issue such

equity to cover its outflow of cash. Separately, GM said a Japanese tool and die maker will help the U.S. company improve efficiency in its metal die-making operation.

GM and AT&T may benefit from a recent U.S.-Chinese trade pact's provisions giving them the opportunity to catch up with rivals that beat the companies into the Chinese market.

The U.S. rice industry plans again to seek punitive action against Japan because of its ban on rice imports. The move is a sign of growing frustration with a lack of progress in efforts to reach a new world trade agreement. Such trade brushfires could spread without a breakthrough in talks.

13 Clinton said his first priority will be an economic-recovery bill with a "disciplined" balance of moves to stimulate job growth in the short run and to cut the budget deficit gradually. The president-elect refrained from repeating his call for a middle-class tax cut. Clinton said his proposal will include an investment tax credit, but lobbying for a more generous version could delay the proposal.

Accounting rule makers intend next week to issue a regulation requiring many companies to set aside reserves for certain benefits for their former or inactive employees. The change could slash reported corporate profits by as much as $30 billion.

16 Retail sales jumped 0.9% in October and a survey found that consumer confidence surged this month. The reports suggest tentatively that the economy is improving and that people are starting to believe it. Separately, consumer prices rose 0.4% last month but the sizable gain may be a fluke.

Sales of cars and trucks made in North America climbed 21.6% in early November from a year earlier, led by strong sales of light trucks. But the selling rate of cars alone was off from the pace of the preceding 30 days.

AT&T is expected today to announce alliances with three Japanese electronics giants and two small U.S. companies in the race to provide wireless data services and equipment.

Italy's government unveiled a proposal to raise about $20 billion by 1995 by selling much of its interests in the country's industrial companies.

17 Industrial output rose 0.3% in October after deteriorating throughout much of the summer, although a big part of the gain was due to a surge in auto and truck production. Industry operated at 78.5% of capacity in October, a slight pickup from September's rate. Business inventories remained unchanged in September while sales rose 1.3%.

The Christmas retail outlook is brightening, as a recent strong upturn in consumer sentiment is helping buoy expectations for substantial holiday sales gains. Two forecasting companies raised their estimates of this year's sales increase to 4% or more.

Russia's drive to privatize its biggest companies gained momentum as the government invited bids for shares in a microelectronics factory.

GM released internal documents about its 1973–87 pickup trucks that could mean the company will face more liability claims concerning its trucks with "side-saddle" gas tanks.

Germany's economy is slowing sharply, but its central bank has no leeway to cut interest rates before well into the first half of 1993, said the nation's council of economic advisers.

The stagnant outlook for the German economy gave a lift to the dollar. Despite the U.S. currency's 15% rise against the mark since early September, economists and traders think the dollar has a lot further to climb.

18 General Motors wants to sell a significant part of its 81.5% stake in National Car Rental, further unraveling a costly strategy to use sales to rental fleets to prop up auto output. GM may take a related fourth-quarter charge of about $300 million, to be nearly offset by gains on sales of other assets.

19 Olympia & York abandoned a plan to restructure its Canadian real estate operations and is expected to propose a liquidation of those holdings. Under the new plan, unsecured creditors would get 90% of what remains. The Reichmann family, Olympia's current owners, would get 10%. The move reflects a militant stance by the company's secured creditors.

Fed chief Greenspan said the credit crunch "may finally be retreating." He criticized regulators, Congress, the administration and bankers themselves for worsening the crunch.

The U.S. trade deficit narrowed slightly to $8.31 billion in September as a 6.8% jump in exports more than offset a modest 4% increase in imports. But analysts say the gap could worsen if the U.S. economy improves faster than other national economies do.

Tokyo stocks soared 4.9% Wednesday after the government pressured institutions to buy shares. But analysts said a sustained recovery is unlikely without good economic news.

20 Housing starts fell 1.1% in October after three gains in a row, suggesting a recovery in the housing market requires more than low interest rates.

Sweden said it will let its currency, the krona, float freely. The decision sent investors fleeing to the mark, pushing the dollar lower as a result. The Swedish stock market surged.

Ford was ordered to pay $1.2 million to a woman who was injured when her Bronco II vehicle rolled over. At least 100 such lawsuits involving the Bronco are estimated to be pending.

23 The EC and the U.S. reached a farm-subsidy accord, averting a trade war and unblocking six-year-old world trade talks. But French farmers could torpedo the latest pact. Even if they don't, complex talks remain on such issues as telecommunications and financial services. Japan, meanwhile, indicated it will resist pressure to relax its ban on rice imports.

The Fed isn't likely to cut interest rates soon with the economy showing hints of strength, officials familiar with the agency's deliberations said.

Home mortgage refinancing applications fell to a five-month low, continuing a slide that began in early October after interest rates hit bottom.

European officials devalued the Spanish peseta and the Portuguese escudo by 6%, marking the second realignment of the European exchange rate mechanism in three months.

24 Ernst & Young agreed to pay a record $400 million to settle federal charges that the big accounting firm inadequately audited four large thrifts that failed at a cost to the government of $6.6 billion. The settlement breaks new ground by resolving charges brought by three agencies.

Norway, Denmark, Finland, Spain and Ireland raised interest rates and intervened in the markets to defend their currencies against speculators.

EC finance ministers agreed on a package of measures intended to stimulate Europe's sluggish economy.

25 Orders for durable goods jumped 3.9% in October, the biggest increase since July 1991. But excluding the transportation and defense sectors, orders fell 2.8%. Separately, consumer confidence surged this month but remained relatively weak. While expressing caution, economists said conditions appear to be improving.

Stocks rallied on unexpectedly strong economic data, while bond prices posted small gains. The Dow Jones industrials surged 25.66 points to 3248.70 in active trading. Nasdaq stocks rose sharply to a record.

Boeing is trimming production of its 757 and 767 jetliner models and may lay off as many as 2,500 workers. The company cited a slowdown in orders from the embattled airline industry.

Sales of U.S.-made cars fell in mid-November from the level of the preceding 30 days and were little changed from a dismal year-earlier period. But light-truck sales surged 14.4% from a year earlier and auto dealers report that showroom traffic is picking up.

Russia defaulted for the first time on U.S.-backed grain loans and might miss more payments this month. Grain prices initially fell on news of the default, which led the Agriculture Department to suspend Moscow's eligibility for more credit guarantees.

27 The economy grew at a 3.9% annual rate in the third quarter, far greater than the government's initial estimate and the biggest increase since 1988. But the expansion has been accompanied by very little job growth. Clinton said the new data may compel him to rethink his plan for a short-term package to spur the economy.

Stocks rallied Wednesday on the economic news. The Dow Jones industrials gained 17.56 points to 3266.26 in heavy trading. Bond prices slipped.

Saudi Arabia and Iran refused to cut their oil production despite falling prices, as each country insisted the other should reduce output. The dispute dimmed prospects for OPEC to reach a meaningful production pact. Crude prices slid in London trading.

Sales of existing homes soared 9.1% in October from the month before and were up 14.3% from a year earlier. The sales rate was the highest since 1988, as rising interest rates spurred purchases by people waiting to buy.

U.S. steelmakers expect the government to impose duties averaging 15% or more on many steel imports in a move that would boost domestic steel prices and exacerbate trade tensions.

30 Personal income soared 1% in October, the biggest gain in 10 months, and consumer spending rose 0.7%, as the economy showed more signs of vigor. But much of the rise in income was caused by several unusual events.

Bond prices dropped on the income and spending figures, which exceeded expectations. Stock prices advanced.

Mutual fund officials say surging confidence among small investors this month has resulted in a big inflow of cash into stock funds, especially funds that take more than average risks. Junk bond funds and municipal bond funds are also attracting cash. But interest in other bond funds is low.

Machine tool orders plunged 24.9% in October from September as buyers apparently waited for a possible investment tax credit next year.

December 1992

1 Stocks climbed again, this time led by blue-chip issues. The Dow Jones industrials jumped 22.96 points in heavy trading to close at 3305.16, about 108 points, or 3.2%, short of its record high of 3413.21. The S&P 500 and Nasdaq stock indexes advanced further into record territory. Bonds moved little. The dollar was mixed.

The U.S. imposed tariffs expected to average 15% to 20% on steel from a dozen nations whose governments are accused of subsidizing steelmakers. Domestic steel companies said the preliminary action will let their industry "move toward profitability."

U.S. auto makers are producing safer cars and minivans than their Japanese rivals and are catching up on quality, a consumer guide says.

2 Factories posted unexpectedly strong growth last month, a survey of purchasing managers indicates. Separately, the index of leading indicators climbed 0.4% in October, while construction spending rose 0.5%. The gains in the leading indicators and in the purchasing managers' index were the strongest since May.

A Fed survey found that banks are increasingly interested in lending to consumers while consumers are showing more interest in borrowing. The quarterly survey found little change in the market for loans to businesses.

Japanese job seekers outnumbered the nation's job openings in October for the first time in 4½ years, adding to worries that declining income will forestall an economic recovery.

Hong Kong stocks sank again, falling 5.3% Tuesday after Beijing said contracts signed by the colony without China's consent will be void after 1997. After the two-day, 8.1% drop, the market was still up 27.9% so far in 1992.

3 The French franc sank against the mark after the German central bank's chief questioned its commitment to Europe's fixed exchange-rate system. The French currency stayed barely above its floor in the system.

4 General Motors identified eight more North American factories to be closed, eliminating nearly 14,000 jobs, as the auto maker accelerates the overhaul of its unprofitable domestic business. As part of the retrenchment, GM plans to dispose of 14% of its auto parts operations.

Sales of U.S.-made cars surged in late November to the highest level in nearly two years. But GM's share of the U.S. market plunged last month.

Factory orders jumped 1.7% in October, marking the latest positive report about the industrial sector. Orders for durable goods rose 4.1%, but orders for nondurable goods fell 0.7%.

Big retailers posted respectable sales for November, bolstering expectations that this will be the best Christmas selling period in years. Results were especially strong for Federated and Limited but were disappointing at Kmart and Dayton Hudson.

Japan and Germany reported that their economies shrank in the latest quarter, and the two economic engines no longer look capable of pulling other nations out of the global recession.

7 American Express's chairman and chief executive, James Robinson, is stepping down and leading a search for a successor. Robinson said it would be a "gross exaggeration" to say he was being pushed out after a 15-year tenure. Harvey Golub is the leading internal candidate to succeed him.

The number of jobs grew significantly in November, ending months of little change. The unemployment rate slid to 7.2% from 7.4% in October. Clinton aides say they want more signs of new hiring before dropping the idea of a fiscal boost for the economy.

Two top tax legislators said any investment tax credit passed next year should be retroactive to last week.

8 TWA owner Carl Icahn reached an accord with the U.S. pension guarantee agency, allowing him to hand over the airline to creditors and workers. Icahn agreed to lend TWA $200 million and guarantee up to $240 million in pension payments over eight years.

Japan's new stock market watchdog launched raids in a probe of suspected stock-price manipulation, marking the agency's first pursuit of possible securities-law violations.

10 IBM's triple-A debt rating from S&P is being reviewed for a possible downgrading by the agency, which cited weak market conditions and news of another possible round of write-offs by the computer giant. IBM's stock slid $2.75 to $62.625. Separately, the FAA is threatening to cancel IBM's $4 billion contract to modernize the air traffic-control system.

Economic conditions are improving in most of the nation, but the change continues to be slow and uneven, according to a regional Fed survey. Retailers in particular expressed growing optimism, and consumer confidence also appeared to be increasing.

Detroit's Big Three auto makers are moving quickly toward an agreement to share technology for building an electric vehicle. The alliance could include joint production of parts for an electric car but may stop short of joint production of the actual vehicles. A deal could be announced within days.

11 Sears' debt was downgraded by Moody's, which said the company's proposed spinoff of its financial businesses could weaken the retailer. Separately, Sears said its Allstate unit's losses from Hurricane Andrew would be $1.65 billion, up from $1.15 billion.

Producer prices fell 0.2% in November, signaling that inflation remains under control even as the economy gains momentum. Excluding food and energy, prices edged up 0.1%.

Norway allowed its currency to float freely, becoming the third Scandinavian country to do so in as many months and sparking a new round of foreign-exchange turmoil in Europe.

Banks posted record earnings for the third quarter and boosted lending for the first time in nearly two years, as the banking industry continued to rebuild its strength after years of large losses on real estate loans.

15 Toyota cut by 20% its profit projection for the year that ends in June, in a sign that Japan's economy isn't expected to pick up soon. Separately, the car maker scrapped a move to cut costs by shifting 600 office workers to jobs on the factory floor, in the wake of publicity about the plan.

General Motors and the UAW unveiled an early retirement plan for hourly workers, but it isn't clear if enough people will participate to make a big dent in the auto maker's costs.

The Supreme Court ruled that states can't force employers to give disabled employees the same health insurance offered to active workers. The court's 8–1 decision could make it more difficult for states to regulate employee benefits in general.

The U.S. loosened the Vietnam trade embargo, saying U.S. companies and Vietnam can sign contracts now to take effect after the ban ends. But it appears Bush will leave it to Clinton to actually lift the embargo. U.S. companies can also get permission to open offices in Vietnam.

Toshiba agreed to share its technology for making "flash" memory chips with California's National Semiconductor, in a step that challenges Intel's dominance of the market. The move is the latest in a series of global partnerships in the chip business.

Japan's trade surplus grew 19% in November from a year earlier, largely because the country's slumping economy continued to depress imports. Last month was the 23rd in a row that the surplus grew from a year earlier.

16 IBM announced it expects to make its first layoffs in 50 years and warned that its once-sacrosanct dividend is in danger. The company is taking a $6 billion fourth-quarter pretax charge to pay for trimming its staff by 25,000 more employees and for disposing of assets in its fading mainframe computer business. IBM said it will only break even on operations in the fourth quarter. Its stock price plummeted $6.75, or nearly 11%, to $56.125.

Sales of U.S.-made cars rose moderately in early December from the preceding month but were well ahead of the lethargic level a year earlier. Analysts are still looking for solid signs of a sustained auto recovery.

17 Ford said it will report a loss for 1992 and will eliminate nearly 10,000, or almost 11%, of the jobs at its money-losing European auto operations next year. The job cuts will result in a $419 million fourth-quarter charge. Ford is also taking a $7.5 billion charge to reflect changes in accounting for retiree health benefits.

IBM's stock sank further, dropping $4.25 to $52.875, an 11-year-low, as analysts concluded its latest retrenchment measures, though drastic, aren't enough to turn around the company. Industry professionals said IBM will still have too many employees.

Industrial production climbed 0.4% in November after a revised 0.5% increase in October. Separately, housing starts were up 1.5% last month, marking their second straight rise.

Stocks slid after some economic data disappointed investors. The Dow Jones industrials dropped 29.18 points to 3255.18 in heavy trading. Bond prices rose and the dollar weakened.

18 The U.S. trade gap narrowed sharply in October as exports rose 3.4% to a record while imports edged 0.3% lower. But economists don't expect the improvement to continue.

Banking regulators estimated that their rules cost banks and thrifts between $7.5 billion and $17 billion a year, and suggested 60 initiatives that could ease the regulatory burden.

A proposed accounting change is leading some banks to modify their investing in a way that could hurt their profits and make it harder for consumers to get fixed-rate mortgages.

21 IBM is bringing back two retired executives, Paul Rizzo and Kaspar Cassani, to help Chairman John Akers run the computer giant, in a sign that its current management may not be strong enough to handle a mounting crisis. It isn't clear whether the move reflects weakening support for Akers on IBM's board. The company denied that his authority is being undercut.

22 Holiday retail sales continued at a strong pace last weekend, and some merchants, particularly department stores, are expected to post their best Christmas sales gains in three years.

Baxter International agreed to ship deeply discounted hospital supplies to Syria as a bribe to get off the Arab blacklist of companies with ties to Israel, U.S. investigators believe. A grand jury is intensifying its probe into whether Baxter broke U.S. law.

23 British Air pulled out from its agreement to invest $750 million in USAir, citing Washington's likely opposition to the deal amid concerns about a lack of access to Britain by U.S. airlines. USAir, though unprofitable, said it will survive without the infusion and is expected to renew its search for an overseas partner.

The economy grew at a 3.4% annual rate in the third quarter, less than the 3.9% previously estimated but greater than any quarter's growth since 1988. Analysts said the report shows the economy is gaining momentum after posting increases of 1.5% in the second quarter and 2.9% in the first period.

24 Durable-goods orders fell 1.9% last month, breaking a string of encouraging news about manufacturing. Most of the drop stemmed from a 10.2% decline in transportation orders, mainly for aircraft. Separately, personal income fell 0.1% after inflation last month, while consumer spending rose 0.3%. A private index of consumer confidence is said to have increased this month.

Sales of U.S.-built light trucks surged in mid-December, while sales of domestic cars returned to sluggish levels after showing signs of life in late November and early December. Total sales of domestic and imported vehicles were up 10.4% from a year ago.

28 Retailers posted moderate to sharp gains in their sales for the Christmas season and generally avoided the ruinous markdowns that depleted profits in recent years. But many retailers remain cautious about their industry's outlook in the wake of recent corporate layoffs and continued uncertainty about the economy.

Many analysts are lowering their ratings on retailing stocks even though consumer confidence is rising and the results of retailers are continuing to meet or exceed expectations.

Machine tool orders slid 22% in November from the month before as some big customers canceled orders and others waited for an investment tax credit being considered by Clinton's economic team. So far this year, orders are off 1% from a year earlier.

Research spending in the U.S. by companies, the government and other groups is expected to rise only slightly next year because of tight corporate budgets and a slowdown in weapons development, a survey found. The amount of corporate research is expected to be practically unchanged.

General Motors' finance arm retained Chemical Banking to advise it on renegotiating at least $7 billion in bank credit lines that mature beginning in May. The lenders are expected ultimately to renew the credit lines, but on less favorable terms, because GM has lost its top debt ratings.

29 Lockheed formed a venture with a Russian aerospace concern to market the Russian-built Proton rocket for commercial satellite launches. The move could help make Russia a dominant force in the commercial launch business. The venture would compete primarily with Arianespace, a French consortium that launches about 60% of U.S. satellites.

Tokyo stock prices tumbled 2.1% Monday in trading that was the lightest in more than a decade. The Nikkei average fell 368.42 points to 17188.62. Frankfurt stocks rose, sending the DAX index up 17.66 points to 1544.61.

30 Consumer confidence increased in December to its highest level in more than 1½ years, as optimism continued to rebound across the country. The gain exceeded economists' forecasts, but it largely reflected greater expectations for the future and not a more favorable assessment of current economic conditions.

Sales of existing homes rose 5.8% in November from the month before to the highest level in nearly six years, reflecting growing consumer confidence and the prospect of further increases in mortgage interest rates.

Non-Japanese chip makers held 15.9% of the Japanese semiconductor market in the third quarter, down a bit from the second period and well short of the 20% goal set by the U.S. and Japan for the end of 1992, the U.S. said. Clinton will have to decide whether to give Japan more time or to retaliate.

31 Investors poured a record $9.9 billion into stock mutual funds last month. Equity fund sales slowed in December, but they had already totaled $68.6 billion through the first 11 months of the year, well ahead of 1991's record inflow of $38.3 billion. Bond funds continued to post strong sales, but they were outsold by stock funds for the second month in a row.

Japanese securities firms are bracing for a year that may prove even worse than 1992. Stock trading volume has plunged, hurting revenue, and the industry faces new threats from foreign firms, banks and regulators.

The index of leading indicators jumped 0.8% in November, providing further evidence that the recovery is gaining momentum. The increase was the biggest since January and followed a revised 0.5% rise for October. New-home sales fell 8.3% last month, after a revised 8.2% drop in October.

Visa credit card holders charged 17% more between Thanksgiving and the day after Christmas than a year earlier, while MasterCard posted a 23.4% increase for the same period. The gains exceeded projections. But consumers may decide to retrench after getting a look at their bills.

January 1993

4 The economy will grow moderately this year, with small declines in the unemployment rate, according to a *Wall Street Journal* survey of 44 economists. The U.S. will do better economically than its major trading partners, spelling trouble for U.S. exporters, the forecasters said. They also predicted very slight increases in interest rates, a stronger dollar and continued mild inflation.

The factory sector strengthened in December for the fourth consecutive month, according to a survey of purchasing managers, who noted a particularly strong increase in new orders. But factory orders fell 0.9% in November, their first drop in three months.

Contracts for new construction fell 10% in November, led by a sharp decline in nonresidential construction.

Blue-chip stock prices slid but stocks of smaller companies rallied. The Dow Jones industrials slid 19.99 points to finish the year at 3301.11, up 4.2% from the end of 1991. The S&P 500 index posted a 4.5% gain for the year. Nasdaq stocks ended 1992 at a record high, up 15.5% from a year earlier.

Initial public offerings of stock raised a record $39.4 billion from investors in 1992, fueled by a bull market in over-the-counter stocks. Many analysts think the volume of initial offerings could grow further. Once issued, new stocks did well last year, but not as spectacularly as 1991's new issues.

5 Boeing plans to team with two members of the rival Airbus consortium to pursue development of a 600-seat super-jumbo jetliner. The expected pact with Daimler-Benz and British Aerospace could shake up the world-wide industry, although it wouldn't obligate the European concerns to pull out of Airbus.

The budget-deficit outlook is growing worse, Bush will report tomorrow, with the gap likely to exceed $300 billion in fiscal 1997 unless there are substantial changes in federal policy. Clinton's advisers say the administration is understating the problem.

Bond prices surged, with the yield on the U.S. 30-year issue falling to 7.32%, a three-month low. Stock prices were mixed as the Dow Jones Industrial Average rose 8.11 points to 3309.22. The dollar moved higher.

6 The United Steelworkers will seek innovative agreements with U.S. steelmakers, including long-term accords and ways to cut work forces and relax stringent work rules. Marking a change from its hard-line stance, the union acknowledged steelmakers' difficulties and the need to create a "modern industry."

Germany and France pledged to defend the French franc from speculators as the Bank of France boosted a short-term interest rate to fend off a post-New Year's run on its currency. The dollar eased in New York.

Stocks turned in a mixed showing, with the Dow Jones Industrial Average slipping 1.35 points to 3307.87. Bond prices closed marginally lower.

7 Ford's Taurus ousted Honda's Accord as the bestselling car in the U.S. last year. The victory marks the first time since 1988 that an American car has been No. 1 in its home market.

Stock mutual funds gained an average of 8.88% in 1992, turning the year into a respectable one, even though the return lagged behind the 35.61% increase of 1991. Taxable U.S. bond funds gained 7.87%, outpacing money market funds' 3.31% return.

The budget deficit will be a record $327.3 billion this fiscal year and will still top $300 billion in four years without policy changes, Bush said. Clinton called the figures "unsettling," and aides said the president-elect is now re-examining his fiscal blueprint.

8 Big retail chains posted healthy December sales gains, a further sign that the rebound in consumer spending may be here to stay. Reversing the pattern of bargain hunting, shoppers bought at department stores, specialty stores and discounters alike.

The U.S. economy should see a broad but moderate recovery in 1993 with high-tech industries expected to excel, the Commerce Department said in its annual industrial outlook.

11 Job growth remained sluggish last month as the unemployment rate remained at November's 7.3% rate. The sluggishness came despite recent pickups in consumer confidence, retail sales and manufacturing. But some analysts said the activity level may be enough to reduce the pressure on Clinton to expedite a major economic stimulus package.

Stock prices ended lower on the jobs data and on Middle East tensions. The Dow Jones industrials fell 17.29 points to 3251.67. Bonds finished mixed, and the dollar closed higher.

The ailing housing industry is poised for its best performance in five years, with builders and brokers reporting surprisingly high levels of home-buying activity around the U.S.

Japan's Pioneer Electronic essentially dismissed 35 managers. The move marks a break with the effort by the nation's blue-chip companies to keep up the appearance of their tradition of lifetime employment.

13 Home-office deductions on federal income taxes have been made harder for people who do some, but not most, of their work at home. The Supreme Court ruling yesterday could affect thousands of taxpayers in numerous lines of work, including doctors, financial advisers and salespeople, and raises a host of questions.

Rising U.S. oil demand is shown in an American Petroleum Institute report due out today. The substantial increase of 1.6% in 1992 deliveries—a measure of demand—could augur a boost soon for the weak oil market.

15 IBM was stripped of its prized triple-A credit rating by S&P. In an unusually severe action, the rating agency slashed the embattled computer giant's debt rating three notches to double-A-minus, citing the company's "significantly lower-than-anticipated" results, especially in its core mainframe computer business.

Hefty December retail sales lifted the year's total to 5.1% above 1991, but analysts don't expect the recent pace to continue. Wholesale prices climbed only 0.2% last month, a signal that inflation remains well in check.

The Fed's principal money-supply measure, M2, grew only 2.1% last year, shy of the goal of 2.5% to 6.5%. Despite that, the bank is moving toward lowering the range for 1993.

18 Consumer prices rose only 2.9% in 1992, their smallest increase in six years. Inflation will likely stay in check this year because of the continuing factors of a weak labor market, improved productivity and a global economic slowdown.

Industrial production edged up 0.3% last month in a broad-based gain with no key bright spots. Separately, consumer confidence eased in early January, while in November business inventories increased and the trade deficit stayed about even.

Many U.S. exporters are optimistic about this year's prospects, despite the slumping economies of Japan and Europe. These companies are finding growing demand elsewhere in the Far East and in Latin America.

19 Clinton is preparing with his advisers a plan aimed at stimulating the economy through tax cuts and spending boosts that would widen the budget deficit in the short run. The proposal, to be unveiled next month, would also include measures to reduce the deficit in later years. Aides say no final decisions have been made.

House staff member Consuela Washington is a leading candidate to be Clinton's nominee to head the SEC. She would be the first woman and the first black in the agency's top post.

20 IBM posted its first-ever operating loss, closing out a disastrous year with a $5.46 billion fourth-quarter deficit that highlighted the depth of the computer maker's woes. Analysts were particularly worried by trouble signs in its huge minicomputer line. The results hold little promise that Chairman John Akers will see any relief from pressures by investors.

Germany unveiled an economic plan that envisions new taxes after 1995 and cuts in once-sacred social programs. The move reflects a deepening recession and the costs of rebuilding the eastern part of the country.

21 Medical-device makers that receive the FDA's approval of their products are largely shielded from lawsuits seeking damages for injuries to users, a federal appeals court ruled.

22 British Airways bought a 19.9% voting stake in USAir for $300 million, in a scaled-back version of an alliance the companies scrapped last month. But AMR's American Airlines and UAL's United said they oppose this accord too, giving the Clinton administration a dispute to resolve.

Economic conditions continue to improve across much of the country, a Fed survey found. The gains haven't resulted in much job growth but also haven't caused prices to jump. But California remains a weak spot.

Ford is raising prices on most of its 1993 models in an unusual step for the middle of a model year. The increases come as Ford gains market share in the U.S. but continues to lose money.

General Motors stock climbed $1.25 to $37.50 on the prospect that the car maker will post better-than-expected results for the fourth quarter.

26 Sears is closing its catalog unit, shutting 113 stores and cutting 50,000 jobs, or nearly 15% of the company's merchandising staff. With the overhaul, Sears is backing away from the idea that it should sell all things to all people. The moves are causing a $1.7 billion fourth-quarter charge.

Bond prices surged, pushing long-term interest rates to their lowest levels in more than six years and sending stocks up sharply. The benchmark 30-year Treasury bond's price rose 1¼ points and its yield slid to 7.19%. The Dow Jones industrials climbed 35.39 points to 3292.20. The dollar fell.

The Chicago Board of Trade tentatively agreed to acquire the faltering Commodity Exchange in New York, in what would be the first major consolidation of U.S. commodities markets.

Oil prices rallied, pushing up oil-company stocks, after Saudi Arabia and Iran called for major cuts in OPEC's output. U.S. crude futures jumped 83 cents to $19.66 a barrel. Exxon's stock price rose $2.50 to $60.625. Mobil shares shot up $2.625 to $62.875.

Several big oil companies posted sharp gains in fourth-quarter profits, benefiting from higher natural-gas prices and efforts to hold down costs.

Japan's Finance Ministry is buying Japanese government bonds in an apparent effort to drive down interest rates without the central bank's help.

27 IBM Chairman John Akers is stepping

down, in an about-face from his repeated insistence that he would lead the computer giant out of its crisis. Akers's top two lieutenants are also losing their posts. A committee of outside directors will head the search for Akers's successor, and the panel's leader is calling for a radical change.

Boeing is sharply cutting production rates for all of its aircraft models in response to the airline recession. Output of the highly profitable 747 jumbo jet line is being chopped 40%. Separately, Boeing posted an 11% decline in fourth-quarter net income.

Consumer confidence leveled off this month after increasing sharply at the end of 1992, a survey found, supporting a belief that further gains in confidence and spending won't come without faster job and wage growth.

Sales of existing homes climbed 5% in December from November, hitting their highest level in 13 years. Sales were up 21% from a year earlier. Analysts credit a surge in consumer confidence for December's sales gain.

28 Clinton aides are considering proposals to limit cost-of-living increases for Social Security recipients and for retired government workers to help reduce the federal deficit. Such a move, one of several money-saving options being considered, could be the politically easiest way to cut Social Security outlays.

Steep tariffs on steel from major U.S. trading partners were imposed by the Commerce Department in a victory for domestic steelmakers. Foreign governments assailed the move, which was the first significant U.S. trade action since Clinton took office.

Westinghouse Chairman Paul Lego resigned, becoming the latest in a series of corporate chiefs to quit in the face of financial troubles and pressure from directors and shareholders. A committee of outside directors will lead the search for a successor.

Former General Motors Chairman Roger Smith is stepping down as a GM director in April as part of a plan to overhaul the auto maker's board.

29 Economic growth accelerated in the fourth quarter to an annual rate of 3.8%. The growth, though still sluggish, was the fastest in four years. It was led by a consumer buying binge. But Treasury chief Bentsen cautioned against elation over the growth data.

The White House plans to ask Congress for quick approval of $15 billion to $25 billion in spending to boost the economy. Fed Chairman Greenspan, meanwhile, suggested cutting the deficit would help the economy more than any short-term fiscal stimulus.

Blue-chip stocks advanced, but over-the-counter issues continued their slide. Bond prices rallied, while the dollar was mixed. The Dow Jones industrials climbed 14.86 points. Treasury bond prices rose a half-point.

February 1993

1 RJR Nabisco is considering creating a class of stock linked to its food unit, people close to the company said. The possible move reflects the frustration of KKR and other shareholders about RJR's stagnant stock, which has been held down in part by the taint of the company's tobacco business.

A former smoker's allegation that tobacco companies conspired to play down the risks of smoking was rejected by an Illinois jury. The victory for RJR's tobacco unit keeps intact the industry's record of never paying a cent to a plaintiff in a health lawsuit.

Toyota and Nissan raised prices on many of their car models sold in the U.S., following similar steps by Ford and Chrysler. The moves by the Japanese companies, whose profits are slumping, come amid signs that their Detroit rivals will charge them with selling at unfairly low prices.

Orders for durable goods soared 9.1% in December, more than offsetting a revised 1.6% drop in November. December's broad-based gain was the biggest advance since July 1991. But personal income was more sluggish. It rose 1% in December but was up only 0.3% excluding some special factors.

2 The U.S. threatened the EC with a series of retaliatory trade measures unless the Europeans change their procurement rules favoring the purchase of European goods. The announcement clearly signals that the Clinton administration will pursue an aggressive trade policy.

The factory sector expanded at a healthy rate in January but employment continued to drop, according to a survey of purchasing managers. The purchasers' index rose for the fourth consecutive month to a 4½-year high.

Stocks and the dollar rallied on new signs of economic growth. The Dow Jones industrials gained 22.15 points to 3332.18 in heavy trading. Bond prices, meanwhile, slipped.

3 The index of leading economic indicators jumped 1.9% in December, the biggest rise since 1983. The indicator that increased the most was consumer expectations. The index's price and money-supply components suggest inflation will continue to be low. Separately, new-home sales climbed 6.3%.

Treasury bond prices fell more than ½ point on the economic data. Stocks and the dollar were mixed.

Detroit's Big Three auto makers plan to file February 12 a sweeping trade complaint accusing Japanese, European and Korean rivals of selling cars in the U.S. at unfairly low prices. But some Big Three officials fear the move will hurt the U.S. car makers' image.

European trade ministers warned that the Clinton administration could extinguish world economic recovery by being too tough in trade disputes. While threatening retaliation against recent U.S. moves, the EC officials refrained from taking immediate steps.

4 Sales of U.S.-made cars soared in late January to their highest level in more than two years, providing further evidence that the U.S. economy is pulling out of the doldrums. The share of the U.S. market held by Japanese companies fell to a two-year low.

Japan's central bank cut its discount rate Thursday to 2.5%, matching its record low, from 3.25%, in another effort to revive the nation's economy.

5 Stocks surged, sending the Dow Jones industrials to a record, on growing economic optimism in the U.S. and interest-rate cuts in Germany and Japan. The industrial average jumped 42.95 points, or 1.3%, to 3416.74 in very heavy trading. But Nasdaq stocks rose only slightly. Bond prices and the dollar advanced.

General Motors was ordered by a Georgia jury to pay $101 million in punitive damages to the parents of a 17-year-old boy who died in a fiery crash in his GMC pickup truck in 1989. The verdict is a blow to GM's efforts to defend the safety of its 1973–87 pickups, which had side-mounted gas tanks.

Labor productivity jumped 2.7% in 1992, the largest gain in 20 years, as U.S. businesses responded to intense competition by slashing costs. Separately, factory orders rose 5.3% in December and were up 3.3% for 1992.

Retail chains reported that sales in January rose more than expected as consumers refused to cut back after their holiday spending spree.

Germany's central bank trimmed key interest rates in response to political and economic pressure, cutting the Lombard rate half a point to 9%. But analysts said the cuts were too small to solve the European currency crisis.

8 Job growth accelerated in January, helping lower the unemployment rate to 7.1% from 7.3% in December. But Clinton called the increase in jobs insufficient, and his labor chief said the administration is likely to proceed with plans to stimulate the economy.

The Fed ended in December its predisposition toward lower interest rates, citing positive economic signs.

10 The Big Three U.S. auto makers said they won't file trade complaints accusing their Japanese rivals of selling cars in the U.S. at unfairly low prices. The about-face reflects a concern that such an action would paint Detroit as anti-consumer. The U.S. companies also want to give Clinton time to develop a trade policy.

The dollar tumbled 2% against the yen on speculation that trade-related political pressure would force Japan to act to strengthen its currency as a way to reduce the nation's trade surplus. Tokyo stocks tumbled 1.5% Tuesday.

Home prices rose sharply in the fourth quarter in parts of the Northwest and the Southwest, but continued to fall in New England and California. Prices rose an average of 4.3% in the 125 largest U.S. metropolitan areas.

11 General Motors scored a public relations triumph in the settlement of its suit against NBC over the network's report on exploding gas tanks in GM pickup trucks. In an embarrassing concession, NBC said it erred by using "igniters" in its staged crashes. The General Electric unit is paying GM the roughly $2 million it incurred investigating the report.

GM's three nonautomotive subsidiaries posted a 37% increase in their combined fourth-quarter profit.

Ford posted a fourth-quarter loss of $840 million, as one-time charges and high marketing costs offset the benefits of a surge in U.S. sales. For the year, Ford had a loss of $7.4 billion, a record for any U.S. company. GM is expected to break that record today.

12 General Motors posted a $651.8 million fourth-quarter loss and a world record $23.5 billion deficit for the year. But excluding one-time charges, GM was in the black as its operating performance rebounded sharply despite more conservative accounting. The auto maker hailed what it called the start of a turnaround. GM's stock jumped $1.25 to $40.50.

Retail sales edged up 0.3% in January after a revised 0.8% gain in December. But analysts said the slower rate of increase isn't disturbing.

16 Corporate earnings soared 62% in the fourth quarter from a year earlier, according to a *Wall Street Journal* survey. The results were better than analysts expected, leading many to raise their estimates for 1993 profits and possibly easing fears that stock prices are too high. But stocks sank Friday.

Producer prices rose 0.2% last month after a 0.1% increase in December. Analysts said the data indicate inflation still isn't a problem. Separately, a private index of consumer confidence moved little this month.

Bond prices rallied Friday, lowering the benchmark 30-year Treasury bond's yield to 7.12%, a six-year low. A growing number of money managers contend rates could drop below 7%.

17 Stocks plummeted amid fears that higher taxes could choke off the economic recovery. The Dow Jones Industrial Average fell 82.94 points, or 2.44%, to 3309.49, its biggest one-day point decline since November 15, 1991. The S&P 500-stock index lost 10.67, or 2.40%, while the Nasdaq Composite Index fell 25.15 points to 665.39, its worst decline since October 26, 1987. The Treasury's 30-year bond slipped less than a quarter of a point, or $2.50 for each $1,000 face amount. Shorter-term Treasury issues rose modestly. But the dollar fell.

Drug stocks tumbled in the wake of the president's attack on the pharmaceutical industry. Merck skidded 2½ points, or 6.2%, to 37⅞, and Pfizer plunged 4⅛, or 6.4%, to 60⅛.

OPEC oil ministers agreed to reduce the flow of oil to world markets March 1 in a move intended to support prices. But the plan was met by skepticism in the oil markets, where crude oil futures prices for March delivery fell 45 cents a barrel to $19.53 on the New York Mercantile Exchange.

18 Clinton proposed tax increases for most Americans to pay for new programs and to trim the budget deficit. The package would hit the rich hard, but wouldn't raise the capital-gains tax rate. The top marginal rate for individuals would rise to 36% from 31%, while those with taxable income of more than $250,000 would be subject to a 10% surtax. The plan also would levy a broad tax on energy. Clinton also proposed a major expansion of the earned income tax credit.

The plan calls for $16 billion in extra spending in the current fiscal year, but $138 billion less over the next four years. Clinton proposes cutting defense spending by about $76 billion over four years, and health-care and other mandatory spending by another $76 billion. Analysts said the plan may not lead to sustained growth.

Housing starts fell 7.2% in January after a revised 4.8% rise in December. The chief economist for the Mortgage Bankers Association said the January report could signal that the housing pickup is "petering out."

OPEC's agreement to cut production reflects a goal by Saudi Arabia for oil prices in a range of $18 to $22 a barrel. Crude oil futures prices for March delivery fell 20 cents to $19.33.

19 Bond prices surged as investors bet that Clinton's economic plan will either push the economy back into recession or significantly reduce the budget deficit. Stock prices and the dollar ended mixed, reflecting confusion about the effects of the plan. The Dow Jones industrials fell 10 points to 3302.19 after a wild day that saw an 80-point swing from peak to trough.

Consumer prices jumped 0.5% in January, their biggest rise in two years. The Fed, meantime, said industrial production rose 0.4% in January, its fourth straight monthly increase. New claims for unemployment benefits fell for the third week in a row.

Boeing plans to slash its payroll by 28,000 jobs, or 20%, through 1994. Most of the reductions, which exceeded analysts' expectations, will come during the summer and fall of this year.

22 Bentsen said Clinton is willing to consider delaying higher personal income taxes to protect the economy, but said

he doubts that will be necessary. The president's plan calls for higher income-tax rates for upper-income Americans to be retroactive to January 1. Bentsen said some Democrats fear that could interfere with Clinton's goal of creating 500,000 jobs.

Greenspan generally praised the president's deficit-reduction plan, but wouldn't say if the Fed will keep interest rates low if it is adopted. Clinton also must get Congress to redirect billions toward public investments.

The dollar fell to a post-World War II low of 118.20 yen after Bentsen said he would like to see a stronger yen. But analysts said the dollar should firm once current speculation subsides.

The yield declined to 7% on the Treasury's 30-year bond, the lowest since 1977. Stocks rose, with the Dow Jones industrials climbing 19.99 points to 3322.18. Energy stocks moved up but health-care issues lost more ground.

23 Clinton unveiled an industrial policy in which the government would explicitly back the development of commercially useful technology. The president's plan would shift billions of dollars from military research to civilian purposes, and also fund a variety of projects in manufacturing, next-generation automobiles and computer networks.

The president's tax package appears to give a big boost to capital-intensive companies rather than to the service sector, causing worry that the plan won't generate 500,000 new jobs. Meantime, some new Democratic congressmen expressed concern about the absence of deeper budget cuts.

A sharp bond market rally sent interest rates plunging. The yield on the Treasury's 30-year bond fell to 6.93%, its lowest level in 15 years. Stocks were mixed, with the Dow Jones industrials climbing 20.81 points to 3342.99. But over-the-counter issues tumbled.

Synergen shares fell 68% on news of disappointing results of a major trial of its flagship drug Antril. It was the third time a biotech company has failed to prove broad effectiveness for an experimental treatment for sepsis, an often-lethal blood infection.

24 Bond yields fell as investors rushed to embrace Clinton's economic package. The yield on the Treasury's benchmark 30-year bond skidded to a record low 6.82%, partly reflecting a sharp drop in consumer confidence. Stock prices fell, with the Dow Jones industrials tumbling 19.72 to 3323.27. The dollar was mixed.

The Conference Board's report showed that consumer confidence in February fell to 68.5 from 76.7. But the report was based on a survey taken prior to Clinton's economic address to Congress, and may not reflect the public's favorable reaction to the speech.

Nissan said it will shut one of its plants, apparently the first closing ever of a Japanese car facility. Further reflecting the nation's slump, Matsushita Electric said pretax profit fell 60% in the latest quarter, while NTT may cut 13% of its work force.

Clinton plans to announce soon a series of bank regulatory initiatives to ease the credit crunch, particularly for small businesses. No details were provided, but officials said the changes will focus on how loans are classified.

25 The bond rally stalled, leaving prices sharply lower. The Treasury's benchmark 30-year issue fell ¾ point, pushing the yield up to 6.89%. Stock prices surged, with the Dow Jones industrials climbing 33.23 to 3356.50, as bargain-hunters bought health-care issues. The dollar rose.

The recent tumble in long-term interest rates, if sustained, could give the economy a more powerful lift than Clinton's spending programs.

New-vehicle sales rose in mid-February, although some dealers reported a falloff in showroom traffic after Clinton outlined his plan to raise taxes.

Durable goods orders slipped 1.7% in January, but analysts said the manufacturing sector was still improving.

26 EC ministers backed a plan to restructure Europe's steel industry by slashing excess capacity through cuts agreed upon by the steel companies.

March 1993

1 Bentsen collected plaudits for Clinton's economic policies at the weekend Group of Seven meeting. But he came away without any tangible steps toward lower German interest rates or increased Japanese government spending. Officials said the Treasury secretary succeeded in laying the groundwork for more progress at a July economic summit in Tokyo.

The dollar rose against the yen early Monday, gaining strength from an emphasis at the meeting on fiscal policy, rather than on a stronger yen, as a way to lift Japan's economy.

New York's commodity exchanges plan to resume trading today despite the explosion at the World Trade Center, where the exchanges are housed. Although some trading will begin later than usual, officials said exchange facilities weren't damaged by the blast.

Stock prices rose Friday, despite the explosion which damped trading activity. The Dow Jones industrials climbed 5.67 points to 3370.81.

The Treasury lowered the guaranteed minimum rate on U.S. Savings Bonds to 4% from 6%, effective with sales today. The change removes one of the most attractive interest rates available to ordinary investors.

Machine-tool orders fell 15% to $175.3 million in January amid concern over the economy and the proposed investment tax credit.

The economy grew in the fourth quarter at its strongest pace in five years. Gross domestic product expanded at an annual rate of 4.8%, but many analysts said Clinton's stimulus plan is still needed to create jobs.

Budget Director Panetta said the plan must clear Congress in the next five weeks if it is to generate the 500,000 jobs the administration promised.

2 Manufacturing activity grew at a slower pace in February, a purchasing group said. Separately, the government said construction spending eased 1.3% in January. Disposable income was unchanged in January while Americans spent 0.1% less on goods and services.

Single-family home sales fell 6.4% in January from December, but brokers said the market remains strong.

Canada's economic recovery accelerated in the fourth quarter. Gross domestic product rose at a 3.5% pace, up from 1.2% in the third quarter.

RJR Nabisco is expected to announce today plans to create a separate class of stock tied to the performance of its Nabisco food business.

Bond prices rose, with the Treasury's 30-year issue climbing ⅝ point to yield 6.84%. The Dow Jones industrials fell 15.40 to 3355.41 in heavy trading. The dollar gained ground.

Corporate health costs rose 10.1% in 1992, reflecting managed care programs, a new survey says. It was the lowest rate of increase in five years.

3 Leading economic indicators rose 0.1% in January, indicating the recovery will continue to be slow. New-home sales plummeted 13.8% in January, the biggest decline in 11 years. An industry spokesman cited bad weather and abnormally high sales in December.

Ford and GM face tougher times in Europe. Total industry sales there are expected to fall by more than one million vehicles, or 8%, this year, putting pressure on both U.S. auto makers.

4 Car and truck sales slumped in late February, apparently reflecting uncertainty over Clinton's economic plan. But Ford and Chrysler continued to pick up market share in February from Japanese auto makers, whose steady gains at the expense of U.S. manufacturers may be over.

Mazda and Ford decided against building cars together in Europe, another setback to Mazda's expansion plans. Mazda is 25% owned by Ford.

Bond prices surged, with the Treasury's 30-year issue rising ¾ point to yield 6.78%. Stocks posted moderate gains. The Dow Jones industrials rose 3.51 to 3404.04. The dollar was mixed.

London stocks rallied 1.3% to a record, partly on optimism about Britain's growth prospects. The Financial Times-Stock Exchange 100-share index climbed 36.3 points to 2918.6.

GM said 16,500 hourly workers, more than double the original estimate, took early retirement. The move will save the auto maker about $1 billion in annual employment costs.

5 Bond prices surged and interest rates fell to record lows, as more investors became convinced that lower inflation is here to stay. The Treasury's benchmark 30-year bond rose nearly ¾ point, or $7.50 for a bond with $1,000 face value, as its yield tumbled to 6.73%. Many investors now believe that a 6.5% yield on the 30-year Treasury bond is possible.

Stock market indexes fell, with the Dow Jones Industrial Average slipping 5.13 points to 3398.91. The dollar declined against the mark, reflecting disappointment that Germany's central bank didn't cut interest rates.

New factory orders slipped 1.3% in January, suggesting a more subdued pace of economic growth. The Labor Department said 351,000 people filed first-time claims for unemployment benefits in the week ended February 20, up 26,000 from a week earlier. Separately, new construction rose 7% in January.

Retail sales rose a slim 1% in February at stores open at least one year, ending a string of strong monthly sales gains. Analysts blamed inclement weather and consumer wariness about Clinton's economic proposals.

8 The unemployment rate fell to 7% last month from 7.1% in January. The surprisingly strong jobs report suggests the U.S. economy is now in a solid recovery, but that businesses are still tentative about the future.

Stocks surged on the jobs data but fell back to close mixed, with the Dow Jones Industrial Average gaining 5.67 points to 3404.58. Bond prices finished generally with small losses.

Germany's central bank eased monetary policy unexpectedly by cutting the interest rate on a key open-market financing instrument. The move is a cautious signal that other reductions may follow as that nation's recession deepens.

The dollar rose sharply in reaction to the German rate cut. Separately, speculators are betting that France's conservative opposition, expected to win in the coming elections, will abandon Europe's exchange rate mechanism and devalue the franc.

9 U.S. steelmakers are planning July price increases averaging 5%, marking the industry's third effort at higher prices in as many quarters. The move is the latest effort by companies in a variety of industries to firm prices.

Du Pont intends to phase out U.S. production of chlorofluorocarbons, which destroy the ozone layer, by the end of 1994, a year ahead of schedule.

10 Drug industry officials said they made several concessions in an unpublicized meeting with top White House staffers Monday. The drug executives agreed, for the first time, to go along with new laws that would monitor and enforce voluntary controls on prescription drug prices.

11 New England and the Far West, two of the weakest economic regions of the country, are showing some signs of growth, according to a survey of the 12 Federal Reserve district banks.

12 Primerica's purchase of Shearson Lehman Brothers' brokerage operations for about $1 billion in cash and securities was approved by the boards of Primerica and Shearson's parent, American Express, people familiar with the matter said. S&P and Moody's have raised no objections to the deal, said executives familiar with the credit-rating agencies.

OPEC has cut oil output sharply, suggesting that prices eventually may rise. Outside monitors say early signs indicate production this month already may be down more than the oil ministers pledged in February.

Retail sales rose a modest 0.3% in February, another sign that consumer spending has slowed from its year-end pickup. Initial claims for unemployment insurance rose to a four-month high in the week ended February 27.

Most stock prices dropped on the economic news. The Dow Jones industrials slid 21.34 to 3457.00. Bond prices declined, and the dollar weakened.

15 The pharmaceutical industry proposed to the government a voluntary program under which each drug company's annual average price increase would be limited to the inflation rate. The plan is part of an industry effort to fend off mandatory price controls.

American Express and Primerica announced the $1.15 billion sale of American Express's Shearson unit to Primerica, which will merge its Smith Barney unit with Shearson, creating a securities firm matched only by Merrill Lynch. The deal could lead rivals to merge as well or to focus on niches.

The proceeds from the sale will help bolster American Express's balance sheet and let it move faster in revamping its charge-card business.

Producer prices jumped 0.4% in February from January, the largest increase since 1990. But economists said the increase wasn't enough to warrant panic about inflation.

Stock and bond prices sank in the wake of the price report. The Dow Jones industrials dropped 29.18 points to 3427.82. Long-term Treasury bond prices fell more than 1¼ points.

The U.S. trade chief said the government expects to block European companies from winning certain federal contracts because the EC hasn't agreed to drop "Buy Europe" rules.

16 Bond prices slumped further amid inflation fears fed by surging commodity prices. Stocks posted gains. The Dow Jones industrials climbed 14.59 points to 3442.41 in light trading. Bond prices dropped more than ⅜ point.

17 The U.S. imposed unexpectedly small

duties on computer chips made in South Korea, in a setback to Micron Technology, Texas Instruments and other U.S. makers of certain chips.

Mutual funds would be allowed to sell shares through newspaper ads and mailings without first giving customers a prospectus, under rules expected to be proposed by the SEC.

18 Consumer prices climbed 0.3% in February, adding to worry that inflation may be accelerating. Excluding food and energy, prices rose 0.5%. But analysts said it is too soon to conclude that inflation is returning to a level that could threaten economic growth. Separately, industrial production increased 0.4% in February, marking its fifth advance in a row.

Bond prices edged up as traders apparently concluded inflation is still under control, while stocks slid and the dollar was mixed. The Dow Jones industrials fell 16.21 points to 3426.74. The benchmark 30-year Treasury bond's price rose less than ⅛ point.

House Democrats predicted Clinton's $16 billion-plus stimulus bill is certain to be passed without amendments sought by conservatives to require additional cuts in spending.

Foreigners withdrew $3.95 billion more from direct investments in the U.S. last year than they put in. The net withdrawal, the first in decades, was more than offset by other foreign investments, such as corporate and government debt and bank deposits.

Tokyo stocks jumped 1.1% Wednesday to their highest level in six months, spurred by a rally in telecommunications stocks. The Nikkei Index climbed 205.07 points to 18173.37.

19 Bond prices surged, pushing up blue-chip stocks, as inflation fears waned. The dollar tumbled to a post-World War II low against the yen. The Dow Jones industrials rose 38.90 points to 3465.64, but Nasdaq stocks rose only slightly. The 30-year Treasury bond's price rose nearly 1⅛ points. Its yield fell to 6.78%.

Tokyo stocks jumped 3.1% Thursday, for a two-week advance of 12%, signaling that the market may have pulled out of its three-year plunge. But much of the climb has been orchestrated by the Japanese government.

Germany's central bank cut its discount rate to 7.5% from 8% in a move to combat the nation's deepening recession. But the more closely watched Lombard rate was left unchanged. European stocks had little reaction.

22 NBC is forcing the departure of four employees who were involved in the broadcast of a staged explosion of a pickup truck, insiders said.

23 European stocks sank in reaction to Moscow's political turmoil as well as to domestic economic worries. Equity prices slid 2.2% in Germany and 1.2% in France and Britain. In the U.S., stocks fell slightly while bond prices advanced. The Dow Jones industrials slipped 8.10 points to 3463.48. The dollar ended mixed.

Detroit's car makers won a promise from the head of the EPA to consider altering fuel economy rules the industry has fought for years. Auto executives were pleased by the environmental official's conciliatory signals.

24 Clinton assailed Japan for keeping its markets closed to the U.S., and indicated he is prepared to raise tariffs on Japanese goods, such as minivans, until the trade barriers are reduced. U.S. trade officials are urging Clinton to use tariffs as a bargaining chip to obtain concessions from Japan.

A Senate panel approved Clinton's $16 billion-plus spending program to aid the economy as the White House moved to shore up the plan's support. Meanwhile, some lawmakers questioned the wisdom of the president's proposed investment tax credits.

25 Orders for durable goods rose 2.2% in February, resuming an upward trend after falling 2.3% in January. But much of last month's gain came from transportation orders, which vary widely from month to month.

26 The SEC is taking a tough stance in enforcing its new executive-pay disclosure rules. The agency says many companies aren't giving shareholders enough detail to justify pay levels. Some consultants think the SEC may end up tightening the reporting rules.

Former Chrysler Chairman Lee Iacocca received $11 million in salary and stock awards last year, more than triple his compensation in 1991.

IBM's credit rating was lowered two notches by Moody's amid gloomy forecasts for mainframe computers.

Sales of existing homes sank 6% in February from the month before. Analysts blamed bad weather on both coasts for the unexpected slowdown. But sales last month were still 2.6% higher than they were a year earlier.

30 U.S. trade officials delayed for at least three weeks the imposition of sanctions on the EC, but said difficult talks remain in a bid to avert a trade war over government contracts. The U.S. described the EC's latest offer as constructive but not yet acceptable.

31 Consumer confidence fell in March for the third straight month, raising concern that the economic recovery may stall. But confidence remains far above last year's low levels. Jobs are the chief concern among consumers.

Stocks slumped on the consumer confidence report but rebounded to finish slightly higher. The dollar lost ground and bond prices were mixed. Over-the-counter stocks rose sharply.

IBM agreed to pay its new chairman and CEO, Louis Gerstner, $2 million in salary this year plus a $1.5 million bonus if he reaches certain performance goals. IBM is also giving Gerstner a one-time $5 million payment to reimburse him for benefits he gave up by leaving RJR Nabisco.

April 1993

1 The House and Senate moved toward quick approval of Clinton's plan to cut the budget deficit by $496 billion over five years while increasing spending on long-term "investments" in the economy. But the lawmakers' negotiations suggested that carrying out the deficit-cutting plan will be harder than adopting it.

U.S. companies sold a record $262.4 billion in stocks and bonds in the first quarter, up 18% from a year earlier. Bonds accounted for 47% of the new issues, reflecting low interest rates. Merrill Lynch was once again the No. 1 underwriter of stock and bond issues.

The volume of new mortgage-backed bond issues fell 6% in the first quarter from a year earlier as institutional investors turned away from the once fast-growing market sector.

Factory orders jumped 1.4% in February, their fourth increase in six months. The index of leading indicators, meanwhile, rose 0.5% in February after no change in January.

A U.S. trade report charged Japan and other nations with erecting unfair trade barriers, but tempered the criticism with relatively gentle language.

Separately, Canada imposed levies on additional imports of steel products.

2 The factory sector's growth slowed for the second consecutive month in March after reaching a four-year high in January, according to a survey of corporate purchasing managers. Separately, initial claims for unemployment benefits increased last week.

The dollar slid to another record low against the yen in the wake of the weak economic data while bond prices slumped and stocks ended mixed. The 30-year Treasury bond's price dropped ½ point, lifting its yield to 6.96%.

Lumber futures sank for a second day, signaling the end of a four-month rally that lifted prices 150% and sharply increased trading volume. The market shift reflects stalled home building and fears of changes in U.S. policy on logging or wood exports.

The FCC adopted a regulatory formula for cable TV rates that could lower prices by $1 billion, or more than 10% for some consumers. Cable operators criticized the action. But consumer advocates said steeper cuts would be justified, and the FCC said its move was only a first step.

The three main TV networks won the right to take a share of the proceeds from syndicating the programs they show. Hollywood studios complained the FCC's reversal could destroy independent producers. The networks weren't entirely happy either.

5 Philip Morris is cutting the price of Marlboro cigarettes by up to 20% and plans to forgo increases on other major brands while expanding distribution of discount brands. The moves, reflecting a decline in brand loyalty, could slash the company's tobacco profit by 40%. Its stock plummeted $14.75, or 23%, to $49.375. Other tobacco stocks also tumbled.

Stocks plunged, triggered by sliding tobacco shares and a weak employment report, while bond prices sank. The Dow Jones industrials fell 68.63 points, or 2%, to 3370.81. The benchmark 30-year Treasury bond's price lost more than a point, sending the yield over 7% to finish at 7.06%.

Stock mutual funds posted gains averaging 3.29% for the first quarter, trailing the S&P 500 index's 4.36% total return. Bond funds gained 3.96%.

Payrolls shrank last month while unemployment held steady at 7%, in another sign that economic growth has slowed considerably. Clinton aides said the data demonstrated the need for a stimulus package. Hourly earnings, meanwhile, climbed 0.5%.

Congress postponed its spring recess as Senate Democrats failed to break a Republican filibuster blocking passage of the White House's $16.3 billion economic stimulus proposal.

6 Brand-name companies' stocks tumbled on concerns that an erosion of buyer loyalty will spread from tobacco to food and other consumer goods. Campbell Soup, Dole, Heinz, P&G and Colgate all posted sharp declines.

Sales of U.S.-built cars and light trucks rebounded in late March, despite a reported decline in consumer confidence. The data could add to confusion over the economy's health. GM's market share slid further.

Tokyo stocks rallied further Monday, sending the Nikkei Index up 312.52 points, or 1.6%, to 19759.46. In London, share prices slumped 1.1%.

8 Accounting rule makers took steps to force businesses to deduct the value of employee stock options from their earnings. But in a concession to critics of the rule, the officials won't implement it until 1997 at the earliest. The change comes amid a public outcry over high compensation levels for some executives.

Tokyo stocks rebounded Wednesday. The Nikkei climbed 342.43 points, or 1.8%, to 19829.23, up 18% in the past month. London share prices fell.

Japanese officials expressed concern that stocks have risen higher than warranted by economic factors. They fear another market plunge.

9 Producer prices rose 0.4% in March, the same as in February. But excluding the volatile food and energy sectors, prices increased 0.1%, after jumping 0.3% the month before. The latest figures may help quell worries about inflation. Separately, U.S. businesses plan to increase capital spending 6.6% this year from 1992.

Bond prices soared on the inflation data as stocks were mixed and the dollar fell to a record low against the yen. The 30-year Treasury bond's price rose 1¼ points. Its yield fell to 6.85%.

12 General Motors was asked by federal regulators to recall 4.7 million pickup trucks with side-mounted gas tanks. Although the auto maker has until the end of the month to issue an official response, it immediately rejected as unwarranted the preliminary request. The recall could cost $200 million to $1 billion. The request, which caught the company by surprise, could give new impetus to dozens of civil lawsuits already filed.

The consumer price index climbed 0.1% in March, tempering fears of increasing inflation after larger rises the previous two months. The rise in the cost of medical care slowed to 0.3% last month from February's 0.5% and was the lowest rate since 1984.

Boeing is negotiating a purchase by China of at least $800 million for wide-bodied aircraft. The talks follow the manufacturer's announcement last week of an order from China of similar value for smaller jets. Boeing, in its announcement, signaled support for China's favored nation status.

Russia's central bank is starting to cooperate more closely with the government to curb hyperinflation, according to Vice Premier Fyodorov. He said Saturday that three central bank officials agreed to a plan aimed at curtailing the growth of bank credits this year. He also said the central bank plans to raise interest rates.

13 Stock and bond prices rallied amid growing optimism that inflation will remain in check. The price of the Treasury's benchmark 30-year bond jumped ¾ point, pushing its yield down to 6.79%. The Dow Jones Industrial Average gained 31.61 points to 3428.09. The Nasdaq Composite Index surged 1.01%. The dollar lost ground.

U.S. manufacturers that have established operations in Europe or pushed exports are now slashing sales and profits estimates amid a slump. The recession also is squeezing companies that rushed to form a presence ahead of a single-market community.

14 Retail sales tumbled 1% last month, the largest drop since January 1991, raising concerns about the recovery's pace. February sales fell 0.3%. March marked the third consecutive month that sales haven't risen. Rain and snowstorms were cited for the latest poor results. Sales fell across all sectors except for drugstores, whose receipts grew 0.5%.

RJR slashed by 73% the proposed total dividend it would pay on new shares representing its separate food and tobacco businesses, amid a slumping market for tobacco stocks.

Accounting rule makers decided to force

banks and insurers to value some bonds held for investment at current market prices. Banks and insurers said the rule will make their financial results more volatile and confusing.

Tokyo stocks surged after the ruling party unveiled a $116.4 billion fiscal package Tuesday. The Nikkei shot up 858.15, or 4.3%, to close above 20000 for the first time in more than a year. Most of the buying came from Japanese institutions and individuals.

Japan's stimulus package drew a muted response from the U.S. government. A U.S. cabinet official in Japan called the plan a "useful first step," but stressed that more is expected.

15 Inventories jumped 0.4% in February, the largest rise in seven months, fueled mostly by a drop in car sales and weak retail sales overall. Analysts said it was too early to draw conclusions from the buildup, which usually augurs slower economic growth.

16 Clinton plans to press Japan to increase purchases of some U.S. manufactured goods, including computers and auto parts, when he meets with Prime Minister Miyazawa today. Clinton is also expected to push for more of an increase in government spending over four years than the Japanese have already announced.

19 Clinton's stimulus package has to be stripped down even further to have any shot at passage, said Sen. Dole, who is leading a GOP snub of Clinton's compromise stimulus plan. Dole said the filibuster still holds, despite Clinton's efforts to win Republican votes by proposing to cut the $16 billion-plus plan by $4 billion. But he said he was willing to allow a separate vote on the part of the plan providing for a jobless aid extension.

Industrial production was stagnant in March, after having shown fairly strong gains since October, raising more questions about the strength of the recovery. Analysts cited a severe snowstorm in the East Coast.

Clinton and Miyazawa's meeting ended with a pledge to choose an agenda for trade talks by the time major nations meet in Tokyo for an economic summit. But contentious trade haggling between the U.S. and Japan is seen lasting for months or years.

The U.S. trade gap widened a bit in February as export growth remained sluggish, reflecting flagging overseas economies. The deficit with Japan was the largest, totaling 73% of the gap.

20 The dollar sank more than 1% against the mark and the yen on the Clinton administration's apparent endorsement of a weaker U.S. currency. Stocks fell while bond prices gained. The Dow Jones industrials fell 11.62 points to 3466.99 in heavy trading.

Tokyo stocks declined as the yen's continued surge hurt shares of Japanese exporters, and economists warned that the yen's strength could hinder Japan's economic recovery. Tokyo is said to seek international cooperation to help stem the yen's rise.

The office vacancy rate rose to 19.9%, a six-year high, in the first quarter in the nation's central business districts, reflecting the weak economy and a wave of corporate consolidations and bank mergers.

21 The Supreme Court ruled that companies may deduct from their taxable income over a number of years the value of certain intangible assets such as lists of customers. The high court's 5–4 decision will especially benefit such industries as publishing, financial services and insurance.

The justices partially shielded employers from litigation accusing them of age discrimination because they interfered with pension benefits.

23 Germany lowered key interest rates amid concern over its deepening recession and foreign pressure for lower rates. The Lombard rate was cut to 8.5% from 9%. The discount rate fell to 7.25% from 7.5%. Other European nations followed with their own rate reductions. European stocks rallied on the rate cuts.

Allstate Insurance plans to let policies lapse for 300,000 homeowners and other customers in Florida, as part of an effort by the Sears unit to reduce its exposure to losses from hurricanes. A state official said Allstate's move will help create an insurance shortage.

26 Orders for durable goods fell 3.7% in March, the biggest drop in 15 months, raising new questions about the vitality of the economic recovery. Machine tool orders jumped 15.7%.

Sales of U.S.-made cars climbed in mid-April, reflecting a rebound by General Motors and continued strong sales for Chrysler and Ford. GM's stock price surged $1.875 to $40.50. Chrysler and Ford shares also rose.

Ford's Explorer sport-utility vehicle recorded a drop in sales, despite strong sales of light trucks overall.

Motorola plans to price a personal-computer chip it is developing with IBM and Apple at less than half the initial price of Intel's newest chip.

27 Gold prices soared for a second day, depressing the bond market, while stocks slumped and the dollar ended mixed. Gold futures gained $6.30 an ounce to $353.80, an eight-month high. The Dow Jones industrials fell 15.42 points to 3398.35 amid sharp declines for bank, insurance and transportation shares. Treasury bond prices lost nearly ½ point.

Sales of existing homes fell 2.9% in March to a nine-month low, reflecting the effects of floods and snowstorms. Analysts said underlying demand in the housing market remains strong.

The world economy remains hesitant and uneven, the IMF said, predicting global growth of 2.2% this year, much less than the 3.6% the agency projected just six months ago.

28 The U.S. sold yen for dollars after the dollar hit a postwar low of 109.33 yen. The Clinton administration's first intervention in the foreign-exchange markets was meant to defuse tensions with Japan on the eve of this week's Group of Seven meeting. In late trading, the dollar stood higher at 111.67 yen and 1.5830 marks, up from 110.55 yen and 1.5688 marks.

Consumer confidence jumped in April, reversing three months of fading optimism. But the latest survey also found 41% of respondents said jobs were hard to get. Separately, workers' wages, benefits and salaries rose 1% in the first quarter, compared with a 0.9% rise in the prior quarter.

The SEC cleared the way for U.S.-registered mutual funds to invest in China's fledgling stock markets, a move likely to be interpreted as a vote of confidence in China's markets.

30 Economic growth slowed to an annual rate of 1.8% in the first quarter from a 4.7% rate in the fourth quarter. The results signaled that the recovery remains disconcertingly tenuous. Much of the latest growth merely reflected an inventory buildup, which could restrain future growth.

Bond prices rallied, lifting stocks, in the wake of the economic data. The Dow Jones industrials climbed 11.62 points to 3425.12 in heavy trading. Treasury bond prices gained ½ point. Gold futures extended their rally.

May 1993

3 Corporate profits from continuing operations climbed 19% in the first quarter, according to a *Wall Street Journal* survey of 578 companies. But the increase fell short of the fourth quarter's 57% gain, in part because of bad weather in the period.

Personal income rose 0.5% in March, but consumers cut their spending by 0.4%, the biggest drop in a year. While many analysts blame the decline on the weather, the report adds to concern about the recovery's pace. Separately, factory orders fell 1.5%.

The U.S. trade chief threatened retaliation against Japan for allegedly discriminating against U.S. construction and supercomputer companies. The move is part of an effort to obtain Japanese trade concessions by July.

Chrysler raised prices on most of its best-selling cars and trucks, in the second round of price increases by the auto maker during this model year.

4 The factory sector shrank in April, marking its first contraction in seven months, a survey of purchasing managers indicated. The report, which depicted a broad deterioration, aggravated worries about the industrial economy's health. Separately, construction spending dropped 1.7% in March from February's level.

Bond prices surged on the purchasers' report, boosting stocks, while the dollar declined. The Dow Jones industrials climbed 18.91 points to 3446.46. The price of the Treasury's benchmark 30-year bond jumped more than ⅞ point. Its yield sank to 6.85%.

U.S. investors bought a net $51.5 billion of foreign securities in 1992, a record, up 10% from a year earlier. Stocks, most of them European, accounted for $32.3 billion of the total.

5 The index of leading indicators plunged 1% in March, the biggest drop in 2½ years, adding to signs of a weakening economic recovery. Bad weather may have been partly responsible, but analysts said other factors were probably at work. The Clinton administration said the figures confirm the need for its economic-stimulus and deficit-reducing proposals.

Bond prices surged again on weak economic data and on hopes of a cutback in Treasury bond sales. Prices of big stocks were flat but Nasdaq shares soared. The dollar declined. The 30-year Treasury bond's price jumped ¾ point, lowering its yield to 6.79%.

Some money managers are predicting that the rally in long-term U.S. Treasury bonds is close to an end.

Sales of U.S.-built cars strengthened in late April, raising hopes of a sustained auto industry rebound. Analysts credited warm weather and promotions by dealers for the upturn.

6 The Treasury unveiled plans to slash its sales of 30-year bonds and to stop selling seven-year notes, in a bid to cut costs. The government will instead sell more debt with maturities of three years or less, which carries lower interest rates. Long-term prices edged up on the news, while prices of shorter-term issues fell slightly.

The economy improved somewhat in late March and last month after bad weather knocked it off track, a Fed survey suggested, in contrast with recent signs of a stalling recovery. But the modest rise in economic activity still isn't creating many jobs.

Clinton's business-tax proposals attracted criticism at a House hearing. The Ways and Means panel is expected to modify the energy tax and perhaps drop a tax on overseas royalty income of multinational companies.

Home prices climbed 5.1% in the first quarter in U.S. metro areas, powered by strong demand in the Midwest and parts of the South and West. But housing prices continued to erode in California and in the Northeast.

7 Big retailers posted disappointing sales for April, as cool weather and small tax refunds discouraged consumers from buying spring goods. Sellers of apparel, especially men's clothing, were among the hardest hit.

Labor productivity slipped at a 0.1% annual rate in the first quarter, the first decline in two years, reflecting a drop in consumer demand coupled with rising retail employment.

U.S. defense companies often offer direct financial assistance to help foreign companies export more goods to the U.S. and elsewhere, congressional auditors found. The practice, used to promote sales of weapons overseas, is raising concern in Washington.

Vehicle sales in Japan sank 11% in April, reflecting special factors but also showing that the nation's economic recovery is uncertain. Analysts said a quick sales upturn isn't likely.

10 The unemployment rate remained at 7% in April as uncertainty about the economy and Clinton's tax and health proposals seemed to make employers leery about hiring. Businesses added 119,000 jobs—not enough to boost consumer spending and speed up the recovery, analysts said. The administration, which conceded it may have unwittingly slowed the economy, said the data show the need to expedite a budget plan.

Microsoft's Gates plans to meet Gerstner of IBM to discuss broadening the ties between the two companies. The meeting plans of the two executives, who have never met, come amid signs that a reconciliation between the companies is increasingly possible.

Canada's unemployment rate jumped to 11.4% last month, heightening concern about the strength of the country's recovery. The April figure, up from 11% in March, was the highest rate since December's 11.5%.

13 Producer prices shot up 0.6% last month, the most in 2½ years, raising inflation concerns. Much of the gain came from a weather-related 45% jump in vegetable prices. But even excluding the food and energy sectors, producer prices were up 0.4%, the biggest increase in nearly a year. Bond prices tumbled on the report.

The Dow Jones industrials rose to a record despite rising interest rates, while the dollar gained. The industrial average jumped 13.56 points to 3482.31, but stocks overall were mixed.

Germany's central bank lowered an interest rate, setting the stage for a possible cut next week in the nation's key discount and Lombard rates.

14 Consumer prices jumped 0.4% in April, indicating that inflation is picking up steam faster than economic growth is. Retail sales, meanwhile, climbed 1.2% last month after a 0.8% weather-related drop in March. Analysts said the price pickup is hard to understand given the slow economy.

Stock and bond prices tumbled on the inflation report, while the dollar rose. The Dow Jones industrials sank 34.32 points to 3447.99. The 30-year Treasury bond's price skidded 1¼ points, pushing its yield up to 6.95%. Gold prices and precious-metals stocks rallied on the price data.

European monetary officials devalued the Spanish peseta and the Portuguese escudo in response to speculative pressure on the currencies. Spain's government said the move would allow it to lower interest rates in hopes of aiding the nation's economy.

Sales of U.S.-built cars and light trucks stalled in early May, leaving auto makers unsure about short-term prospects for a solid sales recovery. Sales were up sharply from a year earlier but were down from April's level.

17 Businesses are raising prices significantly despite the slow economy, often for reasons that don't show up in economic textbooks. They include government trade, regulatory and environmental policies, as well as companies' responses to Japanese price increases due to the strong yen.

Production grew 0.1% last month at factories, mines and utilities, after staying flat in March. The main reason for the virtual stagnation, which comes after encouraging growth of 0.3% in January and 0.5% in February, is a 3.6% drop in utilities' output.

The number of companies taking longer to pay bills rose during the first quarter for the first time in six quarters, according to a survey. The figures are a sign that businesses are wary about the pace of the recovery.

18 Bond prices were knocked lower by continuing inflation concerns. The Treasury's benchmark 30-year bond lost three-eighths of a point. Its yield rose to 6.96%, just shy of the psychologically important 7% level. Stocks were mixed and the dollar rose.

The Chicago and New York mercantile exchanges announced plans to jointly develop a standardized system to clear futures trades, marking the first major cooperation between rival futures markets in different cities.

The yen's run-up against the dollar in recent months has focused world attention on the Japanese currency. Central banks around the world are holding more yen in their reserves of foreign currencies than ever before and more foreigners are investing in Japan's financial markets.

19 The yield on Treasury bonds rose above 7% for the first time in more than a month, as interest rates climbed. The price on the benchmark 30-year issue tumbled ⅝ point, pushing its yield to 7.01%. Stock prices were mixed, with the Dow Jones Industrial Average falling 5.54 points to 3444.39 in brisk trading. The dollar rose.

Gold prices soared again to its highest level since January 1991, as investors continued to pour money into the precious-metals markets. Inflation jitters drove the price of gold $8 higher to $376 an ounce, which spurred an increase in silver and platinum prices.

Housing starts increased 6.7% last month from a revised, storm-beset March level. The largest rebound was in the Northeast, where starts jumped 22.6%. The Midwest showed a drop.

Japan's trade surplus soared 44% last month to $10.25 billion, giving the U.S. more grist for its trade battle with Tokyo. The April figure is Japan's 28th consecutive monthly widening. Its surplus with the U.S. widened 23%.

20 The Dow Jones Industrial Average soared 55.64 points, or 1.62%, to a record 3500.03 on the ninth-heaviest trading day ever on the Big Board. Bonds reversed a recent slide to end substantially higher, with the Treasury's 30-year bond price rising nearly five-eighths point and its yield falling back below 7%. Big swings in the stock and bond markets throughout the day were attributed to rapidly shifting perceptions of inflation.

The U.S. trade deficit deteriorated to $10.21 billion in March, the widest gap in nearly four years. The figure stems from an import surge, which analysts say can't be sustained. February's deficit was $7.91 billion.

U.S. oil production is falling faster than expected, and petroleum imports are rising as a result, a report says. Most of the import rise stems from deteriorating domestic supplies rather than strong growth in consumption.

24 Federal Reserve officials voted to lean toward higher short-term interest rates at their closed-door meeting last week, people familiar with the Fed's deliberations said. The shift doesn't mean an increase in rates is imminent, but it underscores the Fed's concerns about signs of growing inflationary pressures despite the economy's uncertain strength.

Owners of the four high-definition television systems competing to be the U.S. standard reached a tentative agreement to combine their systems, said people close to the talks. The owners decided on ways to blend their technologies and split licensing fees.

The U.S., Canada and Mexico reported serious differences in negotiations to reach labor and environmental side accords to the planned North American Free Trade Agreement.

25 House Democrats are urging a delay until next month of this week's vote on

Clinton's deficit-reduction program, amid increasing nervousness after a weekend of media attention to the dangers ahead for the bill in the Senate and Senator Boren's opposition to the proposed energy tax. But House leaders insisted the vote would take place as scheduled.

Only 20% of investors in a survey say they expect business conditions to improve during the next few months, down from 50% in January. Still, 56% of those polled expect to buy stocks and stock mutual funds over the period.

Employers may not contribute property, instead of money, to retirement plans under the federal pension-protection law, the high court said. The court said employers might overvalue the property and shortchange retirees and the IRS, which allows deductions of the value of contributions.

26 Consumer confidence plunged in May to its lowest level since just before the president's election, raising further concerns about the economy. Except for a small rise in April, the confidence index has seen a fairly steady fall since the first of the year.

Sales of U.S.-built cars surged in mid-May to the highest level this year, with nearly every auto maker reporting big jumps from a year earlier.

Sales of existing homes rose a moderate 2.7% in April from the prior month, reversing a three-month slide due to unusually wet weather.

27 Orders for durable goods were flat last month, in another sign that the manufacturing industry is in a rut. The weak performance in April comes after a decline of 3.7% in March.

Stocks soared, partly boosted by surging bond prices. The Dow Jones Industrial Average jumped 23.53 points to a record 3540.16. The benchmark 30-year issue's price climbed more than 1⅛ points, sending its yield down to 6.92%. The dollar dropped to another record low against the yen.

28 Chevron plans to sell nearly a third of its domestic refining capacity, drastically pruning its profile in oil products and emphasizing its Gulf of Mexico and West Coast operations. The U.S.'s largest petroleum refiner and marketer said it will take a $550 million charge in connection with its plans. The company's stock jumped $3.75, or 4.4%, to $88.625, on the news.

Ford Motor announced its third price increase of the 1993 model year, and the second in just four months, putting the base prices of its hottest models as much as $360 more than their introductory prices last fall. But analysts say the car maker's latest boost will hardly affect sales.

Toyota dominated once again the widely watched J. D. Power & Associates quality survey for 1993 cars, despite Detroit's claim that it has closed the quality gap with Japan. Still, GM and Ford both received overall quality scores higher than all but the three largest Japanese auto makers.

June 1993

1 The economy grew at a revised 0.9% annual rate in the first quarter. After such sluggish growth, analysts predict the current period will be better. While the tax increase passed by the House may put a damper on some spending, enactment of the bill could also have a positive effect by lifting the climate of uncertainty. The rate of first-quarter growth had originally been reported at 1.8%.

2 Manufacturing expanded in May after a disappointing setback the month before, according to a survey of purchasing executives. Separately, the Commerce Department said Americans spent more and made less in April. It also said new construction spending declined 1.5% in April.

3 British Telecom agreed to pay $4.3 billion for a 20% stake in MCI as part of a global communications alliance. The move, which is a blow to AT&T, sets off a battle among phone giants that is expected to spur competition, hasten modernization, cut prices and expand global services. The pact will force governments to open markets to foreign investment and allow alliances with national carriers.

Trade ministers from the U.S., Europe, Canada and Japan saw progress in talks to end a GATT stalemate. European officials said they were particularly encouraged by signs Japan is ready to make further concessions.

The index of leading indicators rose just 0.1% in April, suggesting that economic growth is likely to continue at its sluggish pace. The small rise comes after a 1% plunge in March, which was the largest drop in about two years. Separately, though, sales of new houses soared 22.7% in April.

4 Retail sales at major chains improved a bit in May, though gains for some big retailers were smaller than expected, reflecting consumers' continued worries over the economy. Overall, sales climbed 3.7%, after rising 2.6% in April from a year before.

Sales of North American-made vehicles rose sharply in late May, reflecting a steady recovery to respectable, albeit not boom-year, levels.

Japanese companies understated their U.S.-derived income by more than $500 million on 314 tax returns that were examined last year, according to internal IRS briefing papers.

7 The U.S. joblessness rate eased to 6.9% in May from the 7% level of the prior three months. Despite a decline in manufacturing employment, payrolls grew, suggesting that the economy isn't as weak as many thought.

Interest rates shot up following the jobs report, and stocks ended mixed. The Dow Jones Industrial Average edged up 0.27 point to 3545.14. The Treasury's 30-year bond lost ⅝ point as its yield climbed to 6.91%.

U.S. chip makers said Washington should no longer pressure Japan to open its market. The turnaround by the U.S. companies was accompanied by a declaration of victory in their effort to increase sales in Japan.

U.S. auto makers plan to boost third-quarter output by 17.7% from the year-earlier level, a sign that they believe the recent surge in vehicle sales is sustainable. But some analysts caution that demand in the quarter may not meet industry expectations.

8 OPEC oil ministers began efforts to moderate Kuwait's demands to produce significantly more oil in the third quarter, as they expressed concern that the oil market couldn't absorb much higher supplies. But Kuwait insists it had been promised it would be allowed to produce more oil.

The drop in commercial real-estate values is forcing homeowners to pay higher property taxes, a study shows. From 1989 to 1994, taxes on an average commercial building will drop 25%, and rise 40% for an average home.

Seven multinational oil companies are expected to sign a preliminary pact in Kazakhstan that could lead to the development of a potentially huge oil field in the Caspian Sea.

Employers can reduce treatment costs for job-related injuries by nearly 40% if they send workers to HMOs rather than let workers choose their own doctors, a new study shows.

9 The Clinton administration unveiled a broad, tough agenda for trade talks with Japan, but decided to name former Vice President Walter Mondale the new ambassador to Japan as a way to keep tension between the two countries from getting out of hand.

France dropped its opposition to an oilseeds accord between the EC and the U.S., ending a bitter trans-Atlantic dispute and boosting the prospects for a world trade agreement this year.

Spending by foreign investors to acquire or establish businesses in the U.S. in 1992 fell for the fourth straight year, reflecting weak economic conditions in the U.S. and abroad. Foreign direct investment in the U.S. fell 47% last year to $13.5 billion, the lowest level since 1983's $8.09 billion.

Saudi Arabia and Iran are seeking higher oil prices at the OPEC meeting. Though neither of the two largest producers has officially proposed it yet, they apparently intend to postpone significant increases in output, even though demand for OPEC oil is expected to rise in the third quarter.

11 OPEC agreed to freeze oil production quotas for the third quarter while promising Kuwait a moderate rise in its allotment. But Kuwait rejected the quota and said it would begin increasing its output next month to the level it had sought. Light crude fell 35 cents a barrel to $19.28 on the news.

14 Producer prices were unchanged for May, suggesting that fears of rising inflation are unwarranted. If tomorrow's consumer price report is similarly encouraging, the Fed is likely to hold off on any rise in short-term interest rates. Separately, retail sales grew only 0.1% last month, another hint that the economic recovery remains disappointing.

General Motors' Saturn posted an operating profit for May, the unit's first such profit ever. Saturn said the performance means the company is on track to break even for the year, after a loss of $700 million last year. Saturn workers will receive bonuses of $1,000 each because of the May profit.

Ford cut prices by as much as 15.5% on its big Ford Crown Victoria and Mercury Grand Marquis sedans, apparently reacting to the success of heavily advertised "value" pricing deals on large cars made by GM.

15 Inventories rose 0.1% in April, for the

seventh straight monthly rise. They rose a revised 0.6% in March.

16 Honda Motor is doubling the size of a recall to 1.8 million cars, making the notification its largest ever. The recall of some Accords and Preludes, which are susceptible to a defect that could cause gasoline leaks or fires, comes as the auto maker is struggling with thin profits and sluggish sales.

Sales of cars and light trucks made in North America were up 15.5% in early June from last year, reflecting a steady but not spectacular recovery. Separately, Japanese car prices continued to rise as Nissan lifted prices again, pressured by the surging yen.

U.S. merger activity through Friday rose 29% from the year-ago period. But this year's $68.1 billion in announced deals is running at only about half the rate in 1988, the latest year in which announced deal activity rose.

Consumer prices edged up only 0.1% in May, following a 0.4% increase in April that had resulted in fears that inflation was on the rise. Combined with last week's report that producer prices were unchanged for May, the figures mean the Fed isn't likely to boost interest rates immediately.

Japan's trade surplus edged down 0.1% in May, the first drop in 29 months. But analysts said the figures are probably just a blip and the surplus will continue to grow this year.

17 Housing starts climbed by 2.4% and industrial production rose by 0.2% in May, two signs that the economy continued to grow slowly last month. But many forecasters said they are still looking for it to pick up steam.

Small companies are indirectly charging more through a variety of strategies, instead of raising prices like some bigger competitors. Some are reducing discounts and increasing the purchases required to get them.

18 The U.S. trade deficit widened to $10.49 billion in April, only slightly larger than March's $10.45 billion, but still the largest gap in four years. The April figure reflects continued poor health in some trading partners and moderate domestic economic growth.

The delinquency rate on commercial mortgages held by insurers rose to 7.11% in the first quarter from 6.62% at year end, despite an improving domestic economy and better results in the real estate portfolios of banks.

21 Merck raised prices of 23 of its prescription drugs 4.2%, amid intense public scrutiny over possible price inflation in prescription drugs.

22 The yen continued to drop against the dollar and Tokyo stock prices plunged in the wake of Parliament's vote of no confidence in the Japanese ruling party. The Nikkei Index fell 592.11 points, or 3%, to 19212.43, on the worst day for stocks in more than 10 months. The political tumult could spell months of uncertainty as well as lower share prices.

The dollar's rally against the yen pushed stock and bond prices higher. The Dow Jones industrials jumped 16.05 points to 3510.82. The Treasury 30-year benchmark's price gained nearly 3/8 point. Its yield fell to 6.78%.

Antitrust suits alleging a company slashed prices to hurt a competitor will be tougher to win after a Supreme Court ruling in a cigarette case. The justices rejected Brooke Group's plea to reinstate an award in a suit that charged Brown & Williamson Tobacco with using unfair price-cutting.

Short interest on the New York Stock Exchange rose 4.8% at mid-June to a record level, surpassing the billion-share mark for the second time. The American Stock Exchange's interest also rose to a record, up nearly 10% from the prior month.

GM plans to move some small car production to Michigan from Mexico, pleasing its U.S. unions and proponents of free trade, while doing little harm to workers at the Mexican plant, which is slated to get a new car. The move could put 800 to 1,000 laid-off Michigan employees back to work.

23 Steel imports would be hit with tariffs as high as 109.22% under a Commerce Department action. The move, which is still subject to an ITC ruling, heightens trade tensions between the U.S. and major trading partners. The department's decision was a response to U.S. steelmakers' complaints about dumping and unfair subsidies for foreign producers.

Banks are lowering borrowing costs for large and midsize companies, indicating the credit crunch is easing. The lenders have been prompted by their strong balance sheets and a need to find new sources of earnings.

Home building is among the industries being aggressively targeted by banks for new loans. Bank industry officials attribute the turnabout, primarily, to strengthening housing demand in many parts of the country.

The Clinton administration is scaling back its goals in trade talks with Japan in the wake of the Miyazawa government's fall. U.S. officials believe they had their best chances in areas in which Japan's political leaders had already cut deals with that country's powerful bureaucracy.

Lloyd's of London posted a $4.33 billion loss for its latest reporting year, underscoring worries about the insurance market's future. The loss was due in large part to U.S. claims for asbestosis and pollution coverage.

24 Procter & Gamble will soon begin shrinking its work force by as much as 10%, or 10,000 jobs, in an effort to cut costs. The consumer products giant is struggling with flat prices and the loss of market share in some key areas. The company plans to offer voluntary separation packages to hundreds of salaried workers. Hourly employees could face job cuts.

Durable goods orders fell 1.6% in May. The drop followed declines in April and March and points to further weakness in manufacturing. Meanwhile, the economy grew at a tiny 0.7% annual rate in the first quarter.

Business activity is increasing at a "slow to moderate pace" in most of the nation, the Fed reported. Expectations are generally for slow growth with no major hot spots in the economy.

25 Trade ministers from the U.S., Europe, Canada and Japan failed to reach agreement on the tariff and market-access issues that divide them, casting doubt on their ability to give a lift to the world trade talks.

Personal income rose 0.4% in May after a 0.2% drop in April. However, Americans spent only 0.1% more on goods and services last month. Analysts said consumers remain cautious because of uncertainty over prospective legislation in Congress.

28 Existing-home sales jumped a robust 4.6% in May as the housing recovery continued to regain steam amid continued low interest rates and strengthening employment growth.

29 Stocks rallied after long-term interest rates hit their lowest level in 16 years. The Dow Jones Industrial Average surged 39.31 points to 3530.20. The price of the Treasury's benchmark 30-year bond gained nearly ½ point, while its yield fell to 6.67%, its lowest level since the Treasury began regular auctions of the bond in 1977. A rally among economically sensitive transportation stocks was said to confirm a bright economic outlook.

U.S.–Japanese talks to forge a framework for negotiating trade disputes ended in a stalemate. The collapse makes it unlikely the two sides will reach a pact before leaders of the Group of Seven convene in Tokyo. Officials were unable even to set a date for the next round of U.S.–Japan talks.

Alcoa plans to cut a quarter of its U.S. capacity and lay off 750 workers, or about 2% of its domestic work force, citing a world oversupply of aluminum that shows no signs of easing.

30 DuPont officials knew for at least a decade that their Benlate fungicide can kill or damage plants, company memos and court records indicate. The documents surfaced days before the first of hundreds of damage suits goes to trial against DuPont, which denies that Benlate harms plants.

Consumer confidence dropped in June to the lowest level in eight months, raising concern about how much Americans' spending can rise if their mood is down in the dumps. Separately, the index of leading indicators fell 0.3% in May, following April's 0.2% growth and March's 1% drop.

The inflow into stock mutual funds totaled $9.1 billion in May, down from a record $11.6 billion in April. Some mutual-fund companies say they are seeing strong but lower mutual-fund inflows in June compared with May.

Businesses are continuing to scale back capital-spending plans amid uncertainty and disappointment over Clinton's economic plan, two separate surveys taken recently show. Uncertainty over tax and regulatory implications of Clinton's plan were cited as main causes of the nation's malaise.

July 1993

2 IBM is preparing to announce this month a massive new charge of about $2 billion to pay for slashing its work force by about 50,000 people, twice as many as it predicted last year. The computer firm will need the new charge because its current round of buyouts and layoffs greatly exceeds its previous estimate of 25,000.

Germany's central bank cut interest rates for the fourth time this year, acting on the eve of the Tokyo economic summit and amid calls from abroad that it ease monetary policy. The Bundesbank voted to cut the discount rate to 6.75% from 7.25%, and the Lombard rate to 8.25% from 8.5%.

Europe honed its objections to U.S. trade policies and Russian aid proposals days before the G-7 economic summit in Tokyo, posing new conflicts for efforts to coordinate global recovery. A German official said the U.S. sends mixed signals on trade policies.

Many U.S. executives regard a judge's ruling delaying the North American free trade accord as relatively inconsequential. Chiefly worrisome to the executives is the prospect of a disrupted Mexican economy.

It will probably be more than a month before the government gets an appeals hearing on the judge's decision that has jeopardized Nafta.

Many companies are opting to use excess cash to buy their own shares rather than build new plants. Some buybacks have been by firms whose stock prices have been hurt.

6 The economy will strengthen in 1993's second half but probably won't be sturdy enough to trigger a surge in employment, according to a *Wall Street Journal* semiannual survey of 44 economists. Worried about slumping consumer confidence and the likelihood of higher taxes, business leaders are unlikely to go on a hiring binge, the forecasters said.

Only 13,000 jobs were created in June, the latest sign of economic weakness. That follows a 215,000 rise in May and April's 256,000 gain. The unemployment rate, which had declined to 6.9% in May, returned to 7%.

Clinton vowed to convene a world jobs summit this fall, calling chronic unemployment one of the most vexing problems in the industrialized world. The president said that his purpose at this week's G-7 summit was to create more jobs at home through expanded trade and international cooperation.

International stock funds gained an average 5.26% in the second quarter and 14.56% for 1993's first six months. U.S. stock funds were up 1.29% for the quarter, bringing their year-to-date gain to 4.58%. Taxable bond funds gained 2.61% in the latest quarter.

Car makers plan sizable production rises for the third quarter, reflecting confidence that the industry's budding recovery can gather strength. Overall, General Motors, Chrysler and Ford plan to build 1,091,000 cars in the third quarter, up 20.8% from year-earlier levels, people in the industry say.

7 Apple Computer plans to cut its work force by 16%, or 2,500 workers, as the company seeks to revitalize its earnings in the face of a fierce price war that has wreaked havoc with industry profits and forced Apple to streamline operations. The cuts are expected across the board.

Grain prices soared, leading the biggest single-day commodity price rally in nearly five years. The surge in grain prices, a result of the devastating flooding throughout the Midwest, also boosted prices of precious metals and other commodity markets.

Stock and bond prices fell on renewed inflation fears. The Dow Jones industrials tumbled 34.04 points to 3449.93. The price of the Treasury's benchmark 30-year issue fell nearly ¼ point. Its yield rose to 6.68%.

The U.S. and Japan reconvened trade talks but remained at odds over Clinton's demand that Japan agree to set benchmarks for measuring progress on shrinking its trade surplus. The talks are expected to continue this week as Clinton and Miyazawa meet counterparts from other G-7 nations.

U.S. sales of North American-made cars and trucks rose 6.7% in the late June period, concluding the industry's strongest first half since 1990. But Europe's June car sales plunged 18.4%.

8 Trade negotiators from major industrialized nations agreed to lower tariffs on a range of manufactured products, pushing long-stalled world trade talks a step forward and averting a potentially disastrous deadlock. But the U.S., the European Community and Japan failed to resolve the most contentious issues, which would have required the governments to face down powerful domestic lobbies.

Major banks expect to report another strong quarter as they continue to be helped by sharply lower bad-debt costs and wide profit margins. Banks are expected to report an average 18% net rise for the second quarter, according to a First Boston forecast.

Union militancy appears to be surging, after more than a decade of retreat, but the new activism may just be a last stand for labor. Though membership has shown small gains, it's still shrinking as a portion of workers, to 15.8% last year from 1980's 23%.

9 Big retailers reported mixed sales results for June as consumers concentrated purchasing on home goods and steered clear of apparel, underscoring their cautiousness about spending. Sears and J. C. Penney posted respectable gains, while the Gap and Limited had more disappointing results.

Auto loans in May rose a healthy $1.73 billion, or 7.9% at an annual rate, while credit cards and other revolving credit were up $942 million, or an annual rate of 4.3%, another sign that consumers are borrowing again.

12 The U.S. and Japan agreed on a new framework for bilateral trade talks. The U.S. didn't win a pledge from Japan to set numerical goals for reducing its overall trade surplus or boosting total imports, but did obtain a commitment to use objective criteria to evaluate progress in opening specific Japanese markets.

The Fed confirmed that its policy makers voted to lean toward higher short-term interest rates at their May meeting. Two officials dissented for totally opposite reasons, underscoring the recent difficulty in discerning how serious a threat inflation is.

China raised interest rates and unveiled a plan to tighten central control over the country's banks, as China's economic czar aims at damping speculation and cooling China's economy.

14 General Motors said it will hold price increases on its 1994 vehicles to an average of 1.8%, well below the expected rate of inflation, in an aggressive attempt to raise sales volume.

Damage from record rain and flooding in the Midwest might top $5 billion, possibly depressing retail sales and increasing unemployment across the region this summer, initial economists' estimates indicate.

The Midwestern flooding is expected to put more pressure on lenders to require homeowners in vulnerable areas to have flood insurance.

Producer prices fell 0.3% last month, the second month in a row of encouraging inflation data and further evidence that the spurt in price rises earlier this year was only temporary.

The meager job growth of the first half will continue at a slower pace for the rest of the year as more companies cut staff, the Conference Board said.

Procter & Gamble is slashing prices of liquid laundry detergent, fabric softener and liquid dish soap by as much as 15%, in response to rival brands and private-label competition.

15 A bond rally triggered by two days of reassuring inflation data sent small and large stocks higher. A report showing consumer prices unchanged in June sent the yield on the Treasury's benchmark 30-year issue down to 6.56%. The Nasdaq Composite jumped 4.02 to a record 712.49, while the Dow Jones Industrial Average gained 27.11 to 3542.55.

The consumer price index was unchanged in June after rising a tiny 0.1% the month before, the best back-to-back report on prices in two years. The report was widely interpreted as proof that the inflation rate isn't accelerating, despite a surge early in the year. Retail sales were up 0.4%.

U.S. crude-oil production fell 5.5% to a 35-year low during the first half, and few in the petroleum industry see much chance of a turnaround soon. Imports of crude oil and petroleum products jumped 9.2% in the first half to the highest level since 1990.

Petroleum prices fell more than 60 cents a barrel on hints of a breakthrough in talks between the U.N. and Iraq over a one-time sale of Iraqi oil.

16 Procter & Gamble plans to slash 13,000 jobs, or 12% of its work force, and close 30 plants, reflecting competition from lower-priced and private-label rivals. The cost-cutting moves, P&G's largest ever, will result in a $1.5 billion charge in fiscal 1993. It said it expects a loss for the year.

Inventories rose in May for the eighth consecutive month, climbing 0.2%, but economists don't seem to be worried about the steady increase.

19 Industrial production fell 0.2% last month, signaling that the manufacturing sector is showing no signs of emerging from its protracted slump. Output for May was flat, down from an initial report of a slight increase.

20 The former House postmaster pleaded guilty to embezzlement charges in the cash-for-stamps scandal, a move that could hurt Democrat Rostenkowski at a time when he is focusing on final negotiations shaping Clinton's deficit-cutting plan.

Support for dropping any form of energy tax from the deficit-reduction bill has spread from the House to the Senate, as two senior Democratic senators have begun pushing the idea.

Oil futures initially plunged to three-year lows on renewed indications Iraq may begin exporting crude again soon. But prices rebounded after OPEC announced an emergency meeting to cope with the prospect of Iraq's exports. Some crude futures were up more than 70 cents a barrel.

21 Fed Chairman Greenspan laid the foundation for a move to raise interest rates if the economy continues to strengthen, saying that the inflation news of this year has been disappointing. Greenspan said that, adjusted for inflation, the short-term interest rates that the Fed controls are close to zero and indicated that they can't remain that low indefinitely.

Bond and stock prices fell on Greenspan's comments, but later recovered some of the losses. The Treasury benchmark 30-year issue's price, which had fallen more than half a point, ended over ⅛ point lower.

Sears's net more than tripled in the second quarter, signaling a long-awaited turnaround of retail operations. The company's share price surged $4.125, or 9%, to $50.125, giving a boost to the overall stock market.

The Clinton administration is pressing ahead to complete side deals to the North American Free Trade Agreement in the next few weeks and begin selling the deal in Congress.

Housing starts were flat in June, despite the lowest mortgage-interest rates in more than 20 years.

22 The FTC failed again to reach a conclusion on allegations that Microsoft unfairly uses its dominant market power against competitors. That led the company to declare a qualified victory in the three-year-old investigation. The panel split 2-2 on whether to accept staff recommendations that it take action against Microsoft. The tie vote means the company may continue operating as it has.

Short interest fell slightly on the New York Stock Exchange at mid-July, after a record a month earlier.

France named the first companies to be sold in its privatization plan. The first in the batch will be Banque Nationale de Paris and Rhone-Poulenc.

The Dow Jones industrials climbed 10.62 points to a record 3555.40. But bond prices tumbled on concerns about the deficit reduction package. The price of the Treasury's benchmark 30-year bond plunged more than ⅞ point. Its yield rose to 6.62%.

23 Volkswagen's Lopez was linked directly by German prosecutors to a cache of sensitive General Motors documents found in a German apartment. The prosecutors' link bolsters GM's contention that its former purchasing chief Lopez stole company secrets when he jumped to the German car maker. The prosecutors also said they will widen their probe of suspected industrial espionage to VW.

Fed Chairman Greenspan said that although he doesn't see any major threat of inflation now, the central bank will undoubtedly be forced to raise interest rates in the future. The comments were an attempt to clarify his testimony to a House panel earlier in the week that roiled markets.

Stock prices tumbled on profit-taking and weakness in the bond market, after Greenspan's remarks. The Dow industrials sank 30.18 points to 3525.22. The dollar tumbled against the yen. The price of the Treasury's benchmark 30-year issue fell ⅜ point. The issue's yield increased to 6.65%.

26 IBM's Gerstner appears to have a two-pronged strategy for reviving the ailing computer giant. He is putting the brakes on decentralization, while also encouraging an entrepreneurial spirit. IBM will post second-quarter results tomorrow and is expected to take a charge of $2 billion or more.

Machine-tool orders fell 2.2% in June as orders from auto makers slowed for a second month in a row. Despite the drop, the month's orders were up 46% from a year earlier.

27 Stocks rallied amid hopes that Germany will cut its interest rates when the Bundesbank meets later this week. The Dow Jones industrials jumped 20.96 points to 3567.70, its second record in less than a week. Bond prices also rose. The price of the Treasury's benchmark 30-year issue rose nearly ⅜ point. Its yield fell to 6.67%.

Frankfurt stock prices climbed 1.3% to the highest level since August 1990, amid speculation that Germany will lower exchange rates this week to support the role of the French franc in the European Monetary System.

Sales of existing homes rose 1.9% last month as the national housing recovery maintained a slow but steady momentum, fueled by low interest rates and pent-up consumer demand.

28 IBM announced an $8.9 billion pretax charge and plans to shed 35,000 more

workers and shutter buildings around the world. The computer maker also slashed its dividend in half, its second cut this year, and posted a second-quarter net loss of $8.04 billion. Chairman Gerstner said he believes the latest cuts are finally the last IBM will need. The company's stock rose $3.25, or 7.7%, to $45.625.

U.S. steel companies were dealt a blow when a trade panel cleared foreign steel producers of most pending claims of unfair trading. The decision effectively invalidates last month's average duties of 37% on 20 nations. Bethlehem Steel's stock dropped 21%, and National Steel's fell 27%.

USX reported a $311 million second-quarter loss on a big charge at its U.S. Steel unit, while steel minimill Nucor posted a 75% profit rise.

Consumer confidence fell in July, showing that Americans are still uncertain about the economic future. Separately, though, the employment cost index rose at a slower pace in the latest quarter, indicating that inflation seems to be under control.

29 Merck agreed to buy Medco Containment, the nation's largest marketer of discount prescription medicines, for $6 billion in stock and cash. The acquisition makes Merck by far the biggest integrated producer and distributor of pharmaceuticals. The deal is expected to trigger a wave of alliances and mergers among drug makers and other prescription-drug marketers. Medco's stock price surged $4.375, or 15%, to $34.125.

Orders for durable goods jumped 3.8% last month, the first increase since February, but analysts said the manufacturing sector is still weak.

The U.S. steel industry's defeat by a federal trade panel's decision that foreign rivals are not dumping in the U.S. already has begun to put pressure on steel prices and to ease inflationary fears elsewhere in the economy.

The Clinton administration and steel producers in the U.S. are expected to renew a push to settle trade spats plaguing the world steel market, in the wake of the surprise decision yanking many foreign steel tariffs.

August 1993

2 Foreign-exchange markets braced for another day of turmoil after senior European monetary officials apparently failed to find a cure for the difficulties that pushed Europe's Exchange Rate Mechanism to the brink of collapse. A weekend meeting of finance ministers and central bankers continued well into last night with no sign of concrete progress.

House and Senate leaders hope a conference committee will finish work by tomorrow on a deficit-reduction plan that can be put to a vote in Congress this week. The plan includes a gasoline tax rise of 4.3 cents a gallon.

Boeing is bracing for possible further cuts in jetliner production, depending largely on whether it lands a pivotal order from Saudi Arabia.

3 Crude oil output by OPEC members is rising despite an oversupplied oil market. As a result, the oil market is expected to remain weak, with prices under pressure, at least until the fourth quarter when an increase in petroleum demand normally occurs.

Gold futures hit a record, then fell to settle at $410.20 an ounce, down $1.10 for December, as turmoil in world currency markets spawned a wild day of precious metals trading. Platinum prices surged. Silver fell.

The FDA struck a blow against the drug industry's use of expensive promotions and ad campaigns for doctors, saying they help inflate health-care costs and possibly harm patients.

Europe's turbulent currency markets turned surprisingly calm in the first trading day under the newly loosened monetary system. Several European stock and bond markets rose, some very strongly, on speculation that interest rates will soon fall.

Some U.S. companies expect to be insulated from Europe's tumult by currency hedging and other strategies, but others are taking additional steps to protect their businesses.

4 Airlines based in the U.S. are suspending service on some trans-Atlantic routes, after spending billions of dollars for the right to fly to Europe, signaling that the market probably won't turn around any time soon. AMR's American Airlines carrier said it will suspend service on three European routes this fall.

European central banks seemed to be regaining the upper hand over currency traders for the first time in weeks as calm settled over European currency markets. Europe's weaker currencies regained lost ground on the mark and Germany's central bank cut a key interest rate a bit.

Stocks jumped on many European bourses as rate cuts began to emerge from the foreign-exchange shakeup. Frankfurt shares soared 1.6%, as a rally in bond markets again more than offset bearish effects of the appreciating German currency on equities.

The government's index of leading economic indicators rose a tiny 0.1% in June after falling 0.4% in May, suggesting the future of the economic recovery still looks quite sluggish. Analysts said the weakness in the index reflects weakness in manufacturing.

Business failures in the U.S. fell 9.9% in the first half, reflecting widespread recovery for U.S. businesses. Failures in finance, insurance and real-estate businesses showed the largest decline, decreasing 17.8%.

5 Economic activity continues to expand slowly to moderately across the nation, according to a Federal Reserve survey of its 12 district banks. Most Fed districts reported that manufacturers have not raised employment and don't plan to for the rest of 1993.

6 Gold futures plummeted nearly 6%, in the biggest single-day rout in precious-metals markets since 1991. Platinum and silver prices also sank.

Big retailers reported mixed sales results for last month, as consumers continued to spend selectively. Chains with heavy discounts generally outperformed others in getting shoppers. Retail sales at stores open at least one year increased an average of 5.6%. Home goods sold better than apparel.

Factory orders jumped 2.6% in June, the first rise in four months, but analysts are still wary about the health of the manufacturing sector.

Estimates for world petroleum demand for 1993 were lowered again, this time by 100,000 barrels a day. But some analysts say prices could firm in the fourth quarter because the need for oil from OPEC members remains above OPEC's current output levels.

9 Clinton plans to sign into law his $496 billion deficit-reduction package this week. The bill will raise taxes on the wealthy and corporations, while trimming defense, Medicare and other programs. At the same time, the measure will provide billions of dollars in tax incentives for businesses and the poor. The Senate passed the bill Friday after Gore broke a tie.

The consensus, among some leading forecasters is that Clinton's plan will slightly crimp economic performance in the short run, while providing a modest boost over the long term. The bill gives investors in some small firms a capital-gains tax break.

The economy generated 162,000 new jobs last month, but conditions still suggest the economy is sluggish. Most of the growth was in lower-paying jobs. The unemployment rate fell to 6.8%, but rounding made the drop look larger than it actually was.

London and Paris shares rose sharply to records, as investors continued to hope for lower European interest rates to spur economic rebounds.

10 Cars and light trucks are selling at a record pace in Latin America, thanks to an economic recovery, trade liberalization and lower prices. GM predicts that 1993 sales will shatter the 1980 record of 2.4 million units, marking the sixth yearly rise in a row.

Defense Department audits cited in a government report show a pattern of questionable commissions paid by American companies selling military equipment to Egypt under a U.S.-financed foreign-aid program.

11 Long-term interest rates fell to another 16-year low, as bond prices rose. The price of the Treasury's benchmark 30-year issue gained over ¼ point, while its yield fell to 6.44%.

The productivity of U.S. workers fell in the second quarter, marking the second consecutive three-month drop and raising doubts about whether impressive gains made last year really signaled a long-term trend.

12 Agriculture officials lowered their forecast of the corn crop 5.4% to reflect record rain damage in the Midwest. The deeper-than-expected cut could lift U.S. corn prices today.

France cut interest rates cautiously, in what could be a model for other countries seeking to stimulate economic recovery without capsizing Europe's currency system. European stock prices posted sizable gains.

The Dow Jones industrials rose 10.62 points to a record 3583.35, boosted by strong overseas stock markets and a surge in semiconductor shares. Bond prices rose, sending long-term interest rates to another 16-year low.

13 Producer prices fell 0.2% in July, and retail sales increased 0.1%, suggesting that inflation isn't a problem and that the economy is continuing to grow at

a very moderate pace. The producer price decline, after a 0.3% decrease in June, makes it the first back-to-back decline in two years.

Positive inflation news sparked a bond rally, but long-term bond prices ended lower because of soft demand for the Treasury's long bond sale. Stock prices slumped and gold futures were hammered, falling $8 an ounce.

Exxon's chairman said world oil supplies are tight and prices should rise through the rest of 1993. He predicted the U.N. won't give Iraq permission soon to sell oil, a move that would flood the market and depress prices.

Demand for motor fuel isn't as robust as energy traders think, despite this week's big rally in the gasoline market, according to oil industry figures to be released next week.

16 Trade negotiators for the U.S., Canada and Mexico resolved labor and environmental issues that were stalling the North American free trade pact, but the arrangements seemed to alienate more U.S. lawmakers than they converted. Getting the pact through Congress is likely to require an all-out effort by Clinton, which he doesn't seem ready to make. House Majority Leader Gephardt said he couldn't support the present pact.

Consumer prices edged up 0.1% last month, suggesting that inflation is in check and that a boost in short-term interest rates isn't imminent. While the consumer price report comes on top of other encouraging inflation news, a recent survey found consumer confidence fell again in early August.

The dollar fell to 101.80 yen Friday, its eighth record low in 11 trading days. Traders expect Japan's currency to keep strengthening in the near term, and the so-called parity level of 100 yen to a dollar could come in the currency market this week.

17 Reynolds Metals said it plans to cut capacity by 9%, in an effort to shrink the world-wide aluminum glut. The move, after other cutbacks by Alcoa and some overseas producers, raised the likelihood of a recovery.

The Nasdaq Composite Index rose 8.63 points to a record 726.89, on surging telecommunications stocks. Long-term bond prices rallied sharply, with the Treasury's benchmark 30-year issue soaring almost ⅝ point. Its yield fell to a 16-year low, ending at 6.30%.

The U.S. appears unlikely to act to halt the yen's surge, even as the Japanese currency approaches the 100 yen to a dollar level. The dollar fell to a record 100.80 yen yesterday, but officials in Washington apparently see no reason to be concerned, as long as currency movements remain orderly.

Industrial production rose in July, suggesting the lethargic manufacturing sector is showing signs of growth.

18 Stock prices climbed to record levels as long-battered consumer-growth stocks moved higher. The Dow Jones Industrial Average climbed 7.83 points to a record 3586.98. Bond prices slipped, and the dollar was mixed. The Nasdaq Composite Index rose 4.12 to 731.01, a second consecutive high.

Housing starts fell 2.7% last month, following a revised 0.2% June drop, as low interest rates failed to overcome a persistent reluctance in consumers and an ailing California economy.

19 The Dow broached the 3600 level, amid a plunge in long-term interest rates. The Dow Jones Industrial Average climbed 17.88 points to a record 3604.86. The price of the Treasury's benchmark 30-year bond soared ¾ of a point. Its yield fell to 6.25%, a 16-year low. The Nasdaq Composite Index advanced 3.82 points to 734.83, its third consecutive record.

As stock prices climb steadily, the debate among Wall Street's savviest and best-paid analysts and money managers over where the market goes from here is becoming more heated. Investors have been spending a lot on stocks of companies that until this week had been spurned as risky.

Kodak's chairman said the company will cut 10,000 jobs, or about 8% of its work force, by 1995 and cut spending to increase cash flow. But the move by Whitmore, who was ousted in July and will step down when a successor is named, is viewed as a first step in a plan to be carried out by a successor.

Germany said its recession may have bottomed out in the second quarter, but that outlook was overshadowed by a separate forecast of a sluggish recovery that could eliminate an additional 700,000 jobs by late 1994.

General Electric plans to announce another major round of layoffs at its big jet-engine division near Cincinnati, industry executives said. The layoffs may total as many as 4,000.

20 U.S. exports fell 3.3% in June, helping to widen the U.S. trade deficit to its biggest level in more than five years. Imports climbed 5.1% to a record. The poor results will almost certainly cause the Commerce Department to reduce its estimate for economic growth in the second quarter.

Long-term bond prices rallied, sending interest rates plunging, in response to the trade-deficit report.

24 Wal-Mart sells some products at below cost, but it isn't breaking the law because it isn't trying to destroy competition, Wal-Mart's chief executive said in a predatory pricing trial brought by Arkansas pharmacies.

Japanese car makers in the U.S. have raised the number of U.S.-made parts they use because the yen's rising value makes imports more expensive.

25 Stocks surged to a high, boosted by a rally in economically sensitive issues. Strong gains in heavy machinery and auto stocks helped send the Dow Jones industrials climbing 32.98 points to a record 3638.96. Bond prices also rose, sending long-term interest rates to a 16-year low. The price of the Treasury's benchmark 30-year issue gained nearly ⅜ point. Its yield fell to 6.19%.

Oil production by OPEC members remains high despite sluggish demand, resulting in a rise in inventories that maintains price pressures.

Daimler-Benz's Mercedes plans to eliminate 14,000 jobs from its German operations in 1994, amid a downturn in Europe's car and truck markets.

Honda Motor posted a 55% drop in group pretax profit for the latest quarter, reflecting the effects of the strong yen and a steep decline in car sales.

The selling pace of North American-built cars and light trucks picked up in mid-August, as auto makers used cash incentives to sell 1993 models to make room for newer models.

26 The U.S. imposed on China a package of trade sanctions, but the limited actions don't immediately jeopardize U.S. business plans to cash in on China's economic boom. The move against China, which is accused of selling missile and other weapons technology to Pakistan, mainly blocks the transfer of U.S.-made equipment used in satellites that the U.S. either sells or sends to China for launches.

An influential accounting group is expected to call for a sharp increase in the amount of information companies must disclose in their annual reports, a prospect that is already alarming corporate financial officers.

27 National Medical's facilities were raided by hundreds of agents from the FBI and other U.S. agencies armed with search warrants and subpoenas in a broad investigation of possible criminal misconduct by the hospital operator. The case is the latest sign of the government's heightened interest in fraud and abuse in the health-care industry.

Gold futures prices tumbled nearly $5, and traders said gold appears vulnerable to further declines as investor sentiment seems clearly focused on roaring stock and bond markets.

30 National Medical's policies and directives are being examined by federal agents, who are seeking evidence linking suspected criminal misconduct by many of the firm's hospitals with its top executives. Meanwhile, the company acted to try to restore confidence following Thursday's raid by U.S. agents of more than 20 of its facilities. On August 27th, its stock plunged $3.375, or 30%, to $7.75.

Banks' lending terms seem to be easing, according to a Fed survey. Equally important, the lenders found businesses and households increasingly willing to borrow money.

Mortgage lending to minorities improved last year at many of the nation's biggest banks. However, the disparity between minority and white applicants is still significant.

Machine-tool orders fell 20% in July from June as seasonal plant closings slowed activity, but orders stayed well above the year-earlier level.

Construction contracting declined in July following a surge in June. The retrenchment was seen as a return to a more sustainable level of activity.

31 Bond-fund inflows leaped 22% in July from June to a monthly record of $13 billion, while July's stock-fund inflows rose 5% to $9.7 billion. The gains result from investors accelerating their flight from low-yielding bank deposits and money-market funds.

Two hundred top-paid CFOs received average 25% compensation increases last year as companies recognized their broader talents and moved to keep the headhunters at bay.

Toyota, Nissan and Honda face credit-rating downgrades from S&P, which cited a sharp worsening of industry conditions. Japan's economic slump and the yen's gains against the dollar have hurt the firms' profits.

The oil industry would have to spend a minimum of $166 billion over 20 years to meet environmental rules, a study said. On an annual basis, that amounts to twice the yearly environmental outlays of the industry over the second half of the last decade.

September 1993

1 The economy's recovery is stronger than previously thought and the recession was less severe, according to government statistics. The economy grew at a 2.4% average annual rate from the trough of the recession in 1991 through the second quarter of 1993. Officials had previously put the rate at 2.0%. GDP grew 2.6% in 1992, more than the 2.1% first reported. Job growth seems even weaker now in light of the new GDP numbers.

Consumer confidence slipped in August, according to the Conference Board, wiping out all the gains made since the presidential election.

Kuwait is holding talks with several Western oil companies that could lead to precedent-setting agreements on sharing production in its vast oil fields. The accords would represent a historic reversal of Kuwait's nationalization of its oil fields in 1975.

Chevron got essential Russian government backing for a proposed $1.2 billion pipeline across southern Russia to export oil from the company's giant Tengiz field in Kazakhstan. But despite the progress, big financial, technical and diplomatic hurdles remain.

Many U.S. companies' profits will be cut by a higher-than-expected 33% this year and as much as 45% next year, under a retiree health-benefits accounting rule, a survey shows.

Canada's economy recorded a moderate advance in the April–June period, but job prospects remained bleak for the unemployed. Gross domestic product rose 0.8% in the second quarter, or at an annual rate of 3.4%.

2 The budget deficit will fall to about $180 billion by the end of Clinton's term under the new deficit-reduction law, the White House predicted. The White House also said that despite the disappointing economy so far this year, the basic prognosis for a slow but steady expansion with low inflation remains unchanged. Administration economists expect the economy to grow by 2% this year. For next year, they anticipate 3% growth.

Manufacturing contracted last month for the third month in a row, a purchasing manager's index showed. According to the index, production and new orders did improve a bit, but employment continued to contract.

Stock investors in Europe cashed in on the recent broad run-up in prices. Frankfurt stocks tumbled 1.4%, while Paris's record-setting rally ended as the market lost 1.1%. Madrid plummeted 2.6% and Stockholm fell 1.5%.

3 Toyota raised 1994-model car prices in the U.S. between 2.5% for its cheapest vehicles and a hefty 12.7% for its more expensive cars, reflecting the effects of the strong yen. The Japanese auto maker is also apparently heeding threats from Detroit auto makers that if prices didn't go up substantially, the Big Three would bring on charges of dumping.

Factory orders plunged 2.1% in July, the steepest decline since December 1991, raising more concerns about the strength of the manufacturing sector. Orders rose 2.9% in June.

Big U.S. retailers reported lackluster August sales as the combination of consumer uncertainty, hot weather and full-priced fall apparel kept shoppers away from the nation's malls.

U.S. workers have little loyalty to employers and are deeply divided by race and gender, a survey found. The study, the most comprehensive look so far at employees' lives, also reflects broader-than-expected conflict between work and family life.

Businesses seem considerably more eager to purchase a new piece of equipment than to hire a new employee, amid skyrocketing labor costs compared with equipment costs.

7 Top Clinton advisers are looking for ways to stimulate the economy without widening the deficit, amid a recovery that is shakier than hoped. Meanwhile, employers cut 39,000 jobs in August. But the unemployment rate declined to 6.7% from 6.8% in July.

8 Bond prices rallied, sending long-term interest rates to record lows, while stocks fell. The price of the Treasury's benchmark 30-year issue rose nearly ¾ point, amid a drop in gold and oil prices. Its yield dropped to 5.89%. The Dow Jones industrials tumbled 26.83 points to 3607.10.

Gold futures prices fell sharply on heavy selling by large investors and persistent rumors that European central banks were also selling gold. The December gold contract declined $14.60 to settle at $352.50 an ounce.

Ford Motor's European unit chief said the worst downturn in European car sales in decades may be bottoming out, and he predicted a 1% to 2% upturn in the market for next year.

10 Bond prices plunged after a sell-off that began overseas swept through the U.S. bond market. The price of the Treasury's benchmark 30-year issue fell nearly 1½ points. Its yield rose to 5.96%. Analysts said foreign investors began dumping U.S. bonds overnight on rumors that Congress planned to consider reimposing a 30% withholding tax on foreign investments in U.S. Treasurys.

Clinton health officials will propose that the government absorb most of the cost of providing health benefits for the nation's early retirees, potentially handing a windfall to Big Three car makers and other industries.

Germany's central bank lowered its two key lending rates, triggering a round of interest-rate cuts throughout Europe. The rate reductions were welcome news to both the U.S. and Europe, but the cuts are probably too small to give much stimulus to Europe's recession-hit economies.

Ford plans to raise the base price of 1994-model vehicles from 0.9% on its least expensive vehicles to as much as 13.3% on best-selling F-Series pickups. But Ford cut the price of its Crown Victoria LX by 3.9% in a move to jump-start sales of slower-selling vehicles.

U.S. companies expect to increase capital spending 7.1% this year, a survey taken in July and August shows.

11 Viacom agreed to acquire Paramount Communications for $8.2 billion, a move that would create a multimedia behemoth. But yesterday's accord essentially puts Paramount in play, and there may be other deep-pocketed suitors ready to top Viacom's $69.14-a-share offer. Paramount stock rose $4.25, or 7.5%, to finish at $61.125 in Friday's trading.

Producer prices tumbled 0.6% in August, the fourth consecutive monthly decline and the largest since February 1991. Last month's decline reflected a huge 25.6% drop in tobacco prices, as cigarette makers continue to battle for a shrinking consumer base.

Stocks and bonds rose on the news, with the Dow Jones industrials climbing 32.14 points to 3621.63. The 30-year Treasury bond rose more than 1⅛ points, as its yield fell to 5.88%.

Japan is preparing new measures to pump life back into its economy. Prime Minister Hosokawa called for a $9.49 billion spending package for "new social outlays." Japan's foreign minister sent positive signals about cutting the nation's big trade surplus.

14 DuPont said it will cut 4,500 U.S. jobs, or 3.6% of its world-wide work force, by mid-1994 and plans to trim its European staff over the next year. The company plans a $375 million charge.

Many Japanese companies are selling chunks of stock holdings in other firms or cutting dividends to help meet corporate expenses.

15 American Airlines said it will lay off 5,000 workers this year and ground 19 more jets than originally planned. Robert Crandall, chairman of AMR Corp., American's parent, said labor costs must come down if the carrier is to remain a "viable" competitor. He said he would welcome an employee stake in the company in return for concessions.

USAir slashed ticket prices by 27% to 40% on four North Atlantic routes. The nonrefundable fares are for travel starting November 1. United said it planned similar cuts, while American followed suit on three of the routes.

Clinton launched his campaign to win approval of Nafta, signing labor and environmental deals that provide political cover for supporters. But the moves don't go far enough to win over opponents or to ease fears that Nafta may cost the U.S. millions of jobs.

A new *Wall Street Journal*/NBC News poll found that 36% of Americans surveyed oppose the trade pact, while just 25% approve of the accord.

Retail sales rose at a slower 0.2% pace in August, while consumer prices climbed 0.3% after rising 0.1% in July. However, analysts said the rise in prices last month came mainly from one-time factors. Meanwhile, real average weekly earnings rose 0.8% in August, after rising 0.3% in July.

Bond prices slid on the consumer price data, with the Treasury's 30-year issue falling more than 1⅜ points to yield 5.97%. The Dow Jones industrials tumbled 18.45 points to 3615.76.

Japan's economy shrank at an annual rate of 2% in the second quarter. The government is likely to announce a stimulus package tomorrow. Meantime, Japan also said that its trade surplus widened 7.5% in August.

16 Small manufacturers have turned upbeat about the business outlook for the first time since March, but don't see prices or employment rising anytime soon, a survey found.

Business inventories fell 0.5% in July, the first decline in 10 months and the largest since March 1991.

17 Ford's tentative pact with the UAW represents a setback for General Motors. GM President John Smith had tried to convince union leaders that GM needs fundamental changes in its labor-cost structure to make its U.S. vehicle operations competitive. But those changes aren't included in the Ford pact, which the UAW plans to use as the pattern for contracts with GM and Chrysler.

U.S. auto makers plan to build 12.7% more vehicles in the fourth quarter than a year earlier, a gamble the industry's recovery will strengthen.

Japan unveiled a $58.57 billion spending and deregulation package to spur the economy. But the plan doesn't include an income-tax cut, sought by Japanese business leaders and Washington as a way to boost spending.

Investors reacted negatively, as the Nikkei stock index fell 2.1%, its steepest drop since mid-June, even before the package was announced. The yen climbed against the dollar.

Industrial output climbed 0.2% in August, following a 0.4% rise in July and a revised 0.2% gain in June. Other reports showed that the nation's trade deficit narrowed slightly in July and that claims for unemployment benefits were little changed last week.

20 U S West will lay off 9,000 employees and take $3.8 billion in third-quarter charges as it attempts to turn its telephone network into a modern phone, data and video superhighway.

A special accounting panel is expected today to assert that disclosure in corporate annual reports must be greatly increased to make them relevant to investors and creditors.

Honda will halt exports of its best-selling models to the U.S., another sign the yen's strength is pinching Japanese manufacturers. Honda will sell Accords and Civics made at its North American factories. Separately, Nissan and Mitsubishi plan hefty U.S. price increases on 1994 models.

GM said it sold five parts-making plants employing 6,800 UAW workers. UAW officials are suspicious of the timing of the sale, which came just three days after GM's three-year contract with the union expired.

21 QVC offered $9.5 billion for Paramount, challenging Viacom's $7.5 billion agreement to acquire Paramount and setting the stage for a 1980s-style takeover battle. The battle pits the most powerful moguls in the entertainment industry against each other in a contest for one of the only remaining independent U.S. entertainment and media companies.

The Bank of Japan cut its discount rate to 1.75% from 2.5% in an effort to spur the country's faltering economy and curb the strong yen. The action is sure to please the U.S. government, which wants Japan to stimulate its economy, thereby increasing its appetite for imports of U.S. goods.

More than half of Europe's largest corporations plan to cut their work forces in the next two years, as global competition and high wage rates take their toll, a survey shows.

22 Stocks tumbled amid news that Russian President Yeltsin dissolved Parliament. Long-term bond prices slipped, although shorter-term government notes rose moderately as investors sought a safe harbor. The Dow Jones Industrial Average plunged 38.56 to 3537.24. The dollar rose. Gold futures rose $9.50 to $365 an ounce.

Housing starts jumped 7.8% last month to the highest level in over three years, suggesting low interest rates are finally encouraging construction. Starts fell a revised 1.7% in July.

23 The economic output of the G-7 nations will grow an anemic 1.3% this year and 2.3% next year, the International Monetary Fund predicted. None of the finance ministers from the G-7, who plan to meet on Saturday, see any ready means of stirring their economies out of the current torpor.

The falling market share of U.S. chip makers in Japan must be reversed immediately, the U.S. trade representative said after Japan disclosed that foreign market share slipped in the second quarter.

24 The job outlook will remain gloomy in 1994 as many U.S. companies intend to cut more positions, a survey says.

About 22% of 870 employers surveyed plan to cut workers by June 1994. The finding suggests the weak recovery won't gain strength any time soon.

28 Corporate executives are growing more nervous about the economy and less willing to make capital expenditures, new surveys suggest.

Growth in existing-home sales leveled off in August, but continued to strongly outpace last year's sales.

Ford is recalling 1.2 million 1990–93 pickups to fix fuel-pressure regulators and check valves that may cause gas to leak through the tank cover.

Clinton's health plan could hasten the exodus of small insurers from the business under the proposal's interim controls on the industry, but big insurers would feel little impact.

30 Stock mutual funds attracted a record $12.1 billion in August, a 24% rise from July, with almost half the money going into funds that invest abroad.

Highlights of the 1993 U.S. Industrial Outlook

*by Jonathan C. Menes**

The industry sector forecasts are consistent with stronger economic growth in 1993 than in the previous year. For manufacturers' shipments, average growth of about 2.7 percent is expected—well above the estimated 1992 median growth rate of 1.9 percent. Contrary to usual developments during economic recovery, manufacturers' shipments are expected to expand less rapidly than the assumed 3 percent real growth in the Gross Domestic Product (GDP).

Table 1 summarizes median and mean growth rates for manufacturing industries that are covered in the *1993 Outlook*. These industries represent about 70 percent of total manufactures shipments. More than four-fifths of the sectors covered, representing about 87 percent by value of covered industries, show growth. While comparable data for service industries are not available, the general picture is not much different. Traditional cyclical sectors such as retailing show only moderate growth.

Table 1: Growth Rates of Manufacturers' Shipments

(in constant dollars)

Item	Percent Change (1989–1993)			
	89-90	90-91[1]	91-92[1]	92-93[2]
Median	0.4	−1.3	1.9	2.7
Mean	0.1	−1.6	2.2	2.7

1 Estimate.
2 Forecast.
SOURCE: U.S. Department of Commerce, International Trade Administration.

No consistent pattern emerges in looking at major industry groups. In general, basic industrial materials—chemicals, rubber and plastic products, and wood products—are expected to have modest growth (Table 2). The forecasts for high-tech sectors, such as computers and semiconductors, are especially favorable. The strength of the technology sectors is even more apparent when growth rates of individual industries are compared. After several negative and slow growth years, computers have again moved into a higher growth range. Among other sectors, motor vehicles and parts industries are recovering, with much of the strength coming from rising sales of light trucks. Construction will continue to be a drag on GDP expansion. Non-residential

Table 2: Growth Rates for Selected Industry Groups

(in constant dollars)

Sector	Chapter	Percent Change (1987–1993)					
		87–88	88–89	89–90	90–91[1]	91–92[1]	92–93[2]
Construction	5	1.2	−1.3	−2.9	−9.8	4.1	0.7
Food and beverages	31	2.5	−1.9	1.0	1.4	2.6	1.6
Wood products	6	−0.9	−1.1	−3.0	−6.0	2.6	1.8
Paper and allied products	10	3.0	1.7	0.2	1.1	3.8	4.0
Chemicals	11	3.8	1.1	3.6	1.8	1.9	3.2
Rubber and plastic products	12	2.7	2.7	2.4	1.7	1.3	3.1
Construction materials	7	−0.7	−0.1	0.8	−8.5	1.2	1.1
Steel mill products	13	13.8	−2.6	−1.5	−7.4	4.1	2.4
Production machinery	17	10.5	4.7	−1.0	−2.3	−1.6	2.1
Metal working equipment	16	5.6	7.4	−1.7	−10.9	−0.5	3.5
Electrical equipment	15	6.7	−0.5	−2.5	−3.2	−0.3	1.4
Electronic components	15	11.6	4.3	3.4	1.9	6.2	7.9
Computers	26	12.4	−4.8	−1.3	−2.0	4.0	8.2
Telecommunications and navigation equipment	29	3.0	−4.7	5.5	−3.2	−1.4	−0.4
Motor vehicles and parts	35	6.4	−0.8	−7.2	−8.4	8.2	6.5
Aerospace	20	2.7	2.6	6.4	−0.5	−5.5	−5.3
Instruments, controls and medical equipment	22,44	5.1	−1.2	1.5	1.7	1.9	2.6
Durable consumer goods	36,37	2.7	0.3	−1.1	−4.2	3.2	4.3
Printing and publishing	24	0.5	−1.2	0.6	−2.2	0.7	1.9

[1]Estimate.
[2]Forecast.
NOTE: All data are based on shipments in constant 1987 dollars, except construction and computers (current dollars).
SOURCE: U.S. Department of Commerce: Bureau of the Census, International Trade Administration (ITA). Estimates and forecasts by ITA.

* Director, Office of Trade and Economic Analysis.

Source: *U.S. Industrial Outlook 1993*, U.S. Department of Commerce, International Trade Administration.

construction will continue to drop, with growth coming from private residential construction, home improvement, and public works. The aerospace industry will experience a second straight year of decline in shipments as a result of continued reductions in defense production and a leveling off in backlogs for large commercial aircraft; however, production levels for large commercial aircraft will still be at relatively high levels. Traditional capital goods sectors, such as machinery and machine tools, are showing only modest growth. Consumer durables, which started to pick up in 1992, should continue to improve.

Trade

Compared with the recent past, exports are likely to play a smaller role in promoting industry growth in 1993. Export growth of manufacturers is likely to be in the same range as in 1992, but well below the high rates achieved in 1990 and 1991. This is principally because of the slow growth expected in many major overseas markets. Despite the weaker overall export performance, some industries should benefit from rapidly expanding markets within their own sectors, including medical equipment, instruments and supplies, household appliances, and motor vehicles.

Manufacturing Industries

High-technology industries dominate the list of fastest-growing industries with semiconductors at the top of the list (Table 3). Despite weakness in the Japanese market, semiconductors began a strong recovery in 1992 that is expected to continue in 1993.

Table 3: Ten Fastest-Growing Manufacturing Industries in 1993

(percent change based on constant-dollar shipments)

SIC	Industry	Percent Change 1992–93
3674	Semiconductors	12.0
3841	Surgical and medical instruments	8.5
3842	Surgical appliances and supplies	8.5
357A	Computers and peripherals (SIC 3571, 3572, 3575, 3577)	8.2*
3845	Electromedical equipment	7.8
3711	Motor vehicles and car bodies	6.8
3633	Household laundry equipment	6.7
3632	Household refrigerators and freezers	6.5
371A	Automotive parts and accessories	6.1
3844	X-ray apparatus and tubes	5.6

*Percent change based on current-dollar shipments.

SOURCE: U.S. Department of Commerce, International Trade Administration.

Table 4: Ten Slowest-Growing Manufacturing Industries in 1993

(percent change based on constant-dollar shipments)

SIC	Industry	Percent Change 1992–93
3172	Personal leather goods, NEC	−3.4
3171	Women's handbags and purses	−3.6
2386	Leather and sheep-lined clothing	−3.8
3724	Aircraft engines and engine parts	−3.8
3728	Aircraft parts and equipment, NEC	−4.8
3764	Space propulsion units and parts	−5.0
3554	Paper industries machinery	−5.2
3761	Guided missiles and space vehicles	−5.7
3769	Space vehicle equipment, NEC	−6.0
3721	Aircraft	−6.0

SOURCE: U.S. Department of Commerce, International Trade Administration.

Health-related equipment and materials continue to be among the leading growth industries. Health-related industries have been the most consistent high performers; they have been among the top four in growth during the past five years. The motor vehicles and automotive parts sector returns to the list of the 10 fastest growing industries in 1993. By historical standards, however, unit sales will still be low, an estimated 8.9 million cars and 13.9 million light vehicle sales.

Among the slowest-growing industries, aircraft and other aerospace industries stand out (Table 4). They are traditionally among the fastest growing, but there are several factors causing the anticipated decline in shipments: the decline in defense expenditures; and a dip in orders for large commercial aircraft for the last several years that has brought a pause to the rapid growth in commercial aircraft production and deliveries. Despite the anticipated decline in production in 1993, the level of output will still be very high.

Service Industries

Service industries' performance is more difficult to gauge because of differences in measurement of output and, particularly, the lack of constant-dollar data for most service industries. As in past years, information- and health-based industries should be the leading performers in 1993. Growth in these industries has been little affected by the 1990–91 recession. Expenditures on health services will continue to accelerate faster than the growth in GDP, regardless of efforts to control costs.

Other industries that are expected to grow more strongly are cyclical in nature, such as prerecorded music, home entertainment, apparel stores, and eating and drinking establishments. On the other hand, a number of service industries appear to be growing just above their industries' inflation rate, which has generally exceeded that of manufacturing in recent years. There are also changes in demand and structure in the financial services industry that have been especially noticeable in rapid asset growth for credit unions, moderate asset growth for banks, and an asset decline for savings institutions.

Table 5: Trends In Selected Service Industries

(in billions of current dollars except as noted)

Industry	Chapter	Unit of Measure	1993 Value	Percent Change (1990–1993) 90-91	91-92[1]	92-93[2]
Accounting	54	Receipts	37.5	2.2	2.9	4.2
Advertising	54	Receipts	21.5	1.5	2.5	3.6
Banks	45	Assets	3,788.0	4.0	3.0	4.0
Computer professional services	26	Revenues	61.0	12.2	9.9	9.3
Credit unions	47	Assets	274.5	14.5	12.0	8.0
Data processing	26	Revenues	45.7	14.1	12.9	13.7
Electronic information services	26	Revenues	13.5	13.2	13.7	16.4
Equipment leasing	53	Original equipment cost	126.3	−3.3	0.0	5.0
Health services	42	Revenues	939.9	11.4	11.5	12.1
Home entertainment	31	Revenues	26.7	7.6	7.7	7.7
Legal services	54	Receipts	106.5	4.3	5.3	6.5
Life insurance	52	Premiums	284.8	−0.1	3.3	4.5
Management consulting	54	Receipts	70.0	3.8	4.7	5.3
Motion picture theaters	31	Receipts	4.7	−4.4	−1.3	0.0
Prerecorded music	31	Manufacturers' value	9.4	3.9	7.5	11.3
Property/casualty insurance	52	Net premiums written	239.3	2.4	3.2	4.0
Railroads (class 1)	40	Revenue ton-miles	29.5	0.6	2.4	3.3
Retail sales, total	39	Sales	2,038.0	0.9	4.9	5.4
Apparel and accessories stores	39	Sales	106.0	1.1	4.2	7.1
Department stores	39	Sales	196.0	3.5	6.2	3.7
Eating and drinking places	39	Sales	219.0	4.3	5.7	6.8
Food retailing	39	Sales	395.9	2.5	1.6	2.3
Savings institutions	46	Assets	800.0	−12.9	−7.0	−1.8
Space commerce	41	Revenues	4.9	24.7	14.1	2.0
Telecommunications	28	Revenues	176.4[3]	5.3	4.0	6.3
Travel services	41	Expenditures	393.0	3.1	8.0	5.7
Trucking	40	Cargo ton-miles	296.0	3.1	1.6	1.9
Venture capital	50	Capital commitments	3.2	−31.2	96.7	28.0

[1]Estimate.
[2]Forecast.
[3]In billions of constant dollars.
SOURCE: U.S. Department of Commerce, International Trade Administration.

Table 6: Forecast Growth Rates for 156 Manufacturing Industries and Groups

(in billions of 1987 dollars except as noted)

SIC	Industry	Chapter	Shipments 1993	Growth Rate 1992-93 Percent	Growth Rate 1992-93 Rank	Compound Annual Growth 1988-93 Percent	Compound Annual Growth 1988-93 Rank
2015	Poultry slaughtering and processing	31	21.500	3.5	47	6.7	7
201A	Red meat	31	64.350	1.9	104	0.0	82
2021	Creamery butter	31	1.913	1.6	113	0.7	74
2022	Cheese, natural and processed	31	14.619	1.6	112	2.3	38
2023	Dry, condensed, and evaporated products	31	5.003	0.9	123	−4.2	144
2024	Ice cream and frozen desserts	31	4.916	3.5	50	2.7	34
2026	Fluid milk	31	19.364	−1.3	134	−1.8	122
203A	Canned foods	31	27.055	1.7	108	1.8	48
203B	Frozen foods	31	14.185	1.8	107	3.3	24
2051	Bread, cake, and related products	31	14.423	0.8	124	−1.1	110
2052	Cookies and crackers	31	6.689	1.5	116	1.6	53
2053	Frozen bakery products, except bread	31	1.014	−1.5	135	−4.4	147
2064	Candy and other confectionery products	31	8.082	2.9	73	2.2	42
2082	Malt beverages	31	15.730	1.5	114	2.7	33
2084	Wines, brandy, and brandy spirits	31	3.213	0.4	127	−1.4	114
2085	Distilled and blended liquors	31	2.735	−1.6	137	−4.3	145
2086	Bottled and canned soft drinks	31	22.896	1.3	119	0.0	80
2386	Leather and sheep-lined clothing	33	0.127	−3.8	149	−9.3	155
2411	Logging	6	9.065	−1.0	133	−2.7	135
2421	Sawmills and planing mills, general	6	16.259	2.0	97	−1.7	120
2431	Millwork	6	8.915	2.5	83	−0.4	93
2435	Hardwood veneer and plywood	6	1.885	1.9	105	−1.5	116

(continued)

Table 6: Forecast Growth Rates for 156 Manufacturing Industries and Groups *(continued)*

(in billions of 1987 dollars except as noted)

SIC	Industry	Chapter	Shipments 1993	Growth Rate 1992-93 Percent	Growth Rate 1992-93 Rank	Compound Annual Growth 1988-93 Percent	Compound Annual Growth 1988-93 Rank
2436	Softwood veneer and plywood	6	4.630	4.4	30	−0.4	94
2448	Wood pallets and skids	6	1.863	2.5	85	2.9	27
2451	Mobile homes	5	4.100	5.1	16	0.3	78
2493	Reconstituted wood products	6	3.115	3.7	46	1.4	60
2511	Wood household furniture	36	7.237	3.5	49	−1.8	121
2512	Upholstered household furniture	36	5.410	4.6	25	0.9	70
2514	Metal household furniture	36	1.991	3.9	45	−1.6	119
2515	Mattresses and bedsprings	36	2.715	4.5	27	2.8	29
2611	Pulp mills	10	5.204	4.0	39	4.0	19
2653	Corrugated and solid fiber boxes	10	18.735	4.0	40	2.7	31
2657	Folding paperboard boxes	10	5.965	1.2	121	0.5	75
2676	Sanitary paper products	10	13.850	3.5	53	3.2	25
2677	Envelopes	10	2.578	2.8	76	−0.2	88
26PM	Paper and paperboard mills	10	48.790	4.5	28	1.8	50
2711	Newspapers	24	24.495	−1.8	139	−4.5	148
2721	Periodicals	24	16.623	2.4	86	−1.1	107
2731	Book publishing	24	14.035	3.4	55	1.9	46
2732	Book printing	24	3.955	2.7	78	3.0	26
2741	Miscellaneous publishing	24	8.315	3.2	57	1.5	58
275	Commercial printing	24	49.725	3.0	62	1.5	56
2761	Manifold business forms	24	6.686	−1.0	132	−1.5	117
2771	Greeting cards	24	3.822	5.0	19	5.8	13
2782	Blankbooks and looseleaf binders	24	2.860	2.7	79	−0.5	95
2789	Bookbinding and related work	24	1.305	2.0	103	2.1	43
2791	Typesetting	24	1.988	3.5	52	1.3	65
2796	Platemaking services	24	2.802	3.5	48	2.3	40
281A	Industrial inorganic chemicals, except pigments	11	21.938	3.0	70	3.8	22
2821	Plastics materials and resins	12	28.737	3.0	63	1.3	62
2822	Synthetic rubber	12	3.900	4.0	37	1.6	55
2833	Medicinals and botanicals	43	4.538	3.0	65	2.8	30
2834	Pharmaceutical preparations	43	37.737	5.2	14	2.7	32
2835	Diagnostic substances	43	2.432	3.0	69	1.7	52
2836	Biological products, except diagnostic	43	2.174	3.0	68	4.4	17
2841	Soap and other detergents	34	15.622	2.5	82	5.8	12
2842	Polishes and sanitation goods	34	5.537	2.0	95	−0.3	89
2843	Surface active agents	34	2.917	4.5	26	−1.1	109
2844	Toilet preparations	34	17.178	2.3	89	1.5	59
2851	Paints and allied products	11	11.961	1.5	117	−1.6	118
2873	Nitrogenous fertilizers	11	2.621	−1.5	136	2.1	44
2874	Phosphatic fertilizers	11	5.195	5.0	20	5.7	14
2879	Agricultural chemicals, NEC	11	8.006	2.0	99	3.6	23
2891	Adhesives and sealants	11	5.117	3.0	64	2.6	35
2911	Petroleum refining	4	122.827	0.4	126	−0.2	86
3011	Tires and inner tubes	12	11.588	4.0	36	1.3	63
3069	Fabricated rubber products, NEC	12	6.443	3.0	66	1.6	54
3088	Plastic plumbing fixtures	7	1.100	1.9	106	6.3	9
308A	Miscellaneous plastic products, except bottles and plumbing	12	66.500	2.9	71	2.4	37
3111	Leather tanning and finishing	33	2.151	5.0	23	0.0	81
3142	House slippers	33	0.249	2.0	93	1.8	49
3143	Men's footwear, except athletic	33	1.724	3.0	67	−3.2	138
3144	Women's footwear, except athletic	33	1.079	0.0	129	−4.2	143
3149	Footwear, except rubber, NEC	33	0.273	−2.8	143	−9.4	156
3151	Leather gloves and mittens	33	0.118	−3.3	146	−7.7	154
3161	Luggage	33	0.953	0.0	130	1.0	67
3171	Women's handbags and purses	33	0.407	−3.6	148	−5.4	150
3172	Personal leather goods, NEC	33	0.282	−3.4	147	−6.3	151
3211	Flat glass	7	2.050	2.0	101	−3.0	136
3241	Cement, hydraulic	7	4.175	3.3	56	−0.2	87
3253	Ceramic wall and floor tile	7	0.747	5.4	12	0.4	77
3261	Vitreous plumbing fixtures	7	0.750	1.4	118	−3.9	142
3275	Gypsum products	7	3.076	3.9	44	2.5	36
331A	Steel mill products (SIC 3312, 3315–17)	13	54.860	2.4	87	−1.1	111
3431	Metal sanitary ware	7	0.875	0.6	125	−0.6	98
3432	Plumbing fixture fittings and trim	7	2.250	2.3	90	−0.7	99
3441	Fabricated structural metal	7	7.510	−2.0	140	−2.5	132
3451	Screw machine products	14	2.892	4.0	41	−1.0	105
3452	Bolts, nuts, rivets, and washers	14	5.127	3.5	51	−0.8	101
349A	Valves and pipe fittings	14	7.210	2.5	81	0.0	83
3523	Farm machinery and equipment	17	8.266	−2.5	141	−0.6	96

Table 6: Forecast Growth Rates for 156 Manufacturing Industries and Groups *(concluded)*

(in billions of 1987 dollars except as noted)

SIC	Industry	Chapter	Shipments 1993	Growth Rate 1992-93		Compound Annual Growth 1988-93	
				Percent	Rank	Percent	Rank
3524	Lawn and garden equipment	36	4.291	3.2	58	−2.0	127
3531	Construction machinery	17	14.650	3.0	61	0.7	72
3532	Mining machinery	17	1.675	3.1	60	2.0	45
3533	Oil and gas field machinery	17	4.488	2.0	100	6.5	8
3541	Machine tools, metal cutting types	16	2.864	4.3	33	−1.0	104
3542	Machine tools, metal forming types	16	1.229	5.0	17	−6.4	152
3544	Special dies, tools, jigs and fixtures	16	7.932	2.8	74	0.0	84
3546	Power-driven handtools	16	2.602	4.2	34	1.2	66
3552	Textile machinery	17	1.300	2.8	75	−1.9	126
3554	Paper industries machinery	17	2.235	−5.2	153	2.9	28
3555	Printing trades machinery	17	2.786	2.0	94	−2.5	130
3556	Food products machinery	17	2.083	4.4	32	0.8	71
3562	Ball and roller bearings	14	3.675	4.5	29	−1.3	113
3565	Packaging machinery	17	2.569	5.0	22	3.8	21
357A	Computers and peripherals (SIC 3571, 3572, 3575, 3577)	26	65.000*	8.2	4	0.7	73
3585	Refrigeration and heating equipment	17	17.334	4.0	35	−1.0	106
3612	Transformers, except electronic	18	3.317	−1.7	138	−2.5	131
3613	Switchgear and switchboard apparatus	18	4.715	2.0	102	−2.2	128
3621	Motors and generators	18	6.351	1.0	122	−2.6	134
3625	Relays and industrial controls	18	6.950	2.7	77	1.4	61
3631	Household cooking equipment	36	3.205	4.0	42	−3.2	140
3632	Household refrigerators and freezers	36	4.195	6.5	8	1.5	57
3633	Household laundry equipment	36	3.395	6.7	7	1.7	51
3634	Electric housewares and fans	36	2.845	1.6	111	0.4	76
3635	Household vacuum cleaners	36	1.925	5.4	11	5.8	11
3639	Household appliances, NEC	36	2.955	5.2	15	5.6	15
3643	Current-carrying wiring devices	8	4.358	2.5	84	0.9	68
3644	Noncurrent-carrying wiring devices	8	2.790	−0.5	131	−1.9	125
364A	Lighting fixtures (SIC 3645, 3646, 3648)	8	5.937	1.5	115	−1.1	108
3651	Household audio and video equipment	36	7.856	1.7	110	4.0	20
3661	Telephone and telegraph apparatus	29	17.075	2.0	98	−1.4	115
3663	Radio and TV communications equipment	29	19.100	2.0	96	4.2	18
3674	Semiconductors	15	35.571	12.0	1	9.5	4
367A	Electronic parts, except semiconductors (SIC 3671-2, 3675-9)	15	35.071	3.9	43	0.9	69
3711	Motor vehicles and car bodies	35	137.500	6.8	6	−0.4	92
3715	Truck trailers	35	3.219	5.0	21	−1.8	124
371A	Automotive parts and accessories	35	96.311	6.1	9	−0.8	100
3721	Aircraft	20	41.416	−6.0	156	0.3	79
3724	Aircraft engines and engine parts	20	17.878	−3.8	150	−1.8	123
3728	Aircraft parts and equipment, NEC	20	16.443	−4.8	151	−0.6	97
3731	Ship building and repairing	21	9.554	−3.2	145	2.2	41
3732	Boat building and repairing	37	4.113	2.6	80	−6.5	153
3751	Motorcycles, bicycles, and parts	37	1.461	3.4	54	7.5	5
3761	Guided missiles and space vehicles	20	22.927	−5.7	154	−0.3	90
3764	Space propulsion units and parts	20	3.145	−5.0	152	−4.4	146
3769	Space vehicle equipment, NEC	20	1.390	−6.0	155	−4.8	149
3812	Search and navigation equipment	29	30.768	−3.1	144	−3.2	139
3821	Laboratory apparatus and furniture	22	1.892	3.2	59	−1.0	103
3822	Environmental controls	22	2.213	0.3	128	−0.3	91
3823	Process control instruments	22	5.419	1.7	109	1.3	64
3824	Fluid meters and counting devices	22	1.399	−2.8	142	−3.0	137
3825	Instruments to measure electricity	22	8.636	5.0	18	1.8	47
3826	Analytical instruments	22	5.052	4.7	24	6.0	10
3827	Optical instruments and lenses	22	1.915	2.2	91	−0.8	102
3829	Measuring and controlling devices, NEC	22	4.052	2.3	88	2.3	39
3841	Surgical and medical instruments	44	13.133	8.5	2	10.0	3
3842	Surgical appliances and supplies	44	13.449	8.5	3	6.9	6
3843	Dental equipment and supplies	44	1.489	5.3	13	−0.2	85
3844	X-ray apparatus and tubes	44	3.252	5.6	10	16.0	1
3845	Electromedical equipment	44	7.269	7.8	5	11.9	2
3861	Photographic equipment and supplies	23	17.000	1.2	120	−3.7	141
3911	Jewelry, precious metal	37	3.900	4.0	38	−1.2	112
3931	Musical instruments	37	0.736	2.9	72	−2.5	133
3949	Sporting and athletic goods, NEC	37	7.014	4.4	31	4.7	16
3961	Costume jewelry	37	1.210	2.1	92	−2.3	129

*In billions of current dollars.

SOURCE: U.S. Department of Commerce, International Trade Administration.

Industry Surveys[1]

Aerospace

The U.S. aerospace industry, still a global leader, is a critical part of this country's domestic and export economies. In 1991, aerospace ranked sixth in value of shipments and fourteenth in employment among all U.S. industries. More important, aerospace is the nation's leading exporter of manufactured goods, sending abroad products worth $43 billion in 1991 to 135 countries around the world. Aerospace produces the largest trade surplus of any U.S. industry ($30 billion in 1991). The aerospace industry also accounts for more than 25 percent of all the nation's research and development expenditures, making it the country's leader in R&D spending on new technologies.

Industry Sales Continue Down

The aerospace industry is facing dramatic changes. As a result of continuing defense cuts, a weak global economy, and increasing international competition, industry shipments (in constant dollars) will decline in 1993 for the third year in a row. Aerospace shipments peaked in 1991 at $129 billion. Shipments in 1992 fell 6 percent, in real terms, and shipments in 1993 are expected to be 5 percent lower than 1992. Historically, at least half of the industry's revenues were derived from the military sector. Cuts in the defense budgets for aerospace products, both in the United States and in other developed countries, have reduced requirements for military aircraft, missiles, and related equipment from U.S. suppliers. Total U.S. defense spending peaked in 1985, and current budget requests indicate an annual average 4 percent decline in real spending between fiscal year (FY) 1992 and FY 1997. Relatively stable spending on research and development will help maintain the military technology leadership of the aerospace industry, but the defense industry's production will continue to fall.

In the past, significant growth in the civil sector sustained the aerospace industry during periodic downturns in defense spending. Between 1985 and 1991, when defense aerospace shipments were declining at a rate of approximately 2 percent per year, commercial aerospace shipments increased more than 11 percent per year. In 1991, civil orders represented 65 percent of the industry's total order backlog, up dramatically from 37 percent in 1985. Steady sales of large commercial transport aircraft led this growth.

This counter-cyclical characteristic of the industry seems to have disappeared. The civil sector faces the cumulative effect of the worldwide economic downturn. For the first time in the history of the airline industry, worldwide airline passenger traffic declined between 1990 and 1991, dropping 4 percent. During the first half of 1992, domestic traffic was stimulated by price discounts and international traffic resumed its pre-Desert Shield growth. But the poor financial condition of many airlines in 1992 stifled aircraft, engine, and parts purchases. In 1991, the world's airlines lost almost $4 billion; they are expected to lose another $2 billion in 1992. With airline finances weak, aircraft and parts orders during 1993 should be well below the boom that occurred in the late 1980's.

The financial performance of the aerospace industry has not been significantly better than that of the airlines. Throughout the past decade, the financial performance of the aerospace industry lagged behind that of other U.S. industries. In 1991, the industry as a whole earned 1.8 percent return on sales, compared with 2.5 percent for all manufacturing industries. The profitability of aerospace companies involved in the defense sector fell by more than half in 5 years—from return on sales of 5 percent in 1985 to just 2 percent in 1990—according to the Aerospace Industries Association (AIA). Losses on fixed-price development contracts were a major factor in reducing defense contractors' profitability, while increasing international competition keep profit margins modest in the civil sector of the industry.

Employment Off

Declining shipments and profitability are reflected in a severe decline in employment. Between 1989 and 1992, total aerospace industry employment fell from 823,000 to

[1] Relevant tables are at the end of each industry section. A glossary is on page 155.

Source: *U.S. Industrial Outlook 1993*, U.S. Department of Commerce.

The U.S. Industrial Outlook contains more complete discussions of the industries excerpted for the *Almanac* as well as discussions of many more. The *Outlook* is available for purchase from the Superintendent of Documents (202) 783-3238.

685,000. According to Bureau of Labor statistics, between December 1989 and May 1992, total aerospace employment declined at an average rate of almost 6,200 jobs *per month*. The employment drops have affected both production and nonproduction workers. Production workers employment dropped 4 percent in 1992. Layoffs have occurred in both the commercial and military sectors, although the military sector has suffered the larger cuts. Capacity utilization for the industry, as calculated by the Federal Reserve, has fallen from 85 percent in mid-1990 to only 69 percent by July 1992. As long as capacity utilization remains low, prospects for employment trends to stabilize or improve are poor.

INTERNATIONAL COMPETITIVENESS

The U.S. aerospace industry faces not only the challenge of weaker demand for its products, but also the growing strength of its foreign competition. Although the United States retains both market and technology leadership within the global aerospace industry, its position has eroded. In 1970, the United States led the global aerospace market with a share of almost 80 percent (excluding the former members of the Council for Mutual Economic Assistance, or COMECON, a group of nations led by the former Soviet Union). In 1990, 20 years later, U.S. aerospace shipments still led the world, but had shrunk to less than 60 percent of the worldwide market. This decline reflects the success of other countries in their efforts to foster the development and growth of their national aerospace industries. Many foreign governments have ambitious plans for competitive aerospace industries and support the growth of their industries with subsidies for product development and production. They also have required U.S. aerospace companies to provide offsets and technology transfers, and made sales contingent upon their own firms supplying some of the components. In addition, some governments have encouraged consolidation and cooperation among domestic companies to reduce competition within their borders, enabling them to compete more effectively with established U.S. companies.

The European aerospace industry is the principal competitor responsible for much of the erosion of global U.S. market share. The European Community (EC) aerospace industry produced approximately $60 billion dollars worth of products during 1990, or about 30 percent of the worldwide aerospace production. According to EC statistics, the EC aerospace industry was one-third the size of the U.S. industry in 1985. In 1990, EC industry was nearly half the size of the U.S. industry. Some countries' industries, such as Germany's, grew three times faster than the U.S. industry during the 1980's. The creation and nurturing of the Airbus Industrie consortium by its member governments (France, Germany, Spain, and the United Kingdom) provided the European industry with a worldwide backlog of orders worth $70 billion. U.S. companies, which do not receive such government assistance, must compete for this business. European governments also support commercial space, smaller aircraft, rotorcraft, engine, and parts industries. Most individual EC governments have encouraged concentration in their aerospace industries, leading to diversified, national monoliths such as Deutsche Aerospace, Aerospatiale, Alenia, Fokker, and British Aerospace. Now, the trend toward intra-EC ventures threatens to lead to even larger industry combines as the EC governments work to integrate their economies.

Japan will be a serious future competitor in certain segments of the industry, such as aircraft parts, propulsion systems, and space vehicles. Small by global standards, the Japanese aerospace industry had products worth only $7 billion in 1989. The Japanese aerospace industry is growing, however, at a much faster rate than any other of the country's established industries. Targeted by the Japanese Government, government and industry research and development (R&D) efforts have focused on aircraft fuselage and systems components, electronics, high speed propulsion systems, and space launch vehicles. In nearby Taiwan, the government there believes that its recent efforts to bolster its aerospace industry will generate aerospace shipments of $6 billion in the year 2000, up from only $500 million today. Other countries also seek bigger shares of the global industry: Canada, Brazil, South Korea, China, Singapore, Sweden, Israel, and Australia.

The newly independent states of what was once the Soviet Union and the former Soviet Bloc countries present both opportunities and challenges for the U.S. aerospace industry. A market that contains the world's largest airline, largest space industry, and greatest pent-up consumer demand certainly provides new long-term opportunities for U.S. aerospace companies. Yet it also presents the challenge of new competition. In 1989, Soviet aerospace factories produced at least as many aircraft, missiles, and spacecraft as the United States. Today, most of those same facilities are operating at less than 30 percent capacity. Desire for new orders for those factories, for technology, and for hard currency, will force the industries of the newly independent states to both collaborate and compete in the international market.

LONG-TERM PROSPECTS

Continued overcapacity in the military aerospace sector will force the industry into significant restructuring. Defense spending will continue to decline throughout the decade. The industry will continue to consolidate operations and reduce R&D and capital investment. Layoffs are expected to continue but the rate will slow. A strong world economy and recovery from the 1990–1992 economic uncertainty worldwide will ensure continued steady demand for airline, corporate, and general aviation aircraft and equipment. Space exploration and commercialization face unreliable Government funding and uncertain commercial demand. Some areas of the aerospace industry will grow, while others face market maturation plus severe international competition. Continued efforts to reduce government supports to international aerospace industries will help level the playing field for U.S. manufacturers.

Aircraft

The large transport sector includes all passenger and cargo aircraft weighing more than 15,000 kilograms, typically two- and four-engine jetliners. In contrast to the booming production rates and bursting orderbooks of the late 1980's, the large transport industry is beginning to adjust itself to lower demand from the airline industry, declining orders, reduced production on narrow body aircraft, and fierce competition from Europe. U.S. manufacturers are forecast to ship 480 large transport aircraft valued at $26 billion in 1993, down from their peak of 567 aircraft valued at $27 billion in 1992.

Large Transport Sector Begins to Restructure

The combined backlog of Boeing and McDonnell Douglas was $106 billion at the end of June 1992, down 5 percent from June 1991. The weakness in 1992 orders highlighted a continuing period of uncertainty in the airline industry. The economic recession in the United States and other industrial nations, combined with the fear of terrorism during the crisis in the Middle East, brought growth in airline traffic to a halt between 1990 and 1991. Although international traffic recovered during 1992, and U.S. domestic traffic was stimulated by significant price discounting, the airline industry remained in dire financial straits. International Air Transport Association members lost a combined $2 billion in 1990, $4 billion in 1991, and an estimated $2 billion in 1992. Three major U.S. carriers—Eastern, Pan American, and Midway—disappeared during 1991, and three others—Continental, TWA, and America West—remain under the protection of bankruptcy courts. Though the fare wars have generated a surge of traffic in mid-1992, they have not contributed to the U.S. carriers financial strength. Even the largest, most stable, carriers are rethinking their investment strategies. American, Delta, and United have canceled over $10 billion in new aircraft orders during 1992. Significant international customers, such as Guinness Peat Aviation Group of Ireland, are also reported to be canceling or rescheduling orders.

Market share erosion caused by the European-based Airbus Industrie is exacerbating the effects of lower demand. Airbus Industrie maintained 40 percent of the total value of the backlog for large transport aircraft at the end of 1991. Airbus is increasing its production, introducing three new aircraft models, the A321, A330, and A340. Increased production by Airbus will cut into international sales of Boeing and McDonnell Douglas, and increase aircraft imports into the United States, detracting from the otherwise stellar trade performance of U.S. aircraft producers. During the first half of 1992, Boeing and McDonnell Douglas exported 70 percent of their combined output, and were the most significant contributors to the trade performance of the U.S. aerospace industry. Large transport exports are expected to fall 5 percent in 1993; imports will rise 35 percent.

Declining demand, production overcapacity, and government-supported foreign competition have seriously affected the two U.S. producers. Both McDonnell Douglas and Boeing have announced reduced production rates for their narrow body aircraft. McDonnell Douglas has delayed the launching of its new MD-12 widebody. Both manufacturers have resorted to layoffs. McDonnell Douglas has eliminated over 10,000 jobs since 1990, and planned another 4,000 layoffs during 1992. Boeing has initiated plans to layoff about 8,000 employees between 1992 and 1993.

U.S. manufacturers continue to turn to Asia for partnerships to increase their competitiveness. McDonnell Douglas attempted a joint venture with the newly created Taiwan Aerospace Corporation, in which 49 percent of the Douglas Aircraft Company would have been owned by Taiwanese and other international investors. McDonnell Douglas also increased its ties with the People's Republic of China. Boeing has established a closer relationship with its Japanese partners on the 777, and is also expanding its relationships with smaller Asian countries like Taiwan.

Asian countries are attracting U.S. aircraft manufacturers with access to inexpensive capital, high quality manufacturing, and lower production costs.

Long-term, this segment should see continued growth. The International Civil Aviation Organization (ICAO) forecasts that worldwide airline traffic should grow by 5 percent in 1993, and 6.5 percent in 1994. Growth will be higher overseas, especially in Asia. About one-third of the demand for new aircraft over the next decade should arise from the retirement of older aircraft. Already, over 45 percent of Boeing's firm backlog is for aircraft to be delivered after 1994. As the delivery of new and existing higher value, widebody aircraft increases during this decade, the dollar value of this market will once again experience healthy growth.

The U.S. industry, however, will also continue to face difficult competition from Airbus Industrie. In July 1992 the U.S. and EC governments signed an agreement which will reduce direct government supports to Airbus Industrie. No production supports and no government inducements to customers will be allowed, and development supports will be limited to 33 percent of the development cost of the program (down from 70 to 90 percent of existing Airbus aircraft). This agreement is a critical step in leveling the competitive playing field for U.S. large transport manufacturers, who have suffered significantly from the competition of government-supported Airbus.—*Aircraft and Equipment: Hugh Walsh; Office of Aerospace Policy and Analysis, (202) 482-4222.*

Trends and Forecasts: Aerospace (SIC 372, 376)

(in millions of dollars except as noted)

Item	1987	1988	1989	1990	1991[1]	1992[2]	1993[3]	Percent Change (1987–1993) 87–88	88–89	89–90	90–91	91–92	92–93
Industry Data													
Value of shipments[4]	103,589	107,746	113,477	125,194	128,610	125,749	120,516	4.0	5.3	10.3	2.7	−2.2	−4.2
Value of shipments (1987$)	103,589	106,355	109,070	116,019	115,390	109,021	103,199	2.7	2.6	6.4	−0.5	−5.5	−5.3
Total employment (000)	810	820	823	816	752	695	652	1.2	0.4	−0.9	−7.8	−7.6	−6.2
Production workers (000)	407	399	400	396	361	330	308	−2.0	0.3	−1.0	−8.8	−8.6	−6.7
Average hourly earnings ($)	14.92	15.35	15.84	16.36	—	—	—	2.9	3.2	3.3	—	—	—
Capital expenditures	3,612	3,388	3,921	3,490	—	—	—	−6.2	15.7	−11.0	—	—	—
Product Data													
Value of shipments[5]	97,185	102,242	106,320	118,141	115,345	112,643	107,964	5.2	4.0	11.1	−2.4	−2.3	−4.2
Value of shipments (1987$)	97,185	100,643	101,659	108,635	101,852	96,995	91,748	3.6	1.0	6.9	−6.2	−4.8	−5.4
Trade Data													
Value of imports	—	—	9,755	11,194	12,603	12,718	14,533	—	—	14.8	12.6	0.9	14.3
Value of exports	—	—	30,948	37,599	42,635	42,208	41,681	—	—	21.5	13.4	−1.0	−1.2

[1]Estimated, except exports and imports.
[2]Estimate.
[3]Forecast.
[4]Value of all products and services sold by establishments in the aerospace industry.
[5]Value of products classified in the aerospace industry produced by all industries.

SOURCE: U.S. Department of Commerce: Bureau of the Census, International Trade Administration (ITA). Estimates and forecasts by ITA.

U.S. Aerospace Industry: Military and Civil Sector Shares of Shipments/Backlog

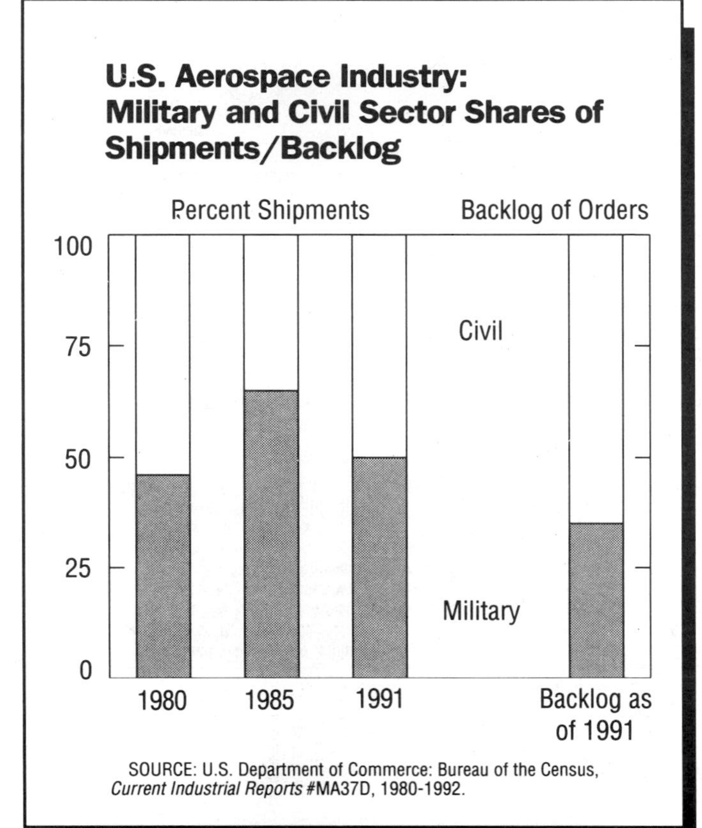

SOURCE: U.S. Department of Commerce: Bureau of the Census, *Current Industrial Reports* #MA37D, 1980-1992.

U.S. Aerospace Trade with the World, 1980–92

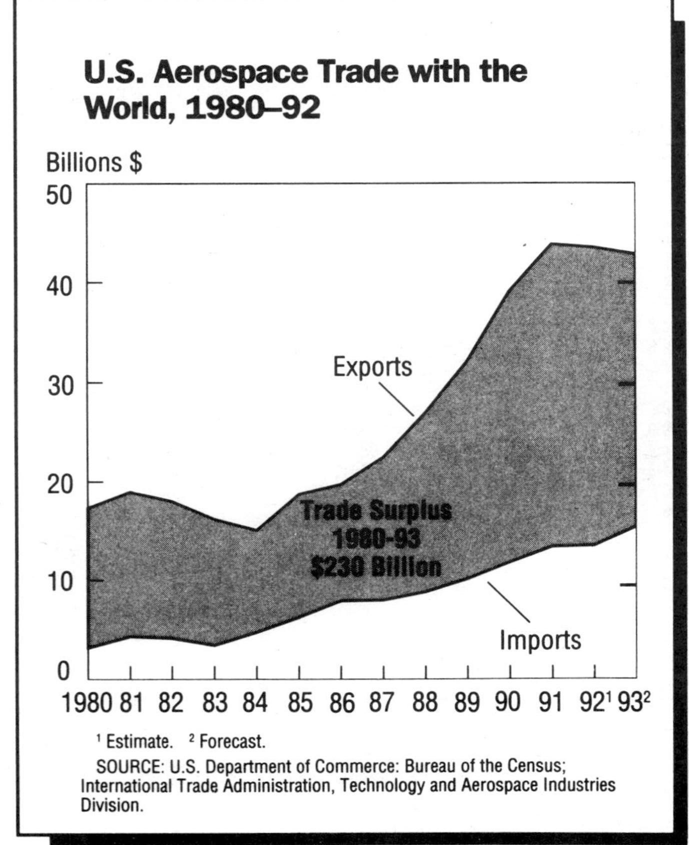

[1] Estimate. [2] Forecast.

SOURCE: U.S. Department of Commerce: Bureau of the Census; International Trade Administration, Technology and Aerospace Industries Division.

U.S. Exports of Aerospace Vehicles and Equipment, 1989–93

(values in millions of dollars)

Items	1989		1990		1991[1]		1992[2]		1993[3]	
	Units	Value	Units	Value	Units	Value	Units	Value	Units	Value
Aerospace vehicles and equipment, total	—	32,884	—	39,030	—	43,783	—	43,423	—	43,089
Civilian aircraft	3,940	14,257	3,446	18,110	2,954	22,387	2,402	22,126	2,374	21,140
Under 4,536 kg. unladen weight, new	1,638	265	799	318	536	304	402	288	426	240
4,536–15,000 kg. unladen weight, new	48	164	79	245	69	279	64	259	70	282
Over 15,000 kg. unladen weight, new	260	13,122	306	16,691	385	20,881	374	20,589	319	19,555
Rotorcraft, new	294	155	349	161	318	168	264	156	285	168
Other aircraft, nec, new	—	18	—	15	—	21	—	19	—	20
Used or rebuilt	1,700	533	1,913	680	1646	734	1,298	815	1,274	875
Military aircraft	846	892	445	1,481	490	1,784	340	1,987	395	2,330
New	647	836	387	1,406	355	1,640	307	1,908	315	2,138
Used	199	56	58	75	135	144	33	79	80	192
Aircraft engines and parts	—	6,629	—	6,870	—	7,039	—	6,719	—	6,872
Piston engines and parts	—	438	—	421	—	417	—	302	—	348
Complete engines, new and used	8,653	131	6,411	110	7,452	111	6,941	96	7,288	101
Engine parts	—	307	—	311	—	306	—	206	—	247
Turbine engines and parts	—	6,191	—	6,449	—	6,622	—	6,417	—	6,524
Complete engines, new and used	3,917	2,053	3,008	1,846	3,199	2,221	3,269	2,237	3,432	2,260
Engine parts	—	4,138	—	4,603	—	4,401	—	4,180	—	4,264
Propellers and parts	—	271	—	343	—	317	—	287	—	301
Landing gear and parts	—	273	—	276	—	333	—	414	—	422
Aircraft parts, nec	—	8,198	—	8,982	—	9,386	—	8,823	—	8,990
Avionics	—	732	—	747	—	780	—	819	—	835
Flight simulators	—	206	—	255	—	245	—	180	—	200
Guided missiles and parts	—	1,042	—	1,306	—	1,204	—	1,660	—	1,585
Space launch equipment	—	384	—	660	—	308	—	408	—	414

[1]Revised.
[2]Estimate.
[3]Forecast.

NOTE: Totals do not correspond to SIC-based trade statistics because of slightly broader coverage. Data shown for certain products for 1989–1993 are not comparable to previous year because of category changes made under the Harmonized System.

SOURCE: U.S. Department of Commerce: International Trade Administration (ITA) and Bureau of the Census. Estimates and forecasts by ITA.

U.S. Imports of Aerospace Vehicles and Equipment, 1989–93

(customs values in millions of dollars)

Items	1989		1990		1991[1]		1992[2]		1993[3]	
	Units	Value	Units	Value	Units	Value	Units	Value	Units	Value
Aerospace vehicles and equipment, total	—	10,508	—	12,124	—	13,468	—	13,435		14,701
Civilian aircraft	1,591	2,775	636	2,774	768	3,412	628	4,730	688	5,993
Under 4,536 kg. unladen weight, new	1,127	142	146	228	156	200	120	140	130	190
4,536–15,000 kg. unladen weight, new	131	1,018	163	1,354	143	1,368	120	1,210	145	1,400
Over 15,000 kg. unladen weight, new	36	1,282	30	737	44	1,285	76	2,900	83	3,900
Rotocraft, new	124	103	167	162	244	289	200	170	210	200
Other aircraft, nec, new	—	2	—	1	—	3	—	3	—	3
Used or rebuilt	173	228	130	292	181	267	112	307	120	300
Military aircraft	29	16	28	44	16	22	20	45	22	50
Aircraft engines and parts	—	3,910	—	4,743	—	4,988	—	4,676	—	4,633
Piston engines and parts	—	184	—	101	—	102	—	72	—	75
Complete engines, new and used	2,833	43	3,152	36	9,379	53	2,626	34	2,652	35
Engine parts	—	141	—	65	—	48	—	38	—	40
Turbine engines and parts	—	3,726	—	4,642	—	4,886	—	4,604	—	4,558
Complete engines, new and used	2,283	1,921	5,007	2,407	2,032	2,370	2,000	2,200	1,980	2,178
Engine parts	—	1,805	—	2,235	—	2,516	—	2,404	—	2,380
Aircraft parts, nec	—	3,339	—	3,688	—	4,391	—	3,300	—	3,400
Avionics	—	252	—	280	—	290	—	190	—	200
Flight simulators	—	68	—	200	—	173	—	180	—	190
Guided missiles and parts	—	118	—	83	—	106	—	92	—	85
Space launch equipment	—	30	—	312	—	86	—	222	—	150

[1]Revised.
[2]Estimate.
[3]Forecast.
NOTE: Totals do not correspond to SIC-based trade statistics because of slightly broader coverage. Data shown for certain products for 1989–1993 are not comparable to previous years because of category changes made under the Harmonized System.
SOURCE: U.S. Department of Commerce, International Trade Administration (ITA) and Bureau of the Census. Estimates and forecasts by ITA.

Trends and Forecasts: Aircraft (SIC 3721)

(in millions of dollars except as noted)

Item	1987	1988	1989	1990	1991[1]	1992[2]	1993[3]	Percent Change (1987–1993) 87–88	88–89	89–90	90–91	91–92	92–93
Industry Data													
Value of shipments[4]	39,093	41,494	43,339	51,370	55,120	54,073	51,315	6.1	4.4	18.5	7.3	−1.9	−5.1
Value of shipments (1987$)	39,093	40,760	40,166	45,180	46,242	44,069	41,416	4.3	−1.5	12.5	2.4	−4.7	−6.0
Total employment (000)	268	274	278	289	264	253	240	2.2	1.5	4.0	−8.7	−4.2	−5.1
Production workers (000)	142	140	140	140	126	119	112	−1.4	0.0	0.0	−10.0	−5.6	−5.9
Average hourly earnings ($)	15.38	16.16	16.40	17.02	—	—	—	5.1	1.5	3.8	—	—	—
Capital expenditures	1,052	1,030	1,270	1,021	—	—	—	−2.1	23.3	−19.6	—	—	—
Product Data													
Value of shipments[5]	36,003	37,765	39,531	46,885	50,380	49,370	46,800	4.9	4.7	18.6	7.5	−2.0	−5.2
Value of shipments (1987$)	36,003	37,097	36,637	41,236	42,265	40,235	37,771	3.0	−1.2	12.6	2.5	−4.8	−6.1
Trade Data													
Value of imports	—	—	2,805	2,838	3,438	4,088	5,920	—	—	1.2	21.1	18.9	44.8
Value of exports	—	—	14,339	19,631	24,173	24,030	23,250	—	—	36.9	23.1	−0.6	−3.2

[1]Estimated, except exports and imports.
[2]Estimate.
[3]Forecast.
[4]Value of all products and services sold by establishments in the aircraft industry.
[5]Value of products classified in the aircraft industry produced by all industries.

SOURCE: U.S. Department of Commerce: Bureau of the Census, International Trade Administration (ITA). Estimates and forecasts by ITA.

Shipments of Complete U.S. Aircraft, 1971–93

(values in millions of dollars)

Year	Aircraft Total		Civil								Military Total	
			Total		Large Transports		General Aviation[1]		Rotorcraft			
	Units	Value	Units	Value	Units	Value	Units	Value	Units	Value	Units	Value
1971	11,056	6,593	8,142	2,971	223	2,580	7,466	322	453	69	2,914	3,622
1972	13,072	6,220	10,542	3,417	199	2,787	9,774	558	569	72	2,530	2,803
1973	16,509	8,176	14,688	4,814	274	3,873	13,646	828	768	113	1,821	3,362
1974	16,810	8,381	15,297	5,056	322	3,993	14,166	909	809	154	1,513	3,325
1975	17,030	9,136	15,251	5,086	315	3,779	14,072	1,033	864	274	1,779	4,050
1976	17,747	8,888	16,429	4,592	222	3,078	15,450	1,229	757	285	1,318	4,296
1977	19,047	9,031	17,913	4,451	155	2,649	16,910	1,551	848	251	1,134	4,580
1978	19,958	10,177	18,962	6,458	241	4,308	17,817	1,822	904	328	996	3,719
1979	19,297	15,074	18,460	10,644	376	8,030	17,055	2,211	1,029	403	837	4,430
1980	14,681	18,950	13,634	13,058	387	9,895	11,881	2,507	1,366	656	1,047	5,892
1981	11,978	20,093	10,916	13,223	387	9,706	9,457	2,920	1,072	597	1,062	6,870
1982	6,244	19,257	5,085	8,610	232	6,246	4,266	1,999	587	365	1,159	10,647
1983	4,409	22,519	3,356	9,773	262	8,000	2,691	1,470	403	303	1,053	12,746
1984	3,935	21,933	2,999	7,717	185	5,689	2,438	1,698	376	330	936	14,216
1985	3,610	28,386	2,691	10,385	278	8,448	2,029	1,431	384	506	919	18,001
1986	3,258	34,809	2,151	11,857	330	10,308	1,495	1,262	326	287	1,107	22,952
1987	3,010	35,925	1,800	12,148	357	10,507	1,085	1,364	358	277	1,210	23,777
1988	3,254	34,875	1,949	15,855	423	13,603	1,143	1,918	383	334	1,305	19,020
1989	3,675	34,229	2,448	17,129	398	15,074	1,535	1,804	515	251	1,227	17,100
1990	3,486	39,206	2,268	24,476	521	22,215	1,144	2,007	603	254	1,218	14,730
1991	2,934	40,776	2,181	29,035	589	26,856	1,021	1,968	571	211	753	11,741
1992[2]	2,444	42,102	1,807	28,800	567	27,000	780	1,580	460	220	637	13,302
1993[3]	2,430	39,923	1,830	27,379	480	25,500	850	1,650	500	229	600	12,544

[1]Excludes off-the-shelf military aircraft.
[2]Estimate.
[3]Forecast.

SOURCE: U.S. Department of Commerce, International Trade Administration (ITA); general aviation (through 1991), General Aviation Manufacturers Association; rotocraft (through 1991), Aerospace Industries Association. Estimates and forecasts by ITA.

Apparel and Textile Products

The apparel and fabricated textile products industry (SIC 23) consists primarily of firms that produce wearing apparel, both cut and sewn and knit to shape, for all population groups. Apparel accounted for about 73 percent of total industry shipments in 1992. However, fabricated textile products, which include home furnishings, canvas products, and automotive trimmings, are a growing segment of the industry.

The apparel and fabricated textile products industry increased shipments by nearly 1 percent (in constant dollars) in 1992, after four annual declines. The upturn primarily resulted from a moderate pickup in consumer spending for clothing and some rebuilding in inventories in anticipation of economic recovery. By the end of 1991, apparel and fabricated textile products production had recovered to close to the peak levels of a few years earlier, but then eased off in mid-1992 as inventory levels rose when consumer demand did not grow as quickly as anticipated. Prices increased by a modest 2 percent in 1992 (slightly below the average of the past several years) because of heavy competition, particularly from abroad, and only a slight pickup in demand. The industry's capacity utilization increased following three years of decline.

Total employment in the apparel and fabricated textile products industry is about 986,000. It grew by about 2 percent in 1992, the first increase since 1977. The average number of hours worked weekly by production workers increased to its 1989 level, but remained well below earlier years. Manufacturing processes in this industry are labor intensive. Production workers constitute 85 percent of the work force, which compares with 68 percent for all U.S. manufacturing. Wages and profit margins in this sector are low relative to other manufacturing industries. In 1992, the hourly earnings of production workers averaged $6.94, 3 percent above 1991. Earnings of apparel and fabricated textile product workers were about 40 percent below the average for all U.S. manufacturing employees.

Apparel

Personal consumption expenditures on clothing expanded sharply at the beginning of 1992, following declines the two prior years, but then tapered off somewhat after mid-year. Retail sales of apparel and accessory stores, which were flat in 1991, picked up in 1992. Inventories increased to the high levels of two years ago, when the recession began. The ratio of inventory to sales for 1992 is below previous year levels.

In 1991, sales of the larger apparel firms continued to account for an increasing share of all apparel sales, and their profits increased. The contrast between the performance of the larger firms and many of the smaller companies intensified, as profits of the latter group declined in 1991. Consequently, the availability of funds needed for reinvestment in the industry was concentrated in relatively few companies.

Men's and Boys' Apparel

These shipments outperformed the apparel industry as a whole in 1992. According to some industry executives, consumers that have delayed buying apparel for so long need to buy replacement items now, despite the lackluster economy. Growth in domestic demand, coupled with sharply expanding exports, led to the first increase in menswear manufacturing employment in several years. Average hourly earnings also grew moderately. In terms of sales, brand-name apparel performed above the average, as did sales of casual wear such as jeans, T-shirts, and fleecewear. Men's sportswear and activewear are mostly made by the bigger apparel companies in large plants, employing 100 or more workers.

Women's, Girls', and Children's Apparel

Women's wear shipments, which generally outperform the industry, were much lower than the industry average in 1992. This led to employment declines in some women's apparel categories. The bright side of this sector has been exports, which were particularly strong in 1992. In addition to traditional markets, U.S. fashions have recently found new popularity in Europe. As European women increasingly adopt the busier U.S. lifestyle, more are also developing a taste for the clothes U.S. women wear. They are looking for sophisticated styles that feel comfortable and are easy to care for.

Demographic trends have had a major impact on this segment of the market. Apparel expenses are becoming a lower proportion of total personal expenditures for the large part of the population that has reached the age where mortgages and the education of children are main concerns. In addition, a leveling off of the number of women entering the work force, and a shift in consumer buying habits to discounters and off-price stores have significantly affected the value of shipments of women's and girls' apparel. In the domestic market, the fleece and T-shirt segments have been the steadiest performers.

Domestic manufacturers of children's wear have generally been able to increase shipments during the past few years, and in 1991 this sector outperformed the market as a whole. In 1992, children's apparel shipments grew at the same rate as for the entire industry. Retail buying in this sector is particularly dependent on price.

Children's wear shipments will continue to perform well, largely as the result of demographic trends. More children have been born in recent years, and more first births are to older, better educated, and more affluent parents who can and do spend more on their children. Grandparents, who are living longer and have more discretionary income, are also playing an increasingly significant role in purchases of children's clothing.

Fabricated Textile Products

The fabricated textile products industry (SIC 239) consists of eight industry groups: curtains and draperies (SIC 2391), housefurnishings (SIC 2392), textile bags (SIC 2393), canvas and related products (SIC 2394), pleating and stitching (SIC 2395), automotive and apparel trimmings (SIC 2396), schiffli machine embroideries (SIC 2397), and fabricated textile products, nec (SIC 2399). Products in the last group include badges, sleeping bags, nondisposable diapers, fishing nets, parachutes, and seat belts. These industries account for a significant share of total SIC 23 industry shipments—about 27 percent in 1992. Textile housefurnishings and automotive and apparel trimmings constitute the largest shares of SIC 239 industry shipments—28 percent and 30 percent, respectively.

Industry shipments of fabricated textile products increased about 3 percent in current dollars in 1992, with strong performances in canvas products, pleating and stitching, and miscellaneous fabricated products. In 1991, the textile home furnishings market was adversely affected by a contraction in the housing market. Shipments by the industry declined 4 percent. By mid-1992, shipments had almost recovered to their peak level of 1990, while personal consumption and residential construction showed signs of improvement. New product lines that have received favorable responses from consumers are all-in-one sets, such as bed in a bag that contains sheets and pillowcases; and kitchen in a bag that contains kitchen towels, pot holders, dish cloths, oven mitts, chair pads, and vinyl place mats.

Domestic industry shipments of pleating and stitching and apparel trimmings have expanded because apparel manufacturers are using more embroideries, trimmings, and appliques to add value to garments and make them more individualized. The most popular trims and embroideries are fringe for western themes, chenille, geometric shapes, and lace and ruffles. Popular appliques include venice lace for children's wear, baseball nostalgia, motorcycle motifs, and western themes. Moderate improvement in the automotive market augmented demand for automotive trimmings and seat belts.

Employment in the fabricated textile industry improved in 1992, following almost continuous declines since 1987. The industry is still relatively labor intensive, with production workers accounting for more than 80 percent of total employment. Fabricated textile product manufacturers, especially in the home furnishing sector, are using computer technologies to increase productivity, design capability, and quality.

Technological Advances

Innovative new technology has been adopted rather unevenly in the overall apparel and fabricated textile products industry because of the large number of firms and the wide variety in size and operations. Almost universally, larger firms have undertaken capital investment programs, resulting in more efficient operations and greater responsiveness to the marketplace. Companies with large-scale operations have the best opportunities for cost-saving improvements and have the financial resources to invest in the sizable expenditures required. Most of the large apparel firms were able to continue technology investments in 1992, but many smaller and mid-size firms had to curtail or postpone planned new equipment expenditures. Virtually all firms, regardless of size, have realized the need to improve the quality of their products as consumers become more demanding.

An area where companies are investing heavily in new technology is communications systems that provide faster ways of determining and responding to consumer preferences in the marketplace. This concept, known as "quick response," involves shortening the production cycle, improving productivity, reducing inventories, and speeding the feedback of consumer preferences to the manufacturing level. Quick response is accomplished by introducing computers to track materials and sales, and also by expanding the use of consumer surveys to determine what should be produced. Major department stores and clothing manufacturers have also been working more closely together to speed restocking time and to determine more efficient ways to reduce order turnaround. In addition to reducing manufacturing costs and raising efficiency, these improvements increase operational flexibility to respond more quickly to changing apparel marketing styles and preferences. Systems designed to work with more standardized products, other than high fashion such as underwear and children's wear, tend to be the most successful, although great strides are being made in quick response by many companies.

All sizes of companies have made major investments in computerization, particularly in information systems. Although the U.S. apparel industry has not been able to reduce its labor needs as extensively as other industries, certain tasks can be automated. Computers and computer-controlled machines have also been used to increase productivity and production efficiency in design, sewing, embroidery, finishing, ticketing, distribution, and other operations. Large and mid-size firms place the most emphasis on high technology machinery, while the smaller companies often buy basic, non-computerized equipment.

INTERNATIONAL COMPETITIVENESS

Exports of apparel and fabricated textile products have grown sharply in recent years, from more than 2 percent of product shipments in 1987 to more than 7 percent in 1992. However, a substantial portion of the gain represents components that are sent abroad for assembly and then reenter the United States under the 9802 provision of the Harmonized Tariff Schedule of the United States (HTSUS). The importer pays duty only on the value-added abroad under HTSUS 9802. Assisted by the weakness of the U.S. dollar, exports of finished apparel products in 1992 were quite strong to Japan and Canada, and also rose sharply to Europe and the Middle East. Men's and women's clothing exports have experienced particularly strong growth. Children's wear exports are relatively insignificant and have declined the past two years. Exports of fabricated textile products continued to expand in 1992, although at a slower pace than in previous years. Mexico and Canada accounted for more than 55 percent of total SIC 239 exports in 1991–92.

Apparel and fabricated textile products imported into the United States are governed by the Arrangement Regarding International Trade in Textiles, known as the Multifiber Arrangement (MFA), which provides guidelines for member nations regarding international trade in textiles and apparel. The MFA is scheduled to expire at the end of December 1992. Apparel trade is also covered under the General Agreement on Tariffs and Trade (GATT), under whose auspices multilateral trade negotiations (the Uruguay Round) are currently taking place. If an agreement is reached in the Uruguay Round, its textile provisions will gradually supplant the MFA; if not, the MFA will probably be extended.

An increased portion of U.S. apparel imports enter the United States under the HTSUS 9802 (formerly 807) program. In 1989, factories abroad that assembled garments from U.S. components accounted for almost 10 percent of apparel imports. By 1992, this share had increased to about 14 percent. Mexico and the Caribbean Basin countries shipped most HTSUS 9802 imports. Apparel trade will also be affected by the North American Free Trade Agreement (NAFTA) among the United States, Canada, and Mexico. If and when the agreement is implemented, apparel trade is expected to increase among the three countries. Many Caribbean Basin countries are concerned about a shift in apparel production from their countries to Mexico as a result of NAFTA.

Imports of apparel expanded in 1992, mainly because of greater arrivals of men's and women's outerwear. The largest increase was from China, which replaced Hong Kong as the largest foreign apparel supplier to the U.S. market. In addition to the countries with a large portion of HTSUS 9802 trade, imports grew rapidly from India, Indonesia, Malaysia, Thailand, Sri Lanka, Bangladesh, Macao, and Canada.

Measured by the degree of U.S. market penetration, imports have not affected fabricated textile products as much as the overall apparel industry. In 1992, imports of fabricated textile products, which accounted for only about 8 percent of total SIC 23 imports, rose 5 percent. Significant increases came from the major suppliers, Mexico and China, while Malaysia, Spain, and Bangladesh also improved their supply positions.

LONG-TERM PROSPECTS

The resumption of moderate growth in the U.S. apparel and fabricated textile products industry will continue during the next few years. Factors contributing to a favorable long-term outlook include higher consumer spending, housing starts, and new car purchases. Demographic changes will continue to play an important role in determining demand for both apparel and fabricated textile products, as will continuing growth in international trade and investment. Growing concerns about environmental and health issues are among the challenges these industries face.

During the next several years, the U.S.

apparel marketplace will become increasingly competitive, with more overseas producers vying with U.S. manufacturers for a share of the market.

International markets will become increasingly more important to the industry. With the help of a favorably valued dollar, innovative and aggressive producers can expand exports to opening markets in Eastern Europe, the newly independent states of the former Soviet Union, and the Middle East. The industry also has the opportunity to take advantage of the growing demand of Western European consumers for fashionable, high-quality clothing.—*Joanne Tucker (Apparel) and Maria D'Andrea (Fabricated Textile Products), Office of Textiles and Apparel, (202) 482-4058.*

Trends and Forecasts: Apparel and Other Textile Products (SIC 23)

(in millions of dollars except as noted)

Item	1987	1988	1989	1990	1991[1]	1992[2]	Percent Change (1987-1992) 87-88	88-89	89-90	90-91	91-92
Industry Data											
Value of shipments[3]	64,243	65,032	63,398	64,414	64,543	66,479	1.2	−2.5	1.6	0.2	3.0
Value of shipments (1987$)	64,243	63,129	60,185	59,483	58,057	58,603	−1.7	−4.7	−1.2	−2.4	0.9
Total employment (000)	1,081	1,066	1,018	993	965	986	−1.4	−4.5	−2.5	−2.8	2.2
Production workers (000)	912	895	865	845	819	839	−1.9	−3.4	−2.3	−3.1	2.4
Average hourly earnings ($)	6.11	6.34	6.46	6.54	6.74	6.94	3.8	1.9	1.2	3.1	3.0
Product Data											
Value of shipments[4]	62,119	62,750	61,447	61,962	62,086	63,949	1.0	−2.1	0.8	0.2	3.0
Value of shipments (1987$)	62,119	60,940	58,349	57,236	55,847	56,372	−1.9	−4.3	−1.9	−2.4	0.9
Trade Data											
Value of imports	—	—	22,704	24,498	25,351	28,176	—	—	7.9	3.5	11.1
Value of exports	—	—	2,354	2,849	3,667	4,717	—	—	21.0	28.7	28.6

[1]Estimated, except exports and imports.

[2]Estimate.

[3]Value of all products and services sold by establishments in the apparel and other textile products industry.

[4]Value of products classified in the apparel and other textile products industry produced by all industries.

SOURCE: U.S. Department of Commerce: Bureau of the Census, International Trade Administration (ITA). Estimates and forecasts by ITA.

Trends and Forecasts: Selected Men's and Boys' Apparel (SIC 231, 2321, 2323, 2325, 2326)

(in millions of dollars except as noted)

Item	1987	1988	1989	1990	1991[1]	1992[2]	Percent Change (1987–1992) 87–88	88–89	89–90	90–91	91–92
Industry Data											
Value of shipments[3]	14,969	15,101	14,772	14,484	14,522	15,127	0.9	−2.2	−1.9	0.3	4.2
2311 Men/boys' suits/coats	2,863	3,169	2,918	2,622	2,614	2,804	10.7	−7.9	−10.1	−.3	7.3
2321 Men's and boys' shirts	4,075	4,031	3,873	4,243	4,153	4,320	−1.1	−3.9	9.6	−2.1	4.0
2323 Men's and boys' neckwear	476	500	534	500	494	455	5.0	6.8	−6.4	−1.2	−7.9
2325 Men/boys' trousers	6,014	5,767	5,983	5,657	5,809	5,987	−4.1	3.7	−5.4	2.7	3.1
2326 Men/boys' work clothing	1,542	1,633	1,464	1,462	1,452	1,561	5.9	−10.3	−0.1	−0.7	7.5
Value of shipments (1987$)	14,969	14,508	13,719	13,070	12,773	13,141	−3.1	−5.4	−4.7	−2.3	2.9
2311 Men/boys' suits/coats	2,863	3,010	2,596	2,239	2,180	2,308	5.1	−13.8	−13.8	−2.6	5.9
2321 Men's and boys' shirts	4,075	3,876	3,613	3,836	3,638	3,650	−4.9	−6.8	6.2	−5.2	0.3
2323 Men's and boys' neckwear	476	490	496	447	431	368	2.9	1.2	−9.9	−3.6	−14.6
2325 Men/boys' trousers	6,014	5,562	5,655	5,224	5,246	5,459	−7.5	1.7	−7.6	0.4	4.1
2326 Men/boys' work clothing	1,542	1,570	1,360	1,324	1,278	1,356	1.8	−13.4	−2.6	−3.5	6.1
Total employment (000)	266	270	258	239	236	246	1.5	−4.4	−7.4	−1.3	4.2
2311 Men/boys' suits/coats	55.2	60.0	54.5	48.4	46.0	44.0	8.7	−9.2	−11.2	−5.0	−4.3
2321 Men's and boys' shirts	76.7	77.4	73.7	69.7	68.0	73.0	0.9	−4.8	−5.4	−2.4	7.4
2323 Men's and boys' neckwear	7.4	7.5	8.0	7.4	7.0	8.0	1.4	6.7	−7.5	−5.4	14.3
2325 Men/boys' trousers	93.3	91.9	88.0	81.7	84.3	88.2	−1.5	−4.2	−7.2	3.2	4.6
2326 Men/boys' work clothing	33.1	33.3	34.0	31.5	30.9	32.7	0.6	2.1	−7.4	−1.9	5.8
Production workers (000)	232	236	225	208	207	217	1.7	−4.7	−7.6	−0.5	4.8
2311 Men/boys' suits/coats	48.1	51.7	47.0	41.3	39.0	38.0	7.5	−9.1	−12.1	−5.6	−2.6
2321 Men's and boys' shirts	66.6	68.0	65.1	61.7	60.8	65.6	2.1	−4.3	−5.2	−1.5	7.9
2323 Men's and boys' neckwear	6.2	6.2	6.6	6.0	6.0	7.0	0.0	6.5	−9.1	0.0	16.7
2325 Men/boys' trousers	82.3	80.8	76.7	71.6	73.7	77.7	−1.8	−5.1	−6.6	2.9	5.4
2326 Men/boys' work clothing	29.0	29.5	30.0	27.8	27.2	28.6	1.7	1.7	−7.3	−2.2	5.1
Average hourly earnings ($)	5.92	6.18	6.42	6.61	6.84	7.08	4.4	3.9	3.0	3.5	3.5
2311 Men/boys' suits/coats	6.95	7.09	7.58	7.84	7.96	8.08	2.0	6.9	3.4	1.5	1.5
2321 Men's and boys' shirts	5.45	5.77	6.29	6.46	6.72	7.06	5.9	9.0	2.7	4.0	5.1
2323 Men's and boys' neckwear	6.98	7.15	7.04	7.28	7.24	7.16	2.4	−1.5	3.4	−0.5	−1.1
2325 Men/boys' trousers	5.88	6.26	6.17	6.43	6.68	6.98	6.5	−1.4	4.2	3.9	4.5
2326 Men/boys' work clothing	5.17	5.17	5.41	5.46	5.67	5.89	0.0	4.6	0.9	3.8	3.9

(continued)

Trends and Forecasts: Selected Men's and Boys' Apparel (SIC 231, 2321, 2323, 2325, 2326) *(concluded)*

(in millions of dollars except as noted)

Item	1987	1988	1989	1990	1991[1]	1992[2]	Percent Change (1987–1992) 87–88	88–89	89–90	90–91	91–92
Product Data											
Value of shipments[4]	14,035	14,174	14,383	13,771	13,817	14,392	1.0	1.5	−4.3	0.3	4.2
2311 Men/boys' suits/coats	2,877	2,977	2,915	2,633	2,625	2,816	3.5	−2.1	−9.7	−.3	7.3
2321 Men's and boys' shirts	3,842	3,728	3,681	3,740	3,661	3,808	−3.0	−1.3	1.6	−2.1	4.0
2323 Men's and boys' neckwear	422	457	526	498	492	453	8.3	15.1	−5.3	−1.2	−7.9
2325 Men/boys' trousers	5,474	5,475	5,889	5,544	5,693	5,868	0.0	7.6	−5.9	2.7	3.1
2326 Men/boys' work clothing	1,420	1,537	1,372	1,355	1,346	1,447	8.2	−10.7	−1.2	−0.7	7.5
Value of shipments (1987$)	14,035	13,617	13,355	12,422	12,151	12,509	−3.0	−1.9	−7.0	−2.2	2.9
2311 Men/boys' suits/coats	2,877	2,827	2,593	2,248	2,189	2,318	−1.7	−8.3	−13.3	−2.6	5.9
2321 Men's and boys' shirts	3,842	3,584	3,433	3,382	3,206	3,217	−6.7	−4.2	−1.5	−5.2	0.3
2323 Men's and boys' neckwear	422	448	489	445	430	367	6.2	9.2	−9.0	−3.4	−14.7
2325 Men/boys' trousers	5,474	5,279	5,566	5,119	5,141	5,350	−3.6	5.4	−8.0	0.4	4.1
2326 Men/boys' work clothing	1,420	1,478	1,274	1,228	1,185	1,257	4.1	−13.8	−3.6	−3.5	6.1
Trade Data											
Value of imports	—	—	5,289	5,374	5,677	6,792	—	—	1.6	5.6	19.6
2311 Men/boys' suits/coats	—	—	777	683	695	680	—	—	−12.1	1.8	−2.2
2321 Men's and boys' shirts	—	—	2,519	2,523	2,703	3,324	—	—	0.2	7.1	23.0
2323 Men's and boys' neckwear	—	—	104	112	142	150	—	—	7.7	26.8	5.6
2325 Men/boys' trousers	—	—	1,885	2,052	2,133	2,634	—	—	8.9	3.9	23.5
2326 Men/boys' work clothing	—	—	4.6	4.1	4.0	4.2	—	—	−10.9	−2.4	5.0
Value of exports	—	—	757	958	1,230	1,661	—	—	26.6	28.4	35.0
2311 Men/boys' suits/coats	—	—	104	140	168	216	—	—	34.6	20.0	28.6
2321 Men's and boys' shirts	—	—	246	322	435	605	—	—	30.9	35.1	39.1
2323 Men's and boys' neckwear	—	—	10.1	9.8	14.5	16.0	—	—	−3.0	48.0	10.3
2325 Men/boys' trousers	—	—	397	486	612	824	—	—	22.4	25.9	34.6
2326 Men/boys' work clothing	—	—	0.0	0.0	0.0	0.0	—	—	—	—	—

[1]Estimated, except exports and imports.

[2]Estimate.

[3]Value of all products and services sold by establishments in the selected men's and boys' apparel industry.

[4]Value of products classified in the selected men's and boys' apparel industry produced by all industries.

SOURCE: U.S. Department of Commerce: Bureau of the Census, International Trade Administration (ITA). Estimates and forecasts by ITA.

Trends and Forecasts: Selected Women's Outerwear (SIC 2331, 2335, 2337)

(in millions of dollars except as noted)

Item	1987	1988	1989	1990	1991[1]	1992[2]	Percent Change (1987–1992) 87–88	88–89	89–90	90–91	91–92
Industry Data											
Value of shipments[3]	13,726	14,316	13,009	13,810	14,200	14,360	4.3	−9.1	6.2	2.8	1.1
2331 Women's/misses' blouses	3,831	3,574	3,402	3,733	3,763	3,777	−6.7	−4.8	9.7	0.8	0.4
2335 Women's/misses' dresses	5,448	6,037	5,366	5,915	6,106	6,203	10.8	−11.1	10.2	3.2	1.6
2337 Women's suits and coats	4,447	4,705	4,241	4,163	4,331	4,380	5.8	−9.9	−1.8	4.0	1.1
Value of shipments (1987$)	13,726	13,818	12,277	12,688	12,686	12,576	0.7	−11.2	3.3	−0.0	−0.9
2331 Women's/misses' blouses	3,831	3,473	3,219	3,375	3,283	3,198	−9.3	−7.3	4.8	−2.7	−2.6
2335 Women's/misses' dresses	5,448	5,856	4,968	5,314	5,348	5,432	7.5	−15.2	7.0	0.6	1.6
2337 Women's suits and coats	4,447	4,489	4,089	3,999	4,055	3,946	0.9	−8.9	−2.2	1.4	−2.7
Total employment (000)	241	235	215	217	209	203	−2.5	−8.5	0.9	−3.7	−2.9
2331 Women's/misses' blouses	73.4	67.0	64.6	64.4	62.1	62.1	−8.7	−3.6	−0.3	−3.6	0.0
2335 Women's/misses' dresses	113	115	105	106	99.8	96.5	1.8	−8.7	1.0	−5.8	−3.3
2337 Women's suits and coats	55.2	53.3	46.1	45.9	47.4	44.6	−3.4	−13.5	−0.4	3.3	−5.9
Production workers (000)	199	191	180	184	178	174	−4.0	−5.8	2.2	−3.3	−2.2
2331 Women's/misses' blouses	63.2	56.7	55.2	54.3	52.4	52.9	−10.3	−2.6	−1.6	−3.5	1.0
2335 Women's/misses' dresses	91.5	91.8	89.2	93.3	86.8	84.5	0.3	−2.8	4.6	−7.0	−2.6
2337 Women's suits and coats	44.6	42.2	36.0	36.6	38.5	36.4	−5.4	−14.7	1.7	5.2	−5.5
Average hourly earnings ($)	5.95	6.20	6.16	6.13	6.45	6.60	4.2	−0.6	−0.5	5.2	2.3
2331 Women's/misses' blouses	5.38	5.65	5.70	5.85	6.10	6.28	5.0	0.9	2.6	4.3	3.0
2335 Women's/misses' dresses	6.08	6.40	6.10	5.93	6.13	6.30	5.3	−4.7	−2.8	3.4	2.8
2337 Women's suits and coats	6.53	6.57	7.02	7.00	7.20	7.32	0.6	6.8	−0.3	2.9	1.7

(continued)

Trends and Forecasts: Selected Women's Outerwear (SIC 2331, 2335, 2337) *(concluded)*

(in millions of dollars except as noted)

Item	1987	1988	1989	1990	1991[1]	1992[2]	Percent Change (1987–1992) 87–88	88–89	89–90	90–91	91–92
Product Data											
Value of shipments[4]	13,410	13,927	12,500	12,817	13,167	13,316	3.9	−10.2	2.5	2.7	1.1
2331 Women's/misses' blouses	4,178	3,983	3,635	3,660	3,689	3,703	−4.7	−8.7	0.7	0.8	0.4
2335 Women's/misses' dresses	5,347	5,810	5,245	5,746	5,931	6,026	8.7	−9.7	9.6	3.2	1.6
2337 Women's suits and coats	3,885	4,134	3,620	3,410	3,547	3,587	6.4	−12.4	−5.8	4.0	1.1
Value of shipments (1987$)	13,410	13,450	11,786	11,748	11,734	11,644	0.3	−12.4	−0.3	−0.1	−0.8
2331 Women's/misses' blouses	4,178	3,871	3,439	3,309	3,218	3,135	−7.3	−11.2	−3.8	−2.8	−2.6
2335 Women's/misses' dresses	5,347	5,636	4,856	5,163	5,195	5,277	5.4	−13.8	6.3	0.6	1.6
2337 Women's suits and coats	3,885	3,944	3,491	3,276	3,321	3,232	1.5	−11.5	−6.2	1.4	−2.7
Trade Data											
Value of imports	—	—	7,784	8,127	8,168	9,386	—	—	4.4	0.5	14.9
2331 Women's/misses' blouses	—	—	2,857	2,850	2,734	3,270	—	—	−0.2	−4.1	19.6
2335 Women's/misses' dresses	—	—	884	970	945	1,094	—	—	9.7	−2.6	15.8
2337 Women's suits and coats	—	—	4,043	4,307	4,490	5,022	—	—	6.5	4.2	11.8
Value of exports	—	—	321	370	501	752	—	—	15.3	35.4	50.1
2331 Women's/misses' blouses	—	—	36.8	37.8	45.8	76.0	—	—	2.7	21.2	65.9
2335 Women's/misses' dresses	—	—	49.0	56.2	69.0	108	—	—	14.7	22.8	56.5
2337 Women's suits and coats	—	—	235	276	386	568	—	—	17.4	39.9	47.2

[1]Estimated, except exports and imports.
[2]Estimate.
[3]Value of all products and services sold by establishments in the selected women's outerwear industry.
[4]Value of products classified in the selected women's outerwear industry produced by all industries.
SOURCE: U.S. Department of Commerce: Bureau of the Census, International Trade Administration (ITA). Estimates and forecasts by ITA.

Trends and Forecasts: Women's and Children's Undergarments (SIC 234)

(in millions of dollars except as noted)

Item	1987	1988	1989	1990	1991[1]	1992[2]	Percent Change (1987–1992) 87–88	88–89	89–90	90–91	91–92
Industry Data											
Value of shipments[3]	3,738	3,884	3,366	3,424	3,356	3,391	3.9	−13.3	1.7	−2.0	1.0
2341 Women/child's underwear	2,658	2,621	2,301	2,337	2,282	2,299	−1.4	−12.2	1.6	−2.4	0.7
2342 Bras and allied garments	1,080	1,263	1,064	1,087	1,074	1,092	16.9	−15.8	2.2	−1.2	1.7
Value of shipments (1987$)	3,738	3,764	3,190	3,199	3,087	3,005	0.7	−15.2	0.3	−3.5	−2.7
2341 Women/child's underwear	2,658	2,543	2,189	2,180	2,099	2,072	−4.3	−13.9	−0.4	−3.7	−1.3
2342 Bras and allied garments	1,080	1,221	1,000	1,019	988	933	13.1	−18.1	1.9	−3.0	−5.6
Total employment (000)	67.5	66.8	61.2	60.3	59.1	57.0	−1.0	−8.4	−1.5	−2.2	−3.4
2341 Women/child's underwear	53.7	53.9	49.4	48.7	48.1	45.9	0.4	−8.3	−1.4	−1.2	−4.6
2342 Bras and allied garments	13.8	12.9	11.8	11.6	11.0	11.2	−6.5	−8.5	−1.7	−5.2	1.8
Production workers (000)	56.2	56.0	51.6	50.8	49.0	48.0	−0.4	−7.9	−1.6	−3.5	−2.0
2341 Women/child's underwear	46.5	46.7	43.2	42.3	41.2	39.5	0.4	−7.5	−2.1	−2.6	−4.1
2342 Bras and allied garments	9.7	9.3	8.4	8.5	8.1	8.6	−4.1	−9.7	1.2	−4.7	6.2
Average hourly earnings ($)	5.70	5.87	5.75	6.02	6.30	6.51	3.0	−2.0	4.7	4.7	3.3
2341 Women/child's underwear	5.72	5.83	5.68	5.96	6.25	6.41	1.9	−2.6	4.9	4.9	2.6
2342 Bras and allied garments	5.63	6.03	6.16	6.34	6.59	7.01	7.1	2.2	2.9	3.9	6.4
Product Data											
Value of shipments[4]	3,575	3,644	3,365	3,322	3,258	3,292	1.9	−7.7	−1.3	−1.9	1.0
2341 Women/child's underwear	2,591	2,513	2,303	2,119	2,069	2,084	−3.0	−8.4	−8.0	−2.4	0.7
2342 Bras and allied garments	983	1,131	1,062	1,203	1,189	1,208	15.1	−6.1	13.3	−1.2	1.6
Value of shipments (1987$)	3,575	3,531	3,189	3,104	2,997	2,912	−1.2	−9.7	−2.7	−3.4	−2.8
2341 Women/child's underwear	2,591	2,438	2,191	1,976	1,904	1,879	−5.9	−10.1	−9.8	−3.6	−1.3
2342 Bras and allied garments	983	1,094	998	1,127	1,093	1,033	11.3	−8.8	12.9	−3.0	−5.5
Trade Data											
Value of imports	—	—	928	1,078	1,256	1,282	—	—	16.2	16.5	2.1
2341 Women/child's underwear	—	—	601	726	829	794	—	—	20.8	14.2	−4.2
2342 Bras and allied garments	—	—	327	352	427	488	—	—	7.6	21.3	14.3
Value of exports	—	—	254	266	355	442	—	—	4.7	33.5	24.5
2341 Women/child's underwear	—	—	88.4	95.9	136	178	—	—	8.5	41.8	30.9
2342 Bras and allied garments	—	—	165	170	219	264	—	—	3.0	28.8	20.5

[1]Estimated, except exports and imports.
[2]Estimate.
[3]Value of all products and services sold by establishments in the women's and children's undergarments industry.
[4]Value of products classified in the women's and children's undergarments industry produced by all industries.
SOURCE: U.S. Department of Commerce: Bureau of the Census, International Trade Administration (ITA). Estimates and forecasts by ITA.

Apparel Producers Use Offshore Assembly

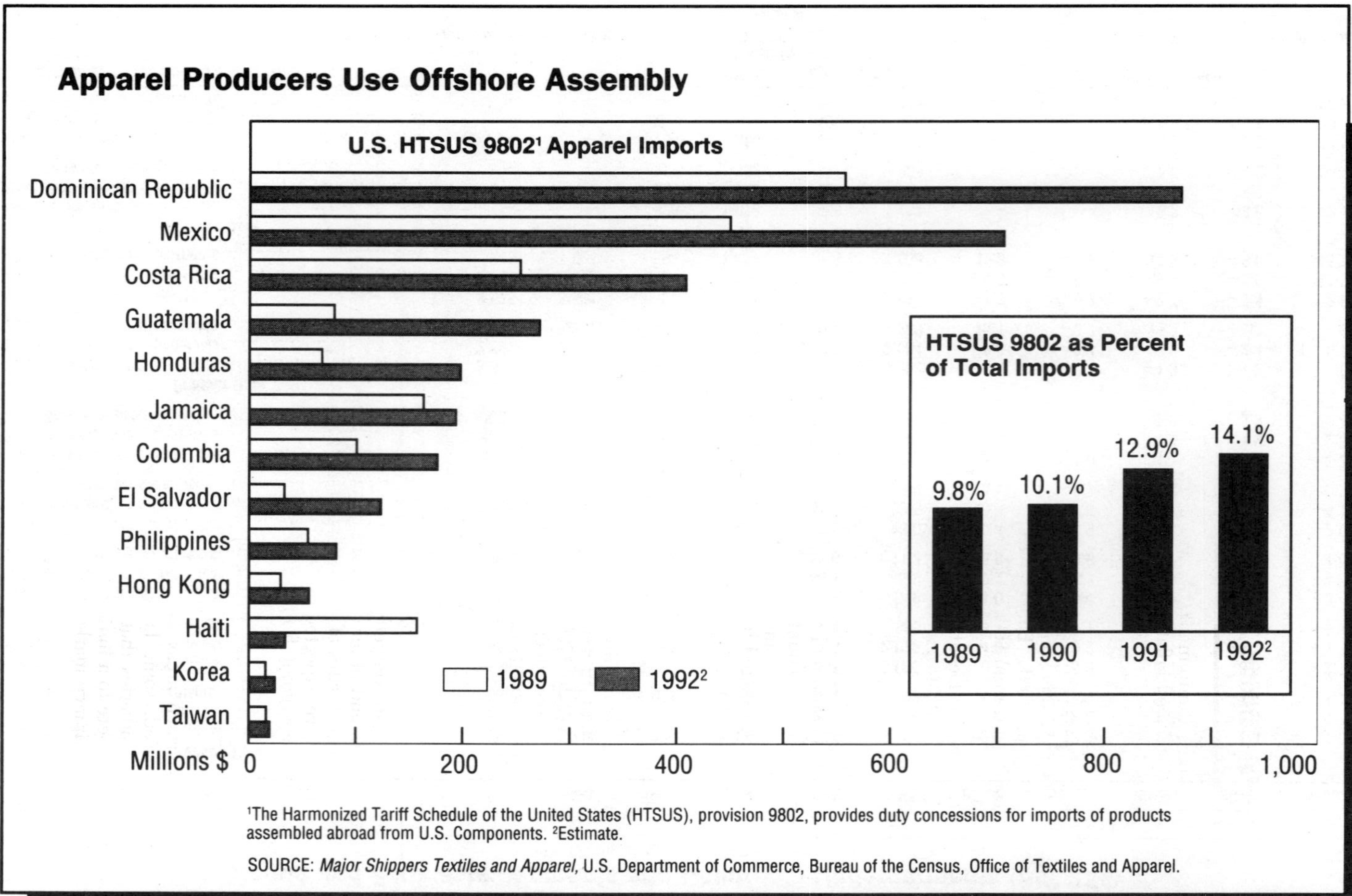

[1]The Harmonized Tariff Schedule of the United States (HTSUS), provision 9802, provides duty concessions for imports of products assembled abroad from U.S. Components. [2]Estimate.

SOURCE: *Major Shippers Textiles and Apparel*, U.S. Department of Commerce, Bureau of the Census, Office of Textiles and Apparel.

Banking

Commercial Banking

The economic slump in 1991, lower interest rates, and reduced inflationary pressures, induced corporations to eschew banks and to return to the stock and bond markets to fund their short-term liabilities. For that reason, aggregate commercial bank loans dropped from $2,309 billion in 1990 to $2,284 billion in 1991. Bank investments jumped 16 percent, from $606 billion to $705 billion.

Following the 1991 cautious credit stance on the part of both lenders and borrowers, 1992 saw a slight rebound in loan demand in such areas as residential mortgages, home equity loans, and consumer lending. On the other hand, credit standards for commercial real estate loans continued to be tight while banks throughout the country maintained a wary attitude towards loans to underdeveloped countries, leveraged buyouts, and junk bonds. Consequently, as long as economic activity maintained its steady but slow upward trend, bank loans in 1992 were expected to fare a little better, rising a modest 2 percent from $2,284 billion in 1991 to $2,330 billion in 1992. Bank investments are expected to rise about 12 percent, going from $705 billion in 1991 to $790 billion in 1992.

Furthermore, the decrease in interest rates on savings accounts and certificates of deposit in 1991 and 1992 has had a dampening effect on the level of bank deposits. Bank deposits increased 1.2 percent in 1991, going from $2,363 billion in 1990 to $2,392 billion in 1991.

As banks tried to compete with other savings instruments and other financial institutions offering higher rates of return, bank deposits in 1992 were expected to show only a 3 percent increase, going from $2,392 billion in 1991 to $2,465 billion in 1992.

Competition from other financial institutions is pressuring banks to continue fighting the numerous regulations that restrict them from entering such areas as insurance and securities. Indeed, some larger banks have established subsidiaries that bank regulators allowed to compete to a limited extent in securities and insurance markets.

Profitability of Banks

As a result of declines in short-term interest rates and of gains in securities transactions, commercial bank profitability rates edged up slightly in 1991 but not enough to lift banks out of their 1989–1991 depressed profit picture. Banks, however, improved their capital and liquidity position during the first half of 1992, eased credit standards, and are in a better position to respond effectively to a livelier rate of loan demand.

The average return on assets, measured by net income as a percentage of average fully consolidated assets went from 0.49 percent in 1990 to 0.54 in 1991. The most progress was experienced by large banks, other than the 10 largest, their return on assets going from 0.28 to 0.58 percent. The 10 largest banks suffered the biggest decline, going from 0.47 to 0.21 percent.

The average return on equity, measured by net income as a percentage of average equity capital, also grew slightly for the industry as a whole, going from 8.02 percent in 1990 to 8.09 in 1991. As with the return on assets, the most progress was experienced by large banks, other than the 10 largest, their return on equity jumping from 5.82 percent to 9.40. The 10 largest banks suffered the biggest decline, falling from 10.11 percent to 4.26.

Failures and Problem Banks

The improvement in the financial health of commercial banks is also reflected by the number of failed banks in 1991 that dropped to 124, from 168 in 1990, and 206 in 1989. The number of banks on the problem list of the Federal Deposit Insurance Corporation (FDIC), however, were slightly up, going from 1,046 in 1990 to 1,090 in 1991. This compares to 1,110 in 1989, 1,415 in 1988, 1,575 in 1987, and 1,484 in 1986.

As a consequence of these bank failures and the depletion of the Bank Insurance Fund, the FDIC increased the premium rates it charges banks from a flat 23 cents for each $100 of insured deposits to an average of 25.4 cents beginning January 1, 1993, with healthy banks continuing to pay 23 cents and weak ones as much as 31 cents. A report by the FDIC, required by Congress, predicts that the premiums will remain constant for at least four years before starting to decline. It also predicts that the Fund will show a deficit through 1999 then start edging up to the prescribed level by 2006. The prescribed level has been mandated by Congress and is 1.25 percent of insured deposits.

INTERNATIONAL ACTIVITIES

The number of foreign bank offices in the United States rose steadily throughout the past two decades, reaching 747 at the beginning of 1992.

These offices include 385 branches, 231 agencies, 99 subsidiaries more than 25 percent owned by foreign banks, 19 Edge Act and Agreement Corporations, and 13 New York State Investment Companies. Nearly one-half of the offices are in New York, with most of the rest in California, Illinois, and Florida. Japan, Canada, France, and the United Kingdom have the largest number of bank offices in the United States. Assets of foreign bank offices in the United States have increased significantly in recent years, rising from $198 billion in 1980 to $864 billion in 1991 or approximately one-fourth of the total banking assets.

In contrast to foreign banks in the United States, U.S. banks abroad have been restructuring and consolidating their activities during the past several years. By the end of 1991, 123 Federal Reserve member banks were operating 794 branches in foreign countries and overseas areas of the United States, a decline from 916 branches at the end of 1985. Of the 123 banks, 92 were national banks operating 674 branches, and 31 were state banks operating the remaining 120 branches.

Legislative Issues

Both the Administration and Congress in 1991 considered sweeping new proposals to modernize and strengthen the commercial banking industry. The proposals represented the most far-reaching restructuring of the industry since the 1930's and included abolishing restrictions related to interstate banking and investment banking.

The bill that would have reformed the U.S. banking industry, entitled Financial Institutions Safety and Consumer Choice Act (see *1992 U.S. Industrial Outlook*) failed to garner the support needed and instead a much narrower bill entitled the Federal Deposit Insurance Corporation Improvement Act (FDICIA) of 1991, was passed in the final hours of the 1st Session of the 102nd Congress. This bill, which contains the Foreign Bank Supervision Enhancement Act of 1991, provided, among other things, for FDIC authority to borrow from the Treasury enough to bail out the Bank Insurance Fund, for instituting a number of reforms to the deposit insurance system, for restricting Federal Reserve ability to extend credit to undercapitalized banks, and for increasing the authority of the Federal Reserve Board to approve, terminate, supervise, and examine branches and agencies of foreign banks.

Mid-1992 saw two legislative proposals being considered by Congress, although there were serious doubts as to their immediate passage. The first of the bills was the result of repeated discussions between some of the largest regional banks on the one hand and insurance agent groups on the other. The former were pushing for interstate banking while the latter were arguing for restricted bank insurance activities as a price for ending their opposition to nationwide banking. To add to the difficulties of such a bill being passed, neither the banking nor the insurance factions in these discussions represented the views of the totality of their respective industries.

The second of the bills was an Administration effort to roll back some of the regulations incorporated in the FDICIA of 1991. Among other things, it would have repealed certain provisions that require regulators to establish specific operational standards on loan underwriting and executive compensation; accept bank examinations from state agencies regulators every year rather than every other year; allow regulators to skip a bank's annual examination if they have already examined 80 percent of its holding company's assets; simplify compliance with the Community Reinvestment Act; and delay the effective dates that some of the new regulations take effect.

LONG-TERM PROSPECTS

There will be constant pressure on legislators and regulators alike in 1993 and beyond to address many of the problems afflicting the U.S. banking industry. The decade of the 1990's will see increased competition not only from other financial institutions both domestic and foreign, but also from nonfinancial corporations that are eager to enter the banking field. Competition will most likely take the form of innovation, such as new products and delivery systems; of securitization, such as converting assets into marketable certificates; and of internationalization, such as the elimination of geographic barriers. These challenges have always been the mainstay of the banking community and the result can only be the establishment of a more efficient, customer-oriented, and globally-attuned financial system.—*Wray O. Candilis, Office of Service Industries, (202) 482-0339.*

Savings Institutions

The savings industry's profitability continues to be held down by losses associated with credit-quality problems. "Bad" loans written off at Savings Association Insurance Fund-insured thrifts during the first quarter of 1992 were one-half percent of total assets—still quite high in historical perspective. Other indicators also suggest that such problems are not entirely behind the industry. For instance, thrifts reported almost 2 percent of total loans were delinquent at the end of the quarter, including nearly 12 percent of construction and land loans.

Lingering earnings problems have made it difficult for thrifts—which have been more thinly capitalized, on average, than commercial banks—to strengthen their capital positions. However, as troubled institutions are closed and many private-sector thrifts address their problems, capital ratios are continuing to improve. The average ratio of tangible capital to total assets for existing thrifts increased to 5.2 percent at the end of the first quarter of 1992, from 4.2 percent a year earlier and 3.5 percent in March 1990.

The savings industry, for purposes of this chapter, includes Federal- and state-chartered firms engaged in deposit banking or closely related functions, including fiduciary activities, and lending activities that are primarily associated with home mortgages under the following Standard Industrial Classification (SIC) categories: Federal and state chartered mutual savings banks; savings institutions, federally chartered; savings institutions, not federally chartered (6035, 6036).

The thrift industry currently includes about 2,000 saving institutions insured by the Savings Association Insurance Fund (SAIF) and about 400 savings banks insured by the Bank Insurance Fund (BIF). These institutions hold approximately $850 billion and $235 billion of assets, respectively, at the time of this writing. The industry arguably has entered the final stage of its longstanding consolidation. During the year ending in the first quarter of 1992, 219 thrifts that were in operation a year earlier were either transferred to the Resolution Trust Corporation (RTC), merged, or converted into another type of financial institution. Private sector savings and loans decreased by 10 percent, and operating savings banks were down by 6 percent.

As failed thrifts fell by the wayside, the savings industry generally has been characterized by stronger, healthier institutions. In the first quarter of 1992, the remaining private sector thrifts earned $1.6 billion. This was the fifth consecutive profitable quarter for the industry. However, a sizable number of these thrifts continue to be plagued by low profitability and inadequate capital. Many also continue to be under pressure to downsize in order to meet capital requirements. Overall assets held by SAIF-insured thrifts fell to $858 billion in the first quarter of 1992—down 10.5 percent from a year earlier. Over the same period, tangible capital for the industry grew from $40.5 billion to $45 billion.

The financial condition of the institutions still operating outside of government control varies greatly. This diversity can be illustrated by comparing performance among the four classifications based on the overall health of institutions that the Office of Thrift Supervision uses to analyze industry trends.

Seventy Percent of Assets in Healthiest Thrifts

The healthiest four-fifths of SAIF-insured thrifts—Group I and Group II—have above-average earnings and capital levels. (These groups hold more than 70 percent of the assets of privately controlled thrifts.) During the first quarter of 1992, Group I institutions reported a net income of $772 million, which translated into an average return on assets (ROA) of 1.03 percent. Group II earned $303 million with an average return on assets of 0.91 percent. Taken together, these thrifts reported a $514 million increase in their net income from first quarter 1991 to first quarter 1992. The average ratio of tangible capital to total assets was 7.1 percent for Group I and 5.4 percent for Group II at the end of the first quarter of 1991.

Despite a highly favorable interest rate environment, the remaining 400 SAIF-insured thrifts continue to experience difficulties. Group III, which includes about 350 thrifts holding 17 percent of the industry's assets, had a net income of $115 million (average ROA of 0.21 percent) in the first quarter of 1992, $58 million higher than in the first quarter of 1991. Tangible capital averaged 3.3 percent of total assets. Twenty percent were unprofitable during the first quarter of 1992.

The remaining 54 institutions classified Group IV as of this writing are targeted for transfer to the RTC. They had an average ROA during the first quarter of 1992 of 0.18 percent, which was boosted by total gains due to asset sales of $172 million. Their tangible capital ratio was negative. The highest concentration of Group IV thrifts at the end of 1991 was in Virginia with seven, followed by Florida, Illinois, and Texas, with five each.

Despite the large number of troubled savings associations still operating outside of government control, industry-wide statistics show that—in the aggregate—SAIF-insured, private-sector thrifts improved profitability during the first quarter of 1992. The figure nearly equaled total profits for the entire year of 1991. Moreover, the percentage of unprofitable thrifts fell to 7 percent, from 15 percent in March 1991 and from 23 percent in March 1990. The average return on assets in the first quarter of 1992 was 0.74 percent—up from 0.25 percent a year earlier.

Overall, net income after taxes—bolstered by the most favorable interest rate spreads since the 1970's—rose from $627 million for the 2,283 SAIF-insured savings institutions in the first quarter of 1991 to $1,588 million for the 2,064 savings institutions still operating outside government control, a year later. The same 2,064 thrifts reporting those profits had an aggregate net income of $792 million during the first quarter of 1991.

Yields and Spreads

The recent increase in the SAIF-insured institutions' earnings reflect a sharp decline in the cost of funds relative to the yield thrifts earn on mortgage portfolios. This development stemmed from falling rates of interest and an unusually steep yield curve. During the first quarter of 1992, SAIF-insured thrifts had a cost of funds of 3.9 percent, down 216 basis points from a year earlier. During the same period, the mortgage portfolio yield declined just 40 basis points to 7.8 percent. This 390 basis point spread is the highest since the early 1970's.

Balance Sheet Developments

As troubled institutions have closed, the thrift industry's share of the mortgage market has declined. Moreover, even the remaining private-sector, SAIF-insured savings associations have lost market share recently, with holdings of home and multi-family mortgages each down 1 percent in the year ending March 31, 1992. Commercial real estate mortgages on the books of savings associations declined 10 percent during the same period. These recent cutbacks likely are part of an effort of many institutions to downsize in order to improve their capital positions. The weakness in commercial real estate lending also may reflect the higher risk-based capital requirements assessed on such assets rather than on residential mortgages and other assets.

Nonetheless, mortgages are still the backbone of savings associations' portfolios. Sixty percent of their assets were home-mortgage-related assets at the end of the first quarter of 1991; another 13 percent were in multi-family and commercial real estate loans.

On the liability side of the balance sheet, retail direct customer deposits continue to be the mainstay of the thrift industry, comprising 80 percent of their liabilities. Nonetheless, SAIF-insured, private-sector thrifts held almost $60 billion less deposits in March 31, 1992 than a year earlier, and $275 billion less than the peak levels of late 1988. As the industry has contracted, it has cut back on other sources of funds more aggressively than direct customer deposits. "Broker deposits," which are deposits of individuals and businesses placed through an intermediary to earn higher interest rates, fell from 2.9 percent to 1.7 percent of total deposits in the year ending in the first quarter of 1991. These "broker" accounts are now restricted by the Financial Institutions Reform, Recovery, and Enforcement Act of 1989 (FIRREA). Borrowing from the Federal Home Loan Bank System also was down 24 percent during the same period.

Mutual Savings Banks Post Profit

The more than 400 mutual savings banks currently insured by the Bank Insurance Fund also are experiencing difficulties. BIF-insured savings institutions earned $176 million in the first quarter of 1992—the first quarterly profit since March 1989. Most of the improvement is due to the resolution of the most troubled institutions. Twenty-seven percent of all BIF-insured savings institutions lost money during the first quarter of 1992. Most of these institutions were in New England, where aggressive entry into commercial real estate markets hurt many savings banks subsequent to their conversion to stock charters in the mid-1980's. Average first-quarter return on assets for the 321 institutions in New England was 0.21 percent, compared with 0.27 percent for the 99 savings banks in the remainder of the Northeast and with 1.43 percent in the 15 institutions elsewhere in the country.

Savings banks, like other thrifts, are contracting as an industry, with total assets down 8.3 percent in the year ending in March 1992. (The industry's capital-to-asset ratio was 7.1 percent at the end of the first quarter. The comparable figure a year earlier was 6.6 percent.)

LONG-TERM PROSPECTS

After the thrift industry—along with most other financial intermediaries—works through its current credit quality problems, its future role in the financial services industry will depend upon the profitability of originating, holding, and servicing home mortgages and related products. A new regulatory environment in which capital requirements are higher and are correlated with the risk of the institution's investments will put an emphasis on providing stockholders—and potential stockholders—a stable and acceptable rate of return. Whether that can be achieved, in turn, depends on the ability of surviving thrifts to efficiently compete in increasingly open mortgage markets. The size and character of the industry will be determined by whether savings institutions are successful as providers of community-oriented financial services, as players in nationwide mortgage markets, or as both.—*Jeanine M. Rossi and James L. Freund, Federal Deposit Insurance Corporation, (202) 898-3960.*

Trends and Forecasts: Commercial Banking (SIC 602)

(in billions of dollars except as noted)

Item	1987	1988	1989	1990	1991	1992[1]	1993[2]	Percent Change 1987–88	1988–89	1989–90	1990–91	1991–92	1992–93
Assets	2,847	3,036	3,246	3,400	3,536	3,642	3,788	6.6	6.9	4.7	4.0	3.0	4.0
Loans	1,899	2,040	2,207	2,309	2,284	2,330	2,423	7.4	8.2	4.6	−1.1	2.0	4.0
Investments	514	533	551	606	705	790	853	3.7	3.4	10.0	16.3	12.1	8.0
Deposits	2,009	2,143	2,270	2,363	2,392	2,465	2,564	6.7	5.9	4.1	1.2	3.0	4.0
Employment (000)	1,540	1,535	1,556	1,565	1,539	1,518	1,503	−0.3	1.4	0.6	−1.7	−1.4	−1.0

[1]Estimate.
[2]Forecast.

SOURCES: Board of Governors of the Federal Reserve System and U.S. Department of Labor, Bureau of Labor Statistics. Estimates and forecasts by U.S. Department of Commerce, International Trade Administration.

Trends and Forecasts: Savings Institutions (SIC 603)

(in billions of dollars except as noted)

Item	1989	1990	1991	1992*	1993*	Percent Change 1989–90	1990–91	1991–92	1992–93
Assets	1,157	1,006	876	815	800	−13.1	−12.9	−7.0	−1.8
Mortgages held	882	728	640	610	615	−17.5	−12.1	−4.7	0.8
Mortgage-backed securities	162	146	126	122	126	−9.9	−13.7	−3.2	3.3
Deposits	856	768	695	660	660	−10.3	−9.5	−5.0	0.0
Number of institutions	2,527	2,342	2,096	2,010	1,950	−7.3	−10.5	−4.1	−3.0

*Estimate.
NOTE: Data are for Savings Association Insurance Fund-insured only.

SOURCE: U.S. Office of Thrift Supervision

Foreign Bank Offices in the United States

(as of December 31, 1991)

Country	U.S. Offices	Country	U.S. Offices
Japan	162	Australia	15
Canada	51	Mexico	14
France	37	Taiwan	14
United Kingdom	36	Thailand	11
Hong Kong	31	Indonesia	10
South Korea	29	India	9
Italy	26	Ireland	9
Brazil	25	Singapore	9
Israel	25	Philippines	8
Germany	23	Colombia	7
Netherlands	23	Pakistan	7
Spain	23	Other	106
Switzerland	19	Total	747
Venezuela	18		

SOURCE: Board of Governors of the Federal Reserve System.

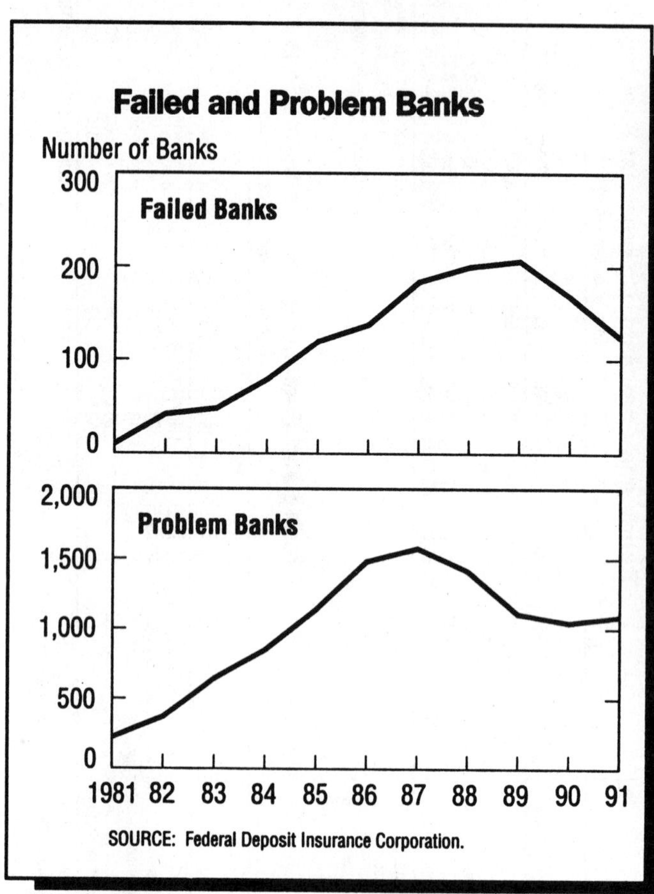

Glossary

Types of Foreign Banks in U.S.

Branches of foreign banks—Full-service banking offices that compete directly with local banks and are subject to all local banking laws and regulations.

Agencies—Agencies make commercial and industrial loans, and finance international transactions, but cannot accept deposits or perform trust functions; not subject to reserve requirements or loan limits.

Commercial bank subsidiary—Any bank that is majority-owned or effectively controlled by a foreign bank. Unlike branches, which are administratively and legally integral parts of a foreign bank, subsidiaries are separate entities.

Edge Act corporations—Banks chartered by the Federal Reserve to engage only in international banking and financing. They are allowed to have offices in more than one state.

Agreement corporations—State-chartered Edge Act corporations.

New York State Investment Companies—New York State charters only for wholesale international commercial banking activities. Like agencies, the companies cannot accept deposits and they are limited to short- and medium-term lending.

Representative offices—These maintain contact with correspondent banks, monitor local business conditions, and serve as a contact point for clients, but handle no banking business.

Principal U.S. Banking Laws

McFadden Act of 1927—Prevents interstate deployment of bank branches and gives states authority to set branching standards for banks within their jurisdictions.

Bank Holding Company Act of 1956—Known as the Douglas Amendment, this prohibits multibank holding companies and one-bank holding companies from acquiring a bank in another state, unless the law of the state in which the bank to be acquired is domiciled affirmatively provides for such entry.

National Banking Act of 1933—Known as the Glass-Steagall Act, this bans affiliations between banks and securities firms, and generally prevents banks from engaging in the issue, flotation, underwriting, public sale, or distribution of stocks, bonds, debentures, notes, or other securities.

Chemicals and Allied Products

The chemical industry is one of the largest industries in the United States and is the largest exporting sector. The industry has a work force of about 850,000, almost 5 percent of all U.S. manufacturing workers. Ten percent of U.S. scientists and engineers work for chemical companies, a reflection of the industry's high-technology products, and capital-intensive, complex manufacturing processes.

The chemical industry is the largest energy consumer in the industrial sector of the U.S. economy. The industry's primary energy sources—natural gas, natural gas liquids, and crude petroleum—are feedstock requirements for organic chemicals. Crude petroleum provides 53 percent of the feedstock requirement for primary petrochemicals; natural gas liquids, 38 percent; and natural gas, 8 percent. The United States and Canada are the world's second and third largest producers of natural gas. The U.S. chemical industry enjoys a natural advantage not shared by the world's other major chemical production centers in Western Europe and Japan.

The U.S. chemical industry has experienced strong growth since the 1981–82 recession. It maintained a positive trade balance during the 1980's as exports contributed greatly to the industry's growth. During 1991–92, the increase in exports contributed a larger percentage to industry growth than did the increase in domestic sales.

Beginning in the mid-1980's, the U.S. chemical industry experienced a massive restructuring, including major acquisitions, spin-offs, plant closings, and extensive early retirement and layoff programs. Companies in the United Kingdom, West Germany, France, and Japan were the major purchasers of U.S. firms. As a result of this restructuring, about 29 percent of the $68 billion in international trade is estimated to be intra-company shipments.

The chemical industry operates under stringent environmental regulations. About 20 percent of the industry's 1992 capital expenditures of $25 billion were for environmental abatement or compliance. Regulatory costs are the fastest-growing components of most companies' capital budgets. In addition to their effect on pricing and competitiveness, Federal and state government regulations influence production processes. For example, full implementation of the Clean Air Act that will take place in 1995 has caused investment in methanol facilities to increase production of methanol-based fuel oxygenates. Further information on major environmental legislation and Federal regulations affecting the chemical industry is in the *1992 U.S. Industrial Outlook*, pages 11–4 to 11–6.

The constant-dollar value of shipments by the chemical industry increased by 2 percent in 1992, and was affected by the domestic and global economic slowdown during the latter part of the year.

INTERNATIONAL COMPETITIVENESS

The chemical industry is truly global in nature. One hundred and seventy U.S. chemical companies have more than 2,800 affiliates abroad, and there are about 1,700 foreign subsidiaries or affiliates operating in the United States.

In 1992, exports exceeded $44 billion, and imports were $23.7 billion, resulting in a trade surplus of $20.5 billion. This was the fourth successive year that the industry's positive trade balance reached new highs. While the United States suffered a cumulative trade deficit of more than $1 trillion during 1981–91, only the chemical industry maintained a trade surplus each year. During this period, chemical exports exceeded imports by more than $126 billion.

More than two-thirds of the U.S. chemical industry's direct foreign investment is in Europe and Canada. About 94 percent of foreign direct investment in the U.S. chemical industry is by European or Canadian companies. Consequently, U.S. industry growth in 1993 is partly dependent upon world economic conditions. The most important markets for U.S. chemical exports are the European Community (EC), with about 26 percent of total exports in 1991, followed by Canada and Mexico (21 percent) and Japan (12 percent).

The North American Free Trade Agreement (NAFTA), when implemented, will spur investment in energy-rich Mexico. Primary petrochemicals from Mexico will permit the U.S. industry to further its effort to concentrate production on higher value-added products. At the same time, development of petrochemical complexes in Southeast Asia will increase competition among building-block chemicals there. The response of the U.S. chemical industry to these supplier and buyer shifts will be to produce high unit-price products rather than low price, high volume chemicals. The move toward higher-value products will be facilitated by the ready availability of lower cost commodity chemicals becoming available from energy-rich countries in the Middle East.

LONG-TERM PROSPECTS

The chemical industry will become increasingly important for technological progress in the United States, especially in the fields of aerospace, electronics, agriculture, and medicine. As a whole, the industry will maintain its historical expansion rate of about 1.5 times GDP growth. Domestic shipments of basic petrochemicals will experience little growth until 1995, when worldwide supply and demand are forecast to move toward equilibrium. Production of downstream petrochemical products needed by the automotive and construction industries is expected to increase as those industries rebound. The plastics and pharmaceutical sectors will increase the fastest during the next five years, and should contribute more than their share to the overall industry growth rate.

Two sectors with strong growth potential are fuel oxygenates and biotechnical applications to agricultural chemicals. Post-1995 fuel oxygenate demand will be determined by the number of non-attainment areas in the United States that will require cleaner fuel to reach Clean Air Act standards. Similarly, regulatory decisions over the next few years will determine the pace of the introduction of biotech agricultural products into the domestic marketplace.

Most U.S. chemical exports go to other industrialized countries. The fastest-growing export markets, although from a relatively small base, are Asia and Latin America. Government policies in Malaysia and Indonesia, for example, seek self-sufficiency in many consumer products and raw materials by 1995. China intends to double ethylene capacity to 3.7 million metric tons by then. This drive by developing countries to free themselves from import dependence on basic building-block chemicals will spur the U.S. industry to develop new products for the aerospace, automotive, electronic, and construction materials industries.

Another emerging global factor affecting the long-term development of the chemical industry is environmental safety. "Green" concerns will affect future plant sites and force new manufacturing, recycling, and disposal processes. In turn, these developments will influence future capital investment decisions, increase R&D expenditures, and tighten profit margins.

Organic Chemicals

Organic chemicals are compounds of carbon and can be derived from several sources, mostly petroleum and natural gas, but also agricultural products and coal. Primary organic chemicals are frequently components of fuels and can be obtained by separation and purification of petroleum refinery products or natural gas constituents. Many of the primary products can be used either as fuel or as basic materials from which other chemicals are derived.

Petrochemicals account for 75–80 percent of organic chemicals on a weight or volume basis, and about 50 percent on a value basis. This is due to the high value of pharmaceutical and drug products, the other large, non-petrochemical segment of organic chemicals.

Petrochemicals account for more than 20 percent of all the chemicals in world trade. The United States, Western Europe, and Japan have historically dominated production of the primary petrochemicals—methanol, ethylene, propylene, butadiene, benzene, toluene, and xylene. Beginning in the 1980's, countries rich in crude oil and natural gas, such as Saudi Arabia, Canada, and Singapore, began construction of world-scale petrochemical facilities. Other developing countries, such as South Korea and Taiwan, strove to develop self-sufficiency in petrochemical products to meet increasing domestic demand and enhance their economic independence. Because these countries had small domestic markets, a significant portion of their production went to export markets. Although the United States, Western Europe, and Japan have experienced declining shares of world production, they continue to be the dominant primary petrochemical producers.

The primary petrochemicals are precursors to a variety of plastics, fibers, elastomers, fertilizers, and chemical intermediates, which are converted into consumer and industrial products. Due to this relationship with consumer and industrial products, the petrochemical industry's well-being is highly dependent upon economic conditions at home and throughout the world. The industry is also sensitive to currency fluctuations because small price differentials of its commodity products can determine whether it is better to produce or import primary petrochemicals.

The value of petrochemical industry shipments increased about 2 percent in constant dollars in 1992, to $129 billion. Total employment in petrochemicals, slightly more than 30 percent of the chemical industry, remained steady at about 264,000 employees. Exports increased 10 percent to $25.4 billion, while imports increased 7 percent to $10.7 billion, resulting in a positive trade balance of $14.8 billion in 1992.

INTERNATIONAL COMPETITIVENESS

Over the next five years, the U.S. petrochemical industry will face growing competition in its export markets. The U.S. producers' domestic advantage in feedstock choice disappeared in 1992, as naphtha and natural gas liquid again became competitive with each other. As long as this price relationship between feedstocks continues, European and Japanese dependence on naphtha feeds will not be a disadvantage, and their downstream products will compete head on with U.S. products.

Countries in the Far East that are now U.S. export markets are building their own domestic supplies of primary petrochemicals. Of 28 new ethylene producers set to start up in the 1990's, 18 are in the Far East; only 1 is in Japan. Also, 46 percent of 4.6 million tons of new styrene capacity to be added to global production by 1995 is in the Far East. This new output will increase competition and depress margins and profitability because the United States and the EC will have excess capacity in 1993.

Another factor affecting petrochemicals is the evolving environmental movement worldwide. Some industry experts estimate that up to 12 percent of high density polyethylene (HDPE) will be recycled in the United States by the year 2000. The estimate for Europe is about the same, while Japan is projected to be recycling about 8 percent of its HDPE by the end of the century. Although the precise percentage that will be recycled is uncertain, the trend toward more recycling will affect future production. Domestically, full implementation of the Clean Air Act in 1995 will require reductions in the content of benzene and butane in gasoline. This will bring more of these feedstocks into the chemical industry. In turn, this development will affect the supply/demand balance of other important chemical feedstocks such as propylene, isobutane, and aromatics.

The integration of Eastern Europe and the Commonwealth of Independent States (most of the former republics of the Soviet Union) into the world marketplace poses investment and expansion opportunities. However, it also introduces uncertainties because these countries will produce increasing amounts of commodity petrochemicals.

LONG-TERM PROSPECTS

Increased foreign production of petrochemical feedstocks will produce fierce competition in third-country markets. The United States, Western Europe, and Japan are expected to remain the world's major petrochemical production centers, but their respective shares of the world market will continue to diminish. They will become more dependent on imports of primary petrochemicals for building block materials with which to produce higher-value downstream products. This is a consequence of new production coming on stream around the world. Industry rationalization and realignment will continue in the United States, but will be more extensive in the EC. The U.S. industry will experience minimal real growth of 1 to 1.5 percent annually during the next five years.—*Michael J. Kelly, Chemicals and Allied Products Division, (202) 482-0128.*

U.S. Trade Patterns in 1991
Chemicals and Allied Products
SIC 28
(in millions of dollars, percent)

Exports	Value	Share	Imports	Value	Share
Canada & Mexico	8,538	20.5	Canada & Mexico	4,764	20.5
European Community	10,945	26.2	European Community	9,604	41.4
Japan	4,785	11.5	Japan	2,468	10.6
East Asia NICs	7,767	18.6	East Asia NICs	1,431	6.2
South America	3,431	8.2	South America	566	2.4
Other	6,236	15.0	Other	4,357	18.8
World Total	41,702	100.0	World Total	23,190	100.0

Top Five Countries

Exports	Value	Share	Imports	Value	Share
Canada	6,153	14.8	Canada	4,093	17.6
Japan	4,785	11.5	Germany	3,035	13.1
Belgium	2,469	5.9	Japan	2,468	10.6
Mexico	2,385	5.7	United Kingdom	2,167	9.3
Netherlands	2,209	5.3	France	1,555	6.7

SOURCE: U.S. Department of Commerce: Bureau of the Census, International Trade Administration.

Trends and Forecasts: Chemicals and Allied Products (SIC 28)

(in millions of dollars except as noted)

Item	1987	1988	1989	1990	1991[1]	1992[2]	1993[3]	Percent Change (1987–1993) 87–88	88–89	89–90	90–91	91–92	92–93
Industry Data													
Value of shipments[4]	229,546	259,699	278,085	288,184	295,677	301,886	—	13.1	7.1	3.6	2.6	2.1	—
Value of shipments (1987$)	229,546	239,529	242,930	248,954	254,929	260,027	265,223	4.3	1.4	2.5	2.4	2.0	2.0
Total employment (000)	814	830	848	853	853	853	853	2.0	2.2	0.6	0.0	0.0	0.0
Production workers (000)	463	475	484	484	485	485	485	2.6	1.9	0.0	0.2	0.0	0.0
Average hourly earnings ($)	13.04	13.21	13.82	14.40	14.90	15.42	15.88	1.3	4.6	4.2	3.5	3.5	3.0
Capital expenditures	8,711	10,858	13,480	15,202	—	—	—	24.6	24.1	12.8	—	—	—
Product Data													
Value of shipments[5]	214,618	244,515	260,649	268,105	274,807	279,479	—	13.9	6.6	2.9	2.5	1.7	—
Value of shipments (1987$)	214,618	225,097	227,632	232,030	235,975	239,750	—	4.9	1.1	1.9	1.7	1.6	—
Trade Data													
Value of imports	—	—	20,253	21,798	23,190	23,664	25,084	—	—	7.6	6.4	2.0	6.0
Value of exports	—	—	35,999	38,031	41,702	44,204	45,972	—	—	5.6	9.7	6.0	4.0

[1]Estimated, except exports and imports.

[2]Estimate.

[3]Forecast.

[4]Value of all products and services sold by establishments in the chemicals and allied products industry.

[5]Value of products classified in the chemicals and allied products industry produced by all industries.

SOURCE: U.S. Department of Commerce: Bureau of the Census, International Trade Administration (ITA). Estimates and forecasts by ITA.

Trends and Forecasts: Petrochemicals (SIC 2821, 2822, 2824, 2843, 2865, 2869, 2873, 2895)

(in millions of dollars except as noted)

Item	1987	1988	1989	1990	1991[1]	1992[2]	1993[3]	Percent Change (1987–1993) 87–88	88–89	89–90	90–91	91–92	92–93
Industry Data													
Value of shipments[4]	96,222	113,216	120,851	118,989	127,080	129,367	—	17.7	6.7	−1.5	6.8	1.8	—
Value of shipments (1987$)	96,222	101,036	103,187	103,738	104,716	105,766	106,824	5.0	2.1	0.5	0.9	1.0	1.0
Total employment (000)	254	254	260	264	264	264	264	0.0	2.4	1.5	0.0	0.0	0.0
Production workers (000)	158	159	164	165	165	165	165	0.6	3.1	0.6	0.0	0.0	0.0
Average hourly earnings ($)	14.95	15.39	15.89	16.50	16.83	17.17	17.51	2.9	3.2	3.8	2.0	2.0	2.0
Capital expenditures	4,421	5,926	7,294	9,065	—	—	—	34.0	23.1	24.3	—	—	—
Product Data													
Value of shipments[5]	92,959	111,244	117,634	115,972	118,813	119,407	119,645	19.7	5.7	−1.4	2.4	0.5	0.2
Value of shipments (1987$)	92,959	98,979	100,255	101,007	102,017	102,731	103,245	6.5	1.3	0.8	1.0	0.7	0.5
Trade Data													
Value of imports	—	—	8,911	9,652	9,918	10,651	11,144	—	—	8.3	2.8	7.4	4.6
Value of exports	—	—	20,589	21,094	23,116	25,427	26,190	—	—	2.5	9.6	10.0	3.0

[1]Estimated, except exports and imports.
[2]Estimate.
[3]Forecast.
[4]Value of all products and services sold by establishments in the petrochemicals industry.
[5]Value of products classified in the petrochemicals industry produced by all industries.
SOURCE: U.S. Department of Commerce: Bureau of the Census, International Trade Administration (ITA). Estimates and forecasts by ITA.

Computer Equipment and Software

The computer equipment and software sectors span seven specific industries. The four computer equipment industries are electronic computers (SIC 3571), computer storage devices (SIC 3572), computer terminals (SIC 3575), and computer peripheral equipment, not elsewhere classified (SIC 3577). In computer software, the three industries are computer programming services (SIC 7371), prepackaged software (SIC 7372), and computer integrated systems design (SIC 7373).

Electronic computers include digital computers of all sizes, as well as computer kits assembled by the purchaser. Computer storage devices are such equipment as magnetic and optical disk drives and tape storage units. The category for computer terminals covers teleprinters. Computer peripherals are printers, plotters, graphics displays, and other input/output equipment. Parts and components for computers and peripherals are included, as appropriate, in each of the first four SIC industries. However, the Census Bureau has reclassified some parts, such as printed circuit boards and integrated microcircuits, originally reported in electronic computers, in their respective component industries since 1988.

During the first half of 1992, the U.S. computer equipment industry showed signs of emerging from the most prolonged and severe downturn in domestic demand in its history. Shipments grew strongly through June, and new orders rose 8 percent compared with no growth during the same period in 1991. The revenue results of many leading U.S. firms also showed a marked improvement. Mainframe, disk storage, and printer sales appeared to have rebounded, while workstation, portable PC, and local area network (LAN) equipment shipments continued to increase at a healthy rate. However, demand for minicomputers and desktop personal computers remained sluggish.

Domestic business purchases of computers rose 10 percent during the first quarter of 1992. Surveys of U.S. business spending plans conducted early in the year indicated that a large number of corporate information system directors were beginning to reinstate major computer hardware procurements previously deferred or canceled to relieve substantial pent-up demand for greater processing power. CSX Index, a subsidiary of Computer Sciences Corp., found in its survey that the largest outlays as a percentage of total revenues would occur in the aerospace, electronics, insurance, and telecommunications services industries. Federal spending on computers increased 77 percent in fiscal 1992 to $5.5 billion, led by major purchases at the Departments of Agriculture, Defense, Justice, Treasury, and Transportation, and the National Aeronautics and Space Administration (NASA).

Product shipments were expected to rise 4 percent to about $54 billion in 1992, provided the recovery in the U.S. economy continued. Other factors affecting shipments growth were intense price competition, particularly in personal computers, and a possible overall fall-off in overseas demand.

The U.S. computer equipment industry endured its fourth consecutive year of employment loss in 1992 as companies continued to restructure their operations in an effort to cut costs and improve efficiency. Total employment declined 5 percent to 224,000 workers due to layoffs, early retirement, and attrition. The majority of the 12,000 job losses occurred among computer systems manufacturers, such as Digital Equipment and IBM, which once again substantially reduced their work forces. Plant closings, increased use of automation by the industry, and the contracting out of the manufacturing of some high-volume products to foreign suppliers continued to depress U.S. production worker employment. The number of production workers fell 4.7 percent to 84,500, a much sharper decline than the 1 percent drop recorded in 1991.

According to *Workplace Trends* newsletter, the U.S. computer industry has been hit much harder by layoffs than defense, aerospace, and automobile manufacturers. U.S. computer firms laid off 191,729 workers worldwide between 1988 and early 1992. These reductions were initially confined to factory workers, and support and administration staffs, but eventually spread to researchers, engineers, engineering managers, and marketing executives.

Automation has become an important competitive tool for the industry, helping to raise productivity, lower costs, and bring products to market sooner than in the past. A survey by the Automation Forum shows that the U.S. computer industry's spending on automation reached $1.7 billion in 1989, the latest year for which data is available, and was exceeded only by the automotive and aircraft/aerospace industries. When measured in terms of investment per production worker, the industry ranked second among the top U.S. industries in its automation spending, with $14,116 invested. Investment was concentrated in computer-assisted design (CAD), computer-assisted manufacturing (CAM), and computer-assisted engineering (CAE) hardware and software (31 percent), plant operations software (22), production equipment (20), and automatic materials handling equipment (18). U.S. computer firms have been particularly adept in using their own technologies to design and engineer new products which, in turn, have allowed them to considerably shorten time needed for product development. In manufacturing plants, they have turned to automated assembly equipment and systems, numerical and non-numerical controls, and robots to improve production processes.

Research and development (R&D) expenditures of a combined sample of 92 U.S. computer equipment suppliers were adversely affected by recession in 1991, rising only 5 percent to $14 billion. Although continuing to devote a high percentage of total revenues to research, and surpassing in absolute spending all other major industrial sectors in *Business Weeks'* annual "R&D Scoreboard" for 1991, the industry's growth rate fell below the composite increase of 7 percent for all industries. It lagged well behind increases for health care (16 percent), consumer products (11), and leisure-time products (10). Most of this slowdown was attributable to large-scale and mid-range computer systems firms. The lower spending of computer systems firms was not offset by substantial growth in the R&D budgets of many workstation and personal computer manufacturers.

Faced with escalating R&D costs and the need to perform research across a broad range of technologies, U.S. computer manufacturers have continued to form research alliances within the industry and with companies in other electronics sectors. General Electric, AT&T, Honeywell, and IBM established the Optoelectronic Technology Consortium in July 1992 to conduct research on advanced optical technology for 30 months. Backed by $8 million in initial funding and matching support from the Defense Advanced Research Projects Agency (DARPA), the group will study optical interconnection devices for high-speed data transmission in commercial and military image detection systems, high performance parallel processors, and telecommunications signal switching. The consortium's members will share research already completed in their own corporate laboratories, and will release results of joint efforts to other U.S. computer firms, semiconductor houses, aerospace companies, and government laboratories. Another effort—led by scientists at Conductus, Inc., a Sunnyvale, CA firm, and involving the National Institute of Standards and Technology, the University of California at Berkeley, Stanford University, and several private sector concerns—will try to integrate optical technologies into a prototype computer that may lead to desktop supercomputers.

The Microelectronics and Computer Technology Corp. (MCC) has successfully developed new software tools, production and packaging technologies since its founding in 1982. Its next 10-year strategy, announced in early 1992, calls for the consortium to be involved in enabling technologies applications, and the creation of new standards for advanced materials, integrated circuits, device packaging, networking, and software. One major goal of its Enterprise Integration Division is development of a commercial information infrastructure (EINet) that will help member companies bring products and services to market with unprecedented speed, flexibility, and quality. The MCC has also begun a five-year project on holographic mass-storage subsystems. The research is supported by $10.3 million in U.S. Government funds and $12.7 million from participating companies.

Federal funding of computer science and engineering R&D (basic and applied) for military and civilian purposes totaled $681 million in fiscal 1991, according to the National Research Council. The major sources of these funds in ranking order were the Department of Defense (DOD), the National Science Foundation (NSF), NASA, and the Department of Energy. Although DOD-funded projects have traditionally been directed to military objectives, they have led to advances in computer technologies that have found commercial uses, such as timesharing, networks, artificial intelligence, advanced computer architectures, and graphics. The NSF has been a significant supporter of basic research in academia, which accounted for 46 percent of the Federal fiscal 1991 computer science and engineering R&D budget.

The High Performance Computing and Communications Initiative (HPCCI), which received $657 million in Federal funds during fiscal 1992, has become the centerpiece of the U.S. Government's computer research effort. A substantial amount of funding will be used for development of generic software technology and algorithms that will help scientists address certain "Grand Challenge" problems, such as modeling changes in the global climate, finding a cure for cancer, minimizing air pollution, and improving energy conservation. Other funds will support development of scalable, parallel computer systems with a sustainable performance of one trillion floating point operations per second (teraflops) and one billion bits per second (gigabit per second) for the National Research and Education Network (NREN).

Japan officially ended its 11-year, $415

million Fifth Generation Computer Project in June 1992. Although Japanese researchers did not produce, as originally planned, a knowledge-based computer that could "reason" like a human being, they did gain valuable experience in inference and parallel processing, and fostered cooperation among scientists in business, government, and academia. Products that resulted from this effort included a highly parallel, prototype computer linking together nearly 1,000 processing elements, a parallel inference machine operating system (PIMOS), a concurrent logic programming language (KL1), and specialized expert systems programs.

The Japanese government launched a 10-year, $450 million Real World Computing Project, a follow-on to the Fifth Generation, in the autumn of 1992. It expects to bring together more than 10 domestic computer firms and several foreign research institutions to conduct R&D on massively parallel processing, optical and neural computing, virtual reality, speech/voice recognition, and "fuzzy" logic. U.S. participation in the project was still under examination by both U.S. and Japanese Government officials during 1992.

The National Science Board, a policy analysis division of the National Science Foundation, issued a report in August 1992 warning that the United States was in danger of falling behind other major countries in economic competitiveness if both industry and government spending on non-military research did not recover from an eight-year slump. It noted that the United States was still ahead in artificial intelligence, and high-performance computing, but trailed Japan in advanced semiconductor devices, digital imaging technology, high-density data storage, and optoelectronics. In its report, the board recommended increased Federal funding of engineering research; a permanent R&D tax credit; more cooperation between government and the private sector in science, engineering and management education programs; and NSF support for research to greatly improve manufacturing processes.

INTERNATIONAL COMPETITIVENESS

The world market for information equipment and services has more than doubled since 1984 to a level of nearly $290 billion in 1991, according to Datamation magazine's annual surveys of the top 100 computer companies worldwide. The U.S. supplier's share of this group's total revenues fell 17 percentage points to 62 percent during this 7-year period. In contrast, the Japanese share tripled to 27 percent, while the European share remained at 10 percent. Japan's gain was largely due to the dominant role Japanese manufacturers play in their domestic market, the second largest single country market in the world.

In the systems area, U.S. suppliers had a firm hold on the midrange computer, personal computer, and workstation market segments, but faced a growing challenge from their Japanese rivals in large scale computers. U.S. suppliers also maintained a strong presence in software products, and computer services such as maintenance, consulting, and systems integration. U.S. firms appear to have a significant share of the peripherals segment, but this position may be overstated since some U.S. companies act as marketers for Asian-sourced products, especially floppy disk drives, printers, and monitors.

Despite overall loss of world market share, many leading U.S. computer companies during the past decade have concentrated on penetrating key foreign markets. These companies have increased overseas sales on average from roughly a third of total revenues in the early 1980's to more than half by 1991. The primary focus has been Western Europe, where U.S. subsidiary operations reportedly supply about 60 percent of that market's computer equipment demand. Leading U.S. computer firms have also been active in the Asia/Pacific region.

Representatives of the U.S. and Japanese Governments signed an agreement in January 1992 to open Japanese public sector computer equipment and services purchases to foreign suppliers. Major provisions of the agreement include equal access for foreign firms to pre-solicitation information, participation in technical and other procurement working groups, equal treatment in bid evaluation, and an effective bid protest system. The agreement began covering computer products (equipment and packaged software) on April 1, 1992. The agreement's terms expanded on October 1, 1992 to include procurement of computer services, such as custom software and systems integration, by many Japanese Government entities. Japan's public sector entities will fully implement the agreement by April 1, 1993.

Computer Trade Deficit Hits $5 Billion

The U.S. computer industry in 1992 is expected to post its second trade deficit. While exports increased 2 percent to nearly $26 billion, imports climbed 15 percent to about $31 billion, resulting in a $5 billion deficit. Imports accounted for about half the U.S. consumption of computer equipment and parts in 1992. Imports of computers and peripherals each surged more than 18 percent above 1991 levels. Imports of computer parts advanced 13 percent.

Major gains in exports to some countries were offset by declines to others. For example, a 61 percent increase in computer system shipments to Canada, was effectively nullified by an 8 percent decrease in computer systems going to the European Community (EC). Peripherals was the only export category to show an increase, 5 percent above 1991. Exports to the EC and Latin America led that growth, up 7 and 28 percent, respectively.

Trade in computer parts illustrates the complexity of the global computer industry. Most large computer companies have located manufacturing and assembling operations, especially for smaller systems, near intended markets. Two-way trade in computer parts is larger than that of computer systems and peripherals. The United States maintained a surplus in computer parts, but the amount shrank from a high of $2.4 billion in 1991 to $1.4 billion in 1992. A deficit of $3.4 billion in computer parts trade with the Asian countries was offset by a $3.8 billion surplus with the EC.

In computers, Japan was the largest U.S. trading partner, with 24 percent of the $56 billion in two-way trade. Singapore followed with nearly 11 percent, Canada with 10 percent, and Taiwan at 9 percent. The surplus with Canada that expanded under the U.S.-Canada Free Trade Agreement is expected to continue, as companies take advantage of the preference the agreement makes available. Trade with the EC accounted for more than 26 percent of total U.S. trade in electronic computing equipment in 1989, but dropped to 23 percent in 1992.

A significant increase in trade with Malaysia appeared in both imports and exports. Imports from Malaysia rose 161 percent in 1991, then expanded 119 percent in 1992 to nearly $900 million. The imports were primarily in the peripherals area. Although this is only a small percentage of total U.S. trade, the significant import growth made by Malaysia in a relatively short period of time is an example of the effect that liberal investment policies, a low-wage rate, and a strong domestic technology policy can have on trading patterns.

Foreign investment in the U.S. computer industry has grown at a much faster pace over the past decade than overseas investment of U.S. computer firms. Foreign outlays to acquire promising U.S. computer companies with advanced technologies, and to establish businesses, research facilities, and plants in the United States rose about 9 percent in 1991 to $2.9 billion. European investors were largely responsible for this growth, increasing their spending during the year by nearly $400 million. Japanese investment fell 5 percent below 1990, but still accounted for more than half of total foreign outlays. Fujitsu, one of Japan's leading computer manufacturers, completed two major acquisitions for nearly $76 million, involving a U.S. high performance computer company and a supplier of hand-held computers. Foreign investors have either gained minority stakes in or acquired at least 133 U.S. computer firms since 1988, according to the Economic Strategy Institute, a Washington, DC-based think tank. Japanese investors accounted for 65 percent of the transactions.

The growth in overseas investment of U.S. computer firms slowed appreciably in 1991. Spending on overseas operations and investment in foreign companies increased only 4 percent to $20.6 billion, compared with a nearly 16 percent boost from 1989 to 1990. Most of this investment went to the EC in preparation for unification of that regional market. U.S. involvement in the European computer industry grew through Digital Equipment's purchase of the computer operations of Philips of the Netherlands and Kienzle of Germany during 1991; and IBM's acquisition of a 5.7 percent stake in Groupe Bull of France in early 1992. U.S. firms are also making significant investments in Asia. For example, U.S. personal computer and peripheral equipment suppliers spent $571 million to expand offshore plants and distribution facilities in Singapore.

LONG-TERM PROSPECTS

The U.S. computer industry will continue to gain a higher percentage of revenues and profits from systems design and integration, software, and after-sales service through 1997, but will face growing competition in the world market from European and Japanese suppliers. Hardware revenues will come from desktop and portable computers more than from larger systems, and will be constrained by severe price competition across the product spectrum. Domestic demand for servers and networking equipment and software should remain vibrant as users continue efforts to link disparate computer systems within their organizations. Sales of personal computers, or some type of information/entertainment system that may gradually replace the personal computer, should intensify in the home and educational user sectors. The movement toward open systems should accelerate because users are increasingly demanding the ability to interconnect equipment and applications from different vendors.

Some of the less profitable U.S. companies may abandon hardware production to serve as original equipment manufacturers and systems integrators. Larger U.S. and foreign firms may acquire companies with promising technologies or significant installed bases in key markets. A number of technologically-weak and cash-poor manufacturers will not survive an industry shakeout.

Employment should continue to decline as a result of consolidation, although perhaps at a much slower pace than during the restructuring of the past few years. According to U.S. Bureau of Labor Statistics' projections, the industry will lose jobs at a 0.9 percent annual rate through 2005, primarily in manufacturing. BLS estimates the computer software and services industry will increase hiring 4.4 percent in the same period.

Strategic alliances among firms within the industry and with suppliers in other electronics sectors may grow, given the mounting costs of performing R&D in several component and systems-level technologies, and establishing new manufacturing facilities. The activities of these groups will range from working collectively and sharing advanced technologies to jointly developing, manufacturing, and distributing products. An example of such an alliance is the Apple-IBM-Motorola partnership concluded in 1991. The growth in joint ventures with foreign companies should also continue unabated.

The convergence of computer, consumer electronics, and communications technologies will have a profound effect in shaping the next generation of computers. Other results will be broader computing capabilities, and more information acquisition and sharing in the workplace, the classroom, and the home. Advances in semiconductor devices should result in computer systems with uniprocessor speeds higher than 500 million instructions per second (MIPs), and 64 million bit (megabit) dynamic random access memories (DRAM) by 1997. This increased microprocessor performance and memory density will provide even low-end systems with the capability of handling compute-intensive tasks, such as high quality speech recognition and synthesis, three-dimensional graphics, and image processing.

The use of optoelectronic technologies in computer systems may also become widespread. Optical interconnections should find their way from massively parallel machines into conventional computer architectures, vastly improving the transmission of large amounts of data between circuit boards, and between layers of integrated circuits within processing units. Higher capacity compact disk-read only memory (CD–ROM), or perhaps even three-dimensional (3–D) holographic devices, may provide storage capacity needed for extensive multimedia capabilities that combine audio, video, and text interactively. High speed, fiber optic cable might transmit information through an integrated services digital network (ISDN) to computers in the home, school, and workplace.

Research and development on user interfaces will bring substantial improvements in pen-based computing and broaden use of computers as data collection and processing devices among such professionals as police officers, nurses, insurance claims estimators, and sales, delivery, and repair personnel. Advances in recognizing human speech patterns may lead to computers that accept voice input, and provide machine responses. Virtual reality (VR), or cyberspace technology may also become more well developed. In VR, a human being uses a helmet with a visor display and head phones, a fiber-optic glove, and sensors to interact on a real-time basis with a three-dimensional, computer-generated imaginary world. Apart from use for combat simulations and planning, potential commercial applications of VR systems in the future may include stock market analysis and trading, automobile design and crash testing, architectural design, and surgical simulation.

Progress in areas of artificial intelligence such as fuzzy logic, expert systems, and neural computing is likely to improve computer intelligence. These efforts may produce machines that can provide personalized instruction on a variety of subjects, assist human beings in making decisions, anticipate needs, and help to manage personal affairs and work.—*Tim Miles, Office of Computers and Business Equipment, (202) 482-2990.*

Supercomputers

Supercomputer systems are distinguished from other computers by high processing speeds and ability to handle numerically intensive problems that are too large for conventional machines. There are two principal classes of supercomputers, those with a few high-powered processors and those with many low-powered processors. The former, often referred to as "traditional," or vector supercomputers, are large, expensive, and account for the majority of supercomputer revenues. The latter, called parallel supercomputers, are smaller and less expensive than traditional systems, but account for the majority of supercomputer units shipped annually. Supercomputers in both classes range in price from about $500,000 to $30 million.

In a sense, all supercomputers manufactured in the United States are parallel systems, in that they have multiple processors. Traditional supercomputers, however, currently range between 2 and 16 processors, while parallel computers can support hundreds or even thousands of processors. The moderate level of parallelism available from traditional supercomputers resulted from the sustained effort of both government-funded programs and supercomputer manufacturers' research throughout the 1980's. In the 1990's, research and development in supercomputing is focused on massive parallelism, designing hardware, and developing computer codes and mathematical models that can efficiently split and distribute problems across thousands of processors. Although massive parallelism holds great promise for achieving faster processing speeds in some areas, the number of applications is still small, and some researchers believe there are traditional supercomputer problems that may never be effectively translated into more highly parallel formats.

The U.S. supercomputer industry grew by about 5 percent in 1992, to $1.8 billion, despite an industry shakeout which caused a number of small firms to abandon the business. Overall revenues from traditional, large-scale vector supercomputer sales held steady, despite movement of low-end users to workstations, and recessionary pressures on purchasers of high-end systems. Unit production of those vector systems actually increased slightly in 1992, but the increased sales of low-end, and therefore, low-priced, systems, held total revenues down. As in the rest of the computing industry in 1992, traditional supercomputer manufacturers began to feel the effect of selling larger volumes at lower margins, which greatly reduced profitability.

On the other hand, parallel systems producers have been moving in the opposite direction, focusing on selling larger configurations of their systems at higher prices. Revenues from parallel computer sales, up 34 percent to almost $300 million in 1992, outpaced unit shipments, which rose about 8 percent. Average unit prices for all parallel systems rose from about $800,000 in 1991 to about $900,000 in 1992.

INTERNATIONAL COMPETITIVENESS

The export market is vital for U.S. supercomputer manufacturers, accounting for more than 50 percent of revenues. After the United States, Europe is the single largest market for U.S. firms, due to its important industrial, academic, and government users, absence of local competition, and insignificant barriers to trade. European development of software and applications has also been important for U.S. supercomputer vendors, including investigation into the future of massively parallel systems. These conditions have led to European sales for even the smallest of U.S. vendors, and have caused larger U.S. firms to create marketing and distribution networks in Germany, the United Kingdom, France and elsewhere. Overall supercomputer sales in Europe reached about $510 million in 1992, most of which involved low-end systems. At the high-end, U.S. supercomputers accounted for 84 percent of installations in Europe, and 86 percent of public sector research facility and university sites. Despite several European Community-based massively parallel research efforts, U.S. vendors of these systems account for about 70 percent of installations in the EC.

Japan's market for supercomputers, while similar to the European market in size, has distinguishing characteristics. First, Japan's private sector accounts for almost 70 percent of supercomputer sales. Second, Japan's market is dominated by Japanese manufacturers that account for 75 percent of private sector installations and 89 percent of public sector installations.

The predominance of supercomputers in the Japanese private sector is due both to a commitment by Japanese industry to employ high-performance computers in their drive to maintain a high level of manufacturing competitiveness, and the relatively small amount of funding available for government laboratories. Unlike the United States and Europe, Japan has few major weapons programs, and has not developed large-scale aeronautics research facilities. As a result, government-funded university centers account for fully half of Japan's public sector supercomputer installations. University sites have served as the proving ground for Japanese systems, which account for 90 percent of installations in the academic market. In the private sector, electronics firms, auto makers, and service centers account for 60 percent of Japanese installations. Many firms in those industries buy primarily from other firms within their keiretsu, or corporate family group, effectively shutting out U.S. producers. Japanese auto manufacturers, however, which are among the most highly competitive firms in Japan, have bought several high-end supercomputers from U.S. vendors to reduce the overall time-to-market for their products by eliminating research and design bottlenecks.

The fact that Japan's public sector supercomputer market was effectively closed to U.S. firms caused the U.S. Government to negotiate two supercomputer procurement agreements with Japan, the most recent of which was signed in June 1990. Of the 43 public sector procurements that took place in Japan from 1980 to 1989, there was seldom any competition, and all but two went to Japanese suppliers. Since the 1990 Agreement, the level of competition in procurements has increased, and Cray Research has won three of ten purchases. The pace of supercomputer acquisitions by the Japanese government since signing the 1990 Agreement remains at about 3 per year, down from as many as 10 or 12 annually in the late 1980's. A remaining problem is the large number of institutions that already own Japanese supercomputers are unlikely to switch to U.S. suppliers when they upgrade. The influence of a supplier's incumbency at these sites, if not offset by Japanese agencies adopting fair and open procedures, will likely keep the percentage of U.S. supercomputer systems in the Japanese market to a relatively low level for the near future.

In July 1992, a U.S. supercomputer firm filed the first-ever protest of a government procurement award in Japan. At issue were the methods of performance evaluation, the winning bidder's promise of not-yet-available peripheral equipment, and an alleged overall bias in favor of the winning bidder. The protest underscored the fact that Japanese government procurement practices have come under close scrutiny, and that the 1990 agreement gives foreign suppliers the mechanism to challenge perceived preferential treatment of Japanese bidders.

The generation of Japanese supercomputers that debuted in 1991 continues to experience problems in achieving its potential, as a result of difficulties in operating systems, and applications software. Although Japanese advances in hardware have been impressive, optimal operation has not been reached in some cases. At least one Japanese firm modified its models in 1992 to adjust for input/output problems. A significant cause of these setbacks has been the move to parallel processing, albeit on a small scale, in Japanese vector supercomputers. Sales of the new generation systems, both domestically and outside Japan, have been somewhat less than expected by Japanese manufacturers. In addition, several Japanese machines that were "sold" in 1991 were not installed or operational as of mid-1992. These difficulties are evidence not so much of failure on the part of Japanese manufacturers, but rather of the complexity inherent in obtaining high-level processing speeds from parallel supercomputers, regardless of the hardware's technical sophistication.

Although the U.S. supercomputer industry's technological lead may face challenges, there is still good news for U.S. firms. In fact, in a 1992 survey of Japanese scientists conducted by Japan's Science and Technology Agency, 91 percent stated their belief that U.S. supercomputers were equal to, or better than, Japanese systems, and only 26 percent thought that Japanese companies would pull ahead by the year 2000. Traditional supercomputer performance levels continue to be pushed higher by advances in U.S. systems, and the movement toward parallel systems has been led by U.S. hardware technology. While much has been made of Japanese supercomputer firms' advances in the speed of individual processors, in "real-world" installations U.S. multi-processing supercomputers have consistently outperformed their Japanese competitors. The success of U.S. supercomputers in every market other than Japan is evidence of this performance advantage. The high price of U.S. supercomputers is, in large part, a result of the market's recognition that true high-performance computing is difficult to achieve, and expensive to develop. On the other hand, Japanese firms' discounting practices are due not only to domestic and international competition, but also reflect the inability of Japanese supercomputers to command higher prices because of performance limitations. While Japanese firms are effectively improving their hardware, U.S. hardware and software firms continue to invest hundreds of millions of dollars to improve parallel technology. In fact, some concern has arisen in the scientific community that parallel hardware developments have begun to outpace software capabilities. Researchers and scientists around the world have come to rely on the large base of applications and software available for traditional vector supercomputers. Just as they have been cautious about utilizing Japanese machines without proven capabilities, they are concerned about moving away from traditional supercomputer hardware to parallel computers that may require extensive rewriting and translation of codes.

One solution to this dilemma may be found in the U.S. Government's High-Performance Computing and Communications Initiative (HPCCI), enacted by Congress in November 1991. The HPCCI, whose funding and structure became formalized in 1992, is an important program that will organize the acquisition, use, and development of supercomputing in the U.S. public sector. With a major emphasis on software, networking, and training, the HPCCI will increase the Government's focus on the so-called "Grand Challenges" of computing. In order to solve such immensely difficult problems as global weather modeling, molecular imaging, and ultra-high speed aircraft design, this program will emphasize greater study of the mathematical theories, algorithms, and software adaptable to parallelism. In fact, of the projected $800 million that the Government will spend on supercomputing under HPCCI in 1993, only 23 percent will go for the purchase of hardware. The remainder will be aimed at developing software, and enhancing supercomputing use.

LONG-TERM PROSPECTS

The market research firm Dataquest predicts that long-term growth in the global supercomputer market will be high, but will lose momentum, averaging a 12 percent annual increase in revenues from 1993 to 1996, with a 15 percent annual increase in unit shipments for the period. Supercomputing's high cost makes the industry particularly vulnerable to weak economic periods, despite strong Federal programs.

The most fundamental issue facing the supercomputing industry is the diminishing role of defense-related research in the post-cold war environment. Programs directly or indirectly related to the development of nuclear fission, weapons systems, and military aircraft have been a driving force in expanding supercomputing's frontiers in both hardware and software for the last 15 years. Historically, such spending has formed a solid base for the U.S. supercomputer industry, where virtually every vendor has sold a system, often in prototype or early production form. Early advances in operating systems, applications, and parallelism were largely made possible by work from researchers in the national labs funded by the Department of Energy (DOE). Under the HPCCI, defense-related outlays are projected to increase from 1993–1995, but those funding levels are subject to approval by Congress. As the national defense rationale for such large expenditures becomes less convincing, current projections for the level of supercomputing development may prove overly optimistic. In 1993, supercomputer R&D spending by DOE and the Defense Advanced Research Projects Agency (DARPA) may approach $400 million, or just less than 50 percent of total HPCCI funding for the year. Those figures do not include spending on supercomputers by the large number of research laboratories in the Defense Department that are under the control of the Army, Navy, and Air Force. Congressional review of defense-related programs may lead to cutbacks, or even the elimination, of parts of the HPCCI, which would have a major impact on the supercomputing field. Nevertheless, growth of supercomputing among civilian government, industrial, and academic users will continue to be significant, and could potentially counteract a gradual decrease in the defense sector.

The massively parallel supercomputer revolution predicted for mid-decade may prove somewhat elusive. It is especially dependent upon standardization, and the availability of applications software. The rapid rise in the number of parallel computer installations has not been accompanied by the ability of the user community to efficiently transfer current applications to these new systems. The future growth of demand for parallel computers depends on such moves. Much software development work remains to be done in terms of operating systems, compilers, and libraries, all of which are necessary to make the parallel hardware platform a viable computational tool. As a result of this software question, at least three traditional supercomputer manufacturers have announced programs to develop hybrid computers, which they believe will provide a transition to parallel computing without abandoning applications currently in use. While evolution in computing is notoriously difficult to predict, most industry analysts, scientists, and Government planners believe that the next five years will bring major changes to the high-performance computing arena.—*Jonathan Streeter, Office of Computers and Business Equipment, (202) 482-0572.*

Mainframes

Mainframes are high-performance computers used principally for such large volume, general purpose business applications as on-line transactions, batch, decision support, and interactive processing. Some systems feature attached vector processors for scientific and engineering use, and compete against advanced multiprocessor workstations, minisupercomputers, and low-end supercomputers for these customers. Their list price currently ranges from about $3 million for a low-end system to more than $30 million for a high-end model.

The performance of these computers is often measured in millions of instructions per second (MIPS). Current low-end, uniprocessor mainframes have processing speeds of about 50 MIPS, nearly three times the performance of machines on the market only five years ago. The fastest, high-end, eight-processor system available exceeds 350 MIPS. Demand for mainframe processing power has grown 30 percent on the average each year, according to vendor estimate.

Mainframe disk storage capacity has increased 50 percent over the past two years through the use of thin-film heads and media. The areal density of high performance drives is currently 90 million bits (megabits) per square inch, which translates into a full string of disk drives having a capacity of 90.8 billion bytes (gigabytes). The average seek time of the fastest drive is down to 12.5 thousandths of a second (milliseconds). Storage cost has also improved significantly. The cost of storing a million bytes (megabytes) of information on the latest drives versus older models has declined 20 percent to $11.

Suppliers in this market usually fall into one of two camps: IBM and both U.S. and foreign firms that produce IBM-compatible mainframes and peripherals, representing the majority of the market; and other manufacturers selling machines running their own proprietary operating systems. Competition has intensified in recent years from producers of smaller systems, offering similar performance capabilities at lower cost, such as scalable parallel computers built from hundreds of microprocessors, minicomputers, and networked workstations and personal computers. Dataquest in a 1991 survey of mainframe sites found that 46 percent of the users queried were in the process of "downsizing," that is, shifting applications from a mainframe to a smaller platform.

This "downsizing" phenomenon, and the trend among corporate users toward fewer, large mainframe sites has led to a slight decline in the installed base of these systems worldwide. International Data Corp. estimates the cumulative number of mainframes in use around the world has fallen from a peak of 26,588 units in 1990 to 25,923 units in 1992. Most of this loss has occurred in the U.S. market, where consolidation of corporate mainframe sites has been going on since the mid-1980's. Consolidation in overseas markets, principally European countries, has just begun, and should accelerate through 1996, but not as rapidly as in the United States.

The value of U.S.-based mainframe shipments recovered slightly in 1992, rising an estimated 2 percent to $12.6 billion. Unit deliveries remained essentially flat. Several major suppliers reported firm order backlogs, and stronger U.S. sales of their new generation systems through the first half of the year, reflecting pent-up demand for greater processing power and functionality among users. However, the overall growth of revenues was constrained by continued interest among some users in leasing used computers, and aggressive price discounting of up to 50 percent on certain new models. International sales were down, particularly in Europe, although the bulk of these customers are served by overseas manufacturing facilities of U.S. firms.

INTERNATIONAL COMPETITIVENESS

The position of U.S. suppliers in the $27 billion world mainframe market continued to be eroded by Japanese competitors in 1991. Many of the leading U.S. firms reported substantial declines in global revenues as they made the transition to volume production of new mainframe families, and experienced sluggish domestic demand. As a result, the U.S. share of the world market fell a few percentage points to about 65 percent. The major Japanese mainframers generally increased revenues and, subsequently, world market share to more than 25 percent, due largely to strength in their own market, and Fujitsu's acquisition in late 1990 of International Computers Limited (ICL), Britain's flagship computer manufacturer. The Europeans fared poorly as a group. Groupe Bull, Olivetti, and Siemens/Nixdorf each had revenue declines. Only Comparex, a remarketer of Japanese systems, registered solid revenue growth.

LONG-TERM PROSPECTS

Mainframe manufacturers will continue to enhance their products, and offer users even greater performance and functionality through advances in hardware and software technology. They will follow these "mid-life kickers" with the introduction of the next generation of systems in 1995. At the logic component level, manufacturers will probably begin to use less expensive, more powerful bipolar Complimentary Metal Oxide Silicon (bi-CMOS) technology in their mainframe computers, instead of the current bipolar Emitter Coupled Logic (ECL) devices. Systems will become scalable and more highly parallel, and include specialized co-processors for handling input/output (I/O) functions, data compression, cryptography, expert systems, vector and image processing, and sorting. Processors located in different locations within an enterprise may be coupled together by very high-speed fiber optic channels, and access a stand-alone, shared memory whose capacity could reach 16 trillion bytes (terabytes). Performance at the high-end of these multiprocessor systems could surpass two billion operations per second.

Improvements in the price/performance ratio of these systems, which is currently at 15 to 18 percent per year, may double over the next five years. The Gartner Group estimates that average per-MIPS list price will have to drop from $100,000 in 1992 to roughly $15,000 in 1995 to maintain the mainframe's competitiveness against smaller computers.

Consolidation of mainframe sites and "downsizing" by users should continue to have an adverse affect on unit shipments of these systems. However, vendors will still find strong demand among users who have mission-critical applications that require high volume, on-line processing, and depend on the security, stability, performance, and reliability that only mainframes currently provide. Vendors will also position systems as servers in distributed computing environments that will store and transfer large amounts of data processed by smaller, computers around networks, and manage these network resources. To succeed in this client/server market, mainframe suppliers will have to address open systems requirements through offering interfaces from their proprietary operating systems to such standards as POSIX and the Open Systems Interconnect (OSI).—*Tim Miles, Office of Computers and Business Equipment, (202) 482-2990.*

Personal Computers

Personal computers (PCs) are predominantly single user, general application computers based on microprocessor chips with a resident operating system and local programming capability. They are grouped into two categories—stationary and portables. Stationary systems include desktop and deskside or "tower" configurations. Portables, comprising about 15 percent of the U.S. market, are divided into transportables, A/C and battery-powered laptops, notebooks, handheld, pocket and pen-based models. Typical units with monitor sell for $1,000 to $2,000, although prices range from $500 for some home computers to $25,000 or more for the most sophisticated, fully-configured systems.

PCs are differentiated from more powerful workstations, historically used in engineering and scientific applications, by slower processors, less graphics capabilities and lower display resolutions. Workstations generally run on the UNIX operating system rather than PC operating systems like DOS, OS/2 and Macintosh OS.

The U.S. PC hardware industry in 1991 was composed of more than 40 major U.S. and foreign vendors, which shipped at least 40,000 units, plus hundreds of support manufacturers, original equipment manufacturers, and computer assemblers. The industry also includes a variety of sales and distribution outlets, service companies, peripheral producers, and circuit board and accessory suppliers. Entry into the business has been relatively easy due to standardized technologies and the availability of off-the-shelf components, purchased mainly from U.S. and Asian vendors. But obtaining a sustainable market presence is becoming increasingly difficult as competition for new and replacement sales heats up.

Slowing demand and reduced revenue and profits in 1992 led to severe price competition, and a focus of major PC vendors on the low-end of the market. Despite improvements over 1991, when some major firms lost money for the first time, most suppliers reported unsatisfactory profit and loss statements. This resulted in the continuation in 1992 of employee layoffs and corporate restructuring that had begun in 1991. The two-year period has been marked by shakeout, consolidation and realignment. Industry concentration at the top remained stable, but could increase in the future due to escalating company acquisitions. The U.S. market share of the top 10 vendors, which had steadily dropped during the 1980's, has hovered near 50 percent in recent years. Volatility continues among smaller suppliers. The top three PC suppliers (IBM, Apple and Compaq) have maintained their positions, but market dynamics, and the introduction of new products and distribution channels has caused significant changes among second and third tier producers. Several firms dropped out of the top 10 ranks in 1992.

The continuing industry shakeout is being felt more strongly among smaller firms, and vendors without sufficient capital resources, efficient cost structures, full or differentiated product lines, and broad distribution and customer bases. Weaker players will be candidates for consolidation with healthier rivals. Sales of less established brands priced at razor thin margins will be hurt by major suppliers that are now pricing their "consumer-targeted" models below $1,000. Purchasers generally are more apt to buy competitively priced name brands than unrecognizable clones. The market is dividing into two segments—companies that supply commodity-like low-end PCs with the best quality and lowest prices, and those that operate in the technology vanguard with network servers, graphics workstations, multiprocessors, and the latest in miniaturized computers. Only the strongest companies can exist in both arenas.

Global market competition intensified in 1992, as domestic and foreign suppliers continued to look beyond their home borders for new markets and commercial partners to strengthen their global presence. From 1985 to 1990, foreign vendors doubled their share of the U.S. market, which was about 10 percent in 1985, through strong laptop sales, aggressive marketing and the purchase of domestic companies. These suppliers tended to sell at the low-end of the market, and to exploit new mass merchandising channels. However, foreign penetration has slowed as a result of the sluggish market, and tougher competition from U.S. suppliers. In 1991, according to IDC, almost one-third of the major vendors in the U.S. market were foreign owned, but only two were among the top ten suppliers. Most of these companies experienced declining sales. As a result, several Asian manufacturers moved design and assembly operations to the United States last year to be closer to consumers and the centers of new product development. Accelerating product cycles have made it less commercially viable to supply the world's largest PC market from a distance. U.S. suppliers also improved their positions in overseas markets through increased exports, and the location of production and sales operations abroad to be closer to the end-user. For example, Dell Computer opened a plant in Ireland to improve its chances in the European market, while Compaq Computer launched a new sales subsidiary in the complex Japanese market.

Along with competition, there is also a growing number of research, manufacturing and marketing joint ventures, consortia, partnerships and mergers, as vendors attempt to leverage their R&D and operating budgets, especially during these lean revenue years. Two of the more monumental, formed to develop the next PC generation, occurred in 1991 with the Apple/IBM agreement and the formation of the Advanced Computing Environment (ACE) consortium. However, the defection of key players from ACE in 1992 may weaken its long term influence. This deepening web of inter-company relationships involved both domestic and foreign vendors. U.S. suppliers established original equipment manufacturing and joint development arrangements with Japanese firms to take advantage of their manufacturing technologies, especially in the area of miniaturizing products.

Shipments of personal computers (desktops, desksides and portables) to the U.S. market in 1992 were 11.1 million units, up 9.4 percent over the previous year. This was lower than the two-digit growth rates enjoyed by the industry during most of the 1980's. These estimates include computers manufactured and assembled in the United States by domestic firms and foreign subsidiaries, and imported systems produced offshore by either U.S. or foreign-owned companies. The value of the U.S. market in 1992 decreased slightly to about $24 billion, according to industry sources. Market value has been growing slower than unit shipments, and exhibited negative growth in 1991 and 1992 due to price erosion. This is yet another sign of a maturing market. With heavy discounting of all computer models, sales at the high-end are not offsetting volume sales of less expensive machines.

Although brighter than in 1991, overall demand was curtailed by decreased consumer confidence caused by the recession and relative product saturation in the largest buying segments, government and business. The U.S. installed base of PCs exceeded 60 million units compared to half that many in Europe. Another factor, although less important than in 1991, was buyer wariness caused by a wait-and-see attitude on pricing, new product introductions and new software promises.

The 1992 PC market was most heavily affected by severe price erosion, accelerated product cycles, the increasing popularity of portables and workstations, and the legitimization of new distribution channels. Price wars dominated the PC landscape. Pushed by slowing demand, unsold inventories, and tough competition from a plethora of low-priced Asian clones, vendors slashed list prices and cut dealer margins. The trend began in earnest in 1991, and accelerated last year when the industry set records for price reductions. Prices on some models were cut in half. In addition, major suppliers, like Compaq, IBM and Apple, introduced low-cost lines aimed at the consumer and home markets. Users, retailers, software developers and component suppliers benefitted from lower prices and systems sales, but the net income of many computer manufacturers was severely affected. Increasingly computer literate consumers exhibited more price sensitivity, but instead of pocketing savings from lower PC prices, spent more on enhanced performance and additional software and peripherals.

Quickening product life cycles accompanied rapid price reductions. Dataquest estimates that PC product life has decreased from 5 years in 1981 to one year in today's market, with R&D and market introduction phases shrinking accordingly. Even component suppliers have contributed to this phenomenon. In the face of competition from other chip manufacturers, Intel expanded and stepped up product introductions in 1992, while launching a campaign to move customers to 80486-based PCs with significant reductions of i486 microprocessor prices. The fallout from an industry caught in the grip of falling prices, and product proliferation was strained company budgets and cautious consumers waiting for the next price cut and performance enhancement before buying. To allay fears, suppliers have designed modularity and upgrade features into their machines.

As vendors searched for untapped market segments, they turned to new marketing channels to reach buyers and increase computer awareness. Needing less support, increasingly sophisticated and price-conscious users turned to these same outlets for the best price/performance deals. As a result, sales increased through computer superstores, mail order catalogs, telemarketing operations, consumer electronics stores and retail chains. Shipments through the traditional channels of dealers and direct sales forces dropped from 81 percent in 1987 to 63 percent in 1991, according to Dataquest. This trend should continue, as value added resellers (VAR), providing specialized, high-end solutions, and low-cost consumer channels show the greatest growth at the expense of the traditional dealer channels. Superstores, offering a full line of computers, peripherals, software and accessories, plus product service, have become the hottest channel. It is estimated that there could be up to 150 of these outlets in the United States by the end of 1993. Major suppliers use mass merchandising channels as conduits to the less penetrated home and small business markets. These channels maximize product exposure and require less operational and vendor support costs than dealers and VARs.

The fragmenting of the microcomputer industry continued with the introduction of a growing variety of pen-based and palm-size computers at one end and multiprocessor and multiuser workstations at the other. Although still in the majority and benefiting from price cuts and the rebirth of the home market, traditional desktop PCs faced stiff competition from the portable and workstation ranks. Because desktop sales are projected to decline six percent annually over the next several years, vendors are looking for help from the high growth fringes of the product spectrum.

However, the distinction between the CISC-based PCs and the RISC-based workstations is blurring fast. From a technological view, Intel's P5 microprocessor, available in 1993, will offer more workstation-like power to PCs. Commercially, workstation vendors are venturing from the arcane world of engineers and scientists into the office environment. Future users will need more robust speed, memory, storage and graphics capabilities to handle new 32-bit, multitasking operating systems, while corporations will begin entrusting mission critical functions to PC networks and client server systems. Whether called personal computers or workstations, these machines will compete on the same dealer shelves at similar prices and run the same applications. Whereas PC vendors must offer and support increasingly complex systems and services, workstation suppliers will have to focus on manufacturing efficiencies, software development and new distribution channels.

As the market expands, the user base continues to fragment into more identifiable and distinct application sectors. A breakdown of 1992 PC sales by application showed that business and professional use, including working at home, represented more than two-thirds of the market in terms of units sold and value according to the International Data Corp. (IDC). The spiraling need to become more competitive required businesses of all sizes to purchase productivity enhancing devices; however, this was balanced by the economic dictates of downsizing, restructuring and layoffs that reduced the demand for additional computers. PC saturation in the office and slower employment growth also depressed corporate demand.

But while the recession curbed sales, prospects for the business sector as a whole remained good, as companies continued to upgrade their base of older Intel 8088/86 and 80286 and Motorola-based systems to accommodate new operating systems, such as Windows, OS/2 and MAC System 7. Businesses also continued to downsize segments of their information systems from mainframes and minicomputers to file servers and network-based PCs. Companies attempted to extend PC use into blue collar domains with pen-based and other special application devices. The improved availability of PCs in consumer outlets at attractive prices should increase sales to the volatile market sector of four million small businesses, although small business spending is generally affected more severely by an economic downturn than large corporation purchasing. With leaner budgets and organizations trying to do more with fewer resources, business spending slowed. The International Data Corp. (IDC) estimated only 5 percent growth in shipment value to the business sector in 1992.

While PCs sold for scientific and technical uses represented only 10 percent of the market in 1992, sales grew faster than sales to the business sector, according to IDC. This sector is populated mostly by high-end PCs and low-end, single-user workstations. The market was fueled by the declining prices for high-end systems, the move to multiuser UNIX systems, and technical advances in graphics and networking. The education sector also represented about 10 percent of the market, but growth rates were significantly lower than those for the market as a whole. Adversely affected by budget cuts, reduced government aid, declining enrollments, and traditional long equipment usage cycles, 1992 school expenditures on computers barely increased, despite aggressive discounting and marketing by major vendors, such as Apple and IBM.

Sales to the nearly 100 million U.S. households have not kept up with vendor expectations since the mid-1980's. Home demand for PCs was hurt by the success of Nintendo-like video games, and the lack of a perceived need for family and financial management applications to supplement entertainment and hobby uses. However, several trends point to a resurgence in this neglected and potentially large market. Major suppliers focused more attention on family sales with new entry-level models. Also, the increased use of home PCs for business drove demand. PCs are enabling more people to work at home, whether working after-hours, in self-employed home-based businesses, or as telecommuters during regular hours. Link Resources estimated that there were more than 35 million homeworker households in 1992, which purchased more than two-thirds of the PCs sold to the home market. Today, home users are more knowledgeable, and are spending more on PCs. Households have multiple PC users and uses, software is becoming more useful and easier-to-use, and the popularity of home on-line information services, such as Prodigy, is growing.

Link Resources estimated that more than 25 million U.S. households owned an estimated 30 million personal computers in 1992. Purchases for 1992 exceeded $4.5 billion, while unit sales grew 5 percent to more than 4 million. This was a significant improvement from the sales decline in 1991. Market growth was mostly driven by price cuts of up to 50 percent, and the introduction of new low-cost PCs targeted at the home buyer. However, about 60 percent of the sales went to satisfy pent up demand for more powerful PCs needed to run new graphical operating systems, such as Windows. Because major brands were sold through mass merchandising channels, consumers received greater exposure to the technology. Buyers also spent 5 to 10 percent more on their PCs than the previous year.

Shipments of 16-bit 8088/86 and 80286-based PCs have been declining since 1986 and 1989, respectively. For desktop applications, these systems are mostly limited to lower-priced, less demanding market segments, such as homes, schools, overseas markets, network terminals, and print servers. New system introductions have almost ceased except in less expensive notebook and hand-held models. PC–AT computers based on the 286 processor, the former mainstay of the PC market, represented only 11 percent of the 1992 U.S. market according to IDC, and were selling at prices well below $1,000.

Computers using the 80386 chips, introduced by Intel in 1986, accounted for more than 50 percent of PC sales in 1992, and brought 32-bit computing into the user mainstream. Sales were boosted by declining prices, as new 80386 chip producers, such as Advanced Micro Devices, entered the market, and by the introduction of new low-power 80386sl's used in notebook computers. The 80386sx chip, capable of running new 32-bit software and spurred by the popularity of Windows, has replaced the 80286 as the predominant processor in the market, and is considered the minimum acceptable standard for business use today. Considered the new entry-level computer for the commercial sector, shipments exceeded 3.7 million units in 1992 and, surpassed sales of 80386dx computers.

Market penetration of the new 80486-based PCs continued to expand as prices fell; sales approached 1.2 million units in 1992, according to IDC. As prices broke below $2,000, these computers, originally positioned as LAN servers and multiuser UNIX systems, entered mainstream user environments. Intel's success prompted competition as AMD, Cyrix and Texas Instruments readied their own 486 chips. Responding to market forces, Intel expanded its 486 product line to include a "sl" version for notebooks, speed-doubling chips for midrange machines, and 66 MHz (megahertz) speeds for high-end applications. Competition also accelerated the industry's move to the next PC generation, as Intel announced its intention to introduce the P5 (also called the 586) microprocessor in early 1993. This microprocessor with RISC features will have 3 million transistors, 3 times the number of the 80486, and initially operate at 66 MHz clock speed.

Fueled by sales of Apple's Macintosh computer that represents more than 80 percent of sales in this category, PCs based on Motorola's 680x0 microprocessors held about 16 percent of the 1992 market, growing by 12 percent from the previous year. RISC, 8-bit and other proprietary chips comprised the remainder of the market. RISC-based single-user workstations, a "hot" item in the market, represented 2 percent of systems sold, but 12 percent of market value.

The debate over the merits of 32-bit bus technologies involving IBM's Micro Channel Architecture (MCA), and the Extended Industry Standard Architecture (EISA), initially supported by a consortium of major PC vendors including Compaq, Hewlett-Packard and Zenith, has lapsed as suppliers concentrate more on positioning their products in the market. EISA is an extension of the Industry Standard Architecture (ISA) still used in most Intel-based PCs, while MCA is used in most PCs manufactured by IBM today. The bus is responsible for transferring information and commands among elements of a computer system, so these new standards provide higher input/output bandwidth to meet the need for greater data, graphics or video-intensive applications, along with complex communication and networking functions. According to IDC, MCA- and EISA-compatible computers represented about 21 percent of the PC market in 1992, most of which were MCA PCs made by IBM. However, many PC vendors are moving to support the EISA standard. EISA boards initially were designed for high-end 80486 systems and network servers. However, technology is migrating down into mid-range desktop PCs with resulting price decreases. All three bus architectures will co-exist into the mid-1990's, with ISA and EISA holding the dominant share of sales.

As personal computers become more widely dispersed among all segments of society, the design of human interfaces becomes exceedingly critical to their utility and popularity. Interface issues range from the design of physical input devices like keyboards, mice and pens to a user's mental interaction with the computer. Since the introduction of the Macintosh in 1984, much has been written about its popular graphical user interface (GUI), pictorial displays that use icons to represent functions the computer can perform. These icons are generally manipulated by a point-and-click mouse in conjunction with a keyboard. This approach has been contrasted with the more traditional method of using typed-in commands, and character-based software that has been characteristic of DOS and other operating systems. GUI software, such as Windows 3.x introduced in May 1990 for the DOS system, is increasing in popularity, especially for new users, and should be a key factor in making computers easier to use. This trend is also leading to the development of more GUI-compatible applications software.—*R. Clay Woods, Office of Computers and Business Equipment, (202) 482-3013.*

Revenue Sources of Leading U.S. Computer Firms, 1991

Firm	Source of Total Revenue (in millions of dollars)		Source of Total Revenue (in percent)			
	U.S.	Foreign	U.S.	Europe	Asia/ Pacific	Other
IBM	26,393	36,447	42	40	14	4
Digital Equipment	5,410	8,827	38	46	16	—
Hewlett-Packard	4,350	6,007	42	39	19	—
Unisys	4,080	3,920	51	30	19	—
Apple	3,897	2,598	60	29	11	—
AT&T	6,210	1,961	76	18	3	3
Compaq	1,341	1,930	41	50	7	2
Sun Microsystems	1,693	1,762	49	30	21	—
Xerox	1,465	1,465	50	33	5	12
Microsoft	1,116	1,162	49	30	13	8

SOURCE: *Datamation.*

Trends and Forecasts: Computers and Peripherals (SIC 3571, 3572, 3575, 3577)

(in millions of dollars except as noted)

Item	1987	1988	1989	1990	1991[1]	1992[2]	1993[3]	Percent Change (1987–1993) 87–88	88–89	89–90	90–91	91–92	92–93
Industry Data													
Value of shipments[4]	55,843	62,773	59,758	58,981	57,800	60,100	65,000	12.4	−4.8	−1.3	−2.0	4.0	8.2
Total employment (000)	286	290	263	248	236	224	220	1.4	−9.3	−5.7	−4.8	−5.1	−1.8
Production workers (000)	101	105	96.8	89.6	88.7	84.5	83.7	4.0	−7.8	−7.4	−1.0	−4.7	−0.9
Average hourly earnings ($)	10.47	10.93	11.68	11.72	12.35	12.47	—	4.4	6.9	0.3	5.4	1.0	—
Capital expenditures	2,020	2,213	2,148	1,993	—	—	—	9.6	−2.9	−7.2	—	—	—
Product Data													
Value of shipments[5]	48,801	53,230	54,891	52,628	51,600	53,700	58,000	9.1	3.1	−4.1	−2.0	4.1	8.0
Trade Data													
Value of imports	—	—	21,706	23,321	26,423	30,697	34,380	—	—	7.4	13.3	14.5	13.7
Value of exports	—	—	22,348	24,127	25,175	25,527	27,362	—	—	8.0	4.3	0.2	8.5

[1]Estimated, except exports and imports.
[2]Estimate.
[3]Forecast.
[4]Value of all products and services sold by establishments in the computers and peripherals industry.
[5]Value of products classified in the computers and peripherals industry produced by all industries.

NOTE: Census reclassified some parts for electronic computers (3571) to component industries (367) for 1988–1990.

SOURCE: U.S. Department of Commerce: Bureau of the Census, International Trade Administration (ITA). Estimates and forecasts by ITA.

Supplier's Share of the World Computer Equipment and Services Market

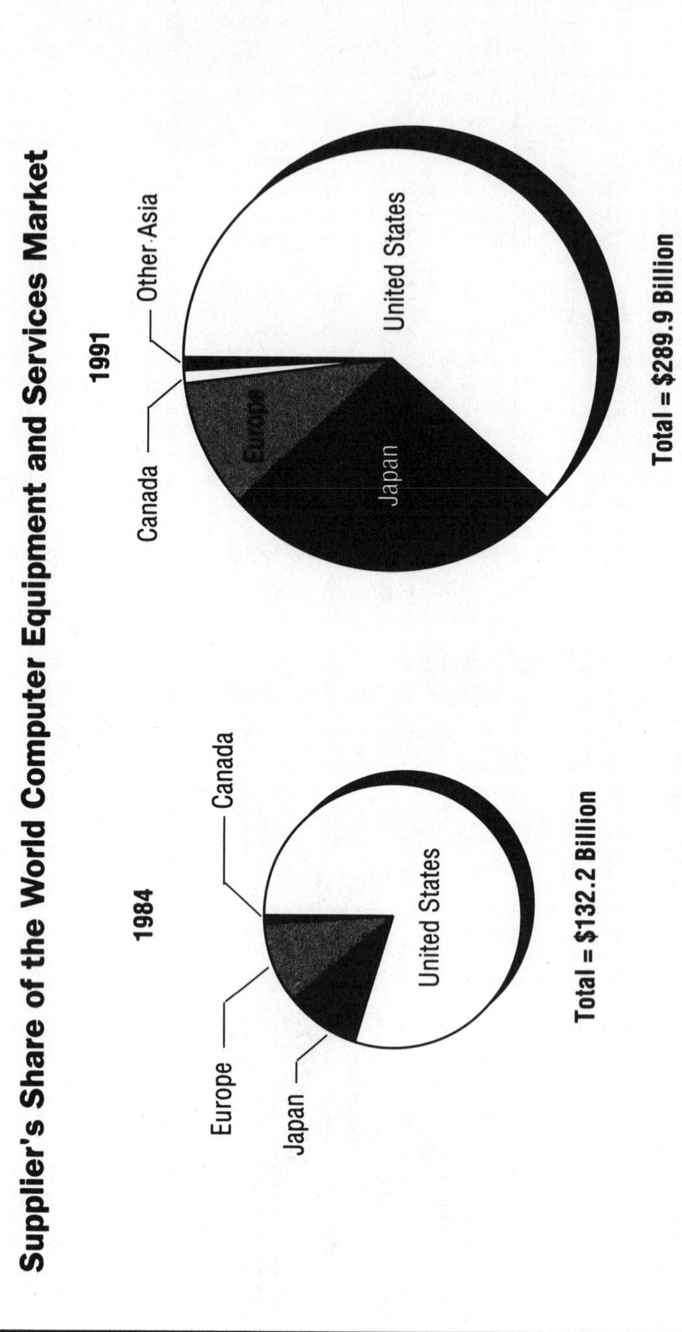

SOURCE: Datamation 100.

Construction

This chapter covers private residential construction (including single unit, multiunit, and manufactured housing); prefabricated building; private nonresidential construction; and publicly owned construction. A final section deals with international construction and engineering.

The inflation-adjusted value of new construction put in place increased about 4 percent in 1992, but was about 10 percent lower than the record level of 1986. (The 1992 current-dollar value of about $423 billion was about 4 percent below the 1990 record.) The number of housing starts increased by about 20 percent to 1.2 million units in 1992. Public works construction increased slightly, led by strong spending for highways and schools. The decline in private nonresidential construction was largely attributable to high vacancy rates for commercial buildings in most cities, as well as tighter lending standards for real estate development.

Remodeling and repair work increased faster than new construction in 1992. Although the data for maintenance and repair construction are not as complete as those for new construction, the available information indicates that 1992 was a record year for maintenance and repair work. Nonresidential building improvements (commercial remodeling and renovation) also reached record levels.

The 1987 Census of Construction showed that about 66 percent of the construction industry's work was for new construction; 19 percent was for additions, alterations, and reconstruction; 10 percent was for maintenance and repair; and 5 percent was unspecified. In 1992, new construction probably accounted for less than 60 percent of the industry's business.

In 1992, the value of new construction put in place was equal to about 7.9 percent of GNP. This is well below the post-World War II peak of 11.9 percent of GNP attained in 1966, and about the same as the cyclical low of 7.7 percent in 1982. Construction's share of GNP is expected to decline in 1993. However, this measure tends to understate the importance of construction in the economy because several types of construction activity that are not included in new construction data have grown rapidly during the past decade. These include maintenance and repair, commercial/industrial renovation, and hazardous waste cleanup.

In 1992, construction costs increased by about 1 percent, as measured by the Census Bureau's composite construction cost index. This is less than half the average annual rate of increase during the past five years, and is considerably less than the rate of increase of the Consumer Price Index. Building materials prices rose an average of about 1 percent in 1992. Land prices, which rose dramatically in many construction markets during the 1980's, were stable in 1992 and even declined in many areas. (Land prices are not included in the construction cost index.) Insurance and bonding costs have continued to increase, although the availability of insurance appears to be better. Labor costs have been relatively steady, with average hourly earnings of construction workers increasing by about 1 percent in 1992. Interest rates declined to 15-year lows, but credit standards were much tighter than they had been, especially for real estate and construction loans.

There were about 4.6 million employees in the construction industry in 1992. This is about 10 percent below the 1990 level, which was a near record. In addition, about 1.4 million people were self-employed as proprietors and working partners. Despite the recent moderation in construction wage increases, construction remained one of the highest-paying industries, as measured by average hourly and weekly earnings.

INTERNATIONAL COMPETITIVENESS

The construction business has become increasingly international during the past 15 years. U.S. contractors continue to be leaders in international contracting. They won $73.1 billion in international construction contracts in 1991, an increase of about 54 percent over 1990. (This amount includes construction contracts won by foreign subsidiaries of U.S. firms.) U.S. international contractors face stiff competition, chiefly from European and Pacific Rim firms, which often have more financial resources at their disposal than U.S. companies. Economic problems in Europe and several countries in the Middle East will make it difficult for U.S. contractors to repeat the remarkable successes of 1991.

Many of the world's largest foreign construction contractors entered the U.S. construction market during the 1980's and are becoming a significant factor in nonresidential construction. Most contractors entering the United States have bought U.S. construction companies, but some of the largest foreign contractors have established their own operations in the United States. Foreign-owned construction firms won about $12.3 billion in U.S. construction contracts in 1991, which was down from the record $15.5 billion in 1990. They accounted for about 6 percent of all construction contracts awarded in the United States during 1990. Most of these foreign entrants are based in Germany, the United Kingdom, Japan, and France, although nearly a dozen additional nations are represented.

International trade and capital flows have become important factors in the domestic construction market. Because of record levels of foreign investment in the United States, an increasing share of U.S. construction projects has been built for foreign owners. Foreign direct investment in the United States has been chiefly in manufacturing facilities, warehouses, office buildings, and hotels. Foreign financial investments, such as U.S. Government bonds and mortgage-backed securities, have greatly benefited U.S. construction demand by keeping interest rates lower than they would have been otherwise. On the other hand, the large foreign trade deficit is reducing U.S. industrial construction by as much as $2 billion annually.

LONG-TERM PROSPECTS

During the 1993–97 period, new construction is expected to increase modestly from current levels, while remodeling and repair construction will increase substantially. Construction is expected to grow more slowly than GDP, despite continued moderation in interest rates.

The slower rate of growth is partly due to the oversupply of commercial buildings, which will be gradually absorbed by attrition and a growing economy. The demand for new housing construction will be limited by demographic factors and by the slower buildup in homeowners equity. The Federal budget deficit will limit spending for public works, despite the well-publicized need for additional infrastructure investment.

The recovery of the U.S. manufacturing sector is expected to result in strong demand for industrial construction during the rest of this decade. Hospital construction will also continue to gain because of demographic and institutional factors. Remodeling and repair work, both residential and nonresidential, is expected to increase more rapidly than the overall economy, as the U.S. stock of structures becomes older and more extensive.

The commercial real estate slump is likely to persist well into the middle of the decade. As measured by the value of new construction put in place, the sector will decline in 1993 and 1994; the bottom may be reached by 1995. Even so, the recovery is likely to be slow, and commercial construction will not reach current levels by 1997. The current downturn has been exacerbated by the record collapse of hundreds of financial institutions. High vacancy rates and weak building prices have made new construction unprofitable in most cases, and reluctance to make real estate loans has further limited opportunities.

In addition to market factors, the U.S. construction industry will face a number of supply-side challenges during the next five years, including foreign competition, the supply of workers, and the cost of insurance. Most of the foreign construction contractors competing in the U.S. market are extremely well-financed and often possess construction expertise equal or superior to that of most U.S. builders. The supply of young workers available to the construction industry is dwindling because of demographic trends. The current recession has eased the construction labor problem, but when construction picks up, shortages of labor and skills could become major problems. The cost of liability insurance has temporarily stabilized, but the cost of health insurance and worker's compensation insurance has continued to increase at rapid rates.—*Patrick MacAuley, Office of Forest Products and Domestic Construction, (202) 482-0132.*

Private Residential Construction

The value of new residential construction in 1992 amounted to about $163 billion, up 15 percent in constant dollars from 1991. This improvement was concentrated in single unit construction, which grew about 20 percent to more than $102 billion, while multiunit construction activity was unchanged at $13.6 billion. Home improvement expenditures increased at a 10 percent rate, to an estimated $46.5 billion. Total new housing starts rose an impressive 20 percent in 1992 to about 1.23 million units. This increase occurred entirely in single units, with multiunit starts remaining at depressed levels.

Interest rates on conventional, 30-year fixed-rate mortgages continued to decline during 1992, to an estimated average of 8.4 percent. The availability of these low rates helped home sales to improve in the face of a sluggish economic recovery and unenthusiastic consumer confidence.

LONG-TERM PROSPECTS

Residential construction will grow more slowly than the overall economy over the next five years. Home improvement expenditures can be expected to remain strong, however, as the housing stock ages and home owners repair and upgrade their existing houses.

A recovery in general economic conditions and a resurgence of consumer confidence will be balanced by demographic factors and housing affordability questions. The demographic support for single family homebuilding is softening because the number of Americans entering the 25-to-35 year age group will decline every year beginning about 1992. Over the 1993–97 period, housing starts are expected to average 1.25 million units annually. The declining number of workers in the 18-to-25 age group, and the effects of the Financial Institutions Reform, Recovery, and Enforcement Act (FIRREA) of 1990 and other regulations will continue to depress the multiunit housing sector through the mid-1990's. These factors will be reinforced if recent unfavorable trends in the ability of potential home buyers to afford such purchases continue. A recent study by the Census Bureau found that a majority of families and individuals in the United States cannot afford to buy a median-priced house in the area where they live.

Single Unit Housing

Private single housing starts were an estimated 1.06 million units in 1992, a significant improvement over the depressed 1991 level of 840,000. Detached houses continue to be the preferred configuration throughout the United States, accounting for about 90 percent of all new single units. The median sales price of a new single unit house declined again in 1992, falling about 2 percent to $117,000.

The average size of houses completed in 1992 remained largely unchanged from the previous two years, and is not expected to change significantly in 1993. This stability contrasts with the upward trend of the late 1980's, when average size increased from 1,785 square feet to 2,080 square feet between 1985 and 1990. The number of new homes containing 2,400 or more square feet of floor area sold in 1991 was 138,000. Although this was a decline from 158,000 in 1989, these homes accounted for 27 percent of total sales in 1991 (up from 24 percent in 1989) because sales of smaller new homes contracted even more during this period.

The recovery in housing construction in 1992 was assisted by low mortgage interest rates. Many homeowners were able to continue the pattern of trading up to larger and better homes. However, the supply of smaller existing houses made available by this process may be a factor in the lower demand for new starter homes.

Multiunit Housing

Multiunit housing consists of two or more unit structures, including certain townhouses and apartment buildings. Apartments account for about 80 percent of multiunit housing starts.

The number of multifamily starts in 1992 was little changed from the previous year—about 170,000 units (14 percent of all private housing units started). Multifamily housing starts have declined more sharply in recent years than single-family starts. In 1985, about 670,000 units were begun in multifamily structures (38 percent of all housing units started that year), and as late as 1990 their volume was 298,000 units.

In addition to diminished demand, the current level of multiunit construction may also be influenced by changes in the regulatory environment. The Fair Housing Act of 1988 imposed handicapped accessibility guidelines on new construction, requiring that all apartment units in elevator buildings be accessible to the disabled. In addition, FIRREA has limited acquisition, development, and construction lending by financial institutions. Therefore, many builders and developers have found it difficult to obtain adequate financing.

Upkeep and Improvement

This category consists of expenditures on maintenance and repairs as well as new construction improvements, but it does not include the value of do-it-yourself labor used in such work. Maintenance and repair consist of property maintenance costs, including activities such as painting and appliance parts replacement and repair. In general, improvements consist of additions and alterations involving major interior and exterior changes to existing residential structures, and the replacement of major individual items such as furnaces and water heaters.

In 1992, total spending for upkeep and improvement was about $103 billion, up from the previous year's level of $97.5 billion. For all residential property, expenditures are now divided roughly in half between maintenance and repair, and improvements. In contrast, during the mid-1980's, improvements accounted for around 60 percent of spending. Expenditures on owner-occupied, single unit properties have been fairly stable during the past five years, holding steady at $58 to $60 billion. During this period, however, maintenance and repair spending has grown by about 50 percent to $24 billion, while improvements have decreased by a similar amount. Similar shifts in the composition of upkeep and improvement spending have also occurred in other owner-occupied structures and in rental properties. In contrast to owner-occupied structures, maintenance and repair spending for rental properties has normally exceeded that for improvements, and this tendency has increased recently. In 1992, only about one-third of the $37 billion spent on rental units was for improvements.

Manufactured Housing

Shipments of manufactured houses (mobile homes) increased more than 15 percent in 1992 to about 197,000 units. Multiwide manufactured homes now amount to about 45 percent of all placements. The average size of multiwides is nearly 1,500 square feet, half more than the average for single wides. Only one-third of multiwide units are located in mobile home communities, while nearly half of single wide units are found in these developments. About 56 percent of new manufactured homes were located in the southern United States in 1991. The Midwest and West absorbed 20 and 16 percent, respectively, of new shipments, while only 8 percent of all placements occurred in the Northeast. The West had the highest proportion of multiwide units and the highest average unit price.

Typical purchasers of manufactured houses include first-time buyers, those living in rural areas, elderly people, and members of nontraditional households. Although the number of potential first-time home buyers in the 25-to-44 age bracket (for whom manufactured houses often are an attractive option) is decreasing, the number of moderate- and low-income retirees is growing.—*Robert M. Shaw, Office of Forest Products and Domestic Construction, (202) 482-0132.*

Value of New Construction Put in Place, 1989–97

(in billions of 1987 dollars except as noted)

Type of Construction	1989	1990	1991	1992[1]	1993[2]	1997[2]	Percent Change, 1991-1997		
							91–92	92–93	92–97[3]
Total New Construction	409.5	397.5	358.6	373.2	375.8	400.2	4	1	1
Residential	181.3	164.0	141.3	162.6	169.0	182.1	15	4	2
Single family	107.8	97.5	85.4	102.5	106.6	113.1	20	4	2
Multifamily	20.6	17.3	13.6	13.6	13.6	15.0	0	0	2
Home improvement	52.9	49.2	42.3	46.5	48.9	53.9	10	5	3
Private Nonresidential	137.4	135.6	118.3	108.4	103.5	109.1	−8	−5	0
Manufacturing facilities	18.9	21.4	20.0	19.4	19.4	23.6	−3	0	4
Office	29.3	25.8	20.6	16.1	13.7	12.4	−22	−15	−5
Hotels and motels	7.8	8.7	5.6	3.4	2.7	2.3	−40	−20	−7
Other commercial	31.5	30.7	22.8	18.7	16.5	16.1	−18	−12	−3
Religious	3.0	3.0	3.1	3.1	3.2	*	0	3	*
Educational	3.4	3.8	3.5	3.6	3.8	4.2	3	5	3
Hospital and institutional	7.7	8.5	8.2	8.6	9.0	10.0	5	5	3
Miscellaneous buildings	4.1	4.1	3.8	3.7	3.7	*	−3	0	*
Telecommunications	8.5	8.5	7.8	8.2	8.2	9.0	5	0	2
Railroads	2.5	2.2	2.4	2.6	2.6	*	7	2	*
Electric utilities	11.8	9.2	9.3	9.8	10.0	10.8	5	2	2
Gas utilities	3.9	4.2	5.5	5.7	5.1	*	3	−10	*
Petroleum pipelines	0.3	0.4	0.5	0.5	0.5	*	0	0	*
Farm structures	2.3	2.4	2.3	2.3	2.3	*	0	2	*
Miscellaneous structures	2.3	2.7	2.9	2.9	2.9	*	0	0	*
Public Works	90.9	97.9	99.0	102.2	103.3	109.0	3	1	1
Housing and redevelopment	3.2	3.1	3.1	3.2	3.2	*	2	2	*
Federal industrial	1.2	1.3	1.6	1.7	1.8	*	5	5	*
Educational	16.0	18.8	21.3	21.7	22.2	24.0	2	2	2
Hospital	2.4	2.4	2.4	2.4	2.3	2.1	0	−3	−3
Other public buildings	14.1	15.9	16.8	18.0	17.1	18.0	7	−5	0
Highways	26.8	28.7	27.2	28.0	29.4	30.9	3	5	2
Military facilities	3.3	2.4	1.7	1.7	1.4	1.2	0	−20	−7
Conservation and development	4.6	4.1	4.3	4.5	4.7	5.0	5	4	2
Sewer systems	8.2	8.9	8.8	8.6	8.6	9.1	−2	0	1
Water supplies	3.5	4.4	4.6	4.8	5.1	5.6	5	5	3
Miscellaneous public structures	7.6	7.8	7.2	7.6	7.6	8.3	0	0	2

[1]Estimate.
[2]Forecast.
[3]Average annual rate.
*Long-term forecast not made separately for this category.

NOTE: Totals may not add due to rounding.
SOURCE: U.S. Department of Commerce: Bureau of the Census, International Trade Administration (ITA). Estimates and forecasts by ITA.

Construction Expenditures by Type of Structure, 1989–97

(in billions of 1987 dollars except as noted)

Item	1989	1990	1991	1992[1]	1993[2]	1997[2]	Percent Change (1991–1997)		
							91–92	92–93	92–97[3]
Total New Construction	409.5	397.5	358.6	373.2	375.8	400.2	4	1	1
New Building Construction	271.0	262.4	231.8	239.5	238.6	252.4	3	0	1
New housing units	128.4	114.8	99.0	116.1	120.2	128.2	17	4	2
Private nonresidential	105.7	106.1	87.6	76.5	71.9	75.4	−13	−6	0
Publicly owned	36.9	41.5	45.2	46.9	46.6	48.9	4	−1	1
Other New Structures	85.6	85.9	84.5	87.1	88.5	93.9	3	1	1
Private nonresidential	31.6	29.5	30.7	31.9	31.6	33.8	4	−1	1
Publicly owned	54.0	56.4	53.8	55.2	56.9	60.1	3	3	2
Home Improvements[4]	52.9	49.2	42.3	46.5	48.9	53.9	10	5	3
Selected Maintenance and Repair[5,8]									
Residential[5]	39.8	41.0	41.0	41.0	42.6	45.3	0	4	2
Nonresidential buildings[5,6]	32.9	34.5	34.5	35.5	36.6	39.2	3	3	2
Highway[5]	20.1	20.7	21.0	21.8	22.5	25.3	4	3	3
Utility[5]	23.1	25.2	26.0	27.3	28.7	33.2	5	5	4
Nonresidential Building Improvements[4,5,6,7,8]	53.8	54.5	55.0	56.0	58.3	61.9	2	4	2

[1]Estimate.
[2]Forecast.
[3]Average annual rate of growth.
[4]Home Improvements are included in Total New Construction, but Nonresidential Building Improvements are not included.
[5]Estimates in constant 1987 dollars were derived by ITA, using current-dollar data developed by the Bureau of the Census, and the Census Fixed-Weight Composite Construction Cost Index as the deflator.
[6]Excludes industrial and agricultural buildings, as well as buildings owned by the Federal Government or private utilities. Also excludes buildings of 1,000 square feet or less.
[7]About half of all nonresidential building improvements are included in the value of new construction.
[8]Not included separately in Total New Construction.

NOTE: Totals may not add due to rounding.

SOURCE: U.S. Department of Commerce: Bureau of the Census, International Trade Administration (ITA). Estimates and forecasts by ITA.

Construction: Trends and Projections, 1989–93

Item	1989	1990	1991	1992[1]	1993[2]
Value of new construction put in place (bil.$)	443.4	442.1	401.0	423.0	—
Value of new construction put in place (bil. 1987$)	409.5	397.5	358.6	373.2	375.8
Number of private housing units (000)	1,376	1,193	1,014	1,230	1,250
Shipments of mobile homes (000 units)	198.1	188.2	170.7	197.0	207.0
Employees (000)[3]	5,187	5,133	4,685	4,600	—
Self-employed workers (000)[4]	1,380	1,400	1,420	1,400	—
Average hourly earnings of construction workers ($)[3]	13.54	13.77	13.99	14.10	—
Construction cost index (1987=100)	107.0	110.2	110.6	111.7	—
Producer price index for all construction materials (1982=100)	113.2	115.3	118.5	121.2	—

[1]Estimate.
[2]Forecast.
[3]Based on establishment surveys by the Bureau of Labor Statistics. Excludes self-employed workers.
[4]Proprietors and working partners, not counted as employees.

NOTE: The data on new construction put in place do not include maintenance and repair work.

SOURCE: U.S. Department of Commerce: Bureau of the Census, International Trade Administration (ITA); U.S. Department of Labor, Bureau of Labor Statistics. Estimates and forecasts by ITA.

Private Housing Starts by Type of House, 1980–93

(in thousands of units)

Year	Total Starts	Single Unit Structures			Multiunit Structures			
		Total	Detached Houses	Townhouses[1]	Total	2–4 Unit Structures	Townhouse-style Apartments[1]	Apartment Units[2]
1980	1,292	852	774	78	440	110	45	285
1981	1,084	705	628	77	379	91	39	249
1982	1,063	663	577	86	400	80	27	293
1983	1,703	1,068	897	171	635	113	44	478
1984	1,750	1,085	875	210	665	121	40	504
1985	1,745	1,075	905	170	670	93	53	524
1986	1,807	1,179	1,013	166	628	84	52	492
1987	1,623	1,146	1,004	142	477	65	35	377
1988	1,488	1,081	968	113	407	59	30	318
1989	1,376	1,003	916	87	373	55	31	287
1990	1,193	895	832	63	298	38	20	240
1991	1,014	840	789	51	174	36	12	126
1992[3]	1,230	1,060	990	70	170	39	13	118
1993[4]	1,250	1,080	—	—	170	—	—	—

[1]A single unit townhouse is one that is separated from adjoining units by a ground-to-roof wall and has separate utilities. Townhouse-style apartments, though attached, are not separated by a ground-to-roof wall, and they may share infrastructural facilities.
[2]Apartment buildings are conventional multifamily buildings in which dwelling units may share a common basement, heating plant, stairs, entrance halls, water supply, or sewage disposal facilities.
[3]Estimate.
[4]Forecast.

SOURCE: U.S. Department of Commerce, Bureau of Census. Estimates and forecasts prepared by the U.S. Department of Commerce, International Trade Administration.

Construction Materials

The demand for construction materials in 1992 reflected the 4 percent rise in constant-dollar construction put-in-place activity. For the first time since the peak level of housing construction in 1986, new residential construction in 1992 rose slightly over the previous year. The increase reflected a rise in single-family construction; multifamily construction remained very weak. The level of new housing starts of slightly more than 1 million units in 1991 was the lowest since 1946. Housing starts in 1992 were up 22 percent to about 1.23 million units. Multifamily housing starts remained at 170,000 units. The long-term slide in shipments of manufactured (mobile) homes continued, with just 171,000 units shipped in 1991. In 1992, shipments increased about 15 percent to 197,000 units.

Over the years, the trend toward larger houses with more amenities has strengthened demand for construction materials. For the first time in many years, the average size of new single-family units in 1991 did not grow but remained at the 1990 level of 2,080 square feet. This compares with 2,035 square feet in 1989 and 1,780 square feet in 1984. Over the years, demand for building materials also benefited from an increase in amenities, such as two-car garages, central air conditioning, additional bedrooms and bathrooms, fireplaces, and full basements. In 1991, the percent of new single-family homes with some of these features declined. For example, the percent of new homes with central air conditioning, 2½ or more bathrooms, 4 or more bedrooms, fireplaces, or garages all declined slightly. Units with full basements rose slightly.

The decline in materials demand from the private nonresidential construction sector continued in 1992. This sector experienced an 8 percent drop in activity on an inflation-adjusted basis, with the important office building segment down about 22 percent, hotels and motels down 40 percent, and the other commercial buildings down 18 percent. The manufacturing segment was down just 3 percent.

In 1992, public construction was up about 3 percent in real terms. Most categories of public building construction rose between 2 and 7 percent, with the hospital subcategory remaining at the 1991 level. The huge highway category went up 3 percent. Most other types of public construction increased modestly, except sewer construction, which was off 2 percent.

Alterations, additions, and repair work continue to be an important market for construction materials. Many building products are produced especially for this market and designed for ease of installation by do-it-yourselfers and small contractors. Residential expenditures in current dollars rose to about $107 million in 1990, but declined sharply to just $97.5 million in 1991. This drop reflected the general weakness in the economy. A 6 percent current dollar rise to about $103 million is expected for 1992. Although similar data on nonresidential renovation and repair work are limited, such construction is also believed to have declined in 1991 and increased modestly in 1992.

With demand still weak, prices of construction materials rose a modest 1.4 percent in 1992, double the rise the year earlier. These data are based on the Bureau of Labor Statistics Producer Price Index for all construction materials. None of the materials covered had 1992 price increases above the 2.1 percent recorded for builders' hardware, and plumbing fixtures and fittings. The largest price declines were for insulation materials (−6.0 percent) and gypsum products (−4.8 percent). Several categories had increases or decreases of 0.5 percent or less (concrete products, metal doors and sash, Portland cement, and prefab metal buildings).

ENVIRONMENTAL PROFILE

Many construction materials are energy-intensive and involve specific environmental issues and problems. Among the more energy intensive industries are cement, clay brick, ceramic tile, construction lime, flat glass, fiber glass, and gypsum board. Many industries get their raw material from the petrochemical or energy/fuel industries. These include various plastics construction materials, asphalt paving, and asphalt roofing. Some industries (particularly cement) burn mainly coal and could be affected by global climate issues and policies. Some are using waste materials (including shredded and whole tires) as fuel in their kilns. Most construction materials industries have some effect on the environment, if only rain water runoff problems.

Recycling is becoming much more common in the construction and materials area. Aggregates are being reused more frequently, more old concrete is being ground up to make aggregates, and asphalt products are being reheated and reused. Broken glass is also being used in pavements as an aggregate; and garbage is now a raw material for a lightweight aggregate product.

INTERNATIONAL COMPETITIVENESS

U.S. exports of non-lumber construction materials increased in 1992 for the sixth consecutive year. Imports, after rising dramatically for many years, declined in 1990 and 1991, but rose again slightly in 1992. Exports were up 5 percent above 1991, while imports grew 3 percent. In 1992, exports totaled about $3.7 billion and imports reached about $3.6 billion, resulting in a trade surplus of about $100 million. This compares with a surplus of about $35 million the year earlier and with a peak annual trade deficit of about $2.1 billion in both 1986 and 1987.

The improving U.S. trade situation for these products in recent years reflects the weakness in the U.S. construction market and the growing long-term market for such products worldwide. Strong construction activity in most Asian countries, Mexico, the Middle East, Spain, and Portugal has helped increase demand for many U.S. construction materials. These factors have affected U.S. imports as well, with foreign producers in many countries concentrating more on their improved domestic markets and third-country markets, rather than exporting to the United States.

Favorable foreign currency exchange rates have played an important role in the trade situation. The U.S. construction materials industries' reputation overseas for quality, innovative products, and superior service were other positive factors. The U.S. trade situation was also aided by sales of prefab homes to other countries, Israel in particular. The U.S.-Canada Free Trade Agreement aided market access both for U.S. and Canadian building products producers. Similar prospects could result from implementation of the North American Free Trade Agreement (NAFTA) with tariff reductions and elimination of nontariff barriers.

Exports are significant in the flat glass, mineral wool, builders hardware, fabricated structural metals, hard-surfaced floor coverings, prefabricated wood and metal buildings, plastics building materials, and cast iron pipe and fittings industries. Industries experiencing large import volumes include flat glass, cement, ceramic wall and floor tile, dimension stone, builders' hardware, fabricated structural metals, and miscellaneous metal work products.

Canada is the largest customer for U.S. non-lumber building products. Other major customers include Mexico, Japan, the United Kingdom, Taiwan, Hong Kong, and Korea.

Major suppliers of these products to the United States are Canada, followed by Italy, Mexico, Taiwan, Japan, Spain, and West Germany.

LONG-TERM PROSPECTS

Demand for construction materials will reflect the expected slow recovery in the construction sector. New residential construction is expected to be the strongest sector at least through 1994. This sector, mainly because of demographics, will not grow to the high levels experienced during the previous housing peaks of the 1970's and 1980's. Overbuilding and problems in commercial real estate and financial institutions will likely result in further declines in most types of private nonresidential building categories until at least 1995. Public construction, despite infrastructure needs, will grow only moderately because of tight Federal, state, and local budgets. As the recovery gets stronger, higher tax revenues should support more public infrastructure renewal and improvement work, although there will be pressure to draw down the Federal budget deficit. The demand for construction materials should rise at a 3- to 4-percent annual rate through 1998.

Housing starts during the peak years in the 1980's and 1970's averaged 1.6 million and 1.8 million units, respectively. Demographics and the affordability problem will result in peak new housing start years in the 1990's at about the 1.4 million unit level. Because of the affordability problem and smaller families, the trend in this decade will likely be toward more modest and less expensive housing. The average size of new units will likely decline, reversing the upward trend of the last 10 to 15 years.

The level of new and renewal infrastructure work will depend not only on government spending at all levels, but also on new types of financing instruments and institutions involving both public and private funding. An expected increase in private sector involvement in building and maintaining public works will follow an easing of Federal, state, and local budget constraints.

The need for additional new electric power and communications facilities should increase demand for utility construction in the 1990's. Financing the facilities will be a problem, as will environmental and other issues surrounding nuclear and coal burning power plants.

Many factors will contribute to the long-term prospects for U.S. construction materials in the world market. Among these are product and price competitiveness, the relative strength of the U.S. and other country markets, and currency exchange rates. Bilateral and multilateral trade negotiations, such as NAFTA, will play an important role. Housing and infrastructure construction is needed in all areas of the world. Canada, Asia, and

Europe have been the U.S.'s major customers. In the future, Mexico and other Latin American countries as well as some African nations also should offer good growth prospects. Approval of NAFTA will offer easier access to the Mexican, Canadian, and U.S. markets for building materials producers in those countries. Initiatives for free trade agreements with other Central and South American countries would further enhance opportunities for exporting U.S.-made goods and, of course, offer opportunities for these countries to sell in the U.S. market.

The fast pace of foreign investment in U.S. construction materials industries in the 1980's is expected to slow in the 1990's. Foreign investment and increased exporting by U.S. firms demonstrate the growing awareness of the many benefits of selling in foreign markets. These include greater sales and growth opportunities, hedging against the cyclical fluctuations of the U.S. market, and greater protection of U.S. markets by competing against foreign producers in their home and third-country markets.—*C. B. Pitcher, Office of Materials, Machinery and Chemicals, (202) 482-0132.*

Construction Materials Price Trends, 1986–92

(annual percent change)

Product	1986–87	1987–88	1988–89	1989–90	1990–91	1991–92[1]
Builders hardware	1.4	4.7	4.3	6.6	3.8	2.1
Ceramic tile	3.4	3.3	2.3	1.8	−1.1	1.0
Clay brick	2.9	2.5	1.2	2.6	1.0	1.2
Concrete products	0.2	0.5	1.1	2.1	2.7	0.5
Fabricated structural steel for buildings	3.6	6.4	3.6	−0.1	−1.3	−2.6
Gypsum products	−8.6	−9.8	−2.6	−4.4	−5.6	−4.8
Hard surfaced floor coverings	2.4	5.5	6.0	2.4	4.7	1.7
Insulation materials	−0.7	−0.8	−0.9	1.6	2.2	−6.0
Metal doors, sash and trim	−0.1	9.3	6.2	1.1	2.4	0.2
Plumbing fixtures and fittings	3.6	7.3	7.0	4.8	3.7	2.1
Portland cement	−1.9	0.1	−0.7	1.6	3.0	−0.3
Prefab metal buildings	2.0	5.6	4.5	1.2	0.6	−0.4
Prepared asphalt roofing	5.1	2.6	1.3	0.1	0.5	−3.8
Sand, gravel, crushed stone	3.4	2.1	1.8	2.1	2.8	1.5
Sheet, plate, and float glass	4.0	4.2	−2.2	−6.5	−4.3	−3.5
All construction materials[2]	2.1	5.7	3.3	0.1	0.7	1.4

[1]Estimate.
[2]Includes lumber, wood products, and other construction products not covered in this chapter.

SOURCE: U.S. Department of Labor, Bureau of Labor Statistics; U.S. Department of Commerce, International Trade Administration (ITA). Estimates by ITA.

Trends and Forecasts: Construction Materials

(in millions of 1987 dollars except as noted)

	Item	1990	1991	1992[1]	1993[2]	Percent Change (1990–1993) Compound Annual 90–93	Annual 90–91	Annual 91–92	Annual 92–93
	Total	23,894	22,026	22,293	22,533	−1.9	−7.8	1.2	1.1
3088	Plastic plumbing fixtures	997	1,080	1,100	1,100	3.3	8.3	1.9	0
3211	Flat glass	2,354	2,177	2,010	2,050	−4.5	−7.5	−7.7	2.0
3241	Hydraulic Cement	4,180	3,804	4,040	4,175	−0.04	−9.0	6.2	3.3
3253	Ceramic wall/floor tile	785	663	709	747	−1.6	−15.5	6.9	5.4
3261	Vitreous plumbing fixtures	771	732	740	750	−0.9	−5.1	1.1	1.4
3275	Gypsum products	2,999	2,747	2,961	3,076	0.8	−8.4	7.8	3.9
3431	Metal sanitary ware	865	823	870	875	0.4	−4.9	5.7	0.6
3432	Plumbing fixture fittings	2,164	2,100	2,200	2,250	1.3	−3.0	4.8	2.3
3441	Fabricated structural metal	8,779	7,900	7,663	7,510	−5.1	−10.0	−3.0	−2.0

[1]Estimate.
[2]Forecast.

SOURCE: U.S. Department of Commerce: Bureau of the Census, International Trade Administration (ITA). Estimates and forecasts by ITA.

Drugs and Biotechnology

The pharmaceutical industry (SIC 283) is composed of four primary components: medicinals and botanicals (SIC 2833), pharmaceutical preparations (SIC 2834), diagnostics (SIC 2835) and biologicals (SIC 2836). Biotechnology is not classified by the Government as a separate Standard Industrial Classification (SIC) code. However, because it is a growing part of the pharmaceutical industry and has applications to other industries as well, it is treated as a separate section in the latter part of this chapter.

The United States remains the world center for research in the pharmaceutical field, and the world's largest single market, accounting for almost 67 percent of world pharmaceutical sales. It possesses the world's leading laboratories and remains the world leader in pharmaceutical innovation, competitiveness and technological development.

Drug industry shipments increased more than 8 percent in 1992 to about $64 billion. In constant dollars, the increase was close to 2.5 percent. New drug discoveries ranging from nicotine patches to non-surgical treatment for prostate enlargement assured the industry a growth year. Fueled in part by demand for new drugs, exports totalled almost $6.8 billion, rising nearly 18 percent above 1991, while imports reached almost $5.5 billion, up nearly 14 percent. For 1992, total employment in the industry reached 195,000, a slight increase over 1991.

The pharmaceutical industry weathered the recent economic slowdown, but a cost-conscious consumer has elevated the generic and over-the-counter (OTC) segments of the industry to the ranks of strong competitors.

The recession heightened consumer interest in personal healthcare and in reducing expenses. This reinforced demographic trends toward an aging population, representing 35 percent of the market, a population that lives on fixed incomes. These developments have also directed the industry's attention to lower-cost medications, particularly for the elderly. Following the trend of self-care through responsible self-medication, the Food and Drug Administration (FDA) for the first time allowed self-diagnosis with its approval of vaginal yeast treatment. While the prescription drug firms did well with the introduction of several blockbuster drugs, producers of OTC and generic drugs continued their intense competition. The trend toward switching prescription drugs to over-the-counter products and generic drugs has increased.

The industry's consistent commitment to invest in research and development is a key to its strong competitive performance. While overall spending on research in the U.S. has declined, the pharmaceutical industry increased spending by 13 percent to about $11 billion on R&D during 1992. Pharmaceutical R&D expenditures amounted to more than 16 percent of its sales, one of the highest proportions of any U.S. industry.

Increasing public concern over healthcare cost has led to numerous legislative proposals to control drug prices. The industry points out, however, that prescription pharmaceuticals accounted for less than 7 cents of the U.S. healthcare dollar, and this represented the most cost-effective medical treatment available. As other healthcare costs have risen, drug costs have decreased as a percentage of total healthcare expenditures, from about 18 percent in 1929 to around 7 percent in 1992. However, because of the cost-containment push throughout the U.S. healthcare system, it is likely that the industry will meet with increasing pressure to contain price increases. Drug purchasing policies for the Medicaid Program and combined purchasing by large hospital groups are having a significant impact on drug prices. Already, six major companies have said they will not raise their prices faster than the Consumer Price Index rate.

During 1992, public policy provided aid as well as anxious concern for the industry. The FDA continues to speed up its approval of new drugs, and to improve harmonization between U.S. and foreign regulation. FDA plans to reduce its approval time to six months for emergency drugs and 12 months for regular ones. The FDA also recently established an Office of OTC Drugs, along with an OTC Advisory Committee to oversee the Rx-to-OTC switch process.

On the other hand, the industry was beset by a barrage of proposed legislation this year to limit drug pricing and to take away tax and orphan drug protection. The Prescription Drug Cost Containment Act of 1991 (S2000) was defeated, but the industry's pricing practices continue to attract the attention of Congress and their largest voting constituency, the elderly.

INTERNATIONAL COMPETITIVENESS

The U.S. pharmaceutical industry has consistently maintained a positive trade balance in international markets. In 1992, the surplus in drug trade exceeded $1.3 billion. Foreign investment in the United States pharmaceutical industry subsided this year after peaking in the late 1980's with large investments by Western European firms. In 1990, foreign investments in the U.S. pharmaceutical industry were $10 billion but U.S. investments in foreign pharmaceutical industries totalled $10.6 billion. Although data is not available, it appears that there were smaller foreign investment flows in 1991 and 1992. The U.K., France, and Switzerland have been the principal sources of foreign investment in the last two years.

In the international arena, the industry firmly supported the use of the Special 301 provisions of the 1988 Omnibus Trade and Competitiveness Act. This led to the breakthrough decision by the People's Republic of China to provide 20 year patent protection for pharmaceuticals.

Because U.S. industry does more than one-half of its foreign business in Western Europe, it is closely following the European Community (EC) 1992 harmonization of regulations to monitor any possible restrictive policies on U.S. imports. A wide range of pharmaceutical pricing and reimbursement constraints in the member states are being consolidated into EC regulations.

Japan remains the United States' second largest pharmaceutical customer. U.S. industry was encouraged by Japan's recent establishment of a new quarterly forum in which industry will be able to discuss priority issues including pricing and reimbursement with high Government officials. The first meeting was held in May 1991.

Intellectual property protection is very important to the industry, and adoption of stronger patent laws by Mexico and China were welcome developments. The trend in Latin America to increase its intellectual property rights protection makes these countries more promising pharmaceutical markets. The North American Free Trade Agreement (NAFTA) also will offer much improved conditions of access to the Mexican market.

Current risks and market opportunities are equally great in the newly independent states of the former Soviet Union. However, with greater political stability, these countries will likely become leading pharmaceutical markets in the future.

LONG-TERM PROSPECTS

The drug market is expected to continue to expand over the next five years, but the industry will face increasing pressure to control prices. The nature of the U.S. healthcare delivery system is also changing with a shift away from the traditional fee-for-service doctor/patient relationship and a corresponding increase in services by large, managed healthcare providers. Growth in the number of older people will boost demand for quality, low cost healthcare services and products. Since R&D costs are expected to continue to rise, the ability of the industry to develop new drugs and new global markets is expected to play an even greater role in determining long-term prospects.

Medicinals and Botanicals

Medicinal and botanical establishments (SIC 2833) are primarily engaged in manufacturing bulk organic and inorganic medicinal chemicals and their derivatives and in processing bulk botanical drugs and herbs. With increasing consumer interest in natural products, companies are increasingly adding herbal ingredients to their products. There are a growing number of new projects dedicated to the screening of plants for potential drug applications. In cancer treatment alone, over 100 U.S. companies are engaged in plant-derived pharmaceutical research.

Pharmaceutical Preparations

The establishments in this industry (SIC 2834) are primarily engaged in manufacturing, fabricating, and processing drugs into pharmaceutical preparations for human or veterinary use. The products of pharmaceutical preparation are usually finished in the form intended for final consumption.

Prescription drug costs in the U.S. continue to remain a much smaller percentage of total healthcare costs than in other industrialized countries. While spending on healthcare has been increasing rapidly as a percentage of the Gross National Product, spending on prescription drugs has remained substantially under 1 percent of GNP, just as it has for the past 25 years. Senior citizens consume 30 percent of all prescription medication dispensed in the United States. The U.S. pharmaceutical industry continues to devote a considerable amount of its resources to discovering new medicines for the cure and treatment of diseases that debilitate older Americans, such as alzheimer's, arthritis, and osteoporosis.

Diagnostic Substances

Diagnostic firms (SIC 2835) are primarily engaged in manufacturing chemicals, biological, and radioactive substances that are used in diagnosing or monitoring the state of human or veterinary health.

The medical diagnostics market is entering a period of flux. It is experiencing slower growth and greater competition as players consolidate and partnerships become more common. The fastest growing area in diagnostics appears to be immunodiagnostics led by sexually transmitted diseases (STD) detection. Also expanding at a good rate are diabetes and cellular diagnostics. Diagnostic kits recorded strong growth and are expected to continue as the self-medication trend continues to expand.

Biological Products

Biological establishments (SIC 2836) are primarily engaged in the production of bacterial and virus vaccines, toxoids, and analogous products (such as allergic extracts), serums, plasmas, and other blood derivatives for human or veterinary use.

In the laboratory, researchers are devising ingenious ways to inject DNA into the body to fight ailments ranging from AIDS and heart problems to cancer and Parkinson's disease. Biologicals are leading the way in technologies that speed bone marrow recovery in patients who undergo the transplantation process to treat certain cancers. New rabies and tetanum toxoids and pertussis vaccines were recently approved by the FDA as vaccines continue to be one of the cheapest and most effective ways to eradicate certain diseases.—*William Hurt, Office of Materials, Machinery, and Chemicals, (202) 482-0128.*

Biotechnology

Biotechnology is revolutionizing the discovery and development of treatments to improve human health. Already, several medicines developed by biotechnology companies founded barely 15 years ago are approaching $500 million in annual sales. Biotechnology is finding applications in other industries as well, to reduce manufacturing costs, improve food quality, reduce reliance on pesticides, and clean up environmental wastes.

Biotechnology refers to biological processes and techniques that use organisms or their cellular, subcellular, or molecular components to make products or modify plants and animals to carry desired traits. Biotechnology broadly defined includes traditional animal and plant breeding, and the long-known use of micro-organisms to make leavened bread and fermented beverages and foods. This discussion focuses on advances in modern biotechnology that have provided powerful new tools to discover new substances, modify with far greater precision and speed the genetic makeup of organisms, and produce rare products in large quantities. Modern biotechnology draws on many scientific and engineering disciplines, including recombinant DNA, monoclonal antibody, gene therapy, DNA amplification, and antisense technologies.

Industrial Structure, Sales and R&D

Because biotechnology consists of processes that are integrated in research and production by a variety of industries, the Government does not classify biotechnology as a separate industry with its own SIC code, nor collect specific production, employment, trade or R&D statistics. Rather, the resulting products and services are categorized under the SIC of the applicable industry.

There are about 1,300 companies applying biotechnology in the United States. About 675 companies, mostly small and new, have been founded to exploit scientific discoveries coming from academic research labs. At least 440 companies supply materials, equipment and services used in research and production. Nearly 200 established firms are involved, mostly pharmaceutical, medical supply, and chemical. These groups are sometimes linked together as the "biotech industry" because they share business alliances and concerns in regulation, patent protection, and R&D needs. About 57,000 people are employed in 572, mainly small biotechnology firms, and 15,000 people in 147 supply firms; total industry employment is not available.

The pace of new company formation has fallen off from the early 1980's. Acquisitions, mergers, equity purchases, and alliances are leading gradually to an industry consolidation. Long development lead times and the high cost of testing, of regulatory approval and the marketing of medical and agricultural products, are driving small companies to form business alliances with established firms. Mergers and acquisitions between biotechnology companies are on the increase.

Sales data on products developed through biotechnology are not broken down in most company reports. Based on unofficial estimates U.S. firms' shipments of biotech-derived products could reach $4 billion by the end of 1992, with medicines and diagnostics accounting for over 90 percent of sales. Estimates for previous years are: 1991, $3.1 billion; 1990, $2.2 billion; 1989, $1.5 billion; 1988, $1 billion; 1987, $600 million; and 1986, $350 million.

The U.S. Government will spend some $4.03 billion in fiscal year (FY) 1993 on R&D, a 7 percent increase over FY 1992. Total industrial R&D investment for the same period is estimated in the $3 billion range. The largest component of government biotech R&D is improvement of human health, an estimated 42 percent; industry spends over 70 percent of its R&D dollars on healthcare.

Biotechnology Advances

To date, 16 new biotech-derived drugs and vaccines have been approved. Sales have grown rapidly because most products offer either the only available treatment or a safer alternative. For example, recombinant human growth hormone replaces the natural hormone extracted from cadavers. The natural hormone was withdrawn from the market because of possible contamination with a deadly virus. Entirely new markets have opened with colony stimulating factors to reduce the threat of infections that afflict patients undergoing chemotherapy and bone marrow transplants, and alpha interferon to treat viral diseases.

As of August 1991, there were 132 biotech-derived medicines in clinical trials, according to the Pharmaceutical Manufacturers Association, a 60 percent increase in 4 years. The major R&D targets are cancers, AIDS, and cardiovascular diseases. Biotechnology has opened new approaches to vaccine design, where much of the focus is on developing both therapeutic and preventative vaccines to combat AIDS. More than 20 biotechnology medicines were awaiting Food and Drug Administration (FDA) approval as of mid-1992, of which six have been recommended for approval by an FDA advisory body. To tackle the large increase in applications of biotech-derived medicines, the FDA is adding 50 staff members solely to review biotech applications. If an agreement between Government and industry reached in August 1992, to speed drug approvals becomes law, the FDA will add 600 new examiners to be paid for by user fees.

Biotechnology has provided research tools to speed the discovery of disease-causing genes. By understanding the biochemical progression of these diseases, drugs or therapies might be developed for early intervention. One mode of treatment is human gene therapy; the first such attempt to correct a rare immune system disorder was carried out in 1990. About two dozen trials are either underway or awaiting permission, to treat brain tumors, AIDS, and other serious diseases. The number of gene therapy applications is expected to quadruple by 1994. The Government's Human Genome Project, a 15-year $3 billion endeavor started in 1990, is intended to map and characterize the 100,000 or so genes that make up the human being. Among the benefits expected are a vast repertoire of information on disease pre-disposing genes that can be used by industry to develop treatments.

Biotech research tools are being used to combat a major public health problem—bacterial diseases that are developing resistance to antibiotics. Using recombinant DNA techniques and DNA probes, researchers identified the genetic change that allows some strains of tuberculosis to become resistant to drugs. This discovery should lead to tests to identify drug-resistant TB cases, and the design of new medicines.

Transgenic animals engineered with conditions that mimic human diseases such as cystic fibrosis are coming on the market to serve as models for studying human diseases and testing experimental drugs and gene therapy protocols. Transgenic animals are now capable of producing rare human proteins in milk such as TPA, blood clotting factors, and hemoglobin. It may take until the late 1990's to extract the targeted proteins in sufficient quantities, and to ensure the necessary purity and efficacy for use in drugs.

As of February 1992, 640 diagnostic kits using monoclonal antibodies, DNA probes and recombinant DNA had been approved by the FDA including screening tests for the AIDS and hepatitis-C viruses. DNA "fingerprinting" of biological materials left at crime scenes is gaining acceptance in the courts to identify suspects.

Veterinary medicine is using biotechnology to improve animal health and reduce diseases that are costly to the livestock industry. Animals produced by new reproductive technologies such as embryo sexing, multiplication and transfer, are available. Growth promoters to increase milk production in dairy cows and produce leaner, faster growing pigs, may be on the market by 1993–94. Transgenic fish and food animals engineered with such traits as lower fat content or resistance to diseases are not expected to become commercially available before 2000.

The food processing industry is benefiting from faster, more accurate diagnostic tests for dangerous contaminants, and realizing improved performance with recombinant DNA-derived enzymes. For example, chymosin, used in coagulating milk products, offers cheese producers a cheaper and purer alternative to the natural product, rennet. Foods made from biotechnology may come on the market faster than expected because of the FDA's proposed policy that it will not require review or labeling of foods produced through genetically engineered plants that are substantially similar to other foods. Regulatory review would be required when a new food raises safety questions, such as a change in levels of nutrients or naturally occurring toxins, or the introduction of allergens or toxins. The first biotech foods expected on the market, in 1993, are tastier and longer-lived tomatoes engineered to retard spoilage.

The first genetically engineered plants are expected to come on the market in two or three years. Closest to the market are plants with resistance to certain herbicides and viral diseases. Plants with engineered resistance to pests are expected in the second half of the decade. Plants resistant to bacteria and fungi, environmental stresses (drought, freeze/thaw climatic changes, saline soils), or higher nutritional content are not expected before 2000.

Engineered crop plants are being used as biological factories to produce such high value-added compounds as drugs, enzymes, flavors, and fragrances. A sunscreen using melanin produced in tobacco plants could be approved in the near future. In specialty chemicals, indigo dye produced through recombinant bacteria could be on the market in 1993.

INTERNATIONAL COMPETITIVENESS

The United States has led in discoveries and the commercial introduction of biotechnology products due to its large investment in biomedical research during the past several decades, and its entrepreneurial environment. The United States is expected to continue to play a preeminent role in the introduction of innovative products, but commercial application of new biotechnologies worldwide still is in its infancy. Other countries have strengths in many related scientific and engineering disciplines, as well as in the industries that utilize biotechnology. For example, six of the world's top ten leading pharmaceutical companies and agrichemical companies are European-based; the balance are U.S. companies.

Some of the factors that will influence future U.S. competitiveness include availability of capital to fund R&D, adequacy of worldwide intellectual property rights and enforceability, the ability of government regulatory agencies and patent offices to review applications on a timely basis, and establishment of domestic and international regulations that do not discriminate against products of biotechnology or pose barriers to trade.

Researchers and firms from many nations can be involved in the discovery, development and marketing of biotech-derived products. U.S. biotechnology firms have initiated alliances with European and Japanese companies to obtain funding and foreign marketing partners. The North Carolina Biotechnology Center estimates that of 1,000 strategic alliances formed between 1975 and 1991, U.S. biotechnology companies had 58 percent of their alliances with other U.S. firms, while 29 percent were with European partners, and 13 percent with Japanese partners.

The increasing globalization of industrial biotechnology activity tends to obscure the national identity of biotech-derived products. Foreign firms have invested in, or acquired some U.S. biotechnology companies. The Department of Commerce estimates that foreign firms made 76 investment transactions involving purchases of 10 percent or more equity in biotech companies between 1981 and the first quarter of 1991. European firms accounted for 82 percent of those transactions, and Japan for the remainder.

Foreign firms also are investing in the building of U.S.-based research facilities. A U.S. site enables them to hire scientific teams that often are unavailable or difficult to assemble at home. Such facilities enhance their ability to monitor research advances and regulatory procedures for biotechnology products in the United States. Restrictions on biotechnology research and manufacturing in Germany have played a major role in the decision by some German firms to locate their research facilities in the U.S. Overall, more than two dozen foreign biotechnology research facilities have been established here, led by firms from Germany, Japan, and Switzerland. In turn, U.S. firms have set up subsidiaries and research facilities, principally in Europe, and have invested in companies.

Although there are no official trade statistics for biotechnology, U.S. companies maintain a favorable trade balance. Many biotech-derived products on the market were developed in the U.S. and earn foreign income from direct exports, from sales by overseas plants, and from royalties from licenses. Income from contract R&D services to foreign clients is another major source of income to U.S. companies.

LONG-TERM PROSPECTS

Sales of biotech-derived products are expected to grow by 15–20 percent annually over the next 5 years. Growth will rely on overcoming research and technical barriers, the timing of regulatory approvals, cost-effectiveness, competitiveness with existing products, and reimbursement limits on medical products. The large number of promising products in the medical development pipeline, some with potentially large markets, indicates that most growth will come from medicines and diagnostics. Sales in non-medical industries will be smaller because of economic and price/performance constraints, research and technical barriers, and lower investment levels by government and industry. Market values will hinge on public acceptance of genetically engineered foods and products used in the environment.—*Emily Arakaki, Basic Industries, (202) 482-3888.*

Products/Services Developed Through Modern Biotechnology on the U.S. Market

Product/Service	Treatment or Use (year first approved)
Human Healthcare	
Alpha interferon	Hairy cell leukemia (1986), Kaposi's sarcoma (1988), venereal warts (1988), Non-A/non-B hepatitis (1991), hepatitis-B (1992)
Granulocyte colony-stimulating factor (G-CSF)	Adjuvant to chemotherapy (1991)
Granulocyte macrophage colony-stimulating factor (GM–CSF)	Adjuvant to certain bone marrow transplants (1991)
Erythropoietin	Anemia associated with kidney disease (1989), AIDS-related anemia (1991)
Gamma interferon	Chronic granulomatous disease (1990)
Human growth hormone	Dwarfism (1985)
Insulin	Diabetes (1982)
Interleukin-2	Kidney cancer (1992)
Tissue plasminogen activator	Acute myocardial infarction (1987), acute pulmonary embolism (1990)
Vaccines	Hepatitis-B (1986)
Therapeutic monoclonal antibodies (MAbs)	Treat kidney transplant rejection (1986); Purify blood clotting agents (1987);
Diagnostic tests (MAbs, rDNA, DNA probes and PCR)	Diagnose pregnancy & fertility; bacterial and viral infections; cancer; genetic diseases; forensic and paternity testing; DNA profiling of military personnel.
Agriculture	
Animals:	
Vaccines	Colibacillosis or scours (1984), pseudorabies (1987), feline leukemia (1990)
Therapeutic MAbs	Canine lymphoma (1991)
Diagnostic tests	Bacterial and viral infections, pregnancy, presence of antibiotic residues
Plants:	
Diagnostic tests	Diagnose plant diseases (turfgrass fungi)
Biopesticides (killed bacteria)	Kills caterpillars, beetles (1991)
Food Processing and Specialty Chemicals	
Diagnostic tests	Diagnose food and feed contaminants (salmonella, aflatoxin, listeria, campylobacter, and Yersinia entercolitica)
Chymosin or rennin	Enzyme used in cheesemaking (1990)
Alpha amylase	Enzyme used in corn syrup and textile manufacturing (1990)
Lipase	Enzyme used in detergents (1991)
Xylanase	Enzyme used in pulp and paper industry (1992)
Luciferase	Luminsecent agent used in diagnostic tests
Other	
Transgenic mice	Medical research
Environmental diagnostic tests	Detect legionella bacteria in water samples

NOTE: Products pending approval at the Food and Drug Administration included a therapeutic MAb to treat graft-versus-host disease associated with bone marrow transplants, a therapeutic MAb to treat septic shock, three MAbs for *in vivo* imaging (of dead heart tissue, colorectal cancer and ovarian cancer), and recombinant Factor VIII to treat hemophilia.

SOURCE: U.S. Department of Commerce, Basic Industries.

Trends and Forecasts: Drugs (SIC 283)

(in millions of dollars except as noted)

Item	1987	1988	1989	1990	1991[1]	1992[2]	1993[3]	Percent Change (1987–1993) 87–88	88–89	89–90	90–91	91–92	92–93
Industry Data													
Value of shipments[4]	39,263	43,987	49,114	53,720	59,032	64,071	—	12.0	11.7	9.4	9.9	8.5	—
2833 Medicinals & botanicals	3,350	4,150	4,753	4,919	5,381	5,865	—	23.9	14.5	3.5	9.4	9.0	—
2834 Pharmaceutical preps	32,094	35,825	40,028	44,182	48,931	53,301	—	11.6	11.7	10.4	10.7	8.9	—
2835 Diagnostic substances	2,205	2,261	2,325	2,462	2,431	2,479	—	2.5	2.8	5.9	−1.3	2.0	—
2836 Bio prod ex diagnostic	1,614	1,750	2,008	2,156	2,289	2,426	—	8.4	14.7	7.4	6.2	6.0	—
Value of shipments (1987$)	39,263	40,942	41,998	42,773	43,723	44,751	46,881	4.3	2.6	1.8	2.2	2.4	4.8
2833 Medicinals & botanicals	3,350	3,960	4,213	4,274	4,359	4,406	4,538	18.2	6.4	1.4	2.0	1.1	3.0
2834 Pharmaceutical preps	32,094	32,988	33,581	34,144	34,998	35,872	37,737	2.8	1.8	1.7	2.5	2.5	5.2
2835 Diagnostic substances	2,205	2,237	2,275	2,282	2,316	2,362	2,432	1.5	1.7	0.3	1.5	2.0	3.0
2836 Bio prod ex diagnostic	1,614	1,757	1,929	2,073	2,050	2,111	2,174	8.9	9.8	7.5	−1.1	3.0	3.0
Total employment (000)	172	175	184	183	—	—	—	1.7	5.1	−0.5	—	—	—
2833 Medicinals & botanicals	11.6	11.3	11.4	10.9	—	—	—	−2.6	0.9	−4.4	—	—	—
2834 Pharmaceutical preps	132	133	142	144	148	152	—	0.8	6.8	1.4	2.8	2.7	—
2835 Diagnostic substances	15.4	16.2	16.1	14.9	—	—	—	5.2	−0.6	−7.5	—	—	—
2836 Bio prod ex diagnostic	13.3	13.7	14.5	13.3	—	—	—	3.0	5.8	−8.3	—	—	—
Production workers (000)	79.6	81.0	82.8	81.4	—	—	—	1.8	2.2	−1.7	—	—	—
2833 Medicinals & botanicals	6.1	6.2	6.6	6.5	—	—	—	1.6	6.5	−1.5	—	—	—
2834 Pharmaceutical preps	59.9	60.8	62.4	61.5	63.4	64.2	—	1.5	2.6	−1.4	3.1	1.3	—
2835 Diagnostic substances	6.8	7.5	6.8	6.6	—	—	—	10.3	−9.3	−2.9	—	—	—
2836 Bio prod ex diagnostic	6.8	6.5	7.0	6.8	—	—	—	−4.4	7.7	−2.9	—	—	—
Average hourly earnings ($)	12.22	12.67	13.48	14.22	—	—	—	3.7	6.4	5.5	—	—	—
2833 Medicinals & botanicals	15.32	16.09	16.29	17.35	—	—	—	5.0	1.2	6.5	—	—	—
2834 Pharmaceutical preps	12.42	12.93	13.83	14.71	—	—	—	4.1	7.0	6.4	—	—	—
2835 Diagnostic substances	10.74	10.93	11.54	11.80	—	—	—	1.8	5.6	2.3	—	—	—
2836 Bio prod ex diagnostic	8.87	9.13	9.30	9.15	—	—	—	2.9	1.9	−1.6	—	—	—

Capital expenditures	1,749	2,058	2,392	2,280	—	—	—	17.7	16.2	−4.7	—	—	—
2833 Medicinals & botanicals	115	151	219	195	—	—	—	31.3	45.0	−11.0	—	—	—
2834 Pharmaceutical preps	1,471	1,725	1,933	1,809	—	—	—	17.3	12.1	−6.4	—	—	—
2835 Diagnostic substances	93.5	93.3	117	147	—	—	—	−0.2	25.4	25.6	—	—	—
2836 Bio prod ex diagnostic	69.9	89.1	124	130	—	—	—	27.5	39.2	4.8	—	—	—
Product Data													
Value of shipments[5]	35,283	39,532	43,796	47,832	48,292	—	—	12.0	10.8	9.2	1.0	—	—
2833 Medicinals & botanicals	4,224	4,948	5,393	5,789	—	—	—	17.1	9.0	7.3	—	—	—
2834 Pharmaceutical preps	26,610	29,555	32,713	35,280	—	—	—	11.1	10.7	7.8	—	—	—
2835 Diagnostic substances	2,683	3,063	3,471	4,234	—	—	—	14.2	13.3	22.0	—	—	—
2836 Bio prod ex diagnostic	1,765	1,966	2,220	2,529	—	—	—	11.4	12.9	13.9	—	—	—
Value of shipments (1987$)	35,283	36,939	37,753	38,649	—	—	—	4.7	2.2	2.4	—	—	—
2833 Medicinals & botanicals	4,224	4,721	4,781	5,030	—	—	—	11.8	1.3	5.2	—	—	—
2834 Pharmaceutical preps	26,610	27,214	27,443	27,264	—	—	—	2.3	0.8	−0.7	—	—	—
2835 Diagnostic substances	2,683	3,030	3,396	3,924	—	—	—	12.9	12.1	15.5	—	—	—
2836 Bio prod ex diagnostic	1,765	1,974	2,132	2,431	—	—	—	11.8	8.0	14.0	—	—	—
Trade Data													
Value of imports	—	—	3,513	3,863	4,785	5,445	5,580	—	—	10.0	23.9	13.8	—
2833 Medicinals & botanicals	—	—	2,336	2,282	2,827	2,775	—	—	—	−2.3	23.9	−1.8	—
2834 Pharmaceutical preps	—	—	868	1,103	1,442	1,883	—	—	—	27.1	30.7	30.6	—
2835 Diagnostic substances	—	—	118	207	191	367	—	—	—	75.4	−7.7	92.1	—
2836 Bio prod ex diagnostic	—	—	191	271	325	420	—	—	—	41.9	19.9	29.2	—
Value of exports	—	—	4,346	5,062	5,746	6,767	6,926	—	—	16.5	13.5	17.8	—
2833 Medicinals & botanicals	—	—	1,797	1,921	2,081	2,384	—	—	—	6.9	8.3	14.6	—
2834 Pharmaceutical preps	—	—	974	1,258	1,478	1,806	—	—	—	29.2	17.5	22.2	—
2835 Diagnostic substances	—	—	739	909	1,160	1,389	—	—	—	23.0	27.6	19.7	—
2836 Bio prod ex diagnostic	—	—	837	973	1,027	1,188	—	—	—	16.2	5.5	15.7	—

[1]Estimated, except exports and imports.
[2]Estimate.
[3]Forecast.
[4]Value of all products and services sold by establishments in the drugs industry.
[5]Value of products classified in the drugs industry produced by all industries.
SOURCE: U.S. Department of Commerce: Bureau of the Census, International Trade Administration (ITA). Estimates and forecasts by ITA.

Electronic Components, Equipment, and Superconductors

Electronic components (SIC 367) represent a broad and distinct category of products in the electronics industry. The products include electronic tubes (SIC 3671), printed circuit boards (SIC 3672), semiconductors/diodes (SIC 3674), capacitors (SIC 3675), resistors (SIC 3676), coils and transformers (SIC 3677), connectors (SIC 3678), and electronic components not elsewhere classified (SIC 3679).

Typically, components are depicted as being either passive or active in nature, i.e., semiconductors, diodes, tubes, and transistors are active components; capacitors, connectors, coils, piezoelectric devices, resistors, switches, and transformers are passive. Printed circuit boards (PCBs) are not necessarily grouped as either because PCBs are the platform upon which active and passive electronic components are mounted.

Components are the fundamental building blocks of the electronics industry. There is an interdependent relationship between supplies of components and sales of application products that use these components. The demand for electronic components is dependent on sales of products in such application markets as consumer electronics, computers, transportation (including automobiles), and telecommunications.

Poor market conditions in 1991 and the first half of 1992 slowly gave way to improved economic signs in the second half of 1992 as orders firmed in key end user sectors such as computers. Sales of electronic components are expected to increase about 6 percent in 1992, compared with a growth of less than 2 percent in 1991. The late-1992 recovery is anticipated to carry forward and strengthen in 1993, driven primarily by predicted global economic improvement. During the 1991–92 period, however, profit margins were down, and are likely to continue to shrink in 1993 due to more intense global competition in the electronic components industry.

Employment losses in the electronic component product sectors continued during the first half of 1992, with semiconductor companies losing 4.1 percent and the rest of components losing 2.9 percent. However, the electronic components industry remained the largest single employer of U.S. workers in the overall electronics industry, accounting for about one-third of total employment. The U.S. Department of Labor estimates employment in components at 618,600 for 1991.

The trade deficit in electronic components increased in 1992 to an estimated $6.6 billion from $4.3 billion in 1991. Export sales of components contributed $14.4 billion to the U.S. economy in 1992.

Due to heightened demand, delivery lead times for components rose 2 percent in 1992, in sharp contrast with a 6 percent decline the previous year. Strongest growth was realized in surface mounted devices (SMDs) with delivery time expansion from 4.5 weeks in June to 10.5 weeks in July. The growth in SMD products was primarily linked to stronger demand from manufacturers of personal computers (PCs), laptop, pen-based, and notebook computers.

Many countries worldwide participate in various aspects of electronic component production. International buying patterns for components are based on manufacturing costs and technology differentials. A range of variables exist in global production costs. These variables include labor and capital inputs, and regulatory enforcement costs for environmental and worker safety standards. Technology differentials relate to variances in the structural development of technology research and the commercialization of research applications.

Research and Development

Research and development (R&D) spending peaked in the U.S. electronic component industry in 1986, when 9.2 percent of sales went into R&D. The most recent data available from the National Science Foundation (NSF) estimates company R&D spending in electronic components to be about $4.4 billion, or 8.3 percent of total sales, in 1989. Despite uncertain economic times in the United States, managers of corporate, government, university, and nonprofit research centers estimate 13-to-25 percent increases in their 1992 R&D spending over the previous year. However, NSF estimates that overall, the United States spends 25 percent less than other industrialized nations on nondefense related R&D.

The sophistication of component technology demands commitments by producers to meet increasingly costly production and product planning expenses. Because of intense international competition, the U.S. industry must: 1) maintain the domestic manufacturing base, 2) be first to market commercial applications of high-quality product innovations, 3) accommodate quick turn-around requests from customers, 4) maintain a leadership role in setting standards, and 5) further penetrate world markets.

Unlike their overseas competition, U.S.

component suppliers do not have long-term supplier relationships with original equipment manufacturers (OEMs) that purchase components and integrate them into electronic systems. OEMs tend to emphasize supplier flexibility, rather than lasting alliances with component suppliers. If the U.S. component industry is to prosper in the face of global competition, better long-term supplier/customer relations are needed.

Today's customers demand higher performance, more functionality, and continued miniaturization of physical characteristics at ultra-competitive prices. Continued product trends toward increased circuit density are strongly related to the overall trend to surface mounted technology (SMT) products, as contrasted with conventional through-the-hole mounting of components.

During the period 1990–96, SMT applications are expected to rise to a $4.6 billion annual market; growth rates are forecast to be 15 to 20 percent per year during this period. Surface mount devices reduce assembly time up to 80 percent over through-hole component mounting. In 1992, surface mounted devices (SMDs) represented an estimated 60 percent of the U.S. market for components.

LONG-TERM PROSPECTS

The product development offices of many companies will expand the search for economically feasible and technologically viable standards for a multichip module (MCM). MCMs may play a major role in the development of other specific downstream technologies, such as voice recognition synthesis, image processing, character recognition, multimedia/video/HDTV processing, and artificial intelligence-based products.

On a related front, advances in electronic packaging will continue to drive markets in low cost, high-volume electronics manufacturing.

An overall transition from through-hole packages to surface mount will continue. The general trends toward surface mounting will include small outline packaging, with innovations to include technologies such as vertical surface mount packaging. In particular, U.S. companies will strive to strengthen electronic packaging technology in North America through combinations of strategic corporate partnering and possible creation of industry led consortia.

The market opportunities for U.S. electronic exports during the next five years will continue to be in the established regional markets of East Asia, North America, and Western Europe. There are longer-term prospects in Eastern Europe and Latin America, providing those areas enjoy sustained economic growth and political stability.

Semiconductors and Related Devices

U.S. semiconductor industry shipments continued to grow in 1992 despite a decline in the Japanese market, with year-end shipments increasing an estimated 12 percent above 1991 levels. Major U.S. companies reported increased sales from 1991 levels in every regional market except Japan. The domestic book-to-bill ratio rose above 1.1 for most of 1992. The ratio is a strongly monitored industry indicator that is a comparison between the registration of orders, and the billing of customers for actual shipments. According to a Shearson Lehman estimate, U.S. semiconductor factory utilization reached 84.8 percent in 1992, another indication of progress toward full recovery. U.S. semiconductor shipments are expected to grow another 12 percent in 1993. The strongest semiconductor markets in 1992 were the United States and the Asia-Pacific region (except Japan), with 18 percent and 11 percent growth, respectively.

Capital and R&D Spending

U.S. semiconductor companies experienced a strong recovery in 1992 that stimulated capital spending. In contrast, Japanese companies' capital spending dropped from last year's levels due to difficult economic conditions there and overcapacity for dynamic random access memory (DRAM) semiconductors.

Dataquest, an authoritative market research company, reported that about one-third of U.S. industry revenues is spent on technology development and capital; 14 percent of revenues is spent on R&D alone. Costs for new semiconductor fabrication facilities (fabs), a major capital consideration for many companies, range from $600 million to $900 million. The cost of capital in the United States has caused semiconductor companies to use various capital-saving strategies. Even though U.S. shipments went up in 1992, many companies were still faced by the need to restructure. Some firms resorted to building "mini-fabs" for smaller, specialized production lines. In addition, some companies that planned to develop larger wafers in 1991, to take advantage of economies of scale, were forced to abandon these plans in 1992 due to overcapacity concerns, especially in DRAMs.

Strategic Alliances

Global corporate connections are becoming a tool of survival for electronics companies, as amply demonstrated by the trend toward industry consolidation in electronics. Corporate partnering and strategic alliances have become a worldwide response for sharing the greater costs of production. These costs, in turn, are driven by the need for constant innovation, an imperative of the electronics industry.

Strategic alliances vary among companies, from joint production, joint development, technology licensing, and fabrication agreements, to full-scale manufacturing integration through company consortia. A majority of U.S. companies of all sizes rate alliances as high or extremely high on the strategic plans for their companies. Challenged by a sagging world economy in 1992, large semiconductor device and systems companies in the United States, Japan, and Europe have joined forces in various combinations to form joint development and production ventures.

Intellectual Property Issues

Corporate alliances have resulted in various arrangements of technology sharing, and pushed issues of intellectual property rights to the forefront. A plethora of cases on licensing and patent coverage continue to be fought out in the courts.

In 1991, Congress extended the Semiconductor Chip Protection Act of 1984 until 1995. The legislation gives the Secretary of Commerce the authority to extend reciprocal protection of semiconductor mask works (glass templates for forming the circuitry on a PCB) to foreign companies in nations that protect U.S. designs. These countries have reciprocal protection under the act: Canada, the 12 countries of the European Community (EC), Austria, Finland, Sweden, Switzerland, Japan, and Australia.

Legislation

The National Advisory Committee on Semiconductors has held that due to the acceleration of technology development, the useful life of semiconductor manufacturing equipment (SME) should be three years, rather than five years. The issue of an accelerated depreciation schedule for SME continues to be important for the semiconductor industry. Parallel bills were introduced in both houses of Congress in 1991 to depreciate SME over three years. In contrast, other countries' depreciation schedules for SME allow a faster write-off than the present U.S. legislation.

In 1984, in order to facilitate joint development activities in the United States, Congress passed the National Cooperative Research Act, which exempts joint development ventures from anti-trust laws. Although passage of this act was intended to prompt U.S. companies to base joint development work in the United States, confusion over the act's application has actually encouraged U.S. companies to move such ventures to Asian countries, where they are not subject to anti-trust restrictions.

Due to high capital costs, the industry also supports a reduction of the Federal capital gains tax. In addition, legislation such as the amended Federal Clean Air Act will greatly affect the semiconductor industry. Because of stronger regulatory requirements to control pollution, U.S.-based semiconductor companies already have had to dramatically increase investment in environmental process control equipment.

Product Development

Semiconductor product segments expected to experience an increase in share of the world semiconductor market in the next few years include metal oxide silicon (MOS) microcomponents, logic, and memory devices.

In MOS memory, two types of semiconductors showed the fastest growth in 1992—DRAMs and flash memories. These product areas also attracted the greatest activity in formation of production alliances between large U.S., Japanese, and European companies.

Although some industry experts have written off U.S. DRAM production, 3 U.S. companies are among the top 15 producers in the world. Global competition is increasing, however, as supply continues to outpace demand, and prices continue to fall faster than U.S. producers can reduce costs. Some DRAM manufacturers suffered losses in 1992 due to severe price competition in this sector. Even as sales volumes climbed, prices fell and profit margins decreased.

Specialization has become increasingly important in DRAMs. While only 3 types of 64 kilobit (64kb) DRAMs were made for computer models in the early 1980's, there now are more than 400 varieties of 4 megabit (4MB) DRAMs on the market and nearly 1,000 varieties of 16MB DRAM products. In 1992, some electronics companies purchasing 4MB DRAM experienced shortages of DRAMs with certain packages, speeds, or configurations, even though there was a components overcapacity. Industry experts now believe that the DRAM industry has split into two distinct segments—application specific memories (ASM) and mass-produced commodity DRAMs.

Questions are being raised as to whether DRAMs are the best technology for submicron research for all types of semiconductors. In 1992, a U.S. company developed a 0.6 micron application specific integrated circuit (a type of MOS logic, see below) without developing a submicron DRAM. Experts are still trying to anticipate the long-term ramifications these changes may bring to the industry.

Commodity DRAMs, however, continue to be the technology of choice for China, Singapore, and other countries wishing to develop indigenous technology for semiconductors. Many companies still believe that DRAMs will continue to be the technology driver for the semiconductor industry.

Flash memory is a Japanese invention, but more than 90 percent of flash memory was being produced by U.S. companies in 1992, prompting Japanese companies to seek joint development and production contracts with U.S. companies.

There are two types of flash memory—flash electronic programmable memory (EPROM), and flash erasable electronic programmable memory (EEPROM). Flash memory retains memory when power is turned off, thus saving data while consuming less power (DRAMs must be electrically powered continuously). Flash memories also can be reprogrammed faster and easier than other types of semiconductors, and are ideally suited for portable equipment applications.

Five U.S. companies, three Japanese companies, and one European company produced flash memory in 1992. More companies are expected to start production soon. In 1992, the industry leader lowered prices per megabyte for flash memory semiconductors and cards to DRAM levels to increase market demand for flash devices and for their use in portable electronic equipment.

Flash semiconductors are used in semiconductor disk drives, a technology that some predict will replace hard drives in portable computers. Flash semiconductor drives are smaller than conventional hard drives, access data more than 100 times faster than floppy disks, and can take hostile environments such as humidity, heat, cold, and shock better than conventional disk drives because they do not have moving parts.

High cost and limited storage capacity have slowed the rise of sales of these drives. But as technology improves, many companies predict that semiconductor drives are the wave of the future for portable, durable drives. Disk drive manufacturers are countering the competition by shrinking the size of their disk drives and increasing their capacity.

Flash memory is also used in auto parts (engine and transmission control electronics), in memory cards, and for storage of BIOS (basic input/output system) in personal computers (PCs). Flash memories are mostly used now in PCs because they require low voltage and power.

Microcomponents

In the MOS microcomponents category, the fastest growing product types are microcontrollers and microprocessors. Dataquest expects the microcomponent market to exceed the MOS memory market in size by the year 2000.

Microcontrollers are used in a variety of electronic goods, including consumer electronics, auto parts, robotics, and telecommunications. Japanese companies have more than 60 percent of the microcontroller market; the United States is second with close to 30 percent. U.S. companies, however, lead in the higher-end (8 and 16 bit) microcontrollers. Sales of microcontrollers to the automotive industry rose dramatically in 1992 because they are an essential part of anti-lock brake systems and dashboard instrument panels.

U.S. companies have more than 80 percent of the world microprocessor market. Three of the top five companies in microprocessors are U.S. companies (6 of the top 10). Microprocessors are the key semiconductors for processing information in computers and workstations.

Microprocessor companies are developing one-chip processor systems. Some computer companies are developing their own systems on chip semiconductors, rather than relying on traditional processor companies. Other computer companies have entered into alliances with semiconductor companies to develop customized systems on a chip for use in their next-generation computers. MOS microcomponents with system-on-silicon (or system on chip) technology is expected to be the fastest growing segment of the microcomponent industry in the 1990's.

In the MOS logic category, the fastest growing segment is application specific integrated circuits (ASICs). ASICs are standard integrated circuits (ICs) customized for specific functions, thus taking advantage of the inherently lower cost of standard parts and the higher performance of custom ICs. U.S. and Japanese industries have nearly equal shares of this segment, while the rest of the world has about 10 percent. Competition in this area was very intense in 1992. In the face of reduced profit margins in DRAMs, Japanese companies switched production from DRAMs to the more profitable microprocessors and ASICs.

In 1992, a U.S. company, in conjunction with the Semiconductor Research Corporation (SRC), developed a submicron (0.6 micron) ASIC using computer simulation-based technology rather than using submicron technology based on traditional DRAM technology. Although submicron technology originally was developed using DRAM technology, the structure of an ASIC is very different.

With DRAMs, producers pack elements as close together as possible, and the pattern has very little variation. With ASICs, the goal is to create as many connections between individual semiconductors as possible using the most efficient pathways (multi-layer, irregular patterns). U.S. ASIC development is geared toward more customized computer simulation applications, while the Japanese focus is on improving the manufacturing processes.

Uses of ASICs are broad because they are tailored for each user. They are used in cellular phones, HDTV, music synthesizers, medical equipment, modems, and speech synthesis. ASIC companies are developing systems on a chip (blurring the line between microprocessors, custom memory, and ASICs). ASICs are also being developed for use in intelligent highways, military mapping, and data compression technology for use in digital systems, the last especially applicable to HDTV. Six of the HDTV systems under U.S. evaluation are digital systems.

Trends toward component miniaturization have renewed interest in the development of multichip modules (MCMs). In general, a MCM is a collection of semiconductor dies as packaged, or bare die, mounted on a common substrate. MCMs occupy about half the space of a conventional PCB, require half the power and are faster (20 percent higher clock rates) than a single-chip application. In addition, MCMs offer a higher packaging efficiency than other technologies.

There are now three substrate options for MCM development: a printed wiring board laminant substrate (MCM–L), a cofired ceramic substrate (MCM–C), or a thin-film multilayer substrate (MCM–D). Each substrate option carries with it certain advantages and disadvantages. MCM substrate selection is determined by the application requirements. Currently, the MCM–L substrate is the most cost effective, but performance limitations are cited by high end users. At the present level of technological development for MCM–C and MCM–D substrates, cost is the primary inhibitor.

Developmental challenges to all MCM substrates are in the areas of solving problems of thermal management, die-testing, and economic feasibility of production. The concept of MCMs has had a major impact on system design because they give higher performance density per dollar. The largest market segments for MCMs are personal computers, workstations, and embedded controllers. The niche markets are in high performance mainframes and portable computers.

INTERNATIONAL COMPETITIVENESS

The U.S. semiconductor trade deficit in 1991 was $2.1 billion. North American semiconductor sales (to the United States, Canada, and Mexico) exhibited strength compared to other regional markets. The dominant regional trading partner continued to be East Asia, despite an economic slowdown in Japan. The North American semiconductor market is estimated to increase by a compound annual growth rate of 9.5 percent over the next 5 years. The recovering U.S. market has become a magnet for imports of semiconductors.

Western Europe

Overall growth prospects for Western Europe are estimated at only 1 to 2 percent in 1993 with unemployment likely to remain between 9 and 10 percent.

The electronics industries of the EC are beginning to show signs of recovery from their disappointing 1992 market performance. Predictions are for steady incremental recovery in the range of 3 to 4 percent annually for the next few years. In the application product sectors, electronic data processing and communications will show the best growth through 1995.

According to the World Semiconductor Trade Statistics (WSTS) organization, the European market for semiconductors was expected to grow by 7.7 percent in 1992. Such growth means an expansion of the European semiconductor market to $10.9 billion in 1992, or about 19 percent of the world market. U.S. imports of semiconductors from the EC countries ranked well below U.S. imports from Asia. These EC countries ranked among the top 20 for U.S. imports: Germany 11th, the United Kingdom (U.K.) 12th, France 14th, Ireland 15th, Spain 16th, Italy 17th, and the Netherlands 18th.

The European semiconductor market is a battleground for competition among the global electronics giants. Both South Korean and Japanese semiconductor companies have increased their presence in the European market, particularly in the semiconductor memory market. However, the United States still holds a sizable market share of the EC market, estimated at 44 percent in 1991 at a value of about $1.7 billion.

The European semiconductor industry is feeling the effects of increased competition. The three largest firms streamlined certain less productive product lines and acquired other lines from smaller sized niche product firms. Consolidation continues to be the trend in the European semiconductor market. The significant costs of reunification contributed to an economic slowdown in Germany in 1992. Nevertheless, Germany continued to be the largest semiconductor market in Europe, accounting for a 4.1 percent increase over the previous year, to a total of $544 million. The German market is forecast to grow to $633 million in 1995.

For U.S. exporters, the German semiconductor market was the 12th largest worldwide in 1991, and the 2nd largest in Europe. Exports to Germany peaked in 1990, and are expected to decline further in 1992. U.S. semiconductor exports to Germany in 1991 were dominated by MOS logic and MOS memory.

The overall electronics sector struggled in the U.K. in 1992, down 5 percent to $328 million. However, the semiconductor market showed a modest second percent increase, the first growth after two years of difficulty. Growth was stimulated by increased demand in the consumer electronics and computer markets.

The U.K. remains the seventh largest market for U.S. exports. Dominant export categories in the U.K. in 1991 were MOS memories, MOS logic, and MOS microprocessors. Both MOS logic and MOS microprocessors were the largest markets worldwide for U.S. exporters, twice the size of any other market.

Prospects for growth in semiconductors are strong due to predicted recovery in the overall U.K. electronics industry in 1993. According to forecasts from Dataquest, the U.K. electronics market will reach $378 million by 1995.

Ireland is an important emerging market in Western Europe, the 16th largest for U.S. semiconductors. MOS logic products dominated U.S. exports in 1991. Growth in Ireland's electronic production capacity should be credited to offshore investments. Ireland is fast becoming a major site in Europe for overseas investment in semiconductor production facilities. In the coming years, increased semiconductor production capacity may dampen Ireland's demand for semiconductor imports.

France ranked third as a major U.S. export market in the EC, and the 13th largest worldwide. Semiconductor exports to France were dominated by sales of MOS memory and MOS logic.

Italy is the fourth largest U.S. semiconductor market in the EC and 14th in the world. U.S. export sales to Italy in 1992 were strongest for MOS memories.

Semiconductor markets in the rest of the EC had sporadic performances in 1992. U.S. exports of semiconductors to Austria, Denmark, the Netherlands, Spain, and Switzerland remained close to 1991 levels.

Eastern Europe

With continued economic and political instability characterizing the region in 1991, the emerging market economies of Eastern Europe have not experienced significant growth in semiconductor production. The former Soviet Union had been the dominant supplier of semiconductors to the region; now Russia has the majority of manufacturing capacity.

Due to continued instability, Eastern Europe does not now offer strong short-term export opportunities for U.S. semiconductor companies. U.S. exports have gone primarily to Poland. Even though market growth is dwarfed in comparison to all other global markets, export levels are increasing in Czechoslovakia, Hungary, and Bulgaria.

Japan

The Japanese semiconductor market experienced a sharp downturn in 1992, with overall consumption declining to about $19.5 billion from a 1991 level of $22.5 billion. The general weakness in the Japanese economy depressed semiconductor demand in key end-user segments of the electronics industry, especially in the computer and consumer electronics segments that account for more than 70 percent of total semiconductor sales. Semiconductor consumption patterns in Japan for 1992 generally were: 39 percent data processing, 32 percent consumer, 14 percent communications, 10 percent industrial, and 5 percent military and transportation.

The Japanese market appeared to have bottomed out by mid-year 1992. The recovery is forecast to continue into 1993 when growth rates are expected to reach 7 to 8 percent. Compound annual growth for the 1992–96 period is forecast at 8 to 10 percent, with the Japanese market continuing to account for about 40 percent of the value of the global semiconductor market during this period.

Strong growth in product demand in the 1992–96 period is expected to occur in the MOS micro and logic sectors, such as microprocessors, gate arrays, programmable logic devices (PLDs) and digital signal processors (DSPs). Sales of PLDs and DSPs have grown steadily, increasing from about 26 percent of domestic Japanese demand in 1986 to 36 percent in 1992. The MOS memory sector has a volatile demand cycle and experienced a sharp decline in pricing between 1989 and 1991, but a strong market for flash memory devices and wide-bit DRAMs should strengthen this sector in 1993. MOS memory accounted for about 20 percent of demand in 1992.

The Japanese market for discrete devices, such as diodes, rectifiers, and transistors, accounted for about 20 percent of overall demand in 1992, down 6 percent from the 1986 level. Analog devices, such as amplifiers, voltage regulators, and data conversion chips, account for about 16 percent of the market, while digital bipolar devices hold about a 6 percent share.

Unlike the U.S. semiconductor industry, which is composed primarily of independent companies such as Intel, Texas Instruments, and LSI Logic, the Japanese industry consists of semiconductor divisions within larger electronics companies such as Sony, NEC, and Fujitsu.

The slump in semiconductor demand in both the domestic data processing and consumer electronics end-use sectors in 1991 and early 1992 translated into intensified price competition and depressed profit margins for Japanese producers. In addition, Japanese companies had invested aggressively in additional production capacity in the late 1980's, primarily for the 4MB and 16MB DRAM generations, and were burdened with overcapacity in 1992 as the expected "silicon cycle" upturn in demand did not materialize.

Japanese semiconductor producers are currently faced with increased capital costs, declining profits, and a reliance on low-margin commodity products where they face increased competition from South Korean suppliers. In addition, the Japanese electronics parent companies have experienced a sharp decline in overall profitability, causing them to place more pressure on their operating units to cut costs and increase profit margins. Net income for the top 10 Japanese electronics companies decreased by about 50 percent for their fiscal year ending March 1992.

This downturn has caused a shift among Japanese semiconductor divisions toward participating more actively in higher value added-product sectors, such as microprocessors, DSPs, and ASICs. This shift will intensify competition with U.S. companies that have traditionally focused on these more design-intensive products.

At the same time the need for reducing cost and lowering financial risk probably will spur alliances between Japanese and foreign companies. These alliances can range from manufacturing joint ventures to joint product development agreements and sales agency agreements. Since 1989, Japanese companies have entered into an average of 88 alliances with foreign companies per year. These alliances have focused on such sectors as HDTV chip development, microprocessor development, ASIC development, and computer-aided design (CAD) projects.

On August 1, 1991, a follow-on agreement to the 1986 U.S.-Japan Semiconductor Arrangement went into effect. The new arrangement lasts five years, with the option to terminate after three years by mutual agreement of the two governments. Both the 1986 and 1991 arrangements are intended to eliminate dumping of Japanese products in world markets and to increase market access for foreign semiconductor suppliers to the Japanese market.

The new agreement reflects U.S. expectations that a more than 20 percent share of the Japanese market can be captured by foreign suppliers by the end of 1992 through efforts by governments and industries. At the time the 1991 arrangement went into effect in 1991, foreign market share in Japan stood at about 13.6 percent. A new statistical system that is part of the arrangement calculated foreign market share for first quarter 1992 at 14.6 percent.

In May 1992, the U.S. Government initiated an interagency review of Japanese compliance with the terms of the arrangement. The review findings, announced on August 4, 1992, were that Japanese efforts had so far resulted in insufficient progress toward increased foreign market access. The review findings noted, however, that a cooperative process had been initiated by U.S. and Japanese industries in June 1992 and that further evaluations should be made.

The Dynamic Asian Economies

The six-country group forming the dynamic Asian economies (DAEs) consists of South Korea, Taiwan, Hong Kong, China, Singapore, and Malaysia. This group of countries sustained growth in semiconductor and electronic component markets in 1992, while the remainder of world markets demonstrated a lackluster performance. DAE countries dominated U.S. imports of semiconductors, ranking among the top 10, as follows: South Korea 2nd, Malaysia 3rd, Singapore 5th, Taiwan 6th, and Hong Kong 10th.

In contrast to consolidation in U.S. electronics industries, DAE electronics companies have expanded. No longer are the newly industrialized DAEs merely sites of test and assembly operations. Rather, companies in these countries have increasingly emphasized development of indigenous technology through joint ventures and licensing agreements with U.S., Japanese, and European firms.

According to Dataquest, for the first time since 1985, North American semiconductor companies lost market share in 1991 in the Asia-Pacific region. North American market share was estimated at 34.7 percent, while Japan slipped to 40.9 percent. In contrast, companies in the DAEs continued to generate increased sales with estimated market share at 17.8 percent in 1991, a 5 percent increase over the three previous years. For the DAEs, microcomponents were the strongest growth area during 1991 with a 38 percent increase over 1990. North American companies continue to dominate this product category with 65.1 percent of the world market, but the Japanese share is growing rapidly.

Evidence of the push by the DAEs' electronic manufacturers is demonstrated by the powerful emergence of South Korean suppliers of DRAMs into top global market positions. Production of electronic parts and components in South Korea increased at an average annual rate of 35 percent between 1980 and 1991. Of these, ICs have been the largest product market. South Korea reportedly produced $6.5 billion worth of semiconductors in 1991, of which $5 billion were exported.

South Korean semiconductor companies hold an 18 percent share of world market production, and challenge both Japan and the United States in the production of memory chips. Current production capability of South Korean memory chip producers is for 4MB and 16MB DRAMs, and commercial development of 64MB DRAMs is planned in 1993.

The South Korean government places a high priority on the semiconductor industry and has fostered its development by committing to contribute 3 percent of GDP for R&D by the year 2000. However, the government's share of R&D funding diminished from 50 percent in 1980 to 20 percent in 1990. South Korean companies, in contrast, have committed larger amounts of sales to R&D budgets; their investment in semiconductor related R&D increased 49 percent in 1991.

Three major semiconductor companies produce a preponderance of South Korean semiconductors. According to In-Stat, a research company, DRAMs account for 70 percent of these companies' sales. In spite of attempts to diversify from semiconductor memory production, they accounted for 78 percent of all South Korean semiconductors produced in 1991.

Semiconductor consumption increased in South Korea by 13.5 percent in 1991. According to Dataquest, this growth was primarily attributable to greater demand in the consumer application and data processing segments. About 55 percent of total semiconductors used in South Korea went to consumer electronic equipment. However, the data processing segment alone consumed 52 percent of all MOS digital ICs in 1991. Growth in semiconductor consumption is likely to level off to 10 percent in 1992 due to slower growth in data processing equipment production and overcapacity of semiconductors worldwide.

U.S. semiconductor exports to South Korea during 1985–91 quadrupled. In 1991, South Korea was the sixth largest U.S. export outlet for semiconductors, primarily for MOS logic and MOS memory. However, Japanese firms remain the major suppliers of semiconductors to South Korea, accounting for more than 58 percent of the import market, followed by the United States with 30 percent.

Semiconductors remain a top priority of the Taiwanese government. It has earmarked substantial funding for companies in the Hsinchu Science-based Industrial Park to encourage expansion in manufacturing technologies, with special emphasis on semiconductors. The government will set aside $428 million to assist R&D for semiconductor manufacturing in 1992. The major initial goals are for development of 8 inch wafers and .35 submicron technology. The large capital investments are in part stimulated by the desire to decrease Taiwan's dependence on foreign supplies of semiconductors.

Even though Taiwan has been more successful than South Korea at expanding and diversifying its semiconductor manufacturing base, it remains dependent on imports to satisfy 80 percent of its total demand. The Taiwanese are openly concerned about heavy reliance on Japanese semiconductors and are seeking to diversify sources for imports and strengthen their indigenous production. The United States ranks a distant second in supplying semiconductors to Taiwan.

Taiwan was the fifth largest market for U.S. exports of semiconductors worldwide in 1991. Semiconductor exports to Taiwan grew 39 percent from 1989 to 1991. Exports were dominated by MOS memories, DRAMs, SRAMs, EEPROMs, and MOS logic. Taiwan was the largest U.S. export outlet for EEPROMs; the second for EPROMs; and the third for DRAMs. The strongest growth area for U.S. exports was in MOS logic with a 600 percent increase between 1989 and 1991.

As reported by Dataquest, Hong Kong's electronics industry has undergone dramatic restructuring in recent years. China has become a central focus in the export and manufacturing strategies of Hong Kong companies. Semiconductor businesses in Hong Kong are actively establishing ties with the neighboring Chinese mainland.

In recent years, Hong Kong electronics firms have increasingly taken advantage of lower production costs and abundant Chinese labor. Hong Kong firms have emphasized investment in co-production facilities in the Special Economic Zones located in Southern China's Guangdong Province, such as Shenzhen. As China's 1997 annexation of Hong Kong nears, these co-production facilities will play an expanded role. Such cooperation maximizes the competitive advantages of capital-intensive Hong Kong and labor-intensive China.

Hong Kong is the strongest growth market for semiconductor consumption in the Asia-Pacific region. According to Dataquest, semiconductor consumption in Hong Kong grew by 22.6 percent in 1991 as an outgrowth of a dramatic 32.2 percent expansion in the data processing segment that, in turn, stimulated production in MOS memory, microcomponents, and logic devices. Consumer electronics was the second fastest growth segment, experiencing 12.6 percent growth. The relatively moderate gains in the consumer segment affected the consumption of analog devices. Analog consumption was up a moderate 8.5 percent to $222 million. Analog devices account for 19.5 percent of the total semiconductor market.

Hong Kong ranked ninth in U.S. exports in 1991, and promises ever-expanding opportunities for U.S. exporters. With their developed ties to the mainland, Hong Kong businesses offer established expertise to U.S. businesses contemplating the Chinese market. U.S. exports to Hong Kong are strongest for MOS memories, microprocessors, DRAMs, and SRAMs. Hong Kong was the third largest market in 1991 and 1992 for U.S. microprocessors.

With the recent approval of the submicron wafer fabrication project, China's semiconductor production and overall market size are likely to expand in the next five years. The submicron project has been proposed since 1990. Site selection is yet to be finalized, but it is likely to be adjacent to China's current largest semiconductor fabrication facility in Wuxi.

The Chinese government has placed high priority on submicron development by the year 2000. CHINATRON, a consortium of Chinese ministries and electronics enterprises, will play a commanding role in the development of submicron technology. China's development of submicron semiconductors, however, is dependent on export license approval by the Coordinating Committee on Multilateral Export Controls (COCOM), and on the acquisition of necessary funding that likely will come from foreign technology partners.

As a market for U.S. semiconductors, China has diminished since 1989, although business confidence there seems to be stabilizing. For 1991, China was the 35th largest U.S. export market; most sales were in monolithic ICs.

Extensive opportunities exist for U.S. exporters in the emerging Southeast Asian markets. Most of the world's major electronic companies have established operations there. Increased production of consumer electronic products, computer systems, peripherals, and communications equipment bodes well for increased semiconductor consumption in the region.

Singapore has traditionally played a major role as a trade axis to the rest of Asia and the West, and it will continue to play a pivotal trade role with the signing of the Asian Free Trade Area pact in 1992. Joint production projects for the electronics area are a major priority. In addition, Singapore will play a decisive role in the "growth triangle," which is a plan to establish manufacturing and financial ties among Singapore, Malaysia's Johore Province, and Indonesia's Batam Islands. Production of electronic products, including semiconductors, will also be a central focus in the growth triangle.

Singapore is the most established semiconductor market in Southeast Asia. Dataquest reports that semiconductor consumption in Singapore increased 15 percent in 1991 to a level of $1.1 billion. However, there are only a few indigenous Singaporean semiconductor manufacturers. As is true of all the Southeast Asian semiconductor markets, production in Singapore is dominated by offshore Japanese and U.S. firms.

Memory devices remain the largest single product area in the Singapore market. Memory consumption accounted for 24 percent of the total semiconductor market in 1991, and is expected to advance 20 percent in 1992 to $362 million. Due to growth from Singapore's globally preeminent disk drive market, microcomponent sales soared in 1991, growing 18.8 percent to $250 million. Singapore's computer and peripheral markets experienced weakened conditions in 1992, tempering microcomponent consumption to an 11 percent increase.

Singapore was the third largest market for U.S. semiconductor exports in 1991. Exports to Singapore are primarily in monolithic ICs, MOS memory, MOS logic, and microprocessors. In 1991, Singapore was ranked as the largest U.S. export market for SRAMs, the second for DRAMs, third for MOS memories, and fourth for microprocessors. Prospects for further U.S. export growth in these product areas remain strong.

Malaysia has achieved strong success in semiconductors and emerged in 1991 as the third largest semiconductor market in the world. Advanced semiconductor production in Malaysia is particularly concentrated in U.S. and Japanese companies. A significant portion of the semiconductors were merely tested and assembled there, with a minor portion actually going through the diffusion process in Malaysia. Malaysia has been a primary site of global offshore semiconductor test and assembly since 1987, and is now likely to become a major site for complete semiconductor fabrication. The Malaysian government has set high priority on development of indigenous semiconductor fabrication capability.

Malaysia boasted the largest market for overall U.S. semiconductor exports in 1991, but the markets were slightly flat for many semiconductor products in 1992. Exports of MOS logic and microprocessors grew strongly in 1991, but peaked in 1992. U.S. exporters may face increased competition over the next few years, with greater Malaysian indigenous manufacturing capacity and increased buying from other Asian sources.—*Judee Mussehl-Aziz, Dorothea Blouin, and Robert Scott, Office of Microelectronics, Medical Equipment and Instrumentation, (202) 482-2470.*

U.S. Trade Patterns in 1991
Semiconductors and Related Devices
SIC 3674
(in millions of dollars, percent)

Exports			Imports		
	Value	Share		Value	Share
Canada & Mexico	1,746	16.1	Canada & Mexico	1,753	13.6
European Community	1,759	16.2	European Community	810	6.3
Japan	1,048	9.7	Japan	3,575	27.6
East Asia NICs	5,329	49.2	East Asia NICs	5,895	45.6
South America	119	1.1	South America	5	0.0
Other	829	7.7	Other	890	6.9
World Total	10,831	100.0	World Total	12,928	100.0
Top Five Countries					
	Value	Share		Value	Share
Malaysia	1,581	14.6	Japan	3,575	27.6
Canada	1,343	12.4	Korea, South	1,779	13.8
Singapore	1,091	10.1	Malaysia	1,584	12.3
Japan	1,048	9.7	Canada	1,420	11.0
Taiwan	887	8.2	Singapore	1,173	9.1

See "How to Get the Most Out of This Book" for definitions of the country groupings.

SOURCE: U.S. Department of Commerce: Bureau of the Census, International Trade Administration.

Trends and Forecasts: Electronic Components and Accessories (SIC 367)

(in millions of dollars except as noted)

Item	1987	1988	1989	1990	1991[1]	1992[2]	1993[3]	Percent Change (1987–1993) 87–88	88–89	89–90	90–91	91–92	92–93
Industry Data													
Value of shipments[4]	50,258	56,999	59,913	60,844	61,998	65,627	70,610	13.4	5.1	1.6	1.9	5.9	7.6
Value of shipments (1987$)	50,258	56,075	58,509	60,514	61,686	65,500	70,642	11.6	4.3	3.4	1.9	6.2	7.9
Total employment (000)	546	552	551	536	524	514	520	1.1	−0.2	−2.7	−2.2	−1.9	1.2
Production workers (000)	329	337	339	325	321	313	318	2.4	0.6	−4.1	−1.2	−2.5	1.6
Average hourly earnings ($)	9.32	9.78	9.96	10.22	10.60	10.83	—	4.9	1.8	2.6	3.7	2.2	—
Product Data													
Value of shipments[5]	46,719	52,874	57,209	59,307	60,066	63,111	69,695	13.2	8.2	3.7	1.3	5.1	10.4
Value of shipments (1987$)	46,719	52,038	55,869	58,843	55,837	58,356	64,349	11.4	7.4	5.3	−5.1	4.5	10.3
Trade Data													
Value of imports	—	—	17,304	17,997	19,228	21,014	19,637	—	—	4.0	6.8	9.3	−6.6
Value of exports	—	—	12,463	14,995	14,915	14,387	14,926	—	—	20.3	−0.5	−3.5	3.7

[1]Estimated, except exports and imports.

[2]Estimate.

[3]Forecast.

[4]Value of all products and services sold by establishments in the electronic components and accessories industry.

[5]Value of products classified in the electronic components and accessories industry produced by all industries.

SOURCE: U.S. Department of Commerce: Bureau of the Census, International Trade Administration (ITA). Estimates and forecasts by ITA.

Trends and Forecasts: Semiconductors and Related Devices (SIC 3674)

(in millions of dollars except as noted)

Item	1987	1988	1989	1990	1991[1]	1992[2]	1993[3]	Percent Change (1987–1993) 87–88	88–89	89–90	90–91	91–92	92–93
Industry Data													
Value of shipments[4]	19,795	22,597	25,708	25,977	26,626	29,821	33,400	14.2	13.8	1.0	2.5	12.0	12.0
Value of shipments (1987$)	19,795	22,574	25,837	27,665	28,357	31,760	35,571	14.0	14.5	7.1	2.5	12.0	12.0
Total employment (000)	185	179	184	182	175	167	170	−3.2	2.8	−1.1	−3.8	−4.6	1.8
Production workers (000)	87.4	86.5	90.5	87.7	86.5	82.0	83.5	−1.0	4.6	−3.1	−1.4	−5.2	1.8
Average hourly earnings ($)	10.57	11.38	12.02	12.58	12.96	13.64	—	7.7	5.6	4.7	3.0	5.2	—
Product Data													
Value of shipments[5]	17,929	20,332	23,488	23,978	24,230	26,839	30,060	13.4	15.5	2.1	1.1	10.8	12.0
Value of shipments (1987$)	17,929	20,312	23,606	25,535	25,805	28,584	32,014	13.3	16.2	8.2	1.1	10.8	12.0
Trade Data													
Value of imports	—	—	12,172	12,023	12,928	15,123	13,611	—	—	−1.2	7.5	17.0	−10.0
Value of exports	—	—	9,531	10,710	10,831	10,417	10,729	—	—	12.4	1.1	−3.8	3.0

[1]Estimated, except exports and imports.

[2]Estimate.

[3]Forecast.

[4]Value of all products and services sold by establishments in the semiconductors and related devices industry.

[5]Value of products classified in the semiconductors and related devices industry produced by all industries.

SOURCE: U.S. Department of Commerce: Bureau of the Census, International Trade Administration (ITA). Estimates and forecasts by ITA.

Food and Beverages

Shipments of the 24 industries covered in this chapter increased an estimated 1.7 percent in 1992, corrected for inflation. Only dairy products, the meat and poultry group, and candy products experienced any significant growth—3 percent or more. Processed fruits and vegetables, soft drinks, and bakery products each expanded less than 2 percent.

The 24 food and beverage industries covered in this chapter are the meat and poultry industry group (SIC 2011, 2013, 2015); dairy goods (SIC 2021, 2022, 2023, 2024, 2026); processed fruits, vegetables, and specialty foods (SIC 2032, 2033, 2034, 2035, 2037, 2038); bakery products (SIC 2051, 2052, 2053); confectionery products (SIC 2064); alcoholic beverages (SIC 2082, 2084, 2085); soft drinks (SIC 2086); and processed fishery products (SIC 2091, 2092). These industries include most high value-added packaged food products and account for 71 percent of the value of all shipments of the food and beverage sector.

New U.S. Food Labeling Laws

Foreign food and beverage makers are likely to react unfavorably to proposed changes in U.S. food labeling requirements. The new labeling, which is required for all packaged foods, covers such topics as nutrition information, serving size, health messages, and descriptive terms such as "light" and "low fat." The U.S. Food and Drug Administration (FDA) and the U.S. Department of Agriculture (USDA) share responsibility for food labeling along product lines. The USDA covers meat and poultry, and the FDA handles all other products.

Effective May 1994, new labels will be required on all packaged foods. Newly labeled products will appear on store shelves later in 1994. The new labels will feature a standardized section (yet to be made final) requiring specific, comparable treatment of key elements, such as serving size. All food products must conform to these requirements. Due to the complexity and extended coverage of the new requirements, it appears likely that most manufacturers will have to design new labels rather than modify existing ones.

The labeling requirements may prove especially difficult for many foreign food manufacturers, especially firms unaccustomed to such extensive product analysis and disclosure. Some industry observers contend that the new requirements constitute a barrier to trade and could be challenged in the General Agreement on Tariffs and Trade (GATT). In contrast, defenders of the requirements observe that all manufacturers, both domestic and foreign, must comply equally, and that the labeling rules are the result of a well-accepted need to improve U.S. health standards. These observers believe that any GATT challenge to the new regulations will be dismissed.

INTERNATIONAL COMPETITIVENESS

In 1992, for the first time since at least 1978, there was a trade surplus in processed food and beverages—an estimated $22.2 billion in exports, 5.9 percent of product shipments, compared to an estimated $21.1 billion in imports. Twenty five U.S. firms with foreign affiliates accounted for nearly one-fourth of the export market in 1990.

About 72 percent of total U.S. processed food and beverage exports are low value-added products such as fats and oils, feed ingredients, corn products, meat, poultry and fish products, while 45 percent of U.S. imports are high value-added consumer-ready products such as confections, bakery goods, alcoholic beverages, and various gourmet fruit and vegetable products. However, exports of higher value-added products grew more rapidly than lower value-added products between 1990 and 1992. This trend will continue for the foreseeable future. Total U.S. food and beverage exports grew 23 percent during the 1990–92 period. Exports of condensed and evaporated milk almost tripled. Canned and frozen specialties exports rose 75 percent. Bakery product exports rose 65 percent. Candy and beverage exports increased 48 percent and 23 percent, respectively.

The cumulative stock of foreign investment has influenced the structure of the U.S. food manufacturing industry through consolidation. Foreign investors have especially affected the bakery and dairy industries, introduced new products, such as European-style cookies and soft-ripened cheeses, and modernized plants. With the latest comparable data from 1987, the ratio of the stock of foreign investment to the gross book value of the U.S. food manufacturing industry stood at 19.8 percent, up from 11.3 percent in 1982. The stock of investment by foreign parties in the U.S. food manufacturing sector grew 1.9 percent in 1991, to $23.4 billion. A recessionary U.S. economy slowed this growth from its average 19 percent annual rate of increase in the 1980's.

Investment by U.S. companies in foreign food manufacturing rose 7.5 percent to a level of $17.1 billion in 1991, slightly above its 6.4 percent average annual increase between 1981 and 1990. About 20 percent of this investment was directed toward Canada and Mexico, spurred by removal of trade and investment barriers in those two countries. U.S. food companies also expanded their investment in the European Community (EC) and Japan. Between 1989 and 1990, foreign affiliates of U.S. food processors increased their sales by 6.6 percent to $74.8 billion, an amount equal to 19.5 percent of domestic industry sales.

LONG-TERM PROSPECTS

Meat shipments are expected to remain constant over the next five years, but the industry will undergo significant consolidation as outdated plants are closed. Meat consumption is expected to remain at current levels, but there will be a difference in the mix. Poultry should increase from just under 37 percent of total meat consumption in 1992 to about 40 percent by 1997. Although commercial fishery landings are expected to remain at or near historic high levels for the next five years, most marine resources are fully utilized and, in some cases, are in a state of overexploitation. In the canned goods sector, the domestic market is maturing, but exports are contributing to production growth. Export markets for dairy products are also expected to continue growing faster than domestic demand. In the beverage industries, prospects are bright for producers of bottled water and "New Age" sweetened waters. Shifting purchasing patterns related to demographic changes will fuel new candy product development and encourage manufacturers' interest in export sales.—*Donald A. Hodgen (202) 482-3346, William V. Janis (202) 482-2250, and Cornelius F. Kenney (202) 482-2428, Office of Consumer Goods.*

Food and Beverage Exports of the Top 25 U.S. Firms With Foreign Affiliates, 1990

Company	Exports (in thousands of dollars)	Percent change 1988–90	Export food sales as a percent of company sales
Philip Morris/Kraft-General Foods	1,232,265	367.6	5.5
Archer Daniels Midland	954,965	−2.5	14.7
Con Agra	536,239	148.9	3.6
Anheuser Busch	445,878	57.9	4.6
Tyson	184,700	21.1	5.0
Coca-Cola	118,000	25.6	3.0
Proctor & Gamble	115,799	−7.0	3.6
General Mills	95,338	28.9	2.3
Heinz	90,718	48.6	2.4
Chiquita Brands	80,046	−6.7	3.8
Ralston Purina	74,670	87.3	2.0
Hershey's	68,000	72.7	2.7
Sara Lee	64,527	68.2	1.3
McCormick	59,500	−3.3	6.0
Kellogg's	54,789	28.4	1.8
Brown Forman	46,224	−10.0	7.0
M&M/Mars	45,000	1.0	1.0
Universal Foods	44,476	23.1	5.8
CPC International	39,477	28.8	1.7
American Brands	39,207	183.7	4.2
Castle & Cooke	35,506	2,510.7	2.0
Borden	35,100	60.5	0.8
International Multifoods	26,168	117.1	1.5
Quaker Oats	23,644	61.7	0.7
PepsiCo	23,304	8.8	0.3
Total	4,533,540	61.8	3.4*

*Average increase in percent of all companies' export sales as a share of all companies' total sales.

SOURCE: Handy, Charles R. and Henderson, Dennis R., "Foreign Direct Investment in Food Manufacturing Industries," International Agricultural Trade Research Consortium symposium, Competitiveness in International Food Markets, Annapolis, MD, August 7–8, 1992.

Food and Beverages Product Shipments and Foreign Trade, 1990–92

(in millions of dollars)

SIC Code	Industry	Product Shipments			Foreign Trade: Imports			Foreign Trade: Exports		
		1990	1991*	1992*	1990	1991	1992*	1990	1991	1992*
201	Meat products	84,432	85,762	89,615	3,156	3,130	3,095	4,963	5,101	5,394
2011	Meat packing plants	47,365	47,825	49,795	3,022	2,980	2,944	4,197	4,169	4,354
2013	Sausage and other prepared meats	16,714	16,900	17,600	102	113	117	49	53	57
2015	Poultry slaughtering and processing	20,353	21,037	22,220	32	37	34	717	879	983
202	Dairy products	45,439	43,539	45,335	783	702	737	439	553	925
2021	Creamery butter	1,480	1,481	1,437	4	2	1	111	45	104
2022	Cheese, natural and processed	13,606	12,890	13,689	439	420	443	39	36	49
2023	Dry, condensed, evaporated products	6,214	6,034	6,112	327	274	288	228	378	635
2024	Ice cream and frozen desserts	5,047	5,276	5,716	0.1	0.2	0.9	30	50	82
2026	Fluid milk	19,092	17,858	18,381	12	6	4	31	43	54
203	Preserved fruits and vegetables	43,125	43,009	46,416	2,591	2,415	2,887	1,756	2,026	2,313
2032	Canned specialties	5,222	5,176	5,328	40	39	44	68	99	108
2033	Canned fruits and vegetables	15,255	15,700	16,960	1,087	1,238	1,451	424	578	645
2034	Dried fruits, vegetables, soups	2,640	2,825	2,977	238	224	255	517	547	571
2035	Pickles, sauces and salad dressings	5,562	6,061	6,560	188	197	240	132	165	205
2037	Frozen fruits and vegetables	7,412	5,943	7,027	1,030	709	888	584	596	718
2038	Frozen specialties, NEC	7,034	7,304	7,564	9	7	8	31	42	65
205	Bakery products	22,756	23,432	24,276	347	381	410	190	233	315
2051	Bread, cake and the like	14,210	14,699	15,354	233	241	262	84	102	128
2052	Cookies and crackers	7,004	7,280	7,473	103	124	125	93	112	162
2053	Frozen bakery products, except bread	1,543	1,453	1,449	11	16	24	13	19	26
206	Sugar and confections									
2064	Candy and other confectionery products	7,915	8,445	8,808	290	340	420	242	271	359
208	Beverages									
2082	Malt beverages	15,111	15,715	16,203	939	840	872	178	207	219
2084	Wine, brandy, and brandy spirits	3,505	3,540	3,583	1,129	1,094	1,196	134	155	197
2085	Distilled and blended liquors	3,248	3,118	3,071	1,305	1,131	1,276	273	300	389
2086	Soft drinks and carbonated water	21,888	22,786	23,582	191	220	262	106	134	173
	Subtotal	247,419	249,346	260,889	10,731	10,252	11,155	8,281	8,990	10,283
2091/92	Processed fishery products	7,048	6,593	6,800	5,088	5,522	5,375	2,696	2,867	3,277
	Total for 24 Sectors	254,467	255,939	267,689	15,819	15,774	16,530	10,977	11,857	13,560
	Estimated total for entire food and beverage industry	358,043	360,094	377,139	19,841	19,786	21,095	18,029	19,324	22,188

*Estimate.
NOTE: Detail may not add to total due to rounding.

SOURCE: U.S. Department of Commerce: Bureau of Census, International Trade Administration.

Health and Medical Services

The healthcare industry consists of public, private and non-profit institutions. These institutions are hospitals; offices and clinics of medical doctors; nursing homes; other specialized healthcare facilities; managed care consisting of pre-paid plans such as health maintenance organizations (HMOs), preferred provider organizations (PPOs), and independent practice associations (IPAs).

The nation's healthcare services industry currently includes thousands of independent medical practices and partnerships, as well as public and non-profit institutions, and many private corporations. The industry is labor intensive, employing approximately 10 million people of whom more than 600,000 are physicians. America's complex healthcare system relies on some of the most sophisticated and expensive technology in use by any domestic industry.

Health Care Expenditures

Total healthcare expenditures rose 11.5 percent from 1991 to 1992, to reach an estimated $838.5 billion. On a per capita basis, these expenditures exceed $3,160. By 1992, the nation's health and medical care sector outlays surpassed 14 percent of the Gross Domestic Product (GDP). This amount is substantially higher than what is found in other leading industrialized countries. The rate of growth for U.S. healthcare expenditures continues to surpass GDP growth rates.

The rising costs of health care are attributable to many factors, including:

- The use of sophisticated and high-priced equipment;
- Increases in variety and frequency of treatments;
- Innovative, but costly treatment of some illnesses such as heart ailments, end stage renal disease, AIDS, and cancer;
- Increased longevity of the population;
- Labor-intensiveness in the health care industry and the high earnings of professional, administrative, and technical workers.

In June 1992, the prospective Payment Assessment Commission in a report submitted to Congress indicated that from 1985 to 1990, population growth, economywide inflation, medical price inflation, utilization, and intensity of services were factors that contributed to the sharp rises in health care costs.

Cost Factors

From 1980–90, the share of household personal income allocated to health care rose from 4 percent to 5 percent. This figure does not include indirect expenditures such as payroll, income taxes, and other taxes that finance public healthcare programs. In 1991 the estimated healthcare bill for the average U.S. family was $4,296. Of this amount, general taxes accounted for 39 percent of the total, out-of-pocket (consumer) costs were 32 percent, insurance premiums 17 percent, Medicare payroll taxes 9 percent, with Medicare premiums accounting for the balance, 3 percent.

Industry sources estimate that, in 1990, the average employer's share of medical and medically-related costs per employee surpassed $3,100. Sharp increases in this amount are cited as a main reason for the rise in uninsured people, from 33.6 million in 1988 to approximately 37 million by 1992.

During the past two decades many strategies have been implemented by the Federal Government, states, and businesses, to control escalating costs. Yet healthcare expenditures have risen from $74.4 billion in 1970 to $838.5 billion in 1992, at an average annual rate of 11.5 percent.

Among measures taken thus far to address this situation are the following:

- strategies to reduce the use of out-of-pocket share of payment;
- programs to restrict choice of provider;
- programs limiting providers' selection of services;
- direct controls over prices of services;
- policies encouraging increased competition in health insurance markets;
- regulatory policies.

Profit Margins

There is no uniform way of reporting the industry's profitability. Fragmentary information indicates that fewer than 13 percent of all hospitals, the dominant group of healthcare providers, are profit-making corporations.

Any analysis of provider services should take into consideration that most hospitals operating for profit or on a non-profit basis *do* make a profit. This enables them to generate sufficient revenues to buy the latest technology, pay competitive salaries, and cover other costs. According to the Prospective Payment Assessment Commission, profit margins have fluctuated since the mid-1970's, when they were 2 percent. They reached 6 percent in 1984, and declined to under 4 percent in 1990.

Profit information on other healthcare providers (physicians, dentists, nursing homes, management care organizations, and health insurance companies) is sparse. Attempts to secure better data are impeded by a wave of industrywide mergers and buyouts. However, HMOs, which are part of managed care organizations, realized after-tax net income of more than $1 billion in 1990 and again in 1991.

Medicare

Medicare is a Federal program that pays hospitals and other medical providers who care for patients aged 65 years and older, for certain disabled people, and most persons with end-stage kidney disease. There are approximately 34 million Medicare enrollees, including more than 3 million afflicted with disabilities. Total Medicare outlays are projected to rise from $131 billion in 1992 to $145.5 billion in 1993 representing an 11 percent increase.

Medicare consists of two parts, Hospital Insurance (HI) and Supplementary Medical Insurance (SMI). HI is funded primarily by Social Security payroll taxes. HI pays for care provided by hospitals, skilled nursing facilities, home health agencies, and hospices. HI outlays are likely to reach $84.8 billion in 1993, an increase of $7.4 billion over the previous year.

SMI pays for physician services, laboratory services, hospital inpatient costs, treatment for end-stage kidney disease, and for durable medical equipment. SMI outlays are expected to grow from $53.6 billion in 1992 to $60.7 billion in 1993, a 13.2 percent rise. Enrollees pay about 35 percent of costs through premiums, but a subsidy from general revenues finances the bulk of the entire program.

Medicaid

Medicaid is a Federally-supported and state-administered assistance program providing medical care for certain low-income individuals and families. Medicaid covered about 28 million people at a cost of $100 billion in 1991.

Medicaid as well as Medicare programs are subject to periodic changes in laws and regulations. All such changes may materially increase or decrease payments to hospitals, physicians, and other medical providers. As Medicaid and Medicare programs have become costlier in recent years, the tendency by Congress and state legislatures has been to reduce Medicaid and Medicare financing.

While Medicaid programs cover a small fraction of the U.S. population, many compare it to a national healthcare program. Medicaid serves many groups. For poor people with Medicare, Medicaid actually serves as a medigap policy, paying coinsurance, deductibles, and services not covered by Medicare. For all income groups, Medicaid is the ultimate payer for long stays in nursing homes or intermediate care facilities for the mentally retarded. Long-term care for these recipients accounts for 44 percent of all Medicaid spending. Medicaid provides catastrophic coverage for people who have episodes of a variety of problems and have no cash assistance. It automatically pays after both family cash reserves and private insurance are exhausted.

Nursing Home Care and Related Care Homes

Nursing homes are an integral feature of the American healthcare system. They provide medical, social, and residential services to chronically disabled people over an extended period of time. Because chronic disability increases with age, the elderly are the primary recipients of nursing home care.

There are 31 million persons aged 65 and over in the United States. An estimated 7 million require continuous assistance for routine daily functions. In cases where family members are absent, an institutional setting becomes essential. In addition, many of the chronically disabled require intensive medical assistance, and often are served by nursing care on an around-the-clock basis.

Long-term care facilities are of three basic types: (1) nursing homes certified by Medicare and Medicaid as skilled nursing care facilities (SNFs); (2) nursing homes certified for chronically disabled patients or the mentally retarded; and (3) all other facilities that furnish some degree of long-term nursing care.

In 1986, the latest year in which data are available, there were 16,388 nursing homes, and 9,258 residential facilities. Also there were 734 hospital-based facilities providing nursing care services in addition to other forms of treatment. In total, there were 1.8 million beds and 1.6 million residents. The occupancy rate for skilled nursing facilities was 94 percent, and for hospital-based facilities it stood at 92 percent.

Medicare payments to SNFs fluctuated from $3.4 billion in 1989 to $2.4 billion in 1990 and $2.5 billion in 1991. The fluctuation was due to the Medicare Catastrophic Coverage Act of 1988. Following its repeal, those payments and services were decreased. State Medicaid programs provide 45 percent of payments and cover more than 60 percent of all nursing home patients. Medicare covers less than 5 percent of nursing home payments. Future Medicaid policies will greatly influence access to nursing home services for prospective beneficiaries.

Home Healthcare Services

Home health care is a method of providing healthcare services to disabled people within their homes. There are more than 5 million people in the United States who require such services. These include physicians' care, part-time or intermittent skilled nursing care, physical therapy, and speech therapy. Medical supplies and durable medical equipment used in providing these services are also elements of this system.

In 1990, there were about 11,000 home health service providers in the United States. More than half, 5,700, were Medicare-certified and about 1,780 were provided by hospitals. Home healthcare expenditures rose from $7.6 billion in 1990 to $9.8 billion in 1991, a 28.9 percent increase. Since 1980, they grew at average annual rates of approximately 26 percent. Government financed three-fourths of the total, while out-of-pocket payments accounted for about 12 percent and most of the balance was paid by private health insurance.

The number of home visits by industry professionals to the afflicted and/or disabled increased from 16.3 million in 1980 to more than 17.8 million in 1991. During the same period, numbers of patients served more than doubled (from 726,000 to an estimated 1.7 million).

Private Health Insurance

Health insurance premiums have increased sharply during the past years. Insurers have raised their rates by 8 to 60 percent, citing escalating healthcare prices, ineffectiveness of cost-cutting efforts, and possible discriminating pricing practices by health providers.

In 1990, private health insurance plans disbursed $216.8 billion, an amount which was more than $20 billion above disbursements for 1989. Private health insurance covers three-fourths of the total non-institutionalized population. There are approximately 71 million workers with 69 million dependents, all of whom obtain coverage as an employment benefit. The remaining 44 million people purchase their own coverage.

More than 1,000 private insurance companies in the United States write individual or group health insurance plans. The private health insurance industry has been growing rapidly because (1) consumers seek to reduce risks of high-out-of-pocket expenses, and (2) business health insurance premiums receive preferential tax treatment, estimated at $60 billion annually.

Private coverage is available through insurance companies, hospitals, through medical service plans, and through group medical plans operating on a prepayment basis. The prepayment plans, such as those that managed care organizations provide, have grown rapidly and are creating competition among healthcare insurers.

Private health insurance companies sometimes deny coverage to individuals because they suffer from AIDS, alcoholism, diabetes, coronary artery disease, or cancer. In addition, coverage may be denied to people in high-risk categories, such as drug abusers, older people, and those in certain occupations. The principal reasons for lack of private insurance coverage are that the offer price is more than the uninsured can pay and/or the coverage is not available at any price.

Hospital Waste Disposal

The contamination of New Jersey beaches in 1988 highlighted potential threats to public health arising from improper medical waste disposal procedures. This issue is having a profound impact on health care. Since then, Federal and state governments are monitoring the situation far more vigorously, focusing on hospital-generated medical waste and disposal practices. The Environmental Protection Agency, has introduced regulations (and mandated penalties) for hospitals which dispose of substances into the environment. Those substances and materials include red bag waste, incinerator emissions, radioactive waste, laboratory waste, and storage tanks.

The Medical Waste Tracking Act of 1988 forces States to enact or modify regulations dealing with disposal of medical and infectious waste. The Clean Air Act imposes tough restrictions on medical waste incinerators that burn over two tons of waste material daily.

One of the few new technologies available to dispose of medical wastes appears to be cost-effective. It compacts potentially dangerous substances, shredding, granulating, and chemically treating the waste material.

Employment

Employment in the healthcare industry rose from 7 million in 1988 to approximately 10 million by 1992. This represents average annual growth rates of 9.3 percent. During the past decade, this industry's employment growth surpassed that of the rest of the private economy—a trend which should continue for the remainder of this decade.

Healthcare workforce totals are exclusive of employment in the health insurance, medical equipment and supplies, and pharmaceuticals industries. There has been positive employment growth in all these sectors, especially in offices and clinics of medical doctors, as well as in nursing and personal care facilities. Hospitals and nursing homes account for about 62 percent of the total number employed in health care.

Allied Health Personnel

Allied health personnel are workers who assist physicians and other specialists. This job category is among the fastest growing occupational sectors of the entire healthcare industry. The Bureau of Health Professionals estimates there were 1.8 million allied health personnel in the United States in 1990, a 44 percent increase from 1980. These professionals play an integral role in the delivery of the nation's health services, with 300,000 employed in clinical laboratory positions. More than one-half of the latter are employed by hospitals.

Healthcare Reform—A Priority for the Nation

Debate over healthcare reform is accelerating. Attention to this issue rose dramatically during the past decade, and major national healthcare associations—representing business, labor, and other constituencies—advocate modifications in existing policy.

Federal and state lawmakers have introduced proposals. One proposal would direct all employers either to provide medical coverage for their workers, or contribute directly to a government insurance fund ("play or pay"). The U.S. Bipartisan Commission on Comprehensive Health Care for All Americans (the Pepper Commission) recommended such a plan. The Commission also suggested overhauling the nation's private insurance system, and suggested ways of restructuring Medicaid.

Other proposed remedies abound. Some emphasize market competition, tax credits, deductions for the uninsured, capping malpractice awards, and encouraging electronic processing of medical claims. Among those who have made proposals are the American Medical Association, American Hospital Association, U.S. Chamber of Commerce, National Governors Association, Heritage Foundation, and academicians such as professors Uwe Reinhardt and Alain C. Enthoven.

Both business and government agree that the United States should seek to accomplish the following objectives:

- provide cost-effective healthcare services in an era when different factors contribute to high costs;
- design a comprehensive healthcare system that will include 37 million uninsured Americans;
- explore the effects of ever-greater reliance on modern medical technologies;
- review the impact of managed care on overall healthcare expenditures;
- examine access of various socio-economic groups to healthcare services;
- determine levels of healthcare in rural America;
- reduce costs of malpractice liability;
- determine what characteristics best assess quality of service;
- restructure Medicare and Medicaid programs;
- improve medical education as necessary;
- assess healthcare planning;
- explore primary care;
- enhance use of preventive care;
- evaluate issues of bioethics.

Factors contributing to escalating costs are waste, fraud, malpractice and limited effective competition. Waste and fraud alone account for billions of dollars. For example, the Federal Bureau of Investigation uncovered evidence in 1992 that some drug companies were defrauding the Medicare/Medicaid system. Awareness of other abuses has spread, and the call for correction of these abuses will doubtless influence prospects of sectors within the nation's healthcare industry.

The International Healthcare Market

The business climate in many foreign countries appears favorable for U.S. healthcare companies to expand into overseas markets. The prospects in Western Europe, Mexico, and in Japan are viewed as particularly promising.

Many foreign governments have designated health care as a cornerstone of their social policy, and they plan to provide steady yearly budget increases over the medium term in order to achieve stated objectives. A number of foreign countries strive to modernize both the public and private health sectors, while offering increased market opportunities for services and medical equipment. Others are contemplating privatization, or exploring options to decentralize existing systems for delivery of services. Despite the problems faced by consumers and institutions bearing the burden of escalating healthcare costs within the United States itself, American companies are recognized globally as industry leaders.

In both Western Europe and Japan, demographics (aging populations as well as increased longevity) and high income levels create growing demand for healthcare services. According to industry specialists, the best prospects in these two regions exist for primary care, home care, and nursing home care services. Also, opportunities in hospital management, and in ancillary services, appear promising.

The newly independent states of the former Soviet Union and countries of Eastern Europe may present some opportunities for U.S. companies. Success in such ventures, however, will demand that U.S. firms tailor their services to the specific needs of each country, while continued efforts by foreign governments to open domestic economies must occur to assure profitability. Although there has been considerable speculation concerning actual healthcare markets across the countries of Eastern Europe and throughout the former Soviet Union, highly volatile commercial and economic conditions prevail in both regions.

In Eastern Europe, U.S. healthcare service providers are frequently in a better position to enter country markets through small, "bite-sized" operations. These undertakings include diagnostic imaging, maternity centers, ambulatory care and surgery, and the sale of computer systems. Several U.S. firms are providing emergency healthcare services, consulting, and insurance coverage in Hungary. In addition, according to some observers, health maintenance organization (HMO) services may offer a prototype for reform of the still largely state-run health sector in these countries. U.S. government agencies are working to facilitate service providers with market entry through organized trade missions and encouraging liberal trade and investment environments in talks with Eastern European counterparts.

LONG-TERM PROSPECTS

Consumers, providers, and policymakers will most likely attempt to devise a healthcare system that could increase competition in the United States. The chief goal of any legislative package to emerge will, of course, be cost containment, access and efficiency. However, healthcare spending will continue to absorb a disproportionately high share of GDP. The elderly population already consumes a large share of total healthcare services.

Providing services to all, including the 37 million uninsured, will ultimately increase both the rate of spending and the volume of healthcare services. Health insurance companies may have to make adjustments in their health coverage to comply with any major national healthcare reform that might arise, while healthcare expenditures will continue to rise but at a slower rate.

Private healthcare institutions may initially realize a lower profit and will have to modify their modus operandi to cope with newly instituted government regulations. Managed care and home healthcare occupy important places in the market, and will undoubtedly continue to do so. Alternatives to institutional care—home health care, personal care services, hospice care, and adult care—will increase. Nursing home care will provide a major market for durable medical equipment, supplies and pharmaceuticals.

Efforts to reduce healthcare costs will generate better collaboration between physicians and hospitals in providing services.—*Simon Francis, Office of Service Industries, (202) 482-2697.*

Trends and Forecasts: Health and Medical Services (SIC 80)

(in billions of dollars)

Item	1987	1988	1989	1990	1991[1]	1992[2]	1993[3]	Percent Change 1987–88	1988–89	1989–90	1990–91	1991–92	1992–93
National Health Expenditures	494.2	546.1	604.3	675.0	751.8	838.5	939.9	10.5	10.7	11.7	11.4	11.5	12.1
Health Services and Supplies	476.9	526.2	583.6	652.4	728.6	813.9	914.0	10.3	10.9	11.8	11.7	11.7	12.3
Personal Health Care	439.3	482.8	530.9	591.5	660.2	739.0	830.2	9.9	10.0	11.4	11.6	11.9	12.3
Hospital	194.2	212.0	232.4	258.1	288.6	323.2	363.4	9.2	9.6	11.1	11.8	12.0	12.4
Physicians' Services	93.0	105.1	116.1	128.8	142.0	157.1	175.2	13.0	10.5	10.9	10.2	10.6	11.5
Dentists' Services	27.1	29.4	31.6	34.1	37.1	40.4	44.2	8.5	7.5	7.9	8.8	9.0	9.5
Other Professional Services	21.1	23.8	27.1	30.7	35.8	41.7	47.4	12.8	13.9	13.3	16.6	16.6	13.7
Home Health	4.1	4.5	5.6	7.6	9.8	12.7	16.5	9.8	24.4	35.7	28.9	29.5	30.0
Non-Durable Medical Products	43.2	46.3	50.5	55.6	60.7	66.4	72.6	7.2	9.1	10.1	9.2	9.4	9.4
Durable Medical Equipment	9.1	10.1	10.4	11.7	12.4	13.2	14.2	11.0	3.0	12.5	6.0	6.3	7.5
Nursing Home Care	39.7	42.8	47.7	53.3	59.8	67.3	76.0	7.8	11.4	11.7	12.2	12.5	13.0
Other Personal Health Care	7.8	8.7	9.8	11.5	14.0	17.0	20.7	11.5	12.6	17.3	21.4	21.7	21.8
Administration	23.0	26.9	33.8	38.9	43.9	48.6	54.3	17.0	25.6	15.1	12.9	10.7	11.7
Government Public Health Activity	14.6	16.6	18.9	22.0	24.5	26.3	29.4	13.7	13.9	16.4	11.4	7.3	11.8
Research and Construction	17.3	19.8	20.7	22.7	23.2	24.6	25.9	14.5	4.5	9.7	1.8	6.0	5.3
Research[4]	9.0	10.3	11.0	11.9	12.6	13.3	14.1	14.4	6.8	8.2	5.8	5.5	6.0
Construction[5]	8.2	9.5	9.7	10.8	10.6	11.3	11.8	15.9	2.1	11.3	−1.8	6.6	4.5

[1]Preliminary.

[2]Estimate.

[3]Forecast.

[4]Research and development expenditures of drug companies and other manufacturers and providers of medical equipment and supplies are excluded from "research expenditures," but they are included in the expenditure class in which the product falls.

[5]Benchmark data by HCFA.

NOTE: Numbers may not add to totals because of rounding.

SOURCE: U.S. Department of Health and Human Services, Health Care Financing Administration (HCFA), Office of the Actuary; U.S. Department of Commerce, International Trade Administration (ITA). Estimates and forecasts by ITA.

Insurance

Premium receipts of life insurance companies grew more than 3 percent in 1992, to surpass $272 billion. Stronger individual annuity sales and growing premiums for health insurance accounted for the bulk of the increase. Premium receipts for life insurance products grew little in 1992. Life insurance in force—the total face value of all policies—grew to more than $10 trillion. For related topics, see chapters 42 (Health and Medical Services), 45 (Commercial Banking), 48 (Mutual Funds), and 49 (Securities Firms).

The life insurance industry consists of more than 2,100 companies that engage in underwriting life insurance and annuities. Life insurers also engage significantly in underwriting accident and health policies, and in managing pension and trust funds. These companies are classified mostly in Life Insurance (SIC 631) and Accident and Health Insurance (SIC 6321). Stock companies, owned by shareholders, and mutual companies, owned by policyholders, are the two main types of insurance providers.

Life insurance companies earn premium income from three major product areas: life insurance, annuities (individual and group pension products), and health insurance. Based on industry surveys, premiums for life insurance products grew about 2.6 percent in 1992. Sales of individual universal policies decreased significantly, countered somewhat by strong growth in variable-type products in which policyholders assume most of the investment risk of the underlying assets.

Premium receipts for term insurance and traditional whole life policies, which make up the bulk of life insurance premiums, increased modestly. There was a small increase in sales of single premium life insurance after several years of sharp drops due to the loss of tax benefits in 1988. About one-fifth of income from life insurance products is from group policies that showed no growth in 1991.

In recent years, sales of life insurance products have shifted from investment-type products, such as universal and variable life insurance, back to traditional whole life and term insurance. Although growth has not been strong, traditional products are typically more profitable and their liabilities more predictable.

Income from both individual and group annuities unexpectedly fell to $123.6 billion in 1991 to 46.9 percent of all premium receipts. Annuities are strongly associated with the well-publicized failures of large life insurance companies in 1991, which likely undermined consumer confidence for these products. Reportedly, group annuities fell again in 1992, although individual annuities rebounded, led by variable annuities. The 1991 decline in individual annuities was primarily due to the drop in sales of single premium deferred annuities.

Insurers writing fewer guaranteed investment contracts, otherwise known as GICs, also contributed to the drop in sales of group annuities. Insurers have deemphasized GICs because the liabilities of GICs clash with the industry's need for higher-grade assets. In addition, a general shift by client companies from defined benefit pension plans to defined contribution pension plans diminished pension business for insurers. In defined benefit plans, current funding is based on expected future benefits, a specialty of insurers. Retirement benefits in defined contribution plans, however, are based solely on actual funds contributed. Most of the lost sales for GICs and defined contribution plans went to mutual funds and banks whose similar products do not require insurance expertise.

Premium growth from health insurance continued to increase in 1991 and 1992, driven almost entirely by cost pressures. Upward cost pressures drove the expansion. These pressures were exacerbated by "cost shifting" where, for instance, health care providers shift unreimbursed fees and expenses from public insurance programs to private insurance programs, such as health insurers, that do not impose cost controls.

The trend toward managed health care and the use of administrative services and self-insurance has also diminished the expansion of health premiums for life insurers. Life insurance companies are major providers of health insurance. Other providers of health insurance include Blue Cross/Blue Shield plans, property/casualty insurers, specialty health insurers, self-funded employer plans, and government programs. Group health, typically provided through employer health plans, accounted for more than three-fourths of health premiums for life insurers.

Investment income for insurers improved in 1991 and 1992 as insurers realized capital gains through falling interest rates and rising equity markets. These gains offset lower earnings from interest-bearing instruments. Insurers also reported growth in income from fee-based activities and other sources. Many insurers sought fee income to conserve capital.

The assets of life insurers increased about 9 percent in 1992 to nearly $1,700 billion. The proportion of corporate bonds decreased slightly in 1991 from 1990, while equities increased. Taken together the mortgage and real estate portfolios of insurers declined both absolutely and as a percentage of assets from 1990 to 1991.

Assets consist mainly of financial instruments such as stocks and bonds. These assets back insurance and annuity contracts required to pay expected claims, and provide the necessary surplus and capital to meet solvency standards. Life insurance companies are major institutional investors. Insurance and pension funds held almost one quarter of the financial assets in the United States in 1991.

The life insurance industry remains financially sound. Year-end 1991 and 1992 balance sheets improved for most companies. In the 1980's, however, basic changes in financial and insurance markets, such as rising interest rates and a shift to investment-type products, set the stage for an increase in insurance company insolvencies. In 1991, the weak economy, the depressed real estate market, the results of earlier investments in low-grade corporate bonds, and a sharp drop in consumer confidence were the immediate causes of several large, well-publicized failures. These insolvent companies did not, or could not, adjust to the changes in the markets, resulting in severe asset and liquidity problems. Many analysts contend that the insolvencies of a few insurers are not indicative of the industry's fiscal health.

In 1992, the bond market improved, stock prices rose, and declines in real estate values abated in many regions. Insurers used gains from bond and stock sales to help offset losses from under-performing assets. As a result, the overall quality of assets in the portfolios of life insurance companies has improved, highlighted by the distinct shift to higher grade bonds. Insurers have shored up their financial positions based on such factors as modest earnings, increased capital gains, use of reinsurance to control liabilities, postponed write-offs of under-performing assets, and slightly reduced dividends to stockholders and policyholders.

General financial improvement, however, does not affect all insurers. The number of insolvencies in 1992 was about the same as 1991, albeit the failures were not as large Because the economy is weak and real estate problems persist, some life insurers remain in jeopardy. Most of the problem real estate loans, however, are concentrated in larger insurance companies with the means to ride out a downturn . . .

Key Developments

The solvency of the insurance industry and its implications for public policy were again the dominant issues of 1992. In 1991, as stated before, several large life insurers became insolvent or were seized by regulators. A downturn in the economy caught these companies overinvested in distressed real estate and low-grade bonds. Even before these high-profile failures, policymakers in Congress and elsewhere had begun looking at financial difficulties in the industry prompted by concerns over the problems in the savings and loan industry and in commercial banking. Congressional inquiries have focused on the ability of the current state regulatory system to protect the public against insurance company failures. This includes detecting and preventing failures before they occur and protecting policyholders, primarily through a guaranty system, if failure occurs.

Critics of state regulation contend that the industry is too big, too diverse and too international for 50 different state regulators to supervise effectively its activities, to prevent insolvencies, and to protect policyholders. As a solution, critics have called for a larger Federal role in insurance regulation. Two congressional bills proposing expanded Federal oversight have advanced the debate.

Senate bill S.1644, The Insurance Protection Act of 1991, would set minimum Federal standards for the certification of state insurance departments. Insurers licensed in certified states could operate nationally. The bill also provides for the regulation of reinsurance, the examination of insurers from certified states, a national guaranty fund, and Federal liquidation procedures.

The other major bill would have the Federal government regulate insurers directly as opposed to setting Federal standards for the states to follow. H.R. 4900, The Federal Insurance Solvency Act of 1992, would give insurance companies the option of obtaining a Federal certificate of solvency. Certified insurers would not be subject to state solvency regulation, although they would be subject to state licensing, rate, and form regulations. The bill would exempt large commercial property/casualty insurers from state rate and form regulation. The bill also would set up a guaranty fund for Federally certified insurers, financial standards for and certification of all foreign insurers and reinsurers, national licensing for agents and brokers, and financial examination and insolvency procedures for all Federally certified insurers. While neither of these bills is likely to be enacted in its present form, they set the direction for future debate.

Other congressional proposals address more narrow aspects of insurance solvency. These proposals include tightening pension regulations, establishing new requirements for foreign insurers and reinsurers, and strengthening Federal laws for insurance fraud and abuse.

Proponents of state regulation, led by the state regulators, claim the current system has done a good job of protecting policyholders and promoting market efficiencies. State regulators cite the success of the current system in handling the large failures of 1991. They contrast this to the problems in the savings and loan, and banking industries that are regulated by the Federal Government.

In a program driven by the National Association of Insurance Commissioners (NAIC), the states are moving to set up improved licensing and financial standards, better screening and surveillance of insurers, and improved guaranty fund programs and insolvency procedures. Improved financial standards may include new risk-based capital requirements based on the amount of asset, underwriting and other risks that an insurer faces, to augment the current minimum capital and surplus requirements.

Under the program, the NAIC will certify any state meeting these standards, thus easing the recognition of insurers from certified states in other states. The NAIC has certified 13 states so far, and more are expected in 1993. Critics of state regulation, however, say that this program is not enough because the NAIC does not have the authority to push it through all states or enforce it.

Banks in insurance remains a key issue. Current banking law restricts banks and bank holding companies to banking and bank-related activities. Banks can provide some types of insurance products such as credit life, but are restricted from selling or underwriting most insurance products, such as annuities, that are primarily savings and investment products.

For years, the banking industry has argued that allowing banks to operate more fully in the insurance and brokerage industries would increase competition in financial services, provide stability to the financial marketplace, improve economic and capital market efficiencies, and provide greater convenience for consumers. In addition, developments in Europe and Japan point to a competitive need to integrate U.S. financial services markets . . .

Other recent events affecting banks in insurance include a 1991 Federal law restricting state-chartered banks from underwriting or selling insurance nationwide except for certain grandfathered banks with insurance subsidiaries. A Supreme Court determination is pending on the right of certain small-town national banks to sell insurance nationwide. Many states have allowed, or are considering allowing, banks to underwrite and sell insurance. In California, Proposition 103 gave state banks the power to sell many kinds of insurance. As of this writing, Pennsylvania was considering permitting state-chartered banks to underwrite and sell insurance.

Health care reform is a key issue. Proposals for reform, some in the form of congressional legislation, range from completely nationalized health insurance to enhancing private markets for the funding and delivery of health care. One hybrid proposal calls for each U.S. business either to provide health insurance to employees or to pay a set amount into a government health insurance plan. Another proposal stresses a plan with tax credits for the underinsured and with legal limits on medical liability costs as elements.

LONG-TERM PROSPECTS

The life insurance industry will go through considerable changes over the next few years. The long-term prospects for life insurance and annuity products of life insurance companies are good. Demographic variables, such as income growth, wealth accumulation, population and workforce changes, and home ownership will determine the demand for insurance products over the long term. The rate of personal savings in the United States is expected to rise with the movement of the baby-boom population into middle age. The ageing of the baby-boom population will raise the demand of individuals for products that provide for retirement income and for health care financing.

Competition for these markets, however, will increase. Banks may get additional powers to sell and underwrite insurance. Banks, mutual funds and other financial institutions will be offering investment and savings products that directly compete with insurance and annuity products. Foreign insurers will continue to expand into the largely unrestricted U.S. market.

Other means of financing and delivering health care—for example, employer self-insurance, government programs, and managed care services—will diminish the growth of private health insurance, especially indemnity insurance. Moreover, new products and markets, such as long-term health care, will not replace business lost elsewhere. Instituting national health insurance could end private health insurance altogether.

On the tax front, the Federal government, in a search for revenue, may tax the investment income of annuity products, the so-called "inside build-up." Lawmakers, however, are also looking at increasing tax benefits of Individual Retirement Accounts to spur long-term investment. This could be a boon to insurers.

Increased competition and lingering problems in real estate for some insurers should keep the rate of insolvencies at the same level as recent years. Real estate problems will persist as commercial mortgages mature over the next couple of years, but diminish as insurers restructure their portfolios and real estate markets recover. Mortgages should become a smaller part of portfolios.

The problem of insolvencies has already prompted state-level action to strengthen financial standards and tighten regulation. A larger Federal role in insurance regulation may follow, if pending congressional legislation is enacted. The Federal government may set basic financial standards for the states to follow or may regulate the industry itself. A national guaranty fund for insurance is possible, although Federal support seems unlikely.

These conflicting forces and issues will change the nature of competition in the industry. Profit margins will likely remain thin and returns on equity will remain below historical levels over the next few years. To compete, life insurance companies may have to consolidate operations, specialize in market segments, reduce operating costs, increase efficiency and service quality, and better manage their assets and liabilities. Larger, better capitalized companies will get a bigger share of the market, but smaller niche players will be strong competitors in selected markets.

To reduce costs there will be much pressure on the distribution system. Agents will have to accept less compensation or increase production. Insurers will look for cost-efficient marketing alternatives, such as direct mail, alliances with other financial institutions, financial advisors, and consultants. Insurers will be seeking new information and communications technology to increase efficiency in underwriting, distributing, investment, claims, and administrative activities.

Diminished returns on life insurance in the United States also will prompt the stronger insurance companies to look for other investment opportunities. Many life insurance companies, mainly through holding companies, have moved, or will move, into related financial services, including securities, banking activities, and real estate. More U.S. life insurance companies will take advantage of expanding foreign markets, especially Europe, Asia, and—with the North American Free Trade Agreement—Mexico.

Property/Casualty Insurance

Net written premiums for property/casualty insurance are expected to increase slightly more than 3 percent in 1992 to about $230 billion. This modest growth has been due mainly to the slow economy and subdued rates in most commercial lines. An overabundance of capital in the industry and the availability of alternative markets has kept rates low. Improvement in underlying cost factors has helped constrain losses from claims. Nevertheless, record catastrophe losses in 1992, led by Hurricane Andrew's $7.8 billion, will severely hurt insurers' operating earnings. Only solid investment performance, mainly from selling assets to capture capital gains, will keep operating earnings positive for 1992.

The property/casualty insurance industry provides financial protection for individuals, commercial businesses and others against losses of property or losses by third parties for which the insured is liable. P/C insurance companies are classified in Fire, Marine and Casualty Insurance (SIC 633). There are an estimated 3,800 P/C companies. Most are organized as stock companies, some as mutual companies.

The biggest premium increases among property/casualty insurers in 1991 was for private automobile insurance that rose $4.4 billion to $82.8 billion. Much of this growth is attributed largely to new rate increases that were needed to offset underwriting losses.

In commercial lines, premiums for workers' compensation inched up only $300 million in 1991 to $31.3 billion, following a decade of strong growth. States that denied requests for rate increases in workers' compensation contributed to the slowdown. Premiums in other commercial lines either fell or changed little in 1991. Most notably, liability insurance other than for automobiles fell for the fifth straight year. The use of captives and other risk funding alternatives has affected premium growth in liability lines for insurers. The overall decline in commercial lines likely continued in 1992 as a direct result of the economy and slowing inflation. A soft economy reduces the number of claims (excluding catastrophe losses). A reduction in inflation produces claims costs that are less than industry projections.

In addition, the abundance of capital kept commercial rates at low levels. The amount of capital available to underwrite business determines the supply of insurance protection. An overabundance of capital sharpens competition for underwriting business and restrains rates (prices) . . .

The overall financial situation of P/C insurers did not improve in 1992. The rate of insolvencies remained at levels of recent years. Losses from catastrophes, such as Hurricane Andrew, helped push many smaller insurers into severe financial difficulties.

Asset quality is not a problem for most

P/C insurers because investments are relatively liquid and secure. There is a concern, however, that insurers have not increased reserves for losses sufficiently. This could affect future performance. Insurers cashed out many of their investments to pay for record losses, but still drew down reserves because of the slow economy and drop in inflation. As a result, realized capital gains supported a small earnings increase in 1992. Unlike 1991, however, operating earnings did not add much to policyholders' surplus in 1992. In addition, some analysts question the reliability of reinsurance recoverables.

Insurers did move to streamline operations and reduce expenses in 1992. Employment fell 1.6 percent to 551,600. This was accompanied by some restructuring and a refocus by many insurers on core business. Merger and acquisition activity was strong in 1991 and 1992, highlighted by several large acquisitions by foreign firms. In addition, agents and brokers reported falling income because of reduced commissions and slower business.

LONG-TERM PROSPECTS

The long-term prospects of the industry will depend mostly on how much and how fast rates increase over the next several years. Commercial rates will head upward, but will be sporadic and limited. Many factors suggest rates are heading upward. Reinsurance rates for catastrophe risks are high and increasing. Rates in the primary markets in Europe are climbing. Premiums for surplus lines insurers increased again, suggesting commercial insurers may be avoiding some risks. (Surplus lines insurers are unlicensed insurers. They underwrite risks that licensed insurers reject.) In addition, there is a general fear that many companies have inadequate loss reserves. Thus, insurers will need to increase rates to bring reserves to adequate levels or face pressure from regulators, rating agencies and stockholders.

Rate increases, however, will be sporadic and limited by line of business. Capital in the industry is relatively strong despite Hurricane Andrew and other catastrophes. There is enough capital for existing premium levels. New capital also keeps coming into the industry as shown by the increase in foreign investment. Alternative markets are strong, as much business would flee from commercial insurers to these markets if rates jumped. In addition, insurance companies may be reluctant to raise rates too far, too fast, fearing a political backlash, as happened during the liability crisis of the mid-1980's. Rates will stay down if low inflation and slow economic growth keep losses in check. Also, political pressure from consumer groups will hold rates in personal lines at lower levels.

In this environment, stronger or more efficient companies with a better capital position will get larger market shares. Weaker companies will need to streamline or consolidate. They may have to join with stronger companies or find other capital sources. Foreign investment, especially from Europe, will provide some of this capital. Thus, merger and acquisition activity will remain high for the next few years.

Many companies will not survive. The rate of insolvencies will remain at current levels. Insolvencies could increase if the economy does not pick up or catastrophe losses jump suddenly. The failure of a large P/C company, although not foreseen, could strain the capacity of state guaranty funds. This could lead to other failures as the effects of the failure move through the industry.

State-level action to improve solvency regulation, now underway, should be largely in place by 1994. This should lessen many of the problems related to solvency. The prospect of Federal regulation of insurance, however, will increase in the next few years, if solvency problems grow. At a minimum, we can expect Federal measures on penalties for insurance fraud and regulating foreign insurers. There is also a good chance of McCarran-Ferguson reform to narrow the antitrust exemptions of the industry.

Finally, the long-term financial health of the industry may depend on resolution of problems with health care costs, environmental liability, workers' compensation and automobile insurance. Federal action may also be taken to reform the product liability system.

INTERNATIONAL COMPETITIVENESS

Insurance and financial markets are becoming increasingly global. Advances in information and communications have made it possible for even the smallest investor to purchase financial instruments from almost anywhere abroad. The rise in personal incomes and savings in many areas around the world and the need to protect this wealth provides significant opportunities for life insurers. This environment makes it possible for life insurance companies to seek premiums and place investments globally.

The growth of multinational companies and international trade and investment has prompted the growth of international nonlife insurance companies and insurance brokers to service the local and global needs of companies for protection from all types of risk. Thus, insurers from Europe, Asia and the United States have expanded internationally through branches, subsidiaries, joint ventures and reinsurance operations. In addition to providing insurance products, insurance companies also transfer services and technologies such as claims adjusting, risk management, actuarial, investment and information technologies.

The United States has the largest insurance market in the world with 35.6 percent of $1,356 billion premiums worldwide. Japan is the second largest market with 20.5 percent of world premiums. The United Kingdom, Germany, and France were the next largest markets as premiums in Europe totaled $460 billion in 1990.

For life insurance, the United States had $205.8 billion in premiums in 1990, followed closely by Japan with $203.3 billion. These figures, which do not include health insurance, show the extent to which the Japanese save through insurance. The United States, with 42.6 percent of world premiums in 1990, leads the world market for nonlife insurance. Japan had 11.6 percent, Germany 8.8 percent and the United Kingdom 5.6 percent. The size of the U.S. nonlife market is due mainly to health insurance and to casualty insurance. Private insurers, rather than the public sector, provide much of the health insurance in the United States. Compared to other countries, the tort-liability system in the United States leans strongly toward fully indemnifying people harmed as the result of the action or products of others.

U.S. insurers have become more active in foreign markets in recent years. U.S.-owned insurers in foreign countries had sales (premium income plus investment income plus other income) of $30.6 billion in 1989, the latest year data was available. Canada, Europe and Japan are key markets for U.S. insurers. Most foreign sales were from nonlife operations, but U.S. life insurers have recently become more active overseas. For example, U.S. life insurers have moved strongly into South Korea, Taiwan and other Asian markets.

Foreign-owned insurers and other insurance services had sales of $54.4 billion in the United States in 1989, up from $39.1 billion in 1987. Foreign-owned property/casualty insurers in the United States earned an estimated $28 billion, or 13.5 percent, of premiums in 1989.

Foreign-owned life insurance companies in the United States had an estimated 6.1 percent of premium receipts of life insurers in 1989. Foreign-owned life insurance companies in the United States had $22.2 billion in sales in 1989, up from $16.8 billion in 1987.

Cross-border trade in insurance is a small, but important part of the U.S. insurance market. U.S.-based insurers earned $6.2 billion in foreign premiums (exports) in 1991. Premiums of $11.4 billion went to foreign-based insurers (imports) to cover risks in the United States. Most premiums sent abroad went to Europe or the off-shore centers, like Bermuda, for reinsurance. In fact, reinsurance premiums sent abroad represent more than 40 percent of the reinsurance market in the United States.

Foreign companies have expanded their insurance activities in the United States over the past few years mainly through acquisitions. Foreign outlays for acquisition or establishment of insurance companies in the United States has totaled more than $16 billion since 1981. This included $5.8 billion in 1988, mostly because of the $5.2 billion invested by Batus Inc. (UK) in the Farmers Group, an insurance company in California. Other recent foreign investments of prominence include the Axa Groupe (France) putting $1 billion in the Equitable Life Assurance Society of New York and the 1991 purchase by Allianz (Germany) of the Fireman's Fund of California valued at $3.1 billion.

Regulatory and trade developments around the world are creating opportunities for U.S. insurance companies. The European Community (EC) is directing its members to liberalize their markets for insurance. Several EC countries, especially in Southern Europe, have opened their insurance sectors more to foreign investment. Insurers in one EC country can write certain nonlife insurance in any other EC country. Recent EC directives harmonize accounting and regulatory standards making it easier to transact business across EC borders. The EC also has formulated directives and proposals that address issues in product liability, pollution liability, pensions, and automobile insurance. Some U.S. insurers have already positioned themselves to take advantage of the business opportunities created by these and other changes in the EC.

U.S. insurers also would gain from a North American Free Trade Agreement (NAFTA). NAFTA would provide U.S. insurers expanded investment opportunities in Mexico; Canada being open already. U.S. insurers would operate equally with Mexican insurers. The NAFTA also liberalizes some types of cross-border insurance among the countries, such as reinsurance and marine insurance. In addition, it will provide broader access to Mexico's insurance market for agents, brokers and insurance service firms such as claims adjusters and actuaries. Although the Mexican insurance market had just $3.5 billion in total premiums in 1991, the market and opportunities for U.S. insurance companies should expand with a NAFTA.—*M. Bruce McAdam, Office of Finance, (202) 482-0346.*

World Insurance Markets,[1] 1990 Premiums

(in billions of dollars)

Country	Total[2]	Life	Nonlife[3]
Total, all countries	1,355.7	707.3	648.5
United States	482.1	205.8	276.4
Canada	31.8	16.0	15.8
Europe	460.0	222.3	237.6
United Kingdom	101.7	65.6	36.1
West Germany	92.5	35.6	56.9
France	74.3	39.1	35.2
Italy	30.2	7.7	22.6
Netherlands	24.1	12.5	11.6
Switzerland	19.6	11.0	8.7
Asia	334.0	239.1	94.9
Japan	278.3	203.3	75.0
South Korea	27.4	22.4	5.0
Taiwan	6.8	4.8	2.1
Latin America	9.4	2.3	7.1
Africa	14.4	9.3	5.1
Oceania[4]	23.9	12.5	11.5

[1]Includes centrally planned economies.
[2]Detail may not add to total due to rounding.
[3]Nonlife business includes accident and health insurance as well as property/casualty insurance.
[4]Includes Australia, New Zealand, and South Pacific Islands.
SOURCE: *Sigma*, 1992, Swiss Reinsurance Co.

Foreign Insurance Affiliates[1] of U.S. Companies

(in billions of dollars except as noted)

Item	1983	1985	1987	1989[2]
All insurance:				
Number of affiliates	621	617	631	610
Total assets	46.9	56.4	80.4	89.6
Sales[3]	16.3	17.9	27.0	30.6
Life insurance:				
Number of affiliates	88	87	86	80
Total assets	20.0	21.3	28.6	27.5
Sales[3]	5.9	5.6	7.8	—
Accident & health insurance:				
Number of affiliates	34	34	39	51
Total assets	2.2	3.0	6.3	—
Sales[3]	0.9	1.0	2.1	—
Other insurance[4]:				
Number of affiliates	499	496	506	479
Total assets	25.1	32.0	45.5	—
Sales[3]	9.5	11.2	17.0	16.8

[1]Affiliates include entities at least 10 percent owned by a nonbank U.S. person.
[2]Preliminary estimates.
[3]Sales equals premium income plus investment income plus other income.
[4]Include nonlife insurers, agencies, brokerage firms and other insurance related companies.
SOURCE: U.S. Department of Commerce, Bureau of Economic Analysis, *U.S. Direct Investment Abroad,* various issues.

Sales[1] of Foreign-Owned Insurance Companies, 1989

(in millions of dollars)

Country[2]	Foreign-owned insurers in the U.S	U.S.-owned insurers abroad
All countries	54,356	30,572
Canada	12,270	6,847
Europe	31,914	10,285
Switzerland	6,965	—
European Community	23,926	—
United Kingdom	10,882	—
Netherlands	6,736	—
West Germany	2,463	—
Latin America[3]	199	5,259
Japan	444	5,851
Australia	—	365

[1]Sales equals premium plus investment plus other income for insurance affiliates that are 10 percent or more owned by any one foreign person.

[2]Country of ultimate beneficial owner (UBO).

[3]Includes offshore centers such as Bermuda and the Bahamas.

SOURCE: U.S. Department of Commerce, Bureau of Economic Analysis, Foreign Direct Investment in the United States, 1991, and U.S. Direct Investment Abroad, 1991.

Foreign-owned Insurers[1] in the United States

(in billions of dollars except as noted)

Item	1983	1985	1987	1989
All insurance:				
Number of companies	—	—	1,071	1,115
Total assets	53.1	67.2	110.1	170.6
Sales[2]	21.9	23.9	39.1	54.4
Life insurance:				
Number of companies	—	—	233	247
Total assets	23.4	33.8	53.3	77.0
Sales[2]	8.8	10.5	16.8	22.2
Other insurance[3]:				
Number of companies	—	—	838	903
Total assets	29.8	33.4	56.8	93.6
Sales[2]	13.0	13.5	22.3	32.1

[1]Companies are members of affiliates which are 10 percent or more owned by any one foreign person. Includes branches and subsidiaries.

[2]Sales equals premium income plus investment income plus other income.

[3]Includes nonlife insurers, agencies, brokerage firms and other insurance related companies.

SOURCE: U.S. Department of Commerce, Bureau of Economic Analysis, *Foreign Direct Investment in the United States*, various issues.

Metals

Steel Mill Products

The U.S. steel industry (SIC 3312, 3315, 3316, and 3317) showed some signs of emerging from a recession-induced slump in 1992. Prompted by a rebound in automotive and appliance demand, domestic shipments of steel mill products reached 41.3 million short tons at mid-year, up more than 7 percent from 1991. If shipments continue this trend, the 1992 level will be less than 3 percent below the peak of the last expansion. Raw steel production through August increased 9 percent, and capacity utilization (output as a percent of raw steelmaking capacity) rose to 82 percent, compared with only 72 percent during the same period of 1991. Import penetration through June declined to 17.9 percent from 19 percent a year earlier, even though after March 31 imports were no longer subject to controls for the first time since 1982.

Despite these positive developments, the steel industry as a whole reported an operating loss of $112 million during the first half of 1992, although by the second quarter some large steel companies became profitable. They attributed the poor earnings largely to an inability to boost depressed prices; higher costs for labor and start-up of new facilities were also cited. Some minimills were able to report higher profits despite declining prices because of reduced operating and raw material costs.

The price decline over the last several years has been substantial. According to the Bureau of Labor Statistics, the composite price for steel mill products declined 7.5 percent between the peak in 1989 and May, 1992. Between February 1991 and May 1992, the price of carbon cold rolled sheet, the bread and butter of many integrated producers, declined 4.6 percent.

The failure of steelmakers to achieve price relief reflects in part the heightened competition among domestic producers that resulted from industry restructuring. During the 1980's, the number of flat-rolled steel producers increased as a result of the entry of small, low-cost firms, the spinoff of some mills by multiplant companies, and the emergence from bankruptcy of a number of slimmed-down companies. As the number and size of these companies grew, the market share of the six largest producers fell from 64 percent to 47 percent. The large number of smaller players operating in a depressed market has made the maintenance of price discipline difficult.

The price discounting was encouraged by overcapacity in many markets as well as by the industry's high capital intensity. Because fixed costs are high, too many producers want to maintain high operating rates to cover those costs and to keep down unit costs.

Shipments are expected to reach 82 million tons in 1992. Imports are likely to decline late in the year, in part because of uncertainty generated by the massive number of trade cases filed by the domestic steel industry (see discussion below). Some price increases were anticipated toward the end of the year.

The flat-rolled market, which accounts for about 60 percent of total shipments, continued to be shaken by Nucor Corporation. This low-cost steelmaker, which began producing one million tons of sheet steel using the revolutionary thin-slab caster technology at its Crawfordsville, Indiana mill in 1988, undercut larger rivals to boost its market share and maintain high operating rates. It was reasonably profitable because of its low costs. The market was expected to be shaken further when Nucor began operation of its new flat-rolled mill at Hickman, Arkansas during the summer of 1992. That mill's production, which is expected to reach 600,000 tons in 1993, will eventually exceed 1.2 million tons annually. Moreover, Nucor may build additional capacity at both mills—at relatively small incremental capital cost. By 2000, the company's capacity may reach 8 million tons or about 15 percent of the current flat-rolled market. The new capacity may influence future prices.

Recognizing profitability was unlikely to be restored through higher prices, many companies took extraordinary measures to reduce costs, including shutting down mills. In the highly competitive structural steel market, which has been affected by the downturn in high-rise construction as well as the entry of low-cost minimills, the U.S. Steel Group closed its 700,000 ton structural steel mill at South Works, Chicago, in April 1992. Another integrated producer, Inland Steel, dropped out of the structural market in 1991 and the remaining integrated producer was under pressure to cut costs in order to remain competitive.

Steel companies are also under pressure to address labor costs, which account for approximately 30 percent of total pretax production costs. Hourly employment costs for the industry rose 19 percent between June 1989 and June 1992. During this period, productivity growth slowed substantially from the rate of the mid and late 1980's, as output dropped more rapidly than employee hours. Labor contracts at four of the major mills expire during the summer of 1993, and management will probably want to take measures to contain costs. Expectation of a strike could boost user inventories, thereby inflating shipments earlier in the year.

INTERNATIONAL COMPETITIVENESS

Massive industry restructuring and investment in new technology over the last decade have made the U.S. steel industry one of the low cost producers among industrialized countries. By one estimate, pretax production costs in early 1992 were lower in the United States than in any other major steel-producing country, except for the United Kingdom. Productivity is currently as high as in any other country. On a quality basis, too, the industry has made extraordinary progress. For example, Ford Motor Company's rejection rate for steel purchases has dropped from 8.8 percent in 1982 to less than 1 percent in 1991.

Reflecting the industry's increased competitiveness, as well as strong demand overseas, exports of steel mill products soared in 1991 to 6.3 million tons, the second highest level ever. Moreover, exports represented a record 8 percent of shipments; over the past 20 years the average was only 3.1 percent. This increase occurred despite a nearly 5 percent drop in demand for steel worldwide.

During the first half of 1992, however, exports fell sharply to 2.3 million tons, or 30 percent below the comparable period of 1991. The decline resulted in part from the collapse of export prices worldwide as steel demand weakened in many countries. Formerly booming markets, especially Japan, began to soften toward the end of 1991 and demand in both Eastern and Western Europe fell sharply. One strong market was Mexico, where demand has been propelled by economic growth and trade liberalization. Exports to that country grew rapidly during the first half of 1992, up 29 percent from the same period in 1991. Mexico nearly replaced Canada as the largest export market for steel mill products for the first time.

Imports of steel mill products rose slightly during the first half of 1992 to 8.3 million tons, an increase of only 1.3 percent compared with the same period of 1991. Import penetration for this period fell to 17.9 percent, down from 19 percent a year earlier.

All controls on imports of steel mill products into the United States were removed on March 31, 1992, following the expiration of the 21 voluntary restraint agreements (VRAs) covering imports from 29 countries. Since October 1982, imports of at least some carbon and alloy steel products had been subject to restraint; coverage was significantly expanded beginning in September 1984. Restraint on imports of stainless steel dated back to 1983. In recent years, these restrictions were not binding as most countries subject to VRAs substantially undershipped their import ceilings because of low prices in the United States and stronger markets elsewhere. The end of VRAs was not expected to result in a surge in imports because of the weak pricing here.

The VRAs were originally instituted for a five-year period beginning in 1984 to address the problem of dumped and subsidized steel imports. VRAs were considered a more effective way of dealing with steel problems than pursuing to conclusion the many antidumping and countervailing duty cases that had been filed. Once the VRAs were signed, unfair trade cases against products covered by VRAs were withdrawn.

President Bush extended the VRAs in 1989 for an additional 2½ years as one part of his Steel Trade Liberalization Program. Another part was the negotiation of an international consensus to eliminate the trade-distorting practices that precipitated the original program. The market instability and worldwide overcapacity that so affected the industry in the 1980's resulted in part from these practices.

In the first step toward reaching the international consensus, nine leading steel exporting nations and the European Community signed bilateral consensus agreements (BCAs) to eliminate subsidies, tariffs, and other trade-distorting practices in the steel sector. They also agreed to support the idea of a multilateral solution to the problem of unfair trade practices.

After two years of negotiations on a multilateral steel agreement (MSA), talks collapsed on March 31, 1992. While negotiators made substantial progress on provisions to eliminate many trade-distorting practices, they were not able to reach an agreement on such fundamental issues as treatment of past subsidies, establishment of a permissible category of subsidies, and consultation before filing of antidumping cases. Participants did agree to continue meeting bilaterally and multilaterally to resolve outstanding issues. The United States remains committed to reaching an agreement.

With the expiration of VRAs and the belief that a future MSA would not address current problems, steelmakers filed a massive number of countervailing duty and dumping cases through the spring and summer of 1992. The first series of cases involved pipe and tube products, followed by rail and leaded bar. On June 30, 12 steel companies filed 48 antidumping and 36 countervailing duty petitions on 4 flat-rolled products against 21 foreign countries. The flat-roll cases affect imports, which totaled 6.5 million tons (41 percent of 1991 imports) valued at nearly $3 billion. In the first hurdle to imposition of supplemental tariffs on these products, the U.S. International Trade Commission voted on August 10 to continue its investigation in all but 12 of these cases.

The petitions threatened to disrupt steel trade. Some fall bookings were reportedly halted because of the uncertainty generated by the cases. Several Japanese companies announced they would stop exporting certain steel products to the United States to avoid possible dumping penalties, which are assessed retroactively. U.S. exports were also affected; in anticipation of the U.S. filings, two Mexican companies filed antidumping suits against seven U.S. flat-rolled producers. Subsequently, some traders in the United States reported difficulty selling those products in Mexico. Canadian producers indicated that they too were preparing antidumping suits against U.S. steelmakers.

Foreign investment in the U.S. steel industry soared during the 1980's but slowed considerably during the early 1990's. The biggest investors were the Japanese steel companies, which established numerous joint ventures with U.S. integrated companies largely to produce a variety of sheet products for the transplant automotive market. By one estimate, foreign steelmakers had obtained a substantial position in almost 25 percent of domestic integrated mills by the late 1980's; total foreign investment was $3 billion during the 1980's. A lack of profitability of these operations, other economic problems in Japan, and the scope of existing assets have discouraged further investment.

One exception to the trend of declining foreign investment was the purchase (expected to be completed by December 1992) of Florida Steel Corporation, one of the largest domestic minimills, by Kyoei Steel, a Japanese minimill, for $330 million. This was the first acquisition of a major minimill by the Japanese, although there are at least three small joint ventures. Florida Steel is a manufacturer of light structural products, wire rod, and reinforcing bar.

ENVIRONMENTAL PROFILE

Amendments to the Clean Air Act passed by Congress in 1990 will have an important impact on the steel industry. Two provisions in particular will effectively boost production costs. The stringent new requirement for toxic coke oven emissions could add $17 per ton of raw steel produced, or 3 percent to production costs for integrated producers according to a Congressional study. Electric furnace-based minimills will see their costs boosted by provisions affecting electric power plants. A more accurate assessment of costs will only be available after the Environmental Protection Agency adopts new regulations in December 1992. (For a more comprehensive assessment of the effect of the Clean Air Act on the steel industry and its efforts to adjust to it, see chapter 14 in the *1992 U.S. Industrial Outlook*.)

As part of its effort to enhance the competitiveness of steel, the industry has actively promoted recyclability. Recycled steel, i.e., scrap largely for electric furnaces, makes up more than one-third of new steel products manufactured each year. To improve the salability of steel cans, a recycling program was established by some of the big integrated producers that has been able to increase the recycling rate of steel cans from 15 percent in 1988 to 34 percent in 1991. Their objective is to reach 66 percent by 1995.

LONG-TERM PROSPECTS

Assuming modest overall economic growth through the mid-1990's, steel demand will likely rebound to the level reached during the peak of the last expansion—in the range of 100 million tons. With the U.S. market expected to be very competitively priced and domestic producers maintaining a cost advantage in their home market, no sizable increase in imports is likely. A pickup in global demand may divert imports to other markets.

Steel is in vigorous competition with lighter weight materials, especially aluminum and plastics, for a future share of its major markets, including motor vehicles and appliances. To retain market share in the auto sector, the industry is continually improving the properties of steel, especially formability, strength, and corrosion resistance. Steels with organic coatings are being developed that are better suited to stamping presses and reduce die wear. New bake hardened steels become more durable as cars are heated to dry the paint. High strength steels mean steel can be thinner, tougher, and lighter. Many of these steels have been developed within the last five years.

One uncertainty is whether growing governmental concern over fuel economy in automobiles will prompt higher corporate average fuel economy standards, forcing auto manufacturers to replace steel with lighter weight materials. Several companies have already announced plans to replace steel with aluminum for body applications, especially hoods. Other parts that may increasingly be replaced by plastic or aluminum are fenders and decks. According to one research project, more than 200,000 tons of steel will be replaced in auto panels by the mid-1990's. Between 1980 and 1992, steel's share of the weight of a typical automobile fell from 60 percent to 54 percent, even as total weight declined by 7 percent, or 228 pounds.

Roofing may become an important market for steel in the 1990's. The standing seam roof, which takes advantage of improvements in coated steels, requires minimal maintenance compared with build-up roofs and typically can be expected to last at least 40 years. Steel's share of the roofing market is now only 2 percent, but demand is expected to grow rapidly during the 1990's.—*Charles Bell, Office of Materials, Machinery, and Chemicals, (202) 482-0606.*

Aluminum

In 1992, shipments of ingot and mill products by the U.S. aluminum industry were estimated to have increased only slightly over 1991, but it was enough to just surpass the previous record level of shipments in 1988. Shipments increased 2.5 percent to 7.49 million metric tons (mt), or 16.5 billion pounds. Although overall shipments increased, the trends of the past few years reversed as domestic shipments increased while total exports decreased. The United States, however, did maintain a positive trade balance for aluminum semifabricated products. Exports of these products, which only accounted for 7.7 percent of industry shipments in 1987, now represent the industry's second largest market, approaching 20 percent of industry shipments. Worldwide, the consumption of aluminum increased negligibly, and key export markets, such as Japan and the EC, actually registered declines. Shipments by aluminum distributors increased at a greater rate than overall shipments.

Domestically, shipments to the three major end-use sectors; containers and packaging, transportation, and building and construction accounted for approximately 60 percent of shipments. A cool summer, which reduced beverage consumption, and the continued light-weighting of cans, the dominant end-use in the containers and packaging sector, resulted in only slight growth in the largest sector. Shipments to the transportation sector increased, benefiting not only from an increase in vehicle production, but also an increase in the amount of aluminum used per vehicle. Residential and commercial building remained very sluggish, and shipments to this sector decreased.

Primary aluminum production capacity in both the United States and worldwide continued to operate at near-capacity levels. U.S. production capacity edged up slightly as improvements in operating efficiency resulted in incremental capacity increases at some smelters. Thus, in spite of the shutdown of the smelter in Troutdale, Oregon, U.S. production was on par with previous years at just over 4 million mt.

The Bonneville Power Administration (BPA), which provides electricity to about 40 percent of the smelting capacity in the United States, imposed a 25 percent power cutback to those smelters the last four months of 1992 due to low water levels and the need to divert water to salmon runs. The affected smelters were able to purchase electricity, albeit at higher prices, from other sources, and there were no reductions in the rate of capacity utilization.

Although aluminum prices in early 1992 rebounded from the historically low year-end levels of 1991, for 1992 as a whole, prices averaged slightly less than 60 cents per pound. Prices were buoyed early in the year by the prospect of supply reductions in conjunction with the expiration of labor contracts at several smelters in the United States. However, a new contract was negotiated without incident, and prices sagged slightly. Prices remained low because of relatively stable Western demand, and a significant increase in supply to Western markets, especially from the continued high level of exports from Russia. Exports from Russia were estimated to be 800,000 to 1,000,000 mt in 1991, and at least 600,000 mt in 1992. Additionally, increases in production capacity from new smelters, especially in Canada, more than offset production cutbacks elsewhere, further exacerbating the supply/demand imbalance. As a result, there has been accumulation of large inventories of primary aluminum, especially of Russian metal in London Metal Exchange warehouses. These historically high inventory levels are likely to continue to have a dampening effect on prices.

Globally, the primary aluminum industry did not cut back production to meet lower demand levels for two principal reasons. First, producers have been very successful in reducing costs, although many producers worldwide still maintain marginal costs above the current price of aluminum. Second, the industry assumed that an increase in demand was imminent.

ENVIRONMENTAL PROFILE

Electricity is the single most costly input to the production of aluminum. The relatively high cost of electricity in the United States is the major reason that new smelting capacity is not constructed domestically, but in areas where there are inexpensive sources of power, such as natural gas in the Middle East and hydropower elsewhere. The competitiveness of the U.S. primary aluminum industry, could be hindered by increased electricity costs due to the reduction in sulfur dioxide emissions required under the amended Clean Air Act of 1990. It is likely that some of the costs of these emission reductions, which will be incurred by electric utilities, will be passed to the consuming aluminum smelters.

Measures to curb potential climate changes caused by the production of greenhouse gases could also adversely affect the aluminum industry. Approximately half of the U.S. smelters (in terms of capacity) are supplied electricity from coal burning power plants, a principal source of greenhouse gas emissions.

INTERNATIONAL COMPETITIVENESS

The combined import volume of ingot and semifabricated aluminum products increased almost 9 percent from the level of 1991. The rate of increase in ingot imports exceeded that of semifabricated products. Conversely, exports of ingot and semifabricated aluminum products decreased by about 6 percent, which was the result of a significant decline (over 20 percent) in ingot exports. Exports of semifabricated products displayed exceptional growth, increasing by approximately 15 percent. Semifabricated product exports were bolstered by an increase in demand for can stock as many overseas markets, especially Japan, increased their use of aluminum beverage cans.

The aluminum mill products industry is a modern and efficient producer of high quality products with an international competitive advantage. From 1981 to 1991, exports by the U.S. aluminum industry achieved an annual growth rate of 9.9 percent. The international competitiveness of the industry would further benefit from reducing the barriers to foreign market access.

LONG-TERM PROSPECTS

U.S. aluminum shipments are expected to increase at a compound annual rate of just under 3 percent through 1997. Beverage cans will remain the largest end use for aluminum. Can stock should also spur exports as aluminum cans become more prevalent in other markets. Exports of semifabricated products will provide the growth as exports of ingot decline. Imports will continue to increase, especially of ingot.

It is expected that the use of aluminum in automobiles could make significant strides in the next decade. In order to meet future fuel efficiency standards automakers are developing several new applications for aluminum in autos, and estimates are that by the end of the decade aluminum usage could increase almost 30 percent to 210 pounds per vehicle. In addition to the current widespread use of cast parts in light vehicles, aluminum should find increasing use in car frames and structural members, as well as in body panels.

Aluminum will also find its way into automobiles in other ways. The typical U.S. car now contains 25 pounds of precision parts made by the powder metallurgy (P/M) process, and auto engineers are specifying more P/M parts for new engines and transmissions. P/M parts have a net-shape advantage over traditional metal forming techniques, requiring less machining and less handling, thereby reducing manufacturing costs. (Net shape means there is little additional machinery necessary for the part to be in usable form.) The use of P/M parts by the automotive industry will aid in improving quality, reducing vehicle weight, designing for recyclability, and trimming costs. The next four years should yield P/M's biggest growth in engines and transmissions. Applications will include pressure plates, sprockets, clutches, clutch hubs, and turbine hubs. P/M could also be a potential candidate for components going into a Ford electric car transmission. Hot forged P/M connecting rods should also have future growth.

The metal injection molding sector of the P/M industry is growing and could reach $100 million in annual sales by 1997. Metal injection molding, a high-volume process, offers very strong economic and engineering advantages especially for medical and dental applications.

The aluminum industry has been developing new materials employing aluminum as a means of ensuring its future. Although the early bright prospects for aluminum-lithium alloys have not been realized, there does seem to be considerable market potential for metal matrix composites (MMC) utilizing aluminum as a matrix material, and typically reinforced with silicon carbide or alumina. The reinforcing materials impart their beneficial characteristics, such as lightweight and high strength, to the overall composite while simultaneously retaining the ease of fabrication of aluminum. Although autos are currently the only significant application for MMC, there are a variety of future applications for these materials such as in high speed commercial aircraft and their engines.—*David Cammarota, Office of Materials, Machinery, and Chemicals, (202) 482-5157.*

Copper

Conditions in the U.S. copper industry (SIC 1021, 3331, 3341, 3351, and 3357) improved during 1992. Spurts of regional demand and pockets of strength in certain end-use sectors emerged. Total copper consumption increased by about 3.2 percent to almost 3 million metric tons (mt). Copper consumption by wire rod mills increased about 2.2 percent to 1.6 million mt; copper consumption by brass mill increased about 5.4 percent to 1 million mt. Replenishing of stocks of manufactured products drawn down during 1991 also lent support to the market, but uncertainty over the future direction of demand kept competition keen, squeezing profits of many producers.

During the first six months of 1992, copper traded between 96 cents and $1.07 per pound compared with a price range of between 99 cents and $1.13 per pound over the same period in 1991. As in 1991, stock levels during the first six months of 1992 generally stayed in the range of six to seven weeks of supply. Financial performance of the major domestic copper mining companies was mixed at mid-year, with some reporting higher sales and profits and others lower. These results did not deter the domestic mining industry from continuing with major renovations and expansions intended to increase the productivity and efficiency of their domestic operations.

Kennecott Corp. announced plans to invest $880 million in a state-of-the-art copper smelter, a 40 percent expansion of its copper refinery, and a new precious metals plant at its facilities in Utah. Kennecott also began operations of a fourth mill line at its Bingham mine in Utah. Asarco Inc. completed a $224 million expansion of its Ray mine, which is expected to increase output by 58 percent. Cyprus began operations at a new, improved smelting facility during 1992. Running counter to the trend, Mitsubishi Materials Corp. announced it would not go forward with its plans to build a new copper smelter on the Texas Gulf Coast following protests from environmental groups and lengthy delays in issuing permits.

INTERNATIONAL COMPETITIVENESS

The trade picture has changed dramatically in the past several years for all segments of the U.S. copper industry. In 1986, the United States reported net imports of refined copper of approximately 489,000 mt. By the end of 1991, net imports had decreased to approximately 17,000 mt. However, the surge in U.S. exports of refined copper that began in 1988 was halted in 1992, due largely to weaker demand from Asian markets, especially Japan. Total exports of refined copper decreased approximately 25 percent by mid-year and are expected to be approximately 37 percent lower for the year. Barring a reoccurrence of production problems that caused an increase in imports of refined copper in 1991, imports are expected to decline in 1992. At mid-year, the brass mill industry appeared to be on its way to a sixth consecutive year of expanding exports and declining imports; exports are expected to increase 19 percent and imports will decrease 4 percent in 1992. Recently, export growth has spread across several product lines, including copper and copper alloy bars, rod, pipe, tube sheet, strip, plate, and foil. Canada, Mexico and Japan are the primary export markets for U.S. brass mills, but these mills have recently made export gains in some EC member countries. Antidumping and countervailing duty orders remained in place on brass sheet and strip during 1992. By mid-year, exports of wire mill products, traditionally a strong export sector, were approximately 30 percent above levels of the prior year and are expected to increase by approximately 23 percent for the entire year. Mexico, Canada, the United Kingdom and the Philippines are the main export markets for these products. A relatively stronger recovery in the U.S. economy compared with several other countries is expected to push imports of wire mill products up by approximately 30 percent in 1992, but the United States is expected to remain a net exporter in this sector.

Historically, the domestic copper mining industry has paid close attention to events in the developing world. Economic and legislative reforms in some developing countries, especially Chile and Peru, are a positive sign for further future U.S. investment in overseas mining. Concern over the practices of state-owned copper mining companies in developing countries, a major issue for the domestic copper mining industry in the past, has largely subsided in the current market. With its enormous copper reserves, Russia may become a much larger force among world copper producers, but when this may occur is still not clear.

Copper is generally mined in the developing countries of the Southern Hemisphere, but is consumed and processed into intermediate and final products in the developed northern countries. The United States is the exception to this rule because it is both a major producer and consumer of copper. Consequently, the economic interests of domestic producers, the mining companies, and the consumers (the brass mills and wire mills) tend to diverge regarding the economic development of Eastern Europe, China, and the newly industrialized countries of Asia. Growth and reconstruction of these economies create demand for raw materials, thereby benefiting producers, but also create new competition in the domestic and foreign markets for producers of mill products and for their customers, the domestic producers of finished products containing copper. The extent to which the domestic mills are able to compete on the basis of quality and serve the high value segment of the market will be a major factor in their future success in the international markets.

During 1992, Phelps Dodge Corp., the largest U.S. copper company, continued with plans to develop the La Candelaria mine in northern Chile. PMX Industries of South Korea opened a new brass and stainless steel mill in Cedar Rapids, Iowa. This is one of the largest investments by a South Korean company in the United States, and existing brass mills are concerned about its effect on competition in the market. During 1992, the United States and 17 other countries, including Chile, Peru, Germany, Italy, France, and China, formed an International Copper Study Group. The group's mission is to improve world statistics on copper production and consumption, and to provide a forum for the exchange of views between producing and consuming countries.

LONG-TERM PROSPECTS

Total world copper consumption is estimated to increase at a compound annual rate of approximately 2 percent to the year 2000. The largest increases are expected in China, provided progress continues on its economic reforms. U.S. copper consumption is estimated to grow at a compound annual rate of approximately 1.5 to 1.7 percent to the year 2000.

U.S. productivity and market development are improving. The domestic copper mining companies, brass mills and wire mills have increased productivity and efficiency, and have controlled costs. These efforts will be important in meeting competition from foreign copper producers and manufacturers of copper substitutes. Market development efforts will be aimed at increasing copper use in existing markets, and finding new applications in construction, telecommunications, and automotive electronics.—*Direct inquiries to Barbara Males, Office of Materials, Machinery, and Chemicals, (202) 482-0606.*

Aluminum Ingot and Mill Products

(in thousands of metric tons)

Item	1989	1990	1991	1992[1]	1993[2]	1997[2]
Total shipments[3]	7,442	7,151	7,307	7,490	7,790	8,940
Primary ingot production	4,030	4,048	4,121	4,020	4,000	4,000
Exports	1,092	1,164	1,374	1,290	1,315	1,470
Ingot	595	686	796	625	595	550
Mill products	497	478	578	665	720	920
Imports	1,353	1,421	1,398	1,520	1,570	1,900
Ingot	926	962	1,029	1,130	1,170	1,350
Mill products	427	459	369	390	400	550

[1]Estimate.

[2]Forecast.

[3]Aluminum ingot and mill products.

SOURCE: U.S. Department of Commerce, International Trade Administration (ITA); The Aluminum Association. Estimates and Forecasts by ITA.

Trends and Forecasts: Steel Mill Products (SIC 3312, 3315, 3316, 3317)

(in millions of dollars except as noted)

Item	1987	1988	1989	1990	1991[1]	1992[2]	1993[3]	Percent Change (1987–1993) 87–88	88–89	89–90	90–91	91–92	92–93
Industry Data													
Value of shipments[4]	50,971	62,783	63,054	60,941	—	—	—	23.2	0.4	−3.4	—	—	—
Value of shipments (1987$)	50,971	57,998	56,464	55,595	51,470	53,580	54,860	13.8	−2.6	−1.5	−7.4	4.1	2.4
Total employment (000)	249	261	256	254	—	—	—	4.8	−1.9	−0.8	—	—	—
Production workers (000)	193	201	199	196	—	—	—	4.1	−1.0	−1.5	—	—	—
Capital expenditures	1,643	2,222	2,961	3,011	—	—	—	35.2	33.3	1.7	—	—	—
Product Data													
Value of shipments[5]	50,058	61,715	62,105	60,065	—	—	—	23.3	0.6	−3.3	—	—	—
Value of shipments (1987$)	50,058	57,056	55,631	54,791	50,730	52,800	54,070	14.0	−2.5	−1.5	−7.4	4.1	2.4
Trade Data													
Value of imports	—	—	9,601	8,915	8,343	8,600	8,900	—	—	−7.1	−6.4	3.1	3.5
Value of exports	—	—	2,954	2,922	3,820	2,500	2,350	—	—	−1.1	30.7	−34.6	−6.0

[1]Estimated, except exports and imports.
[2]Estimate.
[3]Forecast.
[4]Value of all products and services sold by establishments in the steel mill products industry.
[5]Value of products classified in the steel mill products industry produced by all industries.

SOURCE: U.S. Department of Commerce: Bureau of the Census, International Trade Administration (ITA). Estimates and forecasts by ITA.

Steel Mill Products Trends and Projections (SIC 3312, 3315, 3316, 3317)

(in millions of short tons except as noted)

ITEM	1982	1988	1989	1990	1991	1992[1]	1993[2]	Compound annual rate of growth, 82–92	Percent change 92–93
Raw steel production	74.6	99.9	97.9	98.9	87.9	92.0	94.5	2.1	2.7
Continuous casting (percent)	29.0	61.3	64.8	67.3	75.9	77.0	78.0	10.3	1.3
Steel mill product shipments	61.6	83.8	84.1	85.0	78.8	82.0	84.0	2.9	2.4
Exports	1.8	2.1	4.6	4.3	6.3	4.4	4.1	9.3	−6.8
Imports	16.7	20.9	17.3	17.2	15.7	16.5	17.0	−0.1	3.0
Apparent domestic consumption[3]	76.5	102.6	96.8	97.9	88.2	94.1	96.9	2.1	3.0
Exports as a percent of shipments	2.9	2.5	5.5	5.1	8.0	5.4	4.9	6.3	−9.0
Imports as a percent of apparent consumption	21.8	20.4	17.9	17.6	17.8	17.5	17.5	−2.2	0.1

[1]Estimate.
[2]Forecast.
[3]Product shipments plus imports minus exports.

SOURCE: U.S. Department of Commerce: Bureau of the Census. Forecasts by the U.S. Department of Commerce, International Trade Administration; and American Iron and Steel Institute.

Trends and Forecasts: Copper, 1989–93

(in thousands of metric tons except as noted)

	1989	1990	1991	1992[1]	1993[2]	Percent Change (1990–1993) 90–91	91–92	92–93	Compound Growth Rate (89–93)
Copper consumption	3,140.7	3,090.5	2,888.5	2,980.9	2,989.9	−6.5	3.2	.3	−1.3
Copper production	1,956.9	2,017.4	2,000.6	2,020.6	2,121.2	−0.8	1.0	5.0	2.0
Consumption of copper by									
Wire rod mills	1,726.6	1,678.0	1,609.7	1,645.0	1,686.7	−4.1	2.2	2.5	0.6
Brass mills	1,017.1	1,023.4	956.7	1,008.0	986.3	−6.5	5.4	−2.2	0.8
Exports									
Refined	145.5	212.7	271.2	171.4	205.0	27.5	−36.8	19.6	8.9
Wire mill	156.8	161.8	191.7	235.9	200.5	18.5	23.1	−15.0	6.3
Brass mill	133.2	157.0	162.0	192.8	207.3	3.2	19.0	7.5	11.7
Imports									
Refined	303.8	261.6	288.6	226.8	206.4	10.3	−21.4	−9.0	−9.2
Wire mill	139.4	134.3	104.1	135.5	136.4	−22.5	30.2	0.7	−0.5
Brass mill	397.5	347.6	288.1	276.6	262.8	−17.1	−4.0	−5.0	−9.8

[1]Estimate.

[2]Forecast.

NOTE: Production and consumption data include the use of scrap. Trade data on wire mills include insulated wire and cable. Other industries that consume copper include the foundry, powder metallurgy, and chemicals industries.

SOURCE: U.S. Department of the Interior, Bureau of Mines; American Bureau of Metal Statistics; U.S. Department of Commerce, Bureau of the Census; International Trade Administration (ITA); Copper Development Association, Inc. Estimates and forecasts by ITA.

Motor Vehicles and Parts

The motor vehicle industry is one of the largest components of the U.S. economy. The Commerce Department's Bureau of Economic Analysis (BEA) reported that there were 4,341 U.S.-owned companies operating in the United States in the motor vehicle and equipment sector (SIC 371) in 1987. These firms paid $22.8 billion in compensation to their 711,000 employees, while the value of industry shipments totaled $193 billion. In addition, there were 97 companies with some foreign ownership operating in the United States in 1987, the only year for which comparable data have been assembled so far. These companies employed 40,000 individuals, who were paid $1.1 billion, and generated shipments worth $12.9 billion.

In 1991, the Bureau of Labor Statistics (BLS) reported that total direct employment in the motor vehicle industry averaged 776,000 workers, 4.2 percent of total manufacturing employment. Moreover, because the nation depends so heavily upon motor vehicles to satisfy its transportation and recreation needs, nearly one of every seven jobs in the domestic economy is related to the production, sale, operation, or maintenance of motor vehicles. Final sales of cars and trucks to consumers, business, and government buyers in 1991 totaled $189 billion, directly accounting for 3.3 percent of the nation's GDP. In 1991, total personal consumption expenditures for motor vehicles and equipment were $185 billion, 4.4 percent of U.S. disposable personal income.

Challenges of Competition

The U.S. and other major markets for vehicles and components are essentially saturated, with little prospect that annual growth on a long-term basis will exceed more than 1 or 2 percent. Despite (or perhaps because of) this situation, competition in the United States among all foreign and U.S. manufacturers continues to grow more intense, to the immense benefit of vehicle buyers. In 1992, U.S. purchasers could choose from among 31 major domestic and foreign manufacturers offering a total of 618 separate car and light truck models, almost all of them superior in most respects to those previously offered. Moreover, virtually all new vehicles sold today were developed and brought to market more quickly than those produced only five years ago, and were manufactured more efficiently and with less negative impact upon the environment.

There are probably no major vehicle or parts manufacturers anywhere in the world that now do not have at least some involvement in the U.S. market. This situation has profoundly affected the operations of the U.S.-owned industry, from the smallest parts supplier to the largest vehicle manufacturer. While many U.S. firms have declined or disappeared in the face of stiff competition, others have grown and have increased their share of the worldwide automotive market by becoming more competitive.

Recognizing the higher level of competition that exists and the requirement to match or exceed it, General Motors (GM), Ford, and Chrysler—the Big Three—recently initiated several jointly funded "pre-competitive" research projects that seek to develop new product and manufacturing technologies. Under the terms of the National Cooperative Research Act of 1984, these joint efforts cannot focus on the design or production of specific vehicles, but they can and will pursue the development of generic, fundamental technologies to bring vehicles to the market sooner and at less cost to the public.

The Big Three announced in June 1992 the formation of the United States Council for Automotive Research (USCAR), an umbrella organization that will coordinate more effectively their existing and future jointly funded R&D programs. The directorship of the council will rotate every two years among the three companies. Under the council's purview is the Automotive Composites Consortium, which seeks to develop new materials for stronger, lighter, and more durable body panels. This consortium has already generated patents for new methods of fabricating polymer-based components. Other R&D consortia among the Big Three include the Auto Oil/Air Quality Improvement Research Program, the CAD/CAM Partnership, the Environmental Science Research Consortium, the High Speed Serial Data Communications Research and Development Partnership, the Low Emissions Technologies Research and Development Partnership, the Occupant Safety Research Partnership, the U.S. Advanced Battery Consortium, and the Vehicle Recycling Partnership. Federally funded and private industrial research labs are participating in several of the consortia, some of which are pursuing new techniques to further reduce vehicle emissions and to improve fuel economy, as well as to create more environmentally friendly manufacturing and recycling procedures. (The Environmental Profile section later in the chapter has a more complete discussion of this topic.)

Competitive pressures have also resulted in a profusion of cooperative manufacturing and marketing ventures between each of the Big Three and foreign firms. For example, GM uses its Chevrolet network to market Geo nameplate cars throughout the country. The Geo line includes compact sedans made in California in a 50–50 joint venture between GM and Toyota; subcompact and sport utility vehicles made in Canada in a 50–50 joint venture between GM and Suzuki; and a compact made in Japan by Isuzu, of which GM owns 38 percent. Mazda builds Ford-badged cars in Japan for the Japanese market. In 1992, Ford acquired a 50 percent interest in Mazda's Michigan plant, which builds the Mazda MX–6 and the Ford Probe on the same basic platform. Chrysler sold Mitsubishi its half of their 50–50 Illinois joint venture in 1991, but subsequently signed a multimillion dollar contract with Mitsubishi to provide engines to the plant to be used in vehicles that both firms will market in 1993. GM and Toyota operate a joint venture in California that produces the Toyota Corolla and the Geo Prizm (previously the Chevy Nova) on the same platform. During 1992, the two firms agreed to merge their separate manufacturing operations in Australia and now will produce individual models on a common platform in a shared facility.

The interweaving of the passenger car industry is also duplicated in the light and heavy truck industry. In 1992, Chrysler initiated joint-venture production in Austria with Styer Daimler Puch of a slightly modified version of Chrysler's U.S. market-leading minivan for the European markets. Ford began U.S. production in 1990 of a "badge-engineered" light pickup truck for sale in the United States beginning the following year as the Mazda Navajo. This was the first of what may be several instances of Japanese manufacturers purchasing vehicles from a U.S. supplier. In 1993, Mazda will totally replace its B-series light pickup it had imported from Japan with a vehicle produced in the United States by Ford. Ford is now assembling a new small passenger van in Ohio that was designed principally by Nissan and that both manufacturers will sell as a 1993 model. During 1992, Ford also formed a joint venture in Portugal with Volkswagen to produce a minivan for the European markets. VW may also sell the vehicle in the United States.

Volvo and General Motors established the Volvo-GM Heavy Truck Corporation in 1988 to take over the manufacture of GM's Class 8 truck tractors. In 1992, GM sold part of its 27 percent share to Volvo, which now owns the 83 percent balance. Volvo-GM Heavy Truck signed an agreement in 1992 with the Mexican truck manufacturer, Trailers de Monterrey, authorizing that firm to be the sole importer and marketer in Mexico of Volvo-GM trucks.

The intensely competitive U.S. vehicle and parts market not only has taken its toll on profits, it also has propelled the motor vehicle industry on a painful but beneficial quest to reduce operating expenditures by improving manufacturing technology, cutting overhead expenses, and increasing productivity. In 1982, at the bottom of the previous trough in production, the industry assembled 7 million cars and trucks with an average of 221,000 production workers (in SIC 3711), or 31.7 vehicles per worker. In 1991, output totaled 8.8 million units. BLS's average annual production employment in 1991 was 229,000, or 38.4 vehicles per worker.

According to the Labor Department's index of output per SIC 371 production worker, the growth of productivity in the motor vehicle and equipment industry averaged 3.9 percent annually between the 1982 base year and 1990, reaching a level of 136.2. While the long-term employment trend will continue gradually downward and the productivity index upward, short-term anomalies will occur. According to preliminary estimates by the Labor Department, SIC 3711 production employment averaged 235,000 persons during July 1992, a 1.4 percent decrease from June 1992. However, output fell from 914,000 units in June 1992 to 576,000 in July, a drop of 37 percent. The SIC 371 productivity index will probably register declines in both 1991 and 1992.

Financial Performance

New light vehicle sales declined steadily between 1986 and 1991, with the exception of a 3 percent upturn in 1988. Consequently, competition in the market has been intense, producing the inevitable negative impact on industry earnings. Corporate losses on domestic motor vehicle and equipment operations before taxes, inclusive of inventory adjustments, totaled $6.9 billion in 1991, following losses of $2.6 billion in 1990. Nevertheless, motor vehicle and equipment manufacturers invested $11.3 billion in 1990 for new and refurbished manufacturing plant facilities and equipment, and $10.3 billion in 1991. Investments are expected to total $10 billion in 1992.

In 1991, the Big Three suffered global net income losses of $7.5 billion on worldwide sales of $208 billion. (See table on page 122, which includes 1989–91 data and compares 1991 and 1980, two recessionary years for the domestic automobile industry.) GM's $4.5 billion loss, which included a $1.8 billion write-off for restructuring charges to close 21 plants and lay off 74,000 employees in North America during the following 4 years, was the largest in U.S. corporate history. The Big Three lost a combined $1.1 billion in 1990 on worldwide operations totaling $220 billion.

Between 1989 and 1991, the Big Three suffered a steady decline in their sales, revenues, and gross profits, and a drastic drop in net income, which has been reflected in declining profit margins and returns on sales and equity. The liquidity indicators have been more encouraging, showing an increase in cash and marketable securities and a slowing of the previously rapid decline in working capital accounts. In addition, the quick and current ratios (defined in the table on page 122) remained relatively unchanged between 1980 and 1991.

The steady accumulation of cash and marketable securities in the consolidated balance sheets indicates much stronger financial health than is suggested by net income levels. Comparing the two recessions, the total debt-to-equity ratio was lower in 1990–91 than in 1980, working capital was more plentiful, and gross profitability was significantly improved. On the other hand, declining operating profitability indicates that the companies' cost-control efforts must continue and be strengthened.

The Big Three's parts suppliers have suffered less severely. However, many have experienced a sharp drop in profits due to lack of demand, pricing pressures from Detroit, and foreign competition. In recent years, financial pressures on the supplier sector have greatly increased as their customers often have asked them to finance R&D, inventory, tooling, and logistics operations.

Ward's 1992 Automotive Yearbook includes a financial analysis of the 25 leading suppliers—each with annual sales of at least $1 billion. It reports that none of the 25 firms that have automotive-related businesses reported losses in 1989; 4 ended 1990 in the red; and 10 posted losses in 1991.

INTERNATIONAL COMPETITIVENESS

In addition to exporting from the United States, many companies in this industry engage in importing from their foreign subsidiaries and from their competitors. Equally common are arrangements for joint-venture marketing and production activities between U.S.-owned manufacturers and their competitors, both in the United States and abroad.

At the end of 1991, the value of U.S. direct investment in foreign motor vehicle and equipment production facilities was $22.3 billion on a historical cost basis (the market value at the time the investment was made), up from $20.9 billion at the end of 1990. Foreign direct investment in the United States in this sector was valued on the same basis at $3.7 billion at the end of 1991, about the same as the year before.

Foreign subsidiaries of U.S.-owned motor vehicle and equipment manufacturers generated income totaling $2.3 billion in 1991. This sharp decline from $3.6 billion in 1990 was the result of weak markets, increased costs, and expanded competition. Capital outflows from the United States for direct investment abroad were $958 million in 1991 and $385 million in 1990.

U.S. subsidiaries of foreign vehicle and equipment producers reported losses of $366 million in 1991 on their U.S. operations, following negative income of $314 million the year before. Most European firms lost significant sales and market share in the United States in 1990–91. Two firms withdrew completely from the market. Capital outflows from the United States by foreign firms with direct investment in the United States in this sector totaled $94 million in 1991, compared with capital inflows of $579 million in 1990. The Department of Commerce's BEA estimates that foreign motor vehicle and equipment firms spent $350 million in the United States on research and development projects in 1990.

In 1992, the United States recorded an estimated negative trade balance in motor vehicle and car bodies of $44 billion, 2 percent higher than in 1991. (This is based on an imports for consumption accounting.) The estimated 1992 trade balance in automotive parts was a positive $2.3 billion, compared with a $1 billion surplus in 1990. The United States exported more automotive parts than motor vehicles ($21.8 billion vs. $17 billion) in 1992, while importing more vehicles than parts ($61.1 billion vs. $19.5 billion). As has been the case for many years, most of the automotive deficit is the result of trade with Canada and Mexico—where GM, Ford, and Chrysler operate plants producing vehicles for the U.S. market—and with Japan.

Exports of both vehicles and parts are expected to increase significantly over the next few years. The rate of growth in vehicle imports, and to a lesser extent in parts and accessories, will be slowed by more competitive U.S. products and by additional U.S. production by foreign-affiliated manufacturers. Moreover, a deflated dollar has made imports from Europe and Japan more expensive, while lowering the cost to those countries of U.S.-made vehicles and parts. U.S.-owned car and truck makers have all revitalized their U.S. export operations and are assigning them a greater role in their sales strategies. Japanese-owned auto firms are increasing their programs for shipping models made by their U.S. subsidiaries to their homeland, other markets in Asia, and Europe. These firms are increasing their reliance upon U.S.-made components for their U.S. and Japanese plants, and are sourcing some models for world markets exclusively from their U.S. facilities. U.S. parts producers have discovered that the products they make as original equipment for U.S. and foreign vehicles manufactured in the United States and for the local retail aftermarket also have excellent export potential.

ENVIRONMENTAL PROFILE

While a market niche is emerging on its own for environmentally friendly, "green" vehicles, much of the auto industry's current interest in environmental research has been stimulated by the stringent new clean air standards that California introduced in 1990. The new regulations require that, beginning with the 1998 model year (generally the fall of 1997), 2 percent of all new vehicles sold there must emit no harmful particulates. By 2001, 5 percent must be zero emission vehicles (ZEVs) and by 2003, 10 percent. Massachusetts and New York have passed similar regulations, and other states are considering such legislation.

One of the joint ventures formed by the Big Three in response to this challenge is the Low Emissions Technologies Research and Development Partnership. This joint effort will develop techniques to reduce emissions by refining the internal combustion process and improving the performance of catalytic converters and other exhaust-related components. The program also seeks to improve the ability of engines to run on alternative fuels, including ethanol and methanol mixtures combined with gasoline, liquid natural gas (LNG), and liquid petroleum gas. By 1998, 90 percent of all Texas state-owned vehicles must be fueled by LNG. All local Texas governments must comply by 2002.

It appears that the only feasible way to meet California's requirements may be with electric vehicles. This has led the Big Three and the U.S. Department of Energy (DOE) to form the U.S. Advanced Battery Consortium (USABC) to develop new battery storage technology. The private sector and DOE each contributed $130 million to fund the consortium's efforts. In May 1992, USABC awarded an $18.5 million contract to Ovonic Battery Company of Troy, Michigan, to perfect its prototype of a nontoxic, nickel-metal hydride battery. Ovonic's technology may enable a compact-size vehicle to travel 300 miles before needing a mere 15-minute recharge, accelerate from a standing start to 60 miles per hour in a maximum of 8 seconds, and achieve a maximum velocity of 100 miles per hour. These operating capabilities greatly exceed those of existing electric vehicles. Operating costs of the proposed new battery also are expected to be lower.

Another Big Three consortium that focuses on environmental issues is the Vehicle Recycling Partnership (VRP). Although 90 percent of all motor vehicles now pass through a recycling facility, only 75 percent of the weight of a typical motor vehicle is reclaimed. VRP is researching methods to increase that percentage. Plastics, which accounted for about 6 percent of vehicle weight in 1980, and 8 percent (243 pounds) in 1992, represent a growing, major challenge for the industry. About 100 different plastic formulations are present in the typical vehicle. They are difficult to identify and separate during dismantling operations, but if melted together produce a useless, amorphous mess. The Society of Automotive Engineers introduced a plastics labeling standard in 1992 that may help overcome the problem.

Federal regulations now require each manufacturer's fleet of new passenger cars sold in the United States to average 27.5 miles per gallon (mpg). Light truck fleets must average 20.2 mpg. Manufacturers of non-complying fleets are subject to penalties, while individual models are assessed "gas guzzler" taxes of as much as $7,700 per vehicle. According to the Environmental Protection Agency, domestic passenger cars averaged 26.9 mpg in 1992, and imported car fleets averaged 29 mpg. Domestic light truck fleets averaged 20.4 mpg. The imported light truck fleet achieved an average of 22.4 mpg.

The National Academy of Sciences' National Research Council concluded in early 1992 that it is technically feasible for passenger cars to reach a level of 31–33 mpg for model year 2001, and 34–37 mpg by model year 2006. However, this could require additional manufacturing costs of $500 to $2,750 per vehicle while increasing emissions and reducing vehicle safety. The council suggested that increased taxes on gasoline purchases, coupled with a program of rebates to buyers of especially fuel-efficient vehicles and increased gas-guzzler taxes for vehicles not meeting the standards, would be a more viable method of reducing fuel consumption. During 1992, Congress introduced several bills that would raise fuel economy requirements substantially. None passed, but several may be reintroduced in 1993.

Passenger Cars and Light Trucks

Light vehicle sales in 1992 were distributed among 3 American and 8 Japanese manufacturers with U.S. plants, plus 21 other firms with marketing operations in this country. Sales of new imported and domestically made passenger cars and light trucks (collectively, light vehicles) increased about 4.8 percent from 1991 to an estimated 12.9 million units in 1992. Imported light vehicles sales by foreign and U.S.-owned firms accounted for almost 21 percent of light vehicles sales in 1991 and about 18 percent in 1992. Total imports from Japan, including shipments sold by the Big Three, accounted for 16.4 percent of sales in 1991 and an estimated 14.3 percent in 1992.

Total car sales increased slightly in 1992. However, sales of light trucks jumped 13.7 percent. They now account for 36.4 percent of the combined market, compared with 33.6 percent in 1991. Light trucks, which are purchased primarily by consumers for non-commercial passenger use, include all pickups, vans, sport utility, and multipurpose vehicles under 14,000 pounds of gross vehicle weight.

The Big Three (plus AMC/Jeep, later acquired by Chrysler) sold 3.6 million light trucks in 1985, 89 percent of that segment of the market. Their sales fell to 3.4 million units in 1991, an 83 percent share, but increased to an estimated 4.1 million units in 1992, equivalent to 87 percent of the market. In both years, Japanese firms supplied virtually all of the balance.

Nameplate market shares for the 10 leading participants in the new car market, based on new car unit sales, are shown on page 124. Although their individual shares have shifted significantly, these 10 firms supplied 96 percent of the total market in 1985, and 95 percent in 1991. The Japanese nameplate share rose from 20 percent of all units in 1985 to 30 percent in 1991, while the Big Three share dropped from 74 percent to 64 percent. Germany, the second largest foreign-owned source of cars for the U.S. market after Japan, has lost a significant portion of its share over the past several years to U.S. and Japanese competitors. In 1991, German nameplates accounted for less than 3 percent of total unit sales.

During 1992, the competitiveness of the Japanese vehicle makers selling in the United States was adversely affected by their faltering home market, where total sales declined by 4.8 percent in Japan's 1991 fiscal year (April 1—March 31). This reduced operating income and forced engineering, management, and marketing resources to focus more intensely on the home market. The sales decline was the first since 1984. Sales fell an estimated 4.5 percent during JFY 1992. Total net income before taxes for Japan's auto industry was an estimated 431 billion yen in JFY 1992, a drop of 29 percent from JFY 1991 and 54 percent from JFY 1990. Capital costs, which had been as low as 1 percent in calendar year 1990, rose to 6–7 percent in 1992, just as some $6 billion in convertible bonds came due for renewal. According to the Japanese Economic Planning Agency, Japan's auto manufacturers subsequently lowered their JFY 1992 capital spending plans by 19 percent. Some are seeking to implement other cost-control measures, including lengthening their model replacement cycle and reducing parts proliferation, which has run rampant. Conflicting with their cost-control measures are government and worker pressures to reduce overtime and increase pay. The appreciation of the yen against the dollar, which has reduced profit margins, has also complicated the predicament of Japanese auto manufacturers.

In response to these developments, Japanese automakers began to raise prices on their U.S. offerings. This move also was probably in response to bills introduced in the U.S. Congress in 1992 that, if enacted, would have placed limits upon the sale of Japanese vehicles in the United States. According to U.S. industry estimates, there was an average 1992 price differential between comparable Big Three and Japanese nameplate cars of around $2,000 in favor of Detroit. The Japanese share of the U.S. car market dropped slightly to 29.9 percent in 1992, while their light truck share fell an estimated 4.2 percentage points to 12.8 percent. Their overall share of the light vehicle market declined about 2.2 percentage points to 23.6 percent. Daihatsu, the last Japanese firm to enter the U.S. market and also the first to leave it, terminated its sales program in 1992. Another small Japanese firm may also withdraw from direct marketing in the United States in the near future.

Buyers clearly have begun to recognize the improved quality, pricing, and fuel economy of Big Three vehicles in comparison with those from Japanese producers. According to J. D. Power and Associates' consumer ratings, the product quality of cars sold by U.S. automakers improved 23 percent between 1987 and 1991. Asian cars were perceived to have improved 15 percent, and European cars were 25 percent better.

While improving their product offerings and quality, the Big Three are also reducing overhead expenses and direct manufacturing costs. Nonetheless, they also are continuing to spend heavily for new and upgraded manufacturing facilities and technology. Their objective is not only to improve vehicle quality, but also to lower the break-even point on manufacturing operations. Few Big Three facilities can now make a profit on less than 100,000 units of a particular model. The market is fracturing into smaller niche segments, however, and ways must be found to be profitable at lower levels of production.

U.S.-Based Production

One of the most striking changes in the U.S. industry during the past several years has been the steadily increasing local production by Japanese-affiliated firms. Honda, Toyota, Nissan, Mazda, Mitsubishi, and Subaru-Isuzu established automobile plants in the United States during the 1980's. From zero in 1982, production by affiliates reached 1.3 million units in 1989, 12 percent of total domestic output. Their production in 1992 was an estimated 1.6 million units, 17 percent of total light vehicle output. About 200,000 units of their 1992 production were assembled with or for the Big Three. There are seven Japanese-affiliated assembly plants in the United States. Four are wholly owned, one is a joint venture involving two independent Japanese firms, and two are separate joint ventures with GM and Ford.

Japanese investment in the United States for car and light truck assembly, stamping, and foundry facilities was worth $6.4 billion in 1989, according to the Japan Automobile Manufacturers Association. They had an annual capacity of 1.6 million vehicles that year and employed 25,000 workers. The local production capacity of the Japanese affiliates may reach 2.4 million cars and light trucks per year by 1995 because of additional investments by Honda, Nissan, and Toyota. Suzuki (in a joint venture with GM), Honda, Toyota, and Hyundai (the South Korean manufacturer) also produce vehicles in Canada for the U.S. market.

According to Harbour and Associates, as reported by Automotive Industries, Japanese facilities in the United States and Canada in 1991 employed an average of 3.27 final assembly line production workers a day per car produced, compared with a combined average of 4.29 workers for the Big Three. All U.S. factories produced at only a 60–65 percent capacity utilization rate in 1991. Historically, auto assembly plants in the United States have not been profitable below an 85 percent level.

One significant factor that has been holding back the overall domestic market has been the growing price elasticity of auto demand (i.e., vehicles have become a more discretionary purchase). Consumers have stretched their replacement cycle, partially because new vehicles are more reliable and owning them longer represents less of a risk.

According to data compiled by the Motor Vehicle Manufacturers Association (MVMA) from R. L. Polk & Company, the average age of the passenger car fleet in the United States increased from 5.6 years in 1970 to 7.9 years in 1991. During the same period the number of cars that were 9 or more years old increased from 12.7 million units (15.8 percent of the car population) to 43.3 million units (35 percent). Most of these vehicles must now be at the edge of their economically useful life and are ready to be replaced.

The price of vehicles has risen to such an extent that many buyers have found it necessary to lengthen the period of their installment loans in order to reduce their monthly payments. According to the Federal Reserve Board, the average new car loan was 54.6 months in the second half of 1992, down slightly from the previous period. This is still significantly higher than the 50-month average in 1986, the last peak in automobile sales. The average monthly payment has nonetheless risen from $258 in 1986 to $308 in 1992.

The value of the average dealer-buyer transaction for the purchase of a new auto rose from $6,847 in 1979 to $16,695 in 1991. On the other hand, there has been a decrease in the average loan payment as a percentage of per capita disposable income, from 2.27 percent to 1.78 percent during the same period. Nonetheless, the number of weeks of median family earnings needed to equal the total transaction price has risen steadily since 1979. It now stands at 24.5 weeks, according to the MVMA. The association also reports that variable operating costs (gas, oil, tires, maintenance) have risen from 23.97 cents per mile in 1979 to 43.64 cents in 1991. The fixed costs of operating a car (insurance, license and registration fees, depreciation, and finance charges) have jumped from $4.96 to $11.55 per day. Variable operating and fixed costs will probably rise at faster rates in the future, helping to make alternative forms of transportation increasingly more attractive in the long term.

Leasing programs are growing rapidly as one method to reduce consumer resistance to increased loan periods and monthly payments. Leases accounted for only 3 percent of consumer transactions in 1982, but 14 percent in 1991. The expected continued growth of leasing in 1993 should help improve sales.

Part of the softness in new car sales in 1991 was caused when manufacturers decided to keep their factory output running at scheduled rates by selling an estimated 2 million new vehicles to their captive rental companies. This was accomplished by offering to buy the vehicles back after only three months of use. However, since they subsequently shipped those vehicles to their dealers for sale as "nearly new" units, sales of new vehicles by the dealers fell. The producers have now shifted strategies and are seeking other ways to solve their excess productive capacity problems.

INTERNATIONAL COMPETITIVENESS

The worldwide operations of the U.S.-owned motor vehicle manufacturers place them among the world's largest auto producers. In 1991, they ranked first, second, and twelfth overall in motor vehicle production, according to *Automotive News*. In 1991, General Motors produced 7 million vehicles worldwide (7.5 million in 1990), 14.4 percent of the 48.5 million units produced around the world. Ford manufactured 5.4 million units worldwide (5.9 million in 1990), for a world share of 11.1 percent in 1991. Chrysler's production of 1.5 million units (1.7 million in 1990), accounted for a 3.1 percent share of the 1991 world output. Toyota was the third largest producer in 1991 with worldwide output of 4.7 million units. VW was fourth with 3.2 million units, and Nissan was fifth at 3.1 million units.

The Big Three have notable investment positions in several large and small foreign vehicle manufacturers, although there is no direct investment in the Big Three by any foreign vehicle makers. Among its several holdings, GM owns 37.5 percent of the shares of Isuzu, 5.3 percent of Suzuki, 100 percent of Group Lotus (United Kingdom), 50 percent of Saab Automobile (Sweden), and 50 percent of Daewoo Motors (South Korea). Investment in the latter is to be withdrawn in 1994. Ford owns 25 percent of Mazda, 10 percent of Kia Motors (South Korea), 100 percent of Jaguar (United Kingdom), and 75 percent of Aston Martin (United Kingdom). Chrysler owns 100 percent of Lamborghini and 15.6 percent of Maserati (both Italian). Chrysler reduced its investment in Mitsubishi Motors from 24 percent to 5.9 percent in 1992. Wall Street analysts speculate that Chrysler will sell its remaining Mitsubishi shares in 1993.

GM and Ford operate highly successful manufacturing subsidiaries in Germany and the United Kingdom. The two companies are thought to be evaluating manufacturing opportunities in Eastern Europe and in the countries of the former Soviet Union. Chrysler sold its European subsidiaries in the late 1970's, but in March 1990 initiated a joint venture in Austria that began producing minivans for the European markets in 1992. All three producers have substantial manufacturing and marketing subsidiary operations in both Canada and Mexico.

Trade

"General imports" of new automobiles during 1991 declined 5 percent to 3.7 million units, reflecting a greater emphasis on U.S. sourcing by Japanese firms, and the overall softness of the domestic market. (These figures exclude production in free trade zones; see table on page 123 for trade data on all motor vehicles, including used.) The customs value of U.S. new auto imports fell 0.4 percent to $45.6 billion. The volume of cars exported from the United States jumped nearly 7 percent to 835,000 units, while their f.a.s. value rose by 15 percent to $11 billion.

Consequently, the overall new automobile trade deficit dropped 4.4 percent to $34.6 billion in 1991. Bilateral deficits decreased with Belgium, Brazil, Canada, Germany, Italy, South Korea, Sweden, and the United Kingdom, while increasing with Australia, Mexico, and Japan. In the first half of 1992, the overall negative balance in the U.S. auto trade fell to $16.2 billion, an improvement of 0.5 percent over the same period in 1990. The value of exports increased 12 percent to $6.4 billion, while imports rose 3 percent to $22.6 billion.

The bilateral automobile trade deficit with Japan increased 6 percent to $20.1 billion in 1991. The value of Japanese imports grew slightly to $20.6 billion, although unit imports dropped 4 percent to 1.8 million units. U.S. exports to Japan declined 21.4 percent to $553 million in 1991 because of the slowdown in the Japanese economy. Shipments fell 8,000 units to reach 30,000 units. In the first six months of 1992, the value of imports from Japan held steady at $9.8 billion compared with the same 1991 period, and units declined 7 percent to 796,000. Exports to Japan dropped 1 percent to $319 million, while shipments remained unchanged at 18,000 units.

U.S. vehicle exports to Japan have been increasing for the past several years, aided by a number of factors that have made them a better value in Japan. These factors include the lower value of the dollar in relation to the Japanese yen, reduced Japanese taxes, improved U.S. product quality, a better mix of U.S. products appropriate for the market, increased marketing efforts by the Big Three, and "repatriated" production (exports to Japan) by Japanese-affiliated factories in the United States. Official bilateral consultations between the U.S. and Japanese Governments have resulted in relaxations in Japan's import regulations and in Japan's technical standards certification process. Additional consultations are scheduled.

Registration of Big Three U.S.-made vehicles in Japan rose steadily between 1987 and 1990 to 16,000 units. They fell to 13,700 vehicles in 1991, a decrease of 14 percent from 1990, but an increase of 340 percent over 1987. (Total Japanese registrations fell 4.6 percent in 1991, while registrations of all imports were off 11 percent.) Japan also registered 16,000 U.S.-made Japanese nameplate vehicles during 1991, an increase of 127 percent over 1990. In the first six months of 1992, registrations of U.S. Big Three vehicles totaled 7,000 units, equal to the same period in 1991. Registration of U.S.-made Japanese vehicles totaled 7,400 vehicles, off 9 percent. (Total Japanese registrations were off 6 percent during January–June 1992, while registrations of all imports fell 13 percent.)

The realignment of the dollar against the major currencies in Europe that began in 1985 continues to have a marked impact upon the sales of European car companies in the U.S. market. Most European producers chose to increase their U.S. retail prices, attempting to rely upon profit margins rather than volume to maintain their viability. With a doubling of the "gas guzzler tax" and the imposition of a Federal automobile luxury tax (10 percent of the balance above a $30,000 transaction price) in 1991, European sales became especially susceptible to the greatly increased value represented by the several new Japanese luxury models on the market. The rapidly acquired, excellent reputation now enjoyed by the Japanese luxury cars was not anticipated by most of the European makers. Caught off guard, they have found it difficult to recover. Some have already decided to shift their focus elsewhere. Sterling and Peugeot withdrew from the market in 1991 to concentrate on Europe. Big Three divisions that depend on the large/luxury segment of the market also have been affected by Japanese luxury vehicles, but not to the extent experienced by the Europeans.

LONG-TERM PROSPECTS

About 35 percent of the passenger car fleet is 9 years old or more. They are prime candidates for massive replacement, but not necessarily by new cars over the next several years. Since the early 1970's, the long-term sales trend of new cars in the U.S. market has been slightly negative. However, unit sales of light trucks have been growing so rapidly that the overall light vehicle market has a long-term growth rate of about 0.9 percent annually. This situation should persist for several more years, although annual sales will continue to oscillate on either side of the trend line.

Fewer citizens will reach driving age in the next 10 years than in the past decade. The negative implication of this development could be offset somewhat, however, by the baby boom's entry into what has typically been their peak earning years, permitting them to own more expensive cars and more of them. (MVMA reports that in 1988, 52 percent of all households with annual income between $35,000 and $49,999 owned 2 cars, and 27 percent owned 3 or more. Of those with incomes of $50,000 or more, 48 percent owned 2 cars, while 34 percent of them owned 3 or more.)

Another factor affecting the industry's long-term growth is the response of Federal and local governments to increasingly congested urban streets and overburdened, deteriorating interstate highways. If their response is inadequate, or if a preference evolves for giving greater support to mass transit, future vehicle sales could be adversely affected. As part of its initial effort to address the issue of existing road infrastructure, Congress has appropriated $660 million for R&D of "intelligent vehicle highway systems" during FY 1992–97 that could greatly reduce traffic congestion and accidents in several critical regional transportation corridors. The appropriation is part of a larger funding to revive and improve the surface transportation network under the Intermodal Surface Transportation Efficiency Act of 1991.

The domestic light vehicle market will continue to become more competitive, with more producers offering new and revised models on ever-shortening time cycles. Market demand will splinter into smaller segments, aided by the success of the major manufacturers in adopting and refining the high degree of flexibility inherent in the lean manufacturing techniques that were pioneered by Japanese firms. Manufacturers are exploiting their new capabilities by aggressively moving to create and fill new market niches with models constructed specifically for them. This strategy places a heavier burden on product planners, market researchers, design and production engineers, and styling studios to generate new concepts and to compress their development cycles. Although there are risks to such an approach, the risks of not responding may be even greater. Manufacturers must also continue to improve their cost-control procedures so that they can extract profits from relatively small annual production volumes.

The battle for market share may exert downward pressure on prices in the future. However, even more stringent safety, environmental, and fuel economy regulations are likely to increase manufacturer costs and prices. Producers will thus have additional impetus to maximize manufacturing productivity and to keep costs under control. Consequently, labor relations will become increasingly important to the industry. This is especially true since vehicle assembly operations are becoming more vulnerable to total disruption by local strikes. The low parts inventory procedures being implemented as part of the lean manufacturing technique allow for no cushion even for the temporary disruption of supplies. (For example, GM lost the scheduled production of 45,000 vehicles in 1992 because of a strike at one of its own parts plants that lasted only 9 days. GM's Saturn subsidiary, which was built to implement lean manufacturing concepts, was forced to terminate manufacturing operations on the day after the strike began.)

Manufacturers from Eastern Europe and the Far East have expressed interest in entering the U.S. market in the next several years, perceiving it as the world's most lucrative, while apparently ignoring that it is also the world's most competitive. These new entrants may succeed because a certain niche exists in the United States for something new from someplace else. They may also find (as South Korean and Yugoslavian manufacturers did when they entered the U.S. market with subcompacts in the late 1980's) that sales will drop as rapidly as they grew, if the vehicles do not maintain a price advantage or have a unique personality.

The next several years probably will bring more cross-border mergers, takeovers, and cooperative production and marketing arrangements between firms in the United States, Europe, and Asia. The result will be fewer but more equally matched global contestants. Japanese investments will expand in the United States, Europe, and Asia, while U.S. facilities will operate primarily in North America and Europe. Limited Asian production by at least one of the Big Three is a long-term possibility. In general, European auto manufacturers will remain focused on that region. However, BMW announced in 1992 that it will invest $300 million to establish its first foreign plant in South Carolina. It will produce up to 75,000 units per year of a new model that will supply its worldwide markets. Production is scheduled to begin in 1995. Volkswagen and Mercedes-Benz are thought to be considering adding capacity in either the United States or Mexico to bolster their existing facilities in Mexico.

The Big Three will continue to ship limited quantities of their U.S.-made cars to Europe to fill niche markets. The continuing program by the 12 European Community (EC) countries to remove their remaining internal trade and investment barriers will play only a modest role in directly increasing U.S. exports by the Big Three, since they are already effective cross-country players in those markets. Honda has begun to export from the United States to the EC, and Nissan, Toyota, and Mitsubishi have expressed interest in exporting U.S.-built units to Europe. The recently concluded understanding between the EC and Japan regarding Japanese participation in EC markets between 1992 and 1999 does not apply to their production in the United States.

The Big Three are now gearing up to increase their U.S. exports to Mexico and to reinforce their local operations there. They currently have a 55 percent share of the Mexican market. The recently concluded negotiations between the United States, Mexico, and Canada to create a North American Free Trade Agreement (NAFTA) must now be approved and implemented by the three governments. When that is accomplished, U.S. producers will benefit from greatly improved access to the Mexican market, where growth in new car consumption is expanding rapidly. New car sales in Mexico were an estimated 430,000 units in 1992, up 10 percent over 1991. Some industry analysts predict sales of up to 1.5 million units annually by the year 2000. Mexico now has 85 million citizens, but a registered automobile population of fewer than 6.5 million cars.

The Big Three have had no outside competitors in the full-size segment of the light truck market until Toyota's announcement in 1992 that it will offer a "nearly" full-size pickup in 1993. Toyota will first manufacture this vehicle in Japan and is expected to shift production to the United States in 1994–95 if sales warrant. If the Japanese brands are successful in their efforts to gain a significant share of the full-size segment of the light truck market, the Big Three could suffer tangible financial losses. They derive a significant portion of their North American operating income from sales of light trucks. These vehicles typically cost less to engineer and build, and enjoy longer replacement cycles than automobiles. Ford's Econoline van, for example, was marketed successfully between 1975 and 1991 without any major styling or equipment changes.

U.S. imports from Asia will continue to decrease in units, displaced by increased production in North America by manufacturers from Japan and South Korea. The Big Three may also shift sourcing of some vehicles from their Asian suppliers to their own operations in Mexico. On the other hand, U.S. exports to Asia should increase. *Euromotor* predicts that the Asian markets will require 12 million units annually by 2010, a 200 percent increase from 1990. The Big Three, as well as Honda, Toyota, and Mitsubishi, are now shipping certain models to Japan from their plants in the United States. GM, Ford, Toyota, and Nissan export to Taiwan from the United States. The Big Three are also engaged in efforts to expand their efforts in other Far Eastern markets that are emerging. Most notable, perhaps, is Chrysler's joint venture in China, where the company owns 31 percent of Beijing Jeep.—*Randall Miller and Heather West (Financial Performance section), Office of Automotive Affairs, (202) 482-0669.*

Financial Information: General Motors, Ford, and Chrysler, 1980–91

(in billions of dollars except as noted)

Item	1980	1989	1990	1991
Profitability				
Net sales and revenue	103.4	226.6	219.9	208.2
Gross profit	8.0	34.5	26.6	19.7
Operating profit	−4.9	8.8	−3.2	−11.2
Net income	−4.0	8.4	−1.1	−7.5
Gross profit margin[1] (%)	7.7	15.2	12.1	9.5
Operating profit margin[2] (%)	−4.7	3.9	−1.5	−5.4
Return on sales[3] (%)	−3.8	3.7	−0.5	−3.6
Return on equity[4] (%)	−1.4	12.9	−1.7	−12.9
Liquidity				
Cash and marketable securities	6.6	14.9	13.6	16.4
Working capital[5]	3.5	16.5	8.8	7.9
Change in working capital	—	−2.7	−7.6	−0.9
Current ratio[6] (%)	1.1	1.3	1.2	1.1
Quick ratio[7] (%)	0.5	0.8	0.6	0.6
Total debt-to-equity ratio (%)	2.3	0.2	0.3	0.4

[1]Gross profit divided by total net sales and revenue.

[2]Operating profit divided by total net sales and revenue.

[3]Profit after taxes divided by net sales and multiplied by 100.

[4]Profit after taxes divided by equity and multiplied by 100. This ratio expresses the rate of return on stockholders equity.

[5]Current assets minus current liabilities.

[6]Total current assets divided by total current liabilities. This ratio is a rough indication of a firm's ability to service its current obligations.

[7]Cash and cash equivalents plus accounts and notes receivable (trade) divided by total current liabilities. This is a refinement of the current ratio and is a more conservative measure of liquidity.

SOURCE: General Motors, Ford, and Chrysler annual reports.

Trends and Forecasts: Motor Vehicles and Car Bodies (SIC 3711)

(in millions of dollars except as noted)

Item	1987	1988	1989	1990	1991[1]	1992[2]	1993[3]	Percent Change (1987–1993) 87–88	88–89	89–90	90–91	91–92	92–93
Industry Data													
Value of shipments[4]	133,346	142,060	149,315	140,417	128,500	139,800	150,000	6.5	5.1	−6.0	−8.5	8.8	7.3
Value of shipments (1987$)	133,346	140,237	143,572	132,594	118,700	128,800	137,500	5.2	2.4	−7.6	−10.5	8.5	6.8
Total employment (000)	281	250	250	240	228	249	236	−11.0	0.0	−4.0	−5.0	9.2	−3.6
Production workers (000)	236	214	213	200	193	215	205	−9.3	−0.5	−6.1	−3.5	11.4	−4.7
Average hourly earnings ($)	17.33	18.68	19.40	20.31	21.26	22.25	23.30	7.8	3.9	4.7	4.7	5.8	3.6
Capital expenditures	4,121	1,137	2,374	3,004	—	—	—	−72.4	108.8	26.5	—	—	—
Product Data													
Value of shipments[5]	130,857	139,864	144,448	135,741	124,200	135,200	145,000	6.9	3.3	−6.0	−8.5	8.9	7.2
Value of shipments (1987$)	130,857	138,069	138,892	128,178	114,800	124,600	133,000	5.5	0.6	−7.7	−10.4	8.5	6.7
Trade Data													
Value of imports	—	—	58,729	59,790	58,381	61,087	62,770	—	—	1.8	−2.4	4.6	2.8
Value of exports	—	—	12,479	12,838	15,180	16,991	18,190	—	—	2.9	18.2	11.9	7.1

[1]Estimated, except exports and imports.
[2]Estimate.
[3]Forecast.
[4]Value of all products and services sold by establishments in the motor vehicles and car bodies industry; includes trucks of all classes.
[5]Value of products classified in the motor vehicles and car bodies industry produced by all industries.

SOURCE: U.S. Department of Commerce: Bureau of the Census, International Trade Administration (ITA). Estimates and forecasts by ITA.

U.S. Motor Vehicle Trade, 1990–93

(in billions of dollars)

Region	1990 Exports	1990 Imports	1990 Balance	1991 Exports	1991 Imports	1991 Balance	1992[1] Exports	1992[1] Imports	1992[1] Balance	1993[2] Exports	1993[2] Imports	1993[2] Balance
World	13.8	54.9	−41.1	16.9	54.6	−37.7	18.4	54.5	−36.1	19.7	56.0	−36.3
Canada	8.1	20.3	−12.2	9.1	20.6	−11.5	8.1	22.5	−14.4	8.3	23.6	−15.3
Germany	0.7	5.9	-5.2	1.0	4.8	−3.8	1.1	4.5	−3.4	1.2	4.2	-3.0
Japan	1.0	21.5	−20.5	.8	22.6	−21.8	0.8	20.8	−20.0	1.0	22.9	−21.9
Mexico	.3	2.4	−2.1	.3	2.8	−2.5	0.4	3.5	−3.1	0.5	4.2	−3.7

[1]Estimate.
[2]Forecast.

NOTE: Includes cars, trucks, buses, used vehicles and other four-or-more wheeled motor vehicles; all intended primarily for on-road transport of non-military passengers and goods. Import data in this table and in the text are based on "general imports", which exclude motor vehicles produced in U.S. foreign trade zones. This is a better measure of accounting for the motor vehicle industry than "imports for consumption", which overstates the number of completed motor vehicles actually imported from abroad while understating their value. This latter measurement, available from the Bureau of the Census, is the basis for the import data in the Trends and Forecasts tables.

SOURCE: U.S. Department of Commerce, Bureau of the Census. Estimates and forecast by U.S. Department of Commerce, International Trade Administration.

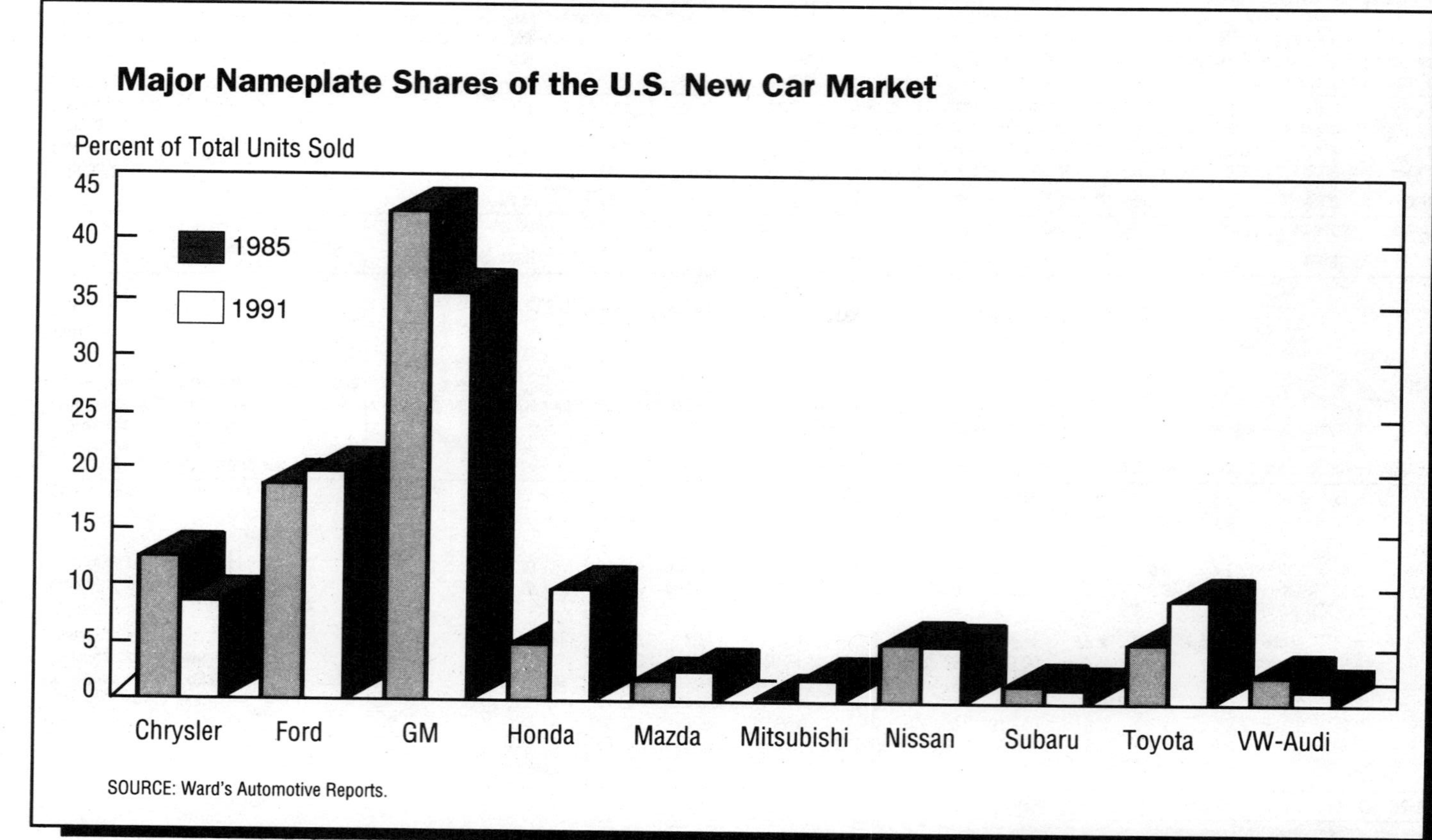
Major Nameplate Shares of the U.S. New Car Market
Percent of Total Units Sold
45
40
35
30
25
20
15
10
5
0
1985
1991
Chrysler
Ford
GM
Honda
Mazda
Mitsubishi
Nissan
Subaru
Toyota
VW-Audi
SOURCE: Ward's Automotive Reports.

U.S. New Light Vehicle Sales by Country of Manufacture, 1991–97

(thousands of units)

Item	1991[1]	1992[2]	1993[3]	1994[3]	1995[3]	1996[3]	1997[3]
Automobiles							
Total	8,175	8,200	8,900	9,400	9,700	9,900	10,000
All local	6,137	6,300	6,755	7,220	7,625	7,800	7,960
Imports	2,038	1,900	2,145	2,180	2,075	2,100	2,040
Japan	1,500	1,450	1,650	1,650	1,550	1,550	1,500
Germany	221	230	210	220	215	210	200
Other	317	220	285	310	310	340	340
Light Trucks							
Total	4,135	4,700	4,970	5,200	5,400	5,600	5,700
All local	3,606	4,300	4,550	4,760	5,000	5,240	5,400
Imports	529	400	420	440	400	360	300
Japan	521	395	417	437	397	357	297
Other	8	5	3	3	3	3	3
Light Vehicles[4]							
Total	12,310	12,900	13,870	14,600	15,100	15,500	15,700
All local	9,743	10,600	11,305	11,980	12,625	13,040	13,360
Imports	2,567	2,300	2,565	2,620	2,475	2,460	2,340
Japan	2,021	1,845	2,067	2,087	1,947	1,907	1,797
Germany (cars)	221	230	210	220	215	210	200
Other	325	225	288	313	313	343	343

[1]Actual.
[2]Estimate.
[3]Forecast.
[4]Automobiles plus light trucks.

NOTE: "Local" includes sales of all vehicles made in the United States and Canada for the U.S. market, plus U.S. sales of Big Three units produced in Mexico.

SOURCE: 1991 data from *Ward's Automotive Reports*. Estimates and forecasts by U.S. Department of Commerce, International Trade Administration.

Plastic Materials and Rubber

Plastic Materials

The plastic materials industry (SIC 282) covers highly moldable materials used singly or in combination, to make a wide variety of plastic products. Plastic materials are usually classified along two criteria: quantity (commodity versus specialty) and structural use (thermoplastic versus thermoset). Most plastics can be grouped accordingly.

Commodity plastics, also termed tonnage plastics, are manufactured according to standard processes, and in large quantities. They are usually sold to a restricted number of large-volume users.

Whether a material is classified as thermoplastic or thermoset depends upon its final processing. Thermoplastics account for at least 80 percent of total U.S. production. In contrast to thermosets, thermoplastics can be repeatedly softened or hardened by heat, even after they have been molded. Frequently used and relatively unspecialized, commodity thermoplastic resins include the polyethylenes (low density, linear low density, high density), polypropylenes, polystyrenes, and polyvinyl chloride. Specialty resins are generally produced on a customized basis, developed to meet specific end-use requirements.

Among the first plastics to have been developed, the thermosets now account for less than one-fifth of total output. Thermosets are characterized by their superior electrical properties and ability to withstand extreme chemical and temperature environments.

In recent years, engineering and specialty thermoplastics emerged as high-growth products, used in situations where high resistance to heat and mechanical stress are important. Typical engineering resins are the cellulosics, the polycarbonates and the polyetheretherketones.

The basic manufacturing sequence is summarized as follows: three primary inputs (petroleum, natural gas and coal) are subjected to various processes (refining, distilling, fractionating). This results in what are normally referred to as petrochemical feedstocks, including gases, light oils, middle fractions, and heavy oils. These basic materials or base stocks are then mixed with other substances (ammonia, formaldehyde)—or are chemically decomposed even further to yield intermediates. The latter can then be catalyzed into monomers and finally to polymers, or resins. Downstream processing into final plastic products is discussed below.

Increased productivity and more efficient processing equipment, resulting from large investment in R&D, allowed U.S. suppliers to become extremely competitive in domestic markets. Industry concentration throughout the 1980's has remained relatively low in comparison with other capital-intensive industries; 8 companies in 1987 controlled 40 percent of output, and the largest 20 about 66 percent. Increased competition has put considerable pressure on prices and made it feasible for plastics to penetrate other material markets (such as wood, glass, and metal). High-performance characteristics, coupled with highly price sensitive demand for most plastic materials, continues to drive material substitution—a fact influencing industry prospects.

INTERNATIONAL COMPETITIVENESS

The United States is still by far the world's largest producer of plastic materials, with nearly 36 percent of total estimated world production, followed by Japan (with 16 percent) and Germany (with 9 percent). Not surprisingly, the United States has been a major exporter in recent years; sales to overseas markets constitute approximately 20 percent of total industry shipments. Exports for SIC 2821 more than doubled throughout the 1980's, from $2.7 billion (4,194 million pounds) in 1980 to $6.3 billion (6,500 million pounds) in 1990. Imports went from $263 million (247 million pounds) to $1.8 billion (2,100 million pounds) during the decade. The bulk of exports were largely tonnage resins (the propylenes, polyvinyl chloride, polyethylene perephthalate and polystyrene). Canada and Japan have maintained their position as major trading partners. Imports represent less than 10 percent of total industry shipments. Recent increases in imports are partly explained by the influx of ethylene-based polymers from Canada and Saudi Arabia. Polyvinyl chloride, acrylonitrile-butadiene-styrene (widely known within the industry as ABS), and specialty polystyrenes were also imported in significant amounts, mostly from Japan, Germany, and the United Kingdom.

LONG-TERM PROSPECTS

An ongoing trend toward highly differentiated resins for very specific uses will continue in the long-term. This trend is largely driven by new assembly and molding techniques coming on line in the automotive and electronics industries. There are signs that conventional thermoplastics used in furniture, automotive, garden products and fluid delivery systems will continue to be replaced by thermoplastic-elastomers, or TPEs. Demand for engineering resins, although still significant, may weaken as even lower-cost alternatives such as thermoplastic olefin elastomers (TPOs) gain acceptance.

Rubber Materials

This SIC, 2822, joins together highly-elastic materials derived from petroleum feedstock, and also materials used to make a wide variety of highly-resistant products. Often referred to as elastomers, synthetic rubber (SR) is normally used by itself or compounded with natural rubber, other thermoplastic materials, and additives. Typical end uses are electrical and thermal insulation; shock, friction, noise and abrasion control; waterproofing and sealing; and load bearing.

Most elastomers fall into two distinct groups: commodity or general purpose, and specialty elastomers. Typical general purpose elastomers include styrene-butadiene latex, polychloropropylene, nitrile, ethylene-propylene diene monomer (or EPDM), carboxylated styrene, butadiene, and polybutadiene. Commodity SR, which accounts for the bulk of SR production, is widely used in the manufacture of tires and fabricated rubber products. Fast-growing, but still minor compared with commodity SR, specialty elastomers—including the thermoplastic elastomers and olefins (TPEs and TPOs)—tend to be used where resistance to extreme temperature and chemical and mechanical stress is required. The value of industry shipments is rising modestly after a stagnant period during 1991–92. Research-intensive TPEs, however, tend to be used where resistance to extreme temperature, chemical and mechanical stress is required.

The early 1980's saw a gradual maturing of the SR industry, and a stagnant end-user market. About one-half of total general-purpose SR is consumed by tire manufacturing. Greater durability, decreasing rates of tire replacement, and a nearly complete change-over to radial design acted to depress demand for SR. Historically a low-margin business, profitability has been dropping. Capacity utilization is now running at 75 percent, compared to 85 percent four years ago. Foreign participation has increased; about half of total SR production is now under foreign ownership.

In contrast to the sagging bulk SR market, smaller-volume high value-added elastomers are expanding into non-auto related sectors. For this reason, they experience growth rates significantly higher than the industry average. For example, TPOs reach growth rates as high as 10 percent annually.

INTERNATIONAL COMPETITIVENESS

Overall, global demand for general purpose SR has remained steady. While some growth is evident in Asia, expectations with respect to Eastern Europe have not been met. Lack of demand in Eastern Europe is generally attributed to problems with quality control, and to obsolete technology.

Foreign trade volumes—as a share of total industry shipments—have remained constant in recent years. Recent trends in foreign exchange rates have benefited U.S. exports. Exports have been running at a ratio of 2:1 over imports. Major export markets for the United States are: Canada, Belgium, Mexico and Japan. Canada's share is about one-third of the total; other major importers include Japan and France.

LONG-TERM PROSPECTS

Future growth in SR depends heavily on technological innovation and speedy commercialization. As more cost-effective elastomer-thermoplastic compounds are developed, commodity SR and other material markets will decline. Material substitution is growing—especially in automotive industries—at the expense of traditional materials. Environmental concerns will also gain prominence as firms are pressured into switching to less toxic chemical processes.

Trends and Forecasts: Plastics Materials and Resins (SIC 2821)

(in millions of dollars except as noted)

Item	1987	1988	1989	1990	1991[1]	1992[2]	1993[3]	Percent Change (1987–1993) 87–88	88–89	89–90	90–91	91–92	92–93
Industry Data													
Value of shipments[4]	26,246	32,110	33,257	31,326	—	—	—	22.3	3.6	−5.8	—	—	—
Value of shipments (1987$)	26,246	26,893	27,622	27,870	27,890	27,900	28,737	2.5	2.7	0.9	0.1	0.0	3.0
Total employment (000)	56.3	58.3	62.0	62.4	62.0	61.4	61.5	3.6	6.3	0.6	−0.6	−1.0	0.2
Production workers (000)	34.9	36.0	37.8	37.9	37.8	37.3	37.4	3.2	5.0	0.3	−0.3	−1.3	0.3
Average hourly earnings ($)	15.24	15.37	15.92	16.88	17.30	17.50	—	0.9	3.6	6.0	2.5	1.2	—
Capital expenditures	1,247	1,606	1,966	2,437	—	—	—	28.8	22.4	24.0	—	—	—
Product Data													
Value of shipments[5]	27,812	34,235	34,692	33,038	—	—	—	23.1	1.3	−4.8	—	—	—
Value of shipments (1987$)	27,812	28,673	28,814	29,393	29,006	29,016	29,886	3.1	0.5	2.0	−1.3	0.0	3.0
Trade Data													
Value of imports	—	—	1,551	1,808	1,772	1,940	1,979	—	—	16.6	−2.0	9.5	2.0
Value of exports	—	—	5,561	6,277	7,398	6,785	6,988	—	—	12.9	17.9	−8.3	3.0

[1]Estimated, except exports and imports.
[2]Estimate.
[3]Forecast.
[4]Value of all products and services sold by establishments in the plastics materials and resins industry.
[5]Value of products classified in the plastics materials and resins industry produced by all industries.

SOURCE: U.S. Department of Commerce: Bureau of the Census, International Trade Administration (ITA). Estimates and forecasts by ITA.

Trends and Forecasts: Synthetic Rubber (SIC 2822)

(in millions of dollars except as noted)

Item	1987	1988	1989	1990	1991[1]	1992[2]	1993[3]	Percent Change (1987–1993) 87–88	88–89	89–90	90–91	91–92	92–93
Industry Data													
Value of shipments[4]	3,283	3,996	4,008	4,210	—	—	—	21.7	0.3	5.0	—	—	—
Value of shipments (1987$)	3,283	3,609	3,630	3,696	3,732	3,750	3,900	9.9	0.6	1.8	1.0	0.5	4.0
Total employment (000)	10.4	11.3	11.2	11.4	11.4	11.3	11.5	8.7	−0.9	1.8	0.0	−0.9	1.8
Production workers (000)	6.7	7.1	7.1	7.2	7.2	7.1	7.3	6.0	0.0	1.4	0.0	−1.4	2.8
Average hourly earnings ($)	15.88	16.36	16.78	17.91	18.60	18.99	—	3.0	2.6	6.7	3.9	2.1	—
Capital expenditures	171	216	266	379	—	—	—	26.3	23.1	42.5	—	—	—
Product Data													
Value of shipments[5]	3,467	3,916	4,070	4,219	—	—	—	13.0	3.9	3.7	—	—	—
Value of shipments (1987$)	3,467	3,537	3,686	3,704	3,769	3,788	3,978	2.0	4.2	0.5	1.8	0.5	5.0
Trade Data													
Value of imports	—	—	527	537	491	532	560	—	—	1.9	−8.6	8.4	5.3
Value of exports	—	—	885	898	917	966	1,005	—	—	1.5	2.1	5.3	4.0

[1]Estimated, except exports and imports.
[2]Estimate.
[3]Forecast.
[4]Value of all products and services sold by establishments in the synthetic rubber industry.
[5]Value of products classified in the synthetic rubber industry produced by all industries.

SOURCE: U.S. Department of Commerce: Bureau of the Census, International Trade Administration (ITA). Estimates and forecasts by ITA.

Trends and Forecasts: Tires and Inner Tubes (SIC 3011)

(in millions of dollars except as noted)

Item	1987	1988	1989	1990	1991[1]	1992[2]	1993[3]	Percent Change (1987–1993) 87–88	88–89	89–90	90–91	91–92	92–93
Industry Data													
Value of shipments[4]	10,427	11,240	11,680	11,861	—	—	—	7.8	3.9	1.5	—	—	—
Value of shipments (1987$)	10,427	10,850	10,947	11,168	11,150	11,142	11,588	4.1	0.9	2.0	−0.2	−0.1	4.0
Total employment (000)	65.4	67.8	68.0	67.7	67.5	67.4	67.6	3.7	0.3	−0.4	−0.3	−0.1	0.3
Production workers (000)	52.6	54.6	54.6	54.7	54.3	54.3	54.4	3.8	0.0	0.2	−0.7	0.0	0.2
Average hourly earnings ($)	15.39	15.52	16.57	16.84	17.85	18.74	—	0.8	6.8	1.6	6.0	5.0	—
Capital expenditures	337	418	785	652	—	—	—	24.0	87.8	−16.9	—	—	—
Product Data													
Value of shipments[5]	10,033	10,841	11,256	11,367	—	—	—	8.1	3.8	1.0	—	—	—
Value of shipments (1987$)	10,033	10,464	10,549	10,704	10,772	10,765	11,196	4.3	0.8	1.5	0.6	−0.1	4.0
Trade Data													
Value of imports	—	—	2,667	2,553	2,271	2,294	2,316	—	—	−4.3	−11.0	1.0	1.0
Value of exports	—	—	854	1,140	1,262	1,386	1,485	—	—	33.5	10.7	9.8	7.1

[1]Estimated, except exports and imports.
[2]Estimate.
[3]Forecast.
[4]Value of all products and services sold by establishments in the tires and inner tubes industry.
[5]Value of products classified in the tires and inner tubes industry produced by all industries.
SOURCE: U.S. Department of Commerce: Bureau of the Census, International Trade Administration (ITA). Estimates and forecasts by ITA.

Printing and Publishing

With establishments in virtually every town and county, products of the U.S. printing and publishing industry serve the country's diverse communication needs. The range of printed materials extends from books to banners, leaflets to ledgers, and pamphlets to playing cards. The industry's 60,000 firms employ 1.5 million persons, the third largest employment roll among the 20 major U.S. manufacturing industry groups.

Shipments of U.S. printed products experienced sluggish growth during the early 1990's, primarily in response to a slowdown in advertising expenditures brought on by the lackluster U.S. economy. Declines in tax revenues cut school and library budgets for textbooks and other educational materials. Fewer new business start-ups cut into demand for newsletters, business service publications, albums and blankbooks, and manifold business forms. As consumers retreated from the marketplace, advertisers scaled back expenditures in newspapers and magazines.

However, both U.S. printers and publishers anticipate a return to prosperity in the mid-1990's, their enthusiasm fueled by a set of favorable demographic factors. By 1997, the population of the United States is expected to increase by 9 million, about 6.4 million new households will be formed, and school enrollments will grow by 4.5 million. Other beneficial trends include growth in the percentage of high school graduates entering colleges, and subsequent growth in the percentage of college graduates in the civilian labor force. In addition to the above factors, printers and publishers note that a recovering U.S. economy, accompanied by gains in disposable personal income, should drive up expenditures for advertising. Ad spending annually supports about two-thirds of total U.S. shipments of printed products.

The tightening of regulations governing the environment will add to printers' and publishers' costs through the balance of the decade. The industry has made considerable progress in developing and applying water-based inks, alcohol-free fountain solutions, and solventless developers and finishers. These chemicals are formulated to remove carcinogens, volatile organic compounds (VOCs), and toxins from the manufacturing process. Continued growth in the percentage of recycled paper used in printed products—particularly newspapers—is an industry priority. An industry concern is potential growth of litigation regarding disposal of waste materials, especially materials disposed of years ago that are only recently classified as hazardous.

Exports generally account for just 2 percent of total U.S. printed product output, a value well below that of most industrialized countries. Although international trade remains a concept alien to many U.S. printers and publishers, in fact 1992 exports of $3.9 billion place the United States second only to Germany in cross-border trade. Books and magazines represent 60 percent of U.S. export volume, but over $1 billion in other printed products—such as decals, labels, calendars, catalogs, posters, and other products—find niche markets overseas. Among the 173 countries purchasing U.S. printed products, Canada, the United Kingdom, Australia, Japan, and Mexico traditionally account for about 75 percent of total U.S. exports.

Imports of printed products totaled $2.2 billion in 1992, representing slightly more than 1 percent of U.S. apparent consumption. Aggregate foreign shipments of books and periodicals account for 50 percent of U.S. import purchases. Printed products from Canada and the United Kingdom represent one-third of total U.S. imports and are purchased primarily for the products' contents. U.S. purchases from Japan and East Asia's newly industrialized countries also account for one-third of the import total, but are desired primarily for reasons of low-cost printing.

Data on U.S. exports and imports are but partial indicators of the extent to which the U.S. printing and publishing industry is tied to the global communications community. Large foreign graphic arts firms have a long history of direct investment and participation in U.S. printed product markets. In recent years, a lethargic domestic economy has led U.S. printers and publishers to expand their foreign sales and acquisition efforts. By the close of this decade, U.S. investments in foreign printing and publishing markets should easily double.—*William S. Lofquist, Office of Consumer Goods, (202) 482-0379.*

Newspapers

For a fifth consecutive year, newspaper industry receipts in 1992 in constant dollars recorded a decline, but at a slower rate than in the previous two years. Newspaper industry (SIC 2711) receipts were down an estimated 3.7 percent in constant dollars in 1992. They totaled an estimated $34.2 billion in current dollars.

While ad pages were down less than in the previous year, newspapers' share of total media advertising expenditures continued to shrink. The slight improvement in advertising receipts in current dollars was due largely to a gain in classified advertising. Circulation revenues were up in 1992, mainly due to increases in both subscription and newsstand prices, although total newspaper circulation remained flat in 1992. The plight of many newspapers was related to lingering uncertainty on the part of both consumers and businesses about the health of the overall economy and continuing economic hardship in many local communities. Aggressive competition from other media for shrinking advertising dollars hurt newspaper publishers' ability to attract advertisers to their papers.

With advertising revenues and circulation at suppressed levels, many newspaper publishers concentrated on cost-cutting measures to improve their profits. Lower-than-expected newsprint prices and labor costs also helped to produce a more favorable profit picture.

Other major industry concerns in 1992 were related to the environment and expected competition from the telecommunications sector. These concerns centered on proposed legislation that would mandate the content of recycled newsprint in newspapers, and other proposals that would reimpose entry restrictions for the Bell companies into the information services market.

Weak Turnaround for Advertising Revenues

Much uncertainty remained concerning the health of newspaper advertising revenues in 1992. With newspaper advertising revenues down slightly in 1990 and reaching a record level loss of nearly 6 percent in current dollars in 1991, newspaper companies were hoping for a stronger recovery than occurred in 1992. Slow recovery in the overall economy, in local housing and employment markets, and in retail sales in many areas of the country, were major factors contributing to the continuing volatile state of newspaper ad revenues.

Projections for total newspaper ad revenues ranged from a decline of 2 percent in current dollars (Standard & Poor) to a gain of more than 4 percent (McCann-Erickson). Ad pages were expected to be down at least 3 percent over the 1991 level. Although newspapers have generally been unwilling to negotiate advertising rates as other media frequently do, more recently some industry analysts report that publishers have initiated new pricing approaches in order to attract badly needed advertising revenues.

Some industry observers are concerned that even as the general economy returns to a healthier state, the newspaper industry's recovery may not bring growth levels achieved earlier because of retail sector restructuring and aggressive competition from other media, including local radio and television stations, cable operators, local magazines, direct mailers, Yellow Pages publishers and shopper papers. According to an annual McCann-Erickson advertising report, during the past decade daily newspapers have seen their share of total media advertising drop from 27.4 percent in 1981 to 24.1 percent in 1991. The Newspaper Association of America (NAA) reported that in 1991 total advertising expenditures in daily newspapers amounted to $30.4 billion.

NAA reported that for the first half of 1992, total ad revenues for dailies were up an estimated 0.2 percent over the 1991 six-month level and were not expected to increase more than 1 percent for the year. Retail advertising receipts declined about 0.4 percent during the same period and classified revenues rose 0.7 percent. The small gain in classified ad revenues during the first half was expected to further improve during the last half of 1992 but still fall short of industry expectations. Retail advertising was expected to remain weak throughout the year. Media analysts' forecasts for all of 1992 were very mixed concerning the major categories of newspaper ad receipts.

Advertising receipts accounted for 78 percent of total newspaper revenues in 1990. Although retail advertising still provides the major portion of newspapers ad revenues, its share of the total dropped from 59 to 52 percent between 1981–91 as classified advertising receipts climbed from 28 to 35 percent. National advertising's share of the total has ranged from 13 to 14 percent throughout the decade.

Continuing Circulation Losses

Both the number and circulation of dailies were expected to show continued reductions in 1992, but at a slower rate than in 1991. The number of dailies fell to 1,586 in 1991, a loss of 25 papers. This was the largest yearly decline during the past decade. Accounting for these losses were a greater number of mergers, closings and conversions from daily to weekly publication. With these losses, total circulation for U.S. dailies also fell significantly, from 62.3 million in 1990 to 60.7 million in 1991. In addition to mergers, closings and conversions, some circulation was lost because of sizable price hikes for both subscriptions and newsstand sales.

Shrinking advertising revenues forced many newspaper publishers to increase both newsstand and home delivery prices. As of January 1992, newspaper circulation prices had risen 9.1 percent from a year earlier, according to the Bureau of Labor Statistics producer price data. NAA figures for single copy sales prices further confirm the sharp increase. In 1990, 656 newspapers still sold for 25 cents, but by 1991 this figure had dropped to 448. Most of the papers lost from this group had increased their price to 35 or 50 cents. Papers selling for 35 cents were the predominant group in 1991; 809 papers, or nearly half, reported that price.

The Audit Bureau of Circulation reported that only 28 of the 100 largest daily newspapers showed circulation gains in the six-month period ending March 31, 1992. During the period, *The New York Times* overtook the *Los Angeles Times* as the largest metropolitan paper. The *Los Angeles Times* saw its circulation drop by 6.3 percent after carrying out planned circulation cutbacks in unprofitable markets. During the past few decades, daily newspaper readership has been slowly declining, especially among young persons. One bright spot for circulation has been the startup of ethnic newspapers, many in native languages which are catering to the broad range of cultural groups found in metropolitan areas. Some of these papers have been very successful in targeting audiences advertisers want to reach.

The number of Sunday newspapers edged upward to 875 in 1991, increasing by 12 even as circulation fell. Sunday circulation has shown sizable gains during much of the past decade, but for the first time in nearly two decades it declined from 62.6 million in 1990 to 62.1 million in 1991.

The number and circulation of weekly newspapers were down in 1992, as they have been for the last two years, according to the National Newspaper Association. Weeklies totaled 7,417 in 1992, a drop of 59 papers. Weekly circulation fell slightly from 54.7 million in 1991 to 54.6 million in 1992.

Decline in Industry Concentration

The number of U.S. daily newspaper chains dropped by 2 in 1991 to 133. These chains owned 75 percent of daily newspapers and 82 percent of Sunday papers in 1991. Circulation for group-owned newspapers also declined, representing 78 percent of total daily U.S. circulation in 1991, down from 81 percent in 1990. The closing of several newspapers accounted for much of the loss.

Papers merged in at least 6 medium-sized metropolitan areas including Ashville, NC, Portland, ME, Durham, NC, Bethlehem, PA, Charleston, SC and Newport News, VA. Nearly a dozen closed, including the *Dallas Times Herald*, and the *Arkansas Gazette* in Little Rock, AK.

INTERNATIONAL COMPETITIVENESS

U.S. exports of newspapers dropped by about 13 percent in 1992 from their 1991 level, to $33 million in current dollars. More foreign printing of U.S. newspapers may account for some of the loss. The major markets for U.S. papers in 1991 were Canada, accounting for 45 percent, followed by the United Kingdom with 35 percent, and Mexico, 7 percent.

Until recently nearly all U.S. papers served local or regional markets, while a few sold nationally in the United States also had limited foreign distribution. Very few U.S. papers had invested in newspaper businesses abroad. Today several U.S. newspapers have international editions printed abroad and a few have begun joint ventures with foreign newspapers. During 1992, both The New York Times Company and the Hearst Corporation launched newspapers in Russia under joint-venture arrangements. Hearst began publishing an English-Russian newspaper with *Izvestia* that will be distributed in the United States and Russia. The Times launched a Russian edition of *The New York Times*, which is printed and distributed in Russia by *Moscow News*.

Two Canadian investors have dominated foreign direct investment in the U.S. newspaper industry. Thomson Corp. and Hollinger, Inc. own more than 200 daily newspapers in the United States. From 1988–91, Canadian investment in the U.S. newspaper sector totaled more than $700 million. Canada does not permit U.S. publishers to purchase Canadian publishing enterprises.

U.S. imports of newspapers rose about 6 percent above their 1991 level, totaling an estimated $51 million (current dollars) in 1992. The major suppliers to the U.S. market in 1991 were Canada, accounting for 81 percent of total imports, followed by Mexico with 9 percent, and France, 5 percent.

LONG-TERM PROSPECTS

Newspaper industry receipts are expected to grow at an average yearly rate of 1–2 percent in constant dollars during the next 5 years, if the economy, retail sales, corporate profits, real disposable personal income and consumer spending rise at moderate rates. Challenges from both old and new competitors throughout the rest of the decade will motivate the newspaper industry to be much more sensitive to advertisers' and consumers' wants and needs.

Newspaper companies will create both electronic and printed products that are more finely tuned to the needs of advertisers, newspaper readers and other information users. Newspapers will have to demonstrate more effectively to both advertisers and readers their capability to deliver advertising and editorial content based on the demographic and lifestyle patterns of readers. Newspapers will concentrate more on conducting quality research for advertisers that provides them with specific reader information needed in planning more effective advertising strategies. Newspapers will give more consideration to the needs and demands of a media-saturated, time-conscious public—a public that is more culturally diverse. Among the groups more newspapers will try to attract are women readers whose numbers have been declining, and teenagers and young adults who could become future newspaper readers.

Competitive Forces

Newspapers will face even more intense competition from a wider range of media competing for limited advertising dollars and media audiences with more leisure choices, but less time. With so many media from which to select, advertisers will choose media that offer the best advertising plans and prices, and that reach more selective audiences. "Free" newspapers, now a rapidly growing market in European countries, may be one answer for some U.S. newspapers. "Free" newspapers permit targeting of audiences more for advertisers. Media users and subscribers will focus more on publications and other media offering vital information for their daily living needs, especially those providing easier access to information.

The biggest potential threat to newspapers over the next few years will be the Bell operating companies (BOCs). The lifting of the ban on the BOCs to provide information services over their telephone lines could have a major impact on newspapers' classified advertising base, as well as result in siphoning off newspaper revenues derived from the papers' present electronic information services. Newspapers will take a harder look at what information services they can best provide to consumers. On the brighter side, some of newspapers' major competitors, including publishers of magazines and catalogs, may turn increasingly to newspapers to distribute their publications. Rising postal costs have already led some publishers to find alternate delivery sources.

Production Improvements

Newspapers will exercise more independence during the next few years in developing their own front-end systems, as well as other production systems. Companies outside the newspaper industry have in the past developed much of the hardware and software newspapers use in their technological and computer applications. This development presented problems for newspapers in integrating the various parts of their editorial, advertising, production, and distribution systems. During the next few years, newspapers are expected to fund more for research and development focused on postpress equipment that would allow them to deliver selective inserts to individual subscribers, and on complete electronic handling of their entire advertising process. These capabilities could create greater revenue opportunities for newspapers because they would improve services to both subscribers and advertisers. A standard model for newspaper color systems that would provide consistent color from editing through printing could become a reality in the next few years. This breakthrough would give a huge boost to the use of color in newspapers and, in turn, help newspapers attract additional readers and advertisers.

Increased Global Interest

With U.S. daily newspapers depending on the major share of their revenues from a more limited U.S. media advertising base, some newspapers will likely explore overseas markets in the next few years in order to expand. Markets closer to home offer limited investment opportunities for U.S. companies since two trade agreements—one with Canada and the other the North America Free Trade Agreement with both Canada and Mexico—have limited the share a U.S. newspaper company may own in a newspaper business located in these other two countries. With the emerging economic community being created in Europe, and the opening up of markets in East European countries, U.S. newspapers will assess what opportunities await them. Advertising expenditures in some European countries have been growing at a significantly faster rate than the overall economies in these countries. Eastern European publishers will seek more joint venture agreements with foreign publishers in order to develop successful and better-financed operations.—*Rose Marie Zummo Bratland, Office of Consumer Goods, (202) 482-0380.*

Trends and Forecasts: Printing and Publishing (SIC 27)

(in millions of dollars except as noted)

Item	1987	1988	1989	1990	1991[1]	1992[1]	1993[2]	Percent Change (1987–1993) 87–88	88–89	89–90	90–91	91–92	92–93
Industry Data													
Value of shipments[3]	136,196	143,907	149,912	157,060	158,628	165,927	176,398	5.7	4.2	4.8	1.0	4.6	6.3
2711 Newspapers	31,850	32,927	34,146	34,642	33,395	34,230	35,839	3.4	3.7	1.5	−3.6	2.5	4.7
2721 Periodicals	17,329	18,612	19,787	20,397	20,254	21,327	22,735	7.4	6.3	3.1	−0.7	5.3	6.6
2731 Book publishing	12,620	13,571	14,074	15,318	16,085	17,050	18,160	7.5	3.7	8.8	5.0	6.0	6.5
2732 Book printing	3,256	3,566	3,839	4,132	4,370	4,610	4,900	9.5	7.7	7.6	5.8	5.5	6.3
2741 Miscellaneous publishing	7,810	8,154	8,021	8,875	9,540	10,110	10,815	4.4	−1.6	10.6	7.5	6.0	7.0
275 Commercial printing	44,786	47,460	50,312	52,904	53,950	57,325	61,625	6.0	6.0	5.2	2.0	6.3	7.5
2761 Manifold business forms	7,397	7,781	7,553	7,808	7,418	7,047	7,153	5.2	−2.9	3.4	−5.0	−5.0	1.5
2771 Greeting cards	2,911	3,082	3,449	3,721	4,037	4,396	4,836	5.9	11.9	7.9	8.5	8.9	10.0
2782 Blankbooks and binders	2,904	3,058	3,058	3,186	3,305	3,450	3,650	5.3	0.0	4.2	3.7	4.4	5.8
2789 Bookbinding	1,176	1,218	1,240	1,363	1,430	1,485	1,575	3.6	1.8	9.9	4.9	3.8	6.1
2791 Typesetting	1,784	1,920	1,776	1,957	1,985	2,010	2,035	7.6	−7.5	10.2	1.4	1.3	1.2
2796 Platemaking services	2,373	2,559	2,657	2,758	2,859	2,887	3,075	7.8	3.8	3.8	3.7	1.0	6.5
Value of shipments (1987$)	136,196	136,941	135,281	136,044	132,935	133,753	136,228	0.5	−1.2	0.6	−2.3	0.6	1.9
2711 Newspapers	31,850	30,859	30,031	28,653	25,902	24,944	24,495	−3.1	−2.7	−4.6	−9.6	−3.7	−1.8
2721 Periodicals	17,329	17,525	17,449	16,815	16,025	16,233	16,623	1.1	−0.4	−3.6	−4.7	1.3	2.4
2731 Book publishing	12,620	12,803	12,455	12,872	13,195	13,575	14,035	1.5	−2.7	3.3	2.5	2.9	3.4
2732 Book printing	3,256	3,409	3,480	3,647	3,755	3,850	3,955	4.7	2.1	4.8	3.0	2.5	2.7
2741 Miscellaneous publishing	7,810	7,707	7,246	7,670	7,880	8,055	8,315	−1.3	−6.0	5.9	2.7	2.2	3.2
275 Commercial printing	44,786	46,065	46,653	47,782	47,320	48,275	49,725	2.9	1.3	2.4	−1.0	2.0	3.0
2761 Manifold business forms	7,397	7,218	6,726	6,971	6,985	6,754	6,686	−2.4	−6.8	3.6	0.2	−3.3	−1.0
2771 Greeting cards	2,911	2,885	3,136	3,241	3,487	3,640	3,822	−0.9	8.7	3.3	7.6	4.4	5.0
2782 Blankbooks and binders	2,904	2,929	2,716	2,714	2,745	2,785	2,860	0.9	−7.3	−0.1	1.1	1.5	2.7
2789 Bookbinding	1,176	1,175	1,155	1,241	1,260	1,280	1,305	−0.1	−1.7	7.4	1.5	1.6	2.0
2791 Typesetting	1,784	1,864	1,675	1,831	1,740	1,655	1,605	4.5	−10.1	9.3	−5.0	−4.9	−3.0
2796 Platemaking services	2,373	2,501	2,559	2,607	2,641	2,707	2,802	5.4	2.3	1.9	1.3	2.5	3.5

[1] Estimate.
[2] Forecast.
[3] Value of all products and services sold by establishments in the printing and publishing industry.

SOURCE: U.S. Department of Commerce: Bureau of the Census, International Trade Administration (ITA). Estimates and forecasts by ITA.

Trends and Forecasts: Newspapers (SIC 2711)

(in millions of dollars except as noted)

Item	1987	1988	1989	1990	1991[1]	1992[2]	1993[3]	Percent Change (1987–1993) 87–88	88–89	89–90	90–91	91–92	92–93
Industry Data													
Value of shipments[4]	31,850	32,927	34,146	34,642	33,395	34,230	35,839	3.4	3.7	1.5	−3.6	2.5	4.7
Value of shipments (1987$)	31,850	30,859	30,031	28,653	25,902	24,944	24,495	−3.1	−2.7	−4.6	−9.6	−3.7	−1.8
Total employment (000)	434	432	431	443	426	415	419	−0.5	−0.2	2.8	−3.8	−2.6	1.0
Production workers (000)	148	146	147	149	144	140	141	−1.4	0.7	1.4	−3.4	−2.8	0.7
Average hourly earnings ($)	11.38	11.42	11.82	12.37	12.52	12.85	13.24	0.4	3.5	4.7	1.2	2.6	3.0
Capital expenditures	1,523	1,631	1,985	1,886	—	—	—	7.1	21.7	−5.0	—	—	—
Product Data													
Value of shipments[5]	30,495	31,461	32,457	32,818	31,637	32,427	33,951	3.2	3.2	1.1	−3.6	2.5	4.7
Value of shipments (1987$)	30,495	29,485	28,546	27,144	24,538	23,630	23,205	−3.3	−3.2	−4.9	−9.6	−3.7	−1.8
Trade Data													
Value of imports	—	—	96.1	62.0	48.3	51.4	54.0	—	—	−35.5	−22.1	6.4	5.1
Value of exports	—	—	28.6	37.7	38.0	33.2	36.0	—	—	31.8	0.8	−12.6	8.4

[1]Estimated, except exports and imports.
[2]Estimate.
[3]Forecast.
[4]Value of all products and services sold by establishments in the newspapers industry.
[5]Value of products classified in the newspapers industry produced by all industries.

SOURCE: U.S. Department of Commerce: Bureau of the Census, International Trade Administration (ITA). Estimates and forecasts by ITA.

Retailing

The retail trade sector (SIC 52–59) is one of the major sources of jobs in the U.S. economy, consistently accounting for more than 20 percent of all jobs in the private sector. Retail establishments are primarily engaged in selling merchandise for personal or household consumption.

Retailing consists of building materials, hardware, garden supply, and mobile home dealers (SIC 52); general merchandise stores (SIC 53); food stores (SIC 54); automobile dealers and gasoline service stations (SIC 55); apparel and accessory stores (SIC 56); home furniture, furnishings, and equipment stores (SIC 57); eating and drinking places (SIC 58); and miscellaneous retail (SIC 59). In general, retail establishments sell durable goods in the first four Standard Industrial Classification (SIC) codes and nondurable goods in the latter four SIC classifications. The Census Bureau designates the several different types of retail stores according to principal merchandise lines or usual trade designations. In 1991, retail stores selling mostly nondurable goods accounted for 60 percent of all retail sales; those selling mostly durable goods accounted for the remaining 40 percent.

Nondurable Goods Merchandise

Sales Performance

Retailers of nondurable goods tend to sell products that are less sensitive to changes in general business conditions than those sold by durable goods retailers. During the 1990–91 recession, total retail sales of nondurable merchandise lines increased 2 percent in current dollars, while total retail sales of durable merchandise declined more than 1 percent.

In 1992, total sales of retail stores exceeded $1.9 trillion, a gain of about 5 percent in current dollars over 1991. However, their payroll of 19.3 million employees remained unchanged from 1991. Department store sales totaled $189 billion in 1992, up over 6 percent in current dollars from the 1991 total of $178 billion. Eating and drinking places sold $205 billion in 1992, almost 6 percent higher than in 1991. Apparel and accessory stores sold $99 billion in 1992, up over 4 percent in current dollars from 1991.

Since the early 1980's, sales of eating and drinking places have consistently set the pace for all retailers by increasing at annual rates that were above the average for the overall economy. At the same time, sales of department stores and apparel and accessory stores had annual increases in sales that were about the same as average growth in the economy. A significant but unknown portion of these different growth patterns is in response to structural changes in retailing and underlying shifts in consumer buying patterns.

Structural Changes

Structural changes in retailing have resulted in increased market shares for the newer types of retailers and decreased shares for traditional retailers. These developments seem to suggest that the type-of-activity categories under which the Bureau of the Census reports retail sales need to be updated. Traditionally, a retail establishment is classified by its principal commodity line or usual trade designation. However, in today's world of "scrambled merchandising" and discount merchandisers, retail sales by merchandise line groupings are becoming increasingly unhelpful indicators of the trends and underlying forces that are changing the face of retailing.

Scrambled merchandising is a relatively new term for a structural change that has been taking place since the 1970's. It denotes the tendency for retail stores to become larger and more diverse in the merchandise lines they carry. For example, during the past two decades, supermarkets have expanded activities from their traditional food product lines to non-food product lines and many services, including "in house" pharmacies.

This important structural change in retailing has paralleled the migration of consumers from the central city to the suburbs. As retailers moved to the suburbs to better serve their customers, they generally built larger stores. During the 1980's, total retail selling space in the United States increased 43 percent, from 3 billion square feet in 1980 to 4.3 billion square feet in 1990. To fill this expanded floor space, traditional retailers have expanded the number of merchandise lines they handle. More drug stores now sell convenience foods and office supplies, and many gasoline service stations offer convenience foods.

The full impact of scrambled merchandising on the traditional retailer is unclear. However, the industry consensus appears to be that the added merchandise lines of a scrambled merchandiser often shift market shares away from the smaller traditional retailer.

Another structural change affecting traditional retailers is the recent rise in importance of discount mass merchandisers in response to changes in consumer buying patterns. Discount merchandisers, also known as off-price retailers, generally offer a specialized merchandise line at discount prices in large superstores or smaller regional discount stores. The small regional discount store usually sells specialty items in a regional shopping mall.

Superstores are large retail establishments usually offering at discount prices a limited product line with an extensive array of complementary merchandise. The average superstore carries an inventory of 40,000 items compared with the 25,000 items carried by an average supermarket. Examples of superstores include Staples (the office supply store), Toys "R" Us, and Wal-Mart.

A new type of superstore is the price club or warehouse store. Price clubs not only have more retail floor space than a superstore, they also offer a broader line of merchandise at discount prices. Nearly all have an "in-house" grocery supermarket. Price clubs are becoming an important part of the U.S. retail market, but data are not readily available to track their market position or their impact on traditional retailing.

A hyperstore is another type of superstore that is several times larger than a warehouse store and carries a significantly larger inventory. Hyperstores account for an important share of the European retail market, but they remain a minor part of the U.S. retail sector.

These ongoing changes in discount mass merchandising are mainly in response to changes in the buying patterns of consumers due to demographic changes and shifts in consumer attitudes. The largest single group of retail customers—those in their 40's—has shifted its priorities toward replacement needs for tangibles, more spending on intangibles such as education for their children and health care, and greater savings for the future. Changes in consumer attitudes include a shift away from status and conspicuous consumption toward price and value consciousness and caution about indebtedness.

Retail sales of "big ticket" items, such as furniture and autos, and discretionary purchases, such as designer apparel, have been especially affected by consumer caution, changes in consumption and savings behavior by the major retail consumer group, and little real growth in credit in 1992. To encourage more consumer spending, retailers have increased their promotion activities, boosted their inventory of off-price merchandise, and invested in sophisticated computer systems to better track market trends and control operating costs.

Technology Advances

State-of-the-art computer system technologies are being used by retailers to maximize operating efficiencies and economies of scale. For instance, registers at checkout counters, in conjunction with coded information attached to the merchandise, are able to generate information on store sales by department, product category, vendor, size, and current price. In addition, these technologies may be programmed to calculate discounts, apply special allowances without the need to update price labels on individual items, approve credit, accept credit cards, and schedule deliveries. The more sophisticated systems also monitor inventory levels and automatically reorder selected merchandise from the vendor, link subsidiary stores to one another and with the home office to give immediate readings on sales and inventory, and calculate turnover by product, store, and sales area. Such an intensive use of computers can lead to dramatically reduced selling and operating costs, and improved employee productivity.

The retailers that have already committed the capital and time needed to install and implement point-of-sale computers and integrate their operations and marketing activities into a computerized system of information indicate that computerization will ultimately revolutionize retailers' marketing and operations activities. Other retailers view computer technology as an unnecessary capital expense.

However, relatively few retail establishments have integrated their operations and marketing activities into a fully integrated system of computerized information. In some cases, the retailer lacks the capital and inclination to use point-of-sale scanners and related technologies. In other cases, the retailer has the capital but not the inclination. In either case, a significant number of retailers could benefit from further computerization of their operation and marketing activities. A review of the productivity trends of the major types of retailers points out the substantial untapped potential for reducing retail selling and operating costs, and improving employee productivity through computerization.

Productivity Trends

The latest U.S. Department of Labor data on the output per manhour for the major types of retail stores show that most stores improved their productivity during the 1980's. Of the 12 major types of retail stores for which this data are available, 8 showed increases in productivity during the period, and 4 showed declines: variety stores, grocery stores, eating and drinking places, and drugs and medicine stores. It is not coincidental that, except for the chain stores in each group, these four groups are among the least computerized of all major types of retail stores.

Output per manhour trends are influenced by many independent factors, of which computerization is only one. Other factors include changes in output of the specified sector, the number of employees and their hours worked, and consumer demand.

Price Issue

Retailers are actively supporting Congressional initiatives to legislate an end to the marketing practice known as manufacturer's suggested retail price (MSRP). The proposed legislation would make it easier for retailers to bring successful lawsuits against manufacturers that refuse to continue supplying merchandise to retailers that fail to adhere to the MSRP. From the producer's point of view, MSRP allows the manufacturer to better target certain niche markets with products differentiated by a combination of quality and price. Manufacturers prefer niche marketing because it allows better projections of consumer demand and, subsequently, more efficiently scheduled production runs.

In contrast, retailers, especially discount mass merchandisers, oppose MSRP practices because they may restrict consumer choice, limit off-price merchandising, and often force price increases that retailers would not otherwise initiate. Retailers believe that MSRP constrains their freedom of action and interferes with their marketing strategies.

INTERNATIONAL COMPETITIVENESS

The retail industry's international competitiveness is difficult to assess because neither the value of merchandise exported by retailers nor the value of retail services incorporated in these exports is reported. Retailers export products and services whenever they sell them to a consumer residing in a foreign country. The export retail sale may be a direct sale to a consumer visiting the United States from a foreign country, particularly Canada and Mexico. The export may also result from a mail order sale from a U.S. retailer to a consumer in a foreign country. For some products, the value of export retail sales may be significant.

For example, thousands of Canadians cross daily into the United States to purchase cigarettes and gasoline, two products heavily taxed in Canada. Others stock up on discount-priced groceries, apparel, and other merchandise sold in U.S. discount stores. Each of these purchases is an export to Canada and confirms the competitive edge U.S. retailers hold over their Canadian counterparts.

Another indication of the international competitiveness of U.S. retailers is the drive to "go global." Retailers, especially discount retailers, have already signed up to participate in privately organized trade missions to Mexico, while others are interested in trade missions to the newly industrializing countries of Asia.

Since the completion of negotiations on the North American Free Trade Agreement (NAFTA) in September 1992, many retailers have investigated investment opportunities in Mexico and Canada to establish a presence there. According to the results of a recent Coopers & Lybrand survey, those looking for investment opportunities in Canada are planning to open their own stores there. In contrast, those planning to invest in Mexico are looking for joint venture or investment partners. The retailers most interested in investment opportunities in the two markets are the discount mass merchandisers. Because the consumer markets in either country are not as large nor as well organized as in the United States, potential investors are looking at regional discount stores rather than superstores.

Some opponents of NAFTA have suggested that its liberalized investment measures will lead to intensified competitive pressures from retailers in Canada or Mexico wishing to invest in the United States. However, a majority of the respondents to the Cooper & Lybrand survey do not view this possibility as a major source of increased competition in U.S. markets.

Despite the interest of retailers in globalization, there are many impediments in foreign markets that will prevent U.S. retailers from fully exercising their competitive edge. Many of these barriers take the form of customary business practices, such as loyalty to local suppliers; others are nontariff measures, such as restrictive standards.

LONG-TERM PROSPECTS

In the long term, the retailing sector is not expected to grow as fast as in the past because of changes in consumer buying patterns and structural shifts in retailing. According to the latest projections of the Department of Labor, retail sales, adjusted for inflation, will show an average annual rate of growth of 2.5 percent during 1990–2005, compared with 3.5 percent annually during the previous 15 years.

The Department of Labor recently projected a near doubling in the rate of worker productivity increase of the retail sector during 1990–2005. Output per employee is expected to increase at an average 0.9 percent annually during the period, compared with a 0.5 percent annual rise during 1975–90. Nearly all of this increase appears to be associated with projected improvements in operating and marketing activities through extensive computerization. During 1990–2005, the average annual rate of increase in consumer demand and the number of employees in retailing are expected to increase at lower rates than in 1975–90, while the number of hours worked per employee will remain unchanged.—*James Walsh, Office of Service Industries, (202) 482-5131.*

Food Retailing

The U.S. food retailing industry (SIC 54) consists mostly of establishments selling fresh and processed/prepared foods to the general public for mainly at-home preparation and consumption. Many food retailers sell a variety of non-food grocery items such as pet supplies, soaps and detergents, paper and plastic goods, and alcoholic beverages. Larger retailers frequently offer fresh fish and other seafood, delicatessen foods, in-store baked goods, flowers, and drugs. Sales data for the industry include food, beverage, and non-food grocery products, and goods sold in service departments such as in-store bakeries, pharmacies, and flower and deli departments.

The food retailing industry encompasses traditional multiline grocery stores, convenience stores, free-standing retail bakeries, meat and fish markets, confectionery stores, and produce and dairy stores. Many of these establishments, especially grocery stores, are owned and operated by corporate chain-store organizations. Industry sales data exclude sales of restaurants, fast-food establishments, or other food service outlets. The data also exclude sales of drug stores, discount department stores, and general merchandise stores, although many of these outlets sell food and non-food grocery items.

In 1992, shipments of the industry (including grocery stores and most other retailers of foods and beverages for consumption at home, but excluding food service) reached an estimated $387 billion. This was an increase of 1.6 percent in current dollars over 1991. Grocery store sales, which account for about 95 percent of industry sector sales, rose more than 1 percent in current dollars to $362 billion in 1992. However, sales of the larger retail grocery firms advanced almost 2 percent, reaching $226 billion. In 1992, these larger grocery retailers captured over 60 percent of the grocery store market and more than 58 percent of total food retailing sales.

INTERNATIONAL COMPETITIVENESS

Food imports play an increasing role in the U.S. food retailing system. They are likely to become even more prominent if two major trade agreements, the North American Free Trade Agreement (NAFTA) and the Uruguay Round of the General Agreement on Tariffs and Trade (GATT), are approved. NAFTA will create the largest free trade area in the world among the United States, Canada, and Mexico.

Both these trade pacts will reduce U.S. and foreign food and beverage tariffs, quotas, and many other marketing restrictions. U.S. food processors are expected to use less costly raw materials for domestic production and to source more finished goods abroad, especially from our NAFTA partners, Canada and Mexico. Foreign-based food and beverage processors are also likely to step up their efforts to market processed and branded products because of improved access to the U.S. market. These trade-liberalizing agreements are expected to result in greater consumer choice and price competition.

The two agreements, when fully implemented, will also provide U.S. retailers, wholesalers, and food/beverage processors with substantially improved access to Mexico and other foreign markets. Under NAFTA, Mexico will bilaterally reduce its current relatively high tariffs on U.S. agricultural and processed foods and beverages over 15 years and replace its restrictive quota system with tariffs. Some Mexican tariffs will be reduced to zero immediately, while the majority will be phased out over 5 to 10 years.

The GATT round of trade negotiations involves virtually all U.S. trading partners. Successful completion of the negotiations will result in generally lower tariffs, reduced trade barriers, and an extension of GATT rules to many service industries and to food, beverage, and agricultural commodities. U.S. food export interests will benefit from a successful Uruguay Round because U.S. food tariffs and trade barriers are now low, while many foreign countries, especially those in the European Community and several Asian nations, maintain high tariffs and other barriers to entry.

New U.S. Food Labeling Laws

Foreign food and beverage makers are likely to react unfavorably to proposed changes in U.S. food labeling requirements. The new labeling, which is required for all packaged foods, both foreign and domestically produced, covers such topics as nutrition information, serving size, health messages, and descriptive terms such as "light" and "low fat." The U.S. Food and Drug Administration (FDA) and the U.S. Department of Agriculture (USDA) share responsibility for food labeling along product lines. The USDA covers meat and poultry, and the FDA handles all other products.

Effective May 1994, new labels will be required on all packaged foods that are produced. Newly labeled products will appear on store shelves later that year. The new labels will feature a standardized section (yet to be made final) requiring specific, comparable treatment of key elements, such as serving size. All food products must conform to these requirements. Due to the complexity and extended coverage of the new requirements, it appears likely that most manufacturers will have to design new labels rather than modify existing ones.

The labeling requirements may prove especially difficult for many foreign food manufacturers, especially firms unaccustomed to such extensive product analysis and disclosure. Some industry observers contend that the new requirements constitute a barrier to trade and could be challenged in GATT. In contrast, defenders of the requirements observe that all manufacturers, both domestic and foreign, must comply equally and that the labeling rules are the result of a well-accepted need to improve U.S. health standards. These observers believe that any GATT challenge to the new regulations will be dismissed.

Consumer Spending

Consumer spending for foods and beverages consumed at home slowed significantly in 1992, reflecting stable-to-declining prices for some staples and U.S. shoppers' concerns about unsettled economic conditions. Nominal personal consumption expenditures (PCE) for all foods and beverages consumed at home rose at an annual rate of less than 1 percent in current dollars during the first six months of 1992. (In contrast, PCE for at-home foods and beverages rose about 2 percent in current dollars in 1991, and increased at an average annual rate of 5 percent during 1988–90.) Adjusted for inflation, PCE for all foods and beverages declined slightly in the first half of 1992, due primarily to a drop of about 2 percent in real PCE for alcoholic beverages consumed at home.

During the first half of 1992, consumer spending for poultry, pork, fresh fruits and vegetables, and non-alcoholic beverages rose by at least 2 percent in current dollars. Sales declined for all types of alcoholic beverages, pet foods, sugar and sweets, bakery products, processed fruits, and other prepared foods.

Industry Issues

In 1992, grocery store operators and food processing firms encountered other problems in addition to slow sales growth. Traditional grocery store operators viewed with concern the incursion of member-only discount clubs into the sale of food and beverages. A recent study by the Food Marketing Institute (FMI) estimates that discount clubs' sales reached $33 billion in 1991 and should capture a 13-percent market share of overall food retailing within the next 10 years. Some retailers have fought back by creating special merchandising sections featuring the large size and no-frills, multipack styles favored by the discount clubs. These actions are viewed as primarily defensive because discount clubs limit their selections to cyclical items in limited sizes, with a high recognition factor and a very low price.

More retailers are directing their anger about discount clubs at food and beverage manufacturers/marketers. The FMI study contends that manufacturers are partially responsible for the grocers' woes and that a new period of tense relations between retailers and manufacturers appears about to occur. Retailers argue that part of the lower selling price of discount clubs results from several factors: lower product and wholesale costs, better promotional deals, and more favorable package sizes and product mixes. The FMI study contends that 6–10 percent of the discounters' lower prices can be attributed to manufacturers' pricing structure.

Retailers appear ready to take a harder line with their suppliers and show interest in pursuing strategies to penalize suppliers believed to be offering special prices and packages to non-traditional retailers. Not surprisingly, grocery product manufacturers react by contending that grocery retailers should not continue to expect to receive substantial promotional funds, special terms, and merchandising monies (including slotting allowances), while demanding low wholesale prices and special packs that are often jumbo size.

Grocery product manufacturers indicate increasing interest in a pricing strategy sometimes referred to as Everyday Low Pricing. This substitutes lower consistent wholesale list prices for complicated pricing schedules encompassing various short-run promotional prices. Many manufacturers believe this pricing strategy will help to cut down substantially on so-called promotional spending, which manufacturers view as required, but unproductive, compared with more direct forms of consumer stimulus. Retailers are generally unsympathetic to this strategy, and the long-range prospects for Everyday Low Pricing remain cloudy.

LONG-TERM PROSPECTS

Between 1993 and 1997, food retailing industry sales are forecast to rise 2 to 4 percent annually in current dollars. Less costly imports resulting from NAFTA and the Uruguay

Round, along with spirited competition among grocery manufacturers and grocery retailers, are expected to restrain food prices. Slow growth of the U.S. population, minimal real increases in disposable personal income, and continuing economic concerns should restrain growth in food purchases. Therefore, the next five years appear difficult for the U.S. food retailing industry.—*Cornelius F. Kenney, Office of Consumer Goods, (202) 482-2428.*

Trends and Forecasts: Retail Sales (SIC 52–59)

(in billions of dollars except as noted)

Type of store	1987	1988	1989	1990	1991	1992[1]	1993[2]	Percent Change (1987–1993) 87–88	88–89	89–90	90–91	91–92	92–93
All stores	1,541	1,650	1,747	1,826	1,843	1,934	2,038	7.1	5.9	4.5	0.9	4.9	5.4
Department stores	149	157	166	172	178	189	196	5.4	5.7	3.6	3.5	6.2	3.7
Eating and drinking	153	167	175	186	194	205	219	9.2	4.8	6.3	4.3	5.7	6.8
Apparel and accessories	79	85	91	94	95	99	106	7.6	7.1	3.3	1.1	4.2	7.1
Employment (millions)	18.5	19.1	19.6	19.7	19.3	19.3	—	3.2	2.6	0.5	−2.0	0.0	—
Average hourly earnings ($)	6.12	6.31	6.53	6.76	7.00	—	—	3.1	3.5	3.5	3.6	—	—

[1]Estimate.
[2]Forecast.

SOURCE: Department of Commerce, Bureau of the Census; Department of Labor, Bureau of Labor Statistics.

Trends and Forecasts: Food Retailing (SIC 54)

(in millions of dollars except as noted)

Item	1987	1988	1989	1990	1991	1992[1]	1993[2]	Percent Change (1987–93) 87–88	88–89	89–90	90–91	91–92	92–93
Sales													
All food stores	309,461	326,504	349,120	371,580	380,927	387,022	395,887	5.5	6.9	6.4	2.5	1.6	2.3
Grocery stores	290,978	307,176	328,075	348,243	357,076	362,075	370,041	5.6	6.8	6.1	2.5	1.4	2.2
Meat, fish markets	6,261	6,399	6,709	6,517	6,478	6,854	7,217	2.2	4.8	−2.9	−0.6	5.8	5.3
Retail bakeries	5,194	5,477	5,753	6,745	7,647	8,029	8,414	5.3	5.2	17.2	13.4	5.0	4.8
Other	7,028	7,458	8,583	10,075	9,726	10,064	10,215	6.1	15.1	17.4	−3.5	3.5	1.5
Chain food stores	176,092	185,100	198,585	216,546	226,010	230,530	236,063	5.1	7.3	9.0	4.4	2.0	2.4
Chain grocery stores	173,857	182,708	195,763	212,922	222,037	226,256	231,912	5.1	7.1	8.8	4.3	1.9	2.5
Employment													
Total employment	2,971	3,089	3,206	3,360	3,480	3,590	—	4.0	3.8	4.8	3.6	3.2	—
Non supervisory employment	2,742	2,841	2,934	3,020	3,095	3,160	—	3.6	3.3	2.9	2.5	2.1	—
Average hourly earnings (dollars)	6.99	7.00	7.14	7.21	—	—	—	0.1	2.0	1.0	—	—	—

[1]Estimate.
[2]Forecast.

SOURCE: U.S. Department of Commerce: Bureau of the Census; International Trade Administration (ITA). Estimates and forecast by ITA.

Telecommunications Services

The U.S. telecommunications services industry serves more than 88 million households and 30 million businesses nationwide, and is expected to have revenues in 1993 exceeding $184 billion. The industry (SIC 4812, 4813, 4822) is broadly divided into providers serving the communications markets for local exchange, long distance (toll), international, cellular and mobile radio, satellite, and data communications, the last including value-added network services (VANs). The more than 2,000 companies, employing more than 860,000 persons, which serve these markets are both regulated common carriers and unregulated private network providers.

Telephone Services

The Federal Communications Commission (FCC) regulates interstate common carrier communications, while individual state public utility commissions regulate communications within their jurisdictions. The FCC also regulates the use of radio frequencies by the U.S. telecommunications industry through a system of spectrum allocation and licensing. Since the break-up of AT&T in 1984, the U.S. common carrier network has been divided into 161 local access transport areas (LATAs). Communications among LATAs are handled by long distance carriers, while intra-LATA telecommunications (both local and toll calling) are the responsibility of the local exchange carriers (LECs). Private telecommunications networks, which serve only specific customers rather than offering services to the public at large, are not regulated as common carriers.

Local telephone services are provided by seven Bell Regional Holding Companies (RHCs) that control 22 local Bell Operating Companies (BOCs), and by GTE, Sprint (United Telecom), Southern New England Telephone Company (SNET), and about 1,300 smaller, independent local telephone companies. Many of these small, local companies operate as rural telephone cooperatives. Long distance service is provided by AT&T, MCI, Sprint, WilTel, Metromedia/ITT, Cable & Wireless, Advanced Telecommunications (ATC), Allnet, and more than 400 smaller carriers.

The United States telephone network is composed of more than 15,373 central telephone offices and 143 million telephone access lines. The United States has about 49 access lines per 100 population; Canada has 53.4, Japan 42.2, Sweden 66.7, and the United Kingdom 41.4 lines. Of the estimated 113 million Bell Company access lines, more than 51 percent are served by digital central office facilities and 48 percent by analog central offices. Nearly all (98 percent) Bell companies' access lines are equipped for equal access (that is, identical interconnection facilities can be provided to all connecting carriers). A common signaling system, called SS7, is used on 59 percent of the access lines, but only about 1 percent of the access lines are equipped to handle services compatible with Integrated Services Digital Network (ISDN). ISDN is a digital system designed eventually to become a global network providing access to all communications services.

Use of the telecommunications network continues to increase rapidly in the United States. The volume of interstate telephone traffic over this giant web of lines has more than doubled since 1983; today, it accounts for 15 percent of total calling minutes. Interstate rate reductions, aggressive telephone company advertising, and expansion of the U.S. economy have led to steady growth in long distance telephone usage since 1984. Long distance minutes-of-use increased 10 percent in 1991, and about 9 percent in 1992. As telephone rates continue to fall, calling volume will increase proportionately because the economic demand for telephone service is highly sensitive to price changes. During 1992, callers made more than 405 billion local calls, 22 billion intra-LATA toll calls, and 46 billion inter-LATA toll calls. On an average business day, there are about 9.5 billion minutes of telephone calling.

The physical telecommunications plant of the United States consists of about 750,000 miles of aerial wire, more than 3.5 million miles of cable, and more than 4.5 million miles of optical fiber. In addition, microwave radio relay systems cover more than 57,000 miles, a network that is the equivalent of 165 million miles of individual telephone circuits. Total cumulative investment in U.S. telecommunications plant and equipment installed by the firms covered in this chapter was about $320 billion in 1992. In 1992 alone, U.S. telephone carriers invested about $22 billion in plant and equipment.

The nation's total number of local telephone lines tends to serve as a basic barometer of the nation's economic growth. Virtually all businesses have telephone lines and more than 93 percent of the nation's households have telephone service. Growth in the number of lines has averaged about 3 percent per year.

Trends

Major developments in 1992 included: increased competition in local exchange telephone service; fast-paced introduction of new mobile radio and satellite technologies; a proliferation of new high-speed data communications services; continued consolidation of long distance markets; and a growing penetration of the U.S. telecommunications market by foreign-based carriers. Continued slow growth in the economy moderated revenues for local and long distance carriers, while price reductions stimulated additional calling volume, especially for international services. Heightened competition and strategic alliances were the watchwords for the international telecommunications service business during 1992. They represented trends that are expected to accelerate as lower prices, increased user demand, an abundant supply of new oceanic fiber optic circuits, private satellite carriers, and accelerating regulatory liberalization create many new opportunities to challenge the old international cartel of government telecommunications organizations—the Postal, Telephone and Telegraph (PTT) monopolies.

Market convergence and vertical integration are important trends now evolving in the domestic telecommunications services industry. Previously distinct market segments and the companies that compete in them, such as private and public communications networks, local and long distance, and cable and telephone communications, are being redefined along more consolidated lines. The proliferation of new radio technologies is moving the industry from point-to-point to person-to-person communications. The interconnection in 1992 of Centel, one of the nation's largest local exchange providers, with Metropolitan Fiber Systems, a private fiber optic network catering to large business users, is a recent example of this trend, as was Centel's acquisition by Sprint, the nation's third largest long distance carrier. Companies such as WilTel that formerly provided only dedicated leased circuit networks are now entering the market for switched telecommunications services in order to compete more directly with AT&T and other major carriers.

Another indication of such convergence during 1992 was evident when Tele-Communications Inc. (TCI), the country's largest cable television system operator, moved emphatically into the data communications market by partnering with Digital Equipment Corporation to test a new fiber optic home communications system. TCI owns fiber systems in many cities, and will push aggressively in the next few years to offer voice as well as data services over its facilities and thus become an alternative carrier to the local telephone companies in regions where it operates. In addition, several cable television companies are investing hundreds of millions of dollars to build networks for cellular telephone service in direct competition with the local telephone industry. Cox Communications acquired a majority interest in Teleport Communication Group in 1992 to solidify its entry into the local telecommunications services market as well. Time-Warner, the second largest U.S. cable television company, is building a fiber optic system in New York capable of delivering voice telephone traffic. Such strategic acquisitions are evidence of strong growth in the market for competitive access providers (CAPs), firms that compete in the local exchange.

The large number of diverse firms competing to provide telecommunications services, coupled with the growing complexity of network technology, also have created serious concerns about the reliability of the country's telecommunications networks. Following a spate of network failures during 1991, a number of companies offering disaster-recovery services experienced solid growth during 1992. As telecommunications systems become increasingly complex, and the economy grows even more dependent on their reliability, the demand for dependable, noninterruptible communications will provide new competitive opportunities. Ironically, the sophistication of today's modern telecommunications infrastructure, with dynamic call routing and self-healing networks, has also resulted in a complexity that makes the system tragically vulnerable to seemingly small problems, such as minor software bugs.

Rates and Tariffs

According to the FCC, the overall Consumer Price Index for telephone service rose 3.5 percent during 1991, the latest year for which data are available, compared with the national inflation rate that year of 3.1 percent. Local service charges increased 5.1 percent, intrastate toll charges declined 1.5 percent, and interstate toll charges rose 1.3 percent. The national average monthly charge for residential local service with unlimited calling was $13.05 in October 1991, and the total cost of local service, including subscriber line access charges and taxes, averaged $18.64, compared with $17.79 one year earlier. Businesses taking single-line service paid an average of $42.42 a month for service, compared with $41.21 the year before.

Since 1984, expenditures for long distance service have increased by about 5 percent each year for the average household, while long distance rates fell about 4 percent a year. The FCC data suggest that residential use of toll service has grown by about 10 percent per year. The average household spent about $35 a month on toll service in 1991, about $14 more than in 1980.

An important predictor of future local telephone rate changes are the decisions of state regulatory commissions. Rate decisions by such commissions have an immediate impact on the price of telephone service, while the number of pending cases and amount of rate increase requests provides an indicator of future change. At the beginning of 1984, just after the divestiture of AT&T, rate cases pending before state commissions totaled nearly $7 billion. Since then, the level of rate activity has diminished substantially, and the current amount of rate increases pending is about $280 million. Such cases typically take more than a year to resolve, so the low number of cases, taken in light of recent price reductions ordered by state commissions, should indicate a low level of state and local rate changes in 1993.

In the long distance market, direct dial rates for interstate service have dropped between 40 and 45 percent since the break-up of AT&T in 1984. The dramatic reductions in long distance charges, however, were due largely to the imposition of subscriber-line access charges on local residential and business customers, reducing the direct subsidy that AT&T used to pay its local operating units from long distance revenues. While competition has had a significant effect on prices, much of the 50 percent drop is attributable to the adjusted subsidy. Long distance carriers pay an additional subsidy to local carriers based on the number of originating and terminating minutes of use, a charge that has been reduced as subscriber line charges have risen. The reduced costs to long distance carriers have enabled them to aggressively lower prices. In 1990, about 35 percent of local telephone company revenue was derived from long distance access charges. In 1984, subscriber access charges were initiated at $6 a line per month for businesses. In 1985, residential users began paying $1 per line. The current access charge per line for residential subscribers is $3.50 a month.

Policy Developments

In a development affecting future market structure and competition in the U.S. enhanced services industry, the FCC decided in 1992 to reaffirm an earlier decision to allow the Bell Companies to offer unregulated enhanced service through the same business units that provide regulated basic telephone service. The decision reinstated rules originally imposed under the 1986 Third Computer Inquiry decision (later overturned in Federal Court) that guaranteed the Bell Companies' competitors equal access to network services used in the provision of enhanced services. Features such as call routing, number identification and traffic data collection can be purchased individually by non-telephone companies, such as voice mail firms, in order to combine them with their own services and compete with the local Bell telephone company.

The FCC also decided in 1992 to allow telephone companies to own cable television systems, although they will be restricted from providing actual programming services. Legislation before Congress in 1992 proposed allowing telephone companies to offer cable television programming services. In the future, there likely will be head-to-head competition between these two previously distinct industries.

Until recently, the FCC considered U.S. international carriers are regulated as "dominant" if they were 15 percent or more owned by a "foreign telecommunications entity." Dominant carriers, such as the U.K.-based firm Cable & Wireless PLC, were subject to a longer approval period for their tariffs (rates), had to justify their tariffs on the basis of costs incurred, and filed quarterly reports, the same rules that the FCC now applies to AT&T. Although the policy placed added requirements on foreign telecom companies, it did not directly hinder a foreign telecom's ability to enter the market or obtain a license.

In October 1992, the FCC adopted a new policy by imposing dominant carrier status only where a foreign carrier has a monopoly bottleneck over telecom facilities in its domestic market. The theory behind such policy is that a competitive market will make it uneconomical for a carrier to favor its foreign partner, since alternative service providers will step in if prices are too high or access discriminatory.

In a closely related decision during 1992, the FCC sanctioned international resale of private leased circuits to provide telephone service in cases where "equivalent opportunities" exist in the foreign market. The decision sparked two companies to file license applications in 1992 to provide resale service between the United States and Canada. Resolution of the dominant carrier decision will likely lead to resale with the United Kingdom as well. Resale will help drive down prices for international telephone service, provided fair competition exists in both telecommunications markets of the countries involved. Competition in basic telecommunications service is beginning to spread to other countries, and in coming years may have similar effects on rates and service innovation as it has in the United States.

Portability of 800 telephone numbers came one step closer to reality in 1992 when the FCC required GTE and the seven RHCs to upgrade their networks and work with the telecom industry to provide mandatory 800 data base access service by March 1993. A new national data base will enable 800 service customers to select or change their carrier without changing their 800 telephone numbers. An interim measure in effect during 1992 enabled individual carriers to assign special 10-digit 800 numbers to customers only within pre-assigned dialing codes. However, most of the large telephone carriers have expressed doubts that they can implement the FCC plan on time in 1993.

The FCC also gave AT&T more freedom to negotiate large service contracts with individual companies under the Tariff 12 option, and initiated an inquiry into the issue of nationwide, universal video dialtone service in which telephone companies would provide on-demand, full-motion image communications to any subscriber.

INTERNATIONAL COMPETITIVENESS

The importance of the international telecommunications market and a growing demand for service in this sector have caused an increasing number of U.S. domestic long distance telephone carriers to begin providing international service. Multinational corporations, using excess capacity on their private networks, are also entering the market. During 1992, for example, the shipping company UPS created a new subsidiary called UPS Telecommunications Inc. to serve the burgeoning market for international data communications. UPS and other companies are taking advantage of regulatory liberalization in Canada, Germany, the United Kingdom, and the United States that has allowed the resale by companies of circuits they have leased from carriers.

U.S. companies will also continue to move into new overseas markets to provide telecommunications services such as cellular, paging and radio communications. Of particular interest during 1993 to U.S. firms will be the developing telecom service markets in the newly independent states of the former Soviet Union, and Eastern European countries. During 1992, US West International inaugurated Moscow's first commercial cellular telephone service, for example, and AT&T acquired 39 percent of a long distance telephone company in the Ukraine.

U.S. telecommunications service providers remain the most competitive in the world, despite recent advances by other countries toward network modernization and regulatory liberalization. Of particular importance is the lengthy lead enjoyed by U.S. firms in providing value-added data communications services, such as wide-area networking, electronic mail, and data processing. However, the United States lags behind several industrialized nations in some categories of public telecommunications infrastructure, such as average investment per line, and deployment of such technologies as digital switches and signaling system 7 (SS7). Such data notwithstanding, the U.S. market supports a much greater number of private communications networks than any other country. The proliferation of private corporate networks in the United States—as contrasted with foreign corporations that must use their national monopoly telephone systems in order to communicate—means that the U.S. communications system is even more competitive than the available data comparing public telecommunications infrastructure might suggest.

U.S. telecommunications firms enjoy the world's most liberal regulatory environment, the most technological experience and the greatest business demand. However, there are concerns over the level of capital investment in some important technologies such as ISDN, where U.S. industry lags behind major trading partners such as Japan. This is likely to lead to new Government policies to encourage telecommunications infrastructure investment over the next few years, and perhaps public funding of projects such as an advanced, nationwide broadband optical fiber system.

Even as U.S. telecommunications providers expand overseas, for example, AT&T's 1992 joint venture in Brazil to provide data communications services, foreign companies are accelerating their entry into the North American market. This underscores the increasingly global nature of the telecommunications services industry. During 1992, there were several key acquisitions that highlighted this trend, notably the sale of Wang Laboratories' value-added data network operations to the British company, Cable & Wireless. Italcable of Italy has also entered the U.S. long distance market. Foreign investment in the U.S. telecommunications market is limited by laws restricting foreign firms from owning more than 25 percent of any common carrier that uses the radio spectrum.

Given the global nature of the telecommunications services industry, however, companies that offer services in their own national markets are looking to provide similar services internationally, often with cooperation of their foreign counterparts. One such example during 1992 was AT&T's announcement that it would provide digital private-line telephone service to the People's Republic of China by satellite. The service is the first stage of a $70 million digital network in which AT&T, KDD of Japan, and the Chinese Ministry of Posts and Telecommunications are participating. Another example is MCI's agreement to license its intelligent network (IN) to the Canadian Stentor telephone group (formerly Telecom Canada). MCI uses its IN system to offer calling card services, virtual network services, and a discounted outbound calling service package for small businesses. With slight software modifications, the Stentor Group companies will be able to offer similar services in Canada, as well as offer future IN services MCI and Stentor will jointly develop. Eventually, both companies will route all their IN traffic over this new integrated network.

A large number of international acquisitions, mergers and privatizations occurred between 1990–1992. A few such ventures include: Bell Atlantic and Ameritech's purchase of 90 percent of the New Zealand telephone company for $2.5 billion; Southwestern Bell's acquisition of a 25 percent position in Telmex of Mexico for $400 million; Bell South, along with Cable & Wireless, acquired 100 percent of Australia's second telephone carrier; and GTE, AT&T, and Telefonica de Espana purchased 40 percent of Venezuela's national telephone system for $1.8 billion.

An even greater level of activity has occurred in the cellular telephone sector. For example, Pacific Telesis is involved in systems in Germany and Portugal; Bell South bought shares of cellular networks in Denmark, Venezuela, and Chile; and US West joined with partners in Hungary, Czechoslovakia, Leningrad, and the United Kingdom. In the area of data communications and networking, AT&T purchased the British firm ISTEL, and MCI acquired a majority of the Infonet global network. US West and Bell Atlantic have set up a joint venture with Czechoslovakia to operate a packet-switching data network there.

International facilities competition will increase in the coming years as global telecommunications carriers compete to build transoceanic optical fiber and satellite links that position their home countries as communications hubs. Such central hubs can serve as links between high-volume traffic regions and economic centers of the world. In the latest such development, Teleglobe Canada, that country's international monopoly, stepped up competition with AT&T by announcing plans to construct two cables down each coast of the United States to vie for trans-Atlantic, trans-Pacific and pan-American telecommunications traffic. The new fiber routes would bypass U.S. networks to link Asia with Canada, and Europe with Latin America and the Caribbean via Canada.

Major segments of the international telecommunications services market include the international message telephone services (IMTS), the traditional telex and telegraph record services, international value-added network services (IVANS), and specialized services such as private line, virtual networks, and ISDN. U.S. revenues from international telecom services revenues are estimated to reach nearly $12 billion in 1993, up from about $10.5 billion in 1992. IMTS revenues account for more than two-thirds of that total.

Although revenues for some international services are not publicly available, international facsimile (including enhanced store-and-forward fax) and IVANs services are expected to grow substantially over the next few years. The U.S. Government continues its efforts to negotiate bilateral IVANS agreements to open up foreign markets to U.S. providers. During 1992, IVAN agreements were reached with the Netherlands and Germany, and prospects are favorable for concluding agreements with Sweden, Australia and France.

LONG-TERM PROSPECTS

Local Exchange Service

Since the divestiture of AT&T in 1984 from its 22 local Bell Operating Companies (BOCs), the "Baby Bells" have emerged as financially strong competitors. The BOCs have won a number of important regulatory freedoms in the past few years that will enable them to enter new markets (e.g., information services) as aggressive competitors, with inherent cost efficiencies due to their ownership of underlying local transmission and switching facilities. The BOCs will also continue their ventures in international telecommunications markets, where they have concentrated on investing in foreign private telephone company opportunities, and providing mobile radio services, cable television, and data communications.

Total revenues from local exchange service will be more than $84 billion in 1993, and are forecast to grow to almost $97 billion by 1997. The market for local telephone service will grow steadily at a rate of about 3 percent annually for the next several years, but market structure will begin to change as competition increases. One of the primary developments of 1992 was introduction of competitive access providers (CAPs) into local exchange competition. CAPs generally provide special, dedicated access between corporate customers and long distance telephone companies. In New York, a watershed decision by the state Public Service Commission created new rules that allow local competitors to sign business customers and then run cables from them to the central office switches of the New York Telephone Company, thereby gaining access to the public network. Such public network interconnection is the critical element in ensuring a competitive local market. In Chicago, Teleport Communications Group has proposed offering actual switched local telephone service in competition with the Illinois Bell Telephone Company, part of a far-reaching plan by the state Commerce Commission to establish a "Telecommunications Free Trade Zone" that would completely deregulate Illinois Bell within a defined downtown region.

Such alternate local access carriers (that provide local exchange services) offer some local business users with high volume telecommunications needs a viable option to the local telephone company. Other competitors in the local loop include satellite-based teleports, personal communications services (PCS), and cellular mobile radio telephone.

Overall penetration of such companies during the next 5 years is not likely to account for more than 3–4 percent of total local exchange revenues; it will amount to about $2 billion in 1993. The Bell Telephone Companies estimated in reports to the FCC during 1992 that revenue loss attributed to bypass from alternative carriers was more than $1 billion annually from switched facility bypass and about $500 million from private line facility bypass. Bypass concerns are important to subscribers, regulators and telephone companies because significant levels could force rate increases in basic residential telephone service. Local exchange competitors generally target only high-volume users, leaving the local telephone company to serve less profitable customers and raising carriers' costs for maintaining the public network.

In the face of such competition, local exchange carriers will continue to engage in mergers and acquisitions to strengthen and expand their customer and technology base. Recent examples of such mergers include: GTE's acquisition of Contel, creating one of the largest local companies with more than 16 million access lines; South Central Bell's merger with Hughes Telephone; Cincinnati Bell Inc. with Automated Phone Exchange of Utah; Pacific Telecom and the Mid Plain Telephone Company of Wisconsin; TDS Inc. with Humphrey and County Telephone Company of Tennessee; Rochester Telephone Company with at least 10 smaller independents; and ALLTEL with CP National.

An important development for the local exchange market has been the move from traditional rate-of-return regulation to a system of price caps, allowing these firms to reap direct profits from productivity gains and to maintain more market-oriented, flexible tariff structures. The phone companies have used their increased flexibility to offer unregulated enhanced services by launching new services such as customer local area signaling services, 700 and 900 number services, voice messaging, store-and-forward facsimile message transmission, electronic mail, audiotex, electronic directories, video conferencing, and caller ID.

An important ruling by the Pennsylvania Supreme Court that caller ID service is illegal, violating state wiretap laws, may have a significant impact on the future regulation of that service. There is currently a diverse number of laws and regulations across the country affecting the provision of caller ID, a service which allows customers to view the originating telephone number of a caller. Privacy advocates have opposed the service as an infringement on personal information. Several bills in Congress during 1992 addressed the issue of caller ID, and the future of the service is in question.

Additional customer services being marketed by local exchange service providers include measured toll service (MTS), pay telephone service, wide area telephone service (outbound WATS), 800 number services, analog and digital private leased lines, and directory and billing services. These services generated about $27 billion in revenues during 1992. The fastest growing segments are the WATS and 800/900 number services, respectively increasing at an annual rate of about 25 and 26 percent. The market for digital private circuits will increase approximately 30 percent in 1993.

The LECs ability to provide such services effectively will depend in large part on technological advances in the local network that will accelerate as more companies implement their plans for the Advanced Intelligent Network (AIN) and ISDN. Bell Atlantic introduced a preliminary version of the AIN service in 1992, allowing users to customize telephone call routing to meet their individual needs. Implementing these new technologies is strategically critical to the LECs because the new enhanced services mentioned above, as well as cellular telephone and PCS, may account for as much as one-third of local telephone company revenue in about five years.

Long Distance Service

In 1992, U.S. long distance carriers generated toll revenues of about $58 billion, an amount that should grow by 6.5 percent in 1993 to almost $62 billion, and to more than $79 billion by 1997. In 1984, the year divestiture took place, AT&T's toll revenues of $35 billion accounted for about 90 percent of all long distance revenues even though the FCC had introduced limited competition years earlier. In 1992, AT&T's share of total interLATA toll revenues had fallen to less than 63 percent, according to the FCC. Although its market share in revenue has fallen to less than two-thirds, AT&T's retained percentage share of minutes of traffic is higher because the company handles a higher number of operator-assisted and international calls than its competition.

The top three long distance service providers—AT&T, MCI and Sprint—have almost a 90 percent combined share of the market; the other 10 percent is shared by medium- and small-sized carriers. MCI's 1992 revenues were about $8.8 billion, a 15 percent market share, and Sprint had revenues of about $5.5 billion and a 9.5 percent market share. Some of the larger second-tier companies are Cable & Wireless Communications (a wholly owned subsidiary of its British parent), Williams Telecommunications Group (WilTel), and Metromedia/ITT, each with revenues of $500 million or less.

Consolidation in the long distance segment during 1992 kept pace with the level of activity in 1991, and will continue or even accelerate during the next few years as the major carriers consolidate their market shares, and smaller competitors face shrinking margins. A development worth noting is that some local facilities-based carriers, such as Rochester Telephone, have begun to absorb long distance resellers and private network carriers in their regions, blurring the boundaries between public and private telecommunications services markets and emphasizing regional one-stop shopping. During 1992, United Telecom purchased the remaining 20 percent of US Sprint owned by GTE and changed its name to Sprint. Sprint, in turn, emerged as the high bidder to acquire Centel Corporation, an independent local service telephone company. If this deal is consummated, Sprint will become the only company to provide local, long distance, and cellular telephone service in the United States. While the Bell Companies are currently prohibited from such activity, more independent LECs are likely to vigorously pursue such strategies to enter other markets, while long distance carriers will target local markets as well. Foreign telecommunications companies will also likely continue their penetration of the lucrative U.S. market.

Competition has also had an important effect on labor issues in the long distance market. The move to price cap rather than rate base regulation has eliminated the incentive for carriers to inflate their rate bases with excessive capital spending and cost structures. Profits are now directly related to productivity gains. Partially in response to this factor, tight budgets and slim profit margins are causing major carriers to scale back personnel and hiring. During 1992, for example, AT&T announced plans to replace up to one-third of its 18,000 long distance telephone operators by 1994 with a computerized voice response system.

Competition in the long distance market has also led to a proliferation of new services, some of which will experience high growth rates for the next few years. Key market segments in the domestic long distance industry include basic toll service (MTS), 800 and 900 number calling, WATS, private line, pay telephones, data communications, ISDN, and enhanced services. With about $7 billion in revenue, the 800 number market is the largest after basic MTS. The explosion of demand for video-conferencing services during the Gulf conflict in 1991 continued during 1992 and is expected to grow throughout the decade. AT&T, MCI and other providers of such services are beginning to offer centralized billing and volume discounts. The current market for such services is about $500 million, and may grow to more than $1 billion by 1995.

The technological foundation for the next generation of long distance services (e.g., ISDN) is composed of the SS7, digital switches, and optical fiber networks. All the major long distance carriers, as well as the LECs, have implemented SS7, an out-of-band signalling technology that sets up calls without first making a physical connection, although deployment is not yet complete. In 1992, the first stage of a U.S. national ISDN network was implemented. During the Transcontinental ISDN Project in November, the first national ISDN call was placed to demonstrate the interconnectivity of ISDN through the local and long distance networks. The RBOCs plan to have more than 60 million ISDN-capable access lines in service by the end of 1994.

Data Communications and Value-Added Network Services

The market for data communications services is evolving as the most dynamic segment of the telecommunications industry, driven in part by a growing demand for contracting with third party vendors for wide-area networking, local area network (LAN) interconnection, data processing, and value-added network services. Increasing numbers of small- and medium-sized businesses with international operations are saving on corporate communications budgets by contracting, or outsourcing, with international value-added network (IVAN) providers. IVANs can provide such services as electronic mail, credit card verification, store-and-forward multipoint facsimile service, point-of-sale transactions, electronic data interchange (EDI), database access and overall private network management. Such IVANs—typified by Electronic Data Systems, General Electric Information Services, and International Business Machines—base their networks largely on high-speed private leased lines purchased from carriers at bulk rate prices. IVANs can link LANs globally and offer efficient, reliable and inexpensive communications by virtue of the economies of scale they gain by maintaining a multinational presence. Customers avoid having to deal with different regulatory and technical standards across international borders by contracting with IVANs for centralized ordering, billing, and nearly seamless networks. The same conditions apply to domestic value-added network services as well.

The distinction between the value-added network services market, characterized by unregulated firms, and that of the data communications services provided by regulated common carriers is beginning to blur. CompuServe, for example, the Ohio-based on-line database provider, has built a global packet-switching network that now offers frame relay data transmission in direct competition with certain long distance and international carriers. Packet switching is a technique to enable the transfer of data among communicating equipment using a shared data network rather than a single physical telephone line connection. Packets of data can be transmitted across network nodes to the correct destination where the packets are reassembled into the proper sequence. Frame relay is a streamlined, fast packet-switching technology made possible by the error-free communications of optical fiber and improved transmission systems. The type of market consolidation exemplified by CompuService has been driven largely by developments in the corporate communications and private network field. Large corporations have typically maintained mid-size or mainframe computer networks with dedicated terminals, but also have allowed individual divisions or offices to operate self-contained LANs. In an effort to consolidate computer network resources and move toward distributed computing, such companies have in recent years begun connecting their disparate LAN and dedicated-user systems into relatively seamless corporate "enterprise" networks by using wide area network (WAN) technology such as routers, bridges and gateways (see the section on Computer Equipment and Software for more information on computer networking). Some estimates project that the number of LANs interconnected via WAN technology will quadruple in the next five years.

The demand to create enterprise networks has created an immediate need for high-speed public and private data communications transmission. These services will generate some of the highest growth in the telecommunications services industry during the next decade: 10–30 percent annually, depending on the service. Computer networks usually operate at very high transmission speeds. In contrast, the public telephone network has been required to operate only at the very low rates necessary to ensure clear, reliable voice transmission. Telephone carriers are now responding with a broad range of high-speed data communications services to meet the exploding demand for wide-area networking and compete in this dynamic data market.

The diversity of data communications standards and computer systems has also created a large demand for network management services to control enterprise networks. The cost of implementing, continually upgrading and operating such data networks has led increasing numbers of corporate communications users to contract their data communications and management needs out to third parties. Value-added network service providers are meeting this need, but telephone carriers have also found it necessary to create new services to serve this segment of the market. Syncordia, the Atlanta-based company owned by British Telecom, offers global network management to large corporate customers. Other carriers such as AT&T are also offering large customers discounted service packages to help manage corporate communications resources. AT&T's Tariff 12 and Tariff 15 service contracts, as well as their Virtual Private Network service, were designed to compete head-on with private VAN suppliers in the corporate telecommunications market.

The principal services introduced in 1992 by carriers to meet the need for such data communications services were frame relay and switched multimegabit data service (SMDS). WilTel was the first long distance carrier to introduce frame relay in 1992, followed by Advanced Telecommunications Corp., British Telecom North America, Glasgal Communications Inc., SP Telecom and Sprint. Until recently, the carriers most interested in offering frame relay have been VAN providers who have traditionally offered low-speed packet switching service based on the international standard known as X.25.

Bell Telephone Companies such as US West and major long-distance carriers have only recently begun to show serious interest in frame relay, which they view as a competitor to SMDS. SMDS uses cell relay technology, which will lead eventually to asynchronous transfer mode (ATM) switching technology deployment, and broadband ISDN. However, SMDS, like ATM switching, requires significant network modifications and is about five years from being widely available. Recognizing that a strong market currently exists for frame relay services, the Bell Operating Companies and other major carriers announced their support in 1992 for nationwide frame relay.

The introduction of frame relay by local and long distance carriers will lead to greater data communications interoperability among frame relay networks, among the Bell Companies themselves, and between the Bell Companies and the long distance companies and VANs. Within five years the carriers will make SMDS available on a nationwide basis. At that time, frame relay services may continue to serve the lower end of the LAN internetworking market, while SMDS may attract customers that demand very high speed networks.

The market sector captured by private companies for value-added services, including electronic data interchange, business communications like electronic mail and enhanced facsimile, managed network services, and consumer services like database access, will reach about $8 billion in 1993. Data communications services provided by telephone carriers, in contrast, will generate revenues of less than $2.5 billion. During the next five years as AT&T and the Bell Companies begin to use their newly acquired regulatory freedom to accelerate entry into the markets for enhanced services, their shares of the entire data communications market will increase. The application-specific enhanced services provided by the value-added carriers today will remain a high growth market that increasingly will attract foreign owned telecom companies to provide those services to and within the United States.—*Ivan H. Shefrin and Daniel W. Edwards, Telecommunications Services, Rates, Trends, and Policy; Linda Gossack, Cellular and Radio Services; and Patricia Cooper, Satellite Services, Office of Telecommunications, (202) 482-4466.*

Largest Local Telephone Companies by Access Lines, 1991

Telephone Companies	Telephone Lines
Bell Atlantic Corp.	17,750,000
BellSouth Corp.	17,614,737
Ameritech Corp.	16,684,000
GTE Corp.	15,632,000
NYNEX	15,409,521
Pacific Telesis Group	14,262,000
US West Communications	12,934,679
Southwestern Bell Corp.	12,129,433
United Telecommunications, Inc.	4,083,205
Contel Service Corp.	1,887,000
Southern New England Telephone Co.	1,593,406
Centel Corp.	1,210,864
ALLTEL Corp.	906,047
Puerto Rico Telephone Co.	852,625
Cincinnati Bell Telephone Co.	796,214
Rochester Telephone Enterprises, Inc.	357,132
Century Telephone Enterprises	314,819
Telephone & Data Systems, Inc.	304,000
Pacific Telecom, Inc.	233,995
Lincoln Telephone & Telegraph Co.	196,622

SOURCE: United States Telephone Association.

Trends and Forecasts: Telecommunications Services (SIC 4812, 4813, 4822)[1]

(in millions of dollars except as noted)

Item	1988	1989	1990	1991	1992[2]	1993[3]	Percent Change 1988–89	1989–90	1990–91	1991–92	1992–93
Operating revenues[4]											
Domestic	136,193	143,086	146,147	153,942	162,475	172,546	5.1	2.1	5.3	5.5	6.2
International	5,754	6,636	7,662	9,296	10,465	11,896	15.3	15.5	21.3	12.6	13.7
Operating revenues (1987$)											
Domestic	134,713	140,349	143,803	151,473	157,559	167,423	4.2	2.5	5.3	4.0	6.3
Total employment (000)[5]	917.7	900.5	925.5	914.8	881.4	868.0	−1.9	2.8	−1.2	−3.7	−1.5
Production workers (000)	654.9	646.3	666.6	670.9	655.7	647.0	−1.3	3.1	0.6	−2.3	−1.3
Average hourly earnings ($)	13.83	14.14	14.17	14.62	14.90	15.04	2.2	0.2	3.2	1.9	0.9

[1]Includes AT&T, BOCs, cellular, independents, mobile radio, VANs, telex and telegraph.
[2]Estimate.
[3]Forecast.
[4]Data include LEC access charge revenues.
[5]Includes telephone and telegraph workers.

SOURCE: U.S. Department of Commerce: Bureau of the Census, Bureau of Economic Analysis, and International Trade Administration (ITA); U.S. Department of Labor, Bureau of Labor Statistics; Federal Communications Commission. Estimates and forecasts by ITA.

Total Toll Service Revenues

(in millions of dollars)

Company	1981	1982	1983	1984	1985	1986	1987	1988	1989	1990	1991
AT&T Communications				34,935	36,770	36,514	35,219	35,407	34,549	33,880	34,384
MCI Telecommunications[1]	413	802	1,326	1,761	2,331	3,372	3,938	4,886	6,171	7,392	8,266
(Telecom*USA)				105	201	291	396	524	713		
US Sprint[2]						1,141	2,592	3,405	4,320	5,041	5,378
(GTE Sprint)	231	393	740	1,052	1,122	779					
(US Telecom)					387	212					
Cable & Wireless					146	171	180	218	275	359	406
Williams Telecommunications Group									300	376	405
Metromedia Communications Corp.[3]									127	381	389
(ITT Communications Services Inc.)	83	128	163	161	241	282	287	379	404		
Advanced Telecommunications Corp.				72	86	124	162	178	326	342	356
Allnet[4]					309	450	395	394	334	326	350
(Lexitel)					127						
ALASCOM	191	238	257	255	271	267	262	272	278	259	338
Telesphere Network, Inc.[5]									192	293	308
(National Telephone Services, Inc.)									150		
LDDS Communications, Inc.									110	154	263
Litel Telecommunications, Inc.									197	215	208
International Telecharge, Inc.									275	230	181
RCI Corporation/RCI Network Services									104	142	155
ComSystems Network Services										130	131
Others[6]	144	263	443	414	639	992	1,352	1,823	2,359	2,582	3,765
TOTAL LONG DISTANCE CARRIERS				38,755	42,630	44,595	44,783	47,486	51,184	52,102	55,283
AT&T COMUNICATIONS SHARE (percent)				90.1	86.3	81.9	78.6	74.6	67.5	65.0	62.2
MCI COMMUNICATIONS SHARE (percent)				4.5	5.5	7.6	8.8	10.3	12.1	14.2	15.0
US SPRINT SHARE (percent)				2.7	2.6	4.3	5.8	7.2	8.4	9.7	9.7
OTHERS (percent)				2.7	5.6	6.2	6.8	7.9	12.0	11.1	13.1
BELL OPERATING COMPANIES				9,037	9,026	9,599	10,268	10,668	10,549	10,578	10,068
OTHER LOCAL EXCHANGE COMPANIES				3,364	3,159	3,304	3,468	4,445	4,402	4,305	4,049
TOTAL: LOCAL EXCHANGE COMPANIES				12,401	12,185	12,903	13,736	15,113	14,951	14,883	14,117
TOTAL: ALL CARRIERS	39,180	43,919	46,970	51,156	54,815	57,498	58,519	62,599	66,135	66,985	69,400

[1]MCI Telecommunications and Telecom*USA merged. Information for 1990 is combined.
[2]In July 1986, GTE Sprint and US Telecom merged and became known as US Sprint.
[3]Metromedia Communicaions and ITT Communications merged during 1988.
[4]Allnet and Lexitel merged at year end 1985.
[5]Telesphere Network and National Telephone Services merged during 1989.
[6]FCC estimate.
SOURCES:Federal Communications Commission, Industry Analysis Division.

Glossary

Antidumping duty A duty imposed by the United States Government to offset any profits that a foreign firm attempts to make by dumping merchandise on the U.S. market. (See dumping.)

Apparent consumption Product shipments plus imports minus exports.

CAD/CAM/CAE Computer-aided design, computer-aided manufacturing, and computer-aided engineering.

Caribbean Basin Initiative (CBI) An inter-American program, led by the United States, of increased economic assistance and trade preferences to Caribbean and Central American countries. CBI provides duty-free access to the U.S. market for most products from the region, and promotes private sector development in the region.

c.i.f. Cost, insurance, and freight.

CIM Computer-integrated manufacturing.

Commonwealth of Independent States (CIS) Twelve countries that were formerly part of the Soviet Union. They are often referred to as the newly independent states. (The three Baltic countries are now considered part of Eastern Europe.)

Compact disc read-only memory (CD–ROM) High-density data storage technology for computer databases and other applications, including entertainment.

Conference Board A nonprofit, nonpolitical group that specializes in the collection, analysis, and reporting of business activity. (845 Third Ave., New York, NY 10022.)

Constant dollars (or "real" dollars) Dollar values converted to a base price level, calculated by dividing current dollars by a deflator. This conversion takes a year's output and values it using the prices of the base (reference) year. Comparison of constant dollar measures permits evaluation of changes in output after adjustment for inflation.

Consumer Price Index (CPI) Measures the average change in prices of goods and services purchased by U.S. consumers.

Countervailing duty A retaliatory charge that a country places on imported goods to counter the subsidies or bounties granted to the exporters of the goods by their home governments.

Current dollars The actual amount paid in sales transactions.

Source: *U.S. Industrial Outlook 1993*, U.S. Department of Commerce, International Trade Administration.

Defense Advanced Research Projects Agency (DARPA) An organization of the Department of Defense responsible for sponsoring advanced research.

Dumping A term used in international trade that means the sale of a product in export markets below the selling price for the same product in domestic markets.

EC92 The economic merger of the 12 countries of the European Community (EC) into a single market by the end of 1992. The process is continuous, however, as EC directives are implemented by member states, and extends beyond 1992.

Eurodollars Deposits denominated in U.S. dollars in commercial banks outside the United States.

European Currency Unit (ECU) An international unit of account created for the European Monetary System (EMS), to be used as the denominator of EMS debts and credits and as a reserve credit in the European Monetary Cooperation Fund (EMCF). The ECU is composed of a weighted basket of currencies of EC members.

Export-Import Bank (Eximbank) An autonomous agency of the U.S. Government created in 1934 to facilitate the export trade of the United States.

Fiscal Year (FY) Designation of a year for budget and accounting purposes.

Foreign trade zones (FTZs) Designated areas in the United States, usually near ports of entry, considered to be outside the customs territory of the United States. Also known as free trade zones.

Free alongside ship (f.a.s.) The transaction price of an export product, including freight, insurance, and other charges incurred in placing the merchandise alongside the carrier in the U.S. port.

Free on board (f.o.b.) Without charge to the buyer for placing goods on board a carrier at the point of shipment.

G–7 (Group of Seven) Seven industrial countries: the United States, Japan, Germany, France, the United Kingdom, Italy, and Canada. G–7 leaders have met at annual economic summits since 1975 to coordinate their economic policies.

General Agreement on Tariffs and Trade (GATT) An international organization and code of tariffs and trade rules that has evolved out of the multilateral trade treaty signed in 1947. GATT is dedicated to equal treatment for all trading nations, reduction of tariffs and nontariff barriers by negotiation, and elimination of import quotas. (See Uruguay Round.)

Generalized System of Preferences (GSP) A system approved by GATT in 1971 that authorizes developed countries to give preferential tariff treatment to developing countries.

Gross domestic product (GDP) The value of all goods and services produced in a country.

Gross national product (GNP) The value of all goods and services produced in a country plus income earned in foreign countries less income payable to foreign sources.

Harmonized System An international convention, implemented by the United States in 1989, for classifying imports and exports so that data from different countries are comparable.

High definition television (HDTV) Commercial television broadcasting and reception without about twice the reception quality of that currently in use.

Industry shipments The total value of all products shipped by establishments classified in the industry, plus the miscellaneous receipts.

Intellectual property Includes trademarks, copyrights, patents, and trade secrets.

International Monetary Fund (IMF) Established in 1945, the IMF is a permanent forum for its member countries to coordinate economic and financial policies. It monitors compliance with agreements to maintain orderly exchange rates, provides resources to members facing balance-of-payments difficulties, and offers technical and policy assistance.

Joint venture A business enterprise undertaken by two business entities.

Just-in-time (JIT) delivery A management technique in which a manufacturer works closely with its suppliers to assure that critical components are delivered as needed in order to avoid disruptions of the production process and the costs of maintaining excessive inventories.

Maquila (maquiladora) Mexican assembly plant; most of its production is exported to the United States.

Ministry of International Trade and Industry (MITI) Japanese government agency with broad powers over the country's trade policies.

Most-favored-nation (MFN) trade status An arrangement in which GATT countries must extend to all other members the most favorable treatment granted to any trading partner, thus assuring that any tariff reductions or other trade concession is automatically extended to all GATT parties.

Multifiber Arrangement (MFA) Trade agreements, under GATT auspices, between major textile importing and exporting countries covering most of the world trade in textiles. The MFA was extended for the fifth time in July 1991, to be in effect through December 1992.

NEC Not elsewhere classified.

National Defense Stockpile Materials deemed critical for national defense, and the amounts of each required to meet national security requirements, administered by the Department of Defense.

NIC Newly industrialized (or industrializing) country. Developing countries that have experienced rapid growth in GDP, industrial production, and exports in recent years.

North American Free Trade Agreement (NAFTA) An agreement to create a free trade area among the United States, Canada, and Mexico. The agreement has not yet been approved by the three governments.

Organization for Economic Cooperation and Development (OECD) Group of 24 industrialized, market economy countries of North America, Europe, the Far East, and the South Pacific. The OECD, which has headquarters in Paris, was established in 1961 to promote economic development and international trade.

Organization of Petroleum Exporting Countries (OPEC) An association of important oil-exporting countries that was formed in 1960. Its major purpose is to coordinate the petroleum production and pricing policies of its 13 members.

Pacific Rim (Pacific Basin) A term that technically means all countries adjoining the Pacific Ocean, although it is normally understood to refer to East Asian countries.

Producers Price Index (PPI) Measures average changes in prices of all commodities produced or imported for sale in commercial transactions in the United States.

Product shipments The total value of specific products shipped by all establishments, irrespective of the industry classification of the establishments.

Real dollars See constant dollars.

Standard Industrial Classification (SIC) system The standard established by the Federal Government for defining industries and classifying individual establishments by industry.

Total quality management (TQM) A management technique to improve the quality of goods and services, reduce operating costs, and increase customer acceptance.

Uruguay Round Eighth round of on-going multilateral trade negotiations held under GATT auspices. Named for the country where initial discussions began in September 1986.

U.S.-Canada Free Trade Agreement (FTA) Implemented in January 1989 to eliminate all tariffs on U.S. and Canadian goods by January 1998 and to reduce or eliminate many nontariff barriers.

Value added The difference between the value of goods produced and the cost of producing them.

Voluntary restraint agreement (VRA) An import relief device to limit foreign trade in a particular commodity and protect domestic industry from injury by foreign competition. Sometimes referred to as a voluntary export restraint or an orderly marketing agreement.

World Bank The International Bank for Reconstruction and Development (IBRD), the most important member of the World Bank Group, was created in 1945 as a companion organization to the IMF. The main purposes of the IBRD are to lend funds at commercial rates and provide technical and policy assistance to foster the economic development of its poorer member countries.

METRIC CONVERSION TABLE

(approximate conversions to metric measures)

This table is included here to help readers who follow U.S. industry and business competition in world markets. A few chapters in this edition of the OUTLOOK present data about production or consumption in both metric and English measurements—chapters (Wood Products)* and (Foods and Beverages), for example. Most chapters, however, report production and consumption only in English measurement. The United States remains one of the few countries in the world still using English measurement.

*The industry standard for wood products converts linear board feet into cubic meters.

Symbol	When You Know	Multiply by	To Find	Symbol
		LENGTH		
in	inches	2.5	centimeters	cm
ft	feet	30	centimeters	cm
yd	yards	0.9	meters	m
mi	miles	1.6	kilometers	km
		AREA		
in^2	square inches	6.5	square centimeters	cm^2
ft^2	square feet	0.09	square meters	m^2
yd^2	square yards	0.8	square meters	m^2
mi^2	square miles	2.6	square kilometers	km^2
	acres	0.4	hectares	ha
		MASS (weight)		
oz	ounces	28	grams	g
lb	pounds	0.45	kilograms	kg
	short tons (2000 lb)	0.9	metric ton	t
		VOLUME		
tsp	teaspoons	5	milliliters	ml
Tbsp	tablespoons	15	milliliters	ml
in^3	cubic inches	16	milliliters	ml
fl oz	fluid ounces	30	milliliters	ml
c	cups	0.24	liters	l
pt	pints	0.47	liters	l
qt	quarts	0.95	liters	l
gal	gallons	3.8	liters	l
ft^3	cubic feet	0.03	cubic meters	m^3
yd^3	cubic yards	0.76	cubic meters	m^3
		TEMPERATURE (exact)		
°F	degrees Fahrenheit	5/9 (after subtracting 32)	degrees Celsius	°C

SOURCE: U.S. Department of Commerce, Metric Program Office.

MEDIA GENERAL P/E DISTRIBUTIONS BY MARKET
(for week ended 07/02/93)

P/E Ratios Now

Rankings as of July 2, 1993

Stocks by P/E Ranking*	Composite Now	Composite 52 Weeks Ago	NYSE Now	NYSE 52 Weeks Ago	ASE Now	ASE 52 Weeks Ago	OTC Now	OTC 52 Weeks Ago
Top 5%	58.0	53.1	46.1	47.3	63.5	60.5	61.5	58.3
10%	40.2	38.3	35.8	33.1	45.0	42.6	43.0	40.6
15%	33.0	31.0	29.3	27.9	34.4	34.6	34.8	33.0
20%	28.2	26.7	25.2	24.3	29.6	29.5	29.2	27.9
25%	24.6	23.6	23.5	22.3	25.4	25.0	25.7	24.4
30%	21.9	21.4	21.2	20.9	21.9	21.3	22.5	21.9
35%	20.1	19.7	19.9	19.6	19.8	19.0	20.3	20.2
40%	18.6	18.2	18.8	18.3	18.2	17.5	18.4	18.2
45%	17.5	16.9	18.0	17.3	17.0	16.0	17.3	16.9
50%	16.4	15.7	17.1	16.2	15.8	14.8	15.9	15.5
55%	15.4	14.5	16.3	15.0	14.6	13.7	14.8	14.3
60%	14.4	13.6	15.4	14.0	13.7	12.9	13.8	13.3
65%	13.6	12.7	14.8	13.2	12.8	12.1	12.9	12.4
70%	12.7	11.9	14.1	12.7	11.8	11.3	11.9	11.4
75%	11.7	11.0	13.3	12.0	11.1	10.3	11.0	10.6
80%	10.8	10.1	12.4	11.1	10.1	9.2	10.2	9.7
85%	9.7	9.0	11.5	10.1	9.1	8.4	9.2	8.8
90%	8.5	7.9	9.9	8.7	8.0	7.3	8.1	7.6
95%	7.0	6.3	8.2	7.2	6.5	5.7	6.7	6.0
No. of Companies	4,146	3,759	1,298	1,237	433	381	2,415	2,141

P/E Ratio Ranges	Composite Now	Composite 52 Weeks Ago	NYSE Now	NYSE 52 Weeks Ago	ASE Now	ASE 52 Weeks Ago	OTC Now	OTC 52 Weeks Ago
0.1 to 1.9	.3%	.2%	.1%	.1%	.4%	.0%	.3%	.2%
2.0 to 2.9	.1	.3	.2	.1	.1	.5	.1	.3
3.0 to 3.9	.2	.4	.1	.1	.1	.2	.2	.6
4.0 to 4.9	.4	.5	.1	.3	.7	.7	.5	.6
5.0 to 5.9	.7	.9	.3	1.0	.8	1.2	.9	.8
6.0 to 6.9	1.1	1.3	.9	.8	1.1	1.3	1.3	1.5
7.0 to 7.9	1.6	1.7	.9	1.6	1.9	1.9	2.0	1.7
8.0 to 8.9	2.2	2.4	1.7	2.3	2.4	2.5	2.5	2.5
9.0 to 9.9	2.6	2.4	1.7	1.7	2.6	1.8	3.0	2.8
10.0 to 11.9	5.8	5.6	4.6	5.6	5.6	5.4	6.4	5.6
12.0 to 13.9	6.3	6.4	6.8	8.7	5.7	5.8	6.1	5.3
14.0 to 15.9	6.3	4.7	8.4	5.3	4.7	3.5	5.5	4.5
16.0 to 17.9	5.1	3.9	6.4	5.1	4.3	3.1	4.7	3.5
18.0 to 19.9	4.3	3.5	6.7	5.1	3.3	3.0	3.2	2.9
20.0 to 24.9	6.3	6.1	8.5	8.2	3.9	3.0	5.6	5.7
25.0 to 29.9	3.8	3.2	3.6	3.4	3.7	2.7	4.0	3.2
30.0 to 39.9	4.4	3.8	4.6	3.4	4.0	3.1	4.4	4.1
40.0 to 49.9	2.0	1.6	1.8	1.3	1.7	2.0	2.2	1.7
50.0 And Over	3.8	3.2	2.3	2.5	4.4	3.4	4.4	3.5
Cannot Calculate	42.7	48.0	40.3	43.1	48.8	55.0	42.6	49.1
No. of Companies	7,231		2,175		846		4,210	

*Excludes negative and zero earnings companies.

Source: Media General Financial Services, Inc., Richmond, Virginia.

MEDIA GENERAL INDUSTRY INDEXES
(for week ended 07/02/93)

Jan. 2, 1970 = 100 — M/G Composite Index 200 days Ago: 432.71

Industry	Index					Percent Change				Fundamental						
	Week's Close	Previous Week's Close	30 Days Ago	90 Days Ago	52-Wk Moving Average	For Week	30 Days	90 Days	Year To Date	P/E Ratio Now	5-Year Average P/E	12 Mos. Earnings Change - (%)	5-Year Earnings Growth - (%)	Dividend Yield - (%)	Return On Equity - (%)	Profit Margin - (%)
Composite	473.44	471.70	475.89	450.42	448.76	.3	-.5	5.1	5.1	26.6	18.7	9	-8	2.4	9.2	3.6
01. Aerospace	725.14	736.40	720.44	646.38	649.36	-1.5	.6	12.1	10.2	10.6	12.4	35	-0	2.5	14.8	3.6
02. Airlines	299.41	291.42	322.35	227.44	253.16	2.7	-7.1	31.6	28.2	NC	NC	NE	NC	.5	NE	-3.0
03. Automotive	246.38	247.40	248.61	210.82	212.61	-.4	-.9	16.8	24.0	NC	NC	NE	NC	1.7	NE	.0
04. Banking	401.57	395.15	383.57	377.73	355.05	1.6	4.6	6.3	12.5	17.7	49.9	39	30	2.4	10.2	6.4
05. Building	342.60	340.66	348.22	345.74	318.59	.5	-1.6	-.9	5.9	29.0	NM	290	-35	2.4	6.6	2.4
06. Building-Heavy	715.79	725.30	730.40	734.73	670.09	-1.3	-2.0	-2.5	4.7	NC	NC	-100	NC	1.5	2.8	.5
07. Business Data Proc	208.77	209.30	219.69	205.11	206.80	-.2	-4.9	1.7	.1	NC	NM	-100	NC	1.0	NE	-1.6
08. Business Equipment	211.99	218.82	220.76	203.32	200.41	-3.1	-3.9	4.2	7.4	NM	46.4	-60	-14	1.3	4.7	1.2
09. Business Services	320.81	319.63	335.47	344.99	339.36	.3	-4.3	-7.0	-10.6	22.5	18.9	12	-6	2.4	12.2	4.5
10. Chemicals	647.66	650.13	681.02	642.85	659.91	-.3	-4.9	.7	-1.6	24.3	13.4	-9	-13	3.0	10.4	3.7
11. Communications	659.52	653.01	638.44	595.29	592.56	1.0	3.3	10.7	12.3	25.0	17.5	11	-4	3.1	14.6	8.6
12. Cosmetic-Personal	388.20	376.69	380.01	408.98	393.17	3.0	2.1	-5.0	-2.6	22.2	NC	29	12	1.7	30.0	6.1
13. Credit	403.08	395.31	382.72	339.66	338.00	1.9	5.3	18.6	9.3	19.0	16.1	26	-4	2.4	11.9	4.3
14. Distillers-Brewers	612.17	608.60	652.23	524.40	558.68	.5	-6.1	16.7	16.2	53.2	17.8	-8	-5	.9	14.0	7.5
15. Drug Manufacturers	782.82	812.23	858.81	803.86	903.51	-3.6	-8.8	-2.6	-17.7	19.8	22.1	6	8	3.0	25.0	14.3
16. Electrical Equip	632.69	631.87	629.98	557.03	575.63	.1	.4	13.5	13.0	21.8	28.1	-19	-6	2.2	11.1	3.6
17. Electronics	544.76	547.61	537.37	455.23	445.39	-.5	1.3	19.6	25.4	31.6	30.9	4	3	.7	7.0	3.0
18. Food Production	837.24	842.23	884.77	928.41	910.82	-.5	-5.3	-9.8	-13.2	24.0	18.9	-26	8	2.6	17.4	4.4
19. Food-Packed Goods	1195.73	1186.74	1211.40	1250.87	1242.60	.7	-1.2	-4.4	-6.1	17.1	16.7	13	11	2.3	25.2	5.3
20. Food-Meats-Dairy	918.43	911.20	948.07	1012.44	978.12	.7	-3.1	-9.2	-12.6	42.2	21.7	-64	-8	2.0	6.9	1.1
21. Food-Confections	1382.46	1381.68	1385.04	1433.92	1401.41	.0	-.1	-3.5	-4.5	22.9	21.1	20	8	1.4	20.4	6.9
22. Freight-Shipping	429.54	419.42	413.64	424.54	401.32	2.4	3.8	1.1	2.6	25.7	22.9	14	-10	1.5	5.9	2.0
23. Health	486.04	481.41	493.94	477.36	511.27	.9	-1.6	1.8	-14.1	26.3	29.7	6	3	1.1	12.2	5.1
24. Hotels-Motels-Res	750.87	746.65	778.84	700.20	691.38	.5	-3.5	7.2	6.2	26.6	22.0	9	-5	1.0	11.5	4.7
25. Housewares-Furn.	494.40	490.05	500.89	478.61	473.67	.8	-1.3	3.3	.7	26.0	16.8	0	-5	1.3	10.2	3.0

26. Insurance	526.29	522.94	513.60	499.33	480.59	.6	2.4	5.4	6.4	23.1	11.9	-33	-4	1.6	6.5	3.8
27. Investments	167.69	165.10	162.73	159.97	156.67	1.5	3.0	4.8	9.8	12.9	11.3	13	15	5.0	19.6	9.2
28. Machinery-Heavy	491.15	435.46	422.77	400.18	386.87	12.7	16.1	22.7	20.9	76.6	NM	NE	NC	1.5	1.6	.8
29. Machine-Lt-Equip	449.64	440.16	449.31	420.93	417.51	2.1	.0	6.8	10.3	NM	39.3	-6	-36	2.0	1.0	.4
30. Metals Fabrication	544.19	534.49	529.52	484.98	465.20	1.8	2.7	12.2	17.3	30.1	NM	111	-15	1.6	6.1	2.0
31. Metals-Iron-Steel	183.18	181.75	182.54	165.84	161.05	.7	.3	10.4	17.5	NC	NC	NE	NC	2.1	NE	-.9
32. Metals-Nonf-Coal	184.60	178.22	179.08	183.12	181.85	3.5	3.0	.8	1.7	NC	59.3	-100	NC	2.2	NE	-.6
33. Metals, Rare	447.84	414.25	402.24	302.43	311.16	8.1	11.3	48.0	70.8	89.3	71.2	-32	-30	1.7	6.2	5.7
34. Multi-Industry	275.89	274.14	276.07	259.41	256.20	.6	-.0	6.3	10.5	35.6	22.1	126	-25	2.7	6.9	1.7
35. Oil, Nat Gas Svcs	483.91	486.75	488.11	447.92	452.81	-.5	-.8	8.0	14.9	23.4	NC	-23	-11	2.6	7.4	3.4
36. Oil, Nat Gas Prod	250.47	249.71	252.76	231.84	232.56	.3	-.9	8.0	17.0	32.4	NC	46	-9	3.4	4.1	1.8
37. Oil Refin, Mkting	620.98	628.04	636.83	601.67	591.95	-1.1	-2.4	3.2	10.1	21.9	17.1	28	-0	4.0	8.5	2.5
38. Paper, Packaging	584.73	584.93	593.46	604.18	593.66	-.0	-1.4	-3.2	-3.5	69.8	17.6	-34	-27	2.1	3.6	1.4
39. Personal Services	315.81	313.29	313.76	300.55	294.29	.8	.6	5.0	5.3	20.5	29.1	-8	6	1.1	9.5	6.4
40. Precision Instruments	184.58	184.24	186.06	180.33	174.20	.1	-.8	2.3	10.1	23.8	21.4	-6	-12	2.5	10.6	3.7
41. Publishing	749.81	747.38	743.72	715.69	696.53	.3	.8	4.7	6.8	34.3	31.5	88	-14	1.5	8.0	5.4
42. Railroads	748.88	737.08	746.96	708.45	673.12	1.6	.2	5.7	12.2	26.8	NC	NE	NC	2.1	7.6	4.4
43. Real Estate Inves	178.38	178.31	171.18	171.55	161.69	.0	4.2	3.9	10.0	23.3	45.5	-13	2	3.5	9.4	8.5
44. Real Estate	74.17	73.62	74.95	69.94	66.32	.7	-1.0	6.0	9.4	NC	NC	NE	NC	3.0	NE	-1.3
45. Recreation-Luxury	281.98	280.80	285.56	262.89	262.06	.4	-1.2	7.2	3.2	29.0	35.9	18	-9	.8	12.3	3.9
46. Recreation-Bdcstg	2708.50	2682.64	2558.40	2410.24	2273.03	.9	5.8	12.3	18.0	63.1	NM	NC	NC	.3	3.5	1.4
47. Recreation-Mov-Sp	1803.76	1816.24	1828.49	1733.30	1646.63	-.6	-1.3	4.0	4.6	29.0	62.2	126	-12	1.2	11.1	6.1
48. Retail-Apparel	1720.49	1733.77	1921.19	1846.87	1856.80	-.7	-10.4	-6.8	-15.3	30.6	20.6	-26	-7	1.3	12.6	2.8
49. Retail-Dept Strs	349.54	349.19	358.63	326.68	316.07	.1	-2.5	7.0	10.1	80.8	18.9	-69	-18	1.9	3.0	.7
50. Retail-Disc, Drug	1187.27	1209.06	1283.85	1356.03	1326.14	-1.8	-7.5	-12.4	-16.5	23.7	22.6	5	9	1.2	14.7	2.3
51. Retail-Food Strs	807.28	808.01	830.75	768.90	764.71	-.0	-2.8	4.9	3.1	25.0	37.9	-34	NC	1.3	16.9	1.0
52. Retail-Misc	963.66	948.93	979.16	943.35	902.44	1.5	-1.5	2.1	-2.1	28.6	20.2	22	2	1.0	11.3	1.8
53. Rubber-Plastic	519.79	523.68	537.05	513.46	515.89	-.7	-3.2	1.2	.5	20.7	16.0	39	-16	2.8	11.9	3.7
54. Savings and Loan	386.03	380.03	374.76	381.79	352.14	1.5	3.0	1.1	9.6	17.4	NC	13	-23	2.0	7.1	5.5
55. Shoes-Leather	847.55	856.17	1053.52	995.81	991.51	-1.0	-19.5	-14.8	-22.3	14.3	15.2	13	13	1.3	14.6	4.5
56. Textile Mfg	539.31	536.28	555.85	535.42	527.08	.5	-2.9	.7	-5.3	23.0	17.6	-1	-7	.6	9.7	3.1
57. Textiles-Apparel	528.55	530.28	568.61	561.56	569.08	-.3	-7.0	-5.8	-8.5	7.3	NM	NE	-17	1.2	8.7	2.5
58. Tobacco	1402.32	1404.74	1447.93	1706.26	1814.67	-.1	-3.1	-17.8	-28.9	9.8	12.0	25	14	5.7	31.3	6.7
59. Utilities-Electric	199.11	197.73	191.90	195.87	186.40	.7	3.7	1.6	9.0	15.4	12.7	13	-2	5.4	11.2	9.4
60. Utilities-Gas-Oth	333.18	327.71	323.91	301.53	302.72	1.6	2.8	10.5	15.8	16.4	24.2	320	-7	4.5	6.0	5.0

Source: Media General Financial Services, Inc., Richmond, Virginia.

General Business and Economic Indicators

SELECTED BUSINESS STATISTICS

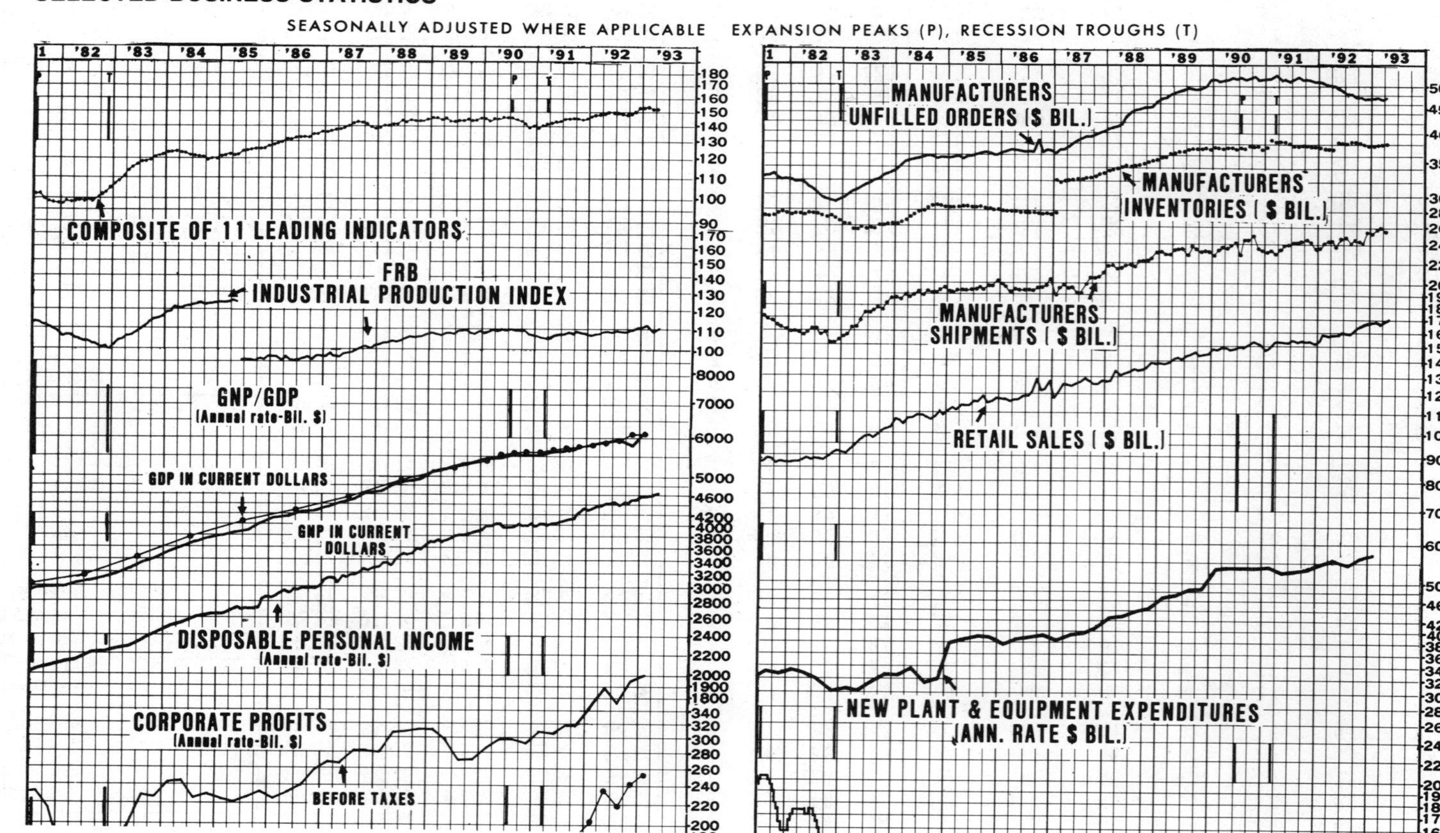

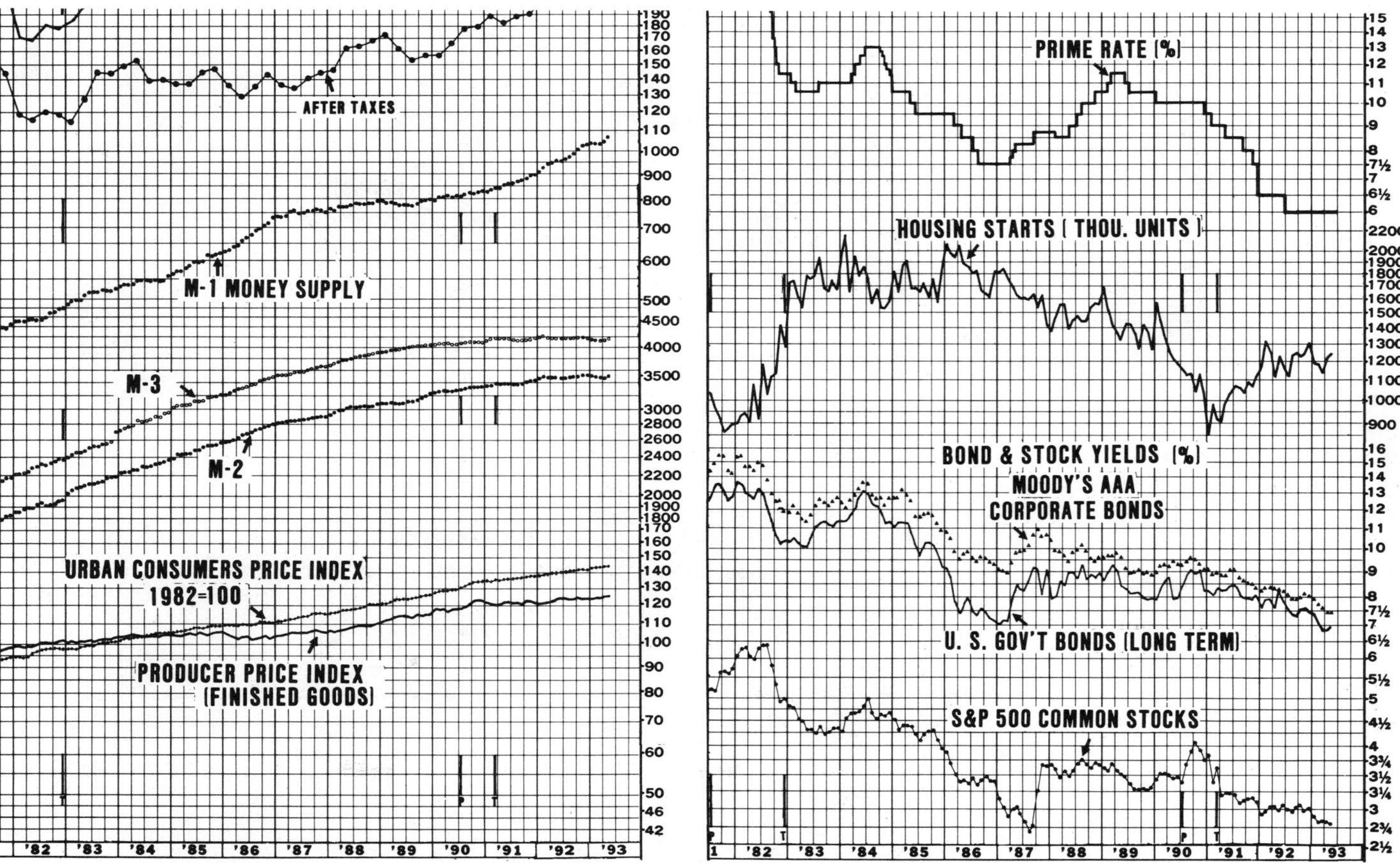

Source: Chart Courtesy of Securities Research Company, a division of Babson-United Investment Advisors, Inc., 101 Prescott St., Wellesley Hills, MA 02181-3319.

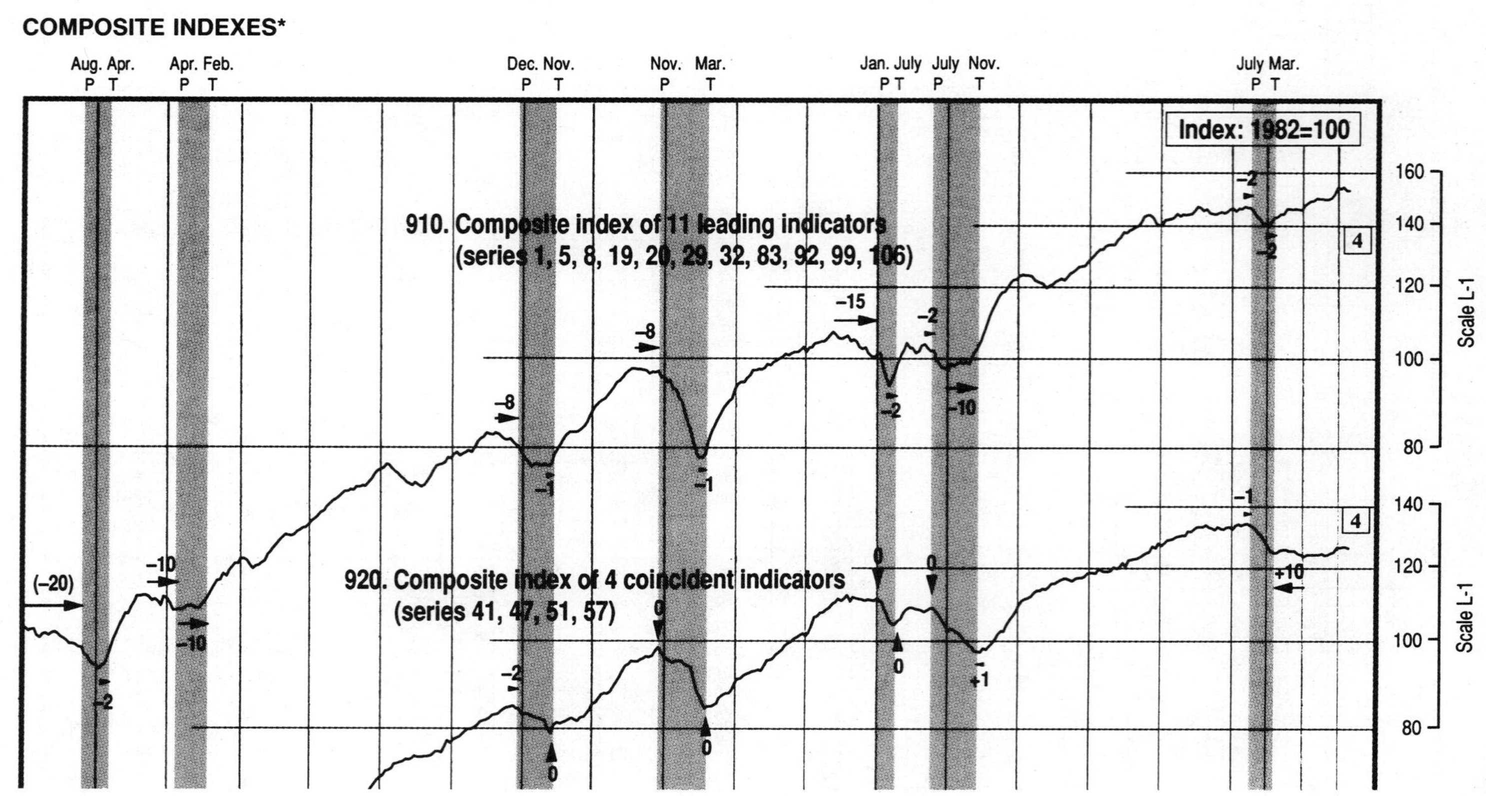
COMPOSITE INDEXES*
Aug. Apr.
P T
Apr. Feb.
P T
Dec. Nov.
P T
Nov. Mar.
P T
Jan. July
P T
July Nov.
P T
July Mar.
P T
Index: 1982=100
910. Composite index of 11 leading indicators
(series 1, 5, 8, 19, 20, 29, 32, 83, 92, 99, 106)
920. Composite index of 4 coincident indicators
(series 41, 47, 51, 57)
Scale L-1
160
140
120
100
80
Scale L-1
140
120
100
80
4
4
(–20)
–2
–10
–10
–8
–1
–8
–1
–15
–2
–2
–2
–10
–2
–2
–2
0
0
0
0
0
0
+1
–1
+10

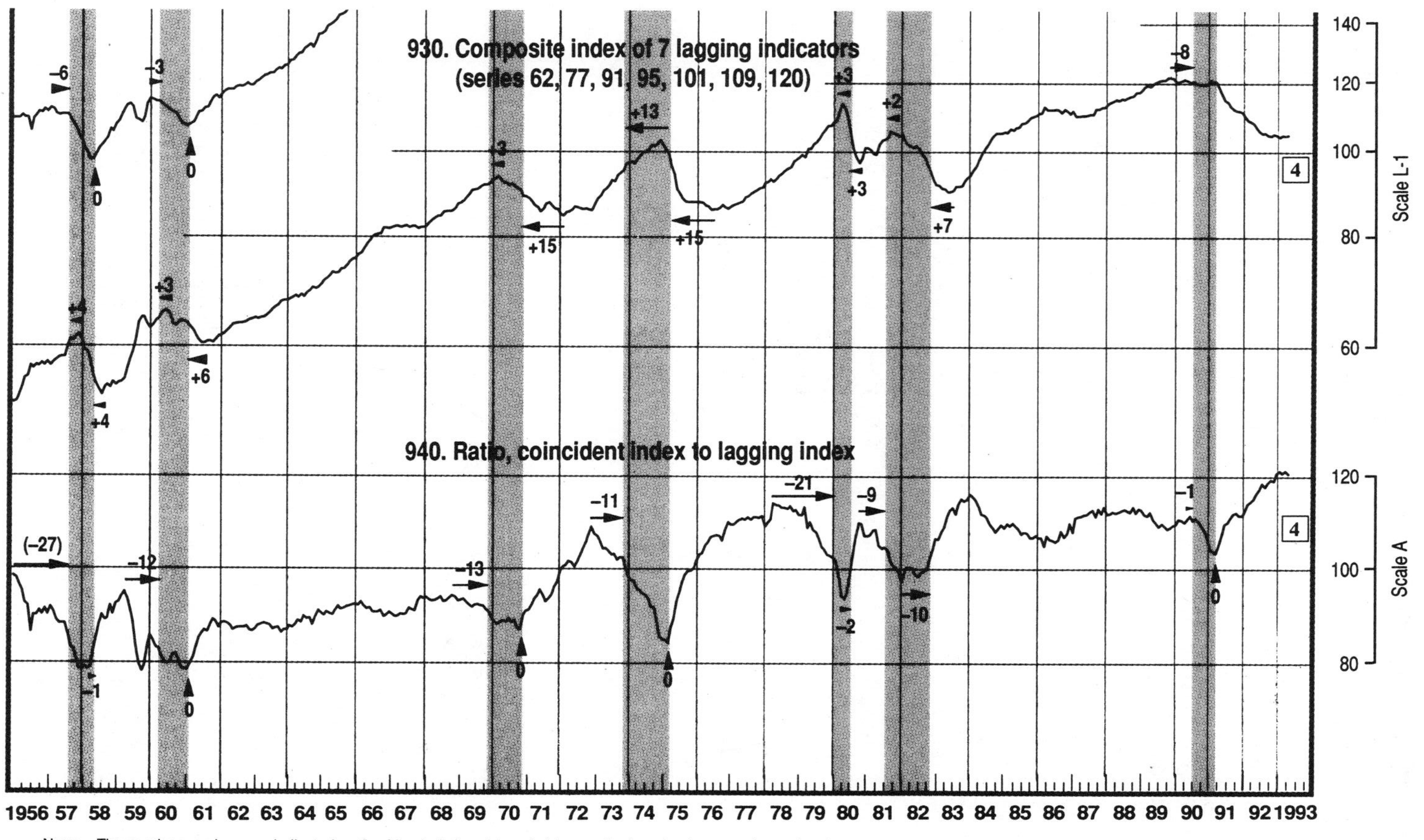

NOTE.—The numbers and arrows indicate length of leads (−) and lags (+) in months from business cycle turning dates.
* For definitions see page 166.

Source: *Survey of Current Business,* U.S. Department of Commerce, Bureau of Economic Analysis.

Composition of Leading, Coincident, and Lagging Indicators

I. THE ELEVEN LEADING INDICATORS

1. Average weekly hours paid to production or non-supervisory workers in manufacturing.
5. Average weekly claims for Unemployment Insurance (inversely related).
8. New orders for consumer goods and materials in 1982 dollars.
19. Index of 500 common stock prices.
20. Contracts and orders for new plant and equipment in 1982 dollars.
29. Index of new private housing starts.
32. Percentage of purchasing agents in greater Chicago area who experience slower deliveries in current month.
83. Index of consumer expectations.
92. Change in manufacturer's unfilled orders for the durable goods industry.
99. Change in index of 28 sensitive materials prices.
106. Money supply (M2 in 1982 dollars).

II. THE FOUR COINCIDENT INDICATORS

41. Employees on non-agricultural payrolls.
47. Index of industrial production, including all stages in manufacturing, mining, gas and electrical utilities.
51. Personal income less transfer payments in 1982 dollars.
57. Monthly volume of sales in manufacturing, wholesale, and retail in 1982 dollars.

III. THE SEVEN LAGGING INDICATORS

62. Index of labor costs per unit of manufacturing output.
77. Ratio of manufacturing and trade inventories to sales in 1982 dollars.
91. Average duration of unemployment in weeks (inversely related).
95. Ratio of consumer installment credit to personal income.
101. Commercial and industrial loans outstanding in 1982 dollars.
109. Average prime rate charged by banks.
120. Change in consumer price index for services.

Source: *Business Conditions Digest*, U.S. Department of Commerce, Bureau of Economic Analysis.

NATIONAL INCOME (Billions of dollars; quarterly data at seasonally adjusted annual rates)

Period	National income	Compensation of employees[1]	Proprietors' income with inventory valuation and capital consumption adjustments		Rental income of persons with capital consumption adjustment	Corporate profits with inventory valuation and capital consumption adjustments					Net interest
						Total	Profits with inventory valuation adjustment and without capital consumption adjustment			Capital consumption adjustment	
			Farm	Nonfarm			Total	Profits before tax	Inventory valuation adjustment		
1985	3,268.4	2,382.8	21.5	238.4	18.7	280.8	225.3	225.0	0.2	55.5	326.2
1986	3,437.9	2,523.8	22.3	261.5	8.7	271.6	227.6	217.8	9.7	44.1	350.2
1987	3,692.3	2,698.7	31.3	279.0	3.2	319.8	273.4	287.9	−14.5	46.4	360.4
1988	4,002.6	2,921.3	30.9	293.4	4.3	365.0	320.3	347.5	−27.3	44.7	387.7
1989	4,249.5	3,100.2	40.2	307.0	−13.5	362.8	325.4	342.9	−17.5	37.4	452.7
1990	4,468.3	3,291.2	41.7	325.2	−12.3	361.7	341.2	355.4	−14.2	20.5	460.7
1991	4,544.2	3,390.8	35.8	332.2	−10.4	346.3	337.8	334.7	3.1	8.4	449.5
1992	4,743.4	3,525.2	39.5	364.9	4.7	393.8	364.2	371.6	−7.4	29.5	415.2
1982: IV	2,551.5	1,940.4	10.2	169.6	24.1	150.3	160.0	168.6	−8.6	−9.6	256.8
1983: IV	2,834.3	2,101.2	6.3	193.8	22.2	229.1	216.2	223.8	−7.6	12.9	281.8
1984: IV	3,134.4	2,288.1	21.9	217.7	24.3	261.3	223.6	220.1	3.5	37.7	321.1
1985: IV	3,341.9	2,442.5	17.8	250.9	14.0	284.9	228.0	231.8	−3.8	56.9	331.9
1986: IV	3,486.0	2,582.5	23.6	260.9	4.7	264.6	225.0	235.7	−10.7	39.6	349.7
1987: IV	3,828.8	2,785.1	42.4	282.6	6.8	343.3	293.4	311.2	−17.8	49.9	368.6
1988: IV	4,127.6	3,004.9	30.9	302.5	2.8	378.3	340.5	372.2	−31.7	37.9	408.1
1989: IV	4,305.2	3,162.8	38.4	311.4	−21.6	354.5	320.6	334.1	−13.5	33.9	459.8
1990: IV	4,517.9	3,339.6	42.8	329.7	−9.6	344.0	333.5	354.7	−21.2	10.5	471.4
1991: III	4,555.4	3,407.0	29.5	337.6	−10.3	341.2	331.9	336.7	−4.8	9.3	450.5
IV	4,599.1	3,433.8	37.9	340.0	−6.6	347.1	333.1	332.3	.7	14.1	446.9
1992: I	4,679.4	3,476.3	40.1	353.6	−4.5	384.0	360.7	366.1	−5.4	23.3	430.0
II	4,716.5	3,506.3	38.5	359.9	3.3	388.4	361.4	376.8	−15.5	27.0	420.0
III	4,719.6	3,534.3	31.5	365.9	6.4	374.1	344.4	354.1	−9.7	29.7	407.3
IV	4,858.0	3,583.7	48.1	380.4	13.6	428.5	390.4	389.4	1.0	38.1	403.6
1993: I	r4,914.2	3,628.4	52.9	389.0	17.7	r424.2	r383.6	r393.0	−9.4	40.6	402.0
II p	....	3,669.4	48.4	394.4	24.6	....	....	....	−16.6	42.6	....

[1] Includes employer contributions for social insurance.

Source: Department of Commerce, Bureau of Economic Analysis.

Source: *Economic Indicators*, Council of Economic Advisers.

Gross Domestic Product as a Measure of U.S. Production

As of late 1991, the Bureau of Economic Analysis (BEA) features gross domestic product (GDP), rather than gross national product (GNP), as the primary measure of U.S. production. This change in emphasis recognizes that GDP is more appropriate for many purposes for which an aggregate measure of the Nation's production is used. GNP will remain a key aggregate in the national income and product accounts (NIPA's) and will continue to be published regularly.

How Do the GDP and GNP Concepts Differ?

Both GDP and GNP are defined in terms of goods and services produced, but they use different criteria for coverage. GDP covers the goods and services *produced by labor and property located in the United States.* As long as the labor and property are located in the United States, the suppliers (that is, the workers and, for property, the owners) may be either U.S. residents or residents of the rest of the world. GNP covers the goods and services *produced by labor and property supplied by U.S. residents.* As long as the labor and property are supplied by U.S. residents, they may be located either in the United States or abroad.

As shown in table 1, to move from GNP to GDP one must subtract factor income receipts from foreigners, which represent the goods and services produced abroad using the labor and property supplied by U.S. residents, and add factor income payments to foreigners, which represent the goods and services produced in the United States using the labor and property supplied by foreigners. Factor incomes are measured as compensation of employees, corporate profits (dividends, earnings of unincorporated affiliates, and reinvested earnings of incorporated affiliates), and net interest.

Why Feature GDP?

GDP refers to production taking place in the United States. It is, therefore, the appropriate measure for much of the short-term monitoring and analysis of the U.S. economy. In particular, GDP is consistent in coverage with indicators such as employment, productivity, industry output, and investment in equipment and structures.

In addition, the use of GDP facilitates comparisons of economic activity in the United States with that in other countries. GDP is the primary measure of production in the System of National Accounts, the set of international guidelines for economic accounting that the U.S. economic accounts will be moving toward in the mid-1990's, and virtually all other countries have already adopted GDP as their primary measure of production. Canada, for example, began featuring GDP in 1986.

The emphasis on GDP is consistent with measurement considerations. Data from BEA's direct investment survey, which is one of the primary sources for estimating factor income payments and receipts, are not available for the first two of the three quarterly estimates of GNP. For these two estimates, factor income payments and receipts are based on judgments about trends in the pace of economic activity in the United States and abroad and about the value of the dollar in foreign countries, on announced profits of individual companies, and on other information. Even when all of the source data become available, BEA does not have the information needed to make a full set of adjustments to reflect the concepts underlying the NIPA's. For example, the profits of foreign affiliates do not include inventory valuation and capital consumption adjustments, and they are affected by intracompany transfer prices and exchange rates. In addition, the deflation of current-dollar factor incomes is problematic because incomes such as interest and dividends cannot be separated into price and quantity components. Lacking a component-specific deflator, BEA uses the implicit price deflator for net domestic product to derive constant-dollar estimates.

GNP, however, continues to be a useful concept. Because it refers to the income available to U.S. residents as the result of their contribution to production, it is appropriate for analyses related to sources and uses of income. For example, saving rates are normally expressed as a percentage of income, and GNP is the more appropriate measure for this purpose. In addition, GNP is better than GDP for analyses that focus on the availability of resources, such as the Nation's ability to finance expenditures on education.

How Much Do the Estimates of GDP and GNP Differ?

For the United States, the dollar levels of GDP and GNP differ little—that is, the net receipts (receipts from foreigners less payments to foreigners) of factor income have been small (tables 1 and 2). The main reason is that the value of the property owned abroad by U.S. residents (U.S. investment abroad) less the value of the property owned by foreigners in the United States (foreign invest-

Source: *Survey of Current Business*, Bureau of Economic Analysis, U.S. Department of Commerce.

Table 1.—Relation of GNP and GDP

	1990	
	Billion of dollars	Billions of 1982 dollars
GNP	5,465.1	4,157.3
Less: Factor income receipts from foreigners	137.4	102.2
Plus: Factor income payments to foreigners	95.7	70.3
GDP[2]	5,423.4	4,125.4

Table 2.—Differences Between GNP and GDP

Year or quarter	GNP less GDP (Billions of dollars)	GNP less GDP, as a per cent of GDP	Growth rate of GNP less growth rate of GDP, based on 1982 dollars (Percentage points)
1980	47.6	1.8	0
1981	52.1	1.7	–.1
1982	51.2	1.6	0
1983	49.9	1.5	–.1
1984	47.4	1.3	–.2
1985	40.7	1.0	–.2
1986	34.4	.8	–.2
1987	29.0	.6	–.2
1988	33.5	.7	.1
1989	37.6	.7	0
1990	41.7	.8	.1
1990: I	41.6	.8	–.1
II	31.6	.6	–.8
III	42.9	.8	.7
IV	50.8	.9	.5
1991: I	54.8	1.0	.2
II	42.4	.8	–.9

NOTE.—The quarterly estimates are based on seasonally adjusted annual rates.

ment in the United States) has been small relative to the size of the U.S. economy. (The value of labor supplied to, and by, foreigners is even smaller.) Since 1929, the receipts by U.S. residents from their investments abroad have exceeded payments to foreigners for their investments here, so GNP has been larger than GDP. The largest percentage difference, 1.8 percent, was in 1980. In 1990, GNP was 0.8 percent larger than GDP.

In some countries, the difference between GDP and GNP is much larger. For example, there is much more foreign investment in Canada than Canadian investment abroad; consequently, its GNP was 3.6 percent smaller than its GDP in 1990. However, the difference in France, Japan, the United Kingdom, and several other industrialized countries is now similar, at 1 percent or less, to that in the United States.

Although the differences between the dollar levels of U.S. GNP and GDP are small, their growth rates sometimes differ. Table 2 shows that the annual growth rate of real GNP was slightly less than that of real GDP in most years of the 1980's. Differences between growth rates tend to be larger and to fluctuate more.

How Will BEA's Presentations Differ?

Although BEA will continue to publish GNP, the emphasis on GDP will change some of the NIPA tables. The several tables that now show GNP and its components will show GDP, with the components adjusted accordingly. For example, in tables showing GNP as the sum of personal consumption expenditures, gross private domestic investment, net exports of goods and services, and government purchases of goods and services, net exports will be adjusted to exclude factor income.

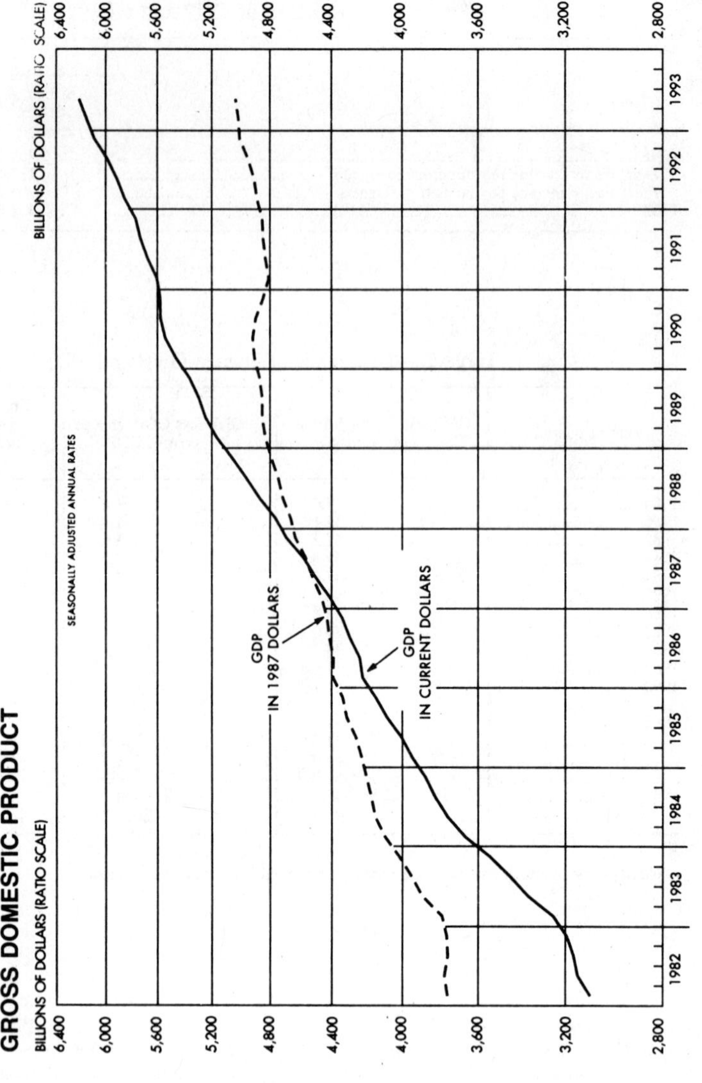
GROSS DOMESTIC PRODUCT
BILLIONS OF DOLLARS (RATIO SCALE)
SEASONALLY ADJUSTED ANNUAL RATES
6,400
6,000
5,600
5,200
4,800
4,400
4,000
3,600
3,200
2,800
GDP IN 1987 DOLLARS
GDP IN CURRENT DOLLARS
1982
1983
1984
1985
1986
1987
1988
1989
1990
1991
1992
1993
SOURCE: DEPARTMENT OF COMMERCE
COUNCIL OF ECONOMIC ADVISERS

[Billions of current dollars; quarterly data at seasonally adjusted annual rates]

Period	Gross domestic product	Personal consumption expenditures	Gross private domestic investment	Exports and imports of goods and services			Government purchases					Final sales of domestic product	Gross domestic purchases [1]	Addendum: Gross national product
				Net exports	Exports	Imports	Total	Federal			State and local			
								Total	National defense	Nondefense				
1984	3,777.2	2,460.3	718.9	−102.7	302.4	405.1	700.8	310.9	233.1	77.8	389.9	3,706.1	3,879.9	3,801.5
1985	4,038.7	2,667.4	714.5	−115.6	302.1	417.6	772.3	344.3	258.6	85.7	428.1	4,014.1	4,154.3	4,053.6
1986	4,268.6	2,850.6	717.6	−132.5	319.2	451.7	833.0	367.8	276.7	91.1	465.3	4,260.0	4,401.2	4,277.7
1987	4,539.9	3,052.2	749.3	−143.1	364.0	507.1	881.5	384.9	292.1	92.9	496.6	4,513.7	4,683.0	4,544.5
1988	4,900.4	3,296.1	793.6	−108.0	444.2	552.2	918.7	387.0	295.6	91.4	531.7	4,884.2	5,008.4	4,908.2
1989	5,250.8	3,523.1	832.3	−79.7	508.0	587.7	975.2	401.6	299.9	101.7	573.6	5,217.5	5,330.5	5,266.8
1990	5,522.2	3,748.4	799.5	−68.9	557.0	625.9	1,043.2	426.4	314.0	112.4	616.8	5,515.9	5,591.1	5,542.9
1991	5,677.5	3,887.7	721.1	−21.8	598.2	620.0	1,090.5	447.3	323.8	123.6	643.2	5,687.7	5,699.3	5,694.9
1992	5,950.7	4,095.8	770.4	−30.4	636.3	666.7	1,114.9	449.1	315.8	133.4	665.8	5,946.3	5,981.1	5,961.9
1982: IV	3,195.1	2,128.7	464.2	−29.5	265.6	295.1	631.6	281.4	205.5	75.9	350.3	3,241.4	3,224.6	3,222.6
1983: IV	3,547.3	2,346.8	614.8	−71.8	286.2	358.0	657.6	289.7	222.8	66.9	367.9	3,527.1	3,619.1	3,578.4
1984: IV	3,869.1	2,526.4	722.8	−107.1	308.7	415.7	727.0	324.7	242.9	81.9	402.2	3,818.1	3,976.2	3,890.2
1985: IV	4,140.5	2,739.8	737.0	−135.5	304.7	440.2	799.2	356.9	268.6	88.3	442.4	4,107.9	4,276.0	4,156.2
1986: IV	4,336.6	2,923.1	697.1	−133.2	333.9	467.1	849.7	373.1	278.6	94.5	476.6	4,355.4	4,469.8	4,340.5
1987: IV	4,683.0	3,124.6	800.2	−143.2	392.4	535.6	901.4	392.5	295.8	96.7	509.0	4,623.7	4,826.2	4,690.5
1988: IV	5,044.6	3,398.2	814.8	−106.0	467.0	573.1	937.6	392.0	296.8	95.2	545.7	5,027.3	5,150.7	5,054.3
1989: IV	5,344.8	3,599.1	825.2	−73.9	523.8	597.7	994.5	405.1	302.5	102.6	589.3	5,314.6	5,418.7	5,365.0
1990: IV	5,561.3	3,818.2	739.0	−67.2	579.7	646.9	1,071.3	438.3	323.2	115.0	633.0	5,592.3	5,628.5	5,592.7
1991: I	5,585.8	3,821.7	705.4	−28.7	573.2	602.0	1,087.5	451.3	332.4	118.8	636.3	5,614.4	5,614.6	5,614.9
II	5,657.6	3,871.9	710.2	−15.3	594.3	609.6	1,090.8	449.9	325.9	124.0	640.8	5,679.4	5,672.9	5,674.3
III	5,713.1	3,914.2	732.8	−27.1	602.3	629.5	1,093.3	447.2	321.9	125.3	646.0	5,712.9	5,740.3	5,726.4
IV	5,753.3	3,942.9	736.1	−16.0	622.9	638.9	1,090.3	440.8	314.7	126.1	649.5	5,744.2	5,769.3	5,764.1
1992: I	5,840.2	4,022.8	722.4	−8.1	628.1	636.2	1,103.1	445.0	313.6	131.4	658.0	5,855.9	5,848.3	5,859.8
II	5,902.2	4,057.1	773.2	−37.1	625.4	662.5	1,109.1	444.8	311.7	133.1	664.3	5,894.1	5,939.4	5,909.3
III	5,978.5	4,108.7	781.6	−36.0	639.0	675.0	1,124.2	455.2	319.6	135.7	669.0	5,963.5	6,014.5	5,992.0
IV	6,081.8	4,194.8	804.3	−40.5	652.7	693.2	1,123.3	451.6	318.2	133.4	671.7	6,071.5	6,122.3	6,086.8
1993: I	6,145.8	4,234.7	844.0	−49.4	649.4	698.9	1,116.6	441.1	304.2	136.9	675.4	6,110.8	6,195.2	r 6,155.1
II p	6,206.9	4,301.0	831.3	−49.9	662.1	712.0	1,124.4	440.6	305.0	135.6	683.8	6,200.5	6,256.8	....

[1] GDP less exports of goods and services plus imports of goods and services.

Source: Department of Commerce, Bureau of Economic Analysis.

Source: *Economic Indicators*, Council of Economic Advisers.

GROSS DOMESTIC PRODUCT IN 1987 DOLLARS (Billions of 1987 dollars; quarterly data at seasonally adjusted annual rates)

Period	Gross domestic product	Personal consumption expenditures	Gross private domestic investment: Nonresidential fixed investment	Gross private domestic investment: Residential fixed investment	Gross private domestic investment: Change in business inventories	Exports and imports of goods and services: Net exports	Exports and imports of goods and services: Exports	Exports and imports of goods and services: Imports	Government purchases: Total	Government purchases: Federal: Total	Government purchases: Federal: National defense	Government purchases: Federal: Nondefense	Government purchases: State and local	Final sales of domestic product	Gross domestic purchases [1]	Addendum: Gross national product
1984	4,148.5	2,746.1	490.2	199.3	67.9	−122.0	305.7	427.7	766.9	331.0	245.8	85.1	436.0	4,080.6	4,270.5	4,174.5
1985	4,279.8	2,865.8	521.8	202.0	22.1	−145.3	309.2	454.6	813.4	355.2	265.6	89.5	458.2	4,257.6	4,425.1	4,295.0
1986	4,404.5	2,969.1	500.3	226.2	8.5	−155.1	329.6	484.7	855.4	373.0	280.6	92.4	482.4	4,395.9	4,559.6	4,413.5
1987	4,539.9	3,052.2	497.8	225.2	26.3	−143.1	364.0	507.1	881.5	384.9	292.1	92.9	496.6	4,513.7	4,683.0	4,544.5
1988	4,718.6	3,162.4	530.8	222.7	19.9	−104.0	421.6	525.7	886.8	377.3	287.0	90.2	509.6	4,698.6	4,822.6	4,726.3
1989	4,838.0	3,223.3	540.0	214.2	29.8	−73.7	471.8	545.4	904.4	376.1	281.4	94.8	528.3	4,808.3	4,911.7	4,852.7
1990	4,877.5	3,260.4	538.1	194.8	6.2	−51.8	510.0	561.8	929.9	383.6	283.3	100.3	546.3	4,871.3	4,929.3	4,895.9
1991	4,821.0	3,240.8	500.2	170.2	−9.3	−21.8	539.4	561.2	941.0	388.3	282.8	105.5	552.7	4,830.3	4,842.8	4,836.4
1992	4,922.6	3,314.0	515.0	192.6	5.0	−41.8	573.2	615.0	937.8	375.6	265.0	110.6	562.2	4,917.6	4,964.4	4,932.8
1982: IV	3,759.6	2,539.3	417.2	131.2	−44.9	−19.0	280.4	299.4	735.9	316.0	229.4	86.6	419.9	3,804.5	3,778.6	3,791.7
1983: IV	4,012.1	2,678.2	449.6	190.6	29.3	−83.7	291.5	375.1	748.1	322.2	242.9	79.3	425.9	3,982.8	4,095.8	4,046.6
1984: IV	4,194.2	2,784.8	509.6	198.8	47.9	−131.4	312.8	444.2	784.3	341.7	254.3	87.4	442.6	4,146.2	4,325.5	4,216.4
1985: IV	4,333.5	2,895.3	525.5	207.4	30.2	−155.4	312.0	467.4	830.5	363.7	272.1	91.6	466.7	4,303.3	4,488.9	4,349.5
1986: IV	4,427.1	3,012.5	495.5	230.5	−20.1	−156.0	342.9	498.9	864.8	377.5	282.2	95.3	487.3	4,447.2	4,583.1	4,430.8
1987: IV	4,625.5	3,074.7	510.6	223.3	59.9	−136.0	386.1	522.1	893.0	391.6	295.0	96.6	501.4	4,565.6	4,761.5	4,633.0
1988: IV	4,779.7	3,202.9	538.8	225.3	20.9	−102.7	438.2	540.9	894.5	378.4	285.7	92.7	516.1	4,758.7	4,882.4	4,789.0
1989: IV	4,856.7	3,242.0	536.7	208.0	24.9	−67.4	487.7	555.0	912.6	376.1	281.5	94.7	536.5	4,831.8	4,924.1	4,875.1
1990: III	4,882.6	3,273.9	542.9	189.1	11.2	−59.3	508.4	567.7	924.8	378.3	277.3	101.0	546.5	4,871.4	4,941.9	4,898.9
IV	4,833.8	3,248.0	529.3	177.5	−26.8	−32.7	522.6	555.3	938.5	387.3	285.8	101.5	551.2	4,860.6	4,866.5	4,861.4
1991: I	4,796.7	3,223.5	507.0	164.1	−25.1	−17.9	515.9	533.8	945.1	394.1	291.8	102.2	551.0	4,821.8	4,814.6	4,822.0
II	4,817.1	3,239.3	503.0	166.9	−20.4	−17.4	536.1	553.5	945.6	393.8	287.6	106.2	551.8	4,837.4	4,834.4	4,831.8
III	4,831.8	3,251.2	498.7	172.6	.6	−31.6	544.2	575.8	940.2	387.2	280.6	106.6	553.0	4,831.2	4,863.4	4,843.7
IV	4,838.5	3,249.0	492.1	177.3	7.5	−20.5	561.4	581.8	933.1	378.2	271.0	107.2	554.9	4,830.9	4,858.9	4,848.2
1992: I	4,873.7	3,289.3	495.8	185.6	−12.6	−21.5	565.4	586.8	937.0	375.3	265.6	109.7	561.8	4,886.3	4,895.2	4,890.7
II	4,892.4	3,288.5	514.7	191.2	7.8	−43.9	563.4	607.3	934.2	372.7	262.1	110.6	561.5	4,884.6	4,936.3	4,899.1
III	4,933.7	3,318.4	518.7	191.3	15.0	−52.7	575.9	628.6	943.0	379.5	267.4	112.1	563.5	4,918.7	4,986.4	4,945.6
IV	4,990.8	3,359.9	530.9	202.3	9.8	−49.0	588.3	637.3	936.8	375.0	265.0	109.9	561.9	4,981.0	5,039.8	4,995.9
1993: I	4,999.9	3,366.5	547.5	203.0	33.5	−70.3	584.2	654.5	919.6	357.0	245.9	111.1	562.6	4,966.3	5,070.1	r 5,008.5
II p	5,019.5	3,398.1	564.9	198.0	8.2	−69.9	593.8	663.6	920.1	354.3	245.0	109.3	565.8	5,011.3	5,089.3	....

[1] GDP less exports of goods and services plus imports of goods and services.

Source: Department of Commerce, Bureau of Economic Analysis.

Source: *Economic Indicators*, Council of Economic Advisers.

PERSONAL CONSUMPTION EXPENDITURES IN 1987 DOLLARS (Billions of 1987 dollars, except as noted; quarterly data at seasonally adjusted annual rates)

Period	Total personal consumption expenditures	Durable goods				Nondurable goods						Services			Retail sales of new passenger cars (millions of units)	
		Total durable goods	Motor vehicles and parts	Furniture and household equipment	Other	Total nondurable goods	Food	Clothing and shoes	Gasoline and oil	Fuel oil and coal	Other	Total services [1]	Housing	Medical care	Domestics	Imports
1984	2,746.1	338.5	160.3	115.3	62.9	934.6	472.3	153.1	77.9	11.2	220.0	1,473.0	426.8	341.9	8.0	2.4
1985	2,865.8	370.1	180.2	123.8	66.1	958.7	483.0	158.8	79.2	11.5	226.2	1,537.0	435.9	353.0	8.2	2.8
1986	2,969.1	402.0	193.3	136.3	72.4	991.0	494.1	170.3	82.9	12.1	231.7	1,576.1	442.1	366.2	8.2	3.2
1987	3,052.2	403.7	183.5	144.0	76.2	1,011.1	500.7	174.5	84.7	12.0	239.1	1,637.4	452.5	384.7	7.1	3.2
1988	3,162.4	428.7	194.8	155.4	78.5	1,035.1	513.4	178.9	86.1	12.0	244.7	1,698.5	461.8	399.4	7.5	3.1
1989	3,223.3	440.7	196.4	165.8	78.5	1,051.6	515.0	187.8	87.3	11.4	250.2	1,731.0	469.2	408.6	7.1	2.8
1990	3,260.4	439.3	192.2	169.5	77.6	1,056.5	520.8	185.9	86.4	10.1	253.4	1,764.6	474.7	423.9	6.9	2.6
1991	3,240.8	414.7	171.0	168.6	75.0	1,042.4	515.8	181.3	85.2	9.7	250.5	1,783.7	478.2	438.8	6.1	2.3
1992	3,314.0	439.1	182.2	179.6	77.4	1,054.1	518.4	188.3	85.5	10.9	251.0	1,820.7	484.4	455.8	6.3	2.1
1982: IV	2,539.3	272.3	123.7	96.4	52.3	880.7	458.3	135.7	73.4	10.5	202.8	1,386.2	411.0	327.8	6.0	2.5
1983: IV	2,678.2	319.1	151.6	109.3	58.1	915.2	467.1	147.7	76.9	11.4	212.2	1,443.9	419.7	334.8	7.4	2.6
1984: IV	2,784.8	347.7	164.3	118.7	64.8	942.9	475.1	154.7	79.0	11.1	222.9	1,494.2	431.3	344.9	7.7	2.6
1985: IV	2,895.3	369.6	173.9	128.6	67.1	968.7	488.2	161.7	79.5	11.4	228.0	1,557.1	438.1	359.1	7.0	3.1
1986: IV	3,012.5	415.7	193.6	141.4	80.7	1,000.9	496.9	171.9	84.6	12.4	235.2	1,595.8	444.8	372.0	7.7	3.4
1987: IV	3,074.7	404.7	183.6	145.9	75.2	1,014.6	502.4	174.5	85.4	11.9	240.4	1,655.5	457.0	390.7	6.6	3.3
1988: IV	3,202.9	439.2	197.7	160.3	81.2	1,046.8	518.0	182.8	87.5	12.0	246.4	1,716.9	465.6	403.0	7.5	3.0
1989: IV	3,242.0	436.8	188.3	167.9	80.5	1,058.9	515.6	190.9	88.6	12.0	251.8	1,746.3	471.3	411.8	6.2	2.6
1990: IV	3,248.0	426.6	182.0	167.5	77.1	1,051.6	522.0	183.2	85.0	8.8	252.7	1,769.8	476.1	428.6	6.6	2.4
1991: I	3,223.5	412.0	169.6	166.9	75.5	1,043.0	516.4	180.8	83.9	9.4	252.5	1,768.5	476.5	431.9	6.1	2.2
II	3,239.3	411.3	167.2	169.3	74.8	1,046.3	516.3	183.2	86.0	9.8	251.0	1,781.8	477.9	435.6	6.1	2.3
III	3,251.2	419.4	173.3	170.4	75.7	1,044.8	515.0	183.7	86.0	10.0	250.0	1,787.0	478.8	440.5	6.3	2.3
IV	3,249.0	416.1	174.0	167.9	74.2	1,035.6	515.3	177.5	84.7	9.4	248.6	1,797.4	479.8	447.2	6.1	2.2
1992: I	3,289.3	432.3	181.5	174.4	76.5	1,049.6	518.9	184.1	85.7	10.2	250.7	1,807.3	481.2	449.6	6.1	2.2
II	3,288.5	430.0	180.2	174.4	75.4	1,045.6	513.5	184.4	85.8	12.0	249.8	1,812.9	483.3	453.7	6.3	2.2
III	3,318.4	439.8	179.0	181.5	79.3	1,052.0	514.3	190.8	86.0	10.9	250.1	1,826.6	485.8	458.1	6.2	2.0
IV	3,359.9	454.4	188.0	188.0	78.3	1,069.4	526.7	193.7	84.6	10.8	253.6	1,836.2	487.2	461.7	6.4	2.0
1993: I	3,366.5	453.5	184.9	189.9	78.8	1,062.2	522.6	188.2	84.8	11.7	254.9	1,850.8	489.2	466.6	6.3	2.0
II p	3,398.1	468.8	196.5	194.1	78.1	1,068.6	523.9	190.8	84.9	11.3	257.7	1,860.7	490.9	471.3	6.9	2.1

[1] Includes other items, not shown separately.

Source: Department of Commerce, Bureau of Economic Analysis.

Source: *Economic Indicators*, Council of Economic Advisers.

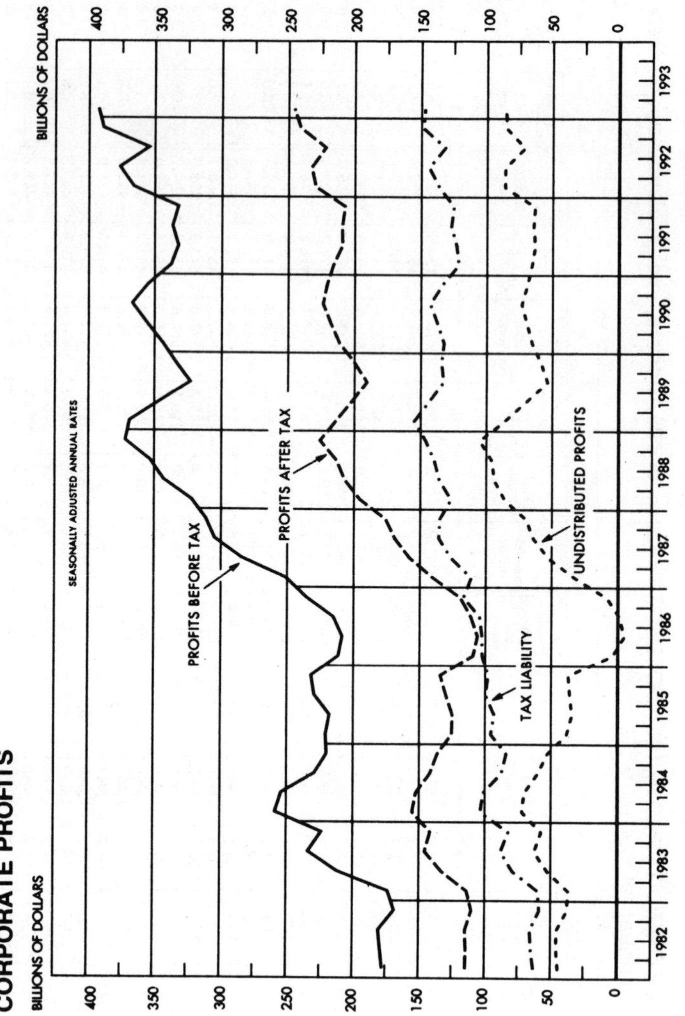

CORPORATE PROFITS
BILLIONS OF DOLLARS
BILLIONS OF DOLLARS
SEASONALLY ADJUSTED ANNUAL RATES
400
350
300
250
200
150
100
50
0
PROFITS BEFORE TAX
PROFITS AFTER TAX
TAX LIABILITY
UNDISTRIBUTED PROFITS
1982
1983
1984
1985
1986
1987
1988
1989
1990
1991
1992
1993
SOURCE: DEPARTMENT OF COMMERCE
COUNCIL OF ECONOMIC ADVISERS

[Billions of dollars; quarterly data at seasonally adjusted annual rates]

Period	Profits (before tax) with inventory valuation adjustment [1]						Profits before tax	Tax liability	Profits after tax			Inventory valuation adjustment
	Total [2]	Domestic industries							Total	Dividends	Undistributed profits	
		Total	Financial	Nonfinancial								
				Total [3]	Manufacturing	Wholesale and retail trade						
1984	236.4	205.2	20.3	185.0	86.7	49.7	240.5	94.0	146.4	82.7	63.8	−4.1
1985	225.3	194.5	28.7	165.8	80.1	43.1	225.0	96.5	128.5	92.4	36.1	.2
1986	227.6	194.6	35.8	158.9	59.0	46.3	217.8	106.5	111.3	109.8	1.6	9.7
1987	273.4	233.9	36.4	197.5	87.0	39.9	287.9	127.1	160.8	106.2	54.6	−14.5
1988	320.3	271.2	41.8	229.4	117.5	37.1	347.5	137.0	210.5	115.3	95.2	−27.3
1989	325.4	266.0	50.6	215.3	108.0	39.7	342.9	141.3	201.6	134.6	67.1	−17.5
1990	341.2	275.5	56.7	218.8	106.9	35.8	355.4	136.7	218.7	149.3	69.4	−14.2
1991	337.8	271.3	60.9	210.4	89.3	44.0	334.7	124.0	210.7	146.5	64.2	3.1
1992	364.2	300.2	56.8	243.5	113.8	47.7	371.6	140.2	231.4	149.3	82.1	−7.4
1982: IV	160.0	130.8	23.0	107.8	50.1	33.8	168.6	58.7	109.9	72.5	37.5	−8.6
1983: IV	216.2	182.6	22.1	160.5	90.5	40.7	223.8	82.2	141.6	84.2	57.4	−7.6
1984: IV	223.6	192.9	20.3	172.6	79.2	50.8	220.1	83.8	136.3	83.4	52.9	3.5
1985: IV	228.0	193.5	29.0	164.5	83.3	39.0	231.8	97.6	134.2	97.4	36.9	−3.8
1986: IV	225.0	192.5	34.7	157.8	63.9	43.1	235.7	116.6	119.2	111.0	8.2	−10.7
1987: IV	293.4	246.3	39.4	207.0	98.7	39.3	311.2	135.2	176.0	106.3	69.7	−17.8
1988: IV	340.5	285.9	46.1	239.7	129.3	39.3	372.2	146.2	226.0	121.0	105.0	−31.7
1989: IV	320.6	254.8	52.5	202.3	94.5	39.2	334.1	134.2	200.0	141.3	58.7	−13.5
1990: IV	333.5	260.2	55.1	205.1	96.3	35.0	354.7	133.7	221.0	151.9	69.1	−21.2
1991: I	344.2	269.4	59.7	209.7	87.6	44.1	337.6	121.3	216.3	150.6	65.7	6.7
II	342.2	275.9	60.7	215.1	90.3	45.5	332.3	122.9	209.4	146.2	63.2	9.9
III	331.9	270.0	63.6	206.4	91.8	41.7	336.7	127.0	209.6	145.1	64.5	−4.8
IV	333.1	270.2	59.7	210.5	87.5	44.5	332.3	125.0	207.4	143.9	63.4	.7
1992: I	360.7	292.0	70.1	221.9	97.5	39.9	366.1	136.4	229.7	143.6	86.2	−5.4
II	361.4	300.4	61.3	239.0	115.2	46.7	376.8	144.1	232.7	146.6	86.1	−15.5
III	344.4	279.3	40.3	239.0	118.0	43.7	354.1	131.8	222.2	151.1	71.1	−9.7
IV	390.4	329.3	55.3	274.0	124.5	60.7	389.4	148.5	241.0	155.9	85.0	1.0
1993: I	r383.6	316.4	64.1	252.3	110.7	51.9	r393.0	147.2	r245.7	160.2	r85.5	−9.4
II p	.....	.....	.....	.....	.....	.....	.....	.....	.....	161.1	.....	−16.6

[1] See p. 167 for profits with inventory valuation and capital consumption adjustments.
[2] Includes rest of the world, not shown separately.
[3] Includes industries not shown separately.

Source: Department of Commerce, Bureau of Economic Analysis.

Source: *Economic Indicators,* Council of Economic Advisers.

Price Data

Definitions are applicable to the exhibits on pages 177–184.

Price data are gathered by the Bureau of Labor Statistics from retail and primary markets in the United States. Price indexes are given in relation to a base period (1982 = 100 for many Producer Price Indexes or 1982–84 = 100 for many Consumer Price Indexes, unless otherwise noted).

DEFINITIONS

The **Consumer Price Index** (CPI) is a measure of the average change in the prices paid by urban consumers for a fixed market basket of goods and services. The CPI is calculated monthly for two population groups, one consisting only of urban households whose primary source of income is derived from the employment of wage earners and clerical workers, and the other consisting of all urban households. The wage earner index (CPI–W) is a continuation of the historic index that was introduced well over a half-century ago for use in wage negotiations. As new uses were developed for the CPI in recent years, the need for a broader and more representative index became apparent. The all urban consumer index (CPI–U) introduced in 1978 is representative of the 1982–84 buying habits of about 80 percent of the noninstitutional population of the United States at that time, compared with 32 percent represented in the CPI–W. In addition to wage earners and clerical workers, the CPI–U covers professional, managerial, and technical workers, the self-employed, short-term workers, the unemployed, retirees, and others not in the labor force.

The CPI is based on prices of food, clothing, shelter, fuel, drugs, transportation fares, doctor's and dentist's fees, and other goods and services that people buy for day-to-day living. The quantity and quality of these items are kept essentially unchanged between major revisions so that only price changes will be measured. All taxes directly associated with the purchase and use of items are included in the index.

Data collected from more than 19,000 retail establishments and 57,000 tenants in 85 urban areas across the country are used to develop the "U.S. city average." Separate estimates for 15 major urban centers are presented in the table on page 184. The areas listed are as indicated in footnote 1 to the table. The area indexes measure only the average change in prices for each area since the base period, and do not indicate differences in the level of prices among cities.

NOTES ON THE DATA

In January 1983, the Bureau changed the way in which homeownership costs are measured for the CPI–U. A rental equivalence method replaced the asset-price approach to homeownership costs for that series. In January 1985, the same change was made in the CPI–W. The central purpose of the change was to separate shelter costs from the investment component of homeownership so that the index would reflect only the cost of shelter services provided by owner-occupied homes. An updated CPI-U and CPI-W were introduced with release of the January 1987 data.

Additional Sources of Information

For a discussion of the general method for computing the CPI, see *BLS Handbook of Methods*, Bulletin 2414 (Bureau of Labor Statistics, 1992). The recent change in the measurement of homeownership costs is discussed in Robert Gillingham and Walter Lane, "Changing the treatment of shelter costs for homeowners in the CPI," *Monthly Labor Review*, July 1982, pp. 9–14. An overview of the recently introduced revised CPI, reflecting 1982–84 expenditure patterns, is contained in *The Consumer Price Index: 1987 Revision*, Report 736 (Bureau of Labor Statistics, 1987).

Additional detailed CPI data and regular analyses of consumer price changes are provided in the *CPI Detailed Report*, a monthly publication of the Bureau. Historical data for the overall CPI and for selected groupings may be found in the *Handbook of Labor Statistics*, Bulletin 2340 (Bureau of Labor Statistics, 1989).

Source: *Monthly Labor Review*, U.S. Department of Labor Statistics, Bureau of Labor Statistics.

CONSUMER PRICE INDEXES FOR ALL URBAN CONSUMERS AND FOR URBAN WAGE EARNERS AND CLERICAL WORKERS: U.S. CITY AVERAGE, BY EXPENDITURE CATEGORY AND COMMODITY OR SERVICE GROUP

(1982-84=100, unless otherwise indicated)

Series	Annual average		1992										1993		
	1991	1992	Mar.	Apr.	May	June	July	Aug.	Sept.	Oct.	Nov.	Dec.	Jan.	Feb.	Mar.
CONSUMER PRICE INDEX FOR ALL URBAN CONSUMERS:															
All items	136.2	140.3	139.3	139.5	139.7	140.2	140.5	140.9	141.3	141.8	142.0	141.9	142.6	143.1	143.6
All items (1967=100)	408.0	420.3	417.2	417.9	418.6	419.9	420.8	422.0	423.2	424.7	425.3	425.2	427.0	428.7	430.1
Food and beverages	136.8	138.7	138.8	138.8	138.3	138.3	138.1	138.8	139.3	139.2	139.1	139.5	140.5	140.7	140.9
Food	136.3	137.9	138.1	138.1	137.4	137.4	137.2	138.0	138.5	138.3	138.3	138.7	139.8	139.9	140.1
Food at home	135.8	136.8	137.5	137.4	136.2	136.1	135.7	136.9	137.4	137.2	137.0	137.5	139.1	139.1	139.4
Cereals and bakery products	145.8	151.5	149.7	150.6	150.7	151.6	152.4	153.1	152.6	152.8	152.7	153.3	153.4	154.9	154.6
Meats, poultry, fish, and eggs	132.6	130.9	130.7	130.3	130.0	130.2	130.1	130.8	131.5	131.5	131.8	132.1	133.5	133.2	134.5
Dairy products	125.1	128.5	127.8	127.4	127.0	127.8	128.3	129.2	129.7	130.1	129.4	129.1	129.5	128.8	128.8
Fruits and vegetables	155.8	155.4	161.3	162.0	155.1	151.9	149.4	153.7	155.5	153.7	154.0	156.2	160.9	159.4	159.1
Other foods at home	127.3	128.8	129.0	128.6	128.9	129.2	128.7	129.1	129.0	129.2	128.2	128.3	129.4	130.3	130.2
Sugar and sweets	129.3	133.1	132.9	133.0	132.9	133.3	133.8	133.8	133.7	133.7	133.0	132.1	133.1	133.3	132.8
Fats and oils	131.7	129.8	129.8	129.6	130.4	130.2	129.9	129.5	129.9	129.9	128.5	128.4	130.2	130.7	130.2
Nonalcoholic beverages	114.1	114.3	115.3	114.4	114.5	115.0	113.9	114.1	114.2	114.1	112.4	112.3	113.5	115.1	114.8
Other prepared foods	137.1	140.1	139.8	139.5	140.0	140.1	139.8	140.8	140.4	140.9	140.6	141.2	142.1	142.7	143.0
Food away from home	137.9	140.7	140.1	140.2	140.4	140.7	140.8	141.0	141.2	141.3	141.5	141.6	142.0	142.2	142.4
Alcoholic beverages	142.8	147.3	146.7	147.2	147.4	147.5	147.7	147.6	148.0	148.2	148.2	148.1	148.7	149.1	149.4
Housing	133.6	137.5	136.6	136.5	136.7	137.7	138.3	138.6	138.4	138.5	138.5	138.5	139.3	139.7	140.2
Shelter	146.3	151.2	150.4	150.2	150.2	151.1	151.8	152.3	151.9	152.5	152.4	152.5	153.7	154.4	154.8
Renters' costs (12/82=100)	155.6	160.9	161.2	160.1	159.5	161.0	162.8	163.5	161.7	161.7	160.6	160.2	162.5	164.4	165.2
Rent, residential	143.3	146.9	146.4	146.2	146.3	146.6	147.0	147.0	147.2	148.0	148.6	148.6	148.9	149.1	149.1
Other renters' costs	174.6	184.8	187.3	183.7	180.9	186.2	192.0	194.7	186.9	184.2	178.3	176.7	184.9	191.6	195.0
Homeowners' costs (12/82=100)	150.2	155.3	154.1	154.2	154.4	155.0	155.5	155.8	156.0	156.8	157.2	157.5	158.2	158.5	158.7
Owners' equivalent rent (12/82=100)	150.4	155.5	154.3	154.4	154.6	155.3	155.7	156.1	156.3	157.1	157.5	157.8	158.5	158.8	159.0
Household insurance (12/82=100)	138.4	142.2	141.0	141.1	141.4	142.0	142.6	142.9	143.1	143.3	143.5	144.3	144.1	144.7	144.9
Maintenance and repairs	126.3	128.6	128.4	128.0	128.1	128.5	128.8	128.1	128.5	129.4	129.5	129.3	129.7	130.5	131.5
Maintenance and repair services	130.3	133.1	132.0	132.2	131.9	133.1	133.4	133.1	133.1	134.7	134.8	135.2	135.1	135.2	135.8
Maintenance and repair commodities	121.0	122.4	123.5	122.4	123.0	122.3	122.6	121.3	122.2	122.2	122.2	121.3	122.5	124.0	125.8
Fuel and other utilities	115.3	117.8	115.8	115.8	116.8	119.0	119.4	119.4	119.8	118.5	118.3	118.7	119.2	118.4	119.5
Fuels	106.7	108.1	105.2	105.1	106.5	110.2	110.4	110.3	111.1	108.7	108.2	108.9	109.2	107.5	108.6
Fuel oil, coal, and bottled gas	94.6	90.7	90.5	89.9	89.8	90.1	90.0	89.7	89.7	91.4	92.1	91.8	92.3	92.5	92.8
Gas (piped) and electricity	112.6	114.8	111.5	111.3	113.0	117.4	117.6	117.5	118.5	115.4	114.8	115.6	115.9	113.8	115.1
Other utilities and public services	137.9	142.5	141.7	142.2	142.4	142.2	143.1	143.3	143.0	143.4	143.7	143.6	144.3	145.3	146.3
Household furnishings and operations	116.0	118.0	117.7	118.0	117.9	118.2	118.4	118.3	118.3	118.4	118.5	118.2	118.2	118.6	118.7
Housefurnishings	107.5	109.0	109.4	109.7	109.2	109.1	109.4	109.0	108.8	109.0	109.1	108.7	108.6	108.9	109.3
Housekeeping supplies	128.9	129.6	128.6	129.0	129.5	129.8	130.1	130.1	129.8	129.9	130.2	129.5	130.0	130.6	129.6
Housekeeping services	127.5	132.1	130.3	130.5	131.0	132.6	132.6	133.0	133.8	133.9	134.0	134.3	134.1	134.5	134.6

(continued)

CONSUMER PRICE INDEXES FOR ALL URBAN CONSUMERS AND FOR URBAN WAGE EARNERS AND CLERICAL WORKERS: U.S. CITY AVERAGE, BY EXPENDITURE CATEGORY AND COMMODITY OR SERVICE GROUP *(continued)*

(1982-84=100, unless otherwise indicated)

Series	Annual average		1992										1993		
	1991	1992	Mar.	Apr.	May	June	July	Aug.	Sept.	Oct.	Nov.	Dec.	Jan.	Feb.	Mar.
Apparel and upkeep	128.7	131.9	133.4	133.3	133.1	131.0	129.2	130.2	133.3	135.0	134.5	131.4	129.7	133.4	136.2
Apparel commodities	126.4	129.4	131.2	131.1	130.9	128.4	126.5	127.6	130.8	132.7	132.1	128.7	126.8	130.9	133.9
Men's and boys' apparel	124.2	126.5	127.4	127.8	127.5	126.2	124.2	124.1	126.8	128.8	128.8	127.1	124.2	126.5	128.7
Women's and girls' apparel	127.6	130.4	133.6	133.1	132.6	128.2	125.1	127.5	132.6	135.1	134.3	129.1	125.7	133.1	138.4
Infants' and toddlers' apparel	128.9	129.3	127.1	131.3	130.3	129.6	128.3	128.8	130.1	130.6	131.9	130.7	127.9	127.0	125.9
Footwear	120.9	125.0	124.9	125.6	126.0	125.4	124.4	124.9	126.3	127.1	126.0	125.1	124.4	125.2	126.3
Other apparel commodities	137.7	142.6	143.9	141.5	142.8	142.7	144.2	143.9	143.6	144.3	142.7	138.9	145.7	145.2	144.6
Apparel services	142.9	147.9	146.6	146.7	146.8	148.6	148.5	148.6	148.8	149.3	149.7	149.7	149.7	150.2	150.6
Transportation	123.8	126.5	124.4	125.2	126.3	126.9	127.2	126.9	126.8	128.0	129.2	129.0	129.1	129.2	129.0
Private transportation	121.9	124.6	122.2	122.9	124.3	125.4	125.5	125.4	125.4	126.1	127.0	126.7	126.6	126.5	126.3
New vehicles	126.0	129.2	129.1	129.1	129.2	129.1	128.6	128.5	128.3	129.1	130.6	131.3	131.8	132.0	132.0
New cars	125.3	128.4	128.2	128.2	128.4	128.2	127.8	127.6	127.4	128.2	129.7	130.5	130.9	130.9	130.9
Used cars	118.1	123.2	115.7	117.9	120.5	123.1	124.8	126.4	127.7	129.1	129.9	129.0	127.4	126.0	126.6
Motor fuel	99.4	99.0	93.4	95.0	99.4	102.9	102.8	101.7	101.7	101.6	102.2	100.2	98.6	98.0	97.3
Gasoline	99.2	99.0	93.2	94.8	99.4	103.0	102.9	101.8	101.8	101.5	102.2	100.1	98.5	97.8	97.1
Maintenance and repair	136.0	141.3	140.3	140.5	140.8	141.2	141.4	141.6	142.2	142.5	142.8	143.2	143.4	144.3	144.7
Other private transportation	149.1	153.2	152.2	152.4	152.5	152.6	153.0	153.1	152.7	154.4	155.3	155.5	156.5	156.8	156.3
Other private transportation commodities	104.1	104.8	105.2	104.8	104.8	104.6	104.4	104.6	104.8	104.5	104.7	104.7	105.0	104.5	103.9
Other private transportation services	159.2	164.2	162.8	163.2	163.2	163.5	164.0	164.1	163.5	165.8	166.8	167.1	168.2	168.8	168.3
Public transportation	148.9	151.4	153.5	154.7	151.6	145.3	148.3	146.7	145.6	152.9	157.4	158.2	161.6	164.1	163.5
Medical care	177.0	190.1	187.3	188.1	188.7	189.4	190.7	191.5	192.3	193.3	194.3	194.7	196.4	198.0	198.6
Medical care commodities	176.8	188.1	186.7	187.9	187.6	188.0	188.6	188.9	189.5	189.8	190.4	191.1	191.8	193.2	193.9
Medical care services	177.1	190.5	187.4	188.1	188.9	189.7	191.1	192.2	192.9	194.2	195.2	195.6	197.5	199.1	199.7
Professional services	165.7	175.8	173.4	174.1	174.7	175.4	176.3	177.1	177.7	178.4	179.1	179.4	180.7	181.7	182.3
Hospital and related services	196.1	214.0	209.7	210.3	211.4	212.3	214.6	216.2	217.1	219.4	221.0	221.4	224.2	227.0	227.4
Entertainment	138.4	142.3	141.2	142.0	142.0	142.0	142.4	142.6	143.2	143.5	143.7	143.8	144.3	144.5	144.8
Entertainment commodities	128.6	131.3	130.7	131.4	131.2	131.3	131.6	131.6	131.3	131.6	132.2	131.9	132.8	132.9	133.1
Entertainment services	150.6	155.9	154.3	155.2	155.3	155.3	155.7	156.2	157.7	158.0	157.8	158.3	158.4	158.7	159.0
Other goods and services	171.6	183.3	179.8	180.3	181.3	181.5	182.3	183.9	187.0	187.9	188.0	189.1	191.0	191.5	192.0
Tobacco products	202.7	219.8	213.5	214.5	219.3	219.2	220.5	221.5	224.0	225.6	225.0	228.9	234.6	235.6	236.3
Personal care	134.9	138.3	137.9	138.5	138.0	137.8	138.8	138.7	138.6	138.7	139.0	139.6	139.8	139.6	140.7
Toilet goods and personal care appliances	132.8	136.5	136.1	137.0	136.1	135.7	137.5	137.3	137.0	136.8	136.9	137.8	137.7	137.0	138.4
Personal care services	137.0	140.0	139.6	139.8	139.8	139.9	140.0	140.1	140.1	140.5	141.1	141.3	141.9	142.2	142.9
Personal and educational expenses	183.7	197.4	193.5	193.9	194.0	194.6	195.2	197.7	202.6	203.6	203.9	204.2	205.4	206.0	206.3
School books and supplies	180.3	190.3	188.6	188.7	188.4	189.1	189.3	189.7	193.0	193.8	193.9	193.8	195.5	195.6	195.7
Personal and educational services	184.2	198.1	194.0	194.5	194.7	195.2	195.8	198.6	203.5	204.6	204.9	205.3	206.4	207.0	207.3

See footnotes at end of table.

All items	136.2	140.3	139.3	139.5	139.7	140.2	140.5	140.9	141.3	141.8	142.0	141.9	142.6	143.1	143.6
Commodities	126.6	129.1	128.4	128.8	129.1	129.2	129.0	129.3	129.9	130.3	130.5	130.1	130.4	130.9	131.4
Food and beverages	136.8	138.7	138.8	138.8	138.3	138.3	138.1	138.8	139.3	139.2	139.1	139.5	140.5	140.7	140.9
Commodities less food and beverages	120.4	123.2	122.1	122.5	123.4	123.5	123.3	123.4	124.1	124.8	125.1	124.3	124.1	124.9	125.5
Nondurables less food and beverages	123.5	126.5	125.0	125.6	126.9	127.0	126.6	126.8	128.0	128.8	128.8	127.4	126.9	128.3	129.2
Apparel commodities	126.4	129.4	131.2	131.1	130.9	128.4	126.5	127.6	130.8	132.7	132.1	128.7	126.8	130.9	133.9
Nondurables less food, beverages, and apparel	124.8	127.9	124.8	125.7	127.9	129.2	129.6	129.3	129.6	129.7	130.1	129.6	129.9	130.0	129.8
Durables	116.0	118.6	117.9	118.2	118.4	118.5	118.6	118.5	118.5	119.2	120.0	120.1	120.0	120.0	120.2
Services	146.3	152.0	150.7	150.8	150.9	151.7	152.5	153.0	153.2	153.7	154.0	154.2	155.2	155.8	156.2
Rent of shelter (12/82=100)	152.1	157.3	156.5	156.3	156.2	157.1	158.0	158.5	158.0	158.6	158.6	158.7	159.9	160.6	161.0
Household services less rent of' shelter (12/82=100)	126.7	130.2	128.0	128.2	129.1	131.4	131.8	131.9	132.4	131.2	131.0	131.4	131.8	131.2	132.2
Transportation services	151.2	155.7	155.2	155.7	155.1	153.9	154.9	154.7	154.3	157.2	158.8	159.2	160.6	161.7	161.4
Medical care services	177.1	190.5	187.4	188.1	188.9	189.7	191.1	192.2	192.9	194.2	195.2	195.6	197.5	199.1	199.7
Other services	159.8	168.5	166.0	166.6	166.7	167.1	167.5	168.9	171.6	172.3	172.4	172.8	173.3	173.8	174.1
Special indexes:															
All items less food	136.1	140.8	139.5	139.7	140.1	140.7	141.1	141.4	141.8	142.4	142.7	142.5	143.1	143.7	144.2
All items less shelter	133.5	137.3	136.2	136.6	136.9	137.2	137.3	137.7	138.4	138.9	139.2	139.1	139.5	140.0	140.5
All items less homeowners' costs (12/82=100)	137.8	141.9	140.8	141.1	141.3	141.8	142.0	142.4	142.9	143.3	143.5	143.4	144.0	144.7	145.2
All items less medical care	133.8	137.5	136.5	136.7	136.9	137.4	137.6	138.0	138.4	138.8	139.0	138.9	139.5	140.0	140.4
Commodities less food	121.3	124.2	123.0	123.5	124.4	124.5	124.3	124.3	125.1	125.7	126.1	125.3	125.1	125.8	126.4
Nondurables less food	124.5	127.6	126.2	126.8	128.0	128.1	127.8	127.9	129.1	129.8	129.8	128.5	128.1	129.4	130.3
Nondurables less food and apparel	125.7	128.9	126.1	127.0	128.9	130.1	130.5	130.2	130.5	130.6	130.9	130.5	130.8	130.9	130.9
Nondurables	130.3	132.8	132.1	132.4	132.8	132.8	132.5	133.0	133.8	134.2	134.2	133.6	133.9	134.7	135.3
Services less rent of' shelter (12/82=100)	150.9	157.6	155.5	156.0	156.3	157.1	157.8	158.3	159.2	159.7	160.3	160.7	161.6	162.0	162.5
Services less medical care	143.3	148.4	147.1	147.2	147.3	148.1	148.8	149.2	149.4	149.9	150.1	150.3	151.2	151.7	152.1
Energy	102.5	103.0	98.9	99.5	102.4	105.9	106.0	105.4	105.9	104.5	104.5	103.9	103.4	102.2	102.5
All items less energy	140.9	145.4	144.7	144.9	144.9	145.0	145.3	145.8	146.2	146.9	147.1	147.1	147.9	148.7	149.1
All items less food and energy	142.1	147.3	146.4	146.6	146.7	146.9	147.3	147.7	148.1	149.0	149.3	149.2	149.9	150.8	151.4
Commodities less food and energy	128.8	132.5	132.1	132.4	132.6	132.2	132.0	132.2	133.1	133.9	134.2	133.6	133.6	134.7	135.5
Energy commodities	99.1	98.3	93.3	94.6	98.6	101.6	101.6	100.5	100.5	100.6	101.2	99.4	98.1	97.6	97.0
Services less energy	149.8	155.9	154.7	154.8	154.8	155.3	156.1	156.6	156.8	157.7	158.0	158.2	159.3	160.1	160.5
Purchasing power of the consumer dollar:															
1982-84=$1.00	73.4	71.3	71.8	71.7	71.6	71.3	71.2	71.0	70.8	70.5	70.4	70.5	70.1	69.9	69.7
1967=$1.00	24.5	23.8	24.0	23.9	23.9	23.8	23.8	23.7	23.6	23.5	23.5	23.5	23.4	23.3	23.3

(continued)

CONSUMER PRICE INDEXES FOR ALL URBAN CONSUMERS AND FOR URBAN WAGE EARNERS AND CLERICAL WORKERS: U.S. CITY AVERAGE, BY EXPENDITURE CATEGORY AND COMMODITY OR SERVICE GROUP *(continued)*

(1982-84=100, unless otherwise indicated)

Series	Annual average		1992										1993		
	1991	1992	Mar.	Apr.	May	June	July	Aug.	Sept.	Oct.	Nov.	Dec.	Jan.	Feb.	Mar.
CONSUMER PRICE INDEX FOR URBAN WAGE EARNERS AND CLERICAL WORKERS:															
All items	134.3	138.2	137.0	137.3	137.6	138.1	138.4	138.8	139.1	139.6	139.8	139.8	140.3	140.7	141.1
All items (1967=100)	399.9	411.5	408.1	408.9	409.9	411.4	412.1	413.3	414.5	415.8	416.5	416.3	417.8	419.2	420.4
Food and beverages	136.5	138.3	138.4	138.5	137.9	137.9	137.8	138.5	138.9	138.8	138.8	139.1	140.1	140.2	140.5
Food	136.0	137.5	137.7	137.7	137.1	137.1	136.9	137.7	138.1	138.0	138.0	138.3	139.4	139.4	139.7
Food at home	135.5	136.4	137.0	136.9	135.8	135.6	135.3	136.5	136.9	136.7	136.6	137.0	138.5	138.5	138.8
Cereals and bakery products	145.6	151.3	149.6	150.5	150.6	151.4	152.2	152.9	152.5	152.6	152.5	153.0	153.1	154.6	154.3
Meats, poultry, fish, and eggs	132.7	130.8	130.6	130.2	130.1	130.2	130.2	130.7	131.6	131.4	131.8	132.1	133.4	133.1	134.4
Dairy products	124.8	128.2	127.5	127.1	126.6	127.4	127.9	128.9	129.5	129.8	129.2	128.9	129.2	128.4	128.5
Fruits and vegetables	155.6	154.8	160.9	161.4	154.4	151.5	149.2	153.4	154.6	152.8	153.3	155.3	159.7	158.1	157.9
Other foods at home	127.2	128.8	128.9	128.5	128.8	129.1	128.6	129.0	129.0	129.1	128.2	128.2	129.4	130.3	130.2
Sugar and sweets	129.2	132.8	132.6	132.6	132.6	133.1	133.5	133.5	133.4	133.3	132.8	131.9	132.9	133.1	132.5
Fats and oils	131.5	129.7	129.7	129.5	130.4	130.1	129.9	129.3	129.8	129.7	128.4	128.3	130.1	130.6	130.1
Nonalcoholic beverages	114.4	114.6	115.7	114.8	114.9	115.4	114.2	114.4	114.6	114.5	112.8	112.7	114.0	115.6	115.3
Other prepared foods	137.0	140.0	139.6	139.4	139.8	139.9	139.6	140.6	140.3	140.7	140.5	141.0	142.0	142.5	142.9
Food away from home	137.8	140.6	139.9	140.1	140.3	140.5	140.7	140.8	141.1	141.2	141.4	141.6	141.8	142.1	142.2
Alcoholic beverages	142.6	147.0	146.6	147.1	147.3	147.4	147.5	147.3	147.7	148.0	147.8	147.7	148.3	148.8	149.0
Housing	131.2	135.0	134.0	133.9	134.1	135.1	135.7	135.9	135.8	135.9	136.0	136.1	136.7	137.0	137.4
Shelter	142.5	147.2	146.4	146.2	146.3	147.0	147.8	148.2	147.9	148.5	148.5	148.7	149.6	150.2	150.5
Renters' costs (12/84=100)	136.9	141.3	141.2	140.6	140.2	141.1	142.3	142.8	141.8	142.0	141.6	141.4	142.8	143.9	144.3
Rent, residential	142.9	146.5	146.0	145.8	145.9	146.1	146.6	146.7	146.9	147.7	148.2	148.2	148.5	148.7	148.7
Other renters' costs	175.0	185.3	188.1	184.2	181.3	186.3	192.7	195.2	187.1	184.5	178.6	176.9	185.0	191.4	194.4
Homeowners' costs (12/84=100)	136.9	141.5	140.4	140.4	140.7	141.3	141.8	142.2	142.2	142.9	143.2	143.5	144.2	144.5	144.7
Owners' equivalent rent (12/84=100)	137.1	141.8	140.6	140.7	140.9	141.6	142.0	142.4	142.4	143.2	143.5	143.8	144.4	144.8	144.9
Household insurance (12/84=100)	126.7	130.2	129.1	129.2	129.5	130.1	130.5	130.9	131.1	131.3	131.3	132.0	131.9	132.3	132.5
Maintenance and repairs	127.8	129.9	130.4	129.6	129.4	129.4	130.2	128.9	129.3	130.1	130.8	129.8	130.0	131.2	131.9
Maintenance and repair services	133.4	136.8	135.7	135.7	134.9	136.6	137.1	136.5	136.5	138.7	138.8	139.0	138.8	139.0	139.9
Maintenance and repair commodities	119.8	120.4	122.7	121.1	121.5	119.7	120.8	118.7	119.6	118.8	120.1	118.0	118.7	120.9	121.3
Fuel and other utilities	114.9	117.5	115.5	115.5	116.5	118.7	119.1	119.1	119.5	118.2	118.0	118.4	118.9	118.2	119.2
Fuels	106.1	107.5	104.7	104.5	105.9	109.7	109.8	109.8	110.7	108.1	107.7	108.4	108.7	106.9	108.0
Fuel oil, coal, and bottled gas	94.4	90.6	90.3	89.7	89.7	89.9	89.9	89.6	89.6	91.3	91.9	91.7	92.2	92.3	92.7
Gas (piped) and electricity	112.1	114.3	111.0	110.8	112.5	116.9	117.0	117.0	118.1	114.8	114.3	115.1	115.4	113.3	114.6
Other utilities and public services	138.4	143.1	142.3	142.7	142.9	142.7	143.7	143.8	143.5	144.0	144.3	144.2	144.9	145.9	147.0
Household furnishings and operations	115.2	116.9	116.7	117.0	116.9	117.0	117.2	117.0	117.1	117.3	117.5	117.2	117.2	117.6	117.5
Housefurnishings	106.5	107.8	108.2	108.4	108.0	107.8	108.1	107.7	107.6	107.8	107.9	107.7	107.7	107.9	108.1
Housekeeping supplies	129.4	130.2	129.2	129.6	130.1	130.3	130.7	130.7	130.4	130.4	130.9	130.0	130.5	131.3	130.0
Housekeeping services	129.0	133.7	132.0	132.3	132.6	133.8	133.7	134.2	135.4	135.4	135.6	135.9	135.7	136.2	136.3

See footnotes at end of table.

Apparel and upkeep	127.4	130.7	132.1	132.1	131.8	129.8	128.1	129.5	132.1	133.8	133.4	130.4	128.4	132.0	134.8
Apparel commodities	125.2	128.3	129.9	129.9	129.6	127.3	125.5	127.0	129.8	131.5	131.1	127.8	125.8	129.5	132.5
Men's and boys' apparel	123.1	125.6	126.5	126.8	126.5	125.1	123.3	123.5	125.9	128.0	128.2	126.4	123.8	126.1	127.7
Women's and girls' apparel	126.0	128.9	132.0	131.5	130.8	126.6	123.8	127.0	131.1	133.4	132.7	127.6	123.8	130.5	136.5
Infants' and toddlers' apparel	131.3	131.6	129.3	133.3	132.6	131.8	130.2	130.8	132.8	133.5	134.6	133.1	130.8	129.6	128.3
Footwear	121.4	125.4	125.4	125.9	126.5	125.6	124.8	125.3	126.5	127.5	126.6	125.6	124.7	125.8	126.5
Other apparel commodities	133.7	140.4	140.8	139.5	140.2	141.2	142.5	141.7	141.5	142.1	141.0	137.3	143.7	144.3	143.7
Apparel services	142.2	147.6	146.4	146.5	146.5	148.2	148.1	148.2	148.5	148.9	149.3	149.2	149.1	149.7	150.2
Transportation	123.1	125.8	123.2	124.1	125.5	126.5	126.7	126.5	126.5	127.5	128.5	128.2	128.0	128.0	127.8
Private transportation	121.7	124.4	121.6	122.4	124.1	125.3	125.4	125.3	125.4	126.1	127.0	126.6	126.3	126.1	125.9
New vehicles	126.2	129.6	129.4	129.5	129.5	129.4	129.0	128.9	128.7	129.6	130.9	131.7	132.1	132.4	132.4
New cars	125.1	128.1	127.9	127.9	128.1	127.9	127.5	127.3	127.2	128.0	129.5	130.1	130.6	130.5	130.5
Used cars	118.1	123.6	115.9	118.1	120.9	123.5	125.3	126.9	128.2	129.7	130.5	129.7	128.0	126.6	127.2
Motor fuel	99.6	99.0	93.4	95.1	99.5	102.9	102.7	101.6	101.6	101.5	102.0	99.9	98.4	97.7	97.1
Gasoline	99.4	99.0	93.2	94.9	99.6	103.1	102.9	101.7	101.8	101.5	102.1	99.9	98.2	97.6	96.9
Maintenance and repair	136.4	141.8	140.8	141.1	141.4	141.7	141.9	142.1	142.8	143.2	143.5	143.9	144.1	145.0	145.4
Other private transportation	146.4	149.9	149.2	149.5	149.5	149.5	149.7	149.6	149.1	150.8	151.6	151.9	152.8	153.0	152.4
Other private transportation commodities	103.5	104.2	104.6	104.1	104.2	104.0	103.8	104.1	104.2	104.0	104.1	104.0	104.4	103.8	103.2
Other private transportation services	156.6	160.9	159.8	160.3	160.3	160.3	160.7	160.5	159.8	162.0	163.1	163.5	164.5	164.9	164.3
Public transportation	146.6	150.0	151.8	152.8	150.3	145.0	147.3	146.2	145.2	151.4	154.9	155.5	158.0	160.8	160.6
Medical care	176.5	189.6	186.8	187.6	188.2	188.9	190.2	191.2	191.9	193.0	193.8	194.3	196.0	197.6	198.2
Medical care commodities	175.4	186.5	185.1	186.3	186.2	186.5	187.2	187.4	188.0	188.3	188.7	189.4	190.0	191.4	192.1
Medical care services	176.7	190.3	187.2	187.9	188.6	189.4	190.9	192.0	192.8	194.0	195.0	195.4	197.3	199.0	199.6
Professional services	166.1	176.3	173.9	174.5	175.2	175.9	176.8	177.7	178.3	179.0	179.7	180.0	181.3	182.3	183.0
Hospital and related services	193.7	211.5	207.3	208.0	208.9	209.8	212.1	213.6	214.6	216.8	218.4	218.9	221.7	224.4	225.0
Entertainment	136.9	140.8	139.7	140.5	140.5	140.5	141.0	141.2	141.6	141.9	142.2	142.2	142.7	142.8	143.1
Entertainment commodities	128.0	130.7	130.0	130.8	130.6	130.8	131.3	131.2	130.9	131.1	131.7	131.5	132.3	132.3	132.5
Entertainment services	150.4	155.7	154.2	155.0	155.2	155.0	155.4	156.0	157.5	157.9	157.6	158.1	158.0	158.4	158.6
Other goods and services	171.7	183.3	179.7	180.3	181.6	181.8	182.7	184.2	186.7	187.7	187.7	189.0	191.2	191.6	192.2
Tobacco products	202.5	219.7	213.2	214.2	219.1	219.0	220.4	221.6	224.1	225.6	225.1	229.0	234.8	235.5	236.1
Personal care	134.7	138.6	138.1	138.8	138.2	138.1	139.1	138.9	138.8	139.0	139.2	139.9	139.9	139.8	140.8
Toilet goods and personal care appliances	132.9	137.2	136.7	137.7	136.7	136.4	138.2	137.9	137.6	137.5	137.5	138.6	138.3	137.7	139.1
Personal care services	136.7	140.0	139.6	139.9	139.8	140.0	140.0	139.9	140.0	140.5	141.0	141.3	141.8	142.2	142.8
Personal and educational expenses	181.8	194.3	190.8	191.1	191.2	191.8	192.3	195.0	199.0	200.0	200.3	200.5	201.5	202.2	202.6
School books and supplies	180.2	190.6	188.4	188.5	188.2	188.9	189.0	189.9	194.1	194.9	195.0	194.9	196.7	196.9	197.0
Personal and educational services	182.2	194.9	191.3	191.6	191.7	192.4	192.9	195.7	199.7	200.7	201.1	201.2	202.2	202.9	203.4
All items	134.3	138.2	137.0	137.3	137.6	138.1	138.4	138.8	139.1	139.6	139.8	139.8	140.3	140.7	141.1
Commodities	126.2	128.7	127.7	128.1	128.6	128.8	128.6	129.0	129.6	130.0	130.2	129.8	130.0	130.4	130.9
Food and beverages	136.5	138.3	138.4	138.5	137.9	137.9	137.8	138.5	138.9	138.8	138.8	139.1	140.1	140.2	140.5
Commodities less food and beverages	119.8	122.7	121.1	121.7	122.8	123.1	123.0	123.2	123.9	124.5	124.9	124.1	123.8	124.4	125.0
Nondurables less food and beverages	123.2	126.2	124.4	125.1	126.7	126.9	126.6	126.9	127.9	128.6	128.7	127.3	126.8	128.0	128.8
Apparel commodities	125.2	128.3	129.9	129.9	129.6	127.3	125.5	127.0	129.8	131.5	131.1	127.8	125.8	129.5	132.5
Nondurables less food, beverages, and apparel	125.1	128.1	124.6	125.6	128.2	129.7	130.0	129.7	130.0	130.1	130.5	129.9	130.2	130.2	130.0
Durables	114.1	116.8	115.6	116.1	116.4	116.8	116.9	117.0	117.2	117.9	118.6	118.7	118.5	118.4	118.5

(continued)

CONSUMER PRICE INDEXES FOR ALL URBAN CONSUMERS AND FOR URBAN WAGE EARNERS AND CLERICAL WORKERS: U.S. CITY AVERAGE, BY EXPENDITURE CATEGORY AND COMMODITY OR SERVICE GROUP *(concluded)*

(1982-84 = 100, unless otherwise indicated)

Series	Annual average		1992										1993		
	1991	1992	Mar.	Apr.	May	June	July	Aug.	Sept.	Oct.	Nov.	Dec.	Jan.	Feb.	Mar.
Services	144.6	150.0	148.7	148.8	149.0	149.8	150.5	150.9	151.1	151.6	151.9	152.1	153.0	153.5	153.9
Rent of shelter (12/84 = 100)	137.0	141.6	140.8	140.7	140.7	141.4	142.1	142.5	142.2	142.8	142.9	143.0	143.9	144.5	144.8
Household services less rent of shelter (12/84 = 100)	116.6	119.7	117.7	117.9	118.7	120.8	121.2	121.3	121.8	120.5	120.4	120.8	121.2	120.6	121.6
Transportation services	149.8	154.3	153.7	154.2	153.9	153.1	153.7	153.4	153.1	155.5	156.7	157.2	158.2	159.2	158.9
Medical care services	176.7	190.3	187.2	187.9	188.6	189.4	190.9	192.0	192.8	194.0	195.0	195.4	197.3	199.0	199.6
Other services	157.8	166.1	163.8	164.3	164.4	164.8	165.1	166.5	168.8	169.5	169.7	169.9	170.4	170.9	171.3
Special indexes:															
All items less food	133.8	138.2	136.7	137.1	137.6	138.2	138.6	138.9	139.3	139.8	140.1	140.0	140.3	140.9	141.3
All items less shelter	132.3	135.9	134.6	135.0	135.5	135.9	136.0	136.4	137.0	137.4	137.7	137.6	137.9	138.4	138.8
All items less homeowners' costs (12/84 = 100)	126.7	130.3	129.2	129.5	129.8	130.3	130.5	130.9	131.3	131.7	131.9	131.8	132.2	132.6	133.1
All items less medical care	132.2	135.7	134.6	134.8	135.2	135.6	135.9	136.2	136.6	137.0	137.2	137.2	137.6	138.0	138.4
Commodities less food	120.7	123.7	122.1	122.7	123.8	124.1	124.0	124.1	124.8	125.4	125.8	125.0	124.7	125.4	125.9
Nondurables less food	124.2	127.4	125.6	126.3	127.8	128.0	127.8	128.0	129.0	129.6	129.7	128.4	128.0	129.1	129.9
Nondurables less food and apparel	125.9	129.0	125.9	126.9	129.1	130.5	130.8	130.5	130.8	130.9	131.2	130.7	131.0	131.1	130.9
Nondurables	130.1	132.5	131.6	132.0	132.5	132.7	132.4	132.9	133.6	133.9	134.0	133.4	133.7	134.3	134.9
Services less rent of shelter (12/84 = 100)	135.3	141.0	139.2	139.6	139.9	140.7	141.3	141.7	142.4	142.7	143.2	143.5	144.3	144.6	145.0
Services less medical care	141.7	146.5	145.3	145.3	145.5	146.3	146.9	147.3	147.5	147.9	148.1	148.4	149.2	149.5	149.9
Energy	102.2	102.6	98.4	99.1	102.1	105.7	105.6	105.0	105.5	104.2	104.2	103.5	102.8	101.7	101.9
All items less energy	138.9	143.2	142.4	142.6	142.7	142.8	143.1	143.6	144.0	144.6	144.9	144.9	145.6	146.2	146.7
All items less food and energy	139.6	144.7	143.7	143.9	144.1	144.3	144.7	145.1	145.5	146.4	146.7	146.6	147.2	148.0	148.5
Commodities less food and energy	127.3	131.2	130.5	130.9	131.2	130.9	130.8	131.3	132.1	132.9	133.2	132.7	132.6	133.5	134.3
Energy commodities	99.4	98.5	93.4	94.9	98.9	102.0	101.9	100.8	100.8	100.9	101.4	99.5	98.1	97.5	97.0
Services less energy	148.2	154.0	152.9	153.0	153.1	153.5	154.2	154.7	154.8	155.7	156.1	156.3	157.2	158.0	158.3
Purchasing power of the consumer dollar:															
1982-84 = $1.00	74.5	72.4	73.0	72.9	72.7	72.4	72.3	72.1	71.9	71.6	71.5	71.5	71.3	71.1	70.9
1967 = $1.00	25.0	24.3	24.5	24.5	24.4	24.3	24.3	24.2	24.1	24.0	24.0	24.0	23.9	23.9	23.8

Source: *Monthly Labor Review*, U.S. Department of Labor, Bureau of Labor Statistics.

CONSUMER PRICE INDEX—U.S. CITY AVERAGE AND AVAILABLE LOCAL AREA DATA: ALL ITEMS

(1982-84=100, unless otherwise indicated)

Area[1]	Pricing schedule[2]	All Urban Consumers							Urban Wage Earners						
		1992				1993			1992				1993		
		Mar.	Apr.	Nov.	Dec.	Jan.	Feb.	Mar.	Mar.	Apr.	Nov.	Dec.	Jan.	Feb.	Mar.
U.S. city average	M	139.3	139.5	142.0	141.9	142.6	143.1	143.6	137.0	137.3	139.8	139.8	140.3	140.7	141.1
Region and area size[3]															
Northeast urban	M	146.2	146.3	149.0	148.9	149.7	150.4	150.9	144.1	144.2	147.1	146.9	147.6	148.2	148.7
Size A - More than 1,200,000	M	146.8	146.8	149.6	149.4	150.3	150.9	151.6	143.6	143.6	146.7	146.6	147.3	147.8	148.4
Size B - 500,000 to 1,200,000	M	145.7	145.8	148.3	147.6	148.0	148.9	149.3	143.8	144.1	146.4	145.7	146.2	147.0	147.3
Size C - 50,000 to 500,000	M	144.2	144.3	146.9	147.2	148.5	149.1	149.1	146.2	146.3	148.8	149.0	150.2	150.7	150.7
North Central urban	M	134.8	135.1	137.6	137.7	138.1	138.6	139.0	132.2	132.6	135.0	135.1	135.4	135.8	136.2
Size A - More than 1,200,000	M	136.0	136.3	138.5	138.9	139.1	139.6	140.1	132.5	132.8	135.2	135.5	135.6	136.1	136.5
Size B - 360,000 to 1,200,000	M	133.4	133.8	136.1	136.3	137.3	137.3	137.3	130.6	131.0	133.1	133.1	134.1	134.0	134.1
Size C - 50,000 to 360,000	M	136.2	136.4	139.4	139.2	139.3	140.1	140.4	134.3	134.5	137.3	137.1	137.2	138.0	138.2
Size D - Nonmetropolitan (less than 50,0000	M	130.0	130.3	133.4	132.8	133.0	133.6	134.7	129.3	129.7	132.7	132.2	132.3	132.7	133.8
South urban	M	135.5	135.9	138.1	137.9	138.4	139.1	139.7	134.2	134.5	136.9	136.8	137.2	137.6	138.3
Size A - More than 1,200,000	M	136.0	136.1	138.3	138.0	138.9	139.8	140.4	134.4	134.6	136.8	136.6	137.2	138.0	138.5
Size B - 450,000 to 1,200,000	M	137.0	137.4	139.7	139.8	139.9	140.3	141.6	133.8	134.2	136.8	136.8	136.8	136.9	138.2
Size C - 50,000 to 450,000	M	134.6	135.1	137.3	137.2	137.8	138.1	138.6	134.5	134.9	137.5	137.4	137.9	138.1	138.5
Size D - Nonmetropolitan (less than 50,000)	M	133.6	134.1	136.0	136.4	136.4	136.7	137.0	133.7	134.2	136.4	136.7	136.6	136.8	137.0
West urban	M	141.1	141.3	143.9	143.9	144.7	145.2	145.2	138.7	139.0	141.6	141.5	142.2	142.7	142.7
Size A - More than 1,250,000	M	143.0	143.2	145.7	145.8	146.7	147.2	147.2	139.0	139.3	141.8	141.8	142.6	143.1	143.0
Size C - 50,000 to 330,000	M	138.3	138.7	142.2	142.1	142.7	143.1	143.8	136.8	137.1	140.4	140.2	140.8	141.3	141.8

(continued)

CONSUMER PRICE INDEX—U.S. CITY AVERAGE AND AVAILABLE LOCAL AREA DATA: ALL ITEMS *(concluded)*

(1982-84 = 100, unless otherwise indicated)

Area[1]	Pricing schedule[2]	All Urban Consumers							Urban Wage Earners						
		1992				1993			1992				1993		
		Mar.	Apr.	Nov.	Dec.	Jan.	Feb.	Mar.	Mar.	Apr.	Nov.	Dec.	Jan.	Feb.	Mar.
Size classes:															
A (12/86=100)	M	126.7	126.8	129.0	129.0	129.7	130.3	130.6	125.8	126.0	128.4	128.3	128.8	129.3	129.7
B	M	138.5	138.8	141.2	141.1	141.5	141.9	142.5	136.3	136.7	139.0	138.9	139.3	139.5	140.1
C	M	137.4	137.7	140.4	140.4	140.9	141.5	141.8	137.0	137.3	140.1	140.0	140.5	141.0	141.3
D	M	134.4	134.8	137.1	137.1	137.3	137.7	138.3	134.0	134.3	136.9	136.8	137.0	137.3	137.8
Selected local areas															
Chicago, IL-Northwestern IN	M	139.7	139.8	142.4	142.9	143.2	143.6	144.1	135.2	135.4	138.2	138.5	138.9	139.1	139.5
Los Angeles-Long Beach, Anaheim, CA	M	145.5	145.8	148.2	148.2	149.2	150.0	149.8	141.0	141.3	143.5	143.5	144.4	145.0	144.8
New York, NY-Northeastern NJ	M	149.1	149.2	152.2	151.9	153.0	153.6	154.1	145.8	145.9	149.2	149.1	149.9	150.3	150.7
Philadelphia, PA-NJ	M	145.4	145.4	147.5	147.5	147.5	148.5	149.3	145.0	145.1	147.6	147.4	147.4	148.6	149.0
San Francisco-Oakland, CA	M	141.9	141.6	144.2	144.3	145.1	145.5	145.7	139.9	139.6	142.3	142.3	143.0	143.5	143.8
Baltimore, MD	1	138.7	-	141.1	-	142.0	-	142.6	137.9	-	140.6	-	141.3	-	141.8
Boston, MA	1	147.9	-	150.2	-	151.8	-	153.9	147.2	-	149.8	-	151.0	-	153.8
Cleveland, OH	1	136.3	-	137.1	-	137.5	-	138.8	129.7	-	130.8	-	130.8	-	131.8
Miami, FL	1	134.5	-	135.9	-	137.8	-	139.2	132.3	-	134.2	-	135.9	-	137.1
St. Louis, MO-IL	1	132.6	-	136.0	-	135.9	-	136.1	132.0	-	135.6	-	135.4	-	135.5
Washington, DC-MD-VA	1	143.0	-	146.9	-	147.8	-	148.5	141.3	-	145.1	-	145.6	-	146.2
Dallas-Ft. Worth, TX	2	-	132.5	-	134.6	-	135.4	-	-	131.5	-	134.1	-	134.8	-
Detroit, MI	2	-	135.3	-	137.1	-	138.3	-	-	131.7	-	133.1	-	134.4	-
Houston, TX	2	-	128.7	-	129.3	-	131.7	-	-	128.4	-	129.2	-	131.3	-
Pittsburgh, PA	2	-	135.1	-	137.3	-	139.2	-	-	129.4	-	131.4	-	133.2	-

[1] Area is the Consolidated Metropolitan Statistical Area (CMSA), exclusive of farms and military. Area definitions are those established by the Office of Management and Budget in 1983, except for Boston-Lawrence-Salem, MA-NH Area (excludes Monroe County); and Milwaukee, WI Area (includes only the Milwaukee MSA). Definitions do not include revisions made since 1983.

[2] Foods, fuels, and several other items priced every month in all areas; most other goods and services priced as indicated:.

M - Every month.

1 - January, March, May, July, September, and November.

2 - February, April, June, August, October, and December.

[3] Regions are defined as the four Census regions.

- Data not available.

NOTE: Local area CPI indexes are byproducts of the national CPI program. Because each local index is a small subset of the national index, it has a smaller sample size and is, therefore, subject to substantially more sampling and other measurement error than the national index. As a result, local area indexes show greater volatility than the national index, although their long-term trends are quite similar. Therefore, the Bureau of Labor Statistics strongly urges users to consider adopting the national average CPI for use in escalator clauses.

Source: *Monthly Labor Review,* U.S. Department of Labor, Bureau of Labor Statistics.

Purchasing Power of the Dollar: 1950–1992

1950 to 1988

[**Indexes: PPI, 1982=$1.00; CPI, 1982-84=$1.00.** Producer prices prior to 1961, and consumer prices prior to 1964, exclude Alaska and Hawaii. Producer prices based on finished goods index. Obtained by dividing the average price index for the 1982=100, PPI; 1982-84=100, CPI base periods (100.0) by the price index for a given period and expressing the result in dollars and cents. Annual figures are based on average of monthly data]

YEAR	ANNUAL AVERAGE AS MEASURED BY—		YEAR	ANNUAL AVERAGE AS MEASURED BY—		YEAR	ANNUAL AVERAGE AS MEASURED BY—	
	Producer prices	Consumer prices		Producer prices	Consumer prices		Producer prices	Consumer prices
1950	$3.546	$4.151	1963	$2.994	$3.265	1976	$1.645	$1.757
1951	3.247	3.846	1964	2.985	3.220	1977	1.546	1.649
1952	3.268	3.765	1965	2.933	3.166	1978	1.433	1.532
1953	3.300	3.735	1966	2.841	3.080	1979	1.289	1.380
1954	3.289	3.717	1967	2.809	2.993	1980	1.136	1.215
1955	3.279	3.732	1968	2.732	2.873	1981	1.041	1.098
1956	3.195	3.678	1969	2.632	2.726	1982	1.000	1.035
1957	3.077	3.549	1970	2.545	2.574	1983	.984	1.003
1958	3.012	3.457	1971	2.469	2.466	1984	.964	.961
1959	3.021	3.427	1972	2.392	2.391	1985	.955	.928
1960	2.994	3.373	1973	2.193	2.251	1986	.969	.913
1961	2.994	3.340	1974	1.901	2.029	1987	.949	.880
1962	2.985	3.304	1975	1.718	1.859	1988	.926	.846

Source: U.S. Bureau of Labor Statistics. Monthly data in U.S. Bureau of Economic Analysis, *Survey of Current Business.*

Source: *Statistical Abstract of the United States,* 1990, U.S. Department of Commerce.

1989 to 1992

YEAR	ANNUAL AVERAGE AS MEASURED BY—	
	Producer prices	Consumer prices
1989	$.880	$.807
1990	.839	.766
1991	.822	.734
1992	.812	.713

Source: U.S. Department of Commerce, U.S. Bureau of Economic Analysis.

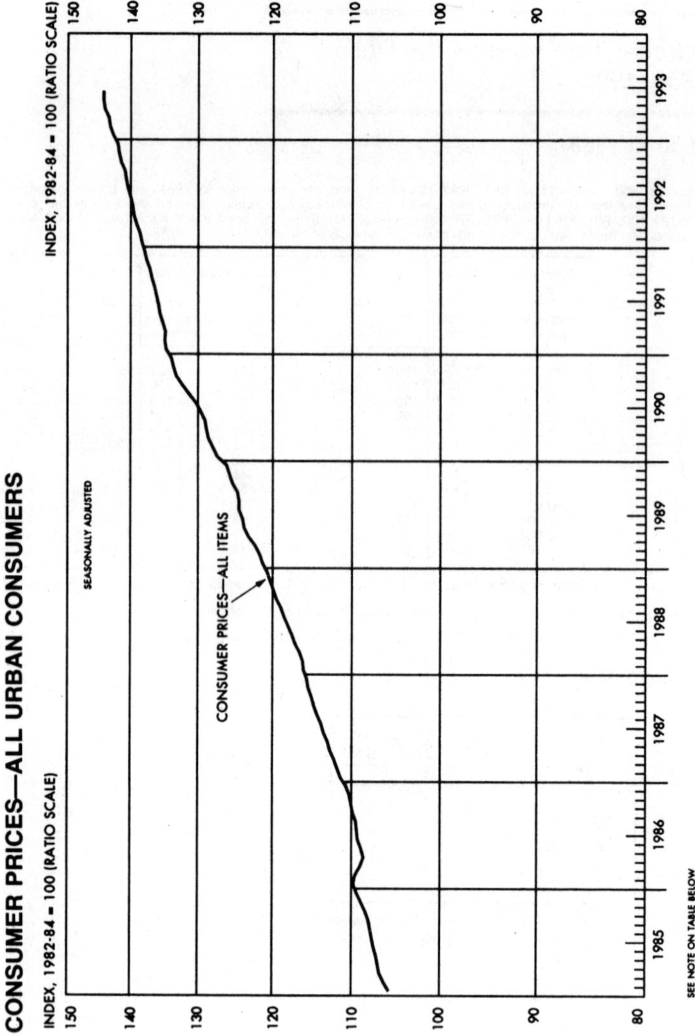
CONSUMER PRICES—ALL URBAN CONSUMERS
INDEX, 1982-84 = 100 (RATIO SCALE)
INDEX, 1982-84 = 100 (RATIO SCALE)
SEASONALLY ADJUSTED
CONSUMER PRICES—ALL ITEMS
150
140
130
120
110
100
90
80
1985
1986
1987
1988
1989
1990
1991
1992
1993
SEE NOTE ON TABLE BELOW
SOURCE: DEPARTMENT OF LABOR
COUNCIL OF ECONOMIC ADVISERS

[1982–84=100, except as noted; monthly data seasonally adjusted, except as noted]

Period	All items [1]		Food	Housing						Apparel and upkeep	Transportation			Medical care	Energy [2]	All items less food and energy
	Not seasonally adjusted (NSA)	Seasonally adjusted		Total [1]	Shelter				Fuel and other utilities		Total [1]	New cars	Motor fuel			
					Total	Renters' costs (Dec. 1982=100)	Homeowners' costs (Dec. 1982=100)	Maintenance and repairs (NSA)								
Rel. imp. [3]	*100.0*		*15.8*	*41.4*	*27.9*	*8.0*	*19.7*	*0.2*	*7.3*	*6.0*	*17.0*	*4.0*	*3.3*	*6.9*	*7.3*	*76.9*
1983	99.6		99.4	99.5	99.1	103.0	102.5	99.9	100.2	100.2	99.3	99.9	99.4	100.6	99.9	99.6
1984	103.9		103.2	103.6	104.0	108.6	107.3	103.7	104.8	102.1	103.7	102.8	97.9	106.8	100.9	104.6
1985	107.6		105.6	107.7	109.8	115.4	113.1	106.5	106.5	105.0	106.4	106.1	98.7	113.5	101.6	109.1
1986	109.6		109.0	110.9	115.8	121.9	119.4	107.9	104.1	105.9	102.3	110.6	77.1	122.0	88.2	113.5
1987	113.6		113.5	114.2	121.3	128.1	124.8	111.8	103.0	110.6	105.4	114.6	80.2	130.1	88.6	118.2
1988	118.3		118.2	118.5	127.1	133.6	131.1	114.7	104.4	115.4	108.7	116.9	80.9	138.6	89.3	123.4
1989	124.0		125.1	123.0	132.8	138.9	137.3	118.0	107.8	118.6	114.1	119.2	88.5	149.3	94.3	129.0
1990	130.7		132.4	128.5	140.0	146.7	144.6	122.2	111.6	124.1	120.5	121.0	101.2	162.8	102.1	135.5
1991	136.2		136.3	133.6	146.3	155.6	150.2	126.3	115.3	128.7	123.8	125.3	99.4	177.0	102.5	142.1
1992	140.3		137.9	137.5	151.2	160.9	155.3	128.6	117.8	131.9	126.5	128.4	99.0	190.1	103.0	147.3
1992:																
June	140.2	140.2	137.6	137.4	150.9	160.2	155.2	128.5	117.4	132.1	126.5	128.3	100.4	189.8	103.1	147.3
July	140.5	140.6	137.5	137.6	151.1	160.2	155.4	128.8	118.1	132.7	127.1	128.5	101.4	190.8	103.8	147.8
Aug	140.9	140.9	138.3	137.9	151.4	160.6	155.7	128.1	118.5	132.4	126.9	128.9	99.8	191.7	103.4	148.1
Sept	141.3	141.1	138.7	138.0	151.6	161.2	155.8	128.5	118.6	131.9	126.9	129.2	99.5	192.6	103.4	148.2
Oct	141.8	141.7	138.7	138.5	152.2	161.8	156.4	129.4	118.9	132.4	127.8	129.2	100.2	193.7	103.9	148.9
Nov	142.0	142.0	138.8	138.8	152.6	162.1	156.8	129.5	119.2	132.3	128.4	129.4	100.3	194.7	104.1	149.3
Dec	141.9	142.2	139.2	138.9	152.9	161.9	157.4	129.3	119.3	131.9	128.5	129.5	99.8	195.5	103.9	149.6
1993:																
Jan	142.6	142.9	139.7	139.3	153.5	161.9	158.2	129.7	119.4	133.0	129.3	129.8	101.2	196.7	104.4	150.3
Feb	143.1	143.4	139.9	139.6	154.0	162.5	158.7	130.5	118.8	135.0	129.9	129.8	101.8	197.7	104.0	151.0
Mar	143.6	143.6	140.1	140.0	154.2	162.8	158.9	131.5	120.2	134.3	130.0	130.1	101.4	198.2	104.7	151.2
Apr	144.0	144.2	140.6	140.7	155.0	163.8	159.6	131.8	120.7	134.3	130.2	130.7	100.8	199.3	104.9	151.8
May	144.2	144.4	141.2	140.8	155.1	164.3	159.7	131.6	120.9	133.6	130.1	131.0	98.4	200.8	103.9	152.1
June	144.4	144.4	140.6	141.2	155.6	164.4	160.3	131.2	121.4	132.9	129.9	131.2	97.3	201.6	103.7	152.3

[1] Includes items not shown separately.
[2] Household fuels—gas (piped), electricity, fuel oil, etc.—and motor fuel. Motor oil, coolant, etc. also included through 1982.
[3] Relative importance, December 1992.

NOTE.—Data beginning 1983 incorporate a rental equivalence measure for homeownership costs and therefore are not strictly comparable with figures for earlier periods.
Data beginning 1987 and 1988 calculated on a revised basis.
Source: Department of Labor, Bureau of Labor Statistics.

Source: *Economic Indicators*, Council of Economic Advisers.

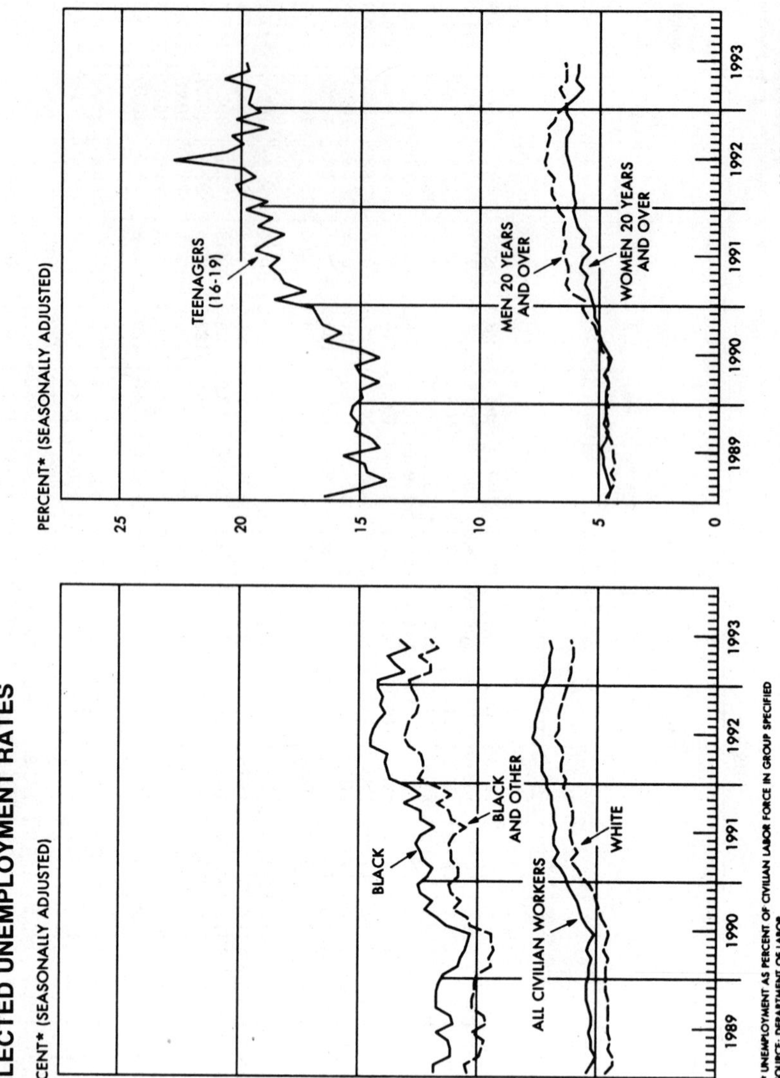
SELECTED UNEMPLOYMENT RATES
PERCENT* (SEASONALLY ADJUSTED)
25
20
15
10
5
0
BLACK
BLACK AND OTHER
ALL CIVILIAN WORKERS
WHITE
1989
1990
1991
1992
1993
* UNEMPLOYMENT AS PERCENT OF CIVILIAN LABOR FORCE IN GROUP SPECIFIED
SOURCE: DEPARTMENT OF LABOR
PERCENT* (SEASONALLY ADJUSTED)
TEENAGERS (16-19)
MEN 20 YEARS AND OVER
WOMEN 20 YEARS AND OVER
COUNCIL OF ECONOMIC ADVISERS

[Monthly data seasonally adjusted]

Period	Unemployment rate, all workers [1]	Unemployment rate (percent of civilian labor force in group)												Labor force time lost (percent) [2]
		All civilian workers	By sex and age			By race			By selected groups					
			Men 20 years and over	Women 20 years and over	Both sexes 16–19 years	White	Black and other	Black	Experienced wage and salary workers	Married men, spouse present	Women who maintain families	Full-time workers	Part-time workers	
1983	9.5	9.6	8.9	8.1	22.4	8.4	17.8	19.5	9.2	6.5	12.2	9.5	10.4	10.9
1984	7.4	7.5	6.6	6.8	18.9	6.5	14.4	15.9	7.1	4.6	10.3	7.2	9.3	8.6
1985	7.1	7.2	6.2	6.6	18.6	6.2	13.7	15.1	6.8	4.3	10.4	6.8	9.3	8.1
1986	6.9	7.0	6.1	6.2	18.3	6.0	13.1	14.5	6.6	4.4	9.8	6.6	9.1	7.9
1987	6.1	6.2	5.4	5.4	16.9	5.3	11.6	13.0	5.8	3.9	9.2	5.8	8.4	7.1
1988	5.4	5.5	4.8	4.9	15.3	4.7	10.4	11.7	5.2	3.3	8.1	5.2	7.6	6.3
1989	5.2	5.3	4.5	4.7	15.0	4.5	10.0	11.4	5.0	3.0	8.1	4.9	7.3	5.9
1990	5.4	5.5	4.9	4.8	15.5	4.7	10.1	11.3	5.3	3.4	8.2	5.2	7.4	6.2
1991	6.6	6.7	6.3	5.7	18.6	6.0	11.1	12.4	6.5	4.4	9.1	6.5	8.3	7.6
1992	7.3	7.4	7.0	6.3	20.0	6.5	12.7	14.1	7.1	5.0	9.9	7.1	9.2	8.3
1992: June	7.6	7.7	7.3	6.3	22.8	6.8	13.1	14.5	7.3	5.1	10.1	7.4	9.3	8.4
July	7.5	7.6	7.2	6.4	20.6	6.6	13.0	14.4	7.2	5.2	10.3	7.3	9.2	8.4
Aug	7.5	7.6	7.2	6.4	19.9	6.6	12.9	14.2	7.2	5.3	10.3	7.3	9.1	8.4
Sept	7.4	7.5	7.1	6.4	20.4	6.6	12.6	13.9	7.2	5.2	9.1	7.2	9.5	8.3
Oct	7.3	7.4	7.2	6.2	18.9	6.5	12.5	14.1	7.1	5.1	9.3	7.1	9.2	8.3
Nov	7.2	7.3	6.9	6.2	20.2	6.4	12.6	14.0	7.0	4.9	10.4	7.0	9.2	8.3
Dec	7.2	7.3	6.8	6.4	19.2	6.3	12.8	14.2	7.0	4.8	10.3	6.9	9.7	8.1
1993: Jan	7.0	7.1	6.4	6.4	19.7	6.2	12.9	14.2	6.8	4.5	10.6	6.7	9.3	7.9
Feb	6.9	7.0	6.5	6.0	19.6	6.1	12.0	13.1	6.7	4.5	10.2	6.6	9.1	7.9
Mar	6.9	7.0	6.7	5.7	19.5	6.1	12.0	13.5	6.6	4.7	9.0	6.6	8.9	7.9
Apr	6.9	7.0	6.4	6.0	20.7	6.0	12.5	13.8	6.7	4.5	9.6	6.6	9.7	7.8
May	6.8	6.9	6.4	5.9	19.7	6.0	11.7	12.9	6.5	4.5	9.9	6.6	8.4	7.9
June	6.9	7.0	6.5	5.9	19.8	6.1	12.0	13.3	6.6	4.4	9.8	6.6	8.9	7.8

[1] Unemployed as percent of total labor force including resident Armed Forces.
[2] Aggregate hours lost by the unemployed and persons on part time for economic reasons as percent of potentially available labor force hours.

Source: Department of Labor, Bureau of Labor Statistics.

Source: *Economic Indicators*, Council of Economic Advisers.

MONEY STOCK, LIQUID ASSETS, AND DEBT MEASURES

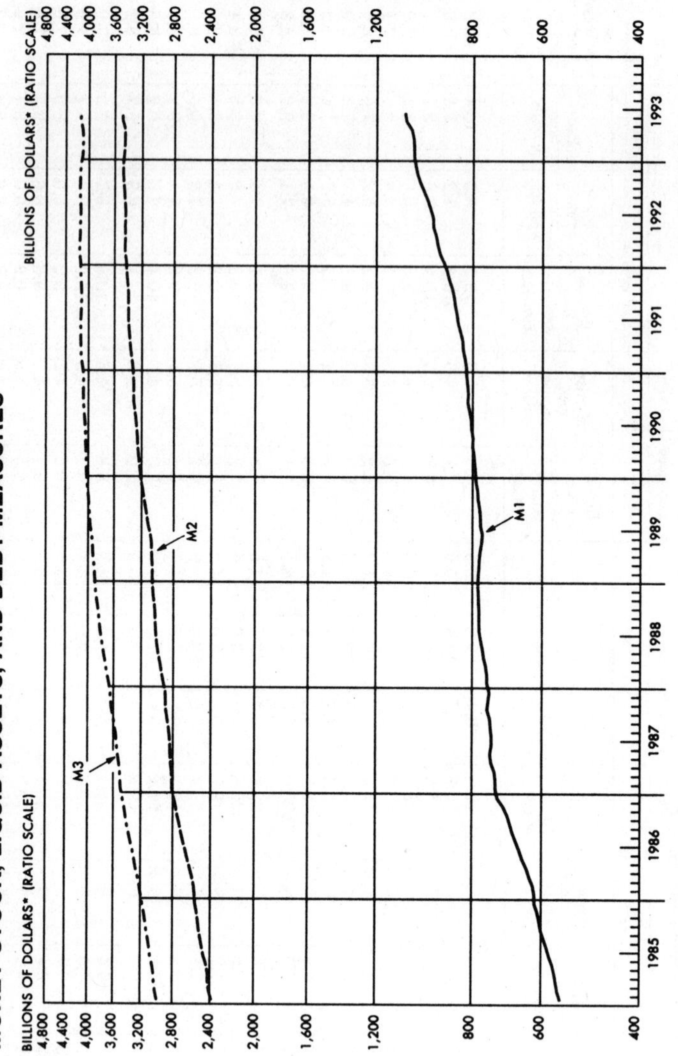

[Averages of daily figures, except as noted; billions of dollars, seasonally adjusted]

Period		M1	M2	M3	L	Debt	Percent change from year or 6 months earlier [2]			
		Sum of currency, demand deposits, travelers' checks, and other checkable deposits (OCDs)	M1 plus overnight RPs and Eurodollars, MMMF balances (general purpose and broker/dealer), MMDAs, and savings and small time deposits	M2 plus large time deposits, term RPs, term Eurodollars, and institution-only MMMF balances	M3 plus other liquid assets	Debt of domestic nonfinancial sectors (monthly average) [1]	M1	M2	M3	Debt
1983:	Dec	521.2	2,186.5	2,693.1	3,154.4	5,244.6	9.9	12.0	10.3	11.6
1984:	Dec	552.4	2,376.0	2,988.2	3,529.6	6,008.2	6.0	8.7	11.0	14.6
1985:	Dec	620.1	2,572.4	3,203.6	3,830.9	6,875.3	12.3	8.3	7.2	14.4
1986:	Dec	724.5	2,816.0	3,491.6	4,131.9	7,795.2	16.8	9.5	9.0	13.4
1987:	Dec	750.0	2,917.2	3,674.8	4,333.5	8,546.2	3.5	3.6	5.2	9.6
1988:	Dec	787.1	3,078.3	3,915.5	4,669.4	9,326.3	4.9	5.5	6.6	9.1
1989:	Dec	794.6	3,233.3	4,056.1	4,886.1	10,086.5	1.0	5.0	3.6	8.2
1990:	Dec	827.2	3,345.5	4,116.7	4,966.6	10,755.3	4.1	3.5	1.5	6.6
1991:	Dec	899.3	3,445.8	4,168.1	4,982.2	11,219.3	8.7	3.0	1.2	4.3
1992:	Dec	1,026.6	[r]3,496.9	[r]4,166.4	[r]5,043.6	11,779.7	14.2	1.5	−.0	5.0
1992:	May	952.2	3,467.5	4,179.8	5,011.0	11,456.5	13.7	1.8	.8	4.6
	June	952.6	3,462.1	4,170.1	5,014.8	11,507.0	11.9	.9	.1	5.1
	July	963.3	3,463.6	4,169.0	5,012.5	11,553.0	11.4	.7	−.2	5.4
	Aug	975.5	3,472.4	[r]4,178.7	5,025.9	11,603.4	10.6	.3	−.5	5.4
	Sept	990.1	3,480.2	4,183.0	5,037.4	11,642.3	11.8	.7	−.1	5.0
	Oct	1,005.9	3,491.4	4,180.0	[r]5,040.5	11,669.4	13.7	1.5	.1	4.5
	Nov	1,019.1	3,498.0	4,178.5	[r]5,050.9	11,724.1	14.1	1.8	−.1	4.7
	Dec	1,026.6	[r]3,496.9	[r]4,166.4	[r]5,043.6	11,779.7	15.5	2.0	−.2	4.7
1993:	Jan	1,033.3	[r]3,486.9	[r]4,141.0	[r]5,018.2	11,810.0	14.5	[r]1.3	−1.3	4.4
	Feb	1,033.1	[r]3,475.4	[r]4,135.4	[r]5,013.0	11,848.6	11.8	.2	−2.1	4.2
	Mar	[r]1,035.3	[r]3,472.9	[r]4,131.0	[r]5,010.6	11,903.2	[r]9.1	−.4	−2.5	4.5
	Apr	1,043.2	[r]3,474.6	[r]4,142.1	[r]5,027.3	[r]11,960.9	7.4	−1.0	[r]−1.8	5.0
	May	1,067.2	[r]3,505.4	[r]4,171.6	[p]5,069.2	[p]12,021.3	9.4	[r].4	[r]−.3	5.1
	June	1,073.7	3,511.6	4,167.2	....	....	9.2	.8	.0	....

[1] Consists of outstanding credit market debt of the U.S. Government, State and local governments, and private nonfinancial sectors; data from flow of funds accounts.

[2] Annual changes are from December to December and monthly changes are from 6 months earlier at a simple annual rate.

Source: Board of Governors of the Federal Reserve System.

Source: *Economic Indicators*, Council of Economic Advisers.

OUTPUT, CAPACITY, AND CAPACITY UTILIZATION[1]

Seasonally adjusted

Series	Output (1987=100) 1992 Q2	Output 1992 Q3	Output 1992 Q4	Output 1993 Q1	Capacity (percent of 1987 output) 1992 Q2	Capacity 1992 Q3	Capacity 1992 Q4	Capacity 1993 Q1	Capacity utilization rate (percent) 1992 Q2	Utilization 1992 Q3	Utilization 1992 Q4	Utilization 1993 Q1
1 **Total industry**	**106.3**	**106.5**	**108.3**	**109.7**	**133.2**	**133.7**	**134.2**	**134.8**	**79.8**	**79.7**	**80.7**	**81.4**
2 Manufacturing	106.7	107.0	108.7	110.4	135.4	136.0	136.6	137.2	78.8	78.7	79.6	80.4
3 Primary processing	103.9	103.7	104.7	106.5	126.1	126.4	126.6	126.8	82.4	82.1	82.7	83.9
4 Advanced processing	108.0	108.5	110.6	112.2	139.8	140.6	141.3	142.1	77.3	77.2	78.3	79.0
5 Durable goods	107.8	108.3	110.8	113.6	141.2	141.9	142.6	143.4	76.3	76.3	77.7	79.2
6 Lumber and products	95.1	96.0	98.5	100.2	112.3	112.4	112.5	112.6	84.7	85.4	87.6	89.0
7 Primary metals	101.3	99.7	101.5	105.1	125.6	125.3	125.0	124.9	80.7	79.6	81.2	84.2
8 Iron and steel	104.7	103.5	105.0	109.6	130.8	130.4	129.9	129.8	80.1	79.4	80.8	84.5
9 Nonferrous	96.7	94.5	96.7	99.0	118.5	118.3	118.2	118.1	81.6	79.8	81.8	83.8
10 Nonelectrical machinery	122.6	126.8	132.4	137.2	159.0	160.6	162.1	163.7	77.1	79.0	81.7	83.8
11 Electrical machinery	119.0	120.9	124.0	126.9	149.9	151.3	152.6	154.1	79.4	80.0	81.2	82.3
12 Motor vehicles and parts	105.7	103.6	111.4	120.8	151.2	152.9	154.5	155.8	69.9	67.7	72.1	77.5
13 Aerospace and miscellaneous transportation equipment	101.3	99.5	97.7	95.7	135.7	135.7	135.8	135.7	74.7	73.3	72.0	70.5
14 Nondurable goods	105.4	105.4	106.1	106.4	128.3	128.7	129.1	129.6	82.2	81.9	82.1	82.1
15 Textile mill products	104.6	105.2	105.2	106.4	116.4	116.6	116.7	116.9	89.8	90.3	90.1	91.0
16 Paper and products	108.7	108.6	107.9	109.7	121.3	121.7	122.1	122.5	89.6	89.2	88.4	89.6
17 Chemicals and products	114.8	114.7	116.9	116.5	141.7	142.6	143.5	144.4	81.0	80.4	81.4	80.7
18 Plastics materials	109.8	110.5	106.6	...	127.8	128.3	128.8	...	85.9	86.2	82.8	...
19 Petroleum products	102.7	100.2	104.2	103.9	116.9	116.6	116.2	115.9	87.8	85.9	89.7	89.7
20 Mining	97.8	97.5	97.9	96.4	112.6	112.3	112.0	111.7	86.9	86.9	87.4	86.3
21 Utilities	111.1	110.9	114.7	115.8	130.9	131.4	131.8	132.2	84.8	84.5	87.1	87.6
22 Electric	110.7	110.6	114.3	115.8	127.4	127.9	128.5	129.0	86.9	86.4	89.0	89.8

Capacity utilization rate (percent)

Series	Previous cycle[2] High	Previous cycle[2] Low	Latest cycle[3] High	Latest cycle[3] Low	1992 Apr.	1992 Sept.	1992 Oct.	1992 Nov.	1992 Dec.	1993 Jan.[r]	1993 Feb.[r]	1993 Mar.[r]	1993 Apr.[p]
1 **Total industry**	**89.2**	**72.6**	**87.3**	**71.8**	**79.9**	**79.3**	**80.2**	**80.8**	**81.0**	**81.2**	**81.5**	**81.4**	**81.4**
2 Manufacturing	88.9	70.8	87.3	70.0	78.8	78.4	79.2	79.7	79.8	80.3	80.5	80.5	80.7
3 Primary processing	92.2	68.9	89.7	66.8	82.3	81.7	82.3	83.0	82.9	83.5	84.4	83.9	84.1
4 Advanced processing	87.5	72.0	86.3	71.4	77.3	77.0	77.9	78.4	78.6	78.9	78.9	79.1	79.2
5 Durable goods	88.8	68.5	86.9	65.0	76.1	76.1	77.1	77.8	78.2	78.9	79.4	79.4	79.5
6 Lumber and products	90.1	62.2	87.6	60.9	84.9	84.3	87.0	88.7	87.1	88.2	90.0	88.7	87.5
7 Primary metals	100.6	66.2	102.4	46.8	81.0	78.2	80.4	81.2	82.0	82.3	86.4	83.9	84.1
8 Iron and steel	105.8	66.6	110.4	38.3	80.6	78.3	80.0	79.7	82.7	82.4	86.9	84.0	84.3
9 Nonferrous	92.9	61.3	90.5	62.2	81.5	78.1	80.8	83.5	80.9	82.2	85.7	83.7	83.9
10 Nonelectrical machinery	96.4	74.5	92.1	64.9	76.2	79.4	80.8	82.0	82.3	82.8	83.7	85.0	86.1
11 Electrical machinery	87.8	63.8	89.4	71.1	79.1	80.1	80.6	81.5	81.6	82.0	82.4	82.6	82.4
12 Motor vehicles and parts	93.4	51.1	93.0	44.5	69.4	66.8	70.1	71.1	74.9	77.7	77.9	76.9	76.8
13 Aerospace and miscellaneous transportation equipment	77.0	66.6	81.1	66.9	75.1	72.7	72.4	72.0	71.5	71.2	70.6	69.8	68.9
14 Nondurable goods	87.9	71.8	87.0	76.9	82.4	81.7	82.0	82.4	82.0	82.2	82.1	82.0	82.2
15 Textile mill products	92.0	60.4	91.7	73.8	90.2	90.1	88.7	90.8	90.8	91.5	91.1	90.4	91.4
16 Paper and products	96.9	69.0	94.2	82.0	90.1	89.9	88.0	88.6	88.6	88.8	90.1	89.8	90.5
17 Chemicals and products	87.9	69.9	85.1	70.1	81.0	80.6	81.1	82.1	81.2	81.1	80.2	80.7	80.9
18 Plastics materials	102.0	50.6	90.9	63.4	85.2	85.4	84.1	83.6	80.5	86.0	85.3	...	...
19 Petroleum products	96.7	81.1	89.5	68.2	88.6	86.8	90.5	89.4	89.1	89.0	90.3	89.7	89.6
20 Mining	94.4	88.4	96.6	80.6	86.5	86.5	87.1	87.4	87.8	87.9	85.5	85.4	86.1
21 Utilities	95.6	82.5	88.3	76.2	85.7	84.5	85.6	87.1	88.5	85.4	88.8	88.6	85.4
22 Electric	99.0	82.7	88.3	78.7	87.9	86.6	87.7	88.8	90.4	87.7	90.8	90.9	87.5

1. Data in this table also appear in the Board's G.17 (419) monthly statistical release. For ordering address, see inside front cover. For a detailed description of the series, see "Recent Developments in Industrial Capacity and Utilization," *Federal Reserve Bulletin*, vol. 76 (June 1990), pp. 411–35. See also "Industrial Production Capacity and Capacity Utilization since 1987," *Federal Reserve Bulletin*, vol. 79, (June 1993), pp. 590–605.

2. Monthly high, 1973; monthly low, 1975.

3. Monthly highs, 1978 through 1980; monthly lows, 1982.

Source: *Federal Reserve Bulletin*, Board of Governors of the Federal Reserve System.

INDUSTRIAL PRODUCTION Indexes and Gross Value[1]

Monthly data seasonally adjusted

Group	1987 proportion	1992 avg.	1992 Apr.	May	June	July	Aug.	Sept.	Oct.	Nov.	Dec.	1993 Jan.[r]	Feb.[r]	Mar.[r]	Apr.[p]
			Index (1987 = 100)												
MAJOR MARKETS															
1 **Total index**	**100.0**	**106.5**	**106.3**	**106.7**	**106.0**	**106.8**	**106.6**	**106.2**	**107.5**	**108.4**	**108.9**	**109.3**	**109.9**	**109.9**	**110.0**
2 Products	60.8	105.6	105.3	105.7	104.8	105.7	105.9	105.3	107.1	107.8	108.2	108.5	109.1	109.1	109.1
3 Final products	46.0	108.2	107.7	108.3	107.1	108.1	108.9	108.1	110.1	111.0	111.5	111.9	112.3	112.3	112.5
4 Consumer goods, total	26.0	105.2	105.4	105.8	104.0	104.9	105.1	104.4	106.4	107.1	107.5	107.6	108.2	108.1	107.9
5 Durable consumer goods	5.6	102.5	102.6	105.6	102.0	102.8	101.9	100.9	104.1	105.7	107.9	110.9	111.7	111.0	111.2
6 Automotive products	2.5	99.4	99.0	102.9	99.0	98.8	99.5	97.3	103.1	104.1	108.7	112.7	112.6	111.4	111.0
7 Autos and trucks	1.5	96.9	97.4	102.1	96.5	95.3	96.0	93.5	101.5	102.9	111.7	116.8	115.7	113.5	112.8
8 Autos, consumer	.9	79.0	79.2	85.3	83.5	81.2	77.0	77.9	78.5	79.6	86.9	86.6	91.9	90.6	88.0
9 Trucks, consumer	.6	127.9	129.1	131.2	119.2	119.8	128.8	120.4	141.3	143.3	154.6	169.1	156.9	153.1	155.9
10 Auto parts and allied goods	1.0	103.7	101.5	104.4	103.2	104.6	105.3	103.7	105.9	106.0	103.8	105.8	107.5	107.9	107.9
11 Other	3.1	105.2	105.8	107.9	104.6	106.3	104.0	104.1	104.9	107.1	107.2	109.3	110.9	110.7	111.4
12 Appliances, A/C, and TV	.8	110.4	111.4	116.8	109.6	109.7	111.0	112.9	110.8	110.8	110.5	116.0	117.6	120.4	120.1
13 Carpeting and furniture	.9	99.9	101.0	102.7	98.0	101.7	97.7	98.2	98.5	103.7	105.4	105.5	107.4	105.2	107.2
14 Miscellaneous home goods	1.4	105.6	105.8	106.3	106.0	107.4	104.1	102.9	105.8	107.1	106.6	108.0	109.4	108.8	109.2
15 Nondurable consumer goods	20.4	105.9	106.1	105.9	104.6	105.5	106.0	105.3	107.1	107.5	107.4	106.7	107.3	107.3	107.0
16 Foods and tobacco	9.1	104.7	104.8	104.7	103.3	105.0	107.0	104.9	105.9	105.2	104.8	104.6	104.9	104.3	104.4
17 Clothing	2.6	95.0	95.0	95.7	94.5	95.1	94.0	94.3	94.5	95.9	96.0	95.7	95.4	95.2	94.9
18 Chemical products	3.5	118.7	118.9	118.1	117.6	117.3	116.5	118.5	121.1	123.3	121.7	122.4	120.4	122.7	123.2
19 Paper products	2.5	100.8	101.2	101.0	100.6	100.1	100.2	100.4	100.1	100.9	100.9	100.2	101.8	101.8	102.2
20 Energy	2.7	108.3	109.0	107.8	105.2	106.3	105.6	104.6	111.1	112.0	114.4	109.5	114.0	113.6	110.2
21 Fuels	.7	104.7	105.2	104.8	103.8	104.1	98.9	103.5	109.8	107.7	106.1	106.5	108.9	107.4	106.0
22 Residential utilities	2.0	109.6	110.5	108.9	105.8	107.2	108.2	105.1	111.6	113.6	117.5	110.7	115.9	116.0	111.8
23 Equipment	20.0	112.7	111.1	112.0	111.6	112.7	114.3	113.5	115.4	116.7	117.2	118.1	118.1	118.4	119.1
24 Business equipment	13.9	123.2	120.6	122.1	121.9	123.7	126.1	125.0	127.5	129.0	129.6	131.2	131.8	132.9	134.0
25 Information processing and related	5.6	134.7	129.6	131.4	134.3	137.4	138.5	138.2	142.2	142.9	143.2	144.4	146.1	149.2	151.9
26 Office and computing	1.9	176.8	168.2	170.5	174.0	178.0	182.0	184.0	187.0	189.0	198.5	205.0	214.1	...	...
27 Industrial	4.0	108.5	106.8	108.4	108.7	109.1	109.2	109.6	110.1	112.0	112.3	113.1	112.5	112.6	112.6
28 Transit	2.5	137.1	137.5	136.9	133.9	135.3	143.3	134.5	137.4	140.4	144.1	146.7	147.1	145.0	143.5
29 Autos and trucks	1.2	117.9	119.5	123.3	117.2	114.2	117.3	114.7	121.7	123.9	131.4	136.7	138.1	135.9	134.6
30 Other	1.9	104.7	104.2	106.5	99.2	100.2	105.6	107.3	108.8	110.7	109.2	112.6	113.0	113.8	114.6
31 Defense and space equipment	5.4	85.9	87.7	87.2	86.5	85.1	84.5	84.4	83.5	83.2	82.5	82.0	81.4	80.9	80.5
32 Oil and gas well drilling	.6	78.3	75.5	75.4	73.1	73.8	75.6	76.3	82.7	86.4	91.2	89.0	77.9	71.1	72.4
33 Manufactured homes	.2	99.7	93.0	92.5	90.1	101.3	96.9	100.9	110.4	118.5	128.6	129.4	127.1	116.2	116.7
34 Intermediate products, total	14.7	97.6	97.9	97.9	97.7	98.6	97.0	96.9	97.8	98.1	98.3	98.2	99.3	99.4	98.6
35 Construction supplies	6.0	93.8	93.6	95.3	93.6	94.3	94.1	93.0	94.7	95.1	94.5	94.8	97.3	97.2	96.3
36 Business supplies	8.7	100.1	100.7	99.6	100.6	101.4	99.0	99.5	99.9	100.0	100.8	100.5	100.6	100.8	100.2
37 Materials	39.2	107.9	107.9	108.0	107.8	108.5	107.6	107.4	108.1	109.3	110.0	110.4	111.0	111.0	111.4
38 Durable goods materials	19.4	108.9	108.8	109.0	108.7	109.3	108.9	107.6	109.7	111.1	111.9	113.3	114.4	114.3	115.0
39 Durable consumer parts	4.2	101.5	102.0	101.5	101.5	100.6	101.4	98.5	101.8	104.3	107.5	110.8	111.8	111.9	112.4
40 Equipment parts	7.3	116.5	115.2	116.1	116.6	117.7	117.1	116.2	118.3	119.3	119.7	120.4	120.9	121.2	122.3
41 Other	7.9	106.0	106.5	106.5	105.4	106.3	105.5	104.6	106.2	107.4	107.5	108.6	110.2	109.7	110.1
42 Basic metal materials	2.8	108.3	109.2	109.2	107.8	108.7	107.7	105.8	108.3	109.8	108.8	110.4	113.1	110.7	111.9
43 Nondurable goods materials	9.0	110.9	111.2	111.5	111.5	111.5	110.7	111.7	110.7	112.0	111.5	112.4	112.1	112.4	113.5
44 Textile materials	1.2	102.8	102.9	102.4	101.8	107.7	101.6	103.3	102.7	103.4	102.9	104.2	103.0	103.8	104.8
45 Pulp and paper materials	1.9	109.9	111.0	109.6	110.8	110.3	108.7	112.3	109.1	110.2	110.7	110.7	111.9	111.1	113.2
46 Chemical materials	3.8	114.2	114.3	115.5	114.8	114.1	114.5	114.5	114.4	115.6	114.6	114.9	114.6	115.4	116.6
47 Other	2.1	110.4	110.4	110.9	111.6	110.0	110.5	110.5	109.7	112.0	111.3	114.1	112.8	113.0	112.7
48 Energy materials	10.9	103.4	103.5	103.3	103.1	104.4	102.5	103.6	103.0	103.9	105.1	103.4	103.9	103.8	102.9
49 Primary energy	7.2	99.7	99.2	99.5	99.6	100.4	99.4	99.6	99.4	100.2	101.3	100.4	98.0	98.1	98.4
50 Converted fuel materials	3.7	110.6	112.1	110.6	109.9	112.3	108.7	111.4	110.0	111.1	112.4	109.1	115.4	115.1	111.7
SPECIAL AGGREGATES															
51 Total excluding autos and trucks	97.3	106.6	106.3	106.6	106.1	107.0	106.7	106.3	107.4	108.4	108.6	108.9	109.5	109.6	109.7
52 Total excluding motor vehicles and parts	95.3	106.6	106.4	106.6	106.1	107.0	106.7	106.4	107.5	108.4	108.6	108.7	109.3	109.4	109.5
53 Total excluding office and computing machines	97.5	105.0	105.1	105.3	104.6	105.3	105.0	104.5	105.7	106.6	107.1	107.3	107.8	107.6	107.5
54 Consumer goods excluding autos and trucks	24.5	105.7	105.9	106.1	104.6	105.5	105.7	105.1	106.8	107.4	107.3	107.0	107.7	107.8	107.6
55 Consumer goods excluding energy	23.3	104.8	104.9	105.6	103.9	104.7	105.0	104.3	105.9	106.6	106.8	107.4	107.6	107.5	107.6
56 Business equipment excluding autos and trucks	12.7	123.7	120.7	122.0	122.3	124.5	126.9	125.9	128.0	129.5	129.5	130.7	131.3	132.7	133.9
57 Business equipment excluding office and computing equipment	12.0	115.7	114.2	115.3	114.3	115.6	118.1	116.1	118.1	119.7	120.1	121.0	120.7	120.7	120.7
58 Materials excluding energy	28.4	109.5	109.5	109.8	109.5	110.0	109.4	108.8	110.0	111.4	111.8	113.0	113.7	113.7	114.5

(continued)

INDUSTRIAL PRODUCTION Indexes and Gross Value *(concluded)*

Group	SIC code	1987 proportion	1992 avg.	1992									1993			
				Apr.	May	June	July	Aug.	Sept.	Oct.	Nov.	Dec.	Jan.[r]	Feb.[r]	Mar.[r]	Apr
				Index (1987 = 100)												
Major Industries																
1 **Total index**	...	**100.0**	**106.5**	**106.3**	**106.7**	**106.0**	**106.8**	**106.6**	**106.2**	**107.5**	**108.4**	**108.9**	**109.3**	**109.9**	**109.9**	**110.**
2 Manufacturing	...	84.3	106.9	106.5	107.1	106.5	107.1	107.0	106.8	108.0	108.9	109.2	109.9	110.5	110.6	111.
3 Primary processing	...	27.1	103.8	103.8	104.2	103.7	104.3	103.5	103.3	104.1	105.1	105.0	105.8	107.1	106.5	106.
4 Advanced processing	...	57.1	108.3	107.8	108.4	107.9	108.4	108.7	108.4	109.9	110.7	111.3	111.9	112.2	112.6	113.
5 Durable goods	...	46.5	108.1	107.2	108.4	107.6	108.2	108.5	108.1	109.8	110.9	111.8	112.9	113.9	114.0	114.
6 Lumber and products	24	2.1	96.4	95.3	96.1	93.8	96.6	96.6	94.7	97.8	99.8	98.0	99.3	101.3	99.9	98.
7 Furniture and fixtures	25	1.5	99.0	99.4	101.0	94.2	97.5	99.2	100.5	100.4	102.3	103.9	105.2	105.2	107.0	107.
8 Clay, glass, and stone products	32	2.4	96.0	94.5	97.4	95.6	96.8	95.7	96.5	96.8	97.6	98.0	97.0	99.1	98.0	98.
9 Primary metals	33	3.3	101.1	101.8	101.1	101.2	100.6	100.5	98.0	100.5	101.6	102.4	102.8	107.9	104.8	105.
10 Iron and steel	331,2	1.9	104.7	105.6	104.8	103.8	104.7	103.8	102.0	104.1	103.6	107.4	107.0	112.8	109.1	109.
11 Raw steel	...	.1	101.2	103.5	101.9	101.6	101.7	99.1	98.9	99.8	102.8	104.6	103.4	105.9	102.0	103.
12 Nonferrous	333–6,9	1.4	96.1	96.6	95.9	97.5	95.0	96.1	92.4	95.6	98.7	95.7	97.1	101.1	98.8	99.
13 Fabricated metal products	34	5.4	96.7	96.8	97.2	97.1	97.0	97.0	96.5	97.5	97.6	97.8	99.8	99.8	100.1	100.
14 Industrial and commercial machinery and computer equipment	35	8.5	124.8	120.9	123.2	123.8	125.7	126.9	127.9	130.6	132.8	133.8	135.0	137.1	139.6	142.
15 Office and computing machines	357	2.3	168.3	158.5	162.1	167.3	171.8	173.7	178.3	183.1	184.5	186.4	192.0	198.0	205.7	212.
16 Electrical machinery	36	6.9	119.8	118.2	119.5	119.3	120.7	120.6	121.5	122.6	124.4	124.8	125.8	127.0	127.8	127.
17 Transportation equipment	37	9.9	102.6	103.2	104.5	102.7	101.4	102.4	100.5	103.0	103.6	106.3	108.4	108.1	107.0	106.
18 Motor vehicles and parts	371	4.8	104.8	104.5	107.9	104.8	103.1	105.0	102.6	108.0	109.9	116.2	120.9	121.3	120.0	120.
19 Autos and light trucks	...	2.2	101.4	102.4	107.9	102.7	100.8	99.7	97.9	104.1	105.4	114.4	118.2	119.2	117.0	115.
20 Aerospace and miscellaneous transportation equipment	372–6,9	5.1	100.6	102.0	101.3	100.8	99.8	100.0	98.6	98.3	97.7	97.1	96.7	95.7	94.7	93.
21 Instruments	38	5.1	104.2	104.9	105.1	104.4	104.9	104.3	103.7	103.7	103.6	103.3	103.0	102.1	102.9	103.
22 Miscellaneous	39	1.3	109.7	108.5	110.2	109.7	111.6	109.1	108.7	110.5	111.4	111.8	110.9	111.9	112.1	112.
23 Nondurable goods	...	37.8	105.4	105.5	105.4	105.2	105.7	105.2	105.2	105.8	106.4	106.0	106.4	106.4	106.4	106.
24 Foods	20	8.8	106.0	106.0	106.1	105.4	105.9	106.3	105.6	106.8	106.4	106.2	105.9	106.3	106.1	106.
25 Tobacco products	21	1.0	99.2	97.3	97.9	96.4	101.5	115.5	101.7	102.4	101.9	96.1	100.5	99.5	97.5	98.
26 Textile mill products	22	1.8	104.7	105.0	105.0	103.8	107.0	103.5	105.1	103.5	106.0	106.0	106.9	106.6	105.7	107.
27 Apparel products	23	2.3	92.3	93.4	93.5	91.7	92.7	91.3	91.5	91.7	92.9	92.7	93.1	92.9	92.5	92.
28 Paper and products	26	3.6	108.2	109.2	108.2	108.7	109.1	107.1	109.5	107.3	108.2	108.3	108.6	110.4	110.1	111.
29 Printing and publishing	27	6.5	95.0	95.8	94.5	95.6	95.7	93.5	94.1	94.5	94.2	94.7	94.7	94.3	94.4	94.
30 Chemicals and products	28	8.8	115.0	114.6	114.8	114.9	114.6	114.4	115.2	116.2	117.7	116.7	116.8	115.8	116.9	117.
31 Petroleum products	29	1.3	102.0	103.7	102.5	101.8	101.5	98.0	101.1	105.3	103.9	103.4	103.2	104.7	103.9	103.
32 Rubber and plastic products	30	3.2	109.7	109.1	110.3	109.7	110.7	110.7	108.5	109.9	111.3	111.3	113.6	114.0	114.3	114.
33 Leather and products	31	.3	92.6	91.1	91.8	92.3	93.6	92.0	93.8	95.1	96.6	96.7	97.1	97.3	97.8	97.
34 Mining	...	8.0	97.6	97.4	98.8	97.1	98.5	97.0	97.1	97.6	97.8	98.2	98.3	95.6	95.4	96.
35 Metal	10	.3	161.7	156.0	172.2	157.8	156.5	165.5	159.8	168.1	171.6	158.1	167.7	163.0	163.5	161.
36 Coal	12	1.2	105.5	106.5	109.5	101.9	108.0	103.9	103.6	103.8	103.5	107.9	108.2	101.7	102.3	108.
37 Oil and gas extraction	13	5.8	92.6	92.4	92.5	93.1	93.6	91.9	92.7	92.7	92.8	93.4	92.7	90.4	90.0	89.
38 Stone and earth minerals	14	.7	93.8	94.8	96.9	92.7	94.1	93.8	91.9	93.6	94.4	92.6	93.8	95.1	95.3	95.
39 Utilities	...	7.7	112.0	112.0	111.2	110.0	111.2	110.4	111.2	112.7	114.7	116.8	112.8	117.4	117.3	113.
40 Electric	491,3PT	6.1	111.6	111.8	110.8	109.5	110.8	110.0	110.9	112.6	114.1	116.4	112.9	117.2	117.4	113.
41 Gas	492,3PT	1.6	113.2	113.0	112.6	112.0	112.8	112.1	112.0	113.2	117.3	118.2	112.4	118.2	116.9	112.
Special Aggregates																
42 Manufacturing excluding motor vehicles and parts	...	79.5	107.0	106.6	107.0	106.6	107.4	107.2	107.1	108.0	108.8	108.8	109.3	109.8	110.0	110.
43 Manufacturing excluding office and computing machines	...	81.9	105.1	105.0	105.5	104.8	105.3	105.1	104.8	105.9	106.7	107.0	107.6	108.0	107.9	108.
				Gross value (billions of 1987 dollars, annual rates)												
Major Markets																
44 **Products, total**	...	**1,707.0**	**1,806.4**	**1,804.4**	**1,814.8**	**1,794.6**	**1,806.8**	**1,802.7**	**1,799.9**	**1,835.6**	**1,846.7**	**1,857.5**	**1,864.9**	**1,878.4**	**1,874.1**	**1,870**
45 Final	...	1,314.6	1,420.1	1,416.2	1,426.9	1,408.8	1,416.7	1,417.8	1,415.7	1,448.1	1,457.1	1,466.8	1,476.4	1,484.1	1,479.7	1,478
46 Consumer goods	...	866.6	913.0	914.7	920.1	906.6	912.6	908.1	905.1	928.4	931.6	936.3	940.0	947.1	942.1	939
47 Equipment	...	448.0	507.1	501.5	506.8	502.2	504.1	509.7	510.6	519.7	525.5	530.5	536.5	537.1	537.6	539
48 Intermediate	...	392.5	386.4	388.2	387.9	385.9	390.1	385.0	384.2	387.4	389.6	390.7	388.4	394.3	394.4	391

1. Data in this table also appear in the Board's G.17 (419) monthly statistical release. For ordering address, see inside front cover.
A revision of the industrial production index and the capacity utilization rates was released in May 1993. See "Industrial Production, Capacity, and Capaci Utilization since 1987," *Federal Reserve Bulletin*, vol. 79 (June 1993), pp. 590–60
2. Standard industrial classification.

Source: *Federal Reserve Bulletin*, Board of Governors of the Federal Reserve System.

PERSONAL INCOME AND SAVING

Billions of current dollars except as noted; quarterly data at seasonally adjusted annual rates

Account	1990	1991	1992	1992				1993
				Q1	Q2	Q3	Q4	Q1
PERSONAL INCOME AND SAVING								
Total personal income	**4,664.2**	**4,828.3**	**5,058.1**	**4,980.5**	**5,028.9**	**5,062.0**	**5,160.9**	**5,237.6**
Wage and salary disbursements	2,742.8	2,812.2	2,918.1	2,877.6	2,901.3	2,923.5	2,969.9	3,006.3
Commodity-producing industries	745.6	737.4	743.2	736.8	743.1	742.4	750.6	754.4
Manufacturing	556.1	556.9	565.7	559.9	564.7	565.5	572.8	576.4
Distributive industries	634.6	647.4	666.8	660.9	662.9	667.7	675.8	685.6
Service industries	847.8	883.9	945.5	925.3	933.9	949.1	973.9	988.2
Government and government enterprises	514.8	543.6	562.5	554.6	561.4	564.3	569.6	578.1
Other labor income	271.0	288.3	305.7	299.2	303.6	307.9	312.2	316.5
Proprietors' income[1]	366.9	368.0	404.5	393.6	398.4	397.4	428.4	442.0
Business and professional[1]	325.2	332.2	364.9	353.6	359.9	365.9	380.4	389.1
Farm[1]	41.7	35.8	39.5	40.1	38.5	31.5	48.1	52.9
Rental income of persons[2]	−12.3	−10.4	4.7	−4.5	3.3	6.4	13.6	17.5
Dividends	140.3	137.0	139.3	133.9	136.6	141.0	145.8	149.9
Personal interest income	694.5	700.6	670.2	684.8	675.2	663.2	657.8	656.4
Transfer payments	685.8	771.1	866.1	842.7	859.7	874.1	888.0	909.4
Old-age survivors, disability, and health insurance benefits	352.0	382.0	414.1	405.7	412.1	417.1	421.6	434.2
LESS: Personal contributions for social insurance	224.8	238.4	250.6	246.8	249.3	251.5	254.8	260.4
EQUALS: Personal income	4,664.2	4,828.3	5,058.1	4,980.5	5,028.9	5,062.0	5,160.9	5,237.6
LESS: Personal tax and nontax payments	621.3	618.7	627.3	619.6	617.1	628.8	643.6	656.3
EQUALS: Disposable personal income	4,042.9	4,209.6	4,430.8	4,360.9	4,411.8	4,433.2	4,517.3	4,581.4
LESS: Personal outlays	3,867.3	4,009.9	4,218.1	4,146.3	4,179.5	4,229.9	4,316.9	4,362.3
EQUALS: Personal saving	175.6	199.6	212.6	214.6	232.3	203.3	200.4	219.0
MEMO								
Per capita (1987 dollars)								
Gross domestic product	19,513.0	19,077.1	19,271.4	19,158.5	19,181.8	19,288.4	19,456.3	19,454.4
Personal consumption expenditures	13,043.6	12,824.1	12,973.9	12,930.2	12,893.3	12,973.3	13,098.4	13,105.3
Disposable personal income	14,068.0	13,886.0	14,035.0	14,017.0	14,021.0	13,998.0	14,105.0	14,165.0
Saving rate (percent)	4.3	4.7	4.8	4.9	5.3	4.6	4.4	4.8
GROSS SAVING								
Gross saving	**718.0**	**708.2**	**686.3[r]**	**677.5**	**682.9**	**696.9**	**687.9[r]**	**736.5**
Gross private saving	854.1	901.5	968.8[r]	950.1	968.1	992.1	965.0[r]	999.0
Personal saving	175.6	199.6	212.6	214.6	232.3	203.3	200.4	219.0
Undistributed corporate profits[1]	75.7	75.8	104.3[r]	104.0	97.7	91.2	124.1[r]	125.2
Corporate inventory valuation adjustment	−14.2	3.1	−7.4	−5.4	−15.5	−9.7	1.0	−9.3
Capital consumption allowances								
Corporate	368.3	383.0	394.8	386.1	391.2	407.2	394.7	399.8
Noncorporate	234.6	243.1	258.6	245.3	247.0	290.4	251.8	261.1
Government surplus, or deficit (−), national income and product accounts	−136.1	−193.3	−282.5[r]	−272.6	−285.2	−295.2	−277.2[r]	−262.5
Federal	−166.2	−210.4	−298.0[r]	−289.2	−302.9	−304.4	−295.5[r]	−273.5
State and local	30.1	17.1	15.5	16.6	17.7	9.2	18.3[r]	11.0
Gross investment	**723.4**	**730.1**	**720.4**	**706.5**	**713.8**	**732.0**	**729.5**	**783.3**
Gross private domestic	799.5	721.1	770.4	722.4	773.2	781.6	804.3	844.1
Net foreign	−76.1	9.0	−49.9	−16.0	−59.4	−49.6	−74.7	−60.8
Statistical discrepancy	**5.4**	**21.9**	**34.1[r]**	**29.0**	**30.9**	**35.1**	**41.7[r]**	**46.8**

1. With inventory valuation and capital consumption adjustments.
2. With capital consumption adjustment.

SOURCE. U.S. Department of Commerce, *Survey of Current Business*.

Source: *Federal Reserve Bulletin*, Board of Governors of the Federal Reserve System.

Largest Companies

The 100 Largest U.S. Industrial Corporations (ranked by sales)

RANK 1992	1991	COMPANY	SALES $ millions	SALES % change from 1991	PROFITS $ millions	PROFITS Rank	PROFITS % change from 1991	ASSETS $ millions	ASSETS Rank	TOTAL STOCKHOLDER EQUITY $ millions	TOTAL STOCKHOLDER EQUITY Rank
1	1	**GENERAL MOTORS** Detroit	132,774.9	7.3	(23,498.3)†	500	—	191,012.8	2	6,225.6	22
2	2	**EXXON** Irving, Texas	103,547.0[E]	0.3	4,770.0	2	(14.8)	85,030.0	5	33,776.0	1
3	3	**FORD MOTOR** Dearborn, Mich.	100,785.6	13.3	(7,385.0)†	476	—	180,545.2	3	14,752.9	5
4	4	**INTL. BUSINESS MACHINES** Armonk, N.Y.	65,096.0	(0.5)	(4,965.0)‡	475	—	86,705.0	4	27,624.0	2
5	5	**GENERAL ELECTRIC** Fairfield, Conn.	62,202.0	3.3	4,725.0	3	79.2	192,876.0	1	23,459.0	3
6	6	**MOBIL** Fairfax, Va.	57,389.0[E]	0.8	862.0†	17	(55.1)	40,561.0	8	16,540.0	4
7	7	**PHILIP MORRIS** New York	50,157.0	4.3	4,939.0	1	64.3	50,014.0	6	12,563.0	9
8	8	**E.I. DU PONT DE NEMOURS** Wilmington, Del.	37,643.0	(3.1)	(3,927.0)†	474	(379.9)	38,870.0	9	11,765.0	10
9	10	**CHEVRON** San Francisco	37,464.0[E]	1.8	1,569.0†	8	21.3	33,970.0	11	13,728.0	7
10	9	**TEXACO** White Plains, N.Y.	37,130.0[E]	(1.1)	712.0†	24	(45.0)	25,992.0	15	9,973.0	11
11	11	**CHRYSLER** Highland Park, Mich.	36,897.0	25.6	723.0‡	22	—	40,653.0	7	7,538.0	17
12	12	**BOEING** Seattle	30,184.0	3.0	552.0†	31	(64.8)	18,147.0	24	8,056.0	16
13	13	**PROCTER & GAMBLE** Cincinnati[1]	29,890.0	9.1	1,872.0	6	5.6	24,025.0	18	9,071.0	12
14	14	**AMOCO** Chicago	25,543.0[E]	(0.2)	(74.0)†	380	(105.0)	28,453.0	13	12,960.0	8
15	17	**PEPSICO** Purchase, N.Y.	22,083.7	11.7	374.3†	47	(65.3)	20,951.2	20	5,355.7	27
16	16	**UNITED TECHNOLOGIES** Hartford	22,032.0	3.6	(287.0)†	440	—	15,928.0	30	3,370.0	51
17	15	**SHELL OIL** Houston[2]	21,702.0[E]	(2.2)	(190.0)†	427	(1,050.0)	26,970.0	14	14,608.0	6
18	19	**CONAGRA** Omaha[3]	21,219.0	8.8	372.4	48	19.7	9,758.7	52	2,232.3	71
19	18	**EASTMAN KODAK** Rochester, N.Y.	20,577.0	4.7	1,146.0‡	12	6,641.2	23,138.0	19	6,557.0	21
20	20	**DOW CHEMICAL** Midland, Mich.	19,177.0	(0.7)	(489.0)†	457	(151.9)	25,360.0	16	8,074.0	15
21	22	**XEROX** Stamford, Conn.	18,261.0	2.4	(1,020.0)†	466	(324.7)	34,051.0	10	3,875.0	40
22	23	**ATLANTIC RICHFIELD** Los Angeles	18,061.0[E]	2.1	801.0†	20	13.0	24,256.0	17	6,721.0	19
23	21	**MCDONNELL DOUGLAS** St. Louis	17,513.0	(6.4)	(781.0)†	464	(284.6)	13,781.0	33	3,022.0	56
24	26	**HEWLETT-PACKARD** Palo Alto, Calif.[4]	16,427.0	13.0	549.0†	33	(27.3)	13,700.0	34	7,499.0	18
25	24	**USX** Pittsburgh	16,186.0[E]	(5.7)	(1,826.0)†	471	—	17,252.0	26	3,709.0	43
26	25	**RJR NABISCO HOLDINGS** New York	15,734.0	5.0	299.0*	58	(18.8)	32,041.0	12	8,376.0	14
27	28	**DIGITAL EQUIPMENT** Maynard, Mass.[1]	14,027.0	0.0	(2,795.5)†	473	—	11,284.3	39	4,930.9	31
28	29	**MINNESOTA MINING & MFG.** St. Paul	13,883.0	4.1	1,233.0	11	6.8	11,955.0	35	6,599.0	20
29	34	**JOHNSON & JOHNSON** New Brunswick, N.J.	13,846.0	10.5	1,030.0†	14	(29.5)	11,884.0	36	5,171.0	28
30	27	**TENNECO** Houston	13,606.0	(3.1)	(1,323.0)†	470	—	16,584.0	28	1,330.0	129
31	32	**INTERNATIONAL PAPER** Purchase, N.Y.	13,600.0	7.1	86.0†	141	(53.3)	16,459.0	29	6,189.0	23
32	39	**MOTOROLA** Schaumburg, Ill.	13,341.0	17.2	453.0†	40	(0.2)	10,629.0	47	5,144.0	29
33	33	**SARA LEE** Chicago[1]	13,321.0	6.9	761.0	21	42.2	9,989.0	51	3,633.0	45
34	37	**COCA-COLA** Atlanta	13,238.0	12.7	1,664.0†	7	2.8	11,052.0	41	3,888.0	39
35	31	**WESTINGHOUSE ELECTRIC** Pittsburgh	12,100.0¶	(5.4)	(1,291.0)†	469	—	10,398.0	50	2,344.0	68
36	36	**ALLIED-SIGNAL** Morris Township, N.J.	12,089.0	1.7	(712.0)†	462	—	10,756.0	46	2,251.0	69
37	30	**PHILLIPS PETROLEUM** Bartlesville, Okla.	11,933.0	(9.7)	180.0†*	84	(30.2)	11,468.0	37	3,045.0	55
38	41	**GOODYEAR TIRE & RUBBER** Akron	11,923.6	7.9	(658.6)†	461	(781.8)	8,563.7	63	1,930.3	90
39	38	**GEORGIA-PACIFIC** Atlanta	11,847.0	2.8	(124.0)†	409	—	10,890.0	43	2,508.0	64
40	40	**BRISTOL-MYERS SQUIBB** New York	11,805.0	4.5	1,962.0†	5	(4.6)	10,804.0	44	6,020.0	24
41	42	**ANHEUSER-BUSCH** St. Louis	11,400.8[E]	3.6	917.5	15	(2.4)	10,537.9	49	4,620.4	35
42	•	**IBP** Dakota City, Neb.	11,129.7	0.9	63.6	174	4,601.8	1,499.4	247	534.1	249
43	35	**ROCKWELL INTERNATIONAL** Seal Beach, Calif.[6]	10,995.1	(8.6)	(1,036.0)†	467	(272.5)	9,731.0	53	2,778.0	59
44	45	**CATERPILLAR** Peoria, Ill.	10,194.0	0.1	(2,435.0)†	472	—	13,935.0	32	1,575.0	109
45	47	**LOCKHEED** Calabasas, Calif.	10,138.0	3.4	(283.0)†	437	(191.9)	6,754.0	73	2,042.0	79
46	49	**COASTAL** Houston	10,062.9	4.8	(126.8)	411	(231.6)	10,579.8	48	2,009.9	83
47	57	**MERCK** Whitehouse Station, N.J.	9,800.8	11.8	1,984.2†	4	(6.5)	11,086.0	40	5,002.9	30
48	52	**ASHLAND OIL** Ashland, Ky.[6]	9,595.8[E]	2.9	(335.7)†	447	(331.5)	5,668.4	86	1,086.0	148
49	46	**ALUMINUM CO. OF AMERICA** Pittsburgh	9,588.4	(3.9)	(1,139.2)†	468	(1,916.9)	11,023.1	42	3,604.3	46
50	60	**ARCHER DANIELS MIDLAND** Decatur, Ill.[1]	9,344.1	9.1	503.8	36	7.9	7,524.5	67	4,492.4	36

The definitions, explanations, and footnotes underlying the figures in this directory are on page 200.

MARKET VALUE 3/5/93		PROFITS AS % OF . . .						EARNINGS PER SHARE				TOTAL RETURN TO INVESTORS					
		SALES		ASSETS		COMMON STOCK-HOLDERS' EQUITY		1992	% change from 1991	1982-92 annual growth rate		1992		1982-92 annual rate		Industry table number	RANK 1992
$ millions	Rank	%	Rank	%	Rank	%	Rank	$		%	Rank	%	Rank	%	Rank		
27,556.0	11	(17.7)	461	(12.3)	453	(397.6)	416	(38.28)	—	—		15.9	167	6.7	281	17	1
78,556.5	1	4.6	166	5.6	155	13.9	124	3.79	(14.8)	4.6	156	5.2	242	22.0	72	18	2
24,090.4	17	(7.3)	427	(4.1)	389	(66.6)	405	(15.61)	—	—		58.4	38	23.1	59	17	3
31,571.8	8	(7.6)	430	(5.7)	409	(18.0)	355	(8.70)	—	—		(39.9)	412	(2.5)	335	6	4
73,353.0	2	7.6	71	2.4	256	20.1	60	5.51	81.8	10.7	88	15.1	173	17.4	132	7	5
27,019.8	12	1.5	281	2.1	270	4.9	261	2.01	(56.8)	(4.9)	211	(2.2)	301	16.1	158	18	6
57,710.1	3	9.8	43	9.9	61	39.3	14	5.45	67.7	21.5	24	(1.2)	292	31.0	18	8	7
31,556.6	9	(10.4)	447	(10.1)	439	(34.2)	376	(5.85)	(381.3)	—		4.8	246	19.8	98	5	8
25,160.3	15	4.2	178	4.6	185	11.4	168	4.63	25.5	1.4	187	5.6	240	14.1	187	18	9
16,301.1	25	1.9	262	2.7	251	6.9	249	2.37	(48.6)	(7.0)	219	2.7	267	15.4	167	18	10
11,557.5	38	2.0	260	1.8	277	9.8	197	2.21	—	10.5	90	181.2	3	19.3	104	17	11
11,753.5	35	1.8	270	3.0	240	6.9	250	1.62	(64.5)	6.1	136	(13.9)	361	17.8	123	1	12
36,501.3	6	6.3	104	7.8	101	19.8	63	2.62	6.5	8.4	120	16.7	159	17.6	128	23	13
26,986.5	13	(0.3)	334	(0.3)	333	(0.6)	302	(0.15)	(105.0)	—		3.8	258	14.9	175	18	14
33,101.4	7	1.7	274	1.8	276	7.0	245	0.46	(65.9)	5.6	146	24.3	115	29.4	26	3	15
5,709.1	74	(1.3)	350	(1.8)	351	(9.8)	332	(2.67)	—	—		(8.0)	338	9.2	252	1	16
N.A.		(0.9)	343	(0.7)	338	—		N.A.	—	—		—		—		18	17
6,675.4	57	1.8	272	3.8	217	30.0	23	1.50	(29.6)	10.4	91	(4.9)	320	26.0	36	8	18
17,435.6	24	5.6	133	5.0	170	17.5	85	3.53	6,960.0	1.1	191	(12.2)	358	5.2	291	22	19
15,128.7	28	(2.5)	366	(1.9)	354	(6.2)	322	(1.83)	(152.9)	—		11.4	205	17.8	124	5	20
7,866.7	49	(5.6)	409	(3.0)	374	(27.9)	368	(11.29)	(388.7)	—		20.6	136	14.1	186	22	21
18,593.9	23	4.4	171	3.3	233	11.9	159	4.96	13.0	(2.8)	207	12.9	192	16.7	147	18	22
2,150.6	167	(4.5)	399	(5.7)	406	(25.8)	364	(20.10)	(282.2)	—		(32.2)	403	4.8	294	1	23
19,358.4	21	3.3	208	4.0	208	7.3	239	2.18	(27.8)	3.6	168	23.9	119	7.5	267	6	24
N.A.		(11.3)	452	(10.6)	442	—		N.A.	—	—		—		—		18	25
9,502.7	42	1.9	264	0.9	297	3.2	272	0.20	(9.1)	—		(19.8)	377	—		25	26
6,149.6	67	(19.9)	466	(24.8)	469	(56.7)	402	(22.39)	—	—		(38.9)	410	(3.8)	338	6	27
23,436.6	18	8.9	51	10.3	54	18.7	75	5.63	7.0	7.7	126	9.2	213	14.4	180	22	28
26,461.8	14	7.4	77	8.7	81	19.9	61	1.56	(28.9)	9.5	107	(10.2)	350	17.7	126	19	29
6,633.9	59	(9.7)	443	(8.0)	427	(163.7)	411	(9.29)	—	—		35.0	70	9.1	253	11	30
7,822.1	50	0.6	303	0.5	312	1.4	283	0.71	(57.2)	(7.0)	218	(3.5)	309	14.5	178	9	31
16,249.4	26	3.4	205	4.3	201	8.8	216	1.70	(50.6)	0.5	194	61.7	33	15.3	169	7	32
14,590.8	32	5.7	125	7.6	107	21.6	48	3.08	186.5	24.8	18	6.0	236	30.8	19	8	33
56,037.6	4	12.6	21	15.1	20	42.8	10	1.26	3.7	14.4	57	5.8	238	29.5	25	3	34
4,590.4	89	(10.7)	449	(12.4)	454	(73.2)	407	(3.81)	—	—		(22.3)	389	7.4	268	7	35
9,399.8	43	(5.9)	412	(6.6)	414	(31.6)	373	(5.05)	—	—		40.4	60	17.1	139	1	36
7,514.2	51	1.5	280	1.6	284	6.7	251	0.69	(30.3)	(6.9)	217	9.5	212	15.5	166	18	37
5,210.6	80	(5.5)	407	(7.7)	424	(34.1)	375	(9.22)	(672.7)	—		28.9	98	11.2	231	21	38
5,815.3	73	(1.0)	346	(1.1)	344	(4.9)	319	(1.43)	—	—		19.5	145	12.4	208	9	39
29,394.5	10	16.6	9	18.2	10	32.6	20	3.79	(4.1)	11.3	78	(20.6)	385	18.8	112	19	40
14,894.4	30	8.0	65	8.7	78	19.9	62	3.22	(1.2)	12.5	67	(2.8)	303	21.0	84	3	41
896.5	288	0.6	306	4.2	203	11.9	158	1.34	4,366.7	—		40.9	59	—		8	42
6,219.8	65	(9.4)	442	(10.6)	443	(37.3)	382	(4.62)	(279.8)	—		9.8	211	14.1	185	7	43
5,931.0	70	(23.9)	473	(17.5)	464	(154.6)	410	(24.12)	—	—		23.6	122	5.0	293	11	44
3,547.2	114	(2.8)	370	(4.2)	391	(13.9)	341	(4.58)	(194.2)	—		31.2	87	12.0	215	1	45
2,646.9	150	(1.3)	348	(1.2)	345	(6.3)	324	(1.23)	(233.7)	—		(1.5)	294	16.8	144	18	46
42,926.3	5	20.2	4	17.9	11	39.7	13	1.72	(53.0)	10.7	87	(20.4)	383	28.0	28	19	47
1,678.9	201	(3.5)	385	(5.9)	412	(30.9)	371	(5.75)	(324.6)	—		(8.4)	340	10.3	241	18	48
5,990.4	69	(11.9)	455	(10.3)	440	(32.2)	374	(13.41)	(1,988.7)	—		13.9	184	12.3	210	15	49
8,532.5	47	5.4	140	6.7	126	11.2	174	1.62	14.2	10.8	85	(15.7)	366	16.9	141	8	50

(continued)

The 100 Largest U.S. Industrial Corporations (ranked by sales) *(concluded)*

RANK 1992	1991	COMPANY	SALES $millions	% change from 1991	PROFITS $millions	Rank	% change from 1991	ASSETS $millions	Rank	TOTAL STOCKHOLDERS' EQUITY $millions	Rank
51	58	**WEYERHAEUSER** Tacoma	9,259.9	6.1	372.0	49	—	18,158.4	23	3,646.0	44
52	56	**UNILEVER U.S.** New York[7]	9,216.8	4.1	N.A.		—	N.A.		N.A.	
53	54	**CITGO PETROLEUM** Tulsa	9,166.7	2.7	33.2†	245	(75.6)	3,488.2	134	1,003.9	158
54	51	**RAYTHEON** Lexington, Mass.	9,118.9	(2.5)	635.1	29	7.3	6,015.1	84	3,843.2	41
55	48	**UNOCAL** Los Angeles	8,948.0[E]	(8.5)	220.0‡	75	201.4	9,452.0	56	3,137.0	54
56	43	**OCCIDENTAL PETROLEUM** Los Angeles	8,940.0	(13.2)	(591.0)†	460	(228.5)	17,877.0	25	3,440.0	49
57	61	**AMERICAN BRANDS** Old Greenwich, Conn.	8,840.3[E]	5.5	883.8	16	9.6	14,963.0	31	4,301.6	38
58	50	**GENERAL DYNAMICS** Falls Church, Va.	8,731.0¶	(8.8)	815.0	18	61.4	4,222.0	115	1,874.0	94
59	44	**SUN** Philadelphia	8,626.0[E]	(15.8)	(559.0)†	459	—	6,061.0	81	1,896.0	91
60	53	**MONSANTO** St. Louis	8,485.0	(5.0)	(88.0)†	396	(129.7)	9,085.0	60	3,005.0	57
61	55	**BAXTER INTERNATIONAL** Deerfield, Ill.	8,471.0	(5.0)	441.0†	41	(25.4)	9,549.0[5]	55	4,345.0[5]	37
62	59	**UNISYS** Blue Bell, Pa.	8,421.9	(3.2)	361.2**	50	—	7,508.6	68	2,244.1	70
63	63	**TEXTRON** Providence	8,347.5	6.5	(355.4)†	448	(218.7)	18,366.8	21	2,487.8	65
64	62	**TRW** Cleveland	8,311.0	5.0	(156.0)†	417	—	5,458.0	89	1,416.0	119
65	70	**HANSON INDUSTRIES NA** Iselin, N.J.[6, 8]	8,288.3	16.7	551.0	32	(16.5)	18,352.4	22	4,704.6	34
66	74	**ABBOTT LABORATORIES** Abbott Park, Ill.	7,894.2	14.0	1,239.1	10	13.8	6,941.2	71	3,347.6	52
67	71	**AMERICAN HOME PRODUCTS** New York	7,873.7	10.9	1,460.8‡	9	6.2	7,141.4	69	3,562.6	47
68	68	**GENERAL MILLS** Minneapolis[3]	7,795.5	8.6	495.6	37	4.8	4,305.0	112	1,370.9	122
69	65	**RALSTON PURINA** St. Louis[6]	7,768.0	5.1	313.2	56	(20.1)	5,150.5	97	655.2	224
70	64	**EMERSON ELECTRIC** St. Louis[6]	7,706.0	3.8	662.9	26	4.9	6,627.0	75	3,729.8	42
71	77	**TEXAS INSTRUMENTS** Dallas	7,470.0	9.7	247.0	64	—	5,185.0	94	1,947.0	86
72	69	**PFIZER** New York	7,414.8	3.8	810.9†	19	12.3	9,590.1	54	4,718.6	33
73	78	**WHIRLPOOL** Benton Harbor, Mich.	7,309.4	8.0	205.0	77	20.6	6,118.0	80	1,600.0	105
74	67	**BORDEN** New York	7,142.6	(1.3)	(439.6)†	454	(249.1)	5,321.4	93	1,051.1	153
75	76	**KIMBERLY-CLARK** Dallas	7,091.1	3.8	135.0†	107	(73.4)	6,029.1	83	2,191.1	73
76	81	**APPLE COMPUTER** Cupertino, Calif.[6]	7,086.5	12.3	530.4	34	71.2	4,223.7	114	2,187.4	74
77	75	**HOECHST CELANESE** Somerville, N.J.[9]	7,044.0	3.7	(7.0)†	337	(104.1)	7,044.0	70	3,454.0	48
78	90	**COLGATE-PALMOLIVE** New York	7,035.4	15.5	477.0	39	281.9	5,434.1	90	2,619.8	63
79	72	**DEERE** Moline, Ill.[4]	6,960.7	(1.3)	37.4	237	—	11,445.6	38	2,650.3	62
80	79	**H.J. HEINZ** Pittsburgh[10]	6,628.5	(0.8)	638.3	28	12.4	5,931.9	85	2,367.4	67
81	84	**CPC INTERNATIONAL** Englewood Cliffs, N.J.	6,599.0	6.4	223.8†	73	(40.0)	5,171.2	95	1,661.8	101
82	85	**MILES** Pittsburgh[11]	6,499.0	4.9	69.8	165	(30.9)	4,973.1	99	2,228.4	72
83	73	**W.R. GRACE** Boca Raton, Fla.	6,329.6¶	(8.9)	(294.5)†	442	(234.7)	5,598.6	88	1,545.0	111
84	95	**ELI LILLY** Indianapolis	6,282.3	7.3	708.7†	25	(46.1)	8,672.8	62	4,892.1	32
85	82	**CAMPBELL SOUP** Camden, N.J.[12]	6,278.5	0.8	490.5	38	22.2	4,353.8	109	2,027.6	80
86	83	**HONEYWELL** Minneapolis	6,254.0	0.5	246.8†	65	(25.5)	4,870.1	101	1,790.4	97
87	92	**KELLOGG** Battle Creek, Mich.	6,190.6	7.0	431.2†	44	(28.8)	4,015.0	121	1,945.2	87
88	66	**UNION CARBIDE** Danbury, Conn.	6,167.0¶	(16.0)	(175.0)†	421	—	4,941.0	100	1,267.0	131
89	86	**COOPER INDUSTRIES** Houston	6,158.5	(0.1)	(228.7)†	433	(158.2)	7,575.6	66	2,866.9	58
90	91	**NORTH AMERICAN PHILIPS** New York[13]	6,138.0	1.2	49.8	200	514.8	3,045.1	153	1,165.6	142
91	80	**AMERADA HESS** New York	5,970.4	(7.0)	7.5	308	(91.1)	8,721.8	61	3,387.6	50
92	88	**MARTIN MARIETTA** Bethesda, Md.	5,970.1	(2.1)	345.4	53	10.3	3,599.6	130	1,945.2	88
93	106	**INTEL** Santa Clara, Calif.	5,922.5	21.0	1,066.5	13	30.3	8,088.6	64	5,444.6	26
94	96	**PPG INDUSTRIES** Pittsburgh	5,857.7	2.3	319.4	55	15.6	5,661.7	87	2,698.9	61
95	99	**LITTON INDUSTRIES** Beverly Hills[12]	5,741.4	8.1	174.4	89	174.7	4,838.7	102	1,364.1	123
96	93	**REYNOLDS METALS** Richmond	5,620.3	(2.8)	(748.8)†	463	(585.9)	6,897.0	72	2,060.0	78
97	100	**WARNER-LAMBERT** Morris Plains, N.J.	5,597.6	8.3	644.0	27	1,750.6	4,077.0	119	1,526.0	112
98	89	**QUAKER OATS** Chicago[1]	5,586.0	(8.4)	247.6	63	20.3	3,039.9	154	850.0	186
99	104	**LEVI STRAUSS ASSOCIATES** San Francisco[14]	5,570.3	13.6	360.8	51	1.2	2,880.7	159	768.2	203
100	97	**NORTHROP** Los Angeles	5,550.0	(2.7)	121.0	119	(39.7)	3,162.0	146	1,254.0	132

E Excise taxes equal to 5% more of total sales have been deducted.
N.A. Not available.
* Reflects an extraordinary change of at least 10%.
** Reflects an extraordinary credit of at least 10%.
† Reflects an SFAS 106 and/or 109 charge of at least 10%.
‡ Reflects an SFAS 109 credit of at least 10%.
¶ Includes sales of discontinued operations of at least 10%.
[1] Figures are for fiscal year ended June 30,1992.
[2] Owned by Royal Dutch/Shell Group (1991 Global 500 rank: 2).
[3] Figures are for fiscal year ended May 31, 1992.
[4] Figures are for fiscal year ended October 31, 1992.

MARKET VALUE 3/5/93		PROFITS AS % OF . . .						EARNINGS PER SHARE				TOTAL RETURN TO INVESTORS					
		SALES		ASSETS		COMMON STOCK-HOLDERS' EQUITY		1992	% change from 1991	1982-92 annual growth rate		1992		1982-92 annual rate			
$ millions	Rank	%	Rank	%	Rank	%	Rank	$		%	Rank	%	Rank	%	Rank	Industry table number	RANK 1992
8,997.3	45	4.0	186	2.0	271	10.2	189	1.83	—	9.4	109	38.8	63	8.8	255	9	51
N.A.		—		—		—		N.A.	—	—		—		—		23	52
N.A.		0.4	314	1.0	296	—		N.A.	—	—		—		—		18	53
7,393.5	52	7.0	85	10.6	51	16.5	95	4.72	5.5	9.6	105	27.0	103	12.0	217	7	54
6,438.6	62	2.5	236	2.3	261	7.7	230	0.85	174.2	(9.5)	228	12.2	198	10.1	244	18	55
6,036.6	68	(6.6)	419	(3.3)	383	(17.3)	353	(1.97)	(229.6)	—		0.2	281	7.2	271	5	56
6,837.0	56	10.0	39	5.9	149	20.4	55	4.29	9.7	10.1	96	(6.4)	328	19.1	106	25	57
3,578.4	112	9.3	48	19.3	9	43.5	9	21.66	79.6	24.6	19	96.6	17	14.4	182	1	58
2,947.4	135	(6.5)	417	(9.2)	436	(29.5)	369	(5.26)	—	—		(1.8)	297	10.9	235	18	59
6,399.7	63	(1.0)	344	(1.0)	342	(2.9)	312	(0.71)	(130.5)	—		(11.9)	356	16.2	157	5	60
8,125.9	48	5.2	145	4.6	186	10.0	194	1.56	(23.2)	1.7	182	(7.5)	336	6.4	285	22	61
2,165.8	166	4.3	174	4.8	176	35.9	19	1.46	—	4.6	157	145.5	8	0.2	326	6	62
3,787.1	105	(4.3)	396	(1.9)	355	(14.4)	343	(4.01)	(217.3)	—		16.4	165	19.0	107	1	63
3,742.5	106	(1.9)	357	(2.9)	372	(11.1)	336	(2.51)	—	—		41.7	57	9.4	250	17	64
N.A.		6.6	91	3.0	242	—		N.A.	—	—		—		—		16	65
21,300.5	19	15.7	11	17.9	12	37.0	16	1.47	15.3	17.4	37	(10.2)	349	22.7	62	19	66
19,362.6	20	18.6	5	20.5	7	41.0	12	4.65	6.7	10.0	99	(17.4)	371	16.6	150	19	67
11,723.9	37	6.4	98	11.5	38	36.2	18	2.99	4.2	10.4	93	(4.8)	319	24.3	49	8	68
5,247.2	78	4.0	185	6.1	142	44.6	8	2.75	(17.7)	23.6	21	(13.4)	360	21.2	82	8	69
12,885.0	34	8.6	58	10.0	60	17.8	83	2.96	4.6	7.3	128	2.7	266	14.3	184	7	70
4,825.9	85	3.3	211	4.8	180	14.2	121	2.50	—	2.1	179	54.5	41	2.2	315	7	71
19,142.7	22	10.9	33	8.5	87	17.2	87	2.41	13.1	8.5	117	(12.0)	357	19.0	108	19	72
3,658.9	107	2.8	223	3.4	232	12.8	140	2.90	18.4	4.2	162	17.9	152	11.4	226	7	73
3,656.7	108	(6.2)	414	(8.3)	429	(41.8)	388	(3.07)	(253.5)	—		(8.7)	343	17.6	129	8	74
8,922.1	46	1.9	263	2.2	267	6.2	255	0.84	(47.2)	4.3	159	20.0	141	24.9	42	9	75
6,509.0	61	7.5	76	12.6	27	24.2	37	4.33	67.8	23.4	22	7.0	227	15.5	165	6	76
N.A.		(0.1)	329	(0.1)	328	—		N.A.	—	—		—		—		5	77
10,255.4	41	6.8	88	8.8	75	20.7	54	2.92	279.2	9.3	111	16.6	160	23.4	55	23	78
4,120.9	98	0.5	307	0.3	318	1.4	282	0.49	—	(4.5)	210	(4.7)	318	7.0	274	11	79
11,310.2	39	9.6	46	10.8	47	27.0	28	2.40	12.7	13.4	61	16.8	156	24.4	47	8	80
7,344.0	53	3.4	206	4.3	200	14.6	110	1.41	(41.3)	1.6	184	14.8	175	21.5	78	8	81
N.A.		1.1	292	1.4	288	—		N.A.	—	—		—		—		5	82
3,415.9	118	(4.7)	400	(5.3)	401	(19.2)	359	3.29	31.6	(0.1)	196	5.7	239	13.4	197	5	83
15,073.3	29	11.3	30	8.2	94	14.5	113	2.41	(46.4)	5.9	141	(24.8)	394	19.2	105	19	84
10,940.3	40	7.8	69	11.3	41	24.2	38	1.95	(38.3)	5.3	151	1.1	277	24.8	43	8	85
4,374.4	94	3.9	189	5.1	169	13.8	127	1.78	(24.3)	1.6	185	4.6	249	15.8	163	22	86
15,725.6	27	7.0	84	10.7	48	22.2	44	1.81	(27.9)	9.3	110	4.4	252	29.9	21	8	87
2,242.1	162	(2.8)	371	(3.5)	385	(15.1)	348	(1.46)	—	—		35.3	68	13.7	192	5	88
5,882.7	71	(3.7)	392	(3.0)	377	(9.9)	333	(2.48)	(181.6)	—		(15.3)	365	16.8	145	7	89
N.A.		0.8	298	1.6	280	—		N.A.	—	—		—		—		7	90
4,825.9	86	0.1	326	0.1	327	0.2	296	0.09	(91.3)	(26.7)	243	(1.5)	295	8.7	256	18	91
3,365.1	119	5.8	118	9.6	65	17.8	84	7.21	14.4	18.7	31	20.1	140	16.8	143	1	92
24,191.8	16	18.0	6	13.2	25	19.6	64	4.97	26.8	36.8	4	77.8	23	21.0	86	7	93
7,161.8	55	5.5	136	5.6	153	11.8	160	3.01	15.8	10.3	94	34.5	72	21.8	76	5	94
2,079.9	176	3.0	217	3.6	224	12.7	141	4.22	192.0	1.1	190	2.1	271	7.0	276	7	95
3,062.7	132	(13.3)	457	(10.9)	445	(36.3)	380	(12.56)	(583.1)	—		(0.2)	285	18.5	115	15	96
9,000.1	44	11.5	28	15.8	19	42.2	11	4.78	1,738.5	15.8	47	(8.1)	339	21.0	87	19	97
4,978.9	83	4.4	172	8.1	96	28.9	24	3.25	22.6	10.6	89	(10.7)	352	24.0	52	8	98
N.A.		6.5	94	12.5	28	46.7	6	N.A.	—	—		—		—		2	99
1,611.5	206	2.2	254	3.8	216	9.6	201	2.56	(39.9)	35.8	6	36.1	67	7.2	272	1	100

[5] FORTUNE estimate.
[6] Figures are for fiscal year ended September 30, 1992.
[7] Owned by Unilever (1991 Global 500 rank: 20).
[8] Owned by Hanson (1991 Global 500 rank: 114).
[9] Owned by Hoechst (1991 Global 500 rank: 34).
[10] Figures are for fiscal year ended April 30, 1992.
[11] Owned by Bayer AG (1991 Global 500 rank: 42).
[12] Figures are for fiscal year ended July 31, 1992.
[13] Owned by Philips Electronics (1991 Global 500 rank: 29).
[14] Figures are for fiscal year ended November 30, 1992).

Source: "Reprinted by permission from FORTUNE magazine; © 1993 Time Inc."

DEFINITIONS AND EXPLANATIONS

Sales All companies on the list must derive more than 50% of their sales from manufacturing and/or mining and must publish financial data. Sales include operating revenues and other income from dividends, interest, royalties, etc. Sales of consolidated subsidiaries are included. So are sales from discontinued operations if these figures are published. If the sales are at least 10% higher for this reason, there is a symbol (¶) next to the sales figure. All figures are for the year ending December 31, 1992, unless otherwise noted. Sales figures do not include excise taxes collected by the manufacturer, so the numbers for some corporations—most of which sell gasoline, liquor, or tobacco—may be lower than those published by the corporations themselves. If they are at least 5% lower for this reason, there is a letter E next to the sales figures.

Profits are shown after taxes and after extraordinary credits or charges if any appear on the income statement, and after cumulative effects of accounting charges. An asterisk (*) signifies an extraordinary charge amounting to at least 10% of the profits shown; a double asterisk (**) an extraordinary credit of at least 10%. A single dagger (†) signifies an SFAS 106 and/or 109 charge amounting to at least 10% of the profits shown; a double dagger (‡) an SFAS 109 credit amounting to at least 10%. Figures in parentheses indicate a loss. Profit declines over 100% reflect swings from 1991 profits to 1992 losses. Cooperatives provide only 'net margin' figures, which are not comparable with the profits figures in these listings, and therefore N.A. is shown in that column.

Assets are those shown at the company's year-end total.

Stockholders' Equity is the sum of capital stock, surplus, and retained earnings at the company's year-end. Preferred stock capital that is technically construed to be debt has been excluded. Redeemable preferred stock whose redemption is either mandatory or outside the control of the company is therefore excluded, as is any portion of an ESOP convertible preferred whose repayment is guaranteed by the company. For purposes of calculating profits as percent of common stockholders' equity, all preferred stock is excluded. The dividends paid on such stock have been subtracted from the profit figures.

Market Value The figure shown was arrived at by multiplying the number of common shares outstanding (at the latest date available) by the price per common share as of March 5, 1993.

Earnings per Share The figures shown for each company are the primary earnings per share that appear on the income statement. Per share earnings for 1991 and 1992 are adjusted for stock splits and stock dividends. They are not restated for mergers, acquisitions, or accounting changes. Nor are the earnings per share numbers marked by any footnotes to indicate extraordinary charges or credits. However, if a company's profits are footnoted to indicate an extraordinary charge or credit, it can be assumed that earnings per share is affected as well. Results are listed as not available (N.A.) if the companies are cooperatives, joint ventures, or wholly owned subsidiaries of other companies; if the figures were not published; or if the stock traded on a limited basis and was not widely held. The 1982–92 growth rate is the average annual growth, compounded.

Total Return to Investors includes both price appreciation and dividend yield to an investor in the company's stock. The figures shown assume sales at the end of 1982 and 1991. It has been assumed that any proceeds from cash dividends, the sale of rights and warrant offerings, and stock received in spinoffs were reinvested when they were paid. Returns are adjusted for stock splits, stock dividends, recapitalizations, and corporate reorganizations as they occur; however, no effort has been made to reflect the cost of brokerage commissions or of taxes. Results are listed as not available (N.A.) if shares are not publicly traded or traded on only a limited basis. If companies have more than one class of shares outstanding, only the more widely held and actively traded has been considered. Total return percentages shown are the returns received by the hypothetical investor described above. The 1982–92 return is the annual rate, compounded.

The World's 100 Biggest Industrial Corporations (ranked by sales)

1992	1991			SALES $ millions	SALES % change from 1991	PROFITS $ millions	PROFITS Rank	PROFITS % change from 1991	ASSETS $ millions	ASSETS Rank	TOTAL STOCKHOLDERS' EQUITY $ millions	TOTAL STOCKHOLDERS' EQUITY Rank	EMPLOYEES Number	EMPLOYEES Rank	Industry table number
1	1	GENERAL MOTORS	U.S.	132,774.9	7.3	(23,498.3)†	500	—	191,012.8	2	6,225.6	68	750,000	1	17
2	3	EXXON	U.S.	103,547.0[E]	0.3	4,770.0	3	(14.8)	85,030.0	6	33,776.0	4	95,000	67	18
3	4	FORD MOTOR	U.S.	100,785.6	13.3	(7,385.0)†	494	—	180,545.2	3	14,752.9	14	325,333	7	17
4	2	ROYAL DUTCH/SHELL GROUP	BRIT./NETH.	98,935.3[E]	(4.7)	5,408.0	1	27.3	100,354.3	4	52,935.3	1	127,000	41	18
5	5	TOYOTA MOTOR[1]	JAPAN	79,114.2	1.3	1,812.6	12	(42.4)	76,131.8	8	37,490.1	2	108,167	54	17
6	7	IRI[G]	ITALY	67,547.4[2]	5.4	(3,811.2)[2]	491	—	N.A.		N.A.		400,000[2]	3	15
7	6	INTL. BUSINESS MACHINES	U.S.	65,096.0	(0.5)	(4,965.0)‡	493	—	86,705.0	5	27,624.0	6	308,010	8	6
8	11	DAIMLER-BENZ	GERMANY	63,339.5	10.5	928.6	36	(17.8)	53,209.9	13	11,416.3	24	376,467	4	17
9	8	GENERAL ELECTRIC	U.S.	62,202.0	3.3	4,725.0	4	79.2	192,876.0	1	23,459.0	8	268,000	12	7
10	9	HITACHI[3]	JAPAN	61,465.5	3.1	619.3	59	(35.4)	76,667.6	7	25,768.3	7	331,505	6	7
11	10	BRITISH PETROLEUM	BRITAIN	59,215.7	1.5	(808.4)	476	(200.7)	52,637.3	14	15,098.2	12	97,650	64	18
12	12	MATSUSHITA ELECTRIC INDUSTRIAL[3]	JAPAN	57,480.8	0.5	307.7	124	(69.1)	75,645.1	9	30,057.6	5	252,075	14	7
13	13	MOBIL	U.S.	57,389.0[E]	0.8	862.0†	40	(55.1)	40,561.0	24	16,540.0	10	63,700	100	18
14	17	VOLKSWAGEN	GERMANY	56,734.1	23.2	49.9	306	(92.5)	46,480.2	20	8,356.5	43	274,103	11	17
15	18	SIEMENS[4]	GERMANY	51,401.9	14.6	1,136.1	25	0.1	50,752.8	15	13,505.3	16	413,000	2	7
16	14	NISSAN MOTOR[3]	JAPAN	50,247.5	2.8	(448.7)	460	(159.0)	62,978.5	10	15,086.0	13	143,754	31	17
17	15	PHILIP MORRIS	U.S.	50,157.0	4.3	4,939.0	2	64.3	50,014.0	16	12,563.0	18	161,000	25	8
18	19	SAMSUNG	SOUTH KOREA	49,559.6	11.5	374.2	105	7.7	48,030.8	19	6,430.8	66	188,558	19	7
19	16	FIAT	ITALY	47,928.7	2.4	446.8	84	(50.3)	58,013.6	11	11,609.5	23	285,482	9	17
20	20	UNILEVER	BRITAIN/NETHERLANDS	43,962.6	6.5	2,278.6	5	11.8	24,267.0	49	6,934.1	57	283,000	10	8
21	21	ENI	ITALY	40,365.5	(1.7)	(767.1)	473	(188.0)	54,790.5	12	11,008.1	25	124,032	46	18
22	24	ELF AQUITAINE[G]	FRANCE	39,717.8	7.0	1,166.4	23	(32.9)	45,129.4	21	15,743.1	11	87,900	74	18
23	26	NESTLÉ	SWITZERLAND	39,057.9	9.8	1,916.9	9	11.3	30,336.3	39	8,891.5	40	218,005	15	8
24	25	CHEVRON	U.S.	38,523.0[E]	4.7	1,569.0†	15	21.3	33,970.0	34	13,728.0	15	49,245	143	18
25	27	TOSHIBA[3]	JAPAN	37,471.6	5.7	164.7	200	(44.5)	49,341.6	18	10,068.5	29	173,000	22	6
26	22	E.I. DU PONT DE NEMOURS	U.S.	37,386.0	(2.5)	(3,927.0)†	492	(379.9)	38,870.0	29	11,765.0	22	125,000	43	5
27	23	TEXACO	U.S.	37,130.0[E]	(1.1)	712.0†	48	(45.0)	25,992.0	44	9,973.0	30	37,582	199	18
28	33	CHRYSLER	U.S.	36,897.0	25.6	723.0‡	46	—	40,653.0	23	7,538.0	48	128,000	39	17
29	32	RENAULT[G]	FRANCE	33,884.9	15.1	1,072.5	28	96.5	23,897.4	54	6,145.3	70	146,604	29	17
30	28	HONDA MOTOR[3]	JAPAN	33,369.6	0.9	306.9	125	(37.0)	26,374.6	43	9,085.2	35	90,900	69	17
31	29	PHILIPS ELECTRONICS	NETHERLANDS	33,269.7	10.1	(511.6)	465	(179.6)	26,853.2	42	4,986.8	90	252,200	13	7
32	34	SONY[3]	JAPAN	31,451.9	7.9	290.5	133	(67.8)	39,700.5	25	12,517.3	19	126,000	42	7
33	30	ABB ASEA BROWN BOVERI	SWITZERLAND	30,536.0	2.8	505.0	73	(17.1)	25,949.0	45	4,095.0	113	213,407	16	7
34	38	ALCATEL ALSTHOM	FRANCE	30,529.1	7.5	1,331.8	18	21.5	44,207.7	22	9,027.5	37	203,000	17	7
35	31	BOEING	U.S.	30,414.0	2.8	552.0†	66	(64.8)	18,147.0	73	8,056.0	46	143,000	32	1
36	40	PROCTER & GAMBLE[1]	U.S.	29,890.0	9.1	1,872.0	10	5.6	24,025.0	53	9,071.0	36	106,200	57	23
37	35	HOECHST	GERMANY	29,570.6	3.0	592.0	63	(10.6)	22,788.8	58	7,308.8	52	177,668	21	5
38	37	PEUGEOT	FRANCE	29,387.4	3.5	636.7	57	(35.0)	23,352.1	56	9,615.3	32	150,800	27	17
39	39	BASF	GERMANY	28,494.3	1.3	393.3	98	(37.3)	24,062.0	52	8,950.3	38	123,254	47	5
40	36	NEC[3,5]	JAPAN	28,376.5	(0.8)	(361.8)	453	(415.5)	34,872.0	32	7,062.5	56	140,969	33	7
41	46	DAEWOO	SOUTH KOREA	28,333.9	11.7	383.9	102	—	39,250.9	27	5,126.1	86	78,727	83	7
42	41	FUJITSU[3]	JAPAN	27,910.7	7.1	(261.2)	436	(385.0)	33,092.3	36	9,651.3	31	161,974	24	6
43	42	BAYER	GERMANY	26,625.3	2.9	970.2	34	(11.8)	23,663.6	55	10,543.9	27	156,400	26	5
44	45	MITSUBISHI ELECTRIC[3]	JAPAN	26,502.3	3.7	228.4	159	(15.7)	30,747.5	38	7,146.7	54	107,859	55	7
45	43	TOTAL	FRANCE	26,141.5	1.5	537.6	69	(47.8)	20,915.5	61	7,382.5	51	51,139	137	18
46	44	AMOCO	U.S.	25,543.0[E]	(0.2)	(74.0)†	390	(105.0)	28,453.0	41	12,960.0	17	46,994	155	18
47	49	MITSUBISHI MOTORS[3]	JAPAN	25,482.2	8.2	207.0	169	(6.6)	20,935.6	60	3,518.6	137	45,000[2]	164	17
48	47	NIPPON STEEL[3]	JAPAN	23,990.8	(2.5)	14.6	356	(97.5)	39,224.4	28	9,162.5	34	51,900	133	15
49	52	MITSUBISHI HEAVY INDUSTRIES[3]	JAPAN	23,011.3	7.1	649.7	54	(18.1)	35,345.8	31	9,344.5	33	66,000[2]	96	11
50	50	THYSSEN[4]	GERMANY	22,731.5	0.6	207.9	168	(29.3)	16,650.1	88	3,415.4	140	147,279	28	15

[E] Excise taxes have been deducted.
[G] Government owned.
N.A. Not available.
* Reflects an extraordinary charge of at least 10%.
** Reflects an extraordinary credit of at least 10%.
† Reflects an SFAS 106 and/or 109 charge of at least 10%.
‡ Reflects an SFAS 109 credit of at least 10%.
[1] Figures are for fiscal year ended June 30, 1992.
[2] FORTUNE estimate.
[3] Figures are for fiscal year ended March 31, 1993.
[4] Figures are for fiscal year ended September 30, 1992.

(continued)

The World's 100 Biggest Industrial Corporations (ranked by sales) *(concluded)*

1992	1991	Company	Country	SALES $millions	SALES % change from 1991	PROFITS $millions	PROFITS Rank	PROFITS % change from 1991	ASSETS $millions	ASSETS Rank	TOTAL STOCKHOLDERS' EQUITY $millions	EQUITY Rank	EMPLOYEES Number	EMPLOYEES Rank	Industry table number
51	56	PEPSICO	U.S.	22,083.7	11.7	374.3†	104	(65.3)	20,951.2	59	5,355.7	82	371,000	5	3
52	55	ROBERT BOSCH	GERMANY	22,036.5	8.7	327.7	118	9.7	15,096.6	95	4,852.1	95	169,804	23	17
53	53	UNITED TECHNOLOGIES	U.S.	22,032.0	3.6	(287.0)†	442	—	15,928.0	94	3,370.0	146	178,000	20	1
54	62	INI	SPAIN	21,654.2	14.2	(273.2)	438	—	39,470.9	26	7,283.3	53	139,712	34	11
55	51	IMPERIAL CHEMICAL INDUSTRIES	BRITAIN	21,548.9	(3.5)	(1,006.0)	480	(205.0)	18,340.6	71	6,484.7	64	114,000	50	5
56	48	PDVSA[G,6]	VENEZUELA	21,375.0	(10.9)	338.0	115	—	33,260.0	35	22,569.0	9	55,137	125	18
57	60	PEMEX (PETRÓLEOS MÉXICANOS)[G]	MEXICO	21,292.8	10.3	1,070.6	29	2.2	49,860.0	17	36,505.4	3	125,000	44	18
58	58	CONAGRA[7]	U.S.	21,219.0	8.8	372.4	106	19.7	9,758.7	172	2,232.3	214	80,787	81	8
59	54	MAZDA MOTOR[3]	JAPAN	20,867.4	1.5	10.3	359	(85.3)	13,944.6	103	3,612.6	131	55,900[2]	123	17
60	64	BMW (BAYERISCHE MOTOREN WERKE)	GER.	20,611.2	11.2	464.6	80	0.8	16,980.9	84	4,091.5	114	73,562	87	17
61	57	EASTMAN KODAK	U.S.	20,577.0	4.7	1,146.0‡	24	6,641.2	23,138.0	57	6,557.0	63	132,600	38	22
62	65	NIPPON OIL[3]	JAPAN	19,863.8[E,2]	7.2	248.7	142	(12.8)	25,166.1	47	5,274.6	83	11,044[2]	433	18
63	59	DOW CHEMICAL	U.S.	19,080.0	(1.2)	(489.0)†	464	(151.9)	25,360.0	46	8,074.0	45	61,353	106	5
64	71	REPSOL	SPAIN	18,618.3	14.8	701.8	51	4.0	11,713.4	130	4,180.9	111	19,632	353	18
65	76	MANNESMANN	GERMANY	18,234.8	21.6	130.8	225	(44.9)	12,797.8	113	3,536.8	136	136,747	36	11
66	66	XEROX	U.S.	18,089.0	1.5	(1,020.0)†	481	(324.7)	34,051.0	33	3,971.0	115	99,300	63	22
67	67	ATLANTIC RICHFIELD	U.S.	18,061.0[E]	2.1	801.0†	43	13.0	24,256.0	50	6,721.0	60	26,800	274	18
68	61	BRITISH AEROSPACE	BRITAIN	17,838.9	(6.0)	(1,567.3)	487	—	16,464.5	91	2,693.1	184	102,500	59	1
69	63	MCDONNELL DOUGLAS	U.S.	17,513.0	(6.4)	(781.0)†	474	(284.6)	13,781.0	105	3,022.0	164	87,377	75	1
70	68	PETROFINA	BELGIUM	17,468.8	(1.0)	144.0	216	(69.8)	10,658.7	152	3,647.5	127	15,490	387	18
71	81	HEWLETT-PACKARD[9]	U.S.	16,427.0	13.0	549.0†	67	(27.3)	13,700.0	107	7,499.0	50	92,600	68	6
72	69	USINOR-SACILOR[G]	FRANCE	16,418.6	(4.7)	(457.2)	463	—	17,336.7	77	3,794.6	121	89,038	73	15
73	92	METALLGESELLSCHAFT[4]	GERMANY	16,390.5	23.0	25.9	341	(8.2)	12,270.4	121	1,205.8	349	62,547	103	15
74	70	USX	U.S.	16,186.0[E]	(5.7)	(1,826.0)†	488	—	17,252.0	78	3,709.0	125	45,582	160	18
75	83	FERRUZZI FINANZIARIA	ITALY	16,136.8	12.4	(1,231.7)	484	(1,427.7)	29,236.0	40	674.6	437	51,769	135	8
76	78	CIBA-GEIGY	SWITZERLAND	16,119.4	7.7	1,079.9	27	21.0	20,873.1	62	12,328.8	20	90,554	71	5
77	74	RHÔNE-POULENC[G]	FRANCE	15,886.5	4.1	412.4	91	16.0	20,327.7	63	4,744.2	97	83,283	80	5
78	82	VIAG	GERMANY	15,784.7	9.5	184.2	184	238.3	12,681.3	115	2,195.2	216	84,543	79	15
79	77	RJR NABISCO HOLDINGS	U.S.	15,734.0	5.0	299.0[*]	130	(18.8)	32,041.0	37	8,376.0	42	64,000	98	25
80	110	BTR	BRITAIN	15,726.1	30.6	1,194.9	22	22.0	13,671.5	108	2,783.9	176	135,133	37	11
81	79	RUHRKOHLE	GERMANY	15,712.0	5.4	32.4	334	(19.3)	17,068.2	81	1,061.0	378	118,337	49	16
82	72	PREUSSAG[4]	GERMANY	15,697.8	(0.9)	297.0	131	(3.2)	9,916.9	168	2,204.3	215	73,680	86	15
83	75	IDEMITSU KOSAN[3]	JAPAN	15,662.9	4.3	19.4	350	(42.5)	16,666.0	86	516.3	459	5,214	482	18
84	84	CANON	JAPAN	15,348.9	7.7	283.3	136	(26.9)	17,226.8	79	5,668.8	78	67,227	94	6
85	88	VOLVO[5]	SWEDEN	14,920.7	11.5	(792.4)	475	(687.0)	17,068.1	82	3,662.9	126	60,115	110	17
86	154	FRIED. KRUPP[10]	GERMANY	14,820.5	62.3	(161.3)	415	(209.1)	12,067.0	124	1,466.9	304	90,588	70	11
87	101	SSANGYONG	SOUTH KOREA	14,609.7	14.3	156.9	203	42.5	12,233.7	122	3,513.4	138	24,000	303	18
88	87	NKK[13]	JAPAN	14,605.5	5.4	60.5	298	(71.1)	24,141.3	51	3,726.1	123	44,291	169	15
89	98	PETROBRÁS[G]	BRAZIL	14,599.8	12.7	4.7	366	—	19,956.9	65	12,129.7	21	56,209	120	18
90	96	SUNKYONG	SOUTH KOREA	14,530.3	11.2	58.7	301	(4.6)	13,321.4	109	3,378.4	145	22,419	322	18
91	93	SAINT-GOBAIN	FRANCE	14,296.9	7.4	448.8	83	0.9	17,161.2	80	5,840.1	76	100,373	62	4
92	91	ELECTROLUX[5]	SWEDEN	14,048.7	5.4	32.6	333	(51.2)	10,436.8	158	2,011.0	236	119,200	48	7
93	86	DIGITAL EQUIPMENT[1]	U.S.	14,027.0	—	(2,795.5)†	490	—	11,284.3	137	4,930.9	92	113,800	51	6
94	73	GRAND METROPOLITAN[4]	BRITAIN	13,964.6[E]	(10.1)	1,132.6	26	44.8	16,656.8	87	6,687.3	61	102,405	60	8
95	90	MINNESOTA MINING & MFG.	U.S.	13,883.0	4.1	1,233.0	21	6.8	11,955.0	127	6,599.0	62	87,015	76	22
96	94	BRIDGESTONE	JAPAN	13,859.8	4.8	224.1	161	303.6	14,788.1	98	3,647.3	128	85,835	77	21
97	104	JOHNSON & JOHNSON	U.S.	13,846.0	10.5	1,030.0†	33	(29.5)	11,884.0	128	5,171.0	84	84,900	78	19
98	97	SUMITOMO METAL INDUSTRIES[13]	JAPAN	13,803.0	6.0	225.7	160	(41.1)	20,113.4	64	4,338.5	108	30,826	237	15
99	85	TENNECO	U.S.	13,606.0	(3.1)	(1,323.0)†	486	—	16,584.0	90	1,330.0	332	79,000	82	11
100	102	INTERNATIONAL PAPER	U.S.	13,600.0	7.1	86.0†	266	(53.3)	16,459.0	92	6,189.0	69	73,000	88	9

[5] Figures prepared in accordance with U.S. Generally Accepted Accounting Principles.
[6] Figures are preliminary.
[7] Figures are for fiscal year ended May 31, 1992.
[9] Figures are for fiscal year ended October 31, 1992.
[10] Merged with Hoesch (1991 rank: 241) on January 1, 1992.
[13] Figures are for fiscal year ended March 31, 1992.

Source: Reprinted by permission from FORTUNE magazine; © 1993 Time Inc.

DEFINITIONS AND EXPLANATIONS

Sales All companies on the list must have derived more than 50% of their sales from manufacturing and/or mining. Sales include operating revenues and other income from dividends, interest, royalties, etc. Sales of consolidated subsidiaries are included as well as sales from discontinued operations. Sales figures do not include excise taxes collected by manufacturers, and so the figures for some corporations—most of which sell gasoline, liquor, or tobacco—may be lower than those published by the corporations themselves. Figures have been converted to dollars using an exchange rate that consists of the official average rate during each company's fiscal year (ended December 31, 1992, unless otherwise noted).

Profits Profits are shown after taxes and after extraordinary credits or charges if any appear on the income statement, and after cumulative effects of accounting changes. An asterisk (*) signifies an extraordinary charge amounting to at least 10% of the profits shown; a double asterisk (**) an extraordinary credit of at least 10%. A single dagger (†) signifies an SFAS 106 and/or 109 charge amounting to at least 10% of the profits shown; a double dagger (‡) an SFAS 109 credit amounting to at least 10%. Figures in parentheses indicate a loss. Profit declines over 100% reflect swings from 1991 profits to 1992 losses. Cooperatives provide only net margin figures, which are not comparable with the profit figures in these listings, and therefore N.A. is shown in that column. Figures have been converted to dollars using the average official exchange rate during each company's fiscal year (ended December 31, 1992, unless otherwise noted).

Assets Assets shown are those at the company's fiscal year-end. Figures have been converted to dollars at the official exchange rate at each company's year-end.

Employees The figure shown is either a fiscal year-end or yearly average number, as published by the corporation.

Stockholders' Equity Stockholders' equity is the sum of capital stock, surplus, and retained earnings at the company's year-end. Minority interest is not included. Figures have been converted to dollars at the official exchange rate at each company's year-end.

Industry Tables Companies are included in the industry that represents the greatest volume of their industrial sales. Industry groups are based on categories established by the U.S. Office of Management and Budget.

The 25 Largest Diversified Service Companies (ranked by sales)

RANK BY SALES 1992	1991	(Major industry)	SALES[1] $ millions	% change from 1991	PROFITS $ millions	Rank	% change from 1991	ASSETS $ millions	Rank	TOTAL STOCKHOLDERS' EQUITY $ millions	Rank
1	1	**AMERICAN TELEPHONE & TELEGRAPH** New York (telecomm.)	65,101.0	2.8	3,807.0	1	629.3	57,188.0	1	18,921.0	1
2	3	**ENRON** Houston (natural gas)	14,126.6¶	4.5	306.2	11	26.6	10,663.9	6	2,546.6	10
3	5	**TIME WARNER** New York (entertainment)	13,070.0	8.7	86.0	39	—	27,366.0	2	8,167.0	2
4	4	**FLEMING** Oklahoma City (wholesale)	12,937.9	0.3	113.0	32	79.4	3,117.7	33	1,060.4	25
5	6	**SUPERVALU** Eden Prairie, Minn. (wholesale)[2, 3]	10,632.3	(8.6)	194.4**	18	25.3	2,484.3	44	1,031.0	27
6	9	**MCI COMMUNICATIONS** Washington, D.C. (telecommunications)	10,562.0	25.2	609.0	6	10.5	9,678.0	8	3,150.0	7
7	10	**MCKESSON** San Francisco (wholesale)[4]	10,345.1	22.1	(78.2)†	87	(177.7)	2,756.9	38	554.5	54
8	7	**SPRINT** Westwood, Mo. (telecommunications)	9,230.4	5.1	457.1	9	24.4	10,188.4	7	2,816.8	9
9	11	**SYSCO** Houston (wholesale)[5]	8,892.8	9.1	172.2	20	12.0	2,301.6	49	1,056.8	26
10	8	**MARRIOTT** Bethesda, Md. (hotels)	8,865.0	1.6	85.0	40	3.7	6,410.0	12	785.0	41
11	12	**WASTE MANAGEMENT** Oak Brook, Ill. (waste)	8,661.0	13.9	850.0†	2	40.2	14,114.2	3	4,319.6	4
12	13	**ELECTRONIC DATA SYSTEMS** Dallas (computing)[6]	8,218.9	15.8	635.5	5	16.1	6,123.5	13	3,063.4	8
13	17	**WALT DISNEY** Burbank, Calif. (theme parks)[7]	7,634.3	21.1	816.7	3	28.3	10,861.7	5	4,704.6	3
14	18	**HUMANA** Louisville, Ky. (managed health care)[8]	6,893.0¶	16.3	122.0‡	29	(65.6)	3,764.0	26	2,016.0	13
15	15	**FLUOR** Irvine, Calif. (engineering, construction)[9]	6,743.7	(0.7)	5.8†	73	(96.4)	2,365.5	47	880.8	35
16	14	**HALLIBURTON** Dallas (engineering, construction)	6,607.9	(6.7)	(137.3)†*	90	(616.2)	4,735.8	20	1,907.3	14
17	25	**BERGEN BRUNSWIG** Orange, Calif. (wholesale)[8]	5,486.7	13.4	60.9	48	(5.1)	1,412.2	62	395.3	65
18	20	**CAPITAL CITIES/ABC** New York (broadcasting)	5,396.1	(1.5)	246.1†	14	(28.4)	6,522.2	11	3,805.7	6
19	16	**PACIFIC ENTERPRISES** Los Angeles (natural gas)	5,232.0¶	(21.5)	(550.0)	93	—	5,414.0	15	969.0	32
20	21	**RYDER SYSTEM** Miami (truck rental)	5,191.5	2.6	123.9	27	784.1	4,930.1	18	1,475.1	17
21	24	**ALCO STANDARD** Wayne, Pa. (wholesale)[7]	5,166.1	5.5	95.8	37	(18.6)	2,444.8	45	860.4	36
22	23	**HOSPITAL CORP. OF AMERICA** Nashville (hospitals)	5,125.7	2.3	28.2	63	—	5,456.1	14	1,415.7	19
23	26	**ARA GROUP** Philadelphia (food service)[7]	4,865.3	1.9	67.4	46	4.9	2,005.0	52	124.2	91
24	27	**DUN & BRADSTREET** New York (information services)	4,750.7	1.4	553.5	7	8.8	4,914.9	19	2,156.0	12
25	28	**PARAMOUNT COMM.** New York (movies)[9]	4,264.9	5.8	261.4	12	113.9	7,054.2	10	4,051.5	5

N.A. Not available.
• Not on last year's list.
* Reflects an extraordinary charge of at least 10%.
** Reflects an extraordinary credit of at least 10%.
† Reflects an SFAS 106 and/or 109 charge of at least 10%.
‡ Reflects an SFAS 109 credit of at least 10%.
¶ Includes sales of discontinued operations of at least 10%.
[1] Sales include all operating revenues, other income, and revenues from discontinued operations when they are published. Sales also incluc consolidated subsidiaries, but they do not include excise taxes. All figures are for the fiscal year ended December 31, 1992, unless otherwis noted. All companies on the list must have derived more than 50% of their revenues from nonmanufacturing and nonmining businesses. Exclude from this list but eligible for those that follow are companies deriving more than 50% of revenues solely from banking, life insurance, financ savings, retail, transportation, or utilities.

DEFINITIONS AND EXPLANATIONS TO THE SERVICE COMPANIES

Assets are those shown at the company's fiscal year-end.

Profits are shown after taxes, after extraordinary credits or charges if any appear on the income statement, and after cumulative effects of accounting charges. An asterisk (*) signifies an extraordinary charge amounting to at least 10% of the profits shown; a double asterisk (**) an extraordinary credit of at least 10%. A single dagger (†) signifies an SFAS 106 and/or 109 charge amounting to at least 10% of the profits shown; a double dagger (‡) an SFAS 109 credit amounting to at least 10%. Figures in parentheses indicate a loss. Profit declines over 100% reflect swings from 1991 profits to 1992 losses. Cooperatives provide only net margin figures, which are not comparable with the profit figures in these listings, and therefore N.A. is shown in that column.

Stockholders' equity is the sum of capital stock, surplus, and retained earnings at the company's year-end. Preferred stock capital that is technically construed to be debt has been excluded. Redeemable preferred stock whose redemption is either mandatory or outside the control of the company, is therefore excluded, as is any portion of an ESOP convertible preferred whose repayment is guaranteed by the company. For purposes of calculating profits as percent of common stockholders' equity, all preferred stock is excluded. The dividends paid on such stock have been subtracted from the profit figure.

Market Value The figure shown was arrived at by multiplying the number of common shares outstanding (at the latest date available) by the price per common share as of April 16, 1993.

MARKET VALUE 4/16/93 $ millions	Rank	PROFITS AS % OF ... SALES %	Rank	ASSETS %	Rank	COMMON STOCKHOLDERS' EQUITY %	Rank	EARNINGS PER SHARE 1992 $	% change from 1991	1982–92 annual growth rate %	Rank	TOTAL RETURN TO INVESTORS 1992 %	Rank	1982–92 annual rate %	Rank	EMPLOYEES Number	Rank	RANK
80,389.9	1	5.8	20	6.7	23	20.1	13	2.86	615.0	(10.2)	46	34.5	18	18.2	18	312,700	1	1
7,157.7	10	2.2	48	2.9	53	12.0	37	2.58	20.0	5.5	23	36.6	16	19.4	13	7,776	61	2
12,865.0	5	0.7	69	0.3	73	(33.1)	84	(1.46)	—	—		35.0	17	12.4	34	44,000	16	3
1,178.9	52	0.9	65	3.6	43	10.7	45	3.16	77.5	(2.2)	40	(4.9)	67	6.4	47	22,800	32	4
2,294.8	37	1.8	54	7.8	19	18.9	17	2.60	26.2	11.4	15	17.4	39	11.6	36	24,406	30	5
12,511.8	6	5.8	22	6.3	24	18.7	18	2.21	10.0	9.3	18	31.4	22	8.2	44	30,964	22	6
1,726.9	45	(0.8)	82	(2.8)	87	(16.9)	82	(2.20)	(194.0)	—		21.9	32	—		14,150	44	7
10,737.7	7	5.0	26	4.5	30	16.2	27	2.07	23.2	5.2	24	12.0	48	15.9	22	43,000	18	8
4,309.8	20	1.9	50	7.5	22	16.3	26	0.93	11.4	15.8	9	14.2	45	19.4	14	22,500	33	9
2,607.6	34	1.0	62	1.3	65	11.6	40	0.64	(20.0)	(0.8)	37	26.9	28	6.9	46	195,000	2	10
16,359.7	4	9.8	11	6.0	25	19.7	15	1.72	39.8	19.1	6	(3.8)	66	21.1	8	67,275	7	11
N.A.		7.7	16	10.4	13	9.1	50	N.A.	—	—		—		—		71,000	5	12
22,055.1	3	10.7	9	7.5	20	17.4	23	1.52	27.2	23.2	3	51.0	8	28.2	2	60,000	11	13
1,072.3	54	1.8	56	3.2	49	6.1	62	0.77	(65.9)	(1.5)	38	(20.9)	76	3.9	54	65,800	9	14
3,521.6	26	0.1	74	0.2	74	0.7	71	0.07	(96.4)	(28.3)	49	(3.4)	65	9.6	42	43,605	17	15
4,374.4	18	(2.1)	87	(2.9)	89	(7.2)	79	(1.28)	(612.0)	—		4.5	58	1.9	59	69,200	6	16
660.9	70	1.1	61	4.3	33	15.4	29	1.62	8.0	10.4	16	22.0	31	8.1	45	2,979	86	17
8,978.4	9	4.6	30	3.8	40	6.5	58	14.82	(27.6)	7.4	20	17.2	40	15.6	24	19,250	37	18
1,856.5	43	(10.5)	91	(10.2)	92	(79.6)	86	(7.57)	—	—		(27.8)	80	3.2	57	9,844	55	19
2,196.4	40	2.4	44	2.5	56	8.2	52	1.51	2,920.0	2.3	33	39.1	15	8.3	43	41,695	20	20
2,215.0	38	1.9	53	3.9	35	11.1	43	2.04	(21.8)	3.3	31	8.8	56	12.5	32	23,500	31	21
3,262.5	27	0.5	70	0.5	71	2.0	69	0.16	—	—		—		—		66,000	8	22
N.A.		1.4	60	3.4	47	54.3	3	5.32	8.4	—		—		—		124,000	3	23
10,522.4	8	11.7	7	11.3	11	25.7	8	3.10	8.8	9.4	17	4.5	59	12.6	31	52,400	12	24
5,971.8	13	6.1	18	3.7	42	6.5	59	2.19	112.6	7.3	21	18.2	36	20.7	10	12,900	46	25

[2] Figures are for fiscal year ended February 28, 1992.
[3] Name changed from Super Valu Stores. Acquired Wetterau (No. 19 on last year's Diversified Service list).
[4] Figures are for fiscal year ended March 31, 1992.
[5] Figures are for fiscal year ended June 30,1992.
[6] Wholly owned by General Motors (No. 1 on FORTUNE Industrial 500).
[7] Figures are for fiscal year ended September 30, 1992.
[8] Figures are for fiscal year ended August 31, 1992.
[9] Figures are for fiscal year ended October 31, 1992.

Earnings per Share The figures shown for each company are the primary earnings per share that appear on the income statement. Per share earnings for 1991 and 1982 are adjusted for stock splits and stock dividends. They are not restated for mergers, acquisitions, or accounting changes. Nor are the earnings per share numbers marked by any footnotes to indicate extraordinary charges or credits. However, if a company's profits are footnoted to indicate an extraordinary charge or credit, it can be assumed that earnings per share is affected as well. Results are listed as not available (N.A.) if the companies are cooperatives, joint ventures, or wholly owned subsidiaries of other companies; if the figures were not published; or if the stock traded on a limited basis and was not widely held. The 1982–92 growth rate is the annual rate, compounded.

Total Return to Investors Total return to investors includes both capital gains or losses plus reinvested dividends. The figures shown assume sales at the end of last year of stock owned at the end of 1982 and 1991. It has been assumed that any proceeds from cash dividends, the sale of rights and warrant offerings, and stock received in spinoffs were reinvested when they were paid. Returns are adjusted for stock splits, stock dividends, recapitalizations, and corporate reorganizations as they occur; however, no effort has been made to reflect the cost of brokerage commissions or of taxes. Results are listed as not available (N.A.) if shares are not publicly traded or are traded on only a limited basis. If companies have more than one class of shares outstanding, only the more widely held and actively traded has been considered. Total return percentages shown are the returns received by the hypothetical investor described above. The 1982–92 growth rate is the average annual growth compounded.

The 25 Largest Life Insurance Companies (ranked by assets)

RANK BY ASSETS 1992	1991	Company	ASSETS[1] $ millions	% change from 1991	PREMIUM AND ANNUITY INCOME[2] $ millions	Rank	NET INVESTMENT INCOME $ millions	Rank	NET GAIN FROM OPERATIONS[3] $ millions	Mutual rank	Stock rank
1	1	**PRUDENTIAL OF AMERICA*** Newark, N.J.	**154,779.4**	**4.3**	**24,762.8**	1	**8,898.2**	1	**904.2**	1	
2	2	**METROPOLITAN LIFE*** New York	**118,178.3**	**6.7**	**19,934.0**	2	**7,312.5**	2	**138.6**	7	
3	3	**TEACHERS INSURANCE & ANNUITY** New York	**61,776.7**	**11.2**	**3,158.1**	21	**5,022.5**	3	**540.6**		1
4	4	**AETNA LIFE** Hartford[8]	**50,896.5**	**(2.8)**	**7,131.4**	6	**2,942.8**	5	**190.5**		5
5	6	**NEW YORK LIFE** New York	**46,925.0**	**9.8**	**8,595.0**	3	**3,470.1**	4	**241.1**	4	
6	5	**EQUITABLE LIFE ASSURANCE*** New York	**46,624.0**	**(7.4)**	**3,856.3**	13	**2,267.7**	10	**(112.0)**	18	
7	7	**CONNECTICUT GENERAL LIFE** Bloomfield, Conn.[9]	**44,075.5**	**5.7**	**3,488.5**	17	**2,521.9**	7	**378.6**		2
8	9	**NORTHWESTERN MUTUAL LIFE*** Milwaukee	**39,666.3**	**11.0**	**4,912.3**	10	**2,745.5**	6	**244.0**	2	
9	8	**JOHN HANCOCK MUTUAL LIFE*** Boston	**39,146.1**	**8.1**	**7,304.7**	5	**2,506.7**	8	**243.9**	3	
10	11	**PRINCIPAL MUTUAL LIFE** Des Moines	**35,124.8**	**11.5**	**8,102.1**	4	**2,396.2**	9	**205.1**	5	
11	10	**TRAVELERS** Hartford[10]	**34,201.7**	**(4.1)**	**5,045.5**	9	**1,983.3**	12	**(188.6)**		32
12	12	**MASSACHUSETTS MUTUAL LIFE*** Springfield, Mass.	**31,164.2**	**6.4**	**4,773.8**	11	**2,096.8**	11	**190.3**	6	
13	13	**LINCOLN NATIONAL LIFE** Fort Wayne	**28,796.3**	**22.4**	**5,977.7**	8	**1,494.4**	14	**152.1**		9[4]
14	14	**IDS LIFE** Minneapolis[11]	**23,278.8**	**19.3**	**3,567.8**	16	**1,421.8**	15	**189.7**		6
15	18	**HARTFORD LIFE** Simsbury, Conn.[12]	**20,756.1**	**27.6**	**6,016.0**	7	**908.9**	22	**16.0**		27
16	15	**ALLSTATE LIFE** Northbrook, Ill.[13]	**20,324.3**	**13.3**	**3,456.1**	18	**1,632.7**	13	**206.8**		4
17	19	**NATIONWIDE LIFE** Columbus, Ohio	**19,259.6**	**20.5**	**3,741.5**	15	**1,042.9**	19	**60.9**		21
18	20	**VARIABLE ANNUITY LIFE** Houston[14]	**17,262.2**	**16.9**	**1,900.9**	27	**1,325.9**	17	**88.7**		16
19	16	**MUTUAL OF NEW YORK*** New York	**16,896.3**	**(3.4)**	**1,643.2**	29	**936.1**	21	**80.5**	10	
20	17	**NEW ENGLAND MUTUAL LIFE*** Boston	**16,351.4**	**(3.5)**	**1,969.3**	26	**866.2**	24	**67.6**	12	
21	21	**STATE FARM LIFE** Bloomington, Ill.	**15,369.9**	**12.6**	**2,173.6**	24	**1,202.9**	18	**137.6**		10
22	23	**AETNA LIFE & ANNUITY** Hartford[8]	**15,183.3**	**13.0**	**2,004.2**	25	**803.4**	25	**55.2**		23
23	22	**JACKSON NATIONAL LIFE** Lansing, Mich.[15]	**14,775.9**	**8.6**	**2,969.8**	22	**1,343.7**	16	**212.1**		3
24	24	**NEW YORK LIFE & ANNUITY** New York	**12,596.6**	**8.5**	**1,069.2**	40	**1,020.7**	20	**171.0**		7
25	27	**PACIFIC MUTUAL LIFE*** Newport Beach, Calif.	**11,546.7**	**8.4**	**1,339.7**	33	**866.8**	23	**69.2**	11	

N.A. Not available.

● Not on last year's list.

* Indicates a mutual company.

1 As of December 31, 1992.

2 Includes premium income from life, accident, and health policies, annuities, and contributions to deposit administration funds.

3 After dividends to policyholders and federal income taxes, excluding realized capital gains and losses. Figures in parentheses indicate loss.

4 After dividends to policyholders and federal income taxes, including realized capital gains and losses. Figures in parentheses indicate loss.

5 Face value of all life policies, including variable life insurance, as of December 31, 1992.

6 Changes between December 31, 1991, and December 31, 1992.

NET INCOME[4] $ millions	Mutual rank	Stock rank	% change from 1991	NET INCOME AS % OF ASSETS %	Rank	LIFE INSURANCE IN FORCE[5] $ millions	Rank	INCREASE IN LIFE INSURANCE IN FORCE[6] $ millions	Rank	%	Rank	EMPLOYEES[7] Number	Rank	RANK
542.6	1		**(60.9)**	**0.4**	33	**824,012.2**	1	**3,303.5**	21	**0.4**	29	**101,600**	1	**1**
225.2	7		**(5.0)**	**0.2**	40	**162,063.8**	20	**114,042.9**	1	**12.0**	6	**50,000**	2	**2**
386.6		1	**16.6**	**0.6**	23	**33,383.3**	35	**3,578.8**	18	**12.0**	7	**3,794**	32	**3**
52.3		5	**(83.1)**	**0.1**	42	**311,826.0**	4	**717.1**	31	0.2	30	**22,033**	5	**4**
176.5	4		**(20.3)**	**0.4**	31	**333,815.6**	3	**22,283.4**	6	**7.2**	17	**17,406**	10	**5**
(260.5)	18		**(445.2)**	**(0.6)**	48	**285,339.4**	5	**(22,872.2)**	50	—		**19,500**	7	**6**
399.2		2	**(12.0)**	**0.9**	12	**482,467.5**	2	**61,091.8**	2	**14.5**	5	**14,280**	14	**7**
349.0	2		**(35.2)**	**0.9**	14	**277,334.9**	6	**26,206.0**	4	**10.4**	10	**10,598**	18	**8**
124.6	3		**(40.3)**	**0.3**	38	**244,813.7**	8	**(1,348.3)**	43	—		**13,903**	15	**9**
236.6	5		**(28.3)**	**0.7**	21	**132,390.6**	14	**10,639.8**	11	**8.7**	12	**12,430**	16	**10**
(317.2)		32	**(265.5)**	**(0.9)**	49	**192,744.1**	10	**(22,126.7)**	49	—		**30,000**	3	**11**
109.9	6		**(37.9)**	**0.4**	32	**132,458.0**	13	**9,523.7**	12	**7.7**	14	**9,314**	19	**12**
163.8		9	**(22.3)**	**0.6**	24	**133,965.0**	12	**(11,588.8)**	48	—		**3,653**	33	**13**
160.1		6	**(8.3)**	**0.7**	20	**35,361.5**	32	**1,410.1**	27	**4.2**	25	**15,637**	13	**14**
68.3		27	**(26.3)**	**0.3**	37	**93,569.6**	23	**56,766.5**	3	**154.2**	2	**2,900**	35	**15**
166.4		4	**19.2**	**0.8**	16	**108,363.0**	18	**6,370.4**	14	**6.2**	21	**17,500**	9	**16**
33.8		21	**66.6**	**0.2**	41	**29,296.1**	38	**2,183.7**	25	**8.1**	13	**8,221**	20	**17**
68.3		16	**(23.5)**	**0.4**	30	**1.8**	50	**(0.1)**	33	—		**1,834**	39	**18**
118.8	10		**(54.3)**	**0.7**	18	**72,932.3**	28	**2,574.6**	24	—		**6,802**	22	**19**
77.7	12		**61.8**	**0.5**	26	**84,296.4**	24	**2,885.6**	23	**3.3**	27	**6,473**	23	**20**
114.5		10	**9.3**	**0.7**	17	**220,546.7**	9	**23,559.1**	5	**12.0**	8	**19,893**	6	**21**
62.5		23	**(35.4)**	**0.4**	28	**33,828.6**	34	**(509.4)**	41	—		**2,709**	38	**22**
147.6		3	**65.8**	**1.0**	10	**127,148.4**	15	**(3,842.8)**	47	—		**1,142**	43	**23**
131.9		7	**44.7**	**1.0**	9	**44,790.7**	31	**1,213.0**	29	**2.8**	28	**17,406**	11	**24**
79.5	11		**2.2**	**0.7**	19	**34,300.5**	33	**3,065.0**	22	**9.8**	11	**4,160**	27	**25**

[7] Includes home office, field force, and full-time agents.
[8] Wholly owned by Aetna Life & Casualty (F-5).
[9] Wholly owned by Cigna (F-8).
[10] Wholly owned by Travelers Corp. (F-11).
[11] Wholly owned by American Express (F-2).
[12] Wholly owned by Sears Roebuck (R-1).
[13] Wholly owned by ITT (F-10).
[14] Wholly owned by American General (F-15).
[15] Wholly owned by Prudential Corp. PLC (No. 7 on last year's Life Insurance list on FORTUNE Global Service 500).

Source: Reprinted by permission from *FORTUNE magazine;* © 1993 Time Inc.

Companies That Rate Insurance Companies

Company	Telephone	Address
A.M. Best & Co.	908-439-2200	A.M. Best Road Oldwich, NJ 08858-9999
Duff & Phelps/ Credit Rating Co.	312-368-3157	55 East Monroe Street Chicago, IL 60603
Moody's Investor's Service, Inc.	212-553-0377	99 Church Street New York, NY 10007
Standard & Poor's Corp.	212-208-1527	25 Broadway New York, NY 10004
Weiss Research, Inc.	800-289-9222	P.O. 2923 West Palm Beach, FL 33402

The 25 Largest Commercial Banking Companies (ranked by assets)

RANK BY ASSETS 1992	1991		ASSETS[1] $ millions	% change from 1991	DEPOSITS $ millions	Rank	LOANS[2] $ millions	Rank	PROFITS $ millions	Rank	% change from 1991
1	1	**CITICORP** New York	213,701.0	(1.5)	144,175.0	1	135,851.0	1	722.0	7	—
2	3	**BANKAMERICA CORP.** San Francisco[3]	180,646.0	56.4	137,883.0	2	120,602.0	2	1,492.0	1	32.7
3	2	**CHEMICAL BANKING CORP.** New York	139,655.0	0.5	94,173.0	3	82,010.0	3	1,086.0	4	605.2
4	4	**NATIONSBANK CORP.** Charlotte, N.C.	118,059.3	7.0	82,726.5	4	72,714.0	4	1,145.2	3	466.9
5	5	**J.P. MORGAN & CO.** New York	102,941.0	(0.5)	32,519.0	12	25,180.0	12	1,382.0	2	20.6
6	6	**CHASE MANHATTAN CORP.** New York	95,862.0	(2.4)	67,224.0	5	60,645.0	5	639.0	8	22.9
7	8	**BANKERS TRUST NEW YORK CORP.** New York	72,448.0	13.3	25,071.0	22	15,698.0	27	761.0	6	14.1
8	12	**BANC ONE CORP.** Columbus, Ohio[4]	61,417.4	32.7	48,464.7	6	37,995.4	6	781.3	5	47.6
9	9	**WELLS FARGO & CO.** San Francisco	52,537.0	(1.9)	42,244.0	8	34,836.0	7	283.0	21	1,247.6
10	15	**PNC BANK CORP.** Pittsburgh[5]	51,379.9	14.5	29,469.5	15	24,919.7	13	426.9†	13	9.5
11	13	**FIRST UNION CORP.** Charlotte, N.C.	51,326.7	11.4	39,389.5	9	32,675.5	8	515.2	9	61.6
12	11	**FIRST INTERSTATE BANCORP** Los Angeles	50,863.1	4.0	43,674.5	7	23,133.2	15	282.3	22	—
13	10	**FIRST CHICAGO CORP.** Chicago	49,281.0	0.6	29,740.0	14	21,901.0	18	93.5	56	(19.6)
14	14	**FLEET FINANCIAL GROUP** Providence[6]	46,938.5	3.3	32,734.8	11	26,246.7	10	279.8	23	186.5
15	17	**NORWEST CORP.** Minneapolis	44,557.1	15.7	26,969.8	19	22,310.0	17	446.7†	10	12.1
16	24	**NBD BANCORP** Detroit[7]	40,937.2	38.7	31,000.8	13	24,725.9	14	300.1†	19	2.4
17	16	**BANK OF NEW YORK CO.** New York	40,909.0	3.8	29,449.0	16	26,388.0	9	369.0	15	202.4
18	20	**BARNETT BANKS** Jacksonville, Fla.[8]	39,464.8	20.6	34,688.6	10	25,503.1	11	207.7	30	67.7
19	22	**REPUBLIC NEW YORK CORP.** New York	37,146.4	19.0	21,102.2	26	7,766.4	43	258.9	26	13.9
20	18	**SUNTRUST BANKS** Atlanta	36,648.6	6.1	28,843.3	17	22,340.9	16	413.3	14	11.5
21	19	**WACHOVIA CORP.** Winston-Salem, N.C.	33,366.5	0.6	23,375.5	24	20,706.1	20	433.2	12	88.7
22	21	**BANK OF BOSTON CORP.** Boston	32,346.1	(1.1)	25,301.6	20	21,150.5	19	263.1**	25	—
23	25	**MELLON BANK CORP.** Pittsburgh	31,574.0	7.6	25,130.0	21	19,450.0	22	437.0	11	56.1
24	23	**FIRST FIDELITY BANCORP.** Lawrenceville, N.J.[9]	31,480.3	4.2	27,004.8	18	17,767.3	24	313.7	17	41.8
25	28	**KEYCORP** Albany, N.Y.[10]	30,114.1	30.1	24,775.1	23	19,734.4	21	290.9†	20	54.7

N.A. Not available.
• Not on last year's list.
** Reflects an extraordinary credit of at least 10%.
† Reflects on SFAS 106 and/or 109 charge of at least 10%.
‡ Reflects an SFAS 109 credit of at least 10%.
1 As of December 31, 1992, all companies on the list must have more than 80% of their assets in chartered commercial banking institutions.
2 Net of unearned discount and loan loss reserves. Figure includes lease financing.
3 Figures reflect acquisition of Security Pacific Corp. (No. 7 on last year's list), April 22, 1992.

TOTAL STOCK-HOLDERS' EQUITY		MARKET VALUE 4/16/93		PROFITS AS % OF				EARNINGS PER SHARE				TOTAL RETURN TO INVESTORS				EMPLOYEES		RANK
				ASSETS		COMMON STOCK-HOLDERS' EQUITY		1992	% change from 1991	1982-92 annual growth rate		1992		1982-92 annual rate				
$ millions	Rank	$ millions	Rank	%	Rank	%	Rank	$		%	Rank	%	Rank	%	Rank	Number	Rank	
11,181.0	2	10,994.6	5	0.3	91	6.5	81	1.35	—	(7.0)	73	114.5	8	8.6	80	81,000	2	1
15,488.0	1	18,693.8	1	0.8	63	10.6	65	4.24	(11.9)	3.4	47	33.4	58	12.5	73	83,235	1	2
9,851.0	3	10,233.0	6	0.8	68	11.7	58	3.90	3,445.5	(3.6)	69	89.1	14	11.6	75	39,687	4	3
7,813.7	4	14,104.2	3	1.0	43	14.4	33	4.60	505.3	11.2	13	30.7	61	23.0	26	50,828	3	4
7,066.0	5	14,250.4	2	1.3	7	20.7	4	6.92	19.3	11.3	12	(0.6)	89	19.6	45	14,368	22	5
6,511.0	6	5,761.2	14	0.7	75	10.2	67	3.46	10.9	(1.1)	63	73.1	18	9.0	77	34,540	5	6
3,809.0	10	6,453.8	12	1.1	27	22.1	2	8.82	13.8	7.8	26	12.4	82	19.6	46	12,917	26	7
5,213.5	7	13,808.9	4	1.3	12	15.4	19	3.28	12.7	12.7	6	13.9	80	21.6	35	32,700	6	8
3,809.0	9	6,622.9	10	0.5	87	7.4	79	4.25	10,525.0	3.9	44	35.7	50	24.4	18	21,300	11	9
3,745.6	11	8,023.8	8	0.8	62	11.3	59	1.90	(51.9)	(2.9)	67	26.1	66	19.0	52	17,809	17	10
3,831.7	8	8,350.9	7	1.0	31	13.7	35	3.72	45.9	10.0	16	50.4	34	22.1	31	23,459	10	11
3,251.1	14	4,585.8	18	0.6	86	8.5	75	3.23	—	(4.9)	72	60.6	24	10.2	76	27,667	8	12
3,401.0	13	3,591.7	25	0.2	94	1.8	84	0.64	(44.3)	(15.2)	78	56.6	29	13.8	68	16,998	19	13
3,010.4	16	4,838.1	16	0.6	84	10.5	66	1.78	165.7	1.3	57	35.5	51	19.4	49	27,500	9	14
3,072.7	15	7,594.7	9	1.0	33	15.3	20	3.48	18.0	13.0	5	21.5	72	23.7	23	28,993	7	15
2,940.9	17	5,593.5	15	0.7	70	10.2	68	1.87	(24.9)	6.6	33	14.0	79	27.1	10	18,543	15	16
3,515.0	12	4,831.4	17	0.9	53	10.8	62	4.45	247.7	2.7	50	81.0	16	18.8	53	14,130	23	17
2,556.1	21	4,566.4	19	0.5	88	8.1	78	1.97	15.2	2.5	54	27.4	65	17.1	59	20,737	12	18
2,263.4	23	2,707.4	31	0.7	73	13.5	38	4.42	11.9	6.6	32	2.6	87	14.1	67	4,900	55	19
2,703.5	19	6,118.6	13	1.1	23	15.3	22	3.28	13.1	10.5	14	12.6	81	19.8	42	18,956	13	20
2,774.8	18	6,521.0	11	1.3	9	15.6	13	5.02	87.3	13.7	4	21.3	74	22.0	34	16,164	21	21
2,230.6	25	2,266.6	37	0.8	64	13.6	36	2.96	458.5	2.9	49	122.6	7	13.7	69	16,900	20	22
2,557.0	20	3,483.3	26	1.4	6	18.5	6	6.96	49.4	0.2	59	57.1	28	9.0	78	18,000	16	23
2,257.6	24	3,696.1	24	1.0	38	14.4	31	3.89	15.4	—		40.1	43	17.3	58	10,600	32	24
2,074.8	27	4,397.0	20	1.0	44	14.4	32	3.17	23.3	11.8	10	34.4	54	29.6	4	17,500	18	25

[4] Figures reflect acquisition of Team Bancshares (No. 90 on last year's list), November 30, 1992.
[5] Name changed from PNC Financial Corp. (No. 15 on last year's list).
[6] Name changed from Fleet/Norstar Financial Group. (No. 14 on last year's list).
[7] Figures reflect acquisition of INB Financial Corp. (No. 80 on last year's list), October 15, 1992.
[8] Figures reflect acquisition of First Florida Banks (No. 89 on last year's list), December 7, 1992.
[9] Figures reflect acquisition of Howard Savings Bank (No. 32 on last year's Savings list).
[10] Figures reflect acquisition of Puget Sound Bancorp (No. 98 on last year's list), January 15, 1993.

Source: Reprinted by permission from *FORTUNE magazine;* © 1993 Time Inc.

The 100 Largest Brokerage Houses*

Rank 1991	Rank 1992	Firm	Total Consolidated Capital ($ millions)	Equity Capital ($ millions)	Long-Term Debt ($ millions)	'Excess' Net Capital ($ millions)	Total Assets ($ millions)
1	1	**Merrill Lynch & Co.**[1]	$15,500.0	$4,600.0	$10,900.0	$1,721.2	$106,000.0
2	2	**Salomon Inc.**	12,841.0	4,308.0	8,533.0	1,201.5	159,459.0
3	3	**Shearson Lehman Brothers**	10,041.0	2,361.0	7,680.0	771.0	85,232.0
4	4	**Goldman, Sachs & Co.**[2]	8,999.0	3,714.0	5,285.0	834.0	83,174.0
5	5	**Morgan Stanley Group**[3]	6,369.0	3,203.0	3,166.0	483.7	76,044.0
8	6	**CS First Boston**	3,024.0	1,069.0	1,955.0	609.0	41,399.0
7	7	**Bear, Stearns & Co.**	2,613.6	1,330.0	1,283.6	688.1	58,155.0
6	8	**PaineWebber**	2,232.0	1,081.0	1,151.0	517.0	26,509.0
10	9	**Prudential Securities**	1,618.0	1,144.0	474.0	564.0	21,572.0
9	10	**Dean Witter Reynolds**	1,336.0	1,036.0	300.0	423.0	11,281.0
11	11	**Smith Barney, Harris Upham & Co.**	1,160.0	895.0	265.0	363.0	9,841.0
12	12	**Donaldson, Lufkin & Jenrette**	1,148.0	455.0	693.0	248.0	22,516.0
16	13	**Shelby Cullom Davis & Co.**	791.0	791.0	—	601.4	2,527.0
15	14	**J.P. Morgan Securities**	782.0	532.0	250.0	436.0	25,000.0
13	15	**Kidder, Peabody & Co.**	776.0	515.0	261.0	405.0	55,180.0
14	16	**Nomura Securities International**	653.7	203.7	450.0	192.4	36,551.7
17	17	**BT Securities Corp.**	647.0	425.0	222.0	308.0	19,128.0
19	18	**A.G. Edwards & Sons**	593.0	593.0	—	348.0	1,862.0
18	19	**UBS Securities**	578.0	253.0	325.0	139.0	12,200.0
25	20	**Charles Schwab & Co.**[4]	357.8	202.6	155.2	157.7	5,823.0
22	21	**Citicorp Securities Markets**	350.0	205.0	145.0	228.0	5,811.0
26	22	**Greenwich Capital Markets**	347.0	152.0	195.0	200.0	18,000.0
20	23	**Chemical Securities**	346.0	346.0	—	289.0	9,466.0
21	24	**Daiwa Securities America**	343.2	193.2	150.0	166.2	24,253.5
24	25	**Deutsche Bank Capital Corp.**	300.0	104.0	196.0	159.0	7,697.0
28		**Van Kampen Merritt**	300.0	300.0	—	47.0	469.0
23	27	**Kemper Securities Group**	284.7	240.4	44.3	63.3	1,721.0
27	28	**Aubrey G. Lanston & Co.**	261.0	261.0	—	136.0	1,165.0
29	29	**Oppenheimer & Co.**	257.0	199.0	58.0	94.0	6,068.0
34	30	**Alex. Brown & Sons**	248.0	228.0	20.0	192.0	1,023.0
30	31	**Yamaichi International (America)**	247.0	147.0	100.0	185.0	15,790.0
37	32	**Chase Securities**	226.0	226.0	—	184.0	4,639.0
31		**Spear, Leeds & Kellogg**	226.0	175.0	51.0	82.0	3,009.0
32	34	**John Nuveen & Co.**	211.0	211.0	—	163.0	294.0
38	35	**Fidelity Brokerage Services**	209.2	209.2	—	131.7	2,533.2
35	36	**Dillon, Read & Co.**	205.4	175.4	30.0	69.0	3,806.2
39	37	**Legg Mason Inc.**	203.2	168.6	34.6	73.6	681.4
33	38	**Allen & Co.**	202.0	202.0	—	62.2	476.5
43	39	**Edward D. Jones & Co.**	199.0	121.0	78.0	132.0	598.0
36	40	**Nikko Securities Co. International**	196.0	96.0	100.0	99.0	10,666.0
40	41	**Gruntal Financial Corp.**	186.6	159.5	27.1	60.5	1,425.9
42	42	**Sanwa-BGK Securities**	177.5	127.5	50.0	90.0	13,317.2
46	43	**Barclays de Zoete Wedd Securities**	171.0	121.0	50.0	150.0	11,460.0
47	44	**Raymond James Financial**	169.0	169.0	—	154.0	818.0
66	45	**D.H. Blair & Co.**	168.0	168.0	—	41.0	218.0
—	46	**Fuji Securities**	158.2	108.2	50.0	117.9	6,338.4
41	47	**Wertheim Schroder & Co.**	157.2	143.6	13.6	63.2	4,180.5
45	48	**M.A. Schapiro & Co.**	154.2	154.2	—	96.3	514.4
50	49	**Quick & Reilly Group**[2]	153.1	152.7	0.4	84.8	1,314.1
52	50	**Jefferies & Co.**	137.6	96.6	41.0	66.7	531.0

* The rankings are based on information supplied by the nation's 200 leading securities firms in response to questionnaires and follow-up phone calls. Where applicable the totals for U.S. commercial banks reflect only their domestic securities affiliates. All figures are for year-end 1992 unless otherwise noted.

The 100 Largest Brokerage Houses *(concluded)*

Rank 1991	Rank 1992	Firm	Total Consolidated Capital ($ millions)	Equity Capital ($ millions)	Long-Term Debt ($ millions)	'Excess' Net Capital ($ millions)	Total Assets ($ millions)
51	51	Brown Brothers Harriman & Co.	$131.0	$131.0	$ —	$ —	$1,340.6
49	52	S.G. Warburg & Co.	129.0	129.0	—	41.0	6,540.0
44	53	Neuberger & Berman	125.0	125.0	—	56.0	1,686.0
48		Stephens	125.0	125.0	—	54.0	471.0
53	55	Arnhold & S. Bleichroeder	123.0	112.0	11.0	79.0	3,071.0
56	56	Piper, Jaffray Cos.[5]	120.0	120.0	—	53.0	481.0
58	57	First Chicago Capital Markets	117.0	82.0	35.0	74.0	4,634.0
55	58	Glickenhaus & Co.	111.0	111.0	—	59.0	459.0
—	59	NYLife Securities	106.0	106.0	—	34.0	137.0
—	60	Toronto Dominion Securities (USA)[3]	103.0	18.0	85.0	99.0	407.0
54	61	Lazard Frères & Co.	100.0	100.0	—	28.0	NA
59	62	Janney Montgomery Scott	93.2	74.2	19.0	55.8	368.1
61	63	Cowen & Co.	93.1	72.6	20.5	30.9	1,023.0
68	64	Dain Bosworth	93.0	88.0	5.0	46.0	910.0
63	65	Tucker Anthony/John Hancock Clearing Corp.	92.8	92.8	—	41.0	919.3
85	66	SBCI Swiss Bank Corp. Investment Banking	92.0	42.0	50.0	25.0	369.0
60	67	J.C. Bradford & Co.	90.6	90.6	—	31.0	599.5
67	68	S.D. Securities	88.4	88.4	—	61.2	209.6
75	69	Morgan Keegan & Co.	88.0	88.0	—	56.0	495.0
70	70	Bernard L. Madoff Investment Securities	86.5	86.5	—	42.8	328.7
65	71	Furman Selz	85.0	80.0	5.0	17.9	218.0
72	72	McDonald & Co. Securities	80.2	80.2	—	26.6	438.4
64	73	Herzog Heine Geduld	78.0	53.0	25.0	29.0	596.0
74	74	Wheat, First Securities	77.0	77.0	—	34.9	507.7
73	75	Montgomery Securities	76.1	45.2	30.9	44.5	270.4
69	76	Interstate/Johnson Lane Corp.	72.3	50.3	22.0	26.9	391.4
70	77	Mabon Securities Corp.	67.9	40.9	27.0	15.8	1,681.7
77	78	Robert W. Baird & Co.	64.0	64.0	—	14.4	384.0
76	79	Weiss, Peck & Greer	60.0	47.0	13.0	14.0	402.0
78	80	Chicago Corp.	59.3	43.1	16.2	28.0	606.5
83	81	Fahnestock & Co.	58.2	45.6	12.6	44.0	315.3
62	82	Advest	58.0	58.0	—	25.0	393.0
79	83	Miller Tabak Hirsch & Co.	53.3	53.3	—	3.1	54.5
80	84	Easton & Co.	51.0	51.0	—	44.6	NA
87	85	J.J.B. Hilliard, W.L. Lyons	50.1	46.5	3.6	17.4	151.6
81	86	William Blair & Co.	50.0	50.0	—	30.8	158.6
92		Rauscher Pierce Refsnes	50.0	50.0	—	21.0	352.0
84	88	The Principal/Eppler, Guerin & Turner	48.0	48.0	—	18.0	168.0
88	89	Sanford C. Bernstein & Co.	47.9	47.9	—	26.9	705.4
85	90	ScotiaMcLeod (USA)	47.0	47.0	—	15.0	1,977.0
91	91	Crowell, Weedon & Co.	46.7	41.1	5.6	18.6	105.2
90	92	ABD Securities Corp.	42.0	42.0	—	17.0	235.0
101	93	BHC Securities	40.1	25.1	15.0	25.8	386.0
82	94	Hambrecht & Quist	40.0	40.0	—	15.0	127.0
95	95	Smith New Court, Carl Marks	38.8	38.8	—	8.8	197.5
95	96	Kankaku Securities (America)	38.0	38.0	—	31.0	39.0
98	97	Commerzbank Capital Markets Corp.	37.0	22.0	15.0	26.0	205.0
97		C.J. Lawrence	37.0	37.0	—	22.0	52.0
99	99	Wedbush Morgan Securities	36.4	36.1	0.3	29.0	409.1
89	100	Crédit Lyonnais Securities (USA)	35.0	35.0	—	8.0	51.0
94		Stifel Nicolaus & Co.	35.0	35.0	—	13.0	273.0

[1] Unaudited 12/25/92.
[2] As of 11/27/92.
[3] As of 10/31/92.
[4] Unaudited.
[5] As of 9/25/92.

Source: "Ranking America's Biggest Brokers" from April 1993 issue of *Institutional Investor;* reprinted by permission.

America's Most Admired Corporations*

THE MOST ADMIRED
The top three remain in place. Old-timers Morgan and Boeing—the only companies that don't sell consumer goods—return, replacing PepsiCo and Johnson & Johnson.

RANK	LAST YEAR	COMPANY	SCORE
1	1	**Merck** Pharmaceuticals	8.74
2	2	**Rubbermaid** Rubber and plastics products	8.58
3	3	**Wal-Mart Stores** Retailing	8.42
4	8	**3M** Scientific, photo & control equipment	8.41
5	7	**Coca-Cola** Beverages	8.19
6	9	**Procter & Gamble** Soaps, cosmetics	8.09
7	5	**Levi Strauss Associates** Apparel	7.96
8	4	**Liz Claiborne** Apparel	7.95
9	15	**J.P. Morgan** Commercial banking	7.93
10	12	**Boeing** Aerospace	7.88

* HOW IT WAS DONE. This Corporate Reputations Survey includes 311 companies in 32 industries that appeared in the 1992 FORTUNE 500 and FORTUNE Service 500 directories. Over 8,000 senior executives, outside directors, and financial analysts were asked to rate the 10 largest companies in their own industry (or sometimes a shorter list) on eight attributes of reputation, using a scale of zero (poor) to ten (excellent).

FORTUNE 500 companies are assigned to a group based on the activity that contributed most to their 1991 industrial sales; Service 500 companies to a group based on the activity contributing most to their service sales.

In addition, the survey firm of Clark Martire & Bartolomeo examined the relationship between poll data and the financial performance of the companies, as published in the FORTUNE 500 and Service 500 directories. Twelve measures of performance were combined with the survey data into a spread-sheet. (Insurance companies were excluded because their data were incompatible.) A multiple regression was run to analyze the relationship between financial performance and the reputation score. The resulting equation was used to predict a reputation score based solely on financial performance.

Source: FORTUNE, "America's Most Admired Corporations,"

America's Best 100 Growth Companies[1]

Rank			Ranking Data				Current Results				Valuation			
			Five-year average		EPS		Latest 12-month			Debt as	Recent	P/E	Price/	Market
This year	Last year	**Company** *Business*	EPS growth	return on equity	1992 (actual)	1993 (est.)	sales (mil.)	profits (mil.)	return on equity	% of equity	stock price	1993 (est.)	book value	value (mil.)
1	2	**Microsoft**	50%	32%	$2.41	$3.12	$3,252	$834	36%	1%	$82.75	26.5	8.4	$22,761
		Makes and markets a variety of computer software, mainly for applications and operating systems												
2	NR	**Techne**	46	20	0.21	0.48	25	4	31	1	15.00	31.3	9.1	135
		Manufactures and sells hematology and biotechnology products for clinical diagnostics market												
3	NR	**SciMed Life Systems**	114	28	3.22E	4.02	211	48	33	6	46.25	11.5	4.1	694
		Designs and makes disposable medical products for treatment of cardiovascular diseases												
4	3	**Ballard Medical Products**	41	26	0.49	0.67	53	15	30	0	17.00	25.4	7.3	447
		Makes disposable medical products for use in critical care and surgical medicine												
5	4	**Novell**	57	24	0.82	1.06	989	268	30	0	30.25	28.5	9.8	9,094
		Produces local area network software, systems and related products												
6	9	**Surgical Care Affiliates**	76	19	0.78	1.04	225	29	25	27	20.88	20.1	6.4	763
		Owns and operates independent surgical centers and owns a health maintenance organization												
7	5	**Rotech Medical**	147	21	0.60	0.75	43	4	24	5	13.25	17.7	4.3	102
		Provides health infusion therapy, home respiratory care and related medical services and equipment												
8	11	**US Surgical**	44	22	2.32	2.99	1,197	138	28	67	59.13	19.8	5.6	3,282
		Makes and markets surgical staples, sutures and laparoscopic surgery products												
9	NR	**PCA International**	28	48	1.03	1.37	159	9	55	0	15.50	11.3	5.2	124
		Producer of color portrait packages operating under license in department and discount stores												
10	NR	**Fastenal**	34	24	0.47	0.63	81	9	27	0	22.50	35.7	11.9	427
		Operates stores selling fasteners and other industrial and construction supplies												
11	20	**US HealthCare**	140	27	1.84	2.21	2,189	200	45	0	42.50	19.2	9.0	4,564
		Owns and operates health maintenance organizations and provides managed-care services												
12	13	**Jean Philippe Fragrances**	26	24	0.48	0.70	38	4	33	0	16.75	23.9	9.6	159
		Makes and distributes cosmetics and fragrances including brand names, proprietary fragrances and copies of designer perfumes												

NR: not rated. E: estimate. Sources: William O'Neil & Co.; Infovest via Global Investment Technologies; First Call via Thomson Financial Services.

(continued)

[1] HOW THE BEST WERE CHOSEN

FOR A COMPANY TO MAKE FW'S AMERICA'S BEST 200 Growth Companies list it must not only have posted stellar results in the past, but it also must have great potential. How did we find such firms.

We began screening Los Angeles-based William O'Neil & Co.'s data base of over 6,500 listings for firms incorporated in the U.S. that have been publicly traded for at least five years and have a stock price of $2 or more. In a stock market overrun by new equity offerings, these two criteria left us with 3,178 companies.

Then we tossed out firms whose earnings per share have not grown by more than 12% annually over the past five years. After all, growing the bottom line is the name of the game. Out went another 2,520 companies.

Next, firms whose sales have not increased over the past five years were dropped. We didn't want companies that had grown earnings simply by cutting costs. Such growth is typically short-lived. This narrowed the list to 609 issues.

Next we looked forward in time. We required that a company's per-share earnings during the latest 12 months be greater than the comparable figures one year ago. Then we used Boston-based First Call, a unit of Thomson Financial Services, a service that collates earnings forecasts from 70 North American brokerage firms, to see what the analysts were expecting. We only kept those companies for which the consensus earnings growth in 1993 versus 1992 was at least 10%. That left only 260 candidates.

To ensure that a company was improving steadily, we stipulated that its return on equity over the most recent four quarters not be lower than its five-year average, and that its debt-to-equity ratio be less than 150%. We then sorted the remaining 207 companies by five-year average ROE and removed the seven lowest. (Note: Companies whose financials are fully consolidated by another U.S. public firm, such as Marion Merrill Dow, were excluded from the survey.) A few more specifics to clarify our methodology follow.

FW's rankings were determined by three equally weighted yardsticks: five-year annual EPS growth, five-year average return on equity and 1993 projected EPS growth. If more than one company had the same final score, tiebreakers were used. These were five-year annual sales growth, 12-month ROE and 12-month EPS growth, in that order.

Stock prices and all pricing information are as of the March 5 close. A company's per-share information has been adjusted for any stock splits with ex-dates on or before the date of this issue, April 27. Any company's fiscal year that ends prior to June will have its earnings shifted to the previous year. For example, SciMed Life Systems' fiscal year ends in February, so the firm's February 1993 EPS estimate of $3.22 falls under the 1992 column and has an "E" next to it, designating that figure as an estimate.

Taken as a group, the companies on FW's Best 200 tables enjoyed a median five-year EPS growth rate of 24% per year, a five-year average ROE of 16% and are expected to grow EPS 21% this year over last.

While these shares are a tad expensive—they trade for 17.4 times 1993's estimated earnings, versus a p/e of 16 for the overall market—they are probably well worth it. Indeed, last year's Best 200 Growth Companies (FW, Aug. 4, 1992) went up an average of 17.7%. In contrast, the Wilshire 5000 index, a measure of the overall stock market, rose only 11.5%.

America's Best 100 Growth Companies *(continued)*

Rank This year	Rank Last year	Company *Business*	Ranking Data: Five-year average EPS growth	Ranking Data: Five-year average return on equity	Ranking Data: EPS 1992 (actual)	Ranking Data: EPS 1993 (est.)	Current Results: Latest 12-month sales (mil.)	Current Results: Latest 12-month profits (mil.)	Current Results: Latest 12-month return on equity	Current Results: Debt as % of equity	Valuation: Recent stock price	Valuation: P/E 1993 (est.)	Valuation: Price/book value	Valuation: Market value (mil.)
13	NR	**HealthCare Compare** *Provides health care utilization services, preferred-provider organization services and cost management*	58	16	0.83	1.21	134	30	27	0	19.88	16.4	5.8	675
14	NR	**Blockbuster Entertainment** *Owns and franchises videotape rental and sales stores*	62	19	0.77	0.98	1,201	142	23	23	18.63	19.0	5.0	3,520
15	NR	**Sierra Health Services** *Owns and operates a health maintenance organization, a life and health insurance company and a multispecialty medical group*	59	25	1.19	1.45	236	14	48	23	14.88	10.3	5.1	181
16	15	**Buffets** *Owns and franchises buffet-style restaurants under the Old Country Buffet name*	38	21	1.03	1.32	248	15	26	6	30.50	23.1	6.8	442
17	12	**Biomet** *Makes and sells joint-reconstruction implants, electrical bone-growth stimulators and other medical products*	39	22	0.58E	0.73	306	58	24	0	13.00	17.8	5.7	1,494
18	6	**Utah Medical Products** *Makes disposable medical products for respiratory care, intravenous therapy and cardiac catheterization*	64	31	0.60	0.71	36	7	34	0	11.33	15.9	5.8	177
19	52	**Atlantic Southeast Air** *Largest regional airline in southeastern U.S.*	34	21	1.08	1.37	236	37	23	81	28.75	21.0	5.8	980
20	17	**Home Depot** *Operates retail warehouse stores selling building and home improvement products*	38	19	0.82	1.09	7,148	363	19	39	47.50	43.6	9.6	20,931
21	NR	**Quantum** *Makes and markets hard disk drives for personal computers, workstations and storage enhancement*	30	21	1.76E	2.24	1,536	85	25	59	15.13	6.8	1.8	649
22	21	**Linear Technology** *Makes integrated circuits for industrial process control, military, measurement and data processing applications*	37	18	0.69	0.92	132	30	23	1	23.00	25.0	5.7	805
23	NR	**Research Industries** *Makes disposable cardiovascular surgery products and pharmaceuticals*	63	14	0.44	0.60	21	5	20	0	11.25	18.8	3.9	103
24	27	**MedStat Group** *Provides insurance companies with data bases and software systems that help control health insurance costs and improve health care quality*	27	20	0.48	0.66	36	3	24	5	22.50	34.1	9.1	125
25	NR	**NovaCare** *Provides rehabilitative speech, physical and occupational therapy services to health care institutions*	51	14	0.75	1.08	455	43	18	74	17.13	15.9	3.3	843
26	NR	**Insituform Mid-America** *Installs and repairs pipelines using trenchless insituform, tile liner and tunneling machine systems*	53	20	0.71	0.87	70	8	24	1	16.50	19.0	5.0	177
27	NR	**Empi** *Makes electrical nerve-stimulation devices for pain control, as well as neuromuscular stimulation devices for muscle tone and mobility*	69%	12%	$0.95	$1.54	$33	$4	19%	0%	$36.50	23.7	6.3	$145
28	NR	**Quality Food Centers** *Largest independent supermarket chain in Seattle area*	40	26	1.28	1.53	480	25	28	0	29.25	19.1	5.6	561
29	NR	**Minntech** *Makes medical devices and sterilants for kidney dialysis and open-heart surgery and water-filtration products for lab and medical use*	68	16	0.73E	0.91	43	5	22	9	15.00	16.5	4.1	90
30	NR	**Conseco** *Holding company for National Life Insurance and five other annuity-writing insurance companies*	50	25	4.41	5.18	1,526	175	36	29	67.00	12.9	3.3	1,936
31	NR	**Synalloy** *Produces stainless steel pipes, process equipment and dyes, specialty chemicals and pigments*	42	19	1.15	1.43	102	6	21	7	24.50	17.1	4.1	147
32	NR	**Merry-Go-Round Enterprises** *Operates fashion apparel stores targeting young men and women*	25	18	0.71	1.06	878	38	18	27	13.75	13.0	3.3	734
33	NR	**Hutchinson Technology** *Makes suspension assemblies for hard disk drives and components for printers and control systems*	81	11	2.72	3.85	176	16	24	14	40.75	10.6	2.5	215
34	NR	**Intel** *Makes semiconductor components and related single-board computers, microcomputer systems and software for OEM market*	21	18	5.03	8.04	5,844	1,067	21	5	115.75	14.4	4.4	24,093
35	24	**Wal-Mart Stores** *Operates discount department stores throughout the U.S.*	25	25	0.86	1.06	55,985	1,995	27	55	32.75	30.9	9.4	75,275
36	NR	**Medical Technology System** *Supplies dispensing systems, forms and labels and provides clinical diagnostic services to health care industry*	28	16	0.58E	0.80	14	2	18	33	9.50	11.9	2.8	37
37	32	**Unifi** *Sells polyester, nylon, spandex and dyed yarns to knitters and weavers in apparel, industrial and home furnishing markets*	18	20	1.04	1.59	1,121	90	22	57	33.63	21.2	4.6	2,008
38	106	**Sunrise Medical** *Makes and markets products used in patient recovery and rehabilitation*	43	13	0.93	1.24	285	15	16	30	24.63	19.9	3.1	398
39	NR	**Mylan Laboratories** *Leading producer of prescription drugs under generic names*	19	20	0.89E	1.17	190	62	27	2	29.75	25.4	8.9	2,306
40	47	**Cracker Barrel Old Country** *Operates restaurants and gift stores in southeastern U.S.*	36	14	0.60	0.79	462	39	18	18	29.00	37.0	6.9	1,710
41	NR	**Komag** *Leading supplier of thin-film data storage disks for use in Winchester disk drives*	83	6	0.78	1.39	327	17	8	4	23.25	16.7	2.1	482

NR: not rated. E: estimate. | *Sources: William O'Neil & Co.; Infovest via Global Investment Technologies; First Call via Thomson Financial Services.*

Rank This year	Rank Last year	Company / Business	Ranking Data: Five-year average EPS growth	Ranking Data: Five-year average return on equity	Ranking Data: EPS 1992 (actual)	Ranking Data: EPS 1993 (est.)	Current Results: Latest 12-month sales (mil.)	Current Results: Latest 12-month profits (mil.)	Current Results: Latest 12-month return on equity	Current Results: Debt as % of equity	Valuation: Recent stock price	Valuation: P/E 1993 (est.)	Valuation: Price/ book value	Valuation: Market value (mil.)
42	**48**	**Stryker** *Makes power surgical instruments, patient-handling equipment and other medical products*	**28**	**17**	**1.00**	**1.25**	**477**	**48**	**24**	**0**	**26.00**	**20.8**	**5.8**	**1,239**
43	**NR**	**Continental Medical Systems** *Operates outpatient centers, rehabilitation hospitals and provides contract therapy services*	**49**	**10**	**0.72**	**1.04**	**778**	**31**	**13**	**120**	**12.13**	**11.7**	**1.7**	**416**
44	**NR**	**SunAmerica** *Sells life insurance and other financial services*	**56**	**8**	**1.80**	**2.88**	**867**	**85**	**13**	**54**	**38.00**	**13.2**	**2.5**	**1,216**
45	**128**	**Meridian Diagnostics** *Makes and markets immunodiagnostic test kits, reagents and related products for hospitals, laboratories and physicians' offices*	**47**	**10**	**0.23**	**0.33**	**14**	**2**	**15**	**12**	**11.00**	**33.3**	**8.1**	**84**
46	**NR**	**ShowBiz Pizza Time** *Operates and franchises pizza parlors and Tex-Mex style restaurants*	**57**	**14**	**1.11**	**1.38**	**253**	**16**	**14**	**9**	**32.00**	**23.2**	**3.1**	**404**
47	**44**	**Crompton & Knowles** *Makes and markets specialty sweeteners, dyes, flavors, food colors, fragrance formulations and pharmaceutical coatings*	**27**	**24**	**0.88**	**1.05**	**518**	**43**	**28**	**45**	**23.00**	**21.9**	**6.6**	**1,167**
48	**NR**	**Fruit of the Loom** *Maker of underwear, active wear and fleece wear*	**24**	**20**	**2.48**	**3.05**	**1,855**	**189**	**25**	**96**	**46.25**	**15.2**	**4.1**	**3,475**
49	**NR**	**Gendex** *Designs and makes dental and medical X-ray systems*	**27**	**13**	**1.37E**	**1.96**	**135**	**12**	**19**	**19**	**42.00**	**21.4**	**6.2**	**424**
50	**NR**	**Insituform Technologies** *Repairs and reconstructs pipelines and sewers using insituform process*	**41**	**10**	**0.81E**	**1.23**	**41**	**5**	**11**	**12**	**25.00**	**20.3**	**3.9**	**215**
51	**38**	**Philip Morris** *Largest maker of cigarettes, second-largest U.S. brewer and major producer of food products*	**24**	**30**	**5.45**	**6.46**	**59,131**	**4,939**	**39**	**118**	**64.63**	**10.0**	**4.6**	**57,929**
52	**71**	**Brinker International** *Owns and operates restaurant franchises in 39 states and Canada*	**30**	**14**	**1.15**	**1.47**	**576**	**41**	**16**	**1**	**46.25**	**31.5**	**4.6**	**1,336**
53	**NR**	**Hon Industries** *Makes office furniture and products, computer accessories and related items*	**16**	**24**	**1.18**	**1.48**	**707**	**39**	**25**	**34**	**28.38**	**19.2**	**5.9**	**919**
54	**NR**	**Artistic Greetings** *Sells stationery, greeting cards and gift items via mail order*	**41**	**15**	**0.60**	**0.73**	**70**	**4**	**21**	**12**	**9.63**	**13.2**	**3.1**	**56**
55	**36**	**Mail Boxes Etc** *Largest franchisor of neighborhood postal and business services in U.S.*	**26**	**17**	**0.57E**	**0.71**	**40**	**7**	**17**	**0**	**13.13**	**18.5**	**3.5**	**160**
56	**NR**	**PDA Engineering** *Develops and markets software for engineering applications*	**40%**	**13%**	**$0.36**	**$0.45**	**$40**	**$4**	**16%**	**0%**	**$9.50**	**21.1**	**3.2**	**$88**
57	**NR**	**Ark Restaurants** *Owns and operates restaurants in New York metropolitan area*	**108**	**9**	**0.48**	**0.60**	**51**	**2**	**14**	**8**	**7.25**	**12.1**	**1.8**	**22**
58	**NR**	**System Software** *Develops, markets and supports business application software for IBM computers*	**43**	**28**	**0.99**	**1.11**	**226**	**20**	**28**	**4**	**12.63**	**11.4**	**4.2**	**334**
59	**NR**	**Albertson's** *Sixth-largest food and drugstore chain in the U.S.*	**16**	**21**	**2.09**	**2.63**	**10,174**	**276**	**22**	**45**	**54.13**	**20.6**	**5.5**	**7,161**
60	**NR**	**Amgen** *Develops health care products*	**204**	**17**	**2.10**	**2.41**	**1,093**	**358**	**47**	**14**	**33.25**	**13.8**	**5.8**	**4,497**
61	**16**	**St Jude Medical** *Makes and markets biomedical devices for cardiovascular applications*	**37**	**25**	**2.12**	**2.43**	**240**	**102**	**27**	**0**	**34.00**	**14.0**	**4.0**	**1,614**
62	**97**	**Invacare** *Manufactures respiratory equipment, wheelchairs, beds and other outpatient aids*	**42**	**15**	**1.25**	**1.51**	**305**	**18**	**19**	**0**	**24.75**	**16.4**	**3.6**	**353**
63	**31**	**Gainsco** *Property and casualty insurer*	**28**	**20**	**0.80**	**0.94**	**86**	**13**	**26**	**0**	**18.38**	**19.6**	**5.7**	**291**
64	**62**	**Schering-Plough** *Makes drugs, skin-care, foot-care and animal health care products*	**21**	**33**	**3.60**	**4.22**	**4,056**	**720**	**50**	**12**	**58.88**	**14.0**	**7.7**	**11,720**
65	**63**	**UST Inc** *Leading producer of smokeless tobacco, wine, pipes and tobacco-related products*	**19**	**46**	**1.39**	**1.64**	**1,044**	**313**	**65**	**0**	**28.13**	**17.2**	**12.4**	**5,859**
66	**165**	**Green Tree Financial** *Buys, pools, sells and services conditional sales contracts on houses and home improvements*	**34**	**20**	**2.38**	**2.75**	**247**	**72**	**28**	**100**	**34.00**	**12.4**	**3.6**	**1,032**
67	**96**	**McCormick** *Produces spices, flavorings, seasonings and convenience foods for retail and food processing markets*	**38**	**17**	**1.13**	**1.33**	**1,471**	**95**	**23**	**46**	**25.75**	**19.4**	**4.7**	**2,065**
68	**NR**	**Dallas Semiconductor** *Designs, makes and markets high-performance integrated circuits*	**37**	**12**	**0.71**	**0.90**	**120**	**19**	**15**	**0**	**15.00**	**16.7**	**2.9**	**366**
69	**109**	**Dahlberg** *Makes and sells hearing aids and related products through owned, franchised and service centers*	**48**	**13**	**0.76**	**0.92**	**89**	**5**	**17**	**3**	**23.13**	**25.1**	**4.6**	**139**
70	**30**	**Raymond James Financial** *Provides brokerage, investment banking, financial planning and other investment advisory services*	**51**	**21**	**2.81**	**3.10**	**374**	**43**	**27**	**8**	**22.13**	**7.1**	**2.0**	**314**
71	**82**	**Coca-Cola** *World's largest producer of soft drink concentrates, syrups, juices and juice drinks*	**18**	**35**	**1.45**	**1.71**	**13,074**	**1,884**	**43**	**22**	**42.88**	**25.1**	**12.2**	**56,169**

NR: not rated. E: estimate. Sources: William O'Neil & Co.; Infovest via Global Investment Technologies; First Call via Thomson Financial Services.

(continued)

America's Best 100 Growth Companies *(concluded)*

Rank This year	Rank Last year	**Company** *Business*	Ranking Data: Five-year average EPS growth	Ranking Data: Five-year average return on equity	Ranking Data: EPS 1992 (actual)	Ranking Data: EPS 1993 (est.)	Current Results: Latest 12-month sales (mil.)	Current Results: Latest 12-month profits (mil.)	Current Results: Latest 12-month return on equity	Current Results: Debt as % of equity	Valuation: Recent stock price	Valuation: P/E 1993 (est.)	Valuation: Price/book value	Valuation: Market value (mil.)
72	95	**Healthsouth Rehabilitation** *Operates outpatient and inpatient rehabilitation centers*	31	10	1.00	1.35	407	30	10	87	16.88	12.5	1.6	476
73	NR	**Syncor International** *Distributes radiopharmaceutical products to clinics and hospitals*	49	10	0.86E	1.07	233	8	15	9	17.25	16.1	3.0	173
74	NR	**Advo** *Largest direct-mail marketing company in U.S.*	25	17	0.89	1.08	816	21	21	0	23.25	21.5	3.7	391
75	34	**Anthem Electronics** *Markets advanced technology semiconductor and subsystem products*	31	16	2.48	2.96	538	30	18	0	37.75	12.8	2.6	453
76	67	**Bridgford Foods** *Makes and distributes refrigerated, frozen and snack food products*	24	24	0.56	0.65	100	5	24	0	17.00	26.2	6.6	160
77	NR	**A&W Brands** *Produces soft drink concentrates and juices*	38	16	1.11	1.30	131	16	18	0	20.63	15.9	3.2	290
78	61	**Adaptec** *Makes optical and tape storage devices and network file-servers*	53	12	1.92E	2.29	274	42	24	7	26.75	11.7	3.2	666
79	23	**Great Lakes Chemical** *World's leading producer of bromine, furfural derivatives and antiknock fuel additives*	23	19	3.27	3.88	1,538	233	24	7	78.00	20.1	5.3	5,551
80	37	**Merck** *Manufactures drugs for humans and animals, and makes specialty chemicals*	22	44	2.14	2.44	9,663	2,447	47	11	37.50	15.4	7.9	43,012
81	NR	**Osmonics** *Manufactures fluid processing equipment, systems and components using reverse osmosis*	29	13	0.68	0.84	51	5	15	41	17.75	21.1	3.3	107
82	NR	**Costar** *Makes disposable plastic products, membrane filters and filtration equipment for life science laboratories and industrial plants*	30	9	0.85	1.10	75	6	14	10	19.25	17.5	2.8	132
83	58	**Cooper Tire & Rubber** *Manufactures and sells car and truck tires, inner tubes, hoses and vibration-control products*	26	18	1.35	1.58	1,176	108	23	10	35.88	22.7	5.9	2,995
84	NR	**InterVoice** *Designs and sells intervoice systems to access computer data bases via touch-tone telephone or verbal commands*	25	11	0.86E	1.13	42	7	16	0	16.13	14.3	3.1	126
85	NR	**TriMas** *Makes specialty containers, towing systems, fasteners and precision tools for industrial use*	26%	18%	$1.76	$2.06	$388	$30	18%	80%	$32.63	15.8	2.2	$471
86	93	**Forest Laboratories** *Develops, makes and sells branded and generic drugs*	24	13	1.41E	1.76	285	60	16	0	34.13	19.4	3.4	1,426
87	NR	**X-Rite** *Produces quality-control instruments for photographic, medical, packaging, finishing and other industries worldwide*	14	18	0.67	0.85	36	7	23	0	24.25	28.5	7.8	253
88	49	**Heartland Express** *Trucking for medium-haul, irregular routes*	24	24	1.16	1.33	97	12	24	0	31.00	23.3	6.2	310
89	99	**Paychex** *Provides computerized payroll accounting services to small businesses*	15	20	0.98E	1.20	175	17	24	2	39.00	32.5	10.1	772
90	151	**Air Express International** *Provides air freight forwarding services and acts as cargo agent for airlines*	19	22	1.60	1.87	672	19	32	15	22.63	12.1	3.9	257
91	NR	**Manor Care** *Owns and operates nursing homes, acute-care hospitals and hotels*	29	13	1.10E	1.32	964	77	25	114	20.75	15.7	3.5	1,188
92	107	**Abbott Laboratories** *Develops and makes a variety of pharmaceuticals, nutritional products and hospital and laboratory products*	16	33	1.46	1.70	7,852	1,239	38	3	25.50	15.0	6.4	21,342
93	NR	**Sbarro** *Owns and franchises family-style Italian restaurants*	26	20	1.78	2.05	238	24	20	0	35.75	17.4	3.7	482
94	131	**Medtronic** *World's leading maker and marketer of cardiac pacemaker systems*	15	20	3.32E	4.04	1,304	201	24	11	75.75	18.8	5.1	4,512
95	NR	**Methode Electronics** *Makes components that connect, control and convey electrical energy*	32	11	0.63E	0.77	166	13	19	0	13.00	16.9	4.0	296
96	NR	**MCI Communications** *Second-largest U.S. long-distance telephone carrier providing voice and data communications services worldwide*	28	20	2.22	2.53	10,562	609	20	116	41.50	16.4	3.6	10,890
97	NR	**Merrill** *Provides computerized typesetting, printing and reproduction services and distributes financial and legal documents*	34	14	1.09E	1.27	143	8	25	6	17.25	13.6	3.4	123
98	NR	**Avon Products** *World's leading direct seller and distributor of beauty products and fashion jewelry*	17	62	3.32	3.81	3,810	175	78	75	62.63	16.4	18.4	4,495
99	78	**Dollar General** *Operates company-owned and franchised discount department stores in southern and eastern U.S.*	44	11	1.01E	1.19	872	31	20	4	25.50	21.4	4.9	829
100	59	**Instrument Systems** *Makes building products, apparel, specialty plastic films and electronic communications equipment*	104	15	0.66	0.73	512	26	18	17	6.50	8.9	1.6	232

NR: not rated. E: estimate. Sources: William O'Neil & Co.; Infovest via Global Investment Technologies; First Call via Thomson Financial Services.

Source: Reprinted from *FINANCIAL WORLD*, 1328 Broadway, New York, N.Y. 10001

Capital Sources for Startup Companies and Small Businesses

Sources of Venture Capital

Small Business Investment Companies (SBICs)

Small Business Administration (SBA)
409 Third Street, S.W.—6th Floor
Washington, D.C. 20416
Telephone: 202-205-7586

The Small Business Investment Companies (SBIC) are licensed by the SBA. They are privately organized and privately managed investment firms, yet they are participants in a vital partnership between government and the private sector economy. With their own capital and with funds borrowed at favorable rates from the Federal government, SBICs provide venture capital to small independent businesses, both new and already established. Today there are two types of SBICs—the original, or regular SBICs and SSBICs (Specialized Small Business Investment Companies). SSBICs are specifically targeted toward the needs of entrepreneurs who have been denied the opportunity to own and operate a business because of social or economic disadvantage.

For further information call your regional SBA office listed below or the Answer Desk at 800-827-5722.

Small Business Administration Regional Structure

Region I 617-451-2020

Connecticut
Maine
Massachusetts
New Hampshire
Rhode Island
Vermont

Region II 212-264-1450

New Jersey
New York
Puerto Rico

Region III 215-962-3700

Delaware
Dist. of Columbia
Maryland
Pennsylvania
Virginia
West Virginia

Region IV 404-347-2797

Alabama
Florida
Georgia
Kentucky
Mississippi
North Carolina
South Carolina
Tennessee

Region V 312-353-5000

Illinois
Indiana
Michigan
Minnesota
Ohio
Wisconsin

Region VI 214-767-7633

Arkansas
Louisiana
New Mexico
Oklahoma
Texas

Region VII 816-426-3208

Iowa
Kansas
Missouri
Nebraska

Region VIII 303-294-7186

Colorado
Montana
North Dakota
South Dakota
Utah
Wyoming

Region IX 415-744-6402

Arizona
California
Hawaii
Nevada

Region X 206-553-5676

Alaska
Idaho
Oregon
Washington

Source: *Directory of Operating Small Business Investment Companies*, U.S. Small Business Administration, Investment Division.

Note: In addition to the companies listed in this section of the *Almanac*, the *Directory of Small Business Investment Companies* includes SBICs designed to assist small businesses owned by socially or economically disadvantaged persons.

Region I

Connecticut

AB SBIC, Inc.
Adam J. Bozzuto, President
275 School House Road
Cheshire, CT 06410
PH: (203) 272-0203

All State Venture
Capital Corporation
Ceasar N. Anquillare, President
The Bishop House
32 Elm Street, P.O. Box 1629
New Haven, CT 06506
PH: (203) 787-5029

Capital Resource Co.
of Connecticut
Morris Morgenstein, General Partner
2558 Albany Avenue
West Hartford, CT 06117
PH: (203) 236-4336

Financial
Opportunities, Inc.
Ms. Robin Munson, Manager
One Vision Drive
Enfield, CT 06082
PH: (203) 741-4444

First New England
Capital, LP
Richard C. Klaffky, President
100 Pearl Street
Hartford, CT 06103
PH: (203) 293-3333

Marcon Capital Corp.
Martin A. Cohen, President
49 Riverside Avenue
Westport, CT 06880
PH: (203) 226-6893

RFE Capital
Partners, L.P.
Robert M. Williams, Managing Partner
36 Grove Street
New Canaan, CT 06840
PH: (203) 966-2800

SBIC of Connecticut
Inc. (The)
Kenneth F. Zarrilli, President
965 White Plains Road
Trumbull, CT 06611
PH: (203) 261-0011

Maine

Maine Capital Corp.
David M. Coit, President
Seventy Center Street
Portland, ME 04101
PH: (207) 772-1001 FAX: NONE

Massachusetts

Advent Atlantic
Capital Company, LP
David D. Croll, Managing Partner
75 State Street, Suite 2500
Boston, MA 02109
PH: (617) 345-7200

Advent Industrial
Capital Company, LP
David D. Croll, Managing Partner
75 State Street, Suite 2500
Boston, MA 02109
PH: (617) 345-7200

Advent V Capital
Company LP
David D. Croll, Managing Partner
75 State Street, Suite 2500
Boston, MA 02109
PH: (617) 345-7200

BancBoston Ventures,
Incorporated
Frederick M. Fritz, President
100 Federal Street
Mail: P.O. Box 2016 Stop 01-31-08
Boston, MA 02110
PH: (617) 434-2442

Business Achievement
Corporation
Michael L. Katzeff, President
1172 Beacon Street, Suite 202
Newton, MA 02161
PH: (617) 965-0550

Chestnut Capital
International II LP
David D. Croll, Managing Partner
75 State Street, Suite 2500
Boston, MA 02109
PH: (617) 345-7200

Chestnut Street
Partners, Inc.
David D. Croll, President
75 State Street, Suite 2500
Boston, MA 02109
PH: (617) 345-7220

First Capital Corp.
of Chicago
(Main Office: Chicago, IL)
One Financial Center
27th Floor
Boston, MA 02111
PH: (617) 457-2500

LRF Capital,
Limited Partnership
Joseph J. Freeman, Manager
189 Wells Avenue, Suite 4
Newton, MA 02159
PH: (617) 964-0049

Mezzanine Capital
Corporation
David D. Croll, President
75 State Street, Suite 2500
Boston, MA 02109
PH: (617) 345-7200

Northeast SBI Corp.
Joseph Mindick, Treasurer
16 Cumberland Street
Boston, MA 02115
PH: (617) 267-3983

Pioneer Ventures
Limited Partnership
Frank M. Polestra, Managing Partner
60 State Street
Boston, MA 02109
PH: (617) 742-7825

Southern Berkshire
Investment Corp.
Henry Thornton, President
P.O. Box 669
Sheffield, MA 01257
PH: (413) 229-3106

UST Capital Corp.
Arthur F.F. Snyder, President
40 Court Street
Boston, MA 02108
PH: (617) 726-7000

Rhode Island

Domestic Capital Corp.
Nathaniel B. Baker, President
815 Reservoir Avenue
Cranston, RI 02910
PH: (401) 946-3310

Fairway Capital Corp.
Paul V. Anjoorian, President
99 Wayland Avenue
Providence, RI 02906
PH: (401) 454-7500

Fleet Venture
Resources, Inc.
Robert M. Van Degna, President
111 Westminster Street
4th Floor
Providence, RI 02903
PH: (401) 278-6770

Moneta Capital Corp.
Arnold Kilberg, President
99 Wayland Avenue
Providence, RI 02906
PH: (401) 454-7500

NYSTRS/NV Capital,
Limited Partnership
Robert M. Van Degna, Managing Partner
111 Westminster Street
Providence, RI 02903
PH: (401) 276-5597

Richmond Square
Capital Corporation
Harold I. Schein, President
1 Richmond Square
Providence, RI 02906
PH: (401) 521-3000

Wallace Capital
Corporation
Lloyd W. Granoff, President
170 Westminister Street
Suite 300
Providence, RI 02903
PH: (401) 273-9191

Vermont

Green Mountain
Capital, L.P.
Michael Sweetman, General Manager
P.O. Box 659
Stowe, VT 05672
PH: (802) 253-8142

Queneska Capital
Corporation
Albert W. Coffrin, III, President
123 Church Street
Burlington, VT 05401
PH: (802) 865-1806

Region II

New Jersey

Bishop Capital, L.P.
Charles J. Irish, General Partner
500 Morris Avenue
Springfield, NJ 07081
PH: (201) 376-0495

CIT Group/Venture
Capital, Inc.
Colby W. Collier, Manager
650 CIT Drive
Livingston, NJ 07932
PH: (201) 740-5429

ESLO Capital Corp.
Leo Katz, President
212 Wright Street
Newark, NJ 07114
PH: (201) 242-4488

First Princeton
Capital Corporation
Michael Lytell, President
One Garret Mountain Plaza
9th Floor
West Paterson, NJ 07424
PH: (201) 278-8111

Fortis Capital
Corporation
Martin Orland, President
333 Thornall Street, 2nd Floor
Edison, NJ 08837
PH: (908) 603-8500

Tappan Zee Capital
Corporation
Jack Birnberg, President
201 Lower Notch Road
Little Falls, NJ 07424
PH: (201) 256-8280

New York

767 Limited
Partnership
H. Wertheim and H. Mallement, G.P.
767 Third Avenue
c/o Harvey Wertheim
New York, NY 10017
PH: (212) 838-7776

ASEA-Harvest
Partners II
Harvey Wertheim, General Partner
767 Third Avenue
New York, NY 10017
PH: (212) 838-7776

American Commercial
Capital Corporation
Gerald J. Grossman, President
600 Third Avenue, Suite 3810
New York, NY 10016
PH: (212) 986-3305

Argentum Capital
Partners, LP
Daniel Raynor, Chairman
405 Lexington Avenue
New York, NY 10174
PH: (212) 949-8272

Atalanta Investment
Company, Inc.
L. Mark Newman, Chairman of the Board
650 5th Avenue, 15th Floor
New York, NY 10019
PH: (212) 956-9100 FAY

BT Capital Corp.
Noel E. Urben, President
280 Park Avenue--32 West
New York, NY 10017
PH: (212) 454-1916

Barclays Capital
Investors Corp.
Graham McGahen, President
222 Broadway, 7th Floor
New York, NY 10038
PH: (212) 412-6784

CIBC Wood Gundy
Ventures, Inc.
Gordon Muessel, Vice President
425 Lexington Avenue, 9th Floor
New York, NY 10017
PH: (212) 856-3713

CMNY Capital II, L.P.
Robert G. Davidoff, General Partner
135 East 57th Street
26th Floor
New York, NY 10022
PH: (212) 909-8432

CMNY Capital L.P.
Robert Davidoff, General Partner
135 East 57th Street
26th Floor
New York, NY 10022
PH: (212) 909-8432

Chase Manhattan
Capital Corporation
Gustav H. Koven, President
1 Chase Plaza--7th Floor
New York, NY 10081
PH: (212) 552-6275

Chemical Venture
Capital Associates
Jeffrey C. Walker, Managing Gen. Partner
275 Park Avenue, 5th Floor
New York, NY 10017
PH: (212) 270-3220

Citicorp
Investments Inc.
David T. King, President
399 Park Avenue
New York, NY 10043
PH: (212) 559-1000

Citicorp Venture
Capital, Ltd.
William Comfort, Chairman of the Board
399 Park Avenue, 6th Floor
New York, NY 10043
PH: (212) 559-1127

Edwards Capital
Company
Edward H. Teitlebaum, President
Two Park Avenue, 20th Floor
New York, NY 10016
PH: (212) 686-5449

Fifty-Third Street
Ventures, L.P.
Patricia Cloherty & Dan Tessler, G.P.
155 Main Street
Cold Spring, NY 10516
PH: (914) 265-4244

First Wall Street
SBIC, LP
Alan Farkas, G.P.
26 Broadway, Suite 1320
New York, NY 10004
PH: (212) 742-3770

Fundex Capital Corp.
Howard Sommer, President
525 Northern Blvd.
Great Neck, NY 11021
PH: (516) 466-8551

Genesee Funding, Inc.
Stuart Marsh, President & CEO
100 Corporate Woods
Rochester, NY 14623
PH: (716) 272-2332

IBJS Capital Corp.
Corbin R. Miller, President
One State Street, 8th Floor
New York, NY 10004
PH: (212) 858-2000

InterEquity Capital
Corporation
Irwin Schlass, President
220 Fifth Avenue, 10th Floor
New York, NY 10001
PH: (212) 779-2022

J.P. Morgan Investment
Corporation
William E. Pike, Chairman
60 Wall Street
New York, NY 10260
PH: (212) 483-2323

Kwiat Capital Corp.
Sheldon F. Kwiat, President
576 Fifth Avenue
New York, NY 10036
PH: (212) 223-1111

M & T Capital Corp.
T. William Alexander, President
One M & T Plaza
Buffalo, NY 14240
PH: (716) 842-5881

MH Capital
Investors, Inc.
Edward L. Kock III, President
270 Park Avenue
New York, NY 10017
PH: (212) 286-3222

NYBDC Capital Corp.
Robert W. Lazar, President
41 State Street
P.O. Box 738
Albany, NY 12201
PH: (518) 463-2268

NatWest USA Capital
Corporation
Orville G. Aarons, General Manager
175 Water Street
New York, NY 10038
PH: (212) 602-1200

Norwood Venture
Corp.
Mark R. Littell, President
1430 Broadway, Suite 1607
New York, NY 10018
PH: (212) 869-5075

Paribas Principal
Incorporated
Steven Alexander, President
787 Seventh Avenue, 33rd Floor
New York, NY 10019
PH: (212) 841-2000

Pyramid Ventures, Inc.
Annmarie O'Shea, Asst. Vice President
280 Park Avenue--29 West
New York, NY 10017
PH: (212) 454-1702

R & R Financial Corp.
Imre Rosenthal, President
1370 Broadway
New York, NY 10036
PH: (212) 356-1400

Rand SBIC, Inc.
Donald Ross, President
1300 Rand Building
Buffalo, NY 14203
PH: (716) 853-0802

Sterling Commercial
Capital, Inc.
Harvey L. Granat, President
175 Great Neck Road--Suite 404
Great Neck, NY 11021
PH: (516) 482-7374

TLC Funding Corp.
Philip G. Kass, President
660 White Plains Road
Tarrytown, NY 10591
PH: (914) 332-5200

Tappan Zee Capital
Corporation
(Main Office: Little Falls, NJ)
120 North Main Street
New City, NY 10956
PH: (914) 634-8890

Vega Capital Corp.
Victor Harz, President
720 White Plains Road
Scarsdale, NY 10583
PH: (914) 472-8550

Winfield Capital Corp.
Stanley M. Pechman, President
237 Mamaroneck Avenue
White Plains, NY 10605
PH: (914) 949-2600

Region III

District of Columbia

Allied Investment
Corporation
Cable Williams, President
1666 K Street, N.W., Suite 901
Washington, DC 20006
PH: (202) 331-1112

Allied Investment
Corporation II
Cable Williams, President
1666 K Street, N.W., Suite 901
Washington, DC 20006
PH: (202) 331-1112

Legacy Fund Limited
Partnership
John Ledecky, Manager & General Partner
1990 M Street, N.W.
Suite 310
Washington, DC 20006
PH: (202) 659-1100

Maryland

American Security
Capital Corp., Inc.
Jim Henry, Investment Officer
100 S. Charles Street, 5th Floor
Baltimore, MD 21203
PH: (410) 547-4205

Greater Washington
Investments, Inc.
Haywood Miller, Manager
5454 Wisconsin Avenue
Chevy Chase, MD 20815
PH: (301) 656-0626

Pennsylvania

CIP Capital, Inc.
Winston Churchill, Jr., Manager
300 Chester Field Parkway
Malvern, PA 19355
PH: (215) 251-5075

Enterprise Venture Cap
Corp of Pennsylvania
Don Cowie, C.E.O.
111 Market Street
Johnstown, PA 15901
PH: (814) 535-7597

Erie SBIC
George R. Heaton, President
32 West 8th Street, Suite 615
Erie, PA 16501
PH: (814) 453-7964

Fidelcor Capital
Corporation
Elizabeth T. Crawford, President
Fidelity Building, 7th Floor
123 South Broad Street
Philadelphia, PA 19109
PH: (215) 985-3722

First SBIC of
California
(Main Office: Costa Mesa, CA)
Daniel A. Dye, Contact
P.O. Box 512
Washington, PA 15301
PH: (412) 223-0707

Meridian Capital Corp.
Joseph E. Laky, President
Horsham Business Center, Suite 200
455 Business Center Drive
Horsham, PA 19044
PH: (215) 957-7520

Meridian Venture
Partners
Raymond R. Rafferty, General Partner
The Fidelity Court Building
259 Radnor-Chester Road
Radnor, PA 19087
PH: (215) 293-0210

PNC Capital Corp.
Gary J. Zentner, President
Pittsburgh National Building
Fifth Avenue and Wood Street
Pittsburgh, PA 15222
PH: (412) 762-2248

Virginia

DC Bancorp Venture
Capital Company
Allen Kendle, Vice President
One Commercial Place, 3rd Floor
Norfolk, VA 23510
PH: (804) 441-4041

Dominion Capital
Markets Corporation
Gregory W. Feldmann, President
213 South Jefferson Street
Mail: P.O. Box 13327; Roanoke, VA 24040
Roanoke, VA 24011
PH: (703) 563-6110

Hampton Roads SBIC
John A. Hornback, Jr., President
420 Bank Street
P.O. Box 327
Norfolk, VA 23510
PH: (804) 622-2312

NationsBanc SBIC
Corporation
Stephen J. Schley, President
12th & Main Streets
Mail: P.O. Box 27025
Richmond, VA 23261
PH: (804) 788-2592

Rural America
Fund, Inc.
Fred Russell, Chief Executive Officer
2201 Cooperative Way
Herndon, VA 22071
PH: (703) 709-6750

Walnut Capital Corp.
(Main Office: Chicago, IL)
8000 Tower Crescent Drive, Suite 1070
Vienna, VA 22182
PH: (703) 448-3771

Region IV

Alabama

First SBIC of
Alabama
David C. DeLaney, President
16 Midtown Park East
Mobile, AL 36606
PH: (205) 476-0700

Hickory Venture
Capital Corporation
J. Thomas Noojin, President
200 W. Court Square, Suite 100
Huntsville, AL 35801
PH: (205) 539-5130

Florida

Allied Investment
Corporation
(Main Office: Washington, DC)
Executive Office Center, Suite 305
2770 N. Indian River Blvd.
Vero Beach, FL 32960
PH: (407) 778-5556

Florida Capital
Ventures, Ltd.
Warren E. Miller, President
111 Madison Street, 26th Floor
Tampa, FL 33602
PH: (813) 229-2294

J & D Capital Corp.
Jack Carmel, President
12747 Biscayne Blvd.
North Miami, FL 33181
PH: (305) 893-0303

Market Capital Corp.
Donald Kolvenbach, President
1102 North 28th Street
Mail: P.O. Box 31667
Tampa, FL 33631
PH: (813) 247-1357

Quantum Capital
Partners, Ltd.
Michael E. Chaney, President
4400 NE 25th Avenue
Fort Lauderdale, FL 33308
PH: (305) 776-1133

Western Financial
Capital Corporation
(Main Office: Dallas, TX)
AmeriFirst Bank Building, 2nd Floor S
18301 Biscayne Boulevard
N. Miami Beach, FL 33160
PH: (305) 933-5858

Georgia

Investor's Equity,
Inc.
I. Walter Fisher, President
945 E. Paces Ferry Road, Suite 1735
Atlanta, GA 30326
PH: (404) 266-8300

North Riverside
Capital Corporation
Tom Barry, President
50 Technology Park/Atlanta
Norcross, GA 30092
PH: (404) 446-5556

Kentucky

Mountain Ventures,
Inc.
Jerry A. Rickett, President
London Bank & Trust Building
400 S. Main Street, Fourth Floor
London, KY 40741
PH: (606) 864-5175

North Carolina

Heritage Capital Corp.
Richard N. Brigden, Vice President
2000 Two First Union Center
Charlotte, NC 28282
PH: (704) 372-5404

Springdale Venture
Partners, LP
S. Epes Robinson, General Partner
212 S. Tryon Street, Suite 960
Charlotte, NC 28281
PH: (704) 344-8290

South Carolina

Charleston Capital
Corporation
Henry Yaschik, President
111 Church Street
P.O. Box 328
Charleston, SC 29402
PH: (803) 723-6464

Floco Investment
Company, Inc. (The)
William H. Johnson, Sr., President
Highway 52 North
Mail: P.O. Box 919; Lake City, SC
Scranton, SC 29561
PH: (803) 389-2731

Lowcountry Investment
Corporation
Joseph T. Newton, Jr., President
4444 Daley Street
P.O. Box 10447
Charleston, SC 29411
PH: (803) 554-9880

Tennessee

Sirrom Capital, LP
George M. Miller, II, Manager
511 Union Street, Suite 2310
Nashville, TN 37219
PH: (615) 256-0701

Region V

Illinois

Business Ventures,
Incorporated
Milton Lefton, President
20 North Wacker Drive, Suite 1741
Chicago, IL 60606
PH: (312) 346-1580

Continental Illinois
Venture Corp.
John Willis, President
209 South LaSalle Street
Mail: 231 South LaSalle Street
Chicago, IL 60693
PH: (312) 828-8023

First Capital Corp.
of Chicago
John A. Canning, Jr., President
Three First National Plaza
Suite 1330
Chicago, IL 60670
PH: (312) 732-5400

Heller Equity
Capital Corporation
John M. Goense, President
500 West Monroe Street
Chicago, IL 60661
PH: (312) 441-7200

Walnut Capital Corp.
Burton W. Kanter, Chairman of the Board
Two North LaSalle Street, Suite 2410
Chicago, IL 60602
PH: (312) 346-2033

Indiana

1st Source Capital
Corporation
Eugene L. Cavanaugh, Jr., Vice President
100 North Michgan Street
Mail: P.O. Box 1602; South Bend 46634
South Bend, IN 46601
PH: (219) 236-2180

Cambridge
Ventures II, LP
Ms. Jean Wojtowicz, President
8440 Woodfield Crossing, #315
Indianapolis, IN 46240
PH: (317) 469-9704

Circle Ventures, Inc.
Carrie Walkup, Manager
26 N. Arsenal Avenue
Indianapolis, IN 46201
PH: (317) 636-7242

Michigan

White Pines Capital
Corporation
Mr. Ian Bund, President & Manager
2929 Plymouth Road, Suite 210
Ann Arbor, MI 48105
PH: (313) 747-9401

Minnesota

FBS SBIC, Limited
Partnership
John M. Murphy, Jr., Managing Agent
601 Second Avenue South
Minneapolis, MN 55402
PH: (612) 973-0988

Northland Capital
Venture Partnership
George G. Barnum, Jr., President
613 Missabe Building
Duluth, MN 55802
PH: (218) 722-0545

Northwest Venture
Partners
Robert F. Zicarelli, Managing G.P.
2800 Piper Jaffray Tower
222 South Ninth Street
Minneapolis, MN 55402
PH: (612) 667-1650

Norwest Equity
Partners IV
Robert Zicarelli, General Partner
2800 Piper Jaffray Tower
222 South Ninth Street
Minneapolis, MN 55402
PH: (612) 667-1650

Norwest Growth Fund,
Inc.
Daniel J. Haggerty, President
2800 Piper Jaffray Tower
222 South Ninth Street
Minneapolis, MN 55402
PH: (612) 667-1650

Ohio

A.T. Capital Corp.
Donald C. Molten, Manager
127 Public Square, 4th Floor
Cleveland, OH 44114
PH: (216) 737-4090

Banc One Capital
Partners Corporation
(Main Office: Dallas, TX)
10 West Broad Street, Suite 200
Columbus, OH 43215

Clarion Capital Corp.
Morton A. Cohen, President
Ohio Savings Plaza, Suite 1520
1801 E. 9th Street
Cleveland, OH 44114
PH: (216) 687-1096

National City Capital
Corporation
William H. Schecter, President & G.M.
1965 East Sixth Street, Suite 400
Cleveland, OH 44114
PH: (216) 575-2491

Society Venture
Capital Corporation
Carl G. Nelson, Chief Inv. Officer
127 Public Square, 4th Floor
Cleveland, OH 44114
PH: (216) 689-5776

Wisconsin

Banc One Venture Corp.
H. Wayne Foreman, President
111 East Wisconsin Avenue
Milwaukee, WI 53202
PH: (414) 765-2274

Bando-McGlocklin
SBIC
George Schonath, Chief Executive Officer
13555 Bishops Court, Suite 205
Brookfield, WI 53005
PH: (414) 784-9010

Capital Investments,
Inc.
James R. Sanler, President
Commerce Building, Suite 540
744 North Fourth Street
Milwaukee, WI 53203
PH: (414) 273-6560

M & I Ventures Corp.
John T. Byrnes, President
770 North Water Street
Milwaukee, WI 53202
PH: (414) 765-7910

MorAmerica Capital
Corporation
(Main Office: Cedar Rapids, IA)
600 East Mason Street
Milwaukee, WI 53202
PH: (414) 276-3839

Polaris Capital Corp.
Richard Laabs, President
One Park Plaza
11270 W. Park Place, Suite 320
Milwaukee, WI 53224
PH: (414) 359-3040

Region VI

Arkansas

Small Business
Inv. Capital, Inc.
Charles E. Toland, President
10003 New Benton Hwy.
Mail: P.O. Box 3627
Little Rock, AR 72203
PH: (501) 455-6599

Southern Ventures, Inc
Jeffrey A. Doose, President & Director
605 Main Street, Suite 202
Arkadelphia, AR 71923
PH: (501) 246-9627

Louisiana

Premier Venture
Capital Corporation
G. Lee Griffin, President
451 Florida Street
Baton Rouge, LA 70821
PH: (504) 389-4421

New Mexico

Albuquerque SBIC
Albert T. Ussery, President
501 Tijeras Avenue, N.W.
P.O. Box 487
Albuquerque, NM 87103
PH: (505) 247-0145

Oklahoma

Alliance Business
Investment Company
Barry Davis, President
17 East Second Street
One Williams Center, Suite 2000
Tulsa, OK 74172
PH: (918) 584-3581

Texas

AMT Capital, Ltd.
Tom H. Delimitros, CGP
8204 Elmbrook Drive, Suite 101
Dallas, TX 75247
PH: (214) 905-9760

Alliance Business
Investment Company
(Main Office: Tulsa, OK)
911 Louisiana
One Shell Plaza, Suite 3990
Houston, TX 77002
PH: (713) 224-8224

Banc One Capital
Partners Corporation
Suzanne B. Kriscunas, President
300 Crescent Court, Suite 1600
Dallas, TX 75201
PH: (214) 979-4360

Capital Southwest
Venture Corp.
William R. Thomas, President
12900 Preston Road, Suite 700
Dallas, TX 75230
PH: (214) 233-8242

Catalyst Fund,
Ltd. (The)
Richard L. Herrman, Manager
Three Riverway, Suite 770
Houston, TX 77056
PH: (713) 623-8133

Central Texas SBI
Corporation
David G. Horner, President
1401 Elm Street, Suite 4764
Dallas, TX 75202
PH: (214) 508-5050

Charter Venture Group,
Incorporated
Winston C. Davis, President
2600 Citadel Plaza Drive, Suite 600
P.O. Box 4525
Houston, TX 77008
PH: (713) 622-7500

Citicorp Venture
Capital, Ltd.
(Main Office: New York, NY)
717 North Harwood
Suite 2920-LB87
Dallas, TX 75201
PH: (214) 880-9670

FCA Investment Company
Robert S. Baker, Chairman
San Felipe Plaza, Suite 850
5847 San Felipe
Houston, TX 77057
PH: (713) 781-2857

First City, Texas
Ventures, Inc.
Mr. J.R. Brlansky, Manager
1001 Main Street, 15th Floor
P.O. Box 4517
Houston, TX 77002
PH: (713) 658-5421

Ford Capital, Ltd.
C. Jeff Pan, President
200 Crescent Court, Suite 1350
Mail: P.O. Box 2140; Dallas, TX 75221
Dallas, TX 75201
PH: (214) 871-5177

HCT Capital Corp.
Vichy Woodward Young, Jr., President
4916 Camp Bowie Boulevard, Suite 200
Fort Worth, TX 76107
PH: (817) 763-8706

Houston Partners, SBIP
Harvard Hill, President, CGP
Capital Center Penthouse, 8th Floor
401 Louisiana
Houston, TX 77002
PH: (713) 222-8600

Jiffy Lube Capital
Corporation
Mark Youngs, Manager
700 Milam Street
Mail: P.O. Box 2967
Houston, TX 77252
PH: (713) 546-8910

Mapleleaf Capital Ltd.
Patrick A. Rivelli, Manager
Three Forest Plaza, Suite 1300
12221 Merit Drive
Dallas, TX 75251
PH: (214) 239-5650

NationsBanc Capital
Corporation
David Franklin, President
901 Main Street, 66th Floor
Dallas, TX 75202
PH: (214) 508-0900

SBI Capital Corp.
William E. Wright, President
6305 Beverly Hill Lane
Mail: P.O. Box 570368; Houston, TX 77257
Houston, TX 77057
PH: (713) 975-1188

Sunwestern Capital,
Ltd.
James L. Leary, President
3 Forest Plaza
12221 Merit Drive, Suite 1300
Dallas, TX 75251
PH: (214) 239-5650

Sunwestern Ventures,
Ltd.
James L. Leary, President
3 Forest Plaza
12221 Merit Drive, Suite 1300
Dallas, TX 75251
PH: (214) 239-5650

UNCO Ventures, Inc.
John Gatti, President
520 Post Oak Blvd., Suite 130
Houston, TX 77027
PH: (713) 622-9595

Ventex Partners, Ltd.
Richard S. Smith, President
1000 Louisiana, Suite 1110
Houston, TX 77002
PH: (713) 659-7860

Victoria Capital Corp.
Kenneth L. Vickers, President
One O'Connor Plaza
Victoria, TX 77902
PH: (512) 573-5151

Victoria Capital Corp.
(Main Office: Victoria, TX)
750 E. Mulberry, Suite 305
Mail: P.O. Box 15616
San Antonio, TX 78212
PH: (512) 736-4233

Western Financial
Capital Corporation
Andrew S. Rosemore, President
17290 Preston Road, Suite 300
Dallas, TX 75252
PH: (214) 380-0044

Region VII

Iowa

MorAmerica Capital
Corporation
David R. Schroder, Vice President
101 2nd Street, SE
Suite 800
Cedar Rapids, IA 52401
PH: (319) 363-8249

Kansas

Kansas Venture
Capital, Inc.
Rex E. Wiggins, President
6700 Antioch Plaza, Suite 460
Overland Park, KS 66204
PH: (913) 262-7117

Kansas Venture
Capital, Inc.
(Main Office: Overland Park, KS)
Thomas C. Blackburn, Vice President
One Main Place, Suite 806
Wichita, KS 67202
PH: (316) 262-1221

Missouri

Bankers Capital Corp.
Raymond E. Glasnapp, President
3100 Gillham Road
Kansas City, MO 64109
PH: (816) 531-1600

CFB Venture Fund I,
Inc.
James F. O'Donnell, Chairman
11 South Meramec, Suite 800
St. Louis, MO 63105
PH: (314) 854-7427

CFB Venture Fund II,
Inc.
Bart S. Bergman, President
1000 Walnut Street, 18th Floor
Kansas City, MO 64106
PH: (816) 234-2357

MBI Venture Capital
Investors, Inc.
Anthony Sommers, President
850 Main Street
Kansas City, MO 64105
PH: (816) 471-1700

Midland Capital Corp.
Neil E. Sprague, Manager
One Petticoat Lane, Suite 110
1020 Walnut Street
Kansas City, MO 64106
PH: (816) 471-8000

MorAmerica Capital
Corporation
(Main Office: Cedar Rapids, IA)
911 Main Street, Suite 2724A
Commerce Tower Building
Kansas City, MO 64105
PH: (816) 842-0114

United Missouri
Capital Corporation
Noel Shull, Manager
1010 Grand Avenue
Mail: P.O. Box 419226; K.C., MO 64141
Kansas City, MO 64106
PH: (816) 556-7333

Nebraska

First of Nebraska
Investment Corp.
Steven Kros, Managing Officer
One First National Center
Suite 701
Omaha, NE 68102
PH: (402) 633-3585

United Financial
Resources Corp.
Joan Boulay, Manager
7401 "F" Street
Mail: P.O. Box 1131; Ohama, NE 68101
Omaha, NE 68127
PH: (402) 339-7300

Region VIII

Colorado

UBD Capital, Inc.
Dennis D. Erickson, President
1700 Broadway
Denver, CO 80274
PH: (303) 861-8811

Region IX

Arizona

First Commerce
& Loan LP
Ross M. Horowitz, GP & Manager
5620 N. Kolb, #260
Tucson, AZ 85715
PH: (602) 298-2500

First Interstate
Equity Corp.
Edmund G. Zito, President
100 West Washington Street
Phoenix, AZ 85003
PH: (602) 528-6647

Sundance Venture
Partners, L.P.
(Main Office: Cupertino, CA)
Gregory S. Anderson, Vice-President
2828 N. Central Avenue, Suite 1275
Phoenix, AZ 85004
PH: (602) 279-1101

California

AMF Financial, Inc.
Ron Arehart, President
4330 La Jolla Village Drive
Suite 110
San Diego, CA 92122
PH: (619) 546-0167

BNP Venture Capital
Corporation
Edgerton Scott II, President
3000 Sand Hill Road
Building 1, Suite 125
Menlo Park, CA 94025
PH: (415) 854-1084

BT Capital Corp.
(Main Office: New York, NY)
300 South Grand Avenue
Los Angeles, CA 90071
PH: NONE

BankAmerica Ventures,
Inc.
Patrick Topolski, President
555 California Street, 12th Floor
c/o Dept. 3908
San Francisco, CA 94104
PH: (415) 953-3001

Citicorp Venture
Capital, Ltd.
(Main Office: New York, NY)
2 Embarcadero Place
2200 Geny Road, Suite 203
Palo Alto, CA 94303
PH: (415) 424-8000

DSC Ventures II, LP
Daniel D. Tompkins, Jr., Managing G.P.
20111 Stevens Creek Boulevard
Suite 130
Cupertino, CA 95014
PH: (408) 252-3800

Developers Equity
Capital Corporation
Larry Sade, Chairman of the Board
1880 Century Park East
Suite 211
Los Angeles, CA 90067
PH: (213) 277-0330

Draper Associates,
a California LP
Bill Edwards, President
c/o Timothy C. Draper
400 Seaport Court, Suite 250
Redwood City, CA 94063
PH: (415) 599-9000

First SBIC of
California
Greg Forrest, President
650 Town Center Drive
Seventeenth Floor
Costa Mesa, CA 92626
PH: (714) 556-1964

First SBIC of
California
(Main Office: Costa Mesa, CA)
5 Palo Alto Square, Suite 938
Palo Alto, CA 94306
PH: (415) 424-8011

First SBIC of
California
(Main Office: Costa Mesa, CA)
155 North Lake Avenue, Suite 1010
Pasadena, CA 91109
PH: (818) 304-3451

G C & H Partners
James C. Gaither, General Partner
One Maritime Plaza, 20th Floor
San Francisco, CA 94110
PH: (415) 981-5252

Hall, Morris
& Drufva II, L.P.
Ronald J. Hall, Managing Director
25401 Cabbot Road, Suite 116
Laguna Hills, CA 92653
PH: (714) 707-5096

Imperial Ventures,
Inc.
H. Wayne Snavely, President
9920 South La Cienega Blvd.
Mail: P.O. Box 92991; L.A. 90009
Inglewood, CA 90301
PH: (310) 417-5928

Jupiter Partners
John M. Bryan, President
600 Montgomery Street
35th Floor
San Francisco, CA 94111
PH: (415) 421-9990

Marwit Capital Corp.
Martin W. Witte, President
180 Newport Center Drive
Suite 200
Newport Beach, CA 92660
PH: (714) 640-6234

Merrill Pickard
Anderson & Eyre I
Steven L. Merrill, President
2480 Sand Hill Road, Suite 200
Menlo Park, CA 94025
PH: (415) 854-8600

New West Partners II
Timothy P. Haidinger, Manager
4350 Executive Drive, Suite 206
San Diego, CA 92121
PH: (619) 457-0723

Northwest Venture
Partners
(Main Office: Minneapolis, MN)
3000 Sand Hill Road
Building 3, Suite 245
Menlo Park, CA 94025

Norwest Equity
Partners IV
(Main Office: Minneapolis, MN)
3000 Sand Hill Road
Building 3, Suite 245
Menlo Park, CA 94025

Norwest Growth Fund,
Inc.
(Main Office: Minneapolis, MN)
3000 Sand Hill Road
Building 3, Suite 245
Menlo Park, CA 94025

Ritter Partners
William C. Edwards, President
150 Isabella Avenue
Atherton, CA 94025
PH: (415) 854-1555

Seaport Ventures, Inc.
Carole H. Catlett, Vice President
525 B Street, Suite 630
San Diego, CA 92101
PH: (619) 232-4069

Sundance Venture
Partners, L.P.
Larry J. Wells, General Manager
10600 N. DeAnza Blvd., Suite 215
Cupertino, CA 95014
PH: (408) 257-8100

Union Venture Corp.
Kathleen Burns, Vice President
445 South Figueroa Street
Los Angeles, CA 90071
PH: (213) 236-5658

VK Capital Company
Franklin Van Kasper, General Partner
50 California Street, Suite 2350
San Francisco, CA 94111
PH: (415) 391-5600

Hawaii

Bancorp Hawaii SBIC
Robert Paris, President
111 South King Street
Suite 1060
Honolulu, HI 96813
PH: (808) 521-6411

Region X

Oregon

Northern Pacific
Capital Corporation
Joseph P. Tennant, President
937 S.W. 14th Street, Suite 200
Mail: P.O. Box 1658
Portland, OR 97207
PH: (503) 241-1255

U.S. Bancorp Capital
Corporation
Gary Patterson, President
111 S.W. Fifth Avenue
Suite 1570
Portland, OR 97204
PH: (503) 275-5860

Directories

Directory of Small Business Investment Companies. Contains a listing of SBICs by state including branch offices, contact persons, and types of businesses funded. Free of charge, the *Directory* is available by calling the Small Business Administration at 202-205-7586.

Pratt's Guide to Venture Capital Sources. Provides extensive information on all leading venture capital firms in the U.S.A. and around the world. Available from:

Venture Economics
40 West 57th Street
New York, NY 10102-0968

Corporate Finance Source Book. This volume provides a listing of thousands of US and world financial sources. Published by:

National Register Publishing Co.
3004 Glenview Road
Wolmette, IL 60091

National Venture Capital Association (NVCA) *Membership Directory* lists members of the association and information about it.

National Venture Capital Association
1655 North Fort Meyer Drive
Arlington, VA 22209
Telephone: 703-528-4370

Small Business Administration (SBA) Field Offices

Type	City	State	Zip Code	Address	Telephone
Region I					
RO	Boston	MA	02110	155 Federal Street	(617)451-2023
DO	Boston	MA	02222-1093	10 Causeway Street	(617)565-5590
DO	Augusta	ME	04330	40 Western Avenue	(207)622-8378
DO	Concord	NH	03302-1257	143 North Main Street	(603)225-1400
DO	Hartford	CT	06106	330 Main Street	(203)240-4700
DO	Montpelier	VT	05602	87 State Street	(802)828-4422
DO	Providence	RI	02903	380 Westminister Mall	(401)528-4561
BO	Springfield	MA	01103	1550 Main Street	(413)785-0268
Region II					
RO	New York	NY	11278	26 Federal Plaza	(212)264-1450
DO	Buffalo	NY	14202	111 West Huron Street	(716)846-4301
DO	Newark	NJ	07102	60 Park Place	(201)645-2434
DO	New York	NY	10278	26 Federal Plaza	(212)264-2454
DO	Hato Rey	PR	00918	Carlos Chardon Avenue	(809)766-5572
DO	Syracuse	NY	13260	100 South Clinton Street	(315)423-5383
BO	Elmira	NY	14901	333 East Water Street	(607)734-8130
BO	Melville	NY	11747	35 Pinelawn Road	(516)454-0750
BO	Rochester	NY	14614	100 State Street	(716)263-6700
POD	Albany	NY	12207	445 Broadway	(518)472-6300
POD	Camden	NJ	08104	2600 Mt. Ephraim Avenue	(609)757-5183
POD	St. Croix	VI	00820-4487	4200 United Shopping Plaza	(809)778-5380
POD	St. Thomas	VI	00802	Veterans Drive	(809)774-8530
Region III					
RO	King of Prussia	PA	19406	475 Allendale Road	(215)962-3700
DO	Baltimore	MD	21202	10 North Calvert Street	(410)962-4392
DO	Clarksburg	WV	26301	168 West Main Street	(304)623-5631
DO	King of Prussia	PA	19406	475 Allendale Road	(215)962-3804
DO	Pittsburgh	PA	15222	960 Penn Avenue	(412)644-2780
DO	Richmond	VA	23240	400 North Eighth Street	(804)771-2400
DO	Washington	DC	20036	1111 18th Street, N.W.	(202)634-1500
BO	Charleston	WV	25301	550 Eagan Street	(304)347-5220
BO	Harrisburg	PA	17101	100 Chestnut Street	(717)782-3840
BO	Wilkes-Barre	PA	18702	20 North Pennsylvania Avenue	(717)826-6497
BO	Wilmington	DE	19801	920 North King Street	(302)573-6295
Region IV					
RO	Atlanta	GA	30367-8102	1375 Peachtree Street, NE	(404)347-2797
DO	Atlanta	GA	30309	1720 Peachtree Road, NW	(404)347-4749
DO	Birmingham	AL	35203-2398	2121 8th Avenue, North	(205)731-1344
DO	Charlotte	NC	28202	200 North College Street	(704)344-6563
DO	Columbia	SC	29201	1835 Assembly Street	(803)765-5376
DO	Jackson	MS	39201	101 West Capitol Street	(601)965-4378
DO	Jacksonville	FL	32256-7504	7825 Baymeadows Way	(904)443-1900
DO	Louisville	KY	40202	600 Dr. M.L. King Jr. Place	(502)582-5971
DO	Coral Gables	FL	33146-2911	1320 South Dixie Highway	(305)536-5521
DO	Nashville	TN	37228-1500	50 Vantage Way	(615)736-5881
BO	Gulfport	MS	39501-7758	One Hancock Plaza	(601)863-4449
POD	Statesboro	GA	30458	52 North Main Street	(912)489-8719
POD	Tampa	FL	33602-3945	501 East Polk Street	(813)228-2594
POD	West Palm Beach	FL	33407-2044	5601 Corporate Way	(407)689-3922
Region V					
RO	Chicago	IL	60606-6617	300 South Riverside Plaza	(312)353-5000
DO	Chicago	IL	60661-2511	500 West Madison Street	(312)353-4528
DO	Cleveland	OH	44199	1240 East 9th Street	(216)522-4180
DO	Columbus	OH	43215-2592	2 Nationwide Plaza	(614)469-6860
DO	Detroit	MI	48226	477 Michigan Avenue	(313)226-6075
DO	Indianapolis	IN	46204-1873	429 North Pennsylvania	(317)226-7272
DO	Madison	WI	53703	212 East Washington Avenue	(608)264-3261
DO	Minneapolis	MN	55403-1563	100 North 6th Street	(612)370-2324
BO	Cincinnati	OH	45202	525 Vine Street	(513)684-2814
BO	Milwaukee	WI	53203	310 West Wisconsin Avenue	(414)297-3941
BO	Marquette	MI	49885	300 South Front Street	(906)225-1108
BO	Springfield	IL	62704	511 West Capitol Street	(217)492-4416

Type	City	State	Zip Code	Address	Telephone
Region VI					
RO	Dallas	TX	75235-3391	8625 King George Drive	(214)767-7633
DO	Albuquerque	NM	87102	625 Silver Avenue, SW	(505)766-1870
DO	Dallas	TX	75242	1100 Commerce Street	(214)767-0605
DO	El Paso	TX	79935	10737 Gateway West	(915)540-5676
DO	Houston	TX	77074-1591	9301 Southwest Freeway	(713)953-5900
DO	Little Rock	AR	72202	2120 Riverfront Drive	(501)324-5278
DO	Harlingen	TX	78550	222 East Van Buren Street	(512)427-8533
DO	Lubbock	TX	79401	1611 Tenth Street	(806)743-7462
DO	New Orleans	LA	70112	1661 Canal Street	(504)589-6685
DO	Oklahoma City	OK	73102	200 North West 5th Street	(405)231-4301
DO	San Antonio	TX	78216	7400 Blanco Road	(512)229-4535
BO	Corpus Christi	TX	78476	606 North Carancahua	(512)888-3331
BO	Ft. Worth	TX	76102	819 Taylor Street	(817)334-3777
POD	Austin	TX	78701	300 Easy 8th Street	(512)482-5288
POD	Marshall	TX	75670	505 East Travis	(903)935-5257
POD	Shreveport	LA	71101	500 Fannin Street	(318)226-5196
Region VII					
RO	Kansas City	MO	64106	911 Walnut Street	(816)426-3608
DO	Cedar Rapids	IA	52402-3147	373 Collins Road, NE	(319)393-8630
DO	Des Moines	IA	50309	210 Walnut Street	(515)284-4422
DO	Kansas City	MO	64105	323 West 8th Street	(816)374-6708
DO	Omaha	NE	68154	11145 Mill Valley Road	(402)221-4691
DO	St. Louis	MO	63101	815 Olive Street	(314)539-6600
DO	Wichita	KS	67202	100 East English Street	(316)269-6273
BO	Springfield	MO	65802-3200	620 South Glenstone Street	(417)864-7670
Region VIII					
RO	Denver	CO	80202	999 18th Street	(303)294-7186
DO	Casper	WY	82602-2839	100 East B Street	(307)261-5761
DO	Denver	CO	80201-0660	721 19th Street	(303)844-3984
DO	Fargo	ND	58108-3086	657 2nd Avenue, North	(701)239-5131
DO	Helena	MT	59626	301 South Park	(406)449-5381
DO	Salt Lake City	UT	84138-1195	125 South State Street	(801)524-5800
DO	Sioux Falls	SD	57102-0527	101 South Main Avenue	(605)330-4231
Region IX					
RO	San Francisco	CA	94105-2939	71 Stevenson Street	(415)744-6402
DO	Fresno	CA	93727-1547	2719 North Air Fresno Drive	(209)487-5189
DO	Honolulu	HI	96850-4981	300 Ala Moana Boulevard	(808)541-2990
DO	Las Vegas	NV	89125-2527	301 East Stewart Street	(702)388-6611
DO	Glendale	CA	91203-2304	330 North Brand Boulevard	(213)894-2956
DO	Phoenix	AZ	85004-1025	2828 North Central Avenue	(602)640-2316
DO	San Diego	CA	92188-0270	880 Front Street	(619)557-7252
DO	San Francisco	CA	94105-1988	211 Main Street	(415)744-6820
DO	Santa Ana	CA	92703-2352	901 West Civic Center Drive	(714)836-2494
BO	Agana	GM	96910	238 Archbishop F.C. Flores St.	(671)472-7277
BO	Sacramento	CA	95814-2413	660 J Street	(916)551-1426
POD	Reno	NV	89505-3216	50 South Virginia Street	(702)784-5268
POD	Tucson	AZ	85701-1319	300 West Congress Street	(602)670-6715
POD	Ventura	CA	93003-4159	6477 Telephone Road	(805)642-1866
Region X					
RO	Seattle	WA	98121	2615 4th Avenue	(206)553-5676
DO	Anchorage	AK	99513-7559	222 West 8th Avenue	(907)271-4022
DO	Boise	ID	83702-5745	1020 Main Street	(208)334-1696
DO	Portland	OR	97201-6605	222 South West Columbia	(503)326-2682
DO	Seattle	WA	98174-1088	915 Second Avenue	(206)553-1420
DO	Spokane	WA	99204-0317	West 601 First Avenue	(509)353-2800

RO = Regional Office **DO** = District Office **BO** = Branch Office **POD** = Post of Duty

Returns on Various Types of Investments

*R. S. Salomon, Jr.**

The Big Picture

One of the crucial decisions an investor must make is: How, among a range of possibilities, should I allocate my assets? Most people choose fairly narrowly. They divide their money among such financial instruments as stocks, bonds and cash, or real estate. Now and then an individual may also decide to sink money into more esoteric—and less liquid—investments such as a barrel of oil or a rare work of art.

Since these different species of investment do not move in unison, it matters greatly how you allocate your money among them. I have tracked a group of assets for many years. The short- and long-term performance of this group is summarized in the table on page 235. If you did not load up on this year's winners, take heart: In the long run the value of all these assets has increased—at least in nominal terms.

The long-term performance data are expressed in compound annual growth rates. To understand the power of reinvesting, note that the 12.2% compound growth in stocks means that $1 invested in stocks in 1973 would be worth $10 today. The arithmetic of compound interest also means that what appear to be small differences in growth rates actually translate into large disparities in the ending value of an investment. Thus, the 2.4-percentage-point difference between the 20-year growth of stocks and bonds means that $1 invested in bonds would be worth roughly one-third less than the same investment in stocks.

The assets break down into two broad categories: financial (stocks, bonds, cash and foreign exchange) and tangible. The latter category can be further subdivided into three groups: collectibles (Chinese ceramics and stamps); commodities (gold, silver, oil and diamonds); and real estate (housing and farmland).

Broadly speaking, every period confronts an investor with the necessity of choosing between financial and tangible assets. An investor who correctly positions a portfolio from one period to the next stands to reap considerably greater returns than an investor who is ignorant of the larger picture.

What are the key factors that drive the performance of these two broad asset classes? Roughly speaking, they can be summarized as follows:

Factors favoring financial assets

1. Declining inflationary expectations
2. Peace and democracy
3. Declining tax rates
4. Deregulation and a shrinking public sector
5. Increased confidence

Factors favoring tangible assets

1. Rising inflationary expectations
2. Political instability
3. Rising tax rates
4. Reregulation and a growing public sector
5. Rising anxiety

Inflation is the most critical factor on this list. The direction and stability of prices affect the future value of money, and the future value of money is what investing is all about. The Consumer Price Index is included in the table of returns to help owners of any of these assets decide whether they are winning or losing in terms of purchasing power.

At present, investors seem to fear higher inflation, and there have been some price increases in certain areas. In spite of this, I remain convinced that the most powerful forces in the system are still exerting deflationary and not inflationary influences.

The price increases thus far are not too worrisome. In the auto industry, where Japanese manufacturers are sizable competitors, price increases by U.S. manufacturers have been a function of currency fluctuations and thus do not appear to reflect underlying inflationary pressures.

Speaking of inflation, I am not as worried about the rise in the gold price as other investors seem to be. Historically, gold has been a bellwether of the overall trend in inflation. Today, however, changes in the price of gold

* Chairman and Chief executive of Salomon Brothers Asset Management, Inc., and portfolio manager of Salomon Brothers Capital Fund, Inc., Research assistant: Caroline Davenport.

are more a function of rising demand—particularly in China—and limited supply.

Meanwhile, the inflation trends in other areas are encouraging. The cost of health care is rising at the slowest rate in the postwar period. Oil—a key commodity—is in abundant supply at present, while demand is being held in check by a sluggish world economy. Finally, price wars seem to be breaking out all over, affecting such products as personal computers, disk drives, airfares, long distance telephone service, diapers and cigarettes.

Judging the direction of the political winds can be even more challenging than figuring out where prices are headed. At the moment, there is a great deal of instability in the world, but there is a positive side. It is that the unrest grows out of the collapse of communism. In the Cold War era, the worst-case scenario was a confrontation between well-armed superpowers. Today's unrest is localized, and it is the inevitable outcome of a very favorable long-term trend—namely, the establishment of more tolerant and democratic political regimes.

There is not much to say about tax rates under the current Administration. It is clear that whatever else may or may not get accomplished in the Clinton era, taxes are going up. Prospects for regulatory change are mixed. Clearly President Clinton is intent on reregulating many areas of the economy.

In spite of this, the government will shrink, largely because of current and anticipated reductions in defense. Over the next few years, the public sector will account for a smaller share of gross national product than it has in the recent past. In addition, most state and local governments are operating in the red, so it seems likely that they will also be forced to shrink the scope of their operations.

Judging how fearful or confident investors are feeling is a subjective exercise. There are surveys of sentiment that are published periodically. And when things get really bleak, people try to get money out of the country altogether. By these measures, I would say that people are uncomfortable and somewhat uncertain, but they are not fearful.

In the Seventies and the Eighties the nature of the confrontation between financial assets and tangible assets was very clear. Investors in tangibles were rewarded with hefty returns in the inflationary Seventies, while financial investors prospered in the Eighties. Of course, these trends are particularly clear with the benefit of hindsight. It is always more difficult to judge a single year than a more extended period.

Given fears about inflation and overall investor uncertainty, it is not too surprising that the figures on my survey for the latest year present a mixed picture. In the 12 months

Investment Clues from the Past*

	20 years		10 years		5 years		1 year	
Asset	**return**	**rank**	**return**	**rank**	**return**	**rank**	**return**	**rank**
Stocks	12.2%	1	14.8%	1	15.1%	1	11.6%	2
Bonds	9.8	2	13.2	2	13.1	2	14.8	1
Stamps	9.6	3	(1.7)	11	0.5	11	8.8	4
3-month Treasury bills	8.8	4	7.3	4	6.6	4	3.3	8
Diamonds	8.5	5	5.9	5	4.3	5	1.5	11
Oil	7.5	6	(4.7)	12	1.7	9	(6.3)	12
Gold	6.9	7	(1.0)	9	(4.2)	12	9.6	3
Housing	6.7	8	4.4	7	3.7	7	1.8	10
Consumer Price Index	6.1	9	3.8	8	4.2	6	3.3	7
Chinese ceramics	5.8	10	7.6	3	9.8	3	(7.5)	13
U.S. farmland	5.4	11	(1.2)	10	2.1	8	2.3	9
Foreign exchange	3.4	12	5.6	6	1.7	10	6.2	6
Silver	2.7	13	(10.1)	13	(8.5)	13	8.4	5

* These rankings for financial and tangible assets can aid investors in deciding how to allocate their funds. The rates of return are compounded annually, based on the latest available data.

Sources: Salomon Brothers Inc; Diamonds, The Diamond Registry; Basket of U.S. stamps, Scott Inc.; Chinese ceramics, Sotheby's; Oil, American Petroleum Institute; Housing, National Association of Realtors; Farmland (excluding income), U.S. government statistics. Note: Old Masters were excluded because current data were unavailable.

ended in June, the top five performing assets include, two financial assets, one collectible and two commodities—hardly a trend-setting year. Without making too many generalizations on a single year's data, it is worth noting that collectibles generally do not conform to the long-term patterns of the tangible asset group as a whole. In part, this is because collectibles do not serve an economic purpose. But more important, people frequently buy them as public emblems of their success: High priced collectibles are a form of conspicuous consumption.

The real estate markets are also showing a mixed picture. Both commercial and residential property prices have been in a prolonged slump. At present it appears as though the residential side of the market is coming to life, but commercial prices remain depressed under the burden of a huge oversupply.

But in contrast with the past 12 months' mixed picture, the long-term trends continue to favor financial assets. Among these, stocks should continue to outperform bonds, based on the improved corporate earnings picture. The market is not cheap, however, and returns will not match the very strong performance of the past ten years. In my view, stock returns could approach 8% to 10% over the next few years, still comfortably outpacing inflation. For the first time in many years, I also think that at least one tangible asset is beginning to look interesting. Prices of residential real estate are likely to improve somewhat in the next few years.

Stock Market: U.S. and Foreign

Investment Returns on Stocks, Bonds, and Bills

Roger G. Ibbotson and Carl G. Gargula***

Our look at history consists of examining the returns of five capital market sectors. We measure total returns (capital gains plus income) on common stocks, long-term corporate bonds, long-term government bonds, U.S. Treasury bills, and rates of inflation on consumer goods. Comparing the returns from the various sectors gives us insights into the returns available from taking risk and the relationships between capital market returns and inflation.

THE RISKS AND REWARDS

We display graphically the rewards and risks available from the U.S. capital markets over the past 67 years. Exhibit 1 shows the growth of an investment in common stocks, long-term government bonds, and Treasury bills as well as the increase in the inflation index over the 67-year period. Each of the series is initiated at $1 at year-end 1925. The vertical scale is logarithmic so that equal distances represent equal percentage changes anywhere along the axis. The graph vividly portrays that despite setbacks such as that of October 1987, common stocks were the big winner over the entire period. If $1 were invested in stocks at year-end 1925 and all dividends reinvested, the dollar investment would have grown to $727.38 by year-end 1992. This phenomenal growth was not without substantial risk, especially during the earlier portion of the period. In contrast, long-term government bonds (with a constant 20-year maturity) exhibited much less risk, but grew to only $23.71.

A virtually riskless strategy (for those with short-term time horizons) has been to buy U.S. Treasury bills. However, Treasury bills have had a marked tendency to track inflation, with the result that their real (inflation adjusted) return is near zero for the entire 1926–1992 period. Note that the tracking is only prevalent over the latter portion of the period. During periods of deflation (such as the late 1920s and early 1930s) the Treasury bill returns were near zero, but not negative, since no one intentionally buys securities with negative yields. Beginning in the early 1940s, the yields (returns) on Treasury bills were pegged by the government at low rates while high inflation was experienced. The government pegging ended with the U.S. Treasury-Federal Reserve Accord in March 1951.

We summarize the investment returns in Exhibit 2 by presenting the average annual returns over the 1926–1992 period. Common stocks returned a compounded (geometric mean) total return of 10.3 percent per year. The annual compound return from capital appreciation alone was 5.4 percent. After adjusting for inflation, annual compounded total returns were 7.2 percent per year.

The average total return over any single year (arithmetic mean) for stocks was 12.4 percent, with positive returns recorded in more than two-thirds of the years (47 out of 67 years). The risk or degree of return fluctuation is measured by standard deviation as 20.6 percent. The frequency distribution (histogram) counts the number of years the returns fell in each 5 percent return increment. Note the wide variations in common stock returns relative to the other capital market sectors. Annual stock returns ranged from 54.0 percent in 1933 to −43.3 percent in 1931.

A simple example illustrates the difference between geometric and arithmetic means. Suppose $1 were invested in a common stock portfolio that experiences successive annual returns of +50 percent and −50 percent. At the end of the first year, the portfolio is worth $1.50. At the end of the second year, the portfolio is worth $0.75. The annual arithmetic mean is 0 percent, whereas the annual geometric mean (compounded return) is −13.4 percent. Naturally, it is the geometric mean that more directly measures the change in wealth over more than one period. On the other hand, the arithmetic mean is a better representation of typical performance over any single annual period.

The other capital market sectors also had returns commensurate with their risks. Long-term corporate bonds outperformed the default-free, long-term government bonds, which in turn outperformed the essentially riskless U.S. Treasury bills. Over the entire period the riskless U.S. Treasury bills had a

* Professor, Yale School of Management, New Haven, Connecticut and President of Ibbotson Associates.

** Managing Director and General Counsel, Communications Resources Group, Ibbotson Associates.

EXHIBIT 1: WEALTH INDICES OF INVESTMENTS IN THE U.S. CAPITAL MARKETS, 1925–1992 (Year-End 1925 = 1.00)

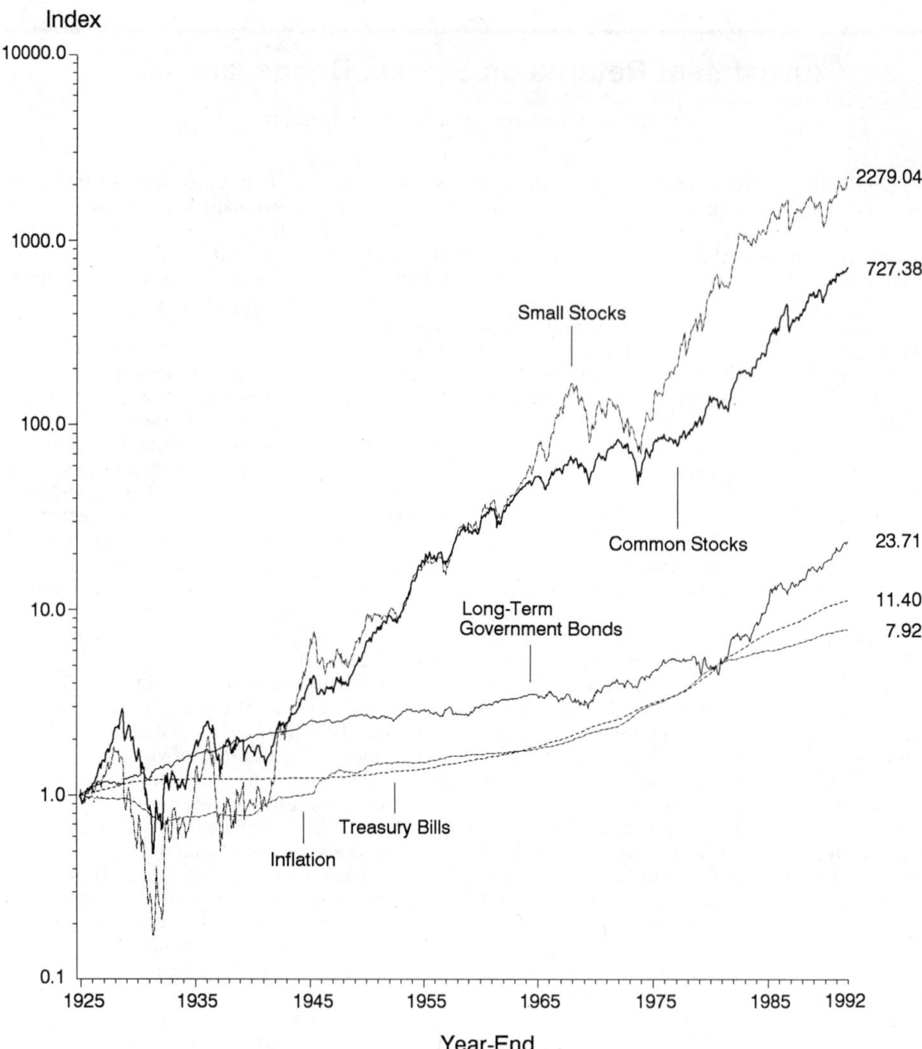

Source: *Stocks, Bonds, Bills, and Inflation: 1993 Yearbook*, published by Ibbotson Associates, Inc., 225 North Michigan Avenue, Suite 700, Chicago, IL. 60601-7676, telephone 312-616-1620. Used with permission. All rights reserved.

return almost identical with the inflation rate. Thus, we again note that the real rate of interest (the inflation-adjusted riskless rate) has been on average very near 0 percent historically.

MEASUREMENT OF THE FIVE SERIES

The returns were computed by compounding monthly returns, with no adjustments made for transactions costs or taxes. We describe each of the five total return series which are listed annually in Exhibit 3. The index numbers in Exhibit 3 are dollar values of a $1 investment made on December 31, 1925. They can be converted to yearly returns by taking the ratio of a given year-end index value to the previous year-end value, then subtracting one (1). For example, the return for common stocks for 1992 equals (727.382 ÷ 675.592) − 1 = .0767, or 7.67 percent.

Common Stocks

The total return index is based upon Standard & Poor's (S&P) Composite Index with

EXHIBIT 2: BASIC SERIES: SUMMARY STATISTICS OF ANNUAL TOTAL RETURNS, 1926–1992

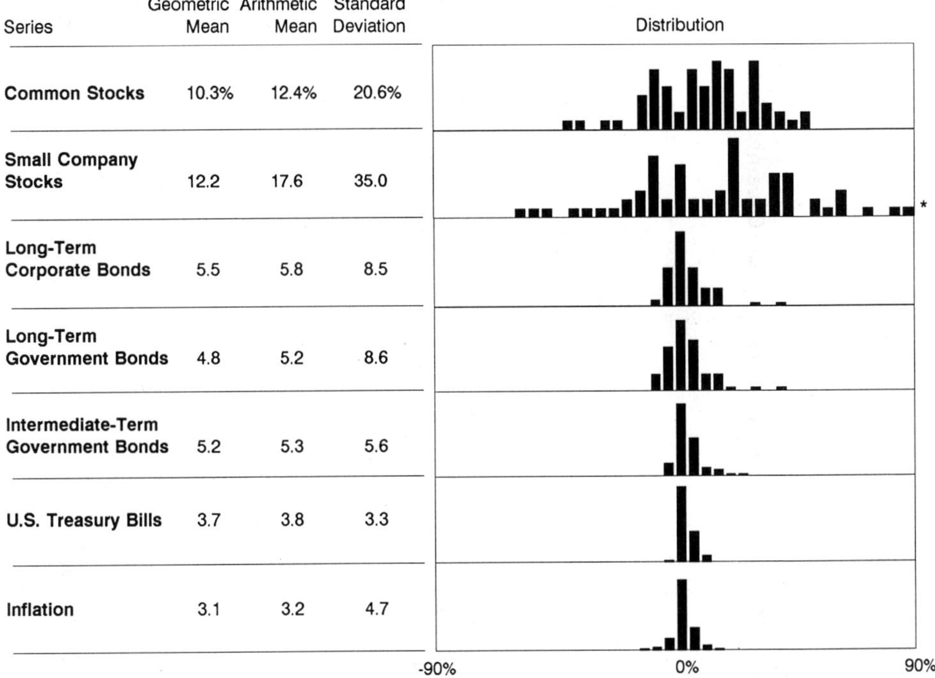

Series	Geometric Mean	Arithmetic Mean	Standard Deviation
Common Stocks	10.3%	12.4%	20.6%
Small Company Stocks	12.2	17.6	35.0
Long-Term Corporate Bonds	5.5	5.8	8.5
Long-Term Government Bonds	4.8	5.2	8.6
Intermediate-Term Government Bonds	5.2	5.3	5.6
U.S. Treasury Bills	3.7	3.8	3.3
Inflation	3.1	3.2	4.7

* The 1933 Small Company Stock Total Return was 142.9 percent.

Source: *Stocks, Bonds, Bills and Inflation 1993 Yearbook,* Ibbotson Associates, Chicago, 1993.

dividends reinvested monthly. To the extent that the 500 stocks currently included in the S&P Composite Index (prior to March 1957, there were 90 stocks) are representative of all stocks in the United States, the market value weighting scheme allows the returns of the index to correspond to the aggregate stock market returns in the U.S. economy.

Long-Term Corporate Bonds

We measure the total returns of a corporate bond index with approximately 20 years to maturity. We use Salomon Brothers' High-Grade Long-Term Corporate Bond Index from its beginning in 1969 through 1992. For the period 1946–68 we backdate Salomon Brothers' index using Salomon Brothers' monthly yield data and similar methodology. For the period 1926–45 we compute returns using Standard & Poor's monthly high-grade corporate composite bond yield data, assuming a 4 percent coupon and a 20-year maturity.

Long-Term Government Bonds

To measure the total returns of long-term U.S. government bonds, we use the bond data obtained from the U.S. Government Bond File (constructed by Lawrence Fisher) at the Center for Research in Security Prices (CRSP) at the University of Chicago. We attempt to maintain a 20-year bond portfolio whose returns do not reflect the potential tax benefits, impaired negotiability, or the special redemption or call privileges frequently characterizing government bond prices and yields.

U.S. Treasury Bills

For the U.S. Treasury bill index, we again use the data in the CRSP U.S. Government Bond File. We measure one-month holding period returns for the shortest-term bills not less than one month in maturity. Since U.S. Treasury bills were not initiated until 1929, we use short-term coupon bonds whenever bill quotes are unavailable.

Consumer Price Index

We utilize the Consumer Price Index for All Urban Consumers (CPI-U), not seasonally adjusted, to measure inflation. The CPI-U, and its predecessor, the CPI (which we use prior to January 1978) is constructed by the Bureau of Labor Statistics, U.S. Department of Labor, Washington, D.C.

EXHIBIT 3: BASIC SERIES, INDICES OF YEAR-END CUMULATIVE WEALTH, 1925–1992 (December 1925 = 1.00)

	Common Stocks		Small Stocks	Long-Term Corp Bonds	Long-Term Government Bonds		Intermediate-Term Government Bonds		U.S. T-Bills	
Year	Total Returns	Capital Apprec	Total Returns	Total Returns	Total Returns	Capital Apprec	Total Returns	Capital Apprec	Total Returns	Inflation
1925	1.000	1.000	1.000	1.000	1.000	1.000	1.000	1.000	1.000	1.000
1926	1.116	1.057	1.003	1.074	1.078	1.039	1.054	1.015	1.033	0.985
1927	1.535	1.384	1.224	1.154	1.174	1.095	1.101	1.025	1.065	0.965
1928	2.204	1.908	1.710	1.186	1.175	1.061	1.112	0.997	1.103	0.955
1929	2.018	1.681	0.832	1.225	1.215	1.059	1.178	1.014	1.155	0.957
1930	1.516	1.202	0.515	1.323	1.272	1.072	1.258	1.048	1.183	0.899
1931	0.859	0.636	0.259	1.299	1.204	0.982	1.228	0.991	1.196	0.814
1932	0.789	0.540	0.245	1.439	1.407	1.109	1.337	1.041	1.207	0.730
1933	1.214	0.792	0.594	1.588	1.406	1.074	1.361	1.031	1.211	0.734
1934	1.197	0.745	0.738	1.808	1.547	1.146	1.483	1.092	1.213	0.749
1935	1.767	1.053	1.035	1.982	1.624	1.171	1.587	1.146	1.215	0.771
1936	2.367	1.346	1.705	2.116	1.746	1.225	1.636	1.165	1.217	0.780
1937	1.538	0.827	0.716	2.174	1.750	1.195	1.661	1.165	1.221	0.804
1938	2.016	1.035	0.951	2.307	1.847	1.229	1.765	1.216	1.221	0.782
1939	2.008	0.979	0.954	2.399	1.957	1.272	1.845	1.255	1.221	0.778
1940	1.812	0.829	0.905	2.480	2.076	1.319	1.899	1.280	1.221	0.786
1941	1.602	0.681	0.823	2.548	2.096	1.306	1.909	1.278	1.222	0.862
1942	1.927	0.766	1.190	2.614	2.163	1.316	1.946	1.293	1.225	0.942
1943	2.427	0.915	2.242	2.688	2.208	1.311	2.000	1.309	1.229	0.972
1944	2.906	1.041	3.446	2.815	2.270	1.315	2.036	1.314	1.233	0.993
1945	3.965	1.361	5.983	2.930	2.514	1.424	2.082	1.327	1.237	1.015
1946	3.645	1.199	5.287	2.980	2.511	1.393	2.102	1.326	1.242	1.199
1947	3.853	1.199	5.335	2.911	2.445	1.328	2.122	1.322	1.248	1.307
1948	4.065	1.191	5.223	3.031	2.529	1.341	2.161	1.326	1.258	1.343
1949	4.829	1.313	6.254	3.132	2.692	1.396	2.211	1.338	1.272	1.318
1950	6.360	1.600	8.677	3.198	2.693	1.367	2.227	1.329	1.287	1.395
1951	7.888	1.863	9.355	3.112	2.587	1.282	2.235	1.307	1.306	1.477
1952	9.336	2.082	9.638	3.221	2.617	1.263	2.271	1.300	1.328	1.490
1953	9.244	1.944	9.013	3.331	2.713	1.271	2.345	1.308	1.352	1.499
1954	14.108	2.820	14.473	3.511	2.907	1.326	2.407	1.322	1.364	1.492

1955	18.561	3.564	17.431	3.527	2.870	1.272	2.392	1.281	1.385	1.497
1956	19.778	3.658	18.177	3.287	2.710	1.165	2.382	1.237	1.419	1.540
1957	17.646	3.134	15.529	3.573	2.912	1.209	2.568	1.287	1.464	1.587
1958	25.298	4.327	25.605	3.494	2.734	1.098	2.535	1.233	1.486	1.615
1959	28.322	4.694	29.804	3.460	2.673	1.030	2.525	1.177	1.530	1.639
1960	28.455	4.554	28.823	3.774	3.041	1.125	2.822	1.264	1.571	1.663
1961	36.106	5.607	38.072	3.956	3.070	1.093	2.874	1.243	1.604	1.674
1962	32.954	4.945	33.540	4.270	3.282	1.124	3.034	1.264	1.648	1.695
1963	40.469	5.879	41.444	4.364	3.322	1.093	3.084	1.237	1.700	1.723
1964	47.139	6.642	51.193	4.572	3.438	1.085	3.209	1.237	1.760	1.743
1965	53.008	7.244	72.567	4.552	3.462	1.048	3.242	1.199	1.829	1.777
1966	47.674	6.295	67.479	4.560	3.589	1.037	3.394	1.194	1.916	1.836
1967	59.104	7.560	123.870	4.335	3.259	0.896	3.428	1.148	1.997	1.892
1968	65.642	8.139	168.429	4.446	3.251	0.847	3.583	1.136	2.101	1.981
1969	60.059	7.210	126.233	4.086	3.086	0.755	3.557	1.054	2.239	2.102
1970	62.465	7.222	104.226	4.837	3.460	0.792	4.156	1.145	2.385	2.218
1971	71.406	8.001	121.423	5.370	3.917	0.844	4.519	1.177	2.490	2.292
1972	84.956	9.252	126.807	5.760	4.140	0.841	4.752	1.168	2.585	2.371
1973	72.500	7.645	87.618	5.825	4.094	0.777	4.971	1.142	2.764	2.579
1974	53.311	5.373	70.142	5.647	4.272	0.750	5.254	1.120	2.986	2.894
1975	73.144	7.068	107.189	6.474	4.665	0.755	5.665	1.121	3.159	3.097
1976	90.584	8.422	168.691	7.681	5.447	0.816	6.394	1.180	3.319	3.246
1977	84.077	7.453	211.500	7.813	5.410	0.752	6.484	1.119	3.489	3.466
1978	89.592	7.532	261.120	7.807	5.346	0.684	6.710	1.069	3.740	3.778
1979	106.113	8.459	374.614	7.481	5.280	0.617	6.985	1.015	4.128	4.281
1980	140.514	10.639	523.992	7.285	5.071	0.530	7.258	0.946	4.592	4.812
1981	133.616	9.605	596.717	7.215	5.166	0.476	7.944	0.903	5.267	5.242
1982	162.223	11.023	763.829	10.374	7.251	0.589	10.256	1.031	5.822	5.445
1983	198.745	12.926	1066.828	10.862	7.298	0.532	11.015	0.997	6.335	5.652
1984	211.199	13.106	995.680	12.642	8.427	0.544	12.560	1.009	6.959	5.875
1985	279.117	16.559	1241.234	16.549	11.037	0.641	15.113	1.100	7.496	6.097
1986	330.671	18.981	1326.275	19.833	13.745	0.737	17.401	1.177	7.958	6.166
1987	347.968	19.366	1202.965	19.780	13.372	0.658	17.906	1.121	8.393	6.438
1988	406.458	21.769	1478.135	21.897	14.665	0.661	18.999	1.096	8.926	6.722
1989	534.456	27.703	1628.590	25.451	17.322	0.718	21.524	1.143	9.673	7.034
1990	517.499	25.886	1277.449	27.178	18.392	0.699	23.618	1.155	10.429	7.464
1991	675.592	32.695	1847.629	32.583	21.941	0.769	27.270	1.240	11.012	7.693
1992	727.382	34.155	2279.039	35.644	23.709	0.772	29.231	1.248	11.398	7.916

Source: *Stocks, Bonds, Bills, and Inflation: 1993 Yearbook,* Ibbotson Associates, Chicago, 1993.

The Constant Dollar Dow

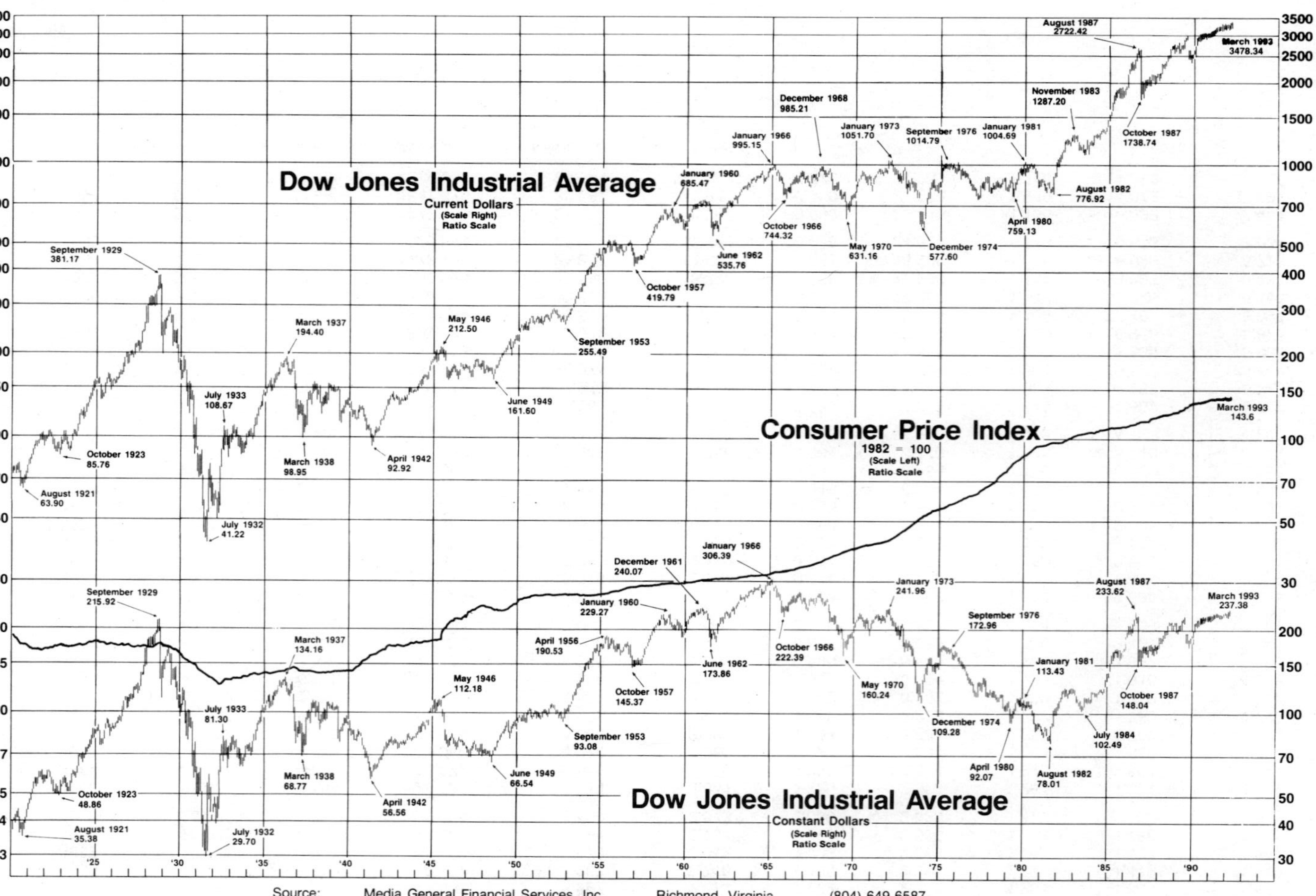

Source: Media General Financial Services, Inc., Richmond, Virginia.

Cash dividends on NYSE listed common stocks

	Number of issues listed at year-end	Common stocks Number paying cash dividends during year	Estimated aggregate cash payments (millions)
1929	842	554	$2,711
1935	776	387	1,336
1940	829	577	2,099
1945	881	746	2,275
1950	1,039	930	5,404
1951	1,054	961	5,467
1952	1,067	975	5,595
1953	1,069	964	5,874
1954	1,076	968	6,439
1955	1,076	982	7,488
1956	1,077	975	8,341
1957	1,098	991	8,807
1958	1,086	961	8,711
1959	1,092	953	9,337
1960	1,126	981	9,872
1961	1,145	981	10,430
1962	1,168	994	11,203
1963	1,194	1,032	12,096
1964	1,227	1,066	13,555
1965	1,254	1,111	15,302
1966	1,267	1,127	16,151
1967	1,255	1,116	16,866
1968	1,253	1,104	18,124
1969	1,290	1,121	19,404
1970	1,330	1,120	19,781
1971	1,399	1,132	20,256
1972	1,478	1,195	21,490
1973	1,536	1,276	23,627
1974	1,543	1,308	25,662
1975	1,531	1,273	26,901
1976	1,550	1,304	30,608
1977	1,549	1,360	36,270
1978	1,552	1,373	41,151
1979	1,536	1,359	46,937
1980	1,540	1,361	53,072
1981	1,534	1,337	60,628
1982	1,499	1,287	62,224
1983	1,518	1,259	67,102
1984	1,511	1,243	68,215
1985	1,503	1,206	74,237
1986	1,536	1,180	76,161
1987	1,606	1,219	84,377
1988	1,643	1,270	102,190
1989	1,683	1,303	101,778
1990	1,741	N/A	103,150*
1991	1,860	N/A	123,385*
1992	2,068	N/A	109,696*

* Estimate based on average annual yield of the NYSE Composite Index.

N/A – Not available

Source: New York Stock Exchange *Fact Book*.

NYSE Composite Index, daily closings, 1992 (December 31, 1965 = 50)

	Jan.	Feb.	Mar.	Apr.	May	June	July	Aug.	Sept.	Oct.	Nov.	Dec.
1	•	•	•	223.42	227.20	229.90	226.75	•	229.02	228.73	•	237.20
2	229.17	•	228.20	221.51	•	228.20	226.41	•	230.01	225.81	232.48	236.74
3	230.35	226.61	228.43	221.86	•	228.65	•	233.66	230.12	•	231.24	236.76
4	•	228.79	226.66	•	229.42	227.90	•	233.39	229.75	•	229.79	237.77
5	•	228.87	224.92	•	229.50	227.88	•	232.29	•	224.14	230.37	•
6	229.85	228.96	223.79	223.79	229.56	•	227.44	231.50	•	224.09	230.09	•
7	229.69	227.65	•	220.00	229.08	•	225.15	230.79	•	222.84	•	239.36
8	230.23	•	•	217.92	230.33	227.71	225.49	•	228.37	224.62	•	240.24
9	230.23	•	224.15	221.10	•	225.95	227.55	•	229.10	222.11	230.63	239.44
10	228.95	228.93	225.02	223.27	•	224.36	227.88	230.86	230.78	•	230.66	238.97
11	•	228.94	223.55	•	230.47	225.10	•	230.61	230.80	•	232.58	238.63
12	•	230.54	223.30	•	229.45	225.51	•	229.99	•	224.28	232.83	•
13	228.47	228.73	224.30	224.16	229.44	•	228.04	229.95	•	225.31	232.64	•
14	231.57	228.16	•	227.31	227.72	•	229.51	231.06	233.73	225.39	•	238.16
15	231.84	•	•	229.15	226.31	225.62	229.20	•	231.04	225.54	•	238.02
16	230.55	•	224.44	228.90	•	224.72	229.49	•	231.07	226.44	231.78	237.26
17	230.89	•	226.01	•	•	221.45	228.51	231.60	230.97	•	231.09	239.12
18	•	225.65	225.94	•	227.59	220.61	•	231.90	232.39	•	232.87	242.08
19	•	225.85	226.25	•	229.32	221.96	•	230.41	•	228.24	233.25	•
20	229.67	228.60	226.96	225.77	228.94	•	227.51	230.38	•	228.58	234.78	•
21	227.64	227.46	•	225.70	227.47	•	227.47	228.61	231.89	228.60	•	241.72
22	230.19	•	•	225.42	228.20	221.56	226.13	•	229.48	228.10	•	241.68
23	228.89	•	226.39	226.16	•	221.99	226.66	•	229.42	227.83	234.11	241.00
24	229.17	227.62	225.89	225.12	•	221.81	226.48	226.34	229.98	•	235.27	241.23
25	•	226.68	225.39	•	•	221.53	•	226.47	227.73	•	236.13	•
26	•	229.23	225.49	•	226.86	221.68	•	227.48	•	229.78	•	•
27	228.94	228.75	223.31	224.94	227.15	•	226.50	227.73	•	230.01	236.72	•
28	228.95	228.21	•	225.12	229.24	•	229.54	228.43	228.70	230.91	•	241.01
29	226.64	•	•	226.58	228.87	224.44	231.95	•	228.90	231.42	•	240.66
30	227.37		222.99	228.30	•	224.33	232.89	•	229.46	230.57	237.45	241.16
31	226.20		223.25		•		233.15	228.03		•		240.21
High	**231.84**	**230.54**	**228.43**	**229.15**	**230.47**	**229.90**	**233.15**	**233.66**	**233.73**	**231.42**	**237.45**	**242.08**
Low	**226.20**	**225.65**	**222.99**	**217.92**	**226.31**	**220.61**	**225.15**	**226.34**	**227.73**	**222.11**	**229.79**	**236.74**
Avg.	**229.34**	**228.12**	**225.21**	**224.55**	**228.61**	**224.68**	**228.17**	**230.07**	**230.13**	**226.97**	**232.84**	**239.47**

• NYSE closed.

Source: New York Stock Exchange *Fact Book*.

NYSE program trading participation in NYSE volume, 1992

	Total program trading as % of NYSE volume	Buy programs as % of NYSE volume	Sell programs as % of NYSE volume	Total program trading as % of twice (TTV) NYSE volume
January	10.8%	5.9%	4.9%	5.4 %
February	10.8	4.3	6.5	5.4
March	13.2	5.7	7.5	6.6
April	10.4	5.8	4.6	5.2
May	12.1	4.9	7.2	6.0
June	15.6	7.7	7.9	7.8
July	11.2	6.3	4.9	5.6
August	9.3	4.7	4.6	4.6
September	11.2	6.0	5.2	5.6
October	9.6	4.5	5.1	4.8
November	9.1	4.5	4.7	4.6
December	14.4	8.7	5.7	7.2
1992	**11.5%**	**5.8%**	**5.7%**	**5.8 %**
1991	11.0	5.9	5.1	5.5
1990	10.7	5.2	5.5	5.3
1989	9.9	5.4	4.5	5.0

Note: Starting June 13, 1991 percentages include Crossing Session II volume.

Source: New York Stock Exchange *Fact Book*.

Compounded growth rates in NYSE Composite Index* (percent)

	Initial year															Index at year
	'77	'78	'79	'80	'81	'82	'83	'84	'85	'86	'87	'88	'89	'90	'91	end
'77																**52.50**
'78	2.1															**53.62**
'79	8.6	15.5														**61.95**
'80	14.0	20.5	25.7													**77.86**
'81	7.9	9.9	7.1	-8.7												**71.11**
'82	9.1	10.9	9.4	2.0	14.0											**81.03**
'83	10.4	12.2	11.3	6.9	15.7	17.5										**95.18**
'84	9.1	10.3	9.2	5.5	10.7	9.1	1.3									**96.38**
'85	11.1	12.4	11.9	9.3	14.3	14.5	13.0	26.1								**121.58**
'86	11.4	12.6	12.2	10.1	14.3	14.4	13.3	19.9	14.0							**138.58**
'87	10.2	11.1	10.6	8.5	11.7	11.3	9.8	12.8	6.6	-0.3						**138.23**
'88	10.4	11.3	10.8	9.1	11.9	11.6	10.4	12.8	8.7	6.2	13.0					**156.26**
'89	11.6	12.5	12.2	10.7	13.4	13.4	12.7	15.1	12.5	12.1	18.8	24.8				**195.04**
'90	10.0	10.6	10.2	8.8	10.9	10.5	9.6	11.0	8.2	6.8	9.3	7.5	-7.5			**180.49**
'91	11.1	11.8	11.5	10.3	12.4	12.3	11.6	13.2	11.2	10.6	13.5	13.7	8.5	27.1		**229.44**
'92	10.7	11.3	11.0	9.8	11.7	11.5	10.8	12.1	10.2	9.6	11.7	11.3	7.2	15.4	4.7	**240.21**

*Index figures taken at year end.

The table on this page presents annual growth rates in the NYSE Composite Index from 1977–92. Growth rate is a term referring to the average rate of increase or decrease, compounded annually, between two periods.

To obtain the growth rate, for example, between 1982 and 1992, go down the vertical column under 1982 to the horizontal row opposite 1992, which shows an 11.5% rate. This means that stock prices, as measured by the NYSE Composite Index, increased at a yearly rate of 11.5%, compounded annually, between the ends of those years. Stock prices showed an increase of 4.7% in 1992.

The price appreciation on stocks is only a partial measure of the return on money invested in stock. To compute a total return, it is necessary to add the dividends received each year—a calculation not included in this table.

Source: New York Stock Exchange *Fact Book.*

NYSE Composite Index—yield and P/E ratio

End of period	Yield•	Price/earnings ratio ★
1992		
December	3.0%	22.7
September	2.9	25.4
June	2.9	26.3
March	2.6	27.1
1991		
December	2.4	25.8
September	3.4	19.7
June	3.4	17.6
March	3.6	17.1
1990		
December	3.7	14.8
September	4.5	13.6
June	3.5	15.5
March	3.7	14.9
1989		
December	3.2	15.0
September	3.4	14.2
June	3.5	13.3
March	3.9	12.5
1988		
December	3.6	12.7
September	3.7	13.1
June	3.4	15.4
March	3.9	15.4
1987		
December	3.4	15.5
September	2.9	22.0
June	2.7	21.1
March	2.8	20.2
1986		
December	3.4	16.1
September	3.3	16.6
June	3.3	16.6
March	3.5	15.5
1985		
December	3.6	13.5
September	4.2	10.7
June	4.2	12.6
March	4.4	11.3
1984		
December	4.5	10.4
September	4.5	10.6
June	4.9	10.1
March	4.5	11.6
1983		
December	4.4%	13.0
September	4.2	13.9
June	4.1	13.9
March	4.9	14.7
1982		
December	5.2	14.7
September	6.1	12.5
June	7.0	11.3
March	7.2	10.3
1981		
December	6.7	11.3
September	7.1	9.9
June	6.0	11.9
March	5.7	12.5
1980		
December	5.4	13.1
September	5.7	12.7
June	6.0	9.8
March	6.8	9.4
1979		
December	6.2	10.1
September	6.0	9.9
June	6.4	9.9
March	5.7	10.5
1978		
December	5.9	10.3
September	5.3	10.9
June	5.5	11.8
March	6.0	10.7
1977		
December	5.7	11.6
September	5.5	11.3
June	5.3	12.7
March	5.2	12.6
1976		
December	4.6	14.3
September	4.6	13.4
June	4.3	14.1
March	4.2	15.2
1975		
December	4.6	13.8
September	5.0	13.8
June	4.3	17.9
March	5.0	13.3

• Total dollar value of dividend payments during latest 12 months—through June 1983 and indicated dollar value through June 1985—divided by market value at end of period and multiplied by 100. Beginning in July 1985, latest quarterly dividend divided by closing price at end of period.

★ Latest closing price divided by trailing 12 months of earnings.

Source: New York Stock Exchange *Fact Book*.

NASDAQ Index Performance

Indexes	Record High	Date Established	12/31/92	12/31/82	10-Year % Change
Composite	676.95	12/31/92	676.95	232.41	+191%
Industrial	741.92	2/12/92	724.94	273.58	+165%
Other Finance	788.81	12/31/92	788.81	207.50	+280%
Bank	532.93	12/31/92	532.93	156.37	+241%
Insurance	803.91	12/31/92	803.91	226.40	+255%
Utility	788.51	10/9/89	734.18	286.23	+157%
Transportation	634.10	12/31/92	634.10	195.48	+224%
Nasdaq/NMS Composite	300.56	12/31/92	300.56	*	*
Nasdaq/NMS Industrial	296.32	2/12/92	291.40	*	*
Nasdaq-100®	723.67	12/7/92	720.37	**	**
Nasdaq-Financial®	699.92	12/31/92	699.92	**	**

*The Nasdaq/NMS indexes began on July 10, 1984, valued at 100.
**The Nasdaq-100® and Nasdaq Financial® indexes began on February 1, 1985, valued at 250.

Source: *1993 NASDAQ FACT BOOK & COMPANY DIRECTORY,* published by the National Association of Securities Dealers, Inc., 1735 K Street, N.W., Washington, D.C. 20006-1500.

50 Most Active NASDAQ National Market Issues in 1992

Symbol	Company Name	Closing Price (12/31/92)	Share Volume (000s)
1. INTC	Intel Corporation	87.000	546,672
2. TCOMA	Tele-Communications, Inc.	21.250	444,621
3. NOVL	Novell, Inc.	28.500	434,405
4. MSFT	Microsoft Corporation	85.375	402,786
5. SGAT	Seagate Technology, Inc.	19.625	391,092
6. SUNW	Sun Microsystems, Inc.	33.625	384,799
7. AAPL	Apple Computer, Inc.	59.750	369,094
8. ORCL	Oracle Systems Corporation	28.375	344,203
9. AMGN	Amgen Inc.	70.625	329,439
10. MCCS	Medco Containment Services, Inc.	37.750	305,942
11. MCIC	MCI Communications Corporation	39.625	300,701
12. COST	Costco Wholesale Corporation	24.500	277,760
13. DELL	Dell Computer Corporation	48.000	268,624
14. CSCO	Cisco Systems, Inc.	78.625	238,850
15. BORL	Borland International, Inc.	22.250	235,522
16. CNTO	Centocor, Inc.	16.250	235,052
17. USHC	U.S. Healthcare, Inc.	44.625	234,816
18. LOTS	Lotus Development Corporation	19.625	227,977
19. QNTM	Quantum Corporation	15.250	204,920
20. MCAWA	McCaw Cellular Communications, Inc.	33.500	178,262
21. BMET	Biomet, Inc.	16.250	177,544
22. ADBE	Adobe Systems Incorporated	31.500	171,583
23. MXTR	Maxtor Corporation	14.375	160,384
24. DIGI	DSC Communications Corporation	22.000	157,895
25. ASTA	AST Research, Inc.	21.000	150,814
26. INEL	Intelligent Electronics, Inc.	12.875	149,939
27. COMS	3Com Corporation	29.625	142,862
28. SYMC	Symantec Corporation	13.625	136,693
29. STJM	St. Jude Medical, Inc.	42.000	136,681
30. GNSA	Gensia Pharmaceuticals, Inc.	24.500	132,582
31. BGEN	Biogen, Inc.	47.000	130,140
32. CMCSK	Comcast Corporation	18.125	129,451
33. SYGN	Synergen, Inc.	64.250	125,918
34. ADPT	Adaptec, Inc.	26.000	125,677
35. SMLS	SciMed Life Systems, Inc.	59.125	124,305
36. PCLB	Price Company (The)	36.250	122,940
37. CHRS	Charming Shoppes, Inc.	18.125	121,310
38. IMNX	Immunex Corporation	51.250	120,432
39. CHIR	Chiron Corporation	56.500	119,786
40. FDLNA	Food Lion, Inc.	7.875	116,689
41. NOBE	Nordstrom, Inc.	38.750	114,882
42. EXBT	Exabyte Corporation	18.250	114,474
43. XOMA	XOMA Corporation	9.625	111,942
44. MIDL	Midlantic Corp.	19.875	111,856
45. PCTL	PictureTel Corporation	25.250	111,068
46. SNPX	SynOptics Communications, Inc.	81.375	110,494
47. ADAC	ADAC Laboratories	5.000	108,442
48. HCCC	HealthCare COMPARE Corp.	30.000	107,280
49. ACAD	Autodesk, Inc.	46.250	105,473
50. AMAT	Applied Materials, Inc.	33.750	104,328

Note: This list includes only securities that had a 1992 closing price of $3 or more.

Source: *1993 NASDAQ FACT BOOK & COMPANY DIRECTORY*, published by the National Association of Securities Dealers, Inc., 1735 K Street, N.W., Washington, D.C. 20006-1500.

Comparison of Share Volumes: NASDAQ, NYSE, and Amex

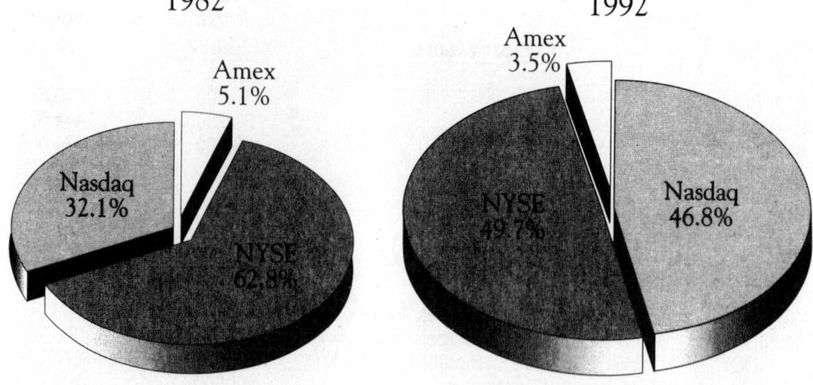

Source: *1993 NASDAQ FACT BOOK & COMPANY DIRECTORY,* published by the National Association of Securities Dealers, Inc., 1735 K Street, N.W., Washington, D.C. 20006-1500.

Ten-Year Comparisons of NASDAQ, NYSE, and Amex

	Companies			Issues			Share Volume (In Millions)		
Year	Nasdaq	NYSE	Amex	Nasdaq	NYSE	Amex	Nasdaq	NYSE	Amex
1992	**4,113**	2,089	814	**4,764**	2,658	942	**48,455**	51,376	3,600
1991	**4,094**	1,885	860	**4,684**	2,426	1,058	**41,311**	45,266	3,367
1990	**4,132**	1,769	859	**4,706**	2,284	1,063	**33,380**	39,665	3,329
1989	**4,293**	1,719	859	**4,963**	2,241	1,069	**33,530**	41,699	3,125
1988	**4,451**	1,681	896	**5,144**	2,234	1,101	**31,070**	40,850	2,515
1987	**4,706**	1,647	869	**5,537**	2,244	1,077	**37,890**	47,801	3,506
1986	**4,417**	1,573	796	**5,189**	2,257	957	**28,737**	35,680	2,979
1985	**4,136**	1,540	783	**4,784**	2,298	940	**20,699**	27,511	2,101
1984	**4,097**	1,543	792	**4,728**	2,319	930	**15,159**	23,071	1,545
1983	**3,901**	1,550	822	**4,467**	2,307	948	**15,909**	21,590	2,081

Source: *1993 NASDAQ FACT BOOK & COMPANY DIRECTORY*, published by the National Association of Securities Dealers, Inc., 1735 K Street, N.W., Washington, D.C. 20006-1500.

THE MAJOR MARKET AVERAGES

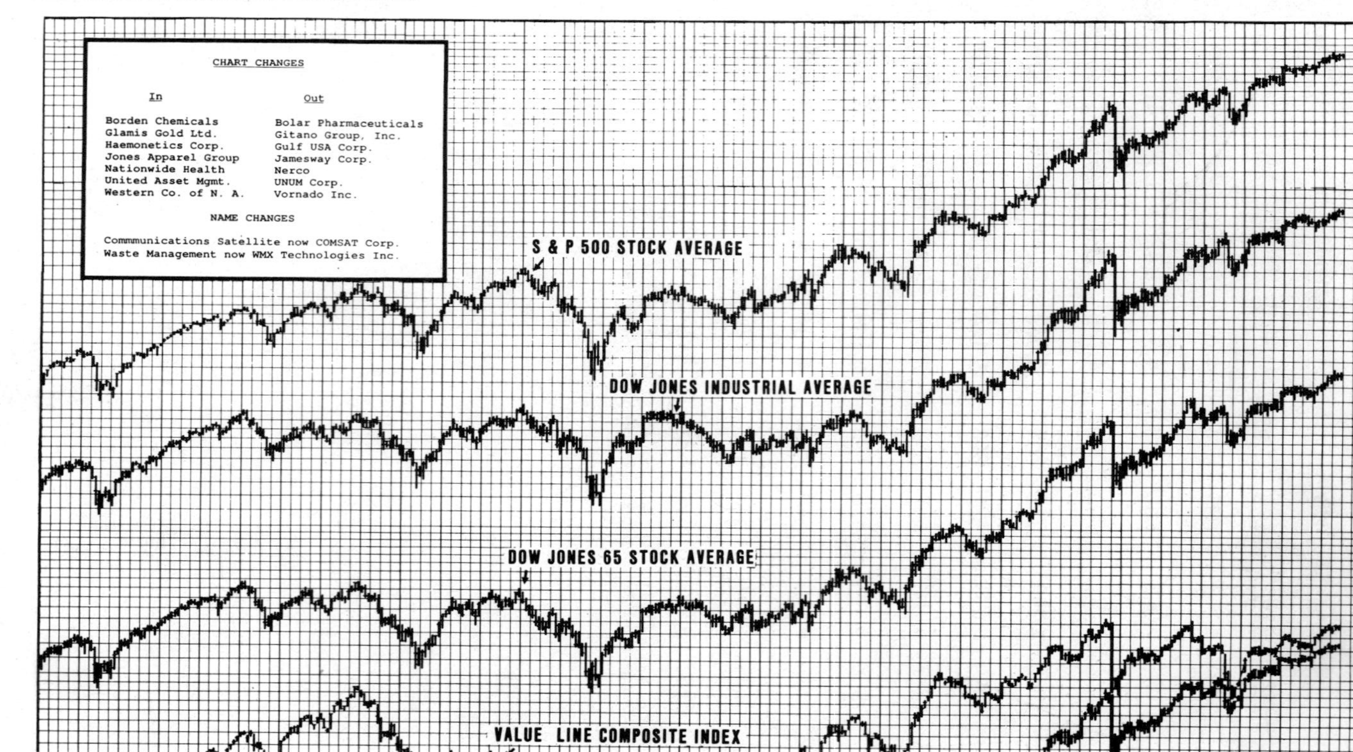
CHART CHANGES
In
Borden Chemicals
Glamis Gold Ltd.
Haemonetics Corp.
Jones Apparel Group
Nationwide Health
United Asset Mgmt.
Western Co. of N. A.
Out
Bolar Pharmaceuticals
Gitano Group, Inc.
Gulf USA Corp.
Jamesway Corp.
Nerco
UNUM Corp.
Vornado Inc.
NAME CHANGES
Commmunications Satellite now COMSAT Corp.
Waste Management now WMX Technologies Inc.
S & P 500 STOCK AVERAGE
DOW JONES INDUSTRIAL AVERAGE
DOW JONES 65 STOCK AVERAGE
VALUE LINE COMPOSITE INDEX

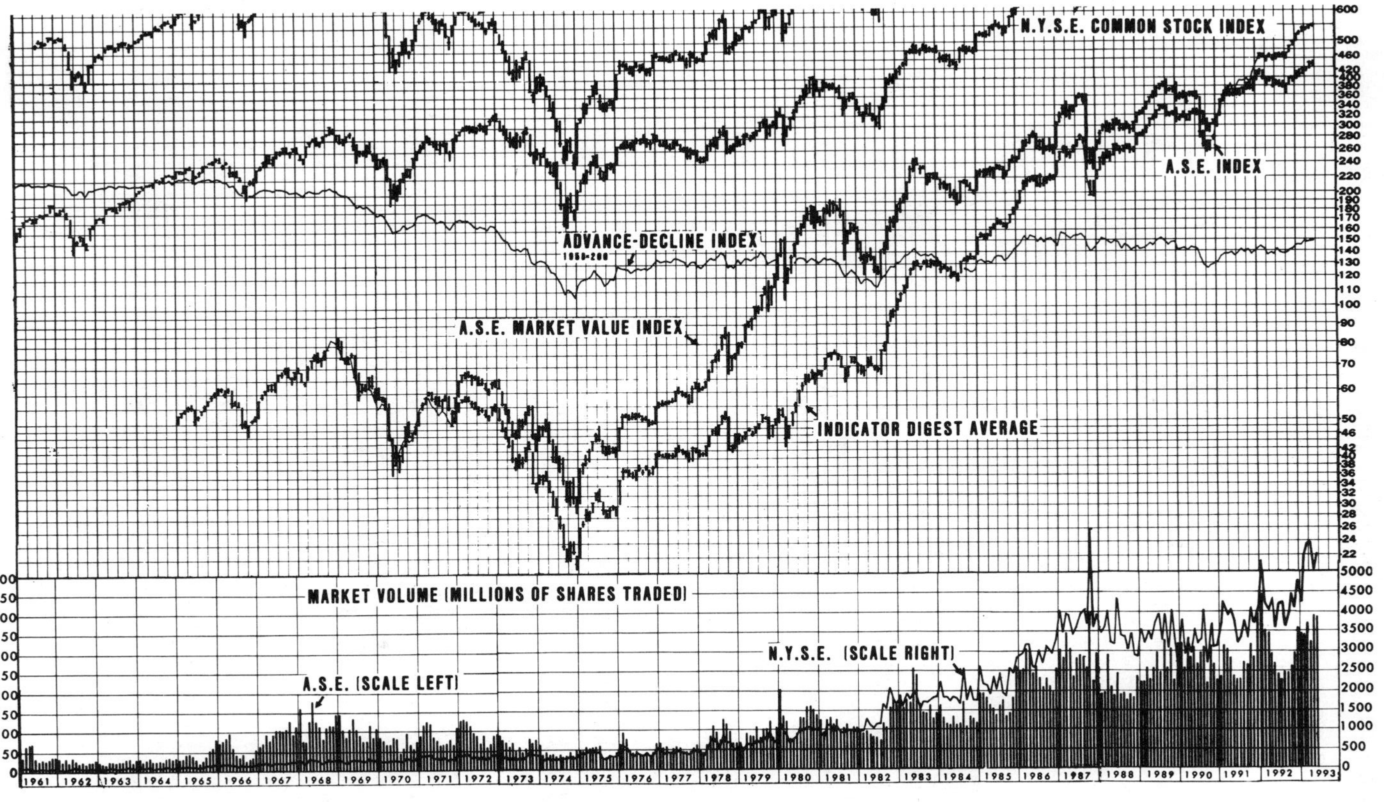

Data in this edition are complete through June 30, 1993; issuance date July 7, 1993

Source: Chart Courtesy of Securities Research Company, a division of Babson-United Investment Advisors, Inc., 101 Prescott St., Wellesley Hills, MA 02181-3319.

QUARTERLY DOW JONES INDUSTRIAL STOCK AVERAGE

The table below lists the total earnings (losses) of the Dow Jones Industrial Average component stocks of record based on generally accepted accounting principles as reported by the company and adjusted by the Dow Divisor in effect at quarter end and the total dividends of the component stocks based upon the record date and adjusted by the Dow Divisor in effect at quarter end. N.A.-Not available. d-Indicates deficit/negative earnings for the quarter.

Year Ended	Quarter Ended	Clos. Avg.	Qtrly Chg.	% Chg.	Qtrly Earns	12-Mth Earns	P/E Ratio	Qtrly Divs	12-Mth Divs	Divs Yield	Payout Ratio
1993	June 30	3516.08	+ 80.97	+ 2.36	N.A.	N.A.	N.A.	25.06	101.84	2.90	N.A.
	Mar. 31	3435.11	+ 134.00	+ 4.06	44.50	113.84	30.2	24.62	102.29	2.98	.8985
1992	Dec. 31	3301.11	+ 29.45	+ 0.90	d1.90	108.25	30.5	26.13	100.72	3.05	.9304
	Sept. 30	3271.66	− 46.86	− 1.41	23.86	84.35	38.8	26.03	97.99	3.00	1.1617
	June 30	3318.52	+ 83.05	+ 2.57	47.38	71.60	46.3	25.51	95.52	2.88	1.3341
	Mar. 31	3235.47	+ 66.64	+ 2.10	38.91	60.62	53.4	23.05	93.28	2.88	1.5388
1991	Dec. 31	3168.83	+ 152.06	+ 5.04	d25.80	49.27	64.3	23.40	95.18	3.00	1.9318
	Sept. 30	3016.77	+ 110.02	+ 3.78	11.11	100.91	29.9	23.56	97.58	3.23	.9670
	June 28	2906.75	− 7.11	− 0.24	36.40	131.42	22.1	23.27	99.37	3.42	.7561
	Mar. 28	2913.86	+ 280.20	+ 10.64	27.56	154.17	18.9	24.95	102.32	3.51	.6637
1990	Dec. 31	2633.66	+ 181.18	+ 7.39	25.84	172.05	15.3	25.80	103.70	3.94	.6027
	Sept. 28	2452.48	− 428.21	− 14.86	41.62	193.17	12.7	25.35	101.40	4.13	.5249
	June 29	2880.69	+ 173.48	+ 6.41	59.15	207.78	13.9	26.22	104.75	3.64	.5041
	Mar. 30	2707.21	− 45.99	− 1.67	45.44	205.60	13.2	26.33	106.67	3.94	.5188
1989	Dec. 29	2753.20	+ 60.38	+ 1.69	46.96	221.48	12.4	23.50	103.00	3.74	.4651
	Sept. 29	2692.82	+ 252.76	+ 10.35	56.23	225.48	11.9	28.70	100.29	3.72	.4447
	June 30	2440.06	+ 146.44	+ 6.38	56.97	226.52	10.8	28.14	92.13	3.77	.4067
	Mar. 31	2293.62	+ 125.05	+ 5.77	61.32	229.75	10.0	22.66	84.17	3.67	.3663
1988	Dec. 30	2168.57	+ 55.66	+ 2.63	50.96	215.46	10.1	20.79	79.53	3.67	.3691
	Sept. 30	2112.91	− 28.80	− 1.34	57.27	181.04	11.7	20.54	76.41	3.62	.4221
	June 30	2141.71	+ 153.65	+ 7.73	60.20	168.54	12.7	20.18	73.92	3.45	.4386
	Mar. 31	1988.06	+ 49.23	+ 2.54	47.03	144.45	13.8	18.02	71.85	3.61	.4974
1987	Dec. 31	1938.83	− 657.45	− 25.32	16.54	133.05	14.6	17.67	71.20	3.67	.5351
	Sept. 30	2596.28	+ 177.75	+ 7.34	44.77	137.99	18.8	18.05	70.62	2.72	.5117
	June 30	2418.53	+ 113.84	+ 4.94	36.11	126.23	19.2	18.11	69.36	2.87	.5494
	Mar. 31	2304.69	+ 408.74	+ 21.56	35.63	126.49	18.2	17.37	68.19	2.96	.5391
1986	Dec. 31	1895.95	+ 128.37	+ 7.26	21.48	115.59	16.4	17.09	67.04	3.54	.5800
	Sept. 30	1767.58	− 125.14	− 6.61	33.01	118.80	14.9	16.79	67.14	3.80	.5652
	June 30	1892.72	+ 74.11	+ 4.08	36.37	103.39	18.3	16.94	65.37	3.45	.6323
	Mar. 31	1818.61	+ 271.94	+ 17.58	24.73	96.43	18.9	16.22	63.38	3.49	.6573
1985	Dec. 31	1546.67	+ 218.04	+ 16.41	24.69	96.11	16.1	17.19	62.03	4.01	.6454
	Sept. 30	1328.63	− 6.83	− 0.51	17.60	90.78	14.6	15.02	61.83	4.65	.6811
	June 28	1335.46	+ 68.68	+ 5.14	29.41	102.26	13.1	14.95	61.53	4.61	.6017
	Mar. 29	1266.78	+ 55.21	+ 4.56	24.41	107.87	11.7	14.87	61.56	4.86	.5707
1984	Dec. 31	1211.57	+ 4.86	+ 0.40	19.36	113.58	10.7	16.99	60.63	5.00	.5338
	Sept. 28	1206.71	+ 74.31	+ 6.56	29.08	108.11	11.2	14.72	58.41	4.84	.5403
	June 29	1132.40	− 32.49	− 2.79	35.02	102.07	11.1	14.98	57.67	5.09	.5650
	Mar. 30	1164.89	− 93.75	− 7.45	30.12	87.38	13.3	13.94	56.39	4.84	.6453
1983	Dec. 30	1258.64	+ 25.51	+ 2.07	13.89	72.45	17.4	14.77	56.33	4.47	.7775
	Sept. 30	1233.13	+ 11.17	+ 0.91	23.04	56.12	22.0	13.98	54.59	4.43	.9727
	June 30	1221.96	+ 91.93	+ 8.13	20.33	11.59	105.4	13.70	54.05	4.42	4.6635
	Mar. 31	1130.03	+ 83.49	+ 7.98	15.19	9.52	118.7	13.88	54.10	4.79	5.6828
1982	Dec. 31	1046.54	+ 150.29	+ 16.77	d2.44	9.15	114.4	13.03	54.14	5.17	5.9169
	Sept. 30	896.25	+ 84.32	+ 10.38	d21.49	35.15	25.5	13.44	55.55	6.20	1.5804
	June 30	811.93	− 10.84	− 1.32	18.26	79.90	10.2	13.75	55.84	6.88	.6989
	Mar. 31	822.77	− 52.23	− 5.97	14.82	97.13	8.5	13.92	56.28	6.84	.5794
1981	Dec. 31	875.00	+ 25.02	+ 2.94	23.56	113.71	7.7	14.44	56.22	6.42	.4944
	Sept. 30	849.98	− 126.90	− 12.99	23.26	123.32	6.9	13.73	56.18	6.61	.4539
	June 30	976.88	− 26.99	− 2.69	35.49	128.91	7.6	14.19	55.98	5.73	.4266
	Mar. 31	1003.87	+ 39.88	+ 4.14	31.40	123.60	8.1	13.86	54.99	5.48	.4449
1980	Dec. 31	963.99	+ 31.57	+ 3.39	33.17	121.86	7.9	14.40	54.36	5.64	.4461
	Sept. 30	932.42	+ 64.50	+ 7.43	28.85	111.58	8.4	13.53	53.83	5.77	.4824
	June 30	867.92	+ 82.17	+ 10.46	30.18	116.40	7.5	13.20	52.81	6.08	.4537
	Mar. 31	785.75	− 52.99	− 6.32	29.66	120.77	6.5	13.23	52.10	6.63	.4314

Source: Reprinted by permission of Barron's *National Business and Financial Weekly,*

Stock Market Averages by Industry Group

These definitions apply to pages 256–271.

All Capitalization figures are based on company's *latest annual* report.

Bonds include other long term debt.

Stocks included in the Dow-Jones Averages are designated by a star "★" placed *before the heading.*

Unless prefaced by a "●" for American Stock Exchange issues, all stocks charted are traded on the New York Stock Exchange.

Earnings and Dividends are read from the left-hand scale of each chart.

Earnings Lines—on a per share 12 months ended basis—are represented by the solid black line. Dots show whether company issues quarterly, semi-annual or only annual earnings reports. Earnings off the range of the charts, and deficits are shown by typed notations.

Dividend Lines—representing the annual rate of interim dividend payments—are shown by the dashed lines. The small circles show the month in which dividend payments are made. Dividends off the range of the charts as well as extra or irregular payments of each year are shown in typed figures.

Monthly Price Ranges represented by the solid vertical bars show the highest and lowest point of each month's transactions. Crossbars indicate the month's closing price.

Price Scale—The price ranges are always read from the scale at the right side of each chart. This scale is equal to 15 times the Earnings and Dividend scale at the left, so when the Price Range bars and the Earnings line coincide, it shows the price is at 15 times earnings. When the price is above the earnings line, the ratio of price to earnings is greater than 15 times earnings; when below, it is less.

Monthly Ratio-Cator: The plottings for this line are obtained by dividing the closing price of the stock by the closing price of the Dow-Jones Industrial Average for the same day. The resulting percentage is then multiplied by a factor of 750 to bring the line closer to the price bars for easier comparison. This line is plotted and read from the right scale. The plotting indicates whether the stock has kept pace, outperformed, or lagged the general market as represented by the DJIA.

Moving Average: This line represents the average of closing prices for the most recent 48-month period. Since our database starts in 1978, the majority of the moving averages begin in 1982. For those companies with shorter records the line begins when there is 48-months of price history.

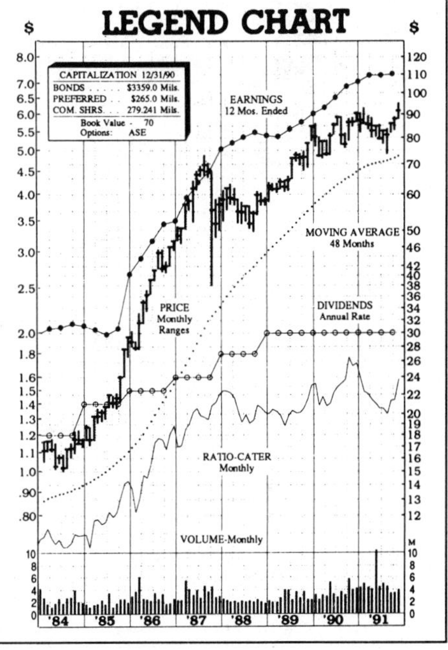

Volume: The number of shares traded each month is shown by vertical bars at the bottom of each chart on an arithmetic scale. Thousands are indicated by a T at the top of the right volume scale and millions by an M.

Source: Chart Courtesy of Securities Research Company, a division of Babson-United Investment Advisors, Inc., 101 Prescott St., Wellesley Hills, MA 02181-3319.

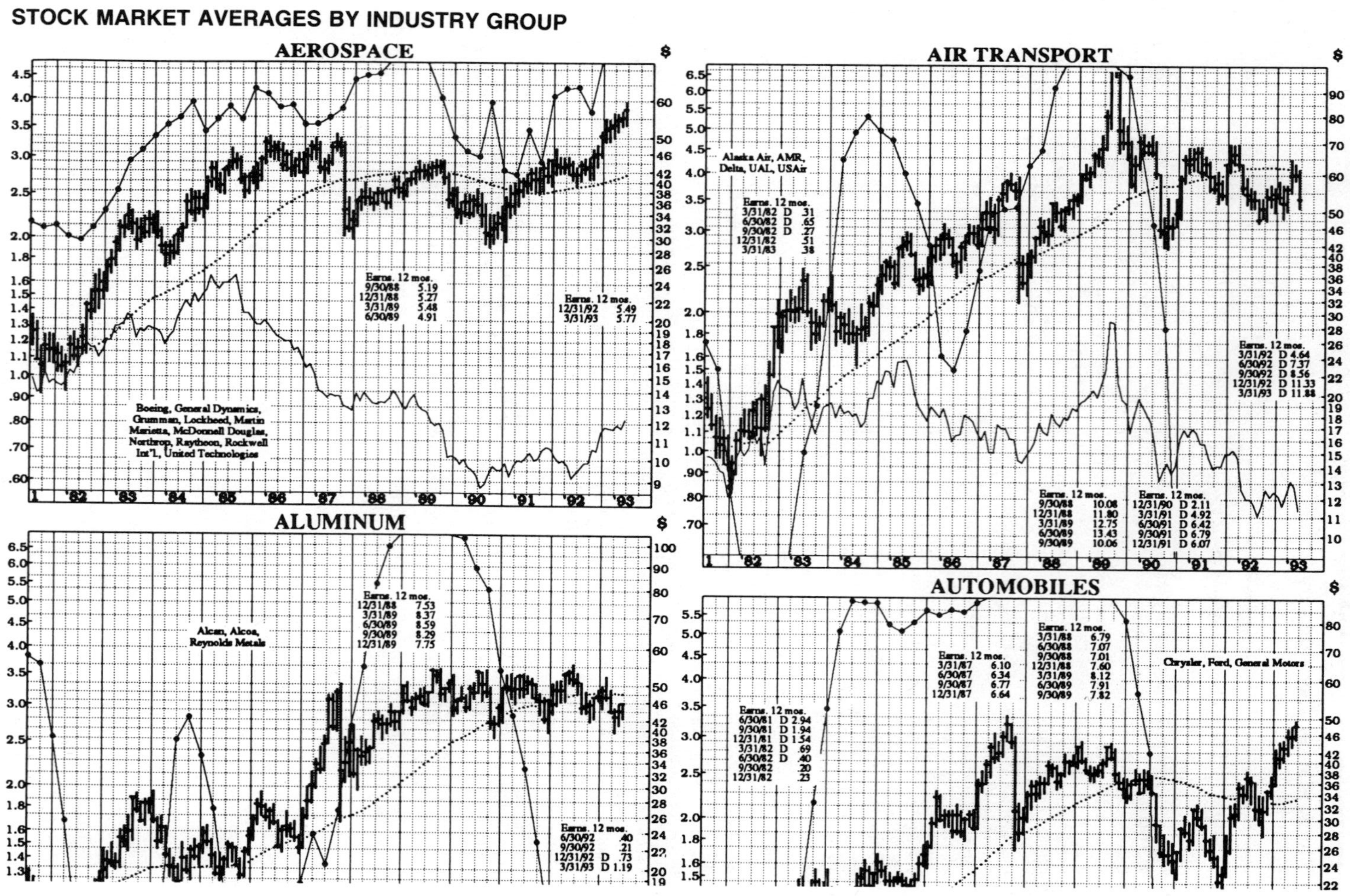
STOCK MARKET AVERAGES BY INDUSTRY GROUP
AEROSPACE
Earns. 12 mos. 9/30/88 5.19 12/31/88 5.27 3/31/89 5.48 6/30/89 4.91
Earns. 12 mos. 12/31/92 5.49 3/31/93 5.77
Boeing, General Dynamics, Grumman, Lockheed, Martin Marietta, McDonnell Douglas, Northrop, Raytheon, Rockwell Int'l, United Technologies
AIR TRANSPORT
Alaska Air, AMR, Delta, UAL, USAir
Earns. 12 mos. 3/31/82 D .31 6/30/82 D .65 9/30/82 D .27 12/31/82 .51 3/31/83 .38
Earns. 12 mos. 9/30/88 10.08 12/31/88 11.80 3/31/89 12.75 6/30/89 13.43 9/30/89 10.06
Earns. 12 mos. 12/31/90 D 2.11 3/31/91 D 4.92 6/30/91 D 6.42 9/30/91 D 6.79 12/31/91 D 6.07
Earns. 12 mos. 3/31/92 D 4.64 6/30/92 D 7.37 9/30/92 D 8.56 12/31/92 D 11.33 3/31/93 D 11.88
ALUMINUM
Alcan, Alcoa, Reynolds Metals
Earns. 12 mos. 12/31/88 7.53 3/31/89 8.37 6/30/89 8.59 9/30/89 8.29 12/31/89 7.75
Earns. 12 mos. 6/30/92 .40 9/30/92 .21 12/31/92 D .73 3/31/93 D 1.19
AUTOMOBILES
Chrysler, Ford, General Motors
Earns. 12 mos. 6/30/81 D 2.94 9/30/81 D 1.94 12/31/81 D 1.54 3/31/82 D .69 6/30/82 D .40 9/30/82 .20 12/31/82 .23
Earns. 12 mos. 3/31/87 6.10 6/30/87 6.34 9/30/87 6.77 12/31/87 6.64
Earns. 12 mos. 3/31/88 6.79 6/30/88 7.07 9/30/88 7.01 12/31/88 7.60 3/31/89 8.12 6/30/89 7.91 9/30/89 7.82

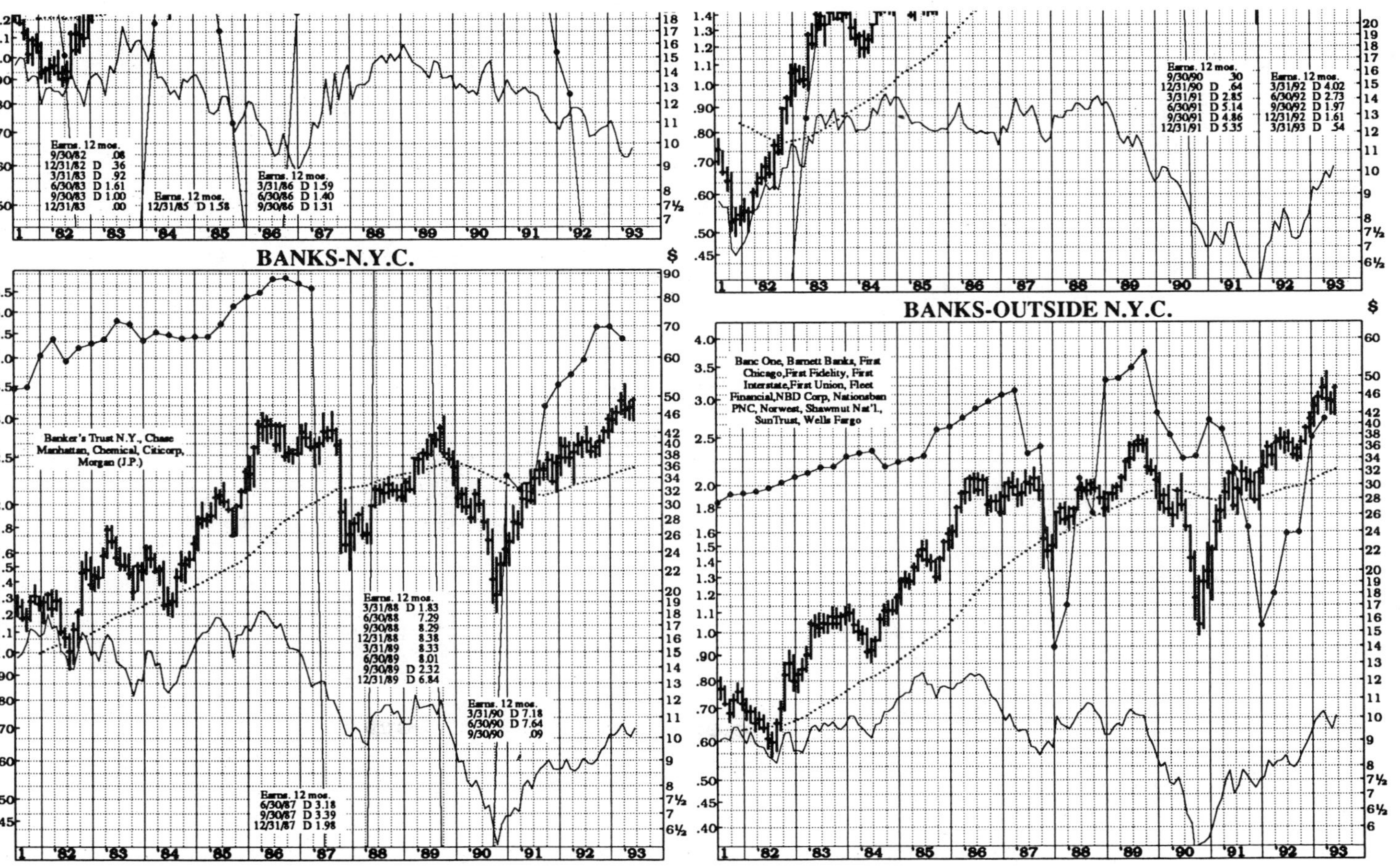
Earns. 12 mos.
9/30/82 .08
12/31/82 D .36
3/31/83 D .92
6/30/83 D 1.61
9/30/83 D 1.00
12/31/83 .00
Earns. 12 mos.
12/31/85 D 1.58
Earns. 12 mos.
3/31/86 D 1.59
6/30/86 D 1.40
9/30/86 D 1.31
BANKS-N.Y.C.
Banker's Trust N.Y., Chase Manhattan, Chemical, Citicorp, Morgan (J.P.)
Earns. 12 mos.
3/31/88 D 1.83
6/30/88 7.29
9/30/88 8.29
12/31/88 8.38
3/31/89 8.33
6/30/89 8.01
9/30/89 D 2.32
12/31/89 D 6.84
Earns. 12 mos.
3/31/90 D 7.18
6/30/90 D 7.64
9/30/90 .09
Earns. 12 mos.
6/30/87 D 3.18
9/30/87 D 3.39
12/31/87 D 1.98
Earns. 12 mos.
9/30/90 .30
12/31/90 D .64
3/31/91 D 2.85
6/30/91 D 5.14
9/30/91 D 4.86
12/31/91 D 5.35
Earns. 12 mos.
3/31/92 D 4.02
6/30/92 D 2.73
9/30/92 D 1.97
12/31/92 D 1.61
3/31/93 D .54
BANKS-OUTSIDE N.Y.C.
Banc One, Barnett Banks, First Chicago, First Fidelity, First Interstate, First Union, Fleet Financial, NBD Corp, Nationsban PNC, Norwest, Shawmut Nat'l, SunTrust, Wells Fargo
$

STOCK MARKET AVERAGES BY INDUSTRY GROUP *(continued)*

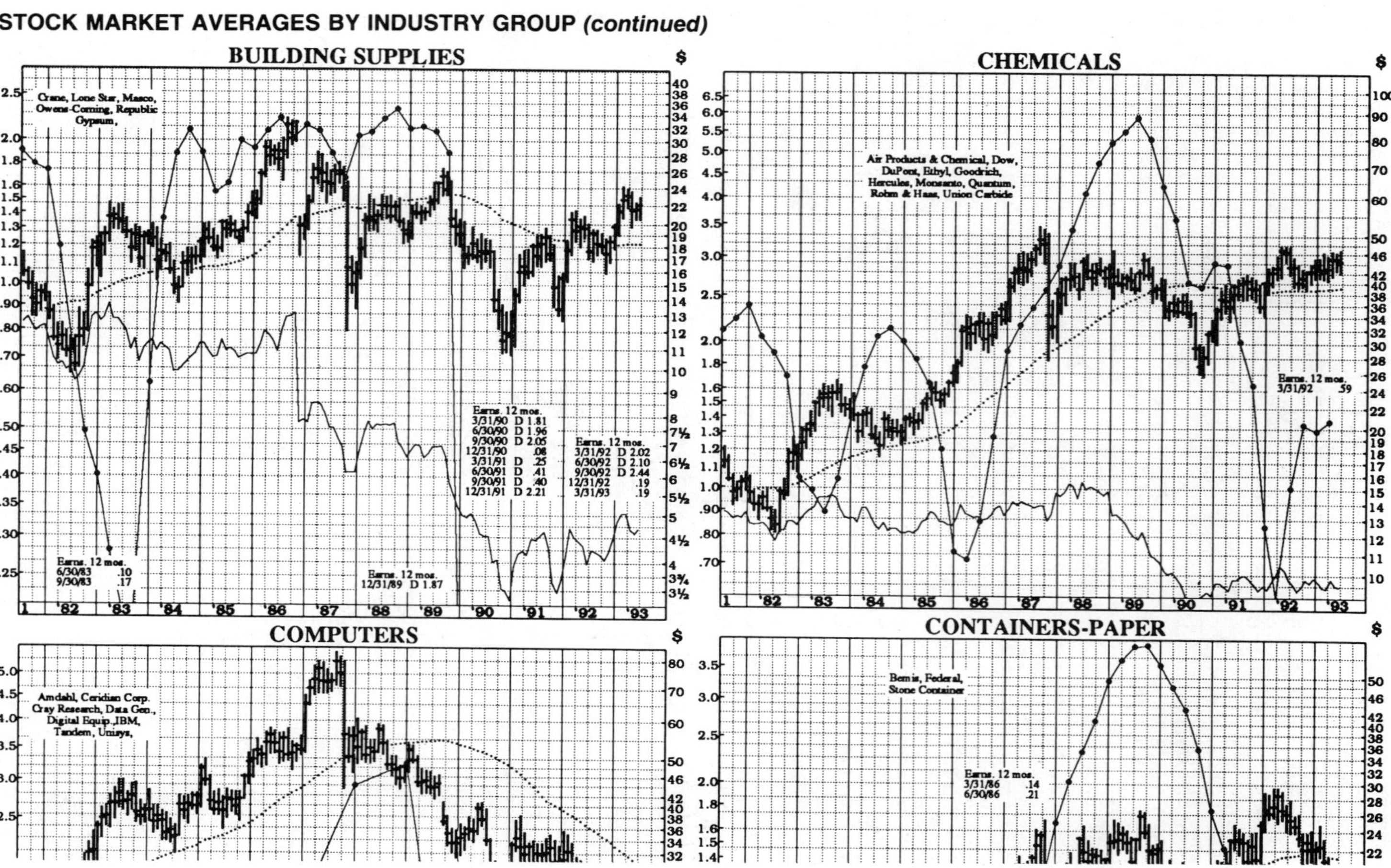

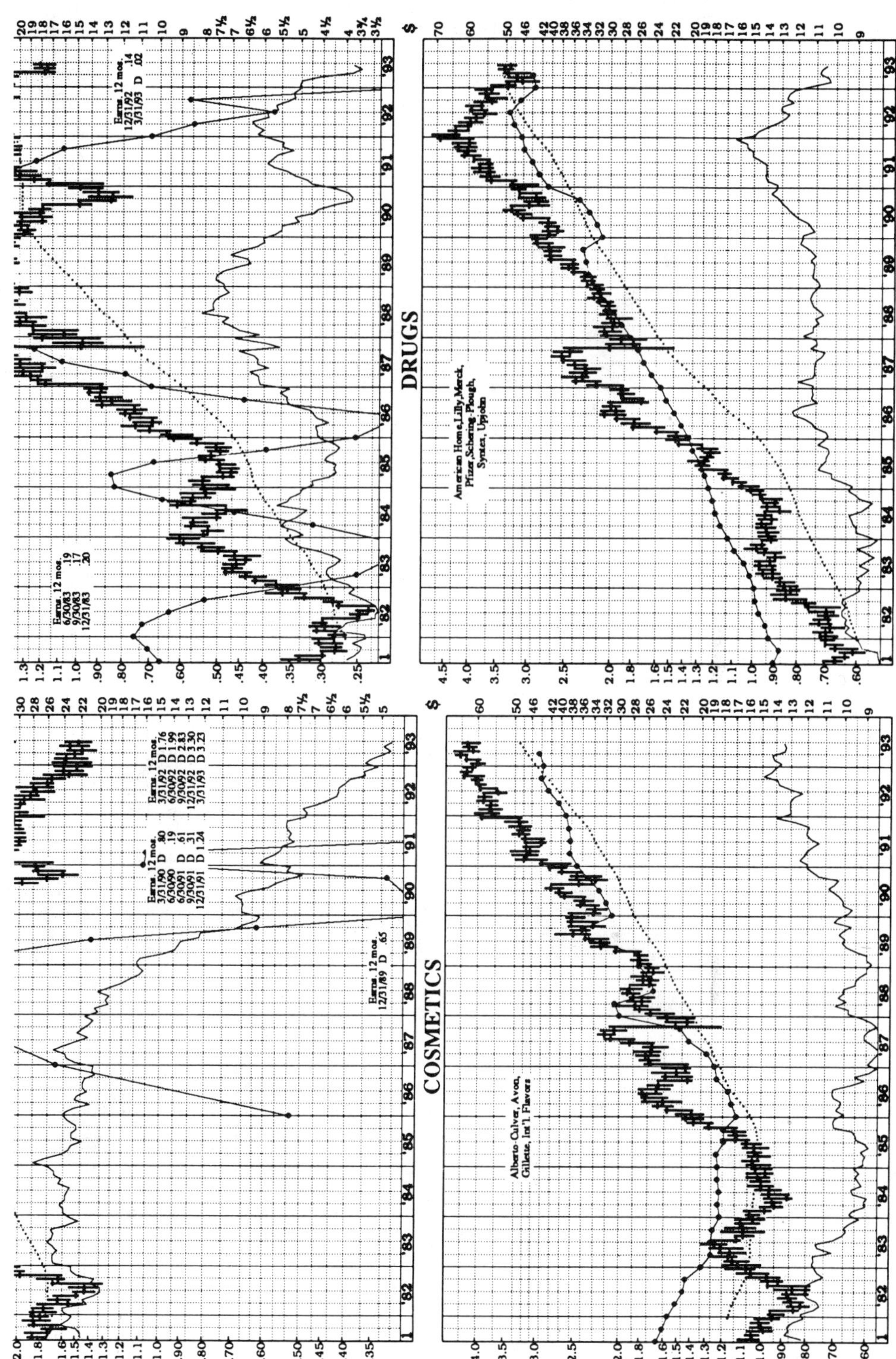
DRUGS
American Home, Lilly, Merck, Pfizer, Schering-Plough, Syntex, Upjohn
COSMETICS
Alberto Culver, Avon, Gillette, Int'l Flavors

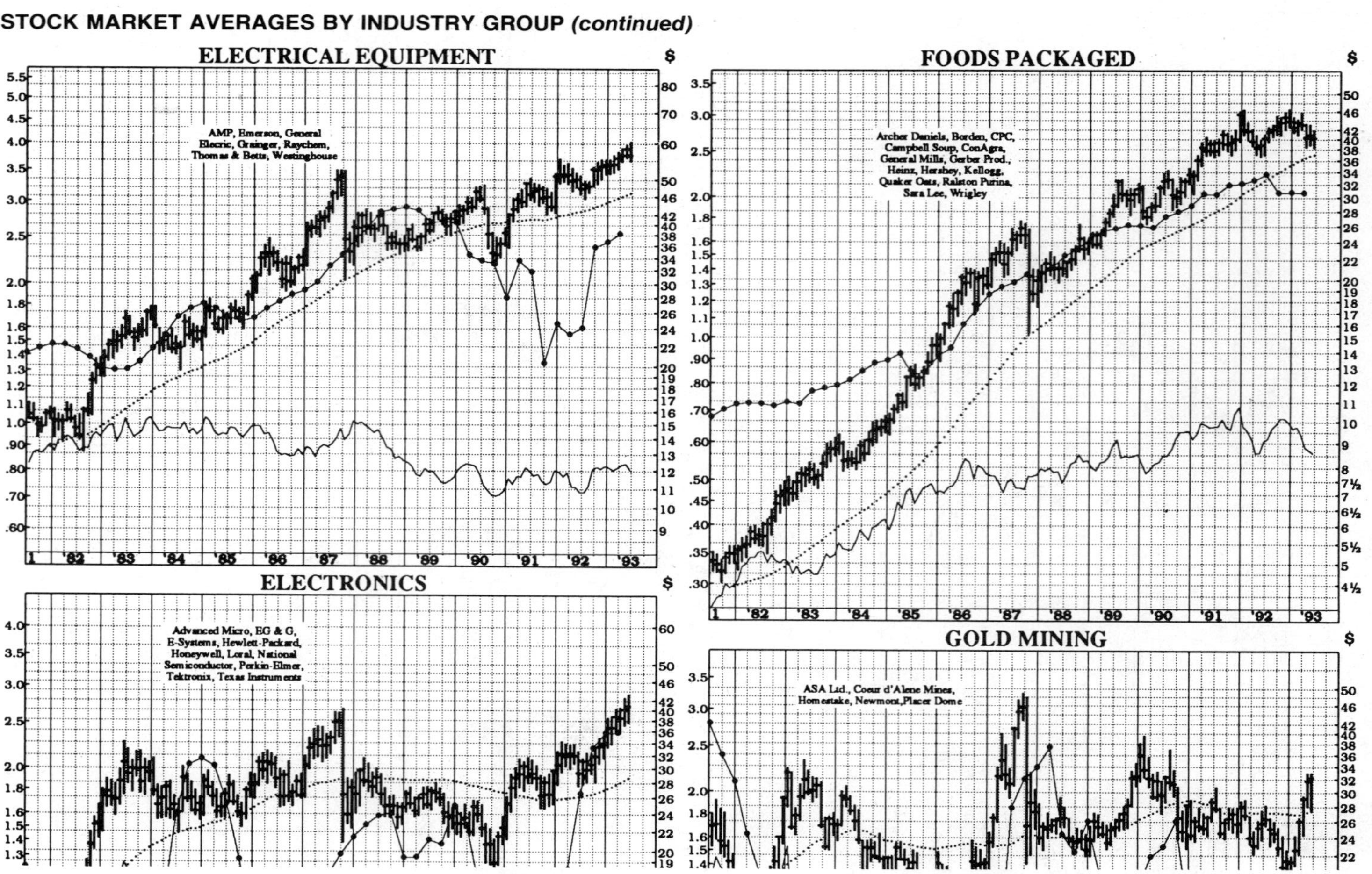
STOCK MARKET AVERAGES BY INDUSTRY GROUP (continued)
ELECTRICAL EQUIPMENT
AMP, Emerson, General Electric, Grainger, Raychem, Thomas & Betts, Westinghouse
ELECTRONICS
Advanced Micro, EG & G, E-Systems, Hewlett-Packard, Honeywell, Loral, National Semiconductor, Perkin-Elmer, Tektronix, Texas Instruments
FOODS PACKAGED
Archer Daniels, Borden, CPC, Campbell Soup, ConAgra, General Mills, Gerber Prod., Heinz, Hershey, Kellogg, Quaker Oats, Ralston Purina, Sara Lee, Wrigley
GOLD MINING
ASA Ltd., Coeur d'Alene Mines, Homestake, Newmont, Placer Dome

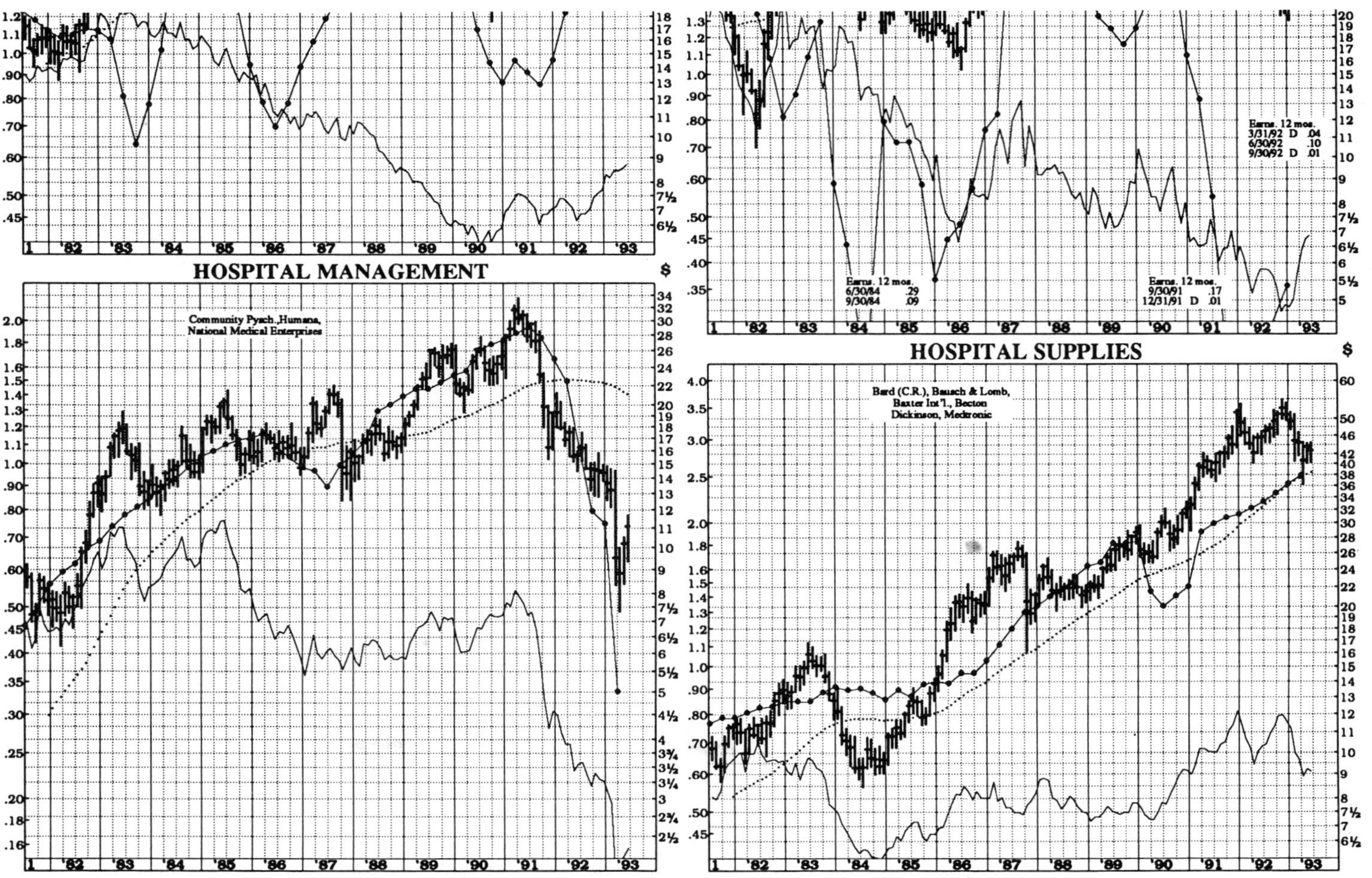
HOSPITAL MANAGEMENT
Community Pysch.,Humana,
National Medical Enterprises
HOSPITAL SUPPLIES
Bard (C.R.), Bausch & Lomb,
Baxter Int'l., Becton
Dickinson, Medtronic
Earns. 12 mos.
6/30/84 .29
9/30/84 .09
Earns. 12 mos.
9/30/91 .17
12/31/91 D .01
Earns. 12 mos.
3/31/92 D .04
6/30/92 .10
9/30/92 D .01

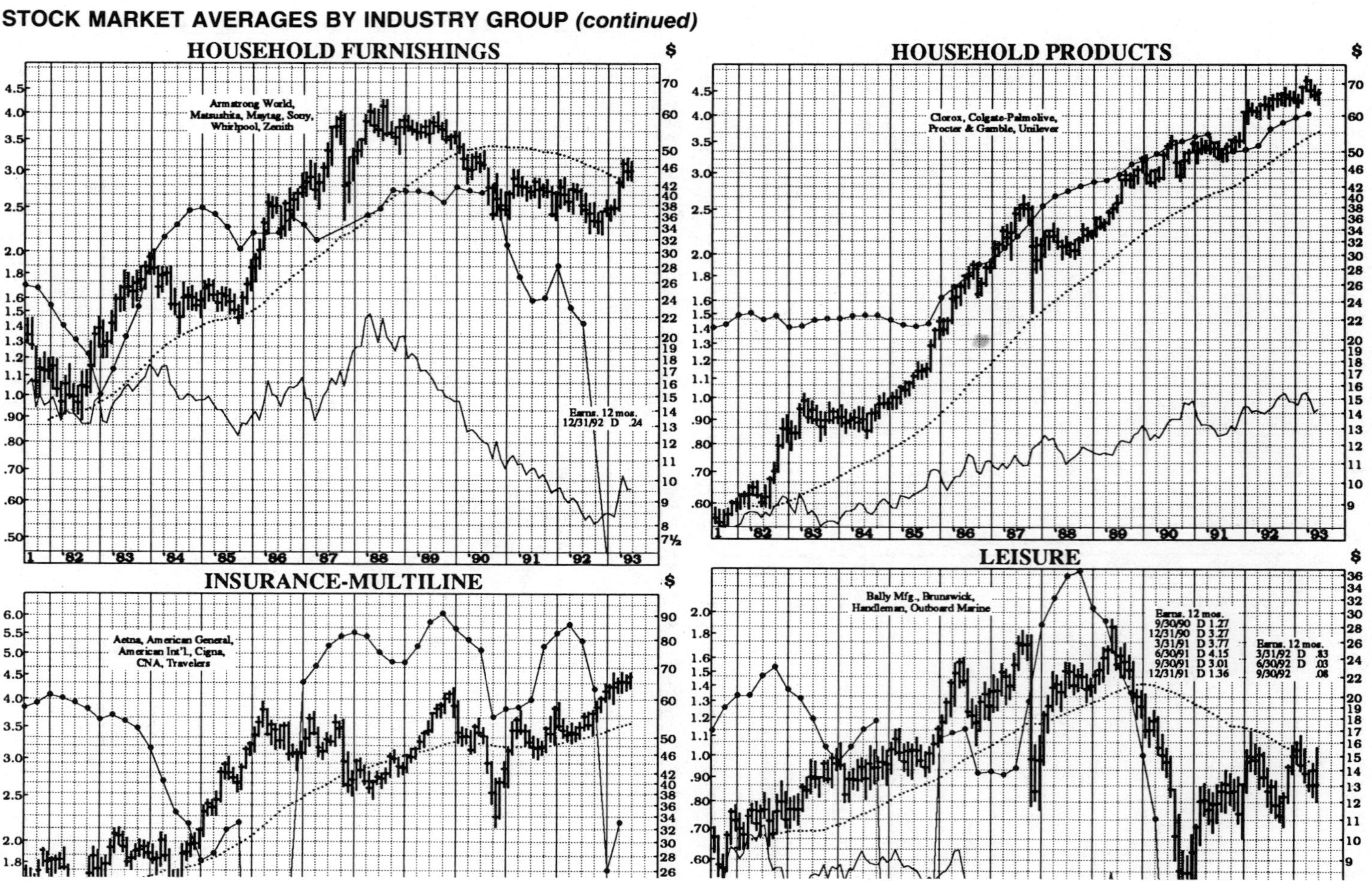
STOCK MARKET AVERAGES BY INDUSTRY GROUP (continued)
HOUSEHOLD FURNISHINGS
Armstrong World, Matsushita, Maytag, Sony, Whirlpool, Zenith
Earns. 12 mos. 12/31/92 D .24
HOUSEHOLD PRODUCTS
Clorox, Colgate-Palmolive, Procter & Gamble, Unilever
INSURANCE-MULTILINE
Aetna, American General, American Int'l., Cigna, CNA, Travelers
LEISURE
Bally Mfg., Brunswick, Handleman, Outboard Marine
Earns. 12 mos.
9/30/90 D 1.27
12/31/90 D 3.27
3/31/91 D 3.77
6/30/91 D 4.15
9/30/91 D 3.01
12/31/91 D 1.36
Earns. 12 mos.
3/31/92 D .83
6/30/92 D .03
9/30/92 .08

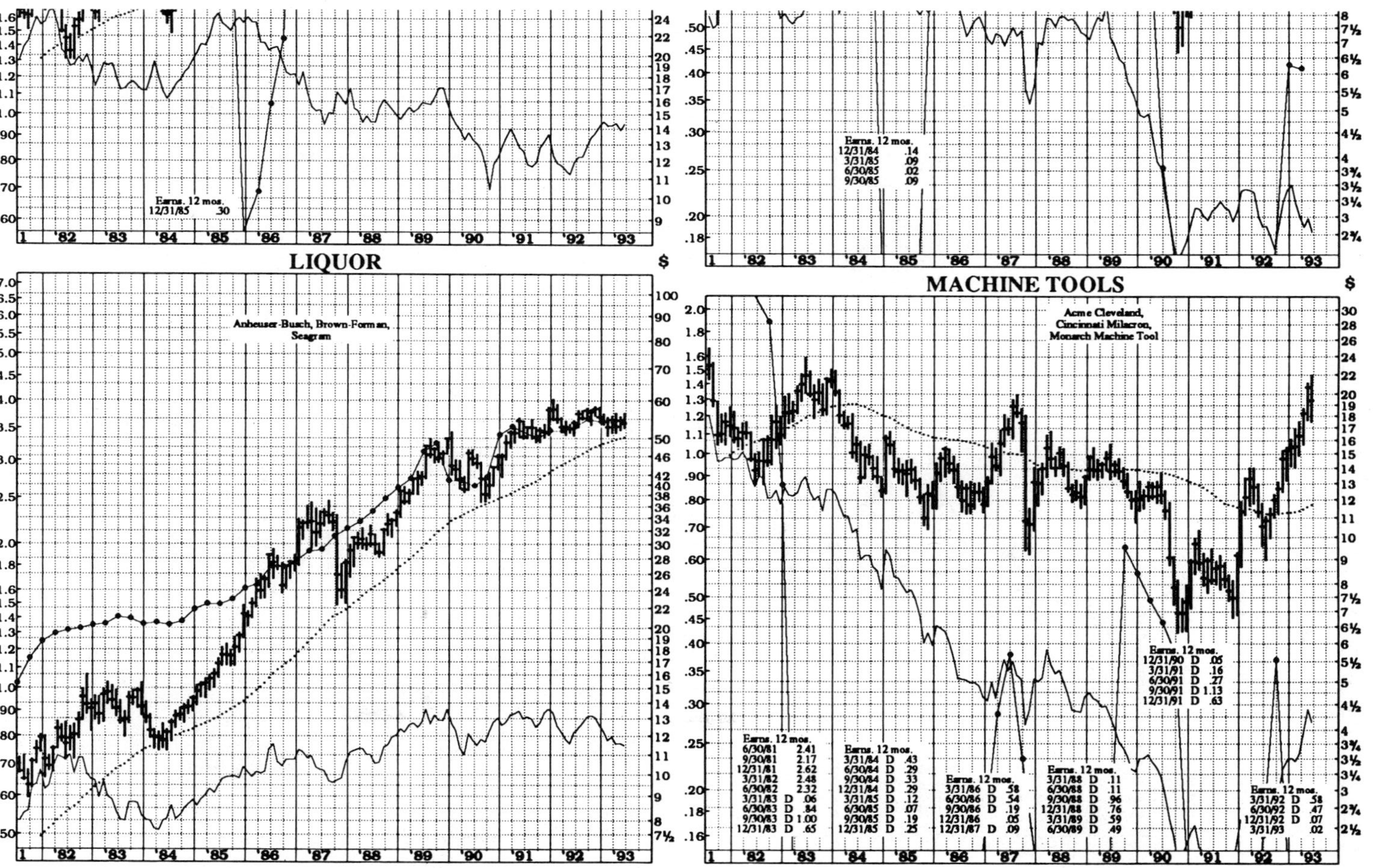
Earns. 12 mos.
12/31/85 .30
Earns. 12 mos.
12/31/84 .14
3/31/85 .09
6/30/85 .02
9/30/85 .09
LIQUOR
Anheuser-Busch, Brown-Forman, Seagram
MACHINE TOOLS
Acme Cleveland, Cincinnati Milacron, Monarch Machine Tool
Earns. 12 mos.
6/30/81 2.41
9/30/81 2.17
12/31/81 2.62
3/31/82 2.48
6/30/82 2.32
3/31/83 D .06
6/30/83 D .84
9/30/83 D 1.00
12/31/83 D .65
Earns. 12 mos.
3/31/84 D .43
6/30/84 D .29
9/30/84 D .33
12/31/84 D .29
3/31/85 D .12
6/30/85 D .07
9/30/85 D .19
12/31/85 D .25
Earns. 12 mos.
3/31/86 D .58
6/30/86 D .54
9/30/86 D .19
12/31/86 .05
12/31/87 D .09
Earns. 12 mos.
3/31/88 D .11
6/30/88 D .11
9/30/88 D .96
12/31/88 D .76
3/31/89 D .59
6/30/89 D .49
Earns. 12 mos.
12/31/90 D .05
3/31/91 D .16
6/30/91 D .27
9/30/91 D 1.13
12/31/91 D .63
Earns. 12 mos.
3/31/92 D .58
6/30/92 D .47
12/31/92 D .07
3/31/93 .02

STOCK MARKET AVERAGES BY INDUSTRY GROUP *(continued)*

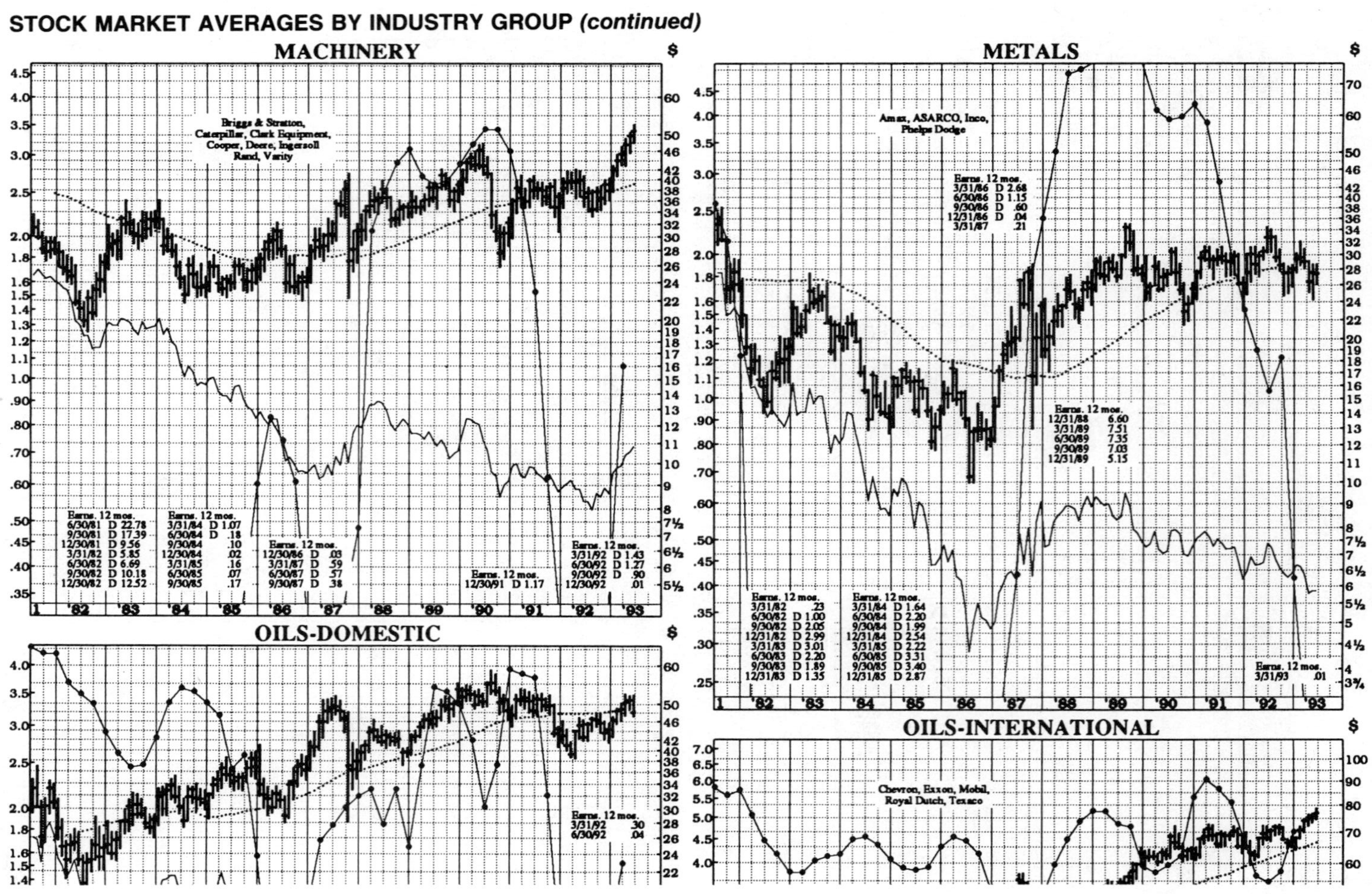

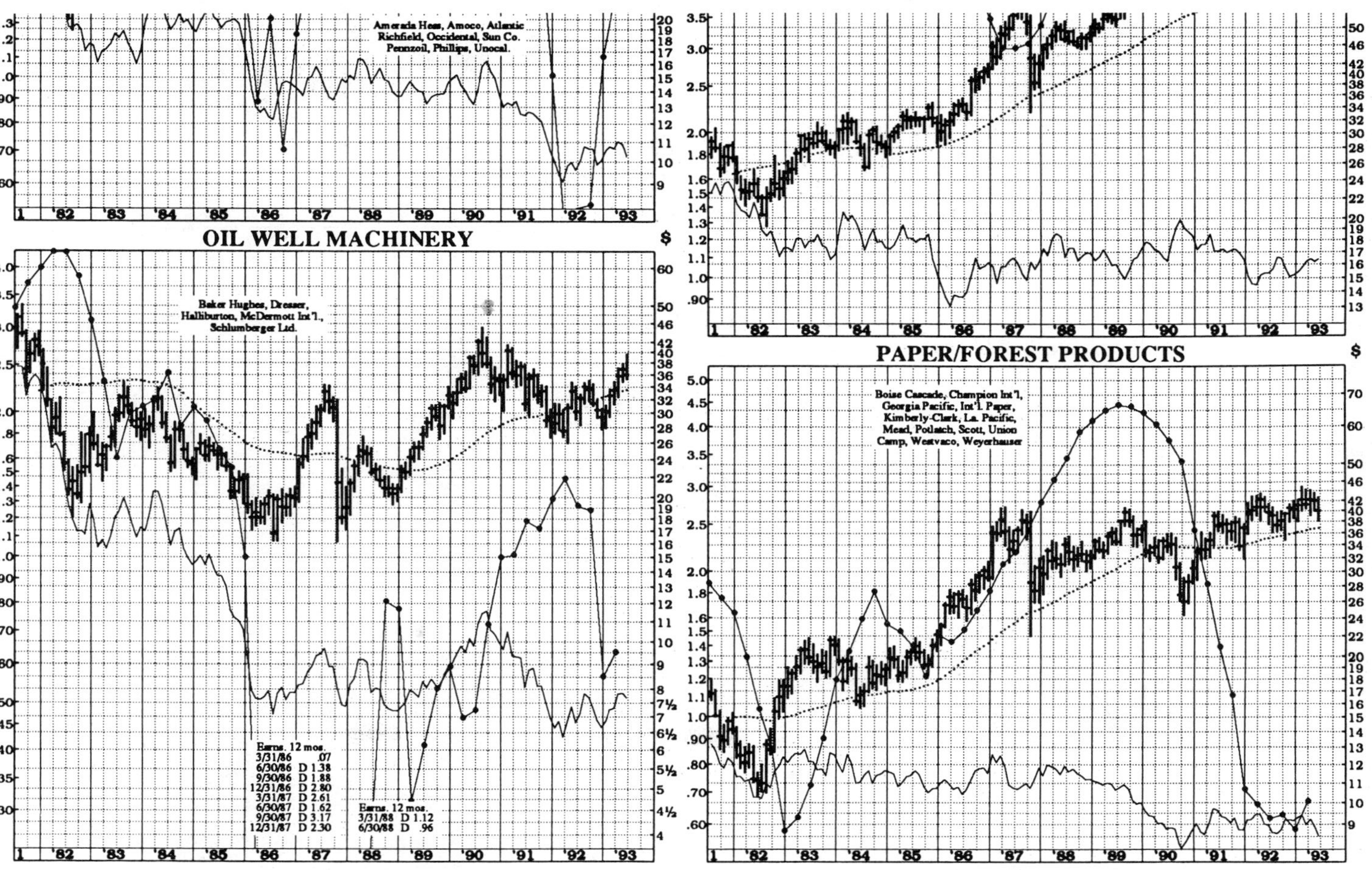
Amerada Hess, Amoco, Atlantic Richfield, Occidental, Sun Co. Pennzoil, Phillips, Unocal.
OIL WELL MACHINERY
Baker Hughes, Dresser, Halliburton, McDermott Int'l., Schlumberger Ltd.
Earns. 12 mos.
3/31/86 .07
6/30/86 D 1.38
9/30/86 D 1.88
12/31/86 D 2.80
3/31/87 D 2.61
6/30/87 D 1.62
9/30/87 D 3.17
12/31/87 D 2.30
Earns. 12 mos.
3/31/88 D 1.12
6/30/88 D .96
PAPER/FOREST PRODUCTS
Boise Cascade, Champion Int'l, Georgia Pacific, Int'l. Paper, Kimberly-Clark, La. Pacific, Mead, Potlatch, Scott, Union Camp, Westvaco, Weyerhaeuser

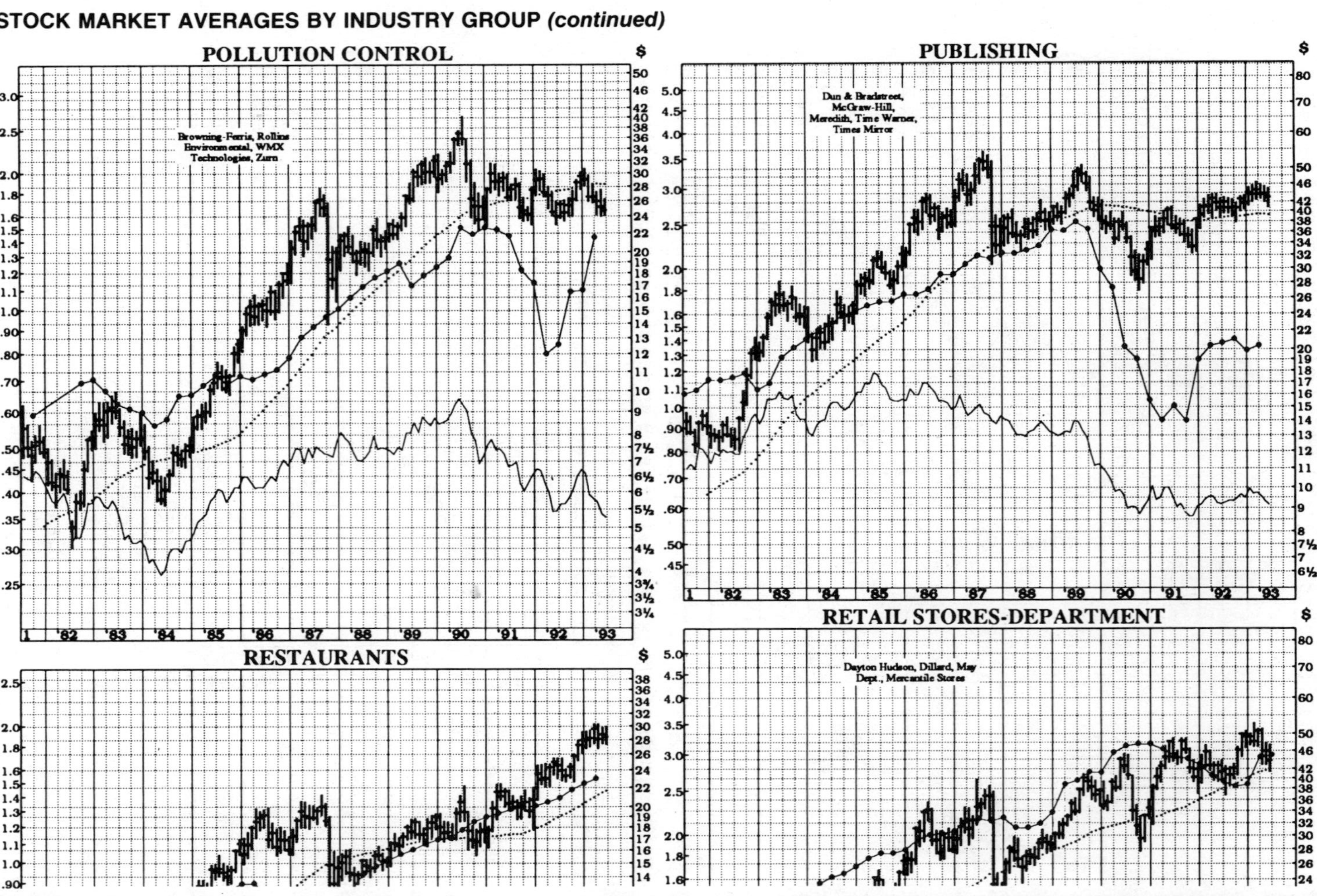
STOCK MARKET AVERAGES BY INDUSTRY GROUP (continued)
POLLUTION CONTROL
Browning-Ferris, Rollins Environmental, WMX Technologies, Zurn
PUBLISHING
Dun & Bradstreet, McGraw-Hill, Meredith, Time Warner, Times Mirror
RESTAURANTS
RETAIL STORES-DEPARTMENT
Dayton Hudson, Dillard, May Dept., Mercantile Stores

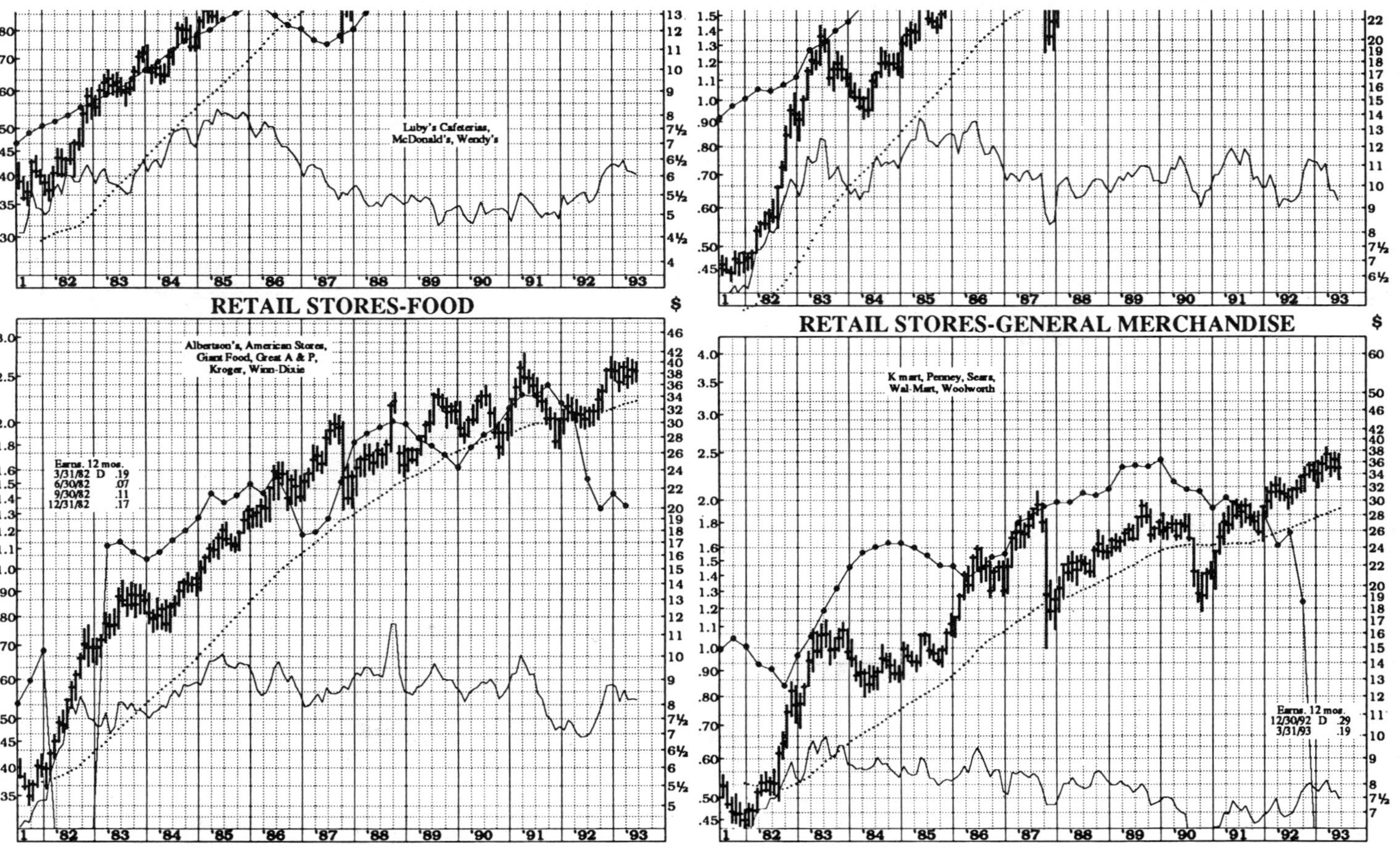
Luby's Cafeterias, McDonald's, Wendy's
RETAIL STORES-FOOD
Albertson's, American Stores, Giant Food, Great A & P, Kroger, Winn-Dixie
Earns. 12 mos.
3/31/82 D .19
6/30/82 .07
9/30/82 .11
12/31/82 .17
RETAIL STORES-GENERAL MERCHANDISE
K mart, Penney, Sears, Wal-Mart, Woolworth
Earns. 12 mos.
12/30/92 D .29
3/31/93 .19

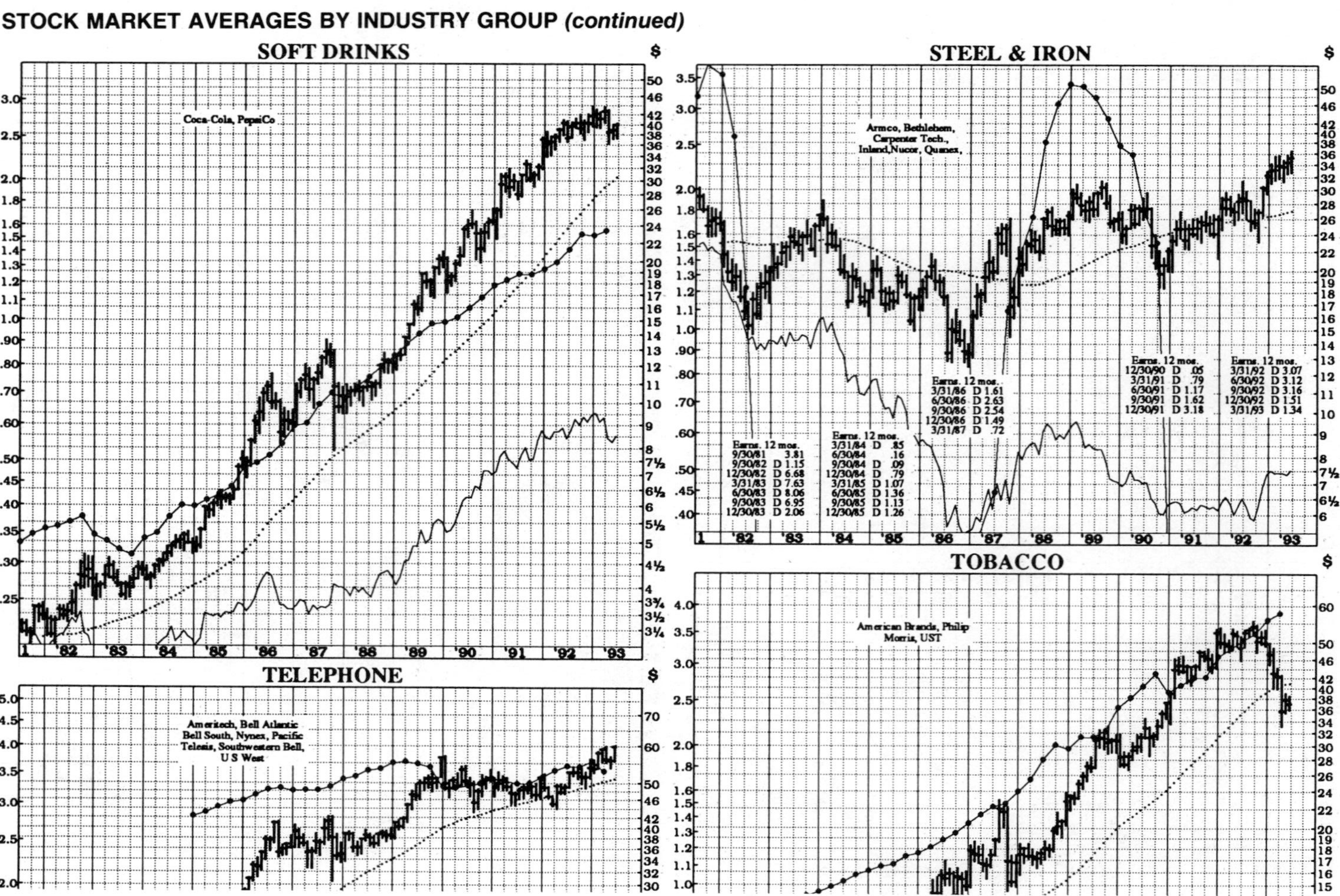
STOCK MARKET AVERAGES BY INDUSTRY GROUP (continued)
SOFT DRINKS
Coca-Cola, PepsiCo
STEEL & IRON
Armco, Bethlehem, Carpenter Tech., Inland, Nucor, Quanex,
Earns. 12 mos. 9/30/81 3.81 9/30/82 D 1.15 12/30/82 D 6.68 3/31/83 D 7.63 6/30/83 D 8.06 9/30/83 D 6.95 12/30/83 D 2.06
Earns. 12 mos. 3/31/84 D .85 6/30/84 .16 9/30/84 D .09 12/30/84 D .79 3/31/85 D 1.07 6/30/85 D 1.36 9/30/85 D 1.13 12/30/85 D 1.26
Earns. 12 mos. 3/31/86 D 1.61 6/30/86 D 2.63 9/30/86 D 2.54 12/30/86 D 1.49 3/31/87 D .72
Earns. 12 mos. 12/30/90 D .05 3/31/91 D .79 6/30/91 D 1.17 9/30/91 D 1.62 12/30/91 D 3.18
Earns. 12 mos. 3/31/92 D 3.07 6/30/92 D 3.12 9/30/92 D 3.16 12/30/92 D 1.51 3/31/93 D 1.34
TELEPHONE
Ameritech, Bell Atlantic Bell South, Nynex, Pacific Telesis, Southwestern Bell, U S West
TOBACCO
American Brands, Philip Morris, UST

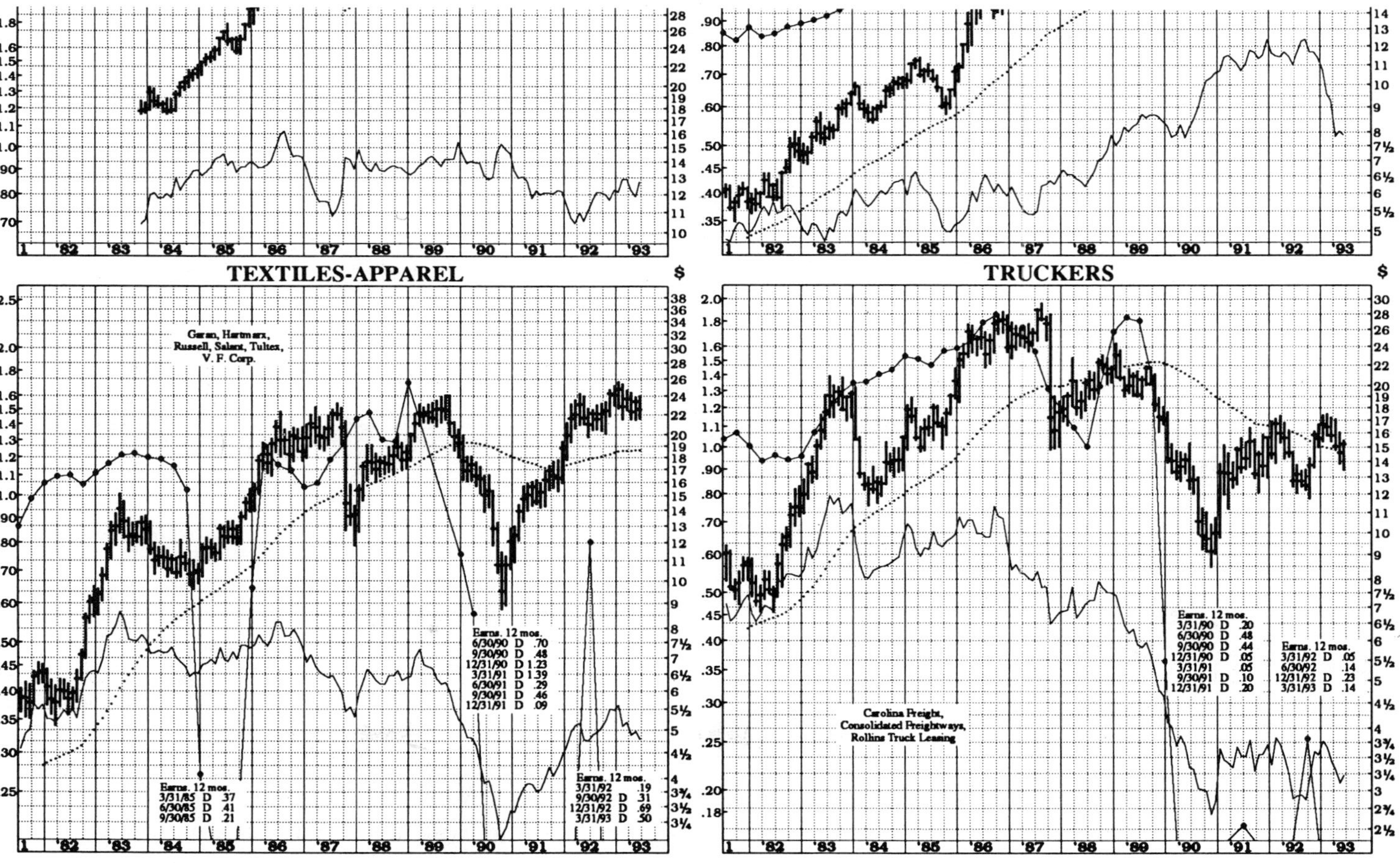
TEXTILES-APPAREL
Garan, Hartmarx,
Russell, Salant, Tultex,
V. F. Corp.
Earns. 12 mos.
3/31/85 D .37
6/30/85 D .41
9/30/85 D .21
Earns. 12 mos.
6/30/90 D .70
9/30/90 D .48
12/31/90 D 1.23
3/31/91 D 1.39
6/30/91 D .29
9/30/91 D .46
12/31/91 D .09
Earns. 12 mos.
3/31/92 .19
9/30/92 D .31
12/31/92 D .69
3/31/93 D .50
TRUCKERS
Carolina Freight,
Consolidated Freightways,
Rollins Truck Leasing
Earns. 12 mos.
3/31/90 D .20
6/30/90 D .48
9/30/90 D .44
12/31/90 D .05
3/31/91 .05
9/30/91 D .10
12/31/91 D .20
Earns. 12 mos.
3/31/92 D .05
6/30/92 .14
12/31/92 D .23
3/31/93 D .14

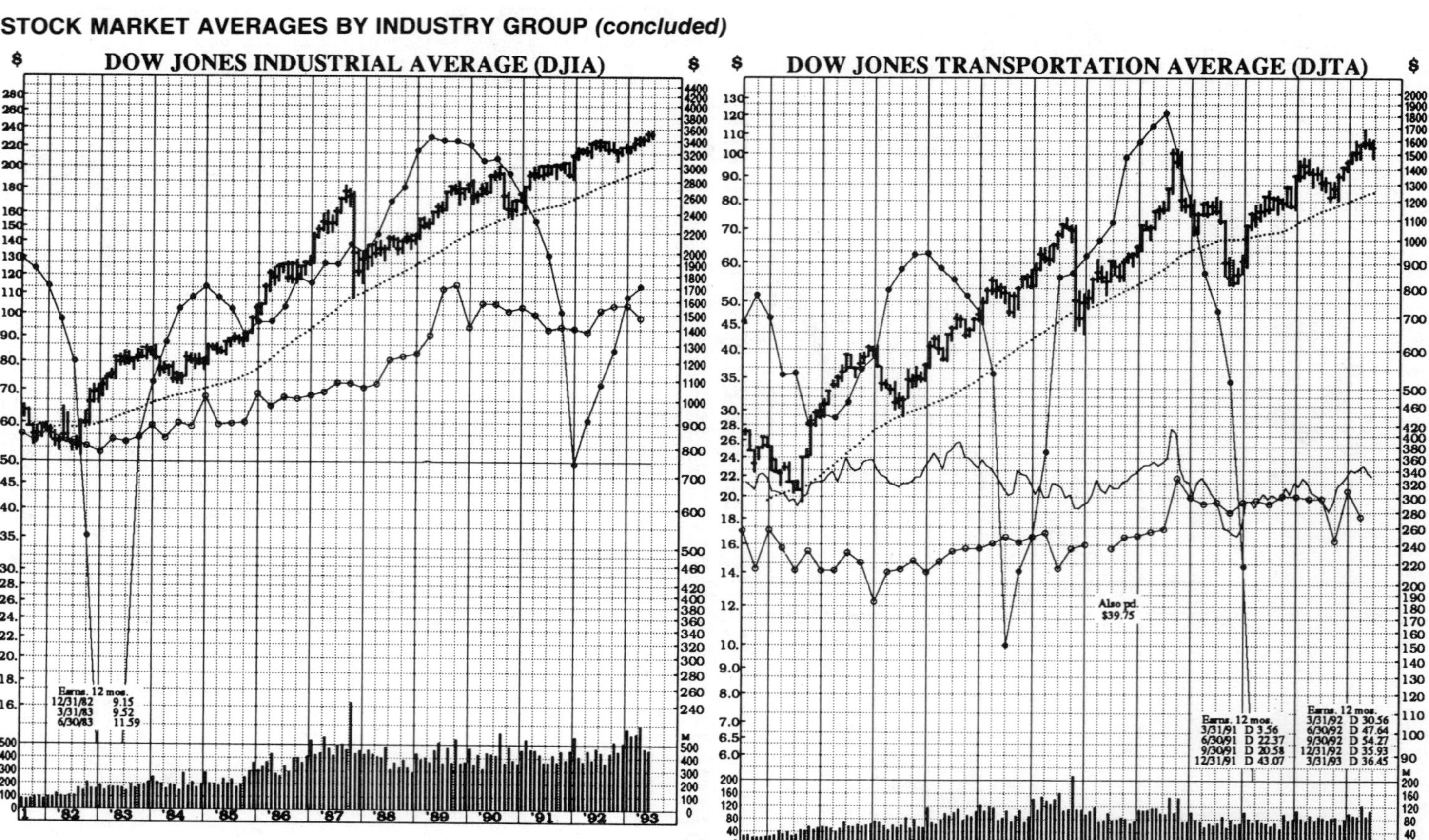
STOCK MARKET AVERAGES BY INDUSTRY GROUP (concluded)
DOW JONES INDUSTRIAL AVERAGE (DJIA)
Earns. 12 mos.
12/31/82 9.15
3/31/83 9.52
6/30/83 11.59
DOW JONES TRANSPORTATION AVERAGE (DJTA)
Also pd. $39.75
Earns. 12 mos.
3/31/91 D 3.56
6/30/91 D 22.37
9/30/91 D 20.58
12/31/91 D 43.07
Earns. 12 mos.
3/31/92 D 30.56
6/30/92 D 47.64
9/30/92 D 54.27
12/31/92 D 35.93
3/31/93 D 36.45

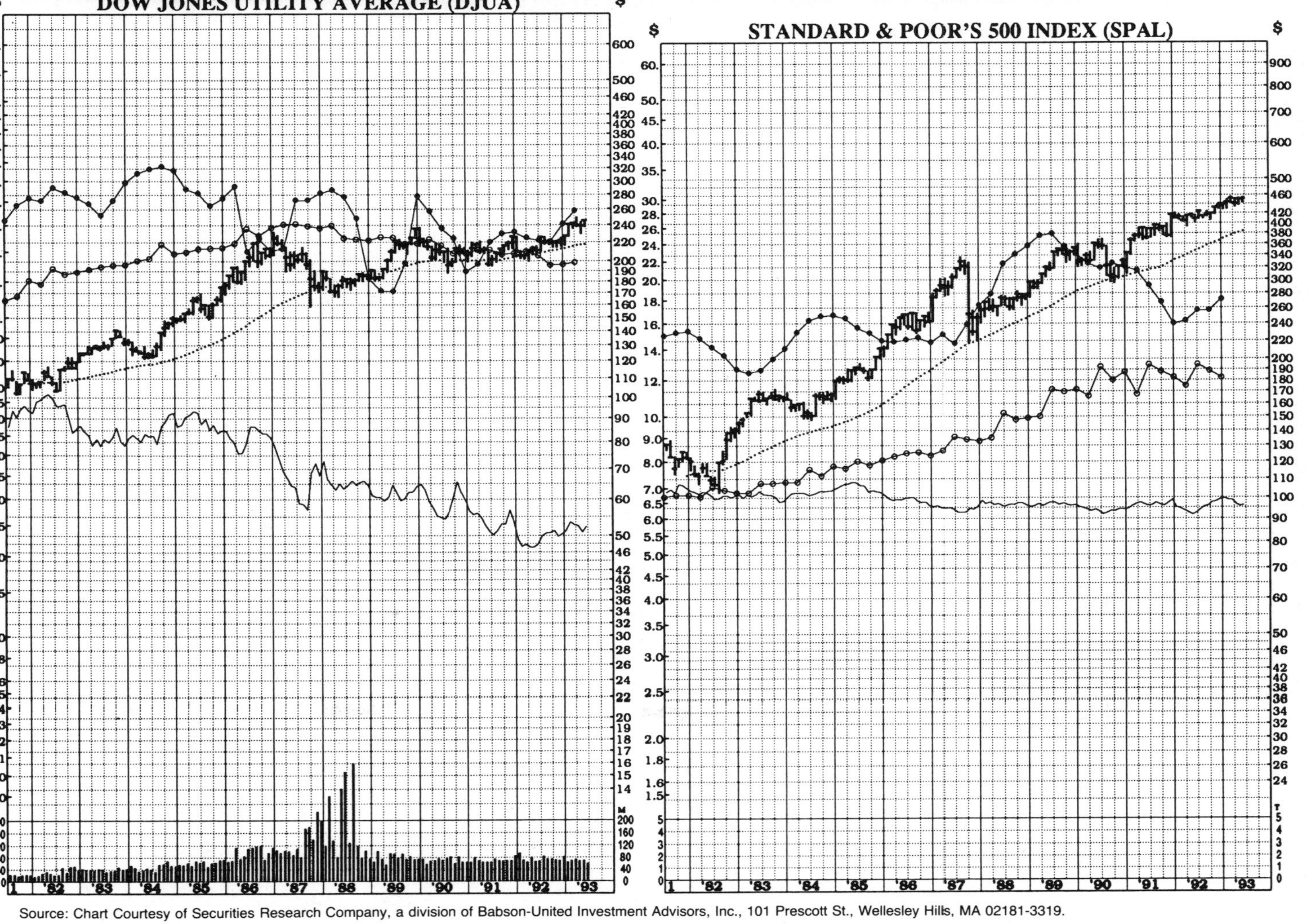

Source: Chart Courtesy of Securities Research Company, a division of Babson-United Investment Advisors, Inc., 101 Prescott St., Wellesley Hills, MA 02181-3319.

Components—Dow Jones 65 Stock Averages

The Dow Jones Stock Averages are compiled by using the New York Stock Exchange only closing prices and adjusting by the then current appropriate divisor. The divisors appear under the Dow Jones Half-Hourly Averages. A list of the stocks on which these averages are based follows:

Industrials

Allied Sig.
Alum Co
Amer Exp
AT&T
Beth Steel
Boeing
Caterpillar
Chevron
Coca-Cola
Disney (Walt)
Du Pont
Eastman
Exxon
Gen Electric
Gen Motors
Goodyear
IBM
Int'l Paper
McDonald's
Merck
Minn M&M
Morgan (J.P.)
Philip Morris
Proc Gamb
Sears
Texaco
Union Carbide
United Tech
Westinghouse
Woolworth

Transportation

AMR Corp.
Airbrn Freigt
Alaska Air
Amer Pres
Burlington
Caro Freight
Cons Freight
Cons Rail
CSX Corp.
Delta Air
Fed Express
Norfolk So
Roadway Svcs
Ryder System
Santa Fe
Southwest Airl
UAL Corp.
Union Pac
USAir
Xtra Corp.

Utilities

Am El Power
Arkla Inc.
Centerior
Comwlth Edis
Cons Edison
Cons N Gas
Detroit Edis
Houston Ind
Niag Mohawk
Pacific G&E
Panhandle
Peoples En
Phila Elec
Pub Serv E
SCEcorp

DOW JONES INDUSTRIAL, TRANSPORTATION AND UTILITY AVERAGES

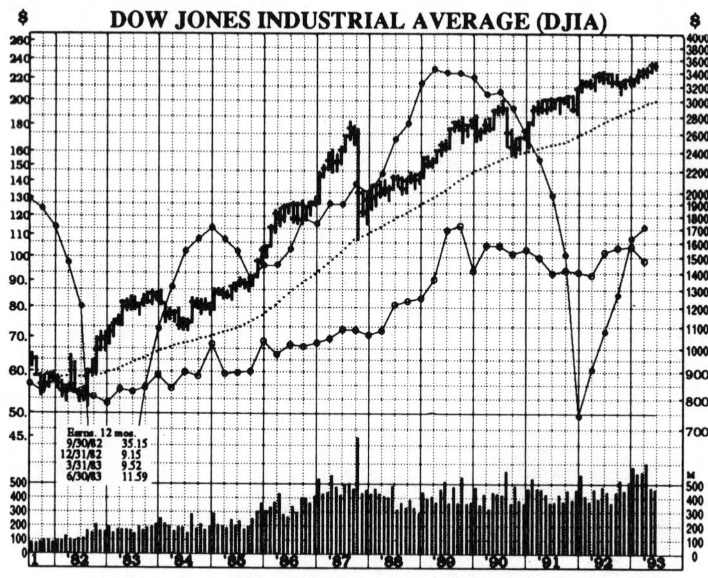

DOW JONES INDUSTRIAL, TRANSPORTATION AND UTILITY AVERAGES *(concluded)*

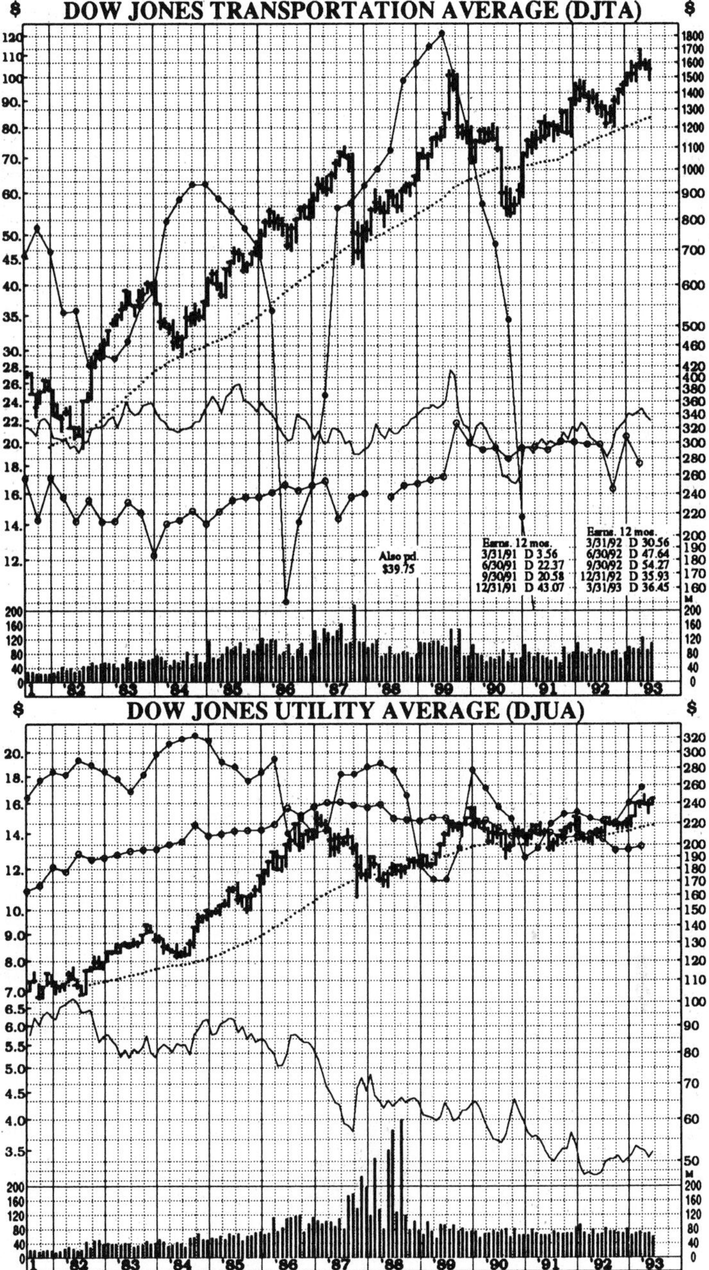

Source: Chart Courtesy of Securities Research Company, a division of Babson-United Investment Advisors, Inc., 101 Prescott St., Wellesley Hills, MA 02181-3319.

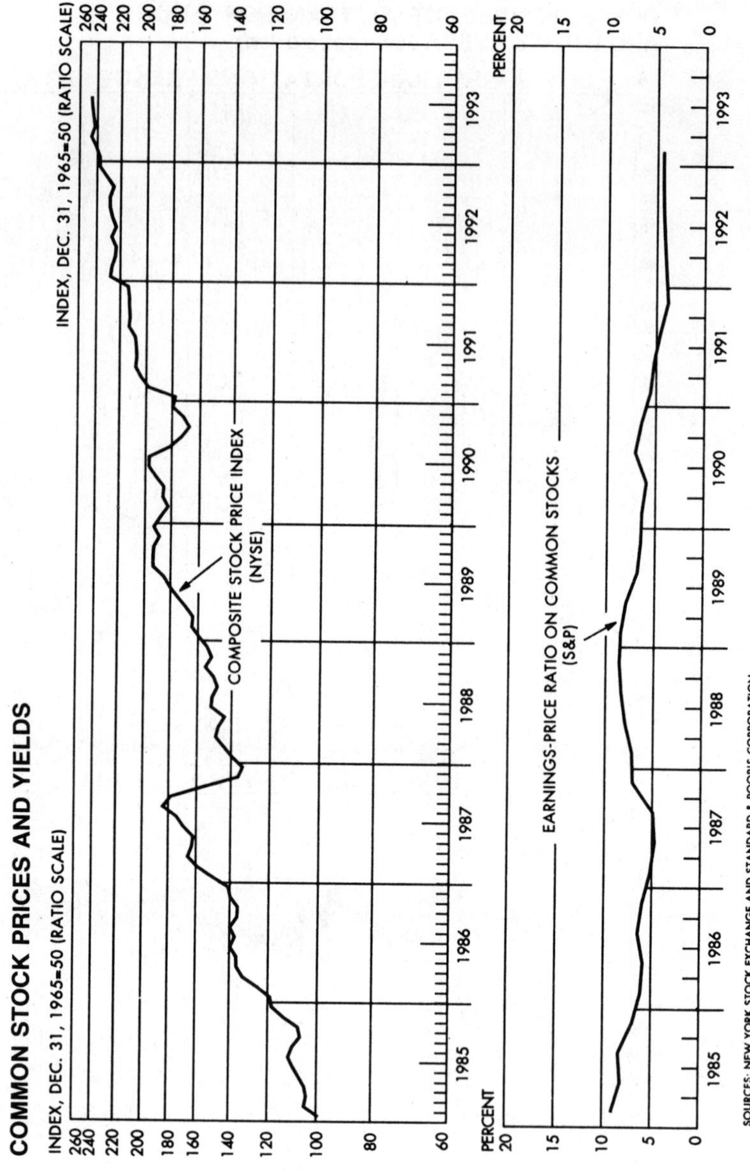
COMMON STOCK PRICES AND YIELDS
INDEX, DEC. 31, 1965=50 (RATIO SCALE)
260
240
220
200
180
160
140
120
100
80
60
COMPOSITE STOCK PRICE INDEX (NYSE)
PERCENT
20
15
10
5
0
EARNINGS-PRICE RATIO ON COMMON STOCKS (S&P)
1985
1986
1987
1988
1989
1990
1991
1992
1993
SOURCES: NEW YORK STOCK EXCHANGE AND STANDARD & POOR'S CORPORATION
COUNCIL OF ECONOMIC ADVISERS

Period	Common stock prices [1]							Common stock yields (percent) [6]	
	New York Stock Exchange indexes (Dec. 31, 1965=50, except as noted) [2]					Dow-Jones industrial average [4]	Standard & Poor's composite index (1941–43=10) [5]	Dividend-price ratio	Earnings-price ratio
	Composite	Industrial	Transportation	Utility [3]	Finance				
1983	92.63	107.45	89.36	94.00	95.34	1,190.34	160.41	4.40	8.03
1984	92.46	108.01	85.63	92.88	89.28	1,178.48	160.46	4.64	10.02
1985	108.09	123.79	104.11	113.50	114.21	1,328.23	186.84	4.25	8.12
1986	136.00	155.85	119.87	142.72	147.20	1,792.76	236.34	3.49	6.09
1987	161.70	195.31	140.39	148.60	146.48	2,275.99	286.83	3.08	5.48
1988	149.91	180.95	134.12	143.54	127.26	2,060.82	265.79	3.64	8.01
1989	180.02	216.23	175.28	174.86	151.88	2,508.91	322.84	3.45	7.41
1990	183.46	225.78	158.62	181.20	133.26	2,678.94	334.59	3.61	6.47
1991	206.33	258.14	173.99	185.32	150.82	2,929.33	376.18	3.24	4.81
1992	229.01	284.62	201.09	198.92	179.26	3,284.29	415.74	2.99	4.22
1992: July	228.17	281.90	198.36	202.36	181.00	3,329.41	415.05	3.00	
Aug	230.07	284.44	191.31	206.82	180.47	3,307.45	417.93	2.97	
Sept	230.13	285.76	191.61	204.52	178.27	3,293.92	418.48	3.00	4.32
Oct	226.97	279.70	192.30	203.24	181.36	3,198.70	412.50	3.07	
Nov	232.84	287.30	204.78	202.26	189.27	3,238.49	422.84	2.98	
Dec	239.47	294.86	212.35	207.70	196.87	3,303.15	435.64	2.90	4.38
1993: Jan	239.67	292.11	221.00	211.04	203.38	3,277.72	435.23	2.88	
Feb	243.41	294.40	226.96	218.89	209.93	3,367.26	441.70	2.81	
Mar	248.12	298.75	229.42	225.06	217.01	3,440.74	450.16	2.76	4.39
Apr	244.72	292.19	237.97	227.56	216.02	3,423.63	443.08	2.82	
May	246.02	297.83	237.80	222.41	209.40	3,478.17	445.25	2.80	
June [r]	247.16	298.78	234.30	226.53	209.75	3,513.81	448.06	2.81	
July	247.85	295.34	238.30	232.55	218.94	3,529.43	447.29	2.81	
Week ended:									
1993: July 3	248.69	297.81	237.74	231.14	217.02	3,511.93	449.59	2.80	
10	246.82	294.21	233.24	231.57	218.22	3,490.27	445.26	2.84	
17	248.56	296.78	234.61	232.24	219.00	3,532.32	448.42	2.79	
24	247.27	294.38	239.50	232.46	218.72	3,541.48	446.43	2.82	
31	248.54	295.38	244.74	234.23	220.48	3,558.70	448.58	2.80	

1 Average of daily closing prices.
2 Includes all the stocks (more than 2,000 in 1992) listed on the NYSE.
3 Dec. 31, 1965=100. Effective April 27, 1993 the NYSE doubled the value of the utility index to facilitate trading of options and futures on the index. Such trading is expected to begin later this year. All indexes shown here reflect the doubling.
4 Includes 30 stocks.
5 Includes 500 stocks.
6 Standard & Poor's series. Dividend-price ratios based on Wednesday closing prices. Earnings-price ratios based on prices at end of quarter.

NOTE.—All data relate to stocks listed on the New York Stock Exchange (NYSE).

Sources: New York Stock Exchange, Dow-Jones & Company, Inc., and Standard & Poor's Corporation.

Source: *Economic Indicators*, Council of Economic Advisers.

NEW SECURITY ISSUES U.S. Corporations
Millions of dollars

Type of issue, offering, or issuer	1990	1991	1992	1992					1993		
				Aug.	Sept.	Oct.	Nov.	Dec.	Jan.	Feb.	Mar.
1 **All issues**[1]	**340,049**	**465,483**	n.a.	**37,091**	**42,849**	**39,280**	**35,525**	**39,424**	**50,793**	**59,623**[r]	**55,272**
2 **Bonds**[2]	**299,884**	**390,018**	**404,992**	**31,815**	**37,539**	**32,314**	**31,026**	**33,375**	**45,559**	**49,563**[r]	**46,434**
By type of offering											
3 Public, domestic	188,848	287,125	377,453	28,561	36,185	30,249	28,774	31,835	41,675	47,165	41,699
4 Private placement, domestic[3]	86,982	74,930	n.a.	n.a.	n.a.	n.a.	n.a.	n.a.	n.a.	n.a.	n.a.
5 Sold abroad	23,054	27,962	27,539	3,254	1,355	2,066	2,252	1,540	3,884	2,397[r]	4,735
By industry group											
6 Manufacturing	51,779	86,628	69,538	4,720	5,974	7,975	3,467	4,232	9,393	8,269[r]	8,067
7 Commercial and miscellaneous	40,733	36,666	30,049	2,159	2,374	2,813	2,396	2,176	3,074	2,268	2,695
8 Transportation	12,776	13,598	6,497	393	677	290	0	611	316	248	1,067
9 Public utility	17,621	23,945	44,643	4,509	5,230	3,700	1,289	2,867	4,282	5,624	7,058
10 Communication	6,687	9,431	13,073	1,053	1,191	427	374	516	3,019	2,890	3,270
11 Real estate and financial	170,288	219,750	241,192	18,982	22,093	17,110	23,499	22,973	25,475	30,264[r]	24,278
12 **Stocks**[2]	**40,165**	**75,467**	n.a.	**5,276**	**5,310**	**6,966**	**4,499**	**6,049**	**5,234**	**10,060**	**8,838**
By type of offering											
13 Public preferred	n.a.	17,408	21,332	1,148	1,233	2,901	1,540	1,608	1,112	1,898	1,647
14 Common	n.a.	47,860	57,099	4,129	4,077	4,065	2,958	4,441	4,122	8,161	7,191
15 Private placement[3]	16,736	10,109	n.a.	n.a.	n.a.	n.a.	n.a.	n.a.	n.a.	n.a.	n.a.
By industry group											
16 Manufacturing	5,649	24,154	n.a.	713	307	1,779	288	1,468	722	2,616	1,741
17 Commercial and miscellaneous	10,171	19,418	n.a.	1,315	602	940	1,366	2,226	1,688	2,021	2,488
18 Transportation	369	2,439	n.a.	n.a.	59	53	304	118	65	64	336
19 Public utility	416	3,474	n.a.	921	595	359	150	92	310	350	743
20 Communication	3,822	475	n.a.	n.a.	1,051	99	22	126	0	0	7
21 Real estate and financial	19,738	25,507	n.a.	2,327	2,695	3,735	2,369	2,019	2,438	5,009	3,522

1. Figures represent gross proceeds of issues maturing in more than one year; they are the principal amount or number of units calculated by multiplying by the offering price. Figures exclude secondary offerings, employee stock plans, investment companies other than closed-end, intracorporate transactions, equities sold abroad, and Yankee bonds. Stock data include ownership securities issued by limited partnerships.

2. Monthly data cover only public offerings.

3. Monthly data are not available.

SOURCES. IDD Information Services, Inc., the Board of Governors of the Federal Reserve System, and, before 1989, the U.S. Securities and Exchange Commission.

Source: *Federal Reserve Bulletin*, Board of Governors of the Federal Reserve System.

A Guide to SEC Corporate Filings

SEC DISCLOSURE STATUTE

The purpose of the Federal securities laws is to provide disclosure of material financial and other information on companies seeking to raise capital through the public offering of their securities, as well as companies whose securities are already publicly held. This enables investors to evaluate the securities of these companies on an informed and realistic basis.

The Securities Act of 1933 is a *disclosure* statute. It generally requires that, before securities may be offered to the public, a registration statement must be filed with the Commission disclosing prescribed categories of information. Before the sale of securities can begin, the registration statement must become "effective," and investors must be furnished a prospectus containing the most significant information in the registration statement.

The Securities Exchange Act of 1934 deals in large part with securities already outstanding and requires the registration of securities listed on a national securities exchange, as well as Over-the-Counter securities in which there is a substantial public interest. Issuers of registered securities must file annual and other periodic reports designed to provide a public file of current material information.

The Exchange Act also requires disclosure of material information to holders of registered securities in solicitations of proxies for the election of directors or approval of corporate action at a shareholder's meeting, or in attempt to acquire control of a company through a tender offer or other planned stock acquisitions. It provides that insiders of companies whose equity securities are registered must report their holdings and transactions in all equity securities of their companies.

The Securities Act of 1933	The Securities Exchange Act of 1934	The Investment Act of 1940
S-1	Form 3	N-1A
S-2	Form 4	N-2
S-3	Form 8	N-5
S-4	8-K	N-14
S-6	10-C	
S-8	10-K	
S-11	10-Q	
S-18	20-F	
F-1	13F	
F-2	13D	
F-3	13E-3	
F-4	13E-4	
F-6	13G	
	14D-1	
	14D-9	
	Proxy Statement	

Source: A *Guide to SEC Corporate Filings*, Disclosure, Inc., 5161 River Road, Bethesda, MD 20816. Provided by Disclosure. To order copies of any SEC filings, call 800–638–8241.

PERIODIC ANNUAL REPORTS

10-K

This report provides a comprehensive overview of the registrant. The report must be filed within 90 days after close of company's fiscal year and contains the following items of disclosure:

Items Reported

COVER PAGE

Lists Fiscal Year End, State or other jurisdiction of incorporation or organization, Title of each class of securities and the exchange on which it is registered and the number of shares outstanding of each of the issuer's classes of common stock, as of the latest practicable date (date is commonly the filing date, NOT the time period covered in the document).

Part I

1. **Business.** Identifies principal products and services of the company, principal markets and methods of distribution and, if "material," competitive factors, backlog and expectation of fulfillment, availability of raw materials, importance of patents, licenses, and franchises, estimated cost of research, number of employees, and effects of compliance with environmental laws.

   If there is more than one line of business, a statement is included for each of the last three years. The statement includes total sales and net income for each line which, during either of the last two fiscal years, accounted for 10 percent or more of total sales or pretax income.
2. **Properties.** Location and character of principal plants, mines, and other important properties and if held in fee or leased.
3. **Legal Proceedings.** Brief description of material legal proceedings pending.
4. **Submission of Matters to a Vote of Secu-**

rity Holders. Information relating to the convening of a meeting of shareholders, whether annual or special, and the matters voted upon.

Part II

5. **Market for the Registrant's Common Stock and Related Security Holder Matters.** Includes principal market in which voting securities are traded with high and low sales prices (in the absence thereof, the range of bid and asked quotations for each quarterly period during the past two years) and the dividends paid during the past two years. In addition to the frequency and amount of dividends paid, this item contains a discussion concerning future dividends.
6. **Selected Financial Data.** These are five-year selected data including net sales and operating revenue; income or loss from continuing operations, both total and per common share; total assets; long-term obligations including redeemable preferred stock; and cash dividend declared per common share. The data also includes additional items that could enhance understanding of trends in financial condition and results of operations. Further, the effects of inflation and changing prices should be reflected in the five-year summary.
7. **Management's Discussion and Analysis of Financial Condition and Results of Operations.** Under broad guidelines, this includes: liquidity, capital resources and results of operations; trends that are favorable or unfavorable as well as significant events or uncertainties; causes of any material changes in the financial statements as a whole; limited data concerning subsidiaries; and discussion of effects of inflation and changing prices.
8. **Financial Statements and Supplementary Data.** Two-year audited balance sheets as well as three-year audited statements of income and cash flow statement.
9. **Changes in and disagreements with Accountants on Accounting and Financial Disclosure.**

Part III*

10. **Directors and Executive Officers.** Name, office, term of office and specific background data on each.
11. **Remuneration of Directors and Officers.** List of each director and highest paid officers with aggregate annual remuneration exceeding $40,000. Also includes total paid all officers and directors as a group.
12. **Security Ownership of Certain Beneficial Owners and Management.** Identification of owners of 5 percent or more of registrant's stock in addition to listing the amount and percent of each class of stock held by officers and directors.
13. **Certain Relationships and Related Transactions.**

* Disclosure normally made via a proxy statement may in some cases be made using Part III of Form 10-K.

Part IV

14. **Exhibits, Financial Statement Schedules and Reports on Form 8-K.** Complete, audited annual financial information and a list of exhibits filed. Also, any unscheduled material events or corporate changes filed in an 8-K during the year.

Form 10-K Schedules (when applicable)

I. Investments other than investments in affiliates
II. Receivables from related parties and underwriters, promoters and employees other than affiliates
III. Condensed financial information
IV. Indebtedness of affiliates (not current)
V. Property, plant and equipment
VI. Accumulated depreciation, depletion and amortization of property, plant and equipment
VII. Guarantees of securities of other issuers
VIII. Valuation and qualifying accounts
IX. Short-term borrowings
X. Supplementary income statement information
XI. Supplementary profit and loss information
XII. Income from dividends (equity in net profit and loss of affiliates)

Annual Report to Shareholders

The Annual Report to Shareholders is the principal document used by most major companies to communicate directly with shareholders. Since it is not a required, official SEC filing, companies have considerable discretion in determining what types of information this report will contain and how it is to be presented.

In addition to financial information, the Annual Report to Shareholders often provides non-financial details of the business which are not reported elsewhere. These may include marketing plans and forecasts of future programs and plans.

20-F

Annual Report/Registration Statement filed by certain foreign issuers of securities trading in the United States. Form 20-F must be filed 6 months after close of fiscal year.

Part I

1. Description of Business
2. Description of Property
3. Material Legal Proceedings
4. Control of Registrant
5. Nature of Trading Market
6. Exchange Controls and Other Limitations Affecting Security Holders
7. Taxation
8. Selected Financial Data
9. Management Discussion and Analysis
10. Directors and Officers
11. Compensation of Directors and Officers
12. Options to Purchase Securities from Registrant or Subsidiaries
13. Interests of Management in Certain Transactions

Part II

14. Description of Securities to be Registered

Part III

15. Defaults upon Senior Securities
16. Changes in Securities and Changes in Security for Registered Securities

Part IV

17.–19. Financial Statements and Exhibits

10-Q

This is the quarterly financial report filed by most companies, which, although unaudited, provides a continuing view of a company's financial position during the year. The 10-Q report must be filed within 45 days after close of fiscal year quarter.

Items Reported

COVER PAGE

Lists time period represented, State of incorporation, former name, address and fiscal year if changed since last report, whether the registrant filed any 1934 Act reports during the past 12 months and has been subject to such filing requirements for the past 90 days, whether the registrant has filed all documents and reports required under the Securities Exchange Act of 1934 subsequent to the distribution of securities, and the number of shares outstanding of each of the company's classes of common stock as of the last practicable date (date is commonly the filing date, NOT the time period covered in the document).

Part I

FINANCIAL STATEMENTS

1. Quarterly Financial Statements
2. Management Discussion and Analysis of material changes in the amount of revenue and expense items in relation to previous quarters, including the effect of any changes in accounting principles.

Part II

1. **Legal Proceedings.** Brief description of material legal proceedings pending; when civil rights or environmental statutes are involved, proceedings must be disclosed.
2. **Changes in Securities.** Material changes in the rights of holders of any class of registered security.
3. **Defaults upon Senior Securities.** Material defaults in the payment of principal, interest, sinking fund or purchase fund installment, dividend, or other material default not cured within 30 days.
4. **Submission of Matters to a Vote of Security Holders.** Information relating to the convening of a meeting of shareholders, whether annual or special, and the matters voted upon, with particular emphasis on the election of directors.
5. **Other Materially Important Events.** Information on any other item of interest to shareholders not already provided for in this form or reported in an 8-K.
6. **Exhibits and Reports on Form 8-K.** Any unscheduled material events or corporate changes reported in an 8-K during the prior quarter.

CORPORATE CHANGES AND VOTING MATTERS

8-K

This is a report of unscheduled material events or corporate changes deemed of importance to the shareholders or to the SEC. Items 1–3 and 8 must be reported in an 8-K within 15 days of the event. Items 4 and 6 must be filed within 5 business days after the event, and Item 5 is optional, meaning there is no mandatory time for filing.

1. Changes in Control of Registrant.
2. Acquisition or Disposition of Assets.
3. Bankruptcy or Receivership.
4. Changes in Registrant's Certifying Accountant.
5. Other Materially Important Events.
6. Resignation of Registrant's Directors.
7. Financial Statements and Exhibits.
8. Change in Fiscal Year.

10-C

Over-the-Counter companies use this form to report changes in name and amount of NASDAQ-listed securities. It is similar in purpose to the 8-K and must be filed within 10 days after the change.

Proxy Statement

A proxy statement provides official notification to designated classes of shareholders of matters to be brought to a vote at a shareholders' meeting. Proxy votes may be solicited for changing the company officers, or many other matters. Disclosures normally made via a proxy statement may in some cases be made using Part III of Form 10-K.

TENDER OFFER/ACQUISITION REPORTS

13-D

Filing required by 5% (or more) equity owners within ten days of acquisition event.
1. Security and issuer
2. Identity and background of person filing the statement
3. Source and amount of funds or other consideration
4. Purpose of the transaction
5. Interest in securities of the issuer
6. Contracts, arrangements or relationships with respect to securities of the issuer
7. Material to be filed as exhibits which may include but is not limited to:
   - Acquisition Agreements
   - Financing Arrangements
   - Contracts, Guarantees and other Agreements

14D-1

Tender offer filing made with the SEC at the time an offer is made to holders of equity securities of the target company, if acceptance of the offer would give the bidder over 5% ownership of the subject securities.
1. Security and subject company
2. Identity and background information
3. Past contacts, transactions or negotiations with subject company
4. Source and amount of funds or other consideration
5. Purpose of the tender offer and plans or proposals of the bidder
6. Interest in securities of the subject company
7. Contracts, arrangements or relationships with respect to the subject company's securities
8. Persons retained, employed or to be compensated
9. Financial statements of certain bidders
10. Additional information
11. Material to be filed as exhibits which may include but is not limited to:
    - Tender Offer Material
    - Loan Agreements
    - Contracts and Other Agreements
    - Legal Opinion on Tax Consequences
    - Prospectus

14D-9

A solicitation/recommendation statement that must be submitted to equity holders and filed with the SEC by the management of a company subject to a tender offer within ten days of the making of the tender offer.
1. Security and subject company
2. Tender offer of the bidder
3. Identity and background
4. The solicitation or recommendation
5. Persons retained, employed or to be compensated
6. Recent transactions and intent with respect to securities
7. Certain negotiations and transactions by the subject company
8. Additional information
9. Material to be filed as exhibits

13E-3

Transaction statement pursuant to the Securities Exchange Act of 1934 with respect to a public company or affiliate going private.
1. Issuer and class of security subject to the transaction
2. Identity and background of the individuals
3. Past contacts, transactions or negotiations
4. Terms of the transaction

5. Plans or proposals of the issuer or affiliate
6. Source and amount of funds or other considerations
7. Purpose, alternatives, reasons and effects
8. Fairness of the transaction
9. Reports, opinions, appraisals and certain negotiations
10. Interest in securities of the issuer
11. Contracts, arrangements or relationships with respect to the issuer's securities
12. Present intention and recommendation of certain persons with regard to the transaction
13. Other provisions of the transaction
14. Financial information
15. Persons and assets employed, retained or utilized
16. Additional information
17. Material to be filed as exhibits
    - Loan Agreements
    - Fairness Opinions and Appraisals
    - Contracts and Other Agreements
    - Disclosure Materials Sent to Security Holders
    - Statement of Appraisal Rights and Procedures

13E-4

Issuer tender offer statement pursuant to the Securities Exchange Act of 1934.

1. Security and issuer
2. Source and amount of funds
3. Purpose of the tender offer and plans or proposals of the issuer or affiliate
4. Interest in securities of the issuer
5. Contracts, arrangements or relationships with respect to the issuer's securities
6. Person retained, employed or to be compensated
7. Financial information
8. Additional information
9. Material to be filed as exhibits
    - Tender Offer Material
    - Loan Agreement
    - Contracts and Other Agreements
    - Legal Opinion on Tax Consequences
    - Prospectus, if applicable

SECURITY HOLDINGS BY INSIDERS AND INSTITUTIONS

13-F

A quarterly report of equity holdings required of all institutions with equity assets of $100 million or more. This includes banks, insurance companies, investment companies, investment advisors and large internally managed endowments, foundations and pension funds. The report must be filed within 45 days after close of fiscal quarter.

13-G

An annual filing which must be filed by all reporting persons (primarily institutions) meeting the 5 percent equity ownership rule within 45 days after the end of each calendar year.

1. Name and address of issuer
2. Identification of reporting person
3. 13D-1 or 13D-2 applicability
4. Amount of shares beneficially owned:
    - Percent of Class Outstanding
    - Sole or Shared Power to Vote
    - Sole or Shared Power to Dispose
5. Ownership of 5 percent or less of a class of stock
6. Ownership of more than 5 percent on behalf of another person
7. Identification of subsidiary which acquired the security being reported on by the parent holding company (if applicable)
8. Identification and classification of members of the group (if applicable)
9. Notice of dissolution of group (if applicable)
10. Certification

Form 3

Initial statement which identifies holdings of registrant's securities owned by directors, officers and 10 percent shareholders. A Form 3 must be filed within 10 days after the event.

Form 4

Amendment to Form 3 reporting a sale or acquisition of registrant's securities. A Form 4 must be filed by the 10th day of the month following the month in which the transaction occurred.

REGISTRATION OF SECURITIES

Registration Statements

Registration statements are of two principal types: (1) "offering" registrations filed under the Securities Act of 1933, and (2) "trading" registrations filed under the Securities Exchange Act of 1934.

"Offering" registrations are used to register securities before they are offered to investors. Part I of the registration, a preliminary prospectus or "red herring," contains preliminary information that will be in the final prospectus. Included in Part I (or incorporated by reference) in many registration statements are:

- Description of Securities to be Registered
- Use of Proceeds
- Risk Factors
- Determination of Offering Price
- Potential Dilution
- Selling Security Holders
- Plan of Distribution
- Interests of Named Experts and Counsel
- Information with Respect to the Registrant (description of business, legal proceedings, market price and dividends on common equity, financial statements, Management Discussion and Analysis, changes in and disagreements with accountants, directors and executive officers, security ownership of certain beneficial owners and management and certain relationships and related transactions).

Part II of the registration contains information not required in the prospectus. This includes:

- Expenses of Issuance and Distribution
- Indemnification of Directors and Officers
- Recent Sales of Unregistered Securities, Undertakings, Exhibits and Financial Statement Schedules

"Offering" registration statements vary in purpose and content according to the type of organization issuing stock:

S-1 Companies reporting under the 1934 Act for less than 3 years. Permits no incorporation by reference and requires complete disclosure in the prospectus.

S-2 Companies reporting under the 1934 Act for 3 or more years but not meeting the minimum voting stock requirement. Reference to 1934 Act reports permits incorporation and presentation of financial information in the prospectus or in an Annual Report to Shareholders delivered with the prospectus.

S-3 Companies reporting under the 1934 Act for 3 or more years and having at least $150 million of voting stock held by non-affiliates, or as an alternative test, $100 million of voting stock coupled with an annual trading volume of 3 million shares. Allows minimal disclosure in the prospectus and maximum incorporation by reference of 1934 Act reports.

S-4 Registration used in certain business combinations or reorganizations.

S-6 Filed by unit investment trusts registered under the Investment Act of 1940 on Form N-8B-2.

S-8 Registration used to register securities to be offered to employees under stock option and various other employee benefit plans.

S-11 Filed by real estate companies, primarily limited partnerships and investment trusts.

S-18 Short form initial registration of up to $7.5 million in securities.

SE Non-electronically filed exhibits made by registrants filing with the EDGAR Project.

N-1A Filed by open-end management investment companies.

N-2 Filed by closed-end management investment companies.

N-5 Registration of small business investment companies.

N-14 Registration of the securities of management investment and business development companies to be issued in business combinations under the Investment Act of 1940.

F-1 Registration of securities by foreign private issuers eligible to use Form 20-F, for which no other form is prescribed.

F-2 Registration of securities by foreign private issuers meeting certain 1934 Act filing requirements.

F-3 Registration of securities by foreign private issuers offered pursuant to certain types of transactions, subject to the 1934 Act filing requirements for the preceding 3 years.

F-4 Registration of securities issued in business combinations involving foreign private registrants.

F-6 Registration of depository shares evidenced by the American Depository Receipts (ADRs).

"Trading" registrations are filed to permit trading among investors on a securities exchange or in the Over-the-Counter market. These Registration Statements do not include a prospectus. Registration statements which serve to register securities for trading fall into three categories:

Quick Reference Chart to Contents of SEC Filings

REPORT CONTENTS	10-K	20-F	10-Q	8-K	10-C	6-K	Proxy Statements	Prospectus	Registration Statements '34 Act F-10	Registration Statements '34 Act 8-A 8-B	Registration Statements '33 Act "S" Type	ARS	Listing Application
Auditor													
□ Name	■	■	░				▨	■	■		■	■	░
□ Opinion	■	■	░						■			■	
□ Changes				■			░						
Compensation Plans													
□ Equity	░		░				▨	▨	■		▨		░
□ Monetary	░		░				■	▨	■		▨		░
Company Information													
□ Nature of Business	■	■				▨		■	■		■	░	░
□ History	▨	■					░	■	▨		■	░	░
□ Organization and Change	▨	▨		■	░	▨	░	■		▨	■	░	
Debt Structure	■					▨		■	■		■	■	
Depreciation & Other Schedules	■	■				▨		■	■		■		
Dilution Factors	■	■		▨		▨		■	■		■	■	
Directors, Officers, Insiders													
□ Identification	▨	■				▨	■	■	■		■	▨	
□ Background	░	░	░	░	░	░	■	■	░		■	░	
□ Holdings	░	■		░			■	■	■		■		
□ Compensation	░	■		░			■	■	■		■		
Earnings Per Share	■	■	■			▨			■			■	
Financial Information													
□ Annual Audited	■	■							■		■	■	
□ Interim Audited		■					░	░			░		
□ Interim Unaudited	░		■	░		▨		▨			▨		
Foreign Operations	■						░	■	■		■	░	▨
Labor Contracts	░	░		░					▨		▨		
Legal Agreements	▨	░		░					▨		▨		
Legal Counsel				░			░	■			■		░
Loan Agreements	▨			░			░		▨		▨		
Plants and Properties	■	▨		░				▨	■		▨	░	
Product-Line Breakout	■							■			■	░	
Securities Structure	■	■			░			■	■		■		
Subsidiaries	■	■					░		■		■		
Underwriting				░				■			■		
Unregistered Securities	░			░			░	░			■		
Block Movements	░			▨			░		■				░

TENDER OFFER/ACQUISITION REPORTS	13D	13G	14D-1	14D-9	13E-3	13E-4
Name of Issuer (Subject Company)	■	■	■	■	■	■
Filing Person (or Company)	■	■	■	■	■	■
Amount of Shares Owned	■	■				
Percent of Class Outstanding	■	■				
Financial Statements of Bidder			▨		▨	▨
Purpose of Tender Offer			■	■	■	■
Source and Amount of Funds	■		■		■	
Identity and Background Information			■	■	■	
Persons Retained, Employed or to be Compensated	░		■	■	■	■
Exhibits	▨		▨	▨	▨	▨

■ *always included* ▨ *frequently included* ░ *special circumstances*

(1) **Form 10** may be used by companies during the first two years they are subject to the 1934 Act filing requirements. It is a combination registration statement and annual report with information content similar to that of SEC required 10-Ks.

(2) **Form 8-A** is used by 1934 Act registrants wishing to register additional securities or classes thereof.

(3) **Form 8-B** is used by "successor issuers" (usually companies which have changed their name or state of incorporation) as notification that previously registered securities are to be traded under a new corporate identification.

Prospectus

When the sale of securities as proposed in an "offering" registration statement is approved by the SEC, any changes required by the SEC are incorporated into the prospectus. This document must be made available to investors before the sale of the security is initiated. It also contains the actual offering price, which may have been changed after the registration statement was approved.

Form 8 (Amendment)

Form 8 is used to amend or supplement any 1934 Act report previously submitted. 1933 Act registration statements are amended by filing an amended registration statement (pre-effective amendment) or by the prospectus itself, as previously noted.

Listing Application

Like the Annual Report to Shareholders, a listing application is not an official SEC filing. It is filed by the company with the NYSE, AMEX or other stock exchange to document proposed new listings. Usually a Form 8-A registration is filed with the SEC at about the same time.

How to Read the New York Stock Exchange and American Stock Exchange Quotations

(1)	(2)	(3)	(4)	(5)	(6)	(7)	(8)	(9)	(10)	(11)	(12)
52 Weeks					Yld		Vol				Net
Hi	Lo	Stock	Sym	Div	%	P-E	100s	Hi	Lo	Close	Chg
42¾	23⅝	WestPtPepri	WPM		. . .	13	47	30¼	29⅝	30¼ +	⅝
18¾	15¾	WestcstEngy	g WE	.80	5.0	15	9	15⅞	15¾	15⅞ +	⅛
17¼	3⅞	WestnCoNA	WSN		. . .	. . .	1026	4¼	4⅛	4¼ −	⅛

Source: Reprinted by permission of THE WALL STREET JOURNAL, © 1992 Dow Jones & Company, Inc. All Rights Reserved Worldwide.

The composite quotations take into account prices paid for a stock on the New York or American Exchanges, plus those prices paid on regional exchanges, Over-the-Counter (OTC) and elsewhere, as shown in the example from the Wall Street Journal. The stock market quotations are explained below:

(1) The highest price per share paid in the past 52 weeks in terms of ⅛ of a dollar, i.e., 10⅛ means $10.125.
(2) The lowest price paid per share in the last 52 weeks.
(3) The name of the company in abbreviated form.
(4) The Stock Exchange symbol used to identify the stock.
(5) The regular annual dividend paid. Special or extra dividends are specified by letters given in the footnotes in the Explanatory Notes shown below.
(6) The yield, that is, the annual dividend divided by the current price of the stock expressed in percent. For example, a stock that sells for $20.00 per share and pays a dividend of $2.00 per share has a yield of 10 percent (2/20).
(7) The P/E ratio is the current price of the stock divided by the company's last reported annual earnings per share. The P/E ratio is generally high for companies which are thought to have a relatively large and persistent earning's growth rate. The average P/E ratio for the Dow Jones stocks varied from 9.8 to 39.5 during the last five years.
(8) The number of shares sold on the day reported in 100s of shares.
(9) The highest price paid per share on the day reported.
(10) The lowest price paid per share on the day reported.
(11) The last price paid per share on the day reported.
(12) The change in the closing price from the previous day's closing price.

EXPLANATORY NOTES

The following explanations apply to New York and American exchange listed issues and the National Association of Securities Dealers Automated Quotations system's over-the-counter securities. Exchange prices are composite quotations that include trades on the Midwest, Pacific, Philadelphia, Boston and Cincinnati exchanges and reported by the NASD and Instinet.

Boldfaced quotations highlight those issues whose price changed by 5% or more from their previous closing price.

Underlined quotations are those stocks with large changes in volume, per exchange, compared with the issue's average trading volume. The calculation includes common stocks of $5 a share or more with an average volume over 65 trading days of at least 5,000 shares. The underlined quotations are for the 40 largest volume percentage leaders on the NYSE and the NASD's National Market System. It includes the 20 largest volume percentage gainers on the Amex.

The 52-week high and low columns show the highest and lowest price of the issue during the preceding 52 weeks plus the current week, but not the latest trading day. These ranges are adjusted to reflect stock payouts of 1% or more, and cash dividends of 10% or more.

Dividend rates, unless noted, are annual disbursements based on the last quarterly, semiannual, or annual declaration. Special or extra dividends, special situations or payments not designated as regular are identified by footnotes.

Yield is defined as the dividends paid by a company on its securities, expressed as a percentage of price.

The P/E ratio is determined by dividing the price of a share of stock by its company's earnings per share of that stock. These earnings are the primary per-share earnings reported by the company for the most recent four quarters. Extraordinary items are usually excluded.

Sales figures are the unofficial daily total of shares traded, quoted in hundreds (two zeros omitted).

Exchange ticker symbols are shown for all New York and American exchange common stocks, and Dow Jones News/Retrieval symbols are listed for Class A and Class B shares listed on both markets. Nasdaq symbols are listed for all Nasdaq NMS issues. A more detailed explanation of Nasdaq ticker symbols appears with the NMS listings.

FOOTNOTES: ▲—New 52-week high. ▼—New 52-week low. **a**—Extra dividend or extras in addition to the regular dividend. **b**—Indicates annual rate of the cash dividend and that a stock dividend was paid. **c**—Liquidating dividend. **e**—Indicates a dividend was declared or paid in the preceding 12 months, but that there isn't a regular rate. **g**—Indicates the dividend and earnings are expressed in Canadian money. The stock trades in U.S. dollars. No yield or P/E ratio is shown. **h**—Indicates a temporary exception to Nasdaq qualifications. **i**—Indicates amount declared or paid after a stock dividend or split. **j**—Indicates dividend was paid this year, and that at the last dividend meeting a dividend was omitted or deferred. **k**—Indicates dividend declared or paid this year on cumulative issues with dividends in arrears. **n**—Newly issued in the past 52 weeks. The high-low range begins with the start of trading and doesn't cover the entire period. **pf**—Preferred. **pp**—Holder owes installment(s) of purchase price. **pr**—Preference. **r**—Indicates a cash dividend declared or paid in the preceding 12 months, plus a stock dividend. **rt**—Rights. **s**—Stock split or stock dividend amounting to 25% or more in the past 52 weeks. The high-low price is adjusted from the old stock. Dividend calculations begin with the date the split was paid or the stock dividend occurred. **t**—Paid in stock in the preceding 12 months, estimated cash value on ex-dividend or ex-distribution date, except Nasdaq listings where payments are in stock. **un**—Units. **v**—Trading halted on primary market. **vj**—In bankruptcy or receivership or being reorganized under the Bankruptcy Code, or securities assumed by such companies. **wd**—When distributed. **wi**—When issued. **wt**—Warrants. **ww**—With warrants. **x**—Ex-dividend or ex-rights. **xw**—Without warrants. **y**—Ex-dividend and sales in full, not in hundreds. **z**—Sales in full, not in hundreds.

Source: Reprinted by permission of THE WALL STREET JOURNAL,

How to Read Over-the-Counter NASDAQ Listings

The notation is the same as that for the New York and American Stock Exchanges on page 284.

(1)	(2)	(3)	(4)	(5)	(6)	(7)	(8)	(9)	(10)	(11)	(12)
52 Weeks					Yld		Vol				Net
Hi	Lo	Stock	Sym	Div	%	P-E	100s	Hi	Lo	Close	Chg
4¾	1⅛	HuntrEnvr	HESI		...	...	158	4⅛	3⅞	4⅛ +	¼
22	14⅜	HuntgBcshr	HBAN	.80b	3.8	11	1231	21¾	21	21¼ −	¼
14¾	7¼	Hurco	HURC	.20	1.8	28	66	11¾	10¾	11 −	¾
32½	8¼	HutchTech	HTCH		...	21	282	28	27¼	27¼ −	¾
8⅜	3⅞	HycorBio	HYBD		...	675	265	6⅞	6½	6¾ −	1/16
3½	1/16	HycorBio wt			...	...	10	3	2¾	3 −	⅛
6⅞	4	HydeAthl	HYDE		...	19	62	5½	4¾	5 +	¼

NASDAQ SYMBOL EXPLANATION

All securities listed in the Nasdaq system are identified by a four letter or five letter symbol. The fifth letter indicates the issues that aren't common or capital shares, or are subject to restrictions or special conditions. Below is a rundown of fifth letter identifiers and a description of what they represent:

A—Class A. **B**—Class B. **C**—Exempt from Nasdaq listing qualifications for a limited period. **D**—New issue. **E**—Delinquent in required filings with SEC, as determined by the NASD. **F**—Foreign. **G**—First convertible bond. **H**—Second convertible bond, same company. **I**—Third convertible bond, same company. **J**—Voting. **K**—Non-voting. **L**—Miscellaneous situations, including second class units, third class of warrants or sixth class of preferred stock. **M**—Fourth preferred, same company. **N**—Third preferred, same company. **O**—Second preferred, same company. **P**—First preferred, same company. **Q**—In bankruptcy proceedings. **R**—Rights. **S**—Shares of beneficial interest. **T**—With warrants or rights. **U**—Units. **V**—When issued and when distributed. **W**—Warrants. **Y**—American Depository Receipt (ADR). **Z**—Miscellaneous situations, including second class of warrants, fifth class of preferred stock and any unit, receipt or certificate representing a limited partnership interest.

Source: Reprinted by permission of THE WALL STREET JOURNAL,

The Ex-dividend Explained

The ex-dividend status of a stock is indicated by an *x* in the newspaper quotation or *xd* on the ticker tape. This is an abbreviation for *without dividend.*

A stock that is purchased during the ex-dividend period will not pay a previously declared dividend to its new owner. The ex-dividend period spans four business days before the so-called record date—the date a dividend issuing corporation uses to tally its shareowners. An ex-dividend stock buyer is not entitled to a dividend because his name is not recorded with the dividend issuing corporation until after the record date.

The New York Stock Exchange requires that the buyer in every transaction be recorded with the issuing corporation on the fifth business day following a trade. A stock buyer, therefore, must purchase his shares at least five business days before the record date in order for the corporation to record his name in time for him to receive his dividend. A purchase one day later disqualifies a buyer from a dividend because the transfer of ownership cannot be completed by the record date. Therefore, on the fourth business day prior to the record date, a stock is sold ex-dividend.

In our example below, the corporation's Board has decided to pay a 50‰ dividend to shareholders of record on Monday, the 10th. A person buying shares up to the close of business on Monday, the 3rd, would be eligible for the dividend because normal settlement (5 business days) will be made on Monday the 10th. On Tuesday, the 4th, however, the stock would begin selling ex-dividend because a stock purchaser as of that date could not settle till after the record date.

On the ex-dividend date, the Exchange specialist will reduce all open buy orders and open sell stop orders by the amount of the dividend. This is done to more equitably reflect the stock's value since purchasers of stock on or after the ex-dividend date are ineligible for a dividend.

EX-DIVIDEND EXPLANATION

Any Month	Date	Calendar Day	Status
	3	Monday	With/Dividend
	4	Tuesday	Ex-Dividend (Without Dividend)
	5	Wednesday	" "
	6	Thursday	" "
	7	Friday	" "
	8	Saturday	Not a trading day
	9	Sunday	Not a trading day
	10	Monday	Record Date/Business Day
	11	Tuesday	Business Day

Source: *Taking The Mystery Out of Ex-Dividend,* The New York Stock Exchange, Inc.

Margin Accounts Explained

Stocks may be purchased by paying the purchase price in full (plus commissions and taxes) or on a margin account. With the margin account, the investors put up part of the purchase price in cash or securities, and the broker lends the remainder. The margin investor must pay the usual commissions as well as interest on the broker's loan. The stocks purchased on margin are held by the broker as collateral on the loan. Dividends are applied to the margin account and help offset the interest payments.

Margin (M) is defined as the market value (V) of the securities less the broker's loan (L), divided by the market value of the securities. The ratio is expressed as a percentage:

$$M = \frac{V - L}{V} \times 100$$

Example: You buy 100 shares of a stock at \$20 per share at a total cost (V) of \$2,000. You put up \$1,200 in cash and borrow (L) \$800 from the broker. The margin at the time of purchase is

$$M = \frac{\$2{,}000 - \$800}{\$2{,}000} \times 100 = 60\%$$

The margin at the time of purchase is called *initial margin.* The smallest allowed value of initial margin (set by the Federal Reserve) is currently 50%. Thus, with the above stock, if you buy 100 shares at \$20 per share on 50% initial margin, you put up \$1,000 (.5 × \$2,000), and the broker's loan is \$1,000.

After the purchase there is a *maintenance margin* (set by the Exchange) below which the margin is not permitted to decrease. The maintenance margin on the New York Stock Exchange is 25%. Some brokers, however, require a higher maintenance margin of about 30%. Thus, if the 100 shares of stocks discussed above decrease in price from \$20 to \$13 per share, then the margin is

$$M = \left(\frac{\$1{,}300 - \$1{,}000}{\$1{,}300}\right) \times 100 = 23\%$$

The margin of 23% is now below the maintenance margin of 25% set by the Exchange. The securities are said to be *under margined,* and a call for additional cash (or securities) is issued by the broker in order to bring up the margin to 25%. If the investor does not meet the call for additional cash (margin call) within a specified time, the stocks in the margin account are immediately sold.

MARGIN REQUIREMENTS (percent of market value and effective date)

	Mar. 11, 1968	June 8, 1968	May 6, 1970	Dec. 6, 1971	Nov. 24, 1972	Jan. 3, 1974
Margin stocks	70	80	65	55	65	50
Convertible bonds	50	60	50	50	50	50
Short sales	70	80	65	55	65	50

Note: Regulations G, T, and U of the Federal Reserve Board of Governors, prescribed in accordance with the Securities Exchange Act of 1934, limit the amount of credit to purchase and carry margin stocks that may be extended on securities as collateral by prescribing a maximum loan value, which is a specified percentage of the market value of the collateral at the time the credit is extended. Margin requirements are the difference between the market value (100 percent) and the maximum loan value. The term "margin stocks" is defined in the corresponding regulation.

Source: *Federal Reserve Bulletin.*

Short Selling Explained

Short selling provides an opportunity to profit from a decline in the price of a stock. If you believe that a stock is due for a substantial decline, you arrange to have your broker borrow the stock from another investor who owns the shares. The borrowed stock is then sold. This cash is held as collateral against the borrowed shares. When (and if) the stock price declines, you purchase the stock at the market price and use it to replace the borrowed shares. The broker arranges the return of your cash collateral less the cost of the repurchased stock. Your profit per share is the price received on the sale of the stock less the purchase price.

There are certain cash outlays and costs associated with the short sale. Generally there is no charge for borrowing the stock, although occasionally stock lenders may charge a premium over the market price. You must deposit $2,000 or the required initial margin, whichever is the greater, at the time the stock is borrowed. Thus, if you borrow 100 shares of a stock priced at $50 per share and the margin required is 50%, you must put up $2,500 (.5 × $50 × 100) in cash or securities. The margin deposit is returned when you close out the short sale. You pay commission when the stock is sold and when it is repurchased. In addition, you must pay the stock lender any dividends which are declared during the period you are short the stock. It is well to remember that if cash is used for the deposit, there is a loss of the interest which you would have obtained if the cash had been invested.

The dividend payments and interest loss can be reduced or eliminated if you short stocks which pay little or no dividends and use interest-bearing securities (such as T-bills or negotiable certificates of deposit) as the margin deposit.

An increase in the price of the stock can result in substantial losses since you may be forced to repurchase at a higher price than you sold. If there are many short sellers seeking to purchase the stock in order to close out their position, prices may be driven to very high levels.

The short sale cannot be executed while the stock price is declining on the exchange. According to the rules of the SEC, the stock must undergo an increase in price prior to the execution of a short sale.

Mutual Fund Reporting Regulations

The new SEC regulations concerning mutual fund reporting practices which went into effect May 1988 require that an easy-to-read table giving all fund charges must appear near the front of all prospectuses. Included must be such items as front end and back end loads, 12b–1 plans to recover marketing and distribution costs, and sales loads imposed on reinvested dividends applied everytime the find reinvest dividends. Typically, fund expense ratios (annual operating expenses to assets) range from .7% to 1%.

Advertisements that contain yields must calculate yields (capital gains plus dividends) on a consistent basis prescribed by the SEC, taking into account any front end sales charges. To put the yield figure into perspective, ads must provide one, five and ten year total return information.

Fund fees are now shown in the newspaper listing by means of the following letters after the fund's name:

- r — indicates a back end load or redemption fee
- p — indicates a 12b–1 plan is in effect
- t — indicates both a back end and a 12b–1 fee
- N.L. — indicates there is no front end or back end load

How to Read Mutual Fund Quotations

The following tables provide explanations of the mutal fund quotations appearing in *The Wall Street Journal.* Note that the performance data provided by Lipper Analytical Services differ depending on the day of the week that the quotation appears. Thus, in the example shown, performance data are given for Wednesday with returns for 13 weeks, 3 years, and YTD (year to date).

The Monday edition of the *Journal* provides information on a fund's initial charges and expenses. The ranking of a fund's total return for each category of investment objective over the longest time period given in the day's quotation is assigned a letter from A (top 20%) to E (bottom 20%).

Extensive mutual fund quotations are also given in the *Investor's Business Daily.* The latter also provides toll free phone numbers and dollar size of the fund families. Rankings of a fund's total return are provided for performance over the prior three year period versus all other mutual funds ranging from A+ for the top 5%, A for the top 10%, B+ for the top 20%, to E below the top 70%. Note that the rankings are against all mutual funds, whereas in *The Wall Street Journal* funds are ranked against other funds with the same investment objective as defined in the table included here.

What These Listings Provide...

		NASD DATA			LIPPER ANALYTICAL DATA			
Monday	Inv. Obj.	NAV	Offer Price	NAV Chg.	%Ret YTD	Max Initl Chrg.	Total Exp Ratio	..
Tuesday	Inv. Obj.	NAV	Offer Price	NAV Chg.	—% Total Return— YTD	4 wk	1 yr	Rank
WEDNESDAY	**Inv. Obj.**	**NAV**	**Offer Price**	**NAV Chg.**	**—% Total Return— YTD**	**13 wk**	**3 yr**	**Rank**
Thursday	Inv. Obj.	NAV	Offer Price	NAV Chg.	—% Total Return— YTD	26 wk	4 yr	Rank
Friday	Inv. Obj.	NAV	Offer Price	NAV Chg.	—% Total Return— YTD	39 wk	5 yr	Rank

EXPLANATORY NOTES

Mutual fund data are supplied by two organizations. The daily Net Asset Value (NAV), Offer Price and Net Change calculations are supplied by the National Association of Securities Dealers (NASD) through Nasdaq, its automated quotation system. Performance and cost data are supplied by Lipper Analytical Services Inc.

Daily price data are entered into Nasdaq by the fund, its management company or agent. Performance and cost calculations are percentages provided by Lipper Analytical Services, based on prospectuses filed with the Securities and Exchange Commission, fund reports, financial reporting services and other sources believed to be authoritative, accurate and timely. Though verified, the data cannot be guaranteed by Lipper or its data sources and should be double-checked with the funds before making any investment decisions.

Performance figures are on a total return basis without regard to sales, deferred sales or redemption charges.

INVESTMENT OBJECTIVE (Inv. Obj.) – Based on stated investment goals outlined in the prospectus. The Journal assembled 10 groups based on classifications used by Lipper Analytical in the daily Mutual Fund Scorecard and other calculations. A detailed breakdown of classifications appears at the bottom of this page.

NET ASSET VALUE (NAV) – Per share value prepared by the fund, based on closing quotes unless noted, and supplied to the NASD by 5:30 p.m. Eastern time.

OFFER PRICE – Net asset value plus sales commission, if any.

NAV CHG. – Gain or loss, based on the previous NAV quotation.

% TOTAL RETURN – Performance calculations, as percentages, assuming reinvestment of all distributions. Sales charges aren't reflected. For funds declaring dividends daily, calculations are based on the most current data supplied by the fund within publication deadlines. A YEAR TO DATE (YTD) change is listed daily, with results ranging from 4 weeks to 5 years offered throughout the week. See chart on this page for specific schedule.

MAXIMUM INITIAL SALES COMMISSION (Max Initl Chrg) – Based on prospectus; the sales charge may be modified or suspended temporarily by the fund, but any percentage change requires formal notification to the shareholders.

TOTAL EXPENSE RATIO (Total Exp Ratio) -- Based on the fund's annual report, the ratio is total operating expenses for the fiscal year divided by the fund's average net assets. It includes all asset based charges such as advisory fees, other non-advisory fees and distribution expenses (12b-1).

RANKING (R) – Funds are grouped by investment objectives defined by The Wall Street Journal and ranked on longest time period listed each day. Percentages are annualized for periods greater than one year. Performance measurement begins at either the closest Thursday or month-end for periods of more than one year. Gains of 100% or more are shown as a whole number, not carried out one decimal place. A=top 20%; B=next 20%; C=middle 20%; D=next 20%; E=bottom 20%.

QUOTATIONS FOOTNOTES

e-Ex-distribution. **f**-Previous day's quotation. **s**-Stock split or dividend. **x**-Ex–dividend.

p-Distribution costs apply, 12b-1 plan. **r**-Redemption charge may apply. **t**–Footnotes p and r apply.

NA-Not available due to incomplete price, performance or cost data. **NE**-Deleted by Lipper editor; data in question. **NL**-No Load (sales commission). **NN**-Fund doesn't wish to be tracked. **NS**-Fund didn't exist at start of period.

k-Recalculated by Lipper, using updated data. **n**-No valid comparison with other funds because of expense structure.

Source: Reprinted by permission of *The Wall Street Journal*,

Example of the Mutual Fund format in *The Wall Street Journal*.

	Inv. Obj.	NAV	Offer Price	NAV Chg.	-% Total Return- YTD	13 wks	3 yrs R
SIBdA	...	20.16	20.16	−0.02	NA	NA	NA ..
SmColnA	...	10.44	10.44	+0.03	NA	NA	NA ..
Benham Group:							
AdjGov	BST	10.04	NL	+0.01	+0.4	+1.2	NS ..
CaTFI	MUN	11.00	NL	...	+1.6	+4.2	+8.6 E
CatfIn	MUN	10.01	NL	...	+1.2	+6.4	+10.0 B
CaTFS	MUN	10.23	NL	+0.01	+0.9	+2.9	NS ..
CatfH	MUN	9.13	NL	−0.01	+0.6	+4.3	+8.9 D
CatfL	MUN	11.26	NL	...	+1.0	+5.5	+9.7 B
EqGro	STK	11.82	NL	+0.02	+1.2	+7.8	NS ..
EurBd	WBD	9.96	NL	−0.02	0.0	−3.1	NS ..
GNMA	BND	10.87	NL	...	+1.4	+3.1	+11.9 B
GoldIn	SEC	7.47	NL	+0.09	−1.1	−5.9	−15.2 E

Source: Reprinted by permission of *The Wall Street Journal*,

MUTUAL FUND OBJECTIVES

Categories used by the Wall Street Journal, based on classifications developed by Lipper Analytical Services Inc., and fund groups included in each:

STOCK FUNDS

General U.S. (STK): Capital Appreciation; Growth and Income; Growth; Equity Income; Option Income.

Small Company (SML): Small Company Growth.

Sector (SEC): Health/Biotechnology; Natural Resources; Environmental; Science & Technology; Speciality & Miscellaneous; Utility; Financial Services; Real Estate; Gold Oriented.

World (WOR): Global; Small Company Global; International; European Region; Pacific Region; Japanese; Latin American; Canadian.

BOND FUNDS

Short Term (BST): Adjustable Rate Preferred; Adjustable Rate Mortgage; Short U.S. Treasury; Short U.S. Government; Short Investment Grade.

Intermediate & Long Term (BND): Intermediate U.S. Treasury; Intermediate U.S. Government; General U.S. Treasury; General U.S. Government; GNMA; U.S. Mortgage; Corporate Debt A-Rated; Corporate Debt BBB-Rated; Intermediate Investment Grade; General Bond; Flexible Income; Target Maturity.

High Yield (BHI): High Current Yield.

World (WBD): Short World Multi-Market; Short World Single-Market; General World Income.

Municipal Bonds, All Maturities (MUN): Short Municipal Debt; General Municipal Debt; Intermediate Municipal Debt; Insured Municipal Debt; High Yield Municipal Debt; Single-State Municipals; Single-State Insured Municipals; Single-State Intermediated Municipals.

STOCK & BOND FUNDS

Blended Funds (S&B): Flexible Portfolio; Global Flexible Portfolio; Balanced; Balanced Target Maturity; Convertible Securities; Income.

Source: Reprinted by permission of *The Wall Street Journal*,

Top 50 No- and Low-Load Mutual Funds *(Based on Five- and 10-Year Performance)*

*What $10,000 Grew To In 5 years (1988 - 1992)***		*What $10,000 Grew To In 10 years (1983 - 1992)***	
Kaufmann Fund	$ 43,658	CGM Capital Development Fund (c)	$ 64,408
Financial Strategic—Health Sciences	38,513	Fidelity Select Health Care	63,767
Fidelity Select Biotechnology	37,155	Fidelity Magellan Fund	60,221
Fidelity Select Retailing	35,020	Fidelity Contrafund	51,637
Financial Strategic—Finl Svcs Port	32,847	Fidelity Select Financial Services	51,203
Fidelity Select Medical Delivery	32,838	Century Shares Trust	50,945
Fidelity Contrafund	32,329	Acorn Fund (c)	49,418
Twentieth Century Ultra Investors	32,043	Sequoia Fund (c)	49,201
Financial Strategic—Tech Port	31,648	Mutual Shares Fund (c)	49,030
Janus Twenty Fund (c)	31,170	Mutual Qualified Fund (c)	48,707
Fidelity Select Regional Banks	31,100	SteinRoe Special Fund	48,700
Twentieth Century Giftrust Investors	30,228	Twentieth Century Ultra Investors	48,688
T Rowe Price Science & Technology	29,903	Sit "New Beginning" Growth Fund	48,289
Financial Strategic—Leisure Port	29,818	Financial Industrial Income Fund	48,287
Thomson Opportunity Fund/Class B	29,805	Berger One Hundred Fund	47,637
Fidelity Select Health Care	29,230	Selected American Shares	47,627
Berger One Hundred Fund	29,181	Neuberger & Berman Manhattan Fund	47,152
Freedom Regional Bank Fund/Class B	29,171	Janus Fund	46,956
Vanguard Splzd Ports—Health Care	28,718	Fidelity Select Utilities	46,861
Fidelity Select Savings & Loan	28,580	Special Portfolios—Stock	45,784
Columbia Special Fund	28,184	Elfun Trusts	45,710
Founders Frontier Fund	28,069	T Rowe Price Intl Stock	45,550
CGM Capital Development Fund (c)	27,901	Twentieth Century Growth Investors	45,520
Fidelity Select Food & Agriculture	27,362	Windsor Fund (c)	45,373
Fidelity Growth Company Fund	27,267	Lindner Dividend Fund	45,125
Brandywine Fund	27,148	State Farm Balanced Fund	45,026
Gabelli Growth Fund	26,819	Dodge & Cox Stock Fund	44,114
Fidelity Select Transportation	26,615	Nicholas Fund	43,875
Janus Venture Fund (c)	26,256	IAI Regional Fund	43,817
Fidelity OTC Portfolio	26,159	Scudder International Fund	43,359
Janus Fund	25,837	Lexington Corporate Leaders Trust	43,155
Strong Discovery Fund	25,649	Vanguard Index Tr—500 Portfolio	43,155
T Rowe Price New America Growth	25,610	Scudder Capital Growth Fund	42,882
Legg Mason Special Invmt Trust	25,565	Salomon Brothers Opportunity Fund	42,482
Special Portfolios—Stock	25,425	Federated Stock Trust	42,439
Century Shares Trust	25,218	CGM Mutual Fund	42,401
Founders Special Fund	25,020	Neuberger & Berman Guardian Fund	42,223
Keystone Custodian Series/S-4	24,663	State Farm Growth Fund	41,577
Nicholas Limited Edition	24,551	Pilgrim MagnaCap Fund	41,168
Fidelity Blue Chip Growth Fund	24,545	Vanguard World—US Growth	40,962
Fidelity Select Insurance	24,433	Pennsylvania Mutual Fund	40,791
Fidelity Select Software & Computer	24,361	SoGen International Fund	40,658
Babson Enterprise Fund (c)	24,323	Fidelity Puritan Fund	40,626
Fidelity Select Telecommunications	24,317	Legg Mason Value Trust	40,559
Parnassus Fund	24,102	Kleinwort Benson Intl Equity Fund	40,077
Fidelity Convertible Securities	24,058	Scudder Japan Fund	39,778
Piper Jaffray Value Fund	24,035	Neuberger & Berman Partners Fund	39,591
Harbor Capital Appreciation Fund	23,952	Fidelity Trend Fund	39,292
SteinRoe Special Fund	23,865	Founders Special Fund	39,149
Fidelity Magellan Fund	23,811	Endowments	39,142

***Does not take into account sales commissions or income taxes that would have to be paid. Includes reinvestment of all dividends and capital gains.*
(c) Fund closed to new investors.

Source: IBC/*Donoghue's 1993 Mutual Funds Almanac.*

Top 10 No- and Low-Load Mutual Funds Listed by Fund Type *(Ranked by 12-month Percentage Gain)***

Bond Funds

Funds	1992 Annual % Gain	Assets ($ Millions) as of 11/30/92
Fidelity Capital & Income	28.0%	$1,818.1
PaineWebber Fxd Incm—High Incm/A	24.1	287.3
American Capital Govt Target—'98	23.4	9.1
American Capital Govt Target—'97	22.1	15.3
Fidelity Spartan High Incm Fund	21.6	526.0
Merrill Lynch Corpt—High Incm/Cl A	20.6	683.8
Merrill Lynch Corpt—High Incm/Cl B	19.6	847.4
Northeast Investors Trust	17.5	452.7
Franklin Tax-Advtgd H-Y Secs	17.0	39.0
Franklin AGE High Income Fund	16.2	1,917.6
Pilgrim High-Yield Trust	16.2	18.6

Growth Funds

Funds	1992 Annual % Gain	Assets ($ Millions) as of 11/30/92
Fidelity Select Savings & Loan	57.8%	$ 91.4
Fidelity Select Regional Banks	48.5	142.3
Freedom Regional Bank Fund/Class B	47.0	53.6
Fidelity Select Financial Services	42.8	95.4
Fidelity Select Automotive	41.6	72.1
Parnassus Fund	36.8	41.7
Fidelity Select Software & Computer	35.5	70.1
Thomson Opportunity Fund/Class B	28.5	179.1
Bull & Bear Special Equities Fund	28.4	45.5
Fidelity Select Electronics	27.4	87.9

Balanced Funds

Funds	1992 Annual % Gain	Assets ($ Millions) as of 11/30/92
Evergreen Foundation Fund	20.0%	$ 40.3
Vanguard Convertible Securities	19.0	87.3
Fidelity Puritan Fund	15.4	5,618.1
Evergreen American Retmt Trust	11.8	23.5
Dodge & Cox Balanced Fund	10.6	246.9
Piper Jaffray Balanced Fund	10.6	27.5
Vanguard STAR Fund	10.5	2,214.5
Fiduciary Total Return Fund	10.4	2.6
Composite Bond & Stock Fund	9.9	99.5
Financial Series Tr—Flex Fund	9.8	121.0

International Bond Funds

Funds	1992 Annual % Gain	Assets ($ Millions) as of 11/30/92
Merrill Lynch Gbl Bond—Invmt & Retmt/A	7.9%	$ 62.4
Scudder International Bond Fund	7.6	729.5
Merrill Lynch Gbl Bond—Invmt & Retmt/B	6.9	621.4
USAA Cornerstone Fund	6.3	567.5
Merrill Lynch World Incm Fund/Cl A	6.2	490.4
Scudder Short Term Gbl Incm Fund	5.5	1,358.4
Merrill Lynch World Incm Fund/Cl B	5.3	1,539.6
Fidelity Global Bond Fund	4.4	348.3
T Rowe Price Gbl Govt Bond Fund	3.7	58.7
Blanchard S-T Global Income	3.6	1,359.1
Prudential Intmd Global Income (A)	3.6	411.1

Tax-Exempt Bond Funds

Funds	1992 Annual % Gain	Assets ($ Millions) as of 11/30/92
Strong Insured Muni Bond Fund	13.1%	$ 18.1
Strong Municipal Bond Fund	12.2	236.6
Rochester Fund Municipals	11.2	865.6
Scudder High-Yield Tax Free Fund	10.9	185.8
Franklin NY Tax-Free Income Fund	10.8	3,818.1
Scudder MA Tax Free Fund	10.8	192.6
Merrill Lynch TX Muni Bond/Cl A	10.7	11.4
Putnam T-F Incm Tr/High Yield Port	10.6	1,067.0
Merrill Lynch NY Muni Bond/Cl A	10.4	18.8
T. Rowe Price NY T-F Bond Fund	10.4	93.2
Voyageur Colorado Tax Free Fund	10.4	173.4

International Stock Funds

Funds	1992 Annual % Gain	Assets ($ Millions) as of 11/30/92
Merrill Lynch Global Alloc/Cl A	12.2%	$ 230.7
T Rowe Price New Asia Fund	11.2	272.6
Merrill Lynch Global Alloc/Cl B	11.1	881.0
Merrill Lynch Global Convt/Cl A	11.1	1.2
Merrill Lynch Global Convt/Cl B	10.0	14.1
Evergreen Gbl Real Estate Equity	9.7	7.7
Janus Worldwide Fund	9.0	130.5
SoGen International Fund	8.4	479.7
Merrill Lynch Gbl Utility Fund/Cl B	8.1	184.1
Fidelity Worldwide Fund	6.2	108.7

Growth & Income Funds

Funds	1992 Annual % Gain	Assets ($ Millions) as of 11/30/92
Merrill Lynch Phoenix Fund/Cl B	31.8%	$ 102.7
Rochester Convertible	31.2	8.1
Century Shares Trust	27.0	204.8
Mutual Beacon Fund	22.9	478.4
Mutual Qualified Fund (c)	22.7	1,170.7
Fidelity Convertible Securities	22.0	332.5
Franklin Balance Sheet Invmt	21.4	4.9
Mutual Shares Fund (c)	21.3	2,729.1
Sound Shore Fund	21.2	35.4
Lindner Dividend Fund	21.1	545.2

Precious Metals/Gold Funds

Funds	1992 Annual % Gain	Assets ($ Millions) as of 11/30/92
US Global Resources Fund	-2.7%	$ 24.2
Fidelity Select American Gold	-3.1	171.3
US World Gold Fund	-4.7	61.8
USAA Gold Fund	-7.9	114.2
Financial Strategic—Gold Port	-8.2	45.6
Benham Gold Equities Index Fund	-8.7	163.3
Scudder Gold Fund	-9.1	31.8
Rushmore—Precious Metals Index	-10.8	4.2
Thomson Precious Metals/Class B	-12.3	6.6
Keystone Precious Metals Holdings	-13.6	116.9

*** Annual percentage gain includes reinvestment of income and capital gains distributions.*

Source: IBC/*Donoghue's 1993 Mutual Funds Almanac.*

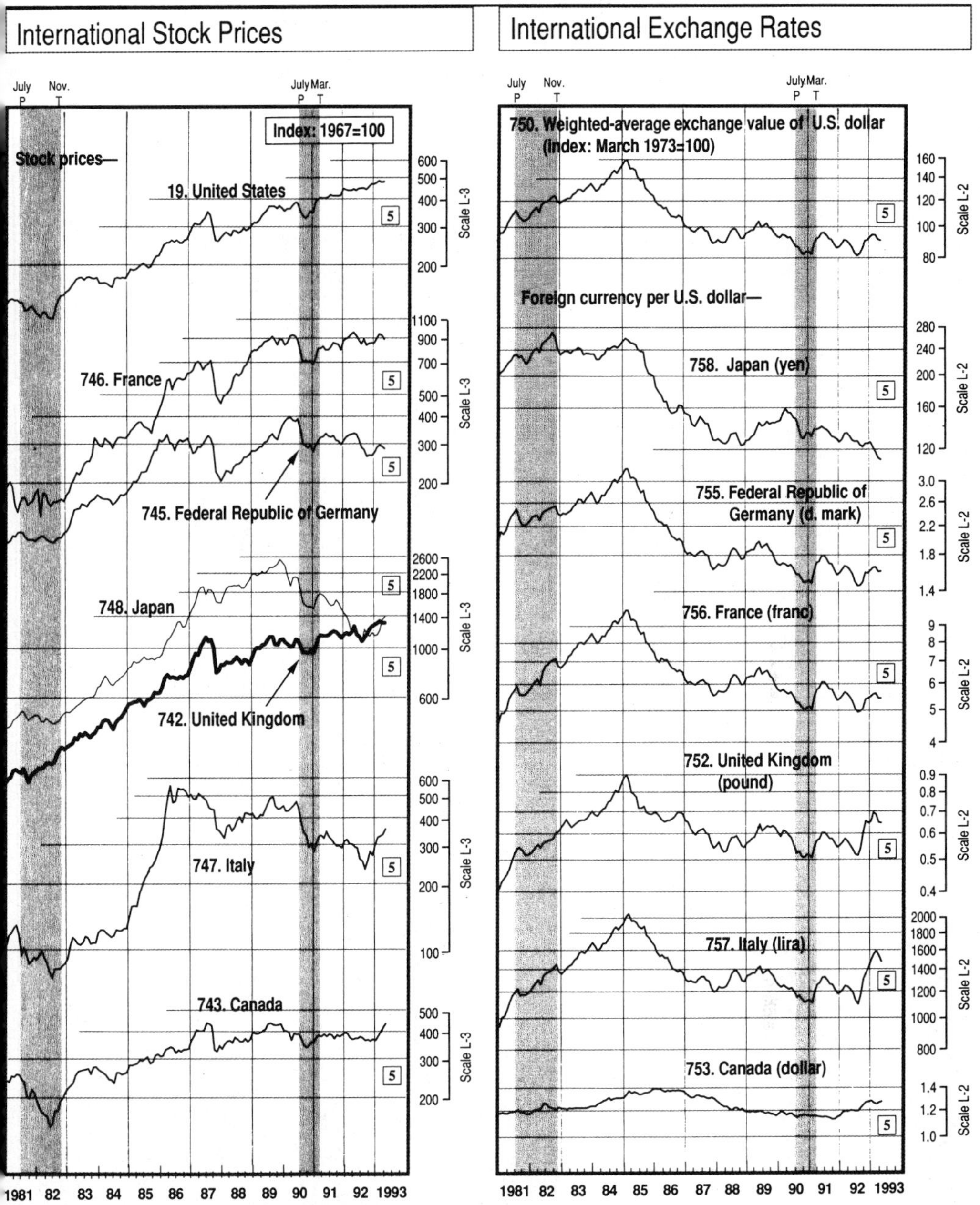

Source: *Survey of Current Business*, U.S. Department of Commerce, Bureau of Economic Analysis.

BARRON'S / LIPPER FUND LISTINGS †

Debt and Equity Funds

Benchmarks

Objective	3/31/93-6/30/93	6/30/92-6/30/93	6/30/88-6/30/93
Growth & Income Funds	10,073.52	11,460.82	18,044.06
Small-Company Growth Funds	10,270.62	12,550.73	19,270.17
International Funds	10,533.85	10,807.83	14,413.14
Gold Funds	12,997.43	13,855.55	11,640,72
Fixed-Income Funds	10,248.14	11,095.97	16,232.77

How a $10,000 investment would have fared in the average fund.

				PERFORMANCE (Return on Initial $10,000 Investment)				PHONE NUMBER		FEES				
FUND NAME	OBJECTIVE	TOTAL NET ASSETS ($ MIL) 5/31/93	NET ASSET $ VALUE 6/30/93	3/31/93-6/30/93	6/30/92-6/30/93	6/30/88-6/30/93	DIVIDEND YIELD % 6/93	800	In-State	Load	12b-1	Redemption	MANAGER	SINCE
AAL BOND★	Fixed Income	375.7	10.68	10,243.50	11,113.80	16,419.80	6.1	553-6319	414-734-5721	4.75	0.25	None	Duff & Phelps	'87
AAL CAPITAL GROWTH★	Growth	744.8	15.03	10,073.70	10,984.00	19,138.00	1.8	553-6319	414-734-5721	4.75	0.25	None	Duff & Phelps	'87
AAL TARGET 2001★	Fixed Income	2.7	12.57	10,428.90	12,167.10	☆	5.9	553-6319	414-734-5721	4.75	0.10	None	Duff & Phelps	'90
AAL TARGET 2006★	Fixed Income	1.9	13.07	10,615.70	12,872.70	☆	6.1	553-6319	414-734-5721	4.75	0.10	None	Duff & Phelps	'90
AARP CAPITAL GROWTH	Growth	540.5	33.76	10,044.60	11,744.90	18,227.20	0.4	253-2277	617-439-4640	None	None	None	Aronoff/Cox	'89/'84

AARP GNMA	Fixed Income	6,335.6	16.09	10,165.40	10,841.70	15,988.70	7.3	253-2277	617-439-4640	None	None	None	Pruyne/Glen	'84/'85
AARP GROWTH & INC	Growth & Income	1,245.6	31.53	10,169.60	11,517.00	18,923.10	2.8	253-2277	617-439-4640	None	None	None	Hoffman/Millard	'90/'85
AARP HIGH QUAL BOND	Fixed Income	504.0	16.79	10,311.60	11,249.80	16,456.30	5.6	253-2277	617-439-4640	None	None	None	Hutchinson/Thorne	'87/'84
ABT EMERGING GROWTH	Capital Appreciation	47.2	13.36	10,136.60	13,472.80	24,614.80	0.0	553-7838	407-655-7255	4.75	0.25	None	Harold Ireland	'83
ABT GROWTH & INCOME TR	Growth & Income	81.7	10.92	9,813.00	11,211.80	14,298.40	2.3	553-7838	407-655-7255	4.75	0.25	None	Ted Wolff	'91
ABT UTILITY INCOME	Utility	149.6	14.10	10,386.00	12,452.20	19,239.30	4.4	553-7838	407-655-7255	4.75	0.25	None	Ted Wolff	'91
ACCESSOR:EQ MKT	Growth & Income	5.9	12.72	9,867.20	☆	☆	0.0	759-3504	206-224-7420	None	None	None	Marilyn Belter	'92
ACCESSOR:GROWTH	Growth	5.2	13.36	9,940.30	☆	☆	0.0	759-3504	206-224-7420	None	None	None	Doug Holmes	'92
ACCESSOR:INT FXD-INC	Fixed Income	17.1	12.57	10,261.30	11,123.10	☆	4.9	759-3504	206-224-7420	None	None	None	Smith Barney	'92
ACCESSOR:MORTGAGE SEC	Fixed Income	27.0	12.36	10,202.70	10,818.80	☆	4.5	759-3504	206-224-7420	None	None	None	John Davis	'92
ACCESSOR:SHT-INT FXD-INC	Fixed Income	29.2	12.41	10,134.80	10,720.60	☆	4.1	759-3504	206-224-7420	None	None	None	John Axten	'92
ACCESSOR:SMALL CAP	Small-Company Growth	5.7	14.21	10,034.70	☆	☆	0.0	759-3504	206-224-7420	None	None	None	Nancy Feld Kiercher	'92
ACCESSOR:VALUE & INCOME	Growth & Income	6.1	13.71	10,160.00	☆	☆	0.0	759-3504	206-224-7420	None	None	None	Martingale Asset Mgmt	'92
ACORN FUND★	Small-Company Growth	1,734.0	64.72	10,672.80	14,109.40	22,964.40	1.1	922-6769	312-634-9200	None	None	2.00	Ralph Wanger	'70
ACORN INV:INTL	International	216.8	12.92	10,766.70	☆	☆	0.0	922-6769	312-634-9200	None	None	2.00	Ralph Wanger	'92
ADDISON CAPITAL	Growth & Income	37.6	22.69	9,908.30	12,100.90	18,058.30	1.1	526-6397	215-665-6000	3.00	0.40	None	Cheston/Kelley	'86/'90
ADVANCE CAP I:BALANCED	Balanced	48.5	10.42	9,913.90	11,186.30	14,945.00	2.8	345-4783	313-350-8543	None	0.25	None	Shoemaker/Cappelli	'87/'91
ADVANCE CAP I:BOND	Fixed Income	4.5	10.96	10,280.90	11,323.60	16,343.10	6.5	345-4783	313-350-8543	None	None	None	Shoemaker/Cappelli	'87/'91
ADVANCE CAP I:EQ UNVERSE	Growth & Income	7.8	9.75	9,784.60	11,049.90	14,434.10	1.0	345-4783	313-350-8543	None	0.25	None	Shoemaker/Cappelli	'87/'91
ADVANCE CAP I:LG TM INC	Fixed Income	0.8	10.73	10,409.60	☆	☆	0.0	345-4783	313-350-8543	None	None	None	Toal/Shoemaker	'92/'92
ADVANCE CAP I:RETIRE INC	Fixed Income	36.8	10.63	10,461.00	☆	☆	0.0	345-4783	313-350-8543	None	0.25	None	Toal/Shoemaker	'92/'92
ADVANTAGE:GOVT SEC	Fixed Income	160.1	10.09	10,570.90	12,097.40	17,166.60	5.7	243-8115	203-525-1421	None	0.40	4.00	Margaret D. Patel	'88
ADVANTAGE:GROWTH	Growth	66.5	16.71	10,010.20	11,470.60	18,989.30	0.2	243-8115	203-525-1421	None	0.70	4.00	Robert Thomas	'89
ADVANTAGE:HIGH YIELD	Fixed Income	88.1	9.69	10,626.80	12,221.20	☆	9.0	243-8115	203-525-1421	None	0.40	4.00	Margaret D. Patel	'89
ADVANTAGE:INCOME	Income	65.0	12.95	10,206.90	11,751.90	17,461.80	3.8	243-8115	203-525-1421	None	0.50	4.00	Susann Stauffer	'86
ADVANTAGE:SPECIAL	Small-Company Growth	17.5	18.18	10,022.10	12,928.20	20,860.10	0.0	243-8115	203-525-1421	None	0.70	4.00	Robert Thomas	'89
ADVISORS FUND LP;A	Flexible	136.9	26.80	10,147.70	12,083.00	☆	0.0	None	212-720-9218	5.00	0.25	None	Hempleman/Jordan/Mark	'90
ADV INNR CIR:CLVR CAP EQ	Growth	13.2	10.83	9,925.00	10,328.20	☆	1.0	932-7781	215-989-6611	None	None	None	Clover Capital Mgt. Inc	'91
ADV INNR CIR:CLVR CAP FX	Fixed Income	10.9	10.63	10,266.90	11,314.30	☆	5.9	932-7781	215-989-6611	None	None	None	Clover Capital Mgt. Inc	'91
ADV INNR CIR:JRK&VYL BAL	Flexible	13.8	12.10	10,177.10	12,136.70	☆	1.3	932-7781	215-989-6611	None	None	None	Jurika & Voyles, Inc.	'92
ADV INNR CIR:PIN OAK	Small-Company Growth	7.4	11.37	10,479.30	☆	☆	0.0	932-7781	215-989-6611	None	None	None	Oak Associates	'92
ADV INNR CIR:TURNER GRO	Capital Appreciation	27.7	11.89	10,175.10	12,109.80	☆	0.7	932-7781	215-989-6611	None	None	None	Turner Invest. Partners	'92
ADV INNR CIR:WHITE OAK	Growth	4.7	10.61	9,817.10	☆	☆	0.0	932-7781	215-989-6611	None	None	None	Oak Associates	'92
AETNA FUND	Flexible	42.4	10.43	10,114.50	10,783.80	☆	3.9	238-6263	None	None	None	None	Charles N. Dawkins	'92
AETNA:BOND	Fixed Income	41.0	10.36	10,273.10	11,147.40	☆	6.4	238-6263	None	None	None	None	Jeanne Wong-Boehm	'92
AETNA:GROWTH & INCOME	Growth & Income	35.3	10.58	9,888.70	11,001.90	☆	1.8	238-6263	None	None	None	None	Team Managed	'92
AETNA:INTL GROWTH	International	31.2	9.97	10,651.70	10,514.90	☆	0.4	238-6263	None	None	None	None	Anna Tong	'92
AFFILIATED FUND	Growth & Income	4,000.7	10.80	10,093.90	11,523.00	17,247.20	3.3	426-1130	212-848-1800	5.75	0.25	None	Thomas S. Henderson	'91
AHA INV:BALANCED★	Balanced	42.0	12.76	10,218.60	11,387.10	☆	3.4	445-1341	708-295-5000	None	None	None	Avatar/Criterion/D&P	'88/'91
AHA INV:DVSD EQUITY★	Growth	20.1	13.95	9,999.60	11,529.80	☆	1.8	445-1341	708-295-5000	None	None	None	Cambiar/Duff&Phelps	'88/'91
AHA INV:FULL MAT FXD INC★	Fixed Income	48.4	10.76	10,302.30	11,260.60	☆	6.6	445-1341	708-295-5000	None	None	None	Bankers Tr/Criterion	'90/'88
AHA INV:LTD MAT FXD INC★	Fixed Income	159.5	10.52	10,155.80	10,604.80	☆	4.7	445-1341	708-295-5000	None	None	None	*Multiple managers*	'88/'92
AIM:AGGRESSIVE GROWTH	Small-Company Growth	87.6	20.46	10,768.40	15,002.40	22,633.60	0.0	347-1919	713-626-1919	5.50	0.25	None	Hutzler *et al.*	'92
AIM CONVERTIBLE SEC	Convertible Securities	16.6	15.27	10,483.30	12,579.70	18,532.90	2.0	347-1919	713-626-1919	4.75	0.25	None	Schoolar/Sachnowitz	'89/'89
AIM EQ:CHARTER;INSTL	Growth & Income	N/A	0.00	N/A	N/A	☆	0.0	347-1919	713-626-1919	None	None	None	Lerner/Sachnowitz	'91/'91

★AAL FUNDS—Limited to Lutherans.

★ACORN FUND—Closed to new investors.

★AHA INVESTMENT FUNDS — Limited to participants of the American Hospital Association Investment Program and to the American Hospital Association.

† For explanations and definitions of terms see pages 380–381.

PERFORMANCE OF MUTUAL FUNDS *(continued)*

FUND NAME	OBJECTIVE	TOTAL NET ASSETS ($ MIL) 5/31/93	NET ASSET $ VALUE 6/30/93	PERFORMANCE (Return on Initial $10,000 Investment) 3/31/93-6/30/93	6/30/92-6/30/93	6/30/88-6/30/93	DIVIDEND YIELD % 6/93	PHONE NUMBER 800	In-State	FEES Load	12b-1	Redemption	MANAGER	SINCE
AIM EQ:CHARTER;RTL	Growth & Income	1,504.7	8.96	10,136.10	11,296.50	22,195.30	2.7	347-1919	713-626-1919	5.50	0.30	None	Lerner/Sachnowitz	'68/'91
AIM EQ:CONSTELTN;RTL	Capital Appreciation	2,150.7	15.85	10,531.60	13,477.90	26,108.60	0.0	347-1919	713-626-1919	5.50	0.30	None	Hutzler *et al.*	'76/'87
AIM EQ:WEINGARTEN;INSTL	Growth	N/A	0.00	N/A	N/A	☆	0.0	347-1919	713-626-1919	None	None	None	Hutzler *et al.*	'91/'91
AIM EQ:WEINGARTEN;RTL	Growth	5,370.4	16.80	9,976.20	10,741.20	20,040.80	0.5	347-1919	713-626-1919	5.50	0.30	None	Hutzler *et al.*	'69/'87
AIM:GOVERNMENT SECS	Fixed Income	133.2	10.36	10,187.70	10,841.50	15,645.70	6.8	347-1919	713-626-1919	4.75	0.25	None	Kelley *et al.*	'92
AIM:GROWTH	Growth	149.5	12.10	10,211.00	10,835.50	16,541.90	0.4	347-1919	713-626-1919	5.50	0.25	None	Barnard/Smith	'92/'92
AIM:HIGH YIELD(C)	Fixed Income	415.0	9.96	10,473.60	11,860.60	18,221.10	10.7	347-1919	713-626-1919	4.75	0.25	None	Petersen/Pessarra	'82/'92
AIM HIGH YIELD SEC	Fixed Income	46.0	5.91	10,451.60	11,478.30	12,403.60	8.8	347-1919	713-626-1919	4.75	0.25	None	John Pessarra	'92
AIM:INCOME	Fixed Income	234.7	8.57	10,348.00	11,611.10	17,013.90	7.1	347-1919	713-626-1919	4.75	0.25	None	Robert G. Alley	'92
AIM INTL:EQUITY	International	173.1	10.29	10,586.40	10,938.90	☆	0.1	347-1919	713-626-1919	5.50	0.30	None	Griffin/Rogge	'92/'92
AIM:INTL GROWTH(C)	International	11.3	10.09	10,643.50	10,759.90	☆	0.2	347-1919	713-626-1919	5.50	0.25	None	Rogge/Griffin	'92/'92
AIM INV:ADJ RATE;RTL	Fixed Income	83.9	9.89	10,124.70	10,483.10	☆	4.7	347-1919	713-626-1919	3.00	0.25	None	Kelley *et al.*	'92
AIM SUMMIT★	Growth	641.0	9.89	10,071.30	11,632.10	20,009.90	1.0	347-1919	713-626-1919	8.50	None	None	Julian Lerner	'88
AIM:UTILITIES	Utility	138.2	14.59	10,282.40	12,142.00	21,181.90	4.3	347-1919	713-626-1919	5.50	0.25	None	Alley/Cody	'92/'92
AIM:VALUE	Growth & Income	393.9	20.02	10,394.60	12,840.90	25,335.40	0.6	347-1919	713-626-1919	5.50	0.25	None	Cody/Dobberpuhl	'92/'92
ALGER:BALANCED	Balanced	1.1	10.59	10,271.60	10,962.70	☆	0.0	992-3863	201-547-3600	None	0.75	5.00	David Alger	'92
ALGER:GROWTH	Growth	30.3	19.96	10,225.40	12,706.60	23,043.00	0.0	992-3863	201-547-3600	None	0.75	5.00	David Alger	'86
ALGER:INCOME & GROWTH	Growth & Income	7.1	13.67	9,855.80	11,910.20	16,323.00	0.0	992-3863	201-547-3600	None	0.75	5.00	David Alger	'86
ALGER:SMALL CAPITAL	Small-Company Growth	256.2	23.03	10,726.60	12,557.30	27,829.40	0.0	992-3863	201-547-3600	None	0.75	5.00	David Alger	'86
ALLIANCE BALANCED;A	Balanced	165.3	14.04	10,122.80	11,319.80	15,101.70	3.1	227-4618	201-319-4000	5.50	0.24	None	Bruce Calvert	'90
ALLIANCE BALANCED;B	Balanced	10.6	13.93	10,112.80	11,237.80	☆	2.7	227-4618	201-319-4000	None	1.00	5.50	Bruce Calvert	'91
ALLIANCE BALANCED;C	Balanced	N/A	13.93	☆	☆	☆	0.0	227-4618	201-319-4000	None	1.00	None	Bruce Calvert	'93
ALLIANCE BD:CORP BD;A	Fixed Income	204.9	14.15	10,667.40	12,962.20	19,493.70	8.8	227-4618	201-319-4000	3.00	0.30	None	Wayne Lyski	'86
ALLIANCE BD:CORP BD;B	Fixed Income	40.6	14.15	10,650.20	☆	☆	0.0	227-4618	201-319-4000	None	1.00	3.00	Wayne Lyski	'93
ALLIANCE BD:CORP BD;C	Fixed Income	N/A	14.15	☆	☆	☆	0.0	227-4618	201-319-4000	None	1.00	None	Wayne Lyski	'93
ALLIANCE BD:US GOVT;A	Fixed Income	519.1	8.64	10,284.00	11,223.40	16,316.10	7.9	227-4618	201-319-4000	3.00	0.30	None	Paul De Noon	'91
ALLIANCE BD:US GOVT;B	Fixed Income	490.3	8.64	10,266.20	11,145.10	☆	7.2	227-4618	201-319-4000	None	1.00	3.00	Paul De Noon	'91
ALLIANCE BD:US GOVT;C	Fixed Income	19.0	8.64	☆	☆	☆	0.0	227-4618	201-319-4000	None	1.00	None	Paul De Noon	'93
ALLIANCE COUNTERPT;A	Growth & Income	68.9	19.06	9,829.80	10,777.30	18,098.80	0.4	227-4618	201-319-4000	5.50	0.30	None	Dutch Handke	'85
ALLIANCE COUNTERPT;B	Growth & Income	0.1	19.05	☆	☆	☆	0.0	227-4618	201-319-4000	None	1.00	5.50	Dutch Handke	'93
ALLIANCE COUNTERPT;C	Growth & Income	0.1	19.04	☆	☆	☆	0.0	227-4618	201-319-4000	None	1.00	None	Dutch Handke	'93
ALLIANCE FUND;A	Growth	812.2	7.08	10,025.50	12,373.80	18,585.20	0.6	227-4618	201-319-4000	5.50	0.18	None	Harrison/Jenkel	'90/'93
ALLIANCE FUND;B	Growth	8.1	7.03	10,014.20	12,282.50	☆	0.0	227-4618	201-319-4000	None	1.00	5.50	Harrison/Jenkel	'92/'93
ALLIANCE FUND;C	Growth	N/A	7.03	☆	☆	☆	0.0	227-4618	201-319-4000	None	1.00	None	Harrison/Jenkel	'93/'93
ALLIANCE GLBL:CANADIAN	Canadian	14.5	5.44	10,522.20	10,772.30	10,922.30	0.0	227-4618	201-319-4000	5.50	0.19	None	Kelly Morgan	'91
ALLIANCE GLBL SM CAP;A	Global Small Company	64.4	10.44	10,295.90	10,764.30	12,266.60	0.0	227-4618	201-319-4000	5.50	0.30	None	Cook/Heisterberg	'90/'93
ALLIANCE GLBL SM CAP;B	Global Small Company	1.0	10.28	10,321.30	10,734.10	☆	0.0	227-4618	201-319-4000	None	1.00	5.50	Cook/Heisterberg	'90/'93
ALLIANCE GLBL SM CAP;C	Global Small Company	0.1	10.24	☆	☆	☆	0.0	227-4618	201-319-4000	None	1.00	None	Cook/Heisterberg	'93/'93
ALLIANCE GRO & INC;A	Growth & Income	436.7	2.49	9,981.30	11,243.60	17,675.00	2.3	227-4618	201-319-4000	5.50	0.19	None	Tom Perkins	'90
ALLIANCE GRO & INC;B	Growth & Income	41.1	2.48	9,921.00	11,128.60	☆	1.7	227-4618	201-319-4000	None	1.00	5.50	Tom Perkins	'91
ALLIANCE GRO & INC;C	Growth & Income	0.4	2.48	☆	☆	☆	0.0	227-4618	201-319-4000	None	1.00	None	Tom Perkins	'93
ALLIANCE INTL;A	International	167.2	16.01	10,609.70	10,786.10	13,968.40	0.2	227-4618	201-319-4000	5.50	0.18	None	Rama Krishna	'92
ALLIANCE INTL;B	International	6.1	15.74	10,599.30	10,698.10	☆	0.0	227-4618	201-319-4000	None	1.00	5.50	Rama Krishna	'92
ALLIANCE INTL;C	International	0.1	15.74	☆	☆	☆	0.0	227-4618	201-319-4000	None	1.00	None	Rama Krishna	'93
ALLIANCE MTGE INC;A	Fixed Income	843.3	9.40	10,284.30	11,240.60	16,724.30	7.9	227-4618	201-319-4000	3.00	0.30	None	Ullman/Young	'92/'92

ALLIANCE MTGE INC;B	Fixed Income	1,348.4	9.40	10,266.20	11,186.50	☆	7.2	227-4618	201-319-4000	None	1.00	3.00	Ullman/Young	'92/'92
ALLIANCE MTGE INC;C	Fixed Income	N/A	9.40	☆	☆	☆	0.0	227-4618	201-319-4000	None	1.00	None	Ullman/Young	'93/'93
ALLIANCE MTGE STR;A	Fixed Income	33.1	10.01	10,189.20	10,696.30	☆	6.3	227-4618	201-319-4000	3.00	0.30	None	Ullman/Young	'92/'92
ALLIANCE MTGE STR;B	Fixed Income	171.1	10.01	10,171.10	10,621.60	☆	5.6	227-4618	201-319-4000	None	1.00	3.00	Ullman/Young	'92/'92
ALLIANCE MTGE STR;C	Fixed Income	N/A	10.01	☆	☆	☆	0.0	227-4618	201-319-4000	None	1.00	None	Ullman/Young	'93/'93
ALLIANCE MU-MK INCOME	World Income	28.5	1.90	10,093.40	10,072.20	☆	3.9	227-4618	201-319-4000	None	0.68	1.00	Sinche/Peebles	'90/'92
ALLIANCE MU-MK INC&GRO	Specialty	123.8	10.24	10,135.60	10,654.20	☆	3.8	227-4618	201-319-4000	1.00	1.00	1.00	Sinche/Perkins	'91/'91
ALLIANCE MU-MK STR;A	World Income	93.4	8.91	10,388.20	10,095.70	☆	7.9	227-4618	201-319-4000	3.00	0.30	None	Sinche/Bloom	'91/'91
ALLIANCE MU-MK STR;B	World Income	500.3	8.91	10,370.00	10,022.50	☆	7.2	227-4618	201-319-4000	None	1.00	3.00	Sinche/Bloom	'91/'91
ALLIANCE MU-MK STR;C	World Income	N/A	8.90	☆	☆	☆	0.0	227-4618	201-319-4000	None	1.00	None	Sinche/Bloom	'93/'93
ALLIANCE NEW EUROPE;A	European Region	85.2	10.30	10,425.10	10,086.10	☆	1.5	227-4618	201-319-4000	5.50	0.30	None	Eric Perkins	'92
ALLIANCE NEW EUROPE;B	European Region	2.2	10.18	10,409.00	10,011.60	☆	1.1	227-4618	201-319-4000	None	1.00	5.50	Eric Perkins	'92
ALLIANCE NEW EUROPE;C	European Region	N/A	10.18	☆	☆	☆	0.0	227-4618	201-319-4000	None	1.00	None	Eric Perkins	'93
ALLIANCE N AM GV INC;A	World Income	152.5	10.11	10,320.80	11,386.80	☆	10.7	227-4618	201-319-4000	3.00	0.30	None	Wayne Lyski	'92
ALLIANCE N AM GV INC;B	World Income	601.1	10.12	10,312.60	11,316.90	☆	9.9	227-4618	201-319-4000	None	1.00	3.00	Wayne Lyski	'92
ALLIANCE N AM GV INC;C	World Income	21.1	10.11	☆	☆	☆	0.0	227-4618	201-319-4000	None	1.00	None	Wayne Lyski	'93
ALLIANCE PREMIER GR;A	Growth	35.4	11.23	9,973.40	☆	☆	0.0	227-4618	201-319-4000	3.00	0.50	None	Al Harrison	'92
ALLIANCE PREMIER GR;B	Growth	122.7	11.19	9,955.50	☆	☆	0.0	227-4618	201-319-4000	None	1.00	3.00	Al Harrison	'92
ALLIANCE PREMIER GR;C	Growth	0.5	11.19	☆	☆	☆	0.0	227-4618	201-319-4000	None	1.00	None	Al Harrison	'93
ALLIANCE QUASAR;A	Small-Company Growth	236.4	22.23	10,296.40	11,760.60	14,358.00	0.0	227-4618	201-319-4000	5.50	0.20	None	Stanley Cook	'92
ALLIANCE QUASAR;B	Small-Company Growth	11.9	21.77	10,273.70	11,661.00	☆	0.0	227-4618	201-319-4000	None	1.00	5.50	Stanley Cook	'92
ALLIANCE QUASAR;C	Small-Company Growth	0.1	21.76	☆	☆	☆	0.0	227-4618	201-319-4000	None	1.00	None	Stanley Cook	'93
ALLIANCE SH-TM MU-MK;A	World Income	1,096.7	9.28	10,281.90	10,226.60	☆	6.7	227-4618	201-319-4000	3.00	0.30	None	Sinche/Bloom	'89/'89
ALLIANCE SH-TM MU-MK;B	World Income	2,104.3	9.28	10,262.10	10,151.10	☆	5.9	227-4618	201-319-4000	None	1.00	3.00	Sinche/Bloom	'90/'90
ALLIANCE SH-TM MU-MK;C	World Income	N/A	9.28	☆	☆	☆	0.0	227-4618	201-319-4000	None	1.00	None	Sinche/Bloom	'93/'93
ALLIANCE TECHNOLOGY;A	Science & Technology	175.9	31.00	10,693.30	14,487.60	17,348.60	0.0	227-4618	201-319-4000	5.50	0.30	None	Peter Anastos	'92
ALLIANCE TECHNOLOGY;B	Science & Technology	0.1	30.99	☆	☆	☆	0.0	227-4618	201-319-4000	None	None	5.50	Peter Anastos	'93
ALLIANCE TECHNOLOGY;C	Science & Technology	0.1	30.98	☆	☆	☆	0.0	227-4618	201-319-4000	None	1.00	None	Peter Anastos	'93
ALLIANCE WORLD INCOME	World Income	181.8	1.91	10,152.40	10,135.30	☆	3.9	227-4618	201-319-4000	None	0.68	None	Sinche/Peebles	'90/'92
ALLMERICA:GROWTH	Growth	2.9	10.83	9,881.40	☆	☆	0.0	828-0540	508-855-1000	4.50	0.25	None	John Duggan	'92
ALLMERICA:GRO & INC	Growth & Income	4.1	10.30	10,103.80	☆	☆	0.0	828-0540	508-855-1000	4.50	0.25	None	Madelyn Wharton	'92
ALLMERICA:INV GRD INC	Fixed Income	7.3	10.20	10,361.40	☆	☆	0.0	828-0540	508-855-1000	4.50	0.25	None	John Grant	'92
AMANA:INCOME	Equity Income	9.4	12.73	10,022.40	11,063.20	15,820.40	2.3	728-8762	206-734-9900	None	None	None	Nicholas Kaiser	'86
AMBASSADOR:BALANCED;FID★	Balanced	16.7	10.07	☆	☆	☆	0.0	892-4366	None	None	None	None	Woodbridge Cap Mgt Inc	'93
AMBASSADOR:BALANCED;INV★	Balanced	0.1	10.07	☆	☆	☆	0.0	892-4366	None	3.00	None	None	Woodbridge Cap Mgt Inc	'93
AMBASSADOR:BALANCED;RET★	Balanced	0.1	10.07	☆	☆	☆	0.0	892-4366	None	3.00	0.25	None	Woodbridge Cap Mgt Inc	'93
AMBASSADOR:BOND;FID★	Fixed Income	151.5	10.08	10,266.20	10,631.40	☆	6.7	892-4366	None	None	None	None	Woodbridge Cap Mgt Inc	'91
AMBASSADOR:BOND;INV★	Fixed Income	9.3	10.08	10,266.20	☆	☆	0.0	892-4366	None	3.00	None	None	Woodbridge Cap Mgt Inc	'92
AMBASSADOR:BOND;RET★	Fixed Income	0.3	10.08	10,266.20	☆	☆	0.0	892-4366	None	3.00	0.25	None	Woodbridge Cap Mgt Inc	'92
AMBASSADOR:CORE GRO;FID★	Growth	60.3	16.50	9,565.20	☆	☆	0.0	892-4366	None	None	None	None	Woodbridge Cap Mgt Inc	'92
AMBASSADOR:CORE GRO;RET★	Growth	3.5	16.50	9,565.20	☆	☆	0.0	892-4366	None	3.00	0.25	None	Woodbridge Cap Mgt Inc	'92
AMBASSADOR:CORE GRO;INV★	Growth	141.9	16.50	9,581.20	10,701.50	18,025.70	0.6	892-4366	None	3.00	None	None	Woodbridge Cap Mgt Inc	'87
AMBASSADOR:GRO STK;FID★	Growth	188.7	12.93	10,146.70	12,934.90	☆	0.3	892-4366	None	None	None	None	Woodbridge Cap Mgt Inc	'91
AMBASSADOR:GRO STK;INV★	Growth	10.3	12.93	10,141.20	☆	☆	0.0	892-4366	None	3.00	None	None	Woodbridge Cap Mgt Inc	'92
AMBASSADOR:GRO STK;RET★	Growth	1.3	12.93	10,141.20	☆	☆	0.0	892-4366	None	3.00	0.25	None	Woodbridge Cap Mgt Inc	'92
AMBASSADOR:INDEXED;FID★	Growth & Income	60.0	11.68	10,037.00	11,319.10	☆	2.6	892-4366	None	None	None	None	Woodbridge Cap Mgt Inc	'91
AMBASSADOR:INDEXED;INV★	Growth & Income	0.3	11.68	10,037.00	☆	☆	0.0	892-4366	None	3.00	None	None	Woodbridge Cap Mgt Inc	'92
AMBASSADOR:INDEXED;RET★	Growth & Income	0.1	11.68	10,037.00	☆	☆	0.0	892-4366	None	3.00	0.25	None	Woodbridge Cap Mgt Inc	'92
AMBASSADOR:INT BD;FID★	Fixed Income	158.5	10.53	10,190.40	10,965.60	☆	5.1	892-4366	None	None	None	None	Woodbridge Cap Mgt Inc	'91
AMBASSADOR:INT BD;INV★	Fixed Income	130.7	10.53	10,190.30	☆	☆	0.0	892-4366	None	3.00	None	None	Woodbridge Cap Mgt Inc	'92

★AIM SUMMIT—Contractual plan fund.

★AMBASSASOR FUNDS—Institutional funds.

PERFORMANCE OF MUTUAL FUNDS *(continued)*

FUND NAME	OBJECTIVE	TOTAL NET ASSETS ($ MIL) 5/31/93	NET ASSET $ VALUE 6/30/93	PERFORMANCE (Return on Initial $10,000 Investment) 3/31/93-6/30/93	6/30/92-6/30/93	6/30/88-6/30/93	DIVIDEND YIELD % 6/93	PHONE NUMBER 800	In-State	FEES Load	12b-1	Redemption	MANAGER	SINCE
AMBASSADOR:INT BD;RET★	Fixed Income	2.5	10.53	10,190.30	☆	☆	0.0	892-4366	None	3.00	0.25	None	Woodbridge Cap Mgt Inc	'92
AMBASSADOR:INTL;FID★	International	46.3	11.33	10,309.40	10,666.30	☆	1.0	892-4366	None	None	None	None	Woodbridge Cap Mgt Inc	'91
AMBASSADOR:INTL;INV★	International	10.9	11.33	10,309.40	☆	☆	0.0	892-4366	None	3.00	None	None	Woodbridge Cap Mgt Inc	'92
AMBASSADOR:INTL;RET★	International	0.2	11.33	10,309.40	☆	☆	0.0	892-4366	None	3.00	0.25	None	Woodbridge Cap Mgt Inc	'92
AMBASSADOR:SM CO;FID★	Small-Company Growth	47.2	13.02	9,848.70	12,660.60	☆	0.1	892-4366	None	None	None	None	Woodbridge Cap Mgt Inc	'91
AMBASSADOR:SM CO;INV★	Small-Company Growth	11.1	13.02	9,848.70	☆	☆	0.0	892-4366	None	3.00	None	None	Woodbridge Cap Mgt Inc	'92
AMBASSADOR:SM CO;RET★	Small-Company Growth	1.4	13.02	9,848.70	☆	☆	0.0	892-4366	None	3.00	0.25	None	Woodbridge Cap Mgt Inc	'92
AMCAP FUND	Growth	3,036.1	12.89	9,979.90	11,322.90	18,213.00	1.2	421-0180	210-530-4000	5.75	0.25	None	Multiple Managers	'67
AMCORE VINTAGE EQUITY	Growth	87.3	10.13	9,988.00	☆	☆	0.0	662-4203	None	4.25	None	None	Darrell Thompson	'92
AMCORE VINTAGE FXD INC	Fixed Income	61.9	10.35	10,220.10	☆	☆	0.0	662-4203	None	3.75	None	None	Dean Countryman	'92
AMELIA EARHART:EAGLE EQ	Growth	0.1	10.45	10,443.60	☆	☆	0.0	525-3863	919-972-9922	4.50	0.25	None	Jill H. Travis	'93
AMER AADVANTAGE:BALANCED★	Balanced	452.1	12.56	10,178.30	11,533.60	17,842.80	5.6	None	817-967-3509	None	None	None	Multiple Managers	'87
AMER AADVANTAGE:EQUITY★	Growth & Income	429.1	13.74	10,073.30	11,517.60	18,968.50	3.8	None	817-967-3509	None	None	None	Multiple Managers	'87
AMER AADVANTAGE:INTL EQU★	International	51.7	10.47	10,407.60	10,684.20	☆	1.1	None	817-967-3509	None	None	None	Multiple Managers	'91
AMER AADVANTAGE:LTD TERM★	Fixed Income	236.2	10.17	10,177.00	10,754.30	15,258.60	6.3	None	817-967-3509	None	None	None	Fields/Mundy	'91/'91
AMERICAN BALANCED	Balanced	1,362.6	12.78	10,231.50	11,333.40	17,807.60	4.7	421-0180	210-530-4000	5.75	0.25	None	Multiple Managers	'75
AMER CAP COMSTOCK;A	Growth & Income	969.0	17.60	10,016.20	11,409.60	18,509.70	2.5	421-5666	713-993-0500	5.75	0.25	None	David Reichert	'89
AMER CAP COMSTOCK;B	Growth & Income	5.7	17.60	9,994.90	☆	☆	0.0	421-5666	713-993-0500	None	1.00	5.00	David Reichert	'92
AMER CAP CORP BOND;A	Fixed Income	184.5	7.16	10,325.00	11,329.00	15,798.80	7.3	421-5666	713-993-0500	4.75	0.25	None	David R. Troth	'79
AMER CAP CORP BOND;B	Fixed Income	4.8	7.17	10,317.70	☆	☆	0.0	421-5666	713-993-0500	None	1.00	4.00	David R. Troth	'92
AMER CAP EMERG GRO;A	Small-Company Growth	458.8	25.26	10,790.30	14,211.40	26,189.30	0.0	421-5666	713-993-0500	5.75	0.25	None	Gary Lewis	'89
AMER CAP EMERG GRO;B	Small-Company Growth	43.9	24.99	10,771.60	14,094.80	☆	0.0	421-5666	713-993-0500	None	1.00	5.00	Gary Lewis	'92
AMER CAP ENTERPRISE;A	Growth	753.3	12.73	10,084.60	11,884.00	20,178.50	1.0	421-5666	713-993-0500	5.75	0.25	None	Stephen Boyd	'89
AMER CAP ENTERPRISE;B	Growth	39.5	12.69	10,060.80	11,776.60	☆	0.1	421-5666	713-993-0500	None	1.00	5.00	Stephen Boyd	'91
AMER CAP EQUITY INC;A	Equity Income	142.5	5.42	10,116.30	11,735.20	17,786.00	3.3	421-5666	713-993-0500	5.75	0.25	None	Jim Gilligan	'90
AMER CAP EQUITY INC;B	Equity Income	45.3	5.42	10,097.40	11,623.40	☆	2.6	421-5666	713-993-0500	None	1.00	5.00	Jim Gilligan	'92
AMER CAP EXCHANGE★	Growth	40.2	107.78	10,079.00	11,218.10	19,007.70	1.5	421-5666	713-993-0500	None	None	None	Stephen Boyd	'90
AMER CAP FED MTGE;A	Fixed Income	89.3	12.58	10,093.50	10,318.80	14,398.20	5.2	421-5666	713-993-0500	2.25	0.25	None	Tom Rogge	'91
AMER CAP FED MTGE;B★	Fixed Income	34.7	12.59	10,074.30	10,240.90	☆	4.5	421-5666	713-993-0500	None	1.00	3.00	Tom Rogge	'91
AMER CAP GOVERNMENT;A	Fixed Income	3,590.1	10.98	10,243.50	11,066.40	16,761.50	7.6	421-5666	713-993-0500	4.75	0.25	None	Jack Reynoldson	'88
AMER CAP GOVERNMENT;B	Fixed Income	299.2	10.98	10,223.70	10,981.80	☆	6.9	421-5666	713-993-0500	None	1.00	4.00	Jack Reynoldson	'91
AMER CAP GROWTH & INCOME	Growth & Income	188.6	13.42	10,081.40	11,641.60	16,541.80	2.1	421-5666	713-993-0500	5.75	0.25	None	Jim Gilligan	'90
AMER CAP HARBOR;A	Convertible Securities	415.7	15.65	10,247.80	11,816.20	18,007.80	4.9	421-5666	713-993-0500	5.75	0.25	None	James Behrman	'84
AMER CAP HARBOR;B	Convertible Securities	36.0	15.59	10,222.20	11,708.50	☆	4.2	421-5666	713-993-0500	None	1.00	5.00	James Behrman	'91
AMER CAP HIGH YIELD;A	Fixed Income	439.5	6.62	10,552.40	11,704.70	14,176.90	10.7	421-5666	713-993-0500	4.75	0.25	None	Ellis Bigelow	'89
AMER CAP HIGH YIELD;B	Fixed Income	25.6	6.63	10,532.30	☆	☆	0.0	421-5666	713-993-0500	None	1.00	4.00	Ellis Bigelow	'92
AMER CAP PACE;A	Growth	2,456.1	12.95	10,148.90	11,519.50	17,722.90	1.0	421-5666	713-993-0500	5.75	0.25	None	Alan Sachtleben	'92
AMER CAP PACE;B	Growth	20.8	12.85	10,118.10	11,412.50	☆	0.3	421-5666	713-993-0500	None	1.00	5.00	Alan Sachtleben	'92
AMER CAP TGT:PORT '97★	Fixed Income	22.9	13.31	10,168.10	11,009.10	☆	0.0	421-5666	713-993-0500	3.00	0.25	None	Jack Reynoldson	'90
AMER CAP US GOVT INC;A	Fixed Income	71.5	9.31	10,159.40	☆	☆	0.0	421-5666	713-993-0500	4.75	0.25	None	Jack Reynoldson	'92
AMER CAP US GOVT INC;B	Fixed Income	158.7	9.31	10,139.90	☆	☆	0.0	421-5666	713-993-0500	None	1.00	4.00	Jack Reynoldson	'92
AMER CAP WRLD:GL EQ;A	Global	12.7	10.42	10,357.90	10,712.00	☆	0.0	421-5666	713-993-0500	5.75	0.25	None	Lash/Armist	'91/'91
AMER CAP WRLD:GL EQ;B	Global	6.9	10.33	10,330.00	10,610.80	☆	0.0	421-5666	713-993-0500	None	1.00	5.00	Lash/Armist	'91/'91
AMER CAP WRLD:GL GOV;A	World Income	36.0	9.13	10,466.30	11,037.40	☆	8.5	421-5666	713-993-0500	4.75	0.25	None	Reynoldson/McHenry	'91/'91
AMER CAP WRLD:GL GOV;B	World Income	56.5	9.17	10,455.20	10,958.50	☆	7.7	421-5666	713-993-0500	None	1.00	4.00	Reynoldson/McHenry	'91/'91

AMER INC:US GOVT	Fixed Income	1,475.3	14.51	10,309.70	11,351.20	16,484.80	7.8	421-0180	210-530-4000	4.75	0.30	None	Multiple Managers	'85
AMERICAN GROWTH	Growth	63.1	9.47	10,128.30	12,335.20	18,425.20	0.8	525-2406	303-623-6137	5.75	None	None	Robert Brody	'58
AMERICAN HERITAGE	Capital Appreciation	65.6	1.47	10,970.10	14,084.30	18,709.20	5.5	828-5050	212-474-7308	None	None	None	Heiko Thieme	'90
AMERICAN HIGH-INCOME TR	Fixed Income	600.9	15.17	10,426.30	11,802.10	18,438.60	8.6	421-0180	210-530-4000	4.75	0.30	None	Multiple Managers	'88
AMERICAN LEADERS;A	Growth & Income	206.1	14.76	10,165.90	11,763.20	17,603.10	1.8	245-4770	412-288-1900	4.50	None	None	Peter R. Anderson	'91
AMERICAN LEADERS;C	Growth & Income	0.3	14.76	☆	☆	☆	0.0	245-4770	412-288-1900	None	0.75	1.00	Peter R. Anderson	'93
AMERICAN MUTUAL	Growth & Income	5,142.4	22.56	10,288.10	11,584.10	17,932.60	3.8	421-0180	210-530-4000	5.75	0.25	None	Multiple Managers	'50
AMERICAN NATIONAL GROWTH	Growth	117.1	4.46	10,056.50	10,791.00	15,740.20	1.7	231-4639	409-763-2767	5.75	None	None	Steven H. Stubbs	'92
AMERICAN NATIONAL INCOME	Equity Income	116.9	22.35	10,073.50	11,004.80	17,818.90	2.4	231-4639	409-763-2767	5.75	None	None	David Zimansky	'91
AMER PERFORM:AGGR GROWTH	Small-Company Growth	13.4	11.74	10,982.20	14,025.40	☆	0.1	762-7085	None	4.00	None	None	Joe Sing	'92
AMER PERFORM:BOND	Fixed Income	34.4	10.84	10,234.50	11,178.40	☆	6.5	762-7085	None	4.00	0.25	None	James Huntzinger	'90
AMER PERFORM:EQUITY	Growth	72.1	12.40	9,992.70	11,014.50	☆	1.1	762-7085	None	4.00	0.25	None	Grafton Potter	'90
AMER PERFORM:INTMDTBOND	Fixed Income	65.0	10.97	10,202.60	11,015.00	☆	5.8	762-7085	None	3.00	0.25	None	James Huntzinger	'90
AMERICA'S UTILITY	Utility	72.9	24.54	10,332.60	12,430.40	☆	3.7	487-3863	804-649-1315	None	None	None	Julie M. Cannell	'92
AMWAY MUTUAL	Growth	62.1	7.87	9,911.80	11,819.00	19,712.40	0.3	346-2670	616-676-6288	3.00	None	None	Bruce Ebel	'89
ANALYTIC OPTIONED EQU	Option Income	89.9	12.34	10,073.00	10,839.70	15,730.60	2.4	374-2633	714-833-0294	None	None	None	Chuck Dobson	'78
ANCHOR CAP ACCUM	Growth	14.3	22.66	9,826.50	10,977.00	16,165.10	1.3	None	802-748-2400	None	1.00	4.00	Paul Jaspard	'83
ANCHOR INTL BOND	World Income	17.8	0.00	N/A	N/A	N/A	0.0	None	802-748-2400	None	1.00	4.00	Paul Jaspard	'88
API TRUST:GROWTH	Capital Appreciation	44.3	11.84	10,367.80	11,797.50	16,391.50	0.0	544-6060	804-846-1361	None	1.00	None	David Basten	'85
API TRUST:TOTAL RETURN	Balanced	4.4	21.67	10,173.70	11,447.40	13,219.40	0.0	544-6060	804-846-1361	None	1.00	None	David Basten	'88
ARCH:EMERGING GRO;INV	Small-Company Growth	3.0	12.08	10,381.10	12,911.70	☆	0.6	452-2724	617-722-7868	4.50	None	None	R. Anthony	'92
ARCH:EMERGING GRO;TR★	Small-Company Growth	39.4	12.08	10,369.10	12,896.80	☆	0.5	452-2724	617-722-7868	None	None	None	R. Anthony	'92
ARCH:GOVT&CORP BOND;INV	Fixed Income	3.2	10.68	10,252.10	11,069.80	15,939.10	6.1	452-2724	617-722-7868	4.50	None	None	David Bethke	'88
ARCH:GR & INC EQUITY;INV	Growth & Income	8.9	14.44	10,146.90	11,632.00	19,273.80	1.7	452-2724	617-722-7868	4.50	None	None	Gene Gillespie	'88
ARCH:US GOVT SEC;INV	Fixed Income	10.3	11.20	10,245.70	11,034.50	16,054.30	5.5	452-2724	617-722-7868	4.50	None	None	David Bethke	'88
ARMSTRONG ASSOCIATES	Growth	9.8	8.26	10,273.60	11,712.30	14,724.50	0.2	None	214-720-9101	None	None	None	C.K. Lawson	'68
ASM FUND	Growth & Income	14.7	9.68	10,274.40	10,619.70	☆	4.3	445-2763	813-963-3150	None	None	0.75	Adler/Tapella	'91/'93
ASO OUTLOOK:BALANCED	Balanced	172.4	11.86	10,284.00	11,511.40	☆	3.8	451-8379	205-326-4732	4.50	None	None	AmSouth Bank	'91
ASO OUTLOOK:BOND	Fixed Income	62.3	11.33	10,236.80	11,269.20	☆	6.2	451-8379	205-326-4732	4.50	None	None	AmSouth Bank	'88
ASO OUTLOOK:EQUITY	Capital Appreciation	144.8	14.34	10,307.20	11,805.00	☆	2.0	451-8379	205-326-4732	4.50	None	None	AmSouth Bank	'88
ASO OUTLOOK:LTD MATURITY	Fixed Income	50.2	10.82	10,188.30	10,761.80	☆	5.8	451-8379	205-326-4732	2.50	None	None	AmSouth Bank	'89
ASO OUTLOOK:REGIONAL EQU	Capital Appreciation	34.6	16.58	9,917.10	12,087.90	☆	1.2	451-8379	205-326-4732	4.50	None	None	AmSouth Bank	'88
ASSET MGMT FINL:ARM★	Fixed Income	1,389.9	10.02	10,135.60	10,464.00	☆	4.3	527-3713	312-856-0715	None	0.25	None	Edward Sammons Jr.	'91
ASSET MGMT FINL:INT LIQ★	Fixed Income	149.7	10.91	10,117.90	10,741.40	15,338.00	6.1	527-3713	312-856-0715	None	0.15	None	Edward Sammons Jr.	'82
ASSET MGMT FINL:INT MTGE★	Fixed Income	100.1	9.99	10,180.70	10,860.10	16,307.20	6.2	527-3713	312-856-0715	None	0.15	None	Edward Sammons Jr.	'86
ASSET MGMT FINL:MTGE SEC★	Fixed Income	73.0	11.37	10,184.80	10,838.80	16,490.40	7.6	527-3713	312-856-0715	None	0.15	None	Edward Sammons Jr.	'84
ATLANTA GROWTH	Specialty	9.1	11.06	9,813.70	11,101.20	☆	0.2	762-0227	404-842-9600	3.75	0.25	None	Shapiro/Astrop	'92/'92
ATLAS:GOVT & MTGE SEC	Fixed Income	256.3	10.76	10,224.00	10,957.10	☆	7.2	933-2852	None	3.00	0.25	None	David Welch	'90
ATLAS:GROWTH & INCOME	Growth & Income	43.8	14.06	10,060.00	11,300.30	☆	1.7	933-2852	None	3.00	0.25	None	Julian Lerner	'90
ATLAS:US TREAS INTMDT	Fixed Income	6.3	10.13	10,231.00	☆	☆	0.0	933-2852	None	3.00	0.20	None	Roberta Conger	'92
AVONDALE TOTAL RETURN	Balanced	7.4	23.50	9,939.80	11,122.10	☆	1.9	424-2295	817-761-3777	None	None	None	Herbert R. Smith Inc.	'88
BABSON BOND:PORTFOLIO L	Fixed Income	156.8	1.68	10,300.30	11,224.60	16,738.10	7.1	422-2766	816-471-5200	None	None	None	Edward L. Martin	'84
BABSON BOND:PORTFOLIO S	Fixed Income	32.5	10.55	10,202.30	10,964.40	15,880.10	7.0	422-2766	816-471-5200	None	None	None	Edward L. Martin	'88
BABSON ENTERPRISE★	Small-Company Growth	198.6	16.12	9,913.90	12,111.50	19,678.10	0.5	422-2766	816-471-5200	None	None	None	Peter C. Schliemann	'85
BABSON ENTERPRISE II	Small-Company Growth	22.1	15.61	9,974.40	12,136.90	☆	0.1	422-2766	816-471-5200	None	None	None	Schliemann/James	'91/'91

★AMER AADVANTAGE FUNDS—Institutional funds.
★AMER CAP EXCHANGE—Closed to new investors.
★AMER CAP FED MTGE; B—Closed to new investors.
★AMER CAP TGT: PORT '97—Closed to new investors.

★ARCH: EMERGING GRO; TR—Institutional fund.
★ASSET MGMT FINL FUNDS—Limited to members of the Federal Home Loan Banking System.
★BABSON ENTERPRISE-Closed to new investors.

PERFORMANCE OF MUTUAL FUNDS (continued)

FUND NAME	OBJECTIVE	TOTAL NET ASSETS ($ MIL) 5/31/93	NET ASSET $ VALUE 6/30/93	PERFORMANCE (Return on Initial $10,000 Investment) 3/31/93-6/30/93	6/30/92-6/30/93	6/30/88-6/30/93	DIVIDEND YIELD % 6/93	PHONE NUMBER 800	In-State	FEES Load	12b-1	Redemption	MANAGER	SINCE
DAVID L BABSON GROWTH	Growth	251.2	12.30	9,933.20	11,428.80	15,761.90	1.5	422-2766	816-471-5200	None	None	None	David G. Kirk	'85
BABSON-STEWART IVORY	International	32.8	13.97	10,324.30	10,305.10	15,718.70	0.7	422-2766	816-471-5200	None	None	None	Begien/Wright	'88/'88
BABSON VALUE	Growth & Income	37.7	22.85	10,150.90	11,229.20	16,578.00	3.9	422-2766	816-471-5200	None	None	None	Nick Whitridge	'84
BAIRD ADJ RATE INCOME	Fixed Income	51.4	9.95	10,124.10	☆	☆	0.0	792-2473	414-765-3500	3.25	0.15	None	Jim Kochan	'92
BAIRD BLUE CHIP	Growth & Income	68.4	18.96	10,005.30	10,843.80	17,594.80	0.9	792-2473	414-765-3500	5.75	0.31	None	Evans/Bosworth	'87/'87
BAIRD CAP DEVELOPMENT	Growth	48.7	22.35	10,182.20	11,812.00	18,462.80	1.0	792-2473	414-765-3500	5.75	0.45	None	Kellner/Wilson	'86/'86
BAIRD QUALITY BOND	Fixed Income	4.2	10.14	10,251.10	☆	☆	0.0	792-2473	414-765-3500	4.00	0.22	None	Jim Kochan	'92
BAKER:US GOVERNMENT	Fixed Income	N/A	0.00	N/A	N/A	N/A	0.0	862-7283	317-634-3300	None	0.50	None	Doug McQueen	'86
BARON ASSET FUND	Small-Company Growth	52.6	19.70	10,467.60	13,012.10	18,519.10	0.0	992-2766	212-759-7700	None	*0.25*	2.00	Ronald Baron	'87
BARTLETT CAP:BASIC VALUE	Growth & Income	99.3	14.50	9,878.00	10,879.10	15,471.90	1.9	800-4612	513-621-4612	None	None	None	Miller/Uible	'90/'93
BARTLETT CAP:FIXED INC	Fixed Income	129.6	10.49	10,155.60	10,904.50	15,674.50	5.2	800-4612	513-621-4612	None	None	None	Dale H. Rabiner	'86
BARTLETT CAP:VALUE INTL	International	32.1	10.23	10,168.30	9,839.80	☆	0.8	800-4612	513-621-4612	None	None	None	Madelynn M. Matlock	'89
BASCOM HILL BALANCED	Balanced	15.1	24.21	10,164.40	11,337.80	14,913.90	2.9	767-0300	608-273-2020	3.00	None	None	Frank Burgess	'86
BASCOM HILL INVESTORS	Growth & Income	10.1	18.56	10,158.70	11,785.40	15,931.20	1.7	767-0300	608-273-2020	None	None	None	Frank Burgess	'78
BAYFUNDS:BOND	Fixed Income	67.4	10.26	10,268.40	☆	☆	0.0	229-3863	None	None	None	None	Rick Vincent	'93
BAYFUNDS:EQUITY	Growth	79.6	10.43	10,121.90	☆	☆	0.0	229-3863	None	None	None	None	Gerri Carrol	'93
BAYFUNDS:SH TM YIELD	Fixed Income	134.7	9.97	10,124.00	☆	☆	0.0	229-3863	None	None	None	None	Eric Letendre	'93
BBK GRP:DIVERSA	Global Flexible	49.6	12.13	10,236.10	11,656.80	13,728.90	2.5	882-8383	415-571-5800	None	None	None	Team Managed	'86
BB&T:GRO & INC;INV	Growth & Income	3.9	10.91	10,072.60	☆	☆	0.0	228-1872	614-899-4668	2.00	0.25	None	Branch Banking & Trust	'93
BB&T:GRO & INC;TR★	Growth & Income	73.4	10.94	10,085.40	☆	☆	0.0	228-1872	614-899-4668	None	None	None	Branch Banking & Trust	'92
BB&T:INTMDT GOVT;INV	Fixed Income	2.9	10.31	10,295.30	☆	☆	0.0	228-1872	614-899-4668	2.00	0.15	None	Branch Banking & Trust	'93
BB&T:INTMDT GOVT;TR★	Fixed Income	62.7	10.27	10,259.10	☆	☆	0.0	228-1872	614-899-4668	None	None	None	Branch Banking & Trust	'92
BB&T:SH-INTMDT GOVT;INV	Fixed Income	10.5	10.23	10,164.20	☆	☆	0.0	228-1872	614-899-4668	2.00	0.15	None	Branch Banking & Trust	'93
BB&T:SH-INTMDT GOVT;TR★	Fixed Income	34.3	10.23	10,168.10	☆	☆	0.0	228-1872	614-899-4668	None	None	None	Branch Banking & Trust	'92
BEACON HILL MUTUAL	Growth	5.4	30.52	9,749.80	9,774.30	15,490.00	0.0	343-0529	617-482-0795	None	None	None	David L. Stone	'64
B STEARNS:EMERG MKT DEBT	World Income	31.0	9.95	☆	☆	☆	0.0	578-8078	None	4.50	None	None	Mark Arnold	'93
BENCHMARK:BOND;A	Fixed Income	158.4	20.87	10,366.30	☆	☆	0.0	621-2550	None	None	None	None	Mark Wirth	'93
BENCHMARK:DVSD GRO;A	Growth	198.0	10.24	9,886.30	☆	☆	0.0	621-2550	None	None	None	None	Karen Adams	'93
BENCHMARK:EQ INDEX;A	Growth & Income	145.5	10.53	10,037.90	☆	☆	0.0	621-2550	None	None	None	None	Robert Mitchell	'93
BENCHMARK:SHORT DURATION	Fixed Income	N/A	10.01	☆	☆	☆	0.0	621-2550	None	None	None	None	Mark Wirth	'93
BENCHMARK:SH INT BD;A	Fixed Income	89.1	20.36	10,133.50	☆	☆	0.0	621-2550	None	None	None	None	Mark Wirth	'93
BENCHMARK:SM CO IDX;A	Small-Company Growth	43.8	10.54	10,125.70	☆	☆	0.0	621-2550	None	None	None	None	Judy Bednar	'93
BENCHMARK:TREAS IDX;A	Fixed Income	70.8	20.97	10,276.10	☆	☆	0.0	621-2550	None	None	None	None	Richard Steck	'93
BENCHMARK:US GOVT SECS;A	Fixed Income	30.2	20.10	☆	☆	☆	0.0	621-2550	None	None	None	None	Richard Steck	'93
BENHAM EQ:EQ GROWTH	Growth	77.5	12.29	10,176.40	11,900.40	☆	2.8	472-3389	415-965-4274	None	None	None	Steve Colton	'91
BENHAM EQ:GOLD EQ INDEX	Gold	316.0	12.34	13,427.60	15,242.80	☆	0.1	472-3389	415-965-4274	None	None	None	Bill Martin	'92
BENHAM EQ:INC & GROWTH	Growth & Income	178.9	14.92	10,229.60	11,981.90	☆	2.8	472-3389	415-965-4274	None	None	None	Steve Colton	'91
BENHAM EQ:UTILITIES INC	Utility	109.1	10.45	10,358.50	☆	☆	0.0	472-3389	415-965-4274	None	None	None	Steve Colton	'93
BENHAM GOVT:ADJ RATE	Fixed Income	1,415.4	9.98	10,136.50	10,460.40	☆	5.6	472-3389	415-965-4274	None	None	None	Merk/Brown	'91/'91
BENHAM GOVT:GNMA	Fixed Income	1,207.7	10.91	10,192.60	10,912.00	16,734.10	7.0	472-3389	415-965-4274	None	None	None	Merk/Tyler	'87/'92
BENHAM GOVT:LG TREAS/AGY	Fixed Income	16.0	10.59	10,513.90	☆	☆	0.0	472-3389	415-965-4274	None	None	None	David W. Schroeder	'92
BENHAM GOVT:SH TREAS/AGY	Fixed Income	16.9	10.05	10,110.40	☆	☆	0.0	472-3389	415-965-4274	None	None	None	David W. Schroeder	'92
BENHAM GOVT:TREAS NOTE	Fixed Income	390.2	10.81	10,191.10	11,011.30	15,894.20	4.9	472-3389	415-965-4274	None	None	None	David W. Schroeder	'90
BENHAM INTL:EURO GOVT	World Income	380.5	10.39	9,942.60	10,357.30	☆	4.6	472-3389	415-965-4274	None	None	None	Tyler/Graham	'92/'92
BENHAM TARGET:1995	Fixed Income	87.8	92.78	10,127.70	10,954.00	16,918.30	0.0	472-3389	415-965-4274	None	None	None	David W. Schroeder	'90

BENHAM TARGET:2000	Fixed Income	266.0	69.52	10,455.70	12,132.60	19,789.40	0.0	472-3389	415-965-4274	None	None	None	David W. Schroeder	'90
BENHAM TARGET:2005	Fixed Income	148.1	48.61	10,773.50	12,942.00	21,385.80	0.0	472-3389	415-965-4274	None	None	None	David W. Schroeder	'90
BENHAM TARGET:2010	Fixed Income	53.8	35.05	10,936.00	13,352.40	22,324.80	0.0	472-3389	415-965-4274	None	None	None	David W. Schroeder	'90
BENHAM TARGET:2015	Fixed Income	86.1	25.69	11,030.50	13,464.40	22,051.50	0.0	472-3389	415-965-4274	None	None	None	David W. Schroeder	'90
BENHAM TARGET:2020	Fixed Income	38.9	17.63	10,998.10	13,551.10	☆	0.0	472-3389	415-965-4274	None	None	None	David W. Schroeder	'90
BERGER ONE HUNDRED	Growth	1,015.8	15.04	10,820.10	13,549.50	30,468.50	0.0	333-1001	303-329-0200	None	0.75	None	Berger/Linafelter	'74/'91
BERGER ONE HUNDRED & ONE	Growth & Income	61.5	10.56	10,388.70	11,747.00	20,231.70	0.3	333-1001	303-329-0200	None	0.75	None	Berger/Linafelter	'74/'91
S BERNSTEIN:GOVT SH DUR	Fixed Income	234.9	12.80	10,131.00	10,552.80	☆	3.6	None	212-756-4097	None	None	None	Investment Policy Group	'89
S BERNSTEIN:INTMDT DUR	Fixed Income	609.0	13.67	10,323.90	11,216.90	☆	5.6	None	212-756-4097	None	None	None	Investment Policy Group	'89
S BERNSTEIN:INTL VALUE	International	295.9	14.33	10,622.70	11,647.30	☆	0.3	None	212-756-4097	None	None	None	Investment Policy Group	'92
S BERNSTEIN:SH DUR PLUS	Fixed Income	539.1	12.88	10,162.00	10,626.40	☆	4.6	None	212-756-4097	None	None	None	Investment Policy Group	'88
BERWYN FUND	Growth & Income	43.7	16.65	10,097.00	12,208.30	17,039.10	0.3	824-2249	215-640-4330	None	None	1.00	Robert Killen	'84
BERWYN INCOME FUND	Income	24.4	12.05	10,387.90	11,735.20	18,826.30	5.1	824-2249	215-640-4330	None	None	None	Robert Killen	'87
BFM INSTL:CORE FIXED INC	Fixed Income	7.6	10.37	10,259.90	☆	☆	0.0	227-7236	None	None	None	None	Team Managed	'92
BFM INSTL:SHORT DURATION	Fixed Income	50.8	9.96	10,169.20	☆	☆	0.0	227-7236	None	None	None	None	Team Managed	'92
BHIRUD MID CAP GROWTH	Growth	5.2	10.55	10,487.10	☆	☆	0.0	845-8406	None	5.75	0.25	None	Suresh L. Bhirud	'92
BJB GLOBAL INCOME	World Income	40.8	12.27	10,471.80	11,137.70	☆	5.3	435-4659	None	None	0.25	None	Urs Schwytter	'92
BLACKROCK GOVT INC;A	Fixed Income	116.5	9.65	9,976.40	10,213.10	☆	6.5	225-1852	None	3.00	0.25	None	Team Managed	'91
BLACKROCK GOVT INC;B	Fixed Income	5.6	9.66	9,963.70	☆	☆	0.0	225-1852	None	None	1.00	1.00	Team Managed	'92
BLANCHARD:AMER EQUITY	Growth	31.5	9.59	9,815.80	☆	☆	0.0	922-7771	212-779-7979	None	0.50	None	Jeff Miller	'92
BLANCHARD:FLEX INCOME	Fixed Income	349.5	5.15	10,319.30	☆	☆	0.0	922-7771	212-779-7979	None	0.25	None	Jack Burks	'92
BLANCHARD:GLBL GRO	Global Flexible	86.1	10.42	10,535.90	11,154.50	13,778.20	4.7	922-7771	212-779-7979	None	0.75	None	Team Managed	'86
BLANCHARD PREC METALS	Gold	44.1	8.18	13,431.90	14,607.10	☆	0.0	922-7771	212-779-7979	None	0.75	None	Peter Cavelti	'88
BLANCHARD:SH-TM GLBL INC	World Income	694.7	1.89	10,434.00	10,700.30	☆	6.7	922-7771	212-779-7979	None	0.25	None	Thomas Berger	'91
BNY HAMILTON:EQ INC	Equity Income	79.1	11.08	10,199.10	☆	☆	0.0	426-9363	None	None	0.25	None	Robert G. Knott, Jr.	'92
BNY HAMILTON:INTMDT GOVT	Fixed Income	52.0	10.22	10,239.30	☆	☆	0.0	426-9363	None	None	0.25	None	Mark A. Hemenetz	'92
BOND FUND OF AMERICA	Fixed Income	4,645.6	14.73	10,360.70	11,592.50	17,309.00	7.7	421-0180	210-530-4000	4.75	0.25	None	Multiple Managers	'74
BOND PORT FOR ENDOWMENTS★	Fixed Income	65.0	19.49	10,352.40	11,448.50	17,661.40	7.5	421-0180	210-530-4000	None	None	None	Multiple Managers	'75
BOSTON CO:AST MGR;INST	Growth & Income	62.6	11.99	10,007.20	11,127.10	☆	2.2	221-7930	None	None	0.15	None	Eric Baggeson	'91
BOSTON CO:CAP APP;INSTL	Growth	N/A	27.48	10,118.20	☆	☆	0.0	221-7930	None	None	0.15	None	Guy Scott	'93
BOSTON CO:CAP APP;RET	Growth	355.8	27.47	10,112.60	11,493.10	15,397.70	1.2	225-5267	None	None	0.25	None	Guy Scott	'91
BOSTON CO:INTMDT;INSTL	Fixed Income	N/A	13.27	10,254.70	☆	☆	0.0	221-7930	None	None	0.15	None	Almond Goduti	'93
BOSTON CO:INTMDT;RET	Fixed Income	9.0	13.27	10,259.10	11,109.60	15,603.10	5.6	225-5267	None	None	0.25	None	Almond Goduti	'90
BOSTON CO:MGD INC;INSTL	Fixed Income	N/A	12.01	10,353.60	☆	☆	0.0	221-7930	None	None	0.15	None	David Gray	'93
BOSTON CO:MGD INC;INV	Fixed Income	10.6	12.01	10,359.70	☆	☆	0.0	225-5267	None	None	None	None	David Gray	'93
BOSTON CO:MGD INC;RET	Fixed Income	56.2	12.01	10,351.50	11,276.90	15,860.40	7.4	225-5267	None	None	0.25	None	David Gray	'90
BOSTON CO:SPEC GRO;INSTL	Growth	19.2	18.90	10,482.50	☆	☆	0.0	221-7930	None	None	0.15	None	Guy Scott	'93
BOSTON CO:SPEC GRO;INV	Growth	9.3	18.92	10,487.80	☆	☆	0.0	225-5267	None	None	None	None	Guy Scott	'93
BOSTON CO:SPEC GR;RET	Growth	60.3	18.87	10,471.70	14,843.50	21,894.80	0.0	225-5267	None	None	0.25	None	Guy Scott	'90
BOSTON CO INV:ASST;INSTL	Flexible	20.3	15.55	10,071.20	☆	☆	0.0	221-7930	None	None	0.15	None	Edgar Peters	'93
BOSTON CO INV:ASST;RET	Flexible	12.9	15.54	10,064.80	11,314.60	☆	1.5	225-5267	None	None	0.25	None	Edgar Peters	'88
BOSTON CO INV:CONT;INSTL	Growth	0.1	16.49	10,280.50	☆	☆	0.0	221-7930	None	None	0.15	None	Guy Scott	'93
BOSTON CO INV:CONT;RET	Growth	3.1	16.49	10,280.50	12,903.00	☆	0.0	225-5267	None	None	0.25	None	Guy Scott	'91
BOSTON CO INV:INTL;INSTL	International	0.2	11.71	10,446.00	☆	☆	0.0	221-7930	None	None	0.15	None	Bruce Clark	'93
BOSTON CO INV:INTL;RET	International	15.4	11.71	10,446.00	11,089.00	☆	0.0	225-5267	None	None	0.25	None	Bruce Clark	'90

★BB&T TR FUNDS—Institutional funds.

★BOND PORT FOR ENDOWMENTS—Limited to tax-exempt institutions.

PERFORMANCE OF MUTUAL FUNDS (continued)

FUND NAME	OBJECTIVE	TOTAL NET ASSETS ($ MIL) 5/31/93	NET ASSET $ VALUE 6/30/93	PERFORMANCE (Return on Initial $10,000 Investment) 3/31/93-6/30/93	6/30/92-6/30/93	6/30/88-6/30/93	DIVIDEND YIELD % 6/93	PHONE NUMBER 800	In-State	FEES Load	12b-1	Redemption	MANAGER	SINCE
BOSTON CO INV:SHTM;INSTL	Fixed Income	0.1	12.52	10,087.00	☆	☆	0.0	221-7930	None	None	0.15	None	Roberta Shea	'93
BOSTON CO INV:SHTM;RET	Fixed Income	3.4	12.52	10,086.70	10,542.70	☆	5.3	225-5267	None	None	0.25	None	Roberta Shea	'89
BOULEVARD:BLUE CHIP GR	Growth & Income	30.5	9.14	9,552.10	☆	☆	0.0	285-3263	412-288-0525	4.00	0.25	None	Boulevard Bank	'92
BOULEVARD:MGD INCOME	Fixed Income	67.7	9.92	10,068.50	☆	☆	0.0	285-3263	412-288-0525	3.00	0.25	None	Boulevard Bank	'92
BOULEVARD:STRAT BALANCE	Specialty	26.5	9.92	10,054.50	☆	☆	0.0	285-3263	412-288-0525	4.00	0.25	None	Boulevard Bank	'92
BRANDYWINE BLUE	Growth	5.4	16.89	10,974.70	13,970.20	☆	0.0	338-1579	302-656-6200	None	None	None	Friess Associates	'91
BRANDYWINE FUND	Growth	1,077.4	24.48	10,597.40	13,688.10	23,418.80	0.0	338-1579	302-656-6200	None	None	None	Friess Associates	'85
BRIDGES INVESTMENT	Growth & Income	18.3	17.75	9,988.60	10,910.80	16,321.20	3.6	None	402-397-4700	None	None	None	Edson L. Bridges II	'63
BRINSON:GLOBAL	Global Flexible	179.1	10.87	10,244.40	☆	☆	0.0	448-2430	312-220-7100	None	None	None	Gary P. Brinson	'92
BROWN CAP BALANCED	Flexible	0.7	10.60	10,009.40	☆	☆	0.0	525-3863	919-972-9922	4.00	0.20	None	Brown Capital Mgt	'92
BROWN CAP EQUITY	Capital Appreciation	0.3	10.89	9,857.00	☆	☆	0.0	525-3863	919-972-9922	4.00	0.20	None	Brown Capital Mgt	'92
BROWN CAP SMALL COMPANY	Small-Company Growth	1.2	10.64	9,974.70	☆	☆	0.0	525-3863	919-972-9922	4.00	0.20	None	Brown Capital Mgt	'92
BRUCE FUND★	Capital Appreciation	2.3	109.61	10,445.00	12,554.80	13,381.10	2.3	872-7823	312-236-9160	None	None	None	Robert Bruce	'83
BSR TR:GROWTH & INCOME	Growth & Income	18.3	12.15	10,024.70	10,936.40	☆	0.9	543-8721	513-629-2000	None	0.25	None	Brandon Reid	'91
BSR TR:SH/INTMDT FXD INC	Fixed Income	38.1	10.83	10,195.70	10,897.00	☆	6.1	543-8721	513-629-2000	None	0.25	None	H. Dean Benner	'91
BT INSTL:EQ 500 INDEX	Growth & Income	23.5	10.43	10,067.70	☆	☆	0.0	545-1074	None	None	0.25	None	Frank Salerno	'93
BT INV:CAPITAL APPREC	Growth	N/A	10.53	10,519.50	☆	☆	0.0	545-1074	None	None	0.20	None	William Newman	'93
BT INV:CAPITAL GROWTH	Growth	8.1	10.38	9,801.80	☆	☆	0.0	545-1074	None	None	0.20	None	Paul Phillips	'92
BT INV:INTL EQUITY	International	11.6	11.25	10,633.30	☆	☆	0.0	545-1074	None	None	0.20	None	Francis Ledwidge	'92
BT INV:SH/INT US GOVT	Fixed Income	10.8	10.07	10,094.50	☆	☆	0.0	545-1074	None	None	0.20	None	Goodchild/Hudson	'93/'93
BT INV:UTILITY	Utility	25.7	11.02	10,213.30	☆	☆	0.0	545-1074	None	None	0.20	None	Maurice Stahl	'92
BT PYRAMID:INV EQ 500	Growth & Income	1.5	10.42	10,043.50	☆	☆	0.0	545-1074	None	None	0.20	None	Frank Salerno	'93
BT PYRAMID:LTD GOVT SECS	Fixed Income	N/A	10.07	10,090.90	☆	☆	0.0	545-1074	None	None	0.20	None	Louis Hudson	'92
BULL&BEAR FINCL NEWS CMP	Growth & Income	6.0	18.71	10,229.60	10,654.00	16,155.30	1.1	847-4200	212-363-1100	None	0.25	None	Thomas B. Winmill	'90
BULL&BEAR:GLBL INC	World Income	49.0	9.39	10,627.30	11,938.60	14,591.40	8.0	847-4200	212-363-1100	None	0.50	None	C.Clifford McCarthy Jr.	'90
BULL&BEAR GOLD INVESTORS	Gold	46.8	16.98	13,486.90	14,612.70	12,140.40	0.0	847-4200	212-363-1100	None	1.00	None	Robert W. Radsch	'82
BULL&BEAR SPL EQUITIES	Capital Appreciation	67.8	27.87	11,170.30	14,263.10	18,816.20	0.0	847-4200	212-363-1100	None	1.00	None	Brett B. Sneed	'88
BULL&BEAR:US GOVT SEC	Fixed Income	22.3	15.53	10,344.30	11,073.80	15,442.50	5.2	847-4200	212-363-1100	None	0.50	None	C.Clifford McCarthy Jr.	'90
BULL&BEAR US & OVERSEAS	Global	9.7	8.49	10,774.10	11,030.20	14,413.60	0.0	847-4200	212-363-1100	None	1.00	None	Robert W. Radsch	'87
BURNHAM FUND	Growth & Income	117.5	21.70	10,217.20	11,525.50	16,794.90	4.0	874-3863	212-262-3100	3.00	None	None	Burnham/Ferguson	'61/'75
CALDWELL FUND	Growth & Income	3.5	14.75	9,880.50	11,048.30	17,247.30	1.3	338-9477	813-485-0654	None	None	None	Roland Caldwell	'85
CALDWELL GOVT	Fixed Income	3.5	10.15	10,209.00	☆	☆	0.0	338-9477	813-485-0654	None	None	None	Roland Caldwell	'92
CALDWELL GROWTH	Growth	1.6	10.12	9,702.80	☆	☆	0.0	338-9477	813-485-0654	None	None	None	Roland Caldwell	'92
C & O:AGGRESSIVE GROWTH	Small-Company Growth	15.9	13.66	10,194.00	☆	☆	0.0	237-7073	404-239-0707	None	None	None	Orkin/Faulkenberry	'92/'92
CA INV TR II:S&P 500	Growth & Income	9.5	10.97	10,052.50	11,292.90	☆	2.5	225-8778	415-398-2727	None	None	None	Philip McClanahan	'92
CA INV TR II:S&P MIDCAP	Growth	14.4	11.83	10,232.00	12,093.50	☆	2.0	225-8778	415-398-2727	None	None	None	Bank of America	'92
CA INV TR II:US GOVT SEC	Fixed Income	28.8	11.25	10,500.90	11,814.00	17,674.10	6.3	225-8778	415-398-2727	None	None	None	Philip McClanahan	'85
CALVERT-ARIEL:APPREC	Small-Company Growth	202.3	20.66	9,814.70	10,992.60	☆	0.4	368-2748	301-951-4820	4.75	0.35	None	Eric McKissack	'89
CALVERT-ARIEL:GROWTH★	Small-Company Growth	245.7	28.84	9,440.30	10,876.60	15,586.80	2.5	368-2748	301-951-4820	4.75	0.35	None	John W. Rogers	'86
CALVERT INCOME	Fixed Income	48.3	18.10	10,345.60	11,450.30	17,259.40	6.9	368-2748	301-951-4820	4.75	0.25	None	Patterson/Gilkison	'82/'82
CALVERT US GOVERNMENT	Fixed Income	11.6	15.88	10,244.90	10,865.50	15,789.70	5.7	368-2748	301-951-4820	4.75	0.25	None	John Nichols	'86
CALVERT SOCIAL INV:BOND	Fixed Income	60.4	17.39	10,265.10	11,335.00	16,824.20	6.3	368-2748	301-951-4820	4.75	0.35	None	Domenic Colasacco	'87
CALVERT SOCIAL INV:EQTY	Growth	83.4	21.18	9,640.40	11,089.20	15,744.20	0.8	368-2748	301-951-4820	4.75	0.35	None	Domenic Colasacco	'87
CALVERT SOCIAL INV:GRO	Balanced	499.3	30.13	10,022.20	11,202.10	15,872.60	3.3	368-2748	301-951-4820	4.75	0.35	None	Colasacco/Trosko	'82/'86
CALVERT WRLD VAL:GLBL EQ	Global	30.1	15.26	10,166.60	10,236.20	☆	0.4	368-2748	301-951-4820	4.75	0.35	None	Murray Johnston Intl Ltd	'92

CAMBRIDGE:CAP GROWTH;A	Growth	31.0	14.83	9,840.30	10,835.00	☆	1.3	934-3883	202-835-4280	5.50	None	None	Cathy Dudley	'92
CAMBRIDGE:CAP GROWTH;B	Growth	51.9	14.83	9,827.70	10,769.20	☆	0.7	934-3883	202-835-4280	None	0.75	None	Cathy Dudley	'92
CAMBRIDGE:GOVT INC;A	Fixed Income	48.7	14.19	10,156.50	10,687.80	☆	8.0	934-3883	202-835-4280	4.75	None	None	Gary Madich	'92
CAMBRIDGE:GOVT INC;B	Fixed Income	119.8	14.21	10,143.20	10,642.20	☆	7.5	934-3883	202-835-4280	None	0.50	None	Gary Madich	'92
CAMBRIDGE:GROWTH;A	Growth	17.3	15.56	9,917.10	11,310.80	☆	0.2	934-3883	202-835-4280	5.50	None	None	Steve Lewis	'92
CAMBRIDGE:GROWTH;B	Growth	27.3	15.50	9,904.20	11,248.20	☆	0.0	934-3883	202-835-4280	None	0.75	None	Steve Lewis	'92
CAMCO INTMDT TM	Fixed Income	0.1	10.02	10,012.20	10,460.90	☆	4.3	423-2345	215-832-1075	None	0.20	None	Daryl L. Hudson	'92
CAMCO SH TM	Fixed Income	0.2	10.13	10,029.00	10,468.90	☆	3.3	423-2345	215-832-1075	None	0.15	None	Daryl L. Hudson	'92
CAMCO TOTAL RETURN	Fixed Income	1.7	10.24	10,019.80	10,655.10	☆	5.3	423-2345	215-832-1075	None	0.20	None	Daryl L. Hudson	'92
CANANDAIGUA CIT:BOND★	Fixed Income	0.5	10.16	10,039.50	☆	☆	0.0	724-2621	716-394-4260	None	None	None	Gregory MacKay	'92
CANANDAIGUA CIT:EQUITY★	Growth & Income	1.8	10.27	9,941.90	☆	☆	0.0	724-2621	716-394-4260	None	None	None	Robert Swartout	'92
CAPITAL EXCHANGE★	Growth	90.0	160.80	9,984.70	11,035.50	17,716.00	1.5	225-6265	617-482-8260	None	None	None	Duncan Richardson	'87
CAPITAL INCOME BUILDER	Equity Income	2,077.1	32.26	10,015.60	11,170.10	19,098.10	5.5	421-0180	210-530-4000	5.75	0.30	None	Multiple Managers	'87
CAPITAL WORLD BOND	World Income	339.4	15.87	10,381.40	10,746.10	15,503.20	5.5	421-0180	210-530-4000	4.75	0.30	None	Multiple Managers	'87
CAPITAL WORLD GRO & INC	Global	589.8	15.26	10,178.90	☆	☆	0.0	421-0180	210-530-4000	5.75	0.30	None	Multiple Managers	'93
CAPITOL EQUITY;A★	Growth & Income	30.4	9.96	9,929.90	11,069.80	☆	2.0	342-5734	215-254-1000	None	None	None	Gene Mulligan	'90
CAPITOL FXD INC;A★	Fixed Income	22.4	10.77	10,264.20	11,131.30	☆	5.5	342-5734	215-254-1000	None	None	None	Gene Mulligan	'90
CAPITOL SPECIAL EQ;A★	Growth	5.2	15.03	10,705.10	☆	☆	0.0	342-5734	215-254-1000	None	None	None	Gene Mulligan	'92
CAPP-RUSH:EMERG GRO	Small-Company Growth	4.0	11.32	10,366.30	☆	☆	0.0	621-7874	301-657-1517	None	None	0.50	Frank Cappiello	'92
CAPP-RUSH:GROWTH	Growth	3.1	10.63	10,350.50	☆	☆	0.0	621-7874	301-657-1517	None	None	0.50	Frank Cappiello	'92
CAPP-RUSH:UTIL INC	Utility	6.5	10.82	10,329.50	☆	☆	0.0	621-7874	301-657-1517	None	None	0.50	Frank Cappiello	'92
CAPSTONE CSHMAN FARRELL	Capital Appreciation	4.7	12.41	10,155.50	12,025.20	14,264.10	0.0	262-6631	713-750-8000	4.75	0.35	None	Dan Cashman	'86
CAPSTONE EUROPEAN	European Region	10.6	11.46	9,973.90	9,190.10	13,185.80	0.0	262-6631	713-750-8000	4.75	0.35	None	Catherine Adibi	'90
CAPSTONE FD OF SOUTHWEST	Capital Appreciation	15.9	18.46	9,919.40	11,814.70	20,215.20	0.0	262-6631	713-750-8000	4.75	0.35	None	Sharon Keith	'87
CAPSTONE GOVT INCOME	Fixed Income	77.1	4.83	10,083.50	10,374.40	12,283.20	2.0	262-6631	713-750-8000	None	0.20	None	Jaroski/Potter	'87/'91
CAPSTONE MED RESEARCH	Health/Biotechnology	10.8	18.32	10,983.20	11,828.50	23,723.00	0.0	262-6631	713-750-8000	4.75	0.25	None	Samuel D. Isaly	'89
CAPSTONE NEW ZEALAND	Pacific Region	1.2	9.85	9,989.90	9,989.90	☆	0.0	262-6631	713-750-8000	4.75	0.35	None	Rob Scharar	'91
CAPSTONE NIKKO JAPAN	Japanese	3.3	7.16	11,834.70	14,066.80	☆	0.0	262-6631	713-750-8000	4.75	0.35	None	Toshihiko Tsuyusaki	'91
CAPSTONE PBHG GROWTH	Capital Appreciation	7.5	12.44	11,561.30	16,913.70	25,322.60	0.0	262-6631	713-750-8000	4.75	None	None	Gary Pilgrim	'85
CAPSTONE US TREND	Growth	100.8	14.37	9,915.50	10,949.80	18,185.10	1.5	262-6631	713-750-8000	4.75	0.35	None	Dan Watson	'86
CARDINAL FUND	Growth & Income	281.4	12.62	9,851.90	10,851.00	17,018.90	2.4	848-7734	614-464-5511	6.00	None	None	John Schlater	'84
CARDINAL GOVT OBLIGATION	Fixed Income	204.2	8.76	10,084.80	10,641.00	15,593.20	8.7	848-7734	614-464-5511	4.50	None	None	John R. Carle	'86
CARILLON INVST:CAPITAL	Flexible	32.2	12.32	10,072.90	10,978.50	17,221.20	3.3	999-1840	513-595-2600	5.00	None	None	Carillon Advisers	'88
CENTENNIAL AMERICA LP★	Fixed Income	4.3	1.00	10,058.10	10,278.50	☆	2.8	525-7048	303-671-3200	None	0.20	None	Warmack/Wolf/Zimmer	'91
CENTURION GROWTH	Growth	4.7	9.11	10,088.60	10,178.80	9,962.30	0.0	947-6984	407-832-3353	4.75	0.25	None	Robert Meeder, Sr.	'93
CENTURY SHARES TRUST	Financial Services	279.3	26.16	9,752.90	12,368.10	23,179.40	1.6	321-1928	617-482-3060	None	None	None	Allan W. Fulkerson	'76
CFB MKTWATCH:EQUITY	Growth & Income	76.2	10.24	10,042.60	☆	☆	0.0	232-9091	None	4.50	0.25	None	Team Managed	'93
CFB MKTWATCH:INT FXD INC	Fixed Income	62.2	10.21	10,181.90	☆	☆	0.0	232-9091	None	4.50	0.25	None	Team Managed	'93
CFB MKTWATCH:S-T FXD	Fixed Income	15.6	10.06	10,083.90	☆	☆	0.0	232-9091	None	4.50	0.25	None	Team Managed	'93
CFS:CALAMOS CONVERTIBLE	Convertible Securities	17.6	13.97	10,325.50	11,923.20	17,171.00	3.2	323-9943	708-571-7115	4.50	0.50	None	Calamos/Calamos	'85/'85
CFS:CALAMOS GROWTH	Growth	2.0	14.33	9,913.30	11,003.10	☆	2.0	323-9943	708-571-7115	4.50	0.50	None	Nick Calamos	'90
CFS:CALAMOS SM/MD CAP CV	Convertible Securities	3.8	13.89	10,339.30	12,461.70	☆	2.4	323-9943	708-571-7115	4.50	0.50	None	Calamos/Calamos	'88/'88
CFS:CALAMOS STRAT INCOME	Fixed Income	2.6	10.96	10,257.40	11,322.90	☆	3.5	323-9943	708-571-7115	4.50	0.50	None	Calamos/Calamos	'90/'90
CGM CAP DEVELOPMENT★	Growth	443.1	30.04	10,323.00	13,830.00	30,262.30	0.6	345-4048	617-859-7714	None	None	None	G. Kenneth Heebner	'76
CGM FIXED INCOME	Fixed Income	16.7	11.16	10,399.70	11,690.10	☆	6.2	345-4048	617-859-7714	None	None	None	Hatch/Hoffmann	'92/'92

★BRUCE FUND—Investment objective changed from Growth to Capital Appreciation, effective 5/13/93.
★CALVERT-ARIEL: GROWTH—Closed to new investors.
★CANANDAIGUA FUNDS—Designed primarily for retirement accounts.
★CAPITAL EXCHANGE—Closed to new investors.

★CAPITOL FUNDS—Institutional funds.
★CENTENNIAL AMERICA LP—Limited to qualifying foreign investors.
★CGM CAP DEVELOPMENT—Closed to new investors.

PERFORMANCE OF MUTUAL FUNDS *(continued)*

FUND NAME	OBJECTIVE	TOTAL NET ASSETS ($ MIL) 5/31/93	NET ASSET $ VALUE 6/30/93	PERFORMANCE (Return on Initial $10,000 Investment) 3/31/93-6/30/93	6/30/92-6/30/93	6/30/88-6/30/93	DIVIDEND YIELD % 6/93	PHONE NUMBER 800	In-State	FEES Load	12b-1	Redemption	MANAGER	SINCE
CGM MUTUAL	Balanced	663.2	29.51	10,482.10	12,462.10	20,774.10	3.1	345-4048	617-859-7714	None	None	None	G. Kenneth Heebner	'80
CHARTER CAP BLUE CHIP	Capital Appreciation	11.1	12.35	9,656.00	10,748.50	14,319.50	0.0	None	414-257-1842	None	None	None	Toll/Mirek	'90/'93
CHESAPEAKE GROWTH	Growth	10.6	11.19	10,811.60	☆	☆	0.0	525-3863	919-972-9922	3.00	None	None	Gardner/Lewis	'93/'93
CHESTNUT ST EXCH LP★	Growth	197.6	137.88	10,078.70	11,350.90	20,031.50	1.8	428-7108	None	None	None	None	Gayland Gee	'90
CHUBB INV:GOVERNMENT SEC	Fixed Income	10.8	10.99	10,294.20	11,257.80	16,987.80	6.6	258-3648	603-226-5000	5.00	None	None	Ned Gerstman	'87
CHUBB INV:GROWTH & INC	Growth & Income	11.0	16.00	10,081.90	11,384.60	18,434.70	1.3	258-3648	603-226-5000	5.00	None	None	Marjorie Raines	'87
CHUBB INV:TOTAL RETURN	Balanced	11.3	14.57	10,147.30	11,407.00	18,277.00	2.7	258-3648	603-226-5000	5.00	None	None	Michael O'Reilly	'87
CIGNA INSTL:INTL STOCK	International	6.3	12.00	10,695.20	☆	☆	0.0	528-6718	None	None	None	None	Chris Carter	'93
CLIPPER FUND	Growth	249.3	53.70	9,962.90	11,663.00	18,901.40	1.7	776-5033	310-247-3940	None	None	None	James H. Gipson	'84
COHEN & STEERS REALTY	Real Estate	108.5	33.48	9,615.50	13,375.10	☆	4.1	437-9912	212-832-3232	None	None	None	Cohen/Steers	'91/'91
COLONIAL ADJ RATE;A	Fixed Income	8.5	9.95	10,115.10	☆	☆	0.0	426-3750	617-426-3750	3.25	0.20	None	Leslie Finnemore	'92
COLONIAL ADJ RATE;B	Fixed Income	0.9	9.95	10,098.60	☆	☆	0.0	426-3750	617-426-3750	None	0.85	4.00	Leslie Finnemore	'93
COLONIAL FED SEC;A	Fixed Income	1,739.7	11.40	10,387.70	11,488.90	17,008.40	7.4	426-3750	617-426-3750	4.75	0.25	None	Helen Peters	'92
COLONIAL FED SEC;B	Fixed Income	52.2	11.40	10,369.00	11,394.80	☆	6.7	426-3750	617-426-3750	None	1.00	5.00	Helen Peters	'92
COLONIAL FUND;A	Growth & Income	484.8	24.15	10,046.10	11,637.70	17,830.20	2.0	426-3750	617-426-3750	5.75	0.35	None	Rie/Palmer	'93/'93
COLONIAL FUND;B	Growth & Income	70.3	24.15	10,028.20	11,573.60	☆	1.3	426-3750	617-426-3750	None	*1.00*	5.00	Rie/Palmer	'93/'93
COLONIAL GLBL EQUITY;A	Global	0.4	10.39	10,183.90	10,733.60	☆	2.1	426-3750	617-426-3750	5.75	0.25	None	Palmer/Lanzendorf	'92/'92
COLONIAL GLBL EQUITY;B	Global	33.9	10.38	10,166.30	10,646.50	☆	1.4	426-3750	617-426-3750	None	1.00	5.00	Palmer/Lanzendorf	'92/'93
COLONIAL GROWTH;A	Growth	165.0	14.41	9,846.90	11,821.20	18,411.60	0.6	426-3750	617-426-3750	5.75	0.35	None	Rie/Lanzendorf	'86/'93
COLONIAL GROWTH;B	Growth	37.6	14.39	9,829.20	11,737.40	☆	0.0	426-3750	617-426-3750	None	0.87	5.00	Rie/Lanzendorf	'92/'93
COLONIAL HI YLD SEC;A	Fixed Income	396.2	6.81	10,509.60	11,860.70	17,172.00	9.7	426-3750	617-426-3750	4.75	0.25	None	Prescott B. Crocker	'82
COLONIAL INCOME;A	Fixed Income	154.0	6.73	10,282.60	11,324.90	16,204.60	7.7	426-3750	617-426-3750	4.75	0.25	None	Carl C. Ericson	'91
COLONIAL INCOME;B	Fixed Income	12.1	6.73	10,263.80	11,242.50	☆	7.0	426-3750	617-426-3750	None	1.00	5.00	Carl C. Ericson	'92
COLONIAL INTL EQ INDEX	International	8.4	17.07	10,643.30	10,935.90	11,724.00	0.9	426-3750	617-426-3750	5.75	0.25	None	Steve Lanzendorf	'89
COLONIAL NATURAL RES;A	Natural Resources	31.4	11.57	11,058.40	11,625.90	☆	1.0	426-3750	617-426-3750	5.75	0.25	None	Orr/Lanzendorf	'92/'93
COLONIAL NATURAL RES;B	Natural Resources	6.3	11.57	11,034.80	11,547.90	☆	0.3	426-3750	617-426-3750	None	1.00	5.00	Orr/Lanzendorf	'92/'93
COLONIAL SMALL STOCK;A	Small-Company Growth	23.9	15.85	10,000.00	12,854.80	12,752.60	0.0	426-3750	617-426-3750	5.75	0.25	None	Lanzendorf/Haynie	'90/'93
COLONIAL SMALL STOCK;B	Small-Company Growth	1.3	15.78	9,981.00	☆	☆	0.0	426-3750	617-426-3750	None	1.00	5.00	Lanzendorf/Haynie	'92/'93
COLONIAL STRAT INC;A	Fixed Income	470.1	7.30	10,333.90	11,175.90	15,986.90	8.9	426-3750	617-426-3750	4.75	0.25	None	Carl C. Ericson	'91
COLONIAL STRAT INC;B	Fixed Income	97.8	7.30	10,315.10	11,110.30	☆	8.2	426-3750	617-426-3750	None	0.75	5.00	Carl C. Ericson	'92
COLONIAL US EQUITY INDEX	Growth & Income	49.8	21.90	10,068.40	11,250.60	18,050.60	2.1	426-3750	617-426-3750	5.75	0.25	None	Steve Lanzendorf	'88
COLONIAL US GRO;A	Capital Appreciation	41.5	11.82	10,250.80	☆	☆	0.0	426-3750	617-426-3750	5.75	0.25	None	State St Asset Mgt	'92
COLONIAL US GRO;B	Capital Appreciation	82.3	11.77	10,239.80	☆	☆	0.0	426-3750	617-426-3750	None	0.25	5.00	State St Asset Mgt	'92
COLONIAL US GOVT;A	Fixed Income	1,225.5	6.89	10,195.40	10,667.00	14,948.20	7.7	426-3750	617-426-3750	4.75	0.25	None	Leslie Finnemore	'87
COLONIAL US GOVT;B	Fixed Income	879.1	6.89	10,176.40	10,588.10	☆	6.9	426-3750	617-426-3750	None	1.00	5.00	Leslie Finnemore	'92
COLONIAL UTILITIES;A	Utility	387.2	14.27	10,245.20	11,971.10	19,558.90	4.8	426-3750	617-426-3750	4.75	0.25	None	Lennon/Haynie	'81/'93
COLONIAL UTILITIES;B	Utility	596.6	14.27	10,226.70	11,885.10	☆	4.1	426-3750	617-426-3750	None	1.00	5.00	Lennon/Haynie	'92/'93
COLUMBIA BALANCED	Balanced	129.1	17.92	10,118.60	11,518.30	☆	2.5	547-1707	503-222-3606	None	None	None	Mike Powers	'91
COLUMBIA COMMON STOCK	Growth & Income	78.8	15.19	10,146.40	11,906.40	☆	1.6	547-1707	503-222-3606	None	None	None	Terry Chambers	'91
COLUMBIA FIXED INCOME	Fixed Income	284.4	13.87	10,287.50	11,270.80	17,276.50	6.4	547-1707	503-222-3606	None	None	None	Tom Thomsen	'83
COLUMBIA GROWTH	Growth	565.6	27.34	10,073.70	12,313.60	19,540.40	0.7	547-1707	503-222-3606	None	None	None	Alec Macmillan	'92
COLUMBIA INTL STOCK	International	29.1	10.73	10,094.10	☆	☆	0.0	547-1707	503-222-3606	None	None	None	James McAlear	'92
COLUMBIA SPECIAL	Capital Appreciation	591.9	20.38	10,565.10	12,886.80	23,803.10	0.0	547-1707	503-222-3606	None	None	None	Alan Folkman	'85
COLUMBIA US GOVT SEC	Fixed Income	36.7	8.52	10,118.50	10,737.50	15,149.80	4.0	547-1707	503-222-3606	None	None	None	Tom Thomsen	'86
COMMON SENSE:GOVERNMENT	Fixed Income	336.4	11.75	10,225.40	11,066.50	16,516.50	6.8	544-5445	404-381-1000	6.75	None	None	Jack Reynoldson	'88

COMMON SENSE:GROWTH	Growth	1,935.5	15.81	10,025.40	11,703.20	19,014.80	0.7	544-5445	404-381-1000	8.50	None	None	Stephen Boyd	'89
COMMON SENSE:GRO & INC	Growth & Income	669.0	16.47	10,034.90	11,503.90	18,664.70	1.7	544-5445	404-381-1000	8.50	None	None	David Reichert	'90
COMMONWEALTH INV TR:GRO	Growth	9.5	20.20	10,057.00	11,285.90	16,582.90	1.4	359-5964	617-345-8200	None	None	None	Stephen J. Kaszynski	'90
COMPASS CAP:AGGRESS EQ	Small-Company Growth	19.4	12.16	9,987.80	12,001.40	☆	0.6	451-8371	215-254-1000	3.75	None	None	Bill Cevallos	'91
COMPASS CAP:EQU INCOME	Equity Income	219.0	12.34	10,195.80	11,331.90	☆	3.2	451-8371	215-254-1000	3.75	None	None	Frank Smith	'89
COMPASS CAP:FIX INCOME	Fixed Income	231.2	11.00	10,274.50	11,349.60	☆	6.1	451-8371	215-254-1000	3.75	None	None	Bill Cavallos	'89
COMPASS CAP:GROWTH	Growth	152.4	10.95	9,718.20	10,582.40	☆	1.0	451-8371	215-254-1000	3.75	None	None	John Lee	'89
COMPASS CAP:INTL EQ	International	15.7	11.70	10,540.50	10,863.60	☆	0.5	451-8371	215-254-1000	3.75	None	None	Sir William Vincent	'91
COMPASS CAP:INTL FIX INC	World Income	39.8	11.24	10,340.40	11,006.30	☆	2.6	451-8371	215-254-1000	3.75	None	None	Morgan Grenfell	'91
COMPASS CAP:SHT/INTMDT	Fixed Income	231.9	10.68	10,159.50	10,853.60	☆	5.9	451-8371	215-254-1000	3.75	None	None	Bill Cavallos	'89
COMPOSITE BOND & STOCK	Balanced	141.6	11.83	10,051.10	11,184.10	16,138.40	4.0	543-8072	509-353-3550	4.50	0.25	None	Randall Yoakum	'91
COMPOSITE GROWTH	Growth & Income	93.6	12.66	9,957.30	11,040.10	15,772.80	1.9	543-8072	509-353-3550	4.50	0.25	None	Randall Yoakum	'91
COMPOSITE INCOME	Fixed Income	91.3	9.33	10,255.10	11,183.50	15,891.60	6.7	543-8072	509-353-3550	4.00	0.20	None	Craig Hobbs	'89
COMPOSITE NRTHWST 50	Growth	182.7	14.37	9,713.20	10,849.70	19,975.70	0.5	543-8072	509-353-3550	4.50	0.25	None	Randall Yoakum	'91
COMPOSITE US GOVT SEC	Fixed Income	236.0	10.91	10,255.90	10,989.40	16,292.40	6.7	543-8072	509-353-3550	4.00	0.20	None	Gary Poker	'93
CMSTOCK PRTNRS STRAT;A	Fixed Income	27.1	9.26	10,321.00	☆	☆	0.0	534-6217	None	4.50	0.25	None	Team Managed	'92
CMSTOCK PRTNRS STRAT;O★	Fixed Income	541.3	9.27	10,329.20	10,696.90	15,531.90	8.6	334-6499	None	4.50	None	None	Team Managed	'88
CONCORD FUND★	Growth	1.1	0.00	N/A	N/A	N/A	0.0	None	617-784-4907	None	None	None	Gerald White	'85
CONCORDE VALUE	Growth & Income	13.5	12.78	10,063.00	11,482.40	12,276.10	1.1	338-1579	214-387-8258	None	None	None	Gary B. Wood	'87
CONESTOGA:EQUITY	Growth	40.3	14.62	10,010.20	11,276.60	☆	1.2	344-2716	None	4.00	None	None	Joe Stocke	'90
CONESTOGA:FIXED INCOME	Fixed Income	21.9	11.05	10,221.30	11,230.30	☆	6.5	344-2716	None	4.00	None	None	Dintino/Moyer	'90/'90
CONESTOGA:LTD MATURITY	Fixed Income	22.9	10.99	10,148.70	10,816.60	☆	5.9	344-2716	None	4.00	None	None	Craig Moyer	'90
CONN MUTUAL:GOVT ACCT	Fixed Income	73.0	11.63	10,317.20	11,107.60	16,662.40	6.1	322-2642	None	4.00	None	None	Steve Libera	'85
CONN MUTUAL:GROWTH ACCT	Growth	52.9	15.69	10,344.70	12,479.60	21,659.30	1.9	322-2642	None	5.00	None	None	Peter Antos	'89
CONN MUTUAL:INCOME ACCT	Fixed Income	43.0	9.94	10,180.60	10,833.30	15,361.50	7.1	322-2642	None	2.00	None	None	Steve Libera	'85
CONN MUTUAL:TOT RTN ACCT	Balanced	130.9	14.85	10,324.70	11,794.50	19,173.50	3.4	322-2642	None	5.00	None	None	Peter Antos	'89
COPLEY FUND★	Growth & Income	47.6	21.50	10,199.20	12,975.30	19,351.90	0.0	None	508-674-8459	None	None	None	Irving Levine	'78
COREFUND:EQUITY INDEX	Growth & Income	49.8	20.97	9,997.00	11,239.20	18,296.10	2.5	342-5734	215-254-1000	None	None	None	Larry Aasheim	'91
COREFUND:GROWTH EQ;A	Growth	66.0	9.95	9,779.70	11,476.00	☆	0.8	342-5734	215-254-1000	None	None	None	Tim Comers	'92
COREFUND:INTMDT BD;A	Fixed Income	42.9	10.18	10,147.00	10,788.90	☆	4.6	342-5734	215-254-1000	None	None	None	Martin Curie, Ltd.	'92
COREFUND:INTL GROWTH;A	International	61.1	11.71	10,568.60	11,205.60	☆	0.6	342-5734	215-254-1000	None	None	None	Martin Curie, Ltd.	'90
COREFUND:VALUE EQ;A	Growth & Income	14.9	13.11	10,169.30	11,831.00	☆	1.3	342-5734	215-254-1000	None	None	None	Roach/Fevell	'90/'90
CORNERSTONE:GROWTH	Capital Appreciation	3.7	7.60	10,039.60	10,998.60	10,955.40	0.0	527-9525	404-240-0666	None	None	None	Cornerstone Capital	'92
CORP ACCUM PROGRAM	Fixed Income	104.4	22.37	10,278.70	11,355.30	16,600.50	7.1	None	609-282-2800	None	None	None	Jay Harbeck	'92
COVENANT PORTFOLIO	Growth & Income	4.9	12.53	9,828.70	11,036.90	☆	1.0	833-4909	None	4.50	0.35	None	Carfang/Bune	'92/'92
COWEN OPPORTUNITY★	Small-Company Growth	15.3	14.83	10,676.70	13,638.80	21,499.70	0.0	262-7116	212-495-6000	4.85	None	None	William Church	'88
COWEN INCOME + GROWTH	Equity Income	34.9	12.97	10,085.50	11,369.30	17,893.80	3.7	262-7116	212-495-6000	4.85	None	None	William Rechter	'86
CRABBE HUSON ASST ALLOC	Flexible	71.6	12.84	10,354.60	11,722.30	☆	2.3	541-9732	503-295-0111	None	0.17	None	Richard Huson	'89
CRABBE HUSON EQUITY	Growth	22.4	14.87	10,405.90	12,375.30	☆	0.9	541-9732	503-295-0111	None	0.08	None	Richard Huson	'89
CRABBE HUSON GOVT INCOME	Fixed Income	12.1	11.01	10,134.70	10,790.80	☆	4.5	541-9732	503-295-0111	None	0.10	None	Jay Willoughby	'89
CRABBE HUSON INCOME	Fixed Income	5.2	10.66	10,096.40	10,853.20	☆	4.8	541-9732	503-295-0111	None	0.16	None	Jay Willoughby	'89
CRABBE HUSON SPECIAL	Small-Company Growth	14.0	10.71	10,132.50	13,660.70	22,086.60	0.0	541-9732	503-295-0111	None	0.06	None	James Crabbe	'87
CRESTFUNDS:BOND;TR	Fixed Income	42.7	10.27	10,273.60	☆	☆	0.0	None	804-782-7222	None	0.15	None	Boyce G. Reid	'92
CRESTFUNDS:CAP APP;TR	Growth	5.8	9.60	9,716.60	☆	☆	0.0	None	804-782-7222	None	0.15	None	David Halloran	'93
CRESTFUNDS:SH/INT;TR	Fixed Income	74.9	10.20	10,216.60	☆	☆	0.0	None	804-782-7222	None	0.15	None	Boyce G. Reid	'92

★CHESTNUT ST EXCH LP—Closed to new investors.
★CMSTOCK PRTNRS STRAT; O—Closed to new investors.
★CONCORD FUND—Closed to new investors.
★COPLEY FUND — On 12/8/92, net asset value increased $1.37 per share due to a decrease in tax reserves.

★COWEN OPPORTUNITY—Fund changed objective from Science & Technology to Small Company Growth on 3/3/93.

PERFORMANCE OF MUTUAL FUNDS (continued)

FUND NAME	OBJECTIVE	TOTAL NET ASSETS ($ MIL) 5/31/93	NET ASSET $ VALUE 6/30/93	PERFORMANCE (Return on Initial $10,000 Investment) 3/31/93-6/30/93	6/30/92-6/30/93	6/30/88-6/30/93	DIVIDEND YIELD % 6/93	PHONE NUMBER 800	In-State	FEES Load	12b-1	Redemption	MANAGER	SINCE
CRESTFUNDS:SPEC EQ;TR	Small-Company Growth	27.6	12.00	10,008.30	☆	☆	0.0	None	804-782-7222	None	0.15	None	Jeffery E. Markunas	'92
CRESTFUNDS:VALUE;TR	Growth & Income	144.6	11.09	10,163.90	☆	☆	0.0	None	804-782-7222	None	0.15	None	Jeffery E. Markunas	'92
CROWLEY:GROWTH	Growth	4.8	10.36	10,000.00	10,743.70	☆	1.6	None	302-529-1717	2.00	None	None	Robert A. Crowley	'89
CROWLEY:INCOME	Fixed Income	4.8	11.29	10,217.20	10,945.40	☆	5.4	None	302-529-1717	2.00	None	None	Robert A. Crowley	'89
CUFUND:ADJ RATE★	Fixed Income	167.8	10.01	10,107.00	10,400.90	☆	3.9	538-9683	215-989-6611	None	None	None	Southwest Corp.	'92
CUFUND:SHORT-TERM★	Fixed Income	20.2	10.02	10,094.00	10,466.10	☆	4.7	538-9683	215-989-6611	None	None	None	Southwest Corp.	'92
CUTLER TR:APPROVED LIST	Growth	2.3	10.09	10,064.70	☆	☆	0.0	228-8537	503-770-9000	None	None	None	Kenneth R. Cutler	'92
CUTLER TR:EQUITY INCOME	Equity Income	2.5	9.95	9,935.30	☆	☆	0.0	228-8537	503-770-9000	None	None	None	Kenneth R. Cutler	'92
CUTLER TR:GOVT SECS	Fixed Income	0.2	10.37	10,188.60	☆	☆	0.0	228-8537	503-770-9000	None	None	None	Kenneth R. Cutler	'92
DEAN WITTER AMER VALUE	Growth	698.5	22.86	10,475.90	12,827.30	22,782.10	0.1	869-3863	212-392-2550	None	1.00	5.00	Anita Kolleeny	'87
DEAN WITTER CAP GROWTH	Growth	902.4	13.00	9,272.50	9,855.60	☆	0.0	869-3863	212-392-2550	None	1.00	5.00	Paul Vance	'90
DEAN WITTER CONVERT	Convertible Securities	209.1	10.26	10,239.60	11,986.20	14,435.30	3.2	869-3863	212-392-2550	None	1.00	5.00	Laura Granger	'93
DEAN WITTER DEV GRO	Small-Company Growth	168.7	17.43	11,209.00	14,405.00	17,192.10	0.0	869-3863	212-392-2550	None	1.00	5.00	Ronald Worobel	'92
DEAN WITTER DIVID GRO	Growth & Income	5,818.2	29.79	10,286.20	11,450.30	19,241.20	2.3	869-3863	212-392-2550	None	1.00	5.00	Paul Vance	'81
DEAN WITTER DVSD INC	Fixed Income	105.7	10.29	10,266.40	11,032.50	☆	7.3	869-3863	212-392-2550	None	0.85	5.00	Gupta/Avelar/Tran	'92/'92
DEAN WITTER EQUITY INC	Equity Income	167.7	8.73	9,760.50	10,630.80	15,783.90	1.5	869-3863	212-392-2550	None	1.00	5.00	Kenton Hinchcliffe	'85
DEAN WITTER EURO GROW	European Region	325.7	10.13	10,719.60	10,486.50	☆	0.0	869-3863	212-392-2550	None	1.00	5.00	John Armitrage	'90
DEAN WITTER FED SEC	Fixed Income	1,135.9	9.94	10,322.80	11,197.50	16,402.40	6.7	869-3863	212-392-2550	None	0.85	5.00	Rajesh Gupta	'87
DEAN WITTER GLBL SH-TM	World Income	349.2	9.36	10,150.20	10,382.90	☆	6.6	869-3863	212-392-2550	None	0.75	3.00	Vihn Tran	'90
DEAN WITTER HEALTH SCI	Health/Biotechnology	228.2	9.33	10,823.70	☆	☆	0.0	869-3863	212-392-2550	None	1.00	5.00	Ronald Worobel	'92
DEAN WITTER HIGH YIELD	Fixed Income	511.0	7.44	10,674.50	12,060.40	13,067.10	14.5	869-3863	212-392-2550	5.50	None	None	Peter Avelar	'90
DEAN WITTER INTMDT INC	Fixed Income	239.0	10.15	10,227.80	10,905.80	☆	6.2	869-3863	212-392-2550	None	0.85	5.00	Rochelle Siegel	'89
DEAN WITTER MGD ASSETS	Flexible	241.4	10.87	10,198.00	11,050.10	15,645.00	2.2	869-3863	212-392-2550	None	1.00	5.00	Kenton Hinchcliffe	'88
DEAN WITTER NTRL RES	Natural Resources	132.0	11.87	10,318.80	11,788.90	15,593.10	1.3	869-3863	212-392-2550	None	1.00	5.00	Diane Lisa Sobin	'90
DEAN WITTER PACIFIC GR	Pacific Region	328.0	15.57	11,356.70	12,204.20	☆	0.0	869-3863	212-392-2550	None	1.00	5.00	Graham Bamping	'90
DEAN WITTER PREC MTLS	Gold	30.7	11.03	12,477.40	13,225.40	☆	0.0	869-3863	212-392-2550	None	1.00	5.00	Diane Lisa Sobin	'90
DEAN WITTER PREMIER INC	Fixed Income	131.7	9.49	10,061.60	10,331.50	☆	6.7	869-3863	212-392-2550	3.00	0.20	None	Scott Amero	'91
DW RET SRS:AMER VALUE★	Growth	0.5	10.10	9,872.90	☆	☆	0.0	869-3863	212-392-2550	None	None	None	Anita Kolleeny	'93
DW RET SRS:CAP GROWTH★	Growth	0.1	9.04	9,358.20	☆	☆	0.0	869-3863	212-392-2550	None	None	None	Paul Vance	'93
DW RET SRS:DIV GROWTH★	Growth & Income	1.8	10.64	10,038.50	☆	☆	0.0	869-3863	212-392-2550	None	None	None	Paul Vance	'93
DW RET SRS:GLOBAL EQUITY★	Global	0.2	10.07	10,039.90	☆	☆	0.0	869-3863	212-392-2550	None	None	None	Thomas Connelly	'93
DW RET SRS:INTMDT INC★	Fixed Income	0.2	10.02	10,167.70	☆	☆	0.0	869-3863	212-392-2550	None	None	None	Rochelle Siegel	'93
DW RET SRS:STRATEGIST★	Flexible	0.4	9.94	10,010.10	☆	☆	0.0	869-3863	212-392-2550	None	None	None	Mark Bavoso	'93
DW RET SRS:US GOVT SECS★	Fixed Income	1.5	10.07	10,122.00	☆	☆	0.0	869-3863	212-392-2550	None	None	None	Rajesh Gupta	'93
DW RET SRS:UTILITIES★	Utility	0.8	11.09	10,353.50	☆	☆	0.0	869-3863	212-392-2550	None	None	None	Edward Gaylor	'93
DW RET SRS:VALUE ADDED★	Growth & Income	0.3	10.01	10,070.20	☆	☆	0.0	869-3863	212-392-2550	None	None	None	Kenton Hinchcliffe	'93
DEAN WITTER SH-TM TREAS	Fixed Income	584.2	10.37	10,106.40	10,634.60	☆	5.2	869-3863	212-392-2550	None	0.35	None	Rajesh Gupta	'91
DEAN WITTER STRATEGIST	Flexible	753.2	14.72	10,031.30	11,221.50	☆	2.1	869-3863	212-392-2550	None	1.00	5.00	Mark Bavoso	'88
DEAN WITTER US GOVT	Fixed Income	12,524.1	9.47	10,228.80	10,924.70	15,292.30	7.3	869-3863	212-392-2550	None	0.75	5.00	Rajesh Gupta	'92
DEAN WITTER UTILITIES	Utility	3,510.2	14.59	10,336.10	12,103.30	18,636.50	4.1	869-3863	212-392-2550	None	1.00	5.00	Edward Gaylor	'88
DEAN WITTER VAL-ADD:EQ	Growth & Income	305.0	19.17	10,084.40	11,850.30	17,401.20	0.7	869-3863	212-392-2550	None	1.00	5.00	Kenton Hinchcliffe	'93
DEAN WITTER WRLDWD INC	World Income	289.8	9.24	10,187.30	10,739.30	☆	6.3	869-3863	212-392-2550	None	0.85	5.00	Vihn Tran	'89
DEAN WITTER WRLDWD INV	Global	230.6	15.87	10,781.30	10,967.30	14,261.90	0.0	869-3863	212-392-2550	None	1.00	5.00	Thomas Connelly	'83
DELAWARE DECATUR I	Equity Income	1,546.8	17.64	10,142.40	11,582.60	16,065.90	3.9	523-4640	215-988-1333	8.50	None	None	John Fields	'93
DELAWARE DECATUR II	Equity Income	438.2	13.99	10,114.90	11,513.20	17,645.10	3.1	523-4640	215-988-1333	5.75	0.30	None	J.B. Fields	'91

DELAWARE DELCAP;RET	Capital Appreciation	1,131.9	23.95	10,376.90	11,981.00	18,266.50	0.0	523-4640	215-988-1333	5.75	0.30	None	Edward N. Antoian	'86
DELAWARE DELCHESTER;RET	Fixed Income	898.5	7.07	10,381.50	11,551.60	17,011.20	10.9	523-4640	215-988-1333	4.75	0.30	None	Matlack/Nichols	'92/'92
DELAWARE FUND;RET	Balanced	538.6	18.96	10,005.20	11,411.70	18,936.40	3.4	523-4640	215-988-1333	5.75	0.30	None	Burwell/Dutton	'92/'92
DELAWARE INTL EQ;RET	International	20.8	10.53	10,173.40	10,564.10	☆	4.2	523-4640	215-988-1333	5.75	0.30	None	Clive A. Gillmore	'91
DELAWARE TREAS RSVS;RET	Fixed Income	1,051.6	10.06	10,130.60	10,709.60	15,289.00	7.0	523-4640	215-988-1333	3.00	0.15	None	David A. Rosenberg	'90
DELAWARE TREND;RET	Capital Appreciation	223.9	13.98	10,401.80	13,524.50	26,501.90	0.0	523-4640	215-988-1333	5.75	0.30	None	Edward N. Antoian	'84
DELAWARE US GOVT;RET	Fixed Income	217.5	9.05	10,254.50	11,020.20	15,997.50	8.5	523-4640	215-988-1333	4.75	0.30	None	Dutton/Taravella	'36/'92
DELAWARE VALUE;RET	Capital Appreciation	102.7	19.01	9,932.10	12,500.20	22,062.30	0.2	523-4640	215-988-1333	5.75	0.30	None	Edward Trumpbour	'87
DEPOSITORS BOSTON★	Growth	61.3	84.69	9,762.20	10,792.30	16,898.00	1.2	225-6265	617-482-8260	None	None	None	Thomas E. Faust, Jr.	'91
DFA GRP:CONTL SMALL CO★	European Region	234.0	11.70	9,906.90	8,599.60	13,825.80	2.7	None	310-395-8005	None	None	None	Dimensional Fund Adv	'88
DFA GRP:DFA/AEW RE SECS★	Real Estate	16.0	10.66	9,888.70	☆	☆	0.0	None	310-395-8005	None	None	None	Scott Thornton	'93
DFA GRP:5 YEAR GOVT★	Fixed Income	131.0	107.58	10,201.00	11,050.40	16,163.80	4.6	None	310-395-8005	None	None	None	Dimensional Fund Adv	'87
DFA GRP:GLOBAL FIXED INC★	World Income	76.0	104.96	10,190.10	10,970.30	☆	3.9	None	310-395-8005	None	None	None	Dimensional Fund Adv	'90
DFA GRP:INTMDT GOVT★	Fixed Income	49.0	116.94	10,305.70	11,448.20	☆	5.9	None	310-395-8005	None	None	None	Dimensional Fund Adv	'90
DFA GRP:JAPAN SMALL CO★	Japanese	274.0	27.38	12,565.40	14,642.80	11,387.00	0.1	None	310-395-8005	None	None	None	Dimensional Fund Adv	'86
DFA GRP:LARGE CAP INTL★	International	54.0	11.33	10,739.30	11,669.60	☆	0.9	None	310-395-8005	None	None	None	Dimensional Fund Adv	'91
DFA GRP:LARGE CAP VALUE★	Growth	53.0	10.52	10,283.50	☆	☆	0.0	None	310-395-8005	None	None	None	Robert Degre	'93
DFA GRP:PAC RIM SMALL CO★	Pacific Region	100.0	13.20	11,548.60	☆	☆	0.0	None	310-395-8005	None	None	None	David Price	'93
DFA GRP:SMALL CAP VALUE★	Small-Company Growth	59.0	9.97	10,050.40	☆	☆	0.0	None	310-395-8005	None	None	None	Robert Degre	'93
DFA GRP:US LARGE CO★	Growth	31.0	13.58	10,030.40	11,290.90	☆	1.8	None	310-395-8005	None	None	None	Dimensional Fund Adv	'90
DFA GRP:1 YEAR FIXED INC★	Fixed Income	578.0	102.74	10,096.90	10,494.30	14,505.30	4.0	None	310-395-8005	None	None	None	Dimensional Fund Adv	'83
DFA GRP:UK SMALL COMPANY★	European Region	174.0	20.94	10,629.40	9,537.50	10,385.50	3.0	None	310-395-8005	None	None	None	Dimensional Fund Adv	'86
DFA GRP:US 6-10 SMALL CO★	Small-Company Growth	166.0	11.02	10,036.40	12,877.00	☆	0.5	None	310-395-8005	None	None	None	Dimensional Fund Adv	'92
DFA GRP:US 9-10 SMALL CO★	Small-Company Growth	599.0	7.83	9,987.20	12,690.70	16,013.20	0.5	None	310-395-8005	None	None	None	Dimensional Fund Adv	'81
DG INV:EQUITY	Growth	240.3	10.29	9,755.20	☆	☆	0.0	344-2488	None	2.00	0.35	None	Ron Lindquist	'92
DG INV:GOVT INCOME	Fixed Income	82.0	10.17	10,241.80	☆	☆	0.0	344-2488	None	2.00	0.35	None	John Mark McKenzie	'93
DG INV:LTD TM GOVT INC	Fixed Income	116.7	10.06	10,126.80	☆	☆	0.0	344-2488	None	2.00	0.35	None	John Mark McKenzie	'93
DIAZ-VERSON:AMERICAS EQ	Global	N/A	9.50	9,490.50	☆	☆	0.0	662-8417	212-309-8400	4.50	0.50	None	Salvador Diaz-Verson	'93
DIVERSIFICATION FUND★	Growth	79.2	168.39	9,901.30	11,343.60	16,632.90	1.1	225-6265	617-482-8260	None	None	None	Robert S. Goodof	'87
DODGE & COX BALANCED	Balanced	361.0	46.23	10,416.50	11,821.50	18,728.70	3.8	None	415-434-0311	None	None	None	Team Managed	'31
DODGE & COX INCOME	Fixed Income	148.6	12.08	10,320.90	11,330.40	☆	6.8	None	415-434-0311	None	None	None	Team Managed	'89
DODGE & COX STOCK	Growth & Income	397.0	53.57	10,483.80	12,191.60	18,416.10	2.0	None	415-434-0311	None	None	None	Team Managed	'65
DOMINI INDEX:SOC INDEX	Growth	16.3	12.01	9,841.90	11,531.70	☆	1.2	762-6814	None	None	0.25	None	Amy Domini	'91
DREMAN:CONTRARIAN PORT	Growth & Income	15.8	13.39	10,022.50	11,406.40	17,378.70	1.8	533-1608	201-332-8228	None	None	None	David N. Dreman	'88
DREMAN:FIXED INCOME PORT	Fixed Income	4.2	10.17	10,128.10	10,676.20	15,022.30	5.8	533-1608	201-332-8228	None	None	None	David N. Dreman	'88
DREMAN:HIGH RETURN PORT	Equity Income	25.6	15.22	10,033.00	11,897.10	21,140.90	1.7	533-1608	201-332-8228	None	None	None	David N. Dreman	'88
DREMAN:SMALL CAP VALUE	Small-Company Growth	5.3	11.30	9,800.80	11,597.80	☆	0.5	533-1608	201-332-8228	None	None	None	Homes/Dreman	'92/'92
DREYFUS A BONDS PLUS	Fixed Income	590.1	15.63	10,303.70	11,605.20	17,501.90	6.6	373-9387	516-338-3300	None	None	None	Barbara Kenworthy	'85
DREYFUS APPRECIATION★	Growth	240.7	14.33	9,822.40	10,274.10	16,709.40	1.1	373-9387	516-338-3300	None	0.20	None	Fayez Sarofim & Co.	'90
DREYFUS BALANCED	Balanced	39.3	13.09	10,115.90	☆	☆	0.0	373-9387	516-338-3300	None	None	None	Dreyfus Mgt. Inc.	'92
DREYFUS CAPITAL GROWTH	Capital Appreciation	576.7	17.70	9,955.00	11,093.80	17,369.90	1.3	373-9387	516-338-3300	3.00	None	None	Howard Stein	'69
DREYFUS CAP VALUE;A	Capital Appreciation	440.8	11.87	10,551.10	9,953.30	13,621.40	5.1	373-9387	516-338-3300	4.50	None	None	Comstock Partners	'87
DREYFUS CONVERTIBLE SEC	Convertible Securities	197.7	8.39	9,871.20	10,599.60	13,686.10	3.7	373-9387	516-338-3300	None	None	None	Catherine Jacobson	'90
DREYFUS EDISON ELEC INDX	Utility	86.6	14.61	10,209.70	12,025.20	☆	4.4	373-9387	516-338-3300	None	None	None	Wells Fargo Nikko Adv.	'91
DREYFUS FUND	Growth & Income	2,921.9	12.98	9,767.20	10,998.20	16,299.00	1.8	373-9387	516-338-3300	None	None	None	Wolodymyr Wronskyj	'86

★CUFUNDS—Institutional funds.
★DW RET SRS FUNDS—Designed primarily for retirement accounts.
★DEPOSITORS BOSTON—Closed to new investors.

★DFA GROUP—Institutional funds.
★DIVERSIFICATION FUND—Closed to new investors.
★DREYFUS: APPRECIATION—On 5/24/93, fund was reclassified from Capital Appreciation to Growth.

PERFORMANCE OF MUTUAL FUNDS *(continued)*

FUND NAME	OBJECTIVE	TOTAL NET ASSETS ($ MIL) 5/31/93	NET ASSET $ VALUE 6/30/93	PERFORMANCE (Return on Initial $10,000 Investment) 3/31/93-6/30/93	6/30/92-6/30/93	6/30/88-6/30/93	DIVIDEND YIELD % 6/93	PHONE NUMBER 800	In-State	FEES Load	12b-1	Redemption	MANAGER	SINCE
DREYFUS GLBL INVEST;A	Global	58.4	14.41	10,292.90	10,745.50	☆	0.6	373-9387	516-338-3300	4.50	0.25	None	Fiona Biggs	'92
DREYFUS GNMA	Fixed Income	1,862.4	15.44	10,201.90	10,960.20	15,844.60	7.1	373-9387	516-338-3300	None	0.20	None	Garitt Kono	'93
DREYFUS GROWTH & INCOME	Growth & Income	649.8	15.49	10,042.30	11,858.00	☆	1.9	373-9387	516-338-3300	None	None	None	Richard Hoey	'92
DREYFUS GRO OPPORTUNITY	Growth	533.5	12.58	10,194.50	10,853.10	15,258.10	0.1	373-9387	516-338-3300	None	None	None	Richard C. Shields	'90
DREYFUS INVSTRS GNMA LP	Fixed Income	53.6	15.60	10,232.50	11,121.20	15,607.30	7.3	373-9387	516-338-3300	None	None	None	Garitt Kono	'93
DREYFUS NEW LEADERS	Small-Company Growth	272.3	33.81	10,026.70	12,046.50	18,914.60	0.4	373-9387	516-338-3300	None	0.25	1.00	Thomas Frank	'85
DREYFUS 100% TREA INT LP	Fixed Income	252.3	13.77	10,309.00	11,408.50	16,714.50	7.0	373-9387	516-338-3300	None	None	None	Barbara Kenworthy	'87
DREYFUS 100% TREA LNG LP	Fixed Income	223.9	15.53	10,537.10	11,962.90	18,380.50	6.8	373-9387	516-338-3300	None	None	None	Barbara Kenworthy	'87
DREYFUS 100% TREA SHT LP	Fixed Income	182.7	16.04	10,140.40	10,881.80	15,760.10	8.0	373-9387	516-338-3300	None	None	None	Barbara Kenworthy	'87
DREYFUS PREM GNMA;A	Fixed Income	185.8	15.29	10,206.00	11,032.50	16,780.90	6.7	373-9387	516-338-3300	4.50	None	None	Garitt Kono	'93
DREYFUS SHT-INTMDT GOVT	Fixed Income	418.6	11.59	10,161.90	10,921.10	15,956.20	6.7	373-9387	516-338-3300	None	None	None	Barbara Kenworthy	'87
DREYFUS SHT-TERM INCOME	Fixed Income	151.7	12.48	10,200.00	☆	☆	0.0	373-9387	516-338-3300	None	0.20	None	Barbara Kenworthy	'92
DREYFUS STRAT GROWTH LP	Flexible	41.6	32.87	10,192.20	10,214.40	12,705.80	0.0	373-9387	516-338-3300	3.00	0.25	None	Howard Stein	'88
DREYFUS STRAT INCOME	Fixed Income	270.4	14.91	10,318.90	11,578.10	17,861.50	6.8	373-9387	516-338-3300	3.00	0.25	None	Barbara Kenworthy	'86
DREYFUS STRAT INVEST;A	Flexible	262.8	21.90	10,148.30	11,360.30	18,503.00	0.2	373-9387	516-338-3300	4.50	None	None	Richard C. Shields	'90
DREYFUS STRAT WLD INV LP	Global Flexible	137.8	31.10	10,264.00	10,190.00	16,257.20	0.0	373-9387	516-338-3300	3.00	0.25	None	Fiona Biggs	'88
DREYFUS THIRD CENTURY	Growth	526.3	8.47	9,906.40	11,250.90	18,384.50	0.5	373-9387	516-338-3300	None	None	None	Tiffany Capital Advisors	'90
DREY-WILSH:LG CO GRO	Growth	8.2	12.65	9,641.80	☆	☆	0.0	373-9387	516-338-3300	None	None	1.00	Wilshire Associates Inc.	'92
DREY-WILSH:LG CO VAL	Growth	6.6	14.49	10,211.40	☆	☆	0.0	373-9387	516-338-3300	None	None	1.00	Wilshire Associates Inc.	'92
DREY-WILSH:SM CO GRO	Small-Company Growth	7.2	15.29	10,324.10	☆	☆	0.0	373-9387	516-338-3300	None	None	1.00	Wilshire Associates Inc.	'92
DREY-WILSH:SM CO VAL	Small-Company Growth	6.4	14.28	9,814.40	☆	☆	0.0	373-9387	516-338-3300	None	None	1.00	Wilshire Associates Inc.	'92
DUPREE:INTMDT GOVT BOND	Fixed Income	5.3	10.60	10,243.60	☆	☆	0.0	866-0614	606-254-7741	None	None	None	Bill Griggs	'92
EAGLE GROWTH SHARES	Growth	2.9	12.62	9,546.10	10,611.90	17,369.70	0.0	749-9933	407-395-2155	8.50	None	None	Donald Baxter	'87
EATON VANCE CHINA GRO★	Pacific Region	N/A	11.60	10,681.40	☆	☆	0.0	225-6265	617-482-8260	4.75	None	1.00	Robert Lloyd George, Mgt	'92
EATON VANCE EQUITY-INC	Equity Income	46.6	11.61	10,063.10	11,250.10	15,763.30	4.0	225-6265	617-482-8260	None	1.00	6.00	Bragdon/Martin	'87/'90
EATON VANCE GOVT:OBLIG	Fixed Income	512.1	11.65	10,186.60	11,063.60	16,218.60	8.2	225-6265	617-482-8260	4.75	0.25	None	Mark S. Venezia	'84
EATON VANCE GOVT:SH TREA★	Fixed Income	N/A	54.95	10,060.40	10,265.30	☆	0.0	225-6265	617-482-8260	None	0.25	None	Michael Terry	'91
EATON VANCE GROWTH	Growth	142.1	7.72	9,449.20	10,505.40	16,615.50	0.0	225-6265	617-482-8260	4.75	0.25	None	Peter Kiely	'90
EATON VANCE HIGH INC	Fixed Income	350.4	7.59	10,429.10	11,425.60	15,847.70	10.9	225-6265	617-482-8260	None	1.00	6.00	Hooker Talcott Jr.	'86
EATON VANCE INC OF BOSTN	Fixed Income	91.5	8.52	10,458.60	11,538.60	17,342.40	11.0	225-6265	617-482-8260	4.75	0.25	None	Hooker Talcott Jr.	'86
EATON VANCE INVESTORS	Balanced	212.7	7.38	10,131.60	11,096.40	16,924.60	4.4	225-6265	617-482-8260	4.75	0.25	None	M. Dozier Gardner	'87
EATON VANCE NTRL RES	Natural Resources	5.0	13.81	10,797.50	11,507.90	14,180.90	0.1	225-6265	617-482-8260	None	1.00	6.00	Thomas E. Faust, Jr.	'90
EATON VANCE SH-TM GLBL	World Income	412.8	9.28	10,215.20	10,105.30	☆	6.6	225-6265	617-482-8260	None	1.00	3.00	Mark S. Venezia	'90
EATON VANCE SPL EQUITIES	Growth	81.3	8.51	9,792.90	11,246.70	19,164.30	0.0	225-6265	617-482-8260	4.75	0.25	None	Clifford Krauss	'87
EATON VANCE STOCK	Growth & Income	88.5	13.25	9,800.30	10,765.40	17,420.10	2.1	225-6265	617-482-8260	4.75	0.25	None	A. Walker Martin	'90
EATON VANCE TOTAL RETURN	Utility	612.0	10.28	10,179.20	12,269.80	20,423.00	4.8	225-6265	617-482-8260	4.75	0.25	None	Edwin W. Bragdon	'81
EBI EQUITY	Growth & Income	93.1	64.69	9,914.20	10,804.50	17,127.90	0.7	972-9030	404-892-0666	None	1.00	5.00	Michael Harhai	'93
EBI INCOME	Fixed Income	49.8	49.00	10,180.80	10,913.70	14,559.10	4.7	972-9030	404-892-0666	None	1.00	5.00	James Baker	'93
EBI FLEX	Flexible	226.9	52.94	10,105.00	11,067.00	16,447.90	2.2	972-9030	404-892-0666	None	1.00	5.00	Edward Mitchell	'88
ECLIPSE:BALANCED	Balanced	17.5	19.08	10,322.00	12,190.80	☆	3.9	872-2710	404-631-0414	None	None	None	Wesley G. McCain	'89
ECLIPSE:EQUITY	Small-Company Growth	173.5	13.84	9,964.00	12,614.70	17,059.40	0.9	872-2710	404-631-0414	None	None	None	Wesley G. McCain	'87
EHRENKRANTZ:GROWTH	Growth	6.2	5.49	9,909.70	10,911.70	14,754.90	0.6	424-8570	212-872-1717	4.50	0.25	None	Jeffrey King	'87
ELFUN:DIVERSIFIED★	Balanced	46.9	14.02	10,050.20	11,226.10	17,722.60	3.2	242-0134	203-326-4040	None	None	None	MacDougall/Carlson	'88/'88
ELFUN:GLOBAL★	Global	51.8	13.99	10,167.20	10,849.20	16,539.80	1.2	242-0134	203-326-4040	None	None	None	Ralph R. Layman	'88
ELFUN:INCOME★	Fixed Income	188.9	12.00	10,264.90	11,130.40	16,849.30	6.7	242-0134	203-326-4040	None	None	None	Robert A. MacDougall	'84

ELFUN:TRUSTS★	Growth	902.5	34.41	9,942.20	11,149.90	19,888.50	2.4	242-0134	203-326-4040	None	None	None	David Carlson	'88
ELITE GROUP:GROWTH & INC	Growth & Income	16.7	14.06	10,122.20	11,470.60	18,665.90	0.8	423-1068	206-624-5863	None	None	None	Richard McCormick	'87
ELITE GROUP:INCOME	Fixed Income	10.9	10.41	10,242.70	11,130.30	15,347.10	4.4	423-1068	206-624-5863	None	None	None	William Church	'93
EMERALD:EQUITY	Growth & Income	151.4	11.70	9,743.40	11,054.30	☆	1.3	637-6336	None	4.50	0.25	None	Murad Antia	'91
EMERALD:US GOVT SEC	Fixed Income	121.9	10.84	10,262.50	11,102.30	☆	6.8	637-6336	None	4.50	0.25	None	Andrew Cantor	'91
ENDOWMENTS INC★	Growth & Income	71.4	18.22	10,051.90	11,293.80	18,452.60	3.7	421-0180	210-530-4000	None	None	None	Multiple Managers	'75
ENTERPRISE:CAPITAL APPR	Capital Appreciation	91.8	29.19	10,069.00	11,318.30	22,965.10	0.0	432-4320	404-396-8118	4.75	0.45	None	Jeff Miller	'87
ENTERPRISE:GOVT SEC	Fixed Income	90.3	12.68	10,205.30	11,147.50	16,018.40	7.7	432-4320	404-396-8118	4.75	0.45	None	Barach/Gundlach	'92/'92
ENTERPRISE:GROWTH	Growth	84.4	7.67	9,770.70	11,080.40	16,847.60	0.0	432-4320	404-396-8118	4.75	0.45	None	Ron Canakaris	'80
ENTERPRISE:GROWTH & INC	Growth & Income	45.3	18.08	10,166.80	11,393.60	16,159.00	2.9	432-4320	404-396-8118	4.75	0.45	None	Rock/Domino	'87/'90
ENTERPRISE:HIGH YLD BOND	Fixed Income	34.3	11.50	10,393.90	11,761.00	15,760.70	8.5	432-4320	404-396-8118	4.75	0.45	None	Jim Caywood	'87
ENTERPRISE:INTL GROWTH	International	13.9	14.73	10,528.90	10,505.00	13,522.30	0.2	432-4320	404-396-8118	4.75	0.45	None	Thomas Maier	'92
EQUITABLE:AGGR GRO;A	Small-Company Growth	2.6	10.99	10,587.70	11,754.00	☆	0.0	852-6860	516-242-4815	5.25	0.25	None	John Callaghan	'92
EQUITABLE:AGGR GRO;B	Small-Company Growth	3.8	10.88	10,563.10	11,648.80	☆	0.0	852-6860	516-242-4815	None	1.00	5.00	John Callaghan	'92
EQUITABLE:BALANCED;A	Balanced	8.6	17.41	10,069.40	11,174.10	☆	2.4	852-6860	516-242-4815	5.25	0.25	None	Judith Taylor	'90
EQUITABLE:BALANCED;B	Balanced	35.9	15.29	10,052.60	11,085.10	18,489.10	1.5	852-6860	516-242-4815	None	1.00	5.00	Judith Taylor	'87
EQUITABLE:CONSV INV;A	Flexible	5.6	10.97	10,255.30	11,271.70	☆	3.5	852-6860	516-242-4815	5.25	0.25	None	Franklin Kennedy III	'92
EQUITABLE:CONSV INV;B	Flexible	10.7	11.07	10,229.00	11,182.20	☆	2.3	852-6860	516-242-4815	None	1.00	5.00	Franklin Kennedy III	'92
EQUITABLE:GOVT SEC;A	Fixed Income	6.3	10.21	10,235.00	10,976.00	☆	5.3	852-6860	516-242-4815	5.25	0.25	None	Johnathan Lieber	'91
EQUITABLE:GOVT SEC;B	Fixed Income	22.2	10.00	10,218.60	10,889.60	14,839.30	4.6	852-6860	516-242-4815	None	1.00	5.00	Johnathan Lieber	'91
EQUITABLE:GROWTH;A	Growth	15.1	24.04	10,548.50	12,860.50	☆	0.6	852-6860	516-242-4815	5.25	0.25	None	Tyler Smith	'90
EQUITABLE:GROWTH;B	Growth	59.6	20.84	10,541.20	12,779.80	23,528.40	0.1	852-6860	516-242-4815	None	1.00	5.00	Tyler Smith	'87
EQUITABLE:GR & INC;A	Growth & Income	13.3	15.29	10,459.80	11,876.80	☆	2.3	852-6860	516-242-4815	5.25	0.25	None	Kennedy/Kuck	'91/'90
EQUITABLE:GR & INC;B	Growth & Income	27.8	15.42	10,436.30	11,784.30	☆	1.5	852-6860	516-242-4815	None	1.00	5.00	Kennedy/Kuck	'91/'90
EQUITABLE:GROWTH INV;A	Flexible	3.9	11.80	10,225.30	12,105.80	☆	1.3	852-6860	516-242-4815	5.25	0.25	None	Franklin Kennedy III	'92
EQUITABLE:GROWTH INV;B	Flexible	9.3	11.86	10,215.30	12,014.00	☆	0.4	852-6860	516-242-4815	None	1.00	5.00	Franklin Kennedy III	'92
EQUITABLE:SH-TM GOVT;A	Fixed Income	6.0	10.21	10,176.30	10,688.30	☆	4.5	852-6860	516-242-4815	3.00	0.25	None	Johnathan Lieber	'92
EQUITABLE:SH-TM GOVT;B	Fixed Income	1.4	10.30	10,146.20	10,610.40	☆	3.7	852-6860	516-242-4815	None	1.00	5.00	Johnathan Lieber	'92
EQUITABLE:SH-TM WRLD;A	World Income	10.7	8.56	10,176.70	10,056.90	☆	5.9	852-6860	516-242-4815	3.00	0.25	None	Paul Larsen	'91
EQUITABLE:SH-TM WRLD;B	World Income	7.5	8.59	10,153.10	9,978.20	☆	4.9	852-6860	516-242-4815	None	1.00	5.00	Paul Larsen	'91
EQUITY STRATEGIES★	Specialty	93.7	43.42	12,629.40	13,430.30	26,294.00	0.0	443-1021	212-888-6685	None	None	None	Martin J. Whitman	'86
EUROPACIFIC GROWTH	International	3,468.2	18.20	10,353.80	10,719.10	17,979.50	1.6	421-0180	210-530-4000	5.75	0.25	None	Multiple Managers	'84
EVERGREEN AMERICAN RET	Balanced	27.8	11.64	10,241.70	11,620.40	16,745.80	5.2	235-0064	914-694-2020	None	None	None	Irene O'Neill	'88
EVERGREEN FOUNDATION	Balanced	121.9	12.85	10,158.10	12,103.70	☆	2.7	235-0064	914-694-2020	None	None	None	Stephen Lieber	'90
EVERGREEN FUND	Growth	731.8	14.00	9,859.20	11,205.50	15,404.70	0.5	235-0064	914-694-2020	None	None	None	Stephen Lieber	'71
EVERGREEN GLBL REAL EST	Real Estate	22.7	11.79	10,526.80	13,772.90	☆	0.0	235-0064	914-694-2020	None	None	None	Sam Lieber	'89
EVERGREEN LIMITED MKT	Small-Company Growth	80.6	20.83	9,679.40	11,604.30	18,385.30	0.0	235-0064	914-694-2020	None	None	None	Lieber/Kelly	'83/'83
EVERGREEN TOTAL RETURN	Equity Income	1,134.4	20.44	10,084.60	11,750.40	16,306.10	6.5	235-0064	914-694-2020	None	None	None	Nola M. Falcone	'78
EVERGREEN VALUE TIMING	Capital Appreciation	68.9	15.10	10,086.80	12,094.80	19,078.30	1.5	235-0064	914-694-2020	None	None	None	Edmund Nicklin	'86
EXCEL MIDAS GOLD SHARES	Gold	7.2	3.99	13,664.40	16,142.00	13,955.50	0.4	783-3444	619-485-9400	4.50	0.25	None	Kgeld Thygesen	'92
EXCEL VALUE	Growth	1.0	4.74	9,753.10	10,085.10	9,251.00	0.0	783-3444	619-485-9400	4.50	0.25	None	Jack Heilbron	'91
EXCHANGE BOSTON★	Growth	68.0	196.10	9,684.30	10,710.40	15,542.50	1.4	225-6265	617-482-8260	None	None	None	Thomas E. Faust Jr.	'91
EXECUTIVE INV:BLUE CHIP	Growth & Income	0.8	14.10	9,929.60	11,073.90	☆	1.8	423-4026	None	4.75	0.50	None	Denise Burns	'90
EXECUTIVE INV:HIGH YIELD	Fixed Income	11.4	7.81	10,419.70	11,614.70	15,785.50	9.7	423-4026	None	4.75	0.50	None	George Ganter	'89
EXETER EQUITY TRUST	Growth	18.4	11.42	9,811.30	10,732.10	☆	0.9	525-3863	919-972-9922	4.75	0.25	None	Branch Cabell & Co	'91

★EATON VANCE CHINA GRO and EATON VANCE GOVT: SH TREA-Fund does not disclose total net assets.

★ELFUN FUNDS—Limited to select Elfun Society members.

★ENDOWMENTS INC—Limited to certain tax-exempt institutions.

★EQUITY STRATEGIES—Closed to new investors.

★EXCHANGE BOSTON—Closed to new investors.

PERFORMANCE OF MUTUAL FUNDS (continued)

FUND NAME	OBJECTIVE	TOTAL NET ASSETS ($ MIL) 5/31/93	NET ASSET $ VALUE 6/30/93	PERFORMANCE (Return on Initial $10,000 Investment) 3/31/93-6/30/93	6/30/92-6/30/93	6/30/88-6/30/93	DIVIDEND YIELD % 6/93	PHONE NUMBER 800	In-State	FEES Load	12b-1	Redemption	MANAGER	SINCE
EXETER FIXED INC TRUST	Fixed Income	1.8	10.34	10,224.60	☆	☆	0.0	525-3863	919-972-9922	3.75	None	None	Branch Cabell & Co	'92
FAHNESTOCK:HUD CAP APPRE	Growth	17.2	12.29	9,887.40	11,666.50	☆	0.0	221-5588	None	5.50	0.50	None	Howard Shawn	'91
FAIRMONT FUND	Capital Appreciation	17.0	20.02	9,920.70	10,839.20	12,383.10	0.0	262-9936	502-636-5633	None	None	None	Morton H. Sachs	'81
FAM VALUE	Growth & Income	172.5	20.09	9,738.20	11,469.70	22,459.50	1.6	932-3271	518-234-4393	None	None	None	Thomas Putnam	'87
FASCIANO FUND	Small-Company Growth	14.6	17.74	10,266.20	11,175.50	☆	0.0	848-6050	312-444-6050	None	None	None	Michael Fasciano	'88
FBL SERIES:BLUE CHIP	Growth & Income	5.3	17.70	10,062.50	10,926.90	17,723.40	0.7	247-4170	515-225-5586	None	0.50	5.00	Roger Grefe	'87
FBL SERIES:GRO COM STK	Growth & Income	49.7	14.71	10,848.10	12,738.80	18,599.40	4.1	247-4170	515-225-5586	None	0.50	5.00	Roger Grefe	'86
FBL SERIES:HI GRADE BD	Fixed Income	8.0	10.69	10,208.00	10,934.60	15,778.80	6.5	247-4170	515-225-5586	None	0.50	5.00	Bob Rummelhart	'90
FBL SERIES:HI YLD BD	Fixed Income	5.8	10.75	10,320.80	11,365.40	17,457.80	7.5	247-4170	515-225-5586	None	0.50	5.00	Bob Rummelhart	'87
FBL SERIES:MANAGED	Flexible	6.5	12.39	10,500.30	12,475.20	17,127.40	4.9	247-4170	515-225-5586	None	0.50	5.00	LouAnn Sandburg	'87
FBP CONTRARIAN	Balanced	17.8	12.11	10,074.40	11,159.20	☆	2.8	525-3863	919-972-9922	None	None	None	Flippin Bruce & Porter	'89
FEDERATED ARMS;INSTL	Fixed Income	2,180.5	9.96	10,123.70	10,509.10	15,563.90	5.3	245-4770	412-288-1900	None	None	None	Gary Madich	'87
FEDERATED ARMS;INT SV	Fixed Income	347.6	9.96	10,117.40	10,475.20	☆	5.0	245-4770	412-288-1900	None	0.25	None	Gary Madich	'92
FEDERATED BOND	Fixed Income	51.6	10.72	10,362.00	11,716.10	17,045.70	5.6	245-4770	412-288-1900	None	None	None	Charles A. Ritter	'89
FEDERATED EXCHANGE	Growth	90.9	70.61	10,153.20	11,761.70	17,558.60	1.9	245-4770	412-288-1900	None	None	None	Peter R. Anderson	'89
FEDERATED GNMA;INSTL	Fixed Income	1,920.7	11.83	10,195.80	10,891.60	16,791.80	7.7	245-4770	412-288-1900	None	None	None	Gary Madich	'87
FEDERATED GNMA;INT SV	Fixed Income	116.2	11.83	10,189.50	10,864.60	☆	7.4	245-4770	412-288-1900	None	0.25	None	Gary Madich	'92
FEDERATED GROWTH TRUST	Growth	448.1	22.99	10,074.90	10,850.20	18,156.30	1.1	245-4770	412-288-1900	None	None	None	Gregory M. Melvin	'87
FEDERATED HIGH YIELD TR	Fixed Income	418.3	9.33	10,382.70	11,539.40	17,790.50	9.6	245-4770	412-288-1900	None	None	None	Mark E. Durbiano	'84
FEDERATED INC;INSTL	Fixed Income	1,604.2	10.68	10,190.00	10,709.60	15,960.80	7.3	245-4770	412-288-1900	None	None	None	Gary Madich	'87
FEDERATED INC;INT SV	Fixed Income	34.8	10.68	10,183.60	10,682.90	☆	7.0	245-4770	412-288-1900	None	0.25	None	Gary Madich	'92
FEDERATED INDEX:MAX-CAP	Growth & Income	372.9	11.78	10,030.20	11,298.50	☆	2.6	245-4770	412-288-1900	None	None	None	Peter R. Anderson	'90
FEDERATED INDEX:MID-CAP	Growth	11.4	11.11	10,202.20	☆	☆	0.0	245-4770	412-288-1900	None	None	None	Peter R. Anderson	'92
FEDERATED INDEX:MINI-CAP	Small-Company Growth	50.3	11.49	10,163.60	☆	☆	0.0	245-4770	412-288-1900	None	None	None	Peter R. Anderson	'92
FEDERATED INT GOV;INSTL	Fixed Income	913.8	10.74	10,160.30	10,882.80	15,829.30	5.0	245-4770	412-288-1900	None	None	None	Susan M. Nason	'91
FEDERATED INT GOV;INT SV	Fixed Income	18.4	10.74	10,154.00	10,855.90	☆	4.7	245-4770	412-288-1900	None	0.25	None	Susan M. Nason	'92
FEDERATED SHT INC;INSTL	Fixed Income	155.9	9.14	10,124.10	10,677.00	14,605.70	5.9	245-4770	412-288-1900	None	None	None	Deborah Cunningham	'86
FEDERATED SHT INC;INT SV	Fixed Income	16.5	9.14	10,117.80	10,653.40	☆	5.7	245-4770	412-288-1900	None	0.25	None	Deborah Cunningham	'92
FEDERATED S-I GOV;INSTL	Fixed Income	992.3	10.52	10,088.90	10,544.10	14,702.70	4.1	245-4770	412-288-1900	None	None	None	Susan M. Nason	'91
FEDERATED S-I GOV;INT SV	Fixed Income	34.9	10.52	10,082.60	10,517.80	☆	3.9	245-4770	412-288-1900	None	0.25	None	Susan M. Nason	'92
FEDERATED STOCK TRUST	Growth & Income	472.1	25.49	10,179.50	11,811.90	16,941.80	2.0	245-4770	412-288-1900	None	None	None	Peter R. Anderson	'82
FFB:EQUITY	Capital Appreciation	4.5	12.61	10,096.10	11,089.50	18,059.10	1.8	522-5219	201-430-4046	2.50	0.25	None	Franklin Tseng	'89
FFB LEXICON:CAP APPREC★	Growth & Income	135.6	11.32	9,887.90	11,261.00	☆	1.6	522-5219	201-430-4046	None	None	None	Donald Demers	'93
FFB LEXICON:FXD INC★	Fixed Income	77.2	10.78	10,323.00	11,377.40	☆	5.8	522-5219	201-430-4046	None	None	None	Mander/Bescker	'91/'91
FFB LEXICON:INTMDT GOVT★	Fixed Income	108.8	10.52	10,141.60	10,913.80	☆	5.5	522-5219	201-430-4046	None	None	None	Robert Cheshire	'91
FFTW:INTL FXD INC HEDGED	World Income	25.1	10.06	10,316.10	☆	☆	0.0	762-4848	212-308-4848	None	None	None	Liaquat Ahamed	'93
FFTW:US SH TM FXD INC	Fixed Income	645.4	10.00	10,078.90	10,326.00	☆	3.2	762-4848	212-308-4848	None	None	None	Adnan Akant	'89
FFTW:WORLDWIDE FI HEDGED	World Income	40.5	9.95	10,246.00	11,260.30	☆	8.0	762-4848	212-308-4848	None	None	None	Liaquat Ahamed	'92
FFTW:WORLDWIDE FXD INC	World Income	138.6	10.09	10,424.30	11,799.10	☆	9.6	762-4848	212-308-4848	None	None	None	Liaquat Ahamed	'92
FIDELITY ADV EQ:GRO;INST	Growth	221.7	28.64	10,460.20	12,831.70	30,606.40	0.3	522-7297	None	None	None	None	Robert Stansky	'87
FIDELITY ADV EQ:GRO;RET	Growth	165.9	28.51	10,439.40	☆	☆	0.0	522-7297	None	4.75	*0.65*	None	Robert Stansky	'92
FIDELITY ADV EQ:INC;INST	Equity Income	173.3	14.50	10,232.60	12,137.80	17,377.10	3.0	522-7297	None	None	None	None	Beth Terrana	'90
FIDELITY ADV EQ:INC;RET	Equity Income	22.0	14.48	10,204.40	☆	☆	0.0	522-7297	None	4.75	*0.65*	None	Beth Terrana	'92
FIDELITY ADV GL NATL RES	Natural Resources	11.3	16.22	11,209.40	13,176.90	20,583.90	0.0	522-7297	None	4.75	0.65	None	Malcolm MacNaught	'87
FIDELITY ADV GOVT	Fixed Income	41.3	10.02	10,289.70	11,170.00	16,005.80	5.8	522-7297	None	4.75	0.25	None	Curt Hollingsworth	'92

FIDELITY ADV GROWTH OPP	Growth	1,286.1	23.62	10,337.00	12,043.00	22,531.40	0.5	522-7297	None	4.75	0.65	None	George Vanderheiden	'87
FIDELITY ADV HI YIELD	Fixed Income	336.2	11.75	10,442.50	11,894.10	21,626.30	8.1	522-7297	None	4.75	0.25	None	Margaret Eagle	'87
FIDELITY ADV INC & GRO	Balanced	904.9	15.25	10,413.50	11,770.50	20,527.80	3.5	522-7297	None	4.75	0.65	None	Robert Haber	'87
FIDELITY ADV LTD TM;INST	Fixed Income	171.7	11.09	10,280.10	11,287.00	16,563.70	7.7	522-7297	None	None	None	None	Michael Gray	'87
FIDELITY ADV LTD TM;RET	Fixed Income	18.3	11.09	10,268.00	☆	☆	0.0	522-7297	None	4.75	*0.25*	None	Michael Gray	'92
FIDELITY ADV OVERSEAS	International	52.1	11.39	10,755.40	10,873.90	☆	0.9	522-7297	None	4.75	0.65	None	*John Hickling*	'93
FIDELITY ADV SHT FXD INC	Fixed Income	381.6	10.06	10,194.60	10,884.00	15,373.90	7.7	522-7297	None	1.50	0.15	None	Donald Taylor	'89
FIDELITY ASSET MANAGER	Flexible	5,403.0	14.47	10,385.20	11,741.10	☆	5.1	544-8888	None	None	None	None	Bob Beckwitt	'88
FIDELITY ASSET MGR:GRO	Flexible	719.2	13.05	10,390.10	12,496.30	☆	1.1	544-8888	None	None	None	None	Bob Beckwitt	'91
FIDELITY ASSET MGR:INC	Income	106.3	10.84	10,245.20	☆	☆	0.0	544-8888	None	None	None	None	Bob Beckwitt	'92
FIDELITY BALANCED	Balanced	2,996.9	13.66	10,494.60	11,843.60	19,104.80	4.8	544-8888	None	None	None	None	Robert Haber	'88
FIDELITY BLUE CHIP GROW	Growth	701.1	25.72	10,793.10	12,583.30	25,891.60	0.5	544-8888	None	3.00	None	None	Michael Gordon	'93
FIDELITY CAPITAL & INC	Fixed Income	2,194.3	9.60	10,681.50	12,424.60	18,777.70	7.9	544-8888	None	None	None	1.50	*Breazzano/Harmetz*	'90
FIDELITY CAPITAL APPREC	Capital Appreciation	1,251.5	16.20	10,792.80	12,175.10	17,478.00	1.1	544-8888	None	3.00	None	None	Thomas Sweeney	'86
FIDELITY CONGRESS STREET★	Growth & Income	64.2	144.44	10,091.60	10,670.80	18,812.60	2.7	544-8888	None	None	None	None	Sandy Cushman	'92
FIDELITY CONTRAFUND	Growth	3,771.2	30.99	10,469.60	12,819.70	31,334.00	0.7	544-8888	None	3.00	None	None	Will Danoff	'90
FIDELITY CONVERTIBLE	Convertible Securities	829.8	16.79	10,329.40	12,330.90	22,961.20	4.2	544-8888	None	None	None	None	Andy Offit	'92
FIDELITY DESTINY I★	Growth	2,854.3	17.22	10,423.70	12,390.40	22,043.90	1.7	544-8888	None	8.24	None	None	George Vanderheiden	'80
FIDELITY DESTINY II★	Growth	1,042.7	26.46	10,437.90	12,328.50	22,715.30	1.3	544-8888	None	8.24	None	None	George Vanderheiden	'85
FIDELITY DISCPLN EQU	Growth	689.4	18.08	10,145.90	11,569.60	☆	1.0	544-8888	None	None	None	0.50	Brad Lewis	'88
FIDELITY DVSD INTL	International	157.0	10.36	10,571.40	10,987.60	☆	1.0	544-8888	None	None	None	None	Greg Fraser	'91
FIDELITY DIVIDEND GROWTH	Growth	N/A	10.67	☆	☆	☆	0.0	544-8888	None	None	None	None	Abigail Johnson	'93
FIDELITY D-MARK PERFORM	World Income	7.3	13.93	9,567.30	9,554.20	☆	0.0	544-8888	None	0.40	None	None	Judy Pagliuca	'89
FIDELITY EMERGING GROW	Small-Company Growth	606.5	18.99	10,901.30	13,982.80	☆	0.1	544-8888	None	3.00	None	None	Lawrence Bowman	'91
FIDELITY EMERGING MKTS	International	77.0	12.71	10,680.70	11,212.00	☆	0.6	544-8888	None	None	None	1.50	John Hickling	'93
FIDELITY EQUITY-INC	Equity Income	5,851.1	31.95	10,282.40	12,124.00	17,371.70	3.3	544-8888	None	2.00	None	None	Beth Terrana	'90
FIDELITY EQUITY-INC II	Equity Income	3,628.4	18.17	10,276.70	12,234.60	☆	2.2	544-8888	None	None	None	None	Brian Posner	'92
FIDELITY EUROPE	European Region	586.4	16.36	10,161.50	9,712.20	14,759.00	1.8	544-8888	None	3.00	None	None	Sally Walden	'92
FIDELITY EXCHANGE★	Growth	189.3	100.21	10,060.10	10,993.70	19,441.60	2.3	544-8888	None	None	None	None	Sandy Cushman	'92
FIDELITY FUND	Growth & Income	1,454.5	20.42	10,260.60	11,688.30	18,373.20	2.4	544-8888	None	None	None	None	Barry Greenfield	'82
FIDELITY GLOBAL BALANCED	Global Flexible	N/A	11.77	10,620.00	☆	☆	0.0	544-8888	None	None	None	None	Robert Haber	'93
FIDELITY GLOBAL BOND	World Income	354.4	11.94	10,487.00	11,083.30	16,490.90	10.4	544-8888	None	None	None	None	Judy Pagliuca	'86
FIDELITY GOVT SECURITIES	Fixed Income	620.2	10.63	10,306.20	11,478.40	17,168.40	6.4	544-8888	None	None	None	None	Curt Hollingsworth	'90
FIDELITY GROWTH COMPANY	Growth	2,178.5	29.84	10,484.90	12,772.00	25,640.60	0.2	544-8888	None	3.00	None	None	Robert Stansky	'87
FIDELITY GROWTH & INCOME	Growth & Income	6,149.8	21.74	10,351.10	12,066.50	22,233.40	2.7	544-8888	None	*3.00*	None	None	Steven Kaye	'93
FIDELITY INC:GNMA	Fixed Income	967.4	11.25	10,190.60	10,818.20	16,281.00	6.2	544-8888	None	None	None	None	Ives	'93
FIDELITY INC:MORTGAGE	Fixed Income	422.0	10.90	10,222.80	10,670.20	16,015.90	6.5	544-8888	None	None	None	None	Ives	'93
FIDELITY INSTL SH-INTMDT	Fixed Income	226.2	9.98	10,138.90	10,772.90	15,503.90	6.3	544-8888	None	None	None	None	Curt Hollingsworth	'87
FIDELITY INTERMEDIATE BD	Fixed Income	1,645.1	10.78	10,267.80	11,184.40	16,165.90	7.3	544-8888	None	None	None	None	Michael Gray	'87
FIDELITY INTL GRO & INC	International	167.7	15.54	10,658.40	10,976.50	15,127.60	2.1	544-8888	None	None	None	None	John Hickling	'87
FIDELITY INV GRADE BOND	Fixed Income	997.4	7.71	10,371.20	11,552.00	17,447.60	7.5	544-8888	None	None	None	None	Michael Gray	'87
FIDELITY INV TR:CANADA	Canadian	68.2	17.70	10,932.70	11,992.20	16,930.60	0.1	544-8888	None	None	None	None	George Domolky	'87
FIDELITY INV TR:JAPAN	Japanese	186.2	13.00	10,979.70	☆	☆	0.0	544-8888	None	None	None	None	*John Hickling*	'93
FIDELITY INV TR:SHT WRLD	World Income	384.7	10.02	10,348.70	10,720.20	☆	6.6	544-8888	None	None	None	None	Judy Pagliuca	'91
FIDELITY LATIN AMERICA	Latin America	22.2	10.70	☆	☆	☆	0.0	544-8888	None	None	None	None	Patti Satterthwaite	'93

★FFB LEXICON FUNDS—Institutional funds.
★FIDELITY CONGRESS STREET—Closed to new investors.

★FIDELITY DESTINY I and FIDELITY DESTINY II—Sold through a contractual plan.
★FIDELITY EXCHANGE—Closed to new investors.

PERFORMANCE OF MUTUAL FUNDS *(continued)*

FUND NAME	OBJECTIVE	TOTAL NET ASSETS ($ MIL) 5/31/93	NET ASSET $ VALUE 6/30/93	PERFORMANCE (Return on Initial $10,000 Investment) 3/31/93-6/30/93	6/30/92-6/30/93	6/30/88-6/30/93	DIVIDEND YIELD % 6/93	PHONE NUMBER 800	In-State	FEES Load	12b-1	Redemption	MANAGER	SINCE
FIDELITY LOW-PRICE★	Small-Company Growth	2,642.9	16.97	10,149.50	12,365.70	☆	0.6	544-8888	None	3.00	None	1.50	Joel Tillinghast	'89
FIDELITY MAGELLAN	Growth	26,537.5	69.80	10,642.30	12,376.90	23,076.00	1.7	544-8888	None	3.00	None	None	Jeff Vinik	'92
FIDELITY MARKET INDEX	Growth & Income	311.7	33.41	10,035.90	11,318.60	☆	2.4	544-8888	None	None	None	0.50	Jonathan Weed	'90
FIDELITY NEW MILLENNIUM	Capital Appreciation	205.9	11.38	10,576.20	☆	☆	0.0	544-8888	None	3.00	None	None	Neal Miller	'92
FIDELITY NC CASH MGT TRM	Fixed Income	79.1	9.94	10,073.20	10,378.00	14,156.70	3.4	544-8888	None	None	0.14	None	Judy Pagliuca	'88
FIDELITY OTC	Small-Company Growth	1,338.2	25.62	9,980.50	11,784.90	21,239.40	1.0	544-8888	None	3.00	None	None	Alan Radlo	'90
FIDELITY OVERSEAS	International	1,088.7	23.84	10,681.00	10,122.60	13,255.80	1.5	544-8888	None	3.00	None	None	John Hickling	'93
FIDELITY PACIFIC BASIN	Pacific Region	352.5	14.68	10,955.20	12,208.20	11,239.60	0.7	544-8888	None	3.00	None	None	*Simon Fraser*	'93
FIDELITY PURITAN	Equity Income	7,324.2	16.35	10,396.90	12,216.30	18,929.10	4.9	544-8888	None	None	None	None	Richard Fentin	'87
FIDELITY REAL ESTATE	Real Estate	380.7	13.82	9,676.40	12,874.10	19,305.20	3.3	544-8888	None	None	None	None	Barry Greenfield	'86
FIDELITY RETIREMENT GR	Capital Appreciation	2,398.8	17.76	10,584.00	12,222.50	20,017.10	0.8	544-8888	None	None	None	None	Harris Leviton	'92
FIDELITY SEL AIR TRANS★	Specialty	28.7	14.90	9,893.90	12,400.40	17,192.30	0.0	544-8888	None	3.00	None	None	*Brenda Reed*	'92
FIDELITY SEL AMER GOLD★	Gold	330.0	20.85	13,246.50	15,308.40	13,006.90	0.0	544-8888	None	3.00	None	None	Malcolm MacNaught	'85
FIDELITY SEL AUTOMOTIVE★	Specialty	103.5	22.69	10,732.10	12,908.60	21,282.50	0.4	544-8888	None	3.00	None	None	*Richard Patton*	'93
FIDELITY SEL BIO TECH★	Health/Biotechnology	583.7	25.20	10,985.20	9,963.20	31,786.10	0.0	544-8888	None	3.00	None	None	Karen Firestone	'92
FIDELITY SEL BROADCAST★	Specialty	29.2	20.04	10,732.10	12,715.20	20,386.00	0.0	544-8888	None	3.00	None	None	*Stephen Dufour*	'93
FIDELITY SEL BROKERAGE★	Financial Services	33.8	16.55	10,781.80	14,812.90	22,893.00	0.1	544-8888	None	3.00	None	None	Scott Offen	'90
FIDELITY SEL CHEMICALS★	Specialty	26.9	28.76	10,080.30	10,524.30	16,575.30	1.0	544-8888	None	3.00	None	None	*Steve Wymer*	'93
FIDELITY SEL COMPUTER★	Science & Technology	37.4	20.87	10,420.00	13,275.30	17,660.20	0.0	544-8888	None	3.00	None	None	Harry Lange	'92
FIDELITY SEL CONST&HOUSE★	Specialty	26.2	16.08	9,987.60	12,143.50	19,403.80	0.0	544-8888	None	3.00	None	None	Katherine Collins	'92
FIDELITY SEL CNSMR PRDCT★	Specialty	11.6	14.73	10,728.30	12,085.90	☆	0.0	544-8888	None	3.00	None	None	*Steve Pesek*	'93
FIDELITY SEL DEFENSE★	Specialty	1.7	17.11	10,774.60	13,151.40	14,244.80	0.0	544-8888	None	3.00	None	None	Steve Binder	'92
FIDELITY SEL DVLP COMM★	Science & Technology	92.6	17.36	10,803.30	14,180.00	☆	0.0	544-8888	None	3.00	None	None	Philip Barton	'93
FIDELITY SEL ELE UTILITY★	Utility	29.1	14.26	10,273.70	12,282.80	20,836.70	2.2	544-8888	None	3.00	None	None	*John Muresianu*	'92
FIDELITY SEL ELECTRONIC★	Science & Technology	45.5	16.19	11,006.70	14,829.40	19,553.30	0.0	544-8888	None	3.00	None	None	Steven Shapiro	'92
FIDELITY SEL ENERGY★	Natural Resources	121.4	17.70	10,637.10	12,329.80	16,416.10	1.4	544-8888	None	3.00	None	None	Bob Bertleson	'92
FIDELITY SEL ENERGY SER★	Natural Resources	163.9	13.02	10,968.70	13,587.90	16,114.40	0.1	544-8888	None	3.00	None	None	Bill Mankivsky	'91
FIDELITY SEL ENVIRONMENT★	Environmental	56.5	10.95	9,882.70	10,798.80	☆	0.0	544-8888	None	3.00	None	None	Tom Sprague	'91
FIDELITY SEL FINANCIAL★	Financial Services	162.1	54.74	9,880.50	13,299.50	23,037.30	0.7	544-8888	None	3.00	None	None	Bruce Herring	'91
FIDELITY SEL FOOD★	Specialty	99.5	29.84	9,815.70	11,289.00	23,831.00	0.3	544-8888	None	3.00	None	None	*Bill Mankivsky*	'93
FIDELITY SEL HEALTH★	Health/Biotechnology	589.4	55.96	10,359.10	9,241.10	24,196.70	0.3	544-8888	None	3.00	None	None	Charles Mangum	'92
FIDELITY SEL HOME FIN★	Financial Services	172.7	21.78	9,528.40	13,131.60	26,887.40	0.1	544-8888	None	3.00	None	None	David Ellison	'85
FIDELITY SEL INDUS EQUIP★	Specialty	23.9	17.02	11,124.20	13,008.40	15,514.20	0.4	544-8888	None	3.00	None	None	Albert Ruback	'91
FIDELITY SEL INDUS MAT★	Specialty	19.4	18.18	10,287.50	10,844.90	13,491.40	0.7	544-8888	None	3.00	None	None	Louis Salemy	'92
FIDELITY SEL INSURANCE★	Financial Services	21.2	21.79	9,612.10	12,910.70	23,432.90	0.0	544-8888	None	3.00	None	None	Bruce Herring	'92
FIDELITY SEL LEISURE★	Specialty	54.2	38.92	10,758.70	12,913.90	19,196.00	0.0	544-8888	None	3.00	None	None	Deborah Wheeler	'92
FIDELITY SEL MEDICAL★	Health/Biotechnology	88.8	15.20	10,284.20	9,010.10	24,829.70	0.0	544-8888	None	3.00	None	None	*Louis Salemy*	'93
FIDELITY SEL NAT GAS★	Natural Resources	N/A	10.26	☆	☆	☆	0.0	544-8888	None	3.00	None	None	*John Muresianu*	'93
FIDELITY SEL PAPER&FRS★	Specialty	14.4	16.47	10,261.80	11,171.40	13,714.40	0.4	544-8888	None	3.00	None	None	Bob Chow	'90
FIDELITY SEL PREC MTLS★	Gold	464.5	14.97	13,366.10	14,381.70	12,990.30	1.0	544-8888	None	3.00	None	None	Malcolm MacNaught	'84
FIDELITY SEL REGL BANKS★	Financial Services	221.4	21.39	9,916.30	13,069.90	28,542.80	0.5	544-8888	None	3.00	None	None	Steve Binder	'90
FIDELITY SEL RETAILING★	Specialty	58.4	24.36	9,709.00	12,220.30	27,095.20	0.0	544-8888	None	3.00	None	None	Jennifer Uhrig	'91
FIDELITY SEL SOFTWARE★	Science & Technology	208.7	28.74	11,505.00	15,648.80	26,103.10	0.0	544-8888	None	3.00	None	None	Arich Coll	'91
FIDELITY SEL TECHNOLOGY★	Science & Technology	166.6	36.51	11,513.40	14,487.80	22,905.70	0.3	544-8888	None	3.00	None	None	Arieh Coll	'92
FIDELITY SEL TELECOMM★	Science & Technology	264.0	37.74	10,874.00	14,010.20	24,310.90	0.5	544-8888	None	3.00	None	None	*Fergus Shiel*	'92

FIDELITY SEL TRANSPORT★	Specialty	11.4	20.61	10,377.90	13,958.40	24,249.90	0.3	544-8888	None	3.00	None	None	Steve Pesek	'92
FIDELITY SEL UTILITIES★	Utility	287.6	43.66	10,348.30	12,460.50	22,279.70	2.2	544-8888	None	3.00	None	None	John Muresianu	'92
FIDELITY SH-INT GOVT	Fixed Income	178.4	10.00	10,121.20	10,635.30	☆	6.6	544-8888	None	None	None	None	Curt Hollingsworth	'91
FIDELITY SHORT-TERM BOND	Fixed Income	2,066.3	9.52	10,175.90	10,816.30	15,396.90	7.5	544-8888	None	None	None	None	Donald Taylor	'89
FIDELITY SOEAST ASIA	Pacific Region	55.6	10.14	☆	☆	☆	0.0	544-8888	None	None	None	1.50	Alan Liu	'93
FIDELITY SPARTAN GNMA	Fixed Income	751.6	10.29	10,202.00	10,773.50	☆	6.5	544-8888	None	None	None	None	Ives	'93
FIDELITY SPARTAN GOV INC	Fixed Income	449.1	10.94	10,286.80	11,013.90	☆	6.2	544-8888	None	None	None	None	Bob Beckwitt	'88
FIDELITY SPARTAN HIINC	Fixed Income	609.1	12.46	10,531.80	11,922.50	☆	8.9	544-8888	None	None	None	1.00	*David Glancy*	'93
FIDELITY SPARTAN INV GRD	Fixed Income	75.0	10.58	10,404.70	☆	☆	0.0	544-8888	None	None	None	None	Michael Gray	'92
FIDELITY SPARTAN LG GOVT	Fixed Income	85.3	12.77	10,430.60	11,883.50	☆	6.7	544-8888	None	None	None	None	Bob Beckwitt	'90
FIDELITY SPARTAN LTD MAT	Fixed Income	1,550.2	10.32	10,203.80	10,789.80	15,305.20	5.9	544-8888	None	None	None	None	Curt Hollingsworth	'88
FIDELITY SPARTAN S-I GOV	Fixed Income	57.3	10.05	10,126.90	☆	☆	0.0	544-8888	None	None	None	None	Curt Hollingsworth	'92
FIDELITY SPARTAN SH-TM	Fixed Income	805.0	9.97	10,196.50	☆	☆	0.0	544-8888	None	None	None	None	Donald Taylor	'92
FIDELITY SP SIT:ADVISOR	Capital Appreciation	223.1	20.81	10,111.80	11,776.00	19,046.90	2.7	522-7297	None	4.75	0.65	None	Daniel Frank	'86
FIDELITY SP SIT:INITL★	Capital Appreciation	19.5	20.98	10,135.30	11,845.70	19,568.50	3.2	544-8888	None	4.75	None	None	Daniel Frank	'83
FIDELITY STRLING PERFORM	World Income	4.1	13.32	9,940.30	8,356.30	☆	0.0	544-8888	None	0.40	None	None	Judy Pagliuca	'89
FIDELITY STOCK SELECTOR	Growth	500.3	19.01	10,160.30	12,126.40	☆	0.5	544-8888	None	None	None	None	Brad Lewis	'90
FIDELITY TREND	Growth	1,285.9	59.31	10,341.80	12,910.80	20,087.20	0.7	544-8888	None	None	None	None	Alan Leifer	'87
FIDELITY US BOND INDEX★	Fixed Income	137.2	11.15	10,262.70	11,232.40	☆	6.9	544-8888	None	None	None	None	Christine Thompson	'90
FIDELITY US EQUITY INDEX	Growth & Income	1,550.3	16.84	10,037.30	11,330.00	19,188.10	2.5	544-8888	None	None	None	None	Jay Weed	'88
FIDELITY UTIL INCOME	Utility	1,285.7	15.31	10,400.10	12,444.50	20,404.30	3.5	544-8888	None	None	None	None	John Muresianu	'92
FIDELITY VALUE	Capital Appreciation	1,274.1	39.31	10,263.70	12,251.20	20,121.10	0.6	544-8888	None	None	None	None	Jeff Ubben	'92
FIDELITY WORLDWIDE	Global	145.3	11.38	10,459.60	11,630.70	☆	2.3	544-8888	None	None	None	None	Penelope Dobkin	'90
FIDELITY YEN PERFORM	World Income	5.2	15.61	10,780.40	11,943.40	☆	0.0	544-8888	None	0.40	None	None	Judy Pagliuca	'89
FIDUCIARY CAPITAL GROWTH	Small-Company Growth	45.0	19.36	10,216.40	11,927.60	16,177.70	0.5	792-2473	414-765-3500	None	None	None	Kellner/Wilson	'81/'81
FIDUCIARY EXCHANGE★	Growth	59.2	145.04	9,643.70	10,882.70	18,565.50	1.0	225-6265	617-482-8260	None	None	None	Duncan Richardson	'87
FIDUCIARY TOTAL RETURN	Growth & Income	2.7	12.02	10,134.90	11,349.80	15,941.50	1.2	792-2473	414-765-3500	None	1.00	None	Kellner/Wilson	'86/'86
59 WALL ST:EUROPEAN	European Region	53.0	26.97	10,063.40	10,335.40	☆	8.5	None	212-493-8100	None	None	1.25	Brown Brothers Harriman	'92
59 WALL ST:PAC BASIN	Pacific Region	62.0	31.81	10,882.70	12,230.70	☆	3.1	None	212-493-8100	None	None	1.25	Brown Brothers Harriman	'92
59 WALL ST:SMALL CO	Small-Company Growth	30.0	12.28	10,165.60	12,478.80	☆	1.1	None	212-493-8100	None	None	0.50	Brown Brothers Harriman	'91
FINANCIAL BD:HIGH YIELD	Fixed Income	291.0	7.35	10,379.40	11,751.20	15,931.70	8.5	525-8085	303-930-6300	None	0.25	None	William B. Veronda	'84
FINANCIAL BD:SELECT INC	Fixed Income	151.7	6.79	10,291.60	11,371.00	16,644.50	7.5	525-8085	303-930-6300	None	0.25	None	Ron Lout	'90
FINANCIAL BD:US GOVT	Fixed Income	33.1	8.00	10,318.10	11,391.40	16,316.40	5.4	525-8085	303-930-6300	None	0.25	None	Ron Lout	'88
FINANCIAL DYNAMICS	Capital Appreciation	273.5	11.85	10,496.70	13,194.90	21,916.80	0.0	525-8085	303-930-6300	None	0.25	None	William Keithler	'89
FINANCIAL EMERGING GR	Small-Company Growth	103.0	10.18	10,560.20	14,060.80	☆	0.0	525-8085	303-930-6300	None	0.25	None	William Keithler	'92
FINL HRZNS:GOVT BOND	Fixed Income	79.3	11.24	10,278.20	11,200.90	☆	7.0	533-5622	None	None	0.35	6.00	Wayne Frisbee	'89
FINL HRZNS:GROWTH	Growth	4.2	13.50	9,963.20	11,251.00	☆	0.7	533-5622	None	None	0.35	6.00	John Schaffner	'89
FINANCIAL INDUST	Growth & Income	465.0	5.47	10,277.80	11,860.50	19,663.10	0.7	525-8085	303-930-6300	None	0.25	None	R. Dalton Sim	'87
FINANCIAL INDUST INCOME	Equity Income	3,338.1	11.53	10,009.70	11,561.10	21,945.30	2.7	525-8085	303-930-6300	None	0.25	None	Kaweske/Lout/Mayer	'85/'92
FINANCIAL PORT:ENERGY	Natural Resources	76.0	11.74	11,013.10	13,665.10	13,433.30	0.2	525-8085	303-930-6300	None	None	None	Tim Miller	'92
FINANCIAL PORT:ENVIRON	Environmental	15.8	6.87	9,703.40	8,641.50	☆	0.0	525-8085	303-930-6300	None	None	None	John Schroer	'93
FINANCIAL PORT:EUROPEAN	European Region	152.6	10.98	10,300.20	9,336.40	14,320.80	1.8	525-8085	303-930-6300	None	None	None	Chamberlain/Mill	'90/'86
FINANCIAL PORT:FINANCIAL	Financial Services	366.1	19.24	9,746.70	13,039.00	30,508.10	0.9	525-8085	303-930-6300	None	None	None	Doug Pratt	'92
FINANCIAL PORT:GOLD	Gold	288.6	6.12	12,697.10	14,676.30	10,980.20	0.0	525-8085	303-930-6300	None	None	None	Dan Leonard	'89
FINANCIAL PORT:HEALTH	Health/Biotechnology	608.4	31.65	10,567.60	8,985.40	29,197.50	0.3	525-8085	303-930-6300	None	None	None	Kaweske/Kurokawa	'85/'92

★FIDELITY LOW-PRICE—Closed to new investors.
★FIDELITY SELECT FUNDS—All redemptions are subject to a minimum $7.50 fee.
★FIDELITY SP SIT:INITL—Closed to new investors.

★FIDELITY US BOND INDEX—Institutional fund.
★FIDUCIARY EXCHANGE—Closed to new investors.

PERFORMANCE OF MUTUAL FUNDS (continued)

FUND NAME	OBJECTIVE	TOTAL NET ASSETS ($ MIL) 5/31/93	NET ASSET $ VALUE 6/30/93	PERFORMANCE (Return on Initial $10,000 Investment) 3/31/93-6/30/93	6/30/92-6/30/93	6/30/88-6/30/93	DIVIDEND YIELD % 6/93	PHONE NUMBER 800	In-State	FEES Load	12b-1	Redemption	MANAGER	SINCE
FINANCIAL PORT:LEISURE	Specialty	155.1	20.51	10,143.40	13,551.80	26,609.60	0.0	525-8085	303-930-6300	None	None	None	Tim Miller	'92
FINANCIAL PORT:PACIFIC	Pacific Region	178.8	13.40	11,037.90	11,746.30	11,531.50	0.4	525-8085	303-930-6300	None	None	None	Somerville/Keithler	'92/'86
FINANCIAL PORT:TECH	Science & Technology	229.3	24.07	11,061.60	13,409.50	26,485.70	0.0	525-8085	303-930-6300	None	None	None	Daniel B. Leonard	'84
FINANCIAL PORT:UTILITIES	Utility	138.1	12.43	10,881.40	12,971.50	20,240.60	1.8	525-8085	303-930-6300	None	None	None	Brian Kelly	'93
FINANCIAL TR:EQUITY	Growth & Income	77.9	17.21	9,880.10	10,856.90	N/A	2.0	525-8085	303-930-6300	None	None	None	Kevin Means	'92
FINANCIAL TR:FLEX	Flexible	189.5	17.79	10,128.20	11,250.00	N/A	3.5	525-8085	303-930-6300	None	None	None	Edward Mitchell	'87
FINANCIAL TR:INTMDT GOVT	Fixed Income	37.9	13.13	10,216.50	11,042.60	N/A	5.4	525-8085	303-930-6300	None	None	None	James Baker	'93
FINANCIAL TR:INTL GROWTH	International	76.5	14.42	10,697.30	10,937.40	N/A	0.8	525-8085	303-930-6300	None	None	None	Davidson/Stevens	'89/'92
FIRST AMER INV:ASST ALLO	Flexible	55.5	10.42	10,069.10	☆	☆	0.0	637-2548	612-973-0166	4.50	None	None	Cory Johnson	'92
FIRST AMER INV:BALANCED	Balanced	85.0	10.59	10,292.50	☆	☆	0.0	637-2548	612-973-0166	4.50	None	None	Jim Rovner	'92
FIRST AMER INV:EQ INDEX	Growth & Income	124.7	10.40	10,049.20	☆	☆	0.0	637-2548	612-973-0166	4.50	None	None	Jim Rovner	'92
FIRST AMER INV:FXD INC	Fixed Income	46.0	11.22	10,232.60	11,119.00	16,177.30	6.2	637-2548	612-973-0166	4.50	0.25	None	Martin Jones	'87
FIRST AMER INV:GOVT	Fixed Income	3.1	9.45	10,107.60	10,630.40	14,576.40	6.2	637-2548	612-973-0166	4.50	0.25	None	Martin Jones	'87
FIRST AMER INV:INT TERM	Fixed Income	58.4	10.19	10,177.40	☆	☆	0.0	637-2548	612-973-0166	4.50	None	None	Martin Jones	'92
FIRST AMER INV:LTD TERM	Fixed Income	129.4	10.01	10,084.00	☆	☆	0.0	637-2548	612-973-0166	3.00	None	None	Martin Jones	'92
FIRST AMER INV:MTGE SECS	Fixed Income	27.4	10.27	10,161.30	☆	☆	0.0	637-2548	612-973-0166	4.50	None	None	Martin Jones	'92
FIRST AMER INV:REGNL EQ	Growth	44.9	11.13	10,072.80	☆	☆	0.0	637-2548	612-973-0166	4.50	None	None	Rick Rinkoff	'92
FIRST AMER INV:SPEC EQU	Capital Appreciation	69.2	15.61	10,327.90	12,293.10	17,064.90	1.7	637-2548	612-973-0166	4.50	0.25	None	Larry Smith	'87
FIRST AMER INV:STOCK	Growth & Income	110.0	15.77	10,346.20	11,415.80	17,236.80	1.7	637-2548	612-973-0166	4.50	0.25	None	Jim Doak	'87
FIRST BOS:INSTL GOVT;A	Fixed Income	67.9	10.46	10,283.70	11,103.40	☆	5.0	545-5799	None	2.50	None	None	Susan Huang	'92
FIRST EAGLE FD OF AMER	Capital Appreciation	93.8	15.12	10,580.80	12,808.40	18,344.70	0.0	451-3623	212-943-9200	None	None	1.00	Levy/Cohen	'87/'89
FIRST INV FD FOR INC	Fixed Income	422.9	4.12	10,396.20	11,731.60	14,804.70	9.6	423-4026	None	6.25	0.30	None	Nancy Jones	'89
FIRST INV GLOBAL	Global	179.1	5.37	10,170.50	10,252.10	14,416.60	0.8	423-4026	None	6.25	0.30	None	Jerry Mitchell	'89
FIRST INV GOVT	Fixed Income	304.3	11.77	10,129.50	10,724.80	15,781.20	6.5	423-4026	None	6.25	0.30	None	Larry Waldorf	'92
FIRST INV GOVT PLUS:I	Balanced Target	1.7	13.20	10,731.70	12,696.30	19,516.70	5.3	423-4026	None	8.00	None	None	Patricia Poitra	'86
FIRST INV HIGH YIELD	Fixed Income	190.4	5.22	10,454.70	11,703.70	13,871.30	9.1	423-4026	None	6.25	0.30	None	George Ganter	'89
FIRST INV SRS:BLUE CHIP	Growth & Income	109.0	15.82	10,012.70	11,407.30	☆	0.6	423-4026	None	6.25	0.30	None	Denise Burns	'89
FIRST INV SRS:INV GRADE	Fixed Income	43.7	10.36	10,273.30	11,336.70	☆	6.7	423-4026	None	6.25	0.30	None	Nancy Jones	'91
FIRST INV SRS:SP SITUAT	Small-Company Growth	37.8	16.45	10,287.70	12,721.40	☆	0.0	423-4026	None	6.25	0.30	None	Patricia Poitra	'90
FIRST INV SRS:TOT RTN	Flexible	62.2	12.67	10,071.60	10,910.70	☆	2.2	423-4026	None	6.25	0.30	None	Team Managed	'92
FIRST INV SRSII:MADE USA	Growth	18.2	12.20	9,838.70	☆	☆	0.0	423-4026	None	6.25	0.30	None	Denise Burns	'92
FIRST INV SRSII:UTIL	Utility	26.4	5.75	☆	☆	☆	0.0	423-4026	None	6.25	0.30	None	Margaret Haggerty	'93
FIRST MUTUAL	Capital Appreciation	18.9	9.29	9,904.10	11,216.70	16,186.50	0.0	257-4414	None	None	0.25	None	David P. Como	'82
FIRST OMAHA EQUITY	Growth & Income	110.9	10.55	10,176.20	☆	☆	0.0	662-4203	None	None	None	None	First Nat. Bk of Omaha	'92
FIRST OMAHA FXD INCOME	Fixed Income	58.4	10.49	10,308.30	☆	☆	0.0	662-4203	None	None	None	None	First Nat. Bk of Omaha	'92
FIRST OMAHA SH-INTMDT	Fixed Income	24.5	10.18	10,155.30	☆	☆	0.0	662-4203	None	None	None	None	First Nat. Bk of Omaha	'92
FIRST PRAIRIE DVRSFD AST	Income	45.0	13.07	10,112.10	11,143.90	18,177.90	5.6	821-1185	None	4.50	0.30	None	Arthur Krill	'86
FIRST PRAIRIE GOVT:INT;A	Fixed Income	0.1	8.31	10,187.00	☆	☆	0.0	821-1185	None	4.50	0.25	None	Annette Furmanski-Cole	'93
1ST PRIORITY EQUITY;INV	Growth & Income	6.4	10.14	9,781.10	10,627.90	☆	1.5	433-2829	205-326-7041	3.00	0.30	None	Charlie Murray	'92
1ST PRIORITY EQUITY;TR	Growth & Income	135.8	10.14	9,787.80	10,659.30	☆	1.8	433-2829	205-326-7041	None	None	None	Charlie Murray	'92
1ST PRIORITY FXD INC;INV	Fixed Income	9.7	10.67	10,201.20	11,145.50	☆	4.8	433-2829	205-326-7041	2.00	0.30	None	Jerry Harris	'92
1ST PRIORITY FXD INC;TR	Fixed Income	128.9	10.67	10,203.80	11,179.00	☆	5.1	433-2829	205-326-7041	None	None	None	Jerry Harris	'92
FIRST UN:BAL;INV B	Balanced	24.8	11.75	10,092.90	11,260.50	☆	3.6	326-3241	704-374-4343	4.00	0.25	None	Dean Hawes	'91
FIRST UN:BAL;INV C	Balanced	26.1	11.75	10,080.80	☆	☆	0.0	326-3241	704-374-4343	None	0.75	4.00	Dean Hawes	'93
FIRST UN:BAL;TR	Balanced	577.6	11.75	10,099.00	11,287.70	☆	3.8	326-3241	704-374-4343	None	None	None	Dean Hawes	'91

FIRST UN:FXD INC;INV B	Fixed Income	22.1	10.69	10,176.60	10,945.00	☆	6.1	326-3241	704-374-4343	4.00	0.10	None	Tom Ellis	'89
FIRST UN:FXD INC;TR	Fixed Income	341.6	10.69	10,182.30	10,973.60	☆	6.4	326-3241	704-374-4343	None	None	None	Tom Ellis	'91
FIRST UN:MGD BD;TR	Fixed Income	125.5	10.79	10,243.90	11,154.50	☆	6.0	326-3241	704-374-4343	None	None	None	John Raithel	'91
FIRST UN:US GOVT;INV C	Fixed Income	131.9	10.21	10,261.50	☆	☆	0.0	326-3241	704-374-4343	None	0.75	None	Rollin Williams	'93
FIRST UN:VALUE;INV B	Growth	181.9	17.56	10,068.50	11,164.00	18,491.90	2.5	326-3241	704-374-4343	4.00	0.25	None	Bill Davis	'85
FIRST UN:VALUE;INV C	Growth	30.1	17.55	10,050.70	☆	☆	0.0	326-3241	704-374-4343	None	0.75	4.00	Bill Davis	'93
FIRST UN:VALUE;TR	Growth	353.0	17.56	10,077.80	11,204.60	☆	2.9	326-3241	704-374-4343	None	None	None	Bill Davis	'91
FIXED INC SEC:LTD TERM	Fixed Income	132.9	10.20	10,190.30	10,819.00	☆	6.4	245-4770	412-288-1900	1.00	0.50	None	Deborah Cunningham	'92
FLAG INV EMERGING GROWTH	Small-Company Growth	36.6	13.36	9,773.20	10,542.70	13,937.80	0.0	645-3923	410-637-6819	4.50	0.25	None	Alec Graham	'92
FLAG INV INTMDT-TM INC	Fixed Income	87.3	10.74	10,203.30	11,006.90	☆	6.5	645-3923	410-637-6819	1.50	0.25	None	Randolph/Corbin	'91/'91
FLAG INV INTL;FLAG	International	13.7	11.01	10,710.10	10,826.00	11,556.60	0.0	645-3923	410-637-6819	4.50	0.25	None	Bessemer Trust/Trott	'86/'92
FLAG INV QUAL GRO;FLAG	Growth	64.6	12.45	9,318.90	10,071.00	☆	0.2	645-3923	410-637-6819	4.50	0.25	None	Killebrow/Brandaleone	'89/'89
FLAG INV TPHONE INC;FLAG	Equity Income	358.1	13.58	10,208.20	13,042.80	22,627.20	3.1	645-3923	410-637-6819	4.50	0.25	None	Behrens/Buppert	'84/'84
FLAG INV VALUE BUILDER★	Balanced	88.6	11.32	10,135.70	11,469.50	☆	1.7	645-3923	410-637-6819	4.50	0.25	None	Buppert/Owen	'92/'92
FLAGSHIP UTILITY;A	Utility	30.3	11.04	10,296.60	☆	☆	6.3	227-4648	513-461-0332	4.20	0.40	None	Bedford/Huber	'92/'92
FLEX-FUNDS:BOND	Fixed Income	11.8	19.94	10,194.00	10,908.70	14,790.30	4.8	325-3539	614-766-7000	None	0.20	None	Philip Voelker	'87
FLEX-FUNDS:GROWTH	Flexible	25.8	12.88	9,756.10	10,727.00	14,467.70	1.6	325-3539	614-766-7000	None	0.20	None	Robert Meeder Jr.	'92
FLEX-FUNDS:MUIRFIELD	Flexible	67.0	5.70	10,142.30	11,133.10	☆	1.1	325-3539	614-766-7000	None	0.20	None	Robert Meeder Jr.	'88
FLEX-FUNDS:SHT GLBL INC	World Income	32.5	9.59	10,044.80	9,979.80	☆	4.9	325-3539	614-766-7000	None	0.20	None	Joseph Zarr	'92
FMB:DVSD EQ;CNSMR	Growth	5.3	11.14	9,733.00	10,546.30	☆	0.7	453-4234	None	4.00	None	None	James Dodge	'91
FMB:DVSD EQ;INSTL	Growth	40.0	11.14	9,733.00	10,550.30	☆	0.8	453-4234	None	None	None	None	James Dodge	'91
FMB:INTMDT GOVT;CNSMR	Fixed Income	9.2	10.50	10,191.90	10,986.80	☆	5.6	453-4234	None	3.00	None	None	Duane Carpenter	'91
FMB:INTMDT GOVT;INSTL	Fixed Income	100.0	10.50	10,191.90	10,993.40	☆	5.7	453-4234	None	None	None	None	Duane Carpenter	'91
FONTAINE:CAPITAL APPREC	Capital Appreciation	12.7	10.48	10,355.70	10,277.10	☆	1.1	247-1550	410-825-7894	None	None	None	Richard H. Fontaine	'89
FONTAINE:GLBL GROWTH	Global	0.4	9.88	10,102.20	9,953.80	☆	0.8	247-1550	410-825-7894	None	None	None	Fontaine/Dyer	'92/'92
FONTAINE:GLBL INCOME	World Income	1.3	9.91	10,050.70	10,001.70	☆	1.7	247-1550	410-825-7894	None	None	None	Richard H. Fontaine	'92
FORTIS ADVTG:ASSET ALLOC	Flexible	100.3	14.62	10,166.70	11,256.90	17,646.80	3.8	800-2638	612-738-4000	4.50	0.45	None	Poling/Ott	'88/'88
FORTIS ADVTG:CAP APPREC	Small-Company Growth	49.0	23.95	10,744.70	13,246.70	22,407.30	0.0	800-2638	612-738-4000	4.50	0.45	None	Stephen Poling	'88
FORTIS ADVTG:GVT TOT RTN	Fixed Income	89.6	9.14	10,260.80	11,048.30	15,335.50	8.0	800-2638	612-738-4000	4.50	0.35	None	Dennis M. Ott	'86
FORTIS ADVTG:HIGH YIELD	Fixed Income	58.3	8.56	10,458.60	11,741.00	16,348.30	10.2	800-2638	612-738-4000	4.50	0.35	None	Dennis M. Ott	'88
FORTIS EQU:CAPITAL	Growth & Income	248.0	17.89	10,039.50	10,972.30	19,513.70	0.5	800-2638	612-738-4000	4.75	0.25	None	Stephen Poling	'83
FORTIS FIDUCIARY	Growth	47.7	29.63	10,081.70	11,168.30	19,914.60	0.0	800-2638	612-738-4000	4.75	0.25	None	Stephen Poling	'83
FORTIS GROWTH	Capital Appreciation	573.2	28.45	10,572.30	12,184.00	23,137.80	0.1	800-2638	612-738-4000	4.75	0.25	None	Stephen Poling	'83
FORTIS INC:US GOVT	Fixed Income	634.1	10.07	10,238.80	10,964.20	16,238.50	8.0	800-2638	612-738-4000	4.50	None	None	Dennis M. Ott	'85
FORTIS WRLDWIDE:GL GRO	Global	16.6	13.24	10,384.30	12,080.30	☆	0.0	800-2638	612-738-4000	4.75	0.25	None	James Byrd	'91
FORTRESS ADJ RT GOVT	Fixed Income	1,063.6	9.88	10,107.20	10,402.40	☆	4.9	245-4770	412-288-1900	None	0.25	1.00	Gary Madich	'91
FORTRESS BOND	Fixed Income	95.0	10.09	10,390.10	11,739.30	17,931.00	8.0	245-4770	412-288-1900	1.00	None	1.00	Mark E. Durbiano	'87
FORTRESS UTILITY	Utility	740.3	13.12	10,193.80	11,973.50	20,268.30	5.1	245-4770	412-288-1900	1.00	None	1.00	Christopher H. Wiles	'90
44 WALL STREET EQUITY	Capital Appreciation	5.0	7.09	10,320.20	12,888.70	19,853.00	0.0	543-2620	212-248-8080	None	None	None	Mark D. Beckerman	'88
FORUM:INVESTORS BOND	Fixed Income	26.9	10.82	10,293.00	11,211.90	☆	7.4	None	207-879-0001	3.75	None	None	Forum Advisors	'89
FORUM:INVESTORS STOCK	Growth & Income	13.3	10.68	10,093.80	10,603.30	☆	2.7	None	207-879-0001	3.75	None	None	Newbolds Asset Mgt	'90
FORUM:PAYSON BALANCED	Balanced	5.7	11.76	10,394.70	11,838.90	☆	2.8	None	207-879-0001	None	None	None	H.M. Payson & Co.	'91
FORUM:PAYSON VALUE	Growth & Income	2.4	11.27	10,272.50	☆	☆	0.0	None	207-879-0001	None	None	None	H.M. Payson & Co.	'92
FOUNDERS:BLUE CHIP	Growth & Income	290.8	7.24	10,182.70	11,361.80	19,258.90	0.9	525-2440	303-394-4404	None	0.25	None	Team Managed	N/A
FOUNDERS:DISCOVERY	Small-Company Growth	180.5	19.99	10,282.90	12,672.60	☆	0.3	525-2440	303-394-4404	None	0.25	None	Team Managed	N/A
FOUNDERS:EQUITY INCOME★	Balanced	40.9	8.99	10,385.10	11,872.30	17,740.10	2.8	525-2440	303-394-4404	None	0.25	None	Team Managed	N/A
FOUNDERS:FRONTIER	Small-Company Growth	198.3	25.78	10,262.70	12,126.50	22,615.10	0.0	525-2440	303-394-4404	None	0.25	None	Team Managed	N/A
FOUNDERS:GOVERNMENT SEC	Fixed Income	31.7	10.63	10,223.60	11,006.50	15,480.50	4.1	525-2440	303-394-4404	None	0.25	None	Team Managed	N/A
FOUNDERS:GROWTH	Growth	199.7	12.13	10,898.50	13,362.90	22,554.10	0.9	525-2440	303-394-4404	None	0.25	None	Team Managed	N/A
FOUNDERS:SPECIAL	Capital Appreciation	454.9	8.11	10,278.80	12,099.30	23,663.40	0.0	525-2440	303-394-4404	None	0.25	None	Team Managed	N/A

★FLAG INV VALUE BUILDER—On 5/15/93, fund was reclassified from Flexible Portfolio to Balanced.

★FOUNDERS: EQUITY INCOME—On 6/28/93, fund was reclassified from Equity Income to Balanced.

PERFORMANCE OF MUTUAL FUNDS *(continued)*

FUND NAME	OBJECTIVE	TOTAL NET ASSETS ($ MIL) 5/31/93	NET ASSET $ VALUE 6/30/93	PERFORMANCE (Return on Initial $10,000 Investment) 3/31/93-6/30/93	6/30/92-6/30/93	6/30/88-6/30/93	DIVIDEND YIELD % 6/93	PHONE NUMBER 800	In-State	FEES Load	12b-1	Redemption	MANAGER	SINCE
FOUNDERS:WORLDWIDE GROW	Global	42.7	14.60	10,436.00	10,703.80	☆	0.0	525-2440	303-394-4404	None	0.25	None	Team Managed	N/A
FOUNTAIN SQ:BALANCED	Balanced	57.7	9.83	9,743.30	☆	☆	0.0	654-5372	513-579-5452	4.50	None	None	Fountain Square Bank	'92
FOUNTAIN SQ:MID CAP	Growth	23.1	9.70	9,522.10	☆	☆	0.0	654-5372	513-579-5452	4.50	None	None	Fountain Square Bank	'92
FOUNTAIN SQ:QUALITY BD	Fixed Income	33.3	10.31	10,192.60	☆	☆	0.0	654-5372	513-579-5452	4.50	None	None	Fountain Square Bank	'92
FOUNTAIN SQ:QUALITY GRO	Growth	66.3	9.63	9,581.90	☆	☆	0.0	654-5372	513-579-5452	4.50	None	None	Fountain Square Bank	'92
FOUNTAIN SQ:US GOVT SECS	Fixed Income	27.3	10.24	10,165.90	☆	☆	0.0	654-5372	513-579-5452	4.50	None	None	Fountain Square Bank	'92
FPA CAPITAL	Growth	133.4	19.11	10,021.00	12,967.50	20,408.00	0.3	982-4372	310-996-5425	6.50	None	None	Robert L. Rodriguez	'84
FPA NEW INCOME	Fixed Income	104.0	11.24	10,264.80	11,311.00	17,372.80	6.4	982-4372	310-996-5425	4.50	None	None	Robert L. Rodriguez	'84
FPA PARAMOUNT★	Growth & Income	333.3	13.93	10,123.50	11,817.60	18,563.10	1.9	982-4372	310-996-5425	6.50	None	None	William M. Sams	'81
FPA PERENNIAL	Growth & Income	85.1	22.98	9,935.10	10,798.00	17,847.70	2.2	982-4372	310-996-5425	6.50	None	None	Christopher Linden	'84
FRANKLIN AGE HI INC	Fixed Income	1,934.9	2.85	10,421.80	11,578.10	16,337.00	9.3	342-5236	415-312-3200	4.00	None	None	Wiskemann/Molumphy	'72/'91
FRANKLIN BALANCE SHEET	Capital Appreciation	10.7	20.06	10,381.70	12,614.20	☆	2.2	342-5236	415-312-3200	1.50	0.50	None	Lippman/Baughman	'90
FRANKLIN CA 250	Specialty	3.6	10.86	10,258.10	11,911.10	☆	1.2	342-5236	415-312-3200	None	None	None	Frank Felicelli	'91
FRANKLIN CUST:DYNATECH	Science & Technology	72.7	9.97	10,152.70	11,187.20	18,135.60	1.2	342-5236	415-312-3200	4.00	None	None	R. Johnson	'68
FRANKLIN CUST:GROWTH	Growth	599.5	14.09	10,191.40	10,819.70	16,580.30	2.6	342-5236	415-312-3200	4.00	None	None	Jerry Palmeieri	'48
FRANKLIN CUST:INCOME	Income	3,407.7	2.40	10,454.60	11,589.20	19,056.60	7.9	342-5236	415-312-3200	4.00	None	None	Matt Avery	'90
FRANKLIN CUST:US GOVT	Fixed Income	14,168.6	7.26	10,211.10	10,935.30	16,342.20	7.8	342-5236	415-312-3200	4.00	None	None	Jack Lemein	'70
FRANKLIN CUST:UTILITIES	Utility	3,080.9	10.41	10,233.10	11,898.10	19,408.90	5.3	342-5236	415-312-3200	4.00	None	None	Johnson/Edwards	'87/'91
FRANKLIN EQUITY	Growth	351.5	7.25	9,976.30	10,970.60	14,292.90	1.6	342-5236	415-312-3200	4.00	None	None	Marvin McClay	'82
FRANKLIN GLOBAL HEALTH	Health/Biotechnology	3.7	9.60	11,041.60	11,145.10	☆	0.9	342-5236	415-312-3200	4.50	0.25	None	R. Johnson	'92
FRANKLIN GOLD	Gold	356.5	14.22	12,730.00	12,491.80	14,200.50	1.6	342-5236	415-312-3200	4.00	None	None	*Team Managed*	'69
FRANKLIN INTL:INTL EQU	International	11.0	10.50	10,350.70	10,333.00	☆	3.9	342-5236	415-312-3200	4.50	0.25	None	Bill Kohli	'91
FRANKLIN INTL:PAC GROWTH	Pacific Region	9.5	11.78	10,969.10	10,870.60	☆	1.6	342-5236	415-312-3200	4.50	0.25	None	Bill Kohli	'91
FRANKLIN INV:ADJ RATE	Fixed Income	22.4	10.05	10,094.10	10,559.00	☆	5.4	342-5236	415-312-3200	2.25	0.25	None	Leman/Coffey	'91
FRANKLIN INV:ADJ US GOVT	Fixed Income	2,455.8	9.86	10,107.10	10,328.10	14,359.10	4.5	342-5236	415-312-3200	2.25	0.25	None	Leman/Coffey	'87/'90
FRANKLIN INV:CONV SEC	Convertible Securities	33.0	11.98	10,362.40	12,394.20	17,810.70	5.7	342-5236	415-312-3200	4.00	None	None	Jamieson/Nori	'87/'92
FRANKLIN INV:GLOBAL GOVT	World Income	172.5	9.14	10,415.90	10,835.40	15,151.20	8.3	342-5236	415-312-3200	4.00	None	None	Bill Kohli	'88
FRANKLIN INV:SH-INT USG	Fixed Income	259.9	10.74	10,152.80	11,018.80	15,504.00	5.0	342-5236	415-312-3200	2.25	None	None	Jack Lemein	'87
FRANKLIN INV:SP EQUITY	Equity Income	31.5	14.15	10,211.50	11,772.30	18,861.10	4.8	342-5236	415-312-3200	4.00	None	None	Frank Felicelli	'88
FRANKLIN MGD:CORP QUAL	Fixed Income	34.5	24.41	10,263.20	10,847.40	16,738.70	4.8	342-5236	415-312-3200	1.50	0.25	None	W. Lippman	'87
FRANKLIN MGD:INV GRADE	Fixed Income	39.1	9.22	10,211.80	11,037.90	15,582.30	6.2	342-5236	415-312-3200	4.00	0.25	None	W. Lippman	'87
FRANKLIN MGD:RISING DIV	Growth & Income	341.0	15.23	9,655.40	10,477.10	17,288.70	1.7	342-5236	415-312-3200	4.00	0.50	None	W. Lippman	'87
FRANKLIN PRT:TX-AD HY	Fixed Income	48.1	8.80	10,373.50	11,619.30	17,644.30	10.0	342-5236	415-312-3200	4.00	None	None	Martin Wiskemann	'87
FRANKLIN PRT:TX-AD INTL	World Income	15.1	11.12	10,171.00	10,090.10	15,691.70	9.5	342-5236	415-312-3200	4.00	None	None	Bill Kohli	'90
FRANKLIN PRT:TX-AD USG	Fixed Income	433.8	11.04	10,252.10	11,061.00	16,618.20	6.9	342-5236	415-312-3200	4.00	None	None	Jack Lemein	'87
FRANKLIN PA:US GOVT	Fixed Income	10.9	10.34	10,230.70	11,037.40	16,456.60	7.2	342-5236	415-312-3200	4.00	None	None	Jack Lemein	'86
FRANKLIN PREMIER RET★	Flexible	21.8	5.86	10,414.50	11,887.40	16,918.70	2.6	342-5236	415-312-3200	4.00	None	None	Costa/Wiskemann	'87/'72
FRANKLIN SM CAP GROWTH	Small-Company Growth	7.0	11.11	10,310.50	12,074.90	☆	0.5	342-5236	415-312-3200	4.50	0.25	None	Ed Jamieson	'92
FRANKLIN STRAT:GLBL UTIL	Utility	16.8	11.50	10,344.40	☆	☆	0.0	342-5236	415-312-3200	4.50	0.25	None	S. Edwards	'92
FRANKLIN STRAT MTGE	Fixed Income	5.1	10.21	10,232.20	☆	☆	0.0	342-5236	415-312-3200	4.50	None	None	Roger Bayston	'93
FREMONT:GLOBAL	Global	141.4	12.30	10,198.90	11,140.90	☆	3.1	548-4539	415-768-9000	None	None	None	Rhodes/Redo/Landini	'88/'88
FREMONT:GROWTH	Growth	38.9	10.76	9,945.20	☆	☆	0.0	548-4539	415-768-9000	None	None	None	Pang/Sit	'92/'92
FT SERIES:INTL EQ;A	International	131.0	15.31	10,289.00	9,926.50	12,643.20	1.2	245-4770	412-288-1900	4.50	None	None	Christopher H. Wiles	'90
FT SERIES:INTL EQ;C	International	0.1	15.30	10,282.30	☆	☆	0.0	245-4770	412-288-1900	None	0.75	1.00	Christopher H. Wiles	'93
FT SERIES:INTL INC;A	World Income	113.7	11.00	10,961.60	10,933.80	☆	6.8	245-4770	412-288-1900	4.50	0.25	None	Randall S. Bauer	'91

FT SERIES:INTL INC;C	World Income	0.1	10.99	10,939.70	☆	☆	0.0	245-4770	412-288-1900	None	0.75	1.00	Randall S. Bauer	'93
FUND FOR US GOVT SEC;A	Fixed Income	1,828.9	8.45	10,141.20	10,660.10	15,762.60	8.1	245-4770	412-288-1900	4.50	None	None	Gary Madich	'87
FUND FOR US GOVT SEC;C	Fixed Income	7.3	8.45	☆	☆	☆	0.0	245-4770	412-288-1900	None	0.75	1.00	Gary Madich	'93
FUNDAMENTAL:GOVT STRAT	Fixed Income	61.1	2.00	10,047.40	10,488.60	☆	8.4	322-6864	212-635-3005	None	0.25	None	Team Managed	'92
FUNDAMENTAL INVESTORS	Growth & Income	1,675.8	18.81	10,233.60	11,903.30	19,046.20	2.2	421-0180	210-530-4000	5.75	0.25	None	Multiple Managers	'78
FUNDTRUST:AGGRESSIVE GRO	Capital Appreciation	30.5	15.75	10,070.30	11,573.30	17,201.40	0.0	638-1896	212-644-1400	1.50	0.50	None	Michael Hirsch	'84
FUNDTRUST:GROWTH	Growth	21.8	13.98	10,115.80	11,438.80	16,491.00	1.6	638-1896	212-644-1400	1.50	0.50	None	Michael Hirsch	'84
FUNDTRUST:GROWTH&INCOME	Growth & Income	39.7	15.94	10,095.00	11,381.50	16,235.90	2.7	638-1896	212-644-1400	1.50	0.50	None	Michael Hirsch	'84
FUNDTRUST:INCOME	Fixed Income	74.4	10.49	10,270.80	11,199.70	15,224.20	6.3	638-1896	212-644-1400	1.50	0.50	None	Michael Hirsch	'84
FUNDTRUST:MGD TOT RETURN	Flexible	24.7	11.66	10,156.80	11,020.30	☆	2.9	638-1896	212-644-1400	1.50	0.50	None	Michael Hirsch	'88
GABELLI ASSET	Growth	739.0	22.10	10,473.90	12,130.80	19,127.30	1.1	422-3554	914-921-5100	None	0.13	None	Mario J. Gabelli	'86
GABELLI:CONVERTIBLE SEC	Convertible Securities	104.1	12.36	10,240.30	11,550.00	☆	5.2	422-3554	914-921-5100	4.50	None	None	Mario J. Gabelli	'89
GABELLI EQ:EQ INCOME	Equity Income	50.1	11.72	10,378.90	11,690.40	☆	2.6	422-3554	914-921-5100	None	0.25	None	Mario J. Gabelli	'92
GABELLI EQ:SM CAP GRO	Small-Company Growth	187.0	15.74	10,181.10	11,887.30	☆	0.2	422-3554	914-921-5100	4.50	0.25	None	Mario J. Gabelli	'91
GABELLI GROWTH	Growth	688.6	21.84	10,059.90	11,406.40	20,481.60	0.4	422-3554	914-921-5100	None	0.18	None	Elizabeth R. Bramwell	'87
GABELLI INV:ABC	Growth	9.7	10.10	☆	☆	☆	0.0	422-3554	914-921-5100	2.00	0.25	None	Mario J. Gabelli	'93
GABELLI VALUE	Capital Appreciation	448.4	11.93	10,699.60	12,785.80	☆	4.6	422-3554	914-921-5100	5.50	0.25	None	Mario J. Gabelli	'89
GALAXY:ASSET ALLOC;RTL	Flexible	55.6	10.84	10,044.20	11,446.60	☆	2.3	828-0450	800-628-0414	None	None	None	Fred Thompson	'91
GALAXY:EQUITY GROWTH;RTL	Growth	402.7	13.44	9,905.20	11,141.60	☆	1.2	828-0450	800-628-0414	None	None	None	Bob Armknecht	'90
GALAXY:EQUITY INCOME;RTL	Equity Income	104.8	12.43	10,036.70	11,113.60	☆	2.2	828-0450	800-628-0414	None	None	None	Edward Klieziewicz	'90
GALAXY:EQUITY VALUE;RTL	Growth & Income	159.3	12.43	10,218.20	11,441.00	☆	1.7	828-0450	800-628-0414	None	None	None	G. Jay Evans	'92
GALAXY:HI QUAL BOND;RTL	Fixed Income	137.7	11.07	10,335.80	11,420.50	☆	6.0	828-0450	800-628-0414	None	None	None	Ken Thomae	'90
GALAXY:INTMDT BOND;RTL	Fixed Income	408.4	10.94	10,191.60	11,095.70	☆	5.8	828-0450	800-628-0414	None	None	None	Bruce R. Barton	'92
GALAXY:INTL EQU;RTL	International	20.1	10.58	10,423.60	10,326.60	☆	0.6	828-0450	800-628-0414	None	None	None	James Knauf	'91
GALAXY:SHT-TM BOND;RTL	Fixed Income	63.2	10.24	10,154.80	10,757.40	☆	5.1	828-0450	800-628-0414	None	None	None	Ken Thomae	'91
GALAXY:SM CO EQUITY;RTL	Small-Company Growth	36.5	10.91	10,706.60	13,740.60	☆	0.0	828-0450	800-628-0414	None	None	None	Steve Barbaro	'91
GAM:EUROPE	European Region	12.0	76.24	9,928.40	9,814.70	☆	0.7	None	212-888-4200	5.00	None	None	Bennett/Crerar	'93/'93
GAM:GLOBAL	Global	21.3	117.96	10,375.60	10,755.70	15,813.30	0.9	None	212-888-4200	5.00	None	None	John Horseman	'90
GAM:INTERNATIONAL	International	39.1	157.68	10,560.60	11,319.10	19,117.70	2.1	None	212-888-4200	5.00	None	None	John Horseman	'90
GAM:NORTH AMERICA	Capital Appreciation	6.8	123.96	9,752.20	10,044.50	☆	0.6	None	212-888-4200	5.00	None	None	Fayez Sarofim & Co.	'90
GAM:PACIFIC BASIN	Pacific Region	28.8	154.28	10,974.20	12,336.70	19,084.10	0.5	None	212-888-4200	5.00	None	None	Bunker/Kirkby	'87/'87
GATEWAY:GOVT BOND PLUS	Fixed Income	25.1	10.52	10,197.10	10,745.80	15,461.30	5.7	354-6339	513-248-2700	None	None	None	Walter Sall	'88
GATEWAY:INDEX PLUS	Growth & Income	216.5	15.89	10,178.60	10,575.50	18,037.00	1.7	354-6339	513-248-2700	None	None	None	Peter W. Thayer	'77
GE FIXED INCOME★	Fixed Income	8.1	12.18	10,215.30	☆	☆	0.0	242-0134	203-326-4040	None	0.25	None	Robert A. MacDougall	'93
GE GLOBAL EQUITY★	Global	7.5	15.92	10,172.50	☆	☆	0.0	242-0134	203-326-4040	None	0.25	None	Ralph R. Layman	'93
GE STRATEGIC INV★	Flexible	8.9	15.53	10,123.90	☆	☆	0.0	242-0134	203-326-4040	None	None	None	MacDougall/Carlson	'93/'93
GE US EQUITY★	Growth & Income	19.9	15.83	10,153.90	☆	☆	0.0	242-0134	203-326-4040	None	0.25	None	Eugene Bolton	'93
GENERAL SECURITIES	Capital Appreciation	27.4	12.56	10,111.60	10,622.70	17,987.50	8.8	331-4923	612-332-1212	5.00	None	None	Jack Robinson	'51
GE S&S PRGRM:LG-TM INTST★	Fixed Income	3,248.0	12.23	10,276.50	11,130.30	17,038.10	6.9	242-0134	203-326-4040	None	None	None	Robert A. MacDougall	'87
GE S&S PRGRM:MUTUAL★	Growth	1,728.0	39.48	10,175.30	11,552.30	19,374.10	2.7	242-0134	203-326-4040	None	None	None	Eugene Bolton	'90
GIBRALTAR EQUITY GROWTH	Growth & Income	1.0	12.72	9,492.50	9,627.40	14,733.10	0.0	None	215-525-6102	None	None	None	Norman McAvoy	'90
GIBRALTAR US GOVT	Fixed Income	1.5	10.01	10,137.50	☆	☆	5.5	None	215-525-6102	4.50	None	None	Joseph Waltman	'92
GINTEL ERISA	Growth & Income	54.6	35.18	9,707.50	10,954.70	15,105.60	1.8	243-5808	203-622-6400	None	0.20	None	Gintel/Godman	'82/'92
GINTEL FUND	Growth	150.5	16.37	9,606.80	11,217.10	18,039.80	0.8	243-5808	203-622-6400	None	None	None	Gintel/Godman	'81/'92
GIT EQUITY:EQUITY INCOME	Equity Income	3.5	16.40	10,050.40	11,089.90	16,596.20	2.2	336-3063	703-528-6500	None	None	None	Kevin Moore	'93

★FPA PARAMOUNT—Closed to new investors.
★FRANKLIN PREMIER RET — On 5/1/93, fund was reclassified from Option Income to Flexible Portfolio.

★GE FUNDS—Limited to selected General Electric employees.

PERFORMANCE OF MUTUAL FUNDS *(continued)*

FUND NAME	OBJECTIVE	TOTAL NET ASSETS ($ MIL) 5/31/93	NET ASSET $ VALUE 6/30/93	PERFORMANCE (Return on Initial $10,000 Investment) 3/31/93-6/30/93	6/30/92-6/30/93	6/30/88-6/30/93	DIVIDEND YIELD % 6/93	PHONE NUMBER 800	In-State	FEES Load	12b-1	Redemption	MANAGER	SINCE
GIT EQUITY:SELECT GROWTH	Growth	5.5	17.93	9,917.20	10,853.70	15,971.30	0.7	336-3063	703-528-6500	None	None	None	Kevin Moore	'93
GIT EQUITY:SPEC GROWTH	Small-Company Growth	40.6	19.81	10,031.60	11,249.70	14,565.30	0.5	336-3063	703-528-6500	None	None	None	Richard Carney	'83
GIT INCOME:GOVERNMENT	Fixed Income	9.7	10.41	10,251.00	11,325.00	15,797.80	4.2	336-3063	703-528-6500	None	None	None	John Edwards	'89
GIT INCOME:MAXIMUM INC	Fixed Income	7.2	7.53	10,299.60	11,340.30	15,097.70	8.7	336-3063	703-528-6500	None	None	None	John Edwards	'88
GLENMEDE:EQUITY	Growth	33.9	13.23	10,153.70	12,012.10	☆	2.4	441-7450	215-875-3200	None	None	None	John Church	'93
GLENMEDE:INSTL INTERNATL	International	11.8	10.96	10,469.60	☆	☆	0.0	441-7450	215-875-3200	None	None	None	Andrew B. Williams	'92
GLENMEDE:INTMDT GOVT	Fixed Income	475.8	10.96	10,235.20	11,007.50	☆	6.3	441-7450	215-875-3200	None	None	None	Durham/Manganaro	'88/'88
GLENMEDE:INTERNATIONAL	International	208.0	11.42	10,487.80	10,600.60	☆	2.4	441-7450	215-875-3200	None	None	None	Andrew B. Williams	'88
GLENMEDE:INTL FIXED INC	World Income	15.9	10.39	10,124.50	☆	☆	0.0	441-7450	215-875-3200	None	None	None	Nicholas Manganaro	'92
GLENMEDE:MODEL EQUITY	Growth	10.8	10.95	10,111.10	☆	☆	0.0	441-7450	215-875-3200	None	None	None	John Church	'93
GLENMEDE:SMALL CAP EQU	Small-Company Growth	51.8	13.46	10,346.30	13,512.00	☆	1.2	441-7450	215-875-3200	None	None	None	Anderson/Manaiso	'92/'93
GLOBAL UTILITY;A	Utility	119.6	13.64	10,178.60	11,695.30	☆	3.4	225-1852	None	5.25	0.30	None	Jack Ryan	'91
GLOBAL UTILITY;B	Utility	95.9	13.65	10,159.80	11,607.00	☆	2.7	225-1852	None	None	1.00	5.00	Jack Ryan	'91
GMO CORE TR:PELICAN	Growth	92.5	12.22	10,489.10	12,239.50	☆	3.0	None	617-330-7517	None	None	None	Richard Mayo	'89
GNA INVESTORS:US GOVT	Fixed Income	1,110.3	10.19	10,320.50	11,011.20	16,079.10	7.0	426-5520	206-625-1755	None	0.98	5.00	David W. Hoyle	'87
GOLDEN RNBOW A JAMES ADV	Growth & Income	172.5	17.81	10,164.30	11,809.30	☆	4.1	227-4648	513-461-0332	None	0.20	None	Team Managed	'91
GOLDMAN SACHS:ADJ AGCY★	Fixed Income	2,295.2	10.02	10,118.40	10,461.00	☆	4.7	526-7384	212-902-0800	None	None	None	Team Managed	'91
GOLDMAN SACHS:ADJ MTGE★	Fixed Income	1.0	14.68	10,149.30	☆	☆	0.0	526-7384	212-902-0800	3.00	None	None	Team Managed	'93
GOLDMAN SACHS EQ:CAP GRO★	Growth	693.1	15.25	10,112.70	11,959.80	☆	0.5	526-7384	212-902-0800	5.50	0.25	None	Team Managed	'92
GOLDMAN SACHS EQ:G&I★	Growth & Income	12.3	14.40	9,822.60	☆	☆	0.0	526-7384	212-902-0800	5.50	0.25	None	Team Managed	'93
GOLDMAN SACHS EQ:INTL★	International	93.9	15.00	10,176.40	☆	☆	0.0	526-7384	212-902-0800	5.50	0.25	None	Team Managed	'92
GOLDMAN SACHS EQ:SEL EQU★	Growth	90.9	15.87	9,875.50	11,237.80	☆	1.4	526-7384	212-902-0800	5.50	0.25	None	Team Managed	'91
GOLDMAN SACHS EQ:SM CAP★	Small-Company Growth	86.6	18.37	10,437.50	☆	☆	0.0	526-7384	212-902-0800	5.50	0.25	None	Team Managed	'92
GOLDMAN SACHS:GLBL INC★	World Income	621.3	14.71	10,399.90	11,054.60	☆	6.3	526-7384	212-902-0800	4.50	0.25	None	Team Managed	'91
GOLDMAN SACHS:GOV AGENCY★	Fixed Income	45.8	10.07	10,129.00	☆	☆	0.0	526-7384	212-902-0800	None	None	None	Team Managed	'92
GOLDMAN SACHS:GOVT INC★	Fixed Income	6.5	14.77	10,238.00	☆	☆	0.0	526-7384	212-902-0800	4.50	0.25	None	Team Managed	'93
GOVERNMENT INCOME SEC	Fixed Income	3,823.9	9.36	10,157.70	10,693.20	15,766.20	7.9	245-4770	412-288-1900	1.00	None	1.00	Gary Madich	'87
GOVETT:EMERG MKT	International	34.1	13.08	11,094.10	11,858.60	☆	0.0	634-6838	415-393-0333	4.95	0.50	None	Rachael Maunder	'92
GOVETT:GLBL GOVT INC	World Income	77.0	10.10	10,422.50	11,449.90	☆	9.4	634-6838	415-393-0333	4.95	0.35	None	Simon Osborne	'92
GOVETT:INTL EQUITY	International	32.7	11.49	10,688.40	11,579.50	☆	0.3	634-6838	415-393-0333	4.95	0.50	None	Gareth Watts	'92
GOVETT:SMALLER COMPANIES	Global Small Company	1.3	12.72	11,723.50	☆	☆	0.0	634-6838	415-393-0333	4.95	0.50	None	Watts/Van Wagoner	'93/'93
GRADISON-MCDONALD:EST	Growth	207.2	21.97	10,380.70	12,901.10	16,730.70	1.3	869-5999	513-579-5700	None	0.50	None	William Leugers	'83
GRADISON-MCDONALD GOVT	Fixed Income	251.8	13.58	10,217.90	10,978.50	16,178.10	6.1	869-5999	513-579-5700	2.00	0.25	None	Michael Link	'87
GRADISON-MCDONALD:OPPTY	Small-Company Growth	68.9	17.77	10,122.00	12,033.60	17,663.20	0.7	869-5999	513-579-5700	None	0.50	None	William Leugers	'83
GREEN CENTURY BALANCED	Balanced	2.7	10.14	9,826.20	10,369.00	☆	0.6	934-7336	None	None	0.50	None	Team Managed	'92
GREENFIELD FUND	Flexible	0.8	0.00	N/A	N/A	N/A	0.0	None	212-986-2600	None	None	1.00	R.F. Nichols	'81
GREENSPRING FUND	Growth	24.8	15.06	10,107.40	12,186.40	16,107.60	3.3	366-3863	410-823-5353	None	None	None	C. Carlson	'87
GROWTH FUND OF AMERICA	Growth	4,651.0	25.29	10,293.00	11,657.50	18,857.30	0.7	421-0180	210-530-4000	5.75	0.25	None	Multiple Managers	'73
GROWTH FD OF WASHINGTON	Growth	39.1	15.34	10,263.80	12,790.90	16,132.50	0.8	648-4782	202-842-5665	4.75	0.25	None	Prabha S. Carpenter	'86
GS SHORT-TERM GOVT AGNCY★	Fixed Income	330.5	10.20	10,130.70	10,656.80	☆	5.9	526-7384	212-902-0800	None	None	None	Team Managed	'93

GT GLOBAL AMERICA	Growth	146.5	15.62	9,768.60	12,271.70	19,338.70	7.9	824-1580	415-392-6181	4.75	0.35	None	Team Managed	'91
GT GLOBAL EMERGING MKTS	International	112.4	12.12	10,566.70	10,873.40	☆	0.7	824-1580	415-392-6181	4.75	0.50	None	Team Managed	'92
GT GLOBAL EUROPE	European Region	766.2	9.41	10,502.20	9,611.80	13,231.30	0.0	824-1580	415-392-6181	4.75	0.35	None	Team Managed	'85
GT GLOBAL GOVT INC;A	World Income	636.0	10.54	10,576.80	11,445.40	16,409.70	8.3	824-1580	415-392-6181	4.75	0.35	None	Team Managed	'91
GT GLOBAL GOVT INC;B	World Income	62.3	10.54	10,558.40	☆	☆	0.0	824-1580	415-392-6181	None	1.00	5.00	Team Managed	'92
GT GLOBAL GRO & INC;A	Global	192.5	5.74	10,300.50	11,014.50	☆	4.8	824-1580	415-392-6181	4.75	0.35	None	Team Managed	'90
GT GLOBAL GRO & INC;B	Global	24.6	5.75	10,302.20	☆	☆	0.0	824-1580	415-392-6181	None	1.00	5.00	Team Managed	'92
GT GLOBAL HEALTH CARE	Health/Biotechnology	510.0	16.90	10,696.20	9,679.30	☆	0.0	824-1580	415-392-6181	4.75	0.50	None	Team Managed	'89
GT GLOBAL HIGH INC;A	World Income	39.1	13.23	11,035.30	☆	☆	0.0	824-1580	415-392-6181	4.75	0.35	None	Team Managed	'92
GT GLOBAL HIGH INC;B	World Income	42.0	13.21	11,010.00	☆	☆	0.0	824-1580	415-392-6181	None	1.00	5.00	Team Managed	'92
GT GLOBAL INTERNATIONAL	International	442.8	9.11	10,483.30	10,035.50	15,281.40	0.2	824-1580	415-392-6181	4.75	0.35	None	Team Managed	'87
GT GLOBAL JAPAN	Japanese	120.2	10.91	11,189.70	12,057.60	10,999.90	0.5	824-1580	415-392-6181	4.75	0.35	None	Team Managed	'91
GT GLOBAL LATIN AMER	Latin American	94.7	16.67	10,245.90	10,198.60	☆	7.2	824-1580	415-392-6181	4.75	0.50	None	Team Managed	'91
GT GLOBAL PACIFIC	Pacific Region	356.4	12.10	10,784.30	10,632.80	16,837.80	0.7	824-1580	415-392-6181	4.75	0.35	None	Team Managed	'87
GT GLOBAL STRAT INC;A	World Income	119.4	12.25	10,944.60	12,301.10	17,111.00	10.4	824-1580	415-392-6181	4.75	0.35	None	Team Managed	'88
GT GLOBAL STRAT INC;B	World Income	51.7	12.25	10,927.90	☆	☆	0.0	824-1580	415-392-6181	None	1.00	5.00	Team Managed	'92
GT GLOBAL TELECOMM;A★	Global	636.5	14.01	11,057.60	12,660.80	☆	1.1	824-1580	415-392-6181	4.75	0.50	None	Team Managed	'92
GT GLOBAL WORLDWIDE	Global	160.6	16.12	10,326.70	11,194.30	17,347.20	0.4	824-1580	415-392-6181	4.75	0.35	None	Team Managed	'87
GUARDIAN PARK AVENUE	Growth	450.2	28.06	10,354.20	13,524.30	20,096.10	2.0	221-3253	212-598-1291	4.50	0.15	None	Charles E. Albers	'72
GUARDIAN US GOVT SECS	Fixed Income	30.5	10.83	10,249.10	11,242.70	☆	5.2	221-3253	212-598-1291	4.50	0.25	None	Michelle Babakian	'89
J HANCOCK ASSET ALLOC	Flexible	34.3	13.81	10,208.90	11,773.60	☆	0.9	225-5291	None	5.00	0.50	None	Robert Freedman	'88
J HANCOCK DISCOVERY;A	Small-Company Growth	4.3	10.67	10,379.40	12,294.60	☆	0.0	225-5291	None	5.00	0.30	None	Chapman/Hazard	'92/'92
J HANCOCK DISCOVERY;B	Small-Company Growth	39.6	10.52	10,374.80	12,220.90	☆	0.0	225-5291	None	None	1.00	4.00	Chapman/Hazard	'91/'91
J HANCOCK DIVERSIFIED	Growth & Income	11.2	12.41	10,234.70	11,752.10	☆	1.9	225-5291	None	2.00	0.50	None	Paul McManus	'91
J HANCOCK FR ENVIRO;A	Environmental	21.0	8.36	9,510.80	9,905.20	☆	0.0	225-5291	None	5.00	1.00	None	David Beckwith	'89
J HANCOCK FR ENVIRO;B	Environmental	1.0	8.30	9,507.40	9,857.50	☆	0.0	225-5291	None	None	1.00	4.00	David Beckwith	'92
J HANCOCK FR GLOBAL;A	Global	79.8	12.02	10,415.90	10,684.40	☆	0.0	225-5291	None	5.00	0.30	None	David Beckwith	'93
J HANCOCK FR GLOBAL;B	Global	13.1	11.93	10,401.00	10,632.80	14,451.30	0.0	225-5291	None	None	0.75	4.00	David Beckwith	'93
J HANCOCK FR GLB INC;A	World Income	12.5	9.42	10,071.00	9,908.70	☆	9.0	225-5291	None	4.50	0.25	None	Robert Kowit	'92
J HANCOCK FR GLB INC;B	World Income	197.5	9.42	10,068.70	9,868.80	14,032.90	8.4	225-5291	None	None	0.75	4.00	Robert Kowit	'90
J HANCOCK FR GLOBAL RX	Health/Biotechnology	16.7	13.72	10,660.50	10,888.90	☆	0.0	225-5291	None	5.00	0.50	None	Benjamin Williams	'92
J HANCOCK FR GLBL TECH	Science & Technology	35.1	17.37	10,965.90	13,596.30	15,346.00	0.0	225-5291	None	5.00	None	None	Barry Gordon	'83
J HANCOCK FR GLD&GOV;A	Gold	18.5	16.49	10,542.30	11,381.00	☆	3.9	225-5291	None	5.00	0.25	None	Arace/Hudson	'92/'92
J HANCOCK FR GLD&GOV;B	Gold	41.8	16.48	10,542.80	11,353.10	15,101.50	3.6	225-5291	None	None	0.75	4.00	Arace/Hudson	'84/'92
J HANCOCK FR NATL AV&T	Science & Technology	81.2	11.78	10,508.50	13,066.50	18,369.40	0.0	225-5291	None	5.00	None	None	Barry Gordon	'73
J HANCOCK FR PAC BASIN	Pacific Region	9.0	12.13	11,118.20	13,085.20	14,254.50	0.0	225-5291	None	5.00	0.50	None	Geoff Ho	'91
J HANCOCK FR REG BNK;A	Financial Services	69.2	20.06	9,913.80	13,578.10	☆	0.9	225-5291	None	5.00	0.25	None	Jim Schmidt	'92
J HANCOCK FR REG BNK;B	Financial Services	123.1	20.00	9,903.40	13,510.70	26,581.60	0.7	225-5291	None	None	0.75	4.00	Jim Schmidt	'85
J HANCOCK FR SH WRLD;A	World Income	17.1	9.20	10,083.20	10,243.60	☆	7.5	225-5291	None	3.00	0.25	None	Robert Kowit	'92
J HANCOCK FR SH WRLD;B	World Income	167.0	9.19	10,063.90	10,153.40	☆	6.7	225-5291	None	None	1.00	3.00	Robert Kowit	'91
J HANCOCK GROWTH	Growth	157.1	17.87	10,223.10	12,348.50	18,452.50	0.0	225-5291	None	5.00	0.50	None	Robert Freedman	'93
J HANCOCK SOVER ACHV;A	Growth	15.6	11.84	9,813.00	11,391.60	☆	0.3	225-5291	None	5.00	0.25	None	Team Managed	'92
J HANCOCK SOVER ACHV;B	Growth	72.7	11.77	9,794.50	11,307.50	15,097.20	0.2	225-5291	None	None	0.75	4.00	Team Managed	'90
J HANCOCK SOVER BAL;A	Balanced	18.2	10.68	10,204.80	☆	☆	0.0	225-5291	None	5.00	0.70	None	Team Managed	'92
J HANCOCK SOVER BAL;B	Balanced	49.6	10.67	10,186.80	☆	☆	0.0	225-5291	None	None	1.00	4.00	Team Managed	'92

★GOLDMAN SACHS FUNDS—Institutional funds.
★GS SHORT-TERM GOVT AGNCY—Institutional fund.

★GT GLOBAL TELECOMM; A — Investment objective changed from Science & Tech to Global, effective 4/22/93.

PERFORMANCE OF MUTUAL FUNDS (continued)

FUND NAME	OBJECTIVE	TOTAL NET ASSETS ($ MIL) 5/31/93	NET ASSET $ VALUE 6/30/93	PERFORMANCE (Return on Initial $10,000 Investment) 3/31/93-6/30/93	6/30/92-6/30/93	6/30/88-6/30/93	DIVIDEND YIELD % 6/93	PHONE NUMBER 800	In-State	FEES Load	12b-1	Redemption	MANAGER	SINCE
J HANCOCK SOVER BOND	Fixed Income	1,460.6	16.04	10,320.60	11,331.20	16,987.70	7.4	225-5291	None	4.50	0.50	None	Ho/Evans	'88/'88
J HANCOCK SOVER GOVT;A	Fixed Income	359.6	10.76	10,250.50	11,089.70	☆	6.5	225-5291	None	4.50	0.30	None	Anne C. Hodson	'92
J HANCOCK SOVER GOVT;B	Fixed Income	221.3	10.75	10,246.50	11,059.10	16,615.30	6.3	225-5291	None	None	0.75	4.00	Anne C. Hodson	'92
J HANCOCK SOVER INVSTRS	Growth & Income	1,129.5	14.82	9,899.90	10,882.60	18,895.00	3.0	225-5291	None	5.00	0.25	None	Team Managed	'79
J HANCOCK SPEC EQ;A	Small-Company Growth	154.0	14.20	10,948.30	15,411.90	29,297.40	0.0	225-5291	None	5.00	0.50	None	Michael DiCarlo	'88
J HANCOCK SPEC EQ;B	Small-Company Growth	32.8	14.18	10,932.90	☆	☆	0.0	225-5291	None	None	1.00	4.00	Michael DiCarlo	'93
J HANCOCK STRAT:INCOME	Fixed Income	261.8	7.64	10,346.20	10,874.50	14,680.90	9.4	225-5291	None	4.50	0.50	None	Frederick L. Cavanaugh	'86
J HANCOCK US GOVT SEC	Fixed Income	260.3	9.05	10,180.30	10,878.60	15,208.90	5.7	225-5291	None	3.00	0.50	None	Anne C. Hodson	'90
HANOVER:BLUE CHIP GROWTH	Growth & Income	62.7	10.06	9,719.90	☆	☆	0.0	821-2371	None	3.00	1.00	None	Steve Duff	'93
HANOVER:GOVT SECS	Fixed Income	87.5	10.20	10,256.30	☆	☆	0.0	821-2371	None	3.00	1.00	None	Pam Wooster	'93
HANOVER:SHORT-TM US GOVT	Fixed Income	7.7	9.96	10,118.30	☆	☆	0.0	821-2371	None	1.50	1.00	None	Guy Barba	'93
HANOVER:SMALL CAP GROWTH	Small-Company Growth	7.4	10.13	☆	☆	☆	0.0	821-2371	None	3.00	1.00	None	Francis Lane	'93
HARBOR:BOND	Fixed Income	116.2	11.66	10,336.20	11,405.10	17,883.30	6.2	422-1050	419-247-2477	None	None	None	William Gross	'87
HARBOR:CAPITAL APPREC	Growth	126.7	15.84	10,102.00	11,995.40	20,973.40	0.1	422-1050	419-247-2477	None	None	None	Spiros Segalas	'90
HARBOR:GROWTH	Growth	208.5	12.52	10,601.20	11,515.90	16,496.50	0.1	422-1050	419-247-2477	None	None	None	Arthur E. Nicholas	'93
HARBOR:INTERNATIONAL	International	1,316.4	19.71	10,636.80	10,850.80	20,692.00	1.1	422-1050	419-247-2477	None	None	None	Hakan Castegren	'87
HARBOR:SHORT DURATION	Fixed Income	151.1	10.08	10,161.50	10,566.60	☆	4.0	422-1050	419-247-2477	None	None	None	Adnan Akant	'92
HARBOR:VALUE	Growth & Income	80.3	13.93	9,802.60	10,842.70	18,319.10	2.6	422-1050	419-247-2477	None	None	None	John Strauss	'87
HARRIS INSIGHT:CONVERT	Convertible Securities	8.5	9.64	10,105.30	11,604.00	14,527.90	5.4	441-7379	302-792-6400	4.50	0.25	None	Mary Ann Gassner	'92
HARRIS INSIGHT:EQUITY	Growth & Income	38.4	13.02	10,474.10	12,444.30	18,640.50	1.8	441-7379	302-792-6400	4.50	0.25	None	Cindy Galor	'92
HARRIS INSIGHT:MGD FI	Fixed Income	83.4	10.69	10,298.70	10,983.30	☆	5.6	441-7379	302-792-6400	4.50	0.25	None	Barbara Downey	'91
HARTWELL EMRG GRO;A	Small-Company Growth	190.7	26.33	10,621.20	13,251.10	23,700.20	0.0	343-2898	617-621-6100	5.75	0.25	None	John M. Hartwell	'68
HARTWELL GROWTH;A	Capital Appreciation	26.3	23.43	9,828.00	11,167.80	18,458.50	0.0	343-2898	617-621-6100	5.75	0.25	None	William Miller	'84
HAWTHORNE INV:BOND	Fixed Income	2.7	10.93	10,256.40	11,236.70	☆	5.5	272-4548	617-245-5400	None	None	None	John H. Abbott	'91
HAWTHORNE INV:SEA	Growth	1.5	10.65	9,763.10	10,022.50	☆	1.7	272-4548	617-245-5400	None	None	None	Charles G. Dyer	'90
HEARTLAND:US GOVT	Fixed Income	41.8	10.86	10,543.20	12,092.30	18,082.90	5.4	432-7856	414-347-7777	None	0.30	3.00	Retzer/Nasgovitz	'89/'87
HEARTLAND:VALUE	Small-Company Growth	129.1	21.61	9,845.10	13,672.30	20,089.20	0.0	432-7856	414-347-7777	None	0.30	3.00	Nasgovitz/Denison	'85/'88
HENLOPEN FUND	Growth	0.9	11.55	10,684.60	☆	☆	0.0	792-2473	414-765-3500	None	None	None	Michael Hershey	'92
HERITAGE CAPITAL APPREC	Capital Appreciation	71.2	14.67	10,215.90	11,956.70	17,339.20	0.5	421-4184	813-573-8143	4.00	0.50	None	Herb Ehlers	'85
HERITAGE INC:DIVERSIFIED	Fixed Income	39.3	10.81	10,222.60	11,176.00	☆	7.8	421-4184	813-573-8143	4.00	0.35	None	Kirschbaum/Ross	'90/'90
HERITAGE INCOME-GROWTH	Equity Income	32.4	11.76	10,019.10	11,606.90	16,481.80	2.4	421-4184	813-573-8143	4.00	0.25	None	Lou Kirschbaum	'90
HERITAGE INC:LTD MAT GOV	Fixed Income	118.0	9.55	10,049.30	10,291.00	☆	5.8	421-4184	813-573-8143	None	0.35	None	Ivan Ross	'90
HERITAGE:SMALL CAP STK	Small-Company Growth	22.8	14.30	☆	☆	☆	0.0	421-4184	813-573-8143	None	0.35	None	Lou Kirschbaum	'93
HIGHMARK:BOND	Fixed Income	31.7	11.11	10,277.80	11,165.10	16,411.50	6.0	433-6884	None	None	None	None	Merus Capital Mgmt	'88
HIGHMARK:INCOME EQUITY	Equity Income	101.9	11.99	10,063.60	11,290.30	18,214.20	3.2	433-6884	None	None	None	None	Merus Capital Mgmt	'88
HIGHMARK:SPEC GRO EQUITY	Small-Company Growth	5.1	12.26	10,140.60	10,850.90	15,448.80	0.0	433-6884	None	None	None	None	Merus Capital Mgmt	'88
HILLIARD LYONS GROWTH	Growth	27.0	15.41	9,993.50	10,898.60	☆	0.6	444-1854	502-588-8400	4.75	0.25	None	Harvey/Norman	'92/'92
HODGES FUND	Capital Appreciation	7.2	11.52	9,779.30	☆	☆	0.0	388-8512	214-954-1177	2.50	0.50	None	Hodges Capital Mgt	'92
HOMESTATE:PA GROWTH	Growth	2.9	10.97	9,972.70	☆	☆	0.0	232-0224	717-396-7864	5.00	0.35	None	Kenneth G. Mertz II	'92
HOMESTEAD:SHORT-TERM BD	Fixed Income	22.5	5.20	10,149.10	10,804.50	☆	5.0	258-3030	None	None	None	None	Peter Morris	'91
HOMESTEAD:VALUE	Growth & Income	34.7	13.75	10,301.90	11,811.20	☆	1.7	258-3030	None	None	None	None	Peter Morris	'90
HUNTINGTON:GERMAN GOVT	World Income	10.9	12.15	9,601.20	☆	☆	0.0	354-4111	213-681-3700	3.00	None	None	Bankers Trust Company	'92
HUNTINGTON ICP:GLBL CURR	World Income	64.2	13.85	10,150.80	10,590.50	15,284.30	4.4	354-4111	213-681-3700	2.25	0.45	None	Bankers Trust Company	'86
HUNTINGTON ICP:HARD CURR	World Income	49.9	12.56	9,969.90	10,399.80	☆	5.3	354-4111	213-681-3700	2.25	0.45	None	Bankers Trust Company	'89
HUNTINGTON ICP:HIGH INC	World Income	32.3	11.58	9,911.60	9,267.10	☆	7.5	354-4111	213-681-3700	2.25	0.45	None	Bankers Trust Company	'89

HYPRN:HYPRN SH DUR I	Fixed Income	115.1	9.22	10,089.80	10,062.00	☆	5.6	497-3746	212-980-8400	3.00	0.25	None	Hyperion Capital Mgt.	'92
HYPRN II:HYPRN SHDUR 2	Fixed Income	128.1	9.50	10,065.30	9,955.30	☆	4.6	497-3746	212-980-8400	None	1.00	3.00	Hyperion Capital Mgt.	'92
IAA TRUST ASSET ALLOC	Fixed Income	6.6	11.60	10,199.20	10,958.30	15,701.40	4.9	245-2100	215-834-3500	3.00	0.25	None	John Jacobs	'78
IAA TRUST GROWTH	Growth	70.9	17.47	9,960.10	11,119.80	17,019.30	1.6	245-2100	215-834-3500	3.00	0.25	None	Gregory Turner	'79
IAI:BALANCED	Balanced	71.8	10.88	10,092.80	11,266.50	☆	1.9	945-3863	612-376-2700	None	0.16	None	John Phillips	'92
IAI BOND	Fixed Income	124.5	10.46	10,382.40	11,555.40	17,286.90	5.6	945-3863	612-376-2700	None	0.24	None	Larry R. Hill	'84
IAI:EMERGING GROWTH	Small-Company Growth	158.5	14.50	10,784.60	14,322.80	☆	0.0	945-3863	612-376-2700	None	0.12	None	Leggott/Press	'91/'91
IAI:GOVERNMENT	Fixed Income	40.5	10.56	10,238.60	10,960.10	☆	5.3	945-3863	612-376-2700	None	0.13	None	Scott Bettin	'91
IAI INTERNATIONAL	International	67.8	11.32	10,354.90	10,750.70	14,378.30	2.3	945-3863	612-376-2700	None	0.25	None	Roy Gillson	'90
IAI:MIDCAP GROWTH	Growth	22.3	11.91	10,025.30	12,120.90	☆	0.2	945-3863	612-376-2700	None	None	None	Chuck Webster	'92
IAI REGIONAL	Growth	656.7	21.58	10,007.40	11,136.40	19,449.60	1.2	945-3863	612-376-2700	None	0.21	None	Julian P. Carlin	'80
IAI RESERVE	Fixed Income	75.2	10.08	10,079.70	10,339.50	13,829.00	3.5	945-3863	612-376-2700	None	None	None	Tim Palmer	'91
IAI STOCK	Capital Appreciation	132.8	14.48	9,980.90	11,068.20	16,707.50	0.7	945-3863	612-376-2700	None	0.18	None	Julian P. Carlin	'91
IAI VALUE	Capital Appreciation	22.7	11.93	10,354.30	11,446.80	16,572.90	0.8	945-3863	612-376-2700	None	None	None	Douglas Platt	'91
IBM FDS:LARGE CO INDEX	Growth & Income	137.4	14.55	10,037.70	11,311.40	☆	2.4	426-9876	None	None	None	None	IBM Credit Invt Mgt	'90
IBM FDS:SMALL CO INDEX	Small-Company Growth	222.1	17.53	10,063.10	11,957.60	☆	1.3	426-9876	None	None	None	None	IBM Credit Invt Mgt	'90
IBM FDS:TREAS INDEX	Fixed Income	144.8	11.18	10,289.80	11,027.60	☆	5.5	426-9876	None	None	None	None	IBM Credit Invt Mgt	'91
IBM FDS:UTILITY INDEX	Utility	54.5	11.31	10,439.30	☆	☆	0.0	426-9876	None	None	None	None	IBM Credit Invt Mgt	'93
IDEX FUND	Growth	348.2	18.89	10,086.10	11,026.50	24,913.00	0.7	624-4339	813-587-1800	8.50	None	None	Thomas F. Marsico	'85
IDEX 3★	Growth	201.8	16.54	10,135.20	11,266.50	24,534.90	0.5	624-4339	813-587-1800	8.50	None	None	Thomas F. Marsico	'87
IDEX TOTAL INCOME	Fixed Income	28.8	9.40	10,367.80	11,424.80	15,979.70	8.4	624-4339	813-587-1800	7.00	None	None	Ronald V. Speaker	'87
IDEX II:GLOBAL	Global	9.3	12.42	9,833.70	☆	☆	0.0	624-4339	813-587-1800	5.50	0.35	None	Helen Young-Hayes	'92
IDEX II:GROWTH	Growth	521.8	17.74	10,068.50	11,030.60	25,225.10	0.4	624-4339	813-587-1800	5.50	0.25	None	Thomas F. Marsico	'86
IDEX II:HIGH YIELD	Fixed Income	67.9	10.85	10,395.80	11,481.40	18,037.70	7.8	624-4339	813-587-1800	4.75	0.35	None	David Halfpap	'85
IDS BLUE CHIP ADVNTG	Growth & Income	131.1	6.40	10,157.90	11,399.70	☆	1.5	328-8300	612-671-3733	5.00	None	None	Stuart Sedlack	'90
IDS BOND	Fixed Income	2,351.6	5.36	10,391.50	11,625.50	17,640.40	7.6	328-8300	612-671-3733	5.00	None	None	Frederick C. Quirsfeld	'85
IDS DISCOVERY	Small-Company Growth	435.3	11.35	10,451.20	12,383.50	19,587.80	0.0	328-8300	612-671-3733	5.00	None	None	Ray Hirsch	'88
IDS DVSD EQUITY INCM	Equity Income	333.1	7.42	10,407.30	12,035.50	☆	3.5	328-8300	612-671-3733	5.00	None	None	Richard Lazarchic	'90
IDS EQUITY PLUS	Growth & Income	580.5	11.73	10,025.60	11,904.90	19,100.80	1.0	328-8300	612-671-3733	5.00	None	None	Joseph M. Barsky III	'83
IDS EXTRA INCOME	Fixed Income	1,454.3	4.45	10,422.80	11,758.10	16,736.50	9.8	328-8300	612-671-3733	5.00	None	None	John A. Utter	'83
IDS FEDERAL INCOME	Fixed Income	1,014.2	5.30	10,188.80	10,887.40	15,557.20	6.2	328-8300	612-671-3733	5.00	None	None	Stuart Sedlack	'89
IDS GLOBAL BOND	World Income	148.9	6.08	10,340.70	11,371.80	☆	7.1	328-8300	612-671-3733	5.00	None	None	Ray S. Goodner	'89
IDS GLOBAL GROWTH	Global	123.1	5.55	10,183.50	10,442.30	☆	0.6	328-8300	612-671-3733	5.00	None	None	Edward Korff	'90
IDS GROWTH	Growth	939.2	18.09	9,934.10	11,985.20	22,438.80	0.0	328-8300	612-671-3733	5.00	None	None	Mary J. Malevich	'92
IDS INTERNATIONAL	International	288.4	8.89	10,471.10	10,687.10	13,912.00	0.2	328-8300	612-671-3733	5.00	None	None	Peter L. Lamaison	'84
IDS MANAGED RETIREMENT	Flexible	1,623.4	11.50	10,028.10	11,708.60	21,873.60	1.7	328-8300	612-671-3733	5.00	None	None	Richard Lazarchic	'93
IDS MUTUAL	Balanced	2,569.4	12.68	10,262.20	11,618.50	17,453.00	4.4	328-8300	612-671-3733	5.00	None	None	Medcalf/Labenski	'83/'87
IDS NEW DIMENSIONS	Growth	3,110.2	13.90	10,220.60	12,047.50	23,071.70	0.3	328-8300	612-671-3733	5.00	None	None	Gordon Fines	'91
IDS PRECIOUS METALS	Gold	68.4	7.82	13,033.30	14,401.00	11,594.40	0.3	328-8300	612-671-3733	5.00	None	None	Richard Warden	'91
IDS PROGRESSIVE	Capital Appreciation	254.3	6.88	9,856.70	11,477.80	14,553.50	1.3	328-8300	612-671-3733	5.00	None	None	Michael W. Garbish	'91
IDS SELECTIVE	Fixed Income	1,655.5	9.72	10,366.70	11,623.90	17,370.60	7.5	328-8300	612-671-3733	5.00	None	None	Ray S. Goodner	'85
IDS STOCK	Growth & Income	1,851.4	19.92	10,159.50	11,536.10	19,634.40	2.8	328-8300	612-671-3733	5.00	None	None	Joseph M. Barsky III	'93
IDS STR:AGGR EQUITY	Capital Appreciation	600.4	15.22	10,066.10	11,227.60	18,956.60	0.0	328-8300	612-671-3733	None	1.00	5.00	Ray Hirsch	'90
IDS STRATEGY:EQUITY	Growth & Income	811.3	9.56	10,163.70	11,442.10	18,574.70	2.0	328-8300	612-671-3733	None	1.00	5.00	Tom Medcalf	'90
IDS STRATEGY:INCOME	Fixed Income	619.5	6.56	10,367.20	11,544.10	16,762.30	6.8	328-8300	612-671-3733	None	1.00	5.00	John A. Utter	'91

★IDEX 3—Closed to new investors.

PERFORMANCE OF MUTUAL FUNDS (continued)

FUND NAME	OBJECTIVE	TOTAL NET ASSETS ($ MIL) 5/31/93	NET ASSET $ VALUE 6/30/93	PERFORMANCE (Return on Initial $10,000 Investment) 3/31/93-6/30/93	6/30/92-6/30/93	6/30/88-6/30/93	DIVIDEND YIELD % 6/93	PHONE NUMBER 800	In-State	FEES Load	12b-1	Redemption	MANAGER	SINCE
IDS STR:SHRT-TRM INC	Fixed Income	176.5	1.03	10,108.20	10,472.30	14,210.00	4.4	328-8300	612-671-3733	None	1.00	5.00	Stuart Sedlack	'92
IDS STR:WRLDWD GROW	International	65.3	4.73	10,487.80	10,677.20	11,734.60	0.0	328-8300	612-671-3733	None	1.00	5.00	Peter L. Lamaison	'91
IDS UTILITIES INCOME	Utility	618.2	7.05	10,246.20	12,003.20	☆	4.7	328-8300	612-671-3733	5.00	None	None	Richard Lazarchic	'89
IFT:FR INST ADJ RATE	Fixed Income	35.5	10.04	10,112.40	10,576.60	☆	5.6	342-5236	415-312-3200	None	None	None	Leman/Coffey	'92/'92
IFT:FR INST ADJ USG	Fixed Income	993.1	9.86	10,122.90	10,363.60	☆	4.9	342-5236	415-312-3200	None	None	None	Leman/Coffey	'91/'91
INCOME FUND OF AMERICA	Equity Income	8,385.9	14.49	10,238.70	11,616.70	18,868.50	6.7	421-0180	210-530-4000	5.75	0.25	None	Multiple Managers	'73
INDEPND CAP:OPPORTUNIT	Capital Appreciation	32.8	11.40	9,939.00	11,520.90	☆	0.0	950-4243	None	4.50	0.50	None	William Ferdinand	'90
INDEPND CAP:SHT-INT GOVT	Fixed Income	15.6	10.06	10,067.80	10,604.10	☆	5.9	950-4243	None	3.00	0.25	None	Joseph Carwile	'92
INDEPND CAP:TOT RTN BOND	Fixed Income	32.8	10.91	10,350.00	11,434.50	☆	5.9	950-4243	None	4.50	0.30	None	Peter Sherman	'90
INDEPND CAP:TOT RTN GRO	Growth	33.6	12.22	10,391.20	11,753.90	☆	0.0	950-4243	None	4.50	0.40	None	Paul G. Secord	'93
INFINITY:BEA SH DUR;CLT	Fixed Income	115.7	5.04	10,134.80	☆	☆	0.0	833-4909	212-492-1600	None	None	None	Gordon Bennett	'92
INFINITY:BEA SH DUR;SVC	Fixed Income	19.5	5.04	10,123.20	☆	☆	0.0	833-4909	212-492-1600	None	0.25	None	Gordon Bennett	'92
INSTL INTL:FOREIGN EQU	International	341.8	11.35	10,509.30	10,613.90	☆	1.6	638-5660	410-547-2308	None	None	None	Martin G. Wade	'89
INSTL INVSTRS CAP APPREC	Growth & Income	47.9	149.14	10,091.10	11,733.10	16,107.40	1.1	None	212-551-1920	None	None	None	McCabe/Trautman	'93/'93
INSTL INVSTRS CONVRT SEC	Convertible Securities	2.6	97.13	10,033.80	11,244.60	13,288.40	4.3	None	212-551-1920	None	None	None	Mark F. Trautman	'93
INSTL INVSTRS OPTION INC	Option Income	3.5	86.73	10,326.20	11,763.10	15,141.20	1.6	None	212-551-1920	None	None	None	Mark F. Trautman	'93
INSTL INVSTRS TX-ADV INC	Fixed Income	9.9	100.99	10,083.50	10,540.30	14,458.50	4.0	None	212-551-1920	None	None	None	Trautman/Keasler	'93/'93
INTERMEDIATE BD FD AMER	Fixed Income	1,541.9	14.53	10,251.80	11,152.20	15,816.00	7.1	421-0180	210-530-4000	4.75	0.30	None	Multiple Managers	'88
INVESTMENT CO OF AMERICA	Growth & Income	17,494.3	18.46	10,114.40	11,222.10	18,984.00	2.5	421-0180	210-530-4000	5.75	0.25	None	Multiple Managers	'33
INVMNT SRS:CAP GR;A	Capital Appreciation	11.6	12.73	10,039.70	10,730.80	☆	0.9	245-4770	412-288-1900	4.50	0.25	None	Gregory M. Melvin	'92
INVMNT SRS:CAP GR;INVMNT	Capital Appreciation	13.3	12.73	10,047.80	10,765.40	☆	1.2	245-4770	412-288-1900	5.75	None	None	Gregory M. Melvin	'89
INVMNT SRS:HI QUAL STOCK	Growth & Income	26.9	13.72	10,137.00	11,630.10	17,241.60	1.9	245-4770	412-288-1900	5.75	None	None	Peter R. Anderson	'87
INVMNT SRS:US GOVT BOND	Fixed Income	40.1	10.32	10,162.20	10,726.10	15,768.20	7.3	245-4770	412-288-1900	5.75	None	None	Kathy Foody-Malus	'90
INVESTORS PREFERENCE INC	Fixed Income	54.9	10.44	10,143.70	10,660.00	16,389.20	7.6	832-1373	509-353-3400	1.50	0.20	None	Robert Hennes	'87
INVESTORS RESEARCH	Capital Appreciation	50.2	4.94	10,123.00	10,901.80	14,834.90	1.4	732-1733	805-569-1011	5.75	None	None	Investors Research Co.	'59
IVY EMERGING GROWTH	Small-Company Growth	N/A	14.87	☆	☆	☆	0.0	456-5111	None	5.75	0.25	None	James Broadfoot	'93
IVY GROWTH	Growth	263.4	15.38	9,993.50	11,233.10	17,700.50	0.9	456-5111	None	5.75	0.25	None	M. Peers	'74
IVY GROWTH WITH INCOME	Growth & Income	18.4	9.61	10,180.10	11,447.20	17,808.50	0.7	456-5111	None	5.75	0.25	None	M. Peers	'84
IVY INTERNATIONAL	International	124.1	22.50	10,739.90	10,942.40	17,292.20	1.2	456-5111	None	5.75	0.25	None	Boston Overseas Invest	'86
JACKSON NATL:GROWTH	Growth & Income	29.2	10.76	10,028.00	☆	☆	0.0	888-3863	None	4.75	None	None	PPM America	'92
JACKSON NATL:INCOME	Fixed Income	27.4	10.55	10,261.20	☆	☆	0.0	888-3863	None	4.75	None	None	PPM America	'92
JACKSON NATL:TOTAL RET	Flexible	29.1	11.11	10,239.60	☆	☆	0.0	888-3863	None	4.75	None	None	PPM America	'92
JANUS BALANCED	Balanced	54.6	11.83	10,008.40	☆	☆	0.0	525-3713	303-333-3863	None	None	None	Warren B. Lammert	'92
JANUS ENTERPRISE	Growth	228.6	19.87	9,900.30	☆	☆	0.0	525-3713	303-333-3863	None	None	None	James P. Goff	'92
JANUS FLEXIBLE INCOME	Fixed Income	358.6	9.78	10,382.90	11,489.30	16,458.70	8.0	525-3713	303-333-3863	None	None	None	Ronald V. Speaker	'92
JANUS FUND	Capital Appreciation	7,864.1	19.64	9,989.80	11,501.60	24,889.30	1.5	525-3713	303-333-3863	None	None	None	James P. Craig	'86
JANUS GROWTH AND INCOME	Growth & Income	437.4	14.64	10,265.70	11,804.90	☆	0.9	525-3713	303-333-3863	None	None	None	Thomas F. Marsico	'91
JANUS INTMDT GOVT SECS	Fixed Income	71.7	5.20	10,063.20	10,486.50	☆	4.5	525-3713	303-333-3863	None	None	None	Ronald V. Speaker	'91
JANUS MERCURY	Capital Appreciation	30.8	10.78	☆	☆	☆	0.0	525-3713	303-333-3863	None	None	None	Warren B. Lammert	'93
JANUS SHORT-TERM BOND	Fixed Income	40.1	3.01	10,128.50	☆	☆	0.0	525-3713	303-333-3863	None	None	None	Ronald V. Speaker	'92
JANUS TWENTY★	Capital Appreciation	3,765.7	24.93	10,229.80	11,672.00	29,087.60	0.7	525-3713	303-333-3863	None	None	None	Thomas F. Marsico	'88
JANUS VENTURE★	Small-Company Growth	1,841.8	51.68	9,870.10	11,894.50	23,798.80	2.2	525-3713	303-333-3863	None	None	None	James P. Craig	'85
JANUS WORLDWIDE	Global	397.7	21.37	10,056.50	11,419.50	☆	1.0	525-3713	303-333-3863	None	None	None	Helen Hayes	'92
JAPAN FUND	Japanese	563.2	11.57	11,287.80	12,853.80	11,727.30	0.1	535-2726	617-439-4640	None	None	None	Allan/Kwak	'90/'89
JENSEN PORTFOLIO	Growth & Income	9.5	8.91	9,168.20	☆	☆	0.0	221-4384	503-274-2044	None	None	None	Val E. Jensen	'92

JP GROWTH	Growth	36.1	17.11	10,058.80	11,529.20	18,112.40	1.3	458-4498	919-691-3448	4.50	None	None	J. Scott Jeffords	'92
JP INCOME	Fixed Income	21.9	9.94	10,298.50	11,168.00	16,115.70	6.5	458-4498	919-691-3448	4.50	None	None	Robert E. Whalen	'92
KAUFMANN FUND	Small-Company Growth	664.0	3.04	10,270.30	13,333.30	30,831.60	0.0	237-0132	212-344-2661	None	0.75	0.20	Utsch/Auriana	'86/'86
KEMPER ADJ RATE US GOVT	Fixed Income	202.5	8.66	10,141.50	10,657.10	15,220.20	5.2	621-1048	816-421-4100	3.50	None	None	Beimford/Schumacher	'91/'92
KEMPER BLUE CHIP	Growth & Income	200.9	13.61	9,993.40	11,253.70	17,770.90	1.1	621-1048	816-421-4100	5.75	None	None	James Neel	'90
KEMPER DIVERSIFIED INC	Fixed Income	292.6	8.25	10,514.20	11,661.40	18,827.50	9.6	621-1048	816-421-4100	4.50	None	None	McNamara/Resis	'89/'92
KEMPER ENVIRONMENTAL	Environmental	46.8	13.21	9,770.70	10,091.70	☆	0.0	621-1048	816-421-4100	5.75	None	None	Frank Korth	'90
KEMPER GLOBAL INCOME	World Income	79.3	9.21	10,197.20	10,615.90	☆	7.8	621-1048	816-421-4100	4.50	None	None	Johns/Wilson	'89/'92
KEMPER GROWTH	Growth	1,754.1	14.32	9,841.90	11,340.50	21,873.20	0.2	621-1048	816-421-4100	5.75	None	None	Lewis/Arends	'91/'91
KEMPER HIGH YIELD	Fixed Income	2,138.3	10.04	10,496.80	11,540.30	17,116.50	9.6	621-1048	816-421-4100	4.50	None	None	McNamara/Resis	'90/'92
KEMPER INCOME & CAP PRES	Fixed Income	528.6	8.81	10,319.00	11,370.10	16,552.20	7.2	621-1048	816-421-4100	4.50	None	None	Harry Resis	'89
KEMPER INTERNATIONAL	International	194.4	9.08	10,632.30	10,460.60	13,751.30	2.0	621-1048	816-421-4100	5.75	None	None	Gordon Wilson	'89
KEMPER PT:DVRSFD;INL	Fixed Income	249.7	6.12	10,488.50	11,534.00	17,684.70	8.3	621-1048	816-421-4100	None	0.75	4.00	McNamara/Resis	'89/'92
KEMPER PT:DVRSFD;PREM	Fixed Income	81.1	6.12	10,508.20	11,620.10	☆	9.1	621-1048	816-421-4100	None	None	None	McNamara/Resis	'92/'92
KEMPER PT:GOVT;INL	Fixed Income	4,344.5	7.56	10,151.60	10,663.70	15,328.10	7.7	621-1048	816-421-4100	None	0.75	4.00	Beimford/Schumacher	'92/'91
KEMPER PT:GOVT;PREM	Fixed Income	1,311.6	7.57	10,184.70	10,745.60	☆	8.5	621-1048	816-421-4100	None	None	None	Beimford/Schumacher	'92/'92
KEMPER PT:GROWTH;INL	Growth	772.5	17.78	9,877.80	11,271.60	20,021.30	0.0	621-1048	816-421-4100	None	0.75	4.00	Lewis/Arends	'87/'89
KEMPER PT:GROWTH;PREM	Growth	155.1	18.01	9,906.50	11,386.10	☆	0.0	621-1048	816-421-4100	None	None	None	Lewis/Arends	'92/'92
KEMPER PT:HI YLD;INL	Fixed Income	1,004.9	8.24	10,465.70	11,437.30	15,741.40	8.7	621-1048	816-421-4100	None	0.75	4.00	McNamara/Resis	'90/'92
KEMPER PT:HI YLD;PREM	Fixed Income	121.1	8.25	10,484.30	11,520.70	☆	9.4	621-1048	816-421-4100	None	None	None	McNamara/Resis	'92/'92
KEMPER PT:SH GLBL;INL	World Income	146.3	7.67	9,991.30	8,825.20	☆	8.0	621-1048	816-421-4100	None	0.75	4.00	Johns/Wilson	'91/'92
KEMPER PT:SH GLBL;PREM	World Income	3.3	7.69	10,007.80	8,913.60	☆	8.8	621-1048	816-421-4100	None	None	None	Johns/Wilson	'92/'92
KEMPER PT:S-I GOVT;INL	Fixed Income	261.3	8.63	10,129.50	10,694.70	☆	5.4	621-1048	816-421-4100	None	0.75	4.00	Beimford/Schumacher	'92/'91
KEMPER PT:S-I GOVT;PREM	Fixed Income	6.2	8.65	10,147.60	10,783.90	☆	6.1	621-1048	816-421-4100	None	None	None	Beimford/Schumacher	'92/'92
KEMPER PT:SM CP EQ;INL	Small-Company Growth	73.4	10.40	10,558.40	☆	☆	0.0	621-1048	816-421-4100	None	0.75	4.00	C. Beth Cotner	'92
KEMPER PT:SM CP EQ;PREM	Small-Company Growth	2.1	10.45	10,587.60	☆	☆	0.0	621-1048	816-421-4100	None	None	None	C. Beth Cotner	'92
KEMPER PT:TOT RTN;INL	Balanced	1,222.7	14.06	10,210.90	11,366.70	18,974.60	2.3	621-1048	816-421-4100	None	0.75	4.00	C. Beth Cotner	'86
KEMPER PT:TOT RTN;PREM	Balanced	86.5	14.10	10,228.90	11,461.10	☆	3.0	621-1048	816-421-4100	None	None	None	C. Beth Cotner	'92
KEMPER RETIRE:SRS I★	Balanced Target	120.8	12.57	10,236.20	11,746.80	☆	3.2	621-1048	816-421-4100	5.00	None	None	Lewis/Arends	'91/'91
KEMPER RETIRE:SRS II★	Balanced Target	199.0	13.95	10,280.00	11,818.20	☆	3.5	621-1048	816-421-4100	5.00	None	None	Lewis/Arends	'90/'90
KEMPER RETIRE:SRS III★	Balanced Target	139.9	10.72	10,347.50	11,996.40	☆	1.7	621-1048	816-421-4100	5.00	None	None	Lewis/Arends	'92/'92
KEMPER RETIRE:SRS IV	Balanced Target	50.8	9.57	10,390.90	☆	☆	0.0	621-1048	816-421-4100	5.00	None	None	Lewis/Arends	'93/'93
KEMPER SH-TM GLBL INC	World Income	155.8	7.67	10,026.10	8,901.20	☆	8.4	621-1048	816-421-4100	3.50	None	None	Johns/Wilson	'90/'92
KEMPER SMALL CAP EQUITY	Small-Company Growth	446.1	5.64	10,681.80	11,977.70	20,145.90	0.0	621-1048	816-421-4100	5.75	None	None	C. Beth Cotner	'87
KEMPER TECHNOLOGY	Science & Technology	604.0	10.07	10,446.10	12,088.00	17,098.00	0.0	621-1048	816-421-4100	5.75	None	None	Richard Goers	'91
KEMPER TOTAL RETURN	Balanced	1,381.5	10.43	10,185.80	11,334.40	19,270.20	2.5	621-1048	816-421-4100	5.75	None	None	Gordon Wilson	'71
KEMPER US GOVT SEC	Fixed Income	6,846.7	9.33	10,199.20	10,722.50	16,263.60	7.8	621-1048	816-421-4100	4.50	None	None	Beimford/Schumacher	'81/'91
KENT EXP MKT EQ;INST	Small-Company Growth	117.5	11.67	10,125.80	☆	☆	0.0	343-2898	617-621-6100	None	None	None	Old Kent Bank	'92
KENT EXP MKT EQ;INV	Small-Company Growth	2.4	11.68	10,013.00	☆	☆	0.0	343-2898	617-621-6100	4.00	0.25	None	Old Kent Bank	'92
KENT FIXED INC;INST	Fixed Income	290.2	10.35	10,243.20	☆	☆	0.0	343-2898	617-621-6100	None	None	None	Old Kent Bank	'92
KENT FIXED INC;INV	Fixed Income	2.5	10.39	10,212.40	☆	☆	0.0	343-2898	617-621-6100	4.00	0.25	None	Old Kent Bank	'92
KENT INDEX EQ;INST	Growth & Income	189.6	10.77	10,117.40	☆	☆	0.0	343-2898	617-621-6100	None	None	None	Old Kent Bank	'92
KENT INDEX EQ;INV	Growth & Income	2.6	10.80	10,023.60	☆	☆	0.0	343-2898	617-621-6100	4.00	0.25	None	Old Kent Bank	'92
KENT INTL EQ;INST	International	121.6	11.76	10,671.50	☆	☆	0.0	343-2898	617-621-6100	None	None	None	Old Kent Bank	'92
KENT INTL EQ;INV	International	0.8	11.73	10,664.40	☆	☆	0.0	343-2898	617-621-6100	4.00	0.25	None	Old Kent Bank	'92

★JANUS TWENTY—Closed to new investors.
★JANUS VENTURE—Closed to new investors.

★KEMPER RETIRE: SRS I, SRS II, SRS III—Closed to new investors.

PERFORMANCE OF MUTUAL FUNDS *(continued)*

FUND NAME	OBJECTIVE	TOTAL NET ASSETS ($ MIL) 5/31/93	NET ASSET $ VALUE 6/30/93	PERFORMANCE (Return on Initial $10,000 Investment) 3/31/93-6/30/93	6/30/92-6/30/93	6/30/88-6/30/93	DIVIDEND YIELD % 6/93	PHONE NUMBER 800	In-State	FEES Load	12b-1	Redemption	MANAGER	SINCE
KENT LTD MAT;INST	Fixed Income	209.0	9.96	10,075.40	☆	☆	0.0	343-2898	617-621-6100	None	None	None	Old Kent Bank	'92
KENT LTD MAT;INV	Fixed Income	0.7	9.98	10,055.00	☆	☆	0.0	343-2898	617-621-6100	4.00	0.25	None	Old Kent Bank	'92
KENT VALUE PLUS;INST	Growth	109.1	10.89	10,198.30	☆	☆	0.0	343-2898	617-621-6100	None	None	None	Old Kent Bank	'92
KENT VALUE PLUS;INV	Growth	1.9	10.86	10,113.90	☆	☆	0.0	343-2898	617-621-6100	4.00	0.25	None	Old Kent Bank	'92
KEYSTONE AM CAP P&I	Fixed Income	64.1	9.87	10,133.70	10,397.00	☆	4.8	343-2898	617-621-6100	3.00	0.25	None	Christopher Conkey	'91
KEYSTONE AM CAP P&I2;B	Fixed Income	162.3	9.90	10,104.20	10,298.30	☆	4.0	343-2898	617-621-6100	None	1.00	3.00	Christopher Conkey	'91
KEYSTONE AM EQ INC;A	Equity Income	26.5	13.08	10,123.00	11,481.90	18,097.40	1.8	343-2898	617-621-6100	5.75	0.25	None	Walter McCormick	'87
KEYSTONE AM EQ INC;B	Equity Income	1.7	13.08	10,096.10	☆	☆	0.0	343-2898	617-621-6100	None	1.00	3.00	Walter McCormick	'93
KEYSTONE AM EQ INC;C	Equity Income	2.7	13.10	10,103.70	☆	☆	0.0	343-2898	617-621-6100	None	1.00	1.00	Walter McCormick	'93
KEYSTONE AM GLBL OPP;A	Global Small Company	15.8	16.09	11,111.90	13,870.70	19,831.30	0.0	343-2898	617-621-6100	5.75	0.25	None	Roland W. Gillis	'91
KEYSTONE AM GLBL OPP;B	Global Small Company	1.4	16.05	11,091.90	☆	☆	0.0	343-2898	617-621-6100	None	1.00	3.00	Roland W. Gillis	'93
KEYSTONE AM GLBL OPP;C	Global Small Company	0.5	16.06	11,098.80	☆	☆	0.0	343-2898	617-621-6100	None	1.00	1.00	Roland W. Gillis	'93
KEYSTONE AM GOVT SEC;A	Fixed Income	48.8	10.43	10,215.30	11,261.30	16,263.80	6.9	343-2898	617-621-6100	4.75	0.25	None	Christopher Conkey	'88
KEYSTONE AM GOVT SEC;B	Fixed Income	5.8	10.42	10,187.00	☆	☆	0.0	343-2898	617-621-6100	None	1.00	3.00	Christopher Conkey	'93
KEYSTONE AM GOVT SEC;C	Fixed Income	8.5	10.42	10,187.00	☆	☆	0.0	343-2898	617-621-6100	None	1.00	1.00	Christopher Conkey	'93
KEYSTONE AM INT BD;A	Fixed Income	18.0	9.47	10,227.00	11,201.90	15,485.00	6.8	343-2898	617-621-6100	4.75	0.25	None	Christopher Conkey	'88
KEYSTONE AM INT BD;B	Fixed Income	5.5	9.46	10,185.90	☆	☆	0.0	343-2898	617-621-6100	None	1.00	3.00	Christopher Conkey	'93
KEYSTONE AM INT BD;C	Fixed Income	4.2	9.46	10,185.90	☆	☆	0.0	343-2898	617-621-6100	None	1.00	1.00	Christopher Conkey	'93
KEYSTONE AM OMEGA;A	Capital Appreciation	80.8	17.15	10,275.60	11,993.20	22,738.10	0.0	343-2898	617-621-6100	5.75	0.25	None	Maureen E. Cullinane	'89
KEYSTONE AM STR INC;A	Fixed Income	74.6	7.82	10,911.10	12,455.70	15,913.40	9.6	343-2898	617-621-6100	4.75	0.25	None	Keller/Gunn/Conkey	'87/'87
KEYSTONE AM STR INC;B	Fixed Income	15.7	7.81	10,881.80	☆	☆	0.0	343-2898	617-621-6100	None	1.00	3.00	Keller/Gunn/Conkey	'93/'93
KEYSTONE AM STR INC;C	Fixed Income	8.4	7.80	10,877.90	☆	☆	0.0	343-2898	617-621-6100	None	1.00	1.00	Keller/Gunn/Conkey	'93/'93
KEYSTONE AM WORLD BD;A	World Income	6.9	9.35	10,603.00	11,160.00	15,426.00	12.8	343-2898	617-621-6100	4.75	0.25	None	Gilman Gunn	'92
KEYSTONE AUSSIE:INCOME	World Income	7.0	9.15	9,928.70	10,029.40	☆	7.2	343-2898	617-621-6100	4.75	0.25	None	David Manor	'89
KEYSTONE AUSSIE:SHT INC	World Income	5.9	8.37	9,676.50	9,313.40	☆	4.0	343-2898	617-621-6100	3.00	0.25	None	David Manor	'89
KEYSTONE B-1	Fixed Income	450.0	16.20	10,234.50	10,862.90	15,523.30	7.3	343-2898	617-621-6100	None	*1.00*	4.00	Barbara McCue	'86
KEYSTONE B-2	Fixed Income	952.1	16.68	10,385.30	11,417.60	15,221.50	8.2	343-2898	617-621-6100	None	*1.00*	4.00	Kristine R. Cloyes	'85
KEYSTONE B-4	Fixed Income	921.7	5.08	10,776.80	12,115.30	14,841.70	9.8	343-2898	617-621-6100	None	*1.00*	4.00	Donald Keller	'89
KEYSTONE INSTL ADJ RATE	Fixed Income	48.9	9.92	10,142.10	10,507.60	☆	5.1	343-2898	617-621-6100	None	None	None	Christopher Conkey	'91
KEYSTONE INTERNATIONAL	International	79.7	6.59	10,427.20	11,020.30	11,458.70	0.6	343-2898	617-621-6100	None	*1.00*	4.00	Gilman Gunn	'91
KEYSTONE K-1	Income	1,446.9	10.10	10,141.40	11,038.70	16,635.20	3.9	343-2898	617-621-6100	None	*1.00*	4.00	McCormick/McCue	'84/'84
KEYSTONE K-2	Growth	366.4	8.27	10,337.50	11,972.10	18,882.40	0.4	343-2898	617-621-6100	None	*1.00*	4.00	Walter McCormick	'89
KEYSTONE PREC METALS	Gold	166.5	21.78	13,528.00	14,145.40	12,911.90	0.2	343-2898	617-621-6100	None	*1.00*	4.00	Pirnie/Thorne	'79/'74
KEYSTONE S-1	Growth & Income	232.2	24.44	10,103.00	10,924.00	16,907.80	1.1	343-2898	617-621-6100	None	*1.00*	4.00	Maureen E. Cullinane	'89
KEYSTONE S-3	Growth	291.0	9.55	9,958.30	11,460.50	17,342.90	0.0	343-2898	617-621-6100	None	*1.00*	4.00	Jill Lyndon	'87
KEYSTONE S-4	Small-Company Growth	966.4	7.37	10,942.50	13,788.20	23,138.50	0.0	343-2898	617-621-6100	None	*1.00*	4.00	Roland W. Gillis	'86
KIDDER EQUITY INCOME	Equity Income	142.7	27.78	10,031.90	10,721.60	18,641.70	2.3	238-7753	212-656-1640	5.75	0.50	None	John D. Chadwick	'85
KIDDER GOVT INCOME;A	Fixed Income	89.7	14.97	10,180.80	10,846.60	15,337.10	6.7	238-7753	212-656-1640	2.25	0.50	None	John F. Green	'93
KIDDER INV:ADJ RATE;A	Fixed Income	190.4	12.08	10,122.20	☆	☆	0.0	238-7753	212-656-1640	2.25	0.25	None	John F. Green	'92
KIDDER INV:ASST ALLO;B	Flexible	102.6	13.11	9,981.40	☆	☆	0.0	238-7753	212-656-1640	1.00	1.00	1.00	John D. Chadwick	'92
KIDDER INV:GLBL EQ;A	Global	138.9	13.55	10,142.20	10,690.50	☆	0.0	238-7753	212-656-1640	5.75	0.25	None	Ralph R. Layman	'91
KIDDER INV:GLBL FXD;A	World Income	163.9	12.66	10,255.30	☆	☆	0.0	238-7753	212-656-1640	2.25	0.25	None	Kenneth A. Windheim	'92
KIDDER INV:INTMDT;A	Fixed Income	57.8	12.66	10,218.50	10,998.70	☆	6.1	238-7753	212-656-1640	2.25	0.25	None	Robert A. MacDougall	'92
KLEINWORT BENSON:INTL EQ	International	61.0	13.03	10,251.80	10,173.00	13,806.10	0.2	233-9164	212-687-2515	None	0.20	None	Team Managed	'87
LANDMARK I:BALANCED	Balanced	19.7	13.99	10,025.30	11,422.90	☆	1.9	223-4447	212-564-3456	3.50	0.20	None	Halley/Hyde	'90/'92

LANDMARK II:EQUITY	Growth	11.2	13.89	10,023.90	11,881.60	☆	0.2	223-4447	212-564-3456	3.50	0.20	None	Dwight Hyde	'92
LANDMARK FXD:US GOVT INC	Fixed Income	62.2	9.94	10,139.90	10,715.20	15,332.80	4.9	223-4447	212-564-3456	1.50	0.20	None	Tom Halley	'88
LANDMARK INTL EQUITY	International	12.6	10.77	10,276.70	10,193.20	☆	0.2	223-4447	212-564-3456	5.00	0.15	None	Henry deVismes	'91
LAUREL INTMDT INC	Fixed Income	27.2	10.97	10,197.60	10,990.20	☆	5.2	235-4331	412-364-1746	None	0.35	None	Laurie Carroll	'91
LAUREL STOCK	Growth & Income	66.4	17.88	10,100.30	11,679.30	20,906.80	1.6	235-4331	412-364-1746	None	0.35	None	Burt Mullins	'87
LEEB INV:PERSONAL FIN★	Growth	58.2	10.84	10,000.00	10,629.90	☆	1.4	543-8721	513-629-2000	None	0.25	None	Stephen Leeb	'92
LEGG MASON GL:GLBL GOVT	World Income	N/A	9.95	☆	☆	☆	0.0	822-5544	410-539-0000	None	0.75	None	Keith Gardner	'93
LEGG MASON INC:GOVT INT	Fixed Income	296.6	10.91	10,163.00	10,812.20	15,928.20	5.1	822-5544	410-539-0000	None	0.50	None	Stephen A. Walsh	'91
LEGG MASON INC:INV GRADE	Fixed Income	57.0	11.03	10,381.20	11,210.60	16,376.10	5.6	822-5544	410-539-0000	None	0.50	None	Kent S. Engel	'87
LEGG MASON SPECIAL INV	Small-Company Growth	352.3	19.14	10,704.60	12,571.70	21,608.30	0.2	822-5544	410-539-0000	None	1.00	None	William H. Miller III	'85
LEGG MASON TOTAL RETURN	Growth & Income	143.9	13.27	9,991.30	11,466.30	16,635.00	2.4	822-5544	410-539-0000	None	1.00	None	Miller/Dennin	'85/'90
LEGG MASON VALUE TRUST	Growth	857.3	17.62	9,922.40	11,395.30	15,649.10	1.0	822-5544	410-539-0000	None	0.95	None	William H. Miller III	'82
LEPERCQ-ISTEL TR:L-I	Growth & Income	17.4	15.33	10,065.70	11,805.50	15,507.10	2.7	338-1579	212-698-0749	None	1.00	None	Bruno Desforges	'74
LEXINGTON CONVERTIBLE	Convertible Securities	7.0	13.29	9,339.90	11,639.50	16,676.60	1.1	526-0056	201-845-7300	None	0.25	None	Richard Russell	'88
LEXINGTON CORP LEADERS	Growth & Income	116.4	12.68	10,241.10	12,137.80	19,631.40	4.5	526-0056	201-845-7300	None	None	None	Lexington Mgmt	'88
LEXINGTON GLOBAL	Global	78.8	12.81	10,448.60	11,327.50	13,982.20	0.5	526-0056	201-845-7300	None	None	None	Caesar Bryan	'87
LEXINGTON GNMA INCOME	Fixed Income	129.0	8.41	10,226.90	10,873.10	16,579.90	7.1	526-0056	201-845-7300	None	None	None	Denis P. Jamison	'81
LEXINGTON GOLDFUND	Gold	127.2	6.10	13,436.10	13,450.30	10,996.30	0.3	526-0056	201-845-7300	None	0.25	None	Caesar Bryan	'86
LEXINGTON GROWTH & INC	Growth & Income	135.9	17.35	9,994.40	11,996.90	17,368.20	1.6	526-0056	201-845-7300	None	0.25	None	William S. Stack	'91
LEXINGTON STRAT INVMENTS★	Gold	40.7	2.30	17,293.20	18,254.00	7,694.20	0.0	526-0056	201-845-7300	5.75	None	None	Caesar Bryan	'91
LEXINGTON STRAT SILVER★	Specialty	13.6	3.52	12,846.70	12,661.90	7,787.60	0.0	526-0056	201-845-7300	5.75	None	None	Caesar Bryan	'91
LEXINGTON WRLDWD EMERG	International	36.3	9.52	10,427.20	10,889.40	15,151.40	1.1	526-0056	201-845-7300	None	None	None	Stack/Bryan	'91/'91
LIBERTY EQUITY INC;A	Equity Income	35.3	11.09	10,264.50	12,019.20	19,236.50	4.5	245-4770	412-288-1900	4.50	0.50	None	Christopher H. Wiles	'91
LIBERTY EQUITY INC;C	Equity Income	1.1	11.09	☆	☆	☆	0.0	245-4770	412-288-1900	None	0.75	1.00	Christopher H. Wiles	'93
LIBERTY FINL:GRO & INC	Growth & Income	17.3	10.35	9,849.10	☆	☆	0.0	872-5426	617-722-6000	4.50	None	None	Robert A. Christensen	'92
LIBERTY FINL:US GOVT	Fixed Income	931.3	9.52	10,173.90	10,821.50	15,642.40	7.3	872-5426	617-722-6000	4.50	None	None	Michael T. Kennedy	'92
LIBERTY FINL:UTILITIES	Utility	220.2	11.66	10,228.10	12,063.30	☆	5.2	872-5426	617-722-6000	4.50	None	None	Robert A. Christensen	'91
LIBERTY HIGH INCOME;A	Fixed Income	429.8	11.33	10,369.70	11,643.40	19,098.60	9.9	245-4770	412-288-1900	4.50	None	None	Mark E. Durbiano	'89
LIBERTY HIGH INCOME;C	Fixed Income	0.9	11.33	☆	☆	☆	0.0	245-4770	412-288-1900	None	0.75	1.00	Mark E. Durbiano	'93
LIBERTY UTILITY;A	Utility	818.5	12.43	10,207.20	12,025.20	20,133.00	5.3	245-4770	412-288-1900	4.50	None	None	Christopher H. Wiles	'90
LIBERTY UTILITY;C	Utility	3.1	12.42	☆	☆	☆	0.0	245-4770	412-288-1900	None	0.75	1.00	Christopher H. Wiles	'93
LINDNER DIVIDEND★	Equity Income	1,217.7	27.69	10,310.00	11,996.60	19,122.00	5.9	None	314-727-5305	None	None	2.00	Eric Ernest Ryback	'82
LINDNER FUND	Growth	1,266.4	22.32	10,145.50	11,487.40	16,939.70	2.4	None	314-727-5305	None	None	2.00	Lange *et al.*	'77
LMH FUND	Growth & Income	7.0	18.45	9,935.40	11,030.50	13,146.80	2.0	847-6002	203-226-4768	None	None	None	Heine/Wayne	'83/'91
LOOMIS SAYLES:BOND	Fixed Income	38.1	11.58	10,534.40	11,965.50	☆	6.0	633-3330	617-482-2450	None	None	None	Daniel J. Fuss	'91
LOOMIS SAYLES:GLBL BOND	World Income	16.4	10.72	10,025.30	10,285.00	☆	6.0	633-3330	617-482-2450	None	None	None	John de Beer	'91
LOOMIS SAYLES:GROWTH	Growth	28.3	13.13	10,265.80	12,421.90	☆	0.0	633-3330	617-482-2450	None	None	None	Jerome A. Castellini	'91
LOOMIS SAYLES:GRO & INC	Growth & Income	16.6	12.05	9,942.20	11,551.70	☆	1.0	633-3330	617-482-2450	None	None	None	Jeffrey W. Wardlow	'91
LOOMIS SAYLES:INTL EQU	International	31.1	10.77	10,208.50	9,802.00	☆	0.9	633-3330	617-482-2450	None	None	None	Frank E. Jedlicka	'91
LOOMIS SAYLES:SH-TM BOND	Fixed Income	14.8	10.03	10,136.30	☆	☆	0.0	633-3330	617-482-2450	None	None	None	John Hyll	'92
LOOMIS SAYLES:SMALL CAP	Small-Company Growth	47.9	14.00	10,211.50	12,872.30	☆	0.0	633-3330	617-482-2450	None	None	None	Friedman/Dillon	'91
LOOMIS SAYLES:US GOVT	Fixed Income	15.7	11.39	10,464.70	11,936.70	☆	5.0	633-3330	617-482-2450	None	None	None	Kent P. Newmark	'91
LORD ABBETT BOND-DEB	Fixed Income	831.7	9.84	10,345.40	11,675.70	17,635.90	9.8	426-1130	212-848-1800	4.75	0.25	None	Morais A. Taylor	'92
LORD ABBETT DEVEL GROWTH	Small-Company Growth	137.8	9.81	10,103.00	11,565.20	15,082.50	0.0	426-1130	212-848-1800	5.75	0.25	None	John Gibbons	'89
LORD ABBETT EQU:1990★	Balanced Target	57.1	13.38	10,144.00	11,524.50	☆	0.0	426-1130	212-848-1800	5.50	0.25	None	John Walsh	'90

★LEEB INV: PERSONAL FIN—On 6/16/93, fund was reclassified from Flexible Portfolio to Growth.
★LEXINGTON STRAT INVMENTS & LEXINGTON STRAT SILVER — Funds were managed by a different adviser prior to 12/91.

★LINDNER DIVIDEND—Closed to new investors.
★LORD ABBETT EQU:1990—Closed to new investors.

PERFORMANCE OF MUTUAL FUNDS (continued)

FUND NAME	OBJECTIVE	TOTAL NET ASSETS ($ MIL) 5/31/93	NET ASSET $ VALUE 6/30/93	PERFORMANCE (Return on Initial $10,000 Investment) 3/31/93-6/30/93	6/30/92-6/30/93	6/30/88-6/30/93	DIVIDEND YIELD % 6/93	PHONE NUMBER 800	In-State	FEES Load	12b-1	Redemption	MANAGER	SINCE
LORD ABBETT FUNDMNTL VAL	Growth & Income	30.0	14.17	10,007.10	11,678.90	17,649.90	1.6	426-1130	212-848-1800	5.75	0.25	None	Thomas Hudson	'92
LORD ABBETT GLBL:EQUITY	Global	45.4	11.83	10,278.00	11,384.80	☆	1.0	426-1130	212-848-1800	5.75	0.25	None	E. Wayne Nordberg	'88
LORD ABBETT GLBL:INCOME	World Income	204.9	9.11	10,170.50	10,928.50	☆	11.3	426-1130	212-848-1800	4.75	0.25	None	Zane Brown	'92
LORD ABBETT US GOVT	Fixed Income	3,704.0	3.06	10,304.50	11,291.50	16,962.90	8.4	426-1130	212-848-1800	4.75	0.25	None	Robert S. Dow	'92
LORD ABBETT VALUE APPREC	Growth	188.6	11.93	10,059.00	11,979.80	17,063.60	1.6	426-1130	212-848-1800	5.75	0.25	None	Denise Higgins	'90
LOSANTIVILLE:STELLAR	Global Flexible	48.2	11.05	10,105.90	11,138.30	☆	2.7	667-3863	513-632-5547	4.50	0.25	None	Bob Herzog	'91
LUTHERAN BRO★	Growth & Income	494.2	18.47	10,109.50	11,691.40	18,981.10	1.3	328-4552	612-339-8091	5.00	None	None	Scott Vergin	'92
LUTHERAN BRO HI YLD★	Fixed Income	376.8	9.55	10,524.70	12,034.80	17,296.70	8.9	328-4552	612-339-8091	5.00	None	None	Tom Haag	'92
LUTHERAN BRO INCOME★	Fixed Income	980.7	9.30	10,259.00	11,232.20	16,885.90	7.0	328-4552	612-339-8091	5.00	None	None	Charles E. Heeren	'86
LUTHERAN BRO OPPTY GRO★	Growth	19.0	9.12	10,641.80	☆	☆	0.0	328-4552	612-339-8091	5.00	None	None	Dave Himebrook	'93
MACKENZIE ADJ US GOVT	Fixed Income	42.4	9.92	10,072.70	10,432.50	☆	4.7	456-5111	None	1.00	0.25	None	Team Managed	'91
MACKENZIE AMERICAN	Growth	45.5	12.33	10,695.80	12,297.80	13,754.60	0.0	456-5111	None	5.75	0.25	None	Alex Christ	'85
MACKENZIE CANADA	Canadian	20.8	10.05	11,892.30	14,709.80	10,720.00	0.0	456-5111	None	5.75	0.40	None	Alex Christ	'87
MACKENZIE FIXED INCOME	Fixed Income	129.5	10.34	10,410.60	11,628.90	17,079.40	6.9	456-5111	None	4.75	0.25	None	Team Managed	'88
MACKENZIE GLOBAL	Global	12.4	10.62	10,296.20	10,454.10	☆	0.3	456-5111	None	5.75	0.25	None	Team Managed	'91
MACKENZIE GROWTH & INC	Growth & Income	7.5	9.92	10,172.60	11,100.20	☆	3.6	456-5111	None	2.75	1.00	None	Team Managed	'92
MACKENZIE N AMERICAN	Flexible	39.8	6.84	10,146.20	11,345.50	13,610.80	5.8	456-5111	None	5.75	0.25	None	Team Managed	'89
MADISON BOND	Fixed Income	8.3	21.75	10,125.00	10,774.80	☆	6.9	767-0300	608-273-2020	2.50	0.25	2.00	Frank Burgess	'90
MAIN STREET GOVT SEC	Fixed Income	10.4	9.76	10,239.20	10,811.40	15,949.30	6.3	548-1225	303-671-3691	4.75	0.47	None	Eva A. Zeff	'92
MAIN STREET INC & GR	Growth & Income	54.5	19.86	10,338.00	14,623.40	29,220.70	0.9	548-1225	303-671-3691	4.75	0.47	None	John Wallace	'92
MAINSTAY:CAPITAL APPRE	Capital Appreciation	235.0	18.62	10,293.00	13,260.30	24,627.00	0.0	522-4202	None	None	1.00	5.00	Spelman/Carryl	'91/'92
MAINSTAY:CONVERTIBLE	Convertible Securities	48.0	13.32	10,450.50	12,609.90	18,824.80	2.9	522-4202	None	None	1.00	5.00	LaPlaige/Feinberg	'91/'92
MAINSTAY:EQUITY INDEX	Growth & Income	58.3	13.42	10,022.40	11,409.10	☆	1.4	522-4202	None	5.50	None	None	James Mehling	'92
MAINSTAY:GLOBAL	Global	23.7	10.14	10,378.70	10,640.10	11,309.30	0.0	522-4202	None	None	1.00	5.00	Raymond Stokes	'91
MAINSTAY:GOVT	Fixed Income	1,145.5	8.72	10,161.90	10,702.00	15,086.10	8.2	522-4202	None	None	1.00	5.00	Akhoury/Munshower	'86/'86
MAINSTAY:HI YLD CORP	Fixed Income	686.1	7.86	10,500.70	11,930.10	16,876.80	9.9	522-4202	None	None	1.00	5.00	LaPlaige/Tananbaum	'91/'89
MAINSTAY:NAT RES/GOLD★	Natural Resources	13.3	10.11	11,208.40	12,574.60	10,986.60	0.0	522-4202	None	None	1.00	5.00	Raymond Stokes	'91
MAINSTAY:TOTAL RETURN	Balanced	425.6	14.97	10,217.20	11,653.60	18,356.00	1.8	522-4202	None	None	1.00	5.00	Akhoury/Spelman	'87/'91
MAINSTAY:VALUE	Growth & Income	168.0	15.15	10,094.50	12,008.30	21,928.30	0.6	522-4202	None	None	1.00	5.00	LaPlaige/Kolefas	'86/'91
MANAGERS:BOND	Fixed Income	37.0	22.63	10,372.60	11,189.80	17,100.80	6.1	835-3879	203-857-5321	None	None	None	Multiple Managers	'84
MANAGERS:CAPITAL APPREC	Capital Appreciation	57.1	25.80	10,141.70	11,670.70	18,933.50	0.6	835-3879	203-857-5321	None	None	None	Multiple Managers	'84
MANAGERS:CORE EQUITY	Growth & Income	6.1	12.98	10,086.10	10,704.90	17,002.10	0.5	835-3879	203-857-5321	None	None	None	Multiple Managers	'87
MANAGERS:INCOME EQUITY	Equity Income	48.7	28.73	10,126.60	11,361.50	17,247.20	2.9	835-3879	203-857-5321	None	None	None	Multiple Managers	'84
MANAGERS:INTMDT MTGE	Fixed Income	169.8	21.91	10,249.00	11,816.60	18,580.60	13.0	835-3879	203-857-5321	None	None	None	Multiple Managers	'86
MANAGERS:INTL EQUITY	International	28.9	30.05	10,498.30	11,303.80	15,954.00	0.3	835-3879	203-857-5321	None	None	None	Multiple Managers	'85
MANAGERS:SHORT GOVT	Fixed Income	100.4	19.74	10,154.30	10,333.10	14,048.00	5.5	835-3879	203-857-5321	None	None	None	Multiple Managers	'87
MANAGERS:SH & INT BD	Fixed Income	92.5	21.19	10,195.10	11,112.70	15,762.80	7.7	835-3879	203-857-5321	None	None	None	Multiple Managers	'84
MANAGERS:SPECIAL EQUITY	Small-Company Growth	63.9	38.50	10,023.40	12,688.10	21,879.70	0.0	835-3879	203-857-5321	None	None	None	Multiple Managers	'84
MARINER EURO INDEX;A	European Region	23.1	10.45	10,028.80	9,580.40	☆	2.3	634-2536	212-503-6826	5.00	0.20	None	James Capel Fund Mgrs	'91
MARINER FIXED INCOME	Fixed Income	76.8	10.25	10,271.00	☆	☆	0.0	634-2536	212-503-6826	4.75	0.35	None	Wayne Wong	'93
MARINER SH-TM FXD INC	Fixed Income	23.2	9.97	10,097.00	☆	☆	0.0	634-2536	212-503-6826	2.00	0.35	None	Mary-Jean Maddia	'93
MARINER SMALL CAP	Small-Company Growth	13.0	11.11	10,989.10	☆	☆	0.0	634-2536	212-503-6826	5.00	None	0.35	Joseph Sing	'93
MARINER TOTAL RETURN EQ	Growth & Income	72.3	12.61	10,079.90	11,398.50	18,265.60	1.1	634-2536	212-503-6826	5.00	0.50	None	Leo Grohowski	'86
MARINER NORTH AMERICA	Global	8.6	10.84	10,216.80	11,256.50	☆	0.0	634-2536	212-503-6826	5.00	0.35	None	Timothy Love	'92
MARK TWAIN:EQUITY	Growth	29.6	9.74	9,609.10	☆	☆	0.0	None	314-889-0715	3.50	0.25	None	Mark Twain Bank	'93

MARK TWAIN:FXD INCOME	Fixed Income	40.6	10.49	10,299.30	☆	☆	0.0	None	314-889-0715	3.50	0.25	None	Mark Twain Bank	'93
MARSHALL:GOVT INC	Fixed Income	50.9	10.22	10,114.00	☆	☆	0.0	934-3883	202-835-4280	None	None	None	Marshall & Ilsley Invt.	'92
MARSHALL:INTMDT BD	Fixed Income	323.1	10.31	10,178.50	☆	☆	0.0	934-3883	202-835-4280	None	None	None	Marshall & Ilsley Invt.	'92
MARSHALL:SHORT-TERM INC	Fixed Income	51.5	9.94	10,075.40	☆	☆	0.0	934-3883	202-835-4280	None	None	None	Marshall & Ilsley Invt.	'92
MARSHALL:STOCK	Growth & Income	303.9	9.85	9,665.20	☆	☆	0.0	934-3883	202-835-4280	None	None	None	Tony Leszczinski	'93
MASS INVESTORS GROWTH	Growth	1,078.1	12.08	10,449.80	12,064.30	20,397.90	0.0	225-2606	617-954-5000	5.75	0.25	None	Thomas Cashman	'88
MASS INVESTORS TRUST	Growth & Income	1,623.1	12.71	9,961.40	11,459.20	19,865.10	2.2	225-2606	617-954-5000	5.75	0.25	None	Jeffrey Shames	'92
MAS POOLED:BALANCED★	Balanced	191.8	28.83	10,137.80	☆	☆	0.0	354-8185	215-940-5000	None	None	None	Team Managed	N/A
MAS POOLED:EMERGING GRO★	Growth	266.9	40.93	10,286.50	11,862.10	☆	0.0	354-8185	215-940-5000	None	None	None	Team Managed	'90
MAS POOLED:EQUITY★	Growth	1,084.7	55.89	9,919.40	11,209.40	19,718.30	1.9	354-8185	215-940-5000	None	None	None	Team Managed	'84
MAS POOLED:FXD INC★	Fixed Income	837.4	31.35	10,367.20	11,452.50	17,613.00	6.9	354-8185	215-940-5000	None	None	None	Team Managed	'84
MAS POOLED:FXD INC II★	Fixed Income	82.3	29.38	10,355.90	11,386.50	☆	4.5	354-8185	215-940-5000	None	None	None	Team Managed	'90
MAS POOLED:HIGH YIELD★	Fixed Income	40.9	23.44	10,545.20	12,260.10	☆	6.9	354-8185	215-940-5000	None	None	None	Team Managed	'89
MAS POOLED:INTL EQUITY★	International	800.5	30.67	10,392.70	10,674.00	☆	1.3	354-8185	215-940-5000	None	None	None	Team Managed	'88
MAS POOLED:LTD DUR FXD★	Fixed Income	53.4	26.56	10,125.70	☆	☆	0.0	354-8185	215-940-5000	None	None	None	Team Managed	'92
MAS POOLED:MTGE SECS★	Fixed Income	33.4	26.86	10,315.00	10,914.10	☆	5.0	354-8185	215-940-5000	None	None	None	Team Managed	'92
MAS POOLED:SEL EQUITY★	Growth	275.4	45.36	9,933.50	11,284.00	19,794.70	1.7	354-8185	215-940-5000	None	None	None	Team Managed	'88
MAS POOLED:SEL FXD INC★	Fixed Income	91.0	29.35	10,363.80	11,527.80	17,733.00	6.7	354-8185	215-940-5000	None	None	None	Team Managed	'87
MAS POOLED:SEL VALUE★	Growth & Income	161.2	34.14	10,027.60	12,038.90	18,555.20	2.6	354-8185	215-940-5000	None	None	None	Team Managed	'87
MAS POOLED:SMALL CAP★	Small-Company Growth	145.7	40.00	10,411.20	12,938.30	20,752.40	0.7	354-8185	215-940-5000	None	None	None	Team Managed	'86
MAS POOLED:SPEC PURP FXD★	Fixed Income	270.4	32.65	10,381.70	11,589.80	☆	6.4	354-8185	215-940-5000	None	None	None	Team Managed	'92
MAS POOLED:VALUE★	Growth & Income	688.6	30.75	10,059.80	11,883.40	19,432.10	2.5	354-8185	215-940-5000	None	None	None	Team Managed	'84
MATHERS FUND	Growth	499.7	15.13	10,147.60	10,490.60	13,922.80	3.3	962-3863	708-295-7400	None	None	None	Henry G. Van Der Eb, Jr	'75
MAXUS EQUITY	Flexible	8.4	13.86	10,266.70	12,169.10	☆	5.2	446-2987	216-292-3434	None	0.50	None	Richard Barone	'89
MAXUS INCOME	Income	33.0	11.28	10,106.30	11,162.30	15,788.80	8.2	446-2987	216-292-3434	None	0.50	None	Richard Barone	'85
MEGY INCOME	World Income	0.6	10.69	9,972.40	10,109.10	☆	1.1	933-8637	407-832-7733	None	0.75	1.00	Hector Megy	'91
MENTOR GROWTH	Growth	151.1	13.06	9,819.50	12,183.70	18,199.20	0.0	472-0090	804-782-3207	None	1.00	5.00	Price/Ziglar	'85/'91
MERGER FUND	Capital Appreciation	13.6	12.89	10,548.30	11,249.70	15,032.70	0.0	343-8959	None	None	0.20	None	Frederick W. Green	'89
MERIDIAN FUND	Growth	67.2	23.87	10,218.30	12,962.80	23,145.30	0.1	446-6662	415-461-6237	None	None	None	Richard Aster Jr	'84
MERRILL ADJ RATE SEC;A	Fixed Income	51.4	9.77	10,097.70	10,258.90	☆	4.4	None	609-282-2800	3.00	0.25	None	Maunz/Hewson	'91/'91
MERRILL ADJ RATE SEC;B	Fixed Income	689.6	9.78	10,095.20	10,217.70	☆	3.9	None	609-282-2800	None	0.75	3.00	Maunz/Hewson	'91/'91
MERRILL BL INV & RET;A	Balanced	42.5	12.68	10,031.60	11,221.30	☆	4.2	None	609-282-2800	6.50	None	None	Denis Cummings	'91
MERRILL BL INV & RET;B	Balanced	849.0	12.72	10,015.70	11,111.70	15,588.10	3.1	None	609-282-2800	None	1.00	4.00	Denis Cummings	'91
MERRILL BASIC VALUE;A	Growth & Income	1,991.6	23.31	10,387.70	11,902.90	17,085.40	2.9	None	609-282-2800	6.50	None	None	Paul F. Hoffmann	'77
MERRILL BASIC VALUE;B	Growth & Income	1,340.4	23.04	10,359.70	11,780.80	☆	2.1	None	609-282-2800	None	1.00	4.00	Paul F. Hoffmann	'88
MERRILL CAPITAL;A	Growth & Income	2,093.5	28.12	10,082.50	11,204.40	17,993.60	3.3	None	609-282-2800	6.50	None	None	Ernest S. Watts	'83
MERRILL CAPITAL;B	Growth & Income	2,803.5	27.66	10,061.80	11,092.00	☆	2.5	None	609-282-2800	None	1.00	4.00	Ernest S. Watts	'88
MERRILL CONSULTS INTL	International	30.3	10.70	10,278.60	☆	☆	0.0	None	609-282-2800	None	1.00	None	James Boller	'92
MERRILL CORP:HI INC;A	Fixed Income	841.0	8.20	10,402.90	11,750.40	19,245.70	9.5	None	609-282-2800	4.00	None	None	Vincent T. Lathbury III	'82
MERRILL CORP:HI INC;B	Fixed Income	1,500.8	8.20	10,383.60	11,662.50	☆	8.8	None	609-282-2800	None	0.75	4.00	Vincent T. Lathbury III	'88
MERRILL CORP:HI QUAL;A	Fixed Income	379.0	12.47	10,278.00	11,426.30	17,130.20	7.7	None	609-282-2800	4.00	None	None	Jay Harbeck	'92
MERRILL CORP:HI QUAL;B	Fixed Income	448.5	12.47	10,258.60	11,340.20	☆	6.9	None	609-282-2800	None	0.75	4.00	Jay Harbeck	'92
MERRILL CORP:INTMDT;A	Fixed Income	178.9	12.16	10,254.40	11,330.20	16,730.30	7.4	None	609-282-2800	2.00	None	None	Jay Harbeck	'92
MERRILL CORP:INTMDT;B	Fixed Income	101.7	12.16	10,241.40	☆	☆	0.0	None	609-282-2800	None	0.50	2.00	Jay Harbeck	'92
MERRILL DEVLOP CAP MKT	International	141.0	11.60	10,459.90	10,499.20	☆	4.5	None	609-282-2800	4.00	None	2.00	Grace Pineda	'89

★LUTHERAN BRO FUNDS—Limited to Lutherans.
★MAINSTAY: NAT RES/GOLD — On 5/20/93, fund was reclassified from Gold Oriented to Natural Resources.

★MAS POOLED FUNDS—Designed for certain tax-exempt fiduciary investors.

PERFORMANCE OF MUTUAL FUNDS (continued)

FUND NAME	OBJECTIVE	TOTAL NET ASSETS ($ MIL) 5/31/93	NET ASSET $ VALUE 6/30/93	PERFORMANCE (Return on Initial $10,000 Investment) 3/31/93-6/30/93	6/30/92-6/30/93	6/30/88-6/30/93	DIVIDEND YIELD % 6/93	PHONE NUMBER 800	In-State	FEES Load	12b-1	Redemption	MANAGER	SINCE
MERRILL DRAGON;A	Pacific Region	126.3	12.05	10,787.80	12,039.10	☆	0.7	None	609-282-2800	4.00	0.25	2.00	Kara Tan Bhala	'92
MERRILL DRAGON;B	Pacific Region	404.9	12.02	10,761.00	11,936.80	☆	0.2	None	609-282-2800	None	1.00	4.00	Kara Tan Bhala	'92
MERRILL EUROFUND;A	European Region	87.5	12.07	10,254.90	9,991.70	☆	0.0	None	609-282-2800	6.50	None	None	Alan J. Albert	'88
MERRILL EUROFUND;B	European Region	439.6	11.72	10,226.90	9,890.30	14,650.40	0.0	None	609-282-2800	None	1.00	4.00	Alan J. Albert	'88
MERRILL FEDERAL SEC;A	Fixed Income	1,877.5	10.05	10,220.70	10,820.60	16,312.00	6.0	None	609-282-2800	4.00	0.25	None	Maunz/Hewson	'89/'92
MERRILL FEDERAL SEC;B	Fixed Income	2,183.3	10.05	10,207.90	10,766.10	☆	5.5	None	609-282-2800	None	0.75	4.00	Maunz/Hewson	'91/'92
MERRILL FDMNTL GRO;A	Growth	6.8	9.41	9,741.20	☆	☆	0.0	None	609-282-2800	6.50	0.25	None	Lawrence Fuller	'92
MERRILL FDMNTL GRO;B	Growth	45.1	9.37	9,719.90	☆	☆	0.0	None	609-282-2800	None	1.00	1.00	Lawrence Fuller	'92
MERRILL TOMORROW;A	Growth	11.0	16.43	9,993.90	10,911.90	☆	3.7	None	609-282-2800	6.50	None	None	Vincent P. Dileo	'88
MERRILL TOMORROW;B	Growth	439.7	16.34	9,963.40	10,798.10	17,019.60	2.7	None	609-282-2800	None	1.00	4.00	Vincent P. Dileo	'84
MERRILL GLBL ALLOC;A	Global Flexible	468.6	12.90	10,420.00	11,734.70	☆	6.3	None	609-282-2800	6.50	None	None	Bryan Ison	'89
MERRILL GLBL ALLOC;B	Global Flexible	2,054.2	12.76	10,390.90	11,607.40	☆	5.7	None	609-282-2800	None	1.00	4.00	Bryan Ison	'89
MERRILL GLBL CONV;A★	Convertible Securities	2.0	10.69	10,425.20	11,805.60	☆	2.6	None	609-282-2800	4.00	None	None	Harry Dewdney	'88
MERRILL GLBL CONV;B	Convertible Securities	17.5	10.73	10,398.20	11,676.50	13,637.30	1.6	None	609-282-2800	None	1.00	4.00	Harry Dewdney	'88
MERRILL GL INV & RET;A	World Income	75.2	10.15	10,263.00	11,117.90	☆	12.1	None	609-282-2800	4.00	None	None	David B. Walter	'88
MERRILL GL INV & RET;B	World Income	725.9	10.16	10,253.80	11,044.60	17,293.80	11.3	None	609-282-2800	None	0.75	4.00	David B. Walter	'86
MERRILL GLBL UTILITY;A	Utility	36.1	12.82	10,332.10	12,030.60	☆	3.4	None	609-282-2800	6.50	None	None	Walter D. Rogers	'90
MERRILL GLBL UTILITY;B	Utility	270.7	12.77	10,315.50	11,934.00	☆	2.8	None	609-282-2800	None	0.75	4.00	Walter D. Rogers	'90
MERRILL GR INV & RET;A	Growth & Income	191.2	17.58	10,654.50	14,316.00	☆	0.0	None	609-282-2800	6.50	None	None	Stephen C. Johnes	'88
MERRILL GR INV & RET;B	Growth & Income	928.4	16.93	10,634.40	14,169.90	21,395.80	0.0	None	609-282-2800	None	1.00	4.00	Stephen C. Johnes	'87
MERRILL HEALTHCARE;A	Health/Biotechnology	66.4	3.70	10,452.00	9,840.40	☆	0.0	None	609-282-2800	6.50	None	None	Jordan Schreiber	'92
MERRILL HEALTHCARE;B	Health/Biotechnology	37.7	3.40	10,397.60	9,742.10	☆	0.0	None	609-282-2800	None	1.00	4.00	Jordan Schreiber	'92
MERRILL INSTL INTMDT	Fixed Income	118.8	10.29	10,169.20	10,925.60	15,771.30	5.5	None	609-282-2800	None	0.15	None	Jay Harbeck	'92
MERRILL INTL HOLDNGS;A	Global	204.4	12.17	10,392.80	11,309.40	15,523.70	0.5	None	609-282-2800	6.50	None	None	Frederick P. Ives	'85
MERRILL INTL HOLDNGS;B	Global	23.8	11.92	10,365.20	11,203.70	☆	0.0	None	609-282-2800	None	1.00	4.00	Frederick P. Ives	'88
MERRILL LATIN AMER;A	Latin American	35.2	11.16	10,488.70	10,933.30	☆	2.9	None	609-282-2800	4.00	0.25	2.00	Grace Pineda	'91
MERRILL LATIN AMER;B	Latin American	141.4	11.15	10,469.50	10,845.70	☆	2.0	None	609-282-2800	None	1.00	4.00	Grace Pineda	'91
MERRILL NATURAL RES;A	Natural Resources	11.9	14.06	9,880.50	10,416.70	☆	1.7	None	609-282-2800	6.50	None	None	Richard S. Price	'88
MERRILL NATURAL RES;B	Natural Resources	218.3	14.02	9,852.40	10,310.30	11,985.30	0.6	None	609-282-2800	None	1.00	4.00	Richard S. Price	'85
MERRILL PACIFIC;A	Pacific Region	369.4	19.40	11,060.40	12,036.90	16,190.10	3.8	None	609-282-2800	6.50	None	None	Stephen I. Silverman	'83
MERRILL PACIFIC;B	Pacific Region	259.0	18.75	11,035.90	11,914.80	☆	3.8	None	609-282-2800	None	1.00	4.00	Stephen I. Silverman	'88
MERRILL PHOENIX;A	Growth & Income	190.0	13.61	10,453.10	13,004.30	18,875.40	4.9	None	609-282-2800	6.50	None	None	Robert J. Martorelli	'86
MERRILL PHOENIX;B	Growth & Income	190.1	13.34	10,430.00	12,869.90	☆	4.8	None	609-282-2800	None	1.00	4.00	Robert J. Martorelli	'88
MERRILL SH-TM GLBL;A	World Income	126.0	8.73	10,201.90	9,735.10	☆	7.6	None	609-282-2800	3.00	0.25	None	Joseph Monagle	'92
MERRILL SH-TM GLBL;B	World Income	2,058.6	8.73	10,200.80	9,686.20	☆	7.1	None	609-282-2800	None	0.75	3.00	Joseph Monagle	'92
MERRILL SPEC VALUE;A	Growth	70.8	15.52	10,130.50	11,855.50	13,388.60	0.1	None	609-282-2800	6.50	None	None	Dennis Stattman	'89
MERRILL SPEC VALUE;B	Growth	79.5	15.17	10,106.60	11,732.40	☆	0.0	None	609-282-2800	None	1.00	4.00	Dennis Stattman	'89
MERRILL STRAT DIV;A	Equity Income	34.5	13.57	10,069.60	11,240.70	☆	3.2	None	609-282-2800	6.50	None	None	Walter D. Rogers	'88
MERRILL STRAT DIV;B	Equity Income	229.8	13.53	10,037.10	11,127.50	15,582.40	2.2	None	609-282-2800	None	1.00	4.00	Walter D. Rogers	'87
MERRILL TECHNOLOGY;A	Science & Technology	102.7	5.50	10,826.80	14,729.70	☆	6.1	None	609-282-2800	6.50	None	None	Jim Renck	'92
MERRILL TECHNOLOGY;B	Science & Technology	63.4	5.43	10,795.20	14,586.90	☆	6.2	None	609-282-2800	None	1.00	4.00	Jim Renck	'92
MERRILL WORLD INC;A	World Income	460.5	9.16	10,272.80	10,734.20	☆	9.7	None	609-282-2800	4.00	None	None	Team Managed	N/A

MERRILL WORLD INC;B	World Income	1,790.3	9.16	10,264.90	10,653.40	☆	9.0	None	609-282-2800	None	0.75	4.00	Team Managed	N/A
MERRIMAN:ASSET ALLOC	Global Flexible	26.1	11.48	10,554.00	11,351.00	☆	1.3	423-4893	206-285-8877	None	None	None	Merriman/Notaro	'89/'89
MERRIMAN:BLUE CHIP	Growth & Income	18.4	10.67	9,880.20	10,272.30	☆	1.2	423-4893	206-285-8877	None	None	None	Merriman/Notaro	'88/'88
MERRIMAN:CAP APPREC	Growth	42.2	11.04	10,027.20	10,630.30	☆	0.6	423-4893	206-285-8877	None	None	None	Merriman/Notaro	'89/'89
MERRIMAN:FLEXIBLE BOND	Fixed Income	11.6	10.71	10,342.90	11,443.30	☆	5.1	423-4893	206-285-8877	None	None	None	Merriman/Notaro	'88/'88
MERRIMAN:LVGD GROWTH	Capital Appreciation	6.2	10.16	9,912.50	10,211.90	☆	0.6	423-4893	206-285-8877	None	None	None	Merriman/Notaro	'92/'92
METLIFE PORT:INTL EQ	International	17.1	8.70	11,132.30	12,825.30	☆	1.0	882-3302	617-348-2000	4.50	None	None	Steve Bamford	'92
METLIFE PORT:INTL FXINC	World Income	23.9	7.98	10,151.60	10,682.20	☆	3.5	882-3302	617-348-2000	4.50	None	None	Nick Sanjana	'92
METLIFE SS:CAP APPREC	Capital Appreciation	214.8	10.42	10,451.40	13,577.40	23,474.30	0.0	882-3302	617-348-2000	4.50	0.25	None	Fredrick R. Kobrick	'86
METLIFE SS:EQ INC	Equity Income	41.8	10.78	10,150.30	12,157.20	16,991.70	3.3	882-3302	617-348-2000	4.50	0.25	None	Bartlett R. Geer	'92
METLIFE SS:EQ INVMTS	Growth & Income	45.9	14.52	10,013.80	12,036.50	18,049.40	0.3	882-3302	617-348-2000	4.50	0.25	None	Peter Bennett	'89
METLIFE SS:GLBL ENGY	Natural Resources	32.5	13.53	11,816.60	16,870.30	☆	0.0	882-3302	617-348-2000	4.50	0.25	None	Dan Rice	'90
METLIFE SS:GOVT SEC	Fixed Income	103.3	7.57	10,238.10	11,143.50	16,287.90	5.9	882-3302	617-348-2000	4.50	0.25	None	Jack Kallis	'87
METLIFE SS:HIGH INC	Fixed Income	528.0	6.43	10,495.10	12,050.20	16,587.70	10.1	882-3302	617-348-2000	4.50	0.25	None	Bartlett R. Geer	'87
METLIFE SS:MGD ASSTS	Flexible	102.1	8.82	10,482.20	12,121.00	☆	2.5	882-3302	617-348-2000	4.50	0.25	None	Michael Yogg	'91
MFS BOND	Fixed Income	492.7	14.58	10,346.00	11,199.80	17,007.40	7.1	225-2606	617-954-5000	4.75	0.25	None	Geoff Kurinsky	'86
MFS CAPITAL DEVELOPMENT	Growth	706.2	12.17	10,347.20	12,075.00	17,861.60	0.9	225-2606	617-954-5000	5.75	0.25	None	Paul McMahon	'92
MFS EMERGING GROWTH	Small-Company Growth	327.6	22.14	11,103.30	13,838.30	20,952.10	0.0	225-2606	617-954-5000	5.75	0.25	None	Donald Pitcher	'88
MFS GOVT LTD MATURITY	Fixed Income	275.1	9.18	10,161.80	11,009.30	☆	5.4	225-2606	617-954-5000	2.50	0.45	None	Steve Nothern	'88
MFS GOVT MTGE	Fixed Income	593.0	6.98	10,188.80	11,042.00	15,490.30	6.4	225-2606	617-954-5000	4.75	0.45	None	James Calmas	'93
MFS GOVT SEC	Fixed Income	370.6	10.10	10,283.70	11,291.30	16,177.30	6.9	225-2606	617-954-5000	4.75	0.45	None	Steve Nothern	'86
MFS HIGH INCOME	Fixed Income	623.8	5.34	10,458.40	11,840.80	16,686.30	9.4	225-2606	617-954-5000	4.75	0.25	None	Joan Batchelder	'83
MFS INCOME & OPPTY	Fixed Income	68.7	8.18	10,358.60	10,798.80	15,689.90	6.5	225-2606	617-954-5000	4.75	0.35	None	James Swanson	'92
MFS LIFETIME CAP GRO	Capital Appreciation	471.8	14.41	9,645.20	11,285.30	18,253.20	0.1	225-2606	617-954-5000	None	1.00	5.00	Kevin Parke	'88
MFS LIFETIME EMER GRO	Small-Company Growth	494.1	16.64	11,412.90	13,556.20	25,640.90	0.0	225-2606	617-954-5000	None	1.00	5.00	John Ballen	'87
MFS LIFETIME GOLD&NATL	Gold	24.1	6.69	12,141.60	13,380.00	☆	0.0	225-2606	617-954-5000	None	1.00	5.00	Redmond Patriquin	'88
MFS LIFETIME GOVT MTGE	Fixed Income	1,887.8	7.10	10,191.50	11,001.70	15,116.40	5.8	225-2606	617-954-5000	None	1.00	5.00	James Calmas	'93
MFS LIFETIME GOVT SEC	Fixed Income	102.0	10.32	10,247.40	11,105.00	☆	5.0	225-2606	617-954-5000	None	1.00	5.00	Steve Nothern	'93
MFS LIFETIME HI INC	Fixed Income	337.9	6.29	10,377.50	11,673.50	16,199.50	9.0	225-2606	617-954-5000	None	1.00	5.00	Joan Batchelder	'87
MFS LIFETIME INTMDT IN	Fixed Income	502.8	9.02	10,205.60	10,569.00	☆	6.5	225-2606	617-954-5000	None	1.00	5.00	Steve Nothern	'88
MFS LIFETIME MGD SECTR	Specialty	246.8	15.09	10,127.50	11,776.10	18,972.80	0.0	225-2606	617-954-5000	None	1.00	5.00	George Bennett	'88
MFS LIFETIME TOT RTN	Balanced	446.9	11.21	10,153.70	11,453.40	16,630.80	3.4	225-2606	617-954-5000	None	1.00	5.00	Richard Dahlberg	'93
MFS LIFETIME WRLD EQ	Global	109.6	14.69	10,455.50	11,192.00	14,962.80	0.0	225-2606	617-954-5000	None	1.00	5.00	David Mannheim	'92
MFS LTD MATURITY	Fixed Income	72.0	7.41	10,120.30	10,680.70	☆	6.5	225-2606	617-954-5000	2.50	0.35	None	Geoff Kurinsky	'92
MFS MGD SECTOR TRUST	Specialty	144.1	16.75	10,163.80	11,869.40	19,925.20	0.0	225-2606	617-954-5000	5.75	0.45	None	George Bennett	'88
MFS RESEARCH	Growth & Income	274.5	13.37	10,486.30	12,455.10	19,003.70	0.5	225-2606	617-954-5000	5.75	0.25	None	John Ballen	'91
MFS SPECIAL	Capital Appreciation	128.1	10.38	10,846.40	13,322.70	18,775.20	0.0	225-2606	617-954-5000	5.75	0.25	None	John Brennan	'91
MFS TOTAL RETURN	Balanced	1,504.6	13.25	10,313.60	11,663.40	18,396.20	5.3	225-2606	617-954-5000	4.75	0.25	None	Richard Dahlberg	'84
MFS UTILITIES	Utility	26.6	7.50	10,414.60	12,394.30	☆	5.2	225-2606	617-954-5000	4.75	0.45	None	Maura Shaugnhnessy	'92
MFS WORLDWIDE GOVT	World Income	376.0	12.57	10,492.50	10,787.20	16,945.10	10.3	225-2606	617-954-5000	4.75	0.25	None	Leslie Nanberg	'84
MFS WORLDWIDE TOT RTN	Global	56.4	10.28	10,271.80	10,974.50	☆	4.6	225-2606	617-954-5000	4.75	0.45	None	Frederick Simmons	'91
MIDWEST INC:INTMDT GOVT	Fixed Income	78.9	11.40	10,275.50	11,294.50	15,960.10	5.5	543-8721	513-629-2000	1.00	0.35	None	Anthony Trotta	'93
MIDWEST STRT:GOVT LG MAT	Fixed Income	11.6	8.74	10,431.40	11,843.30	☆	6.1	543-8721	513-629-2000	4.00	0.25	None	Thomas Mench	'91
MIDWEST STRT:GOVT SEC	Fixed Income	31.3	10.57	10,260.60	11,025.40	15,699.50	6.3	543-8721	513-629-2000	4.00	0.25	None	Anthony Trotta	'92
MIDWEST STRT:GROWTH	Growth	8.1	14.45	9,951.90	10,489.60	12,724.00	1.1	543-8721	513-629-2000	4.00	0.25	None	Susan Flischel	'92
MIDWEST STRT:TREAS ALLOC	Fixed Income	41.8	9.86	10,266.30	11,576.50	15,742.60	5.1	543-8721	513-629-2000	4.00	0.25	None	Thomas Mench	'88
MIDWEST STRT:UTILITY INC	Utility	43.6	11.41	10,149.90	11,723.70	☆	4.0	543-8721	513-629-2000	4.00	0.25	None	Thomas Mench	'89
MIM MUTUAL:AFA EQU INC	Equity Income	3.9	11.54	10,010.40	10,669.20	☆	0.9	233-1240	216-642-3000	None	0.97	None	AFA Financial, Inc.	'91

★MERRILL GLBL CONV; A—Institutional fund.

PERFORMANCE OF MUTUAL FUNDS *(continued)*

FUND NAME	OBJECTIVE	TOTAL NET ASSETS ($ MIL) 5/31/93	NET ASSET $ VALUE 6/30/93	PERFORMANCE (Return on Initial $10,000 Investment) 3/31/93-6/30/93	6/30/92-6/30/93	6/30/88-6/30/93	DIVIDEND YIELD % 6/93	PHONE NUMBER 800	In-State	FEES Load	12b-1	Redemption	MANAGER	SINCE
MIM MUTUAL:BOND INCOME	Fixed Income	3.9	9.26	10,156.90	10,326.60	13,139.30	3.4	233-1240	216-642-3000	None	0.97	None	Harvey M. Salkin	'86
MIM MUTUAL:STOCK APPREC	Capital Appreciation	46.9	16.17	10,874.20	12,142.20	22,910.50	0.0	233-1240	216-642-3000	None	0.97	None	Arthur Bonnel	'87
MIM MUTUAL:STOCK GROWTH	Growth	9.1	10.93	10,064.50	10,312.10	12,817.10	0.0	233-1240	216-642-3000	None	0.97	None	Martin A. Weisberg	'93
MIM MUTUAL:STOCK INCOME	Option Income	10.3	10.14	9,941.20	10,069.80	12,860.30	0.9	233-1240	216-642-3000	None	0.97	None	Harvey M. Salkin	'86
MIMLIC ASSET ALLOCATION	Flexible	52.1	13.69	10,090.90	11,187.00	17,603.40	3.6	443-3677	None	5.00	0.35	None	Thomas Gunderson	'87
MIMLIC FIXED INCOME SEC	Fixed Income	12.5	10.96	10,244.90	11,337.80	16,459.80	6.0	443-3677	None	5.00	0.10	None	Wayne Schmidt	'88
MIMLIC INVESTORS I	Growth & Income	28.5	17.12	10,048.40	11,076.80	18,284.80	0.4	443-3677	None	5.00	0.15	None	Jim Tatera	'85
MIMLIC MORTGAGE	Fixed Income	24.4	10.98	10,268.30	11,087.20	16,668.60	5.9	443-3677	None	5.00	0.20	None	Kent Weber	'85
MONETTA FUND★	Growth & Income	533.9	15.04	10,073.70	10,531.30	20,417.00	0.1	666-3882	708-462-9800	None	None	None	Robert S. Bacarella	'86
MONETTA:INTMDT BOND	Fixed Income	N/A	10.32	10,398.20	☆	☆	0.0	666-3882	708-462-9800	None	None	None	James Boves	'93
MONETTA:MID-CAP EQUITY	Growth	N/A	11.88	10,179.90	☆	☆	0.0	666-3882	708-462-9800	None	None	None	John M. Algona	'93
MONITOR:FIXED INC;INV	Fixed Income	1.3	22.25	10,265.10	11,264.30	☆	6.2	253-0412	614-463-5580	2.00	0.25	None	Stephen Geis	'91
MONITOR:FIXED INC;TR	Fixed Income	103.5	22.25	10,272.00	11,295.30	☆	6.5	253-0412	614-463-5580	None	None	None	Stephen Geis	'89
MONITOR:GROWTH;INV	Growth	4.0	25.39	9,802.60	10,669.80	☆	1.9	253-0412	614-463-5580	4.00	0.25	None	Douglas Epp	'91
MONITOR:GROWTH;TR	Growth	100.7	25.39	9,808.30	10,697.50	☆	2.2	253-0412	614-463-5580	None	None	None	Douglas Epp	'89
MONITOR:INC EQUITY;TR	Equity Income	104.7	22.34	10,006.10	11,061.10	☆	3.4	253-0412	614-463-5580	None	None	None	James Buskirk	'89
MONITOR:SHT/INT FXD;TR	Fixed Income	130.0	21.02	10,151.30	10,887.70	☆	6.7	253-0412	614-463-5580	None	None	None	Stephen Geis	'89
MONITREND GOLD	Gold	5.9	12.71	11,682.00	9,719.80	7,421.90	0.1	251-1970	615-298-1000	3.50	0.99	None	Johann DeVilliers	'91
MONITREND GOVERNMENT	Fixed Income	1.9	14.08	10,396.10	10,852.30	13,276.50	4.5	251-1970	615-298-1000	3.50	0.10	None	Pacific Income Advisors	'92
MONITREND GROWTH	Growth	1.1	12.49	10,237.70	10,399.70	☆	0.0	251-1970	615-298-1000	3.50	0.99	None	Robert Bender	'92
MONITREND SUMMATN INDEX	Growth & Income	3.6	18.05	10,000.00	9,333.30	10,587.10	1.0	251-1970	615-298-1000	3.50	0.99	None	McClellan/Verrill	'91/'88
MONTGOMERY:EMERG MKTS	International	186.6	11.07	10,573.10	11,138.20	☆	0.1	428-1871	415-627-2400	None	None	*None*	Jimenez/Sudweeks	'92/'92
MONTGOMERY:SH DURATION	Fixed Income	21.4	10.23	10,208.20	☆	☆	0.0	428-1871	415-627-2400	None	None	None	James I. Midanek	'92
MONTGOMERY:SMALL CAP★	Small-Company Growth	213.2	16.83	10,726.60	13,046.50	☆	0.0	428-1871	415-627-2400	None	None	*None*	Stuart O. Roberts	'90
MORAN EQUITY	Growth	1.9	12.49	10,121.60	10,394.80	☆	1.8	852-0658	203-869-5100	None	0.25	None	Frederick Moran	'90
MORGAN GRENFELL FXD INC	Fixed Income	70.7	10.64	10,315.70	☆	☆	0.0	932-7781	215-989-6611	None	None	None	David Baldt	'92
MORGAN KEEGAN SOUTHERN	Growth	45.5	14.04	9,901.30	11,332.10	15,412.30	5.0	366-7426	901-524-4100	3.00	0.50	None	Timothy Johnson	'90
M STANLEY:GL EQ ALLO;A	Global	N/A	11.09	10,278.00	☆	☆	0.0	548-7786	617-482-9300	4.75	0.25	None	Stephen Bott	'93
M STANLEY:GL EQ ALLO;B	Global	N/A	11.05	10,260.00	☆	☆	0.0	548-7786	617-482-9300	None	1.00	1.00	Stephen Bott	'93
M STANLEY:GL FXD INC;A	World Income	N/A	10.55	10,289.30	☆	☆	0.0	548-7786	617-482-9300	4.75	0.25	None	Smith/Coughlin	'93/'93
M STANLEY:GL FXD INC;B	World Income	N/A	10.56	10,269.80	☆	☆	0.0	548-7786	617-482-9300	None	1.00	1.00	Smith/Coughlin	'93/'93
M STANLEY INSTL:ACTIVE	International	99.4	10.76	10,518.10	10,947.40	☆	1.1	548-7786	617-482-9300	None	None	None	Jackson/Dhar	'93/'93
M STANLEY INSTL:ASIAN EQ	Pacific Region	99.3	15.57	10,995.80	12,214.00	☆	0.9	548-7786	617-482-9300	None	None	None	Chin/Cheng	'91/'91
M STANLEY INSTL:BALANCED	Balanced	38.7	10.88	10,140.80	11,355.40	☆	4.9	548-7786	617-482-9300	None	None	None	Crowe/Sexauer	'92/'91
M STANLEY INSTL:EMRG GRO	Small-Company Growth	85.4	14.57	10,104.00	9,824.70	☆	0.0	548-7786	617-482-9300	None	None	None	Sherva/Bossett	'89/'89
M STANLEY INSTL:EMRG MKT	International	219.8	12.38	11,033.90	☆	☆	0.0	548-7786	617-482-9300	None	None	None	Madhav Dhar	'92
M STANLEY INSTL:EQ GR	Growth	41.4	11.49	9,771.30	10,799.10	☆	1.6	548-7786	617-482-9300	None	None	None	Benjamin/Johnson	'91/'91
M STANLEY INSTL:FXD INC	Fixed Income	189.5	11.08	10,267.90	11,187.40	☆	5.5	548-7786	617-482-9300	None	None	None	J.D. Knox	'91
M STANLEY INSTL:GLBL EQ	Global	15.3	11.50	10,511.90	☆	☆	0.0	548-7786	617-482-9300	None	None	None	Michael Cowan	'92
M STANLEY INSTL:GLBL FXD	World Income	118.7	11.40	10,335.40	10,870.30	☆	5.1	548-7786	617-482-9300	None	None	None	Coughlan/Smith	'91/'91
M STANLEY INSTL:HI YLD	Fixed Income	32.8	10.80	10,543.80	☆	☆	0.0	548-7786	617-482-9300	None	None	None	Robert Angevine	'92
M STANLEY INSTL:INT EQ	International	661.7	11.86	10,723.30	10,931.70	☆	0.9	548-7786	617-482-9300	None	None	None	D. Caldecott	'89
M STANLEY INSTL:INT SM	International	12.7	13.11	11,072.60	☆	☆	0.0	548-7786	617-482-9300	None	None	None	Margaret Noylor	'92
M STANLEY INSTL:SM CAP	Small-Company Growth	N/A	10.68	9,925.70	☆	☆	0.0	548-7786	617-482-9300	None	None	None	C. Stadlinger	'93
M STANLEY INSTL:VALUE EQ	Growth & Income	34.8	11.88	10,035.10	11,457.30	☆	3.2	548-7786	617-482-9300	None	None	None	Crowe/Zyck	'92/'91

MSB FUND	Growth & Income	41.3	17.29	10,187.80	11,786.80	16,387.40	1.4	None	212-551-1920	None	None	None	McCabe/Trautman	'93/'93
MUHLENKAMP FUND	Flexible	6.9	17.01	10,029.50	12,562.00	☆	0.9	860-3863	412-935-5520	None	None	None	Ronald Muhlenkamp	'88
MUTUAL BENEFIT	Growth & Income	48.8	20.88	9,900.40	11,257.60	19,005.80	2.0	323-4726	401-751-8600	4.75	None	None	Stone/Mullarkey/Lob	'81/'81
MUTUAL OF OMAHA AMERICA	Fixed Income	88.0	11.40	10,249.20	11,182.10	16,679.60	5.7	228-9596	402-397-8555	4.75	0.25	None	Shirley Lang	'86
MUTUAL OF OMAHA GROWTH	Growth	128.2	12.58	10,679.10	12,480.20	21,301.70	0.0	228-9596	402-397-8555	4.75	0.25	None	Eugenia M. Simpson	'86
MUTUAL OF OMAHA INCOME	Income	279.2	10.47	10,301.10	11,325.80	16,975.50	6.2	228-9596	402-397-8555	4.75	0.25	None	Eugenia M. Simpson	'86
MUTUAL:BEACON	Growth & Income	758.6	30.17	10,196.00	12,366.60	18,196.60	1.5	448-3863	201-912-2100	None	None	None	Michael F. Price	'85
MUTUAL:DISCOVERY	Small-Company Growth	242.7	11.52	10,258.20	☆	☆	0.0	448-3863	201-912-2100	None	None	None	Michael F. Price	'92
MUTUAL:QUALIFIED★	Growth & Income	1,385.1	26.76	10,136.40	12,175.30	17,828.30	1.8	448-3863	201-912-2100	None	None	None	Michael F. Price	'80
MUTUAL:SHARES★	Growth & Income	3,186.8	80.16	10,118.70	12,106.40	17,677.20	2.0	448-3863	201-912-2100	None	None	None	Michael F. Price	'75
NATIONAL ASSET RSV;A	Fixed Income	6.6	4.89	10,141.00	☆	☆	0.0	223-7757	203-863-5600	2.25	0.30	None	Thomas Ole Dial	'92
NATIONAL ASSET RSV;B	Fixed Income	3.4	4.89	10,129.90	☆	☆	0.0	223-7757	203-863-5600	None	0.75	2.00	Thomas Ole Dial	'92
NATIONAL BOND	Fixed Income	681.3	2.14	10,608.20	11,965.40	17,377.00	10.5	223-7757	203-863-5600	4.75	0.30	None	Thomas Ole Dial	'89
NATIONAL FEDERAL SEC TR	Fixed Income	313.1	9.89	10,250.60	11,074.60	16,573.60	8.0	223-7757	203-863-5600	4.75	0.15	None	Paul Fulenwider	'91
NATIONAL INC & GRO;A	Balanced	533.5	10.11	10,272.20	11,621.60	19,412.80	4.3	223-7757	203-863-5600	5.75	0.30	None	Ernest N. Mysogland	'92
NATIONAL INC & GRO;B	Balanced	242.7	10.11	10,255.60	11,539.90	☆	3.8	223-7757	203-863-5600	None	1.00	5.00	Ernest N. Mysogland	'92
NATIONAL INDUSTRIES	Growth & Income	33.6	12.53	9,968.20	10,193.90	16,029.00	1.1	367-7814	303-220-8500	None	None	None	Richard Barrett	'84
NATIONAL MULTI-SECT;A	Fixed Income	190.8	14.07	10,411.50	11,658.80	☆	8.7	223-7757	203-863-5600	4.75	0.30	None	Thomas Ole Dial	'89
NATIONAL MULTI-SECT;B	Fixed Income	165.6	14.04	10,393.40	11,574.50	☆	8.0	223-7757	203-863-5600	None	1.00	5.00	Thomas Ole Dial	'92
NATIONAL STOCK	Growth & Income	223.8	10.27	10,436.70	12,621.50	19,144.00	0.4	223-7757	203-863-5600	5.75	0.30	None	Geoffrey Wadsworth	'91
NATIONAL TOTAL RETURN	Equity Income	278.5	8.54	10,300.80	11,801.10	18,989.60	2.2	223-7757	203-863-5600	5.75	0.30	None	Ernest N. Mysogland	'92
NATIONAL WORLDWIDE OPP	Global	91.9	8.00	10,025.10	11,142.10	☆	0.0	223-7757	203-863-5600	5.75	0.30	None	Jean Dorey	'93
NATIONS:ADJ RT;INV A	Fixed Income	40.9	10.01	10,108.30	☆	☆	0.0	321-7854	None	2.50	0.75	None	John Swaim	'92
NATIONS:ADJ RT;INV B	Fixed Income	3.5	10.01	10,102.90	☆	☆	0.0	321-7854	None	None	0.75	1.00	John Swaim	'92
NATIONS:ADJ RT;TR A	Fixed Income	10.2	10.01	10,101.60	☆	☆	0.0	321-7854	None	None	None	None	John Swaim	'92
NATIONS:BALANCED;INV A	Balanced	4.3	10.83	10,246.90	☆	☆	0.0	321-7854	None	4.50	0.25	None	Steve Hoeft	'92
NATIONS:BALANCED;INV B	Balanced	1.1	10.80	10,224.70	☆	☆	0.0	321-7854	None	1.00	1.00	1.00	Steve Hoeft	'92
NATIONS:BALANCED;TR A	Balanced	167.4	10.84	10,250.60	☆	☆	0.0	321-7854	None	None	None	None	Steve Hoeft	'92
NATIONS:CAP GRO;INV A	Growth	10.1	10.77	9,899.20	☆	☆	0.0	321-7854	None	4.50	0.25	None	Edwin Riley	'92
NATIONS:CAP GRO;INV B	Growth	2.9	10.75	9,882.40	☆	☆	0.0	321-7854	None	1.00	1.00	1.00	Edwin Riley	'92
NATIONS:CAP GRO;TR A	Growth	700.3	10.78	9,904.90	☆	☆	0.0	321-7854	None	None	None	None	Edwin Riley	'92
NATIONS:DVSD INC;INV A	Fixed Income	10.1	10.75	10,395.00	☆	☆	0.0	321-7854	None	2.50	0.15	None	Mark Ahnrud	'92
NATIONS:DVSD INC;INV B	Fixed Income	3.2	10.75	10,379.80	☆	☆	0.0	321-7854	None	None	0.75	1.00	Mark Ahnrud	'92
NATIONS:DVSD INC;TR A	Fixed Income	27.0	10.75	10,389.00	☆	☆	0.0	321-7854	None	None	None	None	Mark Ahnrud	'92
NATIONS:EMERG GR;INV A	Small-Company Growth	1.6	10.22	10,292.00	☆	☆	0.0	321-7854	None	4.50	0.25	None	Jack Smiley	'92
NATIONS:EMERG GR;INV B	Small-Company Growth	0.4	10.19	10,272.20	☆	☆	0.0	321-7854	None	1.00	1.00	1.00	Jack Smiley	'92
NATIONS:EMERG GR;TR A	Small-Company Growth	93.1	10.23	10,291.80	☆	☆	0.0	321-7854	None	None	None	None	Jack Smiley	'92
NATIONS:EQU INC;INV A	Equity Income	32.7	11.92	10,071.80	11,428.50	☆	2.9	321-7854	None	4.50	0.25	None	Eric Williams	'91
NATIONS:EQU INC;INV B	Equity Income	4.4	11.95	10,054.80	11,393.90	☆	2.3	321-7854	None	1.00	1.00	1.00	Eric Williams	'92
NATIONS:EQU INC;TR A	Equity Income	175.0	11.95	10,076.60	11,460.50	☆	3.1	321-7854	None	None	None	None	Eric Williams	'91
NATIONS:GOVT SEC;INV A	Fixed Income	15.3	10.54	10,205.60	10,820.30	☆	6.4	321-7854	None	2.50	0.15	None	William Brown	'91
NATIONS:GOVT SEC;INV B	Fixed Income	5.9	10.54	10,180.20	10,768.90	☆	5.8	321-7854	None	None	0.75	1.00	William Brown	'92
NATIONS:GOVT SEC;TR A	Fixed Income	39.5	10.54	10,199.60	10,839.80	☆	6.6	321-7854	None	None	None	None	William Brown	'91
NATIONS:INTL EQU;INV A	International	0.8	10.58	10,751.40	10,610.70	☆	1.2	321-7854	None	4.50	0.25	None	Richard Williams	'92
NATIONS:INTL EQU;INV B	International	0.2	10.51	10,715.80	10,533.40	☆	0.9	321-7854	None	1.00	1.00	1.00	Richard Williams	'92

★MONETTA FUND—Closed to new investors.

★MONTGOMERY: SMALL CAP—Closed to new investors.

★MUTUAL: QUALIFIED and MUTUAL: SHARES—Closed to new investors.

PERFORMANCE OF MUTUAL FUNDS (continued)

FUND NAME	OBJECTIVE	TOTAL NET ASSETS ($ MIL) 5/31/93	NET ASSET $ VALUE 6/30/93	PERFORMANCE (Return on Initial $10,000 Investment) 3/31/93-6/30/93	6/30/92-6/30/93	6/30/88-6/30/93	DIVIDEND YIELD % 6/93	PHONE NUMBER 800	In-State	FEES Load	12b-1	Redemption	MANAGER	SINCE
NATIONS:INTL EQU;TR A	International	118.1	10.19	10,319.20	10,218.10	☆	1.3	321-7854	None	None	None	None	Richard Williams	'91
NATIONS:MGD BOND;INV A	Fixed Income	7.9	10.75	10,282.60	11,211.00	☆	6.0	321-7854	None	2.50	0.15	None	William Armes	'89
NATIONS:MGD BOND;INV B	Fixed Income	0.2	10.75	10,267.40	11,133.80	☆	5.4	321-7854	None	None	0.75	1.00	William Armes	'92
NATIONS:MGD BOND;TR A	Fixed Income	201.8	10.75	10,286.40	11,227.70	☆	6.2	321-7854	None	None	None	None	William Armes	'89
NATIONS:MTGE SEC;TR A	Fixed Income	73.8	10.14	10,184.80	☆	☆	0.0	321-7854	None	None	None	None	William Armes	'92
NATIONS:S-I GOVT;INV A	Fixed Income	191.8	4.29	10,153.20	10,823.90	☆	5.6	321-7854	None	2.50	0.15	None	William Brown	'91
NATIONS:S-I GOVT;INV B	Fixed Income	36.3	4.29	10,137.90	10,757.80	☆	5.0	321-7854	None	None	0.75	1.00	William Brown	'92
NATIONS:S-I GOVT;TR A	Fixed Income	392.0	4.29	10,157.00	10,839.00	☆	5.7	321-7854	None	None	None	None	William Brown	'91
NATIONS:SHTM INC;INV A	Fixed Income	20.7	10.01	10,168.60	☆	☆	0.0	321-7854	None	1.50	0.15	None	Garlon Ebanks	'92
NATIONS:SHTM INC;INV B	Fixed Income	26.9	10.01	10,150.50	☆	☆	0.0	321-7854	None	None	0.50	None	Garlon Ebanks	'92
NATIONS:SHTM INC;TR A	Fixed Income	186.0	10.01	10,162.20	☆	☆	0.0	321-7854	None	None	None	None	Garlon Ebanks	'92
NATIONS:STR INC;INV A	Fixed Income	1.1	10.52	10,270.00	☆	☆	0.0	321-7854	None	2.50	0.15	None	William Armes	'92
NATIONS:STR INC;INV B	Fixed Income	0.1	10.52	10,253.30	☆	☆	0.0	321-7854	None	None	0.75	1.00	William Armes	'92
NATIONS:STR INC;TR A	Fixed Income	524.4	10.52	10,273.70	☆	☆	0.0	321-7854	None	None	None	None	William Armes	'92
NATIONS:VALUE;INV A	Growth & Income	30.9	13.21	10,230.30	11,354.90	☆	1.8	321-7854	None	4.50	0.25	None	Sharon Herrmann	'89
NATIONS:VALUE;INV B	Growth & Income	2.8	13.15	10,213.30	11,241.30	☆	1.3	321-7854	None	1.00	1.00	1.00	Sharon Herrmann	'92
NATIONS:VALUE;TR A	Growth & Income	486.8	13.22	10,236.30	11,381.50	☆	1.9	321-7854	None	None	None	None	Sharon Herrmann	'89
NATIONWIDE:BOND	Fixed Income	124.2	9.90	10,173.00	11,324.00	16,894.60	8.2	848-0920	614-249-7855	4.50	None	None	Mike Groseclose	'80
NATIONWIDE:FUND	Growth & Income	747.7	15.91	9,922.40	10,651.60	18,575.00	2.1	848-0920	614-249-7855	4.50	None	None	Charles Bath	'85
NATIONWIDE:GROWTH	Growth	385.6	10.61	10,201.10	11,210.00	16,866.30	1.6	848-0920	614-249-7855	4.50	None	None	John Schaffner	'81
NATIONWIDE II:GOVT INC	Fixed Income	31.7	10.19	10,290.00	11,007.70	☆	5.6	848-0920	614-249-7855	None	0.20	5.00	Wayne Frisbee	'92
NCC EQUITY;INSTL	Growth	85.2	13.63	9,698.60	10,822.90	☆	2.1	622-3863	None	None	0.04	None	Gerald Gray	'89
NCC EQUITY;RETAIL	Growth	7.7	13.64	9,689.70	10,795.50	☆	1.8	622-3863	None	3.75	0.04	None	Gerald Gray	'89
NCC FXD INC;INSTL	Fixed Income	95.1	11.10	10,271.50	11,204.80	☆	6.3	622-3863	None	None	0.05	None	Larry Kekst	'89
NCC FXD INC;RETAIL	Fixed Income	5.2	11.16	10,270.00	11,165.20	☆	5.8	622-3863	None	3.75	0.05	None	Larry Kekst	'91
N&B ADV MGT TR:BALANCED★	Flexible	124.1	14.81	10,006.80	10,898.00	☆	1.3	877-9700	212-476-8800	None	None	None	Havell/Goldstein	'89/'93
N & B GENESIS	Small-Company Growth	111.6	8.29	9,904.40	11,859.80	☆	0.0	877-9700	212-476-8800	None	None	None	Stephen Milman	'88
N & B GUARDIAN	Growth & Income	1,530.5	17.72	10,090.90	12,188.70	20,132.00	1.4	877-9700	212-476-8800	None	None	None	Simons/Marx	'82/'88
N & B LTD MATURITY BOND	Fixed Income	325.8	10.48	10,155.90	10,758.20	15,237.60	5.7	877-9700	212-476-8800	None	None	None	Havell/Giuliano	'86/'86
N & B MANHATTAN	Capital Appreciation	543.5	12.27	10,115.40	12,547.30	19,140.30	0.4	877-9700	212-476-8800	None	None	None	Mark Goldstein	'92
N & B PARTNERS	Growth	1,064.0	20.98	10,150.00	12,178.10	18,432.30	0.9	877-9700	212-476-8800	None	None	None	Michael Kassen	'90
N & B PROF INV:GROWTH★	Growth	8.8	6.04	9,572.10	11,439.60	☆	0.2	877-9700	212-476-8800	None	None	None	Mark Goldstein	'91
N & B SELECTED SECTORS	Growth	542.8	22.81	10,169.40	12,430.80	20,240.40	1.2	877-9700	212-476-8800	None	None	None	Marx/Simons	'88/'88
N & B ULTRA SHORT BOND	Fixed Income	109.3	9.65	10,071.30	10,340.90	13,875.20	4.5	877-9700	212-476-8800	None	None	None	Havell/Giuliano	'86/'86
NEW ALTERNATIVES	Environmental	31.1	29.98	9,730.60	11,131.60	15,999.00	1.1	None	516-466-0808	4.75	None	None	Schoenwald/Schoenwald	'82
NEW ECONOMY	Growth	1,444.8	29.82	10,548.60	13,034.40	20,771.60	0.5	421-0180	210-530-4000	5.75	0.25	None	Multiple Managers	'83
NEW PERSPECTIVE	Global	3,905.0	13.01	10,201.90	10,660.40	17,263.00	1.5	421-0180	210-530-4000	5.75	0.25	None	Multiple Managers	'73
THE NEW USA	Growth	277.0	13.28	10,464.90	11,244.70	☆	0.0	222-2872	310-448-6856	5.00	0.60	None	David Ryan	'92
NY LIFE INSTL:BOND	Fixed Income	206.6	10.88	10,264.20	11,128.20	☆	5.5	695-2126	None	None	None	None	Ravi Akhoury	'91
NY LIFE INSTL:EAFE INDEX	International	51.9	11.46	10,893.50	11,792.70	☆	0.7	695-2126	None	None	None	None	James Mehling	'92
NY LIFE INSTL:GROWTH EQ	Growth	221.0	14.67	10,131.20	12,460.70	☆	0.0	695-2126	None	None	None	None	Edmund Spelman	'92
NY LIFE INSTL:INDEXED BD	Fixed Income	137.9	11.58	10,266.00	11,167.20	☆	6.8	695-2126	None	None	None	None	James Mehling	'91
NY LIFE INSTL:INDEXED EQ	Growth & Income	187.2	13.67	10,029.30	11,293.30	☆	2.2	695-2126	None	None	None	None	James Mehling	'91
NY LIFE INSTL:MULTI-ASST	Flexible	236.4	11.76	10,111.80	11,118.20	☆	4.1	695-2126	None	None	None	None	James Mehling	'91
NY LIFE INSTL:SH-TM BD	Fixed Income	158.3	10.85	10,111.80	10,663.20	☆	6.1	695-2126	None	None	None	None	Ravi Akhoury	'91

NY LIFE INSTL:VALUE EQ	Growth & Income	255.1	12.94	10,117.30	12,071.90	☆	1.5	695-2126	None	None	None	None	Dennis LaPlaige	'91
NEW YORK VENTURE	Growth	673.8	11.92	9,983.20	12,652.80	23,353.30	1.4	279-0279	505-983-4335	4.75	0.25	None	Shelby M.C. Davis	'69
NICH-APP:BALANCED GR;A	Balanced	N/A	13.77	☆	☆	☆	0.0	551-8045	None	5.25	0.25	None	Anslow/Wylie	'93/'93
NICH-APP:BALANCED GR;B	Balanced	N/A	13.78	☆	☆	☆	0.0	551-8045	None	None	0.35	1.00	Anslow/Wylie	'93/'93
NICH-APP:CORE GROWTH;A	Growth	24.0	13.57	☆	☆	☆	0.0	551-8045	None	5.25	0.25	None	Jack Marshall	'93
NICH-APP:CORE GROWTH;B	Growth	23.0	13.54	☆	☆	☆	0.0	551-8045	None	None	0.75	1.00	Jack Marshall	'93
NICH-APP:CORE GR QUAL	Growth	59.0	13.59	☆	☆	☆	0.0	551-8045	None	None	None	None	Jack Marshall	'93
NICH-APP:GOVT INCOME;A	Fixed Income	N/A	12.86	☆	☆	☆	0.0	551-8045	None	4.75	0.25	None	John Wylie	'93
NICH-APP:GOVT INCOME;B	Fixed Income	N/A	12.85	☆	☆	☆	0.0	551-8045	None	None	0.50	1.00	John Wylie	'93
NICH-APP:GR EQUITY;A	Growth	90.0	14.19	10,534.50	13,854.80	22,207.10	0.0	225-1852	None	5.25	0.30	None	Jack Marshall	'91
NICH-APP:GR EQUITY;B	Growth	165.7	13.90	10,514.40	13,733.50	☆	0.0	225-1852	None	None	1.00	5.00	Jack Marshall	'91
NICH-APP:INC & GR;A	Equity Income	8.0	13.58	☆	☆	☆	0.0	551-8045	None	5.25	0.25	None	John Wylie	'93
NICH-APP:INC & GR;B	Equity Income	9.0	13.57	☆	☆	☆	0.0	551-8045	None	None	0.75	1.00	John Wylie	'93
NICH-APP:INC & GR QUAL	Equity Income	11.0	13.57	☆	☆	☆	0.0	551-8045	None	None	None	None	John Wylie	'93
NICH-APP:WRLDWD GR;A	Global	5.0	13.16	☆	☆	☆	0.0	551-8045	None	5.25	0.25	None	Robert Anslow	'93
NICH-APP:WRLDWD GR;B	Global	9.0	13.15	☆	☆	☆	0.0	551-8045	None	None	0.75	1.00	Robert Anslow	'93
NICHOLAS	Growth	3,076.4	52.26	9,999.30	11,452.50	19,183.80	1.3	None	414-272-6133	None	None	None	Albert O. Nicholas	'69
NICHOLAS II	Small-Company Growth	749.3	26.30	10,022.90	11,379.80	16,773.90	0.9	None	414-272-6133	None	None	None	David O. Nicholas	'83
NICHOLAS INCOME	Fixed Income	141.4	3.57	10,263.80	11,298.70	15,588.70	8.2	None	414-272-6133	None	None	None	Albert O. Nicholas	'77
NICHOLAS LTD EDITION★	Small-Company Growth	183.1	18.89	9,968.30	12,179.30	20,095.40	0.4	None	414-272-6133	None	None	None	David O. Nicholas	'87
NOMURA PACIFIC BASIN	Pacific Region	55.0	16.25	11,451.70	12,646.50	14,041.60	0.1	833-0018	212-509-7893	None	None	None	Takeo Nakamura	'85
NTH AM ASSET ALLOC	Flexible	79.5	11.13	10,127.40	☆	☆	0.0	334-0575	203-698-0068	4.00	1.00	None	Goldman Sachs	'92
NTH AM GLBL GROWTH	Global	28.0	12.51	10,925.80	11,295.80	☆	0.1	334-0575	203-698-0068	4.00	1.00	None	Walter Oechsle	'90
NTH AM GROWTH	Growth	56.4	13.63	10,029.40	11,659.50	☆	0.0	334-0575	203-698-0068	4.00	1.00	None	Goldman Sachs	'91
NTH AM GR & INC	Growth & Income	25.3	12.23	9,983.30	11,741.10	☆	1.6	334-0575	203-698-0068	4.00	1.00	None	Wellington Mgmt.	'91
NTH AM INV QUAL	Fixed Income	10.4	11.03	10,268.00	11,307.20	☆	6.2	334-0575	203-698-0068	4.00	0.35	None	Wellington Mgmt.	'91
NTH AM US GOVT SECS	Fixed Income	149.5	10.31	10,172.50	10,950.90	☆	5.8	334-0575	203-698-0068	4.00	0.35	None	Salomon Bros.	'91
NORTHEAST INV GROWTH	Growth	39.0	28.75	9,765.60	10,743.70	18,999.30	0.7	225-6704	617-523-3588	None	None	None	William A. Oates	'80
NORTHEAST INV TRUST	Fixed Income	470.0	9.96	10,502.10	11,840.60	16,067.50	10.5	225-6704	617-523-3588	None	None	None	Ernest E. Monrad	'60
NORTHWEST:NORTHWEST GRO	Growth	1.5	6.48	10,334.90	10,798.60	15,025.60	0.1	728-8762	206-734-9900	None	None	None	Nicholas Kaiser	'90
NOTTINGHAM:GOV STREET BD	Fixed Income	17.2	21.85	10,199.00	11,025.60	☆	6.1	525-3863	919-972-9922	None	None	None	T. Leavell & Assoc.	'91
NOTTINGHAM:GOV STREET EQ	Growth	22.6	22.61	9,830.80	10,794.40	☆	0.0	525-3863	919-972-9922	None	None	None	T. Leavell & Assoc.	'91
NOTTINGHAM:JMSTWN BAL	Balanced	N/A	0.00	N/A	N/A	☆	0.0	525-3863	919-972-9922	None	None	None	Lowe, Brockenbrough	'89
NOTTINGHAM:JMSTWN BOND	Fixed Income	N/A	0.00	N/A	N/A	☆	0.0	525-3863	919-972-9922	None	None	None	Lowe, Brockenbrough	'90
NOTTINGHAM II:CAP VALUE	Flexible	6.1	10.73	10,113.00	11,037.80	☆	1.9	525-3863	919-972-9922	4.50	0.35	None	Capital Investment Group	'91
NOTTINGHAM II:HATTRS EQ	Growth	1.4	9.06	9,640.40	9,876.80	☆	0.2	525-3863	919-972-9922	None	0.75	None	Hatteras Cap. Mgmt	'91
NOTTINGHAM II:HATTRS UTL	Utility	3.1	11.17	10,144.70	11,387.20	☆	1.9	525-3863	919-972-9922	None	0.75	None	Hatteras Cap. Mgmt	'91
NOTTINGHAM II:INVSTK FXD	Fixed Income	7.8	10.66	10,314.90	11,266.30	☆	6.0	525-3863	919-972-9922	None	None	None	Investek Cap. Mgmt.	'91
OAK HALL EQUITY	Capital Appreciation	11.2	14.30	11,877.10	☆	☆	0.0	None	207-879-0001	None	None	None	Oak Hall Cap Adv Inc	'92
OAKMARK	Growth	725.4	21.21	10,271.20	14,113.00	☆	0.2	476-9625	312-621-0600	None	None	None	Robert Sanborn	'91
OAKMARK INTERNATIONAL	International	255.7	11.99	10,345.10	☆	☆	0.0	476-9625	312-621-0600	None	None	None	David Herro	'92
OAK VALUE	Growth	1.2	10.36	10,006.80	☆	☆	0.0	525-3863	919-972-9922	None	None	None	David R. Carr	'93
OBERWEIS EMERGING GROWTH	Small-Company Growth	98.7	20.59	10,178.00	13,249.70	21,817.80	0.0	323-6166	708-897-7100	None	0.50	None	James Oberweis	'87
OLD DOMINION INVESTRS	Equity Income	6.7	20.14	10,058.00	10,649.00	14,254.20	4.6	441-6580	804-539-2396	4.00	0.25	None	Birdsong *et al.*	'64
OLYMPUS:EQUITY INCOME	Equity Income	14.6	13.19	10,302.50	11,646.30	☆	2.9	950-2748	310-553-6740	4.75	None	None	Julian Lerner	'90

★N & B ADV MGT TR: BALANCED—Designed primarily for retirement accounts.

★N & B PROF INV: GROWTH — Available only through an exchange with the N & B Money Market Fund, which has a $10,000 minimum investment.

★NICHOLAS LTD EDITION—Closed to new investors.

PERFORMANCE OF MUTUAL FUNDS (continued)

FUND NAME	OBJECTIVE	TOTAL NET ASSETS ($ MIL) 5/31/93	NET ASSET $ VALUE 6/30/93	PERFORMANCE (Return on Initial $10,000 Investment) 3/31/93-6/30/93	6/30/92-6/30/93	6/30/88-6/30/93	DIVIDEND YIELD % 6/93	PHONE NUMBER 800	In-State	FEES Load	12b-1	Redemption	MANAGER	SINCE
OLYMPUS:GROWTH	Growth	7.5	16.30	10,117.90	12,784.30	18,243.80	0.0	950-2748	310-553-6740	4.75	None	None	Bob Schonbrunn	'92
OLYMPUS:INV QUALITY BOND	Fixed Income	10.7	9.71	10,232.70	11,158.60	16,400.30	6.4	950-2748	310-553-6740	4.75	None	None	Beauchamp/Alley	'86/'92
OLYMPUS:STOCK	Capital Appreciation	49.7	21.20	10,177.60	11,689.00	21,505.20	0.2	950-2748	310-553-6740	4.75	None	None	Julian Lerner	'84
OLYMPIC TR:BALANCED INC	Balanced	28.9	16.68	10,168.80	11,008.60	17,324.00	4.4	346-7301	213-362-8900	None	None	None	Roger DeBard	'85
OLYMPIC TR:EQUITY INC	Equity Income	86.9	15.50	10,130.20	11,168.70	17,308.00	2.8	346-7301	213-362-8900	None	None	None	George Wiley	'87
OLYMPIC TR:INTERNATIONAL	International	6.3	14.63	10,570.80	10,736.40	☆	0.0	346-7301	213-362-8900	None	None	None	Dennis Bouwer	'90
OLYMPIC TR:SMALL CAPITAL	Small-Company Growth	11.0	19.88	10,392.10	11,979.70	17,997.00	0.2	346-7301	213-362-8900	None	None	None	George Davis	'88
OMNI INVESTMENT	Capital Appreciation	14.5	135.92	9,423.80	11,776.70	15,198.10	1.0	223-9790	312-922-0431	None	None	None	Robert Perkins	'85
ONE GROWTH	Growth	4.2	11.63	10,563.20	☆	☆	0.0	578-8078	None	5.00	0.30	None	Steve Williams	'92
ONE INCOME	Fixed Income	5.6	10.43	10,257.30	☆	☆	0.0	578-8078	None	5.00	0.30	None	Michael Boedeker	'92
ONE INC & GRO	Growth & Income	6.4	10.96	10,460.90	☆	☆	0.0	578-8078	None	5.00	0.30	None	Steve Williams	'92
ONE INTERNATIONAL	International	2.9	9.90	☆	☆	☆	0.0	578-8078	None	5.00	None	None	ONIMCO	'93
ONE GROUP:BLUE CHIP;FID	Growth & Income	109.5	12.91	9,678.30	10,142.10	☆	1.8	338-4345	None	None	None	None	Scott Andrews	'90
ONE GROUP:BLUE CHIP;INV	Growth & Income	5.6	12.91	9,672.30	10,123.00	☆	1.6	338-4345	None	4.50	0.25	None	Scott Andrews	'92
ONE GROUP:DISC VAL;FID	Growth	195.6	12.76	9,812.20	11,358.40	☆	2.2	338-4345	None	None	None	None	Terrence Pavlic	'92
ONE GROUP:DISC VAL;INV	Growth	2.8	12.75	9,814.90	11,326.70	☆	2.0	338-4345	None	4.50	0.25	None	Terrence Pavlic	'92
ONE GROUP:EQ INDEX;FID	Growth & Income	93.4	11.92	10,022.90	11,305.40	☆	2.3	338-4345	None	None	None	None	Mark Pelligrino	'91
ONE GROUP:EQ INDEX;INV	Growth & Income	0.4	11.91	10,027.90	11,274.50	☆	2.1	338-4345	None	4.50	0.15	None	Mark Pelligrino	'92
ONE GROUP:GROWTH EQ;FID	Growth	218.8	16.96	10,255.00	12,136.10	☆	0.4	338-4345	None	None	None	None	Richard R. Jandrain	'89
ONE GROUP:GROWTH EQ;INV	Growth	5.2	16.96	10,250.10	12,170.40	☆	0.3	338-4345	None	4.50	0.25	None	Richard R. Jandrain	'92
ONE GROUP:INCOME;FID	Fixed Income	469.4	10.43	10,212.80	11,062.30	15,721.00	6.3	338-4345	None	None	None	None	Thomas Wilson	'89
ONE GROUP:INCOME;INV	Fixed Income	6.8	10.43	10,206.90	11,057.80	☆	6.1	338-4345	None	4.50	0.25	None	Thomas Wilson	'92
ONE GROUP:INCOME EQ;FID	Equity Income	149.4	13.21	9,929.70	11,156.40	18,021.20	3.2	338-4345	None	None	None	None	Ralph Patek	'87
ONE GROUP:INCOME EQ;INV	Equity Income	8.6	13.20	9,925.20	11,138.30	☆	3.1	338-4345	None	4.50	0.25	None	Ralph Patek	'92
ONE GROUP:LTD VOL BD;FID	Fixed Income	387.4	10.87	10,166.10	10,826.80	☆	5.6	338-4345	None	None	None	None	Tim Holihen	'90
ONE GROUP:LTD VOL BD;INV	Fixed Income	15.3	10.87	10,160.50	10,804.10	☆	5.4	338-4345	None	3.00	0.25	None	Tim Holihen	'92
ONE GROUP:QUANT EQ;FID	Capital Appreciation	125.7	11.64	9,642.60	10,673.50	☆	1.5	338-4345	None	None	None	None	Mark Pelligrino	'91
ONE GROUP:QUANT EQ;INV	Capital Appreciation	0.4	11.64	9,639.30	10,340.90	☆	0.7	338-4345	None	4.50	0.25	None	Mark Pelligrino	'92
111 CORCORAN:BOND	Fixed Income	31.8	10.34	10,311.80	10,895.40	☆	5.1	422-2080	919-683-7277	4.50	None	None	Jim Agnew	'92
OPPENHEIMER ASSET ALLOC	Flexible	275.2	12.31	10,281.50	11,384.90	16,290.00	3.6	525-7048	303-671-3200	5.75	0.25	None	Team Managed	'91
OPPENHEIMER CHAMPN HI YD	Fixed Income	84.8	12.99	10,436.70	11,841.60	19,639.10	9.8	525-7048	303-671-3200	4.75	0.25	None	Ralph Stellmacher	'87
OPPENHEIMER DISCOVERY	Small-Company Growth	493.2	35.16	10,461.20	13,399.40	24,006.70	0.0	525-7048	303-671-3200	5.75	0.25	None	Jay Tracey	'91
OPPENHEIMER EQU INCOME	Equity Income	1,760.0	10.01	10,285.90	11,676.50	16,495.70	4.8	525-7048	303-671-3200	5.75	0.25	None	John Doney	'92
OPPENHEIMER FUND	Growth	218.0	10.41	10,225.90	11,332.70	16,803.10	1.0	525-7048	303-671-3200	5.75	0.25	None	Richard Rubinstein	'90
OPPENHEIMER GLO BIO-TECH	Health/Biotechnology	203.8	21.57	11,275.50	9,835.80	20,133.30	0.0	525-7048	303-671-3200	5.75	0.25	None	Sandra Panem	'92
OPPENHEIMER GLBL ENVIRN	Environmental	46.2	9.85	9,859.90	9,318.80	☆	0.0	525-7048	303-671-3200	5.75	0.25	None	John Wallace	'91
OPPENHEIMER GLOBAL	Global	1,244.1	31.24	10,500.80	10,027.00	17,041.20	0.4	525-7048	303-671-3200	5.75	0.25	None	Bill Wilby	'92
OPPENHEIMER GLBL GR&INC	Global Flexible	64.5	12.91	10,511.20	10,743.00	☆	1.5	525-7048	303-671-3200	5.75	0.25	None	Bill Wilby	'91
OPPENHEIMER GLD & SP MIN	Gold	165.6	12.32	11,789.50	11,714.50	12,061.10	1.1	525-7048	303-671-3200	5.75	0.25	None	Bill Wilby	'92
OPPENHEIMER GOVT SEC;A	Fixed Income	160.5	11.03	10,259.70	10,824.50	16,298.50	6.9	525-7048	303-671-3200	4.75	0.25	None	Arthur Steinmetz	'92
OPPENHEIMER HI YLD;A	Fixed Income	1,079.6	14.16	10,483.30	11,531.00	17,025.40	11.0	525-7048	303-671-3200	4.75	0.25	None	Ralph Stellmacher	'88
OPPENHEIMER INV GRD;A	Fixed Income	111.1	11.20	10,260.10	11,199.10	16,271.80	6.5	525-7048	303-671-3200	4.75	0.25	None	Mary Wilson	'88
OPPENHEIMER MTGE INC;A	Fixed Income	97.5	14.16	10,205.90	10,685.40	15,688.80	6.5	525-7048	303-671-3200	4.75	0.25	None	Eva A. Zeff	'92
OPPENHEIMER SPECIAL	Growth	743.9	27.34	9,877.20	11,687.80	19,141.70	0.9	525-7048	303-671-3200	5.75	0.25	None	Robert Doll, Jr.	'87
OPPENHEIMER STR INC;A	Fixed Income	2,373.6	5.17	10,416.00	11,243.20	☆	9.7	525-7048	303-671-3200	4.75	0.25	None	Steinmertz/Negri	'89/'89

OPPENHEIMER STR INC;B	Fixed Income	305.0	5.18	10,413.50	☆	☆	0.0	525-7048	303-671-3200	None	1.00	5.00	Steinmertz/Negri	'92/'92
OPPENHEIMER STR I&G;A	Fixed Income	62.3	5.28	10,175.30	10,957.50	☆	3.6	525-7048	303-671-3200	4.75	0.25	None	Steinmertz/Negri/Doll	'92
OPPENHEIMER STR I&G;B	Fixed Income	9.5	5.27	10,155.00	☆	☆	0.0	525-7048	303-671-3200	None	1.00	5.00	Steinmertz/Negri/Doll	'92
OPPENHEIMER STR INV;A	Fixed Income	28.2	5.12	10,203.40	11,020.60	☆	7.5	525-7048	303-671-3200	4.75	0.25	None	Steinmertz/Negri	'92/'92
OPPENHEIMER STR INV;B	Fixed Income	6.6	5.12	10,202.80	☆	☆	0.0	525-7048	303-671-3200	None	1.00	5.00	Steinmertz/Negri	'92/'92
OPPENHEIMER STR SHRT;A	Fixed Income	20.5	4.84	10,114.90	☆	☆	0.0	525-7048	303-671-3200	3.50	0.25	None	Steinmertz/Negri	'92/'92
OPPENHEIMER STR SHRT;B	Fixed Income	1.6	4.84	10,114.80	☆	☆	0.0	525-7048	303-671-3200	None	1.00	4.00	Steinmertz/Negri	'92/'92
OPPENHEIMER TARGET	Capital Appreciation	390.6	25.07	9,956.30	11,617.90	18,455.10	0.7	525-7048	303-671-3200	5.75	0.25	None	Robert Doll, Jr.	'88
OPPENHEIMER TIME	Capital Appreciation	370.3	17.06	10,333.10	12,095.20	17,298.80	0.3	525-7048	303-671-3200	5.75	0.25	None	Jay Tracey	'91
OPPENHEIMER TOT RET;A	Growth & Income	942.4	8.57	10,386.40	12,961.70	19,555.10	2.2	525-7048	303-671-3200	5.75	0.25	None	John Wallace	'90
OPPENHEIMER US GOVT TR	Fixed Income	396.8	9.95	10,260.70	10,956.10	15,796.10	6.8	525-7048	303-671-3200	4.75	0.25	None	Arthur Steinmetz	'87
OPPENHEIMER VALUE;A	Growth & Income	84.6	14.77	9,980.20	11,129.40	17,623.00	2.0	525-7048	303-671-3200	5.75	0.25	None	David Salerno	'87
OVERLAND EXP:ASSET ALLOC	Flexible	45.2	12.12	10,144.50	11,621.30	16,785.10	3.2	552-9612	None	4.50	0.25	None	Derringer/Sakamoro	'88/'88
OVERLAND EXP:DIV INC	Equity Income	0.8	10.30	10,070.60	☆	☆	0.0	552-9612	None	4.50	0.25	None	Wisniewski/Bissell	'93/'93
OVERLAND EXP:GRO & INC	Growth & Income	13.9	15.71	9,817.70	11,245.10	☆	1.9	552-9612	None	4.50	0.25	None	Wisniewski/Bissell	'90
OVERLAND EXP:SH-TM GOVT	Fixed Income	79.4	51.45	10,072.40	10,296.20	☆	0.9	552-9612	None	3.00	0.25	None	Single/Glessman	'92
OVERLAND EXP:STRAT GRO	Capital Appreciation	6.7	11.86	11,019.60	☆	☆	0.0	552-9612	None	4.50	0.25	None	Jon Hickman	'93
OVERLAND EXP:US GOVT INC	Fixed Income	45.4	10.98	10,342.00	11,369.80	17,322.40	6.7	552-9612	None	4.50	None	None	Single/Niedermeyer	'88/'88
OVERLAND EXP:VAR RT GOVT	Fixed Income	2,292.4	10.03	10,141.50	10,449.70	☆	4.9	552-9612	None	3.00	0.25	None	Single/Glessman	'90/'92
P HZN:AGG GRO	Capital Appreciation	173.7	26.61	10,597.40	12,488.60	23,175.70	0.0	332-3863	619-456-9197	4.50	0.10	None	Jeff Mallet	'90
P HZN:CAP INC	Convertible Securities	51.6	14.26	10,508.50	13,004.80	23,419.10	3.5	332-3863	619-456-9197	4.50	None	None	William Hensel	'87
P HZN:US GOVT SEC	Fixed Income	139.9	10.28	10,223.80	10,962.90	16,705.20	6.2	332-3863	619-456-9197	4.50	None	None	Kagawa/Osher	'92/'91
PACIFICA:ASSET PRES	Fixed Income	155.3	10.21	10,093.20	10,487.50	☆	4.9	662-8417	212-309-8400	None	0.11	None	Mark Romano	'90
PACIFICA:BALANCED	Balanced	91.1	12.33	10,272.90	11,809.40	☆	3.4	662-8417	212-309-8400	4.50	0.03	None	Sanchez *et al.*	'90
PACIFICA:EQUITY VALUE	Growth	126.6	12.56	10,285.60	12,302.20	☆	1.7	662-8417	212-309-8400	4.50	0.03	None	Sanchez/Bowden	'90
PACIFICA:GOVT INCOME	Fixed Income	157.7	10.79	10,240.30	10,990.20	☆	6.9	662-8417	212-309-8400	4.50	0.03	None	Mark Romano	'90
PAINEWBR ASST ALLOC;A	Flexible	193.9	11.70	10,112.80	11,188.40	☆	2.8	647-1568	None	4.50	0.25	None	Whitney Merrill	'93
PAINEWBR ASST ALLOC;B	Flexible	105.2	11.76	10,086.50	11,100.10	15,045.00	1.4	647-1568	None	None	1.00	5.00	Whitney Merrill	'93
PAINEWBR ASST ALLOC;D	Flexible	9.2	11.70	10,086.20	☆	☆	0.0	647-1568	None	None	1.00	None	Whitney Merrill	'93
PAINEWBR ATLAS GL GR;A	Global	137.7	14.20	10,668.70	10,604.90	13,626.40	0.0	647-1568	None	4.50	0.25	None	Frank Jennings	'92
PAINEWBR ATLAS GL GR;B	Global	27.6	14.02	10,645.40	10,517.60	☆	0.0	647-1568	None	None	1.00	5.00	Frank Jennings	'92
PAINEWBR ATLAS GL GR;D	Global	12.7	14.10	10,641.50	☆	☆	0.0	647-1568	None	None	1.00	None	Frank Jennings	'92
PAINEWBR BL CHIP GR;A	Growth	56.0	16.13	10,043.60	11,984.90	☆	0.0	647-1568	None	4.50	0.25	None	Karen Levy Finkel	'92
PAINEWBR BL CHIP GR;B	Growth	50.1	15.86	10,025.30	11,879.40	16,899.90	0.0	647-1568	None	None	1.00	5.00	Karen Levy Finkel	'92
PAINEWBR BL CHIP GR;D	Growth	1.9	16.01	10,025.00	☆	☆	0.0	647-1568	None	None	1.00	None	Karen Levy Finkel	'92
PAINEWBR CAP APPREC;A	Small-Company Growth	50.7	10.74	10,199.40	12,190.70	☆	0.0	647-1568	None	4.50	0.25	None	Todger Anderson	'92
PAINEWBR CAP APPREC;B	Small-Company Growth	114.8	11.15	10,192.00	12,106.40	☆	0.0	647-1568	None	None	1.00	5.00	Todger Anderson	'92
PAINEWBR CAP APPREC;D	Small-Company Growth	17.0	10.66	10,181.50	☆	☆	0.0	647-1568	None	None	1.00	None	Todger Anderson	'92
PAINEWBR DIVIDEND GR;A	Growth & Income	388.8	20.43	9,518.40	10,471.40	16,986.80	1.2	647-1568	None	4.50	0.25	None	Whitney Merrill	'87
PAINEWBR DIVIDEND GR;B	Growth & Income	488.9	20.34	9,494.60	10,388.70	☆	0.5	647-1568	None	None	1.00	5.00	Whitney Merrill	'91
PAINEWBR DIVIDEND GR;D	Growth & Income	62.7	20.40	9,502.80	☆	☆	0.0	647-1568	None	None	1.00	None	Whitney Merrill	'92
PAINEWBR EUROPE GR;A	European Region	77.8	8.44	10,710.70	10,047.60	☆	0.0	647-1568	None	4.50	0.25	None	Frank Jennings	'92
PAINEWBR EUROPE GR;B	European Region	11.2	8.34	10,692.30	9,976.10	☆	0.0	647-1568	None	None	1.00	5.00	Frank Jennings	'92
PAINEWBR EUROPE GR;D	European Region	5.1	8.38	10,688.80	☆	☆	0.0	647-1568	None	None	1.00	None	Frank Jennings	'92
PAINEWBR GLOB ENGY;A	Natural Resources	7.7	13.52	10,552.80	11,603.00	☆	2.0	647-1568	None	4.50	0.25	None	William Furth	'91
PAINEWBR GLOB ENGY;B	Natural Resources	29.4	13.54	10,530.90	11,505.00	16,059.00	1.1	647-1568	None	None	1.00	5.00	William Furth	'87
PAINEWBR GLOB ENGY;D	Natural Resources	0.8	13.44	10,535.60	☆	☆	0.0	647-1568	None	None	1.00	None	William Furth	'92
PAINEWBR GL GR&INC;A	Global Flexible	55.9	9.82	10,491.50	10,661.80	☆	0.4	647-1568	None	4.50	0.25	None	Frank Jennings	'92
PAINEWBR GL GR&INC;B	Global Flexible	8.5	9.76	10,483.40	10,591.90	☆	0.1	647-1568	None	None	1.00	5.00	Frank Jennings	'92
PAINEWBR GL GR&INC;D	Global Flexible	2.4	9.78	10,482.30	☆	☆	0.0	647-1568	None	None	1.00	None	Frank Jennings	'92

PERFORMANCE OF MUTUAL FUNDS (continued)

FUND NAME	OBJECTIVE	TOTAL NET ASSETS ($ MIL) 5/31/93	NET ASSET $ VALUE 6/30/93	PERFORMANCE (Return on Initial $10,000 Investment) 3/31/93-6/30/93	6/30/92-6/30/93	6/30/88-6/30/93	DIVIDEND YIELD % 6/93	PHONE NUMBER 800	In-State	FEES Load	12b-1	Redemption	MANAGER	SINCE
PAINEWBR GLOBAL INC;A	World Income	458.4	10.96	10,189.10	10,585.60	☆	5.5	647-1568	None	4.00	0.25	None	Waugh/Fachler	'91/'91
PAINEWBR GLOBAL INC;B	World Income	1,077.7	10.93	10,169.40	10,505.10	15,745.20	4.8	647-1568	None	None	1.00	5.00	Waugh/Fachler	'89/'87
PAINEWBR GLOBAL INC;D	World Income	52.5	10.95	10,176.30	☆	☆	0.0	647-1568	None	None	0.75	None	Waugh/Fachler	'92/'92
PAINEWBR GROWTH;A	Growth	120.6	19.37	10,221.60	11,837.10	20,489.80	0.4	647-1568	None	4.50	0.25	None	Ellen Harris	'85
PAINEWBR GROWTH;B	Growth	51.2	19.07	10,203.30	11,741.40	☆	0.4	647-1568	None	None	1.00	5.00	Ellen Harris	'91
PAINEWBR GROWTH;D	Growth	10.7	19.20	10,196.50	☆	☆	0.0	647-1568	None	None	1.00	None	Ellen Harris	'92
PAINEWBR HIGH INCOME;A	Fixed Income	328.2	8.61	10,676.20	12,350.10	18,871.70	10.8	647-1568	None	4.00	0.25	None	Evan Steen	'91
PAINEWBR HIGH INCOME;B	Fixed Income	196.9	8.60	10,656.80	12,275.80	☆	10.1	647-1568	None	None	1.00	5.00	Evan Steen	'91
PAINEWBR HIGH INCOME;D	Fixed Income	103.1	8.62	10,675.30	☆	☆	0.0	647-1568	None	None	0.75	None	Evan Steen	'92
PAINEWBR INCOME;A	Fixed Income	147.4	10.35	10,310.00	11,534.60	☆	7.4	647-1568	None	4.00	0.25	None	Stuart Richardson	'91
PAINEWBR INCOME;B	Fixed Income	33.6	10.34	10,280.40	11,436.60	17,084.30	6.5	647-1568	None	None	1.00	5.00	Stuart Richardson	'91
PAINEWBR INCOME;D	Fixed Income	8.8	10.35	10,287.40	☆	☆	0.0	647-1568	None	None	0.75	None	Stuart Richardson	'92
PAINEWBR INVEST GR;A	Fixed Income	206.2	11.03	10,302.70	11,434.20	17,384.20	7.2	647-1568	None	4.00	0.25	None	Stuart Richardson	'84
PAINEWBR INVEST GR;B	Fixed Income	38.5	11.02	10,284.00	11,338.90	☆	6.5	647-1568	None	None	1.00	5.00	Stuart Richardson	'91
PAINEWBR INVEST GR;D	Fixed Income	35.7	11.03	10,290.30	☆	☆	0.0	647-1568	None	None	0.75	None	Stuart Richardson	'92
PAINEWBR REG FINL GR;A	Financial Services	56.3	18.67	9,643.50	13,016.80	26,463.50	0.6	647-1568	None	4.50	0.25	None	Karen Levy Finkel	'86
PAINEWBR REG FINL GR;B	Financial Services	11.2	18.55	9,622.70	12,923.80	☆	0.3	647-1568	None	None	1.00	5.00	Karen Levy Finkel	'91
PAINEWBR REG FINL GR;D	Financial Services	4.4	18.55	9,629.20	☆	☆	0.0	647-1568	None	None	1.00	None	Karen Levy Finkel	'92
PAINEWBR SEC:SM CAP;A	Small-Company Growth	N/A	10.22	10,078.90	☆	☆	0.0	647-1568	None	4.50	0.25	None	Quest Management	'93
PAINEWBR SEC:SM CAP;B	Small-Company Growth	N/A	10.18	10,049.40	☆	☆	0.0	647-1568	None	None	1.00	5.00	Quest Management	'93
PAINEWBR SEC:SM CAP;D	Small-Company Growth	N/A	10.18	10,049.40	☆	☆	0.0	647-1568	None	None	1.00	None	Quest Management	'93
PAINEWBR S/T GLOBAL;A	World Income	189.5	9.85	10,134.50	10,339.10	☆	2.9	647-1568	None	3.00	0.25	None	Waugh/Fachler	'91/'91
PAINEWBR S/T GLOBAL;B	World Income	211.1	9.82	10,125.40	10,258.60	☆	2.3	647-1568	None	None	1.00	3.00	Waugh/Fachler	'91/'91
PAINEWBR S/T GLOBAL;D	World Income	98.8	9.82	10,122.20	☆	☆	0.0	647-1568	None	None	0.75	None	Waugh/Fachler	'92/'92
PAINEWBR US GOVT;A	Fixed Income	678.4	10.12	10,136.30	10,777.80	16,148.80	6.9	647-1568	None	4.00	0.25	None	Stuart Richardson	'89
PAINEWBR US GOVT;B	Fixed Income	159.4	10.12	10,117.10	10,685.10	☆	6.1	647-1568	None	None	1.00	5.00	Stuart Richardson	'91
PAINEWBR US GOVT;D	Fixed Income	157.4	10.11	10,114.10	☆	☆	0.0	647-1568	None	None	0.75	None	Stuart Richardson	'92
PAPP AMERICA-ABROAD	Growth	10.0	10.57	9,479.10	10,179.00	☆	0.9	421-4004	602-956-0980	None	None	None	L. Roy Papp	'91
L ROY PAPP STOCK	Growth	35.1	14.48	9,702.60	11,121.80	☆	0.9	421-4004	602-956-0980	None	None	None	L. Roy Papp	'89
PARAGON:GULF SOUTH GRO	Small-Company Growth	66.3	14.93	10,006.70	12,637.20	☆	0.1	None	504-332-5968	4.50	None	None	Allred/Chauvin Jr	'91/'91
PARAGON:INTMDT-TERM BOND	Fixed Income	322.6	10.93	10,243.40	11,168.30	☆	6.7	None	504-332-5968	4.50	None	None	Keith Mooney	'89
PARAGON:SHORT-TERM GOVT	Fixed Income	150.2	10.42	10,121.70	10,657.90	☆	5.8	None	504-332-5968	4.50	None	None	Keith Mooney	'89
PARAGON:VALUE EQUITY INC	Equity Income	94.9	12.33	10,032.50	11,356.00	☆	2.3	None	504-332-5968	4.50	None	None	Richard Chauvin, Jr.	'89
PARAGON:VALUE GROWTH	Growth & Income	158.3	14.95	10,021.20	11,959.60	☆	1.2	None	504-332-5968	4.50	None	None	Don Allred	'89
PARIBAS INSTL:QUANT EQ	Growth	N/A	10.62	9,916.00	11,867.50	19,460.90	0.0	None	212-841-3200	None	1.00	4.00	Paribas Asset Mgmt	'86
PARIBAS INSTL:QUANTUS II	Flexible	N/A	11.67	9,864.80	11,514.60	17,005.10	1.0	None	212-841-3200	None	None	None	Paribas Asset Mgmt	'86
PARKSTONE:BALANCED;A	Balanced	5.7	11.09	☆	☆	☆	0.0	451-8377	None	4.50	0.10	None	First of Amer Invt Corp	'93
PARKSTONE:BALANCED;C	Balanced	42.6	11.08	10,253.10	11,765.60	☆	2.6	451-8377	None	None	None	None	First of Amer Invt Corp	'92
PARKSTONE:BOND;A	Fixed Income	17.9	10.54	☆	☆	☆	0.0	451-8377	None	4.00	0.10	None	First of Amer Invt Corp	'93
PARKSTONE:BOND;C	Fixed Income	435.4	10.53	10,283.40	11,181.00	☆	6.9	451-8377	None	None	None	None	First of Amer Invt Corp	'88
PARKSTONE:EQUITY;A	Growth	25.0	15.11	☆	☆	☆	0.0	451-8377	None	4.50	0.10	None	First of Amer Invt Corp	'93
PARKSTONE:EQUITY;C	Growth	584.4	15.10	10,195.80	12,134.60	☆	0.2	451-8377	None	None	None	None	First of Amer Invt Corp	'88
PARKSTONE:GOVT INC;A	Fixed Income	28.7	10.04	☆	☆	☆	0.0	451-8377	None	4.00	0.10	None	First of Amer Invt Corp	'93
PARKSTONE:GOVT INC;C	Fixed Income	66.6	10.04	10,205.20	☆	☆	0.0	451-8377	None	None	None	None	First of Amer Invt Corp	'92
PARKSTONE:HI INC EQ;A	Equity Income	46.6	14.69	☆	☆	☆	0.0	451-8377	None	4.50	0.10	None	First of Amer Invt Corp	'93

PARKSTONE:HI INC EQ;C	Equity Income	370.3	14.69	10,219.70	11,671.00	☆	3.1	451-8377	None	None	None	None	First of Amer Invt Corp	'88
PARKSTONE:INT GOVT;A	Fixed Income	35.0	10.53	☆	☆	☆	0.0	451-8377	None	4.00	0.10	None	First of Amer Invt Corp	'93
PARKSTONE:INT GOVT;C	Fixed Income	268.3	10.53	10,192.30	10,893.20	☆	6.9	451-8377	None	None	None	None	First of Amer Invt Corp	'88
PARKSTONE:INTL DISC;A	International	7.0	11.50	☆	☆	☆	0.0	451-8377	None	4.50	0.10	None	Ivory & Sime	'93
PARKSTONE:LTD MAT BD;A	Fixed Income	17.0	10.18	☆	☆	☆	0.0	451-8377	None	3.00	0.10	None	First of Amer Invt Corp	'93
PARKSTONE:LTD MAT BD;C	Fixed Income	139.0	10.18	10,157.50	10,797.00	☆	6.7	451-8377	None	None	None	None	First of Amer Invt Corp	'88
PARKSTONE:SMALL CAP;A	Small-Company Growth	26.0	20.31	☆	☆	☆	0.0	451-8377	None	4.50	0.10	None	First of Amer Invt Corp	'93
PARKSTONE:SMALL CAP;C	Small-Company Growth	280.5	20.31	10,763.10	14,577.50	☆	0.0	451-8377	None	None	None	None	First of Amer Invt Corp	'88
PARNASSUS FUND	Growth	78.6	31.65	10,066.80	13,292.60	18,313.70	7.0	999-3505	415-362-3505	3.50	None	None	Jerome L. Dodson	'85
PARNASSUS:BALANCED	Balanced	6.3	18.13	10,289.40	☆	☆	0.0	999-3505	415-362-3505	None	None	None	Jerome L. Dodson	'92
PARNASSUS:FXD INC	Fixed Income	3.3	16.01	10,223.10	☆	☆	0.0	999-3505	415-362-3505	None	None	None	Jerome L. Dodson	'92
PASADENA INV:BALANCED	Balanced	79.7	21.32	9,847.60	10,528.10	19,689.50	0.6	648-8050	818-351-9686	5.50	None	None	Roger Engemann	'87
PASADENA INV:GROWTH	Growth	603.6	15.19	9,464.20	9,864.70	21,462.60	1.2	648-8050	818-351-9686	5.50	None	None	Roger Engemann	'86
PASADENA INV:NIFTY FIFTY	Growth	176.1	16.37	9,726.70	10,387.10	☆	0.0	648-8050	818-351-9686	5.50	None	None	Roger Engemann	'90
PAX WORLD	Balanced	502.8	14.16	9,881.40	10,266.00	17,122.70	4.7	767-1729	603-431-8022	None	0.25	None	Anthony S. Brown	'71
PDC&J PERFORMANCE	Capital Appreciation	17.4	18.83	10,261.60	11,995.20	18,583.60	0.5	None	513-223-0600	None	None	None	Johnson/Carlson	'84/'84
PDC&J PRESERVATION	Fixed Income	14.9	11.96	10,283.70	11,019.70	15,733.60	6.9	None	513-223-0600	None	None	None	Johnson/Carlson	'85/'85
PENNSYLVANIA MUTUAL★	Small-Company Growth	1,089.9	8.32	9,893.00	11,529.80	16,801.40	1.2	221-4268	212-355-7311	None	None	1.00	Royce/Ebright	'73/'78
PENN SQUARE MUTUAL	Growth & Income	245.4	10.88	10,064.90	11,258.00	18,173.20	2.1	523-8440	215-670-1031	4.75	0.12	None	James E. Jordan, Jr	'86
PEOPLES INDEX	Growth & Income	257.4	16.14	10,031.10	11,327.70	☆	2.5	373-9387	516-338-3300	None	None	1.00	Wells Fargo Nikko Adv.	'90
PEOPLES S&P MIDCAP	Small-Company Growth	55.0	16.75	10,232.10	12,238.90	☆	1.6	373-9387	516-338-3300	None	None	1.00	Woodbridge Cap Mgt Inc	'91
PERFORM:EQUITY;CNSMR	Growth	3.3	11.40	10,258.80	11,887.50	☆	1.8	524-2276	None	4.70	0.35	None	C. Windham	'92
PERFORM:EQUITY;INSTL	Growth	87.8	11.40	10,268.30	11,900.70	☆	1.9	524-2276	None	None	None	None	C. Windham	'92
PERFORM:INT INC;CNSMR	Fixed Income	2.0	10.75	10,300.00	11,324.30	☆	5.6	524-2276	None	3.50	0.35	None	P. Farnsley	'92
PERFORM:INT INC;INSTL	Fixed Income	150.0	10.75	10,306.80	11,334.40	☆	5.7	524-2276	None	None	None	None	P. Farnsley	'92
PERFORM:SHT INC;CNSMR	Fixed Income	1.1	10.13	10,097.80	10,611.80	☆	4.1	524-2276	None	2.00	0.35	None	Robert H. Spaulding	'92
PERFORM:SHT INC;INSTL	Fixed Income	138.8	10.13	10,104.00	10,620.60	☆	4.2	524-2276	None	None	None	None	Robert H. Spaulding	'92
PERKINS OPPORTUNITY	Capital Appreciation	1.2	16.70	10,489.90	☆	☆	0.0	None	612-473-8367	4.75	0.25	None	Richard W. Perkins	'93
PERMANENT PORT:AGGR GR	Capital Appreciation	3.8	29.01	10,808.50	13,824.20	☆	0.4	531-5142	707-778-1000	None	0.25	None	Terry Coxon	'90
PERMANENT PORT:PERMANENT	Global Flexible	74.8	16.77	10,461.60	11,395.10	12,385.50	1.7	531-5142	707-778-1000	None	0.25	None	Terry Coxon	'82
PERMANENT PORT:TREASURY	Fixed Income	171.7	64.99	10,051.00	10,233.30	13,128.20	3.7	531-5142	707-778-1000	None	0.25	None	Terry Coxon	'87
PERMANENT PORT:VERSATILE	Fixed Income	31.9	54.27	10,053.70	10,493.00	☆	0.0	531-5142	707-778-1000	None	0.25	None	Terry Coxon	'91
PERRITT CAPITAL GROWTH	Small-Company Growth	7.3	12.08	9,534.30	11,194.00	12,629.40	0.0	326-6941	312-649-6940	None	None	None	Gerald W. Perritt	'88
PFAMCO:BALANCED	Flexible	113.5	10.94	10,045.50	11,245.00	☆	2.4	800-7674	714-760-4449	None	None	None	PIMCO *et al.*	'92
PFAMCO:CAPITAL APPREC	Capital Appreciation	65.2	13.34	10,360.80	12,720.00	☆	0.8	800-7674	714-760-4449	None	None	None	Cadence Cap Mgmt Corp.	'91
PFAMCO:DVSFD LOW P/E	Growth & Income	21.4	11.54	10,034.40	11,923.30	☆	2.4	800-7674	714-760-4449	None	None	None	NFJ Investment Grp Inc	'91
PFAMCO:ENHANCED EQUITY	Growth & Income	43.6	12.24	9,850.80	11,183.30	☆	1.5	800-7674	714-760-4449	None	None	None	Parametric Port. Assoc	'91
PFAMCO:EQUITY INCOME	Equity Income	54.2	12.03	10,055.10	11,477.00	☆	5.2	800-7674	714-760-4449	None	None	None	NFJ Investment Grp Inc	'91
PFAMCO:INTL EQUITY	International	62.2	10.77	10,934.00	11,573.40	☆	1.0	800-7674	714-760-4449	None	None	None	Parametric Port. Assoc	'90
PFAMCO:MGD BOND & INCOME	Fixed Income	313.8	10.59	10,350.30	11,496.60	☆	5.7	800-7674	714-760-4449	None	None	None	Pacific Investment Mgt Co	'91
PFAMCO:MID CAP GROWTH	Growth	47.3	13.31	10,456.70	12,566.30	☆	0.7	800-7674	714-760-4449	None	None	None	Cadence Cap Mgmt	'91
PFAMCO:SMALL CAP GROWTH★	Small-Company Growth	40.5	20.43	10,339.10	14,003.30	☆	0.0	800-7674	714-760-4449	None	None	None	Cadence Cap Mgmt	'91
PFAMCO:SMALL CAP VALUE	Small-Company Growth	27.9	12.60	9,810.80	11,835.40	☆	2.1	800-7674	714-760-4449	None	None	None	NFJ Investment Grp	'91
PHILADELPHIA	Growth & Income	94.4	7.03	10,057.50	11,576.70	16,522.70	1.3	749-9933	407-395-2155	None	0.50	None	Donald Baxter	'87
PHILLIPS CAPITAL INV	Growth	5.2	13.61	9,927.10	10,787.60	☆	2.4	None	214-458-2448	None	None	1.00	Guy F. Phillips Jr.	'89

★PENNSYLVANIA MUTUAL—Closed to new investors.

★PFAMCO: SMALL CAP GROWTH—Closed to new investors.

PERFORMANCE OF MUTUAL FUNDS *(continued)*

FUND NAME	OBJECTIVE	TOTAL NET ASSETS ($ MIL) 5/31/93	NET ASSET $ VALUE 6/30/93	PERFORMANCE (Return on Initial $10,000 Investment) 3/31/93-6/30/93	6/30/92-6/30/93	6/30/88-6/30/93	DIVIDEND YIELD % 6/93	PHONE NUMBER 800	In-State	FEES Load	12b-1	Redemption	MANAGER	SINCE
PHOENIX BALANCED	Balanced	2,834.0	16.18	9,945.60	11,015.50	18,953.50	2.9	243-4361	203-253-1000	4.75	0.25	None	Patricia Bannan	'86
PHOENIX CAPITAL APPREC	Growth	335.5	17.86	9,814.40	11,465.00	☆	0.7	243-4361	203-253-1000	4.75	0.25	None	Cathy Dudley	'89
PHOENIX CONVERTIBLE	Convertible Securities	231.6	18.60	10,135.40	11,308.10	16,907.80	4.0	243-4361	203-253-1000	4.75	0.25	None	John Hamlin	'92
PHOENIX GROWTH	Growth	2,588.3	20.78	9,850.40	10,707.60	18,471.00	1.5	243-4361	203-253-1000	4.75	0.25	None	Chesek/Dudley	'80/'90
PHOENIX HIGH QUAL BOND	Fixed Income	60.8	10.15	10,287.40	11,326.70	16,293.20	6.2	243-4361	203-253-1000	4.75	0.25	None	Michael Haylon	'90
PHOENIX HIGH YIELD	Fixed Income	157.2	8.83	10,446.60	11,811.60	16,798.40	8.6	243-4361	203-253-1000	4.75	0.25	None	Curtis Barrows	'85
PHOENIX INTERNATIONAL	International	40.0	9.92	10,409.20	9,920.00	☆	0.0	243-4361	203-253-1000	4.75	0.25	None	Jean Dorey	'93
PHOENIX STOCK	Capital Appreciation	139.0	13.94	10,257.30	11,632.30	16,281.40	1.6	243-4361	203-253-1000	4.75	0.25	None	Michael Matty	'90
PHOENIX TOTAL RETURN	Flexible	74.0	15.56	10,026.00	11,436.60	18,516.60	1.2	243-4361	203-253-1000	4.75	0.25	None	Robert Milnamow	'89
PHOENIX US GOVT SEC	Fixed Income	52.0	9.91	10,210.50	11,189.50	16,154.30	5.9	243-4361	203-253-1000	4.75	0.25	None	Christopher Kelleher	'90
PIC ENDEAVOR GROWTH	Growth	68.6	10.88	9,981.70	☆	☆	0.0	None	818-449-8500	None	None	None	Provident Invt Counsel	'92
PIC PINNACLE BALANCED	Balanced	2.8	11.16	9,928.80	11,216.80	☆	0.8	None	818-449-8500	None	None	None	Provident Invt Counsel	'92
PIC PINNACLE GROWTH	Growth	38.4	10.99	9,963.70	11,010.70	☆	0.1	None	818-449-8500	None	None	None	Provident Invt Counsel	'92
PILGRIM CORP UTILITIES★	Utility	16.5	8.82	9,326.20	9,160.90	☆	9.2	334-3444	310-551-0833	3.00	0.25	None	Howard N. Kornblue	'91
PILGRIM GL:SH MU-MK★	World Income	43.3	6.92	9,864.90	8,186.30	☆	8.4	334-3444	310-551-0833	3.00	0.30	None	S.G. Warburg & Co.	'92
PILGRIM GL:SH MU-MK II	World Income	12.0	7.96	10,055.70	8,892.80	☆	7.7	334-3444	310-551-0833	None	0.75	4.00	S.G. Warburg & Co.	'92
PILGRIM GNMA	Fixed Income	86.6	13.96	10,097.40	10,981.80	15,334.00	7.9	334-3444	310-551-0833	3.00	0.25	None	Brian Carrico	'93
PILGRIM MAGNACAP★	Growth & Income	204.0	12.05	9,860.90	10,821.40	17,020.80	1.1	334-3444	310-551-0833	5.00	0.30	None	Howard N. Kornblue	'89
PILGRIM:ADJ GOVT I★	Fixed Income	736.1	7.25	10,126.90	10,546.40	☆	6.5	334-3444	310-551-0833	None	1.00	4.00	Brian Carrico	'91
PILGRIM:ADJ GOVT I-A	Fixed Income	349.5	7.27	10,126.90	10,561.10	☆	6.5	334-3444	310-551-0833	None	None	4.00	Brian Carrico	'92
PILGRIM:ADJ GOVT II	Fixed Income	87.5	7.31	10,140.90	10,620.30	☆	6.5	334-3444	310-551-0833	3.00	0.25	None	Brian Carrico	'91
PILGRIM:ADJ GOVT III	Fixed Income	56.6	7.30	10,147.00	10,644.80	☆	6.7	334-3444	310-551-0833	5.00	None	None	Brian Carrico	'91
PILGRIM:ADJ RT I★	Fixed Income	57.3	7.22	10,148.10	10,707.20	☆	7.6	334-3444	310-551-0833	None	1.00	4.00	Brian Carrico	'91
PILGRIM:ADJ RT I-A	Fixed Income	132.2	7.24	10,148.20	10,707.60	☆	7.6	334-3444	310-551-0833	None	None	4.00	Brian Carrico	'92
PILGRIM:ADJ RT II	Fixed Income	34.1	7.30	10,162.30	10,780.70	☆	7.5	334-3444	310-551-0833	3.00	0.25	None	Brian Carrico	'91
PILGRIM:ADJ RT III	Fixed Income	36.8	7.27	10,169.80	10,792.80	☆	7.8	334-3444	310-551-0833	5.00	None	None	Brian Carrico	'91
PILGRIM:HIGH YIELD	Fixed Income	18.5	6.41	10,469.00	11,639.20	16,135.10	8.5	334-3444	310-551-0833	3.00	0.25	None	Randolph Birkman	'93
PILLAR:BALANCED GRO;A★	Flexible	19.3	10.64	10,106.30	11,021.30	☆	3.6	932-7782	None	None	None	None	Fernando Garip	'92
PILLAR:BALANCED GRO;B	Flexible	5.0	10.65	10,091.10	10,983.20	☆	3.6	932-7782	None	4.00	0.25	None	Fernando Garip	'92
PILLAR:EQUITY AGGR GRO;A★	Small-Company Growth	31.4	11.03	9,999.10	11,458.80	☆	1.0	932-7782	None	None	None	None	Richard Bodenstein	'92
PILLAR:EQUITY AGGR GRO;B	Small-Company Growth	1.6	11.02	10,002.70	11,427.50	☆	0.8	932-7782	None	4.00	0.25	None	Richard Bodenstein	'92
PILLAR:EQUITY GRO;A★	Growth	60.5	10.48	9,909.70	10,895.50	☆	1.8	932-7782	None	None	None	None	Tom Hesslein	'92
PILLAR:EQUITY GRO;B	Growth	N/A	10.50	9,904.20	10,875.50	☆	1.6	932-7782	None	4.00	0.25	None	Tom Hesslein	'92
PILLAR:EQUITY INC;A★	Income	33.7	11.28	10,144.60	11,453.30	☆	2.5	932-7782	None	None	None	None	Richard Bodenstein	'92
PILLAR:EQUITY INC;B	Income	1.7	11.29	10,139.20	11,419.00	☆	2.5	932-7782	None	4.00	0.25	None	Richard Bodenstein	'92
PILLAR:FIXED INC;A★	Fixed Income	104.9	10.94	10,302.10	11,365.30	☆	5.6	932-7782	None	None	None	None	Bob Lowe	'92
PILLAR:FIXED INC;B	Fixed Income	2.4	10.93	10,285.90	11,337.60	☆	5.4	932-7782	None	4.00	0.25	None	Bob Lowe	'92
PILLAR:INT-TERM GOVT;A★	Fixed Income	20.9	10.61	10,222.10	10,913.90	☆	4.9	932-7782	None	None	None	None	Frances Tendall	'92
PILLAR:INT-TERM GOVT;B	Fixed Income	4.0	10.61	10,215.80	10,887.50	☆	4.7	932-7782	None	4.00	0.25	None	Frances Tendall	'92
PILLAR:SHORT-TERM;A★	Fixed Income	39.7	10.01	10,054.30	10,309.20	☆	3.0	932-7782	None	None	None	None	Bob Lowe	'92
PILLAR:SHORT-TERM;B	Fixed Income	0.2	10.02	10,057.70	10,292.60	☆	2.8	932-7782	None	1.00	0.25	None	Bob Lowe	'92
PIMCO FOREIGN★	World Income	207.2	10.54	10,329.10	☆	☆	0.0	927-4648	714-760-4880	None	None	None	John Hague	'92
PIMCO GROWTH STOCK★	Capital Appreciation	22.6	14.16	9,898.30	11,339.20	18,008.10	1.4	927-4648	714-760-4880	None	None	None	Ben Ehlert	'87
PIMCO HIGH YIELD★	Fixed Income	31.3	10.60	10,408.50	☆	☆	0.0	927-4648	714-760-4880	None	None	None	Ben Trosky	'92
PIMCO LONG-TERM US GOVT★	Fixed Income	22.7	11.89	10,619.00	12,524.30	☆	5.3	927-4648	714-760-4880	None	None	None	Frank Rabinovitch	'91

PIMCO LOW DURATION★	Fixed Income	1,570.8	10.30	10,160.20	10,874.70	16,046.30	6.9	927-4648	714-760-4880	None	None	None	William Gross	'87
PIMCO LOW DURATION II★	Fixed Income	114.0	10.26	10,162.90	10,769.40	☆	6.0	927-4648	714-760-4880	None	None	None	William Gross	'91
PIMCO SHORT-TERM★	Fixed Income	41.3	10.02	10,120.40	10,395.60	13,968.80	4.0	927-4648	714-760-4880	None	None	None	William Gross	'87
PIMCO TOTAL RETURN★	Fixed Income	3,519.6	11.10	10,331.00	11,459.60	18,109.60	6.6	927-4648	714-760-4880	None	None	None	William Gross	'87
PIMCO TOTAL RETURN III★	Fixed Income	67.6	9.98	10,326.30	11,355.00	☆	6.1	927-4648	714-760-4880	None	None	None	William Gross	'91
PINNACLE FUND	Capital Appreciation	15.1	21.83	9,986.30	11,061.40	17,504.30	0.6	None	*317-633-4080*	None	None	None	Heartland Cap. Mgmt	'85
PIONEER BOND	Fixed Income	108.6	9.81	10,295.50	11,266.80	16,563.30	7.2	225-6292	617-742-7825	4.50	0.25	None	Sherman Russ	'87
PIONEER CAPITAL GROWTH	Growth	154.8	15.09	10,086.90	12,797.90	☆	0.0	225-6292	617-742-7825	5.75	0.25	None	Warren Isabelle	'90
PIONEER EQUITY-INCOME	Equity Income	101.0	16.21	10,156.40	12,163.60	☆	3.1	225-6292	617-742-7825	5.75	0.25	None	John Carey	'90
PIONEER EUROPE	European Region	41.7	15.85	10,082.70	9,595.60	☆	0.6	225-6292	617-742-7825	5.75	0.25	None	Norman Kurland	'91
PIONEER FUND	Growth & Income	1,902.1	22.79	10,115.30	11,518.90	16,674.40	2.1	225-6292	617-742-7825	5.75	0.25	None	John Carey	'86
PIONEER GOLD SHARES	Gold	7.6	7.46	13,250.40	14,209.50	☆	0.0	225-6292	617-742-7825	5.75	0.25	None	David Tripple	'90
PIONEER INTL GROWTH	International	6.0	16.85	☆	☆	☆	0.0	225-6292	617-742-7825	5.75	0.25	None	Norman Kurland	'93
PIONEER SH-TM INC TR	Fixed Income	24.8	3.98	10,159.20	☆	☆	0.0	225-6292	617-742-7825	2.50	0.25	None	Richard Schlanger	'92
PIONEER II	Growth & Income	4,257.4	19.80	10,153.90	11,543.20	16,318.20	1.9	225-6292	617-742-7825	5.75	0.25	None	Tripple/Boggan	'80/'91
PIONEER THREE	Growth & Income	980.0	20.20	9,893.00	12,130.00	18,688.10	1.4	225-6292	617-742-7825	5.75	0.25	None	Robert W. Benson	'86
PIONEER US GOVT TRUST	Fixed Income	97.2	10.61	10,257.00	11,067.80	15,903.40	6.5	225-6292	617-742-7825	4.50	0.25	None	Richard Schlanger	'88
PIPER GLBL:PAC-EURO GRO	International	84.9	11.88	10,683.50	11,040.90	☆	0.0	866-7778	612-342-6402	4.00	0.32	None	Ian Watt	'92
PIPER INSTL:ENHANCED 500	Growth & Income	15.4	10.08	10,029.90	☆	☆	0.0	866-7778	612-342-6402	None	None	None	Tony Elavia	'93
PIPER INSTL:GOVT ADJ	Fixed Income	37.9	10.04	10,054.60	☆	☆	0.0	866-7778	612-342-6402	1.00	None	None	Griffin/McGlinch	'93/'93
PIPER JAFFRAY:BALANCED	Balanced	49.0	12.20	10,008.30	11,174.90	16,954.50	2.9	866-7778	612-342-6402	4.00	0.32	None	Rinkey/Elavia/Dow	'87/'89
PIPER JAFFRAY:EMERG GR	Small-Company Growth	163.8	17.87	10,293.80	12,620.10	☆	0.0	866-7778	612-342-6402	4.00	0.30	None	Tauer *et al.*	'90
PIPER JAFFRAY:GOVT INC	Fixed Income	148.5	9.90	10,305.30	11,055.80	16,255.30	8.4	866-7778	612-342-6402	4.00	0.32	None	Rinkey/Griffin/Stone	'87/'87
PIPER JAFFRAY:GRO & INC	Growth & Income	98.6	10.11	9,951.30	☆	☆	0.0	866-7778	612-342-6402	4.00	0.32	None	Dow/Schonberg	'92/'92
PIPER JAFFRAY:INSTL GOVT	Fixed Income	641.9	12.02	10,344.80	12,049.50	☆	7.4	866-7778	612-342-6402	1.50	0.22	None	Bruntjen/Goldstein	'88/'88
PIPER JAFFRAY:SECTOR	Capital Appreciation	12.6	16.12	10,196.10	12,039.00	19,172.00	0.4	866-7778	612-342-6402	4.00	0.32	None	Ed Nicoski	'87
PIPER JAFFRAY:VALUE	Growth	242.5	18.51	9,788.90	11,049.80	21,169.80	0.7	866-7778	612-342-6402	4.00	0.32	None	John A. Tauer Jr.	'87
PNC:BALANCED;INV	Flexible	34.3	12.15	10,226.60	11,615.50	☆	2.4	428-7108	None	4.50	0.55	None	Gayland Gee	'90
PNC:GROWTH EQUITY;INV	Growth	85.2	10.48	10,325.20	11,169.50	☆	1.2	428-7108	None	4.50	0.55	None	Mike Clark	'92
PNC:INDEX EQUITY;INV	Growth & Income	195.4	10.83	10,018.90	11,284.80	☆	2.2	428-7108	None	4.50	0.55	None	Francis X. Morris	'92
PNC:INTMDT GOVT;INV	Fixed Income	146.5	10.52	10,209.80	10,915.00	☆	5.2	428-7108	None	4.50	0.55	None	Rena Williams	'92
PNC:INTL EQUITY;INV	International	97.1	11.40	10,584.60	11,125.60	☆	1.4	428-7108	None	4.50	0.55	None	Herve Van Caloen	'92
PNC:MGD INCOME;INV	Fixed Income	324.3	10.98	10,309.90	11,336.10	☆	6.1	428-7108	None	4.50	0.55	None	Lowry/Williams	'92/'92
PNC:SM CAP VAL EQ;INV	Small-Company Growth	119.7	12.11	9,869.90	12,655.30	☆	0.4	428-7108	None	4.50	0.55	None	Edwin B. Powell	'92
PNC:VALUE EQUITY;INV	Capital Appreciation	402.5	11.12	10,063.90	11,611.30	☆	2.0	428-7108	None	4.50	0.55	None	Edwin B. Powell	'92
PORT DVSD INV:FX INC;SHS★	Fixed Income	37.8	10.41	10,242.40	11,241.60	16,640.40	6.4	821-7432	None	None	None	None	Rena Williams	'91
PORTICO BALANCED	Balanced	66.2	21.59	9,963.30	11,347.50	☆	2.2	982-8909	414-287-3710	None	None	None	Halford/Westman	'92/'92
PORTICO BOND IMMDEX	Fixed Income	234.9	28.33	10,312.40	11,337.50	☆	6.1	982-8909	414-287-3710	None	None	None	Stanek/Westman	'89/'92
PORTICO EQUITY INDEX	Growth & Income	76.8	31.81	9,998.20	11,251.60	☆	2.3	982-8909	414-287-3710	None	None	None	Stanek/Tranchita	'89/'92
PORTICO INCOME & GRO	Equity Income	145.6	23.40	10,041.20	10,958.10	☆	2.6	982-8909	414-287-3710	None	None	None	Marian Zentmyer	'93
PORTICO INT BD MKT	Fixed Income	32.9	10.34	10,210.10	☆	☆	0.0	982-8909	414-287-3710	None	None	None	Stanek/Westman	'93/'93
PORTICO MIDCORE GRO	Growth	57.8	19.64	9,804.50	☆	☆	0.0	982-8909	414-287-3710	None	None	None	Bart Wear	'92
PORTICO SH-TM BD MKT	Fixed Income	130.6	10.57	10,142.80	10,798.40	☆	5.7	982-8909	414-287-3710	None	None	None	Stanek/Tranchita	'89/'93
PORTICO SPECIAL GRO	Small-Company Growth	288.6	29.67	9,669.60	11,390.90	☆	0.4	982-8909	414-287-3710	None	None	None	Harkness/Docter	'89/'89
PRA:REAL ESTATE	Real Estate	102.9	9.93	9,453.80	13,203.80	☆	4.3	435-1405	312-915-3600	None	None	None	Michael T. Oliver	'89

★PILGRIM CORP UTLITIES — On 6/4/93, the fund's NAV was reduced by $0.73 as a result of the RTC takeover of one of its holdings, Western Federal S&L Assoc.
★PILGRIM GL: SH MU-MK — On 6/4/93, the fund's NAV was reduced by $0.73 as a result of the RTC takeover of one of its holdings, Western Federal S&L Assoc.
★PILGRIM MAGNACAP—On 6/16/93, fund was reclassified from Growth to Growth & Income.

★PILGRIM ADJ GOVT I & PILGRIM ADJ RT I—Closed to new investors.
★PILLAR CLASS A FUNDS—Institutional funds.
★PIMCO FUNDS—Designed primarily for retirement accounts. Minimum investment is $500,000.
★PORT DVSD INV: FX INC; SHS—Institutional fund.

PERFORMANCE OF MUTUAL FUNDS (continued)

FUND NAME	OBJECTIVE	TOTAL NET ASSETS ($ MIL) 5/31/93	NET ASSET $ VALUE 6/30/93	PERFORMANCE (Return on Initial $10,000 Investment) 3/31/93-6/30/93	6/30/92-6/30/93	6/30/88-6/30/93	DIVIDEND YIELD % 6/93	PHONE NUMBER 800	In-State	FEES Load	12b-1	Redemption	MANAGER	SINCE
PREFERRED ASSET ALLOC	Flexible	46.6	10.90	10,086.50	☆	☆	3.1	662-4769	309-675-1205	None	None	None	Mellon/PanAgora	'92/'92
PREFERRED FXD INC	Fixed Income	34.6	10.60	10,262.70	☆	☆	4.8	662-4769	309-675-1205	None	None	None	J.P. Morgan Inv Mgt Inc	'92
PREFERRED GROWTH	Growth	114.8	12.42	10,367.30	☆	☆	0.0	662-4769	309-675-1205	None	None	None	Jennison Assoc Cap Corp	'92
PREFERRED INTL	International	38.9	9.59	10,378.80	☆	☆	0.3	662-4769	309-675-1205	None	None	None	Mercator Asset Mgt, Inc	'92
PREFERRED SHT-TM GOVT	Fixed Income	26.5	10.08	10,137.10	☆	☆	3.8	662-4769	309-675-1205	None	None	None	Caterpillar Inv Mgt Ltd	'92
PREFERRED VALUE	Growth & Income	119.8	11.52	10,114.10	☆	☆	1.0	662-4769	309-675-1205	None	None	None	Oppenheimer Capital	'92
T ROWE PRICE ADJ RATE	Fixed Income	372.8	4.81	10,077.40	10,212.90	☆	5.4	638-5660	410-547-2308	None	None	None	Peter Van Dyke	'91
T ROWE PRICE BALANCED	Balanced	283.3	11.38	10,105.60	11,374.70	18,393.50	3.8	638-5660	410-547-2308	None	None	None	Richard T. Whitney	'91
T ROWE PRICE CAP APPREC	Capital Appreciation	449.4	12.23	10,277.30	11,351.40	17,743.30	4.1	638-5660	410-547-2308	None	None	None	Richard P. Howard	'89
T ROWE PRICE DIV GROWTH	Growth & Income	28.2	10.85	10,101.80	☆	☆	0.0	638-5660	410-547-2308	None	None	None	Bill Stromberg	'92
T ROWE PRICE EQU INCOME	Equity Income	2,539.4	16.43	10,159.50	11,440.50	17,426.20	3.4	638-5660	410-547-2308	None	None	None	Brian C. Rogers	'89
T ROWE PRICE GNMA	Fixed Income	906.9	9.91	10,182.10	10,835.20	16,255.80	7.4	638-5660	410-547-2308	None	None	None	Peter Van Dyke	'87
T ROWE PRICE GROWTH &INC	Growth & Income	1,077.2	16.56	9,970.00	12,040.60	18,259.90	3.2	638-5660	410-547-2308	None	None	None	Stephen W. Boesel	'87
T ROWE PRICE GROWTH STK	Growth	1,790.9	19.41	10,157.00	11,472.10	17,483.90	0.9	638-5660	410-547-2308	None	None	None	M. David Testa	'84
T ROWE PRICE HIGH YIELD	Fixed Income	1,630.5	9.05	10,578.40	12,019.50	15,892.80	9.0	638-5660	410-547-2308	None	None	None	Richard Swingle	'84
T ROWE PRICE INDEX:EQU★	Growth & Income	148.4	13.02	10,030.40	11,285.40	☆	2.4	638-5660	410-547-2308	None	None	None	Richard T. Whitney	'90
T ROWE PRICE INTL:ASIA	Pacific Region	637.9	14.69	10,777.70	11,216.70	☆	1.3	638-5660	410-547-2308	None	None	None	Martin G. Wade	'90
T ROWE PRICE INTL:BOND	World Income	611.1	10.26	10,380.50	11,002.60	15,941.70	7.4	638-5660	410-547-2308	None	None	None	David Boardman	'86
T ROWE PRICE INTL:DISC	International	226.9	13.74	10,618.20	10,345.40	☆	0.9	638-5660	410-547-2308	None	None	None	Rochelle Siegel	'89
T ROWE PRICE INTL:EU STK	European Region	192.3	9.96	10,101.40	9,423.60	☆	1.7	638-5660	410-547-2308	None	None	None	Martin G. Wade	'90
T ROWE PRICE INTL:GL GVT	World Income	50.9	10.30	10,303.20	10,970.20	☆	6.3	638-5660	410-547-2308	None	None	None	David Boardman	'90
T ROWE PRICE INTL:JAPAN	Japanese	91.9	10.99	11,146.00	12,050.40	☆	0.0	638-5660	410-547-2308	None	None	None	Robert Howe	'91
T ROWE PRICE INTL:SH GL	World Income	71.8	4.83	10,259.70	☆	☆	7.5	638-5660	410-547-2308	None	None	None	David Boardman	'92
T ROWE PRICE INTL:STOCK	International	2,510.4	10.04	10,502.10	10,622.90	15,519.50	1.6	638-5660	410-547-2308	None	None	None	Testa/Wade	'80/'80
T ROWE PRICE MID-CAP GRO	Growth	37.4	13.49	10,530.80	13,692.00	☆	0.0	638-5660	410-547-2308	None	None	None	Brian Berghuis	'92
T ROWE PRICE NEW AMER	Growth	516.2	25.74	10,374.80	12,649.20	22,061.80	0.0	638-5660	410-547-2308	None	None	None	John H. Laporte	'85
T ROWE PRICE NEW ERA	Natural Resources	751.1	20.39	10,189.90	11,147.40	14,066.30	2.2	638-5660	410-547-2308	None	None	None	George A. Roche	'79
T ROWE PRICE NEW HORIZON	Small-Company Growth	1,424.0	16.09	10,641.50	13,008.10	18,760.50	0.0	638-5660	410-547-2308	None	None	None	John H. Laporte	'87
T ROWE PRICE NEW INCOME	Fixed Income	1,536.0	9.31	10,259.10	11,007.40	16,223.80	6.0	638-5660	410-547-2308	None	None	None	Charles P. Smith	'86
T ROWE PRICE OTC	Small-Company Growth	186.8	15.24	10,318.20	12,321.30	16,103.50	0.4	638-5660	410-547-2308	None	None	None	Greg A. McCrickard	'92
T ROWE PRICE SCI & TECH	Science & Technology	346.2	18.83	11,005.30	14,000.40	27,721.20	0.0	638-5660	410-547-2308	None	None	None	Laporte/Morris	'87/'91
T ROWE PRICE SH-TERM BD	Fixed Income	579.6	5.10	10,183.80	10,735.20	14,930.30	6.5	638-5660	410-547-2308	None	None	None	Veena A. Kutler	'84
T ROWE PRICE SM CAP★	Small-Company Growth	400.6	13.72	10,277.20	12,753.80	☆	0.7	638-5660	410-547-2308	None	None	None	Preston G. Athey	'88
T ROWE PRICE SPCTRM:GRO	Growth & Income	442.8	11.32	10,300.30	11,729.00	☆	1.7	638-5660	410-547-2308	None	None	None	Van Dyke/Notzen	'90/'90
T ROWE PRICE SPCTRM:INC	Fixed Income	486.8	11.16	10,287.60	11,150.20	☆	6.4	638-5660	410-547-2308	None	None	None	Van Dyke/Notzen	'90/'90
T ROWE PRICE TREAS:INTMD	Fixed Income	165.4	5.43	10,176.30	11,036.10	☆	5.7	638-5660	410-547-2308	None	None	None	Smith/Kutler	'89/'89
T ROWE PRICE TREAS:LONG	Fixed Income	59.6	10.98	10,394.10	11,578.90	☆	6.2	638-5660	410-547-2308	None	None	None	Peter Van Dyke	'89
PRIMARY INC:INCOME	Income	2.8	11.68	10,218.40	11,273.80	☆	4.4	443-6544	414-271-7870	None	None	None	David Aushwitz	'89
PRIMARY INC:US GOVT	Fixed Income	1.3	10.60	10,222.30	10,900.30	☆	5.2	443-6544	414-271-7870	None	None	None	James Dean	'89
PRIMARY TREND	Growth & Income	25.2	11.22	10,274.70	10,815.00	14,032.30	3.6	443-6544	414-271-7870	None	None	None	David Aushwitz	'89
PRIME VALUE:ALTURA ARM	Fixed Income	77.4	10.14	10,140.60	10,650.00	☆	4.8	338-1348	612-667-8833	1.50	None	None	Roger Adams	'92
PRIME VALUE:ALTURA GOVT	Fixed Income	131.7	9.91	10,167.60	11,043.00	☆	7.1	338-1348	612-667-8833	3.25	None	None	Mark Karstom	'88
PRIME VALUE:ALTURA INC	Fixed Income	85.3	10.70	10,207.10	11,155.70	16,877.20	7.1	338-1348	612-667-8833	3.25	None	None	Mark Karstom	'87
PRIME VALUE:ALTURA VALGR	Capital Appreciation	109.7	17.21	9,762.40	11,195.50	19,197.90	1.0	338-1348	612-667-8833	4.00	None	None	David Beeck	'88
PRINCIPAL PRES:BALANCED	Balanced	18.8	10.33	9,914.20	☆	☆	2.6	826-4600	414-334-5521	4.50	0.25	None	R. Douglas Ziegler	'92

PRINCIPAL PRES:DIV ACHVR	Growth & Income	26.4	13.48	9,568.00	10,678.70	16,957.80	1.0	826-4600	414-334-5521	4.50	0.25	None	R. Douglas Ziegler	'92
PRINCIPAL PRES:GOVT	Fixed Income	46.1	10.09	10,291.50	11,348.80	16,721.50	6.5	826-4600	414-334-5521	4.50	0.25	None	Vern Van Vooren	'85
PRINCIPAL PRES:S&P 100 +	Growth & Income	33.9	14.69	10,077.20	11,086.20	17,731.40	1.5	826-4600	414-334-5521	4.50	0.25	None	Willaim Zink	'89
PRINCIPAL SP MKT:INTL	Global	10.1	10.00	☆	☆	☆	0.0	247-4123	515-247-5711	None	None	None	Chuck Bastyr	'93
PRINCIPAL SP MKT:MBS	Fixed Income	19.7	10.14	☆	☆	☆	0.0	247-4123	515-247-5711	None	None	None	Martin Schafer	'93
PRINCOR BLUE CHIP	Growth & Income	22.8	11.89	9,941.50	10,808.80	☆	1.3	247-4123	515-247-5711	5.00	0.25	None	Williams/Opsal	'91/'92
PRINCOR BOND	Fixed Income	73.8	11.44	10,252.60	11,359.90	16,982.60	7.2	247-4123	515-247-5711	5.00	0.25	None	Don Brattebo	'87
PRINCOR CAPITAL ACCUM	Growth & Income	224.5	21.45	10,103.60	11,315.80	15,545.20	2.0	247-4123	515-247-5711	5.00	0.15	None	White/Green	'92/'93
PRINCOR EMERGING GROWTH	Capital Appreciation	37.9	21.94	10,004.60	12,048.80	19,708.40	0.6	247-4123	515-247-5711	5.00	0.25	None	Hamilton/Craven	'87/'93
PRINCOR GOVT SEC INCOME	Fixed Income	203.8	11.77	10,258.30	11,112.90	17,104.70	6.4	247-4123	515-247-5711	5.00	0.20	None	Martin Schafer	'85
PRINCOR GROWTH	Growth	73.6	29.02	10,122.10	11,151.50	19,240.20	1.2	247-4123	515-247-5711	5.00	0.22	None	Hamilton/Craven	'87/'93
PRINCOR HIGH YIELD	Fixed Income	17.4	8.51	10,316.50	11,325.50	14,357.50	8.5	247-4123	515-247-5711	5.00	0.25	None	Ken Hovey	'87
PRINCOR MANAGED	Flexible	36.4	13.15	10,162.30	11,211.10	15,883.20	3.0	247-4123	515-247-5711	5.00	0.23	None	Green/Vogal	'93/'93
PRINCOR UTILITIES	Utility	29.7	11.46	10,214.10	☆	☆	0.0	247-4123	515-247-5711	5.00	0.25	None	Green/Vogal	'93/'93
PRINCOR WORLD	International	47.3	5.82	10,620.40	10,730.60	14,038.50	0.8	247-4123	515-247-5711	5.00	0.25	None	Chuck Bastyr	'89
PROGRESSIVE:AGGR GROWTH	Capital Appreciation	0.6	7.54	10,013.30	8,213.50	10,018.70	0.0	275-2382	303-985-9999	4.00	0.50	None	James R. Lampson	'92
PROGRESSIVE:ENVIRONMENT	Environmental	3.3	4.87	9,838.40	11,299.30	☆	0.0	275-2382	303-985-9999	4.50	0.50	None	George R. Gay	'92
PROGRESSIVE:VALUE	Growth	1.0	9.43	10,139.80	11,627.60	8,179.80	0.0	275-2382	303-985-9999	4.00	0.50	None	Stephen K. Bache	'92
PRUDENT SPECULATOR	Small-Company Growth	4.9	6.76	9,754.70	10,674.70	9,268.90	0.0	444-4778	213-252-9000	None	0.25	None	Ed Bernstein	'89
PRUDENTIAL ADJ RATE;A	Fixed Income	193.9	9.84	10,073.90	10,328.40	☆	4.9	225-1852	None	1.00	0.50	None	Kay Willcox	'92
PRUDENTIAL ADJ RATE;B	Fixed Income	35.2	9.87	10,102.60	10,319.00	☆	4.5	225-1852	None	None	1.00	1.00	Kay Willcox	'92
PRUDENTIAL EQUITY;A	Growth	187.7	13.63	10,310.10	12,060.80	☆	1.5	225-1852	None	5.25	0.30	None	Tom Jackson	'90
PRUDENTIAL EQUITY;B	Growth	1,500.3	13.59	10,295.50	11,977.00	19,509.20	0.9	225-1852	None	None	1.00	5.00	Tom Jackson	'82
PRUDENTIAL EQU INC;A	Equity Income	71.2	13.79	10,378.60	12,484.70	☆	3.3	225-1852	None	5.25	0.30	None	Warren Spitz	'90
PRUDENTIAL EQU INC;B	Equity Income	303.1	13.77	10,352.40	12,380.90	18,389.10	2.6	225-1852	None	None	1.00	5.00	Warren Spitz	'87
PRUDENTIAL FLX:CONSV;A	Flexible	18.9	11.69	10,276.00	11,733.10	☆	3.1	225-1852	None	5.25	0.30	None	Guidone/McHugh	'90/'90
PRUDENTIAL FLX:CONSV;B	Flexible	304.5	11.67	10,267.80	11,643.00	16,953.90	2.4	225-1852	None	None	1.00	5.00	Guidone/McHugh	'89/'90
PRUDENTIAL FLX:STRAT;A	Flexible	27.4	11.80	10,189.50	11,319.10	☆	3.1	225-1852	None	5.25	0.30	None	Gleason/Smith	'90/'93
PRUDENTIAL FLX:STRAT;B	Flexible	354.3	11.77	10,163.90	11,225.50	16,643.90	2.4	225-1852	None	None	1.00	5.00	Gleason/Smith	'89/'93
PRUDENTIAL GLOBAL;A	Global	22.0	10.97	10,507.70	11,047.30	☆	0.0	225-1852	None	5.25	0.30	None	Dan Duane	'91
PRUDENTIAL GLOBAL;B	Global	181.4	10.80	10,485.40	10,975.60	11,756.40	0.0	225-1852	None	None	1.00	5.00	Dan Duane	'84
PRUDENTIAL GL GENSIS;A	Global Small Company	3.4	14.60	10,541.50	11,967.20	☆	0.0	225-1852	None	5.25	0.30	None	Dan Duane	'90
PRUDENTIAL GL GENSIS;B	Global Small Company	36.0	14.20	10,526.30	11,882.80	14,036.90	0.0	225-1852	None	None	1.00	5.00	Dan Duane	'88
PRUDENTIAL GL NT RES;A	Natural Resources	1.9	12.07	11,259.30	12,155.10	☆	0.0	225-1852	None	5.25	0.30	None	Leigh Goering	'90
PRUDENTIAL GL NT RES;B	Natural Resources	35.7	11.91	11,235.80	12,066.90	13,530.10	0.0	225-1852	None	None	1.00	5.00	Leigh Goering	'87
PRUDENTIAL GNMA;A	Fixed Income	10.0	15.18	10,161.90	10,794.80	☆	7.3	225-1852	None	4.50	0.30	None	Kay Willcox	'90
PRUDENTIAL GNMA;B	Fixed Income	336.2	15.14	10,147.40	10,732.70	15,081.00	6.7	225-1852	None	None	0.75	5.00	Kay Willcox	'82
PRUDENTIAL GOVT:INTMDT	Fixed Income	322.6	10.20	10,180.90	10,921.30	15,504.20	7.2	225-1852	None	None	0.25	None	Kay Willcox	'92
PRUDENTIAL GOVT PLUS;A	Fixed Income	53.4	9.44	10,258.70	11,095.30	☆	6.9	225-1852	None	4.50	0.30	None	Marty Lawlor	'90
PRUDENTIAL GOVT PLUS;B	Fixed Income	2,570.5	9.44	10,236.70	11,001.40	15,774.70	6.0	225-1852	None	None	1.00	5.00	Marty Lawlor	'85
PRUDENTIAL GROWTH;A	Growth	4.0	15.64	9,755.60	11,323.90	☆	1.1	225-1852	None	5.25	0.30	None	Greg Smith	'90
PRUDENTIAL GROWTH;B	Growth	227.3	15.60	9,734.60	11,238.00	14,633.40	0.4	225-1852	None	None	1.00	5.00	Greg Smith	'83
PRUDENTIAL GR OPPTY;A	Small-Company Growth	79.5	18.04	10,221.00	12,623.70	☆	0.0	225-1852	None	5.25	0.30	None	Bob Fetch	'90
PRUDENTIAL GR OPPTY;B	Small-Company Growth	322.8	17.63	10,196.60	12,517.70	18,534.80	0.0	225-1852	None	None	1.00	5.00	Bob Fetch	'81
PRUDENTIAL HI YLD;A	Fixed Income	150.9	8.64	10,429.40	11,678.10	☆	10.1	225-1852	None	4.50	0.30	None	Lars Berkman	'90

★T ROWE PRICE INDEX: EQU—Available only through retirement funds.

★T ROWE PRICE SM CAP—Closed to new investors.

PERFORMANCE OF MUTUAL FUNDS *(continued)*

FUND NAME	OBJECTIVE	TOTAL NET ASSETS ($ MIL) 5/31/93	NET ASSET $ VALUE 6/30/93	PERFORMANCE (Return on Initial $10,000 Investment) 3/31/93-6/30/93	6/30/92-6/30/93	6/30/88-6/30/93	DIVIDEND YIELD % 6/93	PHONE NUMBER 800	In-State	FEES Load	12b-1	Redemption	MANAGER	SINCE
PRUDENTIAL HI YLD;B	Fixed Income	3,366.3	8.63	10,402.50	11,597.50	15,615.40	9.5	225-1852	None	None	0.75	5.00	Lars Berkman	'79
PRUDENTIAL INCOMVRT;A	Specialty	14.7	11.92	10,170.00	11,744.50	☆	4.5	225-1852	None	5.25	0.30	None	Anne Mosley	'90
PRUDENTIAL INCOMVRT;B	Specialty	333.5	11.93	10,165.70	11,663.30	15,658.60	3.8	225-1852	None	None	1.00	5.00	Anne Mosley	'85
PRUDENTIAL INSTL:ACT BAL★	Balanced	9.1	10.72	10,297.80	☆	☆	0.0	225-1852	None	None	None	None	Jennison Assoc Cap Corp	'93
PRUDENTIAL INSTL:BAL★	Flexible	17.4	11.27	10,301.60	☆	☆	0.0	225-1852	None	None	None	None	Prudential Invstmnt Corp	'93
PRUDENTIAL INSTL:GROWTH	Growth	19.3	11.47	10,268.60	☆	☆	0.0	225-1852	None	None	None	None	Jennison Assoc Cap Corp	'93
PRUDENTIAL INSTL:INCOME	Fixed Income	25.2	10.17	10,305.60	☆	☆	0.0	225-1852	None	None	None	None	Prudential Invstmnt Corp	'93
PRUDENTIAL INSTL:INTL ST	International	15.3	11.69	10,308.60	☆	☆	0.0	225-1852	None	None	None	None	Mercator Asset Mgt, Inc	'93
PRUDENTIAL INSTL:STK IDX	Growth & Income	19.6	10.86	10,027.70	☆	☆	0.0	225-1852	None	None	None	None	Prudential Invstmnt Corp	'93
PRUDENTIAL INT GL;A	World Income	360.4	8.34	10,512.90	11,190.70	15,036.50	7.6	225-1852	None	3.00	0.30	None	Jeff Brummette	'90
PRUDENTIAL INT GL;B	World Income	34.8	8.36	10,509.40	11,128.40	☆	6.9	225-1852	None	None	0.75	3.00	Jeff Brummette	'92
PRUDENTIAL MULTI-SEC;A	Capital Appreciation	44.8	14.01	10,605.60	12,323.10	☆	2.3	225-1852	None	5.25	0.30	None	Mosely/Smith	'92/'92
PRUDENTIAL MULTI-SEC;B	Capital Appreciation	95.0	13.94	10,584.70	12,176.80	☆	1.3	225-1852	None	None	1.00	5.00	Mosely/Smith	'92/'92
PRUDENTIAL PAC GR;A	Pacific Region	26.7	13.47	11,234.40	☆	☆	0.0	225-1852	None	5.25	0.30	None	Dan Duane	'92
PRUDENTIAL PAC GR;B	Pacific Region	70.4	13.36	11,208.10	☆	☆	0.0	225-1852	None	None	1.00	5.00	Dan Duane	'92
PRUDENTIAL SHT GLBL;A	World Income	65.5	9.46	10,404.60	10,327.30	☆	6.7	225-1852	None	3.00	0.30	None	Jeff Brummette	'90
PRUDENTIAL SHT GLBL;B	World Income	451.7	9.45	10,381.80	10,230.10	☆	5.8	225-1852	None	None	1.00	3.00	Jeff Brummette	'90
PRUDENTIAL S GL:AST;A	World Income	163.6	1.92	10,221.70	10,224.30	☆	5.3	225-1852	None	0.99	0.50	None	Jeff Brummette	'91
PRUDENTIAL S GL:AST;B	World Income	24.7	1.93	10,283.40	10,247.50	☆	5.0	225-1852	None	None	1.00	1.00	Jeff Brummette	'91
PRUDENTIAL STRUC MAT;A	Fixed Income	115.0	11.97	10,169.20	10,868.50	☆	6.4	225-1852	None	3.25	0.10	None	Annamarie Carlucci	'93
PRUDENTIAL STRUC MAT;B	Fixed Income	63.9	11.97	10,147.50	☆	☆	0.0	225-1852	None	None	1.00	3.00	Annamarie Carlucci	'93
PRUDENTIAL US GOVT;A	Fixed Income	6.1	10.37	10,366.50	11,499.00	☆	6.4	225-1852	None	4.50	0.30	None	Annamarie Carlucci	'90
PRUDENTIAL US GOVT;B	Fixed Income	161.6	10.38	10,358.00	11,405.60	16,151.50	5.7	225-1852	None	None	1.00	5.00	Annamarie Carlucci	'86
PRUDENTIAL UTILITY;A	Utility	265.1	10.05	10,359.10	12,371.40	☆	3.4	225-1852	None	5.25	0.30	None	Warren Spitz	'90
PRUDENTIAL UTILITY;B	Utility	4,095.0	10.03	10,339.10	12,278.00	20,322.10	2.8	225-1852	None	None	1.00	5.00	Warren Spitz	'84
PUTNAM ADJ RT GOVT;A	Fixed Income	283.1	10.73	9,999.40	10,139.10	13,574.00	5.1	225-1581	617-292-1000	3.25	0.35	None	Diane Wheeler	'92
PUTNAM ADJ RT GOVT;B	Fixed Income	46.8	10.71	9,984.40	10,072.50	☆	4.6	225-1581	617-292-1000	None	1.00	3.00	Diane Wheeler	'92
PUTNAM AMERICAN GOVT INC	Fixed Income	3,703.5	9.22	10,197.00	10,854.60	15,091.30	7.6	225-1581	617-292-1000	4.75	0.25	None	Kenneth Taubes	'92
PUTNAM ASIA PAC GROWTH★	Pacific Region	4.5	10.48	11,196.60	12,257.30	☆	0.0	225-1581	617-292-1000	5.75	0.35	None	David Thomas	'91
PUTNAM BALANCED GOVT;A	Fixed Income	41.3	4.99	10,142.10	☆	☆	0.0	225-1581	617-292-1000	3.25	0.35	None	Christopher Ray	'93
PUTNAM BALANCED GOVT;B	Fixed Income	7.1	4.99	10,126.00	☆	☆	0.0	225-1581	617-292-1000	None	0.85	3.00	Christopher Ray	'93
PUTNAM CONV INC-GRO TR	Convertible Securities	674.3	19.43	10,261.60	12,114.30	18,191.20	4.9	225-1581	617-292-1000	5.75	0.35	None	Hugh H. Mullin	'86
PUTNAM CORPORATE ASSET	Equity Income	150.3	43.80	10,235.20	11,282.50	16,421.00	7.2	225-1581	617-292-1000	2.50	None	None	Sheldon N. Simon	'92
PUTNAM DIVIDEND GROWTH	Growth & Income	45.2	10.25	9,942.60	10,984.00	☆	2.7	225-1581	617-292-1000	5.75	0.35	None	Michael Mach	'90
PUTNAM DVSFD INCOME;A	Fixed Income	588.7	12.71	10,363.40	11,522.40	☆	7.5	225-1581	617-292-1000	4.75	0.35	None	Jennifer Leichter	'89
PUTNAM DVSFD INCOME;B	Fixed Income	N/A	12.69	10,346.60	☆	☆	0.0	225-1581	617-292-1000	None	1.00	5.00	Jennifer Leichter	'93
PUTNAM ENERGY-RESOURCES	Natural Resources	132.5	19.82	11,056.30	12,759.10	18,551.70	1.2	225-1581	617-292-1000	5.75	0.35	None	Douglas Terreson	'92
PUTNAM EQUITY INCOME;A	Equity Income	9.6	9.76	10,230.60	11,399.80	☆	2.8	225-1581	617-292-1000	5.75	0.35	None	Edward Bousa	'91
PUTNAM EUROPE GROWTH	European Region	15.9	9.84	10,020.40	10,059.90	☆	2.6	225-1581	617-292-1000	5.75	0.35	None	Justin Scott	'90
PUTNAM FEDERAL INCOME	Fixed Income	639.1	10.62	10,199.70	10,874.20	16,035.60	7.9	225-1581	617-292-1000	4.75	0.35	None	Kenneth Taubes	'92
GEORGE PUTNAM BOSTON;A	Balanced	735.2	14.21	10,164.90	11,203.00	17,693.10	4.6	225-1581	617-292-1000	5.75	0.35	None	Thomas V. Reilly	'84
GEORGE PUTNAM BOSTON;B	Balanced	68.4	14.17	10,144.30	11,115.90	☆	4.1	225-1581	617-292-1000	None	1.00	5.00	Thomas V. Reilly	'92
PUTNAM GLOBAL GOVT INC	World Income	509.4	15.02	10,258.50	11,268.30	17,135.60	10.3	225-1581	617-292-1000	4.75	0.35	None	Larry J. Daly	'89
PUTNAM GLOBAL GROWTH;A	Global	738.1	8.31	10,426.60	10,933.60	15,711.70	0.8	225-1581	617-292-1000	5.75	0.35	None	Anthony Regan	'88
PUTNAM GLOBAL GROWTH;B	Global	66.3	8.24	10,404.00	10,840.20	☆	0.7	225-1581	617-292-1000	None	1.00	5.00	Anthony Regan	'92

PUTNAM GROWTH;A	Growth	2.2	8.86	☆	☆	☆	0.0	225-1581	617-292-1000	5.75	None	None	Chuck Swanberg	'93
PUTNAM GRO & INC;A	Growth & Income	4,544.3	13.60	10,186.60	11,422.30	18,779.70	3.8	225-1581	617-292-1000	5.75	0.35	None	King/Kreisel/Zukowski	'83/'86
PUTNAM GRO & INC;B	Growth & Income	1,068.2	13.53	10,173.20	11,333.40	☆	3.3	225-1581	617-292-1000	None	1.00	5.00	King/Kreisel/Zukowski	'92/'92
PUTNAM HLTH SCIENCES;A	Health/Biotechnology	857.4	25.15	10,358.30	9,973.10	20,531.50	0.5	225-1581	617-292-1000	5.75	0.35	None	Cheryl D. Alexander	'86
PUTNAM HLTH SCIENCES;B	Health/Biotechnology	N/A	25.07	10,329.60	☆	☆	0.0	225-1581	617-292-1000	None	1.00	5.00	Cheryl D. Alexander	'93
PUTNAM HIGH YIELD;A	Fixed Income	3,061.1	13.10	10,429.40	11,560.90	17,645.30	11.5	225-1581	617-292-1000	4.75	0.35	None	Edward H. D'Alelio	'85
PUTNAM HIGH YIELD;B	Fixed Income	N/A	13.08	10,410.80	☆	☆	0.0	225-1581	617-292-1000	None	1.00	5.00	Edward H. D'Alelio	'93
PUTNAM HIGH YIELD ADVTG	Fixed Income	606.3	10.30	10,457.30	11,578.50	17,902.90	11.5	225-1581	617-292-1000	4.75	0.35	None	Jin Ho	'86
PUTNAM INCOME;A	Fixed Income	754.2	7.27	10,329.60	11,343.20	17,109.20	8.0	225-1581	617-292-1000	4.75	0.35	None	John Geissinger	'86
PUTNAM INCOME;B	Fixed Income	N/A	7.26	10,318.60	☆	☆	0.0	225-1581	617-292-1000	None	1.00	5.00	John Geissinger	'93
PUTNAM INVESTORS;A	Growth	792.5	8.88	10,278.60	12,445.40	19,710.30	1.1	225-1581	617-292-1000	5.75	0.35	None	Brooke Cobb	'88
PUTNAM INVESTORS;B	Growth	N/A	8.86	10,263.70	☆	☆	0.0	225-1581	617-292-1000	None	1.00	5.00	Brooke Cobb	'93
PUTNAM MANAGED INCOME	Income	570.9	9.00	10,250.00	11,660.20	17,535.90	4.0	225-1581	617-292-1000	5.75	0.35	None	Edward Bousa	'92
PUTNAM NEW OPPTY;A	Growth	304.4	20.83	11,068.00	14,638.60	☆	0.2	225-1581	617-292-1000	5.75	0.35	None	Daniel Miller	'90
PUTNAM NEW OPPTY;B	Growth	N/A	20.80	11,069.70	☆	☆	0.0	225-1581	617-292-1000	None	1.00	5.00	Daniel Miller	'93
PUTNAM OTC EMERGING GRO	Small-Company Growth	361.8	10.56	10,943.00	13,844.20	19,549.50	0.0	225-1581	617-292-1000	5.75	0.35	None	Douglas Foreman	'92
PUTNAM OVERSEAS GRO★	International	2.9	9.58	10,504.40	10,861.70	☆	0.0	225-1581	617-292-1000	5.75	0.35	None	Justin Scott	'91
PUTNAM STRATEGIC INCOME	Equity Income	316.2	8.35	10,206.90	11,775.30	15,814.60	4.3	225-1581	617-292-1000	5.75	0.35	None	Edward Bousa	'92
PUTNAM US GOVT INC;A	Fixed Income	4,834.9	13.80	10,153.60	10,821.40	15,737.40	8.0	225-1581	617-292-1000	4.75	0.35	None	Diane Wheeler	'92
PUTNAM US GOVT INC;B	Fixed Income	1,741.6	13.76	10,135.50	10,738.60	☆	7.4	225-1581	617-292-1000	None	1.00	5.00	Diane Wheeler	'92
PUTNAM UTIL GR & INC;A	Utility	550.4	10.14	10,282.80	11,944.50	☆	5.3	225-1581	617-292-1000	5.75	0.35	None	Sheldon N. Simon	'91
PUTNAM UTIL GR & INC;B	Utility	309.5	10.12	10,264.90	11,877.30	☆	4.9	225-1581	617-292-1000	None	1.00	5.00	Sheldon N. Simon	'92
PUTNAM VISTA;A	Growth	429.2	7.42	10,096.90	12,406.50	20,521.50	1.5	225-1581	617-292-1000	5.75	0.35	None	Silver/D'Alelio	'91/'92
PUTNAM VISTA;B	Growth	N/A	7.41	10,077.80	☆	☆	0.0	225-1581	617-292-1000	None	1.00	5.00	Silver/D'Alelio	'93/'93
PUTNAM VOYAGER;A	Capital Appreciation	2,262.2	10.86	10,342.90	12,198.50	22,282.80	0.0	225-1581	617-292-1000	5.75	0.35	None	Matthew A. Weatherbie	'83
PUTNAM VOYAGER;B	Capital Appreciation	338.0	10.74	10,326.90	12,093.00	☆	0.0	225-1581	617-292-1000	None	1.00	5.00	Matthew A. Weatherbie	'92
QUANTUM FUND	Capital Appreciation	0.3	8.54	10,082.60	10,504.30	9,467.80	0.0	None	606-491-4271	6.50	None	1.00	E. Stanley Foster	'87
QUEST FOR VALUE	Capital Appreciation	224.5	12.25	10,149.10	11,886.60	18,286.30	0.4	232-3863	None	5.50	0.50	None	Eileen Rominger	'89
QUEST VALUE GLBL:EQUITY	Global	129.3	12.97	10,536.10	11,260.80	☆	0.7	232-3863	None	5.50	0.50	None	R.J. Glasebrook II	'90
QUEST VALUE GLBL:INCOME	World Income	20.5	9.31	10,324.30	9,932.40	☆	7.6	232-3863	None	3.00	0.25	None	Robert J. Bluestone	'91
QUEST VALUE:GRO & INC	Growth & Income	27.6	11.01	10,198.00	11,002.90	☆	2.5	232-3863	None	4.75	0.40	None	Colin Glinsman	'92
QUEST VALUE:INV QUAL INC	Fixed Income	52.5	11.13	10,368.00	11,509.10	☆	6.5	232-3863	None	4.75	0.40	None	Robert J. Bluestone	'90
QUEST VALUE:OPPORTUNITY	Flexible	94.6	18.22	10,282.20	11,628.40	☆	0.4	232-3863	None	5.50	0.50	None	R.J. Glasebrook II	'89
QUEST VALUE:SMALL CAP	Small-Company Growth	81.8	16.75	10,163.80	12,353.40	☆	0.0	232-3863	None	5.50	0.50	None	Jenny Beth Jones	'89
QUEST VALUE:US GOVT INC	Fixed Income	182.5	12.11	10,215.60	10,966.20	15,976.70	6.1	232-3863	None	4.75	0.30	None	Robert J. Bluestone	'88
RAINBOW FUND	Capital Appreciation	1.9	5.46	9,578.90	10,036.80	12,984.80	0.0	None	212-983-2980	None	None	None	Robert M. Furman	'74
RBB:BALANCED	Balanced	0.8	11.31	10,062.20	11,446.10	☆	4.5	888-9723	212-878-0600	4.75	0.40	None	Gayland Gee	'92
RBB:BEA;EMERG MARKETS	Global Small Company	16.2	16.46	10,551.30	☆	☆	0.0	888-9723	212-878-0600	None	None	1.50	Emilio Bassini	'93
RBB:BEA;INTL EQ	International	186.9	17.07	10,648.80	☆	☆	0.0	888-9723	212-878-0600	None	None	1.00	Emilio Bassini	'92
RBB:EQ GRO&INC	Growth & Income	50.8	16.47	11,793.80	13,840.60	☆	1.0	888-9723	212-878-0600	4.75	0.40	None	Anthony G. Orphanos	'92
RBB:GOVT SECS	Fixed Income	27.0	10.61	10,260.80	11,085.50	☆	7.2	888-9723	212-878-0600	4.75	0.40	None	Robert Morgan	'92
RBB:HIGH YIELD BOND	Fixed Income	10.6	10.42	10,106.20	11,038.90	☆	9.3	888-9723	212-878-0600	4.75	0.40	None	Stuart M. Goode	'91
REA-GRAHAM:BALANCED	Global Flexible	24.0	13.60	9,941.50	10,518.30	12,447.80	1.9	433-1998	310-208-2282	4.75	0.35	None	Rea/Rea	'82/'82
REGIS:C&B BALANCED	Balanced	41.6	12.53	10,065.40	10,888.10	☆	3.5	638-7983	617-482-9300	None	None	None	Thompson/Medveckis	'89/'89
REGIS:C&B EQUITY	Growth	181.9	12.79	9,969.70	10,627.10	☆	2.1	638-7983	617-482-9300	None	None	None	Thompson/Medveckis	'90/'90

★PRUDENTIAL INSTL: ACT BAL—On 6/2/93, fund was reclassified from Flexible Portfolio to Balanced.
★PRUDENTIAL INSTL: BAL—On 6/2/93, fund was reclassified from Balanced to Flexible Portfolio.

★PUTNAM ASIA PAC GROWTH—Available only to Putnam employees.
★PUTNAM OVERSEAS GRO—Available only to Putnam employees.

PERFORMANCE OF MUTUAL FUNDS (continued)

FUND NAME	OBJECTIVE	TOTAL NET ASSETS ($ MIL) 5/31/93	NET ASSET $ VALUE 6/30/93	PERFORMANCE (Return on Initial $10,000 Investment) 3/31/93-6/30/93	6/30/92-6/30/93	6/30/88-6/30/93	DIVIDEND YIELD % 6/93	PHONE NUMBER 800	In-State	FEES Load	12b-1	Redemption	MANAGER	SINCE
REGIS:DSI DISCIP VALUE	Equity Income	39.3	12.03	10,059.40	11,512.40	☆	2.1	638-7983	617-482-9300	None	None	None	Ronald L. McCullough	'89
REGIS:DSI LTD MAT BOND	Fixed Income	33.4	10.20	10,230.70	10,734.40	☆	6.6	638-7983	617-482-9300	None	None	None	Michael H. Porreca	'89
REGIS:FMA SMALL COMPANY	Small-Company Growth	14.0	12.98	10,350.90	13,735.40	☆	0.0	638-7983	617-482-9300	None	None	None	Patricia Falkowski	'92
REGIS:FMA SPECTRUM	Flexible	21.2	10.21	9,587.00	10,144.30	☆	8.3	638-7983	617-482-9300	None	None	None	Robert Thornburgh, Jr.	'90
REGIS:ICM FIXED INCOME	Fixed Income	9.8	10.47	10,225.00	☆	☆	0.0	638-7983	617-482-9300	None	None	None	John Evans	'92
REGIS:ICM SMALL COMPANY	Small-Company Growth	70.6	17.48	10,145.20	13,994.70	☆	0.5	638-7983	617-482-9300	None	None	None	Robert D. McDorman, Jr.	'89
REGIS:SAMI PRFD STK INC	Utility	61.1	9.98	10,080.30	10,460.30	☆	4.5	638-7983	617-482-9300	None	None	None	Scott T. Fleming	'92
REGIS:SIRACH SPEC EQ	Small-Company Growth	448.3	17.36	10,742.60	13,066.30	☆	0.2	638-7983	617-482-9300	None	None	None	Harvey Bateman	'89
REGIS:STRLG PTNR BAL	Balanced	44.4	11.28	10,126.80	11,174.30	☆	2.9	638-7983	617-482-9300	None	None	None	Paul Ersham	'91
REGIS:STRLG PTNR EQ	Equity Income	13.2	11.94	10,034.80	11,488.80	☆	1.2	638-7983	617-482-9300	None	None	None	Paul Ersham	'91
REGIS:STRLG PTNR SHT FXD	Fixed Income	16.5	10.13	10,152.80	10,602.10	☆	5.2	638-7983	617-482-9300	None	None	None	Dave Ralston	'92
REGIS:TS&W EQUITY	Growth	20.8	10.73	10,393.10	☆	☆	0.0	638-7983	617-482-9300	None	None	None	Whitworth/Ferwerda	'92/'92
REGIS:TS&W FIXED INCOME	Fixed Income	21.6	10.62	10,154.00	☆	☆	0.0	638-7983	617-482-9300	None	None	None	Charles Goemer	'92
REGIS:TS&W INTL EQUITY	International	12.1	10.71	10,190.30	☆	☆	0.0	638-7983	617-482-9300	None	None	None	G.D. Rothenberg	'92
REICH & TANG EQUITY	Growth	103.2	17.93	10,210.10	12,027.20	17,783.00	1.2	221-3079	212-476-5055	None	None	None	Robert Hoerle	'85
REICH & TANG GOVT SEC★	Fixed Income	20.4	0.00	N/A	N/A	N/A	0.0	221-3079	212-476-5055	None	None	None	Molly Flewharty	'88
RET SYS:CORE EQUITY	Growth & Income	1.5	11.88	10,330.40	12,384.20	☆	2.3	772-3615	212-503-0160	None	0.25	None	Retirement System Inv.	'91
RET SYS:EMERG GROWTH EQ	Small-Company Growth	1.2	13.11	10,339.10	13,115.40	☆	0.0	772-3615	212-503-0160	None	0.25	None	Friess Associates	'91
RET SYS:INT FXD-INC	Fixed Income	1.1	11.28	10,217.00	11,272.50	☆	4.6	772-3615	212-503-0160	None	0.25	None	Retirement System Inv.	'91
RETIRE PLAN AMER:BOND	Fixed Income	53.8	6.54	10,103.70	10,530.70	14,192.20	8.0	279-0279	505-983-4335	None	1.00	5.00	B. Clark Stamper	'90
RETIRE PLAN AMER:CV SEC	Convertible Securities	36.3	17.17	10,076.50	12,150.60	☆	2.3	279-0279	505-983-4335	4.75	0.25	None	Shelby M.C. Davis	'92
RETIRE PLAN AMER:EQU	Growth	43.9	25.68	10,098.30	11,331.10	17,026.00	0.7	279-0279	505-983-4335	None	1.00	5.00	Graham Tanaka	'87
RETIRE PLAN AMER:GL VAL	Financial Services	42.4	24.12	9,785.00	13,147.80	☆	0.4	279-0279	505-983-4335	4.75	0.25	None	Shelby M.C. Davis	'91
REYNOLDS:BLUE CHIP GRO	Growth & Income	43.9	14.61	9,649.90	10,083.40	☆	0.6	338-1579	415-461-7860	None	None	None	Frederick L. Reynolds	'88
REYNOLDS:OPPORTUNITY	Growth	3.6	9.43	10,512.80	10,273.40	☆	0.0	338-1579	415-461-7860	None	None	None	Frederick L. Reynolds	'92
REYNOLDS:US GOVT BOND	Fixed Income	5.8	10.56	10,259.10	10,958.40	☆	5.0	338-1579	415-461-7860	None	None	None	Frederick L. Reynolds	'92
RIGHTIME:BLUE CHIP	Growth & Income	223.6	31.87	9,990.60	11,098.10	15,326.40	0.7	242-1421	215-887-8111	4.75	0.50	None	Rights/Soslow/Houser	'87/'88
RIGHTIME:FUND	Growth & Income	174.2	35.24	10,109.00	11,256.10	14,692.50	0.1	242-1421	215-887-8111	None	0.75	None	Rights/Soslow/Houser	'85/'88
RIGHTIME:GOVERNMENT SEC	Fixed Income	31.9	13.81	9,985.70	11,417.00	13,793.10	5.2	242-1421	215-887-8111	4.75	0.25	None	Rights/Soslow/Houser	'86/'86
RIGHTIME:GROWTH	Growth	41.5	25.73	9,629.50	10,696.30	12,449.60	0.5	242-1421	215-887-8111	4.75	0.50	None	Rights/Soslow/Houser	'88/'88
RIGHTIME:MIDCAP	Small-Company Growth	50.3	29.71	10,160.70	11,849.60	☆	0.2	242-1421	215-887-8111	4.75	0.50	None	Rights/Soslow/Houser	'92/'92
RIGHTIME:SOC AWARENESS	Growth	10.4	29.09	9,712.90	11,663.80	☆	0.1	242-1421	215-887-8111	4.75	0.50	None	Rights/Soslow/Houser	'90/'90
RIMCO:BOND	Fixed Income	45.9	10.54	10,301.30	11,260.10	☆	5.6	934-3883	202-835-4280	3.50	None	None	Roger Marshall	'92
RIMCO:STOCK	Growth & Income	40.4	11.05	10,379.60	11,912.80	☆	2.4	934-3883	202-835-4280	3.50	None	None	Philip Tasho	'92
RIVERFRONT:INCOME EQUITY	Equity Income	21.5	11.10	9,991.10	☆	☆	0.0	343-2898	617-621-6100	4.50	0.25	None	SunBank	'92
RIVERFRONT:US GOVT INC	Fixed Income	25.2	10.02	10,197.20	☆	☆	0.0	343-2898	617-621-6100	2.25	0.25	None	Provident Bank	'92
RIVERSIDE CAP EQUITY	Growth	52.7	11.57	10,110.70	11,098.40	☆	1.9	662-4203	None	3.00	0.25	None	John Ray	'91
RIVERSIDE CAP FXD INC	Fixed Income	35.4	10.44	10,271.00	10,964.90	☆	6.6	662-4203	None	3.00	0.25	None	Alfred Jordan	'91
RBRTSN STEPH:EMERGING	Small-Company Growth	192.3	14.64	9,966.00	10,447.40	20,153.80	0.0	766-3863	415-781-9700	None	0.25	None	Robert Czepiel	'87
RBRTSN STEPH:VALUE PLUS	Small-Company Growth	19.8	11.95	10,008.40	12,184.70	☆	0.5	766-3863	415-781-9700	None	None	None	Ron Elijah	'92
ROCHESTER:BOND	Convertible Securities	29.6	12.07	10,143.10	12,771.60	17,380.00	6.2	None	716-383-1300	3.25	0.75	None	Michael S. Rosen	'86
ROCHESTER TAX MANAGED	Specialty	13.5	10.21	9,696.10	10,850.20	13,203.20	0.0	None	716-383-1300	6.25	0.25	None	Ronald H. Fielding	'80
ROCKWOOD GROWTH	Capital Appreciation	0.7	15.84	10,199.60	13,714.30	12,952.70	0.0	None	208-522-5593	None	None	None	Ross H. Farmer	'86
ROD SQ INTL SEC:INTL EQ	International	11.8	10.87	10,594.50	10,313.10	11,497.50	0.0	336-9970	302-651-8418	4.00	0.25	None	Multiple Managers	'87
ROD SQ MULTI-MGR:GROWTH	Growth	59.1	16.08	10,196.60	11,872.40	18,667.50	0.0	336-9970	302-651-8418	4.00	0.25	None	Multiple Managers	'87

ROD SQ MULTI-MGR:GRO&INC	Growth & Income	6.1	11.06	10,195.40	11,639.20	17,693.40	2.2	336-9970	302-651-8418	4.00	0.25	None	Multiple Managers	'87
ROD SQ STRAT:DVSD INC	Fixed Income	35.6	13.41	10,202.60	10,976.50	☆	5.8	336-9970	302-651-8418	3.50	0.25	None	Wilmington Trust Co.	'91
ROYCE EQUITY INCOME	Equity Income	79.2	5.83	10,034.70	12,085.90	☆	3.9	221-4268	212-355-7311	None	None	1.00	Royce/Ebright	'90/'90
ROYCE OTC	Small-Company Growth	6.3	6.40	10,015.60	13,275.80	☆	10.0	221-4268	212-355-7311	2.50	None	1.00	Royce/Ebright	'92/'92
ROYCE PREMIER	Growth	5.4	5.99	10,363.30	12,392.50	☆	4.5	221-4268	212-355-7311	None	None	1.00	Royce/Ebright	'92/'92
ROYCE VALUE	Small-Company Growth	185.6	9.90	9,909.90	11,599.50	16,031.10	0.4	221-4268	212-355-7311	None	0.75	1.00	Royce/Ebright	'82/'82
RSI TR:ACTIVELY MGD BD★	Fixed Income	155.5	26.61	10,306.00	11,376.70	16,709.90	0.0	772-3615	212-503-0160	None	0.10	None	Criterion/Ret. Sys. Inv	'83/'90
RSI TR:CORE EQUITY★	Growth & Income	150.9	33.57	10,166.60	11,746.00	18,489.30	0.0	772-3615	212-503-0160	None	0.10	None	Retirement System Inv.	'83
RSI TR:EMERG GROWTH EQ★	Small-Company Growth	51.6	30.78	10,290.90	13,827.50	18,239.50	0.0	772-3615	212-503-0160	None	0.10	None	Friess/Putnam	'90/'90
RSI TR:INTMDT-TERM BOND★	Fixed Income	105.8	25.53	10,207.90	10,975.90	16,032.00	0.0	772-3615	212-503-0160	None	0.10	None	Retirement System Inv.	'83
RSI TR:INTERNATL EQUITY★	International	22.6	32.05	10,532.40	10,987.30	12,594.30	0.0	772-3615	212-503-0160	None	0.10	None	Morgan Grenfell Inv.	'84
RSI TR:SHORT-TERM INVEST★	Fixed Income	40.8	17.74	10,056.70	10,266.20	13,484.30	0.0	772-3615	212-503-0160	None	0.10	None	Retirement System Inv.	'90
RSI TR:VALUE EQUITY★	Growth & Income	38.5	25.62	10,019.60	11,422.20	15,454.30	0.0	772-3615	212-503-0160	None	0.10	None	NFJ Investment Grp Inc	'92
RUSHMORE AMER GAS INDEX	Natural Resources	221.8	12.59	10,424.00	13,157.70	☆	3.1	621-7874	301-657-1517	None	None	None	Team Managed	'92
RUSHMORE:NOVA	Capital Appreciation	10.4	10.36	9,691.30	11,379.30	☆	1.0	621-7874	301-657-1517	None	None	None	Team Managed	'92
RUSHMORE:OTC INDEX	Growth	7.7	15.76	10,200.60	12,021.40	14,285.90	0.0	621-7874	301-657-1517	None	None	0.50	Team Managed	'92
RUSHMORE:PREC MTL INDEX	Gold	8.8	9.12	12,225.20	12,781.50	☆	0.2	621-7874	301-657-1517	None	None	None	Team Managed	'92
RUSHMORE:STK MKT INDEX	Growth & Income	9.9	17.76	10,147.80	10,897.00	16,341.50	2.3	621-7874	301-657-1517	None	None	0.50	Team Managed	'92
RUSHMORE:USG INT TERM	Fixed Income	20.5	10.02	10,355.30	11,650.30	17,071.00	5.8	621-7874	301-657-1517	None	None	None	Team Managed	'92
RUSHMORE:USG LONG TERM	Fixed Income	21.0	11.02	10,501.30	11,978.90	17,816.60	5.9	621-7874	301-657-1517	None	None	None	Team Managed	'92
SAFECO EQUITY	Growth & Income	107.6	12.49	10,619.00	13,254.20	20,952.80	1.2	426-6730	206-545-5530	None	None	None	Doug Johnson	'84
SAFECO GROWTH	Growth	146.2	17.48	10,174.60	11,966.50	17,200.80	0.0	426-6730	206-545-5530	None	None	None	Thomas Maguire	'89
SAFECO HIGH-YIELD BOND	Fixed Income	27.0	9.24	10,418.10	11,657.40	☆	9.7	426-6730	206-545-5530	None	None	None	Ron Spaulding	'88
SAFECO INCOME	Equity Income	199.5	17.45	10,046.10	11,548.00	16,143.50	4.5	426-6730	206-545-5530	None	None	None	Arley N. Hudson	'78
SAFECO INTMDT-TM US TRES	Fixed Income	13.7	10.97	10,281.70	11,265.80	☆	5.8	426-6730	206-545-5530	None	None	None	Ron Spaulding	'88
SAFECO NORTHWEST	Growth	41.4	12.12	9,707.80	11,052.10	☆	0.4	426-6730	206-545-5530	None	None	None	Charles Driggs	'92
SAFECO US GOVT	Fixed Income	61.2	10.03	10,233.40	10,963.60	16,439.70	6.9	426-6730	206-545-5530	None	None	None	Paul Stevenson	'88
SAGAMORE:BOND	Fixed Income	3.5	11.27	10,359.10	11,394.90	☆	5.8	321-7442	812-421-3213	2.75	0.25	None	Ramsey *et al.*	'91
SAGAMORE:GROWTH	Growth	16.3	11.60	10,208.00	10,879.10	☆	0.8	321-7442	812-421-3213	2.75	0.50	None	Ramsey *et al.*	'91
SAGAMORE:TOTAL RETURN	Balanced	8.0	11.28	10,151.10	10,936.10	☆	2.9	321-7442	812-421-3213	2.75	0.38	None	Ramsey *et al.*	'91
SALOMON BROS CAPITAL	Capital Appreciation	108.8	20.41	9,970.70	11,540.40	16,199.50	0.5	725-6666	212-783-1301	None	None	None	Robert S. Salomon, Jr.	'90
SALOMON BROS INVESTORS	Growth & Income	383.2	17.10	10,283.60	11,899.40	17,728.50	1.9	725-6666	212-783-1301	None	None	None	Fleischmann/White	'92/'92
SALOMON BROS OPPORTUNITY	Capital Appreciation	113.2	31.00	10,022.60	11,848.10	16,989.20	1.1	725-6666	212-783-1301	None	None	None	Irving Brilliant	'79
SAM:SMALL-CAP	Small-Company Growth	67.4	12.62	10,369.80	12,181.50	☆	0.0	445-9469	901-761-2474	None	None	None	O. Mason Hawkins	'91
SAM:VALUE TRUST	Growth	315.9	16.06	10,094.30	12,443.70	20,990.70	0.4	445-9469	901-761-2474	None	None	None	O. Mason Hawkins	'87
SBSF CONVERTIBLE SEC	Convertible Securities	60.3	11.89	10,405.90	11,952.40	17,760.30	5.3	422-7273	212-903-1200	None	0.25	None	Louis R. Benzak	'88
SBSF FUND	Growth	114.8	16.26	10,371.80	12,166.40	18,909.10	2.4	422-7273	212-903-1200	None	0.25	None	Louis R. Benzak	'83
SCHAFER VALUE	Growth & Income	18.0	33.76	10,245.80	12,316.80	21,906.40	1.3	343-0481	212-644-1800	None	None	None	David Schafer	'85
SCHRODER CAP:INTLEQUITY	International	241.7	17.48	10,743.70	10,898.90	13,752.10	0.7	344-8332	212-841-3848	None	None	None	Mark J. Smith	'89
SCHRODER CAP:US EQUITY	Growth	20.7	10.40	9,895.30	12,334.30	19,598.80	0.4	344-8332	212-841-3848	None	None	None	Fariba Talebi	'91
SCHWAB INV:1000	Growth & Income	479.6	12.38	10,048.10	11,513.80	☆	2.0	526-8600	415-395-6323	None	None	0.50	Dimensional Fund Adv	'91
SCHWAB INV:SHORT/INTMDT	Fixed Income	262.0	10.55	10,201.90	10,972.20	☆	5.4	526-8600	415-395-6323	None	None	None	Regan/Ward	'91/'91
SCM PORTFOLIO	Flexible	0.7	10.76	10,247.60	10,843.10	☆	2.8	None	404-834-5839	None	None	1.00	Stephen McCutcheon	'89
SCOTTISH WIDOWS INTL	International	35.1	12.15	10,331.60	10,412.30	☆	0.7	243-8115	203-525-1421	5.50	0.25	None	Allan McKenzie	'90
SCUDDER BALANCED	Balanced	51.3	11.82	9,876.10	☆	☆	0.0	535-2726	617-439-4640	None	None	None	Ward/Beatty	'93/'93

★REICH & TANG GOVT SEC—Fund's 12b-1 fee is currently being waived.

★RSI FUNDS—Designed primarily for retirement accounts.

PERFORMANCE OF MUTUAL FUNDS *(continued)*

FUND NAME	OBJECTIVE	TOTAL NET ASSETS ($ MIL) 5/31/93	NET ASSET $ VALUE 6/30/93	PERFORMANCE (Return on Initial $10,000 Investment) 3/31/93-6/30/93	6/30/92-6/30/93	6/30/88-6/30/93	DIVIDEND YIELD % 6/93	PHONE NUMBER 800	In-State	FEES Load	12b-1	Redemption	MANAGER	SINCE
SCUDDER CAP GROWTH	Growth	1,330.0	21.22	10,162.80	12,031.60	19,147.80	0.5	535-2726	617-439-4640	None	None	None	Aronoff/Cox	'89/'84
SCUDDER DEVELOPMENT	Small-Company Growth	838.6	34.60	10,294.60	12,235.40	20,481.70	0.0	535-2726	617-439-4640	None	None	None	McKay/Moran	'88/'82
SCUDDER GLOBAL	Global	548.2	21.62	10,495.10	11,340.20	18,223.80	0.7	535-2726	617-439-4640	None	None	None	Holzer/Garrett	'86/'86
SCUDDER GLBL SMALLCO	Global Small Company	99.1	14.35	10,567.00	11,333.30	☆	0.5	535-2726	617-439-4640	None	None	None	Moran/Economos	'91/'91
SCUDDER GNMA	Fixed Income	627.9	15.44	10,161.60	10,896.80	16,295.60	8.4	535-2726	617-439-4640	None	None	None	Glen/Pruyne	'85/'85
SCUDDER GOLD	Gold	82.9	12.14	12,375.10	13,210.00	☆	0.0	535-2726	617-439-4640	None	None	None	Donald/Wallace	'88/'88
SCUDDER GROWTH & INC	Growth & Income	1,390.9	17.20	10,130.20	11,438.70	19,287.90	2.9	535-2726	617-439-4640	None	None	None	Hoffman/Thorndike	'90/'87
SCUDDER INCOME	Fixed Income	483.9	14.27	10,347.30	11,333.20	17,214.30	6.3	535-2726	617-439-4640	None	None	None	Hutchinson/Thorne	'86/'90
SCUDDER INTRN'L BOND	World Income	957.0	13.57	10,444.20	11,218.70	19,838.50	7.5	535-2726	617-439-4640	None	None	None	Teitelbaum/Greshin	'93/'88
SCUDDER INTRN'L- STK	International	1,335.7	37.03	10,473.30	10,947.30	15,388.90	1.0	535-2726	617-439-4640	None	None	None	Bratt/Franklin	'76/'89
SCUDDER LATIN AMERICA	Latin American	76.8	14.72	10,682.10	☆	☆	0.0	535-2726	617-439-4640	None	None	2.00	Games/Truscott	'92/'92
SCUDDER PACIFIC OPPTY	Pacific Region	26.7	13.32	10,538.00	☆	☆	0.0	535-2726	617-439-4640	None	None	None	Economos/Bratt/Cheng	'92
SCUDDER QUALITY GROW	Growth	131.2	15.33	9,599.20	10,896.80	☆	0.2	535-2726	617-439-4640	None	None	None	Ward/Beatty	'91/'91
SCUDDER SHRT TRM BND	Fixed Income	2,926.7	12.12	10,195.00	10,836.40	16,077.70	7.1	535-2726	617-439-4640	None	None	None	Poor/Gootkind	'89/'89
SCUDDER ST GLBL INC	World Income	1,024.4	11.89	10,413.50	10,722.40	☆	8.4	535-2726	617-439-4640	None	None	None	Craddock/Teitelbaum	'91/'93
SCUDDER VALUE FUND	Growth	22.9	13.08	9,969.50	☆	☆	0.0	535-2726	617-439-4640	None	None	None	Wallace/Hall	'92/'92
SCUDDER ZERO CP 2000	Fixed Income	31.9	13.99	10,518.80	12,221.30	19,272.30	6.1	535-2726	617-439-4640	None	None	None	Thorne/Heisler	'86/'88
SEAFIRST:ASSET ALLOC	Flexible	134.7	13.58	10,221.80	10,918.30	16,968.80	3.4	323-9919	206-358-6234	None	None	None	Team Managed	'88
SEAFIRST:BLUE CHIP FUND	Growth	114.6	16.53	10,224.40	10,825.80	18,122.00	1.9	323-9919	206-358-6234	None	None	None	Team Managed	'88
SEAFIRST:BOND FUND	Fixed Income	83.1	11.27	10,179.10	10,926.90	16,030.10	5.8	323-9919	206-358-6234	None	None	None	Team Managed	'88
SECOND FID EXCHANGE★	Growth	69.0	124.05	9,876.00	10,875.40	16,628.90	1.3	225-6265	617-482-8260	None	None	None	Robert S. Goodof	'87
SECURITY EQUITY FUND	Growth	362.2	6.36	9,922.00	11,675.00	21,140.20	0.8	888-2461	913-295-3127	5.75	None	None	Terry Millberger	'81
SECURITY INC:CORP BOND	Fixed Income	113.8	8.21	10,370.10	11,596.50	16,864.70	7.1	888-2461	913-295-3127	4.75	0.25	None	Jane Tedder	'85
SECURITY INC:US GOVT	Fixed Income	10.1	5.31	10,382.60	11,185.80	16,204.80	6.2	888-2461	913-295-3127	4.75	0.25	None	Jane Tedder	'85
SECURITY INVESTMENT FUND	Income	77.0	7.54	10,090.90	11,377.60	15,934.10	3.2	888-2461	913-295-3127	5.75	None	None	John Cleland	'66
SECURITY ULTRA FUND	Capital Appreciation	67.9	7.66	9,961.00	12,447.80	13,892.40	0.0	888-2461	913-295-3127	5.75	None	None	Ron Niedziela	'87
SEI CASH +:GNMA;A★	Fixed Income	221.2	10.28	10,200.60	10,962.80	16,887.30	7.1	342-5734	215-254-1000	None	0.06	None	Paul Kaplan	'87
SEI CASH +:INTMDT GOVT;A★	Fixed Income	298.8	10.33	10,153.40	10,898.80	15,800.50	5.7	342-5734	215-254-1000	None	0.06	None	Paul Kaplan	'87
SEI CASH +:SHT-TM GOVT;A★	Fixed Income	104.6	10.16	10,099.40	10,585.70	14,785.60	4.4	342-5734	215-254-1000	None	0.06	None	Paul Kaplan	'87
SEI CASH +:SHT-TM GOVT;B★	Fixed Income	1.5	10.16	10,092.00	10,554.50	☆	4.1	342-5734	215-254-1000	None	0.36	None	Paul Kaplan	'90
SEI INDEX:BOND★	Fixed Income	61.9	10.54	10,249.90	11,128.40	16,404.40	6.1	342-5734	215-254-1000	None	0.05	None	Paul Sloan	'86
SEI INDEX:S&P 500★	Growth & Income	712.7	15.78	10,044.80	11,340.80	19,217.10	2.5	342-5734	215-254-1000	None	0.04	None	Bruce George	'85
SEI INSTL:BALANCED;A★	Flexible	19.3	12.01	10,172.40	11,593.20	☆	2.7	342-5734	215-254-1000	None	0.13	None	Anthony Gray	'92
SEI INSTL:BOND;A★	Fixed Income	79.6	11.86	10,461.60	11,944.40	18,428.60	5.9	342-5734	215-254-1000	None	0.09	None	Paul Repponetti	'87
SEI INSTL:CAP APPREC;A★	Growth	738.2	16.21	10,064.70	11,519.70	21,098.20	1.7	342-5734	215-254-1000	None	0.09	None	Anthony Gray	'88
SEI INSTL:CAPITAL GROWTH★	Capital Appreciation	190.2	13.22	10,288.10	12,289.10	☆	1.6	342-5734	215-254-1000	None	0.01	None	Anthony Gray	'90
SEI INSTL:EQU INC;A★	Equity Income	269.3	14.19	10,059.70	11,333.40	18,497.20	3.7	342-5734	215-254-1000	None	0.09	None	John Brown	'88
SEI INSTL:LTD VOLAT;A★	Fixed Income	267.3	10.75	10,207.10	11,075.80	15,926.80	5.8	342-5734	215-254-1000	None	0.08	None	Jacqueline Weitz	'87
SEI INSTL:SM CAP GRO;A★	Small-Company Growth	142.8	13.34	10,680.50	13,225.70	☆	0.2	342-5734	215-254-1000	None	0.14	None	Rick Leggot	'92
SEI INSTL:VALUE;A★	Growth & Income	243.1	11.52	9,961.00	10,600.90	16,702.90	2.8	342-5734	215-254-1000	None	0.08	None	Clyde Bartter	'92
SEI INTL:INTERNATIONAL★	International	266.7	9.86	10,400.80	11,182.80	☆	3.6	342-5734	215-254-1000	None	0.16	None	Richard Carr	'89
SELECTED AMERICAN SHARES	Growth & Income	475.1	17.31	10,081.40	11,235.70	19,148.80	1.0	279-0279	505-983-4335	None	0.25	None	Shelby M.C. Davis	'93
SELECTED CAP:GOVT INC	Fixed Income	12.7	9.58	10,222.00	11,051.30	15,075.70	6.0	279-0279	505-983-4335	None	0.25	None	B. Clark Stamper	'93
SELECTED SPECIAL SHARES	Small-Company Growth	62.5	21.38	10,142.30	11,564.30	16,692.70	0.6	279-0279	505-983-4335	None	0.25	None	Shelby M.C. Davis	'93
SELIGMAN CAPITAL;A	Capital Appreciation	200.9	17.02	9,895.30	11,825.10	22,285.60	0.0	221-2450	212-488-0200	4.75	0.25	None	Loris D. Muzzatti	'88
SELIGMAN COMMON STK;A	Growth & Income	537.8	13.56	10,241.20	11,629.50	18,805.10	2.7	221-2450	212-488-0200	4.75	0.25	None	Charles C. Smith	'91
SELIGMAN COMMUNICATN;A	Science & Technology	62.4	14.03	11,251.00	14,422.30	23,716.20	0.0	221-2450	212-488-0200	4.75	0.25	None	Paul Wick	'90
SELIGMAN FRONTIER;A	Small-Company Growth	36.9	11.29	10,721.70	13,798.00	20,582.00	0.0	221-2450	212-488-0200	4.75	0.25	None	Paul Wick	'91
SELIGMAN GROWTH;A	Growth	586.1	5.81	9,684.20	11,516.40	18,597.30	0.5	221-2450	212-488-0200	4.75	0.25	None	David Watts	'92
SELIGMAN HEND GL EMER CO	Global Small Company	7.0	8.95	10,718.60	☆	☆	0.0	221-2450	212-488-0200	4.75	0.25	None	Iain Clark	'92

SELIGMAN HI INC:BOND	Fixed Income	48.7	6.81	10,415.40	11,901.70	17,450.30	9.8	221-2450	212-488-0200	4.75	0.25	None	Dan Charleston	'89
SELIGMAN HI INC:SEC MTGE	Fixed Income	16.4	6.63	10,103.00	10,413.00	14,494.40	6.7	221-2450	212-488-0200	4.75	0.25	None	James Auchterlonie	'87
SELIGMAN HI INC:US GOVT	Fixed Income	56.2	7.29	10,227.60	10,941.50	15,093.10	7.3	221-2450	212-488-0200	4.75	0.25	None	James Auchterlonie	'87
SELIGMAN INCOME;A	Income	268.1	14.55	10,251.40	11,748.80	17,866.70	5.6	221-2450	212-488-0200	4.75	0.25	None	Charles C. Smith	'91
SELIGMAN INTL★	International	19.0	14.02	10,597.10	11,430.50	☆	0.2	221-2450	212-488-0200	None	None	None	Iain Clark	'92
SENTINEL:AGGRESSIVE GRO★	Small-Company Growth	115.7	6.61	10,107.00	☆	☆	0.0	233-4332	802-229-3761	5.00	0.30	None	Louis E. Conrad II	'93
SENTINEL:BALANCED	Balanced	214.5	15.05	10,106.90	11,134.60	17,329.00	4.1	233-4332	802-229-3761	5.00	0.30	None	Rodney A. Buck	'82
SENTINEL:BOND	Fixed Income	70.0	6.91	10,314.40	11,417.40	17,320.50	6.1	233-4332	802-229-3761	5.00	0.20	None	Richard D. Temple	'85
SENTINEL:COMMON STOCK	Growth & Income	875.0	28.83	10,023.60	11,036.80	18,738.70	2.9	233-4332	802-229-3761	5.00	0.30	None	Christopher E. Martin	'85
SENTINEL:GOVERNMENT SEC	Fixed Income	132.0	10.52	10,227.90	11,220.30	16,705.00	6.2	233-4332	802-229-3761	5.00	0.20	None	William Vautin	'86
SENTINEL:GROWTH	Growth	62.7	17.35	9,692.70	11,161.00	16,532.90	0.2	233-4332	802-229-3761	5.00	0.30	None	William M. Hedberg	'87
SENTINEL:WORLD FUND	International	8.0	10.82	10,494.70	☆	☆	0.0	233-4332	802-229-3761	5.00	0.30	None	Sandor Cseh	'93
SENTRY FUND	Growth	75.3	15.14	9,895.60	10,924.20	18,154.30	1.5	533-7827	None	None	None	None	Keith Ringberg	'77
SEQUOIA FUND★	Growth	1,496.0	60.59	10,724.30	12,114.70	21,365.60	2.8	None	212-245-4500	None	None	None	Ruane/Cuniff	'70/'70
SEVEN SEAS:MATRIX SYNTH	Growth	38.2	11.50	10,379.50	12,071.80	☆	1.1	None	617-542-9049	None	0.25	None	Doug Holmes	'92
SEVEN SEAS:S&P 500 INDEX	Growth & Income	187.2	10.44	10,045.00	☆	☆	0.0	None	617-542-9049	None	0.25	None	State Street Bank	'93
SEVEN SEAS:S&P MIDCAP	Growth	11.5	11.81	10,240.10	☆	☆	1.2	None	617-542-9049	None	0.25	None	Lynn Symanski	'92
SEVEN SEAS:S-T GOVT	Fixed Income	30.6	10.20	10,084.20	10,605.70	☆	4.7	None	617-542-9049	None	0.25	None	Steve Boxer	'93
SEVEN SEAS:YIELD PLUS	Fixed Income	317.8	10.02	10,082.20	☆	☆	0.0	None	617-542-9049	None	0.25	None	Steve Boxer	'93
SHADOW STOCK	Small-Company Growth	33.5	11.66	9,951.00	11,936.00	15,542.60	0.9	422-2766	816-471-5200	None	None	None	Schliemann/Whitridge	'87/'87
SHAWMUT:FXD INCOME	Fixed Income	86.6	10.41	10,256.40	☆	☆	0.0	742-9688	508-626-7877	2.00	None	None	Shawmut Bank	'92
SHAWMUT:GROWTH EQUITY	Growth	23.3	9.97	10,145.50	☆	☆	0.0	742-9688	508-626-7877	4.00	None	None	Shawmut Bank	'92
SHAWMUT:GRO & INC EQ	Growth & Income	132.1	10.36	10,075.60	☆	☆	0.0	742-9688	508-626-7877	4.00	None	None	Shawmut Bank	'92
SHAWMUT:INTMDT GOVT INC	Fixed Income	59.7	10.22	10,170.00	☆	☆	0.0	742-9688	508-626-7877	2.00	None	None	Shawmut Bank	'92
SHAWMUT:LTD TM INCOME	Fixed Income	57.0	10.04	10,105.00	☆	☆	0.0	742-9688	508-626-7877	2.00	None	None	Shawmut Bank	'92
SHAWMUT:SMALL CAP EQ	Small-Company Growth	85.6	10.08	9,863.00	☆	☆	0.0	742-9688	508-626-7877	4.00	None	None	Shawmut Bank	'92
SHEARSON ADJ RT GOVT;A	Fixed Income	312.6	9.96	10,076.30	10,374.80	☆	4.6	None	212-720-9218	None	0.75	None	Blackrock Financial Mgt	'92
SHEARSON ADJ RT GOVT;B	Fixed Income	3.6	9.96	10,076.30	☆	☆	0.0	None	212-720-9218	None	0.75	5.00	Blackrock Financial Mgt	'92
SHEARSON AGGR GRO;A	Capital Appreciation	151.0	22.05	10,709.10	11,538.50	18,173.00	0.0	None	212-720-9218	5.00	0.25	None	Richard Freeman	'83
SHEARSON AGGR GRO;B	Capital Appreciation	15.6	21.95	10,686.50	☆	☆	0.0	None	212-720-9218	None	1.00	5.00	Richard Freeman	'92
SHEARSON APPREC;A	Growth	1,713.0	10.93	9,945.40	11,125.00	18,470.40	1.4	None	212-720-9218	5.00	0.25	None	Williamson *et al.*	'79
SHEARSON APPREC;B	Growth	1,232.9	10.88	9,927.00	☆	☆	0.0	None	212-720-9218	None	1.00	5.00	Williamson/Cohen/Novello	'93
SHEARSON EQ:GR & INC;A	Growth & Income	3.8	9.70	9,952.30	☆	☆	0.0	None	212-720-9218	5.00	0.25	None	Caruso/Gerken	'92/'92
SHEARSON EQ:GR & INC;B	Growth & Income	53.6	9.70	9,950.20	☆	☆	0.0	None	212-720-9218	None	0.75	5.00	Caruso/Gerken	'92/'92
SHEARSON EQ:GRO&OPP;A	Growth	2.5	21.86	9,986.30	☆	☆	0.0	None	212-720-9218	5.00	0.25	None	Brilliant/Fleischmann	'92/'92
SHEARSON EQ:GRO&OPP;B	Growth	141.8	21.78	9,968.00	12,021.60	16,303.20	0.5	None	212-720-9218	None	1.00	5.00	Brilliant/Fleischmann	'86/'86
SHEARSON EQ:SECTOR;A	Capital Appreciation	4.7	14.74	9,833.20	☆	☆	0.0	None	212-720-9218	5.00	0.25	None	Elaine M. Garzarelli	'92
SHEARSON EQ:SECTOR;B	Capital Appreciation	167.7	14.70	9,819.60	10,673.50	15,059.60	0.0	None	212-720-9218	None	1.00	5.00	Elaine M. Garzarelli	'87
SHEARSON EQ:STRAT;A	Flexible	4.5	17.70	10,179.10	☆	☆	0.0	None	212-720-9218	5.00	0.25	None	William Carter	'92
SHEARSON EQ:STRAT;B	Flexible	297.8	17.70	10,168.70	11,319.50	17,966.30	1.9	None	212-720-9218	None	1.00	5.00	William Carter	'87
SHEARSON FDMNTL VAL;A	Growth	103.2	7.97	10,391.10	12,194.70	19,044.00	0.7	None	212-720-9218	5.00	0.25	None	John Goode	'90
SHEARSON FDMNTL VAL;B	Growth	55.6	7.94	10,365.50	☆	☆	0.0	None	212-720-9218	None	1.00	5.00	John Goode	'92
SHEARSON GLOBAL OPP;A	Global	29.6	26.31	10,127.00	10,656.10	12,150.50	0.0	None	212-720-9218	5.00	0.25	None	Robert Penneils	'90
SHEARSON GLOBAL OPP;B	Global	32.4	26.18	10,104.20	☆	☆	0.0	None	212-720-9218	None	1.00	5.00	Robert Penneils	'92
SHEARSON INC:CONVRT;A	Convertible Securities	1.3	14.86	10,125.00	☆	☆	0.0	None	212-720-9218	5.00	0.25	None	Levande/Swab	'92/'92
SHEARSON INC:CONVRT;B	Convertible Securities	72.7	14.86	10,116.50	11,416.40	15,281.60	4.5	None	212-720-9218	None	0.75	5.00	Levande/Swab	'90/'90
SHEARSON INC:DVSD;A	Fixed Income	37.2	8.41	10,302.30	☆	☆	0.0	None	212-720-9218	4.50	0.25	None	Conroy/Bianchi	'92/'92
SHEARSON INC:DVSD;B	Fixed Income	1,938.4	8.41	10,289.90	10,849.80	☆	8.0	None	212-720-9218	None	0.75	4.50	Conroy/Bianchi	'90/'90
SHEARSON INC:GLBL BD;A	World Income	2.0	16.53	10,314.80	☆	☆	0.0	None	212-720-9218	4.50	0.25	None	Pauline Barrett	'92
SHEARSON INC:GLBL BD;B	World Income	62.8	16.53	10,301.50	11,010.60	15,908.00	6.9	None	212-720-9218	None	0.75	4.50	Pauline Barrett	'86
SHEARSON INC:HI INC;A	Fixed Income	236.4	12.00	10,507.10	☆	☆	0.0	None	212-720-9218	4.50	0.25	None	John Bianchi	'92
SHEARSON INC:HI INC;B	Fixed Income	405.8	12.00	10,493.80	12,024.10	15,570.40	9.3	None	212-720-9218	None	0.75	4.50	John Bianchi	'88
SHEARSON INC:L TREAS	Fixed Income	48.3	8.12	10,109.00	10,979.50	☆	4.9	None	212-720-9218	1.25	0.15	1.00	James Conroy	'91
SHEARSON INC:TOT RT;A	Growth & Income	32.3	15.51	10,144.90	☆	☆	0.0	None	212-720-9218	5.00	0.25	None	John Fullerton	'92
SHEARSON INC:TOT RT;B	Growth & Income	1,100.9	15.51	10,132.10	11,237.70	19,117.70	7.7	None	212-720-9218	None	0.75	5.00	John Fullerton	'85

★SECOND FID EXCHANGE—Closed to new investors.
★SEI FUNDS—Institutional funds.
★SELIGMAN INTL—Closed to new investors.

★SENTINEL: AGGRESSIVE GRO — On 6/9/93, fund was reclassified from Growth to Small Company Growth.
★SEQUOIA FUND—Closed to new investors.

PERFORMANCE OF MUTUAL FUNDS (continued)

FUND NAME	OBJECTIVE	TOTAL NET ASSETS ($ MIL) 5/31/93	NET ASSET $ VALUE 6/30/93	PERFORMANCE (Return on Initial $10,000 Investment) 3/31/93-6/30/93	6/30/92-6/30/93	6/30/88-6/30/93	DIVIDEND YIELD % 6/93	PHONE NUMBER 800	In-State	FEES Load	12b-1	Redemption	MANAGER	SINCE
SHEARSON INC:UTIL;A	Utility	45.7	15.67	10,232.90	☆	☆	0.0	None	212-720-9218	5.00	0.25	None	Levande/Mueller/Battaglia	'92
SHEARSON INC:UTIL;B	Utility	2,564.3	15.67	10,221.30	11,722.10	18,494.10	5.4	None	212-720-9218	None	0.75	5.00	Levande/Mueller/Battaglia	'88
SHEARSON INV:DIR VAL;A	Growth	3.4	13.62	10,101.60	☆	☆	0.0	None	212-720-9218	5.00	0.25	None	Caruso/Gerken	'92/'92
SHEARSON INV:DIR VAL;B	Growth	178.4	13.63	10,085.10	11,031.20	15,673.50	0.3	None	212-720-9218	None	1.00	5.00	Caruso/Gerken	'90/'91
SHEARSON INV:EURO;A	European Region	0.7	12.11	9,910.00	☆	☆	0.0	None	212-720-9218	5.00	None	None	Erich Stock	'92
SHEARSON INV:EURO;B	European Region	24.7	12.11	9,910.00	9,112.10	12,949.00	0.0	None	212-720-9218	None	1.00	5.00	Erich Stock	'90
SHEARSON INV:GOVT;A	Fixed Income	7.4	10.10	10,247.30	☆	☆	0.0	None	212-720-9218	4.50	0.25	None	James Conroy	'92
SHEARSON INV:GOVT;B	Fixed Income	947.6	10.09	10,235.40	11,241.00	16,356.80	5.8	None	212-720-9218	None	0.75	4.50	James Conroy	'84
SHEARSON INV:INV GRD;A	Fixed Income	7.3	12.80	10,512.10	☆	☆	0.0	None	212-720-9218	4.50	0.25	None	George Mueller	'92
SHEARSON INV:INV GRD;B	Fixed Income	454.4	12.80	10,491.50	11,705.10	18,091.60	6.9	None	212-720-9218	None	0.75	4.50	George Mueller	'85
SHEARSON INV:SPEC EQ;A	Small-Company Growth	2.8	17.95	11,107.70	☆	☆	0.0	None	212-720-9218	5.00	0.25	None	George Novello	'92
SHEARSON INV:SPEC EQ;B	Small-Company Growth	81.1	17.89	11,084.30	15,148.20	15,916.10	0.0	None	212-720-9218	None	1.00	5.00	George Novello	'90
SHEARSON MGD GOVTS;A	Fixed Income	459.8	13.15	10,211.70	11,104.00	16,350.40	6.7	None	212-720-9218	4.50	0.25	None	James Conroy	'84
SHEARSON MGD GOVTS;B	Fixed Income	471.0	13.15	10,199.00	☆	☆	0.0	None	212-720-9218	None	0.75	4.50	James Conroy	'92
SHEARSON MTLS & MIN;A	Gold	22.9	18.70	12,246.20	13,580.20	10,203.50	0.0	None	212-720-9218	5.00	0.25	None	A. O'Duffy	'90
SHEARSON MTLS & MIN;B	Gold	46.0	18.61	12,219.30	☆	☆	0.0	None	212-720-9218	None	1.00	5.00	O'Duffy/Barrett	'92/'92
SHEARSON 1990S;A	Growth	34.0	9.45	10,523.40	10,139.50	☆	0.0	None	212-720-9218	5.00	0.25	None	Richard Freeman	'90
SHEARSON 1990S;B	Growth	0.5	9.41	10,502.20	☆	☆	0.0	None	212-720-9218	None	1.00	5.00	Richard Freeman	'92
SHEARSON PRIN:1996★	Balanced Target	103.3	11.19	10,072.00	11,078.40	☆	6.3	None	212-720-9218	5.00	None	None	Williamson/Cohen	'89/'89
SHEARSON PRIN:1998★	Balanced Target	154.8	9.14	10,133.00	11,372.80	☆	4.5	None	212-720-9218	5.00	None	None	Williamson/Cohen	'91/'91
SHEARSON PRIN:2000★	Balanced Target	106.9	8.37	10,662.40	11,537.30	☆	3.5	None	212-720-9218	5.00	None	None	Richard Freeman	'91
SHEARSON SH WRLD INC;A	World Income	82.6	6.81	10,054.10	9,671.30	☆	5.4	None	212-720-9218	3.00	0.25	None	Alan Brown	'90
SHEARSON SH WRLD INC;B	World Income	47.2	6.81	10,038.60	☆	☆	0.0	None	212-720-9218	None	0.75	3.00	Alan Brown	'92
SHEARSON SMALL CAP;A	Small-Company Growth	46.6	15.16	10,759.40	10,261.30	12,341.40	0.0	None	212-720-9218	5.00	0.25	None	Richard Freeman	'87
SHEARSON SMALL CAP;B	Small-Company Growth	5.6	15.10	10,739.70	☆	☆	0.0	None	212-720-9218	None	1.00	5.00	Richard Freeman	'92
SHEARSON TELECOM:GRO;A	Science & Technology	44.8	11.61	10,800.00	14,472.40	21,155.00	0.2	None	212-720-9218	5.00	0.25	None	Guy Scott	'88
SHEARSON TELECOM:GRO;B	Science & Technology	9.7	11.56	10,763.50	☆	☆	0.0	None	212-720-9218	None	1.00	5.00	Guy Scott	'92
SHEARSON TELECOM:INC★	Specialty	N/A	111.03	10,163.70	12,464.00	19,658.60	5.2	None	212-720-9218	None	None	None	Guy Scott	'91
SHEARSON WRLD PRIME;A	World Income	128.9	1.79	10,037.70	9,692.40	☆	4.0	None	212-720-9218	None	0.90	None	Alan Brown	'91
SHEARSON WRLD PRIME;B	World Income	0.1	1.79	☆	☆	☆	0.0	None	212-720-9218	None	0.90	5.00	Alan Brown	'93
SHEFFIELD:INTMDT TM BOND	Fixed Income	8.8	10.22	10,171.30	10,923.90	☆	5.8	None	404-953-1597	None	0.50	None	Roger Sheffield	'90
SHEFFIELD:TOTAL RETURN	Growth & Income	25.4	11.93	9,916.90	11,514.80	☆	0.9	None	404-953-1597	None	0.50	None	Roger Sheffield	'90
SHERMAN, DEAN	Capital Appreciation	2.2	7.00	9,234.80	9,277.70	10,161.30	0.6	None	210-735-7700	None	None	None	J. Walter Sherman	'68
SH-TM INV:L M TREAS;AIM	Fixed Income	333.3	10.21	10,086.20	10,537.60	14,682.10	4.3	347-1919	713-626-1919	1.00	0.15	None	Beauchamp/Walsh	'87/'92
SH-TM INV:L M TREAS;INST	Fixed Income	100.0	10.22	10,101.50	10,571.00	14,873.10	4.5	347-1919	713-626-1919	None	None	None	Beauchamp/Walsh	'87/'92
SIERRA:CORP INCOME	Fixed Income	373.6	11.33	10,437.00	11,664.40	☆	7.7	222-5852	818-725-0200	4.50	0.25	None	James Goldberg	'90
SIERRA:EMERGING GROWTH	Small-Company Growth	95.2	13.76	10,014.60	11,984.80	☆	0.0	222-5852	818-725-0200	4.50	0.25	None	James Rothenberg	'90
SIERRA:GROWTH & INCOME	Growth & Income	109.2	12.09	9,910.10	10,919.60	☆	1.0	222-5852	818-725-0200	4.50	0.25	None	James Rothenberg	'89
SIERRA:INTL GROWTH	International	56.3	9.76	10,713.50	11,106.00	☆	0.3	222-5852	818-725-0200	4.50	0.25	None	Doug Dooley	'90
SIERRA:SHT GLBL GOVT	World Income	202.1	2.48	10,268.80	10,607.10	☆	7.8	222-5852	818-725-0200	3.50	0.25	None	Margaret Craddock	'92
SIERRA:US GOVT	Fixed Income	818.6	10.65	10,198.20	10,886.60	☆	7.2	222-5852	818-725-0200	4.50	0.25	None	Robert Davidson	'89
SIFE TRUST	Financial Services	383.3	3.90	9,638.70	12,270.50	19,946.40	3.7	524-7433	510-937-3964	6.25	None	None	Sam A. Marchese	'84
SIG SELECT:GOVT;INV	Fixed Income	95.6	10.86	10,158.50	10,987.00	☆	6.3	444-7123	None	None	0.15	2.00	E. Christian Goetz	'91
SIG SELECT:GOVT;TR	Fixed Income	105.8	10.86	10,162.40	10,994.40	☆	6.4	444-7123	None	None	None	None	E. Christian Goetz	'91
SIG SELECT:VALUE;INV	Growth & Income	13.2	12.37	9,760.10	10,915.50	☆	2.1	444-7123	None	None	0.10	2.00	Charles B. Arrington	'91
SIG SELECT;VALUE;TR	Growth & Income	62.4	12.37	9,763.20	10,922.50	☆	2.1	444-7123	None	None	None	None	Charles B. Arrington	'91
SIT NW BEGIN GROWTH	Small-Company Growth	359.6	47.63	10,006.30	11,388.20	20,446.80	0.4	332-5580	612-334-5888	None	None	None	Sit/Anderson	'82/'85
SIT NW BEGIN INC & GRO	Growth & Income	37.6	25.61	9,828.30	10,951.60	17,570.80	1.4	332-5580	612-334-5888	None	None	None	Mitchelson/Sit	'82/'82
SIT NW BEGIN:INTL GRO	International	33.1	11.99	10,772.70	11,237.10	☆	0.3	332-5580	612-334-5888	None	None	None	Kim/Sit	'91/'91
SIT NW BEGIN INV RSV	Fixed Income	9.9	9.98	10,084.20	10,305.90	13,491.00	3.0	332-5580	612-334-5888	None	None	None	Brilley/Rogers	'85/'91

SIT NW BEGIN US GOVT	Fixed Income	31.4	10.73	10,191.90	10,751.90	15,690.30	6.6	332-5580	612-334-5888	None	None	None	Briley/Sit	'87/'91
SKYLINE:EUROPE	European Region	N/A	10.14	☆	☆	☆	0.0	458-5222	312-670-6035	None	None	None	MGH Advisers	'93
SKYLINE:MONTHLY INCOME	Fixed Income	19.5	10.14	10,394.20	11,439.80	☆	8.0	458-5222	312-670-6035	None	None	None	Thomas Paprocki	'88
SKYLINE:SPECIAL EQ★	Small-Company Growth	220.0	18.59	10,086.80	14,045.30	25,704.70	0.0	458-5222	312-670-6035	None	None	None	William Dutton	'87
SKYLINE:SPECIAL EQ II★	Small-Company Growth	38.0	10.05	9,990.10	☆	☆	0.0	458-5222	312-670-6035	None	None	None	Kenneth S. Kailin	'93
SMALLCAP WORLD	Global Small Company	1,851.6	20.44	10,255.90	11,639.10	☆	0.4	421-0180	210-530-4000	5.75	0.30	None	Multiple Managers	'90
SM BARNEY:CAP APP;A	Capital Appreciation	61.0	13.83	10,236.90	☆	☆	0.0	544-7835	212-698-5349	4.50	None	None	Thomas F. Marsico	'92
SM BARNEY:CAP APP;B	Capital Appreciation	79.3	13.77	10,222.70	☆	☆	0.0	544-7835	212-698-5349	None	None	None	Thomas F. Marsico	'92
SM BARNEY:CAP APP;C	Capital Appreciation	11.1	13.77	10,192.50	☆	☆	0.0	544-7835	212-698-5349	None	None	None	Thomas F. Marsico	'92
SM BARNEY EQUITY;A	Growth	88.6	15.04	10,230.90	11,847.60	17,129.30	1.6	544-7835	212-698-5349	4.50	0.25	None	Ayako Weissman	'92
SM BARNEY EQUITY;B	Growth	0.1	15.03	10,205.60	☆	☆	0.0	544-7835	212-698-5349	None	None	None	Ayako Weissman	'93
SM BARNEY:INC & GRO;A	Growth & Income	612.3	13.48	10,242.00	11,416.90	17,364.80	3.4	544-7835	212-698-5349	4.50	0.25	None	Bruce Sargent	'74
SM BARNEY:INC & GRO;B	Growth & Income	7.1	13.48	10,230.90	☆	☆	0.0	544-7835	212-698-5349	None	None	None	Bruce Sargent	'92
SM BARNEY:INC RET;A	Fixed Income	57.8	9.68	10,082.90	10,580.70	14,989.00	4.9	544-7835	212-698-5349	1.50	None	None	Patrick Sheehan	'92
SM BARNEY:INC RET;B	Fixed Income	1.8	9.68	10,084.60	☆	☆	0.0	544-7835	212-698-5349	None	None	None	Patrick Sheehan	'92
SM BARNEY:MTHLY GOVT;A	Fixed Income	52.2	13.15	10,192.60	10,954.30	16,946.40	7.3	544-7835	212-698-5349	4.00	None	None	Patrick Sheehan	'92
SM BARNEY:MTHLY GOVT;B	Fixed Income	1.4	13.14	10,166.90	☆	☆	0.0	544-7835	212-698-5349	None	None	None	Patrick Sheehan	'92
SM BARNEY:SH-TM TRES;A	Fixed Income	175.6	4.20	10,134.50	10,810.80	☆	4.8	544-7835	212-698-5349	None	0.35	None	Patrick Sheehan	'92
SM BARNEY:US GOVT;A	Fixed Income	482.9	14.02	10,203.00	10,924.90	16,940.50	8.0	544-7835	212-698-5349	4.00	None	None	Patrick Sheehan	'92
SM BARNEY:US GOVT;B	Fixed Income	10.8	14.01	10,177.90	☆	☆	0.0	544-7835	212-698-5349	None	None	None	Patrick Sheehan	'92
SM BARNEY:UTILITY;A	Utility	130.4	14.04	10,347.10	11,963.20	☆	5.5	544-7835	212-698-5349	4.50	0.25	None	Phil Miller	'90
SM BARNEY:UTILITY;B	Utility	4.0	14.03	10,320.50	☆	☆	0.0	544-7835	212-698-5349	None	None	None	Phil Miller	'92
SM BARNEY WLD:GLBL;A	World Income	111.2	12.58	10,516.90	11,055.90	☆	7.3	544-7835	212-698-5349	4.00	0.25	None	Team Managed	'91
SM BARNEY WLD:INTL;A	International	139.1	13.83	10,573.40	10,864.60	18,230.10	0.1	544-7835	212-698-5349	4.50	0.25	None	Mauritis Edershein	'86
SM BARNEY WLD:INTL;B	International	3.9	13.77	10,543.60	☆	☆	0.0	544-7835	212-698-5349	None	1.00	1.00	Mauritis Edershein	'93
SM BREEDEN INST INT GVT/	Fixed Income	N/A	10.82	10,360.20	11,418.60	☆	6.5	221-3138	None	None	None	None	Daniel C. Dektar	'92
SM BREEDEN INSTL SH GVT/	Fixed Income	N/A	10.12	10,159.20	10,576.10	☆	5.0	221-3138	None	None	None	None	Daniel C. Dektar	'92
SM BREEDEN:INTMDT GOVT	Fixed Income	3.8	10.74	10,363.00	11,360.50	☆	7.4	221-3138	None	3.50	0.25	None	Daniel C. Dektar	'92
SM BREEDEN:SHORT GOVT	Fixed Income	52.0	10.05	10,156.30	10,517.10	☆	4.9	221-3138	None	2.75	0.25	None	Daniel C. Dektar	'92
SM&R:AMER NATL GOVT INC	Fixed Income	16.4	10.59	10,142.20	11,010.50	☆	4.9	231-4639	409-763-2767	4.50	None	None	Terry E. Frank	'92
SM&R:AMER NATL PRIMARY	Fixed Income	15.0	1.00	10,060.10	10,269.30	☆	2.7	231-4639	409-763-2767	None	None	None	Vera M. Young	'92
SOCIETY:EARN MOMENTUM EQ	Growth	18.9	10.83	9,431.00	10,384.90	☆	0.8	362-5365	None	4.00	None	None	Bruce McCain	'89
SOCIETY:INTMDT GOVT OBLG	Fixed Income	109.8	11.33	10,185.80	11,044.90	☆	6.0	362-5365	None	4.00	None	None	James Heintschel	'91
SOCIETY:INTL GROWTH	International	15.8	10.44	10,841.10	10,886.30	☆	0.0	362-5365	None	4.00	None	None	Julius Bear Inv Mgt.	'91
SOCIETY:OH REGIONAL EQ	Capital Appreciation	31.6	13.66	10,093.80	11,790.90	☆	1.4	362-5365	None	4.00	None	None	Lynn Hamilton	'89
SOCIETY:RELATIVE VALUE	Growth	244.4	12.78	10,099.70	11,462.10	☆	1.5	362-5365	None	4.00	None	None	Larry Babin	'89
SOCIETY:SH/INTMDT FXDINC	Fixed Income	70.2	10.52	10,162.20	10,699.60	☆	5.6	362-5365	None	4.00	None	None	Steve Moore	'89
SOCIETY RIT:BALANCED	Balanced	38.4	17.77	10,177.50	11,232.60	17,119.50	0.0	362-5365	None	None	None	None	Michael Cobb	'87
SOCIETY RIT:US GOVT	Fixed Income	18.6	17.91	10,275.40	11,285.40	16,707.10	0.0	362-5365	None	None	None	None	Paul Lehman	'87
SOGEN INTERNATIONAL	Global	772.6	20.97	10,422.50	11,493.20	17,272.10	3.0	334-2143	212-399-1141	3.75	0.21	None	Jean-Marie Eveillard	'79
SOUND SHORE	Growth	50.6	17.01	9,912.80	12,205.60	19,790.10	0.7	None	207-879-0001	None	None	None	Kane/Burn	'85/'85
SPECIAL PORTFOLIOS:CASH★	Fixed Income	25.7	9.82	10,098.40	10,540.50	☆	7.4	800-2638	612-738-4000	None	None	None	Poling/Ott	'89/'89
SPECIAL PORTFOLIOS:STOCK★	Capital Appreciation	72.7	35.77	10,508.20	12,214.90	23,317.70	0.1	800-2638	612-738-4000	None	None	None	Stephen Poling	'83
STAGECOACH:ASSET ALLOC	Flexible	732.7	19.14	10,341.70	11,717.80	17,556.90	4.4	222-8222	None	4.50	0.05	None	Derringer/Sakamoro	'87/'87
STAGECOACH:CORP STOCK	Growth & Income	250.6	32.46	10,023.80	11,248.30	18,371.20	1.9	222-8222	None	None	0.05	None	Hom/Gashman	'84/'84
STAGECOACH:DVSD INCOME	Income	10.7	10.70	10,154.10	☆	☆	0.0	222-8222	None	4.50	0.05	None	Bisell/Wisnieski	'92/'92
STAGECOACH:GINNIE MAE	Fixed Income	270.3	11.46	10,215.60	10,939.70	☆	7.4	222-8222	None	4.50	0.05	None	Single/Glessman	'91/'91
STAGECOACH:GOVT ALLOC	Fixed Income	196.7	16.75	10,530.40	11,955.30	16,972.70	5.2	222-8222	None	4.50	0.05	None	Daifotis/Sakamoto	'87/'87
STAGECOACH:GROWTH & INC	Growth & Income	92.7	13.80	9,799.20	10,964.80	☆	1.8	222-8222	None	4.50	0.05	None	Wisniewski/Bissell	'90/'90
STAGECOACH:VAR RATE GOVT	Fixed Income	32.0	10.78	10,111.50	10,396.40	☆	4.8	222-8222	None	3.00	0.05	None	Single/Glessman	'91/'92

★SHEARSON PRIN: 1996, SHEARSON PRIN: 1998 and SHEARSON PRIN: 2000 — Closed to new investors.
★SHEARSON TELECOM: INC—Closed to new investors.
★SKYLINE: SPECIAL EQ—Closed to new investors.

★SKYLINE: SPECIAL EQ II — On 4/29/93, fund was reclassified grom Growth to Small Company Growth.
★SPECIAL PORTFOLIOS FUNDS—Available only through employee retirement plans.

PERFORMANCE OF MUTUAL FUNDS (continued)

FUND NAME	OBJECTIVE	TOTAL NET ASSETS ($ MIL) 5/31/93	NET ASSET $ VALUE 6/30/93	PERFORMANCE (Return on Initial $10,000 Investment) 3/31/93-6/30/93	6/30/92-6/30/93	6/30/88-6/30/93	DIVIDEND YIELD % 6/93	PHONE NUMBER 800	In-State	FEES Load	12b-1	Redemption	MANAGER	SINCE
STAR:RELATIVE VALUE	Growth	40.3	11.06	9,946.80	11,146.60	☆	2.3	667-3863	513-632-5547	4.50	None	None	Joseph Belew	'91
STARBURST:GOVT INC;INV	Fixed Income	87.4	10.33	10,205.20	10,825.40	☆	6.6	239-6669	205-558-6702	4.50	0.17	None	Dan Davidson	'92
STATE BOND COMMON STOCK	Growth	44.4	8.36	9,929.30	10,649.30	19,462.30	1.1	437-6663	612-835-0097	4.75	0.25	None	Keith Martens	'84
STATE BOND DIVERSIFIED	Growth & Income	37.6	9.39	9,958.50	10,799.40	17,945.50	2.5	437-6663	612-835-0097	4.75	0.25	None	Keith Martens	'84
STATE BOND PROGRESS	Growth	9.7	12.55	9,968.20	10,674.70	17,634.00	0.5	437-6663	612-835-0097	4.75	0.25	None	Keith Martens	'84
STATE BOND US GOVT SEC	Fixed Income	15.8	5.34	10,202.80	10,918.40	16,288.70	6.5	437-6663	612-835-0097	5.00	0.25	None	Keith Martens	'85
STATE FARM BALANCED★	Balanced	304.3	30.46	9,986.30	10,906.80	21,111.50	3.3	None	309-766-2029	None	None	None	Kurt Moser	'91
STATE FARM GROWTH★	Growth	724.0	22.00	9,758.20	10,560.30	20,182.70	2.0	None	309-766-2029	None	None	None	Kurt Moser	'91
STATE FARM INTERIM★	Fixed Income	92.2	10.65	10,154.60	10,851.50	15,680.60	7.0	None	309-766-2029	None	None	None	Kurt Moser	'91
STATE STREET MSTR:INVEST	Growth & Income	768.0	9.10	10,077.30	11,365.20	18,771.30	1.7	882-3302	617-348-2000	None	None	None	Peter Bennett	'88
SS RESEARCH:CAPITAL;C	Capital Appreciation	15.6	9.16	10,601.90	13,929.20	23,426.90	0.0	882-3302	617-348-2000	None	None	None	Fredrick R. Kobrick	'86
SS RESEARCH:GOVT INC	Fixed Income	930.7	12.80	10,270.50	11,169.20	16,524.40	6.8	882-3302	617-348-2000	4.50	0.25	None	Jack Kallis	'87
SS RESEARCH:GROWTH;C	Growth	268.8	9.39	9,864.20	11,283.50	18,217.40	1.4	882-3302	617-348-2000	None	None	None	Peter Woodworth	'93
STEADMAN AMER INDUSTRY★	Capital Appreciation	N/A	1.46	9,068.30	11,406.30	6,517.90	0.0	424-8570	202-223-1000	None	0.25	None	Team Managed	N/A
STEADMAN ASSOCIATED FD★	Equity Income	N/A	0.81	9,878.00	12,857.10	13,836.10	0.0	424-8570	202-223-1000	None	0.25	None	Team Managed	N/A
STEADMAN INVESTMENT★	Growth	N/A	1.43	9,662.20	10,833.30	10,592.60	0.0	424-8570	202-223-1000	None	0.25	None	Team Managed	N/A
STEADMAN OCEANOGRAPHIC★	Growth	N/A	2.69	8,621.80	11,594.80	7,173.30	0.0	424-8570	202-223-1000	None	0.25	None	Team Managed	N/A
STEINROE INC:GOVT INCOME	Fixed Income	60.3	10.46	10,163.80	10,959.30	16,149.20	6.1	338-2550	None	None	None	None	Michael T. Kennedy	'88
STEINROE INC:INCOME	Fixed Income	146.2	10.10	10,346.20	11,464.80	16,433.30	7.4	338-2550	None	None	None	None	Ann Henderson	'90
STEINROE INC:INTMDT BOND	Fixed Income	303.6	9.26	10,186.30	11,060.00	16,275.80	7.0	338-2550	None	None	None	None	Michael T. Kennedy	'88
STEINROE INC:LTD MAT INC	Fixed Income	5.4	10.01	10,104.30	☆	☆	0.0	338-2550	None	None	None	None	Lisa Wilhelm	'93
STEINROE INV:CAPITAL OPP	Capital Appreciation	125.8	27.25	10,615.50	12,243.90	15,339.10	0.3	338-2550	None	None	None	None	Dunn/Santella	'91/'91
STEINROE INV:PRIME EQ	Growth & Income	87.0	14.09	9,964.90	11,645.20	19,613.30	1.1	338-2550	None	None	None	None	Ralph Segall	'87
STEINROE INV:SPECIAL	Growth	911.6	23.61	10,278.60	12,567.10	22,324.80	0.7	338-2550	None	None	None	None	Dunn/Peterson	'91/'91
STEINROE INV:STOCK	Growth	387.6	24.44	9,776.00	10,997.00	20,031.70	0.5	338-2550	None	None	None	None	Capital Management Grp	'91
STEINROE INV:TOTAL RTN	Equity Income	200.4	26.62	10,045.70	11,343.40	17,761.50	4.7	338-2550	None	None	None	None	Robert A. Christensen	'81
STI CLASSIC:CAP GRO;INV	Growth	131.4	11.98	10,058.60	11,730.20	☆	0.8	428-6970	None	3.75	0.49	None	Anthony Gray	'92
STI CLASSIC:CAP GRO;TR	Growth	503.5	11.99	10,072.70	☆	☆	1.3	428-6970	None	None	None	None	Anthony Gray	'92
STI CLASSIC:INV GRD;INV	Fixed Income	24.2	10.61	10,254.30	11,113.10	☆	4.5	428-6970	None	3.75	0.30	None	Earl Denney	'92
STI CLASSIC:INV GRD;TR	Fixed Income	328.5	10.61	10,264.50	☆	☆	0.0	428-6970	None	None	None	None	Earl Denney	'92
STI CLASSIC:VAL INC;INV	Equity Income	24.7	10.11	10,009.80	☆	☆	0.0	428-6970	None	3.75	0.30	None	Gregory DePrive	'93
STI CLASSIC:VAL INC;TR	Equity Income	24.6	10.11	10,019.70	☆	☆	0.0	428-6970	None	None	None	None	Gregory DePrive	'93
STOCK & BOND FUND;A	Balanced	112.0	16.35	10,218.40	11,189.70	15,556.70	3.6	245-4770	412-288-1900	None	None	None	Charles A. Ritter	'89
STRATTON GROWTH FUND	Growth & Income	25.3	20.80	9,947.40	11,015.40	16,060.20	2.7	634-5726	215-941-0255	None	None	None	Stratton/Affleck	'72/'79
STRATTON MONTHLY DIV	Utility	147.2	31.11	10,097.40	11,984.50	18,399.50	6.2	634-5726	215-941-0255	None	None	None	Stratton/Heffernan	'80/'80
STRATTON:SMALL-CAP YIELD	Small-Company Growth	4.4	25.33	☆	☆	☆	0.0	634-5726	215-941-0255	None	None	None	Stratton/Reichel	'93/'93
STRATUS:CAP APPREC	Growth	0.6	9.40	9,690.70	☆	☆	0.0	279-7437	402-476-3000	None	None	None	Dunlap/Norris	'93/'93
STRATUS:GROWTH/INCOME	Growth & Income	3.2	9.99	9,762.90	9,827.00	☆	1.4	279-7437	402-476-3000	None	None	None	Union Bank & Trust Co.	'91
STRATUS:INTMDT GOVT BOND	Fixed Income	6.5	10.84	10,173.10	10,886.10	☆	4.5	279-7437	402-476-3000	None	None	None	Union Bank & Trust Co.	'91
STRONG ADVANTAGE	Fixed Income	310.3	10.13	10,179.30	10,814.80	☆	6.4	368-1030	414-359-1400	None	None	None	Koch/Tank	'91/'90
STRONG COMMON STOCK	Growth	600.1	16.62	10,143.00	13,689.70	☆	0.2	368-1030	414-359-1400	None	None	None	Weiss/Murphy	'91/'91
STRONG DISCOVERY FUND	Capital Appreciation	220.6	16.42	10,012.40	11,563.80	21,558.00	7.0	368-1030	414-359-1400	None	None	None	Richard S. Strong	'87
STRONG GOVERNMENT	Fixed Income	133.7	10.89	10,299.90	11,522.40	17,293.90	6.9	368-1030	414-359-1400	None	None	None	Koch/Tank	'91/'90
STRONG INCOME	Fixed Income	112.0	9.97	10,404.70	11,491.40	13,505.10	7.3	368-1030	414-359-1400	None	None	None	Koch/Tank	'91/'90
STRONG INTL STOCK	International	31.5	11.12	10,363.50	10,967.70	☆	0.4	368-1030	414-359-1400	None	None	None	Dillon, Read Intl Ast Mgt	'92
STRONG INVESTMENT★	Flexible	217.9	19.28	10,206.70	11,185.50	15,854.60	4.9	368-1030	414-359-1400	None	None	None	Tank/Stephens/Mueller	'93
STRONG OPPORTUNITY	Growth	300.2	26.54	10,190.20	12,913.30	18,382.20	0.2	368-1030	414-359-1400	None	None	None	Murphy/Weiss	'91/'91
STRONG SHORT-TERM BOND	Fixed Income	975.1	10.21	10,191.80	10,846.80	15,280.20	6.9	368-1030	414-359-1400	None	None	None	Koch/Tank	'91/'90
STRONG TOTAL RETURN	Growth & Income	549.9	22.12	10,272.10	11,850.50	14,856.70	1.5	368-1030	414-359-1400	None	None	None	Ronald C. Ognar	'93
SUN EAGLE EQUITY GROWTH	Growth & Income	41.5	10.92	10,269.00	11,392.90	☆	2.1	752-1823	614-899-4668	None	None	None	Lynn Yturri	'92

SUN EAGLE GOVT SEC	Fixed Income	34.9	10.11	10,101.80	10,600.80	☆	5.2	752-1823	614-899-4668	None	None	None	Ann Kirk	'92
SUN EAGLE INTMDT FXD INC	Fixed Income	43.2	10.51	10,211.20	11,067.40	☆	6.0	752-1823	614-899-4668	None	None	None	Lars Barker	'92
SUNAMER BAL ASSETS	Balanced	101.0	15.86	10,231.20	12,028.90	16,424.30	1.8	858-8850	212-551-5125	None	1.00	5.00	Feeley/Leary	'92/'91
SUNAMER CAP APPREC	Growth	79.2	15.48	10,424.20	12,585.40	14,117.40	0.0	858-8850	212-551-5125	None	1.00	5.00	Stan Feeley	'92
SUNAMER EMERGING GRO	Small-Company Growth	32.7	20.27	10,535.30	14,105.80	17,540.60	0.0	858-8850	212-551-5125	None	1.00	5.00	Audrey Snell	'91
SUNAMER EQ:AGG GROWTH	Small-Company Growth	35.7	17.58	10,501.80	13,772.00	17,842.60	0.0	858-8850	212-551-5125	5.75	0.35	None	Audrey Snell	'91
SUNAMER EQ:GROWTH	Growth	30.6	16.63	10,303.60	13,240.30	19,152.30	0.0	858-8850	212-551-5125	5.75	0.35	None	Dudley/Snell	'93/'93
SUNAMER FEDERAL SEC	Fixed Income	117.4	10.82	10,116.10	10,599.40	15,492.00	5.5	858-8850	212-551-5125	None	0.95	5.00	Paul G. Sullivan	'83
SUNAMER HIGH INCOME	Fixed Income	132.4	8.33	10,464.10	11,609.10	16,289.20	10.8	858-8850	212-551-5125	None	1.00	5.00	Charles Dudley	'91
SUNAMER INC:GOVT INCOME	Fixed Income	72.8	10.00	10,200.60	10,816.30	14,870.40	7.6	858-8850	212-551-5125	4.75	0.35	None	Christopher Leary	'90
SUNAMER INC:HI YIELD	Fixed Income	33.2	9.71	10,448.30	11,608.60	17,215.50	12.4	858-8850	212-551-5125	4.75	0.35	None	Charles Dudley	'90
SUNAMER MUL-AST:DVSD	Fixed Income	35.5	5.06	10,210.40	☆	☆	0.0	858-8850	212-551-5125	None	0.75	3.00	Leary/Dudley	'92/'92
SUNAMER MUL-AST:TOT RTN	Flexible	26.9	15.79	10,253.20	11,721.30	15,228.40	2.6	858-8850	212-551-5125	5.75	0.35	None	Feeley/Leary	'92/'91
SUNAMER US GOVT SEC	Fixed Income	1,268.0	8.74	10,129.80	10,539.60	14,406.00	6.9	858-8850	212-551-5125	None	1.00	5.00	Paul G. Sullivan	'90
SWISSKEY:SBC SH-TM WORLD	World Income	41.6	9.99	10,244.00	☆	☆	0.0	524-9984	212-644-1400	None	0.35	None	Fabio Salvoldeli	'92
SWISSKEY:SBC WORLD GRO	Global	8.7	14.19	10,335.00	☆	☆	0.0	524-9984	212-644-1400	None	0.35	None	Miller/Grimm	'92/'92
SWRW GROWTH PLUS	Growth	20.2	14.78	9,879.70	11,849.30	18,322.00	0.6	877-3344	513-621-2975	None	None	None	Peter Williams	'88
TCW/DW CORE EQUITY	Growth & Income	525.7	11.59	10,293.10	12,161.60	☆	0.0	869-3863	212-392-2550	None	1.00	5.00	James Tilton	'92
TCW/DW INCOME & GROWTH	Equity Income	33.0	10.36	10,480.80	☆	☆	0.0	869-3863	212-392-2550	None	0.75	None	Howard Marks	'93
TCW/DW LATIN AMER GR	Latin American	77.8	9.80	9,879.00	☆	☆	0.0	869-3863	212-392-2550	None	1.00	5.00	Philip Wargnier	'92
TCW/DW NTH AMER GOVT INC	World Income	1,924.1	10.18	10,216.20	☆	☆	0.0	869-3863	212-392-2550	None	0.75	None	Philip Barach	'92
TEMPLETON AMERICAN TR	Global	31.9	12.69	10,135.80	11,355.10	☆	0.9	237-0738	813-823-8712	None	1.00	5.00	Gary Motyl	'92
TEMPLETON CAP ACCUMULATR★	Global Flexible	14.9	12.62	10,543.00	11,587.30	☆	1.6	237-0738	813-823-8712	None	None	None	Thomas Hansberger	'91
TEMPLETON DEVELP MRKTS	International	357.3	11.28	11,371.00	11,349.90	☆	0.7	237-0738	813-823-8712	5.75	0.35	None	Mark Mobius	'91
TEMPLETON FOREIGN	International	2,166.2	24.06	10,438.20	10,393.50	18,355.10	2.3	237-0738	813-823-8712	5.75	0.25	None	Mark G. Holowesko	'87
TEMPLETON WORLD	Global	4,344.6	14.68	10,426.10	11,122.60	16,206.00	2.5	237-0738	813-823-8712	5.75	0.25	None	Mark G. Holowesko	'87
TEMPLETON GLOBAL OPP	Global	293.5	12.15	10,384.60	11,082.90	☆	1.1	237-0738	813-823-8712	5.75	0.25	None	Thomas Hansberger	'90
TEMPLETON GROWTH	Global	3,818.9	16.13	10,467.20	11,052.20	18,148.00	2.1	237-0738	813-823-8712	5.75	0.25	None	Mark G. Holowesko	'87
TEMPLETON INC:INCOME	World Income	198.6	9.87	10,171.80	10,515.80	15,636.60	7.7	237-0738	813-823-8712	4.50	0.25	None	Samuel J. Forester Jr.	'90
TEMPLETON REAL ESTATE	Real Estate	51.5	12.09	10,125.60	11,538.90	☆	2.9	237-0738	813-823-8712	5.75	0.25	None	Jeffrey Everett	'92
TEMPLETON SMALL CO GROW	Global Small Company	1,060.9	6.94	10,190.90	11,086.10	16,713.30	2.0	237-0738	813-823-8712	5.75	0.25	None	Dan Jacobs	'92
TEMPLETON VALUE	Global	105.7	9.26	10,220.80	10,751.80	☆	1.6	237-0738	813-823-8712	5.75	0.25	None	Dan Jacobs	'92
TX COMMERCE RIT:BALANCED★	Balanced	56.2	17.14	10,082.40	11,202.60	16,480.80	0.0	392-3936	713-236-4865	None	None	None	William Leszienski	'88
TX COMMERCE RIT:CORE EQ★	Capital Appreciation	1.5	10.01	☆	☆	☆	0.0	392-3936	713-236-4865	None	None	None	William Leszienski	'93
TX COMMERCE RIT:EQU GRO★	Growth	29.8	18.17	9,929.00	11,250.80	17,304.80	0.0	392-3936	713-236-4865	None	None	None	Charles Mehlhouse	'88
TX COMMERCE RIT:EQU INC★	Equity Income	29.1	17.84	10,136.40	11,607.00	17,153.80	0.0	392-3936	713-236-4865	None	None	None	Robert Heintz	'88
TX COMMERCE RIT:INCOME★	Fixed Income	68.1	15.71	10,268.00	11,141.80	15,402.00	0.0	392-3936	713-236-4865	None	None	None	H. Mitchell Harper	'91
TX COMMERCE RIT:SH-INT★	Fixed Income	4.6	10.09	☆	☆	☆	0.0	392-3936	713-236-4865	None	None	None	William Leszienski	'93
TX COMMERCE RIT:SM CAP★	Small-Company Growth	2.3	9.90	☆	☆	☆	0.0	392-3936	713-236-4865	None	None	None	William Leszienski	'93
TX COMMERCE RIT:US GOVT★	Fixed Income	1.0	10.53	☆	☆	☆	0.0	392-3936	713-236-4865	None	None	None	John Miller	'93
THIRD AVENUE VALUE	Specialty	85.5	16.78	10,088.90	13,374.40	☆	1.4	443-1021	212-888-6685	5.75	None	None	Martin J. Whitman	'90
T U & P:BALANCED	Balanced	21.8	13.79	9,935.20	10,819.80	15,804.70	2.0	999-0887	608-831-1300	None	None	None	Thompson, Unger & Plumb	'87
T U & P:BOND	Fixed Income	5.3	10.70	10,189.00	10,933.90	☆	4.4	999-0887	608-831-1300	None	None	None	Thompson, Unger & Plumb	'92
T U & P:GROWTH	Growth	7.2	19.80	9,792.30	11,012.20	☆	0.0	999-0887	608-831-1300	None	None	None	Thompson, Unger & Plumb	'92
THOMSON:EQUITY INC;A	Equity Income	3.9	11.70	10,362.00	11,555.30	☆	3.1	227-7337	203-352-4946	5.50	0.25	None	I. Smith/A. Hogan	'91/'92
THOMSON:EQUITY INC;B	Equity Income	69.4	11.68	10,340.00	11,464.60	15,048.00	2.4	227-7337	203-352-4946	None	1.00	1.00	I. Smith/A. Hogan	'90/'92
THOMSON:GOVERNMENT;A	Fixed Income	18.0	9.61	10,244.50	10,837.40	☆	7.1	227-7337	203-352-4946	4.75	0.25	None	Team Managed	'92
THOMSON:GOVERNMENT;B	Fixed Income	549.5	9.58	10,215.20	10,749.40	15,267.40	6.3	227-7337	203-352-4946	None	1.00	1.00	Team Managed	'92
THOMSON:GROWTH;A	Growth	93.8	22.55	10,134.80	11,374.30	☆	0.0	227-7337	203-352-4946	5.50	0.25	None	Irwin Smith	'91
THOMSON:GROWTH;B	Growth	1,018.0	22.29	10,118.00	11,289.70	20,331.30	0.0	227-7337	203-352-4946	None	1.00	[illegible]	Irwin Smith	'86

★STATE FARM FUNDS—Open to State Farm agents and employees.
★STEADMAN FUNDS—Closed to new investors.
★STRONG INVESTMENT—On 5/20/93, fund was reclassified from Income to Flexible Portfolio.

★TEMPLETON CAP ACCUMULATR—Sold only on a contractual plan.
★TX COMMERCE RIT FUNDS—Designed primarily for retirement accounts.

PERFORMANCE OF MUTUAL FUNDS *(continued)*

FUND NAME	OBJECTIVE	TOTAL NET ASSETS ($ MIL) 5/31/93	NET ASSET $ VALUE 6/30/93	PERFORMANCE (Return on Initial $10,000 Investment) 3/31/93-6/30/93	6/30/92-6/30/93	6/30/88-6/30/93	DIVIDEND YIELD % 6/93	PHONE NUMBER 800	In-State	FEES Load	12b-1	Redemption	MANAGER	SINCE
THOMSON:INCOME;A	Fixed Income	5.4	8.63	10,180.70	11,071.50	☆	8.6	227-7337	203-352-4946	4.75	0.25	None	Team Managed	'92
THOMSON:INCOME;B	Fixed Income	257.1	8.60	10,162.00	10,978.10	14,176.50	7.9	227-7337	203-352-4946	None	1.00	1.00	Team Managed	'92
THOMSON:INTL;A	International	3.6	11.13	10,490.10	11,750.60	☆	0.0	227-7337	203-352-4946	5.50	0.25	None	Martin Currie, Inc.	'92
THOMSON:INTL;B	International	62.0	10.93	10,479.40	11,665.80	14,319.10	0.0	227-7337	203-352-4946	None	1.00	1.00	Martin Currie, Inc.	'92
THOMSON:OPPORTUNITY;A	Capital Appreciation	76.9	28.69	11,068.70	15,420.80	☆	0.0	227-7337	203-352-4946	5.50	0.25	None	Donald Chiboucas	'91
THOMSON:OPPORTUNITY;B	Capital Appreciation	472.0	28.18	11,051.00	15,303.70	29,447.30	0.0	227-7337	203-352-4946	None	1.00	1.00	Donald Chiboucas	'86
THOMSON:PREC MTLS;A	Gold	5.4	11.46	13,610.50	14,941.30	☆	0.0	227-7337	203-352-4946	5.50	0.25	None	Bingham/Van Eck	'91/'91
THOMSON:PREC MTLS;B	Gold	18.9	11.25	13,603.40	14,841.70	☆	0.0	227-7337	203-352-4946	None	1.00	1.00	Bingham/Van Eck	'88/'88
THOMSON:SH-INT GOVT;A	Fixed Income	6.5	9.85	10,094.80	10,351.80	☆	5.0	227-7337	203-352-4946	3.00	0.25	None	Team Managed	'92
THOMSON:SH-INT GOVT;B	Fixed Income	136.0	9.85	10,072.20	10,300.90	☆	4.5	227-7337	203-352-4946	None	0.75	1.00	Team Managed	'92
THOMSON:TARGET;A	Capital Appreciation	26.8	11.42	10,692.90	☆	☆	0.0	227-7337	203-352-4946	5.50	0.25	None	Columbus Circle Equity	'92
THOMSON:TARGET;B	Capital Appreciation	154.5	11.38	10,675.40	☆	☆	0.0	227-7337	203-352-4946	None	1.00	1.00	Columbus Circle Equity	'92
THORNBURG LTD TERM INC	Fixed Income	N/A	12.38	10,202.80	☆	☆	0.0	847-0200	505-984-0200	2.50	0.25	None	Steven Bohlin	'92
THORNBURG LTD US GOVT	Fixed Income	N/A	12.87	10,151.90	10,906.40	15,496.50	6.0	847-0200	505-984-0200	2.50	0.25	None	Steven Bohlin	'87
TNE ADJ RATE US GOVT	Fixed Income	407.2	7.51	10,131.40	10,484.60	☆	4.5	343-7104	None	3.00	0.35	None	Scott Nicholson	'91
TNE BALANCED	Balanced	122.6	11.72	10,173.20	11,583.80	15,622.70	2.6	343-7104	None	5.75	0.25	None	Ramos/Beck	'90/'90
TNE BOND INCOME	Fixed Income	162.9	12.72	10,309.50	11,383.20	16,918.00	6.5	343-7104	None	4.50	0.25	None	Catherine Bunting	'89
TNE CAPITAL GROWTH	Growth	72.8	14.66	10,131.30	☆	☆	0.0	343-7104	None	5.75	0.25	None	Hurckes/Pape	'92/'92
TNE GLOBAL GOVERNMENT	World Income	17.6	12.37	10,304.90	10,786.80	14,704.10	6.1	343-7104	None	4.50	0.25	None	Andrea Burke	'91
TNE GOVERNMENT SEC	Fixed Income	185.1	12.05	10,287.20	11,106.90	15,826.60	5.3	343-7104	None	4.50	0.25	None	Michael Martino	'85
TNE GROWTH★	Growth	1,195.0	10.49	10,096.20	10,786.60	18,958.90	0.8	343-7104	None	6.50	0.25	None	G. Kenneth Heebner	'76
TNE GROWTH OPPORTUNITIES	Growth & Income	101.8	12.56	10,008.30	11,252.70	18,422.50	1.8	343-7104	None	5.75	0.35	None	Charles Glueck	'88
TNE HIGH INCOME	Fixed Income	26.6	10.01	10,438.40	11,590.20	15,613.00	9.3	343-7104	None	4.50	0.35	None	Charles Glueck	'88
TNE INTL EQUITY;A	International	35.9	13.91	10,659.00	11,383.80	☆	0.6	343-7104	None	5.75	0.25	None	Nick Carn	'92
TNE LTD TERM US GOVT	Fixed Income	521.3	12.68	10,174.70	10,832.00	☆	5.5	343-7104	None	3.00	0.35	None	Michael Martino	'89
TNE VALUE	Growth & Income	170.4	7.73	10,131.10	11,625.60	16,461.00	1.3	343-7104	None	5.75	0.25	None	Ramos/McMurry/Mills	'93/'93
TOCQUEVILLE:TOCQ EUR-PAC	International	3.6	9.83	10,102.80	9,534.10	☆	0.0	697-3863	212-698-0851	None	0.25	None	Frederic Navellou	'91
TOCQUEVILLE:TOCQ	Capital Appreciation	25.7	12.92	10,487.00	11,943.20	17,121.20	1.2	697-3863	212-698-0851	None	0.25	None	Sicart/Kleinschmidt	'87/'91
TORCHMARK GOVT SECS	Fixed Income	1.1	10.20	☆	☆	☆	0.0	733-3863	913-236-2050	None	None	None	John E. Sundeen	'93
TORRAY FUND	Flexible	15.6	13.90	9,924.80	11,065.80	☆	1.2	None	301-493-4600	None	None	None	Robert E. Torray	'90
TOT RTN TREA;FLAG INV	Fixed Income	223.3	11.06	10,432.20	11,552.40	☆	7.3	645-3923	410-637-6819	4.50	0.25	None	R. Alan Medaugh	'88
TOT RTN TREA;ISI	Fixed Income	220.1	11.06	10,432.20	11,552.40	☆	7.3	645-3923	410-637-6819	4.45	0.25	None	R. Alan Medaugh	'88
TOWER:CAPITAL APPREC	Capital Appreciation	143.3	14.13	10,210.00	11,587.10	☆	2.0	999-0124	504-585-5180	4.50	None	None	Paul Mangus	'91
TOWER:TOTAL RETURN BOND	Fixed Income	57.4	10.37	10,239.00	☆	☆	0.0	999-0124	504-585-5180	4.50	None	None	John Hall	'92
TOWER:US GOVT INCOME	Fixed Income	80.1	10.74	10,212.10	10,841.70	☆	7.1	999-0124	504-585-5180	4.50	None	None	Jeff Tanguis	'92
TRANSAM BD:ADJ GOVT;A	Fixed Income	32.1	10.06	10,119.80	10,437.30	☆	5.2	472-3863	713-751-2800	3.50	0.25	None	Team Managed	'91
TRANSAM BD:ADJ GOVT;B	Fixed Income	14.7	10.06	10,103.50	10,369.90	☆	4.5	472-3863	713-751-2800	None	1.00	3.00	Team Managed	'91
TRANSAM BD:GOVT INCOME	Fixed Income	18.7	8.52	10,223.40	11,098.20	15,744.40	8.0	472-3863	713-751-2800	None	0.25	1.00	Team Managed	'85
TRANSAM BD:GOVT SEC	Fixed Income	702.3	8.43	10,222.70	11,090.50	16,113.80	8.1	472-3863	713-751-2800	4.75	0.25	None	Team Managed	'84
TRANSAM BD:INTMDT GOVT	Fixed Income	2.1	10.28	10,191.20	10,813.50	15,614.80	5.5	472-3863	713-751-2800	None	None	1.00	Team Managed	'86
TRANSAM BD:INVEST QUAL	Fixed Income	108.0	9.31	10,254.20	11,037.70	16,303.50	8.1	472-3863	713-751-2800	4.75	0.25	None	Team Managed	'80
TRANSAM CAP APPRECIATION	Capital Appreciation	86.2	11.28	9,616.40	11,133.70	15,224.20	0.0	472-3863	713-751-2800	5.75	0.25	None	Roger Young	'85
TRANSAM INV:GR & INC;A	Growth & Income	104.4	11.69	10,062.40	11,362.80	18,352.50	3.4	472-3863	713-751-2800	5.75	0.25	None	Jeffrey Talley	'92
TRANSAM INV:GR & INC;B	Growth & Income	51.6	11.74	10,047.50	11,270.90	☆	2.5	472-3863	713-751-2800	None	1.00	6.00	Jeffrey Talley	'92
TRANSAM INV:INSTL GOVT	Fixed Income	43.5	25.32	10,071.60	☆	☆	0.0	472-3863	713-751-2800	None	0.25	None	Team Managed	'93
TRANSAM SPEC:BLUE CHIP	Growth	43.8	11.68	9,831.60	10,962.30	16,327.90	0.0	472-3863	713-751-2800	None	1.00	6.00	Robert Arnold	'90
TRANSAM SPEC:EMER GR;A	Small-Company Growth	71.5	23.29	10,134.90	12,917.40	☆	0.0	472-3863	713-751-2800	5.75	*1.22*	None	Edgar Larsen	'91
TRANSAM SPEC:EMER GR;B	Small-Company Growth	177.1	22.85	10,115.10	12,794.00	22,833.60	0.0	472-3863	713-751-2800	None	1.00	6.00	Edgar Larsen	'87
TRANSAM SPEC:GOVT INC	Fixed Income	266.6	9.94	10,180.00	10,946.80	15,409.50	7.4	472-3863	713-751-2800	None	1.00	6.00	Team Managed	'88
TRANSAM SPEC:HI YIELD	Fixed Income	137.1	8.10	10,443.10	11,818.50	15,655.80	9.2	472-3863	713-751-2800	None	1.00	6.00	Team Managed	'87

TRANSAM SPEC:NATRL RES	Natural Resources	14.6	14.69	10,530.50	12,354.90	16,084.80	0.0	472-3863	713-751-2800	None	1.00	6.00	Robert Arnold	'90
TRENT:EQUITY	Capital Appreciation	4.1	10.78	9,670.00	☆	☆	0.0	525-3863	919-972-9922	None	None	None	May/Holderness	'92/'92
TRIFLEX FUND	Balanced	20.6	15.86	10,099.40	10,910.70	15,285.40	2.2	231-4639	409-763-2767	5.75	None	None	David Zimansky	'91
TRUST CO OF SO CORE EQ	Growth & Income	0.7	9.62	9,968.90	☆	☆	0.0	525-3863	919-972-9922	None	None	None	Bill Dameron	'93
TRUST CO OF SO GROWTH	Growth	1.1	10.37	10,098.30	☆	☆	0.0	525-3863	919-972-9922	None	None	None	Bill Dameron	'93
TRUST CO OF SO MGD BOND	Fixed Income	1.6	10.51	10,296.10	☆	☆	0.0	525-3863	919-972-9922	None	None	None	Bill Dameron	'93
TRUST CO OF SO SH TM BD	Fixed Income	0.3	10.05	10,094.60	☆	☆	0.0	525-3863	919-972-9922	None	None	None	Bill Dameron	'93
TRUST CO OF SO SOEAST EQ	Small-Company Growth	0.6	9.80	9,781.40	☆	☆	0.0	525-3863	919-972-9922	None	None	None	Bill Dameron	'93
TR CREDIT UNION:GOVT★	Fixed Income	1,183.8	9.96	10,120.70	10,412.00	☆	4.8	526-7384	212-902-0800	None	None	None	Team Managed	'93
TR CREDIT UNION:MTGE SEC★	Fixed Income	187.5	10.11	10,161.60	☆	☆	0.0	526-7384	212-902-0800	None	None	None	Team Managed	'93
TR FED SEC:INT GOVT;SHS	Fixed Income	13.5	11.02	10,184.30	10,912.60	☆	6.4	821-7432	None	None	None	None	Rena Williams	'88
TR FED SEC:SHT GOVT;SHS	Fixed Income	6.2	10.49	10,142.60	10,746.70	15,217.30	5.8	821-7432	None	None	None	None	Rena Williams	'88
TWENTIETH CENT:BALANCED	Balanced	694.3	15.65	10,270.30	10,832.00	☆	2.4	345-2021	816-531-5575	None	None	None	Team Managed	'88
TWENTIETH CENT:GIFTRUST	Growth	112.9	15.75	10,493.00	15,114.90	26,712.30	0.0	345-2021	816-531-5575	None	None	None	Team Managed	'83
TWENTIETH CENT:GROWTH	Capital Appreciation	4,803.7	23.82	9,966.50	10,739.20	20,697.40	0.0	345-2021	816-531-5575	None	None	None	Team Managed	'58
TWENTIETH CENT:HERITAGE	Growth	584.3	10.17	10,039.50	12,753.60	19,904.70	0.9	345-2021	816-531-5575	None	None	None	Team Managed	'87
TWENTIETH CENT:LNG-TM BD	Fixed Income	166.9	100.49	10,258.40	11,088.00	16,580.40	6.6	345-2021	816-531-5575	None	None	None	Team Managed	'87
TWENTIETH CENT:SELECT	Growth	4,873.1	42.43	10,273.60	11,671.20	18,592.50	1.1	345-2021	816-531-5575	None	None	None	Team Managed	'58
TWENTIETH CENT:ULTRA INV	Capital Appreciation	6,184.5	20.00	11,402.50	13,927.60	29,955.90	0.0	345-2021	816-531-5575	None	None	None	Team Managed	'87
TWENTIETH CENT:US GOVT	Fixed Income	519.4	96.74	10,084.90	10,529.40	14,437.60	3.9	345-2021	816-531-5575	None	None	None	Team Managed	'82
TWENTIETH CENT:VISTA INV	Capital Appreciation	877.5	11.56	10,471.00	11,988.80	19,886.00	0.0	345-2021	816-531-5575	None	None	None	Team Managed	'83
TWENTIETH CENT WRLD:INTL	International	422.1	6.44	10,420.70	10,583.40	☆	3.0	345-2021	816-531-5575	None	None	None	Kopinski/Tyson	'91/'91
UNION:BALANCED	Flexible	115.5	11.74	10,145.30	11,350.10	☆	3.4	634-1100	213-236-5698	None	None	None	Carl J. Colombo	'91
UNION:GRO EQU;INSTL	Growth	138.2	13.40	9,949.90	11,758.40	☆	0.7	634-1100	213-236-5698	None	None	None	Clyde Powers	'91
UNION:INT-TM BOND;INSTL	Fixed Income	112.4	10.84	10,238.40	11,174.40	☆	5.7	634-1100	213-236-5698	None	None	None	Jim Atkinson	'91
UNION:VAL MOMENTUM;INSTL	Growth & Income	99.9	13.15	10,021.20	11,571.50	☆	2.3	634-1100	213-236-5698	None	None	None	Richard H. Earnest	'91
UNITED:ACCUMULATIVE	Growth	1,026.2	7.78	10,117.30	11,614.30	17,654.50	1.8	733-3863	913-236-2050	8.50	None	None	Antonio Intagliata	'79
UNITED:BOND	Fixed Income	616.2	6.69	10,340.90	11,556.00	16,743.50	6.4	733-3863	913-236-2050	8.50	None	None	James C. Cusser	'92
UNITED CONTL INCOME	Balanced	393.2	20.85	10,285.00	11,487.80	17,817.30	4.0	733-3863	913-236-2050	8.50	None	None	Cynthia Price-Fox	'93
UNITED GOLD & GOVERNMENT	Gold	40.6	8.58	12,432.90	12,949.90	11,598.40	0.7	733-3863	913-236-2050	8.50	None	None	John Olsen	'85
UNITED GOVERNMENT	Fixed Income	179.3	5.49	10,236.70	11,276.40	16,675.20	5.9	733-3863	913-236-2050	4.25	None	None	John E. Sundeen	'91
UNITED HIGH INCOME	Fixed Income	999.9	9.40	10,430.20	11,650.90	14,518.50	8.8	733-3863	913-236-2050	8.50	None	None	Louise D. Rieke	'90
UNITED HIGH INCOME II	Fixed Income	370.5	4.23	10,437.50	11,634.10	15,768.70	8.5	733-3863	913-236-2050	8.50	None	None	Louise D. Rieke	'92
UNITED:INCOME	Equity Income	2,773.2	23.42	10,257.90	11,575.50	19,628.80	1.8	733-3863	913-236-2050	8.50	None	None	Russell E. Thompson	'79
UNITED INTL GROWTH	International	345.7	7.16	10,140.90	10,261.70	12,896.30	1.0	733-3863	913-236-2050	8.50	None	None	Mark Yockey	'90
UNITED MISSOURI BK BOND	Fixed Income	84.5	11.53	10,205.40	10,984.00	15,640.10	5.9	422-2766	816-471-5200	None	None	None	George Root	'82
UNITED MISSOURI BK HRTLD	Small-Company Growth	16.4	9.02	9,918.30	10,550.20	☆	1.1	422-2766	816-471-5200	None	None	None	David Anderson	'91
UNITED MISSOURI BK STOCK	Growth & Income	102.3	15.74	10,057.20	11,134.00	16,747.40	2.1	422-2766	816-471-5200	None	None	None	David Anderson	'82
UNITED NEW CONCEPTS	Small-Company Growth	188.9	10.47	10,793.80	11,978.80	19,645.20	0.1	366-5465	913-236-2050	8.50	None	None	Mark G. Seferovich	'89
UNITED RETIREMENT SHARES	Growth & Income	371.4	7.70	10,198.00	11,345.40	18,735.60	2.9	366-5465	913-236-2050	8.50	None	None	James D. Wineland	'88
UNITED:SCIENCE & ENERGY	Science & Technology	413.4	14.59	10,641.70	11,423.70	18,623.80	0.2	366-5465	913-236-2050	8.50	None	None	Abel Garcia	'84
UNITED VANGUARD	Growth	873.6	6.64	10,374.80	11,529.70	15,068.20	0.5	366-5465	913-236-2050	8.50	None	None	James D. Wineland	'92
UNIVERSAL CAPITAL GROWTH	Capital Appreciation	4.8	11.45	10,035.10	10,876.70	☆	4.0	223-9100	708-932-3000	4.75	0.50	None	Dreher/Biscan	'91/'91
US BOS:BOS FRN G&I;SHS	International	18.9	8.54	10,635.10	10,560.70	10,828.40	0.8	331-1244	617-259-1144	None	0.50	1.00	Lyle H. Davis	'87
US BOS:BOS GR&INC;A	Growth & Income	6.5	17.48	10,115.70	11,682.50	☆	1.5	331-1244	617-259-1144	None	None	None	Stonberg/Esielonis	'91/'93
US BOS:BOS GR&INC;SHS	Growth & Income	42.7	17.45	10,104.20	11,626.00	19,903.90	1.0	331-1244	617-259-1144	None	0.50	1.00	Stonberg/Esielonis	'85/'93
US BOS:BOS NUMERIC;SHS	Small-Company Growth	15.9	14.85	10,517.00	☆	☆	0.0	331-1244	617-259-1144	None	0.50	1.00	John C. Bogle, Jr.	'92
US:ALL AMERICAN EQUITY	Growth & Income	12.8	20.60	10,038.70	11,090.80	☆	2.2	873-8637	210-308-1234	None	None	None	David Edwards	'87
US:EUROPEAN INCOME	European Region	1.9	4.16	9,859.80	8,905.00	☆	1.7	873-8637	210-308-1234	None	None	None	Ralph Aldis	'91
US:GLOBAL RESOURCES	Natural Resources	23.9	6.11	10,444.40	10,646.20	10,653.70	0.7	873-8637	210-308-1234	None	None	None	Ralph Aldis	'92
US:GOLD SHARES	Gold	319.1	2.49	14,101.10	11,670.40	8,058.40	2.0	873-8637	210-308-1234	None	None	None	Victor Flores	'92
US:GROWTH	Capital Appreciation	3.7	6.12	10,461.50	10,680.60	11,765.70	0.0	873-8637	210-308-1234	None	None	None	David Edwards	'87
US:INCOME	Utility	10.1	14.06	10,313.60	12,068.10	18,651.60	1.9	873-8637	210-308-1234	None	None	None	David Edwards	'87
US:INTMDT TREASURY	Fixed Income	4.1	11.21	10,347.30	11,494.60	☆	4.9	873-8637	210-308-1234	None	None	None	Allen Parker	'92
US:REAL ESTATE	Real Estate	21.7	10.96	9,581.50	10,945.00	14,194.70	1.6	873-8637	210-308-1234	None	None	None	Allen Parker	'87

★TNE GROWTH—Closed to new investors.

★TR CREDIT UNION FUNDS—Institutional funds.

PERFORMANCE OF MUTUAL FUNDS (continued)

FUND NAME	OBJECTIVE	TOTAL NET ASSETS ($ MIL) 5/31/93	NET ASSET $ VALUE 6/30/93	PERFORMANCE (Return on Initial $10,000 Investment) 3/31/93-6/30/93	6/30/92-6/30/93	6/30/88-6/30/93	DIVIDEND YIELD % 6/93	PHONE NUMBER 800	In-State	FEES Load	12b-1	Redemption	MANAGER	SINCE
US:SPECIAL TERM GOVT	Fixed Income	4.8	10.02	10,146.80	☆	☆	0.0	873-8637	210-308-1234	None	None	None	Allen Parker	'93
US:WORLD GOLD	Gold	99.6	14.59	13,648.30	15,357.90	10,495.90	0.0	873-8637	210-308-1234	None	None	None	Victor Flores	'90
USAA INV TR:BALANCED	Balanced	107.1	12.82	10,405.80	11,230.80	☆	3.6	382-8722	None	None	None	None	John W. Saunders, Jr.	'89
USAA INV TR:CORNERSTONE	Global Flexible	650.3	22.42	10,346.10	11,947.20	15,675.40	2.8	382-8722	None	None	None	None	Harry W. Miller	'90
USAA INV TR:GNMA	Fixed Income	276.5	10.56	10,227.60	11,040.60	☆	7.5	382-8722	None	None	None	None	Carl W. Shirley	'91
USAA INV TR:GOLD	Gold	185.1	9.21	13,063.80	14,551.40	10,638.80	0.4	382-8722	None	None	None	None	Stuart H. Wester	'92
USAA INV TR:INTL	International	60.5	13.37	10,437.20	10,850.40	☆	1.0	382-8722	None	None	None	None	David Peebles	'88
USAA INV TR:WORLD GROWTH	Global	45.8	11.05	10,193.70	☆	☆	0.0	382-8722	None	None	None	None	David Peebles	'92
USAA MUTUAL:AGGR GROWTH	Small-Company Growth	281.5	19.20	9,866.40	11,503.30	15,048.60	0.0	382-8722	None	None	None	None	Mark Johnson	'92
USAA MUTUAL:GROWTH	Growth	576.9	19.26	10,068.00	11,682.60	18,724.50	1.6	382-8722	None	None	None	None	William V. Fries	'89
USAA MUTUAL:GRO & INC	Growth & Income	N/A	9.99	☆	☆	☆	0.0	382-8722	None	None	None	None	R. David Ullom	'93
USAA MUTUAL:INCOME	Fixed Income	1,723.6	13.22	10,294.60	11,430.30	18,127.90	7.0	382-8722	None	None	None	None	John W. Saunders, Jr.	'85
USAA MUTUAL:INCOME STOCK	Equity Income	837.3	14.45	10,133.30	11,445.70	19,493.50	4.9	382-8722	None	None	None	None	Harry W. Miller	'89
USAA MUTUAL:SH-TM BOND	Fixed Income	N/A	10.04	☆	☆	☆	0.0	382-8722	None	None	None	None	Paul Lundmark	'93
USAFFINITY:GOVT INC	Fixed Income	1.8	10.28	10,303.00	☆	☆	0.0	800-3030	None	4.50	0.35	None	F. Horton	'92
USAFFINITY:GREEN	Environmental	1.3	10.46	9,640.60	☆	☆	0.0	800-3030	None	4.50	0.35	None	M. Stansky	'92
USAFFINITY:GROWTH	Growth	2.2	11.34	10,197.80	☆	☆	0.0	800-3030	None	4.50	0.35	None	R. Turner	'92
USAFFINITY:GROWTH & INC	Growth & Income	1.9	10.70	10,142.10	☆	☆	0.0	800-3030	None	4.50	0.35	None	Tengler/Spare	'92/'92
UST MSTR:AGING OF AMER	Growth	3.0	6.97	9,942.90	☆	☆	0.0	233-1136	619-456-9394	4.50	None	None	Roger F. Schaefer	'92
UST MSTR:BUS & INDUST	Growth	2.5	8.07	10,466.90	☆	☆	0.0	233-1136	619-456-9394	4.50	None	None	David J. Williams	'92
UST MSTR:COMMUN & ENTER	Growth	8.1	8.13	10,669.30	☆	☆	0.0	233-1136	619-456-9394	4.50	None	None	John J. Apruzese	'92
UST MSTR:EARLY LIFE	Small-Company Growth	7.3	8.08	10,904.20	☆	☆	0.0	233-1136	619-456-9394	4.50	None	None	Timothy W. Evnin	'92
UST MSTR:EMERGING AMER	Latin American	4.9	7.34	10,411.30	☆	☆	0.0	233-1136	619-456-9394	4.50	None	None	Harry C. Rowney	'92
UST MSTR:ENVIRONMENTAL	Environmental	2.4	6.36	9,151.10	☆	☆	0.0	233-1136	619-456-9394	4.50	None	None	Victor Sapuppo	'92
UST MSTR:EQUITY	Capital Appreciation	106.7	18.66	10,223.70	12,308.80	18,965.30	0.4	233-1136	619-456-9394	4.50	None	None	Laird Grant	'89
UST MSTR:GLBL COMPETITOR	Growth	2.6	7.37	10,193.60	☆	☆	0.0	233-1136	619-456-9394	4.50	None	None	Wendy S. Popowich	'92
UST MSTR:INC & GROWTH	Growth & Income	57.7	11.60	10,131.00	12,759.60	17,694.90	2.3	233-1136	619-456-9394	4.50	None	None	Richard L. Bayles	'90
UST MSTR:INT-TM MGD;ORIG	Fixed Income	28.1	7.28	10,236.40	☆	☆	0.0	233-1136	619-456-9394	4.50	None	None	Charles E. Rabus	'92
UST MSTR:INTL	International	32.8	9.09	10,496.50	10,571.40	13,328.80	0.1	233-1136	619-456-9394	4.50	None	None	Harry C. Rowney	'87
UST MSTR:L-T SPPLY ENERG	Natural Resources	2.1	8.28	10,601.80	☆	☆	0.0	233-1136	619-456-9394	4.50	None	None	Richard L. Bayles	'92
UST MSTR:MGD INC;ORIG	Fixed Income	105.3	9.77	10,326.10	11,522.60	17,603.10	5.7	233-1136	619-456-9394	4.50	None	None	Henry Milkewicz	'86
UST MSTR:MGD INC;PLAN	Fixed Income	1.7	9.77	10,315.40	11,475.00	☆	5.3	233-1136	619-456-9394	4.50	None	None	Henry Milkewicz	'91
UST MSTR:PACIFIC/ASIA	Pacific Region	13.6	8.27	10,968.20	☆	☆	0.0	233-1136	619-456-9394	4.50	None	None	Harry C. Rowney	'92
UST MSTR:PAN EUROPEAN	European Region	4.7	7.13	9,727.10	☆	☆	0.0	233-1136	619-456-9394	4.50	None	None	Harry C. Rowney	'92
UST MSTR:PRODUCTIVITY	Growth	5.3	7.29	10,504.30	☆	☆	0.0	233-1136	619-456-9394	4.50	None	None	Ronald C. Steele	'92
UST MSTR:SH-TM GOVT;ORIG	Fixed Income	15.8	7.07	10,098.50	☆	☆	0.0	233-1136	619-456-9394	4.50	None	None	Charles E. Rabus	'92
VALLEY FORGE	Growth	9.7	10.35	10,433.50	11,779.60	14,684.80	2.5	548-1942	215-688-6839	None	None	None	Bernard B. Klawans	'72
VALUE LINE ARM	Fixed Income	38.2	10.04	10,180.40	10,610.00	☆	5.5	223-0818	212-687-3965	None	None	None	Team Managed	'92
VALUE LINE AGGR INCOME	Fixed Income	37.2	7.63	10,367.10	11,573.60	15,930.90	8.7	223-0818	212-687-3965	None	None	None	Team Managed	'86
VALUE LINE CONVERTIBLE	Convertible Securities	45.7	14.29	10,330.30	12,475.90	17,655.80	4.1	223-0818	212-687-3965	None	None	None	Team Managed	'85
VALUE LINE	Growth & Income	329.0	19.13	10,351.80	12,546.80	21,183.20	0.6	223-0818	212-687-3965	None	None	None	Team Managed	'50
VALUE LINE INCOME	Equity Income	170.9	7.71	10,333.90	11,350.30	18,046.60	3.1	223-0818	212-687-3965	None	None	None	Team Managed	'52
VALUE LINE LVGE GROWTH	Capital Appreciation	290.1	23.91	10,382.10	12,486.40	19,551.60	0.6	223-0818	212-687-3965	None	None	None	Team Managed	'72
VALUE LINE SPECIAL SIT	Growth	87.7	15.82	10,689.20	11,711.60	14,363.60	0.0	223-0818	212-687-3965	None	None	None	Team Managed	'56
VALUE LINE US GOVT SEC	Fixed Income	440.0	13.07	10,287.80	11,160.60	16,601.30	6.8	223-0818	212-687-3965	None	None	None	Team Managed	'81
VAN ECK:ASIA DYNASTY	Pacific Region	14.5	10.50	11,017.80	☆	☆	0.0	221-2220	212-687-5201	4.75	0.25	None	Peter Soo	'93
VAN ECK:GOLD/RESOURCES	Gold	178.6	5.83	13,589.70	15,151.40	11,258.50	0.0	221-2220	212-687-5201	5.75	0.25	None	L. Palermo	'92
VAN ECK:INTL GROWTH	Global	1.3	9.37	9,884.00	9,880.00	☆	1.4	221-2220	212-687-5201	4.75	0.25	None	David Kenerson	'92
VAN ECK:INTL INVESTORS	Gold	639.6	14.26	13,906.70	14,226.50	13,597.20	0.8	221-2220	212-687-5201	5.75	None	None	Harry Bingham	'84
VAN ECK:SH-TM WRLD INC-C	World Income	23.5	8.56	9,910.40	8,999.80	☆	9.2	221-2220	212-687-5201	None	1.00	None	Kenerson/Buescher	'92/'92

VAN ECK TR:S-T WRLD;A	World Income	1.3	8.21	9,953.70	☆	☆	0.0	221-2220	212-687-5201	3.00	0.30	None	Buescher/Kenerson	'93/'93
VAN ECK TR:S-T WRLD;B	World Income	1.6	8.76	9,943.30	☆	☆	0.0	221-2220	212-687-5201	None	1.00	3.00	Buescher/Kenerson	'93/'93
VAN ECK:WORLD INCOME	World Income	312.9	9.06	9,889.80	9,591.80	15,784.20	9.9	221-2220	212-687-5201	4.75	0.25	None	Buescher/Kenerson	'87/'87
VAN ECK:WORLD TRENDS	Global	28.7	13.14	9,939.50	9,917.80	11,823.40	0.2	221-2220	212-687-5201	4.75	0.25	None	Klaus Buescher	'85
VANCE SANDERS EXCHANGE★	Growth	193.5	241.71	9,901.80	11,009.30	18,212.20	1.1	225-6265	617-482-8260	None	None	None	Thomas E. Faust, Jr.	'91
VANGUARD ADM:INT TREAS	Fixed Income	186.8	10.64	10,294.90	☆	☆	0.0	662-7447	215-669-1000	None	None	None	Ian A. MacKinnon	'92
VANGUARD ADM:LG TM TREAS	Fixed Income	82.1	10.89	10,527.20	☆	☆	0.0	662-7447	215-669-1000	None	None	None	Ian A. MacKinnon	'92
VANGUARD ADM:SH TM TREAS	Fixed Income	139.6	10.26	10,130.40	☆	☆	0.0	662-7447	215-669-1000	None	None	None	Ian A. MacKinnon	'92
VANGUARD ASSET ALLOC	Flexible	812.8	14.51	10,210.30	11,627.60	☆	4.0	662-7447	215-669-1000	None	0.20	None	Thomas Hazuka	'88
VANGUARD BALANCED INDEX	Balanced	232.8	10.70	10,142.10	☆	☆	0.0	662-7447	215-669-1000	None	0.20	None	George U. Sauter	'92
VANGUARD BOND INDEX	Fixed Income	1,233.6	10.22	10,270.00	11,172.10	16,788.50	6.5	662-7447	215-669-1000	None	0.20	None	Ian A. MacKinnon	'86
VANGUARD CONVERTIBLE	Convertible Securities	188.6	12.20	10,115.90	11,943.30	18,135.50	4.0	662-7447	215-669-1000	None	0.20	None	Rohit M. Desai	'86
VANGUARD EQUITY INCOME	Equity Income	989.6	13.96	10,256.20	11,620.50	17,850.80	4.2	662-7447	215-669-1000	None	0.20	None	Roger Newell	'88
VANGUARD EXPLORER	Small-Company Growth	684.6	44.32	10,128.00	12,097.90	17,595.50	0.3	662-7447	215-669-1000	None	0.20	None	Wisnewski/Granahan	'79/'90
VANGUARD FXD:GNMA PORT	Fixed Income	7,528.5	10.53	10,165.40	10,867.10	16,892.60	6.9	662-7447	215-669-1000	None	0.20	None	Paul G. Sullivan	'80
VANGUARD FXD:HI YLD	Fixed Income	2,364.3	7.90	10,446.30	11,745.20	16,422.90	8.9	662-7447	215-669-1000	None	0.20	1.00	Earl E. McEvoy	'84
VANGUARD FXD:INTMDT TREA	Fixed Income	827.0	11.16	10,299.80	11,511.60	☆	5.9	662-7447	215-669-1000	None	0.20	None	Ian A. MacKinnon	'91
VANGUARD FXD:INV GR CORP	Fixed Income	3,067.6	9.41	10,386.40	11,746.50	18,690.30	7.0	662-7447	215-669-1000	None	0.20	None	Paul G. Sullivan	'76
VANGUARD FXD:LG-TM TREAS	Fixed Income	825.6	10.61	10,535.60	12,031.50	18,347.50	6.6	662-7447	215-669-1000	None	0.20	None	Ian A. MacKinnon	'86
VANGUARD FXD:SHT-TM CORP	Fixed Income	3,077.4	11.00	10,150.20	10,818.40	15,862.30	5.9	662-7447	215-669-1000	None	0.20	None	Ian A. MacKinnon	'82
VANGUARD FXD:SHT-TM FED	Fixed Income	1,727.8	10.45	10,153.10	10,811.50	15,589.20	5.5	662-7447	215-669-1000	None	0.20	None	Ian A. MacKinnon	'87
VANGUARD FXD:SHT-TM TREA	Fixed Income	604.0	10.47	10,128.60	10,815.90	☆	4.9	662-7447	215-669-1000	None	0.20	None	Ian A. MacKinnon	'91
VANGUARD INDEX:EXTND MKT	Small-Company Growth	666.3	18.28	10,133.00	12,103.90	17,942.30	1.4	662-7447	215-669-1000	None	0.20	None	George U. Sauter	'87
VANGUARD INDEX:500 PORT	Growth & Income	7,709.8	42.45	10,043.30	11,340.70	19,233.40	2.6	662-7447	215-669-1000	None	0.20	None	George U. Sauter	'87
VANGUARD INDEX:S&P GRO	Growth & Income	43.7	9.89	9,793.80	☆	☆	0.0	662-7447	215-669-1000	None	0.20	None	George U. Sauter	'92
VANGUARD INDEX:S&P VALUE	Growth & Income	108.4	11.41	10,278.80	☆	☆	0.0	662-7447	215-669-1000	None	0.20	None	George U. Sauter	'92
VANGUARD INDEX:TOT STOCK	Growth	430.7	11.22	10,072.50	11,551.50	☆	3.1	662-7447	215-669-1000	None	0.20	None	George U. Sauter	'92
VANGUARD INSTL INDEX	Growth & Income	1,856.9	42.93	10,045.10	11,353.00	☆	2.7	662-7447	215-669-1000	None	0.20	None	George U. Sauter	'90
VANGUARD INTL EQ IDX:EUR	European Region	360.1	10.12	10,232.60	9,768.00	☆	2.6	662-7447	215-669-1000	None	0.20	None	George U. Sauter	'90
VANGUARD INTL EQ IDX:PAC	Pacific Region	370.9	10.38	11,728.80	14,557.40	☆	0.5	662-7447	215-669-1000	None	0.20	None	George U. Sauter	'90
VANGUARD/MORGAN GROWTH	Growth	1,163.5	12.80	10,031.30	11,566.80	17,427.70	1.4	662-7447	215-669-1000	None	0.20	None	Team Managed	'93
VANGUARD PREFERRED STK	Fixed Income	273.5	9.50	10,310.40	11,343.00	18,703.40	9.3	662-7447	215-669-1000	None	0.20	None	Earl E. McEvoy	'82
VANGUARD PRIMECAP	Growth	737.7	17.39	10,259.60	12,209.40	17,792.60	0.7	662-7447	215-669-1000	None	0.20	None	Howard B. Schow	'84
VANGUARD QUANTITATIVE	Growth & Income	449.4	17.45	10,175.20	11,823.70	19,863.00	3.3	662-7447	215-669-1000	None	0.20	None	John Nagorniak	'86
VANGUARD SMALL CAP STK	Small-Company Growth	342.4	15.00	10,155.70	12,499.00	16,453.40	1.2	662-7447	215-669-1000	None	0.20	None	George U. Sauter	'89
VANGUARD SPL:ENERGY	Natural Resources	248.7	17.38	10,781.60	13,706.50	20,361.40	1.9	662-7447	215-669-1000	None	0.20	1.00	Ernst Von Metzsch	'84
VANGUARD SPL:GOLD	Gold	469.8	11.96	13,128.40	13,563.20	13,549.40	1.5	662-7447	215-669-1000	None	0.20	1.00	David Hutchins	'87
VANGUARD SPL:HEALTH	Health/Biotechnology	530.3	32.48	10,597.10	10,576.40	22,634.20	2.1	662-7447	215-669-1000	None	0.20	1.00	Edward Owens	'84
VANGUARD SPL:SERVICE	Specialty	31.2	22.61	9,826.20	12,006.00	17,854.30	0.8	662-7447	215-669-1000	None	0.20	1.00	Matthew E. Megargel	'84
VANGUARD SPL:TCHNLGY	Science & Technology	57.7	18.54	10,158.90	12,610.20	16,803.40	0.6	662-7447	215-669-1000	None	0.20	1.00	Perry Traquina	'84
VANGUARD SPL:UTILITIES	Utility	576.6	12.07	10,288.10	12,590.40	☆	4.5	662-7447	215-669-1000	None	0.20	None	John R. Ryan	'92
VANGUARD STAR	Balanced	3,162.5	13.41	10,128.70	11,318.40	17,355.50	5.6	662-7447	215-669-1000	None	0.20	None	The Vanguard Group	'85
VANGUARD/TRUST EQ:INTL	International	844.8	28.55	10,713.30	10,851.90	13,970.80	2.0	662-7447	215-669-1000	None	0.20	None	Jarrod Wilcox	'91
VANGUARD/TRUST EQ:US	Growth & Income	77.2	30.84	10,415.20	12,239.60	16,463.20	1.8	662-7447	215-669-1000	None	0.20	None	John Geewax	'92
VANGUARD WELLESLEY INC	Income	4,281.0	19.41	10,305.30	11,763.90	19,005.90	6.2	662-7447	215-669-1000	None	0.20	None	Ryan/McEvoy	'87/'82
VANGUARD WELLINGTON	Balanced	6,803.9	20.30	10,276.80	11,421.20	17,594.80	4.6	662-7447	215-669-1000	None	0.20	None	Bajakian/Sullivan	'72/'75
VANGUARD WINDSOR★	Growth & Income	9,951.5	13.86	10,139.90	11,685.50	16,583.70	2.8	662-7447	215-669-1000	None	0.20	None	John C. Neff	'64
VANGUARD WINDSOR II	Growth & Income	6,602.2	16.91	10,084.90	11,570.20	19,024.30	3.1	662-7447	215-669-1000	None	0.20	None	Multiple Managers	'85
VANGUARD WORLD:INTL GRO	International	1,146.0	10.88	10,729.80	10,694.30	13,341.20	1.9	662-7447	215-669-1000	None	0.20	None	Richard R. Foulkes	'81
VANGUARD WORLD:US GROWTH	Growth	1,949.5	14.56	9,771.80	10,360.60	20,506.70	1.2	662-7447	215-669-1000	None	0.20	None	J. Parker Hall, III	'87
VANKAMP ADJ RT GOVT;A	Fixed Income	4.3	9.79	10,120.40	☆	☆	0.0	225-2222	708-684-6503	3.00	0.30	None	Laura Alter	'92
VANKAMP ADJ RT GOVT;B	Fixed Income	14.0	9.80	10,124.40	☆	☆	0.0	225-2222	708-684-6503	None	1.00	3.00	Laura Alter	'92
VANKAMP GRO & INC;A	Growth & Income	36.0	21.28	10,147.80	11,560.00	16,812.70	1.6	225-2222	708-684-6503	4.65	0.30	None	Dan Smith	'92
VANKAMP HIGH YIELD;A	Fixed Income	245.4	10.38	10,426.00	11,808.40	15,109.80	10.9	225-2222	708-684-6503	4.65	0.30	None	Kevin G. Mathews	'87
VANKAMP SHORT GLBL;A	World Income	202.4	9.11	10,449.80	10,285.70	☆	8.7	225-2222	708-684-6503	3.00	0.30	None	Tom Slefinger	'90

★VANCE SANDERS EXCHANGE—Closed to new investors.

★VANGUARD WINDSOR—Closed to new investors.

PERFORMANCE OF MUTUAL FUNDS (continued)

FUND NAME	OBJECTIVE	TOTAL NET ASSETS ($ MIL) 5/31/93	NET ASSET $ VALUE 6/30/93	PERFORMANCE (Return on Initial $10,000 Investment) 3/31/93-6/30/93	6/30/92-6/30/93	6/30/88-6/30/93	DIVIDEND YIELD % 6/93	PHONE NUMBER 800	In-State	FEES Load	12b-1	Redemption	MANAGER	SINCE
VANKAMP SHORT GLBL;B	World Income	386.0	9.10	10,419.40	10,201.60	☆	8.0	225-2222	708-684-6503	None	1.00	3.00	Tom Slefinger	'91
VANKAMP US GOVT;A	Fixed Income	3,634.3	16.06	10,246.90	11,011.30	16,810.60	8.3	225-2222	708-684-6503	4.65	0.30	None	J. Doyle	'84
VANKAMP US GOVT;B	Fixed Income	256.2	16.04	10,226.20	☆	☆	0.0	225-2222	708-684-6503	None	1.00	4.00	J. Doyle	'92
VENTURE INCOME (+) PLUS	Fixed Income	43.2	5.24	10,413.90	12,022.50	13,208.00	11.5	279-0279	505-983-4335	4.75	0.25	None	B. Clark Stamper	'90
VISTA:BALANCED	Balanced	6.8	11.13	10,387.60	☆	☆	0.0	348-4782	None	4.50	0.25	None	Joseph DeSautis	'92
VISTA:BOND	Fixed Income	59.0	11.13	10,273.00	11,239.80	☆	6.9	348-4782	None	None	None	None	Mark Buonaugurio	'91
VISTA:CAPITAL GROWTH	Growth	111.9	29.39	10,173.10	12,781.20	30,197.60	0.3	348-4782	None	4.75	0.25	None	Mark Tincher	'91
VISTA:EQUITY	Growth	117.8	13.14	10,001.50	11,202.70	☆	2.8	348-4782	None	None	0.05	None	Christina Michael	'92
VISTA:GLBL FXD INC	World Income	1.0	10.15	10,022.60	☆	☆	0.0	348-4782	None	4.50	0.25	None	Madis Sener	'92
VISTA:GOVT INCOME	Fixed Income	74.2	11.90	10,278.80	11,187.40	16,608.40	5.8	348-4782	None	4.50	0.25	None	Tom Nelson	'92
VISTA:GROWTH & INCOME	Growth & Income	498.2	30.11	10,330.50	12,246.70	32,852.60	1.1	348-4782	None	4.75	0.25	None	Mark Tincher	'91
VISTA:INTL EQUITY	International	2.8	10.76	10,346.20	☆	☆	0.0	348-4782	None	4.75	0.25	None	Greg Adams	'92
VISTA:SH-TM BD	Fixed Income	68.5	10.18	10,092.40	10,509.50	☆	6.0	348-4782	None	None	None	None	Linda Struble	'90
VOLUMETRIC FUND	Growth	11.7	16.15	10,093.80	11,540.70	16,756.90	0.5	541-3863	914-623-7637	None	None	None	Gabriel Gibs	'86
VOYAGEUR US GOVT SEC	Fixed Income	104.0	10.99	10,338.20	11,425.20	17,371.40	7.5	553-2143	612-376-7000	4.75	0.25	None	Jane M. Wyatt	'90
VOYAGEUR GROWTH STOCK	Growth	27.7	17.76	9,406.80	10,209.70	18,724.10	0.0	553-2143	612-376-7000	4.75	0.25	None	James C. King	'92
VULCAN:BOND	Fixed Income	26.2	10.75	10,252.40	11,300.90	☆	6.1	441-7379	302-792-6400	4.00	None	None	Trust Investment Dept.	'92
VULCAN:STOCK	Growth	33.2	10.43	9,840.60	10,970.10	☆	2.0	441-7379	302-792-6400	4.50	None	None	Trust Investment Dept.	'92
WADDELL & REED:GL INC	World Income	8.0	9.58	9,992.50	☆	☆	0.0	366-5465	913-236-1303	None	1.00	3.00	John E. Sundeen	'92
WADDELL & REED:GROWTH	Growth	11.2	12.54	10,736.30	☆	☆	0.0	366-5465	913-236-1303	None	1.00	3.00	Mark G. Seferovich	'92
WADDELL & REED:LTD-TM	Fixed Income	7.4	10.14	10,173.30	☆	☆	0.0	366-5465	913-236-1303	None	1.00	3.00	W. Patrick Sterner	'92
WADDELL & REED:TOT RTN	Growth & Income	23.1	11.34	10,243.90	☆	☆	0.0	366-5465	913-236-1303	None	1.00	3.00	Russell E. Thompson	'92
WADE FUND	Growth	0.5	33.57	10,640.30	11,458.90	15,168.70	0.5	None	901-682-4613	None	None	None	Maury Wade	'73
WALL STREET	Growth	10.5	7.39	10,249.70	11,287.30	15,349.30	0.1	443-4693	212-207-1660	4.00	None	None	Robert Morse	'84
WRBG PINCUS CAP APP;COM	Growth	140.7	14.25	10,089.80	11,930.90	17,936.60	0.3	257-5614	212-878-0600	None	None	None	Andrew H. Massie	'89
WRBG PINCUS CAP APP;SR 2	Growth	4.1	14.25	10,080.10	11,892.70	☆	0.0	257-5614	212-878-0600	None	0.50	None	Andrew H. Massie	'91
WRBG PINCUS EMER GR;COM	Small-Company Growth	113.0	21.32	10,466.40	12,972.80	20,412.70	0.0	257-5614	212-878-0600	None	None	None	Elizabeth Dater	'88
WRBG PINCUS EMER GR;SR 2	Small-Company Growth	14.1	21.15	10,449.60	12,909.30	☆	0.0	257-5614	212-878-0600	None	0.50	None	Elizabeth Dater	'91
WRBG PINCUS FXD INC	Fixed Income	82.4	10.28	10,241.20	11,133.00	15,332.60	5.9	257-5614	212-878-0600	None	None	None	Dale C. Christensen	'92
WRBG PINCUS GL FXD;COM	World Income	29.2	10.95	10,286.80	11,165.80	☆	5.9	257-5614	212-878-0600	None	None	None	Dale C. Christensen	'90
WRBG PINCUS INSTL:INT EQ	International	54.0	11.65	10,552.50	☆	☆	0.0	257-5614	212-878-0600	None	None	None	Richard King	'92
WRBG PINCUS INTL EQ;COM	International	180.4	14.77	10,532.80	11,264.00	☆	0.1	257-5614	212-878-0600	None	None	None	Richard King	'89
WRBG PINCUS INTL EQ;SR 2	International	6.6	14.72	10,526.40	11,217.40	☆	0.0	257-5614	212-878-0600	None	0.50	None	Richard King	'91
WRBG PINCUS INTMDT GOVT	Fixed Income	93.9	11.01	10,180.70	11,051.80	☆	5.4	257-5614	212-878-0600	None	None	None	Dale C. Christensen	'92
WASATCH:AGGRESSIVE EQU	Small-Company Growth	18.1	18.04	10,335.60	12,299.40	20,752.10	0.7	551-1700	801-533-0778	None	None	None	Samuel S. Stewart Jr.	'87
WASATCH:GROWTH	Growth	16.4	14.81	10,383.60	11,565.50	19,141.00	2.8	551-1700	801-533-0778	None	None	None	Samuel S. Stewart Jr.	'87
WASATCH:INCOME	Fixed Income	4.4	10.32	10,068.30	10,611.60	16,091.90	5.1	551-1700	801-533-0778	None	None	None	Samuel S. Stewart Jr.	'87
WASATCH:MID-CAP	Growth	2.4	10.37	9,904.50	☆	☆	0.0	551-1700	801-533-0778	None	None	None	Samuel S. Stewart Jr.	'92
WASHINGTON MUTUAL INV	Growth & Income	11,503.0	17.80	10,194.00	11,644.50	18,749.40	3.1	421-0180	210-530-4000	5.75	0.25	None	Multiple Managers	'52
WAYNE HUMMER GROWTH	Growth	95.7	21.38	9,871.30	10,931.50	18,198.20	1.3	621-4477	312-431-1700	None	None	None	Alan Bird	'83
WAYNE HUMMER INCOME	Fixed Income	26.4	15.60	10,293.00	☆	☆	0.0	621-4477	312-431-1700	None	None	None	David Poitras	'92
WEITZ:FIXED INCOME	Fixed Income	19.8	11.17	10,210.60	10,871.30	☆	5.4	232-4161	402-391-1980	None	None	None	Wallace Weitz	'88
WEITZ:VALUE	Growth & Income	75.6	15.54	10,151.90	11,796.80	18,704.30	1.4	232-4161	402-391-1980	None	None	None	Wallace Weitz	'86
WESTCORE:BALANCED	Flexible	64.1	18.52	10,017.00	10,801.20	☆	3.3	392-2673	303-623-2577	4.50	None	None	Fish/Cahill	'91/'91
WESTCORE:BASIC VALUE	Growth & Income	94.3	22.23	9,855.80	10,814.10	15,611.10	1.5	392-2673	303-623-2577	4.50	None	None	Charlie Fish	'87
WESTCORE:BOND PLUS	Fixed Income	61.0	15.90	10,226.40	10,960.90	16,286.20	6.4	392-2673	303-623-2577	4.50	None	None	Warren Hastings III	'90
WESTCORE:EQUITY INCOME	Equity Income	35.8	11.63	10,180.80	11,383.50	17,575.80	1.7	392-2673	303-623-2577	4.50	None	None	Larry Luchini	'88
WESTCORE:GNMA	Fixed Income	31.2	16.47	10,183.80	10,823.00	16,293.00	6.5	392-2673	303-623-2577	4.50	None	None	Warren Hastings III	'90
WESTCORE:INTMDT-TM BOND	Fixed Income	99.5	10.81	10,240.40	11,174.20	16,017.40	5.8	392-2673	303-623-2577	4.50	None	None	John Cormey	'89
WESTCORE:LONG-TERM BOND	Fixed Income	26.3	11.57	10,450.00	11,889.10	18,303.40	6.6	392-2673	303-623-2577	4.50	None	None	John Cormey	'88

WESTCORE:MIDCO GROWTH	Growth	231.4	15.73	10,274.30	12,424.70	23,867.00	0.0	392-2673	303-623-2577	4.50	None	None	Todger Anderson	'86
WESTCORE:MODERN VAL EQU	Growth & Income	28.2	13.92	10,173.70	11,723.30	17,679.10	2.0	392-2673	303-623-2577	4.50	None	None	Varilyn Schock	'88
WESTCORE:SHORT-TERM GOVT	Fixed Income	51.2	15.85	10,099.70	10,544.00	14,940.50	4.6	392-2673	303-623-2577	2.00	None	None	Warren Hastings III	'90
WESTON:NEW CENTURY CAP	Flexible	38.4	11.76	10,111.80	11,582.90	☆	1.3	None	617-239-0445	None	0.25	None	Douglas Biggar	'89
WESTON:NEW CENTURY I	Income	20.8	11.29	10,262.00	11,487.70	☆	3.4	None	617-239-0445	None	0.25	None	Douglas Biggar	'89
WESTWOOD:BALANCED;INSTL	Balanced	4.0	10.40	10,092.70	11,417.50	☆	2.0	253-4510	None	4.00	None	None	Schaer/McCubbins	'91
WESTWOOD:EQUITY;INSTL	Capital Appreciation	7.8	9.27	9,946.40	11,499.30	15,947.80	4.5	253-4510	None	4.00	None	None	P. McCubbins	'92
WESTWOOD:INTMDT BD;INSTL	Fixed Income	2.7	10.49	10,201.30	11,211.10	☆	4.3	253-4510	None	4.00	None	None	J. Schaer	'91
WM BLAIR:GROWTH SHARES	Growth	122.5	9.48	10,063.70	11,623.40	19,763.30	0.5	742-7272	312-853-2424	None	None	None	Neal L. Seltzer	'85
WM BLAIR:INCOME	Fixed Income	162.8	10.81	10,220.40	10,957.10	☆	7.4	742-7272	312-853-2424	None	None	None	Bentley M. Myer	'91
WM BLAIR:INTL GROWTH SHS	International	N/A	11.39	10,674.80	☆	☆	0.0	742-7272	312-853-2424	None	None	None	Framlington Mgmt	'92
WILLIAM PENN:QUALITY INC	Fixed Income	18.2	10.96	10,326.80	11,538.00	17,171.50	8.1	523-8440	215-670-1031	4.75	0.34	None	Miller Anderson & Sherr.	'87
WILLIAM PENN:US GOVT	Fixed Income	43.7	11.00	10,409.70	11,525.20	16,954.20	7.9	523-8440	215-670-1031	4.75	0.42	None	Miller Anderson & Sherr.	'87
WINTHROP FOCUS:AGG GRO★	Small-Company Growth	61.0	14.48	10,233.20	12,486.30	19,169.90	0.3	225-8011	212-504-4000	None	0.50	4.00	Engle/Haubold	'89/'89
WINTHROP FOCUS:FIX INC	Fixed Income	41.6	10.78	10,260.20	11,187.90	16,793.20	6.0	225-8011	212-504-4000	None	0.25	4.00	Cathy Jameson	'86
WINTHROP FOCUS:GROWTH	Growth	48.5	10.46	10,056.50	11,349.40	16,321.60	1.4	225-8011	212-504-4000	None	0.50	4.00	Gary Haubold	'89
WINTHROP FOCUS:GRO&INC★	Growth & Income	48.3	12.79	10,114.00	11,716.00	17,519.00	3.0	225-8011	212-504-4000	None	0.50	4.00	James Engle	'86
WOOD ISLAND GROWTH FUND	Growth	5.4	14.39	10,027.90	11,105.70	17,794.40	2.3	None	415-461-3850	None	None	None	Siebel/Kirk	'84/'84
WOOD ISLAND TOTAL RETURN	Flexible	2.1	9.65	10,115.30	10,993.10	16,613.90	4.6	None	415-461-3850	None	None	None	Siebel/Kirk	'83/'83
WOODWARD:BOND;RTL	Fixed Income	388.2	10.72	10,351.10	11,292.60	☆	7.9	688-3350	None	4.50	0.35	None	Douglas Swanson	'91
WOODWARD:EQ INDEX;RTL	Growth & Income	286.5	10.90	10,041.30	☆	☆	0.0	688-3350	None	None	0.35	None	Frederick R. Neumann	'92
WOODWARD:GRO/VAL;RTL	Growth & Income	345.4	11.09	10,303.80	11,395.80	☆	2.2	688-3350	None	4.50	0.35	None	George Abel	'91
WOODWARD:INTMDT BD;RTL	Fixed Income	304.3	10.56	10,245.40	10,949.80	☆	7.1	688-3350	None	4.50	0.35	None	Douglas Swanson	'91
WOODWARD:INTRINSIC;RTL	Growth & Income	142.4	10.98	10,149.60	11,538.30	☆	7.6	688-3350	None	4.50	0.35	None	Peter Zuger	'91
WOODWARD:OPPTY;RTL	Small-Company Growth	240.4	13.58	10,216.00	13,393.90	☆	1.5	688-3350	None	4.50	0.35	None	Champagne/Doyle	'91/'91
WORKING ASSETS CIT BAL	Balanced	28.3	11.32	10,008.80	11,373.20	☆	0.6	223-7010	603-436-5152	4.00	0.35	None	DiSilva/Janeway	'92/'92
WORKING ASSETS CIT GRO	Growth	39.8	11.40	9,921.70	11,282.80	☆	0.1	223-7010	603-436-5152	4.00	0.35	None	Harold Janeway	'92
WORKING ASSETS CIT INC	Fixed Income	11.7	10.60	10,222.50	11,007.60	☆	4.4	223-7010	603-436-5152	2.00	0.35	None	Linda DiSilva	'92
WRLD FDS:NEWPORT TIGER	Pacific Region	170.5	16.88	10,827.50	12,023.20	☆	0.3	527-9500	804-285-8211	5.00	None	None	John Mussey	'89
WRLD FDS:VNTBEL EUROPAC	International	75.4	13.58	10,280.10	10,557.60	12,786.80	1.0	527-9500	804-285-8211	None	None	None	Felix Rovelli	'90
WRLD FDS:VNTBEL US VALUE	Growth & Income	34.5	12.32	10,016.30	11,481.80	☆	1.3	527-9500	804-285-8211	None	None	None	Ed Walczak	'90
WPG FUNDS TR:DVD INCOME	Equity Income	21.2	13.85	10,355.50	11,852.70	17,106.20	3.9	223-3332	212-908-9500	None	None	None	Nelson Schaenen, Jr.	'89
WPG FUNDS TR:GOVT SEC	Fixed Income	303.4	10.67	10,322.80	11,162.70	16,705.00	7.3	223-3332	212-908-9500	None	None	None	David W. Hoyle	'86
WPG FUNDS TR:QUANT EQ	Growth & Income	28.0	5.45	10,206.00	☆	☆	0.0	223-3332	212-908-9500	None	None	None	Joseph Pappo	'93
WPG GROWTH	Small-Company Growth	167.1	132.52	10,539.20	12,730.90	18,461.10	1.3	223-3332	212-908-9500	None	None	None	Melville Straus	'86
WPG GROWTH & INCOME	Growth & Income	57.2	25.20	10,182.00	12,146.20	18,996.70	1.7	223-3332	212-908-9500	None	None	None	A. Roy Knutsen	'92
WPG INTERNATIONAL	International	10.8	9.48	10,259.70	10,315.60	☆	0.0	223-3332	212-908-9500	None	None	None	Bruce Ackerman	'92
WPG TUDOR FUND	Capital Appreciation	276.3	25.38	10,444.40	11,661.30	18,513.70	0.6	223-3332	212-908-9500	None	None	None	Melville Straus	'73
WRIGHT EQUI:AUSTRALASIAN	Pacific Region	0.2	8.23	9,915.70	9,492.70	☆	1.1	888-9471	203-333-6666	None	0.50	None	Team Managed	'90
WRIGHT EQUI:DUTCH	European Region	2.3	8.60	9,557.90	8,741.00	☆	1.0	888-9471	203-333-6666	None	0.50	None	Team Managed	'90
WRIGHT EQUI:HONG KONG	Pacific Region	5.8	14.46	10,914.10	10,663.70	☆	1.2	888-9471	203-333-6666	None	0.50	None	Team Managed	'90
WRIGHT EQUI:ITALIAN	European Region	0.8	4.95	11,196.50	8,026.00	☆	0.2	888-9471	203-333-6666	None	0.50	None	Team Managed	'90
WRIGHT EQUI:SPANISH	European Region	0.7	5.62	9,477.60	7,341.40	☆	1.2	888-9471	203-333-6666	None	0.50	None	Team Managed	'90
WRIGHT EQUI:UK	European Region	0.3	8.89	10,033.80	8,779.90	☆	0.3	888-9471	203-333-6666	None	0.50	None	Team Managed	'90
WRIGHT EQ:INTL BLUE CHIP	International	76.6	11.35	10,114.90	9,838.10	☆	0.7	232-0013	203-333-6666	None	0.20	None	Team Managed	'89
WRIGHT EQ:JR BLUE CHIP	Small-Company Growth	66.2	11.57	9,772.20	10,931.60	14,011.50	0.2	232-0013	203-333-6666	None	0.20	None	Team Managed	'85
WRIGHT EQ:QUAL CORE EQU	Growth & Income	91.8	12.88	9,714.40	10,922.70	17,431.80	1.1	232-0013	203-333-6666	None	0.20	None	Team Managed	'85
WRIGHT EQ:SEL BLUE CHIP	Growth & Income	175.5	14.36	9,730.00	10,953.50	16,980.10	1.2	232-0013	203-333-6666	None	0.20	None	Team Managed	'83
WRIGHT INC:CURRENT INC	Fixed Income	106.7	10.97	10,198.60	10,956.60	16,688.50	6.9	232-0013	203-333-6666	None	0.20	None	Team Managed	'87
WRIGHT INC:GOVT OBLIG	Fixed Income	30.3	14.27	10,499.90	11,966.90	17,949.70	6.3	232-0013	203-333-6666	None	0.20	None	Team Managed	'83
WRIGHT INC:NEAR TERM BD	Fixed Income	348.9	10.96	10,197.10	10,985.20	15,614.00	6.4	232-0013	203-333-6666	None	0.20	None	Team Managed	'83
WRIGHT INC:TOTAL RETURN	Fixed Income	228.2	13.26	10,298.90	11,382.40	16,435.30	6.1	232-0013	203-333-6666	None	0.20	None	Team Managed	'83
YACKTMAN FUND	Growth	125.2	9.24	9,310.60	☆	☆	0.0	525-8258	None	None	0.15	None	Donald Yacktman	'92
YAMAICHI FDS:GLOBAL FUND	Global	43.5	8.26	10,429.30	11,581.00	11,592.00	0.6	257-0228	212-432-8620	4.75	0.40	None	Edward Burke	'90
ZSA EQUITY	Capital Appreciation	0.6	11.10	10,276.90	☆	☆	0.0	525-3863	919-972-9922	None	0.35	None	Zaske, Sarafa & Assoc.	'92

★WINTHROP FOCUS: AGG GRO — Fund is a result of the reorganization of the Neuwirth fund on 7/10/92. Performance numbers prior to 7/10/92 are those of Neuwirth.

★WINTHROP FOCUS: GRO & INC — Fund is result of reorganization of Pine Street fund on 7/10/92. Performance numbers prior to 7/10/92 are those of Pine Street.

PERFORMANCE OF MUTUAL FUNDS *(continued)*

FUND NAME	OBJECTIVE	TOTAL NET ASSETS ($ MIL) 5/31/93	NET ASSET $ VALUE 6/30/93	PERFORMANCE (Return on Initial $10,000 Investment) 3/31/93-6/30/93	6/30/92-6/30/93	6/30/88-6/30/93	DIVIDEND YIELD % 6/93	PHONE NUMBER 800	In-State	FEES Load	12b-1	Redemption	MANAGER	SINCE
ZSA GROWTH AND INCOME	Growth & Income	2.7	11.42	10,612.80	☆	☆	0.0	525-3863	919-972-9922	None	0.35	None	Zaske, Sarafa & Assoc.	'92
ZWEIG SR TR:APPREC;A	Small-Company Growth	213.0	14.11	10,085.80	11,992.40	☆	0.4	272-2700	212-635-9800	5.50	0.30	None	David Katzen	'91
ZWEIG SR TR:APPREC;B	Small-Company Growth	66.7	14.04	10,064.50	11,898.30	☆	0.0	272-2700	212-635-9800	None	1.00	1.25	David Katzen	'92
ZWEIG SR TR:GOVT SEC;A	Fixed Income	65.1	10.28	10,194.50	11,107.90	15,341.00	6.6	272-2700	212-635-9800	4.75	0.30	None	Timothy Clark	'92
ZWEIG SR TR:GOVT SEC;B	Fixed Income	12.2	10.26	10,149.30	10,999.10	☆	5.9	272-2700	212-635-9800	None	0.75	1.25	Timothy Clark	'92
ZWEIG SR TR:MGD ASST;A	Flexible	62.2	11.93	10,248.30	☆	☆	0.0	272-2700	212-635-9800	5.50	0.30	None	Timothy Clark	'93
ZWEIG SR TR:MGD ASST;B	Flexible	168.5	11.91	10,222.60	☆	☆	0.0	272-2700	212-635-9800	None	1.00	1.25	Timothy Clark	'93
ZWEIG SR TR:PRIORITY;A	Capital Appreciation	57.6	13.81	10,252.40	11,787.70	19,501.60	0.6	272-2700	212-635-9800	5.50	0.30	None	Joe Kalish	'89
ZWEIG SR TR:PRIORITY;B	Capital Appreciation	17.1	13.75	10,223.00	11,682.20	☆	0.0	272-2700	212-635-9800	None	1.00	1.25	Joe Kalish	'92
ZWEIG SR TR:STRATEGY;A	Growth	371.5	13.79	10,117.20	12,148.50	☆	1.2	272-2700	212-635-9800	5.50	0.30	None	David Katzen	'89
ZWEIG SR TR:STRATEGY;B	Growth	101.7	13.81	10,095.00	12,058.40	☆	0.3	272-2700	212-635-9800	None	1.00	1.25	David Katzen	'92

Municipal Bond Funds

FUND NAME	OBJECTIVE	TOTAL NET ASSETS ($ MIL) 5/31/93	NET ASSET $ VALUE 6/30/93	PERFORMANCE (Return on Initial $10,000 Investment) 3/31/93-6/30/93	6/30/92-6/30/93	6/30/88-6/30/93	DIVIDEND YIELD % 6/93	PHONE NUMBER 800	In-State	FEES Load	12b-1	Redemption	MANAGER	SINCE
AAL MUNICIPAL BOND★	General Muni	279.4	11.11	10,274.30	11,097.10	15,304.30	5.1	553-6319	414-734-5721	4.75	0.25	None	Duff & Phelps Inv. Co.	'87
AARP INS TF GEN BOND	Insured Muni	1,853.1	18.54	10,347.40	11,289.00	16,569.00	4.8	253-2277	617-439-4640	None	None	None	Carleton/Condon	'88/'89
ABT FL HIGH INCOME MUNI	Florida Muni	40.6	10.50	10,367.10	11,273.80	☆	7.1	553-7838	407-655-7255	4.75	0.25	None	Steven Eldredge	'92
ABT FL TAX-FREE	Florida Muni	199.9	11.40	10,319.90	11,234.50	15,989.50	5.9	553-7838	407-655-7255	4.75	0.25	None	Steven Eldredge	'89
AIM:MUNICIPAL BOND	General Muni	283.7	8.58	10,314.00	11,159.30	16,213.70	5.9	347-1919	713-626-1919	4.75	0.25	None	Berry/Turman	'92/'92
AIM:TAX-EX BOND OF CT	Connecticut Muni	38.4	11.08	10,323.40	11,169.80	☆	5.7	347-1919	713-626-1919	4.75	0.25	None	Berry/Turman	'92/'92
ALABAMA TAX FREE BOND	Single-State Muni	1.8	10.22	10,281.10	☆	☆	0.0	525-3863	919-972-9922	None	None	None	Timothy S. Healey	'93
ALLIANCE MUNI:CA;A	California Muni	462.5	10.71	10,328.10	11,230.30	16,475.70	5.7	227-4618	201-319-4000	4.50	0.30	None	Susan Peabody	'86
ALLIANCE MUNI:CA;B	California Muni	49.5	10.71	10,310.20	☆	☆	0.0	227-4618	201-319-4000	None	1.00	3.00	Susan Peabody	'92
ALLIANCE MUNI:CA;C	California Muni	13.7	10.71	☆	☆	☆	0.0	227-4618	201-319-4000	None	1.00	None	Susan Peabody	'93
ALLIANCE MUNI:INS CA;A	California Muni	105.5	13.98	10,297.40	11,285.80	16,260.20	5.1	227-4618	201-319-4000	4.50	0.29	None	Susan Peabody	'86
ALLIANCE MUNI:INS CA;B	California Muni	6.5	13.98	10,279.70	☆	☆	0.0	227-4618	201-319-4000	None	1.00	3.00	Susan Peabody	'92
ALLIANCE MUNI:INS CA;C	California Muni	0.9	13.98	☆	☆	☆	0.0	227-4618	201-319-4000	None	1.00	None	Susan Peabody	'93
ALLIANCE MUNI:INS NA;A	Insured Muni	170.9	10.59	10,361.70	11,257.40	16,468.40	5.4	227-4618	201-319-4000	4.50	0.28	None	Susan Peabody	'86
ALLIANCE MUNI:INS NA;B	Insured Muni	18.2	10.58	10,334.00	☆	☆	0.0	227-4618	201-319-4000	None	1.00	3.00	Susan Peabody	'92

ALLIANCE MUNI:INS NA;C	Insured Muni	N/A	10.58	☆	☆	☆	0.0	227-4618	201-319-4000	None	1.00	None	Susan Peabody	'93
ALLIANCE MUNI:NATL;A	General Muni	337.9	10.89	10,383.90	11,245.80	16,812.60	5.8	227-4618	201-319-4000	4.50	0.29	None	Susan Peabody	'86
ALLIANCE MUNI:NATL;B	General Muni	94.8	10.89	10,366.10	☆	☆	0.0	227-4618	201-319-4000	None	1.00	3.00	Susan Peabody	'92
ALLIANCE MUNI:NATL;C	General Muni	N/A	10.88	☆	☆	☆	0.0	227-4618	201-319-4000	None	1.00	None	Susan Peabody	'93
ALLIANCE MUNI:NY;A	New York Muni	189.8	10.05	10,371.00	11,284.40	16,776.60	5.8	227-4618	201-319-4000	4.50	0.29	None	Susan Peabody	'86
ALLIANCE MUNI:NY;B	New York Muni	25.3	10.04	10,342.70	☆	☆	0.0	227-4618	201-319-4000	None	1.00	3.00	Susan Peabody	'92
ALLIANCE MUNI:NY;C	New York Muni	1.9	10.04	☆	☆	☆	0.0	227-4618	201-319-4000	None	1.00	None	Susan Peabody	'93
AMBASSADOR:TX-FR INT;FID	Short-Term Muni	1.2	10.63	10,175.80	☆	☆	0.0	892-4366	None	None	None	None	Tony Cianfaro	'92
AMBASSADOR:TX-FR INT;INV	Short-Term Muni	119.5	10.63	10,175.80	10,739.40	14,038.40	3.6	892-4366	None	3.00	None	None	Woodbridge Cap Mgt Inc	'87
AMBASSADOR:TX-FR INT;RET	Short-Term Muni	1.9	10.63	10,175.80	☆	☆	0.0	892-4366	None	3.00	0.25	None	Tony Cianfaro	'92
AMCORE VINTAGE INT TX-FR	Intermediate Muni	17.4	10.25	10,305.50	☆	☆	0.0	662-4203	None	3.75	0.25	None	Dean Countryman	'93
AMER CAP MUNI BOND;A	General Muni	319.2	10.39	10,294.50	11,145.00	16,318.20	5.9	421-5666	713-993-0500	4.75	0.25	None	Bob Evans	'88
AMER CAP MUNI BOND;B	General Muni	13.3	10.42	10,303.20	☆	☆	0.0	421-5666	713-993-0500	None	1.00	4.00	Bob Evans	'92
AMER CAP TX-EX:HI YD;A	High-Yield Muni	355.0	11.26	10,245.00	11,054.00	15,395.90	7.3	421-5666	713-993-0500	4.75	0.25	None	Wayne Godlin	'91
AMER CAP TX-EX:HI YD;B	High-Yield Muni	54.0	11.26	10,226.00	☆	☆	0.0	421-5666	713-993-0500	None	1.00	4.00	Wayne Godlin	'92
AMER CAP TX-EX:INS;A	Insured Muni	73.0	11.55	10,212.50	10,885.40	15,062.10	5.8	421-5666	713-993-0500	4.75	0.25	None	Bob Evans	'89
AMER CAP TX-EX:INS;B	Insured Muni	25.0	11.55	10,194.00	☆	☆	0.0	421-5666	713-993-0500	None	1.00	4.00	Bob Evans	'92
AMER CAP TEXAS MUNI;A	Texas Muni	18.3	10.14	10,317.70	11,160.90	☆	5.9	421-5666	713-993-0500	4.75	0.25	None	Bob Evans	'92
AMER CAP TEXAS MUNI;B	Texas Muni	5.9	10.14	10,297.30	☆	☆	0.0	421-5666	713-993-0500	None	1.00	4.00	Bob Evans	'92
AMER TX-EX SR I:MD	Maryland Muni	60.7	15.61	10,335.50	11,094.30	15,356.50	5.1	421-0180	210-530-4000	4.75	0.25	None	Multiple Managers	'86
AMER TX-EX SR I:VA	Virginia Muni	75.5	16.09	10,331.50	11,160.40	15,490.30	5.1	421-0180	210-530-4000	4.75	0.25	None	Multiple Managers	'86
AMER TX-EX SR II:CA	California Muni	197.3	16.03	10,358.90	11,285.70	15,689.80	5.2	421-0180	210-530-4000	4.75	0.25	None	Multiple Managers	'86
AMER PERFORM:INTMDT TXFR	Intermediate Muni	15.4	10.63	10,287.50	11,122.60	☆	5.2	762-7085	None	3.00	0.25	None	Bill Bequette	'92
ARCH TX-EX:MO;INV	Missouri Muni	23.0	11.65	10,302.10	11,146.90	☆	4.9	451-2010	617-722-7868	4.50	None	None	Gary Hurlbut	'90
ATLAS:CA MUNI BOND	California Muni	169.2	11.32	10,349.10	11,242.60	☆	5.2	933-2852	None	3.00	0.25	None	Andrew Windmueller	'91
ATLAS:NATL MUNI BOND	General Muni	48.4	11.36	10,377.80	11,282.90	☆	5.2	933-2852	None	3.00	0.25	None	Andrew Windmueller	'91
BABSON TX-FR INC:LONG	General Muni	33.9	9.49	10,337.40	11,184.20	16,040.00	4.8	422-2766	816-471-5200	None	None	None	Joel Vernick	'86
BABSON TX-FR INC:SHORT	Short-Term Muni	28.0	11.05	10,167.80	10,750.30	14,165.10	4.5	422-2766	816-471-5200	None	None	None	Joel Vernick	'86
BB&T:NC INTMDT TX-FR;INV	North Carolina Muni	8.7	10.16	10,185.30	☆	☆	0.0	228-1872	614-899-4668	2.00	0.25	None	Branch Banking & Trust	'93
BB&T:NC INTMDT TX-FR;TR★	North Carolina Muni	16.6	10.16	10,175.20	☆	☆	0.0	228-1872	614-899-4668	None	None	None	Branch Banking & Trust	'92
BENHAM CA TX-FR:HIGH YLD	California Muni	104.2	9.54	10,424.20	11,207.30	16,022.10	5.9	472-3389	415-965-4274	None	None	None	Steve Permut	'88
BENHAM CA TX-FR:INSURED	California Muni	193.4	10.46	10,349.50	11,315.20	16,240.60	5.3	472-3389	415-965-4274	None	None	None	David MacEwen	'88
BENHAM CA TX-FR:INTMDT	California Muni	392.5	11.26	10,268.60	11,041.80	14,830.20	5.0	472-3389	415-965-4274	None	None	None	David MacEwen	'91
BENHAM CA TX-FR:LONG	California Muni	317.5	11.82	10,396.70	11,277.20	16,048.20	5.6	472-3389	415-965-4274	None	None	None	David MacEwen	'88
BENHAM NATL TX-FR:INT-TM	Intermediate Muni	67.5	11.03	10,274.80	11,015.90	15,030.30	4.7	472-3389	415-965-4274	None	None	None	David MacEwen	'88
BENHAM NATL TX-FR:LNG-TM	General Muni	54.1	12.08	10,426.40	11,418.00	16,523.70	5.1	472-3389	415-965-4274	None	None	None	David MacEwen	'88
S BERNSTEIN:CA MUNI	California Muni	128.7	13.66	10,203.00	10,914.00	☆	4.5	None	212-756-4097	None	None	None	Investment Policy Group	'90
S BERNSTEIN:DIV MUNI	Intermediate Muni	403.8	13.60	10,220.40	10,901.20	☆	4.8	None	212-756-4097	None	None	None	Investment Policy Group	'89
S BERNSTEIN:NY MUNI	New York Muni	286.8	13.65	10,235.50	10,914.50	☆	5.0	None	212-756-4097	None	None	None	Investment Policy Group	'89
BILTMORE:SC MUNI	South Carolina Muni	73.7	11.00	10,302.80	11,130.10	☆	5.4	245-2423	412-288-0525	4.50	None	None	George McCall	'91
BNY HAMILTON:INTMDT NY	New York Muni	40.5	10.24	10,223.70	☆	☆	0.0	426-9363	None	None	0.25	None	Colleen M. Frey	'92
BOSTON CO TF:BOND;INST	Intermediate Muni	5.7	12.61	10,270.40	☆	☆	0.0	221-7930	None	None	0.15	None	Andrew Windmueller	'93
BOSTON CO TF:BOND;INV	Intermediate Muni	8.5	12.61	10,277.70	☆	☆	0.0	225-5267	None	None	None	None	Andrew Windmueller	'93
BOSTON CO TF:BOND;RET	Intermediate Muni	18.0	12.61	10,273.00	11,094.80	15,963.70	4.7	225-5267	None	None	0.25	None	Andrew Windmueller	'87
BOSTON CO TF:CA BD;INST	California Muni	0.5	13.38	10,299.00	☆	☆	0.0	221-7930	None	None	0.15	None	Andrew Windmueller	'93

★AAL MUNICIPAL BOND—Limited to Lutherans.

★BB & T: NC INTMDT TX-FR; TR—Institutional fund.

PERFORMANCE OF MUTUAL FUNDS (continued)

FUND NAME	OBJECTIVE	TOTAL NET ASSETS ($ MIL) 5/31/93	NET ASSET $ VALUE 6/30/93	PERFORMANCE (Return on Initial $10,000 Investment) 3/31/93-6/30/93	6/30/92-6/30/93	6/30/88-6/30/93	DIVIDEND YIELD % 6/93	PHONE NUMBER 800	In-State	FEES Load	12b-1	Redemption	MANAGER	SINCE
BOSTON CO TF:CA BD;INV	California Muni	8.4	13.38	10,298.40	☆	☆	0.0	225-5267	None	None	None	None	Andrew Windmueller	'93
BOSTON CO TF:CA BD;RET	California Muni	10.6	13.38	10,297.10	11,064.40	15,180.40	5.0	225-5267	None	None	0.25	None	Andrew Windmueller	'88
BOSTON CO TF:MA BD;INST	Massachusetts Muni	2.1	12.38	10,238.90	☆	☆	0.0	221-7930	None	None	0.15	None	Andrew Windmueller	'93
BOSTON CO TF:MA BD;INV	Massachusetts Muni	8.7	12.38	10,244.20	☆	☆	0.0	225-5267	None	None	None	None	Andrew Windmueller	'93
BOSTON CO TF:MA BD;RET	Massachusetts Muni	19.7	12.38	10,238.40	11,026.90	15,534.30	5.1	225-5267	None	None	0.25	None	Andrew Windmueller	'87
BOSTON CO TF:NY BD;INST	New York Muni	1.9	13.16	10,283.10	☆	☆	0.0	221-7930	None	None	0.15	None	Andrew Windmueller	'93
BOSTON CO TF:NY BD;INV	New York Muni	0.9	13.16	10,282.30	☆	☆	0.0	225-5267	None	None	None	None	Andrew Windmueller	'93
BOSTON CO TF:NY BD;RET	New York Muni	2.0	13.16	10,277.00	11,024.80	14,828.80	5.1	225-5267	None	None	0.25	None	Andrew Windmueller	'88
BOULEVARD:MGD MUNI	Short-Term Muni	13.4	10.01	10,075.30	☆	☆	0.0	285-3263	412-288-0525	3.00	0.25	None	Boulevard Bank	'92
BT INV:INTMDT TAX FREE	Intermediate Muni	18.6	10.35	10,269.40	☆	☆	0.0	545-1074	None	None	0.20	None	Gary Pollack	'92
BULL&BEAR MUNI INCOME	General Muni	21.4	17.80	10,337.20	11,000.60	15,268.00	4.5	847-4200	212-363-1100	None	0.50	None	C.Clifford McCarthy Jr.	'90
CALDWELL TX FR	General Muni	0.7	10.03	10,017.80	☆	☆	0.0	338-9477	813-485-0654	None	None	None	Roland Caldwell	'92
CA INV TR:CA TX-FR INC	California Muni	258.6	13.15	10,383.40	11,328.30	16,425.00	5.2	225-8778	415-398-2727	None	None	None	Philip McClanahan	'85
CALVERT MUNI:CA INTMDT	California Muni	26.0	10.45	10,235.10	10,893.30	☆	4.9	368-2748	301-951-4820	2.00	0.25	None	Reno Martini	'92
CALVERT MUNI:INTMDT MUNI	Intermediate Muni	16.0	10.21	10,335.00	☆	☆	0.0	368-2748	301-951-4820	3.75	0.25	None	Reno Martini	'92
CALVERT TX-FR RSVS:LTD	Short-Term Muni	591.4	10.70	10,102.20	10,446.60	13,362.40	3.9	368-2748	301-951-4820	2.00	None	None	Reno Martini	'81
CALVERT TX-FR RSVS:LONG	General Muni	49.4	16.83	10,288.40	10,982.00	15,427.90	5.7	368-2748	301-951-4820	4.75	0.35	None	Reno Martini	'83
CALVERT TX-FR RSVS:VT	Single-State Muni	58.3	16.39	10,306.60	11,058.20	☆	5.2	368-2748	301-951-4820	3.75	0.35	None	Reno Martini	'91
CAMBRIDGE:MUNI INC;A	General Muni	27.1	15.57	10,411.50	11,361.90	☆	6.2	934-3883	202-835-4280	4.75	None	None	Dave Johnson	'92
CAMBRIDGE:MUNI INC;B	General Muni	44.2	15.59	10,404.20	11,312.50	☆	5.7	934-3883	202-835-4280	None	0.50	1.00	Dave Johnson	'92
CAPITOL MD TX-FR;A	Maryland Muni	3.9	10.77	10,338.70	11,128.20	☆	4.5	342-5734	215-254-1000	None	None	None	Gene Mulligan	'92
CAPITOL MD TX-FR;B	Maryland Muni	1.9	10.73	10,330.00	☆	☆	0.0	342-5734	215-254-1000	4.00	0.30	None	Gene Mulligan	'92
CARNEGIE TX EX:OH MUNI	Ohio Muni	19.0	9.88	10,212.80	11,007.40	14,820.60	5.7	321-2322	216-781-4440	4.50	None	None	Roy Wallace	'86
CASCADES:TX-FR TR OF OR	Oregon Muni	296.8	10.80	10,238.70	10,997.80	15,447.60	5.5	872-6734	212-697-6666	4.00	None	None	Edward Potts	'86
CFB MKTWATCH:VA MUNI	Virginia Muni	17.2	10.29	10,313.10	☆	☆	0.0	232-9091	None	4.50	0.25	None	Team Managed	'93
CHUBB INV:TAX EXEMPT	General Muni	12.3	12.30	10,294.60	11,215.80	16,386.30	4.9	258-3648	603-226-5000	5.00	None	None	Frederick Gaertner	'89
CHURCHILL TX-FR OF KY	Kentucky Muni	222.2	10.84	10,296.40	11,051.30	16,024.60	5.9	872-5859	212-697-6666	4.00	None	None	T. Radford Hazelip	'87
COLONIAL CA TAX-EX;A	California Muni	354.6	7.52	10,260.60	11,003.60	15,463.80	6.1	426-3750	617-426-3750	4.75	None	None	William Loring	'86
COLONIAL CA TAX-EX;B	California Muni	63.0	7.52	10,241.90	☆	☆	0.0	426-3750	617-426-3750	None	1.00	5.00	William Loring	'92
COLONIAL CT TAX-EX;A	Connecticut Muni	80.0	7.72	10,371.30	11,264.70	☆	5.8	426-3750	617-426-3750	4.75	None	None	Jeffrey Augustine	'91
COLONIAL CT TAX-EX;B	Connecticut Muni	45.2	7.72	10,352.50	11,182.60	☆	5.1	426-3750	617-426-3750	None	0.75	5.00	Jeffrey Augustine	'92
COLONIAL FL TAX-EX;A	Florida Muni	16.3	7.72	10,356.50	☆	☆	0.0	426-3750	617-426-3750	4.75	None	None	Michael Hardie	'93
COLONIAL FL TAX EX;B	Florida Muni	21.2	7.72	10,337.50	☆	☆	0.0	426-3750	617-426-3750	None	0.75	5.00	Michael Hardie	'93
COLONIAL HI YLD MUNI;B	High-Yield Muni	94.3	10.29	10,235.50	10,875.40	☆	6.2	426-3750	617-426-3750	None	1.00	5.00	Bonny Boatman	'92
COLONIAL INT TAX-EX;A	Intermediate Muni	10.0	7.75	10,315.20	☆	☆	0.0	426-3750	617-426-3750	3.25	0.20	None	William Loring	'93
COLONIAL INT TAX-EX;B	Intermediate Muni	3.9	7.75	10,298.50	☆	☆	0.0	426-3750	617-426-3750	None	0.85	4.00	William Loring	'93
COLONIAL MA TAX-EX;A	Massachusetts Muni	202.7	7.95	10,304.80	11,257.90	16,025.30	6.0	426-3750	617-426-3750	4.75	None	None	Jeffrey Augustine	'88
COLONIAL MA TAX-EX;B	Massachusetts Muni	29.1	7.95	10,286.30	11,177.10	☆	5.3	426-3750	617-426-3750	None	0.75	5.00	Jeffrey Augustine	'92
COLONIAL MI TAX-EX;A	Michigan Muni	39.2	7.14	10,238.30	11,139.10	15,040.00	5.6	426-3750	617-426-3750	4.75	None	None	Jeffrey Augustine	'87
COLONIAL MI TAX-EX;B	Michigan Muni	10.6	7.14	10,219.60	☆	☆	0.0	426-3750	617-426-3750	None	0.75	5.00	Jeffrey Augustine	'92
COLONIAL MN TAX-EX;A	Minnesota Muni	39.5	7.32	10,275.40	10,975.90	14,937.30	6.0	426-3750	617-426-3750	4.75	None	None	William Loring	'86
COLONIAL MN TAX-EX;B	Minnesota Muni	6.2	7.32	10,256.60	☆	☆	0.0	426-3750	617-426-3750	None	0.75	5.00	William Loring	'92
COLONIAL NY TAX-EX;A	New York Muni	59.6	7.34	10,345.10	11,184.40	15,639.70	6.0	426-3750	617-426-3750	4.75	None	None	Jeffrey Augustine	'87
COLONIAL NY TAX-EX;B	New York Muni	28.0	7.34	10,326.30	☆	☆	0.0	426-3750	617-426-3750	None	0.75	5.00	Jeffrey Augustine	'92
COLONIAL OH TAX-EX;A	Ohio Muni	70.8	7.50	10,309.10	11,091.50	15,660.20	5.9	426-3750	617-426-3750	4.75	None	None	Jeffrey Augustine	'87

COLONIAL OH TAX-EX;B	Ohio Muni	26.0	7.50	10,290.40	☆	☆	0.0	426-3750	617-426-3750	None	0.75	5.00	Jeffrey Augustine	'92
COLONIAL SH-TM TAX-EX;A	Short-Term Muni	4.4	7.54	10,108.20	☆	☆	0.0	426-3750	617-426-3750	1.00	0.15	None	William Loring	'93
COLONIAL TAX-EX;A	General Muni	3,182.6	13.91	10,266.70	11,044.60	15,399.80	6.3	426-3750	617-426-3750	4.75	0.25	None	Michael Hardie	'84
COLONIAL TAX-EX;B	General Muni	284.2	13.91	10,248.00	10,981.80	☆	5.6	426-3750	617-426-3750	None	1.00	5.00	Michael Hardie	'92
COLONIAL TAX-EX INS;A	Insured Muni	235.1	8.43	10,283.70	11,086.30	15,681.30	5.6	426-3750	617-426-3750	4.75	0.25	None	William Loring	'87
COLONIAL TAX-EX INS;B	Insured Muni	31.9	8.43	10,265.10	11,005.80	☆	4.9	426-3750	617-426-3750	None	1.00	5.00	William Loring	'92
COLUMBIA MUNI BOND	Oregon Muni	384.1	12.63	10,255.30	11,087.90	15,342.70	5.4	547-1707	503-222-3606	None	None	None	Tom Thomsen	'84
COMMON SENSE:MUNI BOND	General Muni	79.9	13.83	10,281.00	11,120.00	☆	5.4	544-5445	404-381-1000	4.75	None	None	Bob Evans	'88
COMPASS CAP:MUNI BOND	Intermediate Muni	26.1	11.09	10,318.20	11,027.40	☆	4.6	451-8371	215-254-1000	3.75	None	None	Joseph Donatacci	'89
COMPASS CAP:NJ MUNI BD	New Jersey Muni	60.9	11.35	10,344.00	11,167.80	☆	4.7	451-8371	215-254-1000	3.75	None	None	Joseph Donatacci	'91
COMPOSITE TAX-EXEMPT BD	General Muni	216.4	7.95	10,347.80	11,295.50	15,697.50	5.1	543-8072	509-353-3550	4.00	0.20	None	Craig Hobbs	'92
CONESTOGA:PA TAX-FREE	Pennsylvania Muni	6.2	10.34	10,288.40	☆	☆	0.0	344-2716	None	4.00	None	None	Craig Moyer	'92
CRESTFUNDS:VA MUNI;TR	Virginia Muni	19.1	10.30	10,239.70	☆	☆	0.0	None	804-782-7222	None	0.15	None	Jennifer Constine	'93
DEAN WITTER CAL TAX FR	California Muni	1,085.2	13.22	10,283.60	11,081.70	15,498.10	5.2	869-3863	212-392-2550	None	0.75	5.00	James Willison	'84
DEAN WITTER MUNI:AZ	Arizona Muni	50.7	10.71	10,390.50	11,278.70	☆	5.7	869-3863	212-392-2550	4.00	0.15	None	James Willison	'91
DEAN WITTER MUNI:CA	California Muni	119.2	11.00	10,425.10	11,335.40	☆	5.8	869-3863	212-392-2550	4.00	0.15	None	James Willison	'91
DEAN WITTER MUNI:FL	Florida Muni	72.0	10.87	10,394.90	11,247.70	☆	5.7	869-3863	212-392-2550	4.00	0.15	None	James Willison	'91
DEAN WITTER MUNI:MA	Massachusetts Muni	14.7	10.99	10,412.90	11,310.90	☆	5.7	869-3863	212-392-2550	4.00	0.15	None	James Willison	'91
DEAN WITTER MUNI:MI	Michigan Muni	19.3	10.99	10,423.90	11,319.50	☆	5.8	869-3863	212-392-2550	4.00	0.15	None	James Willison	'91
DEAN WITTER MUNI:MN	Minnesota Muni	8.6	10.72	10,428.10	11,267.10	☆	5.7	869-3863	212-392-2550	4.00	0.15	None	James Willison	'91
DEAN WITTER MUNI:NJ	New Jersey Muni	46.1	10.94	10,431.30	11,342.00	☆	5.7	869-3863	212-392-2550	4.00	0.15	None	James Willison	'91
DEAN WITTER MUNI:NY	New York Muni	13.5	11.04	10,412.40	11,321.80	☆	5.8	869-3863	212-392-2550	4.00	0.15	None	James Willison	'91
DEAN WITTER MUNI:OH	Ohio Muni	18.0	10.90	10,437.80	11,355.20	☆	5.8	869-3863	212-392-2550	4.00	0.15	None	James Willison	'91
DEAN WITTER MUNI:PA	Pennsylvania Muni	43.1	10.99	10,445.00	11,380.10	☆	5.7	869-3863	212-392-2550	4.00	0.15	None	James Willison	'91
DEAN WITTER NY TXFR IN	New York Muni	226.8	12.51	10,319.00	11,208.70	15,812.40	5.2	869-3863	212-392-2550	None	0.75	5.00	James Willison	'85
DW SELECT MUNI REINVEST	General Muni	83.8	12.64	10,350.00	11,164.20	15,822.70	5.4	869-3863	212-392-2550	None	None	None	James Willison	'83
DEAN WITTER TAX-EXEMPT	General Muni	1,438.6	12.30	10,319.00	11,158.10	16,289.90	6.4	869-3863	212-392-2550	4.00	None	None	James Willison	'80
DELAWARE TX-FR INSURED	Insured Muni	92.9	11.56	10,200.10	10,966.90	15,416.00	5.5	523-4640	215-988-1333	4.75	0.30	None	J. Michael Pokorny	'85
DELAWARE TX-FR INTMDT	Intermediate Muni	7.4	10.41	10,297.00	☆	☆	0.0	523-4640	215-988-1333	3.00	0.30	None	Patrick P. Coyne	'93
DELAWARE TX-FR PA	Pennsylvania Muni	970.2	8.65	10,264.10	11,158.30	15,962.40	5.9	523-4640	215-988-1333	4.75	0.30	None	J. Michael Pokorny	'80
DELAWARE TX-FR USA	General Muni	743.6	12.51	10,273.90	11,186.10	16,057.40	6.0	523-4640	215-988-1333	4.75	0.30	None	J. Michael Pokorny	'84
DREYFUS CA INTMDT MUNI	California Muni	189.0	13.56	10,319.00	11,303.70	☆	5.4	373-9387	516-338-3300	None	None	None	Lawrence Troutman	'92
DREYFUS CA TAX EX BOND	California Muni	1,828.8	15.48	10,314.90	11,081.80	15,355.30	5.7	373-9387	516-338-3300	None	None	None	Lawrence Troutman	'86
DREYFUS CT INTMDT MUNI	Connecticut Muni	88.8	13.44	10,325.90	11,137.40	☆	5.0	373-9387	516-338-3300	None	None	None	Stephen Kris	'92
DREYFUS FL INTMDT MUNI	Florida Muni	400.0	13.50	10,365.50	11,290.90	☆	5.4	373-9387	516-338-3300	None	None	None	Stephen Kris	'92
DREYFUS GEN CA MUNI BD	California Muni	427.7	13.99	10,393.20	11,294.50	☆	5.9	373-9387	516-338-3300	None	None	None	Paul Disdier	'89
DREYFUS GEN MUNI BOND	General Muni	1,250.8	15.79	10,445.90	11,261.20	17,394.60	6.0	373-9387	516-338-3300	None	0.03	None	Paul Disdier	'88
DREYFUS GEN NY MUNI BD	New York Muni	377.4	21.04	10,424.80	11,380.50	15,939.30	5.6	373-9387	516-338-3300	None	0.20	None	Monica Wieboldt	'88
DREYFUS INSURED MUNI BD	Insured Muni	280.0	19.49	10,353.20	11,248.30	15,911.90	5.4	373-9387	516-338-3300	None	0.20	None	Lawrence Troutman	'85
DREYFUS INTMDT MUNI	Intermediate Muni	1,697.0	14.48	10,329.60	11,103.80	15,461.50	5.5	373-9387	516-338-3300	None	None	None	Monica Wieboldt	'85
DREYFUS MA INTMDT MUNI	Massachusetts Muni	43.7	13.37	10,300.50	11,184.40	☆	5.0	373-9387	516-338-3300	None	None	None	Lawrence Troutman	'92
DREYFUS MA TAX EX BOND	Massachusetts Muni	182.9	17.22	10,397.60	11,139.60	15,573.40	5.6	373-9387	516-338-3300	None	None	None	Lawrence Troutman	'86
DREYFUS MUNICIPAL BOND	General Muni	4,416.1	13.46	10,378.20	11,192.00	16,102.10	5.8	373-9387	516-338-3300	None	None	None	Richard Moynihan	'76
DREYFUS NJ INTMDT MUNI	New Jersey Muni	151.5	13.62	10,384.40	11,484.10	☆	5.1	373-9387	516-338-3300	None	None	None	Stephen Kris	'92
DREYFUS NJ MUNI BOND	New Jersey Muni	676.3	13.83	10,416.80	11,274.80	16,393.00	5.7	373-9387	516-338-3300	None	0.25	None	Samuel Weinstock	'87
DREYFUS NY INS TAX EX BD	New York Muni	194.8	12.10	10,349.00	11,157.40	15,987.20	5.1	373-9387	516-338-3300	None	0.25	None	Lawrence Troutman	'87
DREYFUS NY INTMDT TAX EX	New York Muni	316.4	18.29	10,317.30	11,104.10	15,560.40	5.1	373-9387	516-338-3300	None	0.25	None	Monica Wieboldt	'87
DREYFUS NY TAX EX BOND	New York Muni	2,090.6	16.27	10,370.00	11,234.80	15,953.90	5.7	373-9387	516-338-3300	None	None	None	Monica Wieboldt	'85
DREYFUS PREM CA MUNI;A	California Muni	234.2	13.37	10,373.00	11,266.80	16,584.00	5.9	373-9387	516-338-3300	4.50	0.25	None	Paul Disdier	'88
DREYFUS PREM MUNI BD;A	General Muni	532.3	14.68	10,396.30	11,230.90	17,194.40	6.2	373-9387	516-338-3300	4.50	0.25	None	Samuel Weinstock	'87

PERFORMANCE OF MUTUAL FUNDS *(continued)*

FUND NAME	OBJECTIVE	TOTAL NET ASSETS ($ MIL) 5/31/93	NET ASSET $ VALUE 6/30/93	PERFORMANCE (Return on Initial $10,000 Investment) 3/31/93-6/30/93	6/30/92-6/30/93	6/30/88-6/30/93	DIVIDEND YIELD % 6/93	PHONE NUMBER 800	In-State	FEES Load	12b-1	Redemption	MANAGER	SINCE
DREYFUS PREM MUNI:AZ;A	Arizona Muni	6.0	13.37	10,460.80	☆	☆	0.0	373-9387	516-338-3300	4.50	0.25	None	Stephen Kris	'92
DREYFUS PREM MUNI:CT;A	Connecticut Muni	363.7	12.51	10,406.40	11,345.80	16,135.40	5.6	373-9387	516-338-3300	4.50	0.25	None	Samuel Weinstock	'87
DREYFUS PREM MUNI:FL;A	Florida Muni	301.5	15.27	10,414.80	11,273.40	16,916.60	5.9	373-9387	516-338-3300	4.50	0.25	None	Paul Disdier	'88
DREYFUS PREM MUNI:GA;A	Georgia Muni	7.5	13.50	10,398.70	☆	☆	0.0	373-9387	516-338-3300	4.50	0.25	None	Stephen Kris	'92
DREYFUS PREM MUNI:MD;A	Maryland Muni	341.2	13.25	10,376.80	11,190.50	16,441.20	5.7	373-9387	516-338-3300	4.50	0.25	None	Paul Disdier	'88
DREYFUS PREM MUNI:MA;A	Massachusetts Muni	80.0	12.30	10,393.70	11,256.70	16,288.30	5.9	373-9387	516-338-3300	4.50	0.25	None	Samuel Weinstock	'87
DREYFUS PREM MUNI:MI;A	Michigan Muni	186.0	15.97	10,432.80	11,310.20	16,763.00	5.7	373-9387	516-338-3300	4.50	0.25	None	Paul Disdier	'88
DREYFUS PREM MUNI:MN;A	Minnesota Muni	149.9	15.53	10,381.00	11,179.40	16,519.30	5.9	373-9387	516-338-3300	4.50	0.25	None	Paul Disdier	'88
DREYFUS PREM MUNI:NC;A	North Carolina Muni	56.6	13.66	10,414.50	11,385.60	☆	5.7	373-9387	516-338-3300	4.50	0.25	None	Samuel Weinstock	'91
DREYFUS PREM MUNI:OH;A	Ohio Muni	297.3	13.29	10,392.60	11,266.90	16,746.00	5.8	373-9387	516-338-3300	4.50	0.25	None	Paul Disdier	'88
DREYFUS PREM MUNI:PA;A	Pennsylvania Muni	224.2	16.90	10,423.80	11,308.30	16,989.80	5.9	373-9387	516-338-3300	4.50	0.25	None	Paul Disdier	'88
DREYFUS PREM MUNI:TX;A	Texas Muni	73.5	21.65	10,473.00	11,318.20	17,190.90	5.9	373-9387	516-338-3300	4.50	0.25	None	Paul Disdier	'88
DREYFUS PREM MUNI:VA;A	Virginia Muni	57.3	17.14	10,462.60	11,440.10	☆	5.8	373-9387	516-338-3300	4.50	0.25	None	Samuel Weinstock	'91
DREYFUS PREM NY MUNI;A	New York Muni	141.5	14.93	10,430.50	11,391.10	17,141.20	5.6	373-9387	516-338-3300	4.50	0.25	None	Paul Disdier	'88
DREYFUS SHT-INT TX EX BD	Short-Term Muni	435.5	13.25	10,143.60	10,708.30	14,009.50	4.6	373-9387	516-338-3300	None	0.10	None	Samuel Weinstock	'87
DUPREE:KY TX-FR INC	Kentucky Muni	232.3	7.60	10,274.80	11,245.30	16,135.90	5.6	866-0614	606-254-7741	None	None	None	Bill Griggs	'89
DUPREE:KY TX-FR SHT-MED	Kentucky Muni	55.0	5.29	10,106.70	10,692.50	13,810.90	4.4	866-0614	606-254-7741	None	None	None	Bill Griggs	'87
EATON VANCE:CA LTD★	California Muni	N/A	10.47	10,250.90	10,981.90	☆	5.2	225-6265	617-482-8260	None	0.75	3.00	Raymond E. Hender	'92
EATON VANCE:FL LTD★	Florida Muni	N/A	10.48	10,240.80	11,031.80	☆	5.2	225-6265	617-482-8260	None	0.75	3.00	Raymond E. Hender	'92
EATON VANCE INV:CA	California Muni	453.2	10.34	10,288.90	10,979.00	14,785.50	6.0	225-6265	617-482-8260	None	1.00	6.00	Robert MacIntosh	'91
EATON VANCE:MA LTD★	Massachusetts Muni	N/A	10.38	10,233.10	10,900.50	☆	5.2	225-6265	617-482-8260	None	0.75	3.00	Raymond E. Hender	'92
EATON VANCE MUNI:AL★	Single-State Muni	N/A	10.85	10,338.20	11,216.40	☆	5.5	225-6265	617-482-8260	None	1.00	6.00	Timothy Browse	'92
EATON VANCE MUNI:AZ★	Arizona Muni	N/A	11.29	10,399.50	11,338.80	☆	5.6	225-6265	617-482-8260	None	1.00	6.00	Thomas M. Metzold	'91
EATON VANCE MUNI:AR★	Single-State Muni	N/A	10.70	10,344.20	☆	☆	0.0	225-6265	617-482-8260	None	1.00	6.00	Timothy Browse	'92
EATON VANCE MUNI:CO★	Colorado Muni	N/A	10.70	10,373.70	☆	☆	0.0	225-6265	617-482-8260	None	1.00	6.00	Cynthia J. Clemson	'92
EATON VANCE MUNI:CT★	Connecticut Muni	N/A	10.82	10,368.60	11,213.90	☆	5.5	225-6265	617-482-8260	None	1.00	6.00	Robert MacIntosh	'92
EATON VANCE MUNI:FL★	Florida Muni	N/A	11.45	10,387.90	11,222.40	☆	5.6	225-6265	617-482-8260	None	1.00	6.00	Thomas J. Fetter	'90
EATON VANCE MUNI:GA★	Georgia Muni	N/A	10.56	10,356.20	11,136.40	☆	5.7	225-6265	617-482-8260	None	1.00	6.00	David Reilly	'92
EATON VANCE MUNI:KY★	Kentucky Muni	N/A	10.62	10,394.30	11,188.10	☆	5.6	225-6265	617-482-8260	None	1.00	6.00	Timothy Browse	'92
EATON VANCE MUNI:LA★	Louisiana Muni	N/A	10.87	10,406.20	☆	☆	0.0	225-6265	617-482-8260	None	1.00	6.00	Thomas M. Metzold	'92
EATON VANCE MUNI:MD★	Maryland Muni	N/A	10.84	10,393.80	11,235.70	☆	5.4	225-6265	617-482-8260	None	1.00	6.00	Timothy Browse	'92
EATON VANCE MUNI:MA★	Massachusetts Muni	N/A	11.05	10,350.70	11,110.30	☆	5.7	225-6265	617-482-8260	None	1.00	6.00	Robert MacIntosh	'91
EATON VANCE MUNI:MI★	Michigan Muni	N/A	10.95	10,347.50	11,114.70	☆	5.6	225-6265	617-482-8260	None	1.00	6.00	Timothy Browse	'92
EATON VANCE MUNI:MN★	Minnesota Muni	N/A	10.72	10,325.40	11,059.70	☆	5.7	225-6265	617-482-8260	None	1.00	6.00	Robert MacIntosh	'91
EATON VANCE MUNI:MO★	Missouri Muni	N/A	11.03	10,372.90	11,399.40	☆	5.5	225-6265	617-482-8260	None	1.00	6.00	Cynthia J. Clemson	'92
EATON VANCE MUNI:NATL	High-Yield Muni	1,835.7	10.33	10,446.00	11,297.80	15,674.80	6.4	225-6265	617-482-8260	None	1.00	6.00	James Bauer	'90
EATON VANCE MUNI:NJ★	New Jersey Muni	N/A	11.19	10,374.90	11,269.70	☆	5.6	225-6265	617-482-8260	None	1.00	6.00	Robert MacIntosh	'91
EATON VANCE MUNI:NY★	New York Muni	N/A	11.65	10,373.90	11,298.10	☆	5.7	225-6265	617-482-8260	None	1.00	6.00	Thomas J. Fetter	'90
EATON VANCE MUNI:NC★	North Carolina Muni	N/A	10.73	10,350.60	11,052.80	☆	5.5	225-6265	617-482-8260	None	1.00	6.00	David Reilly	'92
EATON VANCE MUNI:OH★	Ohio Muni	N/A	11.06	10,385.00	11,212.90	☆	5.6	225-6265	617-482-8260	None	1.00	6.00	Thomas J. Fetter	'91
EATON VANCE MUNI:OR★	Oregon Muni	N/A	10.92	10,353.30	11,301.90	☆	5.3	225-6265	617-482-8260	None	1.00	6.00	Thomas M. Metzold	'92
EATON VANCE MUNI:PA★	Pennsylvania Muni	N/A	11.09	10,304.10	11,097.40	☆	5.8	225-6265	617-482-8260	None	1.00	6.00	David Reilly	'91
EATON VANCE MUNI:SC★	South Carolina Muni	N/A	10.63	10,299.20	☆	☆	0.0	225-6265	617-482-8260	None	1.00	6.00	David Reilly	'92
EATON VANCE MUNI:TX★	Texas Muni	N/A	10.86	10,315.60	11,136.20	☆	5.7	225-6265	617-482-8260	None	1.00	6.00	Timothy Browse	'92
EATON VANCE MUNI:VA★	Virginia Muni	N/A	10.87	10,304.80	11,052.60	☆	5.7	225-6265	617-482-8260	None	1.00	6.00	David Reilly	'92

EATON VANCE MUNI BOND LP	General Muni	108.2	10.42	10,394.90	11,260.80	16,840.30	6.1	225-6265	617-482-8260	4.75	None	None	Thomas J. Fetter	'87
EATON VANCE:NATL LTD★	Intermediate Muni	N/A	10.56	10,231.50	11,025.10	☆	5.3	225-6265	617-482-8260	None	0.75	3.00	Raymond E. Hender	'92
EATON VANCE:NJ LTD★	New Jersey Muni	N/A	10.48	10,248.60	11,006.10	☆	5.1	225-6265	617-482-8260	None	0.75	3.00	Raymond E. Hender	'92
EATON VANCE:NY LTD★	New York Muni	N/A	10.48	10,240.80	11,043.50	☆	5.2	225-6265	617-482-8260	None	0.75	3.00	Raymond E. Hender	'92
EATON VANCE:PA LTD★	Pennsylvania Muni	N/A	10.52	10,251.30	10,991.30	☆	5.2	225-6265	617-482-8260	None	0.75	3.00	Raymond E. Hender	'92
ELFUN:TAX-EX INCOME★	General Muni	1,204.0	12.28	10,339.50	11,194.30	16,033.50	5.9	242-0134	203-326-4040	None	None	None	Robert R. Kaelin	'84
EMERALD:FL TAX-EX	Florida Muni	165.8	11.27	10,432.50	11,423.10	☆	5.8	637-6336	None	4.50	0.25	None	Doug Byrne	'91
EMPIRE BUILDER TAX FR BD	New York Muni	98.2	18.54	10,331.90	11,220.10	15,529.40	5.0	847-5886	212-309-8400	4.25	None	None	James Vaccacio	'87
ENTERPRISE:TAX-EX INCOME	General Muni	34.2	14.14	10,293.50	11,102.20	15,484.40	5.2	432-4320	404-396-8118	4.75	0.45	None	Gerald Barth	'92
EQUITABLE:TAX EX;A	General Muni	7.6	10.52	10,338.80	11,058.30	☆	5.4	852-6860	516-242-4815	4.25	0.25	None	Johnathan Lieber	'91
EQUITABLE:TAX EX;B	General Muni	38.2	10.73	10,315.60	10,984.80	14,900.40	4.6	852-6860	516-242-4815	None	1.00	5.00	Johnathan Lieber	'87
EVERGREEN MUNI:INS NATL	Insured Muni	26.2	10.69	10,461.80	☆	☆	0.0	235-0064	914-694-2020	None	None	None	James Colby III	'92
EVERGREEN MUNI:SHT-INT	Short-Term Muni	66.5	10.56	10,193.10	10,802.40	☆	4.7	235-0064	914-694-2020	None	None	None	Steven Shachat	'91
EXECUTIVE INV:INS TAX EX	Insured Muni	7.5	13.68	10,391.90	11,516.30	☆	5.2	423-4026	None	4.75	0.50	None	Clark Wagner	'91
FEDERATED INTMDT MUN TR	Intermediate Muni	262.8	10.86	10,259.00	10,992.20	14,927.70	5.1	245-4770	412-288-1900	None	None	None	Jonathan C. Conley	'85
FEDERATED SH-INT MUNI	Short-Term Muni	293.8	10.37	10,099.50	10,511.10	13,300.60	4.2	245-4770	412-288-1900	None	None	None	Jonathan C. Conley	'84
FFB:NJ TAX-FREE	New Jersey Muni	32.9	11.06	10,343.00	11,243.00	☆	5.6	522-5219	201-430-4046	4.50	0.25	None	Jocelyn Turner	'92
FIDELITY ADV HI INC MUNI	High-Yield Muni	333.4	12.44	10,353.10	11,365.90	17,583.90	6.0	522-7297	None	4.75	0.25	None	Peter Allegrini	'92
FIDELITY ADV LTD TX;INST	Intermediate Muni	22.2	10.41	10,225.80	10,901.80	14,648.30	5.5	522-7297	None	None	None	None	John Haley Jr.	'89
FIDELITY ADV LTD TX;RET	Intermediate Muni	14.1	10.42	10,219.40	☆	☆	0.0	522-7297	None	4.75	0.40	None	John Haley Jr.	'92
FIDELITY AGGRESSIVE TX	High-Yield Muni	877.8	12.39	10,352.30	11,264.60	16,399.50	6.4	544-8888	None	None	None	1.00	Anne Punzak	'85
FIDELITY CA TX FR HI YLD	California Muni	573.8	12.42	10,311.90	11,237.40	16,093.40	5.9	544-8888	None	None	None	None	John Haley Jr.	'85
FIDELITY CA TX FR INSURD	California Muni	279.0	11.05	10,345.50	11,336.30	16,216.40	5.4	544-8888	None	None	None	None	John Haley Jr.	'86
FIDELITY HIGH YLD TAX-FR	High-Yield Muni	2,148.3	13.16	10,303.10	11,125.90	16,568.50	5.8	544-8888	None	None	None	None	Guy Wickwire	'81
FIDELITY INSURED TAX FR	Insured Muni	417.6	12.35	10,336.60	11,271.30	16,144.40	5.4	544-8888	None	None	None	None	Anne Punzak	'89
FIDELITY LTD TERM MUNI	Intermediate Muni	1,162.0	9.98	10,295.60	11,161.60	15,352.40	5.3	544-8888	None	None	None	None	David Murphy	'89
FIDELITY MA MUNI HI YLD	Massachusetts Muni	1,336.3	12.10	10,320.40	11,170.20	16,140.90	5.9	544-8888	None	None	None	None	Guy Wickwire	'83
FIDELITY MI TX-FR HI YLD	Michigan Muni	518.3	12.28	10,348.80	11,324.80	16,329.00	5.9	544-8888	None	None	None	None	Peter Allegrini	'85
FIDELITY MN TX-FR	Minnesota Muni	314.0	11.29	10,328.70	11,057.40	15,534.40	5.8	544-8888	None	None	None	None	Peter Allegrini	'91
FIDELITY MUNICIPAL BOND	General Muni	1,254.4	8.87	10,360.80	11,258.80	16,268.30	5.6	544-8888	None	None	None	None	Gary Swayze	'85
FIDELITY NY TX-FR:HI YLD	New York Muni	466.2	13.15	10,337.80	11,247.70	16,180.50	5.7	544-8888	None	None	None	None	Gary Swayze	'84
FIDELITY NY TX-FR:INSURD	New York Muni	383.5	12.30	10,319.00	11,227.50	16,157.60	5.4	544-8888	None	None	None	None	David Murphy	'92
FIDELITY OH TX-FR HI YLD	Ohio Muni	426.7	11.99	10,311.30	11,155.30	16,239.90	5.9	544-8888	None	None	None	None	Peter Allegrini	'85
FIDELITY SPARTAN AGGR	High-Yield Muni	3.4	10.20	☆	☆	☆	0.0	544-8888	None	None	1.00	None	Anne Punzak	'93
FIDELITY SPARTAN CA HY	California Muni	583.6	11.26	10,315.50	11,261.90	☆	5.7	544-8888	None	None	None	0.50	John Haley Jr.	'89
FIDELITY SPARTAN CT HY	Connecticut Muni	449.5	11.79	10,331.00	11,237.40	15,991.10	5.8	544-8888	None	None	None	0.50	Peter Allegrini	'87
FIDELITY SPARTAN FL	Florida Muni	383.0	11.21	10,378.60	11,409.90	☆	5.7	544-8888	None	None	None	0.50	Anne Punzak	'92
FIDELITY SPARTAN IN MUNI	Intermediate Muni	17.6	10.16	☆	☆	☆	0.0	544-8888	None	None	None	None	*David Murphy*	'93
FIDELITY SPARTAN MD	Maryland Muni	8.0	10.18	☆	☆	☆	0.0	544-8888	None	None	0.50	None	Steven Harvey	'93
FIDELITY SPARTAN MUNI	General Muni	885.7	11.17	10,352.60	11,242.20	☆	6.0	544-8888	None	None	None	0.50	Norman Lind	'90
FIDELITY SPARTAN NJ HY	New Jersey Muni	401.1	11.73	10,385.10	11,278.00	16,559.90	5.6	544-8888	None	None	None	0.50	David Murphy	'91
FIDELITY SPARTAN NY HY	New York Muni	415.7	11.36	10,350.00	11,308.80	☆	5.6	544-8888	None	None	None	0.50	Gary Swayze	'90
FIDELITY SPARTAN PA HY	Pennsylvania Muni	278.6	11.02	10,321.90	11,241.20	16,580.40	6.3	544-8888	None	None	None	0.50	Peter Allegrini	'86
FIDELITY SPARTAN S-I MUN	Short-Term Muni	840.8	10.05	10,154.20	10,733.10	13,905.90	4.6	544-8888	None	None	None	None	David Murphy	'89
59 WALL ST:TX FR SH/INT	Short-Term Muni	N/A	10.29	10,157.40	☆	☆	0.0	None	212-493-8100	None	None	None	Brown Brothers Harriman	'92

★EATON VANCE FUNDS—Fund does not disclose total net assets.

★ELFUN: TAX-EX INCOME—Limited to select Elfun Society members.

PERFORMANCE OF MUTUAL FUNDS *(continued)*

FUND NAME	OBJECTIVE	TOTAL NET ASSETS ($ MIL) 5/31/93	NET ASSET $ VALUE 6/30/93	PERFORMANCE (Return on Initial $10,000 Investment) 3/31/93-6/30/93	6/30/92-6/30/93	6/30/88-6/30/93	DIVIDEND YIELD % 6/93	PHONE NUMBER 800	In-State	FEES Load	12b-1	Redemption	MANAGER	SINCE
FINL HRZNS:MUNI BOND	General Muni	20.7	11.48	10,363.10	11,285.40	☆	5.1	533-5622	None	None	0.35	6.00	Randy Baney	'89
FINANCIAL TAX-FR INCOME	General Muni	324.8	16.35	10,327.80	11,260.40	17,040.30	5.2	525-8085	303-930-6300	None	0.25	None	William B. Veronda	'84
FIRST AMER INV:MUNI	General Muni	2.4	10.75	10,231.00	10,794.80	13,887.20	4.5	637-2548	612-973-0166	4.50	0.25	None	Lucille Rehkamp	'87
FIRST INV INSURED TAX EX	Insured Muni	1,427.9	10.61	10,251.20	10,968.00	15,325.30	5.9	423-4026	None	6.25	0.30	None	Clark Wagner	'91
FIRST INV MULTI INS:AZ	Arizona Muni	6.6	12.78	10,402.30	11,450.00	☆	5.3	423-4026	None	6.25	0.30	None	Clark Wagner	'91
FIRST INV MULTI INS:CA	California Muni	15.9	12.04	10,368.30	11,364.70	16,701.70	5.3	423-4026	None	6.25	0.30	None	Clark Wagner	'91
FIRST INV MULTI INS:CO	Colorado Muni	1.7	12.24	10,382.80	11,413.30	☆	4.9	423-4026	None	6.25	0.30	None	Clark Wagner	'92
FIRST INV MULTI INS:CT	Connecticut Muni	13.9	12.80	10,376.60	11,459.40	☆	5.1	423-4026	None	6.25	0.30	None	Clark Wagner	'91
FIRST INV MULTI INS:FL	Florida Muni	16.1	12.89	10,403.70	11,419.00	☆	5.4	423-4026	None	6.25	0.30	None	Clark Wagner	'91
FIRST INV MULTI INS:GA	Georgia Muni	0.7	12.10	10,436.40	11,332.10	☆	4.7	423-4026	None	6.25	0.30	None	Clark Wagner	'92
FIRST INV MULTI INS:MD	Maryland Muni	4.8	12.88	10,463.40	11,486.50	☆	5.1	423-4026	None	6.25	0.30	None	Clark Wagner	'91
FIRST INV MULTI INS:MA	Massachusetts Muni	21.8	12.24	10,287.80	11,275.20	16,484.80	5.4	423-4026	None	6.25	0.30	None	Clark Wagner	'91
FIRST INV MULTI INS:MI	Michigan Muni	24.6	12.66	10,378.20	11,455.90	16,995.00	5.2	423-4026	None	6.25	0.30	None	Clark Wagner	'91
FIRST INV MULTI INS:MN	Minnesota Muni	7.0	11.68	10,292.80	11,126.60	16,022.40	5.5	423-4026	None	6.25	0.30	None	Clark Wagner	'91
FIRST INV MULTI INS:MO	Missouri Muni	0.8	12.23	10,365.70	11,395.20	☆	4.7	423-4026	None	6.25	0.30	None	Clark Wagner	'92
FIRST INV MULTI INS:NJ	New Jersey Muni	59.2	13.35	10,362.70	11,380.20	☆	5.1	423-4026	None	6.25	0.30	None	Clark Wagner	'91
FIRST INV MULTI INS:NC	North Carolina Muni	2.4	12.00	10,419.60	11,223.50	☆	4.6	423-4026	None	6.25	0.30	None	Clark Wagner	'92
FIRST INV MULTI INS:OH	Ohio Muni	17.4	12.48	10,340.50	11,332.40	16,873.70	5.3	423-4026	None	6.25	0.30	None	Clark Wagner	'91
FIRST INV MULTI INS:OR	Oregon Muni	1.7	11.96	10,334.50	11,137.70	☆	4.4	423-4026	None	6.25	0.30	None	Clark Wagner	'92
FIRST INV MULTI INS:PA	Pennsylvania Muni	29.5	12.93	10,380.60	11,371.90	☆	5.4	423-4026	None	6.25	0.30	None	Clark Wagner	'91
FIRST INV MULTI INS:VA	Virginia Muni	20.1	12.84	10,359.80	11,350.40	☆	5.2	423-4026	None	6.25	0.30	None	Clark Wagner	'91
FIRST INV NY INS TAX FR	New York Muni	193.1	15.19	10,247.70	11,061.70	15,646.00	5.5	423-4026	None	6.25	0.30	None	Clark Wagner	'91
FIRST PACIFIC:HAWAII	Single-State Muni	50.5	11.29	10,267.60	11,110.90	☆	5.3	None	808-599-2400	None	0.25	None	Terry Lee	'91
FIRST PRAIRIE TX EX:INT	Intermediate Muni	28.0	12.70	10,254.40	10,959.40	15,513.00	5.1	821-1185	None	4.50	0.25	None	John Erickson	'88
FIRST PRAIRIE TX EX:INS	Insured Muni	9.8	13.12	10,298.30	11,169.90	16,488.30	5.3	821-1185	None	4.50	0.25	None	John Erickson	'88
FIRST UN:INS TAX;INV B	Insured Muni	101.4	10.91	10,324.80	11,230.20	☆	5.2	326-3241	704-374-4343	4.00	0.25	None	Bob Drye	'92
FIRST UN:INS TAX;INV C	Insured Muni	29.8	10.91	10,312.00	☆	☆	0.0	326-3241	704-374-4343	None	0.75	4.00	Bob Drye	'93
FLAGSHIP PA TRIPLE TX EX	Pennsylvania Muni	40.7	10.53	10,362.50	11,155.80	15,935.50	5.8	227-4648	513-461-0332	4.20	0.40	None	Michael Davern	'92
FLAGSHIP TX EX:ALL-AMER	General Muni	170.7	11.25	10,426.70	11,429.70	☆	6.0	227-4648	513-461-0332	4.20	0.40	None	Robert Ashbaugh	'88
FLAGSHIP TX EX:AZ DOUBLE	Arizona Muni	72.7	10.96	10,390.60	11,309.00	16,401.70	5.8	227-4648	513-461-0332	4.20	0.40	None	Jan Terbrueggen	'92
FLAGSHIP TX EX:CO DOUBLE	Colorado Muni	26.6	10.16	10,374.50	11,208.40	15,980.60	5.9	227-4648	513-461-0332	4.20	0.40	None	Jan Terbrueggen	'92
FLAGSHIP TX EX:CT DOUBLE	Connecticut Muni	184.6	10.81	10,353.90	11,246.00	15,837.30	5.7	227-4648	513-461-0332	4.20	0.40	None	Rick Huber	'92
FLAGSHIP TX EX:FL DOUBLE	Florida Muni	369.2	10.90	10,362.70	11,212.70	☆	5.8	227-4648	513-461-0332	4.20	0.40	None	Robert Ashbaugh	'90
FLAGSHIP TX EX:GA DOUBLE	Georgia Muni	101.2	10.76	10,382.50	11,073.60	15,733.00	5.7	227-4648	513-461-0332	4.20	0.40	None	Michael Davern	'92
FLAGSHIP TX EX:INTMDT	Intermediate Muni	18.8	10.44	10,315.60	☆	☆	0.0	227-4648	513-461-0332	3.00	0.40	None	Michael Davern	'92
FLAGSHIP TX EX:KS TRIPLE	Kansas Muni	62.4	10.56	10,498.60	11,418.80	☆	5.6	227-4648	513-461-0332	4.20	0.40	None	Michael Davern	'92
FLAGSHIP TX EX:KY TRIPLE	Kentucky Muni	308.9	11.21	10,368.30	11,227.40	16,428.30	5.8	227-4648	513-461-0332	4.20	0.40	None	Robert Ashbaugh	'87
FLAGSHIP TX EX:LA DOUBLE	Louisiana Muni	54.5	11.09	10,378.10	11,298.00	☆	5.7	227-4648	513-461-0332	4.20	0.40	None	Jan Terbrueggen	'92
FLAGSHIP TX EX:LTD TERM	Short-Term Muni	570.5	10.82	10,218.30	10,950.10	14,890.00	5.1	227-4648	513-461-0332	2.50	0.40	None	Robert Ashbaugh	'91
FLAGSHIP TX EX:MI TRIPLE	Michigan Muni	227.3	11.93	10,376.50	11,203.20	16,057.60	5.7	227-4648	513-461-0332	4.20	0.40	None	Robert Ashbaugh	'87
FLAGSHIP TX EX:MO DOUBLE	Missouri Muni	144.7	11.04	10,447.90	11,272.60	16,312.90	5.8	227-4648	513-461-0332	4.20	0.40	None	Michael Davern	'92
FLAGSHIP TX EX:NJ DOUBLE	New Jersey Muni	2.3	10.29	10,499.00	☆	☆	0.0	227-4648	513-461-0332	4.20	0.40	None	Rick Huber	'92
FLAGSHIP TX EX:NJ INTMDT	New Jersey Muni	5.6	10.34	10,359.30	☆	☆	0.0	227-4648	513-461-0332	3.00	0.40	None	Rick Huber	'92
FLAGSHIP TX EX:NM DOUBLE	Single-State Muni	31.2	10.19	10,415.20	☆	☆	0.0	227-4648	513-461-0332	4.20	0.40	None	Jan Terbrueggen	'92
FLAGSHIP TX EX:NY	New York Muni	33.9	11.06	10,426.60	11,536.20	☆	6.0	227-4648	513-461-0332	4.20	0.40	None	Rick Huber	'92

FLAGSHIP TX EX:NC TRIPLE	North Carolina Muni	170.1	10.65	10,352.70	11,154.40	16,058.20	5.6	227-4648	513-461-0332	4.20	0.40	None	Robert Ashbaugh	'87
FLAGSHIP TX EX:OH DOUBLE	Ohio Muni	410.5	11.74	10,361.50	11,129.20	15,896.70	5.7	227-4648	513-461-0332	4.20	0.40	None	Robert Ashbaugh	'87
FLAGSHIP TX EX:VA DOUBLE	Virginia Muni	96.1	10.97	10,425.50	11,237.50	16,135.00	5.6	227-4648	513-461-0332	4.20	0.40	None	Rick Huber	'92
FMB:MI BD;CNSMR	Michigan Muni	9.7	10.58	10,272.80	10,922.50	☆	4.6	453-4234	None	3.00	0.35	None	Dan Van Timmeren	'91
FMB:MI BD;INSTL	Michigan Muni	9.2	10.58	10,272.80	10,928.90	☆	4.6	453-4234	None	None	None	None	Dan Van Timmeren	'91
FORTIS TAX-FREE:MN	Minnesota Muni	51.0	10.65	10,352.80	11,117.30	15,392.90	5.7	800-2638	612-738-4000	4.50	None	None	Dennis M. Ott	'86
FORTIS TAX-FREE:NATL	General Muni	68.1	11.13	10,381.10	11,199.10	15,930.70	5.7	800-2638	612-738-4000	4.50	None	None	Dennis M. Ott	'86
FORTIS TAX-FREE:NY	New York Muni	13.6	11.51	10,289.80	11,218.20	15,974.00	5.7	800-2638	612-738-4000	4.50	None	None	Dennis M. Ott	'88
FORTRESS MUNI INC	General Muni	404.3	11.13	10,375.60	11,060.20	16,029.50	5.7	245-4770	412-288-1900	1.00	0.25	0.75	Jonathan C. Conley	'87
FORUM:MAINE MUNI	Single-State Muni	18.7	10.72	10,288.50	11,072.80	☆	5.2	None	207-879-0001	3.75	None	None	Forum Advisors	'91
FORUM:NH BOND	Single-State Muni	0.7	10.28	10,400.80	☆	☆	0.0	None	207-879-0001	3.75	None	None	Forum Advisors	'92
FORUM:TAXSAVER BOND	General Muni	16.9	10.78	10,279.60	11,048.00	☆	5.6	None	207-879-0001	3.75	None	None	Forum Advisors	'89
FRANKLIN CA TF INC	California Muni	13,660.2	7.44	10,274.30	11,062.30	15,787.30	6.3	342-5236	415-312-3200	4.00	None	None	B. Schroer	'77
FRANKLIN CA TF:INS	California Muni	1,323.0	12.30	10,294.00	11,171.20	16,085.10	5.7	342-5236	415-312-3200	4.00	None	None	Don Duerson	'85
FRANKLIN CA TF:INTMDT	California Muni	32.5	10.55	10,180.10	☆	☆	0.0	342-5236	415-312-3200	2.25	0.05	None	Jeff Handy	'92
FRANKLIN FED TF INC	General Muni	6,462.6	12.38	10,305.20	11,147.10	16,201.00	6.5	342-5236	415-312-3200	4.00	None	None	A. Jennings	'83
FRANKLIN MUNI:CA HI YLD	California Muni	2.2	10.14	☆	☆	☆	0.0	342-5236	415-312-3200	4.50	0.15	None	Andrew Jennings, Sr.	'93
FRANKLIN MUNI:HI	Single-State Muni	18.6	10.96	10,320.60	11,358.90	☆	5.8	342-5236	415-312-3200	4.50	0.15	None	Jennings/Amoroso	'92/'92
FRANKLIN NY TF INC	New York Muni	4,334.8	12.20	10,342.00	11,246.00	16,373.50	6.4	342-5236	415-312-3200	4.00	None	None	John Pinkham	'90
FRANKLIN NY TF:INS	New York Muni	196.1	11.27	10,280.70	11,197.00	☆	5.5	342-5236	415-312-3200	4.00	None	None	Don Duerson	'91
FRANKLIN NY TF:INTMDT	New York Muni	13.3	10.45	10,171.20	☆	☆	0.0	342-5236	415-312-3200	2.25	0.05	None	John Pinkham	'92
FRANKLIN TF:AL	Single-State Muni	155.0	11.74	10,267.10	11,136.70	15,927.60	5.8	342-5236	415-312-3200	4.00	None	None	Pomeroy/Amoroso	'87/'92
FRANKLIN TF:AZ	Arizona Muni	728.2	11.60	10,279.60	11,230.30	16,006.60	5.8	342-5236	415-312-3200	4.00	None	None	Shelia Amoroso	'87
FRANKLIN TF:AZ INSURED	Arizona Muni	2.2	10.27	☆	☆	☆	0.0	342-5236	415-312-3200	4.50	0.15	None	Don Duerson	'93
FRANKLIN TF:CO	Colorado Muni	167.9	11.87	10,281.00	11,267.10	16,257.10	6.0	342-5236	415-312-3200	4.00	None	None	Shelia Amoroso	'87
FRANKLIN TF:CT	Connecticut Muni	137.7	11.21	10,290.60	11,169.90	☆	5.7	342-5236	415-312-3200	4.00	None	None	John Pinkham	'88
FRANKLIN TF:FED INTMDT	Intermediate Muni	20.0	10.65	10,256.80	☆	☆	0.0	342-5236	415-312-3200	2.25	0.05	None	Jeff Handy	'92
FRANKLIN TF:FL	Florida Muni	1,216.1	11.76	10,310.30	11,177.80	16,122.90	6.1	342-5236	415-312-3200	4.00	None	None	Jennings/Amoroso	'87/'92
FRANKLIN TF:FL INSURED	Florida Muni	2.2	10.13	☆	☆	☆	0.0	342-5236	415-312-3200	4.50	0.15	None	Don Duerson	'93
FRANKLIN TF:GA	Georgia Muni	97.5	11.99	10,355.80	11,165.70	16,208.60	5.6	342-5236	415-312-3200	4.00	None	None	Pomeroy/Amoroso	'87/'92
FRANKLIN TF:HI YLD	High-Yield Muni	2,875.5	11.14	10,307.10	11,214.80	16,118.20	7.0	342-5236	415-312-3200	4.00	None	None	A. Jennings	'86
FRANKLIN TF:INSURED	Insured Muni	1,589.1	12.45	10,283.60	11,140.30	16,156.60	6.0	342-5236	415-312-3200	4.00	None	None	Don Duerson	'85
FRANKLIN TF:IN	Single-State Muni	38.9	11.97	10,317.20	11,245.10	16,453.10	5.9	342-5236	415-312-3200	4.00	None	None	S. Wong	'87
FRANKLIN TF:KY	Kentucky Muni	15.5	11.18	10,391.80	11,328.20	☆	5.9	342-5236	415-312-3200	4.00	None	None	Shelia Amoroso	'91
FRANKLIN TF:LA	Louisiana Muni	101.4	11.62	10,302.60	11,170.90	16,215.20	6.0	342-5236	415-312-3200	4.00	None	None	S. Wong	'87
FRANKLIN TF:MD	Maryland Muni	130.3	11.34	10,311.20	11,177.80	☆	5.8	342-5236	415-312-3200	4.00	None	None	Pomeroy/Johnson	'88/'92
FRANKLIN TF:MA INS	Massachusetts Muni	283.5	11.81	10,268.30	11,150.70	15,729.50	5.8	342-5236	415-312-3200	4.00	None	None	Don Duerson	'85
FRANKLIN TF:MI INS	Michigan Muni	934.0	12.26	10,289.10	11,156.30	15,913.80	5.8	342-5236	415-312-3200	4.00	None	None	Don Duerson	'85
FRANKLIN TF:MN INS	Minnesota Muni	464.4	12.42	10,276.70	11,080.30	15,708.60	5.8	342-5236	415-312-3200	4.00	None	None	Don Duerson	'85
FRANKLIN TF:MO	Missouri Muni	182.0	11.84	10,303.10	11,197.80	16,157.80	5.8	342-5236	415-312-3200	4.00	None	None	Shelia Amoroso	'87
FRANKLIN TF:NJ	New Jersey Muni	466.4	11.88	10,286.90	11,128.30	16,182.40	5.9	342-5236	415-312-3200	4.00	None	None	S. Wong	'88
FRANKLIN TF:NC	North Carolina Muni	173.7	11.93	10,271.60	11,215.30	16,131.30	5.6	342-5236	415-312-3200	4.00	None	None	S. Wong	'87
FRANKLIN TF:OH INS	Ohio Muni	596.9	12.45	10,284.60	11,225.90	16,017.20	5.7	342-5236	415-312-3200	4.00	None	None	Don Duerson	'85
FRANKLIN TF:OR	Oregon Muni	324.3	11.73	10,246.80	11,113.10	15,828.50	5.6	342-5236	415-312-3200	4.00	None	None	Shelia Amoroso	'87
FRANKLIN TF:PA	Pennsylvania Muni	532.7	10.59	10,278.20	11,239.80	16,140.60	6.0	342-5236	415-312-3200	4.00	None	None	S. Wong	'86
FRANKLIN TF:P RICO	Single-State Muni	150.3	11.82	10,279.40	11,088.10	15,963.50	5.9	342-5236	415-312-3200	4.00	None	None	Shelia Amoroso	'85
FRANKLIN TF:TX	Texas Muni	142.1	11.68	10,265.00	11,082.70	16,086.60	6.0	342-5236	415-312-3200	4.00	None	None	S. Wong	'87
FRANKLIN TF:VA	Virginia Muni	222.6	11.78	10,311.00	11,202.70	16,170.70	5.7	342-5236	415-312-3200	4.00	None	None	S. Wong	'87
FREMONT:CA INTMDT	California Muni	54.5	11.00	10,277.10	10,980.20	☆	5.0	548-4539	415-768-9000	None	None	None	William M. Feeney	'90
FD T-F INV:RUSHMORE MD	Maryland Muni	51.2	11.08	10,326.10	11,149.20	☆	5.3	621-7874	301-657-1517	None	None	None	Dan Gillespie	'91

PERFORMANCE OF MUTUAL FUNDS *(continued)*

FUND NAME	OBJECTIVE	TOTAL NET ASSETS ($ MIL) 5/31/93	NET ASSET $ VALUE 6/30/93	PERFORMANCE (Return on Initial $10,000 Investment) 3/31/93-6/30/93	6/30/92-6/30/93	6/30/88-6/30/93	DIVIDEND YIELD % 6/93	PHONE NUMBER 800	In-State	FEES Load	12b-1	Redemption	MANAGER	SINCE
FD T-F INV:RUSHMORE VA	Virginia Muni	31.9	11.32	10,378.60	11,191.00	☆	5.3	621-7874	301-657-1517	None	None	None	Dan Gillespie	'91
FUNDAMENTAL:CALIF MUNI	California Muni	13.2	9.34	10,361.00	11,334.40	15,199.20	6.2	322-6864	212-635-3005	None	0.50	None	Lance Brofman	'84
FUNDAMENTAL:HI-YLD MUNI	High-Yield Muni	1.0	7.22	10,056.70	10,511.50	12,595.80	5.5	322-6864	212-635-3005	None	0.50	None	David Wieder	'87
FUNDAMENTAL:NY MUNI	New York Muni	243.6	1.26	10,369.00	11,228.50	16,115.10	4.8	322-6864	212-635-3005	None	0.50	None	Lance Brofman	'81
GALAXY:CT MUNI BOND;RTL	Connecticut Muni	5.9	10.15	10,282.70	☆	☆	0.0	828-0450	800-628-0414	None	None	None	Steve Woodruff	'93
GALAXY:MA MUNI BOND;RTL	Massachusetts Muni	5.7	10.06	10,287.10	☆	☆	0.0	828-0450	800-628-0414	None	None	None	Dave Lindsay	'93
GALAXY:NY MUNI BOND;RTL	New York Muni	41.2	10.87	10,331.90	11,214.80	☆	4.8	828-0450	800-628-0414	None	None	None	Maria C. Schwenžer	'91
GALAXY:TAX-EXEMPT BD;RTL	General Muni	123.0	11.00	10,338.00	11,237.50	☆	4.9	828-0450	800-628-0414	None	None	None	Mary McGoldrick	'91
GE TAX-EXEMPT	General Muni	7.4	12.09	10,335.20	☆	☆	0.0	242-0134	203-326-4040	None	0.25	None	Robert R. Kaelin	'93
GIT TAX-FREE:ARIZONA	Arizona Muni	14.1	10.95	10,366.70	11,171.90	☆	4.6	336-3063	703-528-6500	None	None	None	Ricardo Fontanilla	'91
GIT TAX-FREE:HIGH YIELD	High-Yield Muni	41.0	11.61	10,370.30	11,104.40	14,927.80	4.9	336-3063	703-528-6500	None	None	None	Ricardo Fontanilla	'91
GIT TAX-FREE:MARYLAND	Maryland Muni	2.3	10.17	10,380.40	☆	☆	0.0	336-3063	703-528-6500	None	None	None	Ricardo Fontanilla	'93
GIT TAX-FREE:MISSOURI	Missouri Muni	12.3	10.95	10,320.90	11,112.30	☆	4.6	336-3063	703-528-6500	None	None	None	Ricardo Fontanilla	'91
GIT TAX-FREE:VIRGINIA	Virginia Muni	41.1	12.11	10,353.40	11,161.90	14,869.60	4.7	336-3063	703-528-6500	None	None	None	Ricardo Fontanilla	'91
GLENMEDE:INTMDT MUNI	Intermediate Muni	77.5	10.45	10,238.40	10,804.80	☆	3.6	441-7450	215-875-3200	None	None	None	Mary Ann B. Wirts	'92
GOLDMAN SACHS:SH DUR★	Short-Term Muni	77.5	10.21	10,160.50	☆	☆	0.0	526-7384	212-902-0800	None	None	None	Team Managed	'92
GRADISON-MCDONALD MUN:OH	Ohio Muni	60.7	13.39	10,428.90	☆	☆	0.0	869-5999	513-579-5700	2.00	0.25	None	Steve Dilbone	'92
GREAT HALL:MN INSURED	Minnesota Muni	28.9	10.53	10,277.40	11,082.60	15,662.20	5.4	934-6674	612-371-7981	4.50	0.30	None	Hippen/Kanzenbach	'86/'86
GREAT HALL:NATIONAL	High-Yield Muni	57.1	10.53	10,288.90	11,216.60	16,056.90	6.3	934-6674	612-371-7981	4.50	0.30	None	Hippen/Kanzenbach	'86/'86
J HANCOCK FR MGD TAX;A	General Muni	12.8	11.90	10,369.50	11,189.00	☆	5.8	225-5291	None	4.50	0.25	None	Bud Kingston	'92
J HANCOCK FR MGD TAX;B	General Muni	246.0	11.90	10,355.80	11,132.50	16,059.40	5.3	225-5291	None	None	0.75	4.00	Bud Kingston	'87
J HANCOCK TAX-EXEMPT	General Muni	513.1	11.48	10,354.70	11,133.00	15,927.50	5.2	225-5291	None	4.50	0.50	None	Frank Lucibella	'88
J HANCOCK TX-EX SRS:CA	California Muni	43.4	12.16	10,393.90	11,228.20	16,046.40	5.5	225-5291	None	4.50	0.50	None	Peggy Gartin	'92
J HANCOCK TX-EX SRS:MA	Massachusetts Muni	43.9	12.21	10,445.70	11,253.00	15,826.90	5.5	225-5291	None	4.50	0.50	None	Peggy Gartin	'92
J HANCOCK TX-EX SRS:NY	New York Muni	46.4	12.41	10,388.70	11,306.30	16,394.30	5.6	225-5291	None	4.50	0.50	None	Peggy Gartin	'92
HANIFEN,IMHOFF COL BD TX	Colorado Muni	32.0	9.11	10,208.60	10,874.00	14,065.30	7.4	525-9989	303-291-5414	4.75	None	None	Fred Kelly Jr.	'90
HAWAIIAN TX-FR TR	Single-State Muni	615.5	11.73	10,243.20	11,022.80	15,363.60	5.6	228-4227	212-697-6666	4.00	0.20	None	Lorene Okimoto	'91
HEARTLAND:WI TAX FREE	Single-State Muni	66.3	10.24	10,354.50	10,980.50	☆	4.8	432-7856	414-347-7777	3.00	None	None	Patrick Retzer	'92
IAA TRUST TAX EXEMPT BD	General Muni	19.7	9.11	10,233.40	10,919.30	15,048.10	5.0	245-2100	215-834-3500	3.00	0.25	None	Mary Guinane	'86
IAI:TAX FREE	General Muni	5.8	10.99	10,425.80	11,270.10	☆	4.3	945-3863	612-376-2700	None	0.10	None	Steve Coleman	'92
IBM MUNICIPAL BOND	Intermediate Muni	10.3	10.17	☆	☆	☆	0.0	426-9876	None	None	None	None	IBM Credit Invt Mgt	'93
IDEX II:TAX-EXEMPT	General Muni	29.5	11.91	10,230.30	10,839.50	15,382.50	4.6	624-4339	813-587-1800	4.75	0.35	None	Rachel Dennis	'85
IDS CA TAX-EXEMPT	California Muni	256.4	5.41	10,274.40	11,062.30	15,695.70	5.6	328-8300	612-671-3733	5.00	None	None	Paul Hylle	'93
IDS HIGH YLD TAX-EXEMPT	High-Yield Muni	6,444.7	4.77	10,244.50	10,990.10	15,796.10	6.3	328-8300	612-671-3733	5.00	None	None	Kurt Larson	'79
IDS INSURED TAX-EXEMPT	Insured Muni	445.9	5.63	10,299.00	11,159.50	16,055.90	5.3	328-8300	612-671-3733	5.00	None	None	Paul Hylle	'93
IDS MA TAX-EXEMPT	Massachusetts Muni	62.3	5.49	10,244.20	11,159.00	15,331.50	5.4	328-8300	612-671-3733	5.00	None	None	Paul Hylle	'93
IDS MI TAX-EXEMPT	Michigan Muni	69.6	5.60	10,301.60	11,154.00	15,747.70	5.5	328-8300	612-671-3733	5.00	None	None	Paul Hylle	'93
IDS MN TAX-EXEMPT	Minnesota Muni	393.3	5.44	10,253.30	11,053.30	15,650.80	5.8	328-8300	612-671-3733	5.00	None	None	Paul Hylle	'93
IDS NY TAX-EXEMPT	New York Muni	114.6	5.41	10,272.90	11,170.40	16,072.10	5.6	328-8300	612-671-3733	5.00	None	None	Paul Hylle	'93
IDS OH TAX-EXEMPT	Ohio Muni	61.9	5.58	10,265.50	11,194.40	15,681.10	5.5	328-8300	612-671-3733	5.00	None	None	Paul Hylle	'93
IDS TAX-EXEMPT BOND	General Muni	1,273.9	4.15	10,237.50	11,086.90	15,557.40	5.3	328-8300	612-671-3733	5.00	None	None	Terry Seirstad	'93
INDEPND CAP:MUNI BOND	General Muni	4.4	11.39	10,353.80	11,224.10	☆	5.0	950-4243	None	4.50	0.30	None	Peter Sherman	'90
INDEPND CAP:NY MUNI	New York Muni	4.6	11.81	10,341.10	11,281.50	☆	4.9	950-4243	None	4.50	0.30	None	Peter Sherman	'90
INVMNT SRS:MUNI INCOME	General Muni	7.9	11.90	10,267.60	10,994.40	15,966.70	5.5	245-4770	412-288-1900	5.75	None	None	Jonathan C. Conley	'87
INVESTORS PREFERENCE NY	New York Muni	30.1	13.27	10,304.40	11,164.60	☆	5.5	832-1373	509-353-3400	1.50	None	None	Robert Hennes	'91

JACKSON NATL:TAX-EXEMPT	General Muni	27.1	10.51	10,342.80	☆	☆	0.0	888-3863	None	4.75	None	None	PPM America	'92
JANUS FEDERAL TAX-EXEMPT	General Muni	5.1	7.15	☆	☆	☆	0.0	525-3713	303-333-3863	None	None	None	Ronald V. Speaker	'93
KEMPER MUNICIPAL BOND	General Muni	3,774.1	10.71	10,408.80	11,276.80	16,434.20	5.9	621-1048	816-421-4100	4.50	None	None	Beimford/Mier	'86/'91
KEMPER TAX-FREE INC:CA	California Muni	1,283.6	7.88	10,356.30	11,222.80	16,106.10	5.5	621-1048	816-421-4100	4.50	None	None	Beimford/Mier	'84/'89
KEMPER TAX-FREE INC:FL	Florida Muni	122.8	10.81	10,470.20	11,333.30	☆	5.4	621-1048	816-421-4100	4.50	None	None	Beimford/Mier	'91/'91
KEMPER TAX-FREE INC:NY	New York Muni	327.6	11.41	10,356.40	11,271.20	16,581.80	5.6	621-1048	816-421-4100	4.50	None	None	Beimford/Mier	'85/'89
KEMPER TAX-FREE INC:OH	Ohio Muni	11.7	9.82	10,552.60	☆	☆	0.0	621-1048	816-421-4100	4.50	None	None	Bimford/Mier	'93/'93
KEMPER TAX-FREE INC:TX	Texas Muni	11.2	10.52	10,426.40	11,335.40	☆	5.6	621-1048	816-421-4100	4.50	None	None	Beimford/Mier	'91/'91
KENT MED TX EX;INST	Intermediate Muni	71.0	10.31	10,196.90	☆	☆	0.0	343-2898	617-621-6100	None	None	None	Old Kent Bank	'92
KENT MED TX EX;INV	Intermediate Muni	1.6	10.33	10,196.50	☆	☆	0.0	343-2898	617-621-6100	4.00	0.25	None	Old Kent Bank	'92
KEYSTONE AM TXFR:FL;A	Florida Muni	45.3	11.19	10,378.70	11,196.90	☆	5.6	343-2898	617-621-6100	4.75	0.15	None	Betsy Blacher	'90
KEYSTONE AM TXFR:FL;B	Florida Muni	4.4	11.19	10,359.10	☆	☆	0.0	343-2898	617-621-6100	None	0.90	3.00	Betsy Blacher	'93
KEYSTONE AM TXFR:FL;C	Florida Muni	5.5	11.19	10,365.80	☆	☆	0.0	343-2898	617-621-6100	None	1.00	1.00	Betsy Blacher	'93
KEYSTONE AM TXFR INC;A	General Muni	124.8	10.55	10,286.40	11,075.80	15,672.00	5.7	343-2898	617-621-6100	4.75	0.25	None	Betsy Blacher	'88
KEYSTONE AM TXFR INC;B	General Muni	5.8	10.56	10,267.50	☆	☆	0.0	343-2898	617-621-6100	None	0.90	3.00	Betsy Blacher	'93
KEYSTONE AM TXFR INC;C	General Muni	9.6	10.55	10,267.70	☆	☆	0.0	343-2898	617-621-6100	None	1.00	1.00	Betsy Blacher	'93
KEYSTONE AM TXFR:PA;A	Pennsylvania Muni	33.7	11.69	10,385.70	11,268.30	☆	5.6	343-2898	617-621-6100	4.75	0.15	None	Betsy Blacher	'90
KEYSTONE AM TXFR:PA;B	Pennsylvania Muni	5.9	11.68	10,358.20	☆	☆	0.0	343-2898	617-621-6100	None	0.90	3.00	Betsy Blacher	'93
KEYSTONE AM TXFR:PA;C	Pennsylvania Muni	2.7	11.69	10,364.30	☆	☆	0.0	343-2898	617-621-6100	None	1.00	1.00	Betsy Blacher	'93
KEYSTONE AM TXFR:TX;A	Texas Muni	2.2	10.85	10,348.80	11,198.60	☆	5.7	343-2898	617-621-6100	4.75	None	None	Betsy Blacher	'92
KEYSTONE AM TXFR:TX;B	Texas Muni	0.5	10.88	10,337.50	☆	☆	0.0	343-2898	617-621-6100	None	0.90	3.00	Betsy Blacher	'93
KEYSTONE AM TXFR:TX;C	Texas Muni	0.1	10.85	10,325.80	☆	☆	0.0	343-2898	617-621-6100	None	1.00	1.00	Betsy Blacher	'93
KEYSTONE TAX EXEMPT TR	General Muni	790.4	11.49	10,256.90	10,984.20	15,424.20	5.5	343-2898	617-621-6100	None	1.00	4.00	Betsy Blacher	'88
KEYSTONE TAX FREE	General Muni	1,519.6	8.35	10,283.60	11,037.90	15,592.10	5.7	343-2898	617-621-6100	None	1.00	4.00	Betsy Blacher	'88
LANDMARK NY TX FR INCOME	New York Muni	99.2	11.33	10,265.90	11,139.10	16,118.60	5.0	223-4447	212-564-3456	3.00	0.20	None	Frank Flammino	'92
LEAHI TR:TAX FREE INCOME	General Muni	37.6	14.13	10,323.50	11,227.30	15,575.50	5.1	None	808-522-7777	None	0.25	None	Leahi Management Co.	'93
LEBENTHAL:NY MUNI	New York Muni	56.0	8.00	10,372.70	11,319.40	☆	5.6	221-5822	212-425-6116	4.50	None	None	Thomas P. Moles	'91
LEGG MASON TX-FR:INTMDT	Intermediate Muni	43.0	15.30	10,276.30	☆	☆	0.0	822-5544	410-539-0000	2.00	0.25	None	Victoria M. Schwatka	'92
LEGG MASON TX-FR:MD	Maryland Muni	135.5	16.29	10,335.30	11,219.90	☆	5.3	822-5544	410-539-0000	2.75	0.25	None	Victoria M. Schwatka	'91
LEGG MASON TX FR:PA	Pennsylvania Muni	54.0	16.46	10,407.10	11,313.60	☆	5.4	822-5544	410-539-0000	2.75	0.25	None	Victoria M. Schwatka	'91
LEXINGTON TX EX:NATL	General Muni	14.0	10.87	10,369.80	11,091.40	15,169.80	5.3	526-0056	201-845-7300	None	None	None	Denis P. Jamison	'86
LIBERTY FINL:INS MUNI	Insured Muni	17.8	10.82	10,328.50	11,067.30	☆	4.7	872-5426	617-722-6000	4.50	None	None	M. Jane McCart	'91
LIBERTY FINL:TAX-FR BOND	General Muni	235.9	10.73	10,289.70	11,175.90	15,790.50	5.4	872-5426	617-722-6000	4.50	None	None	M. Jane McCart	'92
LIBERTY MUNI SECS;A	General Muni	731.3	11.80	10,298.10	11,106.10	16,109.20	5.6	245-4770	412-288-1900	4.50	None	None	Jonathan C. Conley	'84
LIBERTY MUNI SECS;C	General Muni	1.0	11.80	☆	☆	☆	0.0	245-4770	412-288-1900	None	0.75	1.00	Jonathan C. Conley	'93
LOOMIS SAYLES:MUNI	General Muni	3.6	11.47	10,368.90	11,253.10	☆	4.5	633-3330	617-482-2450	None	None	None	Martha F. Hodgman	'93
LORD ABBETT CA TX-FR INC	California Muni	303.9	11.60	10,349.50	11,314.20	16,766.30	5.7	426-1130	212-848-1800	4.75	0.25	None	Barbara Grummel	'91
LORD ABBETT TX-FR:CT	Connecticut Muni	80.7	10.77	10,384.50	11,359.00	☆	5.7	426-1130	212-848-1800	4.75	0.25	None	Nicoletta Marinelli	'91
LORD ABBETT TX-FR:FL	Florida Muni	163.9	5.18	10,450.80	11,408.00	☆	5.8	426-1130	212-848-1800	4.75	0.25	None	Barbara Grummel	'91
LORD ABBETT TX-FR:HI	Single-State Muni	75.1	5.20	10,386.90	11,358.50	☆	5.9	426-1130	212-848-1800	4.75	0.25	None	Nicoletta Marinelli	'91
LORD ABBETT TX-FR:MI	Michigan Muni	18.9	5.12	10,414.10	☆	☆	0.0	426-1130	212-848-1800	4.75	None	None	Nicoletta Marinelli	'92
LORD ABBETT TX-FR:MO	Missouri Muni	92.0	5.40	10,352.10	11,278.90	☆	5.6	426-1130	212-848-1800	4.75	0.25	None	Barbara Grummel	'91
LORD ABBETT TX-FR:NATL	General Muni	647.0	12.10	10,342.10	11,289.50	16,530.70	5.7	426-1130	212-848-1800	4.75	0.25	None	Nicoletta Marinelli	'91
LORD ABBETT TX-FR:NJ	New Jersey Muni	153.4	5.44	10,332.90	11,420.90	☆	5.6	426-1130	212-848-1800	4.75	0.25	None	Nicoletta Marinelli	'91
LORD ABBETT TX-FR:NY	New York Muni	351.6	12.02	10,333.00	11,261.80	16,530.30	5.7	426-1130	212-848-1800	4.75	0.25	None	Barbara Grummel	'91

★GOLDMAN SACHS: SH DUR—Institutional fund.

PERFORMANCE OF MUTUAL FUNDS *(continued)*

FUND NAME	OBJECTIVE	TOTAL NET ASSETS ($ MIL) 5/31/93	NET ASSET $ VALUE 6/30/93	PERFORMANCE (Return on Initial $10,000 Investment) 3/31/93-6/30/93	6/30/92-6/30/93	6/30/88-6/30/93	DIVIDEND YIELD % 6/93	PHONE NUMBER 800	In-State	FEES Load	12b-1	Redemption	MANAGER	SINCE
LORD ABBETT TX-FR:PA	Pennsylvania Muni	63.8	5.20	10,428.60	11,397.20	☆	5.9	426-1130	212-848-1800	4.75	None	None	Nicoletta Marinelli	'92
LORD ABBETT TX-FR:TX	Texas Muni	99.3	10.58	10,323.10	11,163.30	16,676.40	5.8	426-1130	212-848-1800	4.75	0.25	None	Barbara Grummel	'91
LUTHERAN BRO MUNI BOND★	General Muni	574.5	8.81	10,333.20	11,242.20	16,207.50	5.8	328-4552	612-339-8091	5.00	None	None	Paul Hylle	'85
MACKENZIE CA MUNICIPAL	California Muni	46.5	10.45	10,268.50	10,955.50	15,456.00	5.5	456-5111	None	4.75	0.25	None	Team Managed	'83
MACKENZIE LTD MUNICIPAL	Intermediate Muni	87.9	10.47	10,171.70	10,696.80	☆	6.0	456-5111	None	3.00	0.25	None	Team Managed	'91
MACKENZIE NATL MUNICIPAL	General Muni	42.1	10.17	10,295.30	10,947.70	15,246.20	5.6	456-5111	None	4.75	0.25	None	Team Managed	'83
MACKENZIE NY MUNICIPAL	New York Muni	41.2	10.10	10,256.60	11,006.80	15,455.10	5.4	456-5111	None	4.75	0.25	None	Team Managed	'83
MAIN STREET CA TX-EX	California Muni	69.1	12.66	10,335.50	11,237.10	☆	6.4	548-1225	303-671-3691	4.75	None	None	Robert Patterson	'93
MAINSTAY:CA	California Muni	12.9	10.29	10,357.70	11,296.60	☆	5.8	522-4202	None	4.50	None	None	Ravi Akhoury	'91
MAINSTAY:NY	New York Muni	13.6	10.34	10,316.50	11,208.90	☆	6.3	522-4202	None	4.50	None	None	Ravi Akhoury	'91
MAINSTAY:TAX FREE BD	General Muni	422.4	10.34	10,291.30	11,105.20	15,160.70	5.9	522-4202	None	None	0.50	5.00	Ravi Akhoury	'85
MANAGERS:MUNI BOND	General Muni	16.9	0.00	N/A	N/A	N/A	0.0	835-3879	203-857-5321	None	None	None	Multiple Managers	'84
MANAGERS:SHORT MUNI	Short-Term Muni	6.9	0.00	N/A	N/A	N/A	0.0	835-3879	203-857-5321	None	None	None	Multiple Managers	'84
MGD MUNI;FLAG INV	General Muni	50.1	10.94	10,378.00	11,132.30	☆	5.6	645-3923	410-637-6819	4.50	0.25	None	R. Alan Medaugh	'90
MGD MUNI;ISI	General Muni	71.2	10.94	10,378.00	11,132.30	☆	5.6	645-3923	410-637-6819	4.45	0.25	None	R. Alan Medaugh	'90
MARINER NY TAX FREE BD	New York Muni	46.7	11.62	10,370.40	11,387.10	☆	5.4	634-2536	212-503-6826	4.75	0.20	None	Lucia Dunbar	'90
MARK TWAIN:MUNI INCOME	General Muni	21.6	10.35	10,314.20	☆	☆	0.0	None	314-889-0715	3.50	0.25	None	Randi Scofield	'93
MAS POOLED:MUNI FXD INC	General Muni	18.3	27.20	10,393.40	☆	☆	0.0	354-8185	215-940-5000	None	None	None	Team Managed	'92
MAS POOLED:PA MUNI FXD	Pennsylvania Muni	8.0	27.64	10,442.00	☆	☆	0.0	354-8185	215-940-5000	None	None	None	Team Managed	'92
MERRILL CA MUNI:BOND;A	California Muni	56.3	12.19	10,347.80	11,249.40	☆	5.8	None	609-282-2800	4.00	None	None	Vincent Giordano	'88
MERRILL CA MUNI:BOND;B	California Muni	781.2	12.20	10,343.40	11,192.80	15,679.70	5.3	None	609-282-2800	None	0.50	4.00	Vincent Giordano	'85
MERRILL CA MUNI:INS;A	California Muni	16.0	9.99	10,396.60	☆	☆	0.0	None	609-282-2800	4.00	None	None	Vincent Giordano	'93
MERRILL CA MUNI:INS;B	California Muni	61.9	9.99	10,383.90	☆	☆	0.0	None	609-282-2800	None	0.50	4.00	Vincent Giordano	'93
MERRILL MULTI MUN:AZ;A	Arizona Muni	17.2	11.06	10,385.50	11,376.20	☆	5.4	None	609-282-2800	4.00	None	None	Vincent Giordano	'9[illegible]
MERRILL MULTI MUN:AZ;B	Arizona Muni	77.3	11.06	10,372.50	11,319.30	☆	4.9	None	609-282-2800	None	0.50	4.00	Vincent Giordano	'9[illegible]
MERRILL MULTI MUN:FL;A	Florida Muni	68.7	10.88	10,429.70	11,230.20	☆	5.5	None	609-282-2800	4.00	None	None	Vincent Giordano	'9[illegible]
MERRILL MULTI MUN:FL;B	Florida Muni	207.3	10.88	10,416.70	11,174.00	☆	5.0	None	609-282-2800	None	0.50	4.00	Vincent Giordano	'91
MERRILL MULTI MUN:MA;A	Massachusetts Muni	6.1	11.13	10,505.30	11,480.50	☆	5.6	None	609-282-2800	4.00	None	None	Vincent Giordano	'92
MERRILL MULTI MUN:MA;B	Massachusetts Muni	65.9	11.13	10,492.10	11,423.10	☆	5.1	None	609-282-2800	None	0.50	4.00	Vincent Giordano	'92
MERRILL MULTI MUN:MI;A	Michigan Muni	12.0	10.36	10,439.00	☆	☆	0.0	None	609-282-2800	4.00	None	None	Vincent Giordano	'93
MERRILL MULTI MUN:MI;B	Michigan Muni	38.6	10.36	10,426.00	☆	☆	0.0	None	609-282-2800	None	0.50	4.00	Vincent Giordano	'93
MERRILL MULTI MUN:MN;A	Minnesota Muni	11.4	10.84	10,401.80	11,259.30	☆	5.4	None	609-282-2800	4.00	None	None	Vincent Giordano	'92
MERRILL MULTI MUN:MN;B	Minnesota Muni	52.0	10.84	10,388.80	11,202.40	☆	5.0	None	609-282-2800	None	0.50	4.00	Vincent Giordano	'92
MERRILL MULTI MUN:NJ;A	New Jersey Muni	43.8	11.28	10,376.30	11,148.20	☆	5.5	None	609-282-2800	4.00	None	None	Vincent Giordano	'90
MERRILL MULTI MUN:NJ;B	New Jersey Muni	161.3	11.28	10,363.20	11,092.40	☆	5.0	None	609-282-2800	None	0.50	4.00	Vincent Giordano	'90
MERRILL MULTI MUN:NY;A	New York Muni	28.6	12.22	10,346.80	11,270.20	☆	5.7	None	609-282-2800	4.00	None	None	Vincent Giordano	'90
MERRILL MULTI MUN:NY;B	New York Muni	679.3	12.22	10,333.90	11,213.90	15,972.70	5.3	None	609-282-2800	None	0.50	4.00	Vincent Giordano	'90
MERRILL MULTI MUN:NC;A	North Carolina Muni	8.4	10.70	10,424.90	☆	☆	0.0	None	609-282-2800	4.00	None	None	Vincent Giordano	'92
MERRILL MULTI MUN:NC;B	North Carolina Muni	34.8	10.70	10,412.00	☆	☆	0.0	None	609-282-2800	None	0.50	4.00	Vincent Giordano	'92
MERRILL MULTI MUN:OH;A	Ohio Muni	7.1	11.08	10,512.30	11,428.90	☆	5.2	None	609-282-2800	4.00	None	None	Vincent Giordano	'92
MERRILL MULTI MUN:OH;B	Ohio Muni	48.3	11.08	10,499.20	11,371.50	☆	4.8	None	609-282-2800	None	0.50	4.00	Vincent Giordano	'92
MERRILL MULTI MUN:PA;A	Pennsylvania Muni	26.6	11.45	10,392.20	11,299.30	☆	5.6	None	609-282-2800	4.00	None	None	Vincent Giordano	'90
MERRILL MULTI MUN:PA;B	Pennsylvania Muni	102.7	11.45	10,379.10	11,242.50	☆	5.1	None	609-282-2800	None	0.50	4.00	Vincent Giordano	'90
MERRILL MULTI MUN:TX;A	Texas Muni	13.5	11.14	10,448.90	11,310.50	☆	5.6	None	609-282-2800	4.00	None	None	Vincent Giordano	'91
MERRILL MULTI MUN:TX;B	Texas Muni	70.0	11.14	10,435.80	11,254.00	☆	5.1	None	609-282-2800	None	0.50	4.00	Vincent Giordano	'91

MERRILL MUNI:INS;A	Insured Muni	2,156.4	8.64	10,383.30	11,241.50	16,193.00	5.7	None	609-282-2800	4.00	None	None	Vincent Giordano	'79
MERRILL MUNI:INS;B	Insured Muni	887.1	8.63	10,351.80	11,144.30	☆	5.0	None	609-282-2800	None	0.75	4.00	Vincent Giordano	'88
MERRILL MUNI:LTD MAT;A	Short-Term Muni	837.3	10.01	10,107.10	10,527.60	13,479.40	4.1	None	609-282-2800	0.75	None	None	Vincent Giordano	'79
MERRILL MUNI:LTD MAT;B	Short-Term Muni	85.8	10.01	10,098.30	☆	☆	0.0	None	609-282-2800	None	0.35	1.00	Vincent Giordano	'92
MERRILL MUNI:NATL;A	General Muni	1,337.3	11.02	10,404.00	11,219.00	16,170.80	6.0	None	609-282-2800	4.00	None	None	Vincent Giordano	'79
MERRILL MUNI:NATL;B	General Muni	408.6	11.02	10,384.60	11,145.50	☆	5.3	None	609-282-2800	None	0.75	4.00	Vincent Giordano	'88
MERRILL MUNI SRS:INC;A	Intermediate Muni	18.9	10.23	10,287.30	11,094.90	☆	5.5	None	609-282-2800	2.00	None	None	Vincent Giordano	'88
MERRILL MUNI SRS:INC;B	Intermediate Muni	143.6	10.23	10,279.40	11,061.30	14,803.70	5.2	None	609-282-2800	None	0.30	2.00	Vincent Giordano	'88
METLIFE SS TAX-EX:TX-EX	General Muni	258.9	8.34	10,345.50	11,263.70	16,143.00	4.9	882-3302	617-348-2000	4.50	0.25	None	Susan Drake	'90
MFS CA MUNI	California Muni	298.4	5.87	10,318.00	11,303.20	16,348.50	5.8	225-2606	617-954-5000	4.75	0.35	None	David Smith	'93
MFS HIGH YIELD MUNI ★	High-Yield Muni	760.6	9.41	10,269.60	11,071.50	15,267.60	7.8	225-2606	617-954-5000	4.75	None	None	Robin Huntley	'84
MFS LIFETIME MUNI BOND	General Muni	500.0	8.99	10,285.00	11,075.80	15,365.00	5.5	225-2606	617-954-5000	None	1.00	5.00	Robert Dennis	'87
MFS MULTI-STATE:AL	Single-State Muni	76.0	10.71	10,313.50	11,232.80	☆	5.3	225-2606	617-954-5000	4.75	0.35	None	David Smith	'92
MFS MULTI-STATE:AR	Single-State Muni	157.0	10.23	10,302.10	11,239.20	☆	5.8	225-2606	617-954-5000	4.75	0.35	None	Cindy Brown	'92
MFS MULTI-STATE:FL	Florida Muni	90.2	10.43	10,447.80	11,423.50	☆	5.7	225-2606	617-954-5000	4.75	0.35	None	Cindy Brown	'92
MFS MULTI-STATE:GA	Georgia Muni	74.7	10.96	10,331.20	11,160.60	15,724.20	5.4	225-2606	617-954-5000	4.75	0.35	None	David Smith	'92
MFS MULTI-STATE:LA	Louisiana Muni	8.2	9.80	10,415.40	☆	☆	0.0	225-2606	617-954-5000	4.75	0.35	None	Cindy Brown	'93
MFS MULTI-STATE:MD	Maryland Muni	159.4	11.69	10,287.10	11,038.30	15,321.40	5.8	225-2606	617-954-5000	4.75	0.35	None	David Smith	'92
MFS MULTI-STATE:MA	Massachusetts Muni	283.9	11.68	10,255.00	11,126.70	15,624.20	6.0	225-2606	617-954-5000	4.75	0.35	None	Cindy Brown	'92
MFS MULTI-STATE:MS	Single-State Muni	59.8	9.75	10,410.90	☆	☆	0.0	225-2606	617-954-5000	4.75	0.35	None	Cindy Brown	'92
MFS MULTI-STATE:NY	New York Muni	161.1	11.18	10,318.70	11,316.30	16,347.20	5.7	225-2606	617-954-5000	4.75	0.35	None	Cindy Brown	'93
MFS MULTI-STATE:NC	North Carolina Muni	437.6	12.15	10,304.10	11,083.10	15,362.80	5.4	225-2606	617-954-5000	4.75	0.35	None	Cindy Brown	'92
MFS MULTI-STATE:PA	Pennsylvania Muni	8.8	9.76	10,478.20	☆	☆	0.0	225-2606	617-954-5000	4.75	0.35	None	Cindy Brown	'93
MFS MULTI-STATE:SC	South Carolina Muni	162.7	12.42	10,300.00	11,057.80	15,659.70	5.4	225-2606	617-954-5000	4.75	0.35	None	David Smith	'92
MFS MULTI-STATE:TX	Texas Muni	11.3	10.50	10,436.30	11,366.90	☆	5.8	225-2606	617-954-5000	4.75	0.35	None	David Smith	'92
MFS MULTI-STATE:VA	Virginia Muni	432.1	11.93	10,294.90	11,078.30	15,713.30	5.7	225-2606	617-954-5000	4.75	0.35	None	Cindy Brown	'92
MFS MULTI-STATE:WV	Single-State Muni	127.8	11.87	10,312.30	11,117.10	15,777.80	5.6	225-2606	617-954-5000	4.75	0.35	None	Cindy Brown	'92
MFS MUNICIPAL BOND	General Muni	2,090.5	11.44	10,306.00	11,337.00	16,484.30	6.1	225-2606	617-954-5000	4.75	0.35	None	Robert Dennis	'84
MFS MUNI LTD MATURITY	Short-Term Muni	65.0	7.67	10,219.10	10,863.20	☆	4.2	225-2606	617-954-5000	2.50	0.35	None	Robert Dennis	'92
MIDWEST TX FR:INTMDT	Intermediate Muni	78.5	10.98	10,277.80	11,074.90	14,542.50	4.8	543-8721	513-629-2000	1.00	0.25	None	John Goetz	'86
MIDWEST TX FR:OH INSURED	Ohio Muni	76.9	12.41	10,370.10	11,223.50	15,657.60	5.2	543-8721	513-629-2000	4.00	0.25	None	John Goetz	'86
MONITOR:OH TAX-FR;INV	Ohio Muni	1.9	21.78	10,204.20	10,770.30	☆	4.2	253-0412	614-463-5580	4.00	0.25	None	William Doughty	'91
MONITOR:OH TAX-FR;TR	Ohio Muni	52.6	21.78	10,211.20	10,800.40	☆	4.5	253-0412	614-463-5580	None	None	None	William Doughty	'88
MORGAN GRENFELL MUNI	Intermediate Muni	120.8	11.20	10,334.20	11,366.80	☆	5.9	932-7781	215-989-6611	None	None	None	David Baldt	'91
MUIR:CA TAX FREE BOND	California Muni	16.5	16.97	10,315.30	11,189.00	☆	4.0	648-3448	415-677-8500	4.50	None	None	Kieschnick/Seneca	'91/'91
MUNI CAL:INTMDT;INTER	California Muni	17.3	10.77	10,230.10	10,927.40	☆	5.1	821-7432	None	None	None	None	Cathryn Allen	'88
MUNI TEMP:INTMDT;SHS	Intermediate Muni	23.7	11.16	10,212.00	10,882.20	14,622.30	4.8	821-7432	None	None	None	None	Robert Morgan	'92
MUNI SECS INC:CA;FORT	California Muni	9.8	10.74	10,390.10	☆	☆	0.0	245-4770	412-288-1900	1.00	0.50	1.00	Jonathan C. Conley	'92
MUNI SECS INC:MI	Michigan Muni	45.5	10.89	10,314.30	11,123.50	☆	5.0	245-4770	412-288-1900	3.00	None	None	Jonathan C. Conley	'91
MUNI SECS INC:NY;FORT	New York Muni	11.2	10.75	10,446.60	☆	☆	0.0	245-4770	412-288-1900	1.00	0.50	1.00	Jonathan C. Conley	'92
MUNI SECS INC:OH;FORT	Ohio Muni	66.5	11.47	10,415.80	11,230.80	☆	5.1	245-4770	412-288-1900	1.00	0.40	1.00	Jonathan C. Conley	'90
MUNI SECS INC:OH;TR	Ohio Muni	5.3	11.47	10,424.00	11,263.20	☆	5.4	245-4770	412-288-1900	None	None	None	Jonathan C. Conley	'92
MUNI SECS INC:PA;INV	Pennsylvania Muni	63.9	11.53	10,400.50	11,260.90	☆	5.2	245-4770	412-288-1900	3.00	0.40	None	Jonathan C. Conley	'90
MUNI SECS INC:PA;TR	Pennsylvania Muni	11.6	11.54	10,417.70	11,304.10	☆	5.5	245-4770	412-288-1900	None	None	None	Jonathan C. Conley	'92
MUTUAL OF OMAHA TAX-FREE	General Muni	507.7	12.66	10,328.80	11,238.10	16,559.50	5.4	228-9596	402-397-8555	4.75	0.25	None	Mark Winter	'86
NARRAGANSETT INS TX-FREE	Single-State Muni	12.3	10.07	10,368.40	☆	☆	0.0	453-6864	212-697-6666	4.00	0.15	None	Salvtore DiSanto	'92
NATIONAL CA TAX EXEMPT	California Muni	145.8	13.76	10,265.90	10,956.10	15,775.20	5.7	223-7757	203-863-5600	4.75	0.15	None	John DeJong	'83
NATIONAL SEC TAX EXEMPT	General Muni	112.1	10.76	10,270.90	11,015.30	15,921.40	5.9	223-7757	203-863-5600	4.75	0.15	None	John DeJong	'76
NATIONS:FL INT;INV A	Florida Muni	2.0	10.43	10,296.90	☆	☆	0.0	321-7854	None	2.50	0.15	None	Michelle Poirier	'92
NATIONS:FL INT;INV B	Florida Muni	0.5	10.43	10,281.60	☆	☆	0.0	321-7854	None	None	0.75	1.00	Michelle Poirier	'92

★LUTHERAN BRO MUNI BOND—Limited to Lutherans.

★MFS HIGH YIELD MUNI—Closed to new investors.

PERFORMANCE OF MUTUAL FUNDS (continued)

FUND NAME	OBJECTIVE	TOTAL NET ASSETS ($ MIL) 5/31/93	NET ASSET $ VALUE 6/30/93	PERFORMANCE (Return on Initial $10,000 Investment) 3/31/93-6/30/93	6/30/92-6/30/93	6/30/88-6/30/93	DIVIDEND YIELD % 6/93	PHONE NUMBER 800	In-State	FEES Load	12b-1	Redemption	MANAGER	SINCE
NATIONS:FL INT;TR A	Florida Muni	23.2	10.43	10,300.60	☆	☆	0.0	321-7854	None	None	None	None	Michelle Poirier	'92
NATIONS:GA INT;INV A	Georgia Muni	15.9	10.74	10,286.60	11,103.10	☆	4.7	321-7854	None	2.50	0.15	None	Michelle Poirier	'92
NATIONS:GA INT;INV B	Georgia Muni	2.7	10.74	10,281.80	11,037.60	☆	4.2	321-7854	None	None	0.75	1.00	Michelle Poirier	'92
NATIONS:GA INT;TR A	Georgia Muni	25.6	10.74	10,290.50	11,119.90	☆	4.9	321-7854	None	None	None	None	Michelle Poirier	'92
NATIONS:MD INT;INV A	Maryland Muni	23.4	11.04	10,264.50	10,952.90	☆	4.5	321-7854	None	2.50	0.15	None	Cynthia Seibert	'90
NATIONS:MD INT;INV B	Maryland Muni	4.2	11.04	10,249.50	10,888.00	☆	3.9	321-7854	None	None	0.75	1.00	Cynthia Seibert	'92
NATIONS:MD INT;TR A	Maryland Muni	58.6	11.04	10,277.90	10,969.00	☆	4.7	321-7854	None	None	None	None	Cynthia Seibert	'90
NATIONS:MUNI INC:INV A	General Muni	27.2	11.27	10,396.80	11,284.40	☆	5.0	321-7854	None	2.50	0.15	None	Michelle Poirier	'91
NATIONS:MUNI INC;INV B	General Muni	6.7	11.27	10,381.50	11,217.30	☆	4.4	321-7854	None	None	0.75	1.00	Michelle Poirier	'92
NATIONS:MUNI INC;TR A	General Muni	87.9	11.27	10,410.20	11,301.30	☆	5.2	321-7854	None	None	None	None	Michelle Poirier	'91
NATIONS:NC INT;INV A	North Carolina Muni	10.8	10.43	10,292.70	☆	☆	0.0	321-7854	None	2.50	0.15	None	Michelle Poirier	'92
NATIONS:NC INT;INV B	North Carolina Muni	1.5	10.43	10,267.40	☆	☆	0.0	321-7854	None	None	0.75	1.00	Michelle Poirier	'92
NATIONS:NC INT;TR A	North Carolina Muni	10.8	10.43	10,296.50	☆	☆	0.0	321-7854	None	None	None	None	Michelle Poirier	'92
NATIONS:SC INT;INV A	South Carolina Muni	19.4	10.56	10,248.10	10,970.20	☆	4.8	321-7854	None	2.50	0.15	None	Michelle Poirier	'92
NATIONS:SC INT;INV B	South Carolina Muni	7.7	10.56	10,233.40	10,905.20	☆	4.2	321-7854	None	None	0.75	1.00	Michelle Poirier	'92
NATIONS:SC INT;TR A	South Carolina Muni	54.5	10.56	10,251.80	10,986.60	☆	4.9	321-7854	None	None	None	None	Michelle Poirier	'92
NATIONS:TX INT;INV A	Texas Muni	0.9	10.30	10,231.70	☆	☆	0.0	321-7854	None	2.50	0.15	None	Melinda Lestyan	'93
NATIONS:TX INT;TR A	Texas Muni	17.2	10.30	10,235.40	☆	☆	0.0	321-7854	None	None	None	None	Melinda Lestyan	'93
NATIONS:VA INT;INV A	Virginia Muni	92.8	10.96	10,298.80	10,979.70	☆	4.7	321-7854	None	2.50	0.15	None	Cynthia Seibert	'89
NATIONS:VA INT;INV B	Virginia Muni	10.3	10.96	10,293.10	10,913.90	☆	4.1	321-7854	None	None	0.75	1.00	Cynthia Seibert	'92
NATIONS:VA INT;TR A	Virginia Muni	177.8	10.96	10,312.30	10,996.10	☆	4.8	321-7854	None	None	None	None	Cynthia Seibert	'89
NATIONWIDE II:TX-FR	General Muni	218.7	10.65	10,309.80	11,250.20	15,961.80	5.1	848-0920	614-249-7855	None	0.20	5.00	Alpha Benson	'86
NCC OH;INSTL	Ohio Muni	40.1	10.94	10,251.90	10,987.60	☆	4.5	622-3863	None	None	0.14	None	Stephen P. Carpenter	'90
NCC OH;RETAIL	Ohio Muni	1.5	10.90	10,252.50	10,979.00	☆	4.5	622-3863	None	3.00	0.14	None	Stephen P. Carpenter	'91
ND TAX-FREE	Single-State Muni	74.2	9.56	10,235.20	10,550.60	☆	5.9	562-6637	701-852-5292	None	0.25	4.00	W. Dan Korgel	'89
N & B MUNI SECURITIES	Intermediate Muni	63.3	10.97	10,267.10	10,977.60	14,716.90	4.7	877-9700	212-476-8800	None	None	None	Havell/Giuliano	'87/'87
NORTH CAROLINA TX FR BD	North Carolina Muni	1.9	10.29	10,243.90	☆	☆	0.0	525-3863	919-972-9922	None	None	None	T. Leavell	'93
NORTHWEST:IDAHO TAX-EX	Single-State Muni	6.3	5.23	10,167.10	10,817.80	14,240.30	5.0	728-8762	206-734-9900	None	None	None	Vern Clemenson	'87
NUVEEN AZ VALUE	Arizona Muni	10.7	10.49	10,404.70	11,288.80	☆	4.9	621-7227	312-917-7810	4.75	None	None	Steve Krupa	'92
NUVEEN CA INSURED VALUE	California Muni	180.8	10.85	10,350.10	11,223.80	16,399.90	5.2	621-7227	312-917-7810	4.75	None	None	Steve Krupa	'91
NUVEEN CA VALUE	California Muni	193.6	10.88	10,319.10	11,133.50	16,230.50	5.6	621-7227	312-917-7810	4.75	None	None	Steve Krupa	'91
NUVEEN FL VALUE	Florida Muni	31.0	10.39	10,376.20	11,247.30	☆	4.9	621-7227	312-917-7810	4.75	None	None	Tom Futfell	'92
NUVEEN INSURED MUNI BOND	Insured Muni	613.2	10.90	10,397.70	11,311.20	16,784.90	5.2	621-7227	312-917-7810	4.75	None	None	William Norris	'87
NUVEEN MD VALUE	Maryland Muni	35.0	10.37	10,396.40	11,245.80	☆	5.0	621-7227	312-917-7810	4.75	None	None	Ted Neild	'92
NUVEEN MA INSURED VALUE	Massachusetts Muni	50.6	10.47	10,373.40	11,209.70	15,986.50	5.0	621-7227	312-917-7810	4.75	None	None	William Norris	'87
NUVEEN MA VALUE	Massachusetts Muni	59.6	9.97	10,388.50	11,238.70	16,120.70	5.6	621-7227	312-917-7810	4.75	None	None	William Norris	'87
NUVEEN MI VALUE	Michigan Muni	18.7	10.55	10,414.10	11,347.90	☆	5.0	621-7227	312-917-7810	4.75	None	None	Ted Neild	'92
NUVEEN MUNI BOND	General Muni	2,453.2	9.46	10,235.30	10,923.40	15,779.70	5.6	621-7227	312-917-7810	4.75	None	None	Thomas Spalding	'77
NUVEEN NJ VALUE	New Jersey Muni	22.4	10.30	10,331.00	11,106.40	☆	5.1	621-7227	312-917-7810	4.75	None	None	Steve Peterson	'92
NUVEEN NY INSURED VALUE	New York Muni	337.6	10.72	10,398.80	11,330.70	16,505.90	5.1	621-7227	312-917-7810	4.75	None	None	William Norris	'87
NUVEEN NY VALUE	New York Muni	116.5	10.72	10,350.60	11,274.90	16,466.50	5.4	621-7227	312-917-7810	4.75	None	None	William Norris	'87
NUVEEN OH VALUE	Ohio Muni	141.4	10.69	10,397.20	11,252.20	16,641.40	5.4	621-7227	312-917-7810	4.75	None	None	William Norris	'87
NUVEEN PA VALUE	Pennsylvania Muni	32.1	10.48	10,428.80	11,259.60	☆	5.0	621-7227	312-917-7810	4.75	None	None	Tom O'Shaughnessy	'92
NUVEEN VA VALUE	Virginia Muni	43.8	10.46	10,407.30	11,276.70	☆	4.9	621-7227	312-917-7810	4.75	None	None	Bill Fitzgerald	'92
OLYMPUS:CA INTMDT TX-FR	California Muni	41.2	10.19	10,196.80	10,788.50	14,872.20	5.0	950-2748	310-553-6740	4.75	None	None	Richard Berry	'88

OLYMPUS:NATL TAX-FREE	General Muni	7.4	7.77	10,217.10	10,841.60	14,264.00	6.5	950-2748	310-553-6740	4.75	None	None	Robert Washer	'89
ONE GROUP:INT TX-FR;FID	Intermediate Muni	163.1	11.15	10,254.80	10,979.30	☆	4.7	338-4345	None	None	None	None	Mike Graham	'90
ONE GROUP:INT TX-FR;INV	Intermediate Muni	4.2	11.14	10,240.10	10,946.70	☆	4.5	338-4345	None	4.50	0.25	None	Mike Graham	'92
ONE GROUP:OH MUNI BD;FID	Ohio Muni	72.1	11.11	10,296.20	11,142.70	☆	4.8	338-4345	None	None	None	None	Roberta Olsen	'91
ONE GROUP:OH MUNI BD;INV	Ohio Muni	12.1	11.13	10,299.60	11,139.70	☆	4.6	338-4345	None	4.50	0.25	None	Roberta Olsen	'92
ONE GROUP:TX-FR BD;FID	General Muni	36.3	10.11	10,201.30	☆	☆	0.0	342-5734	215-254-1000	None	None	None	Patrick Morrissey	'93
111 CORCORAN:NC MUNI	North Carolina Muni	28.1	10.52	10,340.30	10,955.90	☆	3.9	422-2080	919-683-7277	4.50	None	None	Jim Agnew	'92
OPPENHEIMER CA TX-EX;A	California Muni	243.7	10.82	10,322.00	11,254.90	☆	5.7	525-7048	303-671-3200	4.75	0.25	None	Robert Patterson	'88
OPPENHEIMER NY TX-EX;A	New York Muni	701.1	13.15	10,339.80	11,240.80	15,886.40	5.3	525-7048	303-671-3200	4.75	0.25	None	Robert Patterson	'85
OPPENHEIMER PA TX-EX;A	Pennsylvania Muni	49.5	12.62	10,327.90	11,285.30	☆	5.5	525-7048	303-671-3200	4.75	0.15	None	Robert Patterson	'89
OPPENHEIMER TX-EX:INS;A	Insured Muni	49.9	17.63	10,353.80	11,340.00	16,535.90	5.5	525-7048	303-671-3200	4.75	0.25	None	Robert Patterson	'92
OPPENHEIMER TX-EX:INTMDT	Intermediate Muni	57.5	15.07	10,231.10	11,036.00	16,215.20	5.2	525-7048	303-671-3200	3.50	0.25	None	Robert Patterson	'92
OPPENHEIMER TX-FR BD;A	General Muni	566.8	10.36	10,366.70	11,262.70	16,025.50	5.7	525-7048	303-671-3200	4.75	0.25	None	Robert Patterson	'85
OREGON MUNICIPAL BOND	Oregon Muni	24.1	12.66	10,218.10	10,886.10	14,605.40	4.7	541-9732	503-295-0111	None	0.14	None	Jay Willoughby	'84
OVERLAND EXP:CA TX-FR BD	California Muni	378.6	11.47	10,379.70	11,240.30	☆	5.7	552-9612	None	4.50	None	None	Wines/Klug	'88/'88
OVERLAND EXP:MUNI INCOME	General Muni	78.7	11.07	10,384.70	11,303.20	☆	6.0	552-9612	None	3.00	0.25	None	Wines/Sabrell	'91/'91
P HZN:CA TX-EX BOND	California Muni	210.4	15.12	10,345.40	11,223.20	15,742.30	5.6	332-3863	619-456-9197	4.50	0.10	None	Kim Michalski	'84
PACIFICA:CA TAX-FREE	California Muni	209.7	11.30	10,336.70	11,154.10	☆	5.1	662-8417	212-309-8400	4.50	0.03	None	Kelli Chaux	'90
PAINEWBR CALIF TX-FR;A	California Muni	235.9	11.78	10,288.40	11,114.30	15,481.90	5.3	647-1568	None	4.00	0.25	None	Gregory Serbe	'85
PAINEWBR CALIF TX-FR;B	California Muni	39.9	11.79	10,268.90	11,030.30	☆	4.6	647-1568	None	None	1.00	5.00	Gregory Serbe	'91
PAINEWBR CALIF TX-FR;D	California Muni	47.7	11.77	10,275.50	☆	☆	0.0	647-1568	None	None	0.75	None	Gregory Serbe	'92
PAINEWBR MUNI HI INC;A	High-Yield Muni	81.1	11.01	10,368.50	11,203.70	16,535.40	5.8	647-1568	None	4.00	0.25	None	Gregory Serbe	'87
PAINEWBR MUNI HI INC;B	High-Yield Muni	26.3	11.01	10,348.80	11,129.30	☆	5.1	647-1568	None	None	1.00	5.00	Gregory Serbe	'91
PAINEWBR MUNI HI INC;D	High-Yield Muni	26.8	11.01	10,355.10	☆	☆	0.0	647-1568	None	None	0.75	None	Gregory Serbe	'92
PAINEWBR NATL TX-FR;A	General Muni	419.5	12.18	10,383.20	11,195.20	15,786.00	5.5	647-1568	None	4.00	0.25	None	Gregory Serbe	'84
PAINEWBR NATL TX-FR;B	General Muni	57.2	12.18	10,372.60	11,111.50	☆	4.7	647-1568	None	None	1.00	5.00	Gregory Serbe	'91
PAINEWBR NATL TX-FR;D	General Muni	168.7	12.18	10,370.30	☆	☆	0.0	647-1568	None	None	0.75	None	Gregory Serbe	'92
PAINEWBR NY TX-FR;A	New York Muni	44.7	11.11	10,365.20	11,305.60	☆	5.5	647-1568	None	4.00	0.25	None	Gregory Serbe	'88
PAINEWBR NY TX-FR;B	New York Muni	14.9	11.11	10,355.40	11,231.70	☆	4.7	647-1568	None	None	1.00	5.00	Gregory Serbe	'91
PAINEWBR NY TX-FR;D	New York Muni	25.0	11.11	10,351.70	☆	☆	0.0	647-1568	None	None	0.75	None	Gregory Serbe	'92
PARAGON:LA TAX-FREE	Louisiana Muni	171.1	10.92	10,259.10	11,026.60	☆	5.2	None	504-332-5968	4.50	None	None	Keith Mooney	'89
PARKSTONE:MI MUNI;A	Michigan Muni	30.2	10.97	☆	☆	☆	0.0	451-8377	None	4.00	0.10	None	First of Amer Invt Corp	'93
PARKSTONE:MI MUNI;C	Michigan Muni	162.0	10.97	10,265.40	10,941.90	☆	4.9	451-8377	None	None	None	None	First of Amer Invt Corp	'90
PARKSTONE:MUNI BOND;A	Intermediate Muni	9.0	10.92	☆	☆	☆	0.0	451-8377	None	4.00	0.10	None	First of Amer Invt Corp	'93
PARKSTONE:MUNI BOND;C	Intermediate Muni	144.4	10.92	10,236.20	10,947.60	☆	4.9	451-8377	None	None	None	None	First of Amer Invt Corp	'88
PARNASSUS:CA TX-FR	California Muni	2.2	15.84	10,310.90	☆	☆	0.0	999-3505	415-362-3505	None	None	None	David Pogran	'92
PHOENIX TAX-EXEMPT BOND	General Muni	53.1	11.50	10,354.80	11,333.40	☆	5.5	243-4361	203-253-1000	4.75	0.25	None	James Wehr	'88
PILGRIM TX-FR:CA;A	California Muni	2.2	7.62	10,281.20	☆	☆	0.0	334-3444	310-551-0833	3.00	0.25	None	Leschner Financial	'93
PILGRIM TX-FR:CA;B	California Muni	0.3	7.60	10,267.90	☆	☆	0.0	334-3444	310-551-0833	None	1.00	4.50	Leschner Financial	'93
PILGRIM TX-FR:FL;A	Florida Muni	3.4	7.56	10,500.70	☆	☆	0.0	334-3444	310-551-0833	3.00	0.25	None	Leschner Financial	'93
PILGRIM TX-FR:FL;B	Florida Muni	2.1	7.47	10,390.20	☆	☆	0.0	334-3444	310-551-0833	None	1.00	4.50	Leschner Financial	'93
PILGRIM TX-FR:NY;A	New York Muni	0.6	7.48	10,354.00	☆	☆	0.0	334-3444	310-551-0833	3.00	0.25	None	Leschner Financial	'93
PILGRIM TX-FR:NY;B	New York Muni	1.9	7.47	10,354.40	☆	☆	0.0	334-3444	310-551-0833	None	1.00	4.50	Leschner Financial	'93
PILLAR:NJ MUNI;A★	New Jersey Muni	16.7	10.67	10,288.20	11,040.00	☆	4.5	932-7782	None	None	0.25	None	Charlene Palmer	'92
PILLAR:NJ MUNI;B	New Jersey Muni	11.6	10.66	10,261.00	10,991.70	☆	4.1	932-7782	None	1.00	0.25	None	Charlene Palmer	'92
PIONEER CA DOUBLE TX-FR	California Muni	3.2	11.36	10,312.80	☆	☆	0.0	225-6292	617-742-7825	3.50	0.15	None	Kathy McClaskey	'93
PIONEER MA DOUBLE TX-FR	Massachusetts Muni	2.7	11.31	10,378.80	☆	☆	0.0	225-6292	617-742-7825	3.50	0.15	None	Kathy McClaskey	'93
PIONEER MUNICIPAL BOND	General Muni	69.0	10.71	10,363.90	11,101.70	16,036.50	5.3	225-6292	617-742-7825	4.50	0.15	None	Kathy McClaskey	'86
PIONEER NY TRIPLE TX-FR	New York Muni	2.4	11.32	10,402.60	☆	☆	0.0	225-6292	617-742-7825	3.50	0.15	None	Kathy McClaskey	'93
PIPER JAFFRAY:MINN TX-EX	Minnesota Muni	158.2	11.22	10,322.70	11,147.30	☆	5.6	866-7778	612-342-6402	4.00	0.22	None	Reuss/White	'88/'88

★PILLAR: NJ MUNI; A—Institutional fund.

PERFORMANCE OF MUTUAL FUNDS *(continued)*

FUND NAME	OBJECTIVE	TOTAL NET ASSETS ($ MIL) 5/31/93	NET ASSET $ VALUE 6/30/93	PERFORMANCE (Return on Initial $10,000 Investment) 3/31/93-6/30/93	6/30/92-6/30/93	6/30/88-6/30/93	DIVIDEND YIELD % 6/93	PHONE NUMBER 800	In-State	FEES Load	12b-1	Redemption	MANAGER	SINCE
PIPER JAFFRAY:NATL TX-EX	General Muni	71.8	11.46	10,357.60	11,314.90	☆	5.4	866-7778	612-342-6402	4.00	0.22	None	Reuss/White	'88/'88
PNC:OH TX-FR INC;INV	Ohio Muni	2.4	10.32	10,282.50	☆	☆	0.0	428-7108	None	4.50	0.55	None	T. Radford Hazelip	'92
PNC:PA TX-FR INC;INV	Pennsylvania Muni	25.3	10.50	10,301.90	☆	☆	0.0	428-7108	None	4.50	0.55	None	T. Radford Hazelip	'92
PNC:TX-FR INCOME;INV	General Muni	9.1	11.06	10,348.40	11,221.40	☆	5.0	428-7108	None	4.50	0.55	None	W. Donald Simmons	'90
PORTICO TX-EX INTMDT	Intermediate Muni	16.0	10.11	10,214.20	☆	☆	0.0	982-8909	414-287-3710	None	None	None	Elfe	'93
T ROWE PRICE CA TX-FR:BD	California Muni	145.7	10.69	10,326.40	11,204.40	15,811.70	5.3	638-5660	410-547-2308	None	None	None	Mary J. Miller	'90
T ROWE PRICE TX-FR:FL IN	Florida Muni	N/A	10.27	10,370.50	☆	☆	0.0	638-5660	410-547-2308	None	None	None	William T. Reynolds	'93
T ROWE PRICE TX-FR:GA BD	Georgia Muni	N/A	10.29	10,406.70	☆	☆	0.0	638-5660	410-547-2308	None	None	None	Carol Anne Miller	'93
T ROWE PRICE TX-FR:HI YD	High-Yield Muni	866.3	12.42	10,387.70	11,268.00	16,394.70	6.1	638-5660	410-547-2308	None	None	None	C. Stephen Wolfe	'93
T ROWE PRICE TX-FR INC	General Muni	1,435.1	9.90	10,368.70	11,322.70	15,807.30	5.5	638-5660	410-547-2308	None	None	None	William T. Reynolds	'90
T ROWE PRICE TX-FR INS	Intermediate Muni	63.4	10.57	10,357.50	☆	☆	0.0	638-5660	410-547-2308	None	None	None	William T. Reynolds	'92
T ROWE PRICE TX-FR:MD BD	Maryland Muni	737.2	10.59	10,389.90	11,262.90	15,812.50	5.4	638-5660	410-547-2308	None	None	None	Mary J. Miller	'90
T ROWE PRICE TX-FR:NJ BD	New Jersey Muni	43.2	11.28	10,450.10	11,415.90	☆	5.0	638-5660	410-547-2308	None	None	None	William T. Reynolds	'91
T ROWE PRICE TX-FR:NY BD	New York Muni	114.6	11.10	10,370.60	11,357.10	16,110.00	5.5	638-5660	410-547-2308	None	None	None	William T. Reynolds	'86
T ROWE PRICE TX FR SH-IN	Short-Term Muni	477.6	5.35	10,166.10	10,674.30	13,691.00	4.4	638-5660	410-547-2308	None	None	None	Mary J. Miller	'89
T ROWE PRICE TX-FR:SH MD	Short-Term Muni	28.0	5.08	10,134.80	☆	☆	0.0	638-5660	410-547-2308	None	None	None	Mary J. Miller	'93
T ROWE PRICE TX-FR:VA BD	Virginia Muni	125.6	11.16	10,418.20	11,307.90	☆	5.2	638-5660	410-547-2308	None	None	None	Mary J. Miller	'91
PRIME VALUE:ALTURA MN	Minnesota Muni	10.9	10.77	10,315.70	10,986.50	14,994.70	5.1	338-1348	612-667-8833	3.00	None	None	Pat Hovanetz	'88
PRIME VALUE:ALTURA TX-FR	General Muni	110.0	10.18	10,293.10	10,843.70	☆	6.4	338-1348	612-667-8833	3.25	None	None	Bill Jackson	'93
PRINCIPAL PRES:INS TX-EX	Insured Muni	19.4	10.68	10,308.40	11,208.60	15,793.70	5.0	826-4600	414-334-5521	4.50	0.25	None	Vern Van Vooren	'86
PRINCIPAL PRES:TAX-EX	General Muni	63.2	9.16	10,338.10	11,274.90	15,510.30	5.4	826-4600	414-334-5521	4.50	0.25	None	Vern Van Vooren	'84
PRINCOR TAX-EX BOND	General Muni	144.3	12.42	10,310.10	11,294.10	16,408.50	5.3	247-4123	515-247-5711	5.00	0.22	None	Dan Garrett	'91
PRUDENTIAL BD:HI YLD;A	High-Yield Muni	45.2	11.28	10,336.00	11,131.10	☆	6.8	225-1852	None	4.50	0.30	None	Liz Forsyth	'90
PRUDENTIAL BD:HI YLD;B	High-Yield Muni	1,052.8	11.28	10,325.70	11,086.90	15,901.90	6.4	225-1852	None	None	0.50	5.00	Liz Forsyth	'87
PRUDENTIAL BD:INS;A	Insured Muni	30.1	11.63	10,364.10	11,185.50	☆	5.2	225-1852	None	4.50	0.30	None	Liz Forsyth	'90
PRUDENTIAL BD:INS;B	Insured Muni	781.5	11.64	10,362.80	11,141.40	15,960.60	4.8	225-1852	None	None	0.50	5.00	Liz Forsyth	'87
PRUDENTIAL BD:MODIFD;A	Intermediate Muni	3.7	11.23	10,296.10	11,075.30	☆	4.9	225-1852	None	4.50	0.30	None	Liz Forsyth	'90
PRUDENTIAL BD:MODIFD;B	Intermediate Muni	51.9	11.23	10,276.50	11,009.20	15,134.70	4.4	225-1852	None	None	0.50	5.00	Liz Forsyth	'87
PRUDENTIAL CA MUNI:INC	California Muni	181.4	10.53	10,407.70	11,302.80	☆	6.4	225-1852	None	4.50	0.30	None	Jerry Webman	'90
PRUDENTIAL MUNI:AZ;A	Arizona Muni	5.5	12.30	10,364.40	11,153.90	☆	5.4	225-1852	None	4.50	0.30	None	Jerry Webman	'90
PRUDENTIAL MUNI:AZ;B	Arizona Muni	55.3	12.30	10,354.20	11,109.90	15,375.00	5.0	225-1852	None	None	0.50	5.00	Jerry Webman	'84
PRUDENTIAL MUNI:CA;A	California Muni	9.8	12.03	10,349.50	11,171.80	☆	5.7	225-1852	None	4.50	0.30	None	Jerry Webman	'90
PRUDENTIAL MUNI:CA;B	California Muni	199.6	12.02	10,339.50	11,128.10	15,230.80	5.3	225-1852	None	None	0.50	5.00	Jerry Webman	'84
PRUDENTIAL MUNI:FL	Florida Muni	137.2	10.71	10,377.30	11,288.30	☆	5.8	225-1852	None	4.50	0.30	None	Jerry Webman	'91
PRUDENTIAL MUNI:GA;A	Georgia Muni	0.8	11.95	10,354.80	11,305.80	☆	5.1	225-1852	None	4.50	0.30	None	Jerry Webman	'90
PRUDENTIAL MUNI:GA;B	Georgia Muni	18.9	11.94	10,335.60	11,252.10	15,193.20	4.7	225-1852	None	None	0.50	5.00	Jerry Webman	'84
PRUDENTIAL MUNI:MD;A	Maryland Muni	2.4	11.50	10,388.10	11,140.10	☆	5.4	225-1852	None	4.50	0.30	None	Jerry Webman	'90
PRUDENTIAL MUNI:MD;B	Maryland Muni	55.5	11.51	10,377.60	11,095.90	15,129.10	5.0	225-1852	None	None	0.50	5.00	Jerry Webman	'85
PRUDENTIAL MUNI:MA;A	Massachusetts Muni	1.7	12.00	10,321.50	11,152.90	☆	5.6	225-1852	None	4.50	0.30	None	Jerry Webman	'90
PRUDENTIAL MUNI:MA;B	Massachusetts Muni	58.1	12.00	10,311.20	11,109.00	15,282.30	5.3	225-1852	None	None	0.50	5.00	Jerry Webman	'84
PRUDENTIAL MUNI:MI;A	Michigan Muni	2.4	12.40	10,378.50	11,250.30	☆	5.3	225-1852	None	4.50	0.30	None	Jerry Webman	'90
PRUDENTIAL MUNI:MI;B	Michigan Muni	65.7	12.40	10,368.20	11,205.90	15,667.50	5.0	225-1852	None	None	0.50	5.00	Jerry Webman	'84
PRUDENTIAL MUNI:MN;A	Minnesota Muni	0.8	12.19	10,329.80	10,997.10	☆	5.1	225-1852	None	4.50	0.30	None	Jerry Webman	'90
PRUDENTIAL MUNI:MN;B	Minnesota Muni	26.2	12.20	10,328.10	10,976.30	14,808.20	4.8	225-1852	None	None	0.50	5.00	Jerry Webman	'84
PRUDENTIAL MUNI:NJ;A	New Jersey Muni	14.8	11.58	10,406.70	11,218.00	☆	5.5	225-1852	None	4.50	0.30	None	Jerry Webman	'90

PRUDENTIAL MUNI:NJ;B	New Jersey Muni	333.4	11.58	10,396.60	11,173.70	16,230.80	5.1	225-1852	None	None	0.50	5.00	Jerry Webman	'88
PRUDENTIAL MUNI:NY;A	New York Muni	10.4	12.37	10,375.60	11,290.80	☆	5.6	225-1852	None	4.50	0.30	None	Jerry Webman	'90
PRUDENTIAL MUNI:NY;B	New York Muni	341.9	12.37	10,356.80	11,246.10	15,680.40	5.2	225-1852	None	None	0.50	5.00	Jerry Webman	'84
PRUDENTIAL MUNI:NC;A	North Carolina Muni	1.6	11.89	10,379.30	11,181.50	☆	5.5	225-1852	None	4.50	0.30	None	Jerry Webman	'90
PRUDENTIAL MUNI:NC;B	North Carolina Muni	70.8	11.90	10,368.90	11,137.00	15,345.70	5.1	225-1852	None	None	0.50	5.00	Jerry Webman	'85
PRUDENTIAL MUNI:OH;A	Ohio Muni	3.3	12.25	10,352.20	11,192.70	☆	5.6	225-1852	None	4.50	0.30	None	Jerry Webman	'90
PRUDENTIAL MUNI:OH;B	Ohio Muni	115.8	12.25	10,341.90	11,147.30	15,490.20	5.2	225-1852	None	None	0.50	5.00	Jerry Webman	'84
PRUDENTIAL MUNI:PA;A	Pennsylvania Muni	8.6	11.07	10,373.40	11,286.40	☆	5.5	225-1852	None	4.50	0.30	None	Jerry Webman	'90
PRUDENTIAL MUNI:PA;B	Pennsylvania Muni	245.5	11.06	10,353.60	11,231.70	15,797.00	5.1	225-1852	None	None	0.50	5.00	Jerry Webman	'87
PRUDENTIAL NATL MUNI;A	General Muni	11.3	16.68	10,385.90	11,216.80	☆	5.4	225-1852	None	4.50	0.30	None	Patricia Dolan	'90
PRUDENTIAL NATL MUNI;B	General Muni	851.5	16.71	10,375.30	11,178.20	15,606.00	5.1	225-1852	None	None	0.50	5.00	Patricia Dolan	'80
PUTNAM AZ TAX EX INC	Arizona Muni	133.1	9.37	10,334.50	11,167.00	☆	5.9	225-1581	617-292-1000	4.75	None	None	James Erickson	'91
PUTNAM CA TXEX INC;A	California Muni	3,330.1	8.73	10,316.70	11,258.50	16,440.80	6.5	225-1581	617-292-1000	4.75	0.35	None	William H. Reeves	'86
PUTNAM CA TXEX INC;B	California Muni	105.4	8.73	10,310.20	☆	☆	0.0	225-1581	617-292-1000	None	1.00	5.00	William H. Reeves	'93
PUTNAM FL TXEX INC;A	Florida Muni	268.4	9.54	10,285.80	11,255.60	☆	5.8	225-1581	617-292-1000	4.75	None	None	Richard P. Wyke	'90
PUTNAM FL TXEX INC;B	Florida Muni	14.2	9.53	10,251.00	☆	☆	0.0	225-1581	617-292-1000	None	1.00	5.00	Richard P. Wyke	'93
PUTNAM MA TAX EX INC II	Massachusetts Muni	215.5	9.67	10,321.70	11,265.80	☆	6.0	225-1581	617-292-1000	4.75	0.35	None	Triet N. Nguyen	'89
PUTNAM MI TAX EX INC II	Michigan Muni	113.0	9.42	10,321.10	11,251.90	☆	5.9	225-1581	617-292-1000	4.75	0.35	None	Richard P. Wyke	'89
PUTNAM MN TAX EX INC II	Minnesota Muni	86.7	9.16	10,303.30	11,059.60	☆	6.0	225-1581	617-292-1000	4.75	0.35	None	Richard P. Wyke	'89
PUTNAM MUNI INCOME;A	General Muni	709.4	9.28	10,331.30	11,292.60	☆	6.4	225-1581	617-292-1000	4.75	0.35	None	James E. Erickson	'89
PUTNAM MUNI INCOME;B	General Muni	154.6	9.27	10,303.50	☆	☆	0.0	225-1581	617-292-1000	None	1.00	5.00	James E. Erickson	'93
PUTNAM NJ TXEX INC;A	New Jersey Muni	225.7	9.46	10,395.20	11,289.00	☆	5.8	225-1581	617-292-1000	4.75	0.35	None	Triet N. Nguyen	'90
PUTNAM NJ TXEX INC;B	New Jersey Muni	12.0	9.46	10,376.40	☆	☆	0.0	225-1581	617-292-1000	None	1.00	5.00	Triet N. Nguyen	'93
PUTNAM NY TXEX INC;A	New York Muni	2,184.2	9.41	10,350.30	11,381.80	16,571.30	6.2	225-1581	617-292-1000	4.75	None	None	David J. Eurkus	'83
PUTNAM NY TXEX INC;B	New York Muni	72.3	9.40	10,332.00	☆	☆	0.0	225-1581	617-292-1000	None	1.00	5.00	David J. Eurkus	'93

(continued)

PERFORMANCE OF MUTUAL FUNDS *(continued)*

NAME CHANGES

FROM	TO
AIM: AGGRESSIVE GRO (C)	AIM: AGGRESSIVE GROWTH
AIM: GOVERNMENT SEC (C)	AIM: GOVERNMENT SECS
AIM: GROWTH (C)	AIM: GROWTH
AIM: INCOME (C)	AIM: INCOME
AIM: MUNICIPAL BOND (C)	AIM: MUNICIPAL BOND
AIM: TAX-EX BOND OF CT (C)	AIM: TAX-EX BOND OF CT
AIM: UTILITIES (C)	AIM: UTILITIES
AIM: VALUE (C)	AIM:VALUE
ALLIANCE COUNTERPOINT	ALLIANCE COUNTERPT; A
ALLIANCE TECHNOLOGY	ALLIANCE TECHNOLOGY; A
AMERICAN LEADERS	AMERICAN LEADERS; A
ARCH: CAP APPREC; INV	ARCH: GR & INC EQUITY; INV
ARCH: DVSFD FXD INC; INV	ARCH: GOVT & CORP BOND; INV
CRESTFUNDS	CRESTFUNDS; TR
DELAWARE FUNDS	DELAWARE FUNDS; RET
EVERGREEN MUNI: NAT TX-FR	EVERGREEN MUNI: INS NATL
FEDERATED INC: MI	MUNI SECS INC: MI
FEDERATED INC: OH; TR	MUNI SECS INC: OH; TR
FEDERATED INC: PA; INV	MUNI SECS INC: PA; INV
FEDERATED INC: PA; TR	MUNI SECS INC: PA; TR
FEDERATED STOCK & BOND	STOCK & BOND; A
FLAGSHIP UTILITY INC	FLAGSHIP UTILITY; A
FREMONT: EQUITY	FREMONT: GROWTH
FREMONT: MULTI ASSET	FREMONT: GLOBAL
FRANKLIN INV: GLOBAL OPP	FRANKLIN INV: GLOBAL GOVT
FT SERIES: INTL EQUITY	FT SERIES: INTL EQ; A
FT SERIES: INTL INCOME	FT SERIES: INTL INC; A
FUND FOR US GOV SEC	FUND FOR US GOVT SEC; A
GT GLOBAL TELECOMM	GT GLOBAL TELECOMM; A
HARTWELL EMERGING GROWTH	HARTWELL EMRG GRO; A
HARTWELL GROWTH FUND	HARTWELL GROWTH; A
HELMSMAN FUNDS	ONE GROUP FUNDS
HELMSMAN: TX-FR INC; INV	ONE GROUP: INT TX-FR; INV
IAA TRUST INCOME	IAA TRUST ASSET ALLOC
INVMNT SRS: CAP GR; LBRTY	INVMNT SRS: CAP GR; A
KEYSTONE AM OMEGA	KEYSTONE AM OMEGA; A
KEYSTONE AM WORLD BD	KEYSTONE AM WORLD BD; A
KIDDER GOVT INCOME	KIDDER GOVT INCOME; A
KIDDER INV: ADJ RATE GOVT	KIDDER INV: ADJ RATE; A
KIDDER INV: ASST ALLOC	KIDDER INV: ASST ALLO; B
KIDDER INV: GLBL FXD INC	KIDDER INV: GLBL FXD; A
KIDDER INV: GLOBAL EQUITY	KIDDER INV: GLBL EQ; A
KIDDER INV: INTMDT	KIDDER INV: INTMDT; A
LIBERTY EQUITY INCOME	LIBERTY EQUITY INC; A
LIBERTY HIGH INCOME BOND	LIBERTY HIGH INCOME; A
LIBERTY MUNI SECURITIES	LIBERTY MUNI SECS; A
LIBERTY UTILITY	LIBERTY UTILITY; A
LOSANTIVILLE: REL VALUE	STAR: RELATIVE VALUE
M STANLEY INSTL: CTY ALLO	M STANLEY INSTL: ACTIVE
MANAGERS: FXD INCOME SEC	MANAGERS: BOND
MANAGERS: SH INT FXD INC	MANAGERS: SH & INT BD
MANAGERS: SHORT GOVT INC	MANAGERS: SHORT GOVT
METLIFE SS EQ FUNDS	METLIFE SS FUNDS
METLIFE SS INC FUNDS	METLIFE SS FUNDS
MFS GOVT PREMIUM	MFS GOVT LTD MATURITY
NICH-APPLEGATE FUNDS	NICH-APP FUNDS
NTH AM SEC TR FUNDS	NTH AM FDS
OPPENHEIMER CA TX-EX	OPPENHEIMER CA TX-EX; A
OPPENHEIMER GNMA	OPPENHEIMER MTGE INC; A
OPPENHEIMER GOVT SEC	OPPENHEIMER GOVT SEC; A
OPPENHEIMER HIGH YIELD	OPPENHEIMER HI YLD; A
OPPENHEIMER INV GRADE BD	OPPENHEIMER INV GRD; A
OPPENHEIMER NY TX-EX FD	OPPENHEIMER NY TX-EX; A
OPPENHEIMER PA TX-EX FD	OPPENHEIMER PA TX-EX; A
OPPENHEIMER TAX-FREE BD	OPPENHEIMER TX-FR BD; A
OPPENHEIMER TOTAL RETURN	OPPENHEIMER TOT RET; A
OPPENHEIMER TX-EX: INS	OPPENHEIMER TX-EX: INS; A
OPPENHEIMER VALUE STOCK	OPPENHEIMER VALUE; A
OVERLAND EXP: VAR RATE II	OVERLAND EXP: SH-TM GOVT
PARK AVE: GUARDIAN GOVT	GUARDIAN US GOVT SECS
PARK AVE: GUARDIAN PARK	GUARDIAN PARK AVENUE
PRU SPEC LEV FUND	PRUDENT SPECULATOR FUND
PUTNAM TOTAL RETURN	PUTNAM: EQUITY INCOME; A
RBB: INCOME OPP; HI YLD	RBB: HIGH YIELD BOND
RBB: TX-FR; RBB	RBB: TAX-FREE
ROCHESTER CONVERTIBLE	ROCHESTER: BOND FD FOR GR
SBSF FDS: GROWTH	SBSF FDS: SBSF
SCHWAB INV: CA TX-FR BOND	SCHWAB INV: CA LT TXFR BD
SCHWAB INV: NATL TAX-FREE	SCHWAB INV: LT TXFR BD
SELIGMAN CAPITAL	SELIGMAN CAPITAL; A
SELIGMAN COMM & INFORMTN	SELIGMAN COMMUNICATN; A
SELIGMAN FRONTIER	SELIGMAN FRONTIER; A
SELIGMAN COMMON STOCK	SELIGMAN COMMON STK; A
SELIGMAN GROWTH	SELIGMAN GROWTH; A
SELIGMAN INCOME FUND	SELIGMAN INCOME; A
SHEARSON INC: INT CA; A	SHEARSON INC: INT CA
SHEARSON INC: INT NY; A	SHEARSON INC: INT NY
SHEARSON INC: L MUNI; A	SHEARSON INC: L MUNI
STATE STREET GR: GRO; C	SS RESEARCH: GROWTH; C
STATE STREET: CAPITAL	SS RESEARCH: CAPITAL; C
TNE PREMIUM INCOME	TNE LTD TERM US GOVT
TNE RETIREMENT EQUITY	TNE VALUE
VANGUARD TRUSTEES: INTL	VANGUARD/TRUST EQ: INTL
VANGUARD TRUSTEES: US	VANGUARD/TRUST EQ: US
VANKAMP CA INSURED	VANKAMP CA INSURED; A
VANKAMP INS TAX FREE	VANKAMP INS TAX FREE; A
VANKAMP PA TAX FREE	VANKAMP PA TAX FREE; A
VANKAMP TAX FREE HIGH	VANKAMP TAX FREE HIGH; A
WEXFORD TR: MUHLENKAMP	MUHLENKAMP FUND
WOODWARD FUNDS; INSTL	WOODWARD FUNDS; RTL

NEW FUNDS ADDED

ALLIANCE BALANCED; C
ALLIANCE BD: CORP BD; C
ALLIANCE BD: US GOVT; C
ALLIANCE COUNTERPT; B
ALLIANCE COUNTERPT; C
ALLIANCE FUND; C
ALLIANCE GLBL SM CAP; C
ALLIANCE GRO & INC; C
ALLIANCE INTL; C
ALLIANCE MTGE INC; C
ALLIANCE MTGE STR; C
ALLIANCE MU-MK STR; C
ALLIANCE MUNI: CA; C
ALLIANCE MUNI: INS CA; C
ALLIANCE MUNI: INS NA; C
ALLIANCE MUNI: NATL; C
ALLIANCE MUNI: NY; C
ALLIANCE N AM GV INC; C
ALLIANCE NEW EUROPE; C
ALLIANCE PREMIER GR; C
ALLIANCE QUASAR; C
ALLIANCE SH-TM MU-MK; C
ALLIANCE TECHNOLOGY; B
ALLIANCE TECHNOLOGY; C
AMBASSADOR: BOND; INV
AMBASSADOR: BOND; RET
AMBASSADOR: CORE GROWTH; FID
AMBASSADOR: CORE GRO; RET
AMBASSADOR: GROWTH STK; INV
AMBASSADOR: GROWTH STK; RET
AMBASSADOR: INDEXED; INV
AMBASSADOR: INDEXED; RET
AMBASSADOR: INT BD; INV
AMBASSADOR: INT BD; RET
AMBASSADOR: INTL; INV
AMBASSADOR: INTL; RET
AMBASSADOR: SM CO; INV
AMBASSADOR: SM CO; RET
AMBASSADOR: TX-FR INT; FID
AMBASSADOR: TX-FR INT; RET
AMCORE VINTAGE INT TX-FR
AMELIA EARHART: EAGLE EQ
AMER FDS INC: US GOVT
AMERICAN LEADERS; C
B STEARNS: EMERG MKT DEBT
BBK GRP: DIVERSA
BB&T: SH-INTMDT GOVT; TR
BENCHMARK: SHORT DURATION
BENCHMARK: US GOVT SECS; A
BENHAM EQ: UTILITIES INC
BOSTON CO INV: ASST; INSTL
BOSTON CO INV: CONT; INSTL
BOSTON CO INV: INTL; INSTL
BOSTON CO INV: SHTM; INSTL
BOSTON CO TF: BOND; INV
BOSTON CO TF: CA BD; INV
BOSTON CO TF: MA BD; INV
BOSTON CO TF: NY BD; INV
BOSTON CO: CAP APP; INSTL
BOSTON CO: INTMDT; INSTL
BOSTON CO: MGD INC; INSTL
BOSTON CO: MGD INC; INV
BOSTON CO: SPEC GRO; INSTL
BOSTON CO: SPEC GRO; INV
BT INSTL: EQ 500 INDEX
BT INV: CAPITAL APPREC
BT INV: CAPITAL GROWTH
BT INV: INTL EQUITY
BT INV: INTMDT TAX FREE
BT INV: SH/INT US GOVT
BT INV: UTILITY
BT PYRAMID: INV EQ 500
BT PYRAMID: LTD GOVT SECS
CAPITAL WORLD GRO & INC
CFB MKTWATCH: EQUITY
CFB MKTWATCH: INT FXD INC
CFB MKTWATCH: S-T FXD
CFB MKTWATCH: VA MUNI
COLONIAL ADJ RATE; B
COLONIAL INT TAX-EX; A
COLONIAL INT TAX-EX; B
COLONIAL SH-TM TAX-EX; A
DELAWARE TX-FR INTMDT
DFA GRP: DFA/AEW RE SECS
DFA GRP: LARGE CAP VALUE
DFA GRP: PAC RIM SMALL CO
DFA GRP: SMALL CAP VALUE
DIAZ-VERSON: AMERICAS EQ
FFTW: INTL FXD INC HEDGED
FFTW: US SH TM FXD INC
FIDELITY DIVIDEND GROWTH
FIDELITY GLOBAL BALANCED
FIDELITY LATIN AMERICA R
FIDELITY SEL NAT GAS
FIDELITY SOEAST ASIA
FIDELITY SPARTAN AGGR
FIDELITY SPARTAN IN MUNI
FIDELITY SPARTAN MD
59 WALL ST: TX FR SH/INT
FIRST AMER INV: ASST ALLO
FIRST AMER INV: BALANCED
FIRST AMER INV: EQ INDEX
FIRST AMER INV: INT TERM
FIRST AMER INV: LTD TERM
FIRST AMER INV: MTGE SECS
FIRST AMER INV: REGNL EQ
FIRST INV SRS II: UTIL
FIRST PRARIE GOVT: INT; A
FIRST UN: BAL; INV C
FIRST UN: INS TAX; INV C
FIRST UN: US GOVT; INV C
FIRST UN: VALUE; INV C
FRANKLIN MUNI: CA HI YLD
FRANKLIN STRAT MTGE
FRANKLIN TF: AZ INSURED
FRANKLIN TF: FL INSURED
FT SERIES: INTL EQ; C
FT SERIES: INTL INC; C
FUND FOR US GOVT SEC; C
GABELLI INV: ABC
GALAXY: CT MUNI BOND; RTL
GALAXY: MA MUNI BOND; RTL
GIT TAX-FREE: MARYLAND
GLENMEDE: INTL FIXED INC
GLENMEDE: MODEL EQUITY
GOVETT: SMALLER COMPANIES
HANOVER: BLUE CHIP GROWTH
HANOVER: GOVT SECS
HANOVER: SHORT-TM US GOVT
HANOVER: SMALL CAP GROWTH
HERITAGE: SMALL CAP STK
IBM FDS: MUNICIPAL BOND
IVY EMERGING GROWTH
J HANCOCK SPEC EQ; B
JANUS FEDERAL TAX-EXEMPT
JANUS MERCURY
KEMPER TAX-FREE INC: OH
LEGG MASON GL: GLBL GOVT
LIBERTY EQUITY INC; C
LIBERTY HIGH INCOME; C
LIBERTY MUNI SECS; C
LIBERTY UTILITY; C
M STANLEY INSTL: HI YLD
M STANLEY INSTL: INT SM
M STANLEY INSTL: SM CAP
M STANLEY: GL EQ ALLO; A
M STANLEY: GL EQ ALLO; B
M STANLEY: GL FXD INC; A
M STANLEY: GL FXD INC; B
MONETTA: INTMDT BOND
MONETTA: MID-CAP EQUITY
MONTGOMERY: SH DURATION
NICH-APP: BALANCED GR; A
NICH-APP: BALANCED GR; B
NICH-APP: CORE GR QUAL
NICH-APP: CORE GROWTH; A
NICH-APP: CORE GROWTH; B
NICH-APP: GOVT INCOME; A
NICH-APP: GOVT INCOME; B
NICH-APP: INC & GR QUAL
NICH-APP: INC & GR; A
NICH-APP: INC & GR; B
NICH-APP: WRLDWD GR; A
NICH-APP: WRLDWD GR; B
NORTH CAROLINA TAX FR BD
ONE FUND: INTERNATIONAL
ONE GROUP: TX-FR BD; FID
PAINEWBR SEC: SM CAP; A
PAINEWBR SEC: SM CAP; B
PAINEWBR SEC: SM CAP; D
PARKSTONE: BALANCED; A
PARKSTONE: BOND; A
PARKSTONE: EQUITY; A
PARKSTONE: GOVT INC; A
PARKSTONE: HI INC EQ; A
PARKSTONE: INT GOVT; A
PARKSTONE: INTL DISC; A
PARKSTONE: LTD MAT BD; A
PARKSTONE: MI MUNI; A
PARKSTONE: MUNI BOND; A
PARKSTONE: SMALL CAP; A
PILGRIM TX-FR: CA; A
PILGRIM TX-FR: CA; B
PILGRIM TX-FR: FL; A
PILGRIM TX-FR: FL; B
PILGRIM TX-FR: NY; A
PILGRIM TX-FR: NY; B
PIONEER INTL GROWTH
PRINCIPAL PRES: BALANCED
PRINCIPAL SP MKT: INTL
PRINCIPAL SP MKT: MBS
PRUDENTIAL STRUC MAT; B
PUTNAM DVSFD INCOME; B
PUTNAM GROWTH FUND; A
PUTNAM HIGH YIELD; B
PUTNAM HLTH SCIENCES; B
PUTNAM INCOME; B
PUTNAM INVESTORS; B
PUTNAM NEW OPPTY; B
PUTNAM VISTA; B
SAFECO INSURED MUNI BOND
SAFECO INTMDT MUNI BOND
SCHWAB INV: SH/INT TX-FR
SHEARSON 1990s; B
SHEARSON ADJ RT GOVT; B
SHEARSON AGGR GRO; B
SHEARSON APPREC; B
SHEARSON AZ MUNI; B
SHEARSON CA MUNI; B
SHEARSON EQ: GR & INC; A
SHEARSON EQ: GR & INC; B
SHEARSON EQ: GRO & OPP; A
SHEARSON EQ: SECTOR; A
SHEARSON EQ: STRAT; A
SHEARSON FL MUNI; A
SHEARSON FL MUNI;B
SHEARSON FDMNTL VAL; B
SHEARSON GLOBAL OPP; B
SHEARSON INC: CONVRT; A
SHEARSON INC:DVSD; A
SHEARSON INC: GLBL BD; A
SHEARSON INC: HI INC; A
SHEARSON INC: TOT RET; A
SHEARSON INC: TX-EX; A
SHEARSON INC: UTIL; A
SHEARSON INV: DIR VAL; A
SHEARSON INV: EURO; A
SHEARSON INV: GOVT; A
SHEARSON INV: INV GRD; A
SHEARSON INV: SPEC EQ; A
SHEARSON MGD GOVTS; B
SHEARSON MGD MUNI; B
SHEARSON MA MUNI; B
SHEARSON MTLS & MIN; B
SHEARSON NJ MUNI; B
SHEARSON NY MUNI; B
SHEARSON SH WRLD INC; B
SHEARSON SMALL CAP; B
SHEARSON TELECOM: GRO; B
SHEARSON WRLD PRIME; B
SKYLINE: EUROPE
SM BARNEY MUNI: CA; C
SM BARNEY MUNI: NY; B
SM BARNEY WLD: INTL; B
SM BARNEY: CAP APP; A
SM BARNEY: CAP APP; B
SM BARNEY: CAP APP; C
SM BARNEY: EQUITY; B
SM BARNEY: INC & GR; B
SM BARNEY: INC RET; B
SM BARNEY: MNTHLY GOVT; B
SM BARNEY: US GOVT; B
SM BARNEY: UTILITY; B
STEINROE INC: LTD MAT INC
STRATTON: SMALL-CAP YIELD
STRATUS: CAP APPREC
T ROWE PRICE TX-FR: FL IN
T ROWE PRICE TX-FR: GA BD
TCW/DW INCOME & GROWTH
THORNBURG LTD TERM INC
TNE INTMDT TM TX FR CA
TNE INTMDT TM TX FR NY
TX COMMERCE RIT: CORE EQ
TX COMMERCE RIT: SH-INT
TX COMMERCE RIT: SM CAP
TX COMMERCE RIT: US GOVT
TORCHMARK GOVT SECS
TORCHMARK INS TAX- FREE
US: NEAR TERM TAX FREE
USAA MUTUAL: GRO & INC
USAA MUTUAL: SH-TM BOND
VAN ECK TR: S-T WRLD; A
VAN ECK TR: S-T WRLD; B
VAN ECK: ASIA DYNASTY
WM BLAIR: INTL GROWTH SHS

LIQUIDATIONS

ENTERPRISE: PREC METALS
FORUM: CORE PORTFOLIO PLUS

MERGERS

AMER CAP TGT: PORT '96	Merged into AMER CAP TGT: PORT '97
CITIBANK CIT: BALANCED	Merged into LANDMARK I BALANCED
CITIBANK CIT: EQUITY	Merged into LANDMARK II EQUITY
CITIBANK CIT: INCOME	Merged into LANDMARK IV FIXED INCOME
DREYFUS INDEX	Merged into PEOPLES INDEX
EXTER BAL TR	Merged into EXTER EQ TR & EXTR FX INC TR
44 WALL ST	Merged into 44 WALL ST EQUITY
SKYLINE VALUE	Merged into SKYLINE: SPEC EQ II

(continued)

PERFORMANCE OF MUTUAL FUNDS (continued)

FUND NAME	OBJECTIVE	TOTAL NET ASSETS ($ MIL) 5/31/93	NET ASSET $ VALUE 6/30/93	PERFORMANCE (Return on Initial $10,000 Investment) 3/31/93-6/30/93	6/30/92-6/30/93	6/30/88-6/30/93	DIVIDEND YIELD % 6/93	PHONE NUMBER 800	In-State	FEES Load	12b-1	Redemption	MANAGER	SINCE
PUTNAM NY TX EX OPPTNIES	New York Muni	148.4	9.05	10,207.30	10,985.20	☆	6.5	225-1581	617-292-1000	4.75	0.25	None	David J. Eurkus	'90
PUTNAM OH TAX EX INC II	Ohio Muni	177.8	9.35	10,299.30	11,172.60	☆	5.8	225-1581	617-292-1000	4.75	0.35	None	Richard P. Wyke	'89
PUTNAM PA TAX EX INC	Pennsylvania Muni	153.5	9.39	10,288.70	11,201.40	☆	5.9	225-1581	617-292-1000	4.75	None	None	Richard P. Wyke	'89
PUTNAM TXEX INC;A	General Muni	2,246.7	9.48	10,369.60	11,368.00	16,864.70	6.1	225-1581	617-292-1000	4.75	None	None	David J. Eurkus	'85
PUTNAM TXEX INC;B	General Muni	73.0	9.48	10,351.70	☆	☆	0.0	225-1581	617-292-1000	None	1.00	5.00	David J. Eurkus	'93
PUTNAM TX-FR INC:HI YD	High-Yield Muni	1,399.9	15.04	10,349.80	11,320.00	15,746.20	6.3	225-1581	617-292-1000	None	0.75	5.00	Triet N. Nguyen	'88
PUTNAM TX-FR INC:INSUR	Insured Muni	557.1	15.60	10,285.50	11,102.20	15,618.70	4.8	225-1581	617-292-1000	None	1.00	5.00	Richard P. Wyke	'88
PUTNAM TX TAX EX INC	Texas Muni	14.8	9.30	10,353.60	11,283.10	☆	5.6	225-1581	617-292-1000	4.75	0.35	None	James Erickson	'92
QUEST VALUE:CA	California Muni	37.3	11.20	10,379.20	11,251.50	☆	5.8	232-3863	None	4.75	0.25	None	Robert J. Bluestone	'90
QUEST VALUE:NATL	General Muni	107.8	11.36	10,364.00	11,269.80	☆	6.0	232-3863	None	4.75	0.25	None	Robert J. Bluestone	'90
QUEST VALUE:NY	New York Muni	33.1	11.32	10,396.70	11,379.70	☆	5.8	232-3863	None	4.75	0.25	None	Robert J. Bluestone	'90
RANSON MGD:KANSAS	Kansas Muni	91.4	12.73	10,364.20	11,326.80	☆	5.4	345-2363	316-262-4955	4.25	0.25	None	Ranson/Meitzner	'90/'90
RANSON MGD:KANSAS INS	Kansas Muni	16.7	12.34	10,323.50	☆	☆	0.0	345-2363	316-262-4955	3.40	None	None	Ranson/Meitzner	'92/'92
RBB:TAX-FREE	General Muni	6.3	11.31	10,366.80	11,386.20	☆	5.9	888-9723	212-878-0600	4.75	0.40	None	W. Donald Simmons	'88
ROCHESTER MUNICIPALS	New York Muni	1,382.8	18.71	10,436.50	11,507.80	17,022.80	6.4	None	716-383-1300	4.00	0.10	None	Ronald H. Fielding	'83
ROCHESTER:LTD TM NY	New York Muni	274.3	3.28	10,257.40	11,061.40	☆	5.3	None	716-383-1300	2.00	0.25	None	Ronald H. Fielding	'91
SAFECO CA TX-FR INCOME	California Muni	81.9	12.44	10,378.60	11,236.60	16,499.60	5.4	426-6730	206-545-5530	None	None	None	Stephen C. Bauer	'83
SAFECO INSURED MUNI BOND	Insured Muni	3.1	10.57	10,396.20	☆	☆	0.0	426-6730	206-545-5530	None	None	None	Stephen C. Bauer	'93
SAFECO INTMDT MUNI BOND	Intermediate Muni	4.2	10.41	10,245.30	☆	☆	0.0	426-6730	206-545-5530	None	None	None	Stephen C. Bauer	'93
SAFECO MUNICIPAL BOND	General Muni	565.1	14.38	10,404.60	11,270.90	16,765.70	5.5	426-6730	206-545-5530	None	None	None	Stephen C. Bauer	'81
SCHWAB INV:CA LT TXFR BD	California Muni	120.9	11.11	10,354.70	11,250.00	☆	5.2	526-8600	415-395-6323	None	None	None	Keighley/Ward	'92/'92
SCHWAB INV:LT TXFR BD	General Muni	44.7	10.42	10,381.80	☆	☆	0.0	526-8600	415-395-6323	None	None	None	Keighley/Ward	'92/'92
SCHWAB INV:SH/INT TX-FR	Short-Term Muni	41.2	10.06	☆	☆	☆	0.0	526-8600	415-395-6323	None	None	None	Ward/Keighley	'93/'93
SCUDDER CAL TXFREE	California Muni	315.3	10.98	10,357.00	11,385.60	16,704.30	5.0	535-2726	617-439-4640	None	None	None	Ragus/Carleton	'89/'83
SCUDDER HI YLD TXFR	High-Yield Muni	265.3	12.51	10,373.40	11,344.00	16,945.60	5.5	535-2726	617-439-4640	None	None	None	Manning/Condon	'87/'87
SCUDDER MGD MUNI BOND	General Muni	879.4	9.17	10,331.60	11,304.40	16,629.40	5.3	535-2726	617-439-4640	None	None	None	Carleton/Condon	'86/'87
SCUDDER MASS TXFREE	Massachusetts Muni	295.4	13.86	10,403.80	11,417.10	16,523.50	6.0	535-2726	617-439-4640	None	None	None	Condon/Meany	'89/'91
SCUDDER MED TRM TXFR	Intermediate Muni	870.4	11.20	10,264.80	11,100.90	14,819.30	5.7	535-2726	617-439-4640	None	None	None	Carleton/Patton	'86/'87
SCUDDER NY TXFREE	New York Muni	206.8	11.35	10,380.40	11,337.80	16,465.20	4.9	535-2726	617-439-4640	None	None	None	Ragus/Carleton	'90/'86
SCUDDER OHIO TXFREE	Ohio Muni	72.7	13.40	10,370.50	11,223.60	16,117.30	5.3	535-2726	617-439-4640	None	None	None	Manning/Condon	'87/'88
SCUDDER PENN TXFREE	Pennsylvania Muni	64.3	13.73	10,365.20	11,256.70	16,370.60	5.5	535-2726	617-439-4640	None	None	None	Manning/Condon	'87/'87
SECURITY TAX-EXEMPT	General Muni	31.2	10.48	10,382.00	11,088.10	14,860.30	5.5	888-2461	913-295-3127	4.75	None	None	Jane Tedder	'84
SEI TX EX:INT-TM MUNI★	Intermediate Muni	106.4	10.73	10,203.70	10,829.30	☆	4.9	342-5734	215-254-1000	None	0.08	None	Blake Miller	'89
SEI TX EX:KS;A★	Kansas Muni	53.6	10.83	10,258.50	11,045.10	☆	5.5	342-5734	215-254-1000	None	None	None	Michael Colgan	'90
SEI TX EX:MA INTMDT★	Massachusetts Muni	6.3	10.32	10,227.50	☆	☆	0.0	342-5734	215-254-1000	None	0.12	None	Janet Fiorenza	'92
SEI TX EX:PA MUNI★	Pennsylvania Muni	143.4	10.87	10,221.10	10,887.90	☆	5.1	342-5734	215-254-1000	None	0.08	None	Peter Pellett	'89
SELIGMAN NJ TAX-EXEMPT	New Jersey Muni	78.3	8.07	10,388.50	11,264.80	16,375.70	5.2	221-2450	212-488-0200	4.75	0.25	None	Thomas P. Moles	'88
SELIGMAN PA TAX-EX:QUAL	Pennsylvania Muni	40.7	8.38	10,374.50	11,284.50	16,082.90	5.1	221-2450	212-488-0200	4.75	0.25	None	Thomas P. Moles	'86
SELIGMAN TAX-EX:CA HIYLD	California Muni	49.4	6.67	10,285.30	11,027.60	15,783.60	5.8	221-2450	212-488-0200	4.75	0.25	None	Thomas P. Moles	'84
SELIGMAN TAX-EX:CA QUAL	California Muni	106.2	7.13	10,302.90	11,224.40	16,119.30	5.2	221-2450	212-488-0200	4.75	0.25	None	Thomas P. Moles	'84
SELIGMAN TAX-EX:CO	Colorado Muni	65.7	7.62	10,319.70	11,126.40	15,376.20	5.1	221-2450	212-488-0200	4.75	0.25	None	Thomas P. Moles	'86
SELIGMAN TAX-EX:FL	Florida Muni	47.0	8.02	10,428.70	11,316.60	16,667.70	5.7	221-2450	212-488-0200	4.75	0.25	None	Thomas P. Moles	'86
SELIGMAN TAX-EX:GA	Georgia Muni	56.0	8.15	10,334.60	11,137.70	16,120.70	5.3	221-2450	212-488-0200	4.75	0.25	None	Thomas P. Moles	'87
SELIGMAN TAX-EX:LA	Louisiana Muni	63.2	8.64	10,299.40	11,078.70	15,914.30	5.4	221-2450	212-488-0200	4.75	0.25	None	Thomas P. Moles	'85
SELIGMAN TAX-EX:MD	Maryland Muni	61.8	8.43	10,341.60	11,159.90	15,880.20	5.2	221-2450	212-488-0200	4.75	0.25	None	Thomas P. Moles	'85

SELIGMAN TAX-EX:MA	Massachusetts Muni	134.7	8.39	10,357.80	11,206.90	15,799.80	5.6	221-2450	212-488-0200	4.75	0.25	None	Thomas P. Moles	'84
SELIGMAN TAX-EX:MI	Michigan Muni	157.4	8.92	10,364.20	11,228.60	16,206.70	5.3	221-2450	212-488-0200	4.75	0.25	None	Thomas P. Moles	'84
SELIGMAN TAX-EX:MN	Minnesota Muni	143.2	8.13	10,373.70	11,160.00	15,448.80	5.7	221-2450	212-488-0200	4.75	0.25	None	Thomas P. Moles	'84
SELIGMAN TAX-EX:MO	Missouri Muni	53.4	8.13	10,345.00	11,051.20	15,789.00	5.1	221-2450	212-488-0200	4.75	0.25	None	Thomas P. Moles	'86
SELIGMAN TAX-EX:NATL	General Muni	132.2	8.50	10,387.90	11,342.10	16,188.40	5.3	221-2450	212-488-0200	4.75	0.25	None	Thomas P. Moles	'84
SELIGMAN TAX-EX:NY	New York Muni	100.0	8.56	10,373.80	11,314.40	16,282.70	5.3	221-2450	212-488-0200	4.75	0.25	None	Thomas P. Moles	'84
SELIGMAN TAX-EX:NC	North Carolina Muni	32.4	8.01	10,353.00	11,256.00	☆	5.3	221-2450	212-488-0200	4.75	0.25	None	Thomas P. Moles	'90
SELIGMAN TAX-EX:OH	Ohio Muni	181.6	8.60	10,350.80	11,146.90	15,871.90	5.4	221-2450	212-488-0200	4.75	0.25	None	Thomas P. Moles	'84
SELIGMAN TAX-EX:OR	Oregon Muni	57.5	7.93	10,326.70	11,086.60	15,877.90	5.3	221-2450	212-488-0200	4.75	0.25	None	Thomas P. Moles	'86
SELIGMAN TAX-EX:SC	South Carolina Muni	105.2	8.34	10,337.90	11,098.50	16,057.70	5.1	221-2450	212-488-0200	4.75	0.25	None	Thomas P. Moles	'87
SENTINEL PA TAX-FREE	Pennsylvania Muni	33.7	13.53	10,282.00	11,093.30	15,517.80	5.4	233-4332	802-229-3761	5.00	0.20	None	Kenneth J. Hart	'93
SENTINEL:TAX-FREE INCOME	General Muni	100.6	13.75	10,358.40	11,250.30	☆	5.5	233-4332	802-229-3761	5.00	0.20	None	Kenneth J. Hart	'90
SHEARSON AZ MUNI;A	Arizona Muni	43.9	10.53	10,326.20	11,313.70	16,147.40	5.6	None	212-720-9218	4.50	0.15	None	Larry McDermott	'88
SHEARSON AZ MUNI;B	Arizona Muni	8.1	10.53	10,312.80	☆	☆	0.0	None	212-720-9218	None	0.65	4.50	Larry McDermott	'92
SHEARSON CA MUNI;A	California Muni	418.1	16.61	10,349.50	11,166.80	16,073.60	6.0	None	212-720-9218	4.50	0.15	None	Deane/Fare	'89/'89
SHEARSON CA MUNI;B	California Muni	59.2	16.61	10,337.50	☆	☆	0.0	None	212-720-9218	None	0.65	4.50	Deane/Fare	'92/'92
SHEARSON FL MUNI;A	Florida Muni	10.9	10.31	10,406.30	☆	☆	0.0	None	212-720-9218	4.50	0.15	None	Larry McDermott	'92
SHEARSON FL MUNI;B	Florida Muni	28.4	10.31	10,394.10	☆	☆	0.0	None	212-720-9218	None	0.65	4.50	Larry McDermott	'92
SHEARSON INC:INT CA	California Muni	17.9	8.47	10,359.90	11,168.70	☆	4.7	None	212-720-9218	1.25	0.15	1.00	Joseph Deane	'91
SHEARSON INC:INT NY	New York Muni	42.7	8.53	10,290.40	11,165.40	☆	4.8	None	212-720-9218	1.25	0.15	1.00	Larry McDermott	'91
SHEARSON INC:L MUNI	Short-Term Muni	62.3	8.25	10,198.50	10,852.60	☆	4.6	None	212-720-9218	1.25	0.15	1.00	Larry McDermott	'91
SHEARSON INC:TX-EX;A	General Muni	10.4	18.28	10,328.50	☆	☆	0.0	None	212-720-9218	4.50	0.15	None	Larry McDermott	'92
SHEARSON INC:TX-EX;B	General Muni	1,070.5	18.28	10,315.90	11,158.00	15,692.00	5.8	None	212-720-9218	None	0.65	4.50	Larry McDermott	'85
SHEARSON MGD MUNI;A	General Muni	1,786.9	16.87	10,455.40	11,599.00	16,944.20	6.0	None	212-720-9218	4.50	0.15	None	Joseph Deane	'88
SHEARSON MGD MUNI;B	General Muni	127.5	16.87	10,441.30	☆	☆	0.0	None	212-720-9218	None	0.65	4.50	Joseph Deane	'92
SHEARSON MA MUNI;A	Massachusetts Muni	30.6	13.27	10,353.20	11,290.90	16,121.10	5.9	None	212-720-9218	4.50	0.15	None	Larry McDermott	'87
SHEARSON MA MUNI;B	Massachusetts Muni	13.6	13.27	10,341.50	☆	☆	0.0	None	212-720-9218	None	0.65	4.50	Larry McDermott	'92
SHEARSON NJ MUNI;A	New Jersey Muni	116.1	13.44	10,354.80	11,284.90	16,585.50	5.6	None	212-720-9218	4.50	0.15	None	Larry McDermott	'88
SHEARSON NJ MUNI;B	New Jersey Muni	21.2	13.44	10,342.20	☆	☆	0.0	None	212-720-9218	None	0.65	4.50	Larry McDermott	'92
SHEARSON NY MUNI;A	New York Muni	559.7	17.66	10,285.90	11,139.90	16,050.10	6.2	None	212-720-9218	4.50	0.15	None	Larry McDermott	'89
SHEARSON NY MUNI;B	New York Muni	71.4	17.66	10,274.10	☆	☆	0.0	None	212-720-9218	None	0.65	4.50	Larry McDermott	'92
SIERRA:CA MUNICIPAL	California Muni	486.9	11.23	10,367.70	11,384.30	☆	5.5	222-5852	818-725-0200	4.50	0.25	None	Joe Piraro	'89
SIERRA:NATL MUNICIPAL	General Muni	375.8	11.65	10,418.70	11,341.40	☆	5.7	222-5852	818-725-0200	4.50	0.25	None	David Johnson	'90
SIG SELECT:MD MUNI;INV	Maryland Muni	27.3	10.91	10,311.10	11,113.40	☆	4.6	444-7123	None	None	0.10	2.00	E. Christian Goetz	'91
SIG SELECT:MD MUNI;TR	Maryland Muni	8.0	10.91	10,314.70	11,120.40	☆	4.7	444-7123	None	None	None	None	E. Christian Goetz	'91
SIG SELECT:VA MUNI;INV	Virginia Muni	48.7	10.96	10,342.30	11,141.70	☆	4.7	444-7123	None	None	0.10	2.00	E. Christian Goetz	'91
SIG SELECT:VA MUNI;TR	Virginia Muni	33.0	10.96	10,345.60	11,148.10	☆	4.8	444-7123	None	None	None	None	E. Christian Goetz	'91
SIT NW BEGIN TX-FR:INC	General Muni	337.5	10.02	10,281.00	10,981.20	☆	6.0	332-5580	612-334-5888	None	None	None	Brilley/Sit	'88/'91
SM BARNEY MUNI:CA;A	California Muni	164.1	12.98	10,312.20	11,202.30	16,687.50	6.0	544-7835	212-698-5349	4.00	None	None	Peter Coffey	'87
SM BARNEY MUNI:CA;C	California Muni	4.6	12.98	10,316.60	☆	☆	0.0	544-7835	212-698-5349	None	0.15	1.50	Peter Coffey	'93
SM BARNEY MUNI:FL;A	Florida Muni	104.8	13.46	10,340.30	11,308.70	☆	5.9	544-7835	212-698-5349	4.00	None	None	Peter Coffey	'91
SM BARNEY MUNI:LTD;A	Intermediate Muni	251.8	6.76	10,263.50	10,949.80	☆	5.7	544-7835	212-698-5349	2.00	None	None	Peter Coffey	'88
SM BARNEY MUNI:NATL;A	General Muni	395.1	14.07	10,351.60	11,327.50	17,052.60	6.3	544-7835	212-698-5349	4.00	None	None	Peter Coffey	'86
SM BARNEY MUNI:NJ;A	New Jersey Muni	57.1	14.01	10,371.20	11,309.90	☆	5.8	544-7835	212-698-5349	4.00	None	None	Peter Coffey	'90
SM BARNEY MUNI:NY;A	New York Muni	63.3	13.51	10,351.40	11,338.00	16,870.60	6.0	544-7835	212-698-5349	4.00	None	None	Peter Coffey	'87
SM BARNEY MUNI:NY;B	New York Muni	1.8	13.50	10,334.10	☆	☆	0.0	544-7835	212-698-5349	None	0.70	1.00	Peter Coffey	'93
SOCIETY:OH TAX-FREE BOND	Ohio Muni	38.3	11.26	10,392.70	11,197.90	☆	4.8	362-5365	None	4.00	None	None	Robert Moore	'91
STAGECOACH:CA TX FR BD	California Muni	439.3	11.01	10,403.40	11,372.60	☆	5.4	222-8222	None	4.50	0.05	None	Wines/Klug	'92/'92
STARBURST:MUNI INCOME	General Muni	25.7	10.62	10,305.40	11,008.50	☆	4.6	239-6669	205-558-6702	1.00	0.15	None	Dan Davidson	'91
STATE BOND TAX EXEMPT	General Muni	79.0	11.09	10,278.70	10,930.10	15,664.20	5.7	437-6663	612-835-0097	4.50	0.25	None	Keith Martens	'84

★SEI TX EX FUNDS—Institutional funds.

PERFORMANCE OF MUTUAL FUNDS *(continued)*

FUND NAME	OBJECTIVE	TOTAL NET ASSETS ($ MIL) 5/31/93	NET ASSET $ VALUE 6/30/93	PERFORMANCE (Return on Initial $10,000 Investment) 3/31/93-6/30/93	6/30/92-6/30/93	6/30/88-6/30/93	DIVIDEND YIELD % 6/93	PHONE NUMBER 800	In-State	FEES Load	12b-1	Redemption	MANAGER	SINCE
STATE BOND TAX-FR INC:MN	Minnesota Muni	15.0	10.94	10,311.00	11,005.90	15,374.80	5.3	437-6663	612-835-0097	4.50	0.25	None	Keith Martens	'88
STATE FARM MUNICIPAL★	General Muni	245.1	8.59	10,278.20	11,011.70	15,642.50	6.0	None	309-766-2029	None	None	None	Kurt Moser	'91
SS RESEARCH:CAL TAX	California Muni	31.4	8.33	10,347.70	11,307.10	☆	5.1	882-3302	617-348-2000	None	0.25	None	Susan Drake	'90
SS RESEARCH:NY TAX	New York Muni	57.4	8.30	10,391.20	11,329.00	☆	5.2	882-3302	617-348-2000	None	0.25	None	Susan Drake	'90
STEINROE MUNI:HI YLD	High-Yield Muni	358.1	11.84	10,245.90	10,786.60	15,658.80	5.9	338-2550	None	None	None	None	Jim Grabovac	'91
STEINROE MUNI:INTMDT	Intermediate Muni	236.5	11.57	10,266.30	11,091.50	15,131.00	4.7	338-2550	None	None	None	None	Joanne Costopoulos	'91
STEINROE MUNI:MANAGED	General Muni	770.1	9.38	10,268.10	11,078.60	16,125.90	5.5	338-2550	None	None	None	None	M. Jane McCart	'91
STI CLASSIC:INV TX;INV	Intermediate Muni	15.6	10.99	10,379.90	11,392.40	☆	3.4	428-6970	None	3.75	0.38	None	Ron Schartz	'92
STRONG INS MUNI BD	Insured Muni	47.6	11.36	10,338.50	11,387.80	☆	5.3	368-1030	414-359-1400	None	None	None	Conlin/Bourbulas	'91/'91
STRONG MUNICIPAL BOND	General Muni	394.9	10.39	10,300.40	11,242.80	15,786.10	5.8	368-1030	414-359-1400	None	None	None	Conlin/Bourbulas	'91/'91
STRONG SH-TM MUNI BD	Short-Term Muni	166.2	10.34	10,196.60	10,747.10	☆	4.6	368-1030	414-359-1400	None	None	None	G. Nolan Smith	'92
SUNAMER TX FR:INSURED	Insured Muni	168.9	12.70	10,350.70	10,803.50	14,702.00	6.0	858-8850	212-551-5125	4.75	0.35	None	John Keough	'85
TAX-EXEMPT BD AMERICA	General Muni	1,192.6	12.27	10,325.00	11,219.20	15,844.30	5.6	421-0180	210-530-4000	4.75	0.25	None	Multiple Managers	'79
TAX-FREE OF CO	Colorado Muni	197.4	10.75	10,287.80	11,169.30	15,411.60	5.5	872-2652	212-697-6666	4.00	None	None	Christopher Johns	'87
TAX-FREE FOR UT	Single-State Muni	11.5	10.00	10,341.30	☆	☆	0.0	882-4937	212-697-6666	4.00	0.20	None	Sterling Jensen	'92
TAX FREE OF VERMONT	Single-State Muni	4.5	9.98	10,183.90	10,736.10	☆	5.5	675-3333	802-773-0674	None	None	None	John Pearson	'91
TAX-FR INV:INTMDT;AIM	Intermediate Muni	78.0	10.87	10,233.80	10,932.10	14,855.30	4.7	347-1919	713-626-1919	3.00	None	None	Berry/Turman	'88/'87
TAX-FREE TRUST OF AZ	Arizona Muni	334.9	10.83	10,271.00	11,134.60	15,935.90	5.7	437-1020	212-697-6666	4.00	None	None	Todd Curtis	'86
TEMPLETON TX FR:INSURED	Insured Muni	30.1	11.68	10,338.80	11,328.60	☆	5.1	237-0738	813-823-8712	4.50	0.25	None	Robert M. Schubert	'91
THOMSON:TAX EXEMPT;A	General Muni	2.5	12.38	10,340.10	11,232.60	☆	5.2	227-7337	203-352-4946	4.75	0.25	None	Norman Seltzer	'92
THOMSON:TAX EXEMPT;B	General Muni	69.0	12.37	10,312.70	11,140.20	15,355.80	4.5	227-7337	203-352-4946	None	1.00	1.00	Norman Seltzer	'92
THORNBURG INT MUNI NATL	Intermediate Muni	N/A	13.15	10,304.70	11,188.00	☆	5.5	847-0200	505-984-0200	3.50	0.12	None	Brian McMahon	'91
THORNBURG INT MUNI NM	Single-State Muni	N/A	13.12	10,260.30	11,032.40	☆	5.1	847-0200	505-984-0200	3.50	0.12	None	Brian McMahon	'91
THORNBURG LTD MUNI NATL	Short-Term Muni	N/A	13.59	10,226.80	10,926.30	14,559.40	5.0	847-0200	505-984-0200	2.50	0.12	None	Brian McMahon	'84
TNE INTMDT TM TX FR CA	California Muni	10.4	7.63	☆	☆	☆	0.0	343-7104	None	2.50	0.25	None	James Welch	'93
TNE INTMDT TM TX FR NY	New York Muni	10.3	7.63	☆	☆	☆	0.0	343-7104	None	2.50	0.25	None	James Welch	'93
TNE MASS TAX FREE INCOME	Massachusetts Muni	113.0	17.39	10,350.20	11,244.20	15,505.70	5.7	343-7104	None	4.25	0.35	None	Nathan Wentworth	'88
TNE TAX EXEMPT INCOME	General Muni	203.4	7.84	10,336.40	11,194.30	15,987.80	5.5	343-7104	None	4.50	0.25	None	Nathan Wentworth	'86
TORCHMARK INS TAX-FREE	Insured Muni	2.1	10.13	☆	☆	☆	0.0	733-3863	913-236-2050	None	0.25	None	John Holiday	'93
TOWER:LA MUNI INCOME	Louisiana Muni	77.4	11.46	10,327.70	11,246.50	☆	5.4	999-0124	504-585-5180	3.00	None	None	Jeff Tanguis	'88
TRANSAM CA TX-FR INC;A	California Muni	244.9	10.95	10,384.10	11,279.80	☆	5.[illegible]	472-3863	713-751-2800	4.75	0.15	None	Team Managed	'89
TRANSAM CA TX-FR INC;B	California Muni	40.7	10.95	10,374.50	11,206.70	☆	5.2	472-3863	713-751-2800	None	0.90	4.00	Team Managed	'91
TRANSAM SPEC:HI YLD TX	High-Yield Muni	90.1	9.83	10,319.10	11,110.60	15,246.50	6.[illegible]	472-3863	713-751-2800	None	1.00	6.00	Team Managed	'86
TRANSAM TAX-FREE BD;A	General Muni	121.0	11.13	10,426.90	11,464.40	☆	5.[illegible]	472-3863	713-751-2800	4.75	0.15	None	Team Managed	'90
TRANSAM TAX-FREE BD;B	General Muni	31.4	11.13	10,407.60	11,380.00	☆	5.[illegible]	472-3863	713-751-2800	None	0.90	4.00	Team Managed	'91
TWENTIETH CENT:TX-EX INT	Intermediate Muni	88.9	106.19	10,236.50	10,877.80	14,349.70	4.4	345-2021	816-531-5575	None	None	None	Team Managed	'87
TWENTIETH CENT:TX-EX LNG	General Muni	63.1	108.77	10,314.10	11,066.50	15,812.80	4.8	345-2021	816-531-5575	None	None	None	Team Managed	'87
UNITED MUNICIPAL BOND	General Muni	988.6	7.65	10,334.00	11,324.50	17,096.00	5.2	366-5465	913-236-2050	4.25	None	None	John Holliday	'80
UNITED MUNICIPAL HI INC	High-Yield Muni	301.1	5.41	10,329.00	11,215.40	16,540.50	6.3	366-5465	913-236-2050	4.25	None	None	John Holliday	'86
US:TAX FREE	General Muni	15.0	12.16	10,346.20	10,996.60	15,218.50	5.2	873-8637	210-308-1234	None	None	None	Allen Parker	'87
USAA TX EX:CA BOND	California Muni	395.5	10.89	10,375.30	11,289.20	☆	5.6	382-8722	None	None	None	None	Kenneth Willmann	'89
USAA TX EX:INTMDT-TERM	Intermediate Muni	1,437.7	13.01	10,307.80	11,097.40	15,443.20	5.5	382-8722	None	None	None	None	Clifford A. Gladson	'93
USAA TX EX:LONG-TERM	General Muni	1,930.6	14.31	10,381.10	11,219.00	16,486.30	6.0	382-8722	None	None	None	None	Kenneth Willmann	'82
USAA TX EX:NY BOND	New York Muni	52.4	11.84	10,326.30	11,248.20	☆	5.4	382-8722	None	None	None	None	Kenneth Willmann	'90
USAA TX EX:SHORT-TERM	Short-Term Muni	865.7	10.67	10,148.80	10,586.90	13,754.80	4.6	382-8722	None	None	None	None	David G. Miller	'92
USAA TX EX:VA BOND	Virginia Muni	216.8	11.33	10,355.90	11,209.90	☆	5.6	382-8722	None	None	None	None	Kenneth Willmann	'90
USAFFINITY:TX-FREE MUNI	General Muni	1.1	10.69	10,438.90	☆	☆	0.0	800-3030	None	4.50	0.35	None	Dow/Grand	'92/'92
UST MSTR TX-EX:INT;ORIG	Intermediate Muni	284.1	9.19	10,255.50	11,070.60	15,066.50	4.2	233-1136	619-456-9394	4.50	None	None	Kenneth M. McAlley	'85

UST MSTR TX-EX:INT;PLAN	Intermediate Muni	3.4	9.19	10,245.50	11,027.00	☆	3.8	233-1136	619-456-9394	4.50	None	None	Kenneth M. McAlley	'91
UST MSTR TX-EX:LONG	General Muni	85.3	9.99	10,370.90	11,467.80	17,251.70	4.3	233-1136	619-456-9394	4.50	None	None	Kenneth M. McAlley	'86
UST MSTR TX-EX:NY INT	New York Muni	90.9	8.67	10,232.00	10,929.10	☆	3.7	233-1136	619-456-9394	4.50	None	None	Kenneth M. McAlley	'90
UST MSTR TX-EX:SH-TM SEC	Short-Term Muni	36.6	7.11	10,140.70	☆	☆	0.0	233-1136	619-456-9394	4.50	None	None	Kenneth M. McAlley	'92
VALUE LINE NY TX EX TR	New York Muni	41.5	10.90	10,411.90	11,286.50	16,037.60	5.4	223-0818	212-687-3965	None	None	None	Team Managed	'87
VALUE LINE TX EX:HI YLD	General Muni	293.7	11.29	10,328.70	11,061.40	15,631.00	5.5	223-0818	212-687-3965	None	None	None	Team Managed	'84
VANGUARD CA TX-FR:INS LG	California Muni	1,005.2	11.31	10,345.40	11,310.00	16,485.00	5.4	662-7447	215-669-1000	None	0.20	None	Ian A. MacKinnon	'86
VANGUARD FL INS TX-FR	Florida Muni	188.9	10.80	10,376.90	☆	☆	0.0	662-7447	215-669-1000	None	0.20	None	Ian A. MacKinnon	'92
VANGUARD MUNI:HIGH YIELD	High-Yield Muni	1,797.4	11.06	10,385.60	11,311.70	17,147.80	6.0	662-7447	215-669-1000	None	0.20	None	Ian A. MacKinnon	'81
VANGUARD MUNI:INS LG-TM	Insured Muni	2,102.5	12.74	10,352.30	11,282.20	16,690.40	5.6	662-7447	215-669-1000	None	0.20	None	Ian A. MacKinnon	'84
VANGUARD MUNI:INTMDT-TM	Intermediate Muni	4,403.7	13.34	10,304.00	11,174.90	16,075.90	5.3	662-7447	215-669-1000	None	0.20	None	Ian A. MacKinnon	'81
VANGUARD MUNI:LIMITED-TM	Short-Term Muni	1,431.7	10.78	10,158.20	10,706.30	14,267.40	4.6	662-7447	215-669-1000	None	0.20	None	Ian A. MacKinnon	'87
VANGUARD MUNI:LONG-TM	General Muni	1,084.6	11.26	10,370.40	11,302.00	16,948.60	5.7	662-7447	215-669-1000	None	0.20	None	Ian A. MacKinnon	'81
VANGUARD MUNI:SHORT-TM	Short-Term Muni	1,218.4	15.65	10,102.10	10,453.70	13,374.80	4.0	662-7447	215-669-1000	None	0.20	None	Ian A. MacKinnon	'81
VANGUARD NJ TX-FR:INS LG	New Jersey Muni	691.8	11.78	10,409.60	11,369.60	16,638.40	5.5	662-7447	215-669-1000	None	0.20	None	Ian A. MacKinnon	'88
VANGUARD NY INS TAX-FR	New York Muni	729.6	10.96	10,391.50	11,304.80	16,728.90	5.5	662-7447	215-669-1000	None	0.20	None	Ian A. MacKinnon	'86
VANGUARD OH TX-FR:INSURE	Ohio Muni	138.2	11.56	10,357.10	11,276.40	☆	5.3	662-7447	215-669-1000	None	0.20	None	Ian A. MacKinnon	'90
VANGUARD PA TX-FR:INS LG	Pennsylvania Muni	1,357.0	11.31	10,361.20	11,322.00	16,681.30	5.7	662-7447	215-669-1000	None	0.20	None	Ian A. MacKinnon	'86
VANKAMP CA INSURED;A	California Muni	101.9	17.88	10,396.50	11,486.30	16,494.30	5.5	225-2222	708-684-6503	3.00	0.30	None	Joe Piraro	'92
VANKAMP INS TAX FREE;A	Insured Muni	1,107.0	19.54	10,343.60	11,257.90	16,243.90	5.8	225-2222	708-684-6503	4.65	0.30	None	Joe Piraro	'92
VANKAMP MUNI INC;A	General Muni	550.7	15.93	10,331.50	11,151.20	☆	6.4	225-2222	708-684-6503	4.65	0.30	None	David Johnson	'90
VANKAMP MUNI INC;B	General Muni	116.4	15.91	10,308.10	☆	☆	0.0	225-2222	708-684-6503	None	1.00	4.00	David Johnson	'92
VANKAMP PA TAX FREE;A	Pennsylvania Muni	186.2	17.76	10,424.30	11,320.50	17,113.60	5.9	225-2222	708-684-6503	4.65	0.30	None	William Grady	'92
VANKAMP TX FR HIGH;A	High-Yield Muni	560.9	14.87	10,368.80	10,509.80	13,917.30	7.7	225-2222	708-684-6503	4.65	0.30	None	David Johnson	'89
VENTURE MUN (+) PLUS	High-Yield Muni	147.5	9.62	10,248.70	10,871.70	15,152.00	6.9	279-0279	505-983-4335	None	1.00	4.00	B. Clark Stamper	'90
VISTA:NY INCOME	New York Muni	110.7	12.04	10,366.80	11,399.60	16,730.90	5.0	348-4782	None	4.50	0.25	None	Pamela Hunter	'87
VISTA:TX FR INCOME	General Muni	42.8	12.41	10,376.50	11,678.00	17,645.60	5.5	348-4782	None	4.50	0.25	None	Pamela Hunter	'87
VLC TR:OCEAN STATE TX-EX	Single-State Muni	41.5	10.75	10,315.80	11,175.60	15,480.00	5.7	992-2207	401-421-1411	4.00	None	None	Samuel Hallowell	'92
VOYAGEUR AZ INSURED	Arizona Muni	180.8	11.23	10,357.50	11,364.20	☆	5.6	553-2143	612-376-7000	4.75	None	None	Andrew M. McCullagh, Jr.	'91
VOYAGEUR CA INSURED	California Muni	5.9	10.88	10,296.70	☆	☆	0.0	553-2143	612-376-7000	4.75	None	None	Andrew M. McCullagh, Jr.	'92
VOYAGEUR CO TAX FREE	Colorado Muni	284.2	11.06	10,358.00	11,422.00	16,240.30	5.7	553-2143	612-376-7000	3.90	None	None	Andrew M. McCullagh, Jr.	'87
VOYAGEUR FL INSURED	Florida Muni	169.5	10.93	10,338.70	11,432.90	☆	6.0	553-2143	612-376-7000	4.75	None	None	Andrew M. McCullagh, Jr.	'92
VOYAGEUR KS TAX FREE	Kansas Muni	1.0	10.57	10,263.10	☆	☆	0.0	553-2143	612-376-7000	4.75	None	None	Dawkins/Howell	'92/'92
VOYAGEUR MN INSURED	Minnesota Muni	214.6	10.77	10,331.40	11,304.10	15,850.20	5.6	553-2143	612-376-7000	4.75	0.25	None	Dawkins/Howell	'87/'90
VOYAGEUR MN INTMDT TX	Minnesota Muni	59.1	11.04	10,152.20	10,829.70	14,066.60	4.5	553-2143	612-376-7000	2.75	0.15	None	Dawkins/Howell	'85/'90
VOYAGEUR MN TAX FREE	Minnesota Muni	393.2	12.73	10,280.70	11,208.00	15,608.00	5.7	553-2143	612-376-7000	4.75	0.25	None	Dawkins/Howell	'84/'90
VOYAGEUR MO INSURED	Missouri Muni	19.7	10.49	10,291.80	☆	☆	0.0	553-2143	612-376-7000	4.75	0.25	None	Dawkins/Howell	'92/'92
VOYAGEUR NATL INSURED	Insured Muni	10.0	10.62	10,336.60	11,327.40	☆	5.9	553-2143	612-376-7000	4.75	None	None	Andrew M. McCullagh, Jr.	'92
VOYAGEUR NM TAX FREE	Single-State Muni	10.0	10.72	10,337.10	☆	☆	0.0	553-2143	612-376-7000	4.75	0.25	None	Andrew M. McCullagh, Jr.	'92
VOYAGEUR ND TAX FREE	Single-State Muni	26.0	10.97	10,279.40	11,268.20	☆	6.1	553-2143	612-376-7000	4.75	0.25	None	Andrew M. McCullagh, Jr.	'91
VOYAGEUR UT TAX FREE	Single-State Muni	2.2	10.85	10,302.40	☆	☆	0.0	553-2143	612-376-7000	4.75	0.25	None	Andrew M. McCullagh, Jr.	'92
WADDELL & REED:MUNI BD	General Muni	11.1	10.83	10,379.50	☆	☆	0.0	366-5465	913-236-1303	None	1.00	3.00	John Holliday	'92
WRBG PINCUS NY MUNI BOND	New York Muni	66.3	10.54	10,244.50	10,994.60	14,523.50	4.5	257-5614	212-878-0600	None	None	None	Dale C. Christensen	'92
WESTCORE:AZ INT TX-FR	Arizona Muni	22.4	10.76	10,284.50	11,060.00	☆	4.6	392-2673	303-623-2577	3.75	None	None	Jack Berryman	'92
WESTCORE:CA INTMDT TX-FR	California Muni	3.2	10.26	10,236.30	☆	☆	0.0	392-2673	303-623-2577	3.50	None	None	Gerry Wagner	'93
WESTCORE:CO TX-EX	Colorado Muni	7.3	10.82	10,265.00	11,018.40	☆	5.2	392-2673	303-623-2577	4.50	None	None	Bob Lindig	'91
WESTCORE:OREGON TX-EX	Oregon Muni	45.5	17.01	10,367.50	11,061.90	15,282.00	5.1	392-2673	303-623-2577	4.50	None	None	Diane Angius	'88
WESTCORE:QUALITY TX EX	Intermediate Muni	7.4	15.38	10,285.70	☆	☆	0.0	392-2673	303-623-2577	3.50	None	None	Mary Gail Walton	'93
WILLIAM PENN:PA TAX-FREE	Pennsylvania Muni	74.7	11.28	10,246.80	11,159.20	15,826.50	5.6	523-8440	215-670-1031	4.75	0.50	None	Miller Anderson & Sherr.	'87
WOODWARD:MI BD;RTL	Michigan Muni	20.7	10.36	10,353.50	☆	☆	0.0	688-3350	None	4.50	0.35	None	Robert Grabowski	'93
WOODWARD:MUNI BD;RTL	General Muni	22.9	10.39	10,377.30	☆	☆	0.0	688-3350	None	4.50	0.35	None	Robert Grabowski	'93
WRIGHT INC:INS TAX FREE	Insured Muni	16.2	11.97	10,238.20	11,052.10	14,616.90	4.8	232-0013	203-333-6666	None	0.20	None	Team Managed	'85

★STATE FARM MUNICIPAL—Open only to State Farm agents and employees.

How To Read Our Listings

MORE, better, faster. As we've said before, that's the motto of the *Barron's*/Lipper mutual-fund quarterly. The "more," truth to tell, is out of our hands; the number of funds continues to explode, reaching 3,826 this quarter—up by about 250 in less than three months! And unlike most of our competitors, we have chosen to include *all* long-term funds, even if they're too small, too new, too exclusive or too obscure to be listed in the daily newspapers.

Under the heading "faster," note that this quarterly hits the newstands just two weeks after the end of the quarter, down from a three-week lag last quarter (and six weeks not so very long ago). In order to speed up the process, we have had to make a few compromises. One, the total net asset numbers now date from the end of May, rather than the end of June. And the names of the funds are also as of June 30. So we're still listing Financial Programs funds under "F," even though they've just taken their parent's name and are called Invesco (you'll find them under "I" in *Barron's* regular weekly listings). Similarly, we still list Equitable funds, though they are joining the Alliance family.

Meanwhile, the stock and taxable-bond funds, listed alphabetically, begin on page 294; the tax-exempt funds start on page 358. If you can't find your fund, check out the lists of name changes, mergers and liquidations on page 374.

So you find your fund—then what? If you see a ★ after the name, look at the footnotes at the bottom of the page. These notes may describe an unusual occurrence that affects performance, or note that the fund isn't open to the general public. Fund names followed by the abbreviation INSTL are generally open only to institutions.

Next to every fund's name you'll find its **objective**, which is defined below. Aside from telling you about a fund's goals or practices, objectives can give you a rough idea of how volatile—and so how risky—a fund is likely to be. The chart on page M12[1] ranks various kinds of stock funds by their volatility over the last five years.

Going back to the listings, in the third column you'll find the fund's **total net assets** on May 31, in millions of dollars. A fund's size can can have a big impact on its performance. Small funds tend to suffer from high expenses, which can drag down performance, and often soar or sink on the basis of a single holding. Huge stock funds—over $1 billion, say—are likely to lumber, though in bond funds, bigger tends to be better.

In the fourth column, you will discover the fund's **net asset value** at quarter's end. This figure, reckoned by dividing the total net assets by the number of shares outstanding, tells you what you would have had to pay for a share (excluding any sales charges).

The most important part, **performance,** comes next. These columns tell you how much you'd have as of June 30 if you invested a net $10,000 in a fund at the beginning of one of three periods: one quarter, 12 months and five years. The result is each fund's **total return:** The amount an investment makes, taking into account both sources of potential gains — dividend payments and share-price appreciation. Total return calculations assume that you reinvest all these distributions, as well as regular dividends, in fund shares, as most investors do.

These total return numbers do not take into account sales charges. Why? Because few people buy a fund at the beginning of a quarter and sell 90 days later; assuming that they did so would skew the performance results and make it hard for people who already own a fund to compare its investment performance to its competitors'. Furthermore, those funds that levy front-end fees usually reduce them for larger purchases, and sometimes waive them for limited periods and special investors. So, like most analysts who track funds, Lipper has chosen to focus on pure investment performance.

To see how your fund stacks up against the competition, begin with the five **benchmarks** on page 294. Similar information for every fund category that Lipper tracks, as well as the major market indexes, appears on page M23[1], expressed in terms of percentage changes. To make this data comparable to the listing's $10,000 presentation, multiply the percentage number by 100 and add it to (or subtract it from, if it's a loss) $10,000.

Next in the listings comes the **dividend yield** column, which tells you the average amount of income dividends a fund has paid in the last 12 months, expressed as a percentage of the NAV. The dividend yield does not reflect any capital-gains distributions; instead, it indicates the income a fund has received—and passed on to shareholders — from dividends or interest payments.

For more info about a fund, you can dial up the listing under **phone numbers**, which includes toll-free 800 numbers where they exist; if the number doesn't work in the fund's home state, use the "in-state" number. ("None" in that column usually means the 800 number works in all states.)

Front-end **fees** represent the *maximum* amount that a fund will charge for sales. Redemption fees often decline the longer you remain invested in the fund; again, our table lists the max. Annual 12b-1 fees generally reflect what funds charged during their last fiscal year; for young

[1] This page number refers to *Barron's National Business and Financial Weekly*, July 19, 1993.

funds, we show the most they can hit you with. In a few cases, when funds have been able to convince Lipper that they're really charging a different fee, that's the number we've used. Expect more such changes as funds comply with new regulatory limits on 12b-1s; while the regs limit these fees, they permit funds to add new ones for "service" — which, of course, they're doing. All these annual fees, by the way, are included in funds' expenses, so they are already reflected in total return numbers.

Finally, we tell you who the fund's **portfolio manager** is, and how long he or she has been in charge. If the captain is really a committee (or competing managers), that's reflected, too.

* * *

The following are the definitions of mutual-fund objectives; Lipper assigns funds to these groups based on both the language in the prospectus and their actual practices.

Debt and Equity Funds

Balanced: Goal is preserving principal; fund maintains a 60%/40% or so ratio of stocks to bonds.

Balanced Target: Invests to provide a guaranteed return of principal at maturity. Some assets are in zero-coupon Treasury bonds, the remainder is in long-term growth stocks.

Canadian: Invests primarily in securities traded in Canadian markets.

Capital Appreciation: Seeks maximum capital appreciation through strategies such as high portfolio turnover, leveraging, purchasing unregistered shares or options; may hold a lot of cash.

Convertibles: Invests primarily in convertible bonds, preferred stock.

Equity Income: Normally has more than 60% of its assets in equities and seeks high income.

European Region: Focuses on one European stock market or several.

Financial Services: Invests 65% of assets in stocks of financial-service companies.

Fixed Income: Typically has more than 75% of assets in fixed-income securities, such as bonds, preferred stocks, money-market instruments.

Flexible: Aims for high total return by allocating its portfolio among a wide range of asset classes.

Global: At least 25% of its portfolio is in non-U.S. securities.

Global Flexible: Similar to flexible; invests at least 25% of assets in securities traded outside the U.S.

Global Small-Company: Invests at least a quarter of its assets outside the U.S.; limits 65% of its holdings on the basis of market capitalization.

Gold: Has at least 65% of its assets in gold-mining or gold-oriented mining finance shares, gold coins or bullion.

Growth: Invests in companies whose long-term earnings it expects to grow faster than those of the stocks in the major market indexes.

Growth & Income: Seeks earnings growth as well as dividend income.

Health/Biotech: Has 65% of its portfolio in health-care, medical companies and biotechnology companies.

Income: Seeks high current income through stocks, bonds and money-market instruments.

International: Invests in securities traded primarily outside the U.S.

Japanese: Concentrates on securities trading in Tokyo.

Latin American: Invests primarily in securities in Mexico, Brazil, Chile and other Latin American countries.

Natural Resource: Usually invests more than 65% of its equity holdings in natural-resource stocks.

Option Income: Writes covered options on at least half its portfolio.

Pacific Region: Concentrates on stocks trading in one or more of the Pacific Basin markets.

Real Estate: Puts 65% of its assets into real-estate company securities.

Small-Company Growth: Limits investment to companies on the basis of their size.

Specialty: Limits its investments to a specific industry, or falls outside other classifications.

Technology: 65% of portfolio is in science and technology stocks.

Utility: Utilities comprise 65% of its equity portfolio.

World Fixed-Income: May own common and preferred, but invests primarily in U.S. and foreign debt.

Municipal Bond Funds

General Muni: Puts at least 65% of its assets in municipal bonds carrying the top four credit ratings.

Insured Muni: At least 65% of its holdings have been insured for timely payment of interest.

Intermediate Muni: Its tax-exempt debt holdings have an average maturity of five to 10 years.

High-Yield Muni: Can put more than half of its assets in low-rated credits.

Short Muni: Invests in tax-exempt debt maturing, on average, in less than five years.

Single-State Muni: Limits investments to securities exempt from taxation in a particular state. States with only a few such funds are lumped together in the Single State category; the following state funds are identified separately:

Ariz.; Calif.; Colo.; Conn.; Fla.; Ga.; Kan.; Ky.; La.; Md.; Mass.; Mich.; Minn.; Mo.; N.J.; N.Y.; N.C.; Ohio; Ore.; Pa.; S.C.; Texas; Va.

Source: Lipper Analytical Services, Inc. Reprinted by permission of *Barron's National Business and Financial Weekly,*

A Brief Guide to Mutual Fund Investing[1]

Sumner Levine

The essentials of good mutual fund investing are not very complicated and are summarized in the following.

1. *Determine Your Goals*

Begin by estimating the amount of cash you will need and when you will need it. Are you investing to purchase a home, to send the kids to college, for retirement—all of these and more? Your estimate must, of course, include the effects of inflation. How to calculate the effects of inflation on costs and hence the future purchasing power of your investments is explained below. The worksheet (Exhibit 1) given below should be helpful in formulating your thoughts.

2. *List Your Current Investments and Estimate Your Savings*

Take inventory of your current cash and investments by identifying and evaluating such items as:

bonds
certificates of deposit
checking accounts
money market funds
mutual funds
savings accounts
stocks

Also list your current and anticipated incomes, including those from salaries, self employment, rentals, royalties, trusts, social security, pensions, and other retirement plans. How much do you expect to save each year?

Using the above information and assuming plausible rates of return, estimate the future resources you expect to have available to meet your goals. The calculation is described below (see *Estimating The Future Value Of Your Investments*).

3. *Understand The Risk-Return Characteristics of Investments*

Different types of investments exhibit different risk return characteristics as shown in the Basic Series Exhibit on page 239. Risk refers to the extent by which the price of an investment fluctuates and is measured by the standard deviation (SD). The larger the SD, the greater the risk. For example, funds consisting of small company growth stocks with an SD of 35.3% are considerably riskier than, say, a Government bond fund with an SD of 8.6%. It is also evident from the Basic Series Exhibit that the greater the risk the greater the return. Over long time periods the greater return provided by more risky investments offsets the fluctuation in value associated with the risk. However, over relatively short time intervals investors in risky assets may experience substantial losses. Hence, it is generally best to reserve investments in riskier (aggressive) assets to money that will not be needed for several years (say, five years or more).

4. *Determine Your Risk Tolerance*

Your risk tolerance and hence the extent to which you elect to expose your portfolio to aggressive investments depend on several considerations. These include where you are in your career cycle (starting out, preparing for retirement, etc.), the number and age of your dependents, and your psychological makeup. The Worksheet provides some helpful guidance in these regards. Generally, as investors approach retirement age, investments are shifted from the more aggressive (riskier) assets to those that are less so, as discussed in the following.

5. *Select a Diversified Investment Portfolio Consistent With Your Risk Tolerance*

The importance of investment diversification in reducing risk for a given return is now well established. No one knows what type of investment will flourish or decline in the future so that a portfolio should have a broad exposure to different types of investments to reduce risk. An important requirement for effective diversification is that the investments composing your portfolio should tend to fluctuate (in price) oppositely to one another—or, at least, independently of one another. Hopefully as one investment decreases another will increase in value. In practice, diversification is achieved by including in your portfolio funds with different investment philosophies; for example, aggressive, growth, growth-income, fixed income, and foreign equity funds (see page 381 for definitions).

As discussed, the proportion of each fund type in your portfolio will depend on your risk tolerance. Since most investors are risk adverse the proportion of aggressive (riskier) funds in most portfolios is usually smaller than that of the more conservative funds. The shift

[1] The material in this section is for informational purposes only. Any portfolio decisions you make should be discussed with your tax and financial advisers.

EXHIBIT 1

YOUR INVESTMENT PROFILE

Before you launch your investment plan, make a realistic analysis of your financial circumstances and your feelings about risk. Answering the following questions will give you a starting point.

Do you have a sufficient financial "safety net" in place?

- ❑ Do you have 3 to 6 months' salary in a liquid investment that can be converted to cash easily, in case of an emergency?
- ❑ Do you have adequate insurance coverage for yourself and your family?

How will your personal circumstances affect your investing approach? How aggressively—or conservatively—you pursue your investing goals will depend on such factors as:

Your age ______________
Number of dependents ______________
Your current net worth ______________
Your annual income ______________
Amount you have to invest ______________

Your investing experience: ❑ None ❑ Limited ❑ Good ❑ Extensive

What specific investing goals do you have?	**How long do you have to achieve them?**
❑ College savings for your children	______________
❑ Home purchase	______________
❑ Retirement savings	______________
❑ Business investment	______________
❑ Wealth building	______________
❑ Other	______________

What is your primary investment objective?

❑ Maximum growth ❑ Growth ❑ Income ❑ Preservation of principal/safety

Should you consider tax-advantaged investments?

Are you in a tax bracket where you could keep more of your earnings if invested in tax-free investments? (Consult your tax advisor if you're unsure.)

How do you feel about investment risk?

For example, which of these descriptions fit you best:

- ❑ You want maximum investment growth. You're willing to risk the loss of some—or even most—of your principal in exchange for the chance to receive higher returns on your money.
- ❑ You seek high returns but not at the expense of too much risk. You're investing primarily for growth, but want to keep some portion of your money in more "secure" investments.
- ❑ You want good investment returns but only moderate exposure to risk. You're willing to accept slower growth of your investments in exchange for somewhat less portfolio risk.
- ❑ You want your returns to keep pace with inflation but keep risk to a minimum. You're still looking out for the future, but you have a low tolerance for risk and would limit your "growth investments."
- ❑ You want to safeguard your principal at all costs. You're extremely averse to risk and don't want to take any more chances than necessary to maintain the value of your portfolio and/or receive the steady income it generates.

Source: The Charles Schwab Guide to *Investing Made Easy*, Charles Schwab & Co., Inc.

into more conservative investments is usually more pronounced as the investor approaches retirement. Representative portfolios illustrating this point are shown below:

	Amount (%)
EARLY TO MID-CAREER	
Aggressive Growth	15–20
Growth	50–30
Fixed Income (Bond) Funds	25–35
International	10–15
PRE-RETIREMENT	
Aggressive Growth	10–
Growth	35–30
Fixed Income	45–50
International	10–
RETIREMENT	
Growth	30–35
Fixed Income	50–45
International	10–
Money Market	10–

For those in the higher tax brackets, tax free (municipal) funds should be considered. Investors with a greater risk tolerance might prefer a somewhat different allocation: for example, a greater proportion in aggressive growth funds. As a rule of thumb, the percentage of your portfolio in equity funds is given by 100 minus your age. Thus, a 65 year old would have 35% in equities.

Selection of funds for inclusion in the portfolio can be made by examining the year to year return of funds with different investment philosophies and picking those with a consistently superior performance (say, among the top 20% over the last 5 years). A simpler and perhaps a more satisfactory approach is to refer to a good service such as Morningstar, which specializes in evaluating fund performance. Several helpful references for selecting funds are given below. Be sure that the same management which achieved the superior performance is still in place. If a management change has occurred then it might be prudent to defer inclusion until the new management has proven itself.

As to the choice between a load fund (which charges a fee for purchasing and/or selling the fund) or a no-load fund, our preference is for a no-load fund since there is no evidence that load funds, as a group, out perform no-load funds. With a no-load fund the full amount of your investment goes to work for you at the outset.

Another item to check is the annual expense ratio charged by the fund. This should be at least consistent (or preferably lower) with that of other funds of the same type.

There are no hard and fast rules concerning the number of funds to own. The number will depend on your need for diversification, the size of your assets, and your tolerance for the paper work involved in keeping tax records and monitoring performance. Typically, a modest portfolio, of say, $50,000.00 to $100,000.00 might consist of two aggressive growth funds, two international equity funds, one conservative growth fund or growth-income fund, and a fixed income fund, giving a total of six funds. Larger portfolios of about one million dollars or more might consist of fifteen to twenty funds.

6. *Time Average Your Purchases*

The market constantly fluctuates; sometime it is up, sometime down. A simple way to average out this effect is to make constant dollar purchases on a monthly basis. Thus every month a fixed amount, say $200.00 is invested. To take inflation into account, the monthly purchase might be increased by the inflation rate. If the inflation rate is, say 4%, the $200.00 purchase would become $208.00.

A second approach to time averaging requires the value of your portfolio to increase by a fixed amount, say $200.00 per month. The amount of your monthly investment contribution would be the difference between the target value you set and the actual increase. Thus, if the value of the portfolio increased $100.00, then you would invest $100.00 assuming a target value of $200.00. If your portfolio increased $200.00 or more, you add nothing.

Another version of this approach requires that you sell shares for portfolio increases over $200.00 and reinvest the cash at a later time when the gain is less than $200.00. However, this approach usually incurs large capital gains taxes.

With this approach, if your portfolio lost money, say $20.00, you would contribute $220.00 to achieve a net increase of $200.00. In this way, you invest more in a weak market and less in a strong one.

7. *Monitor Your Portfolio and Keep Abreast of Developments*

The performance of your portfolio should be reviewed at least twice a year and preferably more often. Determine how well your funds have performed relative to others of the same type. Check to see if there has been a change in investment manager or philosophy.

The total returns on your portfolio should also be calculated. This is done by multiplying the return of each fund over the period in question by the fractional amount of the fund in the portfolio. Add up the results for all the funds to obtain the over all portfolio return.

Alas, the vicissitudes of the Government are such that even the most prudent investor cannot anticipate the changes in the tax law and it is essential therefore to keep informed by reading the financial press and consulting with your tax adviser.

INFORMATION SOURCES

The following is a selected list of information sources to help you evaluate and monitor funds.

1. *The Wall Street Journal*

Probably the most complete daily source of information. For details see page 288.

2. *Morningstar Mutual Funds*

An excellent detailed source of information. This loose leaf service provides updates every two weeks. Over 1240 funds are followed. Try your library or take a trial subscription. Also publishes a newsletter on closed-end funds (i.e., funds traded on one of the Stock Exchanges).

Morningstar
53 West Jackson Boulevard
Chicago, IL 60604
Telephone: 800-876-5005

3. *Mutual Fund Buyer's Guide*

This inexpensive monthly publication is a compact information source on safety ratings, performance, fees, asset size, and more. Covers over 1500 funds.

The Institute for Econometric Research
3471 N. Federal
Fort Lauderdale, FL 33306
Telephone: 800-442-9000

4. *No-Load Fund Investor*

A monthly publication covering 664 no-load and low-load funds. Contains information on returns, risk, asset size, and gives fund fixed diversification suggestions. Also available is the useful publication *Handbook For No-Load Fund Investors.*

The No-Load Fund Investor, Inc.
P.O. Box 283
Hastings-on-Hudson, NY 10706
Telephone: 800-252-2042

5. *Barron's*

This well-known weekly provides information on 52 week high and low prices, latest dividend payouts, and 12 month payouts. Quarterly reports are published on over 3500 funds summarizing extensive data provided by the Lipper organization. The complete 2nd quarter report is included here starting on page 294. Available on most news stands and by subscription.

Barron's
200 Burnett Road
Chicopee, MA 01020

HELPFUL CALCULATIONS

How Inflation Affects Future Costs

Estimating future cash needs is an important aspect of investment planning. The effect of inflation on future costs can be calculated from the expression.

$F = P\,(1 + I)^n$
F is the cost n years from now
P is the present cost
I is the estimated inflation rate

Example:
You want to estimate the cost ten years from now for sending your child to college. The present cost is $6000.00 per year and you estimate the inflation of college costs to be about 6% per year.

Here P = $6000.00 per year
$I = .06$
n = 10 years
so that your future cost estimate is
$F = 6.000\ (1.06) = \$10{,}745/\text{yr}$

Estimating the Portfolio Return Required to Maintain Current Purchasing Power

The return on your portfolio will be decreased by income taxes and the purchasing power of your investment will be reduced by inflation. It is often important to know the before tax return which will just maintain the current purchasing power of your portfolio.

The appropriate expression for the calculation is

$$i = \frac{I}{1 - t}$$

Where

i is the before tax return
t is your income tax bracket
I is the inflation rate

Example:
You want to determine the rate of return on your portfolio required to maintain the current purchasing power of the assets. You are in the 35% tax bracket (Federal and State) and you estimate future inflation to be 4% per year.

The required before tax return is

$$i = \frac{.04}{1 - .35} = 6.15\%$$

Under these assumptions this return will just maintain the purchasing power of your investments over time. The purchasing power will increase if the investment return is greater and decrease if it is less than the calculated rate.

Return Required to Maintain Purchasing Power When Funds Are Withdrawn

In the above example it was assumed that no funds were withdrawn from the portfolio. We now assume that a percentage of the portfolio is withdrawn for, say, living expenses.

The before tax return required to maintain the purchasing power of the remaining portfolio is given by

$$i = \frac{I + w}{1 - t}$$

Where w is the percentage of the portfolio withdrawn.

Example:

Assume the same tax brackets and inflation rate as in the above example. You desire to withdraw 5% of the portfolio each year for living expenses. The required before tax return (i) is

$$i = \frac{.04 + .05}{1 - .35} = 13.8\%$$

At the calculated rate the purchasing power of the remaining portfolio will be preserved. If the rate of return is smaller, the purchasing power will decrease.

Estimating the Future Value of Your Investments

You often want to know how much your portfolio will grow if you invest a fixed amount each month (or other period) and the funds generated by the portfolio investments are reinvested.

The required expression for the size of the portfolio n months from now

$$F = P\,(1 + i)^n + A\left[\frac{(1 + i)^n - 1}{i}\right]$$

Where

P is the current value of the portfolio
A is the fixed amount invested each period (month, year, etc.)
n is the number of months from now at which it is desired to evaluate the portfolio
i is the after tax return per month (the annual after tax return divided by twelve)

Example:

Your current portfolio is valued at $50,000.00. You want to know how much the portfolio will grow 10 years from now if you deposit $200.00 per month over that time period. You assume a before tax return of 12% per year. If you are in the 35% tax bracket, your after tax return will be 7.8% [12 (1 − .35)] per year. The *monthly return* is just the annual return divided by 12 or .65% per month. Ten years corresponds to 120 months so that at ten years the portfolio will have grown to

$$F = 50{,}000(1.0065)^{120}\left[\frac{(1.0065)^{120} - 1}{1.0065}\right]$$

$$F = \$144{,}982$$

Calculations of this type are helpful in forming realistic expectations of portfolio growth possibilities.

Maximum Amount that Can Be Withdrawn Annually from a Portfolio During Retirement

You are now retired and have accumulated a portfolio valued at P dollars. It is invested at a return of i (after income taxes). You want to know the maximum amount you can withdraw each year over your remaining life so that nothing will remain at the end.

The appropriate expression is

$$A = P\left[\frac{i(1 + i)^n}{(1 + i)^n - 1}\right]$$

Where

A is the maximum amount that can be withdrawn each year over n years
P is the value of the portfolio at retirement
i is the after tax return
n is the number of years you expect to live after retirement

Example:

You are retired at the age of 68 with a portfolio of $500,000.00. Life expectancy tables indicate that your remaining expected life is about 13 years. You estimate your after tax return to be about 6.5%. What is the most you can withdraw each year so that nothing remains when you have lived your expected life?

$$A = \frac{500{,}000(.065)(1.065)^{13}}{(1.065)^{13} - 1} = \$58{,}151$$

How Long Will My Savings Last

You want to determine how long your investment savings will last given the after tax rate of return on your investments and a withdrawal rate.

The expression to use is:

$$n = -\frac{\ln\left(1 - \frac{Pi}{A}\right)}{\ln(1 + i)}$$

Where

ln designates the logarithm
n is the years required to use up all of your investment
P = the size of your investment when you start to withdraw
A = the amount to be withdrawn each year
i = the after tax rate of return

EXHIBIT 2: Table for Determining the Longevity of Retirement Savings

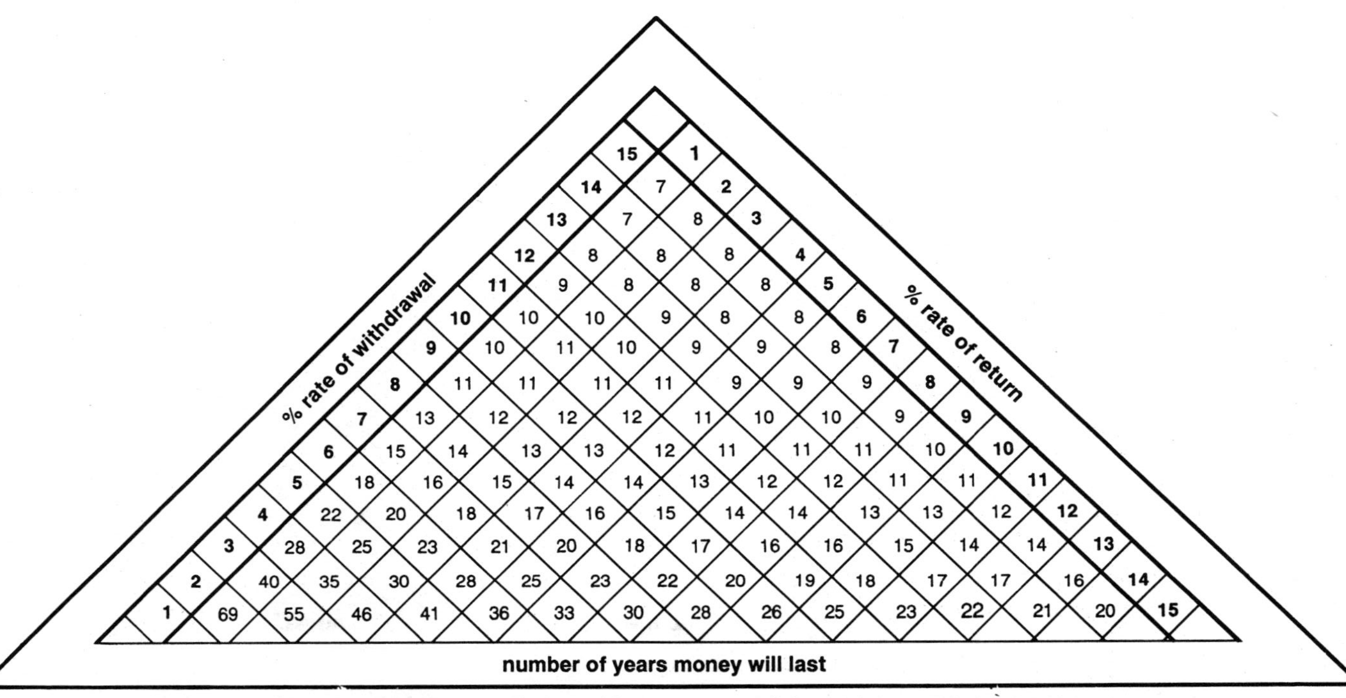

number of years money will last

% rate of withdrawal \ % rate of return	1	2	3	4	5	6	7	8	9	10	11	12	13	14	15
1															
2	69														
3	40	55													
4	28	35	46												
5	22	25	30	41											
6	18	20	23	28	36										
7	15	16	18	21	25	33									
8	13	14	15	17	20	23	30								
9	11	12	13	14	16	18	22	28							
10	10	11	12	13	14	15	17	20	26						
11	10	11	11	12	12	13	14	16	19	25					
12	9	10	10	11	11	11	12	14	16	18	23				
13	8	8	9	9	9	10	11	12	13	15	17	22			
14	7	8	8	8	9	9	10	11	11	13	14	17	21		
15	7	8	8	8	8	8	9	9	10	11	12	14	16	20	

Source: *The Handbook For No-Load Fund Investors,* Sheldon Jacobs, The No-Load Fund Investor, Inc., P.O. Box 318, Irvington-on-Hudson, New York 10533.

An alternative approach is to use Exhibit 2 based on the above equation. Find the rate of withdrawal on the left side and the rate of return on the right. The intersection of the two rows gives the number of years the money will last.

Example:

At retirement your investment savings are $200,000.00 and you want to start withdrawing $20,000.00 each year. You estimate an after tax return of 7%. How long will your savings last?

Here

$$i = .07$$
$$A = \$20{,}000.$$
$$P = \$200{,}000.$$

Therefore

$$n = -\frac{\ln\left(1 - \dfrac{200{,}000}{20{,}000} \times .07\right)}{\ln (1.07)} = 17.7 \text{ years}$$

Note if the withdrawal rate (A/P) is less than the rate of return (i), your savings will last indefinitely.

Foreign Securities Investments

This section provides data on the performance of major foreign securities markets and also listings of foreign stocks traded on the New York and American Exchanges. Over 200 foreign stocks and ADRs are also traded on the Over-The-Counter (OTC) market. A complete listing of foreign OTC stocks is available from the National Association of Securities Dealers, 1735 K Street, Washington, DC 20006.

Foreign securities not traded on the above exchanges may generally be purchased through stock brokers or major foreign banks in the country of interest. Most of these banks, which have U.S. branches in New York and other major cities, provide details concerning opening a foreign brokerage account.

A difficulty associated with foreign stock selection is that of obtaining timely information. The following general information sources may be helpful in this regard.

The Wall Street Journal
The Asian Wall Street Journal
Dow Jones & Company
22 Cortlandt Street
New York, NY 10007

The Asian Wall Street Journal, a weekly, is particularly helpful for the Asian region, including stock market coverage.

Barron's
World Financial Center
200 Liberty Street
New York, NY 10281

The weekly *International Trader* section is of special interest.

Capital International Perspectives
3 Place Des Bergues
1201 Geneva, Switzerland

Capital International Perspectives is a leading monthly publication dealing with international investments.

The Financial Times
Bracken House
10 Cannon Street
London EC4P 4BY, England

The Financial Times provides comprehensive coverage of European businesses and securities markets and is published daily.

Moody's Investor Services, International Manual
Moody's Investor Services
99 Church Street
New York, NY 10007

The International Manual provides financial information on about 5,000 major foreign corporations.

Disclosure
5161 River Road
Bethesda, MD 20816

This service also provides annual reports and filings on foreign firms.

Worldscope provides company financial information in published and compact disk formats. This service is available online through Dow Jones Retrieval.

Contact: Wright Investor Service
P.O. Box 428
Bridgeport, CT 06601

Reuters, based in London, is one of the largest international news agencies. Online services include Newsline which gives current international news, and Company News Year which provides access to one year of news items concerning specific companies.

Contact: Reuters Information Services
60 Broadway
New York, NY 10006

PERFORMANCES OF FOREIGN SECURITIES MARKETS

東証株価指数(日本)
Tokyo Stock Price Index (Japan)

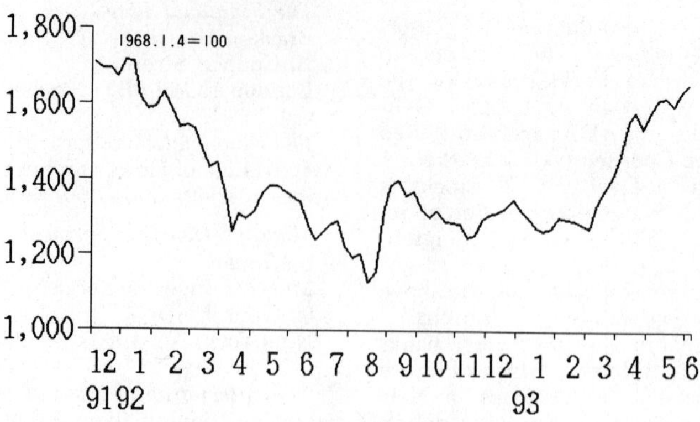

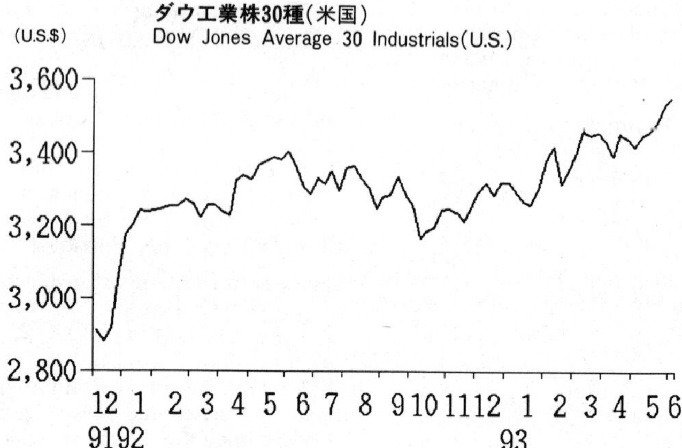

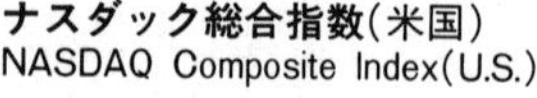

NASDAQ Composite Index (U.S.)

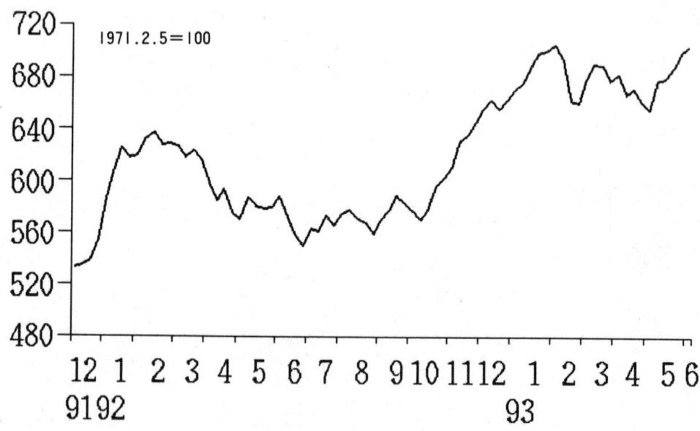

Source: *Investors Guide*, July 1993. Daiwa Securities Co., Ltd.

PERFORMANCES OF FOREIGN SECURITIES MARKETS *(continued)*

FT工業株指数(英国)
Financial Times Index of Industrial Ordinary Shares(U.K.)

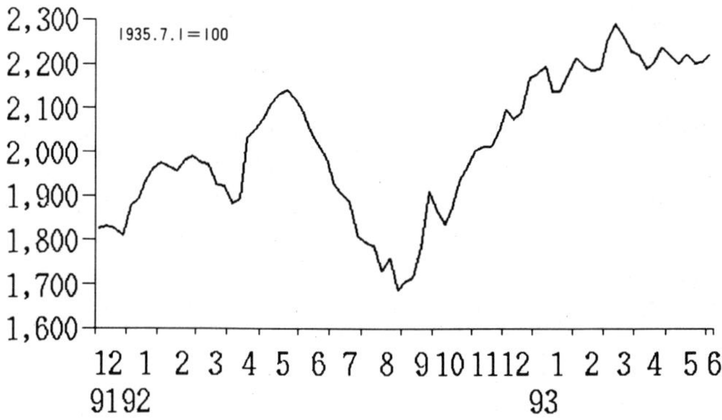

コメルツバンク総合指数(西ドイツ)
Commerzbank Index (West Germany)

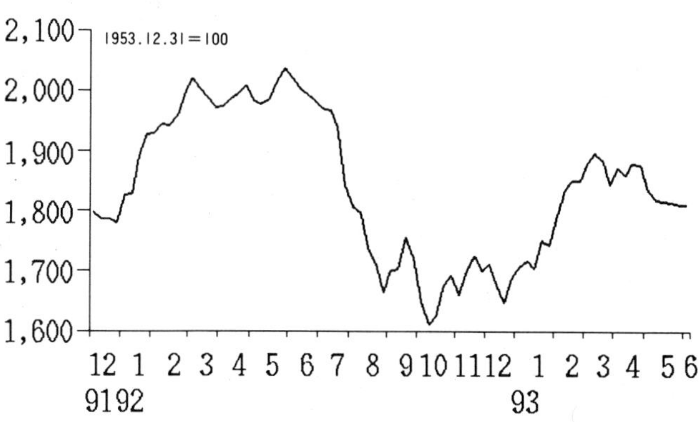

オーストラリア証券取引所全普通株指数
Australia Stock Exchange All Ordinaries Index

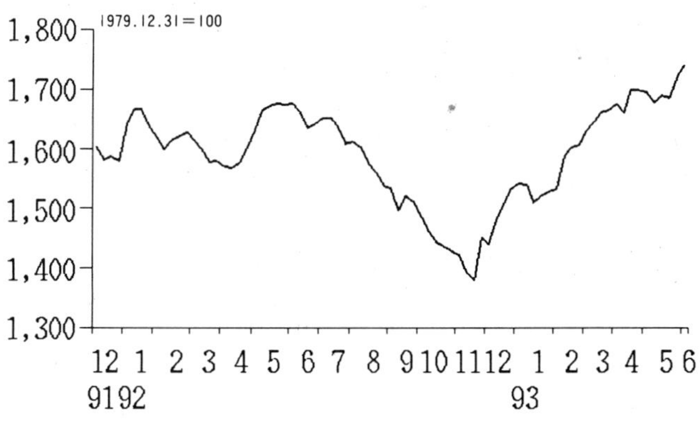

(continued)

PERFORMANCES OF FOREIGN SECURITIES MARKETS *(concluded)*

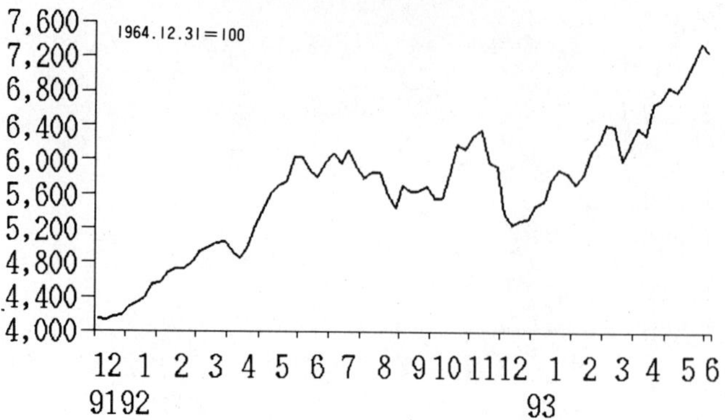

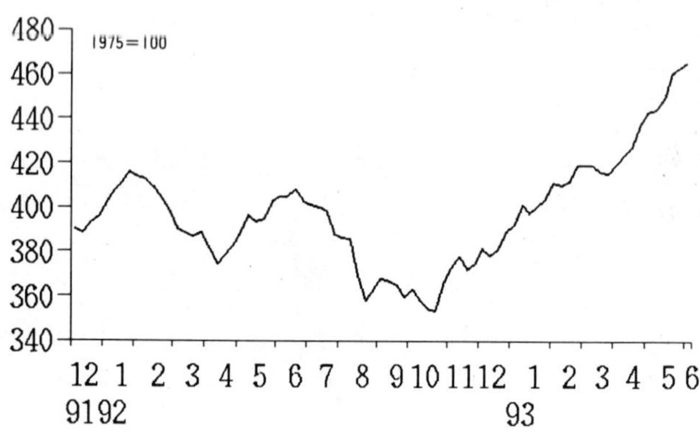

Source: *Investors Guide,* July 1993. Daiwa Securities Co., Ltd.

Stocks of Non–U.S. Corporate Issuers, December 31, 1992 (NYSE)

Country	Company	Symbol	Date Admitted
Australia	Broken Hill Proprietary Company Limited*	BHP	05/28/87
	Coles Myer Ltd.*	CM	10/31/88
	FAI Insurances Limited*	FAI	09/28/88
	National Australia Bank Limited*	NAB	06/24/88
	News Corporation Ltd.*	NWS	05/20/86
	Orbital Engine Corporation Limited*	OE	12/04/91
	Western Mining Corp. Holdings Ltd.*	WMC	01/02/90
	Westpac Banking Corporation* (2 issues)	WBK	03/17/89
Bermuda	ADT Ltd.	ADT	08/21/91
Brazil	Aracruz Celulose, S.A.*	ARA	05/27/92
British W.I.	Club Med, Inc.	CMI	09/25/84
Canada	Abitibi-Price Inc.	ABY	07/01/87
	Alcan Aluminium Limited	AL	05/31/50
	American Barrick Resources Corp.	ABX	02/25/87
	Avalon Corporation	AVL	06/13/83
	BCE Inc.	BCE	08/18/76
	Campbell Resources Inc.	CCH	06/13/83
	Canadian Pacific Limited	CP	01/24/1883
	Cineplex Odeon Corporation	CPX	05/14/87
	Curragh Resources Inc.	CZP	05/24/90
	Domtar Inc.	DTC	09/22/87
	Horsham Corporation	HSM	01/15/90
	Inco Limited	N	12/20/28
	Intertan Inc.	INT	11/01/88
	LAC Minerals Ltd.	LAC	07/30/85
	Laidlaw Inc. (Class A)	LDWA	12/10/90
	Laidlaw Inc. (Class B)	LDWB	12/10/90
	Magna International Inc.	MGA	10/09/92
	Mitel Corporation	MLT	05/18/81
	Moore Corporation Limited	MCL	11/13/80
	Northern Telecom Limited	NT	11/10/75
	Northgate Exploration Limited	NGX	02/03/70
	NOVA Corporation of Alberta	NVA	06/13/88
	Placer Dome Inc.	PDG	08/13/87
	Potash Corporation of Saskatchewan Inc.	POT	11/02/89
	Ranger Oil Limited	RGO	01/28/83
	Seagram Company Ltd.	VO	12/02/35
	TransCanada Pipelines Limited	TRP	05/30/85
	United Dominion Industries Limited	UDI	12/06/83
	Westcoast Energy Inc.	WE	08/15/64
Cayman Islands	Extecapital Ltd.	BEXPR	12/23/92
	News Corp. Cayman Island Ltd.*	NWSPR	05/20/86
Chile	Compania de Telefonos de Chile S.A.*	CTC	07/20/90
Denmark	Novo-Nordisk A/S*	NVO	07/09/81
France	Alcatel Alsthom Compagnie Générale d'Electricité	ALA	05/20/92
	Rhone-Poulenc S.A.* (3 issues)	RPU	11/10/89
	Societe Nationale Elf Aquitaine*	ELF	06/14/91
	TOTAL*	TOT	10/25/91
Hong Kong	Brilliance China Automotive Holdings Limited	CBA	10/09/92
	Hong Kong Telecommunications Ltd.*	HKT	12/08/88
	Tommy Hilfiger Corporation	TOM	09/23/92
Ireland	Allied Irish Banks plc* (2 issues)	AIB	09/12/89
Israel	Elscint Limited	ELT	09/20/84
	Tadiran Limited	TAD	08/06/92
Italy	Benetton Group S.p.A.*	BNG	06/09/89
	Fiat S.p.A.* (3 issues)	FIA	02/14/89
	Luxottica Group S.p.A.*	LUX	01/24/90
	Montedison S.p.A.* (2 issues)	MNT	07/16/87
Japan	Hitachi, Ltd.*	HIT	04/14/82
	Honda Motor Co., Ltd.*	HMC	02/11/77
	Kubota Corporation*	KUB	11/09/76

(continued)

Stocks of Non–U.S. Corporate Issuers, December 31, 1992 *(concluded)*

Country	Company	Symbol	Date Admitted
Japan (continued)	Kyocera Corporation*	KYO	05/23/80
	Matsushita Electric Industrial Co., Ltd.*	MC	12/13/71
	Mitsubishi Bank Ltd.*	MBK	09/19/89
	Pioneer Electronic Corporation*	PIO	12/13/76
	Sony Corporation*	SNE	09/17/70
	TDK Corporation*	TDK	05/15/82
Mexico	Empresas ICA Sociedad Controladora, S.A. de C.V.*	ICA	04/09/92
	Telefonos de Mexico, S.A. de C.V.*	TMX	05/14/91
	Transportacion Maritima Mexicana S.A. de C.V.* (2 issues)	TMM	06/10/92
	Vitro, Sociedad Anonima*	VTO	11/19/91
Netherlands	AEGON N.V.**	AEG	11/05/91
	KLM Royal Dutch Airlines**	KLM	05/22/57
	Philips N.V.**	PHG	04/14/87
	PolyGram N.V.**	PLG	12/14/89
	Royal Dutch Petroleum Co.**	RD	07/20/54
	Unilever N.V.**	UN	12/12/61
Netherlands Antilles	Schlumberger Limited	SLB	02/02/62
	Singer Company N.V.	SEW	07/17/91
New Zealand	Telecom Corporation of New Zealand Ltd.*	NZT	07/17/91
Norway	Hafslund Nycomed AS*	HN	06/24/92
	Norsk Hydro a.s.*	NHY	06/25/86
Panama	Banco Latinoamericano de Exportaciones, S.A.	BLX	09/24/92
Philippines	Benguet Corporation	BE	06/27/49
Portugal	Banco Comercial Portugues, S.A.*	BPC	06/12/92
South Africa	ASA Limited	ASA	12/08/58
Spain	Banco Bilbao Vizcaya, S.A.* (3 issues)	BBV	12/14/88
	Banco Central, S.A.*	BCM	07/20/83
	Banco de Santander, S.A.*	STD	07/30/87
	Empresa Nacional de Electricidad, S.A.*	ELE	06/01/88
	Repsol, S.A.*	REP	05/11/89
	Telefonica de Espana, S.A.*	TEF	06/12/87
United Kingdom	Attwoods PLC*	A	04/12/91
	Automated Security (Holdings) PLC*	ASI	07/22/92
	Barclays PLC* (5 issues)	BCS	09/09/86
	Bass plc*	BAS	02/08/90
	BET Public Limited Company*	BEP	08/06/87
	British Airways Plc*	BAB	02/11/87
	British Gas plc*	BRG	12/08/86
	British Petroleum Co. p.l.c.*	BP	03/23/70
	British Steel plc*	BST	12/05/88
	British Telecommunications plc*	BTY	12/03/84
	Cable and Wireless Public Limited Co.*	CWP	09/27/89
	English China Clays PLC*	ENC	04/30/92
	Enterprise Oil plc (3 issues)	ETP	07/20/92
	Glaxo Holdings p.l.c.*	GLX	06/10/87
	Grand Metropolitan Plc*	GRM	03/13/91
	Hanson PLC*	HAN	11/03/86
	Huntingdon International Holdings plc*	HTD	02/16/89
	Imperial Chemical Industries PLC*	ICI	11/01/83
	National Westminster Bank PLC* (2 issues)	NW	10/22/86
	Royal Bank of Scotland Group plc* (3 issues)	RBS	10/16/89
	RTZ Corporation PLC*	RTZ	06/28/90
	Saatchi & Saatchi Company PLC*	SAA	12/08/87
	"Shell" Transport & Trading Co., p.l.c.**	SC	03/13/57
	SmithKline Beecham plc*	SBE	07/27/89
	SmithKline Beecham plc*	SBH	07/27/89
	Tiphook Plc*	TPH	10/01/91
	Unilever PLC*	UL	12/12/61
	Vodafone Group Plc*	VOD	10/26/88
	Willis Corroon plc*	WCG	10/09/90
	Wellcome PLC*	WEL	07/27/92
	Waste Management International PLC*	WME	04/07/92

* American depository receipts/shares.

** N.Y. shares and/or guilder shares.

Source: New York Stock Exchange *Fact Book.*

TOPIX (Tokyo Stock Price Index)

(Jan. 4, 1968=100)

	Year-end	High		Low	
		Index	Date	Index	Date
1950	11.57	13.24	Aug. 21	9.59	July 3
1951	16.94	17.11	Oct. 20	11.58	Jan. 4
1952	33.35	33.55	Nov. 22	17.07	Jan. 8
1953	33.30	42.18	Feb. 4	28.46	Apr. 1
1954	30.27	33.22	Jan. 11	26.79	Nov. 13
1955	39.06	39.06	Dec. 28	30.00	Mar. 28
1956	51.21	52.95	Dec. 6	38.81	Jan. 25
1957	43.40	54.82	Jan. 21	43.18	Dec. 27
1958	60.95	60.95	Dec. 27	43.48	Jan. 4
1959	80.00	90.14	Nov. 30	61.11	Jan. 9
1960	109.18	112.53	Nov. 15	79.46	Jan. 4
1961	101.66	126.59	July 14	90.86	Dec. 19
1962	99.67	111.45	Feb. 14	83.39	Oct. 30
1963	92.87	122.96	May 10	91.21	Dec. 18
1964	90.68	103.77	July 3	87.94	Nov. 11
1965	105.68	105.68	Dec. 28	81.29	July 15
1966	111.41	114.51	Mar. 24	105.21	Jan. 19
1967	100.89	117.60	May 31	99.17	Dec. 11
1968	131.31	142.95	Oct. 2	100.00	Jan. 4
1969	179.30	179.30	Dec. 27	132.62	Jan. 4
1970	148.35	185.70	Apr. 8	147.08	Dec. 9
1971	199.45	209.00	Aug. 14	148.05	Jan. 6
1972	401.70	401.70	Dec. 28	199.93	Jan. 4
1973	306.44	422.48	Jan. 24	284.69	Dec. 18
1974	278.34	342.47	June 5	251.96	Oct. 9
1975	323.43	333.11	July 2	268.24	Jan. 10
1976	383.88	383.88	Dec. 28	326.28	Jan. 5
1977	364.08	390.93	Sept. 29	350.49	Nov. 24
1978	449.55	452.60	Dec. 13	364.04	Jan. 4
1979	459.61	465.24	Sept. 29	435.13	July 13
1980	494.10	497.96	Oct. 20	449.01	Mar. 10
1981	570.31	603.92	Aug. 17	495.79	Jan. 5
1982	593.72	593.72	Dec. 28	511.52	Aug. 17
1983	731.82	731.82	Dec. 28	574.51	Jan. 25
1984	913.37	913.37	Dec. 28	735.45	Jan. 4
1985	1,049.40	1,058.35	July 27	916.93	Jan. 4
1986	1,556.37	1,583.35	Aug. 20	1,025.85	Jan. 21
1987	1,725.83	2,258.56	June 11	1,557.46	Jan. 13
1988	2,357.03	2,357.03	Dec. 28	1,690.44	Jan. 4
1989	2,881.37	2,884.80	Dec. 18	2,364.33	Mar. 27
1990	1,733.83	2,867.70	Jan. 4	1,523.43	Oct. 1
1991	1,714.68	2,028.85	Mar. 18	1,638.06	Dec. 24
1992	1,307.66	1,763.43	Jan. 6	1,102.50	Aug. 18

Source: Tokyo Stock Exchange *1993 Fact Book.*

TOKYO STOCK EXCHANGE (TOPIX): 30 Most Active Stocks (Volume and Value), 1992

	(mils. of shares)				(¥ bils.)
Rank	Stocks	Volume	Rank	Stocks	Value
1	Meiji Milk Products	865	1	Mochida Pharmaceutical	858
2	NIPPON STEEL	782	2	Meiji Milk Products	830
3	TOSHIBA	655	3	THE GREEN CROSS	709
4	Hitachi	585	4	The Nomura Securities	644
5	Mitsui Mining and Smelting	563	5	SONY	638
6	Mitsubishi Heavy Industries	543	6	OKAMOTO INDUSTRIES	614
7	OKAMOTO INDUSTRIES	518	7	Chiyoda	575
8	NIPPON MINING	509	8	SEGA ENTERPRISES	540
9	THE GREEN CROSS	475	9	NIPPON TELEGRAPH AND TELEPHONE	535
10	The Nomura Securities	453	10	Hitachi	466
11	NKK	441	11	The Industrial Bank of Japan	465
12	Japan Metals & Chemicals	393	12	The Mitsubishi Bank	462
13	Kawasaki Steel	393	13	The Sumitomo Bank	442
14	Sumitomo Metal Industries	391	14	TOYOTA MOTOR	440
15	MORINAGA MILK INDUSTRIES	382	15	Fuji Photo Film	439
16	SUMITOMO CHEMICAL	367	16	Matsushita Electric Industrial	407
17	Nippon Zeon	362	17	TOSHIBA	406
18	RICOH	361	18	PIONEER ELECTRONIC	403
19	TORAY INDUSTRIES	354	19	CANON	396
20	NEC	351	20	TOKYO STEEL MANUFACTURING	360
21	Hitachi Zosen	338	21	The Fuji Bank	347
22	Chiyoda	336	22	The Tokyo Electric Power	345
23	OSAKA GAS	325	23	The Tokio Marine and Fire Insurance	334
24	Mitsubishi Electric	325	24	SANKYO	328
25	Matsushita Electric Industrial	322	25	The Dai-Ichi Kangyo Bank	314
26	FUJITSU	322	26	Mitsubishi Heavy Industries	310
27	Mitsui Engineering & Shipbuilding	314	27	Ito-Yokado	310
28	Ishikawajima-Harima Heavy Industries	313	28	Sharp	308
29	TOYOTA MOTOR	309	29	Japan Storage Battery	306
30	Japan Storage Battery	308	30	NEC	301

Total Trading Volume of the 30 stocks (A)	12,968	A/B	Total Trading Value of the 30 stocks (C)	13,845	C/D
Total Trading Volume of all stocks (B)	66,407	19.5%	Total Trading Value of all stocks (D)	60,110	23.0%

Source: Tokyo Stock Exchange *1993 Fact Book.*

JAPANESE STOCK EXCHANGES: Domestic Companies Listed

Number of Listed Companies on TSE & Other Exchanges

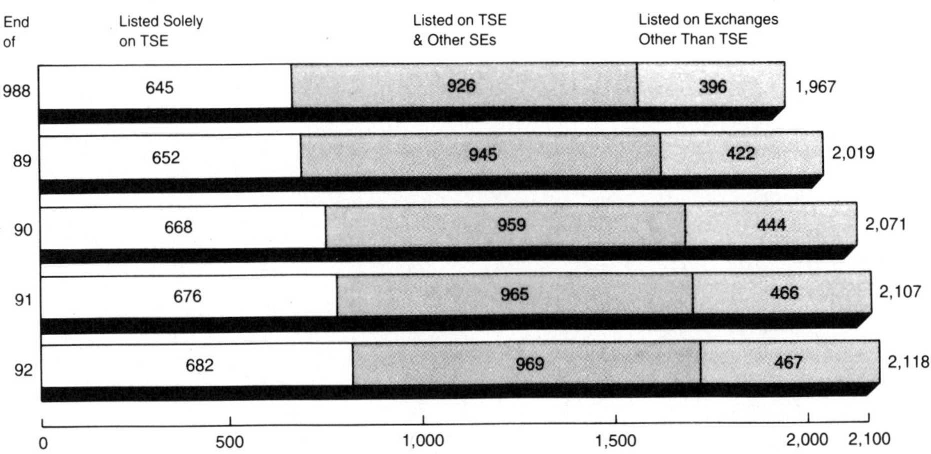

Number of Companies Listed on All Stock Exchanges, End of 1992

	Tokyo 1st Sec.	Tokyo 2nd Sec.	Osaka 1st Sec.	Osaka 2nd Sec.	Nagoya 1st Sec.	Nagoya 2nd Sec.	Kyoto	Hiroshima	Fukuoka	Niigata	Sapporo
No. of Listed Companies	1,229	422	856	307	433	119	238	198	252	198	192
Listed on Single Exchange	350	332	41	187	14	89	1	10	25	10	16
Listed on 2 or more Exchanges;	879	90	815	120	419	30	237	188	227	188	176
Listed on 8 SEs	95	—	95	—	95	—	95	95	95	95	95
〃 7 SEs	23	—	23	—	22	—	18	18	22	19	16
〃 6 SEs	32	—	32	—	29	—	19	20	26	17	17
〃 5 SEs	30	1	30	1	28	1	12	7	18	14	13
〃 4 SEs	55	1	54	1	42	—	18	7	17	17	12
〃 3 SEs	249	11	251	12	150	8	45	25	27	9	8
〃 2 SEs	395	77	330	106	53	21	30	16	22	17	15

Source: Tokyo Stock Exchange *1993 Fact Book.*

DOLLAR VOLUME OF EQUITY TRADING IN MAJOR WORLD MARKETS: 1992

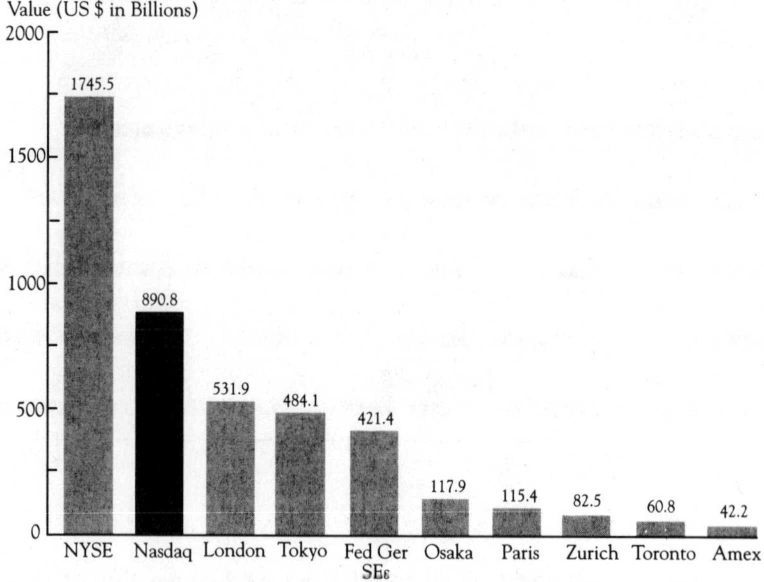

Source: *1993 NASDAQ FACT BOOK & COMPANY DIRECTORY,* published by the National Association of Securities Dealers, Inc., 1735 K Street N.W., Washington, D.C. 20006-1500.

FOREIGN COMPANIES AND ADR ISSUERS—NASDAQ, NYSE, AND AMEX: 1992

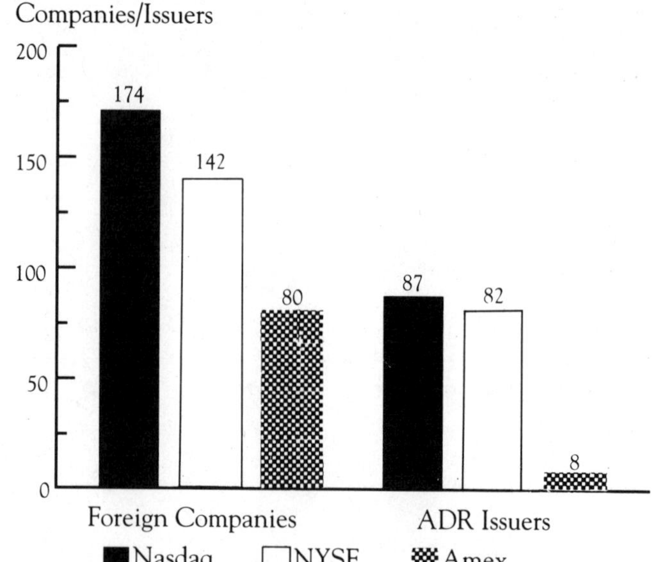

Source: *1993 NASDAQ FACT BOOK & COMPANY DIRECTORY,* published by the National Association of Securities Dealers, Inc., 1735 K Street N.W., Washington, D.C. 20006-1500.

Securities Markets: Notable Dates

1792 Original brokers' agreement subscribed to by 24 brokers (May 17).
1817 Constitution and the name "New York Stock Exchange Board" adopted (March 8).
1830 Dullest day in history of exchange—31 shares traded (March 16).
1840s Outdoor trading in unlisted securities begins at Wall and Hanover Streets, moves to Wall and Broad, then shifts south along Broad Street.*
1863 Name changed to "New York Stock Exchange" (NYSE) (January 29).
1867 Stock tickers first introduced (November 15).
1868 Membership made salable (October 23).
1869 Exchange required registering of securities by listed companies to prevent their over-issuance (February 1).
NYSE and Open Board of Brokers adopted plan of consolidation (May 8).
Gold speculation resulted in "Black Friday" (September 24).
1871 Continuous markets in stocks established.
1873 NYSE closed September 18–29.
Failure of Jay Cooke & Co. and others (September 18).
Trading hours set at 10 A.M. to 3 P.M.; Saturdays, 10 A.M. to noon (December 1).
1878 First telephones introduced in the exchange (November 13).
1881 Annunciator board installed for paging members (January 29).
1885 Unlisted Securities Department established (March 25).
1886 First million-share day—1,200,000 shares traded (December 15).
1895 Exchange recommended that companies listed or traded publish and distribute to stockholders annual statements showing income and balance sheet (January 23).
Exchange occupied new building with present trading floor at 18 Broad Street (April 23).
Call money loaned as high as 125%, following suspension of payments by Knickerbocker Trust Company on previous day. This period was generally known as panic of 1907 (October 23).
1908 E. S. Mendels forms New York Curb Agency in first departure from informal trading.*
1910 Unlisted Securities Department abolished (March 31).
1911 Trading rules established with formation of New York Curb Market Association.*
1914 Exchange closed from July 31 through December 11—World War I.
1915 Stock prices quoted in dollars as against percent of par value (October 13).
1919 Separate ticker system installed for bonds (January 2).
1920 Stock Clearing Corporation established (April 26).
1921 New York Curb Market association moves indoors at 86 Trinity Place; name shortened to New York Curb Market and ticker service initiated (June 21).*
1924 Sliding scale of commission rates adopted.
1927 Start of ten-share unit of trading for inactive stocks (January 3).
1929 Stock market crash; 16,410,000 shares traded (October 29).
New York Curb Market modifies its name to New York Curb Exchange.*
1930 Faster ticker—500 characters per minute—installed (September 2).
1931 Exchange building expanded; Telephone Quotation Department formed to send stock quotes to member firm offices.*
1933 Exchange announced formal adoption of rule requiring independent audit of statements of listed companies (January 6).
New York Stock Exchange closed for bank holiday, March 4–14.
Securities Act of 1933 enacted. Its two basic purposes: to provide full disclosure to investors and to prohibit fraud in connection with the sale of securities (May 27).
1934 Enactment of Securities Exchange Act of 1934 (June 6).
1938 First salaried president elected—Wm. McChesney Martin, Jr. (June 30).
1946 Listed stocks outnumber unlisted stocks for first time since the 1934 act imposed restrictions on unlisted trading.*
1952 Trading hours changed: weekdays, 10 A.M. to 3:30 P.M. Closed Saturdays (September 29).
1953 Name of New York Curb Exchange

---

* Refers to American Exchange (AMEX).

† Applies to both the New York Stock Exchange and the American Exchange.

Sources: New York Stock Exchange *Fact Book*, American Stock Exchange *Data Book* and *The Wall Street Journal*.

changed to American Stock Exchange.*

1958 First member corporation—Woodcock, Hess & Co. (June 4).

Mary C. Roebling becomes first woman governor.*

1962 Committee system of administration replaced by expanded paid staff reporting to president. Specialist system strengthened, surveillance of trading increased, listing and delisting standards introduced, and board restructured to give greater representation to commission and out-of-town brokers.*

1964 New member classification—Registered Trader (August 3).

New ticker—900 characters per minute—put into service (December 1).†

Am-Quote computerized telephone-quotation service was completed as first step in major automation program.*

1965 Fully automated quotation service introduced (March 8).

Electronic Systems Center created (October 15).

First women, Phyllis S. Peterson and Julia Montgomery Walsh, elected to regular membership.*

1966 New NYSE Composite Index inaugurated (July 14).

AMEX Price Change Index System introduced; computer complex installed for ticker, surveillance, and compared-clearance operations.*

1967 First woman member admitted—Muriel F. Siebert (December 28).

1968 Ticker speed increased to maximum 900 characters per minute; transmission begun to six European countries. Trading floor modernized; line capacity for communications doubled. Visitors gallery expanded.*

1969 Central Certificate Service fully activated (February 26).

1970 Public ownership of member firms approved (March 26).

Securities Investor Protection Corporation Act signed (December 30).

1971 New York Stock Exchange Incorporated (February 18).

First negotiated commission rates effective (April 5).

First member organization listed—Merrill Lynch (July 27).

AMEX incorporates and marks 50th anniversary of move indoors; Listed Company Advisory Committee formed, composed of nine chief executives of AMEX-listed companies.

1972 NYSE reorganization, based on Martin Report, approved (January 20).

Board of Directors, with ten public members, replaced Board of Governors (July 13).

Securities Industry Automation Corporation established with AMEX to consolidate facilities of both exchanges (July 17).*

First salaried chairman took office—James J. Needham (August 28).

Board of Governors reorganized to include ten public and ten industry representatives plus full-time salaried chairman as chief executive officer.*

1973 Depository Trust Company succeeded Central Certificate Service (May 11).

Chicago Board of Options Exchange opened with trading in 16 classes of call options (April 26).

AMEX formally adopts affirmative action employment plan; Market Value Index System introduced to replace Price Change Index.

1974 Trading hours extended to 4 P.M. (October 1).

Consolidated tape begun; 15 stocks reported (October 18).

1975 Fixed commission system abolished (April 30).

Full consolidated tape begun (June 16).

AMEX trades call options.

Trading begins in call options and odd lots of U.S. government instruments.*

1976 New data line installed, handling 36,000 characters per minute (January 19).

Specialists began handling odd lots in their stocks (May 24).

Varo, Inc.—first stock traded on both NYSE and AMEX (August 23).

Competition between specialists begun (October 11).

1977 Independent audit committee on listed companies' boards required (January 6).

Competitive Trader category for members approved (January 19).

National Securities Clearing Corporation (NSCC) began merging the clearing operations of the Stock Clearing Corporation of NYSE with American Stock Exchange Clearing Corporation and National Clearing Corporation of the NASD (January 20).

Foreign broker/dealers permitted to obtain membership (February 3).

Full Automated Bond System in effect (July 27).

1978 First 60 million share day in history (63,493,000 shares) (April 17).
Intermarket Trading System (ITS) began.
Registered Competitive Market-Maker category for members approved (May 2).
First 65 million share day in history (66,370,000 shares) (August 3).
Trading in Ginnie Maes inaugurated on the AMEX Commodities Exchange (ACE) (September 12).
AMEX reached an index high of 176.87 (September 13).

1979 Trading began at pilot post on the exchange floor. First stage in a $12-million upgrading of exchange facilities (January 29).
Board of Directors of NYSE approved plan for the creation of the New York Futures Exchange, a wholly owned subsidiary of NYSE. Futures contracts in seven financial instruments will be traded on the NYSE (March 1).
New York Commodities Exchange and NYSE terminated merger talks (March 15).
81,619,000 shares were traded on the NYSE, making it the heaviest trade day in exchange history (October 10).

1980 American Stock Exchange reached an all-time daily stock volume record of 14,980,680 shares sold (January 15).
NYSE volume of 67,752,000 shares traded was second largest volume on record to date (January 16).
NYSE Futures Exchange opened (August 7).
Option seat on the American Stock Exchange sold at an all-time high of $160,000 (December 24).
NYSE index reached an all time high of 81.02 (November 28).

1981 First 90 million share day in the history of the Exchange, 92,881,000 (January 7).
The New York Stock Exchange subsidiary, the New York Futures Exchange, started trading futures in Domestic Bank Certificates of Deposit.

1982 A new AMEX subsidiary, The American Gold Coin Exchange (AGCE), began trading in the Canadian Maple Leaf (January 21).
Trading in NYSE Composite Index Futures began on the New York Futures Exchange (May 6).
Trading started through experimental linkage between ITS operated by NYSE and six other exchanges and Computer Assisted Execution Service (CAES) operated by NASD, in 30 stocks exempted from exchange off-board trading rules under SEC Rule 19c-3. (May 17).
Record advance of 38.81 points reached in NYSE trading as measured by Dow Jones Industrial Average (August 17).
First 100 million share day (132,-681,120 shares. (August 18).
Trading in Interest Rate Options on U.S. Treasury Bills & Notes started in May on the AMEX.
Trading soared to an all time high of 147,081,070 shares on the NYSE (October 7).
All time options high of 340,550 contracts were traded on the AMEX (October 7).
Dow Jones Industrial Average plunged 36.33 points, the largest one-day loss since the record plunge of 38.33 points on October 28, 1929 (October 25).

1983 Trading in options on NYSE Common Stock Index Futures started on New York Futures Exchange (January 28).
NYSE started trading options on the NYSE Common Stock Index (September 23).
Dow Jones Industrial Average reached an all time high of 1260.77 (September 26).
New shares of common stocks of seven regional telephone companies and shares of the "new" AT&T began trading on a "when issued" basis. Divestiture of AT&T effective January 1, 1984 (November 21).
AMEX stock trading went over the two billion share mark for the first time.
The AMEX list of stock options increased by four index options, two on specific industry groups, one on the AMEX Market Value Index.

1984 Largest NYSE trading day of 159,-999,031 shares traded (January 5).
CBOT (Chicago Board of Trade) began trading a futures contract on the Major Market Index (July 23).*
Trading began in NYSE Double Index Options (July 23).
NYSE volume soared to a record 236,565,110 shares traded (August 3).
NYSE opened on Presidential Election Day for first time ever.
Super DOT 250 (electronic order-

routing system) launched on NYSE (November 16).

1985 For the first time the NYSE index went over 100, closing at 101.12 (January 21).

19,091,950 shares were traded on the AMEX, the highest single day volume ever (February 6).

Ronald Reagan visited the NYSE, the first President to do so while in office (March 28).

Trading in options on gold bullion started on AMEX (April 26).

50 billionth share listed in NYSE (May 30).

NYSE began trading options in three over-the-counter stocks (June 3).

NYSE reached an all time index high of 113.49 (July 17).

Amex and Toronto Stock Exchange linked together as part of the first two-way electronic hookup between primary equity markets in different countries (September 24).

Instinet Corporation and the AMEX reached an agreement enabling European institutional investors to have access to the AMEX options market via Reuter's electronic terminals.

The opening trading time on both the NYSE and AMEX went from 10:00 A.M. to 9:30 A.M. (September 30).

The Dow Jones Industrial Average reached an all-time high of 1368.50 (October 16).

Options traded on two listed stocks on the NYSE (October 21).

Tokyo Stock Exchange admitted its first foreign member firms (December 1).

A daily record of 119,969 contracts traded on the AMEX Major Markets Index Option (December 13).

1986 The Dow Jones Industrial Average for the first time closed above 1600 at 1600.69 (February 6).

The Dow Jones Industrial Average for the first time closed above 1700 at 1713.99. (February 27).

The Dow Jones Industrial Average for the first time closed above 1800 at 1804.24 (March 20).

NYSE began trading the NYSE Beta Index Option (May 22).

NYSE Board of Directors expanded to 24 outside directors: 12 public members and 12 industry members (June 5).

New York Futures Exchange (NYFE) began trading the Commodity Research Bureau (CRB) index futures contract (June 12).

The Dow Jones Industrial Average for the first time closed above 1900 at 1903.54 (July 1).

The Directors of the NYSE voted to abandon the one-share-one-vote rule which gives common shareholders equal voting rights (July 3).

The Dow Jones Industrials nose-dived a record 86.61 points on a record volume of 237,600,000 shares traded (September 11).

$600,000.00 (the highest price ever) was paid for membership in the NYSE (December 1).

1987 The Dow Jones industrials passed the 2000 mark, closing at 2000.25 (January 8).

The Dow Jones Industrials closed above 2300 for the first time, up 33.95 points to 2333.52 (March 20).

The Dow Jones Industrials climbed above 2400 for the first time to close at 2405.54 (April 7).

Foreign currency warrants began trading (June 11).

The Chicago Board of Trade and the Chicago Board Options Exchange agreed to permit members of both exchanges to trade financial futures and options contracts side by side (June 25).

For the first time the Dow Jones Industrials closed over 2500 at 2510.04 (July 16).

AMEX Market Value closed at the all-time high of 365.0 (August 13).

A gain of 15.14 points brought the Dow Jones Industrials above 2700 points for the first time with the market closing at 2700.52 (August 17).

Dow Jones industrial average set a record at 2722.42 (August 25).

New York Futures Exchange began to trade the Russell 2000 and Russell 3000® Stock Index futures contracts (September 10).

A price of $1,150,000 was paid for a member of the NYSE, the highest ever (September 21).

The stock market 'crashed' with the Dow Jones Industrials down 508.00 points or 22% to close at 1738.74 on a record volume of 604.3 shares. Other record declines were: Dow Jones transportations off 164.78; utilities off 29.16; the S & P 500 stock index off 57.86; the AMEX index down 41.05, the NYSE down 30.51, and the NASDAQ composite of over-the-counter stocks off 46.12 (October 19).

A record volume of 608,148,710 shares

traded on the NYSE and 43,432,760 on the AMEX (October 20).

The Dow Jones Industrials rocketed 186.84 points, the highest ever, on a volume of 449,350,000 shares (October 21).

The AMEX Market Value Index registered its largest increase ever, 23.81 (October 21).

1988 343,949,330 shares were traded on the NYSE, making it the highest volume day to date since the 'crash' of 1987 (June 17).

The SEC approved a series of initiatives by the NYSE and the Chicago Mercantile Exchange to coordinate procedures between the equities and futures markets, including coordinated circuit breakers; a joint effort against front-running; inter-exchange communications; and shared audit trail and surveillance information (October 19).

The NYSE opened an office in London to assist European companies in gaining access to the U.S. capital markets and listing on the NYSE (November 7).

1989 Dow Jones industrials established a record high of 2734.64 (August 25).

The Dow Jones industrials plunged 190.58 points to 2569.26 (October 13).

The NYSE launched a new trading vehicle, the Exchange Stock Portfolio, which enables the trading of a standardized basket of stocks in a single execution (October 26).

The NYSE created a blue-ribbon panel to study market volatility and investor confidence (December 7).

The DJIA peaked to a record 2810.12 (December 29).

1990 The Dow Jones industrials closed above 2900 for the first time (June 4).

NYSE Market Volatility and Investor Confidence Panel released a study recommending initiatives for reducing market volatility and enhancing investor confidence.

The NYSE implemented a new rule requiring Trade Date + 1 (T+1) for the completion of transactions effected on the NYSE (August 6).

NYSE approved two crossing sessions which will extend trading hours to 5:15 P.M. (September 11).

1991 For the first time the Dow Jones industrials closed above 3,000 at 3,0004.46 on a volume of 246.9 million shares (April 17).

Dow Jones industrials rose to a record 3035.33 (June 4).

NYSE extended trading hours to 5:15 P.M. with two crossing sessions (June 13).

1992 For the first time the Dow Jones industrials closed over 3400 to reach a high of 3413.21 (June 1).

Globex, an after hours electronic system for trading options and futures on the Chicago Board of Trade and the Chicago Mercantile Exchange went into operation (June 25).

The New York Stock Exchange's "clean cross" rule allows large institutional investors to bypass floor trades by "crossing" trades of 25,000 shares or more between customers while ignoring orders placed at the same price by investors on the floor. A broker will have to accept a floor order if it is at a better price (October 26).

1993 Dow Jones Industrials plunged 82.94 to 3309.49, the biggest one day decline since November 15, 1991 (February 16).

The NASDAQ Composite Index had its worst decline since October 26, 1987 and closed at 665.39 (February 16).

The Dow Jones Industrials soared 55.65 points to reach a record of 3500.03 on the ninth heaviest trading day on the "Big Board" to date (May 19).

The Dow Jones Industrial Average hit a record high of 3604.83 (August 18).

Investment and Financial Terms

Accelerated Cost Recovery System (ACRS) A system that specifies the allowable depreciation recovery period for different types of assets. The normal recovery period is generally shorter than that allowed before the passage of the 1981 Economic Recovery Tax Act.*

Accruals Recurring continuous short-term liabilities. Examples are accrued wages and accrued interest.

Accrued interest Interest accrued on a bond since the last interest payment was made. The buyer of the bond pays the market price plus accrued interest. Exceptions include bonds that are in default and income bonds. (See: *Flat income bond.*)†

Acquisition The acquiring of control of one corporation by another. In "unfriendly" takeover attempts, the potential buying company may offer a price well above current market values, new securities and other inducements to stockholders. The management of the subject company might ask for a better price or try to join up with a third company. (See: *Merger, Proxy.*)††

Ad valorem tax A tax based on the value (or assessed value) of property.**

Aging of accounts receivable Analyzing accounts by the amount of time they have been on the books.*

American Depository Receipt (ADR) Issued by American banks, an ADR is a certificate which serves as a proxy for a foreign stock deposited in a foreign bank. For all practical purposes, trading an ADR is equivalent to trading the foreign stock. Hundreds of ADRs are traded on U.S. stock exchange.

Amortization Accounting for expenses or charges as applicable rather than as paid. Includes such practices as depreciation, depletion, write-off of intangibles, prepaid expenses, and deferred charges.†

Annual report The formal financial statement issued yearly by a corporation. The annual report shows assets, liabilities, earnings—how the company stood at the close of the business year, how it fared profit-wise during the year and other information of interest to shareowners.†

Arbitrage A technique employed to take advantage of differences in price. If, for example, ABC stock can be bought in New York for $10 a share and sold in London at $10.50, an arbitrageur may simultaneously purchase ABC stock here and sell the same amount in London, making a profit of 50 cents a share, less expenses. Arbitrage may also involve the purchase of rights to subscribe to a security, or the purchase of a convertible security—and the sale at or about the same time of the security obtainable through exercise of the rights or of the security obtainable through conversion.

Arrearage Overdue payment; frequently omitted dividend on preferred stock.

Assessed valuation The valuation placed on property for purposes of taxation.**

Asset-based public offerings Public offerings backed by receivables as collateral. Essentially, a firm factors (sells) its receivables in the securities markets.*

Assets Everything a corporation owns or due to it: Cash, investments, money due it, materials and inventories, which are called current assets; buildings and machinery, which are known as fixed assets; and patents and good will, called intangible assets. (See: *Liabilities.*)†

Asset utilization ratios A group of ratios that measures the speed at which the firm is turning over or utilizing its assets. We measure inventory turnover, fixed asset turnover, total asset turnover, and the average time it takes to collect accounts receivable.*

Assignment The liquidation of assets without going through formal court procedures. In order to affect an assignment, creditors must agree on liquidation values and the relative priority of claims.*

Assignment Notice to an option writer that an option holder has exercised the option and that the writer will now be required to deliver (receive) under the terms of the contract.††

Ask (See: *Bid and asked.*)†

Auction market The system of trading securities through brokers or agents on an exchange such as the New York Stock Exchange. Buyers compete with other buyers

---

* Entries from *Foundations of Financial Management.*

† Entries from *The Language of Investing Glossary.*

** Entries from *Tax-Exempt Securities & the Investor.*

†† Entries from the *Glossary.*

¶ Entries from the Federal Reserve *Glossary.*

Source: *Foundations of Financial Management*, 5th edition by Stanley B. Block and Geoffrey A. Hirt, Irwin, Homewood, IL 1989.

The *Language of Investing Glossary* published by the New York Stock Exchange, Inc.

The *Glossary* published by the New York Stock Exchange.

Tax-Exempt Securities & the Investor published by the Securities Industry Association.

The *Glossary* published by the Board of Governors of the Federal Reserve System.

while sellers compete with other sellers for the most advantageous price.††

Auditor's report Often called the accountant's opinion, it is the statement of the accounting firm's work and its opinion of the corporation's financial statements, especially if they conform to the normal and generally accepted practices of accountancy.††

Automated clearinghouse (ACH) An ACH transfers information between one financial institution and another and from account to account via computer tape. There are approximately 30 regional clearinghouses throughout the United States that claim the membership of over 10,000 financial institutions.*

Average collection period The average amount of time accounts receivable have been on the books. It may be computed by dividing accounts receivable by average daily credit sales.*

Averages Various ways of measuring the trend of securities prices, one of the most popular of which is the Dow-Jones average of 30 industrial stocks listed on the New York Stock Exchange. The prices of the 30 stocks are totaled and then divided by a divisor which is intended to compensate for past stock splits and stock dividends and which is changed from time to time. As a result point changes in the average have only the vaguest relationship to dollar price changes in stocks included in the average. (See: *NYSE composite index.*)††

Balance of payments The term refers to a system of government accounts that catalogs the flow of economic transactions between countries.*

Balance sheet A condensed financial statement showing the nature and amount of a company's assets, liabilities and capital on a given date. In dollar amounts the balance sheet shows what the company owned, what it owed, and the ownership interest in the company of its stockholders. (See: *Assets, Earnings report.*)†

Bankers acceptance Bankers acceptances are negotiable time drafts, or bills of exchange, that have been accepted by a bank which, by accepting, assumes the obligation to pay the holder of the draft the face amount of the instrument on the maturity date specified. They are used primarily to finance the export, import, shipment, or storage of goods.¶

Bankruptcy The market value of a firm's assets are less than its liabilities, and the firm has a negative net worth. The term is also used to describe in-court procedures associated with the reorganization or liquidation of a firm.*

Basis book A book of mathematical tables used to convert yields to equivalent dollar prices.**

Basis point One gradation on a 100-point scale representing one percent; used especially in expressing variations in the yields of bonds. Fixed income yields vary often and slightly within one percent and the basis point scale easily expresses these changes in hundredths of one percent. For example, the difference between 12.83% and 12.88% is 5 basis points.††

Basis price The price expressed in yield or percentage of return on the investment.**

Bear market A declining market. (See: *Bull market.*)†

Bearer bond A bond which does not have the owner's name registered on the books of the issuer and which is payable to the holder. (See: *Coupon bond, Registered bond.*)†

Bearer security A security that has no identification as to owner. It is presumed to be owned, therefore, by the bearer or the person who holds it. Bearer securities are freely and easily negotiable since ownership can be quickly transferred from seller to buyer.**

Beta A measure of the volatility of returns on an individual stock relative to the market. Stocks with a beta of 1.0 are said to have risk equal to that of the market (equal volatility). Stocks with betas greater than 1.0 have more risk than the market, while those with betas of less than 1.0 have less risk than the market.*

Bid and asked Often referred to as a quotation or quote. The bid is the highest price anyone has declared that he wants to pay for a security at a given time, the asked is the lowest price anyone will take at the same time. (See: *Quote.*)†

Blanket inventory liens A secured borrowing arrangement in which the lender has a general claim against the inventory of the borrower.*

Block A large holding or transaction of stock—popularly considered to be 10,000 shares or more.†

Blue chip A company known nationally for the quality and wide acceptance of its products or services, and for its ability to make money and pay dividends.†

Blue-sky laws A popular name for laws various states have enacted to protect the public against securities frauds. The term is believed to have originated when a judge ruled that a particular stock had about the same value as a patch of blue sky.†

Board room A room for registered representatives and customers in a broker's office where opening, high, low, and last prices of leading stocks used to be posted on a board throughout the market day. Today such price displays are normally electronically controlled although most board rooms have replaced the board with the ticker and/or individual quotation machines.†

Bond Basically an IOU or promissory note of a corporation, usually issued in multiples of $1,000 or $5,000, although $100 and $500 denominations are not unknown. A bond is evidence of a debt on which the issuing company usually promises to pay the bondholders a specified amount of interest for a specified length of time, and to repay the loan on the expiration date. In every case a bond represents debt—its holder is a creditor of the corporation and not a part owner as is the shareholder. (See: *Collateral, Convertible security, Debenture, General Mortgage Bond, Income Bond.*)††

Bond ratings Bonds are rated according to risk by Standard & Poor's and Moody's Investor Service. A bond that is rated Aaa by Moody's has the lowest risk, while a bond with a C rating has the highest risk. Coupon rates are greatly influenced by a corporation's bond rating.*

Book A notebook the specialist in a stock uses to keep a record of the buy and sell orders at specified prices, in sequence of receipt, which are left with him by other brokers. (See *Specialist.*)†

Book value (See: *Net worth.*)

Break-even analysis A numerical and graphical technique that is used to determine at what point the firm will break even (revenue = cost). To compute the break-even point, we divide fixed costs by price minus variable cost per unit.*

Broker An agent, who handles the public's orders to buy and sell securities, commodities, or other property. For this service a commission is charged. (See: *Commission broker, Dealer.*)†

Brokers' loans Money borrowed by brokers from banks or other brokers for a variety of uses. It may be used by specialists and to help finance inventories of stock they deal in; by brokerage firms to finance the underwriting of new issues of corporate and municipal securities; to help finance a firm's own investments; and to help finance the purchase of securities for customers who prefer to use the broker's credit when they buy securities. (See: *Margin.*)†

Bull market An advancing market. (See: *Bear market.*)†

Call (1) The right (option) to buy a share of stock at a specified price within a given time period (see options). (2) The redemption of a bond or preferred stock before its normal maturity.

Call feature Used for bonds and some preferred stock. A call allows the corporation to retire securities before maturity by forcing the bondholders to sell bonds back to it at a set price. The call provisions are included in the bond indenture.*

Call premium The premium paid by a corporation to call in a bond issue before the maturity date.*

Callable A bond issue, all or part of which may be redeemed by the issuing corporation under definite conditions before maturity. The term also applies to preferred shares which may be redeemed by the issuing corporation.†

Capital Sources of long-term financing that are available to the business firm.*

Capital asset pricing model A model that relates the risk-return trade offs of individual assets to market returns. A security is presumed to receive a risk-free rate of return plus a premium for risk.*

Capital gain or capital loss Profit or loss from the sale of a capital asset. A capital gain, under current federal income tax laws, may be either short-term (12 months or less) or long-term (more than 12 months). A short-term capital gain is taxed at the reporting individual's full income tax rate. A long-term capital gain is subject to a lower tax. The capital gains provisions of the tax law are complicated. You should consult your tax advisor for specific information.†

Capital lease A long-term, noncancelable lease that has many of the characteristics of debt. Under FASB *Statement No. 13*, the lease obligation must be shown directly on the balance sheet.*

Capital markets Competitive markets for equity securities or debt securities with maturities of more than one year. The best examples of capital market securities are common stock, bonds, and preferred stock.*

Capital rationing Occurs when a corporation has more dollars of capital budgeting projects with positive net present values than it has money to invest in them. Therefore, some projects that should be accepted are excluded because financial capital is rationed.*

Capital stock All shares representing ownership of a business, including preferred and common. (See: *Common stock, Preferred stock.*)†

Capitalization Total amount of the various

securities issued by a corporation. Capitalization may include bonds, debentures, preferred and common stock, and surplus. Bonds and debentures are usually carried on the books of the issuing company in terms of their par or face value. Preferred and common shares may be carried in terms of par or stated value. Stated value may be an arbitrary figure decided upon by the directors or may represent the amount received by the company from the sale of the securities at the time of issuance. (See: *Par.*)†

Carrying costs The cost to hold an asset, usually inventory. For inventory, carrying costs include such items as interest, warehousing costs, insurance, and material-handling expenses.*

Cash budget A series of monthly or quarterly budgets that indicate cash receipts, cash payments, and the borrowing requirements for meeting financial requirements. It is constructed from the pro forma income statement and other supportive schedules.*

Cash flow Reported net income of a corporation *plus* amounts charged off for depreciation, depletion, amortization, extraordinary charges to reserves, which are bookkeeping deductions and not paid out in actual dollars and cents. (See: *Amortization, Depreciation.*)††

Cash sale A transaction on the floor of the Stock Exchange which calls for delivery of the securities the same day. In "regular way" trades, the seller is to deliver on the fifth business day except for bonds, which is the next day.

Certificate The actual piece of paper which is evidence of ownership of stock in a corporation. Watermarked paper is finely engraved with delicate etchings to discourage forgery.††

Certificate of Deposit (CD) A money market instrument issued by banks. The time CD is characterized by its set date of maturity and interest rate and its wide acceptance among investors, companies and institutions as a highly negotiable short-term investment vehicle.††

CFTC The Commodity Futures Trading Commission, created by Congress in 1974 to regulate exchange trading in futures.††

Clientele effect The effect of investor preferences for dividends or capital gains. Investors tend to purchase securities that meet their needs.*

Coefficient of correlation The degree of associated movement between two or more variables. Variables that move in the same direction are said to be positively correlated, while negatively correlated variables move in opposite directions.*

Coefficient of variation A measure of risk determination that is computed by dividing the standard deviation for a series of numbers by the expected value. Generally, the larger the coefficient of variation, the greater the risk.*

Collateral trust bond A bond secured by collateral deposited with a trustee. The collateral is often the stocks or bonds of companies controlled by the issuing company but may be other securities.†

Combined leverage The total or combined impact of operating and financial leverage.

Commercial paper An unsecured promissory note that large corporations issue to investors. The minimum amount is usually $25,000.*

Commission The broker's basic fee for purchasing or selling securities or property as an agent.†

Commission broker An agent who executes the public's orders for the purchase or sale of securities or commodities.†

Commodities (See: *Futures.*)

Common equity The common stock or ownership capital of the firm. Common equity may be supplied through retained earnings or the sale of new common stock.*

Common stock Securities which represent an ownership interest in a corporation. If the company has also issued preferred stock, both common and preferred have ownership rights. Common stockholders assume the greater risk, but generally exercise the greater control and may gain the greater reward in the form of dividends and capital appreciation. The terms of common stock and capital stock are often used interchangeably when the company has no preferred stock.†

Common stock equivalent Warrants, options, and any convertible securities that pay less than two thirds of the average Aa bond yield at the time of issue.*

Common stockholder Holders of common stock are the owners of the company. Common stockholders elect the members of the board of directors, who in turn help select the top management.*

Compensating balances A bank requirement that business customers maintain a minimum average balance. The required amount is usually computed as a percentage of customer loans outstanding or as a percentage of the future loans to which the bank has committed itself.*

Competitive trader A member of the Exchange who trades in stocks on the Floor for an account in which he has an interest. Also known as a Registered Trader.†

Composition An out-of-court settlement in which creditors agree to accept a fractional settlement on their original claim.*

Compound sum The future value of a single amount or an annuity when compounded at a given interest rate for a specified time period.*

Conglomerate A corporation that has diversified its operations, usually by acquiring enterprises in widely varied industries.†

Consolidated balance sheet A balance sheet showing the financial condition of a corporation and its subsidiaries. (See: *Balance sheet.*)†

Consolidated tape The ticket tape reporting transactions in NYSE listed securities that take place on the NYSE or any of the participating regional stock exchanges and other markets. Similarly, transactions in AMEX-listed securities, and certain other securities listed on regional stock exchanges, are reported and identified on a separate tape.††

Consolidation The combination of two or more firms, generally of equal size and market power, to form an entirely new entity.*

Constant dollar accounting One of two methods of inflation-adjusted accounting that have been approved by the Financial Accounting Standards Board. Financial statements are adjusted to present prices, using the consumer price index. This is shown as supplemental information in the firm's annual report.*

Consumer price index An economic indicator published monthly by the U.S. Commerce Department. It measures the rate of inflation for consumer goods.*

Contribution margin The contribution to fixed costs from each unit of sales. The margin may be computed as price minus variable cost per unit.*

Conversion premium The market price of a convertible bond or preferred stock minus the security's conversion value.*

Conversion price The conversion ratio divided into the par value. The price of the common stock at which the security is convertible. An investor would usually not convert the security into common stock unless the market price were greater than the conversion price.*

Conversion ratio The number of shares of common stock an investor will receive if he exchanges a convertible bond or convertible preferred stock for common stock.*

Conversion value The conversion ratio multiplied by the market price per share of common stock.*

Convertible security A security that may be traded into the company for a different form or type of security. Convertible securities are usually bonds or preferred stock that may be exchanged for common stock.*

Corporate stock repurchase A corporation may repurchase its shares in the market as an alternative to paying a cash dividend. Earnings per share will go up, and if the price-earnings ratio remains the same, the stockholder will receive the same dollar benefit as through a cash dividend. Furthermore, the increase in stock price is a capital gain, whereas the cash dividend would be taxed as ordinary income. A corporation may also justify the repurchase of its stock because it is at a very low price or to maintain constant demand for the shares. Reacquired shares may be used for employee options or as part of a tender offer in a merger or acquisition. Firms may also reacquire part of their shares as a protective device against being taken over as a merger candidate.*

Corporation A form of ownership in which a separate, legal entity is created. A corporation may sue or be sued, engage in contracts and acquire property. It has a continual life and is not dependent on any one stockholder for maintaining its legal existence. A corporation is owned by stockholders who enjoy the privilege of limited liability. There is, however, the potential for double taxation in the corporate form of organization: the first time at the corporate level in the form of profits, and again at the stockholder level in the form of dividends.*

Correlation coefficient Measures the degree of relationship between two variables.*

Correspondent A securities firm, bank, or other financial organization which regularly performs services for another in a place or market to which the other does not have direct access. Securities firms may have correspondents in foreign countries or on exchanges of which they are not members. Correspondents are frequently linked by private wires. Member organizations of the N.Y.S.E. with offices in New York City may also act as correspondents for out-of-town member organizations which do not maintain New York City offices.†

Cost-benefit analysis A study of the incremental costs and benefits that can be derived from a given course of action.*

Cost of capital The cost of alternative sources of financing to the firm. (See: *Weighted average cost of capital.*)*

Cost of goods sold The cost specifically associated with units sold during the time period under study.*

Coupon bond Bond with interest coupons attached. The coupons are clipped as they come due and are presented by the holder for payment of interest. (See: *Bearer bond, Registered bond.*)†

Coupon rate The actual interest rate on the bond, usually payable in semiannual installments. The coupon rate normally stays constant during the life of the bond and indicates what the bondholder's annual dollar income will be.*

Coverage A term usually connected with revenue bonds. It is a ratio of net revenues pledged to principal and interest payments to debt service requirements. It is one of the factors used in evaluating the quality of an issue.**

Covered option An option position that is offset by an equal and opposite position in the underlying security.††

Covering Buying a security previously sold short. (See: *Short sale, Short covering.*)†

Credit terms The repayment provisions that are part of a credit arrangement. An example would be a 2/10, net 30 arrangement in which the customer may deduct 2 percent from the invoice price if payment takes place in the first ten days. Otherwise the full amount is due.*

Cumulative preferred A stock having a provision that if one or more dividends are omitted, the omitted dividends must be paid before dividends may be paid on the company's common stock.†

Cumulative voting A method of voting for corporate directors which enables the shareholder to multiply the number of his shares by the number of directorships being voted on and cast the total for one director or a selected group of directors. A 10-share holder normally casts 10 votes for each of, say 12 nominees to the board of directors. He thus has 120 votes. Under the cumulative voting principle he may do that or he may cast 120 (10 × 12) votes for only one nominee, 60 for two, 40 for three, or any other distribution he chooses. Cumulative voting is required under the corporate laws of some states, is permitted in most others.†

Currency futures contract A futures contract that may be used for hedging or speculation in foreign exchange.*

Current assets Those assets of a company which are reasonably expected to be realized in cash, or sold, or consumed during the normal operating cycle of the business. These include cash, U.S. government bonds, receivables and money due usually within one year, and inventories.†

Current cost accounting One of two methods of inflation-adjusted accounting approved by the Financial Accounting Standards Board in 1979. Financial statements are adjusted to the present, using current cost data rather than an index. This is shown as supplemental information in the firm's annual report.

Current liabilities Money owed and payable by a company, usually within one year.†

Current return (See: *Yield.*)

Current yield A relation stated as a percent of the annual interest to the actual market price of the bond.**

Day order An order to buy or sell which, if not executed expires at the end of the trading day on which it was entered.†

Dealer An individual or firm in the securities business who buys and sells stocks and bonds as a principal rather than as an agent. The dealer's profit or loss is the difference between the price paid and the price received for the same security. The dealer's confirmation must disclose to the customer that the principal has been acted upon. The same individual or firm may function, at different times, either as broker or dealer. (See: *NASD, Specialist.*)††

Debenture A long-term unsecured corporate bond. Debentures are usually issued by large, prestigious firms having excellent credit ratings in the financial community.*

Debit balance In a customer's margin account that portion of purchase price of stock, bonds, or commodities covered by credit extended by the broker to the margin customer.†

Debt limit The statutory or constitutional maximum debt that a municipality can legally incur.**

Debt service Refers to the payments required for interest and retirement of the principal amount of a debt.**

Debt utilization ratios A group of ratios that indicates to what extent debt is being used and the prudence with which it is being managed. Calculations include debt to total assets, times interest earned, and fixed charge coverage.*

Degree of financial leverage A measure of the impact of debt on the earnings capability of the firm. The percentage change in earnings per share is divided by the percentage change in earnings before interest and taxes at a given level of operation. Other algebraic statements are also used.*

Degree of operating leverage A measure of the impact of fixed costs on the operating earnings of the firm. The percentage change in operating income is divided by the percentage change in volume at a given level of operation. Other algebraic statements are also used.*

Denomination The face amount or par value of a security which the issuer promises to pay on the maturity date. Most municipal bonds are issued with a minimum denomination of $5,000, although a few older issues are available in $1,000 denominations.**

Depletion accounting Natural resources, such as metals, oil and gas, and timber, which conceivably can be reduced to zero over the years, present a special problem in capital management. Depletion is an accounting practice consisting of charges against earnings based upon the amount of the asset taken out of the total reserves in the period for which accounting is made. A bookkeeping entry, it does not represent any cash outlay nor are any funds earmarked for the purpose.†

Depository trust company (DTC) A central securities certificate depository through which members effect security deliveries between each other via computerized bookkeeping entries thereby reducing the physical movement of stock certificates.†

Depreciation Normally, charges against earnings to write off the cost, less salvage value, of an asset over its estimated useful life. It is a bookkeeping entry and does not represent any cash outlay nor are any funds earmarked for the purpose.†

Dilution of earnings This occurs when additional shares of stock are sold without creating an immediate increase in income. The result is a decline in earnings per share until earnings can be generated from the funds raised.*

Director Person elected by shareholders to establish company policies. The directors appoint the president, vice presidents, and all other operating officers. Directors decide, among other matters, if and when dividends shall be paid. (See: *Management*, *Proxy*.)†

Discount The amount by which a preferred stock or bond may sell below its par value. Also used as a verb to mean "takes into account" as the price of the stock has discounted the expected dividend cut. (See: *Premium*.)†

Discount rate [1]The interest rate at which future sums or annuities are discounted back to the present.*

The interest rate at which eligible depository institutions may borrow funds, usually for short periods, directly from the Federal Reserve Banks. The law requires the board of directors of each Reserve Bank to establish the discount rate every 14 days subject to the approval of the Board of Governors.¶

Discounted loan A loan in which the calculated interest payment is subtracted or discounted in advance. Because this lowers the amount of available funds, the effective interest rate is increased.*

Discretionary account An account in which the customer gives the broker or someone else discretion, which may be complete or within specific limits, either to the purchases, or sale of securities or commodities including selection, timing, amount, and price to be paid or received.†

Diversification Spreading investments among different companies in different fields. Another type of diversification is also offered by the securities of many individual companies because of the wide range of their activities. (See: *Investment trust*.)†

Dividend The payment designed by the board of directors to be distributed pro rata among the shares outstanding. On preferred shares, it is generally a fixed amount. On common shares, the dividend varies with the fortunes of the company and the amount of cash on hand, and may be omitted if business is poor or the directors determine to withhold earnings to invest in plant and equipment. Sometimes a company will pay a dividend out of past earnings even if it is not currently operating at a profit.†

Dividend information content This theory of dividends assumes that dividends provide information about the financial health and economic expectations of the company. If this is true, corporations must actively manage their dividends to provide the market with information.*

Dividend payment date The day on which a stockholder of record will receive his or her dividend.*

Dividend payout The percentage of dividends to earnings after taxes. It can be computed by dividing dividends per share by earnings per share.*

Dividend record date Stockholders owning the stock on the holder-of-record date are entitled to receive a dividend. In order to be listed as an owner on the corporate books, the investor must have bought the stock before it went ex-dividend.*

Dividend reinvestment plans Plans that provide the investor with an opportunity to buy additional shares of stock with the cash dividends paid by the company.*

Dividend valuation model A model for determining the value of a share of stock by taking the present value of an expected stream of future dividends.*

Dividend yield Dividends per share divided by market price per share. Dividend yield indicates the percentage return that a stockholder will receive on dividends alone.*

Dollar bond A bond that is quoted and traded in dollars rather than in terms of yield.**

Dollar cost averaging A system of buying securities at regular intervals with a fixed dollar amount. Under this system the investor buys by the dollars' worth rather than by the number of shares. If each investment is of the same number of dollars, payments buy more when the price is low and fewer when it rises. Thus temporary downswings in price benefit the investor if he continues periodic purchases in both good times and bad and the price at which the shares are sold is more than their average cost. (See: *Formula investing.*)†

Double-barrelled bond A bond secured by the pledge of two or more sources of repayment, e.g., secured by taxes as well as revenues.**

Double exemption Refers to securities that are exempt from state as well as Federal income taxes.**

Double taxation Short for *double taxation of dividends*. The federal government taxes corporate profits once as corporate income; any part of the remaining profits distributed as dividends to stockholders may be taxed again as income to the recipient stockholder.†

Dow theory A theory of market analysis based upon the performance of the Dow-Jones industrial and transportation stock price averages. The theory says that the market is in a basic upward trend if one of these averages advances above a previous important high, accompanied or followed by a similar advance in the other. When the averages both dip below previous important lows, this is regarded as confirmation of a basic downward trend. The theory does not attempt to predict how long either trend will continue, although it is widely misinterpreted as a method of forecasting future action.†

Down tick (See: *Up tick.*)

Dual trading Exists when one security, such as General Motors common stock, is traded on more than one stock exchange. This practice is quite common between NYSE-listed companies and regional exchanges.*

Dun & Bradstreet A credit-rating agency that publishes information on over 3 million business establishments through its *Reference Book*.*

Du Pont System of Ratio Analysis An analysis of profitability that breaks down return on assets between the profit margin and asset turnover. The second, or modified, version shows how return on assets is translated into return on equity through the amount of debt that the firm has. Actually return on assets is divided by (1 − debt/assets) to arrive at return on equity.*

Earnings per share The earnings available to common stockholders divided by the number of common stock shares outstanding.*

Earnings report A statement—also called an *income statement*—issued by a company showing its earnings or losses over a given period. The earnings report lists the income earned, expenses, and the net result. (See: *Balance sheet.*)†

Economic indicators Hundreds of indicators exist. Each is a specialized series of data. The data are analyzed for their relationship to economic activity, and the indicator is classified as either a lagging indicator, a leading indicator, or a coincident indicator of economic activity.*

Economical ordering quantity (EOQ) The most efficient ordering quantity for the firm. The EOQ will allow the firm to minimize the total ordering and carrying costs associated with inventory.*

Efficient frontier A line drawn through the optimum point selections in a risk-return trade-off diagram. Each point represents the best possible trade-off between risk and return (the highest return at a given risk level or the lowest risk at a given return level).*

Efficient market hypothesis Hypothesis which suggests that markets adjust very quickly to new information and that it is very difficult for investors to select portfolios of securities that outperform the market.

Electronic funds transfer A system in which funds are moved between computer terminals without the use of written checks.*

Employment Act of 1946 An act which specifies the four goals that the Federal Reserve Board should strive to achieve: economic growth, stable prices, high employment, and a balance of trade.*

Equipment trust certificate A type of security, generally issued by a railroad, to pay for new equipment. Title to the equipment, such as a locomotive, is held by a trustee until the notes are paid off. An equipment trust certificate is usually secured by a first claim on the equipment.†

Equity The net worth of a business, consisting of capital stock, capital (or paid-in) surplus, earned surplus (or retained earnings), and occasionally, certain net worth reserves. *Common equity* is that part of the total net worth belonging to the common stockholders. *Total equity* would include preferred stockholders. The terms *common stock, net worth,* and *common equity* are frequently used interchangeably.†

Eurobonds Bonds payable or denominated in the borrower's currency, but sold outside the country of the borrower, usually by an international syndicate.*

Eurodollar loan A loan from a foreign bank denominated in dollars.*

Eurodollars U.S. dollars held on deposit by foreign banks and loaned out by those banks to anyone seeking dollars.*

Exchange acquisition A method of filling an order to buy a large block of stock on the floor of the exchange. Under certain circumstances, a member-broker can facilitate the purpose of a block by soliciting orders to sell. All orders to sell the security are lumped together and crossed with the buy order in the regular action market. The price to the buyer may be on a net basis or on a commission basis.†

Exchange distribution A method of selling large blocks of stock on the floor of the exchange. Under certain circumstances, a member-broker can facilitate the sale of a block of stock by soliciting and getting other member-brokers to solicit orders to buy. Individual buy orders are lumped together and crossed with the sell order in the regular auction market. A special commission is usually paid by the seller; ordinarily the buyer pays no commission.†

Ex-dividend A synonym for "without dividend." The buyer of a stock selling ex-dividend does not receive the recently declared dividend. Every dividend is payable on a fixed date to all shareholders recorded on the books of the company as of a previous date of record. For example, a dividend may be declared as payable to holders of record on the books of the company on a given Friday. Since five business days are allowed for delivery of stock in a "regular way" transaction on the New York Stock Exchange, the Exchange would declare the stock "ex-dividend" as of the opening of the market on the preceding Monday. That means anyone who bought it on and after Monday would not be entitled to that dividend. When stocks go ex-dividend, the stock tables include the symbol "x" following the name. (See: *Cash sale, Net change, Transfer.*)†

Ex-dividend date Four business days before the holder-of-record date. On the ex-dividend date the purchase of the stock no longer carries with it the right to receive the dividend previously declared.*

Expectations theory of interest rates This theory explains the shape of the term structure relative to expectations for future short-term interest rates. It is thought that long-term rates are an average of the expected short-term rates. Therefore, an upward-sloping yield curve would indicate that short-term rates will rise.*

Expected value A representative value from a probability distribution arrived at by multiplying each outcome by the associated probability and summing up the values.*

Export-Import Bank (Eximbank) An agency of the United States government that facilitates the financing of United States exports through its miscellaneous programs. In its direct loan program, the Eximbank lends money to foreign purchasers of U.S. products—such as aircraft, electrical equipment, heavy machinery, computers, and the like. The Eximbank also purchases eligible medium-term obligations of foreign buyers of U.S. goods at a discount from face value. In this discount program, private banks and other lenders are able to rediscount (sell at a lower price) promissory notes and drafts acquired from foreign customers of U.S. firms.*

Expropriation The action of a country in taking away or modifying the property rights of a corporation or individual.*

Ex-rights The situation in which the purchase of common stock during a rights offering no longer includes rights to purchase additional shares of common stock.*

Extension An out-of-court settlement in which creditors agree to allow the firm more time to meet its financial obligations. A new repayment schedule will be developed, subject to the acceptance of creditors.*

External corporate funds Corporate financing raised through sources outside of the firm. Bonds, common stock, and preferred stock fall in this category.*

External reorganization A reorganization under the formal bankruptcy laws in which a merger partner is found for the distressed firm. Ideally, the firm should be merged with a strong firm in its own industry, although this is not always possible.*

Factoring receivables Selling accounts receivable to a finance company or a bank.*

Federal budget deficit Government expenditures are greater than government tax revenues, and the government must borrow to balance revenues and expenditures. These deficits act as an economic stimulus.*

Federal budget surplus Government tax receipts are greater than government expenditures. A rarity during the last 20 years. These surpluses have a dampening effect on the economy.*

Federal National Mortgage Association A government agency that provides a secondary market in mortgages.*

Federal Reserve discount rate The rate of interest that the Fed charges on loans to the banking system. A monetary tool for management of the money supply.*

Federally sponsored agency securities Securities issued by federal agencies such as the Federal Land Bank and Federal Home Loan Board.*

Field warehousing An inventory financing arrangement in which collateralized inventory is stored on the premises of the borrower but is controlled by an independent warehousing company.*

FIFO A system of writing off inventory into cost of goods sold in which the items purchased first are written off first. Referred to as first-in, first-out.*

Financial Accounting Standards Board A privately supported rulemaking body for the accounting profession.*

Financial capital Common stock, preferred stock, bonds, and retained earnings. Financial capital appears on the corporate balance sheet under long-term liabilities and equity.*

Financial disclosure Presentation of financial information to the investment community.*

Financial futures market A market that allows for the trading of financial instruments related to a future point in time. A purchase or sale takes place in the present, with a reversal necessitated in the future to close out the position. If a purchase (sale) takes place initially, then a sale (purchase) will be necessary in the future. The market provides for futures contracts in Treasury bonds, Treasury bills, certificates of deposits, GNMA certificates, and many other instruments. Financial futures contracts may be executed on the Chicago Board of Trade, the Chicago Mercantile Exchange, the New York Futures Exchange, and other exchanges.*

Financial intermediary A financial institution such as a bank or a life insurance company that directs other people's money into such investments as government and corporate securities.*

Financial lease A long-term noncancelable lease. The financial lease has all the characteristics of long-term debt except that the lease payments are a combination of interest expense and amortization of the cost of the asset.*

Financial leverage A measure of the amount of debt used in the capital structure of the firm.*

Financial sweetener Usually refers to equity options, such as warrants or conversion privileges, attached to a debt security. The sweetener lowers the interest cost to the corporation.*

Fiscal policy The tax policies of the federal government and the spending associated with its tax revenues.*

Fixed costs Costs that remain relatively constant regardless of the volume of operations. Examples are rent, depreciation, property taxes, and executive salaries.*

Float The difference between the corporation's recorded cash balance on its books and the amount credited to the corporation by the bank.*

Floating rate bond The interest payment on the bond changes with market conditions rather than the price of the bond.*

Floating rate preferred stock The quarterly dividend on the preferred stock changes with market conditions. The market price is considerably less volatile than it is with regular preferred stock.*

Floor price Usually equal to the pure bond value. A convertible bond will not sell at less than its pure bond value even when its conversion value is below the pure bond value.*

Flotation cost The distribution cost of selling securities to the public. The cost includes the underwriter's spread and any associated fees.*

Forced conversion Occurs when a company calls a convertible security that has a conversion value greater than the call price. Investors will take the higher of the two values and convert the security to common stock rather than take a lower cash call price.*

Foreign Credit Insurance Association (FCIA) An agency established by a group of 60 U.S. insurance companies. It sells credit export insurance to interested exporters. The FCIA promises to pay for the exported merchandise if the foreign importer defaults on payment.*

Foreign exchange rate The relationship between the value of two or more currencies. For example, the exchange rate between U.S. dollars and French francs is stated as dollars per francs or francs per dollar.*

Foreign exchange risk A form of risk that refers to the possibility of experiencing a drop in revenue or an increase in cost in an international transaction due to a change in foreign exchange rates. Importers, exporters, investors, and multinational firms alike are exposed to this risk.*

Formula investing An investment technique. One formula calls for the shifting of funds from common shares to preferred shares or bonds as the market, on average, rises above a certain predetermined point—and the return of funds to common share investments as the market average declines. (See: *Dollar cost averaging.*)†

Founders' stock Stock owned by the original founders of a company. It often carries special voting rights that allow the founders to maintain voting privileges in excess of their proportionate ownership.*

Fourth market A market of stocks and bonds in which there is direct dealing between financial institutions, such as investment bankers, insurance companies, pension funds, and mutual funds.*

Free and open market A market in which supply and demand are freely expressed in terms of price. Contrasts with a controlled market in which supply, demand, and price may all be regulated.†

Fronting loan A parent company's loan to a foreign subsidiary is channeled through a financial intermediary, usually a large international bank. The bank fronts for the parent in extending the loan to the foreign affiliate.*

Fully diluted earnings per share Equals adjusted earnings after taxes divided by shares outstanding, plus common stock equivalents, plus all convertible securities.*

Fundamental research Analysis of industries and companies based on factors such as sales, assets, earnings, products or services, markets, and management. As supplied to the economy, fundamental research includes consideration of gross national product, interest rates, unemployment, inventories, savings, and so on. (See: *Technical research.*)†

Funded debt Usually long-term, interest-bearing bonds or debentures of a company. Could include long-term bank loans. Does *not* include short-term loans, preferred, or common stock.†

Futures contract A contract to buy or sell a commodity at some specified price in the future.*

General mortgage bond A bond which is secured by a blanket mortgage on the company's property, but which may be outranked by one or more other mortgages.†

General obligation bond A bond secured by the pledge of the issuer's full faith, credit and taxing power.**

Gilt-edged High-grade bond issued by a company which has demonstrated its ability to earn a comfortable profit over a period of years and pay its bondholders their interest without interruption.†

Give up A term with many different meanings. For one, a member of the exchange on the floor may act for a second member by executing an order for him with a third member. The first member tells the third member that he is acting on behalf of the second member and "gives up" the second member's name rather than his own.††

Going private The process by which all publicly owned shares of common stock are repurchased or retired, thereby eliminating listing fees, annual reports, and other expenses involved with publicly owned companies.*

Gold fix The setting of the price of gold by dealers (especially in a twice-daily London meeting at the central bank); the fix is the fundamental worldwide price for setting prices of gold bullion and gold-related contracts and products.††

Golden parachute Highly attractive termination payments made to current management in the event of a takeover of the company.*

Good delivery Certain basic qualifications must be met before a security sold on the exchange may be delivered. The security must be in proper form to comply with the contract of sale and to transfer title to the purchaser.†

Good 'til cancelled order (GTC) or open order An order to buy or sell which remains in effect until it is either executed or cancelled.†

Goodwill An intangible asset that reflects value above that generally recognized in the tangible assets of the firm.*

Government bonds Obligations of the U.S. government, regarded as the highest grade issues in existence.†

Growth stock Stock of a company with a record of growth in earnings at a relatively rapid rate.†

Guaranteed bond A bond which has interest or principal, or both, guaranteed by a company other than the issuer. Usually found in the railroad industry when large roads, leasing sections of trackage owned by small railroads, may guarantee the bonds of the smaller road.†

Guaranteed stock Usually preferred stock on which dividends are guaranteed by another company; under much the same circumstances as a bond is guaranteed.†

Hedge (See: *Arbitrage, Option, Short sale.*)

Hedging The purchase or sale of a derivative security (such as options or futures) in order to reduce or neutralize all or some portion of the risk of holding another security.††

Holding company A corporation which owns the securities of another, in most cases with voting control.†

Hurdle rate The minimum acceptable rate of return in a capital budgeting decision.*

Hypothecation The pledging of securities as collateral—for example, to secure the debit balance in a margin account.†

Inactive stock An issue traded on an exchange or in the over-the-counter market in which there is a relatively low volume of transactions. Volume may be no more than a few hundred shares a week or even less. On the New York Stock Exchange many inactive stocks are traded in 10-share units rather than the customary 100. (See: *Round lot.*)†

In-and-out Purchase and sale of the same security within a short period—a day, a week, even a month. An in-and-out trader is generally more interested in day-to-day price fluctuations than dividends or long-term growth.†

Income bond Generally income bonds promise to repay principal but to pay interest only when earned. In some cases unpaid interest on an income bond may accumulate as a claim against the corporation when the bond becomes due. An income bond may also be issued in lieu of preferred stock.†

Income statement A financial statement that measures the profitability of the firm over a period of time. All expenses are subtracted from sales to arrive at net income.*

Indenture A written agreement under which bonds and debentures are issued, setting forth maturity date, interest rate, and other terms.†

Independent broker Members on the floor of the NYSE who execute orders for other brokers having more business at that time than they can handle themselves, or for firms who do not have their Exchange member on the floor. Formerly known as *two-dollar brokers* from the time when these independent brokers received $2 per hundred shares for executing such orders. Their fees are paid by the commission brokers. (See: *Commission broker.*)†

Index A statistical yardstick expressed in terms of percentages of a base year or years. For instance, the Federal Reserve Board's index of industrial production is based on 1967 as 100. An index is not an average. (See: *Averages.*)†

Industrial revenue bond A security backed by private enterprises that have been financed by a municipal issue.**

Inflation The phenomenon of price increase with the passage of time.*

Inflation premium A premium to compensate the investor for the eroding effect of inflation on the value of the dollar. In the 1980s the inflation premium has been 3 to 4 percent. In the late 1970s it was in excess of 10 percent.*

Installment loan A borrowing arrangement in which a series of equal payments are used to pay off the loan.*

Institutional Investor An organization whose primary purpose is to invest its own assets or those held in trust by it for others. Includes pension funds, investment companies, insurance companies, universities, and banks.†

Interest Payments a borrower pays a lender for the use of his money. A corporation pays interest on its bonds to its bondholders. (See: *Bond, dividend.*)†

Interest factor *(IF)* The tabular value to insert into the various formulas. It is based on the number of periods (n) and the interest rate (i).*

Interest rate parity theory A theory based on the interplay between interest rate differentials and exchange rates. If one country has a higher interest rate than another country after adjustments for inflation, interest rates and foreign exchange rates will adjust until the foreign exchange rates and money market rates reach equilibrium (are properly balanced between the two countries).*

Intermarket Trading System (ITS) An electronic communications network now linking the trading floor of seven registered exchanges to foster competition among them in stocks listed on either the NYSE or AMEX and one or more regional exchanges. Through ITS, any broker or market-maker on the floor of any participating market can reach out to other participants for an execution whenever the nationwide quote shows a better price is available.††

Internal corporate funds Funds generated through the operations of the firm. The principal sources are retained earnings and cash flow added back from depreciation and other noncash deductions.*

Internal financing Funds made available for capital budgeting and working-capital expansion through the normal operations of the firm; internal financing is approximately equal to retained earnings plus depreciation.*

Internal rate of return (IRR) A discounted cash flow method for evaluating capital budgeting projects. The IRR is a discount rate which makes the present value of the cash inflows equal to the present value of the cash outflows.*

Internal reorganization A reorganization under the formal bankruptcy laws. New management may be brought in and a redesign of the capital structure may be implemented.*

International diversification Achieving diversification through many different foreign investments that are influenced by a variety of factors.*

International Finance Corporation (IFC) An affiliate of the World Bank established with the sole purpose of providing partial seed capital for private ventures around the world. Whenever a multinational company has difficulty raising equity capital due to lack of adequate private risk capital, the firm may explore the possibility of selling equity or debt (totaling up to 25 percent) to the International Finance Corporation.*

Intrinsic value The dollar amount of the difference between the exercise price of an option and the current cash value of the underlying security. Intrinsic value and time value are the two components of an option premium, or price.††

Inventory profits Profits generated as a result of an inflationary economy in which old inventory is sold at large profits because of increasing prices. This is particularly prevalent under FIFO accounting.*

Inverted yield curve A downward-sloping yield curve. Short-term rates are higher than long-term rates.*

Investment The use of money for the purpose of making more money, to gain income or increase capital, or both.††

Investment banker A financial organization that specializes in selling primary offerings of securities. Investment bankers can also perform other financial functions, such as advising clients, negotiating mergers and takeovers, and selling secondary offerings.*

Investment company A company or trust which uses its capital to invest in other companies. There are two principal types: the closed-end and the open-end, or mutual fund. Shares in closed-end investment companies, some of which are listed on the New York Stock Exchange, are readily transferable in the open market and are bought and sold like other shares. Capitalization of these companies remains the same unless action is taken to change, which is seldom. Open-end funds sell their own new shares to investors, stand ready to buy back their old shares, and are not listed. Open-end funds are so called because their capitalization is not fixed; they issue more shares as people want them.†

Investment counsel One whose principal business consists of acting as investment adviser and a substantial part of his business consists of rendering investment supervisory services.†

Investment tax credit (ITC) A percentage of the purchase price that may be deducted directly from tax obligations.

IRA Individual Retirement Account. A pension plan with major tax advantages. Any worker can begin an IRA by a cash contribution up to $2,000 annually which is not tax deductible; however, the investment return on which is tax deferred. (See: *Keogh Plan.*)

Issue Any of a company's securities, or the act of distributing such securities.†

Issuer A municipal unit that borrows money through the sale of bonds or notes.**

Keogh Plan Tax advantaged personal retirement program that can be established by a self-employed individual. Currently, annual contributions to a plan can be up to $15,000. Such contributions and reinvestments are not taxed as they accumulate but will be when withdrawn (presumably at retirement when taxable income may be less). (See: *IRA.*)††

Leading indicators The most commonly followed series of economic indicators (a series of the 12 leading indicators). These are used to help forecast economic activity.*

Lease A contractual arrangement between the owner of equipment (lessor) and the user of equipment (lessee) which calls for the lessee to pay the lessor an established lease payment. There are two kinds of leases, financial leases and operating leases.*

Legal list A list of investments selected by various states in which certain institutions and fiduciaries, such as insurance companies and banks, may invest. Legal lists are often restricted to high quality securities meeting certain specifications. (See: *Prudent man rule.*)††

Legal opinion An opinion concerning the legality of a bond issue usually written by a recognized law firm specializing in public borrowings.**

Letter of credit A credit letter normally issued by the importer's bank in which the bank promises to pay out the money for the merchandise when delivered.*

Level production Equal monthly production used to smooth out production schedules and employ manpower and equipment more efficiently and at a lower cost.*

Leverage The effect on a company when the company has bonds, preferred stock, or both outstanding. Example: If the earnings of a company with 1,000,000 common shares increases from $1,000,000 to $1,500,000—earnings per share would go from $1 to $1.50, or an increase of 50 percent. But if earnings of a company that had to pay $500,000 in bond interest increased tha, much—earnings per common share would jump from 50 cents to $1 a share, or 100 percent.††

Leveraged buy-out Existing management or an outsider makes an offer to "go private" by retiring all the shares of the company. The buying group borrows the necessary money, using the assets of the acquired firm as collateral. The buying group them repurchases all the shares and expects to retire the debt over time with the cash flow from operations or the sale of corporate assets.*

Liabilities All the claims against a corporation. Liabilities include accounts and wages and salaries payable, dividends declared payable, accrued taxes payable, fixed or long-term liabilities such as mortgage bonds, debentures, and bank loans. (See: *Assets, Balance sheet.*)†

LIBOR (See: *London Interbank Offered Rate.*)*

Life cycle curve A curve illustrating the growth phases of a firm. The dividend policy most likely to be employed during each phase is often illustrated.*

LIFO A system of writing off inventory into cost of goods sold in which the items purchased last are written off first. Referred to as last-in, first-out.*

Limit, limited order, or limited price order An order to buy or sell a stated amount of a security at a specified price, or at a better price, if obtainable after the order is represented in the Trading Crowd.†

Limited partnership A special form of partnership to limit liability for most of the partners. Under this arrangement, one or more partners are designated as general partners and have unlimited liability for the debts of the firm, while the other partners are designated as limited partners and are only liable for their initial contribution.*

Limited tax bond A bond secured by a pledge of a tax or group of taxes limited as to rate or amount.**

Liquidation The process of converting securities or other property into cash. The dissolution of a company, with cash remaining after sale of its assets and payment of all indebtedness being distributed to the shareholders.†

Liquidity The ability of the market in a particular security to absorb a reasonable amount of buying or selling at reasonable price changes. Liquidity is one of the most important characteristics of a good market.†

Liquidity ratios A group of ratios that allows one to measure the firm's ability to pay off short-term obligations as they come due. Primary attention is directed to the current ratio and the quick ratio.*

Listed stock The stock of a company which is traded on a securities exchange. The various stock exchanges have different standards for listing. Some of the guides used by the New York Stock Exchange for an original listing are national interest in the company, a minimum of 1.1-million shares publicly held among not less than 2,000 round-lot stockholders. The publicly held common shares should have a minimum aggregate market value of $18 million. The company should have net income in the latest year of over $2.5-million before federal income tax and $2-million in each of the preceding two years.††

Listing requirements Financial standards that corporations must meet before their common stock can be traded on a stock exchange. Listing requirements are not standard, but are set by each exchange. The requirements for the NYSE are the most stringent.*

Load The portion of the offering price of shares of open-end investment companies in excess of the value of the underlying assets which cover sales commissions and all other costs of distribution. The load is usually incurred only on purchase, there being, in most cases, no charge when the shares are sold (redeemed).†

Lockbox system A procedure used to expedite cash inflows to a business. Customers are requested to forward their checks to a post-office box in their geographic region, and a local bank picks up the checks and processes them for rapid collection. Funds are then wired to the corporate home office for immediate use.*

London Interbank Offered Rate (LIBOR) An interbank rate applicable for large deposits in the London market. It is a bench-mark rate just like the prime interest rate in the United States. Interest rates on Eurodollar loans are determined by adding premiums to this basic rate. Most often LIBOR is lower than the U.S. prime rate.*

Long Signifies ownership of securities: "I am long 100 U.S. Steel" means the speaker owns 100 shares. (See: *Short position, Short sale.*)†

Majority voting All directors must be elected by a vote of more than 50 percent. Minority shareholders are unable to achieve any representation on the board of directors.*

Management The board of directors, elected by the stockholders, and the officers of the corporation, appointed by the board of directors.†

Managing underwriter An investment banker who is responsible for the pricing, prospectus development, and legal work involved in the sale of a new issue of securities.*

Manipulation An illegal operation. Buying or selling a security for the purpose of creating a false or misleading appearance of active trading or for the purpose of raising or depressing the price to induce purchase or sale by others.†

Margin The amount paid by the customer when using a broker's credit to buy or sell a security. Under Federal Reserve regulations, the initial margin required since 1945 has ranged from the current rate 50 percent of the purchase price up to 100 percent. (See: *Brokers' loans, Equity, Margin call.*)††

Margin call A demand upon a customer to put up money or securities with the broker. The call is made when a purchase is made; also if a customer's equity in a margin account declines below a minimum standard set by the exchange or by the firm. (See: *Margin.*)†

Margin requirement A rule that specifies the amount of cash or equity that must be deposited with a brokerage firm or bank, with the balance of funds eligible for borrowing. Margin is set by the Board of Governors of the Federal Reserve Board. For example, margin of 60 percent would mean that a $10,000 purchase would allow the buyer to borrow $4,000 toward the purchase.*

Marginal corporate tax rate The rate that applies to each new dollar of taxable income. For a corporation, the rate in 1986 is 15 percent on the first $25,000, 18 percent on the second $25,000, 30 percent on the third 25,000, 40 percent on the fourth $25,000, and 46 percent on all larger amounts.*

Marginal cost of capital The cost of the last dollar of funds raised. It is assumed that each dollar is financed in proportion to the firm's optimum capital structure.*

Marginal principle of retained earnings The corporation must be able to earn a higher return on its retained earnings than a stockholder would receive after paying taxes on the distributed dividends.*

Market efficiency Markets are considered to be efficient when (1) prices adjust rapidly to new information; (2) there is a continuous market in which each successive trade is made at a price close to the previous price (the faster the price responds to new information and the smaller the differences in price changes, the more efficient the market); and (3) the market can absorb large dollar amounts of securities without destabilizing the prices.*

Market maker (See: *Dealer.*)

Market order An order to buy or sell a stated amount of a security at the most advantageous price obtainable after the order is represented in the trading crowd. (See: *Good 'til cancelled order, Limit order, Stop order.*)††

Market price In the case of a security, market price is usually considered the last reported price at which the stock or bond sold.†

Market risk premium A premium over and above the risk-free rate. It is represented by the difference between the market return (K_m) and the risk-free rate (R_f), and it may be multiplied by the beta coefficient to determine additional risk-adjusted return on a security.*

Market stabilization Intervention in the secondary markets by an investment banker to stabilize the price of a new security offering during the offering period. The purpose of market stabilization is to provide an orderly market for the distribution of the new issue.*

Market value maximization The concept of maximizing the wealth of shareholders. This calls for a recognition not only of earnings per share but also how they will be valued in the marketplace.*

Marketability The measure of the ease with which a security can be sold in the secondary market.**

Maturity The date on which a loan or a bond or debenture comes due and is to be paid off.†

Member corporation A securities brokerage firm, organized as a corporation, with at least one member of the New York Stock Exchange, who is an officer or an employee of the corporation.††

Member firm A securities brokerage firm organized as a partnership and having at least one general partner who is a member of the New York Stock Exchange, Inc. (See: *Member corporation.*)†

Member organization This term includes New York Stock Exchange Member Firm *and* Member Corporation. (See: *Member corporation, Member firm.*)†

Merger The combination of two or more companies in which the resulting firms maintain the identity of the acquiring company.*

Merger arbitrageur A specialist in merger investments who attempts to capitalize on the difference between the value offered and the current market value of the acquisition candidate.*

Merger premium The part of a buy-out or exchange offer which represents a value over and above the market value of the acquired firm.*

Minimum warrant value The market value of the common stock minus the option price of the warrant multiplied by the number of shares of the common stock that each warrant entitles the holder to purchase.*

Monetary policy Management by the Federal Reserve Board of the money supply and the resultant interest rates.*

Money market accounts Accounts at banks, savings and loans, and credit unions in which the depositor receives competitive money market rates on a typical minimum deposit of $1,000. These accounts may generally have three deposits and three withdrawals per month, and are not meant to be transaction accounts, but a place to keep minimum and excess cash balances. These accounts are insured by various appropriate governmental agencies up to $100,000.*

Money market funds A fund in which investors may purchase shares for as little as $500 or $1,000. The fund then reinvests the proceeds in high-yielding $100,000 bank CDs, $25,000–$100,000 commercial paper, and other large-denomination, high-yielding securities. Investors receive their pro rata portion of the interest proceeds daily as a credit to their shares.*

Money markets Competitive markets for securities with maturities of one year or less. The best examples of money market instruments would be Treasury bills, commercial paper, and negotiable certificates of deposit.*

Mortgage agreement A loan which requires real property (plant and equipment) as collateral.*

Mortgage bond A bond secured by a mortgage on a property. The value of the property may or may not equal the value of the bonds issued against it. (See: *Bond, Debenture.*)††

Multinational corporation A firm doing business across its national borders is considered a multinational enterprise. Some definitions require a minimum percentage (often 30 percent or more) of a firm's business activities to be carried on outside its national borders.*

Municipal bond A bond issued by a state or a political subdivision, such as county, city, town, or village. The term also designates bonds issued by state agencies and authorities. In general, interest paid on municipal bonds is exempt from federal income taxes and state and local income taxes within the state of issue.†

Municipal securities Securities issued by state and local government units. The income from these securities is exempt from federal income taxes.*

Mutual fund (See: *Investment company.*)

Mutually exclusive The selection of one choice precludes the selection of any competitive choice. For example, several machines can do an identical job in capital budgeting. If one machine is selected, the other machines will not be used.*

Naked option An option position that is *not* offset by an equal and opposite position in the underlying security.††

NASD The National Association of Securities Dealers, Inc. An association of brokers and dealers in the over-the-counter securities business.††

NASDAQ An automated information network which provides brokers and dealers with price quotations on securities traded over-the-counter. NASDAQ is an acronym for National Association of Securities Dealers Automated Quotations.†

National Market List The list of the best-known and most widely traded securities in the over-the-counter market.*

National market system A system mandated by the Securities Acts Amendments of 1975. The national market system that is envisioned will include computer processing and computerized competitive prices for all markets trading similar stocks. The exact form of the system is yet to be determined.*

Negotiable Refers to a security, title to which is transferable by delivery. (See: *Good delivery.*)†

Negotiable Order of Withdrawal account An interest earning account on which checks may be drawn. Withdrawals from NOW accounts may be subject to a 14-day or more notice requirement although such is rarely imposed. NOW accounts may be offered by commercial banks, mutual savings banks, and savings and loan associations and may be owned only by individuals and certain non-profit organizations and governmental units.¶

Net asset value Usually used in connection with investment companies to mean net asset value per share. An investment company computes its assets daily, or even twice daily, by totaling the market value of all securities owned. All liabilities are deducted, and the balance divided by the number of shares outstanding. The resulting figure is the net asset value per share. (See: *Assets, Investment company.*)††

Net change The change in the price of a security from the closing price on one day and the closing price on the following day on which the stock is traded. The net change is ordinarily the last figure on the stock price list. The mark + 1⅛ means up $1.125 a share from the last sale on the previous day the stock traded.†

Net debt Gross debt less sinking fund accumulations and all self-supporting debt.**

Net present value (NPV) The NPV equals the present value of the cash inflows minus the present value of the cash outflows with the cost of capital used as a discount rate. This method is used to evaluate capital budgeting projects. If the NPV is positive, a project should be accepted.*

Net present value profile A graphical presentation of the potential net present values of a project at different discount rates. It is very helpful in comparing the characteristics of two or more investments.*

Net trade credit A measure of the relationship between the firm's accounts receivable and accounts payable. If accounts receivable exceed accounts payable, the firm is a net provider of trade credit; otherwise, it is a net user.*

Net worth, or book value Stockholders' equity minus preferred stock ownership. Basically, net worth is the common stockholders' interest as represented by common stock par value, capital paid in excess of par, and retained earnings. If you take all the assets of the firm and subtract its liabilities and preferred stock, you arrive at net worth.*

New housing authority bonds A bond issued by a local public housing authority to finance public housing. It is backed by Federal funds and the solemn pledge of the U.S. Government that payment will be made in full.**

New issue A stock or bond sold by a corporation for the first time. Proceeds may be issued to retire outstanding securities of the company, for new plant or equipment, or for additional working capital, or to acquire a public ownership interest in the company for private owners.††

New issue market Market for new issues of municipal bonds and notes.**

New York Futures Exchange (NYFE) A subsidiary of the New York Stock Exchange devoted to the trading of futures products.††

New York Stock Exchange (NYSE) The largest organized securities market in the United States, founded in 1792. The Exchange itself does not buy, sell, own, or set the prices of securities traded there. The prices are determined by public supply and demand. The Exchange is a not-for-profit corporation of 1,366 individual members, governed by a Board of Directors consisting of 10 public representatives, 10 Exchange members or allied members and a full-time chairman, executive vice chairman and president.††

Nominal GNP GNP (gross national product) in current dollars without any adjustments for inflation.*

Nominal yield A return equal to the coupon rate.*

Noncumulative A type of preferred stock on which unpaid dividends do not accrue. Omitted dividends are, as a rule, gone forever. (See: *Cumulative preferred.*)††

Nonfinancial corporation A firm not in the banking or financial services industry. The term would primarily apply to manufacturing, wholesaling, and retail firms.*

Nonlinear break-even analysis Break-even analysis based on the assumption that cost and revenue relationships to quantity may vary at different levels of operation. Most of our analysis is based on *linear* break-even analysis.*

Normal recovery period The depreciation recovery period (3, 5, 10, 15 years) under the Accelerated Cost Recovery System of the 1981 Economic Recovery Tax Act.*

Normal yield curve An upward-sloping yield curve. Long-term interest rates are higher than short-term rates.*

Notes Short-term unsecured promises to pay specified amounts of money. For municipal notes maturities generally range from six to twelve months.**

NYSE composite index A composite index covering price movements of all common stocks listed on the "Big Board." It is based on the close of the market December 31, 1965 as 50.00 and is weighted according to the number of shares listed for each issue. The index is computed continuously and printed on the ticker tape each half hour. Point changes in the index are converted to dollars and cents so as to provide a meaningful measure of changes in the average price of listed stocks. The composite index is supplemented by separate indexes for four industry groups: industries, transportation, utilities, and finances. (See: *Averages.*)††

Odd lot An amount of stock less than the established 100-share unit. (See: *Round lot.*)††

Off-board This term may refer to transactions over-the-counter in unlisted securities, or to a transaction involving listed shares that is not executed on a national securities exchange.††

Offer The price at which a person is ready to sell. Opposed to bid, the price at which one is ready to buy. (See: *Bid and asked.*)†

Official statement Document prepared by or for the issuer that gives in detail the security and financial information about the issue.**

Open-end investment company (See: *Investment company.*)

Open interest In options and futures trading, the number of outstanding option contracts, at a given point in time, which have not been exercised and have not yet reached expiration.††

Open-market operations The purchase and sale of government securities in the open market by the Federal Reserve Board for its own account. The most common method for managing the money supply.*

Open order (See: *Good 'til cancelled order.*)

Operating lease A short-term, nonbinding obligation that is easily cancelable.*

Operating leverage A reflection of the extent to which fixed assets and fixed costs are utilized in the business firm.*

Optimum capital structure A capital structure that has the best possible mix of debt, preferred stock, and common equity. The optimum mix should provide the lowest possible cost of capital to the firm.*

Option A right to buy (call) or sell (put) a fixed amount of a given stock at a specified price within a limited period of time. The purchaser hopes that the stock's price will go up (a call) or down (a put) by an amount sufficient to provide a profit when the stock is sold. If the stock price holds steady or moves in the opposite direction, the price paid for the option is lost entirely. There are several other types of options available to the public but these are basically combinations of puts and calls. Individuals may write (sell) as well as purchase options. Options are also traded on stock indexes, futures, and debt instruments.††

Orders good until a specified time A market or limited price order which is to be represented in the Trading Crowd until a specified time, after which such order or the portion thereof not executed is to be treated as cancelled.†

Overbought An opinion as to price levels. May refer to a security which has had a sharp rise or to the market as a whole after a period of vigorous buying, which it may be argued, has left prices "too high."†

Overseas Private Investment Corporation (OPIC) A government agency that sells insurance policies to qualified firms. This agency insures against losses due to inconvertibility into dollars of amounts invested in a foreign country. Policies are also available from OPIC to insure against expropriation and against losses due to war or revolution.*

Oversold The reverse of overbought. A single security or a market which, it is believed, has declined to an unreasonable level.††

Over-the-counter A market for securities made up of securities dealers who may or may not be members of a securities exchange. The over-the-counter market is conducted over the telephone and deals mainly with stocks of companies without sufficient shares, stockholders, or earnings to warrant listing on an exchange. Over-the-counter dealers may act either as principals or as brokers for customers. The over-the-counter market is the principal market for bonds of all types. (See: *NASD, NASDAQ.*)††

Paper profit (LOSS) An unrealized profit or loss on a security still held. Paper profits and losses become realized profits only when the security is sold. (See: *Profit-taking.*)††

Par In the case of a common share, par means a dollar amount assigned to the share by the company's charter. Par value may also be used to compute the dollar amount of the common shares on the balance sheet. Par value has little relationship to the market value of common stock. Many companies issue no-par stock but give a stated per share value on the balance sheet. In the case of preferred stocks, it signifies the dollar value upon which dividends are figured. With bonds, par value is the face amount, usually $1,000.††

Parallel loan A U.S. firm that wishes to lend funds to a foreign affiliate (such as a Dutch affiliate) locates a foreign parent firm (such as a Dutch parent firm) that wishes to loan money to a U.S. affiliate. Avoiding the foreign exchange markets entirely, the U.S. parent lends dollars to the Dutch affiliate in the United States, while the Dutch parent lends guilders to the American affiliate in the Netherlands. At maturity, the two loans would each be repaid to the original lender. Notice that neither loan carries any foreign exchange risk in this arrangement.*

Participating preferred A preferred stock which is entitled to its stated dividend and, also, to additional dividends on a specified basis upon payment of dividends on the common stock.†

Partnership A form of ownership in which two or more partners are involved. Like the sole proprietorship, a partnership arrangement carries unlimited liability for the owners. However, there is only single taxation for the partners, an advantage over the corporate form of ownership.*

Passed dividend Omission of a regular or scheduled dividend.†

Payback A value that indicates the time period required to recoup an initial investment. The payback does not include the time-value-of-money concept.*

Paying agent Place where principal and interest is payable. Usually a designated bank or the treasurer's office of the issuer.**

Penny stocks Low-priced issues often highly speculative, selling at less than $1 a share. Frequently used as a term of disparagement, although a few penny stocks have developed into investment-caliber issues.†

Percent-of-sales method A method of determining future financial needs that is an alternative to the development of pro forma financial statements. We first determine the percentage relationship of various asset and liability accounts to sales, and then we show how that relationship changes as our volume of sales changes.*

Permanent current assets Current assets that will not be reduced or converted to cash within the normal operating cycle of the firm. Though from a strict accounting standpoint the assets should be removed from the current assets category, they generally are not.*

Perpetuity An investment without a maturity date.*

Planning horizon The length of time it takes to conceive, develop, and complete a project and to recover the cost of the project on a discounted cash flow basis.*

Pledging receivables Using accounts receivable as collateral for a loan. The firm usually may borrow 60 to 80 percent of the value of acceptable collateral.*

Point In the case of shares of stock, a point means $1. If ABC shares rises 3 points, each share has risen $3. In the case of bonds a point means $10, since a bond is quoted as a percentage of $1,000. A bond which rises 3 points gains 3 percent of $1,000, or $30 in value. An advance from 87 to 90 would mean an advance in dollar value from $870 to $900. In the case of market averages, the word point means merely that and no more. If, for example, the NYSE Composite Index rises from 90.25 to 91.25, it has risen a point. A point in this average, however, is not equivalent to $1. (See: *Index.*)††

Point-of-sales terminals Computer terminals in retail stores that either allow digital input or use optical scanners. The terminals may be used for inventory control or other purposes.*

Pooling of interests A method of financial recording for mergers in which the financial statements of the firms are combined, subject to minor adjustments, and goodwill is *not* created.*

Portfolio Holdings of securities by an individual or institution. A portfolio may contain bonds, preferred stocks, common stocks and other securities.††

Portfolio effect The impact of a given investment on the overall risk-return composition of the firm. A firm must consider not only the individual investment characteristics of a project, but also how the project relates to the entire portfolio of undertakings.*

Preemptive right The right of current common stockholders to maintain their ownership percentage on new issues of common stock.*

Preferred stock A class of stock with a claim on the company's earnings before payment may be made on the common stock and usually entitled to priority over common stock if the company liquidates. Usually entitled to dividends at a specified rate—when declared by the board of directors and before payment of a dividend on the common stock—depending upon the terms of the issue. (See: *Cumulative preferred, Participating preferred.*)†

Premium The amount by which a bond or preferred stock, may sell above its par value. For options, the price that the buyer pays the writer for an option contract ("option premium") is synonymous with "the price of an option." (See: *Discount.*)††

Present value The current or discounted value of a future sum or annuity. The value is discounted back at a given interest rate for a specified time period.*

Price-earnings ratio A popular way to compare stocks selling at various price levels. The PE ratio is the price of a share of stock divided by earnings per share for a twelve-month period. For example, a stock selling for $50 a share and earning $5 a share is said to be selling at a price-earnings ratio of 10.††

Primary distribution Also called primary offering. The original sale of a company's securities. (See: *Investment banker.*)††

Primary earnings per share Adjusted earnings after taxes divided by shares outstanding plus common stock equivalents.*

Primary market Market for new issues of securities.

Prime rate The lowest interest rate charged by commercial banks to their most credit-worthy and largest corporate customers; other interest rates, such as personal, automobile, commercial and financing loans are often pegged to the prime.††

Principal The person for whom a broker

executes an order, or dealers buying or selling for their own accounts. The term *principal* may also refer to a person's capital or to the face amount of a bond.††

Private placement The sale of securities directly to a financial institution by a corporation. This eliminates the middleman and reduces the cost of issue to the corporation.*

Productivity The amount of physical output for each unit of productive input.¶

Profitability ratios A group of ratios that indicates the return on sales, total assets, and invested capital. Specifically, we compute the profit margin (net income to sales), return on assets, and return on equity.*

Profit-taking Selling stock which has appreciated in value since purchase, in order to realize the profit. The term is often used to explain a downturn in the market following a period of rising prices. (See: *Paper profit.*)††

Pro forma balance sheet A projection of future asset, liability, and stockholders' equity levels. Notes payable or cash is used as a plug or balancing figure for the statement.*

Pro forma financial statements A series of projected financial statements. Of major importance are the pro forma income statement, the pro forma balance sheet, and the cash budget.*

Pro forma income statement A projection of anticipated sales, expenses, and income.*

Prospectus The official selling circular that must be given to purchasers of new securities registered with the Securities and Exchange Commission. It highlights the much longer Registration Statement filed with the commission.††

Proxy Written authorization given by a shareholder to someone else to represent him and vote his shares at a shareholders' meeting.††

Proxy statement Information given to stockholders in conjunction with the solicitation of proxies.††

Prudent man rule An investment standard. In some states, the law requires that a fiduciary, such as a trustee, may invest the fund's money only in a list of securities designated by the state—the so-called legal list. In other states, the trustee may invest in a security if it is one that would be bought by a prudent man of discretion and intelligence, who is seeking a reasonable income and preservation of capital.††

Public Offering (See: *Primary distribution.*)

Public placement The sale of securities to the public through the investment banker-underwriter process. Public placements must be registered with the Securities and Exchange Commission.*

Public warehousing An inventory financing arrangement in which inventory, used as collateral, is stored with and controlled by an independent warehousing company.*

Purchase of assets A method of financial recording for mergers in which the difference between the purchase price and the adjusted book value is recognized as goodwill and amortized over a maximum time period of 40 years.*

Purchasing power parity theory A theory based on the interplay between inflation and exchange rates. A parity between the purchasing powers of two countries establishes the rate of exchange between the two currencies. Currency exchange rates, therefore, tend to vary inversely with their respective purchasing powers in order to provide the same or similar purchasing power.*

Pure bond value The value of the convertible bond if its present value is computed at a discount rate equal to interest rates on straight bonds of equal risk, without conversion privileges.*

Quote The highest bid to buy and the lowest offer to sell a security in a given market at a given time. If you ask your broker for a "quote" on a stock, he may come back with something like "45¼ to 45½." This means that $45.25 is the highest price any buyer wanted to pay at the time the quote was given on the floor of the exchange and that $45.50 was the lowest price which any seller would take at the same time. (See: *Bid and asked.*)††

Rally A brisk rise following a decline in the general price level of the market, or in an individual stock.†

Ratings Designations used by investors' services to give relative indications of quality.**

Real capital Long-term productive assets (plant and equipment).*

Real GNP GNP (gross national product) in current dollars adjusted for inflation.*

Real rate of return The rate of return that an investor demands for giving up the current use of his or her funds on a noninflation-adjusted basis. It is payment for forgoing current consumption. Historically, the real rate of return demanded by investors has been of the magnitude of 2 to 3 percent. However, throughout the 1980s the real rate of return has been much higher; that is, 5 to 7 percent.*

Record date The date on which you must be registered as a shareholder of a company in order to receive a declared dividend or, among other things, to vote on company affairs. (See: *Ex-dividend, Transfer.*)††

Redemption price The price at which a bond may be redeemed before maturity, at the option of the issuing company. Redemption value also applies to the price the company must pay to call in certain types of preferred stock. (See: *Callable.*)†

Red Herring (See: *Prospectus.*)

Refunding The process of retiring an old bond issue before maturity and replacing it with a new issue. Refunding will occur when interest rates have fallen and new bonds may be sold at lower interest rates.*

Registered bond A bond which is registered on the books of the issuing company in the name of the owner. It can be transferred only when endorsed by the registered owner. (See: *Bearer bond, Coupon bond.*)†

Registered representative The man or woman who serves the investor customers of a broker/dealer. In a New York Stock Exchange Member Organization, a Registered Representative must meet the requirements of the exchange as to background and knowledge of the securities business. Also known as an Account Executive or Customer's broker.††

Registrar Usually a trust company or bank charged with the responsibility of keeping a record of the owners of corporation's securities and preventing the issuance of more than the authorized amount. (See: *Transfer.*)††

Registration Before a public offering may be made of new securities by a company, or of outstanding securities by controlling stockholders—through the mails or in interstate commerce—the securities must be registered under the Securities Act of 1933. A statement is filed with the SEC by the issuer. It must disclose pertinent information relating to the company's operations, securities, management and purpose of the public offering.

Before a security may be admitted to dealings on a national securities exchange, it must be registered under the Securities Exchange Act of 1934. The application for registration must be filed with the exchange and the SEC by the company issuing the securities.††

Regional stock exchanges Organized exchanges outside of New York that list securities. Regional exchanges exist in San Francisco, Philadelphia, and a number of other U.S. cities.*

Regulation T The federal regulation governing the amount of credit which may be advanced by brokers and dealers to customers for the purchase of securities. (See: *Margin.*)†

Regulation U The federal regulation governing the amount of credit which may be advanced by a bank to its customers for the purchase of listed stocks. (See: *Margin.*)†

Reinvestment assumption An assumption must be made concerning the rate of return that can be earned on the cash flows generated by capital budgeting projects. The NPV method assumes the rate of reinvestment to be the cost of capital, while the IRR method assumes the rate to be the actual internal rate of return.*

REIT Real Estate Investment Trust, an organization similar to an investment company in some respects but concentrating its holdings in real estate investments. The yield is generally liberal since REIT's are required to distribute as much as 90 percent of their income. (See: *Investment company.*)†

Repatriation of earnings Returning earnings to the multinational parent company in the form of dividends.*

Replacement cost The cost of replacing the existing asset base at current prices as opposed to original cost.*

Replacement cost accounting Financial statements based on the present cost of replacing assets.*

Repurchase agreements When the Federal Reserve makes a repurchase agreement with a government securities dealer, it buys a security for immediate delivery with an agreement to sell the security back at the same price by a specific date (usually within 15 days) and receives interest at a specific rate. This arrangement allows the Federal Reserve to inject reserves into the banking system on a temporary basis to meet a temporary need and to withdraw these reserves as soon as that need has passed.¶

Required rate of return The rate of return that investors demand from an investment (securities) to compensate them for the amount of risk involved.*

Reserve requirements The amount of funds that commercial banks must hold in reserve for each dollar of deposits. Reserve requirements are set by the Federal Reserve Board and are different for savings and checking accounts. Low reserve requirements are stimulating; high reserve requirements are restrictive.*

Residual dividends This theory of dividend payout states that a corporation will retain as much earnings as it may profitably invest. If any income is left after investments, it will pay dividends. This theory assumes that dividends are a passive decision variable.*

Restructuring Redeploying the asset and liability structure of the firm. This can be accomplished through repurchasing shares with cash or borrowed funds, acquiring other firms, or selling off unprofitable or unwanted divisions.*

Revenue bond A bond payable from revenues derived from tolls, charges, or rents paid by users of the facility constructed from the proceeds of the bond issue.**

Rights When a company wants to raise more funds by issuing additional securities, it may give its stockholders the opportunity, ahead of others, to buy the new securities in proportion to the number of shares each owns. The piece of paper evidencing this privilege is called a right. Because the additional stock is usually offered to stockholders below the current market price, rights ordinarily have a market value of their own and are actively traded. In most cases they must be exercised within a relatively short period. Failure to exercise or sell rights may result in actual loss to the holder. (See: *Warrant.*)†

Rights offering A sale of new common stock through a preemptive rights offering. Usually one right will be issued for every share held. A certain number of rights may be used to buy shares of common stock from the company at a set price that is lower than the market price.*

Rights-on The situation in which the purchase of a share of common stock includes a right attached to the stock.*

Risk A measure of uncertainty about the outcome from a given event. The greater the variability of possible outcomes, on both the high side and the low side, the greater the risk.*

Risk-adjusted discount rate A discount rate used in the capital budgeting process that has been adjusted upward or downward from the basic cost of capital to reflect the risk dimension of a given project.*

Risk averse An aversion or dislike for risk. In order to induce most people to take larger risks, there must be increased potential for return.*

Risk-free rate of interest Rate of return on an asset that carries no risk. U.S. Treasury bills are often used to represent this measure, although longer-term government securities have also proved appropriate in some studies.*

Risk premium A premium associated with the special risks of an investment. Of primary interest are two types of risk, business risk and financial risk. Business risk relates to the inability of the firm to maintain its competitive position and sustain stability and growth in earnings. Financial risk relates to the inability of the firm to meet its debt obligations as they come due. The risk premium will also differ (be greater or less) for different types of investments (bonds, stocks, etc.).*

Risk-return trade-off function (See *Security market line.*)

Round lot A unit of trading or a multiple thereof. On the NYSE the unit of trading is generally 100 shares in stocks and $1,000 or $5,000 par value in the case of bonds. In some inactive stocks, the unit of trading is ten shares. (See: *Odd lot.*)††

Scale order An order to buy (or sell) a security which specifies the total amount to be bought (or sold) and the amount to be bought (or sold) at specified price variations.†

Seat A traditional figure-of-speech for a membership on an exchange.††

SEC The Securities and Exchange Commission, established by Congress to help protect investors. The SEC administers the Securities Act of 1933, the Securities Exchange Act of 1934, the Securities Act Amendments of 1975, the Trust Indenture Act, the Investment Company Act, the Investment Advisers Act, and the Public Utility Holding Company Act.†

Secondary offering The sale of a large block of stock in a publicly traded company, usually by estates, foundations, or large individual stockholders. Secondary offerings must be registered with the SEC and will usually be distributed by investment bankers.*

Secondary trading The buying and selling of publicly owned securities in secondary markets such as the New York Stock Exchange and the over-the-counter markets.*

Secured debt A general category of debt which indicates that the loan was obtained by pledging assets as collateral. Secured debt has many forms and usually offers some protective features to a given class of bondholders.*

Securities Act of 1933 An act that is sometimes referred to as the truth in securities act because it requires detailed financial disclosures before securities may be sold to the public.*

Securities Acts Amendments of 1975 The major feature of this act was to mandate a national securities market. (See: *National market system.*)*

Securities Exchange Act of 1934 Legislation that established the Securities and Exchange Commission (SEC) to supervise and regulate the securities markets.*

Security market line A line or equation that depicts the risk-related return of a security based on a risk-free rate plus a market premium related to the beta coefficient of the security.*

Self-liquidating assets Assets that are converted to cash within the normal operating cycle of the firm. An example is the purchase and sell-off of seasonal inventory.*

Semiannual compounding A compounding period of every six months. For example, a five-year investment in which interest is compounded semiannually would indicate an *n* value equal to 10 and an *i* value at one half the annual rate.*

Semivariable costs Costs that are partially fixed but still change somewhat as volume changes. Examples are utilities and "repairs and maintenance."*

Serial bond An issue which matures in part at periodic stated intervals.†

Settlement Conclusion of a securities transaction when a customer pays a broker/dealer for securities purchased or delivers securities sold and receives from the broker the proceeds of a sale. (See: *Cash sale.*)††

Shelf registration A process which permits large companies to file one comprehensive registration statement (under SEC Rule 415), which outlines the firm's plans for future long-term financing. Then, when market conditions appear to be appropriate, the firm can issue the securities without further SEC approval.*

Short covering Buying stock to return stock previously borrowed to make delivery on a short sale.†

Short position Stocks, options, or futures sold short and not covered as of a particular date. On the NYSE, a tabulation is issued once a month listing all issues on the Exchange in which there was a short position of 5,000 or more shares and issues in which the short position had changed by 2,000 or more shares in the preceding month. Short position also means the total amount of stock an individual has sold short and has not covered, as of a particular date.††

Short sale A transaction by a person who believes a security will decline and sells it, though the person does not own any. For instance: You instruct your broker to sell short 100 shares of XYZ. Your broker borrows the stock so delivery of the 100 shares can be made to the buyer. The money value of the shares borrowed is deposited by your broker with the lender. Sooner or later you must cover your short sale by buying the same amount of stock you borrowed for return to the lender. If you are able to buy XYZ at a lower price than you sold it for, your profit is the difference between the two prices—not counting commissions and taxes. But if you have to pay more for the stock than the price you received, that is the amount of your loss. Stock exchange and federal regulations govern and limit the conditions under which a short sale may be made on a national securities exchange. Sometimes people will sell short a stock they already own in order to protect a paper profit. This is known as selling short against the box.††

Simulation A method of dealing with uncertainty in which future outcomes are anticipated. The model may use random variables for inputs. By programming the computer to randomly select inputs from probability distributions, the outcomes generated by a simulation are distributed about a mean, and instead of generating one return or net present value, a range of outcomes with standard deviations is provided.*

Sinking fund Money regularly set aside by a company to redeem its bonds, debentures or preferred stock from time to time as specified in the indenture or charter.††

SIPC Securities Investor Protection Corporation, which provides funds for use, if necessary, to protect customers' cash and securities which may be on deposit with a SIPC member firm in the event the firm fails and is liquidated under the provisions of the SIPC Act. SIPC is not a government agency. It is a nonprofit membership corporation created, however, by an act of Congress.†

Special bid A method of filling an order to buy a large block of stock on the floor of the New York Stock Exchange. In a special bid, the bidder for the block of stock—a pension fund, for instance, will pay a special commission to the broker who represents him in making the purchase. The seller does not pay a commission. The special bid is made on the floor of the exchange at a fixed price which may not be below the last sale of the security or the current bid in the regular market, whichever is higher. Member firms may sell this stock for customers directly to the buyer's broker during trading hours.†

Special offering Opposite of special bid. A notice is printed on the ticker tape announcing the stock sale at a fixed price usually based on the last transaction in the regular auction market. If there are more buyers than stock, allotments are made. Only the seller pays the commission.†

Special tax bond A bond secured by a special tax, such as a gasoline tax.**

Specialist A member of the New York Stock Exchange, Inc., who has two functions: First, to maintain an orderly market in the securities registered to the specialist. In order to maintain an orderly market, the Exchange expects specialists to buy or sell for the own account, to a reasonable degree, when there is a temporary disparity between supply and demand. Second, the specialist acts as a broker's broker. When a commission broker on the Exchange floor receives a limit order, say, to buy at $50 a stock then selling at $60—he cannot wait at the post where the stock is traded to see if the price reaches the specified level. So he leaves the order with the specialist, who will try to execute it in the market if and when the stock declines to the specified price. At all times the specialist must put his customers' interests above his own. There are about 400 specialists on the NYSE. (See: *Limited order.*)††

Speculation The employment of funds by a speculator. Safety of principal is a secondary factor. (See: *Investment.*)†

Speculative warrant premium The market price of the warrant minus the warrant's intrinsic value.*

Speculator One who is willing to assume a relatively large risk in the hope of gain.††

Spin off The separation of a subsidiary or division of a corporation from its parent by issuing shares in a new corporate entity. Shareowners in the parent receive shares in the new company in proportion to their original holding and the total value remains approximately the same.††

Split The division of the outstanding shares of a corporation into a larger number of shares. A 3-for-1 split by a company with 1 million shares outstanding results in 3 million shares outstanding. Each holder of 100 shares before the 3-for-1 split would have 300 shares, although his proportionate equity in the company would remain the same; 100 parts of 1 million are the equivalent of 300 parts of 3 million. Ordinarily splits must be voted by directors and approved by shareholders. (See: *Stock dividend.*)

Spontaneous sources of funds Funds arising through the normal course of business, such as accounts payable generated from the purchase of goods for resale.*

Standard deviation A measure of the spread or dispersion of a series of numbers around the expected value. The standard deviation tells us how well the expected value represents a series of values.*

Step-up in conversion A feature that is sometimes written into the contract which allows the conversion ratio to decline in steps over time. This feature encourages early conversion when the conversion value is greater than the call price.*

Stock ahead Sometimes an investor who has entered an order to buy or sell a stock at a certain price will see transactions at that price reported on the ticker tape while his own order has not been executed. The reason is that other buy and sell orders at the same price came in to the specialist ahead of his and had priority. (See: *Book, Specialist.*)†

Stock dividend A dividend paid in securities rather than cash. The dividend may be additional shares of the issuing company, or shares of another company (usually a subsidiary) held by the company.††

Stock Index Futures Futures contracts based on market indexes, e.g., NYSE Composite Index Futures Contracts.††

Stock split A division of shares by a ratio set by the board of directors—2 for 1, 3 for 1, 3 for 2, and so on. Stock splits usually indicate that the company's stock has risen in price to a level that the directors feel limits the trading appeal of the stock. The par value is divided by the ratio set, and new shares are issued to the current stockholders of record to increase their shares to the stated level. For example, a two-for-one split would increase your holdings from one share to two shares.*

Stockholder of record A stockholder whose name is registered on the books of the issuing corporation.†

Stockholder wealth maximization Maximizing the wealth of the firm's shareholders through achieving the highest possible value for the firm in the marketplace. It is the overriding objective of the firm and should influence all decisions.*

Stockholders' equity The total ownership position of preferred and common stockholders.*

Stop limit order A stop order which becomes a limit order after the specified stop price has been reached. (See: *Limit order, Stop order.*)†

Stop order An order to buy at a price above or sell at a price below the current market. Stop buy orders are generally used to limit loss or protect unrealized profits on a short sale. Stop sell orders are generally used to protect unrealized profits or limit loss on a holding. A stop order becomes a market order when the stock sells at or beyond the specified price and, thus, may not necessarily be executed at that price.†

Stopped stock A service performed—in most cases by the specialist—for an order given him by a commission broker. Let's say XYZ just sold at $50 a share. Broker A comes along with an order to buy 100 shares at the market. The lowest offer is $50.50. Broker A believes he can do better for his client than $50.50, perhaps might get the stock at $50.25.

But he doesn't want to take a chance that he'll miss the market—that is, the next sale might be $50.50 and the following one even higher. So he asks the specialist if he will stop 100 at ½ ($50.50). The specialist agrees. The specialist guarantees Broker A he will get 100 shares at 50½ if the stock sells at that price. In the meantime, if the specialist or broker A succeeds in executing the order at $50.25, the stop is called off. (See: *Specialist.*)†

Street name Securities held in the name of a broker instead of his customer's name are said to be carried in a *street name.* This occurs when the securities have been bought on margin or when the customer wishes the security to be held by the broker.†

Subchapter S corporation A special corporate form of ownership in which profit is taxed as direct income to the stockholders and thus is only taxed once as would be true of a partnership. The stockholders still receive all the organizational benefits of a corporation, including limited liability. The Subchapter S designation can only apply to corporations with up to 35 stockholders.*

Subdivision Any legal and authorized political entity under a state's jurisdiction (county, city, water district, school district, etc.).**

Subordinated debenture An unsecured bond in which payment to the holder will take place only after designated senior debenture holders are satisfied.*

Swapping Selling one security and buying a similar one almost at the same time to take a loss, usually for tax purposes.††

Switch order or contingent order An order for the purchase (sale) of one stock and the sale (purchase) of another stock at a stipulated price difference.†

Switching Selling one security and buying another.†

Syndicate A group of investment bankers who together underwrite and distribute a new issue of securities or a large block of an outstanding issue.†

Synergy The recognition that the whole may be equal to more than the sum of the parts. The "2 + 2 = 5" effect.

Take-over The acquiring of one corporation by another—usually in a friendly merger but sometimes marked by a "proxy fight." In "unfriendly" take-over attempts, the potential buying company may offer a price well above current market values, new securities, and other inducements to stockholders. The management of the subject company might ask for a better price or fight the take-over or merger with another company. (See: *Proxy.*)†

Tax base The total resources available for taxation.**

Tax-exempt bond Another name for a municipal bond. The interest on a municipal bond is presently exempt from Federal income tax.**

Tax loss carry-forward A loss that can be carried forward for a number of years to offset future taxable income and perhaps be utilized by another firm in a merger or an acquisition.*

Tax shelter A medium or process intended to reduce or eliminate the tax burden of an individual. They range from such conventional ones as tax-exempt municipal securities and interest or dividend exclusion to sophisticated limited partnerships in real estate, cattle raising, equipment leasing, oil drilling, research and development activities and motion picture production.††

Technical insolvency A firm is unable to pay its bills as they come due.*

Technical research Analysis of the market and stocks based on supply and demand. The technician studies price movements, volume, and trends and patterns which are revealed by charting these factors, and attempts to assess the possible effect of current market action on future supply and demand for securities and individual issues. (See: *Fundamental research.*)†

Temporary current assets Current assets that will be reduced or converted to cash within the normal operating cycle of the firm.*

Tender offer A public offer to buy shares from existing stockholders of one public corporation by another company or other organization under specified terms good for a certain time period. Stockholders are asked to "tender" (surrender) their holdings for stated value, usually at a premium above current market price, subject to the tendering of a minimum and maximum number of shares.††

Term issue An issue that has a single maturity.**

Term loan An intermediate-length loan in which credit is generally extended from one to seven years. The loan is usually repaid in monthly or quarterly installments over its life rather than the one single period.*

Term structure of interest rates The relationship between interest rates and maturities for securities of equal risk. Usually government securities are used for the term structure.*

Terms of exchange The buy-out ratio or terms of trade in a merger or an acquisition.*

Thin market A market in which there are

comparatively few bids to buy or offers to sell, or both. The phrase may apply to a single security or to the entire stock market. In a thin market, price fluctuations between transactions are usually larger than when the market is liquid. A thin market in a particular stock may reflect lack of interest in that issue or a limited supply of or demand for stock in the market. (See: *Bid and asked, Liquidity, Offer.*)†

Third market Trading of stock exchange listed securities in the over-the-counter market by non-exchange-member brokers.††

Tight money A term to indicate time periods in which financing may be difficult to find and interest rates may be quite high by normal standards.*

Time order An order which becomes a market or limited price order at a specified time.†

Time value The part of an option premium that is in excess of the intrinsic value.††

Tips Supposedly "inside" information on corporation affairs.†

Trade credit Credit provided by sellers or suppliers in the normal course of business.*

Trader Individuals who buy and sell for their own accounts for short-term profit. Also, an employee of a broker/dealer or financial institution who specializes in handling purchases and sales of securities for the firm and/or its clients. (See: *Investor, Speculator.*)††

Trading market The secondary market for outstanding securities.*

Trading post One of 23 trading locations on the floor of the New York Stock Exchange at which stocks assigned to that location are bought and sold. About 75 stocks are traded at each post.†

Transaction exposure Foreign exchange gains and losses resulting from *actual* international transactions. These may be hedged through the foreign exchange market, the money market, or the currency futures market.*

Transfer This term may refer to two different operations. For one, the delivery of a stock certificate from the seller's broker to the buyer's broker and legal change of ownership, normally accomplished within a few days. For another, to record the change of ownership on the books of the corporation by the transfer agent. When the purchaser's name is recorded, dividends, notices of meetings, proxies, financial reports, and all pertinent literature sent by the issuer to its securities holders are mailed direct to the new owner. (See: *Registrar, Street name.*)††

Transfer agent A transfer agent keeps a record of the name of each registered shareowner, his or her address, the number of shares owned, and sees that certificates presented for transfer are properly cancelled and new certificates issued in the name of the new owner. (See: *Registrar.*)††

Translation exposure The foreign-located assets and liabilities of a multinational corporation, which are denominated in foreign currency units, and are exposed to losses and gains due to changing exchange rates. This is called accounting, or translation, exposure.*

Treasury bills Short-term U.S. Treasury securities issued in minimum denominations of $10,000 and usually having original maturities of 3, 6, or 12 months. Investors purchase bills at prices lower than the face value of the bills; the return to the investors is the difference between the price paid for the bills and the amount received when the bills are sold or when they mature. Treasury bills are the type of security used most frequently in open market operations.¶

Treasury bonds Long-term U.S. Treasury securities usually having initial maturities of more than 10 years and issued in denominations of $1,000 or more, depending on the specific issue. Bonds pay interest semiannually, with principal payable at maturity.¶

Treasury notes Intermediate-term coupon-bearing U.S. Treasury securities having initial maturities from 1 to 10 years and issued in denominations of $1,000 or more, depending on the maturity of the issue. Notes pay interest semiannually, and the principal is payable at maturity.¶

Treasury stock Stock issued by a company, but later reacquired. It may be held in the company's treasury indefinitely, reissued to the public, or retired. Treasury stock receives no dividends, and has no vote while held by the company.††

Trend analysis An analysis of performance that is made over a number of years in order to ascertain significant patterns.*

Trust receipt An instrument acknowledging that the borrower holds the inventory and proceeds for sale in trust for the lender.*

Two-step buy-out An acquisition plan in which the acquiring company attempts to gain control by offering a very high cash price for 51 percent of the shares of the target company. At the same time the acquiring company announces a second lower price that will be paid, either in cash, stock or bonds, at a subsequent point in time.*

Underwriter (See: *Investment banker.*)

Underwriting The process of selling securities and, at the same time, assuring the seller a specified price. Underwriting is done by investment bankers and represents a form of risk taking.*

Underwriting spread The difference between the price that a selling corporation receives for an issue of securities and the price at which the issue is sold to the public. The spread is the fee that investment bankers and others receive for selling securities.*

Underwriting syndicate A group of investment bankers that is formed to share the risk of a security offering and also to facilitate the distribution of the securities.*

Unlimited tax bond A bond secured by pledge of taxes that are not limited by rate or amount.**

Unlisted A security not listed on a stock exchange. (See: *Over-the-counter.*)†

Unsecured debt A loan which requires no assets as collateral, but allows the bondholder a general claim against the corporation rather than a lien against specific assets.*

Up tick A term used to designate a transaction made at a price higher than the preceding transaction. Also called a *plus-tick.* A *zero-plus* tick is a term used for a transaction at the same price as the preceding trade but higher than the preceding different price.

Conversely, a *down tick,* or *minus* tick, is a term used to designate a transaction made at a price lower than the preceding trade.

A plus sign, or a minus sign, is displayed throughout the day next to the last price of each company's stock traded at each trading post on the floor of the New York Stock Exchange. (See: *Short sale.*)†

Variable annuity A life insurance policy where the annuity premium (a set amount of dollars) is immediately turned into units of a portfolio of stocks. Upon retirement, the policyholder is paid according to accumulated units, the dollar value of which varies according to the performance of the stock portfolio. Its objective is to preserve, through stock investment, the purchasing value of the annuity which otherwise is subject to erosion through inflation.††

Variable costs Costs that move directly with a change in volume. Examples are raw materials, factory labor, and sales commissions.*

Volume The number of shares traded in a security or an entire market during a given period. Volume is usually considered on a daily basis and a daily average is computed for longer periods.†

Voting right The common stockholder's right to vote their stock in the affairs of a company. Preferred stock usually has the right to vote when preferred dividends are in default for a specified period. The right to vote may be delegated by the stockholder to another person. (See: *Cumulative voting, Proxy.*)††

Warrant A certificate giving the holder the right to purchase securities at a stipulated price within a specified time limit or perpetually. Sometimes a warrant is offered with securities as an inducement to buy. (See: *Rights.*)††

Warrant intrinsic value (See: *Minimum warrant value.*)*

Weighted average cost of capital The computed cost of capital determined by multiplying the cost of each item in the optimal capital structure by its weighted representation in the overall capital structure and summing up the results.*

When issued A short form of "when, as, and if issued." The term indicates a conditional transaction in a security authorized for issuance but not as yet actually issued. All "when issued" transactions are on an "if" basis, to be settled if and when the actual security is issued and the exchange or National Association of Securities Dealers rules the transactions are to be settled.†

Wire house A member firm of an exchange maintaining a communications network linking either its own branch offices, offices of correspondent firms, or a combination of such offices.†

Working capital management The financing and management of the current assets of the firm. The financial manager determines the mix between temporary and permanent "current assets" and the nature of the financing arrangement.*

Working control Theoretically, ownership of 51 percent of a company's voting stock is necessary to exercise control. In practice—and this is particularly true in the case of a large corporation—effective control sometimes can be exerted through ownership, individually or by a group acting in concert, of less than 50 percent.†

Yield Also known as return. The dividends or interest paid by a company expressed as a percentage of the current price. A stock with a current market value of $3.20 is said to return 8 percent ($3.20 ÷ $40.00). The current yield on a bond is figured the same way.††

Yield curve A curve that shows interest rates at a specific point in time for all securities having equal risk but different maturity dates. Usually government securities are used to construct such curves. The yield curve is also referred to as the term structure of interest rates.*

Yield to maturity The yield of a bond to maturity takes into account the price discount from or premium over the face amount. It is greater than the current yield when the bond is selling at a discount and less than the current yield when the bond is selling at a premium.†

Zero coupon bonds Bonds which do not convey a coupon (i.e., do not pay interest) but which are offered at a substantial discount from par value and appreciate to their full value (usually $1,000) at maturity. However, under U.S. tax law, the imputed interest is taxed as it accrues. The appeal of Zero coupon bonds is primarily for IRA and other tax sheltered retirement accounts.

Acquisition Takeover Glossary

Asset Play[1] A firm whose underlying assets are worth substantially more (after paying off the firm's liabilities) than the market value of its stock.

Bear hug An unnegotiated offer, in the form of a letter made directly to the board of directors of the target company. The price and terms are sufficiently detailed so that the directors are obliged to make the offer public. The offer states a time limit for a response and may threaten a tender offer or other action if it is not accepted.

Breakup value[1] The sum of the values of the firm's assets if sold off separately.

Crown jewel option[1] The strategem of selling off or spinning off the asset that makes the firm an attractive takeover candidate.

Four-nine position[1] A holding of approximately 4.9% of the outstanding shares of a company. At 5%, the holder must file a form [13d] with the SEC, revealing his position. Thus, a four-nine position is about the largest position that one can quietly hold.

Black knight[1] A potential acquirer that management opposes and would prefer to find an alternative to (i.e. a *white knight*).

Going private[1] The process of buying back the publicly held stock so that what was heretofore a public firm becomes private.

Golden handcuffs[1] Employment agreement that makes the departure of upper level managers very costly to them. For instance, such managers may lose very attractive stock option rights by leaving prior to their normal retirement age.

Golden handshake[1] A provision in a preliminary agreement to be acquired in which the target firm gives the acquiring firm an option to purchase its shares or assets at attractive prices or to receive a substantial bonus if the proposed takeover does not occur.

Golden parachute[1] Extremely generous separation payments for upper level executives that are required to be fulfilled if the firm's control shifts.

Greenmail[1] Incentive payments to dissuade the interest of outsiders who may otherwise seek control of a firm. The payment frequently takes the form of a premium price for the outsiders' shares, coupled with an agreement from them to avoid buying more stock for a set period of time.

The firm bears the cost of the payment. The stock price generally falls after the payment and the removal of the outside threat.

In play[1] The status of being a recognized takeover candidate.

Junk bonds[1] High-risk, high-yield bonds that are often used to finance takeovers.

LBO[1] A leveraged buyout. A purchase of a company financed largely by debt that is backed by the firm's own assets.

Loaded laggard[1] A stock of a company whose assets, particularly its liquid assets, have high values relative to the stock's price.

Lockup agreement[1] An agreement between an acquirer and target that makes the target very unattractive to any other acquirer; similar to a *golden handshake*.

Mezzanine financing Debt financing subordinate to the claims of the senior debt. This financing often has equity participation in the form of stock options, warrants or conversion to cheap stock.

Nibble strategy A takeover approach involving the purchase in the public market of minority stock position in the target company and a subsequent tender offer for the rest of the target stock.

PacMan defense[1] The tactic of seeking to acquire the firm that has targeted your own firm as a takeover prospect.

Poison pill[1] A provision in the corporate bylaws or other governance documents providing for a very disadvantageous result for a potential acquirer should its ownership position be allowed to exceed some preassigned threshold. For example, if anyone acquires more than 20% of Company A's stock, the

[1]Source: From the *AAII Journal*, American Association of *Individual Investors*, 612 North Michigan Avenue, Chicago, IL 60611. Excerpted from Ben Branch "White Knight Rescues Investors From Terminology."

acquirer might then have to sell $100 worth of its own stock to other shareholders at $50.

Raider A hostile outside party that seeks to take over other companies.

Saturday night special A seven day cash tender offer for all of the target firm's stock. It is usually launched on a Saturday on the assumption that the target company will have difficulty mobilizing its key advisors in reaction to the offer.

Scorched earth defense[1] A tactic in which the defending company's management engages in practices that reduce their company's value to such a degree that it is no longer attractive to the potential acquirer. This approach is more often threatened than actually employed.

Senior debt financing The issuance of debt instruments having first claim on a firm's assets (secured debt) or cash flow (unsecured debt).

Shark repellant[1] Anti-takeover provisions such as the poison pill.

Short swing profit[1] A gain made by an insider (including anyone with more than 10% of the stock) who holds stock for less than six months. Such gains must be paid back to the company whose shares were sold.

Standstill agreement[1] A reciprocal understanding between a company's management and an outside party that usually owns a significant minority position. Each party gives up certain rights in exchange for corresponding concessions by the other party. For example, the outside group may agree to limit its stock purchases to keep its ownership percentage below some level (for instance, 20%). In exchange, management may agree to a minority board representation by the outsider.

Swipe An unnegotiated offer to purchase the shares of a target company's stock made after the target's board has announced its intention to sell the company (usually in a leverage buyout to management). The swipe price is higher than that initially proposed by the board of directors.

Tender offer An offer by a firm to buy the stock of another firm (target) by going directly to the stockholders of the target. The offer is often made over the opposition of the management of the target firm.

13d[1] A form that must be filed with the SEC when a single investor or an associated group owns 5% or more of a company's stock. The form reveals the size of the holding and the investor's intentions.

Two-tier offer[1] A takeover device in which a relatively high per share price is paid for controlling interest in a target and a lesser per share price is paid for the remainder.

White knight defense[1] Finding an alternative and presumably more friendly acquirer than the present takeover threat.

White squire defense[1] Finding an important ally to purchase a strong minority position (for example, 25%) of the potential acquisition's stock. Presumably this ally (the "white squire") will oppose and hopefully block the efforts of any hostile firm seeking to acquire the vulnerable firm.

Stock Exchanges

Common Stocks (shares of ownership in a corporation) are traded on several exchanges. The best known are the New York Stock Exchange and the American Stock Exchange, both located in Manhattan's financial district. Generally, the stocks of the largest companies are traded on the New York Stock Exchange, while somewhat smaller companies are traded on the American Exchange. There are also a number of regional exchanges such as the Midwest Exchange in Chicago and the Pacific Exchange in San Francisco. These exchanges trade stocks of local corporations as well as stocks listed on the New York and American Exchanges.

In addition, there is the Over-The Counter-Market (OTC) which, unlike the exchanges previously mentioned, does not have a specific location but consists of a network of brokers and dealers linked by telephone and private wires. Smaller or relatively new companies are traded on the OTC. Trading information for many (but far from all) stocks on the OTC market is collected and displayed on a computerized system, the National Association of Security Dealers Automatic Quote System (NASDAQ).

Large institutional traders (mutual and pension funds, insurance companies, etc.) often trade blocks of stocks directly with one another. This information is collected and displayed on the Instinet System.

Major Stock Exchanges*

UNITED STATES

AMERICAN STOCK EXCHANGE, INC.
86 Trinity Place
New York, New York 10006

BOSTON STOCK EXCHANGE, INC.
One Boston Place
Boston, Massachusetts 02109

THE CINCINNATI STOCK EXCHANGE, INC.
205 Dixie Terminal Building
Cincinnati, Ohio 45202

MIDWEST STOCK EXCHANGE, INC.
440 South LaSalle Street
Chicago, Illinois 60603

NEW YORK STOCK EXCHANGE, INC.
11 Wall Street
New York, New York 10005

PACIFIC STOCK EXCHANGE, INC.
618 South Spring Street
Los Angeles, California 90014

301 Pine Street
San Francisco, California 94104

PHILADELPHIA STOCK EXCHANGE, INC.
1900 Market Street
Philadelphia, Pennsylvania 19103

SPOKANE STOCK EXCHANGE, INC.
206 Radio Central Building
Spokane, Washington 99201

FOREIGN

AUSTRALIA

SYDNEY STOCK EXCHANGE
Exchange Centre
20 Bond Street
Australia Square
P.O. Box H224
Sydney, 2000

BELGIUM

BRUSSELS STOCK EXCHANGE
Palais de la Bourse
1000 Brussels

* See page 519 for a listing of futures and options exchanges.

CANADA

ALBERTA STOCK EXCHANGE
300–5th Avenue S.W.
Calgary, Alberta T2P 3C4

BOURSE DE MONTRÉAL
The Stock Exchange Tower
800 Victoria Square
Montreal, Quebec H4Z 1A9

TORONTO STOCK EXCHANGE
2 First Canadian Place
Toronto, Ontario M5X 1J2

VANCOUVER STOCK EXCHANGE
Stock Exchange Tower
P.O. Box 10333
609 Granville Street
Vancouver, B.C. V7Y 1H1

WINNIPEG STOCK EXCHANGE
500 Commodity Exchange Tower
360 Main Street
Winnipeg, Manitoba R3C 324

FRANCE

BOURSE DE PARIS—PARIS STOCK EXCHANGE
4, Place de la Bourse
F-75080 Paris Cedex 02

GERMANY

FRANKFURTER WERTPAPIERBORE—FRANKFORT EXCHANGE
Börsenplatz 6, P.O. 100811
D-6000 Frankfurt am Main 1

HONG KONG

STOCK EXCHANGE OF HONG KONG
One and Two Exchange Square
Central Hong Kong

JAPAN

TOKYO STOCK EXCHANGE
2–1 Nihombashi Kayuto-Cho
Cho-Ku, Tokyo 103

THE NETHERLANDS

AMSTERDAMSE EFFECTENBEURS—AMSTERDAM STOCK EXCHANGE
Beursplein 5
1012 JW Amsterdam

SWITZERLAND

GENEVA STOCK EXCHANGE
Rue de la Confédération 8
CH-1204 Geneva

ZÜRICH STOCK EXCHANGE
Bleicherweg 5
P.O. Box CH-8021
Zürich

UNITED KINGDOM

THE INTERNATIONAL STOCK EXCHANGE OF THE UNITED KINGDOM AND THE REPUBLIC OF IRELAND LIMITED
Old Broad Street
London, England EC 2N 1HP

Securities and Exchange Commission

JUDICIARY PLAZA
450 FIFTH STREET, NW
WASHINGTON, DC 20549
PUBLIC AFFAIRS: 202-272-2650
FREEDOM OF INFORMATION ACT:
202-272-7420
FILINGS BY REGISTERED COMPANIES:
202-272-7450

FULL AND FAIR DISCLOSURE

The Securities Act of 1933 requires issuers of securities and their controlling persons making public offerings of securities in interstate commerce or through the mails, directly or by others on their behalf, to file with the Commission registration statements containing financial and other pertinent data about the issuer and the securities being offered. It is unlawful to sell such securities unless a registration statement is in effect. (There are limited exemptions, such as government securities, nonpublic offerings, and intrastate offerings, as well as offerings not exceeding $1,500,000. The effectiveness of a registration statement may be refused or suspended after a public hearing, if the statement contains material misstatements or omissions, thus barring sale of the securities until it is appropriately amended.

Registration of securities does not imply approval of the issue by the Commission or that the Commission has found the registration disclosures to be accurate. It does not insure investors against loss in their purchase but serves rather to provide information upon which investors may make an informed and realistic evaluation of the worth of the securities.

Persons responsible for filing false information with the Commission subject themselves to the risk of fine or imprisonment or both; and persons connected with the public offering may be liable in damages to purchasers of the securities if the disclosures in the registration statement and prospectus are materially defective. Also, the above act contains antifraud provisions which apply generally to the sale of securities, whether or not registered (48 Stat. 74; 15 U.S.C. 77a et seq.).

Source: This material was abstracted from the United States Government Manual.

REGULATION OF SECURITIES MARKETS

The Securities Exchange Act of 1934 assigns to the commission board regulatory responsibilities over the securities markets, the self-regulatory organizations within the securities industry, and persons conducting a business in securities. Persons who execute transactions in securities generally are required to register with the Commission as broker-dealers. Securities exchanges and certain clearing agencies are required to register with the Commission, and associations of brokers or dealers are permitted to register with the Commission. The Act also provides for the establishment of the Municipal Securities Rulemaking Board to formulate rules for the municipal securities industry.

The Commission oversees the self-regulatory activities of the national securities exchanges and associations, registered clearing agencies, and the Municipal Securities Rulemaking Board. In addition, the Commission regulates industry professionals, such as securities brokers and dealers, certain municipal securities professionals, and transfer agents.

The Securities Exchange Act authorizes national securities exchanges, national securities associations, clearing agencies, and the Municipal Securities Rulemaking Board to adopt rules that are designed, among other things to promote just and equitable principles of trade and to protect investors. The Commission is required to approve or disapprove most proposed rules of these self-regulatory organizations and has the power to abrogate or amend existing rules of the national securities exchanges, national securities associations, and the Municipal Securities Rulemaking Board.

In addition, the Commission has broad rulemaking authority over the activities of brokers, dealers, municipal securities dealers, securities information processors, and transfer agents. The Commission may regulate such securities trading practices as short sales and stabilizing transactions. It may regulate the trading of options on national securities exchanges and the activities of members of exchanges who trade on the trading floors and may adopt rules governing broker-dealer sales practices in dealing with investors. The Commission also is authorized to adopt rules concerning the financial responsibility of brokers and dealers and reports to be made by them.

The Securities Exchange Act also requires the filing of registration statements and annual and other reports with national securities exchanges and the Commission by companies whose securities are listed upon the exchanges, by companies that have assets of $5 million or more and 500 or more shareholders of record. In addition companies that distributed securities pursuant to a registration statement declared effective by the Commission under the Securities Act of 1933, must also file annual and other reports with the Commission. Such applications and reports must contain financial and other data prescribed by the Commission as necessary or appropriate for the protection of investors and to issue fair dealing. In addition, the solicitation of proxies, authorizations, or consents from holders of such registered securities must be made in accordance with rules and regulations prescribed by the commission. These rules provide for disclosures to securities holders of information relevant to the subject matter of the solicitation.

Disclosure of the holdings and transactions by officers, directors, and large (10 percent) holders of equity securities of companies is also required, and any and all persons who acquire more than 5 percent of certain equity securities are required to file detailed information with the Commission and any exchange upon which such securities may be traded. Moreover, any person making a tender offer for certain classes of equity securities is required to file reports with the Commission, if as a result of the tender offer such person would own more than 5 percent of the outstanding shares of the particular class of equity involved. The Commission also is authorized to promulgate rules governing the repurchase by a corporate issuer of its own securities.

REGULATION OF MUTUAL FUNDS AND OTHER INVESTMENT COMPANIES

The Investment Company Act of 1940 (15 U.S.C. 80a–1-80a-64) requires investment companies to register with the Commission and regulates their activities to protect investors. The regulation covers sales and management fees, composition of boards of directors, and capital structure. The act prohibits investment companies from engaging in various transactions, including transactions with affiliated persons unless the Commission first determines that such transactions are fair. In addition, the act provides a somewhat parallel but less stringent regulation of business development companies. Under the act, the Commission may institute court action to enjoin the consummation of mergers and other plans for reorganization of investment companies if such plans are unfair to security holders. It also may impose sanctions by administrative proceedings against investment company managements for violations of the act and other federal securities laws, and file court actions to enjoin acts and practices of management officials involving breaches of fiduciary duty involving personal misconduct and to disqualify such officials from office.

REGULATION OF COMPANIES CONTROLLING UTILITIES

The Public Utility Holding Company Act of 1935 (15 U.S.C. 79–79z-6) provides for regulation by the commission of the purchase and sale of securities and assets by companies in electric and gas utility holding company systems, their intra-system transactions and service and management arrangements. It limits holding companies to a single coordinated utility system and requires simplification of complex corporate and capital structures and elimination of unfair distribution of voting power among holders of system securities.

The issuance and sale of securities by holding companies and their subsidiaries, unless exempt (subject to conditions and terms which the Commission is empowered to impose) as an issue expressly authorized by the state commission in the state in which the issuer is incorporated, must be found by the Commission to meet statutory standards.

The purchase and sale of utility properties and other assets may not be made in contravention of rules, regulations, or orders of the Commission regarding the consideration to be received, maintenance of competitive conditions, fees and commissions, accounts, disclosure of interest, and similar matters. In passing upon proposals for reorganization, merger, or consolidation, the Commission must be satisfied that the objectives of the act generally are complied with and that the terms of the proposal are fair and equitable to all classes of security holders affected.

REGULATION OF INVESTMENT ADVISERS

The Investment Advisers Act of 1940 (15 U.S.C. 80b–1–80b–21) provides that persons who, for compensation, engage in the business of advising others with respect to their security transactions must register with the Commission. The act prohibits certain types of fee arrangements, makes unlawful practices of investment advisers involving fraud or deceit, and requires, among other things, disclosure of any adverse interests the advisers may have in transactions executed for clients. The act authorizes the Commission, by rule, to define fraudulent and deceptive practices and prescribe means to prevent those practices.

REHABILITATION OF FAILING CORPORATIONS

Chapter 11, section 1109(a), of the Bankruptcy Code (11 U.S.C. 1109) provides for Commission participation as a statutory party in corporate reorganization proceedings administered in Federal courts. The principal functions of the Commission are to protect the interests of public investors involved in such cases through efforts to ensure their adequate representation and to participate on legal and policy issues which are of concern to public investors generally.

REPRESENTATION OF DEBT SECURITIES

The interests of purchasers of publicly offered debt securities issued pursuant to trust indentures are safeguarded under the provisions of the Trust Indenture Act of 1939 (15 U.S.C. 77aaa–77bbb). This act, among other things, requires the exclusion from such indentures of certain types of exculpatory clauses and the inclusion of certain protective provisions. The independence of the indenture trustee, who is a representative of the debt holder, is assured by proscribing certain relationships that might conflict with the proper exercise of his duties (15 U.S.C. 77aaa–77bbbb).

ENFORCEMENT ACTIVITIES

The Commission's enforcement activities are designed to secure compliance with the federal securities laws administered by the Commission and the rules and regulations adopted thereunder. These activities include measures to compel obedience to the disclosure requirements of the registration and other provisions of the acts; to prevent fraud and deception in the purchase and sale of securities; to obtain court orders enjoining acts and practices that operate as a fraud upon investors or otherwise violate the laws; to suspend or revoke the registrations of brokers, dealers, investment companies and investment advisers who willfully engage in such acts and practices; to suspend or bar from association persons associated with brokers, dealers, investment companies and investment advisers who have violated any provision of the federal securities laws; and to prosecute persons who have engaged in fraudulent activities, or other willful violations of those laws. In addition, attorneys, accountants, and other professionals who violate the securities laws face possible loss of their privilege to practice before the commission. To this end, private investigations are conducted into complaints or other evidences of securities violations. Evidence thus established of law violations is used in appropriate administrative proceedings to revoke registration or in actions instituted in federal courts to restrain or enjoin such activities. Where the evidence tends to establish fraud or other willful violation of the securities laws, the facts are referred to the Attorney General for criminal prosecution of the offenders. The commission may assist in such prosecutions.

SOURCES OF INFORMATION

Consumer Activities Publications detailing the Commission's activities, which include material of assistance to the potential investor, are available from the Publications Unit. In addition, the Office of Filings, Information and Consumer Services answers questions from investors, assists investors with specific problems regarding their relations with broker-dealers and companies, and advises the Commission and other offices and divisions regarding problems frequently encountered by investors and possible regulatory solutions to such problems. Phone, 202-272-7440.

INVESTOR INFORMATION AND PROTECTION

Complaints and inquiries may be directed to the home office or to any regional office. Registration statements and other public documents filed with the Commission are available for public inspection in the public reference room at the home office. Much of the information also is available in its New York and Chicago regional offices. Copies of the public material may be purchased from the Commission's contract copying service at prescribed rates.

Small Business Activities Information on security laws which pertain to small businesses in relation to securities offerings may be obtained from the Commission. Phone, 202-272-2644.

Reading Rooms The Commission maintains a public reference room (phone, 202-272-7450) and also a library (phone, 202-272-2618) where additional information may be obtained.

REGIONAL OFFICES (Securities and Exchange Commission)

Region	Address
1. New York, New Jersey	75 Park Place, New York, NY 10007 Phone: 212-264-1636
2. Maine, Vermont, New Hampshire, Massachusetts, Connecticut, Rhode Island	90 Devonshire Street, Boston, MA 02109 Phone: 617-223-9900
3. Tennessee, North Carolina, South Carolina, Mississippi, Alabama, Georgia, Florida, Louisiana (southeastern portion only), Virgin Islands	3475 Lenox Road NE, Atlanta, GA 30326 Phone: 404-347-4768
4. Minnesota, Wisconsin, Michigan, Iowa, Missouri, Illinois, Indiana, Ohio, Kentucky	219 S. Dearborn Street, Chicago, IL 60604 Phone: 312-353-7390
5. Kansas, Oklahoma, Texas, Arkansas, Louisiana (except southeastern portion)	411 W. 7th Street, Fort Worth, TX 76102 Phone: 817-334-3821
6. North Dakota, South Dakota, Colorado, Utah, Wyoming, New Mexico	1801 California Street, Denver, CO 80202 Phone: 303-391-6800
7. California, Nevada, Arizona, Hawaii, Guam	5757 Wilshire Boulevard, Los Angeles, CA 90036 Phone: 213-965-3998
8. Washington, Oregon, Alaska, Montana, Idaho	915 Second Avenue, Seattle, WA 98174 Phone: 206-442-7990
9. Pennsylvania, West Virginia, Virginia, Maryland, Delaware, Washington, D.C.	601 Walnut St., Philadelphia, PA 19106 Phone: 215-597-3100

How to Read a Financial Report

If you are a certified public accountant it is most unlikely that you can learn anything from reading this book. You don't need to be told the basics of understanding what's presented in corporate annual reports. If you aren't a certified public accountant, and you find that annual reports are "over your head," this booklet can help you to grasp the facts contained in such reports and possibly become a better informed investor. That is our principal aim in publishing this booklet, but we also hope that it will be useful to other readers who want to understand how business works and to learn more about the companies that provide them with goods and services or that offer them employment.

Most annual reports can be broken down into three sections: the Executive Letter, the Business Review, and the Financial Review. The Executive Letter gives a broad overview of the company's business and financial performance. The Business Review summarizes recent developments, trends, and objectives of the company. The Financial Review is where business performance is quantified in dollars. This is the section we intend to clarify.

The Financial Review has two major parts: Discussion and Analysis, and Audited Financial Statements. A third part might include information supplemental to the Financial Statements.

In the Discussion and Analysis, management explains changes in operating results from year to year. This explanation is presented mainly in a narrative format, with charts and graphs highlighting the comparisons. The operating results are numerically captured and presented in the Financial Statements.

The principal components of the Financial Statements are the balance sheet; income statement; statement of changes in shareholders' equity; statement of cash flows; and footnotes. The balance sheet portrays the financial strength of the company by showing what the company owns and what it owes on a certain date. The balance sheet can be thought of as a snapshot photograph since it reports on financial position as of the end of the year. The income statement, on the other hand, is like a motion picture since it reports on how the company performed during the year and shows whether operations have resulted in a profit or loss. The statement of changes in shareholders' equity reconciles the activity in the equity section of the balance sheet from year to year. Common changes in equity result from company profits or losses, dividends, or stock issuances. The statement of cash flows reports on the movement of cash by the company for the year. The footnotes provide more detailed information on the balance sheet and income statement.

This booklet will focus on illustrating the basic financial statements and footnotes presented in annual reports in accordance with current practice. It will also include examples of financial methods used by investors to better analyze financial statements. In order to provide a framework for illustration, we will invent a company. It will be a public company (one whose shares are freely traded on the open market). The reason for choosing a public company is that it is required to provide the most extensive amount of information in its annual reports in accordance with guidelines issued by the Securities and Exchange Commission (SEC). Our company will represent a typical corporation with the most commonly used accounting and reporting practices. We'll call our company Typical Manufacturing Company, Inc.

A Few Words Before We Begin

The following four pages show a sample Balance Sheet, Income Statement, Statement of Changes in Shareholders' Equity, and a Statement of Cash Flows. These are the statements we will discuss in the first section. To simplify matters, we did not illustrate the Discussion and Analysis nor did we present examples of the Executive Letter or Business Review. In our sample statements, we've presented two years of financial results on the balance sheet and income statement and one year of activity on the statement of changes in shareholders' equity and statement of cash flows. This was also done for ease of illustration. Were we to comply with SEC requirements, we would have had to report the last three years of activity in the Income Statement, Statement of Changes in Shareholders' Equity, and Statement of Cash Flows. Further SEC requirements that we did not illustrate include: presentation of selected quarterly financial data for the past two years, business segment information for the last three years, a listing of company directors and executive officers, and the market price of the company's common stock for each quarterly period within the two most recent fiscal years.

TYPICAL MANUFACTURING COMPANY INC.
CONSOLIDATED BALANCE SHEET
DECEMBER, 19X9 & 19X8 (DOLLARS IN THOUSANDS)

	19X9	19X8
ASSETS		
CURRENT ASSETS		
CASH	$20,000	$15,000
MARKETABLE SECURITIES AT COST WHICH APPROXIMATES MARKET VALUE	40,000	32,000
ACCOUNTS RECEIVABLE - LESS ALLOWANCE FOR DOUBTFUL ACCTS 19X9 $2,375, 19X8 $3,000	156,000	145,000
INVENTORIES	180,000	185,000
	4,000	3,000
		$380,000

Typical
Manufacturing
Company Inc.

Consolidated Balance Sheet

December 31,19X9 and 19X8 *(dollars in thousands)*

Assets	**19X9**	19X8
Current assets		
Cash	**$ 20,000**	$ 15,000
Marketable securities at cost which approximates market value	**40,000**	32,000
Accounts receivable less allowance for doubtful accounts: 19X9: $2,375, 19X8: $3,000	**156,000**	145,000
Inventories	**180,000**	185,000
Prepaid expenses and other current assets	**4,000**	3,000
Total current assets	**$400,000**	$380,000
Property, plant and equipment		
Land	**$ 30,000**	$ 30,000
Buildings	**125,000**	118,500
Machinery	**200,000**	171,100
Leasehold improvements	**15,000**	15,000
Furniture, fixtures, etc.	**15,000**	12,000
Total property, plant and equipment	**$385,000**	$346,600
Less accumulated depreciation	**$125,000**	$97,000
Net property, plant and equipment	**$260,000**	$249,600
Intangibles (goodwill, patents)—less amortization	**$2,000**	$2,000
Total assets	**$662,000**	$631,600

See accompanying notes to consolidated financial statements.

Typical
Manufacturing
Company Inc.

December 31,19X9 and19X8 *(dollars in thousands)*

Liabilities	19X9	19X8
Current liabilities		
Accounts payable	**$ 60,000**	$ 57,000
Notes payable	**51,000**	61,000
Accrued expenses	**30,000**	36,000
Income taxes payable	**17,000**	15,000
Other liabilities	**12,000**	12,000
Total current liabilities	**$170,000**	$181,000
Long-term liabilities		
Deferred income taxes	**$ 16,000**	$ 9,000
12.5% Debentures payable 2010	**130,000**	130,000
Other long-term debt	**0**	6,000
Total liabilities	**$316,000**	$326,000

Shareholders' Equity		
Preferred stock $5.83 cumulative, $100 par value authorized, issued and outstanding 60,000 shares	**$ 6,000**	$ 6,000
Common stock $5.00 par value, authorized 20,000,000 shares, 19X9 issued 15,000,000 shares, 19X8 14,500,000 shares	**75,000**	72,500
Additional paid-in capital	**20,000**	13,500
Retained earnings	**249,000**	219,600
Foreign currency translation adjustments	**1,000**	(1,000)
Less: Treasury stock at cost (19X9–1,000; 19X8–1,000 shares)	**5,000**	5,000
Total shareholders' equity	**$346,000**	$305,600
Total liabilities and shareholders' equity	**$662,000**	$631,600

See accompanying notes to consolidated financial statements.

Typical
Manufacturing
Company Inc.

Consolidated Income Statement

Years ended December 31, 19X9 and 19X8 *(dollars in thousands)*	**19X9**	19X8
Net sales	**$765,000**	$725,000
Cost of sales	**535,000**	517,000
Gross margin	**$230,000**	$208,000
Operating expenses		
Depreciation and amortization	**28,000**	25,000
Selling, general and administrative expenses	**96,804**	109,500
Operating income	**$105,196**	$73,500
Other income (expense)		
Dividends and interest income	**5,250**	9,500
Interest expense	**(16,250)**	(16,250)
Income before income taxes and extraordinary loss	**$94,196**	$66,750
Income taxes	**41,446**	26,250
Income before extraordinary loss	**$52,750**	$40,500
Extraordinary item: Loss on early extinguishment of debt (net of income tax benefit of $750)	**(5,000)**	—
Net income	**$47,750**	$40,500
Common shares outstanding	**$14,999,000**	$14,499,000
Earnings per common share before extraordinary loss	**$3.49**	$2.77
Earnings per share—extraordinary loss	**(.33)**	—
Net income (per common share)	**$3.16**	$2.77

Consolidated Statement Of Changes In Shareholders' Equity

Year ended December 31, 19X9 *(dollars in thousands)*

	Preferred Stock	**Common Stock**	**Additional Paid-in Capital**	**Retained Earnings**	**Foreign Currency Translation Adjustment**	**Treasury Stock**	**Total**
Balance January 1, 19X9	$6,000	$72,500	$13,500	$219,600	($1,000)	($5,000)	$305,600
Net income				47,750			47,750
Dividends paid on:							
preferred stock				(350)			(350)
common stock				(18,000)			(18,000)
Common stock issued		$2,500	$6,500				$9,000
Translation gain					$2,000		2,000
Balance December 31, 19X9	**$6,000**	**$75,000**	**$20,000**	**$249,000**	**$1,000**	**($5,000)**	**$346,000**

See accompanying notes to consolidated financial statements.

Typical
Manufacturing
Company Inc.

Consolidated Statement Of Cash Flows

Year ended December 31, 19X9 *(dollars in thousands)*

Cash flows from operating activities:	
Net income	**$47,750**
Adjustments to reconcile net income to net cash from operating activities:	
Depreciation and amortization	**$28,000**
Increase in marketable securities	**(8,000)**
Increase in accounts receivable	**(11,000)**
Decrease in inventory	**5,000**
Increase in prepaid expenses and other current assets	**(1,000)**
Increase in deferred taxes	**7,000**
Increase in accounts payable	**3,000**
Decrease in accrued expenses	**(6,000)**
Increase in income taxes payable	**2,000**
Total Adjustments	**$19,000**
Net Cash Provided by Operating Activities	**$66,750**
Cash Flows from Investing Activities:	
Purchase of fixed assets	**($38,400)**
Net Cash Used in Investing Activities	**($38,400)**
Cash Flows from Financing Activities:	
Decrease in notes payable	**($10,000)**
Decrease in other long-term debt	**(6,000)**
Proceeds from issuance of common stock	**9,000**
Payment of dividends	**(18,350)**
Net Cash Used in Financing Activities	**($25,350)**
Effect of Exchange Rate Changes on Cash	**$2,000**
Increase in Cash	**$5,000**
Cash at beginning of year	**15,000**
Cash at end of year	**$20,000**

Income tax payments totaled $3,000 in 19X9.
Interest payments totaled $16,250 in 19X9.
See accompanying notes to consolidated financial statements.

The Balance Sheet

(dollars in thousands except per-share amounts)

The balance sheet represents the financial picture as it stood on one particular day, December 31, 19X9, as though the wheels of the company were momentarily at a standstill. Typical Manufacturing's balance sheet not only includes the most recent year, but also the previous year. This lets you compare how the company fared in its most recent years.

The balance sheet is divided into two sides: on the left are shown assets; on the right are shown liabilities and shareholders' equity. Both sides are always in balance. Each asset, liability, and component of shareholders' equity reported in the balance sheet represents an "account" having a dollar amount or "balance." In the assets column, we list all the goods and property owned, as well as claims against others yet to be collected. Under liabilities we list all debts due. Under shareholders' equity we list the amount shareholders would split up if Typical were liquidated at its balance sheet value.

Assume that the corporation goes out of business on the date of the balance sheet. If that occurs, the illustration which follows shows you what Typical Manufacturing's shareholders might expect to receive as their portion of the business.

Total assets (Less: intangibles)	**$660,000**
Amount required to pay liabilities	**316,000**
Amount remaining for the shareholders	**$344,000**

Now, we are going to give you a guided tour of the balance sheet's accounts. We'll define each item, one by one, and explain how they work.

Assets

Current Assets

In general, current assets include cash and those assets which in the normal course of business will be turned into cash in the reasonably near future, i.e., generally within a year from the date of the balance sheet.

Cash

This is just what you would expect—bills and coins in the till (petty cash fund) and money on deposit in the bank.

1 Cash	**$20,000**

Marketable securities

This asset represents investment of excess or idle cash that is not needed immediately. In Typical's case it is invested in preferred stock. Because these funds may be needed on short notice, it is essential that the securities be readily marketable and subject to a minimum of price fluctuation. The general practice is to show marketable securities at cost or market, whichever is lower.

2 Marketable securities at cost which approximates market value	**$40,000**

Accounts receivable

Here we find the amount due from customers but not yet collected. When goods due are shipped prior to collection, a receivable is recorded. Customers are usually given 30, 60, or 90 days in which to pay. The amount due from customers is $158,375. However, experience shows that some customers fail to pay their bills, because of financial difficulties or some catastrophic event (a tornado, a hurricane, or a flood) befalling their business. Therefore, in order to show the accounts receivable item at a figure representing expected receipts, the total is after a provision for doubtful accounts. This year that debt reserve was $2,375.

3 Accounts receivable—less allowance for doubtful accounts of $2,375	**$156,000**

Inventories

The inventory of a manufacturer is composed of three groups: raw materials to be used in the product, partially finished goods in process of manufacture, and finished goods ready for shipment to customers. The generally accepted method of valuation of the inventory is *cost or market, whichever is lower*. This gives a conservative figure. Where this method is used, the value for balance sheet purposes will be cost, or perhaps less than cost if, as a result of deterioration, obsolescence, decline in prices, or other factors, less than cost can be realized on the inventory. Inventory valuation includes an allocation of production and other expenses, as well as the cost of materials.

4 Inventories	**$180,000**

Consolidated Balance Sheet

	December 31, 19X9 and 19X8 (dollars in thousands)		
	Assets	**19X9**	**19X8**
	Current Assets		
1	Cash	**$ 20,000**	$ 15,000
2	Marketable securities at cost which approximates market value	**40,000**	32,000
3	Accounts receivable—less allowance for doubtful accounts: 19X9: $2,375, 19X8: $3,000	**156,000**	145,000
4	Inventories	**180,000**	185,000
5	Prepaid expenses and other current assets	**4,000**	3,000
6	**Total current assets**	**$400,000**	$380,000
	Property, plant and equipment		
	Land	**$ 30,000**	$ 30,000
	Building	**125,000**	118,500
	Machinery	**200,000**	171,100
	Leasehold improvements	**15,000**	15,000
	Furniture, fixtures, etc.	**15,000**	12,000
7	**Total property, plant and equipment**	**$385,000**	$346,600
8	Less accumulated depreciation	**$125,000**	$97,000
9	**Net property, plant and equipment**	**$260,000**	$249,600
10	Intangibles (goodwill, patents)—less amortization	**$2,000**	$2,000
11	**Total assets**	**$662,000**	$631,600

Prepaid expenses

Prepaid expenses may arise for a situation such as this: During the year, Typical prepaid fire insurance premiums and advertising charges for the next year. Those insurance premiums and advertising services are as yet unused at the balance sheet date, so there exists an unexpended item, which will be used up over the next 12 months. If the advance payments had not been made, the company would have more cash in the bank. So payments made in advance from which the company has not yet received benefits, but for which it will receive benefits next year, are listed among current assets as prepaid expenses.

5 Prepaid expenses and other current assets	**$4,000**

Deferred charges for such items as the introduction of a new product to the market, or for moving a plant to a new location, represent a type of asset similar to prepaid expenses. However, deferred charges are not included in current assets because the benefit from such expenditure will be reaped over several years to come. So the expenditure incurred will be gradually written off over the next several years, rather than fully charged off in the year payment is made. Our balance sheet shows no deferred charges because Typical has none. If it had, they would normally be included just before intangibles on the asset side of the ledger.

To summarize, the *total current assets* item includes primarily: cash, marketable securities, accounts receivable, inventories, and prepaid expenses.

6 Total current assets	**$400,000**

You will observe that these assets are mostly *working assets* in the sense that they are in a constant cycle of being converted into cash. Inventories, when sold, become accounts receivable; receivables, upon collection, become cash; cash is used to pay debts and running expenses. We will discover later in the booklet how to make current assets tell a story.

Property, Plant and Equipment

Property, plant and equipment represents those assets not intended for sale that are used over and over again in order to manufacture, display, warehouse, and transport the product. This category includes land, buildings, machinery, equipment, furniture, automobiles, and trucks. The generally accepted and approved method for valuation is *cost minus the depreciation accumulated* by the date of the balance sheet. Depreciation is discussed in the next section.

Property, plant and equipment	
Land	**$ 30,000**
Buildings	**125,000**
Machinery	**200,000**
Leasehold Improvements	**15,000**
Furniture, fixtures, etc.	**15,000**
7 Total property, plant & equipment	**$385,000**

The figure displayed is not intended to reflect market value at present or replacement cost in the future. While it is recognized that the cost to replace plant and equipment at some future date might be higher, that possible cost is obviously variable. For this reason, up to now, most companies have followed a general rule: *acquisition cost less accumulated depreciation based on that cost.*

Depreciation

Depreciation is the practice of allocating the cost of a fixed asset over its useful life. This has been defined for accounting purposes as the decline in useful value of a fixed asset due to wear and tear from use and passage of time.

The cost incurred to acquire the property, plant and equipment must be spread over the expected useful life, taking into consideration the factors discussed above. For example: Suppose a delivery truck costs $10,000 and is expected to last five years. Using a "straight-line" method of depreciation, $2,000 of the truck's cost is allocated to each year's income statement. The balance sheet at the end of one year would show:

Truck (cost)	**$10,000**
Less accumulated depreciation	**2,000**
Net depreciated value	**$ 8,000**

At the end of the second year it would show:

Truck (cost)	**$10,000**
Less accumulated depreciation	**4,000**
Net depreciated value	**$ 6,000**

In our sample balance sheet, a figure is shown for accumulated depreciation. This amount is the total of accumulated depreciation for buildings, machinery, leasehold improvements, and furniture and fixtures. Land is not subject to depreciation, and its listed value remains unchanged from year to year.

8 Less accumulated depreciation	**$125,000**

Thus, *net property, plant and equipment* is the valuation for balance sheet purposes of the investment in property, plant and equipment. As explained before, it consists of the cost of the various assets in this classification, less the depreciation accumulated to the date of the financial statement.

9 Net property, plant and equipment	**$260,000**

Depletion is a term used primarily by mining and oil companies or any of the so-called extractive industries. Since Typical Manufacturing is not in the mining business, we do not show depletion on the balance sheet. To deplete means to exhaust or use up. As the oil or other natural resource is used up or sold, a depletion reserve is set up to compensate for the natural wealth the company no longer owns.

Intangibles

These may be defined as assets having no physical existence, yet having substantial value to the company. Examples? A franchise to a cable TV company allowing exclusive service in certain areas, or a patent for exclusive manufacture of a specific article. It should be noted, however, that only intangibles purchased from other companies are shown on the balance sheet.

Another intangible asset sometimes found in corporate balance sheets is *goodwill*, which represents the amount by which the price of acquired companies exceeds the related values of net assets acquired. Company practices vary considerably in assigning value to this asset. Accounting rules now require one firm that buys another to write off the goodwill over a period not exceeding 40 years.

10 Intangibles (goodwill, patents) less amortization	**$2,000**

All of these items added together produce the figure listed on the balance sheet as *total assets.*

11 Total assets	**$662,000**

Liabilities

	Consolidated Balance Sheet		
	December 31, 19X9 and 19X8 **Liabilities**	**19X9**	19X8
	Current Liabilities		
12	Accounts payable	**$ 60,000**	$ 57,000
13	Notes payable	**51,000**	61,000
14	Accrued expenses	**30,000**	36,000
15	Income taxes payable	**17,000**	15,000
16	Other liabilities	**12,000**	12,000
17	**Total current liabilities**	**$170,000**	$181,000
	Long-term liabilities		
18	Deferred income taxes	**$ 16,000**	$ 9,000
19	12.5% Debentures payable 2010	**130,000**	130,000
20	Other long-term debt	**0**	6,000
21	**Total liabilities**	**$316,000**	$326,000
	Shareholders' Equity		
22	Preferred stock $5.83 cumulative, $100 par value, authorized, issued and outstanding 60,000 shares	**$ 6,000**	$ 6,000
23	Common stock $5.00 par value, authorized 20,000,000 shares, issued 19X9 15,000,000 shares, 19X8 14,500,000 shares	**75,000**	72,500
24	Additional paid-in capital	**20,000**	13,500
25	Retained earnings	**249,000**	219,600
26	Foreign currency translation adjustments	**1,000**	(1,000)
27	Less: Treasury stock at cost (19X9–1,000; 19X8–1,000)	**5,000**	5,000
28	**Total shareholders' equity**	**$346,000**	$305,600
29	**Total liabilities and shareholders' equity**	**$662,000**	$631,600

Current Liabilities

This item generally includes all debts that fall due within 12 months. The *current assets* item is a companion to *current liabilities* because current assets are the source from which payments are made on current debts. The relationship between the two is one of the most revealing things to be learned from the balance sheet, and we will go into that later. For now, we need to define the subgroups within current liabilities.

Accounts payable

The *accounts payable* item represents amounts the company owes to its regular business creditors from whom it has bought goods or services on open account.

12 Accounts payable	**$ 60,000**

Notes payable

If money is owed to a bank, individual, corporation, or other lender, it appears on the balance sheet under *notes payable* as evidence that a promissory note has been given by the borrower.

13 Notes payable	**$ 51,000**

Accrued expenses

Now we have defined accounts payable as the amounts owed by the company to its regular business creditors. The company also owes, on any given day, salaries and wages to its employees, interest on funds borrowed from banks and from bondholders, fees to attorneys, insurance premiums, pensions, and similar items. To the extent that the amounts owed and not recorded on the books are unpaid at the date of the balance sheet, these expenses are grouped as a total under *accrued expenses*.

14 Accrued expenses	**$ 30,000**

Income tax payable

The debt due to the various taxing authorities such as the Internal Revenue Service is the same as any other liability under *accrued expenses*. But because of the amount and the importance of the tax factor, it is generally stated separately as *income taxes payable*.

15 Income taxes payable	**$17,000**

Other Liabilities

Simply stated, *other liabilities* includes all liabilities not captured in the specific categories presented.

16 Other liabilities	**$12,000**

Total current liabilities

Finally, the *total current liabilities* item sums up all of the items listed under this classification.

17 Total current liabilities	**$170,000**

Long-term Liabilities

In the matter of current liabilities, you will recall that we included debts due within one year from the balance sheet date. Here, under the heading of *long-term liabilities* are listed debts due after one year from the date of the financial report.

Deferred income taxes

One of the long-term liabilities on our sample balance sheet is *deferred income taxes.* The government provides businesses with tax incentives to make certain kinds of investments that will benefit the economy as a whole. For instance, a company can take accelerated depreciation deductions for investments in plant and equipment. These rapid write-offs in the early years of investment reduce what the company would otherwise owe in current taxes, but at some point in the future the taxes must be paid. Companies include a charge for deferred taxes in their tax calculations on the income statement and show what taxes would be without the accelerated write-offs. That charge then accumulates as a long-term liability on the balance sheet.

18 Deferred income taxes	**$16,000**

Debentures

The other long-term liability on our balance sheet is the *12.5% debentures* due in 2010. The money was received by the company as a loan from the bondholders, who in turn were given a certificate called a bond, as evidence of the loan. The bond is really a formal promissory note issued by the company, which in this case agreed to repay the debt at maturity in 2010 and also agreed to pay interest at the rate of 12.5% per year. Bond interest is usually payable semiannually. Typical's bond issue is called a debenture because the bonds are backed by the general credit of the corporation rather than by the company's assets. Debentures are the most common type of bond issued by large, well-established corporations today.

Companies can also issue *first mortgage bonds,* which offer bondholders an added safeguard because they are secured by a mortgage on all or some of the company's property. First mortgage bonds are considered one of the highest grade investments because they give investors an undisputed claim on company earnings and the greatest safety. If the company is unable to pay off the bonds in cash when they are due, holders of first mortgage bonds have a claim or lien before other creditors (such as debenture holders) on the mortgaged assets, which may be sold and the proceeds used to satisfy the debt.

19 12.5% Debentures payable 2010	**$130,000**

Other long-term debt

Other *long-term debt* includes all debt other than what is specifically reported on in the balance sheet. In the case of Typical, this debt was extinguished in 1989.

20 Other long-term debt	**0**

Total liabilities

Current and long-term debt are summed together to produce the figure listed on the balance sheet as *total liabilities.*

21 Total liabilities	**$316,000**

Shareholders' Equity

This item is the total equity interest that all shareholders have in this corporation. In other words, it is the corporation's net worth after subtracting all liabilities. This is separated for legal and accounting reasons into the categories discussed below.

Capital Stock

In the broadest sense this represents shares in the proprietary interest in the company. These shares are represented by the stock certificates issued by the corporation to its shareholders. A corporation may issue several different classes of shares, each class having slightly different attributes.

Preferred Stock

These shares have some preference over other shares with respect to dividends and in distribution of assets in case of liquidation. Specific provisions can be obtained from a corporation's charter. In Typical, the preferred stock is a $5.83 *cumulative $100 par value,* which means that each share is entitled to $5.83 in dividends a year, before any dividends are paid to the common shareholders. Cumulative means that if in any year the dividend is not paid, it accumulates in favor of the preferred shareholders and must be paid to them when available and declared before any dividends are distributed on the common stock. Sometimes preferred shareholders have no voice in company affairs unless the company fails to pay them dividends at the promised rate.

22	**Preferred stock $5.83 cumulative, $100 par value, authorized issued and outstanding 60,000 shares**	**$6,000**

Common Stock

Each year before common shareholders receive any dividends, preferred holders are entitled to $5.83 per share, but no more. Common stock has no such limit on dividends payable each year. In good times, when earnings are high, dividends may also be high. And when earnings drop, so may dividends.

23	**Common stock $5.00 par value authorized 20,000,000 shares, issued 15,000,000 shares**	**$75,000**

Additional Paid-In Capital

This is the amount paid in by shareholders over the par or legal value of each share. Typical's common stock has a par value of $5.00 per share. In 1989, Typical sold 500,000 shares of stock for a total of $9,000. The $9,000 was allocated on the balance sheet between capital stock and additional paid-in capital. 500,000 shares at a par value of $5.00 for a total of $2,500 was allocated to common stock. The remaining $6,500 was allocated to additional paid-in capital.

23	**Common stock $5.00 par value authorized 20,000,000 shares issued 15,000,000 shares**	**$75,000**
24	**Additional paid-in capital**	**$20,000**
	Total of capital stock (common) and additional paid-in capital	**$95,000**

Retained Earnings

When a company first starts in business, it has no retained earnings. Retained earnings accumulate as the company earns profits and reinvests or "retains" profits in the company. In other words, retained earnings increase by the amount of profits earned, less dividends declared to shareholders. At the end of its first year, if profits are $80,000 and dividends of $30,000 are paid on the preferred stock but no dividends are declared on the common, the balance sheet will show retained earnings of $50,000. In the second year, if profits are $140,000 and Typical pays $30,000 in dividends on the preferred and $40,000 on the common, the accumulated retained earnings will be $120,000:

Balance at the end of the first year	**$ 50,000**
Net profit for second year	**140,000**
Total	**$190,000**
Less: all dividends	**70,000**
Retained earnings at the end of the second year	**$120,000**

The balance sheet for Typical shows the company has accumulated $249,000 in retained earnings.

25	**Retained earnings**	**$249,000**

Foreign Currency Translation Adjustments

When a company has an ownership interest in a foreign entity and the entity's results are to be captured in the company's consolidated financial statements, the *financial statements* of the foreign entity must be translated to U.S. dollars. Generally, the translation gain or loss should be reflected as a separate component of shareholders' equity called *foreign currency translation adjustment.* This adjustment should be distinguished from adjustments relating to *transactions* which are denominated in foreign currencies. The gain or loss in these cases should be included in a company's net income.

26	**Foreign currency translation adjustments**	**$1,000**

Treasury Stock

When a company reacquires its own stock, it is reported as *treasury stock* and is deducted from shareholders' equity. Of the cost and par methods of accounting, the former method is more commonly applied to treasury stock. Under the cost method, the cost of reacquired stock is deducted from shareholders' equity. Any dividends on shares held in the treasury should never be included as income.

27	**Treasury stock**	**$5,000**

The sum total of stock (net of treasury stock), additional paid-in capital, retained earnings and foreign currency translation adjustments, represents the *total shareholders' equity.*

28	**Total shareholders' equity**	**$346,000**

Just what does the balance sheet show?

In order to analyze balance sheet figures, investors look to certain financial statement ratios for guidance. One of their concerns is whether the business will be able to pay its debts when they come due. They are also interested in the company's inventory turnover and the amount of assets backing corporate securities (bonds, preferred and common stock), along with the relative mix of these securities. In the following section, we will discuss various ratios used for balance sheet analysis.

Net Working Capital

One very important thing to be learned from the balance sheet is *net working capital* or *net current assets,* sometimes called *working capital.* This is the difference between total current assets and total current liabilities. You will recall that current liabilities are debts generally due within one year from the date of the balance sheet. The source from which to pay those debts is current assets. Thus, working capital represents the amount that is left free and clear after all current debts are paid off. For Typical this is:

6	**Current assets**	**$400,000**
17	**Less: current liabilities**	**170,000**
	Working capital	**$230,000**

If you consider yourself a conservative investor, you should invest only in companies that maintain a comfortable amount of working capital. A company's ability to meet obligations, expand volume, and take advantage of opportunities is often determined by its working capital. Moreover, since you want your company to grow, this year's working capital should be larger than last year's.

Current Ratio

What is a comfortable amount of working capital? Analysts use several methods to judge whether a company has a sound working capital position. To help you interpret the current position of a company in which you are considering investing, the *current ratio* is more helpful than the dollar total of working capital. The first rough test for an industrial company is to compare the current assets figure with the total current liabilities. A current ratio of 2 to 1 is generally considered adequate. This means that for each $1 of current liabilities, there should be $2 in current assets.

To find the current ratio, divide current assets by current liabilities. In Typical's balance sheet:

6	**Current assets**	**$400,000**	**2.35**	**or 2.35 to 1**
17	**Current liabilities**	**$170,000**	**1**	

Thus, for each $1 of current liabilities, there is $2.35 in current assets to back it up.

There are so many different kinds of companies, however, that this test requires a great deal of modification if it is to be really helpful in analyzing companies in different industries. Generally, companies that have a small inventory and easily collectible accounts receivable can operate safely with a lower current ratio than those companies having a greater proportion of their current assets in inventory and selling their products on credit.

How Quick is Quick?

In addition to net working capital and current ratio, there are other ways of testing the adequacy of the current position. What are *quick assets*? They're the assets you have to cover a sudden emergency, assets you could take right away to the bank, if you had to. They are those current assets that are quickly convertible into cash. This leaves out merchandise inventories, because such inventories have yet to be sold and are not convertible into cash. Accordingly, quick assets are current assets minus inventories and prepaid expenses.

6	**Current assets**	**$400,000**
4	**Less: inventories**	**180,000**
5	**Less: prepaid expenses**	**4,000**
	Quick assets	**$216,000**

Net quick assets are found by taking the quick assets and subtracting the total current liabilities. A well-fixed industrial company should show a reasonable excess of quick assets over current liabilities. This provides a rigorous and important test of a company's ability to meet its obligations.

	Quick assets	**$216,000**
17	**Less: current liabilities**	**170,000**
	Net quick assets	**$ 46,000**

The *quick assets ratio* is found by dividing quick assets by current liabilities.

	Quick assets	**$216,000**	**1.3**	**or 1.3 to 1**
17	**Current liabilities**	**$170,000**	**1**	

As you see, for each $1 of current liabilities, there is $1.30 in quick assets available.

Debt to Equity

A certain level of debt is acceptable, but too much debt presents a hazardous signal to investors. The *debt-to-equity ratio* is an indicator of whether the company is excessively using debt for financing purposes. For Typical, the debt-to-equity ratio is computed as follows:

21	**Total liabilities**	**$316,000**	**= .91**
28	**Total shareholders' equity**	**$346,000**	

A debt-to-equity ratio of .91 means the company is using 91 cents of liabilities for every dollar of shareholders' equity in the business. Normally, industrial companies maintain a maximum of a 1 to 1 ratio, to keep debt at a level which is less than the investment level of the owners of the business. Utilities and financial companies can operate safely with much higher ratios.

Inventory Turnover

How big an inventory should a company have? That depends on a combination of many factors. An inventory is large or small depending upon the type of business and the time of the year. An automobile dealer, for example, with a large stock of autos at the height of the season is in a strong inventory position; yet that same inventory at the end of the season is a weakness in the dealer's financial condition.

One way to measure adequacy and balance of inventory is to compare it with sales for the year to get *inventory turnover*. Typical's sales for the year are $765,000, and inventory on the balance sheet date is $180,000. Thus turnover is 4.25 times (765÷ 180), meaning that goods are bought and sold out more than four times per year on average. (Strict accounting requires computation of inventory turnover by comparing annual *cost of goods sold* with *average inventory*. This information is not readily available in some published statements, so many analysts look instead for *sales* related to *inventory*.)

Inventory as a percentage of current assets is another comparison that may be made. In Typical, the inventory of $180,000 represents 45% of the total current assets, which amount to $400,000. But there is considerable variation between different types of companies, and thus the relationship is significant only when comparisons are made between companies in the same industry.

Book Value of Securities

The balance sheet will reveal *net book value* (the value on the company's books) or *net asset value* of the company's securities. This value represents the amount of corporate assets backing a bond or a common or preferred share. Here's how we calculate values for Typical's securities.

Net Asset Value Per Bond

To state this figure conservatively, intangible assets are subtracted as if they have no value on liquidation. Current liabilities of $170,000 are considered paid. This leaves $490,000 in assets to pay the bondholders. So, $3,769 in net asset value protects each $1,000 bond.

11	**Total assets**	**$662,000**
10	**Less: intangibles**	**2,000**
	Total tangible assets	**$660,000**
17	**Less: current liabilities**	**170,000**
	Net tangible assets available to meet bondholders' claims	**$490,000**

$490,000 / 130 (bonds outstanding) = $3,769 net asset value per $1,000 bond

Net Asset Value Per Share of Preferred Stock

To calculate net asset value of a preferred share, we take total assets, conservatively stated at $660,000 (eliminating $2,000 of intangible assets). Current liabilities of $170,000 and long-term liabilities are considered paid. This leaves $344,000 of assets protecting the preferred. So, $5,733 in net asset value backs each share of preferred.

11	**Total assets**	**$662,000**
10	**Less: intangibles**	**2,000**
	Total tangible assets	**$660,000**
17	**Less: current liabilities**	**$170,000**
18,19, & 20	**long-term liabilities**	**146,000**
	Net assets backing the preferred stock	**$344,000**

$344,000,000 / 60,000 (shares of preferred stock outstanding) = $5,733 net asset value per share of preferred stock

Net Book Value per Share of Common Stock

The net book value per share of common stock can be looked upon as meaning the amount of money each share would receive if the company were liquidated, based on balance-sheet values. Of course, the preferential shareholders would have to be satisfied first. The answer, $22.54 net book value per share of common stock, is arrived at as follows:

11	**Total assets**		**$662,000**
10	**Less: intangibles**		**2,000**
	Total tangible assets		**$660,000**
17	**Less: current liabilities**	**$170,000**	
18, 19, & 20	**long-term liabilities**	**146,000**	
22	**preferred stock**	**6,000**	
			$322,000
	Net assets available for the common stock		**$338,000**

$338,000,000 / 14,999,000 (shares of common stock outstanding) = $22.54 net asset value per share of common stock

An alternative method of arriving at the common shareholders' equity—conservatively stated at $338,000—is:

23	**Common stock**	**$ 75,000**
24	**Additional paid-in capital**	**20,000**
25	**Retained earnings**	**249,000**
26	**Foreign currency translation adjustments**	**1,000**
27	**Treasury stock**	**(5,000)**
		$340,000
10	**Less: intangible assets**	**(2,000)**
	Total common shareholders' equity	**$338,000**

$338,000,000 / 14,999,000 (shares of preferred stock outstanding) = $22.54 net book value per share of common stock

Do not be misled by book value figures, particularly of common stocks. Profitable companies often show a very low net book value and very substantial earnings. Railroads, on the other hand, may show a high book value for their common stock but have such low or irregular earnings that the stock's market price is much less than its book value. Insurance companies, banks, and investment companies are exceptions. Because their assets are largely liquid (cash, accounts receivable, and marketable securities), the book value of their common stock is sometimes a fair indication of market value.

Capitalization Ratio

The proportion of each kind of security issued by a company is the *capitalization ratio.* A high proportion of bonds sometimes reduces the attractiveness of both the preferred and common stock, and too much preferred can detract from the common's value. That's because bond interest must be paid before preferred dividends, and preferred dividends before common dividends.

To get Typical's *bond ratio* divide the face value of the bonds, $130,000, by the total value of bonds, preferred and common stock, additional paid-in capital, retained earnings, foreign currency translation adjustments and treasury stock, less intangibles, which is $474,000. This shows that bonds amount to about 27% of Typical's total capitalization.

19	**Debentures**	**$130,000**
22	**Preferred stock**	**6,000**
23	**Common stock**	**75,000**
24	**Additional paid-in capital**	**20,000**
25	**Retained earnings**	**249,000**
26	**Foreign currency translation adjustments**	**1,000**
27	**Treasury stock**	**(5,000)**
10	**Less: intangibles**	**(2,000)**
	Total capitalization	**$474,000**

The *preferred stock ratio* is found the same way—divide preferred stock of $6,000 by the entire capitalization of $474,000. The result is about 1%.

The *common stock ratio* will be the difference between 100% and the total of the bond and preferred stock ratio—or about 72%. The same result is reached by combining common stock, additional paid-in capital, retained earnings, foreign currency translation adjustments, and treasury stock.

		Amount	Ratio
19	**Debentures**	**$130,000**	**27%**
22	**Preferred stock**	**6,000**	**1%**
10 & 23 – 27	**Common stock (including additional paid-in capital, related earnings, and foreign currency translation adjustments less: treasury stock and intangibles)**	**338,000**	**72%**
	Total	**$474,000**	**100%**

The Income Statement

(dollars in thousands except per-share amounts)

Now, we come to the payoff for many potential investors: the income statement. It shows how much the corporation earned or lost during the year. It appears on Page 443 of this booklet.

While the balance sheet shows the fundamental soundness of a company by reflecting its financial position at a given date, the income statement may be of greater interest to investors because it shows the record of its operating activities for the whole year. It serves as a valuable guide in anticipating how the company may do in the future. The figure given for a single year is not nearly the whole story. The historical record for a series of years is more important than the figure of any single year. Typical includes two years in its statement and gives a ten-year financial summary as well, which appears on Page 464.

An income statement matches the amounts received from selling goods and services and other items of income against all the costs and outlays incurred in order to operate the company. The result is a *net income* or a *net loss* for the year. The costs incurred usually consist of cost of sales, overhead expenses such as wages and salaries, rent, supplies, depreciation; interest on money borrowed; and taxes.

Consolidated Income Statement

	Years ended December 31, 19X9 and 19X8 (dollars in thousands except per-share amounts)	19X9	19X8
30	Net sales	$765,000	$725,000
31	Cost of sales	535,000	517,000
32	Gross margin	$230,000	$208,000
	Operating Expenses		
33	Depreciation and amortization	28,000	25,000
34	Selling, general and administrative expenses	96,804	109,500
35	Operating income	$105,196	$73,500
	Other income (expense)		
36	Dividends and interest income	5,250	9,500
37	Interest expense	(16,250)	(16,250)
38	Income before income taxes and extraordinary loss	$94,196	$66,750
39	Income taxes	41,446	26,250
40	Income before extraordinary loss	$52,750	$40,500
41	Extraordinary item: Loss on early extinguishment of debt (net of income tax benefit of $750)	(5,000)	—
42	**Net income**	$47,750	$40,500
43	**Common shares outstanding**	$14,990,000	$14,499,000
44	Earnings per share of common stock before extraordinary loss	$3.49	$2.77
45	Earnings per share—extraordinary loss	(.33)	—
46	**Net income (per common share)**	$3.16	$2.77

Net Sales

The most important source of revenue always makes up the first item on the income statement. In Typical Manufacturing, it is *net sales.* It represents the primary source of money received by the company from its customers for goods sold or services rendered. The *net sales* item covers the amount received after taking into consideration returned goods and allowances for reduction of prices. By comparing 19X9 and 19X8, we can see if Typical had a better year in 19X9, or a worse one.

30 Net sales	$765,000	$725,000

Cost of Sales

In a manufacturing establishment, this represents all the costs incurred in the factory in order to convert raw materials into finished products. These costs are commonly known as product costs. Product costs are those costs which can be identified with the purchase or manufacture of goods made available for sale. There are three basic components of product cost: direct materials; direct labor; and manufacturing overhead. Direct materials and direct labor costs can be directly traced to the finished product. For example, for a furniture manufacturer, lumber would be a direct material cost and carpenter wages would be a direct labor cost. Manufacturing overhead costs, while associated with the manufacturing process, cannot be traceable to the finished product. Examples of manufacturing overhead costs are costs associated with operating the factory plant (plant depreciation, rent, electricity, supplies, maintenance and repairs, and production foremen salaries).

31 Cost of sales	$535,000

Gross Margin

Gross Margin is the excess of sales over cost of sales. It represents the residual profit from sales after considering product costs.

32 Gross margin	$230,000

Depreciation and amortization
Each year's decline in value of non-manufacturing facilities would be captured here. Amortization is the decline in useful value of an intangible, such as a 17-year patent.

33 Depreciation and amortization	**$28,000**

Selling, General, and Administrative Expenses
These expenses are generally grouped separately from cost of sales so that the reader of an income statement may see the extent of selling and administrative costs. They include salesmen's salaries and commissions, advertising and promotion, travel and entertainment, executives' salaries, office payroll and office expenses.

34 Selling, general and administrative expenses	**$96,804**

Subtracting all operating expenses from the net sales figure gives us the *operating income.*

35 Operating income	**$105,196**

An additional source of revenue comes from dividends and interest received by the company from its investment in stocks and bonds. This is listed separately under an item called *other income (expense).*

36 Dividends and interest income	**$5,250**

Interest Expense

The interest paid to bondholders for the use of their money is sometimes referred to as a *fixed charge* because the interest must be paid year after year whether the company is making money or losing money. Interest differs from dividends on stocks, which are payable only if the board of directors declares them.

Interest paid is another cost of doing business and is deductible from earnings in order to arrive at a base for the payment of income taxes.

Typical Manufacturing's debentures, carried on the balance sheet as a long-term liability, bear 12.5% interest per year on $130,000. Thus, the interest expense in the income statement is equal to $16,250 per year. It shows up under *other income (expense).*

37 Interest expense	**$16,250**

Income Taxes

Each corporation has a basic tax rate, which depends on the level and nature of its income. Large corporations like Typical Manufacturing are subject to the top corporate income tax rate, but tax credits tend to lower the overall tax rate. Typical's income before taxes is $94,196; the tax comes to $41,446.

38 Income before provision for income taxes	**$94,196**
39 Provision for income taxes	**41,446**

Income Before Extraordinary Loss
After we have taken into consideration all ordinary income (the plus factors) and deducted all ordinary costs (the minus factors), we arrive at *income before extraordinary loss* for the year.

40 Income before extraordinary loss	**$52,750**

Extraordinary Loss

Under ordinary conditions, the above income of $52,750 would be the end of the story. However, there are years in which companies experience unusual and infrequent events called *extraordinary items.* Examples of extraordinary items include debt extinguishments, tax loss carryforwards, pension plan terminations, and litigation settlements. In this case, Typical extinguished a portion of its debt early. This event is isolated on a separate line, net of its tax effect. Its earnings-per-share impact is also segregated from the earnings per share attributable to "normal" operations.

41 Loss on early extinguishment of debt (net of tax benefit of $750)	**($5,000)**

Net Income

Once all income and costs, including extraordinary items, are considered, we arrive at net income.

42	Net income	$47,750

Condensed, the income statement looks like this:

	Plus factors:	
30	Net sales	$765,000
36	Dividends and Interest	5,250
	Total	$770,250
	Minus factors:	
31	Cost of sales	$535,000
33–34	Operating expenses	124,804
37	Interest expense	16,250
39	Provision for income taxes	41,446
	Total	$717,500
40	Net income before extraordinary loss	$ 52,750
41	Extraordinary loss	(5,000)
42	Net income	$ 47,750

Other Items

Two other items that do not apply to Typical could appear on an income statement. First, U.S. companies that do business overseas may have transaction gains or losses related to fluctuations in foreign currency exchange rates.

Second, if a corporation owns more than 20% but less than 51% of the stock of a subsidiary company, the corporation must show its share of the subsidiary's earnings—minus any dividends received from the subsidiary—on its income statement. For example, if the corporation's share of the subsidiary's earnings is $1,200 and the corporation received $700 in dividends from the company, the corporation must include $500 on its income statement under the category *equity in the earnings of unconsolidated subsidiaries.* The corporation must also increase its investment in the company to the extent of the earnings it picks up on its income statement.

Analyzing the income statement

The income statement will tell us a lot more if we make a few detailed comparisons. Before you invest in a company, you want to know its *operating margin of profit* and how it has changed over the years. Typical had sales of $765,000,000 in 19X9 and showed $105,196,000 as the operating income.

35	$105,196 operating income	= 13.8%
30	$765,000 sales	

This means that for each dollar of sales 13.8¢ remained as a gross profit from operations. This figure is interesting but is more significant if we compare it with the profit margin last year.

35	$ 73,500 operating income	= 10.1%
30	$725,000 sales	

Typical's profit margin went from 10.1% to 13.8%, so business didn't just grow, *it became more profitable.* Changes in profit margin can reflect changes in efficiency, product line, or types of customers served.

We can also compare Typical with other companies in its field. If our company's profit margin is very low compared to others, it is an unhealthy sign. If it is high, there are grounds for optimism.

Analysts also frequently use *operating cost ratio* for the same purpose. Operating cost ratio is the complement of the margin of profit. Typical's profit margin is 13.8%. The operating cost ratio is 86.2%.

		Amount	Ratio
30	Net sales	$765,000	100.0%
31, 33, 34	Operating costs	659,804	86.2%
35	Operating income	$105,196	13.8%

Net profit ratio is still another guide to indicate how satisfactory the year's activities have been. In Typical Manufacturing, the year's net income was $47,750. The net sales for the year amounted to $765,000. Therefore, Typical's income was $47,750 on $765,000 of sales or:

42	**$ 47,750 net income**	=	**6.2%**
30	**$765,000 sales**		

This means that this year for every $1 of goods sold, 6.2¢ in profit ultimately went to the company. By comparing the net profit ratio from year to year for the same company and with other companies, we can best judge profit progress.

Last year, Typical's net income was $40,500 on $725,000 in sales:

42	**$ 40,500 net income**	=	**5.6%**
30	**$725,000 sales**		

We can compare the U.S. Department of Commerce's latest available average profit margins for all U.S. manufacturers to the profit margins calculated from Typical's 10-year summary on Page 464.

The margin of profit ratio, operating cost ratio, and net profit ratio, like all those we examined in connection with the balance sheet, give us general information about the company and help us judge its prospects for the future. All these comparisons have significance for the long term, because they tell us about the fundamental economic condition of the company. One question remains: are the securities a good investment for you now? For an answer, we must look at some additional factors.

Profit Margins (After Tax)

	19X3	19X4	19X5	19X6	19X7
Average of U.S. Manufacturers	4.1	4.6	3.8	3.8	4.9
Typical	6.1	5.3	5.0	5.1	5.5

Interest Coverage

The bonds of Typical Manufacturing represent a very substantial debt, but they are due many years in the future. The yearly interest, however, is a fixed charge, and we want to know how readily the company can pay the interest. More specifically, we would like to know whether the borrowed funds have been put to good use so that the earnings are ample and thus available to meet interest costs.

The available income representing the source for payment of the bond interest is $110,446 (operating profit plus dividends and interest). The annual bond interest amounts to $16,250. This means the annual interest expense is covered 6.8 times.

37	**$110,446 available income**	=	**6.8%**
	$ 16,250 interest on bonds		

Before an industrial bond can be considered a safe investment, most analysts say that the company should earn its bond interest requirement three to four times over. By these standards, Typical Manufacturing has a fair margin of safety.

What About Leverage?

A stock is said to have high leverage if the company that issued it has a large proportion of bonds and preferred stock outstanding in relation to the amount of common stock. A simple illustration will show why. Let's take, for example, a company with $10,000,000 of 4% bonds outstanding. If the company is earning $440,000 before bond interest, there will only be $40,000 left for the common stock after payment of $400,000 bond interest ($10,000,000 at 4% equals $400,000). However, an increase of only 10% in earnings (to $484,000) will leave $84,000 for common stock dividends, or an increase of more than 100%. If there is only a small amount of common stock issued, the increase in earnings per share will appear very impressive.

You have probably realized that a decline of 10% in earnings would not only wipe out everything available for the common stock, but also result in the company's being unable to cover its full interest on its bonds without dipping into accumulated earnings. This is the great danger of so-called high-leverage stocks and also illustrates the fundamental weakness of companies that have a disproportionate amount of debt or preferred stock. Conservative investors usually steer clear of them, although these stocks do appeal to people who are willing to assume the risk.

Typical Manufacturing, on the other hand, is not a highly leveraged company. Last year, Typical paid $16,250 in bond interest and its net profit—before this payment—came to $56,750. This left $40,500 for the common stock and retained earnings. Now look what happened this year. Net profit before subtracting bond interest rose by $7,250, or about 13%. Since the bond interest stayed the same, net income after paying this interest also rose $7,250. But that is about 18% of $40,500. While this is certainly not a spectacular example of leverage, 18% is better than 13%.

Preferred Dividend Coverage

To calculate the *preferred dividend coverage* (the number of times preferred dividends were earned), we must use net profit as our base, because federal income taxes and all interest charges must be paid before anything is available for shareholders. Because we have 60,000 shares of $100 par value preferred stock that pays a dividend of $5.83 1/3, the total dividend requirement for the preferred stock is $350,000. Dividing the net income of $47,750,000 by this figure we arrive at approximately 136.4, which means that the dividend requirement of the preferred stock has been earned more than 136 times over. This ratio is so high partly because Typical has only a small amount of preferred stock outstanding.

Earnings Per Common Share

The buyer of common stock is often more concerned with the earnings per share of a stock than with the dividend. This is because earnings per share usually influence stock market prices. Although our income statement separates earnings per share before and after the effect of the extraordinary item, the remainder of our presentation will only consider earnings per share after the extraordinary item. In Typical's case the income statement shows earnings available for common stock.

46	**Earnings per share**	**$3.16**

But if it didn't, we could calculate it ourselves:

42	**Net profit for the year**	**$47,750**
	Less: dividend requirements on preferred stock	**350**
	Earnings available for the common stock	**$47,400**

$$\frac{\$47{,}400{,}000 \text{ earnings available after preferred dividends}}{14{,}999{,}000 \text{ number of outstanding common shares}} = \$3.16 \text{ earnings per share of common}$$

Typical's capital structure is a very simple one, comprised of common and preferred stock. It's earnings-per-share computation will suffice under this scenario. However, if the capital structure is more complex and contains securities which are convertible into common stock, options, warrants or contingently issuable shares, the calculation requires modification. In fact, two separate calculations must be performed. This is called dual presentation. The calculations are primary and fully diluted earnings per common share.

Primary Earnings Per Common Share

This is determined by dividing the earnings for the year not only by the number of shares of common stock outstanding but by the common stock plus *common stock equivalents if dilutive.*

Common stock equivalents are securities, such as convertible preferred stock, convertible bonds, stock options, warrants and the like, that enable the holder to become a common shareholder by exchanging or converting the security. These are deemed to be only one step short of common stock—their value stems in large part from the value of the common to which they relate.

Convertible preferred stock and convertible bonds offer the holder either a specified dividend rate or interest return, or the option of participating in increased earnings on the common stock, through conversion. They don't have to be actually converted to common stock for these securities to be called a common stock equivalent. This is because they are in substance equivalent to common shares, enabling the holder at his discretion to cause an increase in the number of common shares by exchanging or converting. How do accountants determine a common stock equivalent? A convertible security is considered a common stock equivalent if its effective yield at the date of its issuance is less than two-thirds of the then-current average Aa corporate bond yield.

Now, let's put our new terms to work in an example, remembering that it has nothing to do with our own company, Typical Manufacturing. We start with the facts we have available. We'll say we have 100,000 shares of common stock outstanding plus another 100,000 shares of preferred stock, convertible into common on a share-for-share basis. (Assume they qualify as common stock equivalents.) We add the two and get 200,000 shares altogether. Now let's say our earnings figure is $500,000 for the year. With these facts, our primary computation is easy:

$$\frac{\$500{,}000 \text{ earnings for the year}}{200{,}000 \text{ adjusted shares outstanding}} = \$2.50 \text{ primary earnings per share}$$

However, as mentioned earlier, the common stock equivalent shares are only included in the computation if the effect of conversion on earnings per share is dilutive. Dilution occurs when earnings per share decrease or loss per share increases. For example, assume the preferred stock paid $3 a share in dividends. Without conversion, the earnings per share would be $2, as opposed to $2.50 per share, because net income available for common after payment of dividends would be $200,000 ($500,000 less $300,000) divided by the 100,000 common shares outstanding. In this case, the common stock equivalent shares would be excluded from the computation because conversion results in a higher earnings per share (anti-dilutive). Therefore, earnings per share of $2 will be reflected on the income statement.

Fully Diluted Earnings Per Common Share

The primary earnings per share item, as we have just seen in the preceding section, takes into consideration common stock and common stock equivalents. The purpose of *fully diluted earnings per share* is to reflect maximum potential dilution in earnings that would result if all contingent issuances of common stock had taken place at the beginning of the year.

This computation is the result of dividing the earnings for the year by: *common stock* and *common stock equivalents* and *all other securities that are convertible (even though they do not qualify as common stock equivalents).*

How would it work? First, remember that we have 100,000 shares of convertible preferred outstanding, as well as our 100,000 in common. Now, let's say we also have convertible bonds with a par value of $10,000,000 outstanding. These bonds pay 6% interest and have a conversion ratio of 20 shares of common for every $1,000 bond. Assume the current average Aa corporate bond yield is 8%. These bonds are not common stock equivalents, because 6% is not less than two-thirds of 8%. However, for fully diluted earnings per share we have to count them in. If the 10,000 bonds were converted, we'd have another 200,000 shares of stock, so adding everything up gives us 400,000 shares. But by converting the bonds, we could skip the 6% interest payment, which gains us another $600,000 gross earnings. So our calculation looks like this:

Earnings for the year		**$500,000**
Interest on the bonds	**$600,000**	
Less: the income tax applicable to deduction	**300,000**	
		300,000
Adjusted earnings		**$800,000**

$800,000 adjusted earnings / 400,000 adjusted shares outstanding = $2 fully diluted earnings per share

The only remaining step is to test for dilution. Earnings per share without bond conversion would be $2.50 ($500,000 divided by 200,000 shares). Since earnings per share of $2 is less than $2.50 we would assume debt conversion in our calculation of fully diluted earnings per share.

Price-Earnings Ratio

Both the price and the return on common stock vary with a multitude of factors. One such factor is the relationship that exists between the earnings per share and the market price. It is called the *price-earnings ratio*, and this is how it is calculated: If a stock is selling at 25 and earning $2 per share, its price-earnings ratio is 12 1/2 to 1, usually shortened to 12 1/2 and the stock is said to be selling at 12 1/2 times earnings. If the stock should rise to 40, the price-earnings ratio would be 20. Or, if the stock drops to 12, the price-earnings ratio would be 6.

In Typical Manufacturing, which has no convertible common stock equivalents, the earnings per share were calculated at $3.16. If the stock were selling at 33, the price-earnings ratio would be 10.4. This is the basic figure that you should use in viewing the record of this stock over a period of years and in comparing the common stock of this company with other similar stocks.

46 $ 33 market price / $ 3.16 earnings per share = 10.4 : 1 or 10.4 times

This means that Typical Manufacturing common stock is selling at approximately 10.4 times earnings.

Last year, Typical earned $2.77 per share. Let's say that its stock sold at the same price-earnings ratio then. This means that a share of Typical was selling for $28.80 or so, and anyone who bought Typical then would be satisfied now. Just remember, in the real world, investors can never be certain that any stock will keep its same price-earnings ratio from year to year. The historical P/E multiple is a guide, not a guarantee.

In general, a high P/E multiple, when compared with other companies in the same industry, means that investors have confidence in the company's ability to produce higher profits in the future.

Statement of Changes in Shareholders' Equity

(dollars in thousands except per-share amounts)

This statement analyzes the changes from year to year in each shareholder's equity account. From this statement, we can see that during the year additional common stock was issued at a price above par. We can also see that Typical experienced a translation gain. The rest of the components of equity, with the exception of retained earnings which we discuss below, remained the same.

Just as the income statement reflects the payoff for shareholders, retained earnings reflects the payoff for the company itself. It shows how much money the company has plowed back into itself for new growth. The Statement of Changes shows that retained earnings increase by net income less dividends on preferred and common stock. Since we have already analyzed net income, we will now analyze dividends.

Dividends

Dividends on common stock vary with the profitability of the company. Common shareholders were paid $18,000 in dividends this year. Since we know from the balance sheet that Typical has 14,999,000 shares outstanding, the first thing we can learn here is what may be the most important point to some potential investors — dividends per share.

$18,000,000 common stock dividends / **14,999,000 shares**	=	**$1.20 a share**

Once we know the amount of dividends per share, we can easily discover the dividend *payout ratio*. This is simply the percentage of net earnings per share that is paid to shareholders.

46	**$1.20 dividend per common share** / **$3.16 earnings per common share**	=	**38%**

Of course, the dividends on the $5.83 preferred stock will not change from year to year. The word *cumulative* in the balance statement description tells us that if Typical's management someday didn't pay a dividend on its preferred stock, then the $5.83 payment for that year would accumulate. It would have to be paid to preferred shareholders before any dividends could ever be declared again on the common stock.

That's why preferred stock is called preferred. It gets at any dividend money first. We've already talked about convertible bonds and convertible preferred stock. Right now, we're not interested in that aspect because Typical Manufacturing doesn't have any convertible securities outstanding. Chances are its 60,000 shares of preferred stock, with a par value of $100 each, were issued to family members of Mr. Isaiah Typical, who founded the company back in 1923. When he took Typical public, he didn't keep any of the common stock. In those days, the guaranteed $5.83 dividend was more important to Isaiah. He was not interested in taking any more chances on Typical.

During the year, Typical has added $29,400 to its retained earnings. Even if Typical has some lean years in the future, it has plenty of retained earnings from which to keep on declaring those $5.83 dividends on the preferred stock and $1.20 dividends on the common stock.

There is one danger in having a lot of retained earnings. It could attract another company—Shark Fast Foods & Electronics, for instance—to buy up Typical's common stock to gain enough control to vote out the current management. Then Shark might merge Typical into itself. Where would Shark get the money to buy Typical stock? By issuing new shares of its own stock, perhaps. And where would Shark get the money to pay the dividends on all that new stock of its own? From Typical's retained earnings. So Typical's management has the obligation to its shareholders to make sure that its retained earnings are put to work to increase the total earnings per share of the shareholders. Or else, the shareholders might cooperate with Shark if and when it makes a raid.

25	**Retained earnings**	**$249,000**

Return on Equity

Seeing how hard money works, of course, is one of the most popular measures that investors use to come up with individual judgments on how much they think a certain stock ought to be worth. The market itself—the sum of all buyers and sellers—makes the real decision. But the investors often try to make their own, in order to decide whether they want to invest at the market's price or wait. Most investors look for Typical's return on equity, which shows how hard shareholders' equity in Typical is working. In order to find Typical's current return on equity, we look at the balance sheet and take the common shareholders' equity for last year—not the current year—and then we see how much Typical made this year on it. We use only the amount of net profit after the dividends have been paid on the preferred stock. For Typical Manufacturing, that means $47,750 net profit minus $350. Here is what we get:

$47,750 net income — $350 preferred stock dividend
$305,600 last year's stockholders' equity — $6,000 preferred stock value

$ 47,400 / $299,600 = 15.8% return on equity

For every dollar of shareholders' equity, Typical made more than 15¢. Is that good? Well, 15.8¢ on the dollar is better than Typical could have done by going out of business, taking its shareholders' equity and putting that $299,600 in the bank. So Typical obviously is better off in its own line of work. When we consider putting our money to work in Typical's stock, we should compare Typical's 15.8¢ not only to whatever Typical's business competitors make, but to Typical's investment competitors for our money. For instance, the latest available average rate for all U.S. industry, according to the U.S. Federal Trade Commission, was 16¢.

Just remember that 15.8¢ is what Typical itself makes on the dollar. By no means is it what you will make in dividends on Typical's stock. What that return on equity really tells you is whether Typical Manufacturing is relatively attractive as an enterprise. You can only hope that this attractiveness might be translated into demand for Typical stock, and be reflected in its price.

Many analysts also like to see a company's annual return on the total capital available to the company. To get this figure, we use all the equity, plus all available borrowed funds. This becomes the total capital available. And for the total return on this figure we use net income before income taxes and interest charges. This gives us a bigger capital base and a larger income figure. As shareholders, however, what we're most interested in is how hard our own share of the company is working. And that's why we are more interested in return on equity.

Statement of Cash Flows

One more statement needs to be analyzed in order to get the full picture of Typical's financial status. The Statement of Cash Flows examines the changes in cash resulting from business activities. Cash-flow analysis is necessary in order to make proper investing decisions, as well as to maintain operations. Cash flows, although related to net income, are not equivalent. This is because of the accrual concept of accounting. Generally, under accrual accounting, a transaction is recognized on the income statement when the earnings process has been completed or an expense has been incurred. This does not necessarily coincide with the time that cash is exchanged. For example, cash received from merchandise sales often lags behind the time when goods are delivered to customers. However, the sale is recorded on the income statement when the goods are shipped.

Cash flows are separated by business activity. The business activity classifications presented on the statement include investing activities, financing activities, and operating activities. First, we will discuss financing and investing activities. Operating activities basically include all activities not classified as either financing or investing activities.

Financing activities include those activities relating to the generation and repayment of funds provided by creditors and investors. These activities include the issuance of debt or equity securities and the repayment of debt and distribution of dividends. Investing activities include those activities relating to asset acquisition or disposal.

Operating activities involve activities relating to the production and delivery of goods and services. They reflect the cash effects of transactions which are included in the determination of net income. Since many items enter into the determination of net income, the indirect method is used to determine the cash provided by or used for operating activities. This method requires adjusting net income to reconcile it to cash flows from operating activities. Common examples of cash flows from operating activities are interest received and paid, dividends received, salary, insurance, and tax payments.

Qualifying and Certifying

Watch Those Footnotes

The annual reports of many companies contain this statement: "The accompanying footnotes are an integral part of the financial statements." The reason is that the financial reports themselves are kept concise and condensed. Therefore, any explanatory matter that cannot readily be abbreviated is set out in greater detail in footnotes.

Some examples of appropriate footnotes are:

Description of the company's *policy* for depreciation, amortization, consolidation, foreign currency translation, and earnings per share.

Inventory valuation method. This footnote indicates whether inventories shown on the balance sheet or used in determining the cost of goods sold on the income statement are valued on a last in, first out (LIFO) basis or a first in, first out (FIFO) basis. Last in, first out means that the costs on the income statement reflect the actual cost of inventories purchased most recently. First in, first out means the income statement reflects the cost of the oldest inventories. This is an extremely important consideration because a LIFO valuation reflects current costs and does not overstate profits during inflationary times while a FIFO valuation does.

Changes in accounting policy as a result of new accounting rules.

Non-recurring items such as pension-plan terminations or sales of significant business units.

Employment contracts, profit sharing, pension, and retirement plans.

Details of stock options granted to officers and employees.

Long-term leases. Companies which usually lease a considerable amount of selling space must show their lease liabilities on a per-year basis for the next several years and their total lease liabilities over a longer period of time.

Details relating to issuance and maturities of long-term debt.

Contingent liabilities representing claims or lawsuits pending.

Commitments relating to contracts in force that will affect future periods.

Inflation accounting adjustments. Certain companies must show the impact of changing prices on their financial position by adjusting items that appear on the balance sheet and the income statement for current costs and the Consumer Price Index. FASB Statement Number 89 spells out the requirements for presenting inflation-adjusted financial data.

Separate breakdowns of sales and gross profits must be shown for each line of business that accounts for more than 20% of a company's sales. Multinational corporations must also show sales and gross income on a geographic basis by country.

Most people do not like to read footnotes because they may be complicated and are almost always hard to read. This is unfortunate, because footnotes are very informative. Even if they don't reveal that the corporation has been forced into bankruptcy, footnotes can still reveal many fascinating sidelights of the financial story.

Independent Audits

The certificate from the independent auditors, which is printed in the report, says, first, that the auditing steps taken in the process of verification of the account meet the accounting world's approved standards of practice; and second, that the financial statements in the report have been prepared in conformity with generally accepted accounting principles.

As a result, when the annual report contains financial statements that have the stamp of approval from independent auditors, you have an assurance that the figures can be relied upon as having been fairly presented.

However, if the independent accountants' opinion contains words such as "except for," or "subject to," the reader should investigate the reason behind such qualifications. Often the answer can be found by reading the footnotes that pertain to the matter. They are usually referred to in the auditor's opinion.

The Long View

We cannot emphasize too strongly that company records, in order to be very useful, must be compared. We can compare them to other company records, to industry averages or even to broader economic factors, if we want. But most of all, we can compare one company's annual activities to the same firm's results from other years.

This used to be done by keeping a file of old annual reports. Now, many corporations include a ten-year summary in their financial highlights each year. This provides the investing public with information about a decade of performance. That is why Typical Manufacturing included a ten-year summary in its annual report. It's not a part of the statements vouched for by the auditors, but it is there for you to see. A ten-year summary can show you:

- The trend and consistency of sales
- The trend of earnings, particularly in relation to sales and the economy
- The trend of net earnings as a percentage of sales
- The trend of return on equity
- Net earnings per share of common
- Dividends, and dividend policy.

Other companies may include changes in net worth, book value per share, capital expenditures for plant and machinery, long-term debt, capital stock changes by way of stock dividends and splits, number of employees, number of shareholders, number of outlets, and where appropriate, information on foreign subsidiaries and the extent to which foreign operations have been embodied in the financial report.

All of this is really important because of one central point: You are not only trying to find out how Typical is doing *now*. You want to predict how Typical *will* do, and how its stock will perform.

Ten-Year Financial Summary

	19X9	19X8	19X7	19X6	19X5	19X4	19X3	19X2	19X1	19X0
Net Sales	$765,000	$725,000	$690,000	$660,000	$600,000	$520,000	$500,000	$450,000	$350,000	$300,000
Income–before income taxes and extraordinary loss	94,196	66,750	59,750	54,750	50,400	42,000	45,800	40,500	34,350	29,500
Extraordinary loss	(5,000)	–	–	–	–	–	–	–	–	–
Net profit for year	47,750	40,500	37,700	33,650	29,850	27,300	30,360	25,975	21,000	18,100
Earnings per share before extraordinary loss	3.49	2.77	2.57	2.28	2.00	1.83	2.20	1.93	1.69	1.43
Earnings per share after extraordinary loss	3.16	2.77	2.57	2.28	2.00	1.83	2.20	1.93	1.69	1.43
Dividend per share	1.20	1.20	1.20	1.00	1.00	1.00	1.00	.80	.80	.80
Net working capital	230,000	199,000	218,000	223,000	211,000	178,000	136,000	111,000	86,000	96,000
Net plant and equipment	260,000	249,600	205,000	188,000	184,300	187,500	161,600	125,600	92,500	87,600
Long-term debt	130,000	136,000	136,000	–	–	–	–	–	–	–
Preferred stock	6,000	6,000	6,000	6,000	6,000	6,000	6,000	6,000	6,000	6,000
Common stock and surplus	340,000	299,600	275,800	254,700	238,100	220,500	203,250	166,000	133,800	128,000
Book value per share	22.53	20.53	18.39	16.98	15.87	14.70	13.55	11.07	8.92	8.53

Note: All data in thousands except per-share figures.

Selecting Stocks

From the items we've studied in this booklet, Typical Manufacturing appears to be a healthy concern. Which should make Board Chairman Patience Typical, old Isaiah Typical's daughter, and her four nieces, who own most of the shares, happy. But it makes us rather sad, since Typical is fictional, and we can't offer you shares of its stock. When you decide to invest money in real stocks, please remember this:

Selecting common stocks for investment requires careful study of factors other than those we can learn from financial statements. The economics of the country and the particular industry must be considered. The management of the company must be studied and its plans for the future assessed. Information about these other things is rarely in the financial report. These other facts must be gleaned from the press or the financial services or supplied by some research organization. Merrill Lynch's Global Securities Research and Economics Group stands ready to help you get the available facts you need to be an intelligent investor. Ask any Financial Consultant to put Merrill Lynch to work for you.

Tracing Obsolete Securities*

The following is a list of some of the available sources of information on tracing obsolete securities. This list should be useful to those who wonder whether their old securities have any value, to researchers, and to collectors. All of the books listed below should be available in large public libraries or in larger business libraries.

To trace a security, you need to know the name of the company, the date of issue and the state in which the company was incorporated; all three pieces of information should appear on the security. Start with volumes appropriate to the issue date of the security and continue through to the present, if necessary. If the security can not be found, contact the department that registers corporations in the state in which the company was incorporated. In most states this will be the office of the Secretary of State. They maintain records of name changes and bankruptcies and can usually answer your inquiry quickly; some charge a nominal fee for the service. Call the department to see what their procedures and costs are. You may need to send a copy of the certificate. Do not send the original certificate.

For an introduction to searching obsolete securities, the best guide, now out-of-print, is:

Cargiulo, Albert F. and Rocco Carlucci.
The Questioned Stock Manual: A Guide to Determining the True Worth of Old and Collectible Securities. New York: McGraw-Hill, 1979, xiv, 193 p.: ill. tables.
Chapters 3 and 4 deal with locating sources of information on securities. Chapter 6 covers the detection and recognition of fraudulent securities and a description of how securities are printed. The appendix contains a table of the top 100 firms, 1917–1977.

For historical data, beginning with colonial times, the Fisher, Scudder, and Smythe manuals are classics. The manuals are still published and the Smythe firm continues to do research into obsolete securities, charging a fee of $50 for each company. They also serve as dealers and appraisers of obsolete securities for collectors. You can contact them at:

R. M. Smythe & Co.
26 Broadway
New York, NY 10004
(212) 943–1880

Robert D. Fisher
Manual of Valuable & Worthless Securities: Showing Companies That Have Been Reorganized, Merged, Liquidated or Dissolved, Little Known Companies and Oil Leases. New York: R. M. Smythe, 1926–. 15 v.
First published in 1926 as the *Marvyn Scudder Manual . . .* , the series was taken over by Robert D. Fisher with vol. 5 in 1937. It has been published by the R. M. Smythe firm since 1971 under the editorship of Robert D. Fisher, Jr. With vol. 6 the series limited itself to securities and the date on which they became worthless. The earlier volumes present brief corporate obituaries. Volume 15, 1984, includes a price guide for collectors of obsolete certificates.

Smythe, Roland M.
Valuable Extinct Securities: the Secret of the Obsolete Security Business, Unclaimed Money and How to Collect It, With a List of . . . Extinct Securities of Good Value From the Records of the Four Principal Dealers. . . . New York: R. M. Smythe, 1929. v, 398 p.
By the author and publisher of *Obsolete American Securities and Corporations,* later the *Robert D. Fisher Manual of Valuable and Worthless Securities.* This list of over 1,500 securities gives due and foreclosure dates and the dates of sale or merger.

Smythe, Roland M.
Obsolete American Securities and Corporations. New York: R. M. Smythe, 1911. liv, 1166 p.: ill.
(*Obsolete American Securities and Corporations:* vol. 2). Pages 1–28 discuss Continental and other early U.S. state and foreign notes and bonds. Twenty plates illustrate some of the bonds discussed. Volume 1 was published in 1904.
Valuable Extinct Securities Guide. 1939 ed. New York: R. M. Smythe, Inc., 1938. 127 p. The first edition was published in 1929 and was the sequel to *Obsolete American Securities and Corporations.*

The books below can be consulted to trace more recent corporate reorganizations:

Capital Changes Reporter for Federal Income Tax Purposes. Clark, NJ: Commerce Clearing House (NJ), 1949–. 6 v., looseleaf. Securities distributions, taxability of disbursements, splits, offers, rights, etc.

The National Monthly Stock Summary. Jer-

* Frederick N. Nesta, formerly Director, Marymount Manhattan College Library.

sey City, NJ: National Quotation Bureau, 1926–.
Summary data from the daily service, supplied either from the service or from dealers' lists. Name, par value, exchange, closing price, bids and offerings. May also include shares outstanding, control, reorganization, dividend or other information. Monthly, with bound cumulative volumes issued twice yearly.

Capital Adjustments, Reorganizations and Exchanges, Stock Dividends. Rights and Splits. Englewood Cliffs, NJ: Prentice-Hall, 1980–. 2 v. in 3, looseleaf.
Current changes, disbursements, etc. Includes notes on taxability. Supplements the bound volumes below.

Capital Adjustments: Stock Dividends, Stock Rights, Reorganizations. Englewood Cliffs, NJ: Prentice-Hall, 1962–.
The earlier volumes cover corporate and government securities from early in the century. Updated by looseleaf supplements. Includes name changes, incorporation dates, mergers.

Bank & Quotation Record. Arlington, MA: National News Services, 1928–.
"A publication of the Commercial and Financial Chronicle." Monthly opening and closing prices, highs, lows, etc. Includes equipment trusts, public utility bonds, Chicago Board Options Exchange, foreign exchange rates for the month, CDs, Federal funds, prime banker acceptance rates, commercial paper statistics. Published continuously for over sixty years, it is a fascinating document of American financial history.

FOREIGN CORPORATIONS

Canada

Canadian Mines Register of Dormant and Defunct Companies: Third Supplement. Toronto: Northern Miner Press Limited, 1976. 108 p. Originally published in 1960.

Survey of Predecessor and Defunct Companies. 3rd ed. Toronto: The Financial Post Corporation Service Group, 1985. 208 p.
Covers over 12,000 companies and spans over 50 years. Lists name changes, removals, the exchange basis for new shares, along with the addresses and telephone numbers of Canadian Federal and Provincial corporate registry offices.

United Kingdom

The Stock Exchange Official Year-Book. London: Macmillan, 1934–.
Contains substantial information on the London Stock Exchange, foreign securities, municipal securities, regulations and statistics and a directory of International exchanges. The main body lists each company with parent/subsidiary note, background, financial data, stock history, voting, dividends. Includes the *Register of Defunct and Other Companies Removed from the Stock Exchange Official Year-Book,* a listing of over 23,000 companies removed from the Official Year-Book since 1875, along with a list of Commonwealth Government and Provincial stocks redeemed or converted since 1940. The Register was published separately until 1980.

Australia

Register of Companies Removed from the Stock Exchanges Official Lists. Sydney: Stock Exchange Research Pty., 1984? 104 p.
Lists companies that were traded on one or more Australian exchanges. Historical data, with delistings going back to the early 1930s.

Bonds and Money Market Instruments

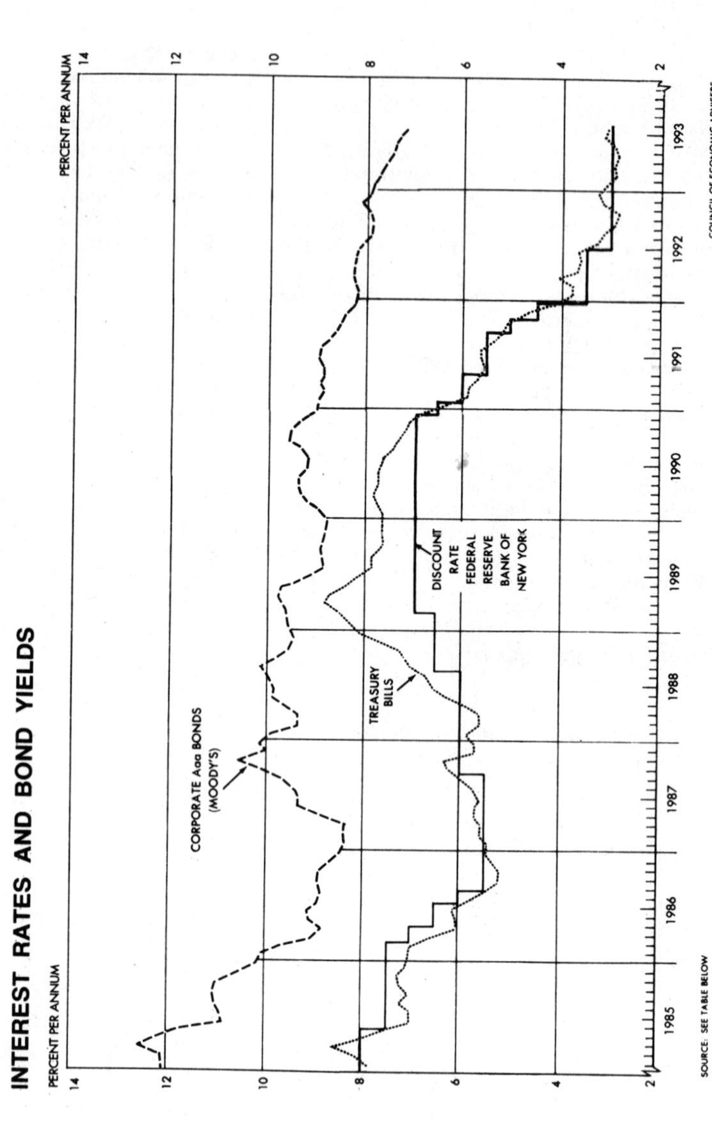

[Percent per annum]

Period	U.S. Treasury security yields			High-grade municipal bonds (Standard & Poor's)[3]	Corporate Aaa bonds (Moody's)	Prime commercial paper, 6 months[1]	Discount rate (N.Y. F.R. Bank)[4]	Prime rate charged by banks[4]	New-home mortgage yields (FHFB)[5]
	3-month bills (new issues)[1]	Constant maturities[2]							
		3-year	10-year						
1983	8.63	10.45	11.10	9.47	12.04	8.89	8.50	10.79	12.57
1984	9.58	11.89	12.44	10.15	12.71	10.16	8.80	12.04	12.38
1985	7.48	9.64	10.62	9.18	11.37	8.01	7.69	9.93	11.55
1986	5.98	7.06	7.68	7.38	9.02	6.39	6.33	8.33	10.17
1987	5.82	7.68	8.39	7.73	9.38	6.85	5.66	8.21	9.31
1988	6.69	8.26	8.85	7.76	9.71	7.68	6.20	9.32	9.19
1989	8.12	8.55	8.49	7.24	9.26	8.80	6.93	10.87	10.13
1990	7.51	8.26	8.55	7.25	9.32	7.95	6.98	10.01	10.05
1991	5.42	6.82	7.86	6.89	8.77	5.85	5.45	8.46	9.32
1992	3.45	5.30	7.01	6.41	8.14	3.80	3.25	6.25	8.24
1992: July	3.28	4.91	6.84	6.12	8.07	3.53	3.50–3.00	6.50–6.00	8.00
Aug	3.14	4.72	6.59	6.08	7.95	3.44	3.00–3.00	6.00–6.00	8.00
Sept	2.97	4.42	6.42	6.24	7.92	3.26	3.00–3.00	6.00–6.00	7.93
Oct	2.84	4.64	6.59	6.43	7.99	3.33	3.00–3.00	6.00–6.00	7.90
Nov	3.14	5.14	6.87	6.35	8.10	3.67	3.00–3.00	6.00–6.00	8.07
Dec	3.25	5.21	6.77	6.24	7.98	3.70	3.00–3.00	6.00–6.00	7.88
1993: Jan	3.06	4.93	6.60	6.18	7.91	3.35	3.00–3.00	6.00–6.00	7.82
Feb	2.95	4.58	6.26	5.87	7.71	3.27	3.00–3.00	6.00–6.00	7.77
Mar	2.97	4.40	5.98	5.65	7.58	3.24	3.00–3.00	6.00–6.00	7.46
Apr	2.89	4.30	5.97	5.78	7.46	3.19	3.00–3.00	6.00–6.00	7.46
May	2.96	4.40	6.04	5.81	7.43	3.20	3.00–3.00	6.00–6.00	7.37
June [r]	3.10	4.53	5.96	5.73	7.33	3.38	3.00–3.00	6.00–6.00	7.23
July	3.05	4.43	5.81	5.60	7.17	3.35	3.00–3.00	6.00–6.00	....
Week ended:									
1993: July 3	3.05	4.37	5.79	5.64	7.24	3.38	3.00–3.00	6.00–6.00	....
10	3.01	4.36	5.79	5.56	7.22	3.33	3.00–3.00	6.00–6.00	....
17	3.04	4.34	5.74	5.55	7.16	3.31	3.00–3.00	6.00–6.00	....
24	3.05	4.49	5.83	5.61	7.17	3.34	3.00–3.00	6.00–6.00	....
31	3.10	4.54	5.88	5.66	7.14	3.39	3.00–3.00	6.00–6.00	....

[1] Bank-discount basis.
[2] Yields on the more actively traded issues adjusted to constant maturities by the Treasury Department.
[3] Weekly data are Wednesday figures.
[4] Average effective rate for year; opening and closing rate for month and week.
[5] Effective rate (in the primary market) on conventional mortgages, reflecting fees and charges as well as contract rate and assumed, on the average, repayment at end of 10 years.

Sources: Department of the Treasury, Board of Governors of the Federal Reserve System, Federal Housing Finance Board, Moody's Investors Service, and Standard & Poor's Corporation.

Source: *Economic Indicators*, Council of Economic Advisers.

INTEREST RATES Money and Capital Markets

Averages, percent per year; weekly, monthly, and annual figures are averages of business day data unless otherwise noted

Item	1990	1991	1992	1993				1993, week ending				
				Jan.	Feb.	Mar.	Apr.	Apr. 2	Apr. 9	Apr. 16	Apr. 23	Apr. 30
MONEY MARKET INSTRUMENTS												
1 Federal funds[1,2,3]	8.10	5.69	3.52	3.02	3.03	3.07	2.96	3.18	3.11	2.93	2.91	2.87
2 Discount window borrowing[2,4]	6.98	5.45	3.25	3.00	3.00	3.00	3.00	3.00	3.00	3.00	3.00	3.00
Commercial paper[3,5,6]												
3 1-month	8.15	5.89	3.71	3.21	3.14	3.15	3.13	3.19	3.16	3.14	3.10	3.10
4 3-month	8.06	5.87	3.75	3.25	3.18	3.17	3.14	3.19	3.17	3.16	3.12	3.11
5 6-month	7.95	5.85	3.80	3.35	3.27	3.24	3.19	3.24	3.23	3.20	3.16	3.16
Finance paper, directly placed[3,5,7]												
6 1-month	8.00	5.73	3.62	3.25	3.18	3.15	3.06	3.10	3.08	3.07	3.05	3.03
7 3-month	7.87	5.71	3.65	3.32	3.27	3.17	3.06	3.10	3.08	3.06	3.06	3.04
8 6-month	7.53	5.60	3.63	3.29	3.21	3.14	3.07	3.09	3.09	3.07	3.07	3.05
Bankers acceptances[3,5,8]												
9 3-month	7.93	5.70	3.62	3.14	3.06	3.07	3.05	3.09	3.07	3.04	3.04	3.04
10 6-month	7.80	5.67	3.67	3.23	3.15	3.14	3.10	3.15	3.13	3.09	3.08	3.09
Certificates of deposit, secondary market[3,9]												
11 1-month	8.15	5.82	3.64	3.14	3.08	3.10	3.08	3.11	3.10	3.07	3.06	3.06
12 3-month	8.15	5.83	3.68	3.19	3.12	3.11	3.09	3.12	3.11	3.09	3.08	3.08
13 6-month	8.17	5.91	3.76	3.33	3.22	3.20	3.16	3.22	3.20	3.16	3.14	3.14
14 Eurodollar deposits, 3-month[3,10]	8.16	5.86	3.70	3.22	3.12	3.11	3.10	3.11	3.11	3.13	3.09	3.06
U.S. Treasury bills												
Secondary market[3,5]												
15 3-month	7.50	5.38	3.43	3.00	2.93	2.95	2.87	2.91	2.91	2.85	2.81	2.91
16 6-month	7.46	5.44	3.54	3.14	3.07	3.05	2.97	3.01	3.00	2.97	2.93	2.98
17 1-year	7.35	5.52	3.71	3.35	3.25	3.20	3.11	3.17	3.16	3.09	3.05	3.12
Auction average[3,5,11]												
18 3-month	7.51	5.42	3.45	3.06	2.95	2.97	2.89	2.96	2.92	2.89	2.82	2.88
19 6-month	7.47	5.49	3.57	3.17	3.08	3.08	3.00	3.04	3.04	3.00	2.96	2.95
20 1-year	7.36	5.54	3.75	3.52	3.32	3.09	3.24	n.a.	3.24	n.a.	n.a.	n.a.
U.S. TREASURY NOTES AND BONDS												
Constant maturities[12]												
21 1-year	7.89	5.86	3.89	3.50	3.39	3.33	3.24	3.32	3.31	3.21	3.18	3.25
22 2-year	8.16	6.49	4.77	4.39	4.10	3.95	3.84	3.95	3.92	3.80	3.77	3.83
23 3-year	8.26	6.82	5.30	4.93	4.58	4.40	4.30	4.43	4.38	4.26	4.23	4.30
24 5-year	8.37	7.37	6.19	5.83	5.43	5.19	5.13	5.25	5.21	5.08	5.06	5.14
25 7-year	8.52	7.68	6.63	6.26	5.87	5.66	5.59	5.75	5.72	5.53	5.48	5.60
26 10-year	8.55	7.86	7.01	6.60	6.26	5.98	5.97	6.07	6.06	5.90	5.87	6.01
27 30-year	8.61	8.14	7.67	7.34	7.09	6.82	6.85	6.95	6.96	6.77	6.76	6.89
Composite												
28 More than 10 years (long-term)	8.74	8.16	7.52	7.17	6.89	6.65	6.64	6.77	6.76	6.56	6.53	6.66
STATE AND LOCAL NOTES AND BONDS												
Moody's series[13]												
29 Aaa	6.96	6.56	6.09	5.91	5.61	5.42	5.47	5.64	5.65	5.44	5.39	5.38
30 Baa	7.29	6.99	6.48	6.28	5.98	5.81	5.88	6.04	6.05	5.85	5.82	5.79
31 *Bond Buyer* series[14]	7.27	6.92	6.44	6.15[r]	5.87	5.64	5.76	5.86	5.84	5.70	5.67	5.75
CORPORATE BONDS												
32 Seasoned issues, all industries[15]	9.77	9.23	8.55	8.24	8.01	7.83	7.76	7.89	7.88	7.71	7.66	7.74
Rating group												
33 Aaa	9.32	8.77	8.14	7.91	7.71	7.58	7.46	7.64	7.61	7.45	7.34	7.40

34 Aa	9.56	9.05	8.46	8.11	7.90	7.72	7.62	7.75	7.75	7.59	7.50	7.59
35 A	9.82	9.30	8.62	8.26	8.03	7.86	7.80	7.92	7.90	7.74	7.72	7.80
36 Baa	10.36	9.80	8.98	8.67	8.39	8.15	8.14	8.23	8.25	8.07	8.05	8.15
37 A-rated, recently offered utility bonds[16]	10.01	9.32	8.52	8.13	7.80	7.61	7.66	7.86	7.64	7.55	7.59	7.76
MEMO												
Dividend–price ratio[17]												
38 Preferred stocks	8.96	8.17	7.46	7.25	7.37	6.70	6.69	6.64	6.74	6.72	6.62	6.67
39 Common stocks	3.61	3.25	2.99	2.88	2.81	2.76	2.82	2.76	2.82	2.78	2.82	2.86

1. The daily effective federal funds rate is a weighted average of rates on trades through New York brokers.
2. Weekly figures are averages of seven calendar days ending on Wednesday of the current week; monthly figures include each calendar day in the month.
3. Annualized using a 360-day year or bank interest.
4. Rate for the Federal Reserve Bank of New York.
5. Quoted on a discount basis.
6. An average of offering rates on commercial paper placed by several leading dealers for firms whose bond rating is AA or the equivalent.
7. An average of offering rates on paper directly placed by finance companies.
8. Representative closing yields for acceptances of the highest-rated money center banks.
9. An average of dealer offering rates on nationally traded certificates of deposit.
10. Bid rates for Eurodollar deposits at 11 a.m. London time. Data are for indication purposes only.
11. Auction date for daily data; weekly and monthly averages computed on an issue-date basis.
12. Yields on actively traded issues adjusted to constant maturities. Source: U.S. Treasury.
13. General obligations based on Thursday figures; Moody's Investors Service.
14. General obligations only, with twenty years to maturity, issued by twenty state and local governmental units of mixed quality. Based on figures for Thursday.
15. Daily figures from Moody's Investors Service. Based on yields to maturity on selected long-term bonds.
16. Compilation of the Federal Reserve. This series is an estimate of the yield on recently offered, A-rated utility bonds with a thirty-year maturity and five years of call protection. Weekly data are based on Friday quotations.
17. Standard and Poor's corporate series. Preferred stock ratio based on a sample of ten issues: four public utilities, four industrials, one financial, and one transportation. Common stock ratios on the 500 stocks in the price index.

NOTE. These data also appear in the Board's H.15 (519) and G.13 (415) releases. For ordering address, see inside front cover.

Source: *Federal Reserve Bulletin*, Board of Governors of the Federal Reserve System.

PRIME RATE CHARGED BY BANKS on Short-Term Business Loans (percent per year)

Date of change	Rate	Period	Average rate	Period	Average rate	Period	Average rate
1990— Jan. 1	10.50	1990	10.01	1991— Jan.	9.52	1992— Jan.	6.50
8	10.00	1991	8.46	Feb.	9.05	Feb.	6.50
		1992	6.25	Mar.	9.00	Mar.	6.50
1991— Jan. 2	9.50			Apr.	9.00	Apr.	6.50
Feb. 4	9.00	1990— Jan.	10.11	May	8.50	May	6.50
May 1	8.50	Feb.	10.00	June	8.50	June	6.50
Sept. 13	8.00	Mar.	10.00	July	8.50	July	6.02
Nov. 6	7.50	Apr.	10.00	Aug.	8.50	Aug.	6.00
Dec. 23	6.50	May	10.00	Sept.	8.20	Sept.	6.00
		June	10.00	Oct.	8.00	Oct.	6.00
1992— July 2	6.00	July	10.00	Nov.	7.58	Nov.	6.00
		Aug.	10.00	Dec.	7.21	Dec.	6.00
		Sept.	10.00				
		Oct.	10.00			1993— Jan.	6.00
		Nov.	10.00			Feb.	6.00
		Dec.	10.00			Mar.	6.00
						Apr.	6.00
						May	6.00

1. Data in this table also appear in the Board's H.15 (519) weekly and G.13 (415) monthly statistical releases. For ordering address, see inside front cover.

Source: *Federal Reserve Bulletin*, Board of Governors of the Federal Reserve System.

NYSE Bond Volume

Annual bond volume (billions of dollars)

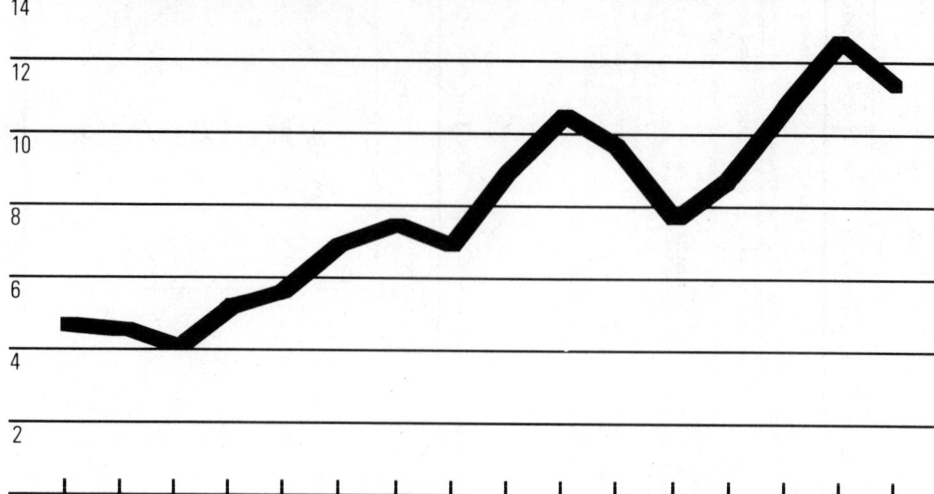

Source: New York Stock Exchange *Fact Book*

Reported bond volume and trades on NYSE, 1992 (par value in thousands)

	Par value		No. of	Avg. daily	Avg. trade size
	Total	Avg. daily	trades	trades	(thousands)
January	$1,274,728	$57,942	60,206	2,737	$21.2
February	1,251,322	65,859	53,804	2,832	23.3
March	1,124,576	51,117	54,286	2,468	20.7
April	924,161	44,008	46,813	2,229	19.7
May	840,556	42,028	41,283	2,064	20.4
June	904,486	41,113	42,968	1,953	21.1
July	999,560	45,435	44,913	2,042	22.3
August	867,662	41,317	40,993	1,952	21.2
September	859,794	40,943	40,612	1,934	21.2
October	981,832	44,629	45,719	2,078	21.5
November	764,175	38,209	37,997	1,900	20.1
December	836,155	38,007	40,932	1,861	20.4
Year	**$11,629,007**	**$45,783**	**550,526**	**2,167**	**$21.1•**

	Par value	
High Day	$95,017	February 7
Low Day	$12,995	November 27
High Month	$1,274,728	January
Low Month	$764,175	November

• New record.

Source: New York Stock Exchange *Fact Book*.

MARKETABLE U.S. TREASURY BONDS AND NOTES Foreign Transactions

Millions of dollars

Country or area	1991	1992	1993	1992				1993		
			Jan.–Mar.	Sept.	Oct.	Nov.	Dec.	Jan.	Feb.	Mar.p
	Transactions, net purchases or sales (−) during period[1]									
1 **Estimated total**	**19,865**	**39,319**	**5,876**	**−5,995**	**3,546**	**17,648**	**8**	**454**	**−1,273r**	**6,695**
2 Foreign countries	19,687	37,966	3,848	−6,204	4,351	17,661	−194	−129	−2,166r	6,143
3 Europe	8,663	19,647	−4,931	−4,655	4,671	7,284	3,163	−585	−382r	−3,964
4 Belgium and Luxembourg	523	1,985	504	−25	232	370	−28	−59	45	518
5 Germany	−4,725	2,076	−3,692	900	−8	−1,584	898	697	−1,632	−2,757
6 Netherlands	−3,735	−2,923	−885	−239	−40	1,827	−804	−1,238	206	147
7 Sweden	−663	−804	−336	−843	202	668	−344	−54	258	−540
8 Switzerland	1,007	481	−2,223	292	769	1,334	213	−199	−455	−1,569
9 United Kingdom	6,218	24,184	2,880	16	4,068	7,209	2,833	2,025	183r	672
10 Other Western Europe	10,024	−6,002	−1,408	−4,761	−551	−2,758	395	−1,759	975	−624
11 Eastern Europe	13	650	229	5	−1	218	0	2	38	189
12 Canada	−3,019	562	5,874	−4,281	458	−1,087	−99	3,302	82	2,490
13 Latin America and Caribbean	10,285	−3,223	−1,668	−1,479	−1,915	7,270	−4,519	−1,495	445	−618
14 Venezuela	10	539	158	31	155	27	11	−175	179	154
15 Other Latin America and Caribbean	4,179	−1,957	−5,436	−2,537	−3,233	2,385	415	−3,309	−1,656	−471
16 Netherlands Antilles	6,097	−1,805	3,610	1,027	1,163	4,858	−4,945	1,989	1,922	−301
17 Asia	3,367	23,526	5,047	4,004	1,416	4,000	1,188	−1,136	−1,032	7,215
18 Japan	−4,081	9,817	3,518	2,448	−339	3,383	2,201	−743	804	3,457
19 Africa	689	1,103	−238	59	−37	119	0	−33	−139	−66
20 Other	−298	−3,649	−236	148	−242	75	73	−182	−1,140	1,086
21 Nonmonetary international and regional organizations	178	1,353	2,028	209	−805	−13	202	583	893	552
22 International	−358	1,018	865	−31	−903	−38	76	228	581	56
23 Latin American regional	−72	533	506	201	219	−31	97	270	235	1
MEMO										
24 Foreign countries	19,687	37,966	3,848	−6,204	4,351	17,661	−194	−129	−2,166r	6,143
25 Official institutions	1,190	6,876	−8,001	−4,483	2,951	−603	−719	−2,965	−4,364	−672
26 Other foreign[2]	18,496	31,090	11,849	−1,721	1,400	18,264	525	2,836	2,198r	6,815
Oil-exporting countries										
27 Middle East[2]	−6,822	4,323	−1,282	750	−271	407	511	−238	−1,855	811
28 Africa[3]	239	11	8	4	0	0	0	8	0	0

1. Official and private transactions in marketable U.S. Treasury securities having an original maturity of more than one year. Data are based on monthly transactions reports. Excludes nonmarketable U.S. Treasury bonds and notes held by official institutions of foreign countries.

2. Comprises Bahrain, Iran, Iraq, Kuwait, Oman, Qatar, Saudi Arabia, and United Arab Emirates (Trucial States).

3. Comprises Algeria, Gabon, Libya, and Nigeria.

Source: *Federal Reserve Bulletin,* Board of Governors of the Federal Reserve System.

Most active bonds on NYSE, 1992

Issue		Par value of reported volume (thousands)
RJR Nabisco Inc.	disc debs '01	$588,584
Chrysler Corporation	12s '15	486,593
General Motors Acceptance	zero coupon '15	334,820
General Motors Acceptance	zero coupon '12	245,420
Walt Disney	LYONS '05	239,355
USG Corporation	16s '08	196,992
Chrysler Corporation	10.95s '99	195,273
American Telephone & Telegraph	8 1/8s '22	192,663
Chrysler Corporation	10.4s '99	162,677
Chrysler Corporation	9.6s '94	154,070
Time Warner	reset notes '02	152,535
Stone Container	10 3/4s '02	141,075
RJR Nabisco Inc.	10 1/2s '98	134,085
Chrysler Corporation	13s '97	126,917
American Telephone & Telegraph	7s '01	126,810
USAir Inc.	12 7/8s '00	124,192
Stone Container	11 1/2s '99	113,208
Federated Department Stores	10s '00	100,996
Chrysler Auburn Hills	12 3/8 exchange certificates '20	95,535
American Telephone & Telegraph	8 5/8s '26	93,256
Owens-Illinois	10 3/4s '99	89,943
Owens-Illinois	11s '03	88,108
RJR Nabisco Inc.	15s '01	83,150
Reliance Group Holdings	11 1/2s '01	81,854
Chrysler Financial Corp.	9.3s '94	80,812
du Pont de Nemours	6s '01	79,145
Reliance Group Holdings	11s '96	78,902
American Telephone & Telegraph	7 1/8s '03	76,414
Mesa Capital Corporation	13½s '99	74,036
International Business Machines	cv 7 7/8s '04	74,035
General Motors Acceptance	8¼s '16	70,782
RJR Nabisco Inc.	13 1/2s '01	66,973
Stone Container	13 5/8s '95	64,461
MGM/UA Communications	13s '96	62,172
American Telephone & Telegraph	8 5/8s '31	61,031
Unisys Corp.	13 7/8s '92	59,639
Eastman Kodak	8 5/8s '16	59,175
Unisys Corp.	10 3/4s '95	59,152
American Telephone & Telegraph	7 1/8s '02	58,785
Chrysler Financial Corp.	8 1/8s '94	57,925
Mesa Capital Corporation	12s '96	57,507
National Gypsum	disc debs '04	55,101
Zenith Electronics	cv 6 1/4s '11	49,778
American Telephone & Telegraph	8 1/8s '24	48,825
Marathon Oil Company	9 1/2s '94	48,193
Orion Pictures Corp.	reset notes '98	47,928
Chiquita Brands International	10 1/2s '04	46,670
Union Carbide Corp.	cv 7 1/2s '12	43,036
International Business Machines	10 1/4s '95	43,019
Eastman Kodak	LYONS '11	42,218

Source: New York Stock Exchange *Fact Book.*

Credit Ratings of Fixed Income and Money Market Securities

KEY TO STANDARD & POOR'S CORPORATE AND MUNICIPAL BOND RATING DEFINITIONS

A Standard & Poor's corporate or municipal debt rating is a current assessment of the creditworthiness of an obligor with respect to a specific debt obligation. This assessment may take into consideration obligors such as guarantors, insurers, or lessees.

The debt rating is not a recommendation to purchase, sell or hold a security, inasmuch as it does not comment as to market price or suitability for a particular investor.

The ratings are based on current information furnished by the issuer or obtained by Standard & Poor's from other sources it considers reliable. Standard & Poor's does not perform an audit in connection with any rating and may, on occasion, rely on unaudited financial information. The ratings may be changed, suspended or withdrawn as a result of changes in, or unavailability of, such information, or for other circumstances.

The ratings are based, in varying degrees, on the following considerations:

I. Likelihood of default—capacity and willingness of the obligor as to the timely payment of interest and repayment of principal in accordance with the terms of the obligation;

II. Nature of and provisions of the obligation;

III. Protection afforded by, and relative position of, the obligation in the event of bankruptcy, reorganization or other arrangement under the laws of bankruptcy and other laws affecting creditor's rights.

AAA

Debt rated **AAA** have the highest rating assigned by Standard & Poor's to a debt obligation. Capacity to pay interest and repay principal is extremely strong.

AA

Debt rated **AA** have a very strong capacity to pay interest and repay principal and differ from the highest rated issues only in a small degree.

A

Debt rated **A** have a strong capacity to pay interest and repay principal although they are somewhat more susceptible to the adverse effects of changes in circumstances and economic conditions than debts in higher rated categories.

BBB

Debt rated **BBB** are regarded as having an adequate capacity to pay interest and repay principal. Whereas they normally exhibit adequate protection parameters, adverse economic conditions or changing circumstances are more likely to lead to a weakened capacity to pay interest and repay principal for debts in this category than for debts in higher rated categories.

BB, B, CCC, CC

Debt rated **BB, B, CCC,** and **CC** are regarded, on balance, as predominantly speculative with respect to capacity to pay interest and repay principal in accordance with the terms of the obligation. **BB** indicates the lowest degree of speculation and **CC** the highest degree of speculation. While such debts will likely have some quality and protective characteristics, these are outweighed by large uncertainties or major risk exposures to adverse conditions.

C

The rating **C** is reserved for income bonds on which no interest is being paid.

D

Debt rated **D** are in default, and payment of interest and/or repayment of principal is in arrears.

Plus (+) or minus (−)

The ratings from **AA** to **B** may be modified by the addition of a plus or minus sign to show relative standing within the major rating categories.

Provisional ratings

The letter *p* indicates that the rating is provisional. A provisional rating assumes the successful completion of the project being financed by the debts being rated and indicates that payment of debt service requirements is largely or entirely dependent upon the successful and timely completion of the project. This rating, however, while addressing credit quality subsequent to completion of the project, makes no comment on the likelihood of, or the risk of default upon failure of, such completion. The investor should exercise his own judgment with respect to such likelihood and risk.

Source: From Standard & Poor's Debt Rating Division.

L*

The letter "L" indicates that the rating pertains to the principal amount of those bonds where the underlying deposit collateral is fully insured by the Federal Savings & Loan Insurance Corp. or the Federal Deposit Insurance Corp.

NR

Indicates that no rating has been requested, that there is insufficient information on which to base a rating or that S&P does not rate a particular type of obligation as a matter of policy.

Debt Obligations

Debt Obligations of issuers outside the United States and its territories are rated on the same basis as domestic corporate and municipal issues. The ratings measure the creditworthiness of the obligor but do not take into account currency exchange and other uncertainties.

Bond Investment Quality Standards

Under present commercial bank regulations issued by the Comptroller of the Currency, bonds rated in the top four categories (**AAA, AA, A, BBB,** commonly known as "Investment Grade" ratings) are generally regarded as eligible for bank investment. In addition, the Legal Investment Laws of various states impose certain rating or other standards for obligations eligible for investment by savings banks, trust companies, insurance companies and fiduciaries generally.

KEY TO STANDARD & POOR'S PREFERRED STOCK RATING DEFINITIONS

A Standard & Poor's preferred stock rating is an assessment of the capacity and willingness of an issuer to pay preferred stock dividends and any applicable sinking fund obligations. A preferred stock rating differs from a bond rating inasmuch as it is assigned to an equity issue, which issue is intrinsically different from, and subordinated to, a debt issue. Therefore, to reflect this difference, the preferred stock rating symbol will normally not be higher than the bond rating symbol assigned to, or that would be assigned to, the senior debt of the same issuer.

The preferred stock ratings are based on the following considerations.

I. Likelihood of payment—capacity and willingness of the issuer to meet the timely payment of preferred stock dividends and any applicable sinking fund requirements in accordance with the terms of the obligation.

II. Nature of, and provisions of, the issue.

III. Relative position of the issue in the event of bankruptcy, reorganization, or other arrangements affecting creditors' rights.

AAA

This is the highest rating that may be assigned by Standard & Poor's to a preferred stock issue and indicates an extremely strong capacity to pay the preferred stock obligations.

AA

A preferred stock issue rated **AA** also qualifies as a high-quality fixed income security. The capacity to pay preferred stock obligations is very strong, although not as overwhelming as for issues rated **AAA.**

A

An issue rated **A** is backed by a sound capacity to pay the preferred stock obligations, although it is somewhat more susceptible to the adverse effects of changes in circumstances and economic conditions.

BBB

An issue rated **BBB** is regarded as backed by an adequate capacity to pay the preferred stock obligations. Whereas it normally exhibits adequate protection parameters, adverse economic conditions or changing circumstances are more likely to lead to a weakened capacity to make payments for a preferred stock in this category than for issues in the **A** category.

BB, B, CCC

Preferred stock rated **BB, B,** and **CCC** are regarded, on balance, as predominately speculative with respect to the issuer's capacity to pay preferred stock obligations. **BB** indicates the lowest degree of speculation and **CCC** the highest degree of speculation. While such issues will likely have some quality and protective characteristics, these are outweighed by large uncertainties or major risk exposures to adverse conditions.

CC

The rating **CC** is reserved for a preferred stock issue in arrears on dividends or sinking fund payments but that is currently paying.

C

A preferred stock rated **C** is a non-paying issue.

* Continuance of the rating is contingent upon S&P's receipt of an executed copy of the escrow agreement or closing documentation confirming investments and the cash flows.

D

A preferred stock rated **D** is a non-paying issue with the issuer in default on debt instruments.

NR

NR indicates that no rating has been requested, that there is insufficient information on which to base a rating, or that S&P does not rate a particular type of obligation as a matter or policy.

Plus (+) **or Minus** (−) To provide more detailed indications of preferred stock quality, the ratings from **AA** to **B** may be modified by the addition of a plus or minus sign to show relative standing within the major rating categories.

The preferred stock rating is not a recommendation to purchase or sell a security, inasmuch as market price is not considered in arriving at the rating. Preferred stock *ratings* are wholly unrelated to Standard & Poor's earnings and dividend *rankings* for common stocks.

MUNICIPAL NOTES

A Standard & Poor's role rating reflects the liquidity concerns and market access risks unique to notes. Notes due in 3 years or less will likely receive a long-term debt rating. The following criteria will be used in making that assessment.

—Amortization schedule (the larger the final maturity relative to other maturities the more likely it will be treated as a note).

—Source of Payment (the more dependent the issue is on the market for its refinancing, the more likely it will be treated as a note).

Note rating symbols are as follows:

SP-1 Very strong or strong capacity to pay principal and interest. Those issues determined to possess overwhelming safety characteristics will be given a plus (+) designation.

SP-2 Satisfactory capacity to pay principal and interest.

SP-3 Speculative capacity to pay principal and interest.

TAX-EXEMPT DEMAND BONDS

Standard & Poor's assigns "dual" ratings to all long-term debt issues that have as part of their provisions a demand or double feature.

The first rating addresses the likelihood of repayment of principal and interest as due, and the second rating addresses only the demand feature. The long-term debt rating symbols are used for bonds to denote the long-term maturity and the commercial paper rating symbols are used to denote the put option (for example, "AAA/A-1+"). For the newer "demand notes," S&P's note rating symbols, combined with the commercial paper symbols, are used (for example, "SP-1+/A-1+").

KEY TO STANDARD & POOR'S COMMERCIAL PAPER RATING DEFINITIONS

A Standard & Poor's Commercial Paper Rating is a current assessment of the likelihood of timely payment of debt having an original maturity of no more than 365 days.

Ratings are graded into four categories, ranging from **A** for the highest quality obligations to **D** for the lowest. The four categories are as follows:

A

Issues assigned this highest rating are regarded as having the greatest capacity for timely payment. Issues in this category are further refined with the designations 1, 2, and 3 to indicate the relative degree of safety.

A-1 This designation indicates that the degree of safety regarding timely payment is very strong.

A-2 Capacity for timely payment on issues with this designation is strong. However, the relative degree of safety is not as overwhelming as for issues designated **A-1.**

A-3 Issues carrying this designation have a satisfactory capacity for timely payment. They are, however, somewhat more vulnerable to the adverse effects of changes in circumstances than obligations carrying the higher designations.

B

Issues rated **B** are regarded as having only an adequate capacity for timely payment. However, such capacity may be damaged by changing conditions for short-term adversities.

C

This rating is assigned to short-term obligations with a doubtful capacity for payment.

D

This rating indicates that the issue is either a default or is expected to be in default upon maturity.

The Commercial Paper Rating is not a recommendation to purchase or sell a security. The ratings are based on current information furnished to Standard & Poor's by the issuer or obtained from other sources it considers reliable. The ratings may be changed, suspended, or withdrawn as a result of changes in, or unavailability of, such information.

KEY TO MOODY'S MUNICIPAL RATINGS*

Aaa

Bonds which are rated **Aaa** are judged to be of the best quality. They carry the smallest degree of investment risk and are generally referred to as "gilt edge." Interest payments are protected by a large or by an exceptionally stable margin and principal is secure. While the various protective elements are likely to change, such changes as can be visualized are most unlikely to impair the fundamentally strong position of such issues.

Aa

Bonds which are rated **Aa** are judged to be of high quality by all standards. Together with the **Aaa** group they comprise what are generally known as high grade bonds. They are rated lower than the best bonds because margins of protection may not be as large as in **Aaa** securities or fluctuation of protective elements may be of greater amplitude or there may be other elements present which make the long term risks appear somewhat larger than in **Aaa** securities.

A

Bonds which are rated **A** possess many favorable instrument attributes and are to be considered as upper medium grade obligations. Factors giving security to principal and interest are considered adequate, but elements may be present which suggest a susceptibility to impairment sometime in the future.

Baa

Bonds which are rated **Baa** are considered as medium grade obligations; i.e., they are neither highly protected nor poorly secured. Interest payments and principal security appear adequate for the present but certain protective elements may be lacking or may be characteristically unreliable over any great length of time. Such bonds lack outstanding investment characteristics and in fact have speculative characteristics as well.

Ba

Bonds which are rated **Ba** are judged to have speculative elements; their future cannot be considered as well assured. Often the protection of interest and principal payments may be very moderate, and thereby not well safeguarded during both good and bad times over the future. Uncertainty of position characterizes bonds in this case.

B

Bonds which are rated **B** generally lack characteristics of the desirable investment. Assurance of interest and principal payments or of maintenance of other terms of the contract over any long period of time may be small.

Caa

Bonds which are rated **Caa** are of poor standing. Such issues may be in default or there may be present elements of danger with respect to principal or interest.

Ca

Bonds which are rated **Ca** represent obligations which are speculative in a high degree. Such issues are often in default or have other marked shortcomings.

C

Bonds which are rated **C** are the lowest rated class of bonds, and issues so rated can be regarded as having extremely poor prospects of ever attaining any real investment standing.

Con.(—)

Bonds for which the security depends upon the completion of some act or the fulfillment of some condition are rated conditionally. These are bonds secured by (a) earnings of projects under construction, (b) earnings of projects unseasoned in operation experience, (c) rentals which begin when facilities are completed, or (d) payments to which some other limiting condition attaches. Parenthetical rating denotes probable credit stature upon completion of construction or elimination of basis of condition.

KEY TO MOODY'S CORPORATE RATINGS*

Aaa

Bonds which are rated **Aaa** are judged to be of the best quality. They carry the smallest degree of investment risk and are generally referred to as "gilt edge." Interest payments are protected by a large or by an exceptionally

* **Note:** Those bonds in the **Aa, A, Baa, Ba** and **B** groups which Moody's believes possess the strongest investment attributes are designated by the symbols **Aa 1, A 1, Baa 1, Ba 1** and **B 1.**

Source: Moody's Investors Service, Inc.

* ***Note:*** Moody's applies numerical modifiers, **1, 2** and **3** in each generic rating classification from **Aa** through **B** in its corporate bond rating system. The modifier **1** indicates that the security ranks in the higher end of its generic rating category; the modifier **2** indicates a mid-range ranking; and the modifier **3** indicates that the issue ranks in the lower end of its generic rating category.

stable margin and principal is secure. While the various protective elements are likely to change, such changes as can be visualized are most unlikely to impair the fundamentally strong position of such issues.

Aa

Bonds which are rated **Aa** are judged to be of high quality by all standards. Together with the **Aaa** group they comprise what are generally known as high grade bonds. They are rated lower than the best bonds because margins of protection may not be as large as in **Aaa** securities or fluctuation of protective elements may be of greater amplitude or there may be other elements present which make the long term risks appear somewhat larger than in **Aaa** securities.

A

Bonds which are rated **A** possess many favorable investment attributes and are to be considered as upper medium grade obligations. Factors giving security to principal and interest are considered adequate but elements may be present which suggest a susceptibility to impairment sometime in the future.

Baa

Bonds which are rated **Baa** are considered as medium grade obligations, i.e., they are neither highly protected nor poorly secured. Interest payments and principal security appear adequate for the present but certain protective elements may be lacking or may be characteristically unreliable over any great length of time. Such bonds lack outstanding investment characteristics and in fact have speculative characteristics as well.

Ba

Bonds which are rated **Ba** are judged to have speculative elements; their future cannot be considered as well assured. Often the protection of interest and principal payments may be very moderate and thereby not well safeguarded during both good and bad times over the future. Uncertainty of position characterizes bonds in this class.

B

Bonds which are rated **B** generally lack characteristics of the desirable investment. Assurance of interest and principal payments or of maintenance of other terms of the contract over any long period of time may be small.

Caa

Bonds which are rated **Caa** are of poor standing. Such issues may be in default or there may be present elements of danger with respect to principal or interest.

Ca

Bonds which are rated **Ca** represent obligations which are speculative in a high degree. Such issues are often in default or have other marked shortcomings.

C

Bonds which are rated **C** are the lowest rated class of bonds and issues so rated can be regarded as having extremely poor prospects of ever attaining any real investment standing.

KEY TO MOODY'S COMMERCIAL PAPER RATINGS

The term "Commercial Paper" as used by Moody's means promissory obligations not having an original maturity in excess of nine months. Moody's makes no representation as to whether such Commercial Paper is by any other definition "Commercial Paper" or is exempt from registration under the Securities Act of 1933, as amended.

Moody's Commercial Paper ratings are opinions of the ability of issuers to repay punctually promissory obligations not having an original maturity in excess of nine months. Moody's makes no representation that such obligations are exempt from registration under the Securities Act of 1933, nor does it represent that any specific note is a valid obligation of a rated issuer or issued in conformity with any applicable law. Moody's employs the following three designations, all judged to be investment grade, to indicate the relative repayment capacity of rated issuers:

Issuers rated **Prime-1** (or related supporting institutions) have a superior capacity for repayment of short-term promissory obligations. Prime-1 repayment capacity will normally be evidenced by the following characteristics:

- -Leading market positions in well established industries.
- -High rates of return on funds employed.
- -Conservative capitalization structures with moderate reliance on debt and ample asset protection.
- -Broad margins in earnings coverage of fixed financial charges and high internal cash generation.
- -Well established access to a range of financial markets and assured sources of alternate liquidity.

Issuers rated **Prime-2** (or related supporting institutions) have a strong capacity for short-term promissory obligations. This will normally be evidenced by many of the characteristics cited above but to a

Source: Moody's Investors Service, Inc.

lesser degree. Earnings trends and coverage ratios, while sound, will be more subject to variation. Capitalization characteristics, while still appropriate, may be more affected by external conditions. Ample alternate liquidity is maintained.

Issuers rated **Prime-3** (or related supporting institutions) have an acceptable capacity for repayment of short-term promissory obligations. The effect of industry characteristics and market composition may be more pronounced. Variability in earnings and profitability may result in changes in the level of debt protection measurements and the requirement for relatively high financial leverage. Adequate liquidity is maintained.

Issuers rated **Not Prime** do not fall within any of the Prime rating categories.

If an issuer represents to Moody's that its Commercial Paper obligations are supported by the credit of another entity or entities, the name or names of such supporting entity or entities are listed within parenthesis beneath the name of the issuer. In assigning ratings to such issuers, Moody's evaluates the financial strength of the indicated affiliated corporations, commercial banks, insurance companies, foreign governments or other entities, but only as one factor in the total rating assessment. Moody's makes no representation and gives no opinion on the legal validity or enforceability of any support arrangement. You are cautioned to review with your counsel any questions regarding particular support arrangements.

KEY TO MOODY'S PREFERRED STOCK RATINGS*

Moody's Rating Policy Review Board Extended its rating services to include quality designations on preferred stocks on October 1, 1973. The decision to rate preferred stocks, which Moody's had done prior to 1935, was prompted by evidence of investor interest. Moody's believes that its rating of preferred stocks is especially appropriate in view of the ever-increasing amount of these securities outstanding, and the fact that continuing inflation and its ramifications have resulted generally in the dilution of some of the protection afforded them as well as other fixed-income securities.

Because of the fundamental differences between preferred stocks and bonds, a variation of our familiar bond rating symbols is being used in the quality ranking of preferred stocks. The symbols, presented below, are designed to avoid comparison with bond quality in absolute terms. It should always be borne in mind that preferred stocks occupy a junior position to bonds within a particular capital structure.

Preferred stock rating symbols and their definitions are as follows:

aaa

An issue which is rated **aaa** is considered to be a top-quality preferred stock. This rating indicates good asset protection and the least risk of dividend impairment within the universe of preferred stocks.

aa

An issue which is rated **aa** is considered a high-grade preferred stock. This rating indicates that there is reasonable assurance that earnings and asset protection will remain relatively well maintained in the foreseeable future.

a

An issue which is rated **a** is considered to be an upper-medium grade preferred stock. While risks are judged to be somewhat greater than in the "**aaa**" and "**aa**" classifications, earnings and asset protection are, nevertheless, expected to be maintained at adequate levels.

baa

An issue which is rated **baa** is considered to be medium grade, neither highly protected nor poorly secured. Earnings and asset protection appear adequate at present but may be questionable over any great length of time.

ba

An issue which is rated **ba** is considered to have speculative elements and its future cannot be considered well assured. Earnings and asset protection may be very moderate and not well safeguarded during adverse periods. Uncertainty of position characterized preferred stocks in this class.

b

An issue which is rated **b** generally lacks the characteristics of a desirable investment. Assurance of dividend payments and maintenance of other terms of the issue over any long period of time may be small.

caa

An issue which is rated **caa** is likely to be in arrears on dividend payments. This rating designation does not purport to indicate the future status of payments.

***Note:** Moody's applies numerical modifiers **1**, **2** and **3** in each rating classification from **1** indicates that the security ranks in the higher end of its generic rating category; the modifier **2** indicates a mid-range ranking; and the modifier **3** indicates that the issue ranks in the lower end of its generic rating category.

Source: Moody's Investors Service, Inc.

"ca"

An issue which is rated "**ca**" is speculative in a high degree and is likely to be in arrears on dividends with little likelihood of eventual payment.

"c"

This is the lowest rated class of preferred or preference stock. Issues so rated can be regarded as having extremely poor prospects of ever attaining any real investment standing.

KEY TO SHORT-TERM LOAN RATINGS

MIG 1/VMIG 1

This designation denotes best quality. There is present strong protection by established cash flows, superior liquidity support or demonstrated broadbased access to the market for refinancing.

MIG 2/VMIG 2

This designation denotes high quality. Margins of protection are ample although not so large as in the preceding group.

MIG 3/VMIG 3

This designation denotes favorable quality. All security elements are accounted for but there is lacking the undeniable strength of the preceding grades. Liquidity and cash flow protection may be narrow and market access for refinancing is likely to be less well established.

MIG 4/VMIG 4

This designation denotes adequate quality. Protection commonly regarded as required of an investment security is present and although not distinctly or predominantly speculative, there is specific risk.

Issues or the features associated with **MIG** or **VMIG** ratings are identified by date of issue, date of maturity or maturities or rating expiration date and description to distinguish each rating from other ratings. Each rating designation is unique with no implication as to any other similar issue of the same obligor. **MIG** ratings terminate at the retirement of the obligation while **VMIG** rating expiration will be a function of each issue's specific structural or credit features.

Collateralized Mortgage Obligation (CMO) Volatility Ratings

Fitch announces ratings of collateralized mortgage obligation (CMO) volatility. V-Ratings offer a balanced view of the relative volatility of total return, price, and maturity for each CMO tranche.

CMOs are fixed income investments supported by U.S. government agency or whole loan collateral and structured into specific classes of securities known as tranches. All CMOs have high credit quality reflecting their support by federal agency certificates of Fannie Mae, Freddie Mac, or Ginnie Mae, or backing from whole loan collateral rated 'AAA.'

Individual tranches, however, have varying degrees of market risk. CMOs differ from pass-through certificates because cash flows from the collateral are structured to prioritize payment among tranches. Pass-through certificates are sold and priced with an expected yield and maturity based on an assumed mortgage prepayment rate. All pass-through certificate holders share symmetrically in this prepayment risk. CMO tranches are individually priced for expected return, maturity, and assumed prepayment rates based on their unique characteristics. Because cash flows are specifically allocated as part of structuring a new issue CMO, there is an asymmetrical distribution of prepayment risk among the tranches.

V-Rating Definitions

Fitch Indicated Volatility: Low to Moderate

Securities rated V1, V2, or V3 perform predictably over a range of various interest rate scenarios. On balance, total return, price, and cash flow indicators are less volatile than current coupon agency certificates.

V1 The security exhibits relatively small changes in total return, price, and cash flow in all modeled interest rate scenarios.

V2 The security exhibits relatively small changes in total return, price, and cash flow in most modeled interest rate scenarios. Under certain adverse interest rate scenarios, one or more of the indicators are more volatile than securities rated V1.

V3 The security exhibits relatively larger changes in total return, price, and cash flow in all modeled interest rate scenarios. However, on balance, total return, price, and cash flow indicators are less volatile than current coupon agency certificates.

Fitch Indicated Volatility: High

Securities rated V4 or V5 perform less predictably over a range of various interest rate scenarios. On balance, total return, price, and cash flow indicators are more volatile than current coupon agency certificates.

V4 The security exhibits greater changes in total return, price, and cash flow than current coupon agency certificates in all modeled interest rate scenarios. However, most indicators show less volatility than securities rated V5.

V5 The security exhibits substantial changes in total return, price, and cash flow in all modeled interest rate scenarios compared to current coupon agency certificates. Under the most stressful interest rate scenario tests, negative total returns may result.

Source: Fitch Investors Service, Inc., One State Street Plaza, New York, NY 10004.

MAJOR MONEY MARKET AND FIXED INCOME SECURITIES

Type	Interest: When Paid	Marketability	Denominations	Maturity
A. Interest Fully Taxable				
Corporate Bonds and Notes	S[1]	Very good to poor depending on quality	$1,000	1 to 50 years
Corporate Preferred Stock (Pays dividends as a fixed percentage of face value. Dividends not obligatory, but if declared must be paid before that of the common stock. Dividends fully taxable for individuals, but 85% exempt from federal tax for corporations)	Generally quarterly	Good to poor depending on quality	$100 or less	No maturity
Federal Home Loan Mortgage Corporate Bonds	S	Fair	$25,000	Up to 25 years
Federal Home Loan Mortgage Certificates	S	Fair	$100,000	Up to 3 years
Farmers' Home Administration Notes and Certificates	Annual	Fair	$25,000	1 to 25 years
Federal Housing Administration Debentures (Guaranteed by the U.S. Government)	S	Very good	$50	1 to 40 years
Federal National Mortgage Association Bonds	S	Fair	$25,000	2 to 25 years
Government National Mortgage Modified Pass through Certificates (interest plus some repayment of principal, guaranteed by U.S. Government)	Monthly	Good	$25,000	30 years; average life 12 years
Federal Home Loan Bank Bonds and Notes	S	Good	$10,000	1 to 20 years
Export-Import Bank Debentures and Certificates	S	Good	$5,000	3 to 7 years
International Bank for Reconstruction Development (World Bank), Inter-American Development Bank, Asia Development Bank	S	Fair to poor	$1,000	3 to 25 years
Foreign and Eurodollar Bonds and Notes	May be Annual or S	Poor	$1,000 (amounts vary in foreign currencies)	1 to 30 years
Bankers Acceptances (short-term debt obligations (resulting from international trade and guaranteed by a major bank)	Discounted[2] on a 360-day year basis	Fair	$5,000	1 to 270 days
Commercial Paper (short-term debt issued by a major corporation)	Discounted on a 360-day year basis	No secondary market	$100,000 (occasionally smaller)	1 to 270 days
Negotiable Certificates of Deposit (short-term debt issued by banks and which can be sold on the open market)	Interest paid on maturity; 360-day year basis	Fair	$100,000 (occasionally smaller)	30 days to 1 year
Non-negotiable Certificate of Deposit (savings certificates)	Interest paid on maturity; 360-day year basis	Non-negotiable	$500 $10,000	30 months 6 months
Collateralized Mortgage Obligations (CMO)	S or monthly	Good	$1,000	typically 2 to 20 years
Repurchase Agreements (generally short term loans by large investors, secured by U.S. Government or other high quality issues)[3]	Interest paid on maturity; 360-day year basis	No secondary market	$100,000	1 to 30 days (sometimes more)

(continued)

MAJOR MONEY MARKET AND FIXED INCOME SECURITIES *(concluded)*

Type	Interest: When Paid	Marketability	Denominations	Maturity
Zero Coupon Bonds (Bonds stripped of coupons)	Bonds issued at deep discount. Full yield realized at maturity	Good	$1,000 on maturity	1 to 30 years
B. Interest Exempt from State and Local Income Taxes				
U.S. Treasury Bonds and Notes	S	Very good	$1,000	1 to 20 years
U.S. Treasury Bills	Discounted on a 360-day basis	Very good	$10,000	90 days to 1 year
U.S. Series EE Savings Bonds[4]	Issued at discount, full interest, paid on maturity	No secondary market: available for resale	$50 minimum $10,000 maximum	10 years (can be redeemed before maturity at reduced yields
U.S. Series HH Savings[5] Bonds	S	No secondary market	$10,000 $15,000 maximum	10 years
Federal Land Bank Bonds	S	Good	$1,000	1 to 10 years
Federal Financing Bank Notes and Bonds	S	Good	$1,000	1 to 20 years
Tennessee Valley Authority Notes and Bonds	S	Fair	$1,000	5 to 25 years
Banks for Cooperatives Bonds	Interest: 360-day year basis	Good	$5,000	180 days
Federal Intermediate Credit Bank Bonds	Interest: 360-day year basis	Good	$5,000	270 days
Federal Home Loan Bank Notes and Bonds	Discounted: 360-day year basis	Good	$10,000	30 to 360-day year basis (some more)
Farm Credit Bank Notes and Bonds	Interest: 360-day year basis	Good	$50,000	270 days (some more)
C. Interest Exempt from Federal Income Tax				
State and Local Notes and Bonds (in-State issues, usually exempt from State and local income taxes)	S	Good to fair depending on rating	$5,000	1 to 50 years
Housing Authority Bonds (in-State issues usually exempt from State and local income taxes)	S	Good to fair	$5,000	1 to 40 years

[1] S means semiannually.

[2] A discount means interest paid in advance, thus a 10% discounted security maturing at $10,000 would cost $9,000 to purchase.

[3] Recently some banks have issued repurchase agreements for smaller amounts of money, i.e., several thousands of dollars.

[4] Since November 1982, U.S. Savings Bonds pay variable interest equal to 85% of the 5 year Treasury securities' rate adjusted semi-annually and have a minimum guaranteed rate which is adjustable. The rate applies to bonds held 5 years or more.

[5] Issued in exchange for EE bonds.

U.S. Treasury Bonds, Notes, and Bills: Terms Defined*

U.S. Treasury bonds, notes and bills are interest paying securities representing a debt on the part of the U.S. Government. Treasury bonds have a maturity of over 5 years, while notes mature within 5 to 7 years. Bills are discussed below. Both Treasury bonds and notes are generally issued in minimum denominations of $1,000 and pay interest semiannually. The amount of semiannual interest paid is determined by the coupon rate specified on the bond and is calculated on a 365-day year basis. For a $1,000 face value† bond the interest is given by:

$$\text{semiannual interest} = 1/2\ (\$1{,}000 \times \text{coupon rate})$$

Bonds may be priced higher (at a premium) or lower (at a discount) than the face value (par) depending on current interest rates. The *current yield* is the rate the investor receives based on the prices actually paid for a bond. The price is given by:

$$\text{current yield} = \frac{\$1{,}000 \times \text{coupon rate}}{\text{purchase price}}$$

Thus, a $1,000 face value bond with an 8% coupon rate purchased at $850 has a current yield by:

$$\text{current yield} = \frac{\$1{,}000 \times 8\%}{\$850} = 9.41\%$$

The *yield to maturity* (YTM) is the yield obtained on taking into account the years remaining to maturity, annual interest payments, and the capital gain (or loss) realized at maturity. It is obtained from special tables.

However, the yield to maturity (YTM) may be found approximately from the formula

$$\text{YTM} = \frac{I + A}{B}$$

$$I = \text{annual interest rate}$$

$$A = \frac{\$1{,}000 - M}{N}$$

$$B = \frac{\$1{,}000 + M}{2}$$

where M = current market price of the bond

N = years remaining to maturity

As an example, a bond ($1,000 face value) has a 10% coupon and is currently priced at $1,100 with 10 years remaining to maturity. What is the approximate YTM?

$$I = \$1{,}000 \times .1 = \$100 \text{ interest per year}$$

$$A = \frac{\$1{,}000 - \$1{,}100}{10} = \$ - 10$$

$$B = \frac{\$1{,}000 + \$1{,}100}{2} = \$1{,}050$$

$$\text{YTM} = \frac{\$100 - \$10}{\$1{,}050} = .0857 = 8.57\%$$

U.S. Treasury bills (T-bills) are U.S. Government debt obligations which mature within one year. They are offered by the Federal Reserve Bank with maturities of 90 days (3 month bills) and 182 days (six month bills). Nine-month bills and one-year bills are also available. Treasury bills are sold in a minimum denomination of $10,000. Interest is paid by the discount method based on a 360-day year. With the discount method, interest is, in effect, paid at the time the bill is purchased. Thus a 91-day $10,000 bill (face value) with an 8% discount interest rate would provide the buyer with $202.22 ($10,000 × .08 × 91/360) interest at the time of purchase. This amount is deducted from the face value of the bill at the time of purchase so the buyer actually pays a net amount of $9,797.78 ($10,000 − $202.22). When the bill matures, the buyer receives $10,000 on redemption.

Since T-bills pay interest at the time of purchase (discount basis) on a 360-day year basis, while bonds (and notes) pay interest semiannually on a 365-day year basis, the two rates cannot be compared directly. To compare the two rates, the discount rate must be converted to the so-called *bond equivalent yield*, given by

$$\text{bond equivalent yield} = \frac{365 \times \text{discount rate}}{360 - (\text{discount rate} \times \text{days to maturity})}$$

As an example, a newly issued 91-day note with a discount rate of 12% has a

$$\text{bond equivalent yield} = \frac{365 \times (.12)}{360 - (.12 \times 91)} = 12.55\%$$

Interest from U.S. Treasury bonds, notes, and bills are subject to federal income tax,

* The terms *current yield*, *yield to maturity*, etc. defined in this section are generally applicable to all fixed incomes.

† Face value is the amount of the bond or note payable upon maturity.

but are exempt from state and local income taxes.

a bond maturing in June of 1985 and bearing a 10⅜% coupon is indicated by *May '85 10⅜.*

How to Read U.S. Government Bond and Note Quotations

TREASURY BONDS AND NOTES

(1) Rate	Maturity (2) Mo/yr	(3) Bid	(4) Asked	(5) Chg	(6) Ask Yld
8½	Feb 92n	100:00	100:02 –	1	0.00
7⅞	Mar 92n	100:11	100:13	...	3.25
8½	Mar 92n	100:13	100:15	...	3.18
11¾	Apr 92n	101:00	101:02 –	1	3.46
8⅞	Apr 92n	100:27	100:29	...	3.51
6⅝	May 92n	100:18	100:20 +	1	3.62

Source: Reprinted by permission of THE WALL STREET JOURNAL,

The above exhibit is an example of U.S. Government bond and note quotations as it appears in *The Wall Street Journal.*

(1) Indicates the coupon rate of interest. Rates are quoted to ⅛ of a percent. Thus 8⅜ means 8.375%. The semiannual interest payments are calculated, as described elsewhere, using this rate.

(2) Indicates the year of maturity and the month in which the bond or note matures. The letter *n* means the security is a note. Otherwise a bond is implied.

(3) The *bid price* per bond or note (the price at which the bond can be sold to the dealer), expressed as a percentage of the face value ($1,000) of the bond. Prices are quoted in terms of 1/32 of a percent. Thus 98.5 means 98 5/32. To find the dollar value of the price, convert 98 5/32 to a decimal (98 5/32 = .98156) and multiply by the face value of the bond to give $981.56 (.98156 × $1,000).

(4) The *ask price* per bond or note (the price at which the dealer will sell the bond). The dollar value is found as indicated above.

(5) The change in the bid price from the closing price of the previous day.

(6) The yield if the bond is held to maturity, based on the ask price.

Some U.S. Treasury bonds can be called back for redemption prior to maturity. These are shown with two dates (under item 2 for example)—*1993–98* indicating that the bonds mature in 1998, but may be called back and redeemed any time after 1993.

Some newspapers (such as *The New York Times*) use a slight modification of the above arrangement, though the various terms have the same meaning as defined above. Thus, a bond maturing in June of 1985 and bearing a 10⅜% coupon is indicated by *May '85 10⅜.*

How to Read U.S. Treasury Bill Quotations

(1) Rate	(2) Days to Mat.	(3) Bid	(4) Asked	(5) Chg	(6) Ask Yld
Feb 27 '92	0	3.59 –	3.49 +	0.09	0.00
Mar 05 '92	7	3.92	3.82 +	0.09	3.89
Mar 12 '92	14	3.93	3.83 +	0.04	3.90
Mar 19 '92	21	3.93	3.83 +	0.06	3.90
Mar 26 '92	28	3.84	3.80 +	0.04	3.87
Apr 02 '92	35	3.92	3.88 +	0.06	3.96

Source: Reprinted by permission of THE WALL STREET JOURNAL,

The above exhibit is an example of Treasury bill quotations as it appears in *The Wall Street Journal.*

(1) The date of maturity.

(2) Days to maturity.

(3) The bid price at market close quoted as a *discount* rate in percent. This bid price is the price at which the dealer will buy the bill. To convert the discount rate to a dollar price use the formula

$$\text{dollar price} = \$10{,}000 - (\text{discount rate} \times \text{days to maturity} \times .2778)$$

In the above, the discount must be expressed in percent. For example, if the dealer bids 3.82% discount for a bill which matures in 50 days, the dollar price is given by

$$\text{dollar price} = \$10{,}000 - [3.82 \times 50 \times .2778] = \$9{,}946.94$$

(4) The asked price at market close expressed as a discount rate in percent. The asked price is the price at which the dealer will sell a bill to a buyer. To convert to a dollar price use the above formula.

(5) The bond equivalent yield expressed in percent. This is calculated (as explained elsewhere) from the asked price expressed as a discount rate. This rate is used to compare T-bill yields to that of bonds, notes and certificates of deposit.

Some newspapers (e.g., *The New York Times*) use a somewhat different arrangement, though the meaning of the terms is the same as defined above. Thus, a bill maturing on June 4, 1981, is indicated as such. Also included in some newspapers is the change in bid price expressed as a discount rate.

How to Read Corporate Bond Quotations*

Corporate bonds are debt securities issued by private corporations. They generally have a face value (the amount due on maturity) of $1,000 and a specified interest rate (coupon rate) paid semiannually. Many corporate bonds have a *call* provision which permits the company to recall and redeem the bond after a specified date. Call privileges are usually exercised when interest rates fall sufficiently. Investors, therefore, cannot count on *locking in* high interest rates with corporate bonds. Bond quality designations used by Moody's and Standard & Poor's are given elsewhere in the Almanac (pp. 438–444).

The following is an example of price quotations for bonds traded on The New York Stock Exchange as they appear in *The Wall Street Journal.*

CORPORATION BONDS

VOLUME, $18,990,000

(1) Bonds		(2) Cur Yld	(3) Vol	(4) High	(5) Low	(6) Close	(7) Net Chg
AlaP	9s2000	14.	6	63	62	63	2
AlaP	8½s01	15.	10	57½	57½	57¼	. . .
AlaP	8⅞s03	15.	25	60	59½	60	+ ½
AlaP	10⅞05	15.	3	72	72	72	− 2¼
AlaP	10½05	15.	12	70½	70½	70½	− 1
AlaP	12⅝10	16.	7	81¼	81⅛	81⅛	− 1⅝

(1) The name of the issue in abbreviated form, followed by the coupon rate of interest in percent (designated by the letter *s*), and the year in which the bond matures. The coupon rate is stated in terms of ⅛ of a percent; 9⅜ means 9.375%.

(2) This is the current yield which is calculated as stated elsewhere. (See U.S. Treasury Bonds, Notes, and Bills, p. 485.)

(3) This item is the number of bonds sold that day.

(4) This is the highest price quoted for the bond sold on that day, expressed as a percentage of face value ($1,000). To convert to dollars, express the price as a decimal and multiply by the face value of the bond. As an example:

$$58\frac{1}{2} = (.5850 \times \$1{,}000.) = \$585$$

(5) This is the lowest price quoted that day. It is converted into dollars as described above.

(6) This is the price at the close of the market that day.

(7) This is the change in the closing price from that of the previous day. To convert to dollars, express as a decimal and multiply by $1,000. Thus, −1⅞ means a decrease per bond of $18.75 (.01875 × $1,000) from that of the previous day.

* Yield terms are the same as those defined in the section on U.S. Treasury Bonds, Notes and Bills, p. 485.

TAX EXEMPT VERSUS TAXABLE YIELDS

tax bracket	To equal a tax-free yield of:											
	5½%	6%	6½%	7%	7½%	8%	8½%	9%	9½%	10%	10½%	11%
	a taxable investment has to earn:											
28%	7.64%	8.33%	9.03%	9.72%	10.42%	11.11%	11.81%	12.50%	13.19%	13.89%	14.58%	15.28%
30	7.86	8.57	9.29	10.00	10.71	11.43	12.14	12.86	13.57	14.29	15.00	15.71
31	7.97	8.70	9.42	10.14	10.87	11.59	12.32	13.04	13.77	14.49	15.22	15.94
32	8.09	8.82	9.56	10.29	11.03	11.76	12.50	13.24	13.97	14.71	15.44	16.18
34	8.33	9.09	9.85	10.61	11.36	12.12	12.88	13.64	14.39	15.15	15.91	16.67
36	8.59	9.38	10.16	10.94	11.72	12.50	13.28	14.06	14.84	15.63	16.41	17.19
37	8.73	9.52	10.32	11.11	11.90	12.70	13.49	14.29	15.08	15.87	16.67	17.47
39	9.02	9.84	10.66	11.48	12.30	13.11	13.93	14.75	15.57	16.39	17.21	18.03

Tax-Exempt Bonds

Tax exempt (municipal) bonds are issued by state and local governments and are free from federal income tax on interest payments. The bonds are often issued in $5,000 denominations and pay interest semiannually. Capital gains are taxable. In addition, holders of out-of-state bonds may be subject to state and local income taxes of the state in which they reside. For example, a New York City resident holding Los Angeles municipal bonds would be subject to New York State and City income taxes on the interest.

The taxable equivalent yield of a tax exempt bond is obtained by means of the expression

$$\text{taxable equivalent yield} = \frac{\text{tax exempt yield}}{1 - (F + S + L)}$$

where

F is the federal tax bracket of the investor
S is the state tax bracket of the investor
L is the local tax bracket of the investor

Thus, an investor in the 50% federal bracket, 10% state bracket and 3% local bracket who holds a bond with a current yield of 6% which is exempt from all income taxes would enjoy a taxable equivalent yield (TEY) given by

$$\text{TEY} = \frac{6\%}{1 - (.5 + .1 + .03)} = 16.21\%$$

A taxable yield of 16.21% would be necessary to provide the same yield as the 6% current yield on the tax exempt security.

TYPES OF TAX EXEMPT BONDS AND NOTES

General Obligation bonds, also known as GO's, are backed by a pledge of a city's or state's full faith and credit for the prompt repayment of both principal and interest. Most city, county and school district bonds are secured by a pledge of unlimited property taxes. Since general obligation bonds depend on tax resources, they are normally analyzed in terms of the size of the resources being taxed.

Revenue bonds are payable from the earnings of a revenue-producing enterprise such as a sewer, water, gas or electric system, airport, toll bridge, college dormitory, lease payments from property rented to industrial companies, and other income-producing facilities. Revenue bonds are analyzed in terms of their earnings.

Limited and Special Tax bonds are payable from the pledge of the proceeds derived by the issuer from a specific tax such as a property tax levied at a fixed rate, a special assessment, or a tax on gasoline.

Municipal notes are short term obligations maturing from 30 days to a year and are issued in anticipation of revenues coming from the sales of bonds (BANS), taxes (TANS), or other revenues (RANS).

Project notes, issued by local housing and urban renewal agencies, are backed by a U.S. Government guarantee and are also tax exempt.

How to Understand Tax-Exempt Bond Quotations

Generally the prices of municipal bonds are quoted in terms of the yield to maturity (defined elsewhere) rather than in percentage of face value, as with other bonds. The yield to maturity can be converted to a dollar price if the years remaining to maturity and the rate of interest due are known. Certain tables used for this purpose are given in the *Basis Book* (published by the Financial Publishing Company, 82 Brookline Avenue, Boston, Massachusetts). The books list the dollar price (per $1,000 face value of the bond) corresponding to a given coupon rate, yield, and years to maturity.

Some municipal bonds, however, are quoted directly in terms of percentage of face value. Thus, a bid price (the price at which the dealer will buy the bonds from the investor) of 98⅝ for a $5,000 face value bond can be converted to a dollar price by first converting the bid to a decimal expression (.98625) and then multiplying by the face value of the bond. The result in this case is $4,931.25 (.98625 × $5,000). The same calculation applies to the ask price (the price at which the dealer will sell the bond to the investor).

Prices of tax exempt bonds are not quoted in the daily press. They can be obtained by calling municipal bond dealers. Extensive quotations are given in some relatively expensive publications:

The Blue List
Standard & Poor's
25 Broadway
New York, New York 10004
(212) 770-4600

The Daily Bond Buyer
and
The Weekly Bond Buyer
The Bond Buyer
1 State Street Plaza
New York, New York 10004
(212) 943-8200

Bond Week (Formerly Money Manager)
Institutional Investor
488 Madison Avenue
New York, New York 10022
(212) 303-3300

Government National Mortgage Association (GNMA) Modified Pass Through Certificates

A GNMA Mortgage-Backed Security is a government-guaranteed security which is collateralized by a pool of federally-underwritten residential mortgages. The investor receives a monthly check for a proportionate share of the principal and interest on a pool of mortgages whether or not the payments have actually been collected from the borrowers.

The GNMA Mortgage-Backed Security offers the highest yield of any federally-guaranteed security. In addition, the GNMA security offers a very competitive return in comparison to private corporation debt issues. Moreover, the investor receives a monthly return on the GNMA guaranteed investment, rather than semi-annual payments as on most bonds. This monthly payment represents a cash flow available for reinvestment and has the effect of increasing the yield on GNMAs by 10 to 18 basis points (a basis point is 0.1%) when compared to the yield equivalent received on a bond investment with the same "coupon" rate but paying interest semi-annually.

On single-family securities (the most popular form) the maturity is typically 30 years. However, statistical studies have determined that the average life of a single-family security is approximately 12 years, due to prepayments of principal. Nevertheless, some of the mortgages in any pool are likely to remain outstanding for the full 30-year period.

The minimum size of original individual certificates is $25,000 with increments of $5,000 above that amount.

Due to the uncertainties in the maturity of the above mentioned pass-through certificates, collateralized mortgage obligations (CMOs) have been introduced. CMOs are bonds backed by Ginnie Maes, Freddie Macs, and other mortgage instruments providing investors with a wide choice of maturities ranging from 2 to 20 years. Essentially, the monthly payments from the underlying mortgage instruments are initially allocated to the nearest maturity CMO and subsequently to CMO maturities of successively longer duration. CMO interest payments are made semiannually or monthly.

Components—Dow Jones 20 Bond Average

The Dow Jones Bond Averages are a simple arithmetic average compiled daily by using the New York Exchange closing bond prices. A list of the bonds on which these averages are based follows:

10 Public Utilities

Name	Coupon	Maturity
Comwlth Ed	8¾%	2005
Cons Ed	7.9%	2001
Cons Nat Gas	7¼%	2015
Duke Power	8⅛%	2007
Duquesne Light	8⅜%	2007
Ill Bell Tel	8%	2004
Mich Bell	7%	2012
Pac G&E	7¾%	2005
Phil Elec	7⅜%	2001
Potomac El Pwr	7%	2018

10 Industrials

Name	Coupon	Maturity
AT&T	7⅛%	2002
BankAm	7⅞%	2003
Beth Steel	6⅞%	1999
Champion Intl	6½%	2011
Eastman Kodak	8⅝%	2016
Exxon	6%	1997
Hercules	8%	2010
Kerr-McGee	7¼%	2012
Proc & Gamble	7%	2002
Union Carbide	7½%	2012

Source: Reprinted by permission of Barron's *Business and Financial Weekly,*

Components—Barron's Confidence Index

Barron's Confidence Index is the ratio of the average yield to maturity on best grade corporate bonds to the intermediate grade corporate bonds average yield to maturity. A list of the bonds on which the confidence index is based follows:

Best Grade Bonds

Name	Coupon	Maturity
AMBAC Inc	9⅜%	2011
Amoco Co	8⅝%	2016
Campbell Soup	8¾%	2021
Ches & Potom T	7⅞%	2022
Genl RE Cp	9%	2009
IBM	8⅜%	2019
McDonalds	8⅞%	2011
Proc & Gamb	8½%	2009
United Parcel	8⅜%	2020
Wisc El Svc	8⅜%	2026

Intermediate Grade Bonds

Name	Coupon	Maturity
Arco Chem	9.80%	2020
Ariz Pub Svc	8¾%	2024
CSX Corp	8⅝%	2022
Dayton Hud	8⅞%	2022
Delta Airl	9¼%	2022
Eastman K	9.20%	2021
GTE Corp	8¾%	2021
NCNB	9⅜%	2009
Philips Pet	9⅜%	2011
Ralston Purina	9¼%	2009

Source: Reprinted by permission of Barron's *Business and Financial Weekly,*

Monetary Aggregates Defined

Money supply data has been revised and expanded to reflect the Federal Reserve's redefinition of the monetary aggregates. The redefinition was prompted by the emergence in recent years of new monetary assets—for example, negotiable order of withdrawal (NOW) accounts and money-market mutual fund shares—and alterations in the basic character of established monetary assets—for example, the growing similarity of and substitution between the deposits of thrift institutions and those of commercial banks.

M1-A has been discontinued with M1-B now designated as "M-1." M-1 is currency in circulation plus all checking accounts including those which pay interest, such as NOW accounts. M-1 excludes deposits due to foreign commercial banks and official institutions.

M-2 as redefined adds to M1-B overnight repurchase agreements (RPs) issued by commercial banks and certain overnight Eurodollars (those issued by Carribbean branches of member banks) held by U.S. nonbank residents, money-market mutual fund shares, and savings and small-denomination time deposits (those issued in denominations of less than $100,000) at all depository institutions. Depository institutions are commercial banks (including U.S. agencies and branches of foreign banks, Edge Act Corporations, and foreign investment companies), mutual savings banks, savings and loan associations, and credit unions.

M-3 as redefined is equal to new M-2 plus large-denomination time deposits (those issued as in denominations of $100,000 or more) at all depository institutions (including negotiable CDs) plus term RPs issued by commercial banks and savings and loan associations.

L, the very broad measure of liquid assets, equals new M-3 plus other liquid assets consisting of other Eurodollar holdings of U.S. nonbank residents, bankers acceptances, commercial paper, savings bonds, and marketable liquid Treasury obligations.

Federal Reserve Banks

Board of Governors of the Federal Reserve System, Washington, D.C. 20551

Federal Reserve Bank	Telephone Number	District	Address
BOSTON*	617-973-3000	1	600 Atlantic Avenue, Boston, Massachusetts 02106
NEW YORK*	212-720-5000	2	33 Liberty Street (Federal Reserve P.O. Station), New York, New York 10045
Buffalo Branch	716-849-5000		160 Delaware Avenue, Buffalo, New York 14202 (P.O. Box 961, Buffalo, New York 14240-0961)
PHILADELPHIA	215-574-6000	3	Ten Independence Mall, Philadelphia, Pennsylvania 19106 (P.O. Box 66, Philadelphia, Pennsylvania 19105)
CLEVELAND*	216-579-2000	4	1455 East Sixth Street, Cleveland, Ohio 44114 (P.O. Box 6387, Cleveland, Ohio 44101)
Cincinnati Branch	513-721-4787		150 East Fourth Street, Cincinnati, Ohio 45202-0999 (P.O. Box 999, Cincinnati, Ohio 45201-0999)
Pittsburgh Branch	412-261-7800		717 Grant Street, Pittsburgh, Pennsylvania 15219 (P.O. Box 867, Pittsburgh, Pennsylvania 15230)
RICHMOND*	804-697-8000	5	701 East Byrd Street, Richmond, Virginia 23219 (P.O. Box 27622, Richmond, Virginia 23261)
Baltimore Branch	301-576-3300		502 South Sharp Street, Baltimore, Maryland 21201 (P.O. Box 1378), Baltimore, Maryland 21203)
Charlotte Branch	704-358-2100		530 Trade Street, Charlotte, North Carolina 28202 (P.O. Box 30248, Charlotte, North Carolina 28230)
Culpeper Communications and Records Center	703-829-1600		Mount Pony Rd., State Rte. 658 (P.O. Drawer 20, Culpeper, Virginia 22701)
ATLANTA	404-521-8500	6	104 Marietta Street, N.W., Atlanta, Georgia 30303-2713
Birmingham Branch	205-731-8500		1801 Fifth Avenue, North, Birmingham, Alabama 35283 (P.O. Box 830447, Birmingham, Alabama 35283-0447)
Jacksonville Branch	904-632-1000		800 Water Street, Jacksonville, Florida 32204 (P.O. Box 929, Jacksonville, Florida 32231-0044)
Miami Branch	305-591-2065		9100 Northwest 36th Street, Miami, Florida 33178 (P.O. Box 520847, Miami, Florida 33152-0847)
Nashville Branch	615-251-7100		301 Eighth Avenue, North, Nashville, Tennessee 37203 (P.O. Box 4407, Nashville, Tennessee 37203-4407)
New Orleans Branch	504-593-3200		525 St. Charles Avenue, New Orleans, Louisiana 70130 (P.O. Box 61630, New Orleans, Louisiana 70161-1630)
CHICAGO*	312-322-5322	7	230 South LaSalle Street, Chicago, Illinois 60604 (P.O. Box 834, Chicago, Illinois 60690-0834)
Detroit Branch	313-961-6880		160 W. Fort Street, Detroit, Michigan 48226 (P.O. Box 1059, Detroit, Michigan 48231)
ST. LOUIS	314-444-8444	8	411 Locust Street, St. Louis, Missouri 63102 (P.O. Box 442, St. Louis, Missouri 63166)
Little Rock Branch	501-324-8300		325 West Capitol Avenue, Little Rock, Arkansas 72201 (P.O. Box 1261, Little Rock, Arkansas 72203)
Louisville Branch	502-568-9200		410 South Fifth Street, Louisville, Kentucky 40202 (P.O. Box 32710, Louisville, Kentucky 40232)
Memphis Branch	901-523-7171		200 North Main Street, Memphis, Tennessee 38103 (P.O. Box 407, Memphis, Tennessee 38101)
MINNEAPOLIS	612-340-2345	9	250 Marquette Avenue, Minneapolis, Minnesota 55480
Helena Branch	406-447-3800		100 Neill Avenue, Helena, Montana 59601

Federal Reserve Bank	Telephone Number	District	Address
KANSAS CITY	816-881-2000	10	925 Grand Avenue, Kansas City, Missouri 64198
Denver Branch	303-572-2300		1020 16th Street, Denver, Colorado 80202 (Terminal Annex-P.O. Box 5228, Denver, Colorado 80217)
Oklahoma City Branch	405-270-8400		226 Dean A. McGee Avenue (P.O. Box 25129) Oklahoma City, Oklahoma 73125
Omaha Branch	402-221-5500		2201 Farnam Street, Omaha, Nebraska 68102 (P.O. Box 3958 Omaha, Nebraska 68103)
DALLAS	214-651-6111	11	400 South Akard Street (Station K), Dallas, Texas 75222
El Paso Branch	915-544-4730		301 East Main Street, El Paso, Texas 79901 (P.O. Box 100, El Paso, Texas 79999)
Houston Branch	713-659-4433		1701 San Jacinto Street, Houston, Texas 77002 (P.O. Box 2578, Houston, Texas 77252)
San Antonio Branch	512-224-2141		126 East Nueva Street, San Antonio, Texas 78204 (P.O. Box 1471, San Antonio, Texas 78295)
SAN FRANCISCO	415-974-2000	12	101 Market Street, San Francisco, California 94105 (P.O. Box 7702, San Francisco, California 94120)
Los Angeles Branch	213-683-2300		950 South Grand Avenue, Los Angeles, California 90015 (Terminal Annex-P.O. Box 2077, Los Angeles, California 90051)
Portland Branch	503-221-5900		915 S.W. Stark Street, Portland, Oregon 97025 (P.O. Box 3436, Portland, Oregon 97208)
Salt Lake City Branch	801-322-7900		120 South State Street, Salt Lake City, Utah 84111 (P.O. Box 30780, Salt Lake City, Utah 84125)
Seattle Branch	206-343-3600		1015 Second Avenue, Seattle, Washington 98104 (P.O. Box 3567, Seattle, Washington 98124)

*Additional offices of these Banks are located at Lewiston, Maine 04240; Windsor Locks, Connecticut 06096; Cranford, New Jersey 07016; Jericho, New York 11753; Utica Oriskany, New York 13424; Columbus, Ohio 43216; Columbia, South Carolina 29210; Charleston, West Virginia 25328; Des Moines, Iowa 50306; Indianapolis, Indiana 46206; and Milwaukee, Wisconsin 53201.

Source: Board of Governors of the Federal Reserve System, Washington, D.C., 20551.

Options and Futures

What Are Stock Options?

There are two types of stock options—call and put. A call option is the right to buy a specified number of shares of a stock at a given price before a specific date. A put option is the right to sell a specific number of shares of a stock at a given price before a specific date. Options, unlike a futures contract, are a right *not an obligation* to buy or sell stock. The price at which the stock may be bought or sold is referred to as the exercise (or striking) price. The date at which the option expires is the *expiration* date. The term "in-the-money" option refers to either a call option with an exercise price less than that of the market price of the stock, or a put option with an exercise price above the market price of the stock.

Expiration months are set at intervals of three months for the cycles: the January–April–July–October cycle, February–May–August–November cycle, and the March–June–September–December cycle. Options expire at 11:59 P.M. Eastern Standard Time on the Saturday immediately following the third Friday of the expiration month.

The exercise prices are set at 5 point (dollar) intervals for stocks trading below $50, 10 point intervals for stocks trading between $50 to $200, and 20 point intervals for securities trading above $200. Initial exercise prices are set above and below the price of the security. Thus, if a security is priced at 32½ on the New York Stock Exchange at the time new options are opened, the opening exercise prices would be set at 30 and 40. If the price of the security is close to a standard exercise price, three prices are set: at the standard price, as well as above and below the latter.

Standard option contracts are written for 100 shares of stock of the underlying security. The price at which the seller (writer) agrees to sell an option to the buyer is called the *premium*. The premium is quoted *per share* of the underlying stock so that the price per contract is 100 times the quote.

After the option is issued, the premium will fluctuate with the price of the stocks. With call options the premium will increase with an increase in the price of stock. With put options the premium will increase when the stock price declines. The reason should be clear from the following examples. Assume that in January a July call option is written at the exercise price of 50 ($50 per share) on the XYZ Corporation stock. We assume that the stock is selling at $51. The call option writer (seller) asks and receives a premium of $2 ($200 per option contract). After brokerage commission on the sale (say $25 per contract) the option writer nets a profit of $175 per contract. The call option buyer pays $200 for the contract plus the commission or $225. Assume that the stock increases to 60 per share. The option holder (buyer) can, in principle, purchase the stock at 50 (the Exercise price) and sell it at 60 netting a profit on transaction of $10 per share (neglecting commissions). Clearly the call option has acquired increased value which will be reflected in the premium (option price). Let us assume that the premium increases from 2 to 10 ($200 to $1,000 per contract). If the option holder now sells the option, he will make a profit (after commissions) of $750 on a $250 investment ($200 premium and $50 commissions).

Alternatively, the option holder may elect to exercise the option and acquire the shares at 50 (the exercise price). The option writer must then deliver 100 shares of XYZ Corporation at $50 per share.

If the stock price drops below the exercise price and remains so until expiration of the option, the call option buyer can lose his entire investment. Sometimes the loss may be reduced if the option is sold before it matures. The holder then is said to have *closed out* his position.

Similar arguments apply to put options. In this case the option holder benefits if the price of the stock decreases below the exercise price. Assume that the above stock drops to 40. The put holder could, in principle, buy the stock at 40 and sell it at 50 (the exercise price) to the put writer. The put holder would make a profit of $10 per share (neglecting commissions). The put premium would reflect this situation and, as a result, increase.

Instead of selling the option and taking a profit, the put holder may elect to exercise the option and sell 100 shares to the put writer who must purchase these shares at the 50 exercise price.

If the market price of the stock is greater than the exercise price when the put option expires, the holder will lose his investment.

Options are traded on the Chicago Board of Options Exchange, the American Stock Exchange, the Pacific Stock Exchange and the Philadelphia Stock Exchange.

How to Read Option Quotations

(1) Option & NY Close	(2) Strike Price	(3) Calls—Last Aug	Nov	Feb	(4) Puts—Last Aug	Nov	Feb
Slb							
94¾	100	2½	7	9½	5⅞	7¾	a
94¾	110	⅝	3⅜	5½	a	16	a
94¾	120	⅛	1⅛	b	a	a	b
94¾	130	1/16	b	b	a	b	b
Skylin	15	3⅜	4	a	a	⅝	a
17⅝	20	⅝	1 11/16	2¼	a	a	a
Southn	10	a	2⅜	2 7/16	b	b	b

Source: Reprinted by permission of *The Wall Street Journal*

(1) The name of the company in abbreviated form. Below the company name is the New York or American Exchange closing price of the stock in terms of ⅛ of a dollar.
(2) The striking (exercise) price of the option.
(3) The expiration month of the call option, beneath which is the option's premium (price) per share of stock. Contracts are for 100 shares of stock so that, for example, the price of a contract quoted as 2⅛ ($2.125 per share) is $212.50. Options expire on the Saturday following the third Friday of the expiration month. The premium does not include commissions.
(4) The same as item 3, but for a put option. The letter *a* means the option was not traded that day, and *b* means the option is not offered.

Stock Market Futures*

Standard & Poor's 500 Stock Index futures† combine the unique aspects of the futures market with the opportunities of stock ownership and stock options by helping many investors manage their inherent stock market risks, and at the same time allowing others to participate in broad market moves. S&P 500 Index futures can play an important role in an individual's or institution's overall market strategy.

Stock ownership is subject to several risks. Lower earnings reports or changes in industry fundamentals can cause severe declines in individual issues. Or, a promising industry or company might drop because the entire market is heading down. A myriad of decisions go into individual stock selection—but the first question is usually what is the state and direction of the entire market.

The introduction of the Standard & Poor's 500 Stock Index contract allows investors to hedge, and therefore, virtually eliminate their portfolio exposure in a declining market without disturbing their holdings. At the same time, others can purchase or sell the contract according to their expectations of future market activity. This simultaneous ability to hedge the risks of stock ownership and to take advantage of broad market moves creates opportunities for everyone with positions in or opinions about the stock market.

A NEW MARKET FOR TODAY'S INVESTOR

S&P 500 Index futures are traded on the Index and Option Market division of the Chicago Mercantile Exchange. One of the largest commodity exchanges in the world, the CME introduced financial futures trading in 1972 when it formed the International Monetary Market to trade contracts in foreign currencies. Later, the IMM added futures contracts in Gold, 90-Day Treasury Bills, Three-Month Domestic Certificates of Deposit, and Three-Month Eurodollar Time Deposits.

THE S&P 500 INDEX

The Standard & Poor's Stock Price Index has been the standard by which professional portfolio managers and individuals have measured their performance for 65 years. Begun in 1917 as an index based on 200 stocks, the list was expanded to 500 issues in 1957.

Currently, the Index is one of the U.S. Commerce Department's 12 leading economic indicators.

The S&P 500 Index is made up of 400 industrial, 40 public utilities, 20 transportation, and 40 financial companies and represents approximately 80% of the value of all issues traded on the New York Stock Exchange.

The S&P 500 Index is calculated by giving more "weight" to companies with more stock issued and outstanding in the market. Basically, each stock's price is multiplied by its number of shares outstanding. This assures that each stock influences the Index with the same importance that it carries in the actual stock market.

* Although every attempt has been made to insure the accuracy of the information in this section, the Chicago Mercantile Exchange assumes no responsibility for any errors or omissions. All matters pertaining to rules and specifications herein are made subject to and are superseded by official Exchange rules.

† Editor's Note: Futures based on the Value Line (Kansas City Exchange) and the New York Stock Exchange (New York Futures Exchange) indices are also traded. The principles are the same as with the S&P 500 futures.

Source: *Opportunities in Stock Futures*, Index and Option Market, Chicago Mercantile Exchange, 444 West Jackson Street, Chicago, IL 60606.

The Index is calculated by multiplying the shares outstanding of each of the 500 stocks by its market price. These amounts are then totaled and compared to a 1941–43 base period.

Calculations are performed continually while the market is open for each of the 500 stocks in the Index. The resulting Index is available minute-by-minute via quote machines throughout the world.

WHAT IS FUTURES TRADING?

The practice of buying or selling goods at prices agreed upon today, but with actual delivery made in the future, dates back to the 12th century. In the United States, organized futures exchanges were active as early as the 1840s. Today, the markets offer futures in grains, meats, lumber, metals, poultry products, currencies and interest-bearing securities.

The ability to contract today at a fixed price for future delivery performs two vital economic functions: risk transfer and price discovery.

For example, suppose a producer of cattle sees that someone is willing to buy his animals for delivery six months hence at a price that insures him an adequate profit. He decides to sell his production, with delivery after the animal matures, at the contracted price. In the process, he has locked in a price that is satisfactory to him and has insulated himself against the risk that the price may fall. In other words, he has transferred the risk of lower prices to someone else. Conversely, the purchaser of his animals has locked in his price and is assured that he will not have to pay a higher price in the future. This transaction could take place directly between the two men, or could be accomplished through futures trading at the CME—without the need for buyer and seller to actually meet. The open public trading system at the CME makes it easy to discover what the market currently considers to be a fair price for future delivery.

If the sale takes place on the Chicago Mercantile Exchange, the Exchange guarantees that both parties adhere to their agreement by placing itself and its resources between them. The Exchange thus becomes the buyer and the seller of the contract. This assures both parties that the contract will be carried out because the Exchange stands behind both parts of the agreement.

When delivery day arrives, the product is delivered to designated delivery points and inspected to make sure it is of the quality stipulated by the contract. The seller receives payment at the agreed price and buyer receives the produce.

Since full payment does not occur until the delivery day, the performance of both parties to the contract requires a good faith deposit or performance bond—known as the margin—when the contract is entered. Margins usually amount to a small percentage of the contract's total face value.

This payment differs from margin for stock purchases in that it is not a partial payment. It serves as a guarantee for both buyer and seller that there are sufficient funds on either side to cover adverse price movements that might otherwise bring the ability to meet contract terms into question.

At the close of business each day, each futures position is revalued at the contract's current closing price. This price is compared to the previous day's close (or if an initial position, the purchase or sale price) and the net gain or loss is calculated. Gains and losses are taken or made from the margin account each day in cash. There are no paper gains or losses in futures trading. If a margin account falls below a specified level, futures traders are required to deposit more money to maintain their positions.

All futures market participants should understand the operation of futures markets and consult with a Registered Commodity Representative before opening a futures trading account.

The S&P 500 Index futures contract is quoted in terms of the actual Index, but carries a face value of 500 times the Index. The contract does not move point-for-point with the actual Index, but it stays close enough to act as an effective proxy for the Index, and by extension, for the stock market as a whole.

If, for example, the futures price is quoted at 108.75, then the face value of the contract would be $54,375 (500 × 108.75). Minimum futures price increments, or movements, are .05 of the Index or $25. So if the futures quote is at 108.75, trades can continue to take place at that level, or move to 108.80 or to 108.70, with each .05 move equal to $25.

Trading opens at 9:00 A.M. and closes at 3:15 P.M. (Chicago time) with contracts trading for settlement in March, June, September and December. The final settlement day is the third Thursday of the contract month. At the close of business on that day all open positions have one final mark-to-market calculation—only on this day the expiration of the contract is marked to the actual closing level of the S&P 500 Index itself. Unlike traditional commodities, there is no physical delivery of the underlying commodity or resulting payment for the commodity in S&P 500 futures.

It is this unique cash settlement feature

of the S&P 500 futures contract that eliminates the prohibitively expensive costs of delivering 500 individual issues in varying amounts. Since there are little or no delivery costs, investors are assured that there will be no institutional factors to influence the futures contract's price. Thus, the price of the futures contract will reflect the current expectations about the direction of future stock prices. The International Monetary Market division of the CME pioneered this innovative concept in 1981, when its Eurodollar Time Deposit contract became the first cash settlement futures contract ever traded.

The S&P 500 futures contract should be viewed as a complement to equity ownership, not a substitute for it. Among the many benefits of S&P futures is the hedging ability that holders of stock can employ to provide an effective, cost efficient means of protecting security holdings against temporary market declines rather than selling and disturbing stock holdings. In addition, investors find the futures market equally as liquid for both buyers and sellers. Unlike the stock exchanges, short sellers do not require an up-tic before a trade can take place and there are no additional margin requirements.

SITUATIONS & STRATEGIES

Outright positions, either long or short, spreading and hedging are all uses for S&P futures. The contract also offers an unusually large number of hedging strategies when combined with equity portfolios and options. The following examples will show some of these uses in more detail.

LONG POSITION

Situation: An individual sees that interest rates are declining, the economy is firming and believes the entire market is undervalued. He notes that the S&P 500 futures contract for September delivery is at 108.85 and the actual S&P 500 Index is at 108.70.

It is apparent that most futures market participants also believe a move up is imminent. As supply and demand factors are bal-

Day	Position	Cost	S&P Future Closing Price	Gain or (Loss) Points × $5 (.01 equals 1 point)		Account Balance	Cumulative Gain or (Loss)
1	Long one contract	108.85	108.90	.05	$ 25	$5,025	$ 25
2	same	108.85	108.60	(.30)	(150)	4,875	(125)
3	same	108.85	108.40	(.20)	(100)	4,775	(225)
4	same	108.85	107.00	(1.40)	(700)	4,075	(925)
5	same	108.85	108.00	1.00	500	4,575	(425)
6	same	108.85	108.70	.70	350	4,925	(75)
7	same	108.85	109.50	.80	400	5,325	325
Sub Total Period one		108.85	109.50	65	$325	$5,325	$325

Period one: Our investor was a little off on his timing and his margin account was debited each day that losses occurred. If his margin balance had fallen to the maintenance minimum ($2,000 per contract) in this example he would have been required to make an additional payment to bring his balance back to the initial margin level ($5.000). As it is, he ended the period with a credit of $325 in cash.

Period two: With minor backing and filling, the trend is up and the S&P futures price closes period two at a level of 115.65.

	Position	Cost	S&P Future Closing Price	Gain or (Loss) Points × $5 (.01 equals 1 point)		Account Balance	Cumulative Gain or (Loss)
Sub Total Period Two	Long one contract	108.85	115.65	6.80	$3,400	$8,400	$3,400

Observations: During the first two weeks our investor's judgment of the market was correct and the S&P futures price advanced 680 index points or 6.25%. This translated into a gain of $3,400 on his initial investment of $5,000 or a gain of 68%.

At this point our investor believes that the market is due for a correction and decides to lock in his profit. He calls his RCR and instructs him to "cover" his September long position. His broker will then enter a sell order. After the close of business, the Exchange Clearing House will match the investor's previous long position and his new short position for a net zero position. All margins will be returned with cash credited to the investor's account with his broker the next day. Brokerage commissions have not been included in this example, but they are usually extremely reasonable and generally are quoted to include *both* the purchase and sale of the contract.

anced in an open marketplace, the intrinsic value of the September contract is established. The market is willing to pay a slight premium (.15) for the futures contract over the actual Index.

He calls his Registered Commodity Representative, enters an order to buy one September S&P 500 futures contract at the market and makes a good faith deposit to his account to guarantee his ability to meet his contractual commitment. For purposes of the following example, a margin account balance of $5,000 will be used. Margin requirements for actual positions vary. Individuals should contact their Registered Commodity Representatives for current information.

SHORT POSITION

If, instead of a rising market our investor believed that tight money would increase interest rates and the economy was weakening, he might have concluded that the S&P 500 Index futures price of 108.85 was an overvaluation and that the price was vulnerable to a decline.

September S&P Index contract to cover his short at the opening.

The opening is down on news that industrial production was weak and his position is covered at 106.55. His gain on his short then amounts to 2.30 at $25 per .05 or $1,150. The money is credited to his account the following day.

REDUCING THE VOLATILITY OF A STOCK PORTFOLIO

One reason for equity ownership is to take advantage of the long-term growth prospects of the company in which stock is purchased. Over time, higher earnings per share might be translated into a higher dividend payout. In the case of a company with a high return on investment and profits that are reinvested in the company's own growth, the expectation is that the growth will be reflected in higher share prices. However carefully constructed and diversified a portfolio may be, it is still subject in varying degrees to the risk that the market will decline. In order to protect principal values in a declining market, investors have traditionally sold stock to raise cash or shifted to more defensive issues with less volatility. These tactics very often are short-run solutions that disturb carefully tailored long-run objectives. S&P 500 Index futures can be used to add protection against a market downturn and allow an investor to maintain his equity holdings based on the prospects of the companies rather than the direction of the market.

Day	Position	Cost	S&P Future Closing Price	Gain or (Loss) Points × $5 (.01 equals 1 point)		Account Balance	Cumulative Gain or (Loss)
1	Short one contract	108.85	110.05	(1.20)	$ 600	$4,400	($ 600)
2	same	108.85	112.50	(2.45)	(1,225)	3,175	(1,825)
3	same	108.85	112.00	(.50)	(250)	3,425	(1,575)
4	same	108.85	109.50	(2.50)	(1,250)	4,675	(325)
5	same	108.85	108.75	.75	375	5,050	50
6	same	108.85	107.40	1.35	675	5,725	725
7	same	108.85	107.05	.35	175	5,900	900
Sub Total		108.85	107.05	1.80	$ 900	$5,900	$ 900

In our hypothetical example, the short position eventually worked. If the price had gone to a closing level of 114.85, the investor's account balance would have dropped to the maintenance margin level of $2,000 and he would have been required to add additional funds to bring his balance back to $5,000.

He decides to call his Registered Commodity Representative and enter a sell order for one September S&P 500 Stock Index future. Selling is just as easy as buying in an open outcry market. All bids to buy and offers to sell must be made publicly in the trading arena and are subject to immediate acceptance by any member. This differs greatly from stock exchanges where specialists or market makers require an up-tic from the previous sale to transact a short sale.

Let's again assume the initial margin required is $5,000. The above table shows the status of the short position over the course of seven trading days.

Our investor decides at this point that he wants to cover his short position and lock in his profit. The next morning before the opening of trading, he enters an order to buy one

SHORT HEDGE AGAINST A DIVERSIFIED PORTFOLIO

Situation: An investor owns a well-diversified portfolio with a current market value of $110,000. The S&P 500 futures contract is at 108.85. The market appears weak and the investor believes that there is substantial downside risk during the next three months. He decides to short S&P 500 futures to protect his portfolio.

Action: The S&P 500 futures contract at 108.85 represents a contract value of $54,425 (500 × 108.85). In order to protect his portfolio, he sells two contracts ($110,000 divided by $54,425 equals 2.02).

This hypothetical example assumed that the volatility of the portfolio very closely matched that of the market as measured by the S&P 500 futures contract prices. In reality, portfolios may be more or less sensitive to market moves. Statistical regression analysis for individual issues and entire portfolios can be calculated to measure past price volatility relative to the market. Expressed as "beta," it is a statistical measure of past movements which may change in the future. However, it is useful when hedging market risk in portfolios that are more volatile than the market.

Day	Position Short 2 Contracts	Closing Price S&P Contract	Gain or (Loss) Contract Points X $5 X 2 Contracts (.01 equals 1 point)		Value of Stock Portfolio	Portfolio Gain or (Loss)
1	108.85	110.05	(1.20)	($1,200)	$111,213	$1,213
18	108.85	109.50	(.65)	(650)	110,657	657
36	108.85	107.40	1.45	1,450	108,535	(1,465)
54	108.85	106.05	2.80	2,800	107,171	(2,829)
72	108.85	103.10	5.75	5,750	104,190	(5,810)
90	108.85	100.65	8.20	8,200	101,714	(8,286)
Position Closed	108.85	100.65	8.20	$8,200	$101.714	($8,286)

Observations: The market dropped and our investor hedged the cash decline in his portfolio with an offsetting gain in his futures position. Of course, if he were wrong about the direction of the market and it went up, he would have had losses in his futures positions but his stocks may have participated in the advance. The investor throughout this period, did not have to disturb his holdings and continued to receive his dividend payments.

Let us assume that the S&P 500 has a beta of 1.00, (that is, a given percentage move in the market gives rise to the same percentage move in the S&P 500) and our hypothetical portfolio has a beta of 1.50. Our portfolio's past market action relative to moves in the market was 50% greater than a given move in the general market. To compensate for this greater volatility, our hedger would require more S&P contracts to offset a greater decline in the value of his portfolio. Known as a hedge ratio, the dollar value of the portfolio is divided by the dollar value of the S&P 500 futures contract, the resulting figure is multiplied by the beta of the portfolio. Using our investor's portfolio and having calculated a beta of 1.5, we arrive at three contracts instead of two when the beta was 1.00:

$$\frac{\$110{,}000}{54{,}425} \times 1.5 = 3.03 \text{ contracts}$$

Thus, our investor would have sold three contracts to offset the portfolio's greater volatility to the market.

The concept of volatility and hedge ratios also may be applied to industry groupings and individual stocks. However, as the number of individual stock holdings that are being hedged decreases, then the greater is the chance that factors affecting that smaller group will make their prices react differently relative to the market than they have in the past.

ADDITIONAL USES OF THE S&P 500 FUTURES CONTRACT

Spreads: The simultaneous purchase and sale of different contract months to take advantage of perceived price discrepancies is called "spreading." The technique is considered by many to be less volatile than an outright long or short position, and as such, spreads generally carry lower margin requirements.

A characteristic of the futures market is that the closest contract date behaves more like the cash market. (In the S&P 500 futures contract, the cash market is the actual S&P 500 Index.) More distant months or back months have a greater component of their price determined by the expectations of what the price will be in the future.

These changing expectations of price levels of the S&P 500 contract into the future creates spreading opportunities. Options strategists will use the S&P 500 futures contract to reduce market risk when writing uncovered puts and calls. Block traders, investment bankers, stock specialists, options principals and anyone with the risk of stock market volatility, now have a vehicle and a well-capitalized liquid market to buy and sell market risk—the Standard & Poor's 500 Stock Index futures contract.

CONTRACT TERMS SUMMARY

Size	500 times the value of the S&P 500 Index
Delivery	Mark-to-market at closing value of the actual S&P 500 Index on Settlement Date
Hours	9:00 am to 3:15 pm Central Time
Months Traded	March, June, September, December
Clearing House Symbol	SP
Ticker Symbol	SP
Prices	Contract quoted in terms of S&P 500 Index
Minimum Fluctuation in Price	05 ($25)
Limit Move	3.00 ($1,500)
Last Day of Trading	3rd Thursday of Contract Month
Settlement Date	Last Day of Trading

Understanding the Commodities Market

COMMODITY EXCHANGES

A Commodity Exchange is an organized market of buyers and sellers of various types of commodities. It is public to the extent that anyone can trade through member firms. It provides a trading place for commodities, regulates the trading practices of the members, gathers and transmits price information, inspects and governs commodities traded on the Exchange, supervises warehouses that store the commodity, and provides means for settling disputes between members. All transactions must be conducted in a pit on the Exchange floor within certain hours.

FUTURES CONTRACT

A futures contract is a contract between two parties where the buyer agrees to accept delivery at a specified price from the seller of a particular commodity, in a designated month in the future, if it is not liquidated before the contract reaches maturity. A futures contract is not an option; nothing in it is conditional. Each contract calls for a specified amount, and grade of product. For example: *A person buying a February Pork Belly contract at 52.40 in effect is making a legal obligation, now, to accept delivery of 38,000 pounds of frozen Pork Bellies, to be delivered during the month of February, for which the buyer will pay 52.40 per pound.*

The average trader does not take delivery of a futures contract, since he normally will close out his position before the futures contract matures. As a matter of fact, a survey conducted by a leading exchange has estimated that less than 3% of the contracts traded are settled by actual delivery.

Editor's Note: The scope of the commodities market has been broadened in recent years to include contracts on financial (debt) instruments (T-bills, bonds, etc.) and composite stock market indices such as Value Line, S&P 500, and the New York Stock Exchange. With the stock market index futures, settlement is made in cash in amount based on the underlying index. Cash, not the securities, is used to offset the long and short positions. The cash value of the contract is defined as the index quotation × 500.

THE HEDGER AND SPECULATOR

A hedger buys or sells a futures contract in order to reduce the risk of loss through price variation. A short hedger sells a futures contract to protect the possible decline in the actual commodity owned by him. A long hedger purchases a futures contract to protect the possible advance in the value of an actual commodity needed to be purchased in the future.

The speculator is an important factor in the volume of future trading today. He, in effect, voluntarily assumes the risk, which the hedger tries to avoid, with the expectations of making a profit. He is somewhat of an insurance underwriter. The largest number of traders on any commodity exchange is the speculator. In order for the hedger to participate, he must have continuous trading interests and activity in the market. This trading activity stems from the role of the speculator, because he involves himself in buying or selling of futures contracts with the idea of making a profit on the advance or decline of prices. The speculator tries to forecast prices in advance of delivery and is willing to buy or sell on this basis. A speculator involves himself in an inescapable risk.

CAN YOU BE A SPECULATOR?

Now, can you be a speculator? Before considering entering into the futures market as a speculator, there are several facts which you should understand about the market and also about yourself. In order to enter into the futures market, you must understand that you are dealing with a margin account. Mar-

Source: Commodity Educational Services, Division of Commodity Cassettes, Inc., 778 Frontage Road, Northfield, IL 60093.

gins are as low as 5 to 10% of the total value of the futures contract, so you are obtaining a greater leverage on your capital.

Fluctuations in price are rapid, volatile, and wide. It is possible to make a very large profit in a short period of time, but also, it is possible to take a substantial loss. In fact, surveys taken by the Agricultural Department have shown that up to 75% of the individuals speculating in commodity markets have lost money. This does not mean that some of their trades were not profitable, but after a period of time with a given sum of money they ended up being a loser.

Now taking you as an individual, let us see whether you have the characteristics to become a commodity trader. Number one and the most important is that you do not take money that you have set aside for your future, or money you need daily to support your family or yourself. Number two, and almost equally important, is that you must be willing to assume losses and be willing to assume these losses with such a temperament that it is not going to affect your everyday life. Money used in the futures market should be money that has been set aside for strictly risk purposes, and if this money is not risk capital, your methods of trading could be seriously affected, because you cannot afford to be a loser.

Another very important factor is that you must not feel that you are going to take a thousand, two thousand, five or ten thousand dollars and place this with a brokerage firm and not follow the daily happenings of the market. Price fluctuations are fast, and as stated before, wide, so you must not only be in contact with your Account Executive daily, but know and study the technical facts that may be affecting the particular market in which you are speculating.

The individual who makes his first trade by buying a contract on Monday and selling this contract on the following Wednesday, making six hundred dollars on a $1,000 investment, in a period of two days, suddenly says to himself, *"Where has this market been all my life? Why am I working? Why not just concentrate on this market, if every two days or so I can make six hundred dollars?"* This is a fallacy, since this is an individual that is going to destroy himself and most likely his family. The next trade he will feel confident that because of his first profitable trade the market will always go his way even though he is now showing a loss in his position. He still feels that the market will turn around in his direction. If you become married to a particular commodity futures contract and constantly feel that the losses you are taking at the present time will reverse into profits, you are really fighting the market and in most cases fighting a losing battle. This could lead to disaster. There is a saying that you let your profits ride, but liquidate your losses fast.

In any way that you are uneasy with a position that you are holding, it is better to liquidate it. If, prior to the time of buying or selling a contract, you are not sure that this is the right step to take, do not take it. To protect yourself against this hazard you should pre-decide on every trade and exactly how much you intend to lose.

Another important point is not to involve yourself in too many markets. It is difficult to know all the technical facts and be able to follow numerous markets. In addition, if you are in a winning position, be conservative as to how you add additional contracts or pyramid your position. Being conservative will sometimes cause you to miss certain moves in certain markets and you may feel this to be wrong, but over a long period of time, this conservatism will be profitable to you.

If at this point you feel that you are ready, both financially and mentally to trade commodities, the next step is to begin the actual mechanics of trading a futures contract.

OPENING AN ACCOUNT

The first important factor is to decide which brokerage firm will afford you the best service. To accomplish this, you should do a little research by checking with the various exchanges about different brokerage firms. You should study their advertising, market letters, and other information. These should all be presented in a business-like manner and have no unwarranted claims, such as a guarantee of profit without indicating the possibility of loss.

The brokerage firm must be able to handle orders on all commodity exchanges. Do not pick just any Account Executive in a firm, but one you feel confident to help you make market decisions. Become acquainted with the Account Executive through phone or personal conversations. His knowledge of the factors entering into the market and the understanding of current market trends are important in your final choice.

After making a decision on the brokerage firm and the Account Executive that would be best for you, contact him and have him send you the literature concerning different contracts, and also, any additional information as to his organization. He will then send you the necessary signature cards required by the firm to open an account, and ask you for a deposit of margin money.

You will be trading in regulated commodities, and margin money will be deposited in a segregated fund at the brokerage firm's bank. A segregated account means that the money will only be used for margin and not for expenses of the brokerage firm.

Now you decide to enter into your first trade. Your Account Executive and you decide to enter into a December Live Cattle contract on the Chicago Mercantile Exchange. Your order will be executed as follows: Your Account Executive will place this order with his order desk who will then transmit the order to the floor of the Chicago Mercantile Exchange. There your order will be executed on the trading floor, in the pit. All technical details connected with the transaction will be handled by the brokerage firm.

Upon filling of your order, the filled order will be transmitted back to your Account Executive, who will then contact you, advising you that you have purchased one December Live Cattle contract at a given price. You will also receive a written confirmation on this transaction. You will now show an open position in December Live Cattle on the books of the brokerage firm.

MECHANICS OF A TRADE

Let us go back one step to explain in detail just how your order to buy one December Cattle was handled on the floor of the exchange. All buying and selling in the pit is done by open out-cry, and every price change is reported on the exchange ticker system. Each firm has brokers in the different pits, a pit meaning a trading area for the purpose of buying and selling contracts.

When your order was received on the exchange floor, it was time stamped and then given to a runner. This is a person who takes the order from the desk on the exchange floor and gives it to one of the brokers in the December Cattle trading pit. He is then responsible to the brokerage firm to fill that order, if possible, at the stated price. After filling the order, he then has the runner return it to the desk where it is time stamped and transmitted back to the order desk at the brokerage house, and the filled order is reported to you.

MARGIN

Futures trading requires the trader to place margin with his brokerage firm. Initial margin is required and this amount varies with each commodity. The minimum margin is established by each commodity exchange. Additional funds are needed when the equity of your account falls below this level. This is known as a maintenance margin call.

All margin calls must be met immediately. Normally you will be given a reasonable amount of time to comply with this request. If you do not comply, the firm has the right to liquidate your trades or a sufficient number of trades to restore your account to margin requirements.

The brokerage firm has the right to raise margin requirements to the customer at any time. This is normally done if the price of the commodity is changing sharply or if it is the brokerage firm's opinion that due to the volatility of the market the margin requirement is not sufficient at that particular time.

Most commodity contracts have a minimum fluctuation and also a maximum fluctuation for any one particular day. For example, if you are trading frozen Pork Bellies on the Chicago Mercantile Exchange the fluctuation is considered in points. A point equals three dollars and eighty cents. this means that if you buy a contract at 52.40 and the next price tick is 52.45, you have made a paper profit of five points or nineteen dollars. The maximum fluctuation on a belly contract is 200 points, so your profit or loss cannot exceed in one day more than 200 points from the previous day's settlement. There are exceptions in some commodity contracts, where the spot month has no limit.

Let us assume that you had originally placed in the hands of your brokerage firm two thousand dollars margin money, and that you and your Account Executive decide to purchase a December Live Cattle contract whose initial margin is $1200 with maintenance of $900.00. After the purchase of the contract your account would show initial margin required $1200 dollars with excess funds of eight hundred dollars. At the end of each day the settlement price of December Cattle would be applied to your purchase price and your account would be adjusted to either an increase due to profit or decrease due to loss in your contract.

Further, assume that in a period of two or three days there is a decline in the price of the December Cattle contract and your account now shows a loss of three hundred dollars. Since maintenance margin is only nine hundred dollars on this contract, you will still show an excess of eight hundred dollars over and above maintenance margin. But, in the next four days suppose there is an additional loss of nine hundred dollars. Your account will now need one hundred dollars to maintain the maintenance margin and four hundred dollars additional in order to bring your account up to initial margin. Your Account Executive, or a man from the margin department of the brokerage firm will then contact you, stating that you must place additional money with the firm in order to maintain the December Cattle contract.

At this point, you must decide whether you should continue with the contract, feeling that it may be profitable in the next few days, and thus sending the brokerage firm the required four hundred dollars to maintain your position, or whether to assume your loss and sell the contract.

Let us assume that you decide to sell your December contract at this point and that the selling price causes a loss of four hundred dollars. Added to this loss would be the commission of forty dollars, so your total loss on the transaction would be four hundred forty dollars. A confirmation and purchase and sales statement will be sent to you, showing the original price paid for the contract, the price for which it was sold, the gross loss of four hundred dollars plus the commission of forty dollars making the total loss four hundred forty dollars, and your new ledger balance on deposit with the firm as fifteen hundred sixty dollars.

As shown in our example, commission was charged only when the contract was closed out. A single commission is charged for each round-turn transaction consisting of the creation and liquidation of a single contract.

CONTROLLED, DISCRETIONARY, AND MANAGED ACCOUNTS

There are two methods of trading your account. The first is the professional approach where you and your Account Executive decide on each trade with no discretion being given directly to your Account Executive. This method was illustrated in the discussion about margins. The second method is called a controlled discretionary or managed account. Under this method, you are giving your Account Executive authorization to trade your account at his discretion at any time and as many times that he considers that a trade should be made. The Chicago Mercantile Exchange, and the Board of Trade have rules governing this type of relationship. The following is an excerpt from the C.M.E. rule regarding controlled, discretionary and managed accounts.

REQUIREMENTS

No clearing member shall accept or carry an account over which any individual or organization, other than the person in whose name the account is carried, exercises trading authority or control, hereinafter referred to as controlled accounts, unless:

> The account is initiated with a minimum of $5000*, and maintained at a minimum equity of $3,750*, regardless of lesser applicable margin requirements. In determining equity the accounts or ledger balances and positions in all commodities traded at the clearing member shall be included. Whenever at the close of any business day the equity, calculated with all open positions figured to the settling price, in any such account is below the required minimum, the clearing member shall immediately notify the customer in person, by telephone or telegraph and by written confirmation of such notice mailed directly to the customer, not later than the close of the following business day. Such notice shall advise the customer that unless additional funds are promptly received to restore the customer's controlled account to no less than $5,000*, the clearing member shall liquidate all of the customer's open futures positions at the Exchange.
>
> In the event the call for additional equity is not met within a reasonable time, the customer's entire open position shall be liquidated. No period of time in excess of five business days shall be considered reasonable unless such longer period is approved in writing by an officer or partner of the clearing member upon good cause shown.

* Minimums can be changed by each exchange, so consult your Account Executive for current regulations.

REVIEWING YOUR CONFIRMATIONS AND STATEMENTS

An important factor in trading is that you must be sure that no errors occur in your account. For every trade made you should receive a confirmation, and for every close-out a profit and loss statement known as a Purchase-and-Sale, showing the financial results of each transaction closed out in your account. In addition, a monthly statement showing your ledger balance, your open position, the net profit or loss in all contracts liquidated since the date of your last previous statement, and the net unrealized profit and loss on all open contracts figured to the market should be sent to you.

You should carefully review these statements. Upon receiving a confirmation of a trade you should immediately check its accuracy as far as type of commodity, month, trading price and quantity of contracts. If this does not agree with your original order, it should be immediately reported to the main office of your brokerage firm, and any differences should be explained and adjustments should be made.

If you do not receive a confirmation on a trade after it was orally reported to you by your Account Executive, be sure to contact him and the main office so that if an error was made it can be corrected immediately.

You should receive written confirmation when you deposit money with your brokerage firm. If within a few days, you have not received this confirmation, report it immediately to the main office of your brokerage firm.

Never assume that an order has been filled until you receive an oral confirmation from your broker. A ticker or a board that you may be observing can be running several minutes behind and is not the determining factor as to whether your trade was executed or not. Until you receive this oral confirmation, never re-enter an order to buy or sell, against that position.

If you receive a confirmation in the mail showing a trade not belonging to you, immediately notify the main office of your brokerage firm and have them explain why this is on a confirmation with your account number. If it is an error, be sure that it is adjusted immediately and a written confirmation sent to you showing the adjustment of the error. If an error is made and it is profitable to you do not consider this any differently than if it was not profitable. Regardless of whether there is a profit or loss, all errors should be immediately reported to the brokerage firm.

Be sure that when you request funds to be mailed from your account that they are received within a few days from the time of your request. If not, contact the accounting department of the brokerage firm to see what is the cause of the delay.

Never make a check out to an individual. Always make your check out to the brokerage firm.

DAY TRADING

Day trading is where there is a buy and sell made during the trading hours on one particular day. Day trading is not considered to be a sound practice for the new speculator and inexperienced trader. Day trading is something that should be executed only by a sophisticated trader who is in frequent communication with the floor, and even then, on a limited basis.

ORDERS

In order to trade effectively in the commodity market there are several basic types of orders. The most common order is a market order. A market order is one which you authorize your Account Executive to buy or sell at the existing price. This is definitely not a predetermined price, but is executed at a bid or offer at that particular moment.

> *Example: Buy 5 Feb Pork Bellies at the market.*

LIMITED OR PRICE ORDERS AND "OB" DESIGNATION

This type of order to buy or sell commodities at a fixed or "limited" price and the ordinary "market" order are the most common types of orders.

> *Example: Buy Three Jan Silver 463.10.* This limit order instructs the floor broker to buy three contracts of January Silver futures at 463.10. Even with this simple order, however, one presumption is necessary—that the market price prevailing when the order enters the pit is 463.10 or higher. If the price is below 463.10, the broker could challenge on the basis that the client may have meant *"Buy Three Jan Silver 463.10 stop."* Therefore, while it is always assumed that a "limit: order means 'or better,'" if possible, it saves confusion and challenges if the "OB" designation is added to the limit price. This is particularly true on orders near the market, or on pre-opening orders with the limit price based on the previous close, because no one knows whether the opening will be higher or lower than the close, *i.e., Buy Three Jan Silver 463.10 OB.*

STOP ORDERS *(Orders having the effect of market orders)*

Buy Stop Buy stop orders must be written at a price higher than the price prevailing at the time of entry. If the prevailing price for December Wheat is 456 per bushel, a buy stop order must designate a price above 456.

> *Example: "Buy 20 Dec Wht 456½ Day Stop."* The effect of this order is that if December Wheat touches 456½ the order to buy 20 December Wheat becomes a market order. From that point, 456½ on, all the above discussion regarding market orders applies.

Sell Stop Sell stop orders must be written at a price lower than the price prevailing at the time of entry in the trading pit. If the prevailing price of December Wheat is 456 per bushel, a sell stop order must designate a price below 456.

> *Example: "Sell 20 Dec Wht 455 Day Stop."* If this order enters the trading pit with the above price of 456 prevailing, the order to sell 20 December Wheat becomes a market order. From that point 455 on, all the above discussion regarding market orders applies.

Buy stop orders have several specific uses. If you are short a December Wheat at 456, and wish to limit your loss to ½ cent per bushel, the above buy stop order at 456½ would serve this purpose. However, it is important to realize that such *"stop loss"* orders do not actually limit the loss to exactly ½ cent when *"elected"* or *"touched off"* because they become market orders and must be executed at whatever price the market conditions dictate.

Another use is when you are without a position and believe that, because of chart analysis or for other reasons, a buy of December Wheat at 456½ would signal the beginning of an important uptrend in Wheat prices. Thus, the same order to *"Buy 20 Dec Wheat 456½ Day Stop"* would serve this purpose.

Sell stop orders have the same uses in reverse. That is, if you are long 20 December Wheat at 456 and wish to limit this loss to 1 cent per bushel, the above sell stop order at 455 would serve this purpose, within the limitations of the market order possibilities. Similarly, if you are without a position and believe that a sale of December Wheat at 455 would signal a downtrend in wheat prices, and you wish to be short the market, you could use the order to *"Sell 20 December Wheat 455 Day Stop"* for this purpose.

STOP LIMIT ORDERS *(Variations of stop orders)*

Stop limit orders should be used by you when you wish to give the floor broker a limit beyond which he cannot go in executing the order which results when a stop price is *"elected."*

> *Example: "Buy 20 Dec Wheat 456½ Day Stop Limit."* This instructs the broker that when the price of 456½ is reached and *"elects"* this stop order, instead of making it a market order, it becomes a limited order to be executed at 456½ *(or lower)*, but no higher than 456½. Another possibility:

> *Example: "Buy One February Pork Belly 58.10 Day Stop Limit 58.25 (or any other price above 58.10)."* This instructs the broker that when the price of 58.10 *"elects"* the stop order instead of making it a market order, it becomes a limited order to buy at 58.25 *(or lower)*, but no higher as with any limit order.

Stop limit orders are particularly useful to you when you have no position and wish to enter a market via the stop order, but want to put some reasonable limit as to what you will pay. On the other hand, stop limit orders are not useful to you when you have an open position and wish to prevent a loss beyond a certain point. The reason is that by limiting the broker to a certain price after a *"stop loss"* order is elected, **you also run the risk that the market may exceed the limit too fast for the broker to execute.** This would leave you with your original position because the broker would have to wait for the return to the limit before executing. With a straight stop *(no limit)* order, the broker must execute *"at the market."*

> *Example: "Buy One February Pork Belly 58.10 Day Stop Limit 58.25."* Suppose the market moves to 58.10 but then only 20 February Pork Bellies are offered at that price. Your broker bids for one at 58.10 but another broker in the pit catches the seller's eye first and buys 20 and your broker misses the sale. Your broker then bids 58.20 but the best offer is 58.30. He bids 58.25, but the offer at 58.30 remains unchanged. Then another broker bids for and buys February Pork Bellies at 58.30 and the market moves on up. Your broker is left with no execution to your order unless the market later declines to your limit making a fill possible.

If you did not have a position you might be disappointed, but you would be unhurt financially. However, if you had a position and were trying to limit your loss you would have defeated your purpose with the stop limit order, if you truly wanted *"out"* after the stop was elected.

Stop limit orders on the sell side have exactly the same uses, advantages and disadvantages as discussed above, but in reverse:

> *Example: "Sell 20 December Wheat 455 Day Stop Limit."* This means that when the market declines to 455 per bushel, the broker may sell at 455 *(or higher)*, but no lower.

> *Another Example: "Sell One February Pork Belly 58.25 Stop Limit 58.10."* This instructs the broker to sell a belly after the stop price of 58.25 is reached and *"elects"* the stop order, but no lower than 58.10

M.I.T. ORDERS *(Market-if-touched)*

By adding MIT *(Market-If-Touched)* to a limit order, the limit order will have the effect of a market order when the limit price is reached or touched. This type of order is useful to you, when you have an open position and if a certain limit price is reached.

> *Example: "Sell One September Sugar 950 MIT."* The floor broker is told that if and when the price of September Sugar rises to 9½¢ per pound, he is to sell one contract at the market. At this price of 9½¢ all prior discussion on market orders applies.

Under certain market conditions, not

enough contracts are bid at 9½ cents to fill all offers to sell. Thus, you may see your straight limit price appear on the ticker, but your broker fails to make the sale.

But by adding MIT to the limit price, you will receive an execution, because the order becomes a market order, if the price is touched. However, the price will not necessarily be a good one in your eyes, since it became a market order when touched.

The same reasoning is true on the buy side of MIT orders but in reverse. Assume you are short one contract of September Sugar, with the prevailing price at 9½¢ per pound and you want to cover or liquidate your short at 9¢.

Example: "Buy One September Sugar 9¢ MIT." If and when the price of September sugar declines to 9¢ per pound, the floor broker must buy one contract at the market. Aside from the disadvantages of any market order, the MIT designation on the buy order prevents the disappointment which might arise if a straight limit buy at 9¢ were entered without the MIT added.

SPREAD ORDERS

As explained in the Glossary, a spread is a simultaneous long or short position in the same or related commodity. Thus a spread order would be to buy one month of a certain commodity and sell another month of the same commodity, or buy one month of one commodity and sell the same or another month of a related commodity.

Example: "Buy 5 July Beans Market and Sell 5 May Beans Market" or "Buy 10 Kansas City Dec Wheat Market and Sell 10 Chicago May Wheat Market."

Another Example: "Buy 5 May Corn Market and Sell 5 May Wheat Market."

In the example of the related commodity spread, normally the reason you would use such a spread, is that you expect to make a profit out of an expected tightness in the Corn Market, in the hope the corn contract will gain in value faster than wheat.

There may be a situation where you have a position either long or short in a commodity and want to change to a nearer or more distant option of the same commodity. For example you are long 5,000 bushels of May Soybeans on May 20 and want to avoid a delivery notice by moving your position forward into the July option. The basic spread order would be:

"Buy 5 July Beans Market and Sell 5 May Beans Market."

Sometimes you may prefer not to use market orders, in which case you use the difference spread.

Example: "Buy 5 July Beans and Sell 5 May Beans July 2¢ Over." Even though the prices of the two options are not specified, the broker is allowed to execute at any time he can do so with July selling at 2¢ or less above May. Over or under designations are a necessity for clarity to the floor broker. Omitting either is like omitting the price.

All orders, except market orders, can be cancelled, prior to execution. Naturally, a market order is executed immediately upon reaching the pit, so its cancellation is almost impossible.

There are other variations of orders, but for you the new speculator, the types mentioned are sufficient for your trading.

Options on Stock Market Indices, Bond Futures, and Gold Futures

STOCK MARKET INDEX OPTIONS

Stock market index related options are options whose prices are determined by the value of a stock market average such as the Standard and Poor (S&P) 500 Index or the New York Stock Exchange Composite Index, among others. Two types of such options are currently traded; index options and index futures options. The former are settled in cash while the latter are settled by delivery of the appropriate index futures contract.

Both types of options move in the same way in response to the underlying market index, thereby providing investors the opportunity to speculate on the market averages. The buyer of a call index option is betting that the underlying market index value will increase significantly above the strike price (before the option expires) so as to provide a profit when the option is sold. On the other hand, the buyer of a put option is speculating that the market index value will fall sufficiently below the strike price before the option expires so as to provide a profit when the put option is sold. Options writers (sellers), on the other hand, assume an opposite position.

While index futures (page 458) also permit speculation on the market averages, index option tend to be less risky since option *buyers* are not subject to margin calls and losses are limited to the price (premium) paid for the option. However, index option writers (sellers), in return for the premium received, are subject to margin calls and are exposed to losses of indeterminate magnitude. However, writers of call options on index *futures* can protect themselves by holding the underlying futures contract.

Index Options

A number of index options based on the broad market averages are now traded:

- S&P 100 Index [Chicago Board of Options Exchange (CBOE)]
- S&P 500 Index (Chicago Board of Options Exchange)
- Major Market Index [American Exchange (Amex)]
- Institutional Index (American Exchange)
- NYSE Options Index (New York Stock Exchange)
- Value Line Index (Philadelphia Exchange)
- National OTC Index (Philadelphia Exchange)

A brief description of some of the more important indices follows.

The S&P 100 Index is a so-called weighted index obtained by multiplying the current price of each of the 100 stocks by the number of shares outstanding and then adding all of the products to obtain the weighted sum. The weighted sum is then multiplied by a scaling factor to provide an index of a convenient magnitude. The S&P 500 Index is calculated similarly except that all of the S&P 500 stocks are included.

The NYSE Index is based on the weighted sum of all of the stocks traded on the New York Exchange while the AMEX Index is based on the weighted sum of all of the issues traded on the American Exchange. The Institutional Index consists of 75 stocks most widely held by institutional investors.

The Major Market Index differs from the above in that it is just the simple (unweighted) sum of 20 blue chip stocks multiplied by a factor of one tenth. This index behaves very similarly to the Dow Jones Index.

Generally index options expire on the Saturday following the third Friday of the expiration month. Hence the last trading day is on the third Friday of the expiration month. The price of an index option contract is $100 times the premium as quoted in the financial press.

Example: The July 120 (an option with a strike price of 120 expiring in July) Major Market Index call option is quoted (Exhibit 1) at 3.00. The cost of an option contract is $300 ($100 × 3).

Option premiums consist of the sum of two components; the intrinsic value and the time value. The intrinsic value of a *call* option

EXHIBIT 1 INDEX OPTIONS QUOTATIONS

CHICAGO BOARD

CBOE 100 INDEX

Strike	Calls—Last			Puts—Last		
Price	June	Sept	Dec	June	Sept	Dec
145	15¼	....	....	1/16	1	....
150	13¾	....	....	⅛	1¾	....
155	9⅛	10	....	7/16	3⅛	....
160	5⅛	9¼	....	17/16	4⅝	8¼
165	2⅛	6½	8⅝	3⅞	7¼	10½
170	11/16	3¾	6	7⅝	12	13½

Total call volume 20846. Total call open int. 62006.
Total put volume 25167. Total put open int. 103733.
The index closed at 163.55, +1.91.

AMERICAN EXCHANGE

MAJOR MARKET INDEX

Strike	Calls—Last			Puts—Last		
Price	Jul	Oct	Jan	Jul	Oct	Jan
115	5¾	8⅝	10	1⅞	3¾	5½
120	3	5¾	7	4	5⅞	7½
125	1⅛	3¼	....	7⅜	....	....
130	7/16	2¼	3⅝	....	....	

Total call volume 2351. Total call open int. 14572.
Total put volume 5276. Total put open int. 9593.
The index closed at 118.69, +1.00.

Source: Reprinted by permission of *The Wall Street Journal*, Dow Jones & Co., Inc.

is $100 times the difference obtained by subtracting the strike price from the current value of the index. The instrinsic value of a *put* option is $100 times the difference obtained by subtracting the current value of the index from the strike price. The time value is the money which an option buyer is willing to pay in the expectation that the option will become more valuable (*increase its intrinsic value*) before it expires. Obviously the time value decreases as the time to expiration decreases.

It should be noted that there is a distinction between exercising an index option and selling an index option to close out a position. Exercising an option gives the holder the right to a cash amount equal to the *intrinsic* value of the option. Hence, the time value of the option is lost. When an option is sold to close out a position, the option holder receives a cash amount equal to the *premium* which contains both the intrinsic value and the time value of the option. Thus, in most cases it is more profitable to sell the option. The profit realized (before commissions and taxes) on the *sale* of an option contract is equal to $100 times the difference obtained by subtracting the premium paid when the option was purchased from the premium received when the option was sold.

Example: On May 24 the CBOE 100 Index

was 163.55. In anticipation of a market decline, an investor buys a September 165-put option quoted at 7¼ for a total premium of \$725 (7.25 × 100) per option. Assume that on August 10 the puts were selling at a total premium of \$850 due to a decline in the CBOE 100 Index to 160.10. If the investor sells the put option he will realize a profit, before commissions and taxes, of \$125 (850 − 725). If the market moves in a contrary direction he could lose his entire investment.

Index Futures Options

Index futures options (also called futures options) are the right to buy (call) or sell (put) the underlying index futures contracts (see page 495). Futures options are currently traded on the New York Futures Exchange and the Chicago Mercantile Exchange. The dollar value of the underlying contract for the New York Futures Exchange option is equal to the New York Stock Exchange Composite Index multiplied by 500 while that for the Chicago Mercantile Exchange option is equal to the S&P 500 Index multiplied by 500. Quotations for futures options as they appear in *The Wall Street Journal* are shown in Exhibit 2. The total futures option premium per option is equal to the quoted value multiplied by 500. Gains and losses are calculated in the same way as index options.

The expiration day of the S&P 500 futures option is on the third Thursday of the expiration month while that for the NYSE futures option is the business day prior to the last business day of the expiration month.

Example: On May 24, 1983, the New York Composite Index is 94.39. An investor expects the Index to increase during the next six months and buys a September 96 futures call option at a total premium of \$1750 (3.50 × 500), as indicated in Exhibit 2. Assume that by August 10 the Index is at 100 and that the September call premium is quoted at 8.00 corresponding to a total premium per option of \$4000 (8.00 × 500). By selling the option at the current value the investor can realize a profit of \$2250 (4000 − 1750) before commissions and taxes.

Example: Assume that on May 24, 1983 when the S&P 500 Index is at 163.43, an investor expects a market decline within six months. He purchases a September 155 S&P put option at a total premium per option of \$1150 (2.30 × 500), as indicated in the quotations shown in Exhibit 2. Assume that the Index declines to 150 on August 10 and that the quoted put premium is 6.50 corresponding to a total premium per option of \$3250 (6.50 × 500). By selling the option at the current value the investor can realize a profit of \$2100 (3250 − 1150), before commissions and taxes.

EXHIBIT 2 FUTURES OPTIONS

CHICAGO MERCANTILE EXCHANGE

S&P 500 STOCK INDEX – Price = \$500 times premium.

Strike	Calls—Settle			Puts—Settle		
Price	Jun	Sep	Dec	Jun	Sep	Dec
135	....	....	....	.05	....	....
140	23.90	24.25	....	.05	.45	....
145	18.90	20.20	....	.05	.90	....
150	13.95	15.25	....	.10	1.25	....
155	9.20	11.50	....	.30	2.30	4.50
160	4.95	8.60	....	1.05	3.60	....
165	1.90	5.50	8.75	3.00	5.75	7.80
170	.45	3.50	....	6.50	9.50	....
175	.10	1.80	....	11.15	14.00	....

Estimated total vol. 1,440
Calls: Fri. vol. 766; open int. 6,216
Puts: Fri. vol 532; open int. 6,552

N.Y. FUTURES EXCHANGE

NYSE COMPOSITE INDEX – Price = \$500 times premium.

Strike	Calls—Settle			Puts—Settle		
Price	Jun	Sep	Dec	Jun	Sep	Dec
84	10.90	11.70	....	.05	.40	.75
86	8.00	10.00	11.00	.05	.70	1.50
88	5.95	8.50	9.70	.05	1.00	1.75
90	5.15	7.00	8.30	.25	1.50	2.30
92	3.35	5.50	7.00	.50	2.00	2.95
94	1.95	4.50	6.00	1.15	3.00	3.75
96	.95	3.50	5.00	2.10	3.90	4.95
98	.40	2.75	3.95	3.50	5.25	6.05
100	.15	1.75	3.25	....	6.25	7.00

Estimated total vol. 1,405
Calls: Fri. vol. 844; open int. 4,836
Puts: Fri. vol. 549; open int. 4,801

S&P 500 Index 163.43
New York Composite Index = 94.39

Source: Reprinted by permission of *The Wall Street Journal*, Dow Jones & Co., Inc.

While a number of the same basic concepts apply to both index options and future options, there are differences between the two because the futures options have underlying index futures contracts which are traded on the open market. This makes possible a number of trading strategies with futures options which are not available with index options; for example, simultaneously buying an index futures contract and writing a corresponding call option. Also, for the reason given above, there is a distinction between selling a futures option, the usual procedure, and exercising the option. When a futures option is exercised, the option is exchanged for a position in the index futures market which may result in a loss in the time value of the option.

Investors planning to trade options should read two free booklets available from any of the options exchanges:

Understanding the Risks and Uses of Options
Listed Options On Stock Indices

Subindex Options

Subindex options are based on an index made up of leading publicly traded companies within a specific industry. These options permit speculation on an industry without the necessity of selecting specific stocks within the industry. As with all stock index options they are settled in cash.

U.S. TREASURY BOND FUTURES OPTIONS

Options on U.S. Treasury Bonds (T-Bonds), traded on the Chicago Board of Trade, are the right to buy (call) or sell (put) a T-Bond futures contract. The T-Bond futures contract underlying the option is for $100,000 of Treasury Bonds, bearing an 8% or equivalent coupon, which do not mature (and are non-callable) for at least 15 years. When long term interest rates decline, the value of the futures contract and the call option increases while the value of a put option decreases. The reverse is true when long term rates increase.

Premiums for T-bond futures *options* are quoted in 1/64 of 1% (point): Hence each 1/64 of a point is equal to $15.63 ($100,000 × .01 × 1/64) per option. Thus a premium quote of 2–16 means 2 16/64 or (2 × 64 + 16) × $15.63 or $2250.72 per option. It should be noted that prices of T-bond *futures* are quoted in 1/32 (of a point) worth $31.25 per futures contract.

As with options trades in general, the profit (before taxes and commissions) is the premium received (per option) when the option is sold minus the premium paid when the option was purchased.

The last trading day for the options is the first Friday, preceded by at least five business days, in the month *prior* to the month in which the underlying futures contract expires. For example, in 1983 a December option stops trading on November 18, 1983.

GOLD FUTURES OPTIONS

The most widely traded gold futures option is on the New York Comex Exchange. The option is the right to buy (call) or sell (put) a gold futures contract for 100 Troy ounces of pure gold. Both the futures contract and the corresponding call option increase or decrease with the price of gold. Put option premiums move in the opposite direction to the price of gold.

Option premiums are in dollars per ounce of gold. Thus a quoted premium of 2.50 corresponds to total premium of $2500 (2.50 × 100) per option.

The profit (before commissions and taxes) to an option buyer is simply the premium received when the option is sold less the premium paid when the option was purchased.

The last trading day for gold futures options is the second Friday in the month *prior* to the expiration date of the underlying gold futures contract. Thus in 1983 a December option expires on Friday November 11, 1983. Example: In August an investor buys a December 400 (an option with a strike price of 400 on a December gold futures contract) Comex call option quoted at 25.00. The total price per option is $2500 (25.00 × 100).

On November 5, the price of gold has increased and the investor sells the option at a quoted premium of 50.00 or $5000.00 (50 × 100) per option. His profit is $2500 (5000 − 2500).

The Commodities Glossary

Acreage allotment The portion of a farmer's total acreage that he can harvest and still qualify for government price supports, low interest crop loans and other programs. It currently applies to specialty crops—tobacco, peanuts and extra long staple cotton—for which complex federal marketing orders have been written to control production closely. Before the 1977 farm bill was passed, the same term also applied more loosely to the portion of a farmer's wheat or feed grain acreage for which government payments would be made. A farmer could harvest 100 acres of wheat, for instance, but he'd receive price support payments only for 70 acres if that was his allotment. The allotment in this sense is called "program acreage" in the new farm bill.

Arbitrage The simultaneous buying and selling of futures contracts to profit from what the trader perceives as a discrepancy in prices. Usually this is done in futures in the same commodity traded on different exchanges, such as cocoa in New York and cocoa in London or silver in New York and silver in Chicago. Some arbitrage occurs between cash markets and futures markets.

Asking price The price offered by one wishing to sell a physical commodity or a futures contract. Sometimes a futures market will close with an asking price when no buyers are around.

Backwardation An expression peculiar to New York markets. It means "nearby" contracts are trading at a higher price, or "premium," to the deferreds. See also *Inverted market.*

Basis A couple of meanings: (1) The difference between the price of the physical commodity (the cash price) and the futures price of that commodity. (2) A geographic reference point for a cash price; for example, the price of a beef carcass is quoted "basic Midwest packing plants."

Bear A trader who thinks prices will decline. "Bearish" is often used to describe news or developments that have, or are expected to have, a downward influence on prices. A bear market is one in which the predominant price trend is down. Some think this term originated with an old axiom about "selling the skin before you've caught the bear."

Bid The price offered by one who wishes to purchase a physical commodity or a futures contract. Sometimes a futures market will close with a bid price when no sellers are around.

Broker An agent who buys and sells futures on behalf of a client for a fee. They work for brokerage firms, some of which have extensive research and analysis departments that occasionally issue trading advice. A few firms have so many customers who follow such advisories that recommendations to buy or sell can influence market prices materially.

Bull A trader who thinks prices will go up. "Bullish" describes developments that have, or are expected to have, an upward influence on prices. A bull market is one in which the predominant price trend is up. Some theorize this term originally related to a bull's habit of tossing its head upward.

Butterfly An unusual sort of spread involving three contract months rather than two. Often used to move profits or losses from one year to the next for tax purposes.

Cash The price at which dealings in the physical commodity take place. Used more sweepingly, it can mean simply the physical commodity itself (as in "cash corn" or "cash lumber"), or refer to a market. For example, the cash hog market is a terminal (or, collectively, all terminals) where live hogs are sold by farmers and bought by meat packers.

Chart A graph of futures prices (and sometimes other statistical trading information) plotted in such a way that the charter believes gives insight into future price movements. Several futures markets regularly are influenced by buying or selling based on traders' price-chart indications.

Clearing house The part of all futures exchanges (usually a separate corporation with its own members, fees, etc.) which clears all trades made on the exchange during the day. It matches the buy transactions with the equal number of sell transactions to provide orderly control over who owns what and who owes what to whom. Although futures traders theoretically trade contracts among themselves, the clearing house technically is in the middle of each transaction—being the buyer to every seller and the seller to every buyer. That's how it keeps track of what is going on.

Close The end of the trading session. On some exchanges, the "close" lasts for several minutes to accommodate customers who have entered buy or sell orders to be consummated "at the close." On those exchanges, the closing price may be a range encompassing the highest and lowest prices of trades consummated at the close. Other exchanges officially use settlement prices as the closing prices.

Source: The *Dow Jones Commodities Handbook*, edited by Dan Ruck, Dow Jones Books, Dow Jones Company, Inc. 1979.

Cold storage Refrigerated warehouses where perishable commodities are stored. In effect, the warehouses are secondary sources of commodities that aren't immediately available from the producers. The Agriculture Department periodically reports the quantities of various commodities stored in warehouses. Futures traders watch these reports to see if the supplies are building or dwindling abnormally fast, which indicates how closely supply and demand are balanced.

Commission The fee charged by a broker for making a trade on behalf of customers.

Contract In the case of futures, an agreement between two parties to make and in turn accept delivery of a specified quantity and quality of a commodity (or whatever is being traded) at a certain place (the delivery point) by a specified time (indicated by the month and year of the contract).

Country Refers to a place relatively close to a farmer where he can sell or deliver his crop or animals. For instance, a country elevator typically is located in a small town and accepts grain from farmers in the immediate vicinity. A country shipping point is a place where farmers in an area combine their marketings for shipment. A country price is the one these elevators, shipping points or whatever pay for the farmers' goods; it's based on the terminal-market prices, less transportation and handling costs.

Covering Buying futures contracts to offset those previously sold. "Short covering" often causes prices to rise even though the overall market trend may be down.

Crop report Estimates issued periodically by the Department of Agriculture on estimated size and condition of major U.S. crops. Similar reports are made on livestock.

Crush The process of reducing the raw, unusable soybean into its two major components, oil and meal. A "crush spread" is a futures spreading position in which a trader attempts to profit from what he believes to be discrepancies in the price relationships between soybeans and the two products. The "crush margin" is the gross profit that a processor makes from selling oil and meal minus the cost of buying the soybeans.

Deferred contracts In futures, those delivery months that are due to expire sometime beyond the next two or three months.

Delivery The tendering of the physical commodity to fulfill a short position in futures. This takes place only during the delivery month and normally takes the form of a warehouse receipt (from an exchange-accredited warehouse, elevator or whatever) that shows where the cash commodity is.

Delivery point The place(s) at which the cash commodity may be delivered to fulfill an expiring futures contract.

Discretionary accounts A futures trading account in which the customer puts up the money but the trading decisions are made at the discretion of the broker or some other person, or maybe a computer. Also known as "managed accounts."

Evening up Liquidating a futures position in advance of a significant crop report or some other scheduled development so as not to be caught on the wrong side of a surprise. In concentrated doses, evening up can cause a bull market to retreat somewhat and a bear market to rebound somewhat.

First notice day The first day of a delivery period when holders of short futures positions can give notice of their intention to deliver the cash commodity to holders of long positions. The number of contracts circulated on first notice day and how they are accepted or not accepted by the longs is often interpreted as an indication of future supply-demand expectations and thus often influence prices of all futures being traded, not just the delivery-month price. This effect also sometimes occurs on subsequent notice days. Rules concerning notices to deliver vary from contract to contract.

F.O.B. Free on Board, meaning that the commodity will be placed aboard the shipping vehicle at no cost to the purchaser, but thereafter the purchaser must bear all shipping costs.

Forward Contract A commercial agreement for the merchandising of commodities in which actual delivery is contemplated but is deferred for purposes of commercial convenience or necessity. Such agreements normally specify the quality and quantity of goods to be delivered at the particular future date. The forward contract may specify the price at which the commodity will be exchanged, or the agreement may stipulate that the price will be determined at some time prior to delivery.

Fundamentalist A trader who bases his buy-sell decisions on supply and demand trends or developments rather than on technical or chart considerations.

Futures Contracts traded on an exchange that call for a cash commodity to be delivered and received at a specified future time, at a specified place and at a specified price. Similar arrangements made directly between buyer and seller are called "forward contracts." They aren't traded on an exchange.

Hedge Using the futures market to reduce the risks of unforeseen price changes that are inherent in buying and selling cash commodities. For example, as an elevator operator buys cash grain from farmer, he can "hedge" his purchases by selling futures contracts; when he sells the cash commodity, he purchases an offsetting number of futures contracts to liquidate his position. If prices rise while he owns the cash grain, he sells the cash grain at a profit and closes out his futures at a loss, which almost always is no greater than his profit in the cash transaction. If prices fall while he owns the cash grain, he sells the cash grain at a loss but recoups all or almost all of the loss by buying back futures contracts at a price correspondingly lower than at which he first sold them. Some users of commodities assure themselves of supplies of their raw materials at a set price by buying futures, which is another form of hedging. When the time comes to acquire inventories, they can either take delivery on their futures contracts or, more likely, simply buy their supplies in the cash market. Futures-contract prices tend to match cash prices at the time the futures expire, so if cash prices have risen the users' higher costs are offset by profits on their futures contracts.

Hedger The Commodity Futures Trading Commission says a hedger in a general sense is someone who uses futures trading as a temporary, risk-reducing substitute for a cash transaction planned later in his main line of business. All other futures traders are classified as speculators. There are more legally specific definitions of hedging and hedgers in such markets as grains, soybeans, potatoes and cotton, where limits are placed on the number of contracts speculators may trade or own. The Commission has broadened these limits to allow hedging in closely related, rather than exactly matching, commodities. A sorghum producer, for instance, can use corn futures as a hedging tool where he couldn't before this rule-broadening. The more general distinction between hedgers and speculators may be important to potential traders. Some may want to use a market like interest rate futures to offset some expected heavy borrowing. The government hasn't set any speculative trading limits in those markets, but lenders or company directors are more apt to back a plan to trade futures for hedging purposes rather than speculation.

Inverted market A futures market where prices for deferred contracts are lower than those for nearby-delivery contracts because of great near-term demand for the cash commodity. Normally, prices of deferred contracts are higher, in part reflecting storage costs.

Last trading day The day when trading in an expiring contract ceases, and traders must either liquidate their positions or prepare to make or accept delivery of the cash commodity. After that, there is no more futures trading for that particular contract month and year.

Life of contract The period of time during which futures trading in a particular contract month and year may take place. This is usually less than a year, but sometimes up to 18 months.

Limit move The maximum that a futures price can rise or fall from the previous session's settlement price. This limit, set by each exchange, varies from commodity to commodity. Some exchanges have variable limits, whereby the limit is expanded automatically if the market moves by the limit for a certain number of consecutive trading sessions. When prices fail to move the expanded limit, or after a specified period of time, the limits revert to normal.

Liquidation Closing out a previous position by taking an opposite position in the same contract. Thus, a previous buyer liquidates by selling, and a previous seller liquidates by buying.

Long A trader who has bought futures, speculating the prices will rise. He is "long" until he liquidates by selling or fulfills his contracts by making delivery.

Margin The amount of "good faith" money that commodity traders must put in order to trade futures. The margins, set by each exchange, usually amount to 5% to 10% of the total value of the commodity contract. The "initial margin" is the amount of money that must be put up to establish a position in a futures market. Exchanges establish this margin, too, but brokerage firms often require even larger amounts to protect their own financial interests. "Maintenance margin" is the money that traders must put up to retain their position in the futures markets.

Margin call A request by a brokerage firm that a customer put up more money. That means the market price has gone against the customer's position and the brokerage firm wants the customer to cover his paper loss, which would become a real loss if the position were liquidated.

Nearby contracts The futures that expire the soonest. Those that expire later are called deferred contracts.

New crop The supply of a commodity that will be available after harvest. The term also is sometimes used in connection with pigs and hogs because the major farrowing periods in the spring and fall are referred to as "crops." There sometimes are substantial price differences between futures contracts related to new-crop supplies and those related to old-crop supplies.

Nominal price An artificial price—usually the midpoint between a bid and an asked price—that gives an indication of the market price level even though no actual transactions may have taken place at that price.

Old crop The supply from previous harvests.

Open The period each session when futures trading commences. Sometimes the open lasts several minutes to accommodate customers who have placed orders to buy or sell contracts "on the open." On these exchanges, opening prices often are reported by the exchange as a range, although these seldom are widely disseminated because of space restrictions in newspapers and periodicals; they are carried on tickers and display panels during that trading day, however.

Open interest Outstanding futures contracts that haven't been liquidated by purchase or sale of offsetting contracts, or by delivery or acceptance of the physical commodity.

Option The right to buy or sell a futures contract over a specified period of time at a set price.

Overbought A term used to express the opinion that prices have risen too high too fast and so will decline as traders liquidate their positions.

Oversold Like "overbought" except the opinion is that prices have fallen too far too fast and so probably will rebound.

Pit The areas on exchange floors where futures trading takes place. Pits usually have three or more levels and can accommodate a large number of traders. On several New York exchanges the trading areas are called rings and consist of open-center, circular tables around which traders sit or stand.

Position A trader's holdings, either long or short. A position limit is the maximum number of contracts a speculator can hold under law; it doesn't apply to bona-fide hedgers, although there really isn't any objective way of telling whether a person in position to hedge actually is hedging or is speculating instead.

Profit taking A trader holding a long position turns paper profits into real ones by selling his contracts. A trader holding a short position takes profits by buying back contracts.

Reaction A decline in prices following a substantial advance.

Recovery An increase in prices following a substantial decline.

Settlement price The single closing price, determined by each exchange's price committee of directors. It is used primarily by the exchange clearing house to determine the need for margin capital to be put up by brokerage-firm members to protect the net position of that firm's total accounts. It's also issued by some exchanges as the official closing price, and it is used to determine the price limits and net price changes on the following trading day. (See also: *Close*.)

Set-aside Acreage withdrawn from crop production for a season and used for soil conservation under a production-control program. Wheat farmers this year must set aside two acreas of land for each 10 acres they plant to wheat in order to get any federal price support or disaster aid. The Agriculture Department has also said corn, sorghum and barley producers similarly may be required to set aside some of their acreage if it appears that surpluses will grow too much otherwise.

Short A trader who has sold futures, speculating that prices will decline. He is "short" until he liquidates by buying back contracts or fulfills his contracts by taking delivery.

Short squeeze A situation in which "short" futures traders are unable to buy the cash commodity to deliver against their positions and so are forced to buy offsetting futures at prices much higher than they'd ordinarily be willing to pay.

Speculation Buying or selling in hopes of making a profit. The word connotes a high degree of risk.

Spot The same as cash commodities. Literally, delivery "on the spot" rather than in the future.

Spreads and straddles Terms for the simultaneous buying of futures in one delivery month and selling of futures in another delivery month (or even the simultaneous buying of futures in one commodity and selling of futures in a different but related commodity). One purpose is to profit from perceived discrepancies in price relationships. Another purpose is to transfer current trading profits to some future time to avoid immediate tax liability.

Stop-loss order An open order given to a brokerage firm to liquidate a position when the market reaches a certain price so as to prevent losses from mounting or profits from eroding. Sometimes market price trends are accelerated when concentrations of stop-loss orders are touched off.

Support price A level below which the government tries to keep the agricultural-commodity prices that farmers receive from falling. They're set basically by Congress when farm legislation is passed and adjusted from time to time by the President or Agriculture Secretary. Subsidy payments, commodity purchases, production controls or commodity-secured loans are among the devices used to make up the difference when market prices dip below the support level. Futures and cash prices often tend to remain near the support level when there are large crop surpluses because lower prices keep commodities off the market and higher ones quickly draw willing sellers.

Switch A trading maneuver in which a trader liquidates his position in one futures delivery and takes the position in another delivery month in expectation that prices will change more rapidly in the second contract than in the first. Thus, a trader might switch out of a position in an October silver futures contract into a position in a December silver futures contract. Warning: Some people use the word "switch" when they mean "spread" or "straddle." Feel free to correct them.

Technical factors Futures prices often are affected by influences related to the market itself, rather than to supply-demand fundamentals of the commodity with which the market is concerned. For example, if a market moves up or down the limit several days in succession there frequently is a subsequent "technical reaction" caused in part by the liquidation of contracts held by traders on the wrong side of the price move.

Terminal Refers to an elevator or livestock market at key distribution points to which commodities are sent from a wide area.

Trading range The amount that futures prices can fluctuate during one trading session—essentially, the price "distance" between limit up and limit down. If, for instance, the soybean futures price can advance or fall by a maximum of 20 cents per bushel in one day, the trading range is double that, or 40 cents per bushel. In one market, cocoa, price movements are restricted to a daily range of six cents a pound.

Visible supply The amount of a commodity that can be accounted for and computed accurately, usually because it is being kept in major known storage places.

Warehouse or elevator receipt The negotiable slip of paper that a short can hand over to fulfill an expiring futures contract's delivery requirement. The receipt shows how much of the commodity is in storage.

Dow Jones Futures and Spot Commodity Indexes

The method for arriving at the Dow Jones Futures and Spot Commodity Indexes differs from some others in the order in which the computations are made. Instead of first weighting each price, then adding them up and finally calculating the percentage or index, this method first turns each price into an index or percentage of its base-year price, then weights each individual index, and finally adds them up. Stated mathematically, the more usual method calculates the percentage relation of one average to another, while the Dow Jones Commodity Index method calculates the average of a set of percentage changes. These two methods do not result in exactly the same figures. However, they are equally valid when used consistently, and the indexes they produce are of the same general magnitude.

The Dow Jones Commodity Index method has two advantages. One is that it saves computation, because the factors or multipliers perform two computations at once. They calculate the individual percentages and weight them at one stroke. The other advantage is that if you have yesterday's index, you can apply the multipliers to today's individual price changes. Then all you do is add the resulting figures to yesterday's index, or subtract them from it, depending on whether they're up or down. That gives today's index. No need to recalculate the whole thing each day.

As for the weights, they were obtained by the usual mathematical methods. Basically, the weight of each commodity is the percentage of its commercial production value to the total commercial production value of all commodities in the index, in this case for the years 1927–31. In calculating the weights, consideration also was given to the relation between volume of trading in each commodity and its commercial production.

A further refinement was necessary because price changes of the various commodities are quoted in different units. Grain prices change in eighths of a cent, wool prices change in tenths of a cent, and all the other staples in the Dow Jones index move in hundredths of a cent. This adjustment merely required appropriate treatment in each case of the multiplier, so that it would give the

Source: The *Dow Jones Commodities Handbook*, edited by Dan Ruck, Dow Jones Books, Dow Jones & Company, Inc.

right figure for any price change. In the case of grains it meant an adjustment of 20%, since one-tenth is that much smaller than one-eighth. In other cases a mere adjustment of decimal points was sufficient.

The twelve commodities, with the weight of each and the multiplier applied to the price changes of each, are:

	Weight	Multiplier
Wheat	19.5	16
Corn	8	11
Oats	5	13
Rye	4	5
Wool Tops	5.5	4
Cotton	23	10
Cottonseed Oil	4.5	4
Coffee	7	3
Sugar	8.5	27
Cocoa	5	5
Rubber	6	3
Hides	4	3

These are the essentials for calculating the spot index. However, the futures index requires one more set of unusual steps. That's because several times a year an actual quoted "future" disappears. For instance, while early in the year it is possible to buy wheat to be delivered in December, when the month of December actually arrives that "delivery" expires and is no longer quoted.

The result is that futures prices are affected not only by market conditions but also by how close the delivery date looms. Interest charges and other such factors influence them. On July 1, the December delivery is just five months off, but a month later it is only four months away, and a five-month delivery should not, in a precise index, be compared with a four-month delivery.

This problem is overcome by the use of two futures quotations for each commodity. They are combined to produce on each market day the calculated price that would apply to a delivery exactly five months off.

On the first day of July, only the December delivery is used, since it is just five months away and thus no adjustment need be made. On the second day, the two quotations used are those for the same December delivery and the one for May of the following year. The quoted price for December is adjusted by one day's proportion of the difference between it and May's quoted price. Since there are 151 days between December and May (except in leap years) the figure for one day's proportion is 1/151 of the price difference between the two. The resulting fraction is added to December's price, or subtracted from it, depending on whether May is quoted above or below December.

The following day 2/151 of the difference are added or subtracted, the third day 3/151 and so on until December 1, on which day only the May contract's price is used. On December 2, the combination used is May and July, and so on around the year.

To facilitate the work of calculating the futures index every hour of each business day and the spot index once a day, tables have been prepared—resembling somewhat tables of logarithms or bond yields—which give the figures arrived at by multiplying the various quotational units of each commodity by its factor or multiplier. For instance, the tables show the proper multiples for one-eighth, one-quarter, three-eighths, etc., when each is multiplied by each grain's factor or multiplier.

The commodity futures index is published once an hour and as of the close of commodity markets each day on the Dow Jones News Service, where also the spot index is published once daily. Both are published likewise in *The Wall Street Journal*.

Futures and Option Contracts by Exchange[1]

American Stock Exchange

Options

Biotechnology Index
Computer Technology Index
Eurotop 100 Index
Institutional Index
Japan Index
Major Market Index (XMI)
Pharmaceutical Index
LT-20 Index
Oil Index
S & P Mid Cap 400

Chicago Board of Trade

Futures

Anhydrous Ammonia
Corn
Diammonium Phosphate
Oats
Soybeans
Soybean Meal
Soybean Oil
Wheat
Gold
Silver
U.S. Treasury Bonds
U.S. Treasury Notes (10 yr)
U.S. Treasury Notes (5 yr)
U.S. Treasury Notes (2 yr)
30-Day Interest Rate
Major Market Index-Maxi
Municipal Bond Index
Wilshire Small Cap Index
3-year Interest Rate Swap
5-year Interest Rate Swap

Options on Futures

Corn
Oats
Soybeans
Soybean Meal
Soybean Oil
Wheat
Gold
Silver
U.S. Treasury Bonds
U.S. Treasury Notes (10 yr)
U.S. Treasury Notes (5 yr)
Major Market Index
Municipal Bond Index
Wilshire Small Cap Index
3-year Interest Rate Swap
5-year Interest Rate Swap
Japanese Government Bonds
Project A Contracts:
  Barge Freight Rate Index
  Ferrous Scrap

[1] Addresses of the Exchanges are given on page 519.

U.S. Treasury Bonds
Zero Coupon Bonds
Zero Coupon Notes

Chicago Board Options Exchange

Options

ADRs
CBOE Biotech Index LEAPS
CBOE Biotech Index
Equities
Equity LEAPS®*
FT-SE 100 Index LEAPS
FT-SE 100 Index
OEX LEAPS®
Interest Rate (Long-Term, Short-Term)
S&P 100 Index
S&P 500 Index
SPX LEAPS
Russell 2000 Index
Russell 2000 Index LEAPS

Chicago Mercantile Exchange

Futures

Broiler Chickens
Live Hogs
Pork Bellies
Live Cattle
Feeder Cattle
Lumber
T-Bills (90-day)
DM/JY Cross Rate
Eurodollar Time Deposit
Dollar/Pound Diff
Dollar/Yen Diff
LIBOR[2]
Eurodollar Time Deposit
British Pound
Canadian Dollar
Deutschemark
Japanese Yen
Swiss Franc
Australian Dollar
Nikkei 225 Stock Average
S&P 500 Index
DM/JY Cross Rate

Options on Futures

Broiler Chickens
Live Hogs
Live Cattle
Pork Bellies
Feeder Cattle
LIBOR[2]
Lumber

* LEAPS® are Long-Term Equity AnticiPation Securities® and are traded on selected blue chips.

[2] LIBOR is an acronym for London Interbank Offered Rate.

Eurodollar Time Deposit
British Pound
BP/DM Cross Rate
Deutschemark
DM/JY Cross Rate
Swiss Franc
Japanese Yen
Canadian Dollar
Australian Dollar
T-Bills (90 day)
Nikkei 225 Stock Average
S&P 500 Stock Index
S & P Mid Cap 400 Index
FT-SE 100 Stock Index
Goldman Sachs Commodity Index

Coffee, Sugar & Cocoa Exchange

Futures

Brazil Differential Coffee
Cocoa
Coffee "C"
Sugar No. 11
Sugar No. 14
Sugar (white)

Options on Futures

Cocoa
Coffee "C"
Sugar No. 11

Commodity Exchange Inc. (COMEX)

Futures

Aluminum
Copper (High Grade)
Eurotop 100 Stock Index
Gold
Palladium
Platinum
Silver

Options

Five Day Gold
Five Day Silver

Options on Futures

Copper (High Grade)
Eurotop 100 Stock Index
Gold
Platinum
Silver

Financial Instrument Exchange (FINEX) of the NY Cotton Exchange

Futures

U.S. Dollar Index
European Currency Unit
U.S. Treasury Auction Notes (2 yr and 5 yr)

Options on Futures

European Currency Unit
U.S. Dollar Index
U.S. Treasury Auction (5 yr)

Kansas City Board of Trade

Futures

Mini Value Line Stock Index
Value Line Stock Index
Wheat

Options on Futures

Mini Value Line
Wheat

MidAmerica Commodity Exchange

Futures

Cattle, Live
Hogs, Live
Corn
Oats
CRCE Rough Rice
Soybeans
Soybean Meal
Wheat
New York Gold
New York Silver
Platinum
British Pound
Canadian Dollar
Deutsche Mark
Eurodollar
Japanese Yen
Swiss Franc
U.S. Dollar Index
U.S. Treasury Bills
U.S. Treasury Bonds
U.S. Treasury Notes

Options on Futures

Corn
Rough Rice
Soybeans
Wheat (Soft red winter)
New York Gold
U.S. Treasury Bonds

Minneapolis Grain Exchange

Futures

Wheat (Hard Red Spring)
Wheat (White)

Options on Futures

Wheat (White)

New York Cotton Exchange

Futures and Options on Futures

Cotton

New York Cotton Exchange, Citrus Associates of the

Futures and Options on Futures

Frozen Concentrated Orange Juice

New York Futures Exchange

Futures

NYSE Composite Stock Index
CRB Futures Price Index

Options on Futures

NYSE Composite Stock Index
CRB Futures Price Index

New York Mercantile Exchange

Futures

Crude Oil
Natural Gas
Heating Oil
Palladium
Platinum
Propane Gas
Residual Fuel Oil
Sour Crude Oil
Unleaded Reg. Gasoline

Options on Futures

Crude Oil (Light sweet)
Heating Oil
Natural Gas
Platinum
Unleaded Gasoline

New York Stock Exchange

Options

NYSE Composite Index

Pacific Stock Exchange

Options

Financial News Composite Index
Wilshire Small Cap Index

Philadelphia Board of Trade

Futures

Australian Dollar
British Pound
Canadian Dollar
Deutsche Mark
European Currency Unit
French Franc
Japanese Yen
National Over-the-Counter Index
Swiss Franc

Philadelphia Stock Exchange

Options

Australian Dollar
Bank Index
BP/DM Cross Rates
British Pound
Canadian Dollar
Deutsche Mark
DM/JY Cross Rates
European Currency Unit
French Franc
Gold/Silver Stock Index
Japanese Yen
National Over-the-Counter Index
Swiss Franc
Utility Index (European-style)
Value Line Index (European-style)

Futures

Australian Dollar
British Pound
Canadian Dollar
Deutsche Mark
European Currency Unit
French Franc
Swiss Franc

Commodity Futures Trading Commission (CFTC)

Federal laws regulating commodity futures trading are enforced by the Commodity Futures Trading Commission. For information on commodity brokers call (202) 254-8630.

National Office

Commodity Futures Trading Commission
2033 K Street, NW
Washington, DC 20581
Telephone: (202) 254-6387
Public Information: 202-254-8630

Regional Offices

Eastern Region
1 World Trade Center
New York, NY 10048
Telephone: (212) 466-2061

Central Region
233 S. Wacker Drive
Chicago, IL 60606
Telephone: (312) 353-5991

Southwestern Region
4900 Main Street
Kansas City, MO 64112
Telephone: (816) 374-6602

Minneapolis Office
510 Grain Exchange Building
Minneapolis, MN 55415
Telephone: (612) 370-2025

Western Region
10880 Wilshire Boulevard
Los Angeles, CA 90024
Telephone: (213) 209-6783

Source: U.S. Government Manual and the Commodity Futures Trading Commission.

The Commodity Futures Trading Commission (CFTC), the Federal regulatory agency for futures trading, was established by the Commodity Futures Trading Commission Act of 1974 (88 Stat. 1389; 7 U.S.C. 4a), approved October 23, 1974. The Commission began operation in April 1975, and its authority to regulate futures trading was renewed by Congress in 1978, 1982, and 1986.

The CFTC consists of five Commissioners who are appointed by the President with the advice and consent of the Senate. One Commissioner is designated by the President to serve as Chairman. The Commissioners serve staggered 5-year terms, and by law no more than three Commissioners can belong to the same political party.

ACTIVITIES

The Commission regulates trading on the 13 U.S. futures exchanges, which offer active futures and options contracts. It also regulates the activities of numerous commodity exchange members, public brokerage houses (futures Commission merchants), Commission-registered futures industry salespeople and associated persons, trading advisers, and commodity pool operators. Some off-exchange transactions involving instruments similar in nature to futures contracts also fall under CFTC jurisdiction.

The Commission's regulatory and enforcement efforts are designed to ensure that the futures trading process is fair and that it protects both the rights of customers and the financial integrity of the marketplace. The CFTC approves the rules under which an exchange proposes to operate and monitors exchange enforcement of those rules. It reviews the terms of proposed futures contracts, and registers companies and individuals who handle customer funds or give trading advice. The Commission also protects the public by enforcing rules that require that customer funds be kept in bank accounts separate from accounts maintained by firms for their own use, and that such customer accounts be marked to present market value at the close of trading each day.

Futures contracts for agricultural commodities were traded in the United States for more than 100 years before futures trading was diversified to include trading in contracts for precious metals, raw materials, foreign currencies, financial instruments, commercial interest rates, and U.S. Government and mortgage securities. Contract diversification has grown in exchange trading in both traditional and newer commodities.

Futures and Options Exchanges: Addresses

UNITED STATES

American Stock Exchange (AMEX)
86 Trinity Place
New York, NY 10006
(212) 306-1000

Chicago Board of Trade (CBOT)
141 West Jackson Boulevard
Chicago, IL 60604
(312) 435-3620

Chicago Board Options Exchange (CBOE)
400 South LaSalle
Chicago, IL 60605
(312) 786-5600

Chicago Mercantile Exchange (CME) and International Monetary Market Division of the CME (IMM) and Index and Option Market Division (IOM) of the CME
30 South Wacker Drive
Chicago, IL 60606
(312) 930-1000

Citrus Associates of the New York Cotton Exchange
4 World Trade Center
New York, NY 10048
(212) 938-2702

Coffee, Sugar & Cocoa Exchange (CSCE)
4 World Trade Center
New York, NY 10048
(212) 938-9863

Commodity Exchange, Inc. (COMEX)
4 World Trade Center
New York, NY 10048
(212) 938-2900

Financial Instrument Exchange (FINEX)
4 World Trade Center
New York, NY 10048
(212) 938-2634

GLOBEX
30 S. Wacker Drive
Chicago, IL 60606
(312) 456-6700

International Monetary Market **(see Chicago Mercantile Exchange)**

Index and Option Market **(see Chicago Mercantile Exchange)**

Kansas City Board of Trade (KCBT)
4800 Main Street
Kansas City, MO 64112
(816) 753-7500
(816) 821-4444 (hotline)

Midamerica Commodity Exchange (MidAm)
141 West Jackson Boulevard
Chicago, IL 60604
(312) 341-3000

Minneapolis Grain Exchange (MGE)
400 S. Fourth Street
Minneapolis, MN 55415
(612) 338-6212

New York Cotton Exchange (NYCE)
4 World Trade Center
New York, NY 10048
(212) 938-2702

New York Futures Exchange (NYFE)
20 Broad Street
New York, NY 10005
(212) 656-4949

New York Mercantile Exchange (NYMEX)
4 World Trade Center
New York, NY 10048
(212) 938-2222

New York Stock Exchange Options (NYSE)
11 Wall Street
New York, NY 10005
(212) 656-8533
(800) 692-6973 (Out-of-State)

Pacific Stock Exchange (PSE)
301 Pine Street
San Francisco, CA 94104
(415) 393-4000

Philadelphia Board of Trade (PHLX)
1900 Market Street
Philadelphia, PA 19103
(215) 496-5000

Philadelphia Stock Exchange (PBOT)
1900 Market Street
Philadelphia, PA 19103
(215) 496-5000

Selected Foreign Exchanges

AUSTRALIA

Australian Options Market
Australian Stock Exchange Derivatives Market
20 Bond Street
Sydney, NSW 2000, Australia
Phone: 61-2-227-0000

Sydney Futures Exchange (SFE)
30-32 Grosvenor St.
Sydney, NSW 2000, Australia
Phone: 61-2-256-0555

CANADA

Montreal Exchange (ME)
800 Victoria Square
Montreal, Quebec, Canada H4Z 1A9
Phone: (514) 871-2424

Toronto Futures Exchange (TFE)
2 First Canadian Place
Exchange Tower
Toronto, Ontario, Canada M5X 1J2
Phone: (416) 947-4487

Toronto Stock Exchange (TSE)
2 First Canadian Place
Exchange Tower
Toronto, Ontario, Canada M5X 1J2
Phone: (416) 947-4700

Vancouver Stock Exchange (VSE)
609 Granville Street
Vancouver, British Columbia
Canada V7Y 1H1
Phone: (604) 689-3334

The Winnipeg Commodity Exchange (WCE)
500 Commodity Exchange Tower
360 Main Street
Winnipeg, Manitoba
Canada R3C 3Z4
Phone: (204) 949-0495

FRANCE

Marche á Terme International de France (MATIF)
176 Rue Montmartre
75002 Paris, France
Fax: 33-1-40-28-80-01

Marche des Options Negociables de Paris (MONEP)
39 Rue Cambon
75001 Paris, France
Fax: 33-1-49-27-18-23

GERMANY

Deutsche Terminböerse (DTB)
Grueneburgweg 102
Postfach 17 02 03
6000 Frankfurt 1, Germany
Fax: 49-69-15-303-310

HONG KONG

Hong Kong Futures Exchange (HKFE)
Asia Pacific Finance Tower
3 Garden Road
Hong Kong
Fax: 852-810-5089

JAPAN

Osaka Securities Exchange
8-16 Kitahama, 1-chome, Chuo-ku
Osaka 541, Japan
Fax: 81-6-231-2639

Tokyo Commodity Exchange (TOCOM)
10-8 Nihonbashi Horidomecho
1-chome, Chuo-ku
Tokyo 103, Japan
Fax: 81-3-3661-7568

Tokyo International Financial Futures Exchange (TIFFE)
NTT Data Otemachi Bldg.
2-2-2 Otemachi, Chiyoda-ku
Tokyo 100, Japan
Fax: 81-3-3275-2862

Tokyo Stock Exchange (TSE)
2-1 Nihombashi-Kabuto-Cho
Chuo-ku, Tokyo 103, Japan
Fax: 81-3-3663-0625

NETHERLANDS

European Options Exchange (EOE)
Rokin 65, Amsterdam
1012 KK, The Netherlands
Fax: 31-20-6230-0012

Financiële Termijnmarkt Amsterdam N.V. (FTA)
Nes 49, Amsterdam
1012 KD, The Netherlands
Fax: 31-20-6245416

SINGAPORE

Singapore International Monetary Exchange Ltd. (SIMEX)
1 Raffles Place, #07-00
OUB Centre, Singapore 0104
Fax: 65-535-7282

SWITZERLAND

Swiss Options and Financial Futures Exchange AG (SOFFEX)
Neumattstrasse 7
8953 Dietikon, Switzerland
Fax: 41-1-740-1776

UNITED KINGDOM

International Petroleum Exchange of London Ltd. (IPE)
International House
1 St. Katharine's Way
London, England E1 9UN
Phone: 44-71-481-0643

London International Financial Futures and Options Exchange (LIFFE)
Cannon Bridge
London, England EC4R 3XX
Phone: 44-71-623-0444

London Fox Futures and Options Exchange
1 Commodity Quay
St. Katharine Docks
London, England E1 9AX
Phone: 44-71-481-2080

London Metal Exchange
Plantation House, Fenchurch Street
London, England EC3M 3AP
Phone: 44-71-626-3311

OM London Ltd. (OML)
107 Cannon Street
London EC4N 5AD
Phone: 44-71-283-0678

Futures and Securities Organizations

UNITED STATES

Chicago Futures/Options Society
50 S. LaSalle Street
Chicago, IL 60675
(312) 444-7810

Futures Industry Association, Inc.
2001 Pennsylvania Avenue, NW
Washington, DC 20006
(202) 466-5460

Futures Industry Institute
2001 Pennsylvania Avenue
Washington, D.C. 20006
(202) 223-1528

Managed Futures Association
182 University Avenue, P.O. Box 287
Palo Alto, CA 94302
(415) 325-4533

1919 Pennsylvania Avenue
Washington, DC 20006
(202) 872-9186

Market Technicians Association Inc.
71 Broadway
New York, NY 10006
(212) 344-1266

National Association of Securities Dealers (NASD)
1735 K Street, NW
Washington, DC 20006
(202) 728-8300

National Futures Association (NFA)
200 West Madison Street
Chicago, IL 60606
(312) 781-1300
(800) 621-3570

National Option & Futures Society Inc.
170 Old Country Road
Mineola, NY 11501
(212) 213-0241

North American Securities Administrators Association, Inc. (NASAA)
1 Massachusetts Avenue, NW
Washington, DC 20004
(202) 737-0900

FOREIGN

Canada

International Organization of Securities Commissions
800 Square Victoria, P.O. Box 4510
Montreal, Quebec, H4Z 1C8 Canada
(514) 875-8278

Investment Dealers Association of Canada
121 King Street West
Toronto, Ontario M5H 3T8
(416) 364-6133

Japan

Federation of Bankers Associations of Japan
3-1 Marunouchi, 1-chome
Chiyoda-ku, Tokyo 100, Japan

Japan Securities Dealers Association
5-8 Kayabacho, 1-chome
Nihonbashi, Chuo-ku
Tokyo 103, Japan

Switzerland

Swiss Commodities, Futures and Options Association
11 Route de Drize
P.O. Box 1181
CH-1227 Carouge/Geneva, Switzerland

United Kingdom

Association for Futures Investment
1 New Inn Square
Bateman's Row
London EC2A 3PY, UK

European Managed Futures Association
St. Katharine's Way
London E1 9, UK

COMMODITY PRICE CHARTS[1]

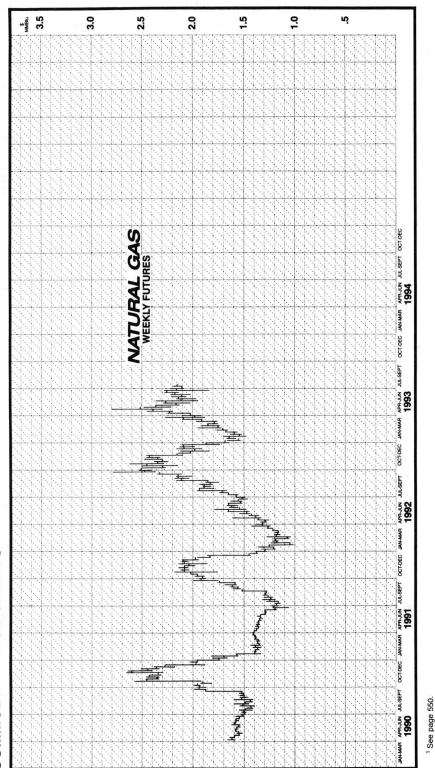

[1] See page 550.

Source: Courtesy of Commodity Price Charts, 219 Parkade, Cedar Falls, Iowa 50613.

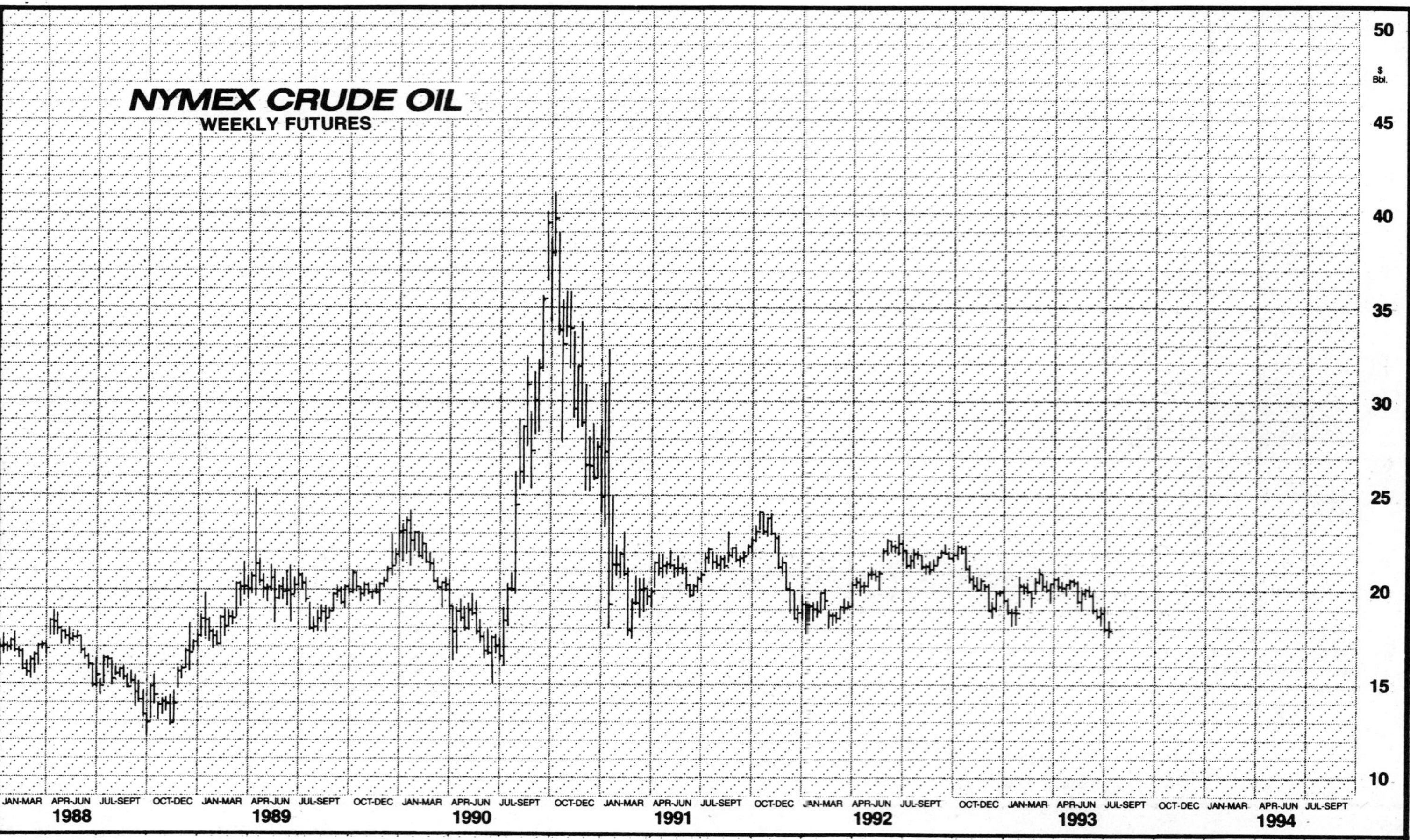
NYMEX CRUDE OIL
WEEKLY FUTURES
$
Bbl.
50
45
40
35
30
25
20
15
10
JAN-MAR APR-JUN JUL-SEPT OCT-DEC
1988
1989
1990
1991
1992
1993
1994

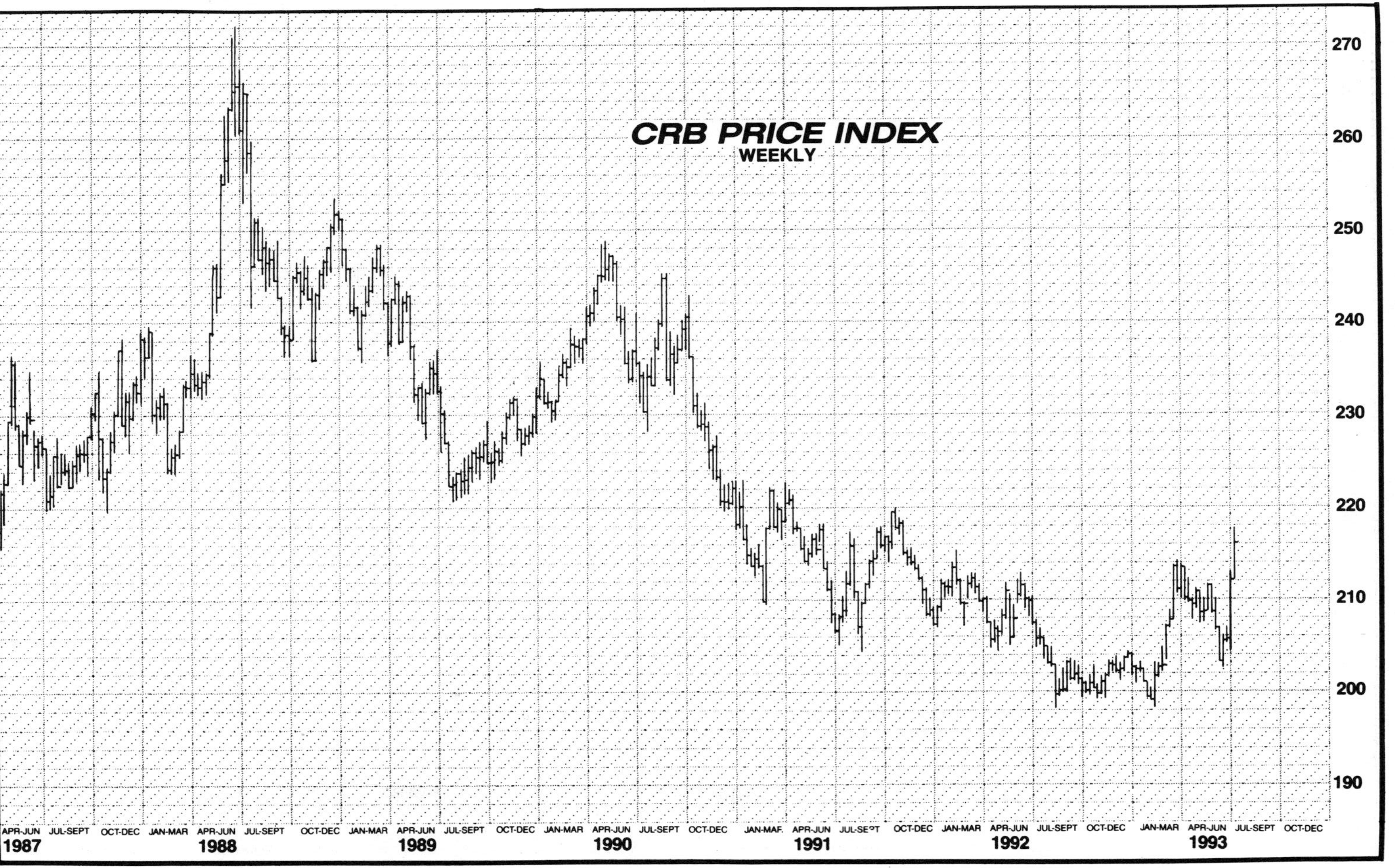

Source: Courtesy of Commodity Price Charts, 219 Parkade, Cedar Falls, Iowa 50613.

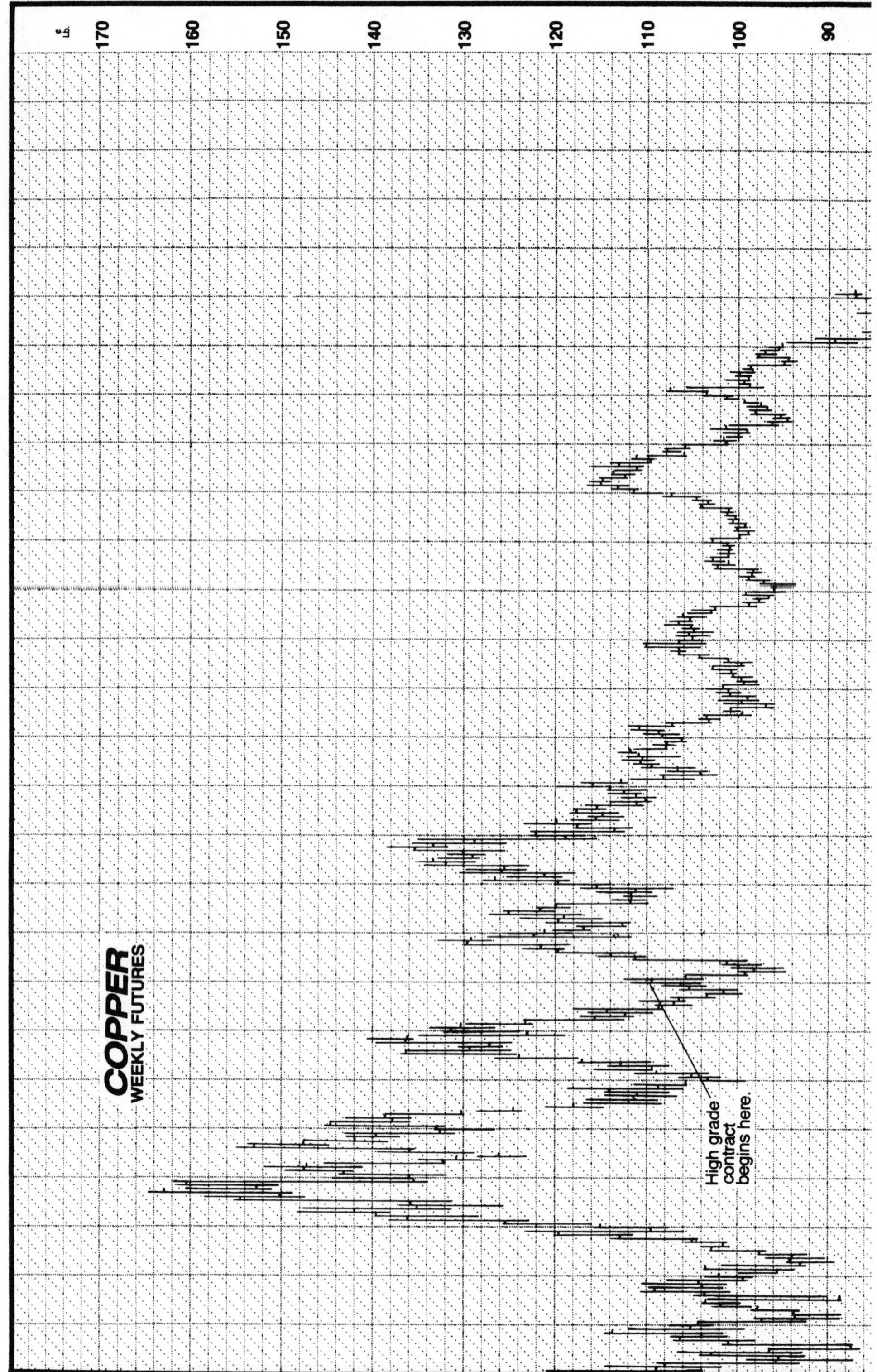
COPPER
WEEKLY FUTURES
High grade contract begins here.
170
160
150
140
130
120
110
100
90

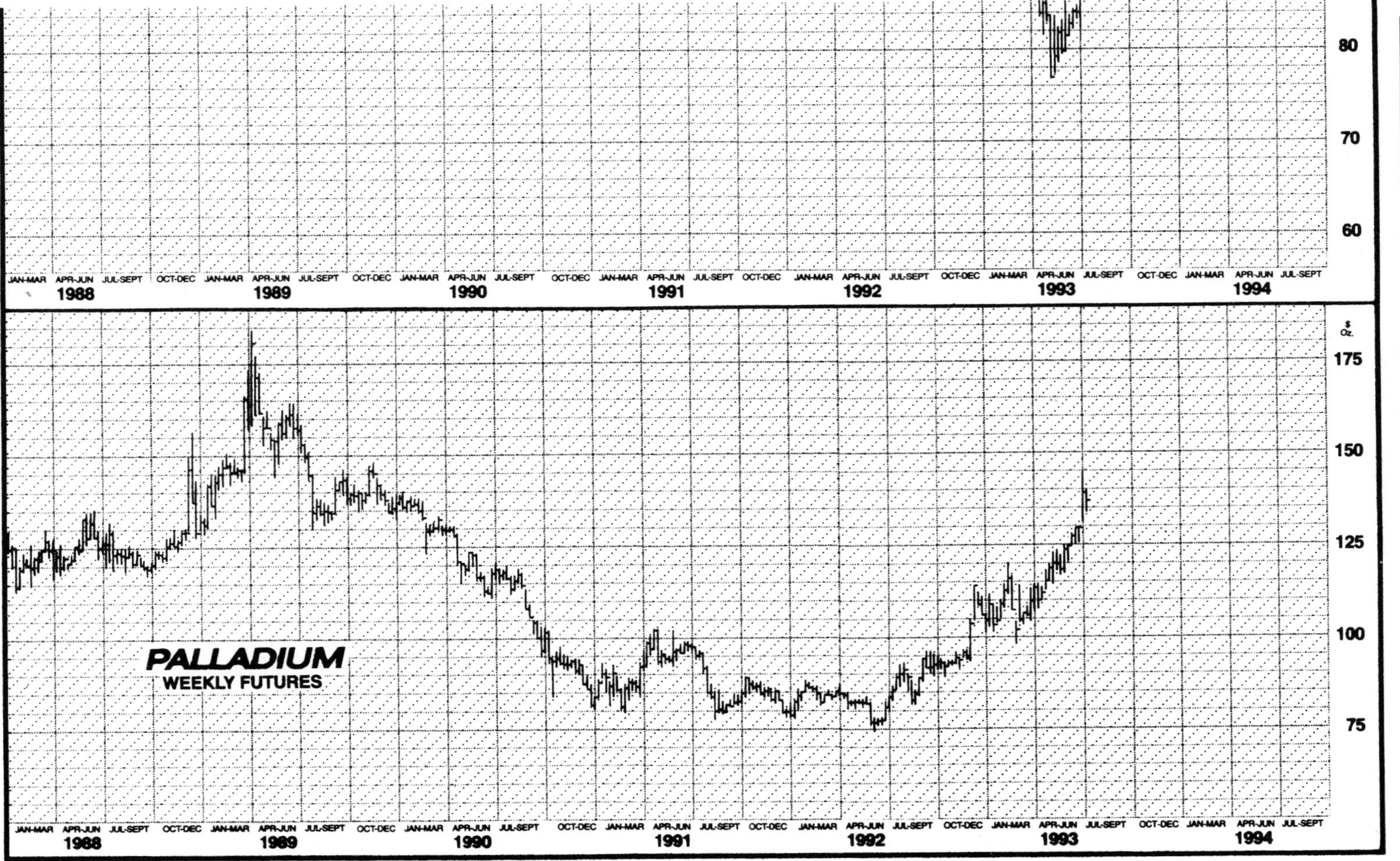

Source: Courtesy of Commodity Price Charts, 219 Parkade, Cedar Falls, Iowa 50613.

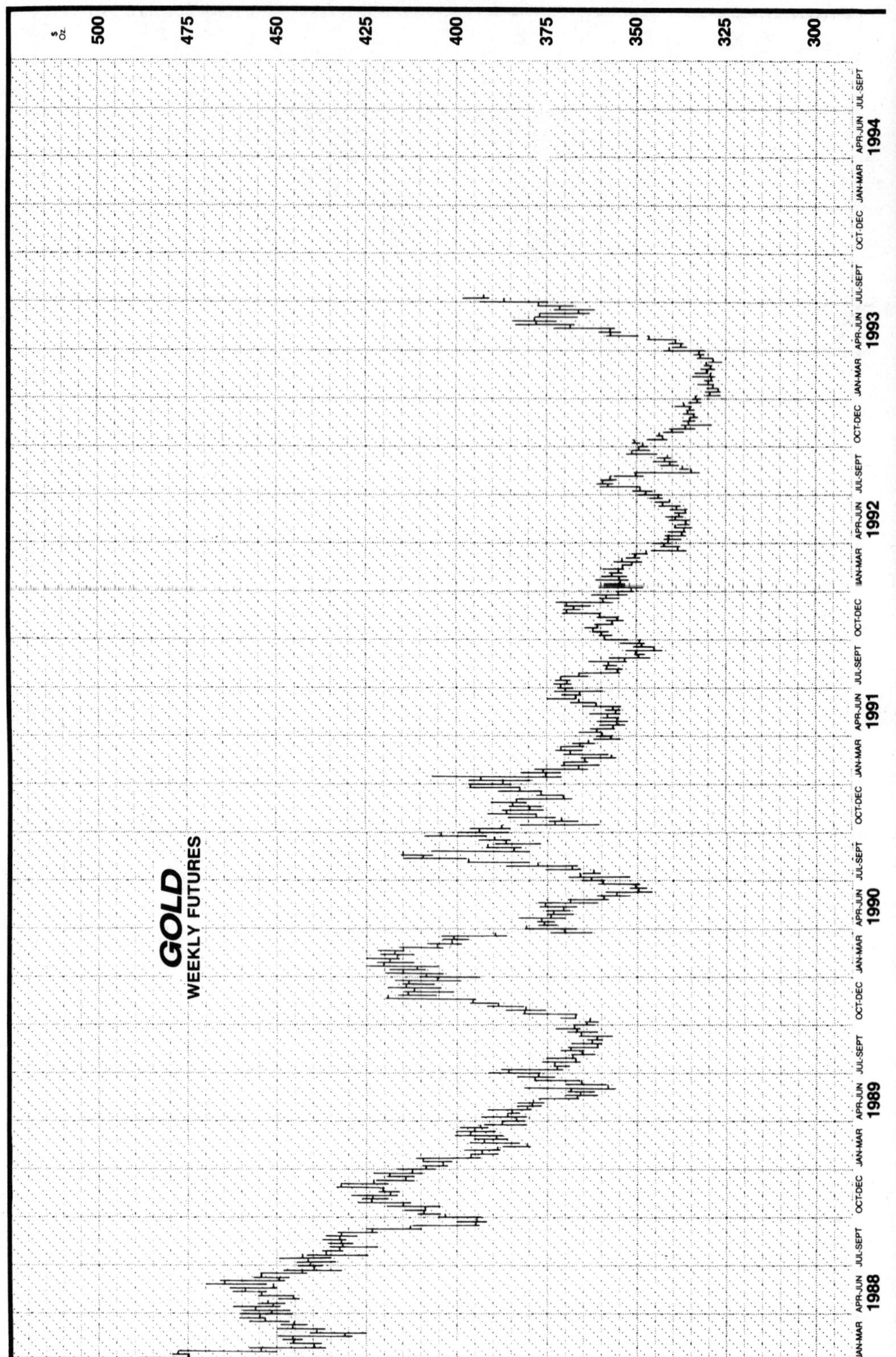
GOLD
WEEKLY FUTURES
$ Oz.
500
475
450
425
400
375
350
325
300
JAN-MAR APR-JUN JUL-SEPT OCT-DEC
1988
1989
1990
1991
1992
1993
1994

Source: Courtesy of Commodity Price Charts, 219 Parkade, Cedar Falls, Iowa 50613.

COMEX SILVER
WEEKLY FUTURES

$/oz.

11.0
10.5
10.0
9.5
9.0
8.5
8.0
7.5
7.0
6.5

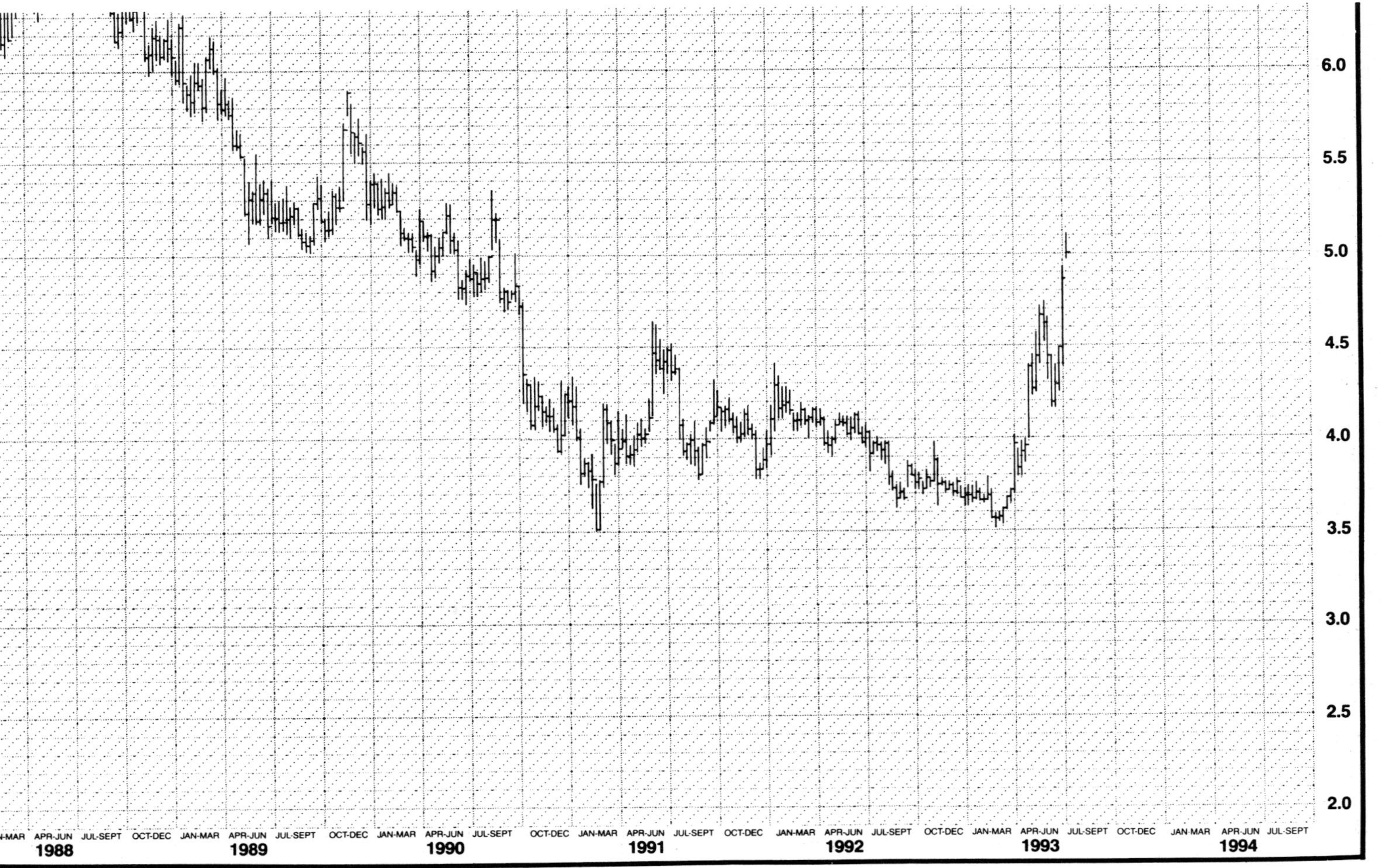

Source: Courtesy of Commodity Price Charts, 219 Parkade, Cedar Falls, Iowa 50613.

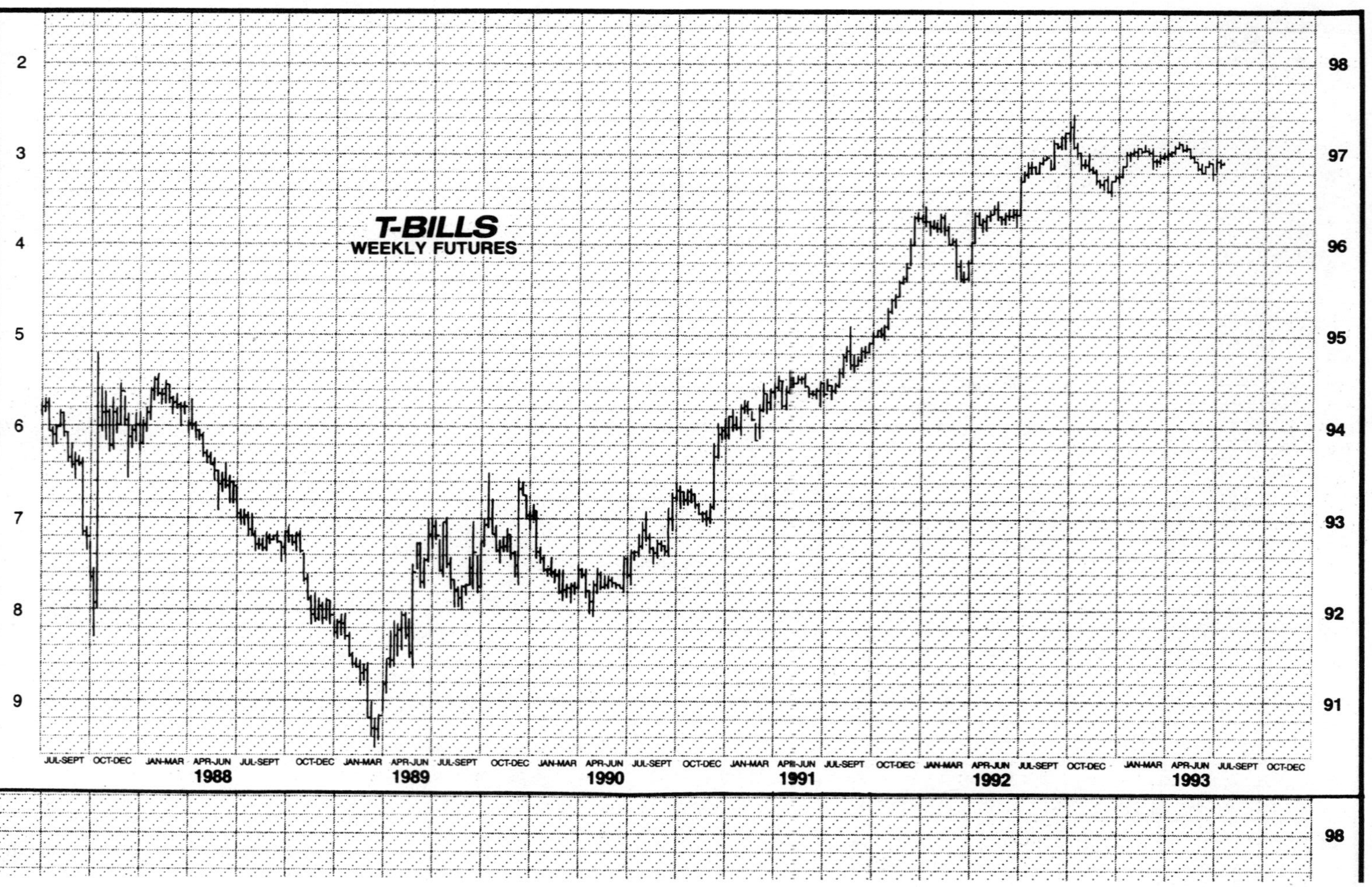
T-BILLS
WEEKLY FUTURES
2
3
4
5
6
7
8
9
98
97
96
95
94
93
92
91
98
JUL-SEPT OCT-DEC JAN-MAR APR-JUN JUL-SEPT OCT-DEC JAN-MAR APR-JUN JUL-SEPT OCT-DEC JAN-MAR APR-JUN JUL-SEPT OCT-DEC JAN-MAR APR-JUN JUL-SEPT OCT-DEC JAN-MAR APR-JUN JUL-SEPT OCT-DEC JAN-MAR APR-JUN JUL-SEPT OCT-DEC
1988
1989
1990
1991
1992
1993

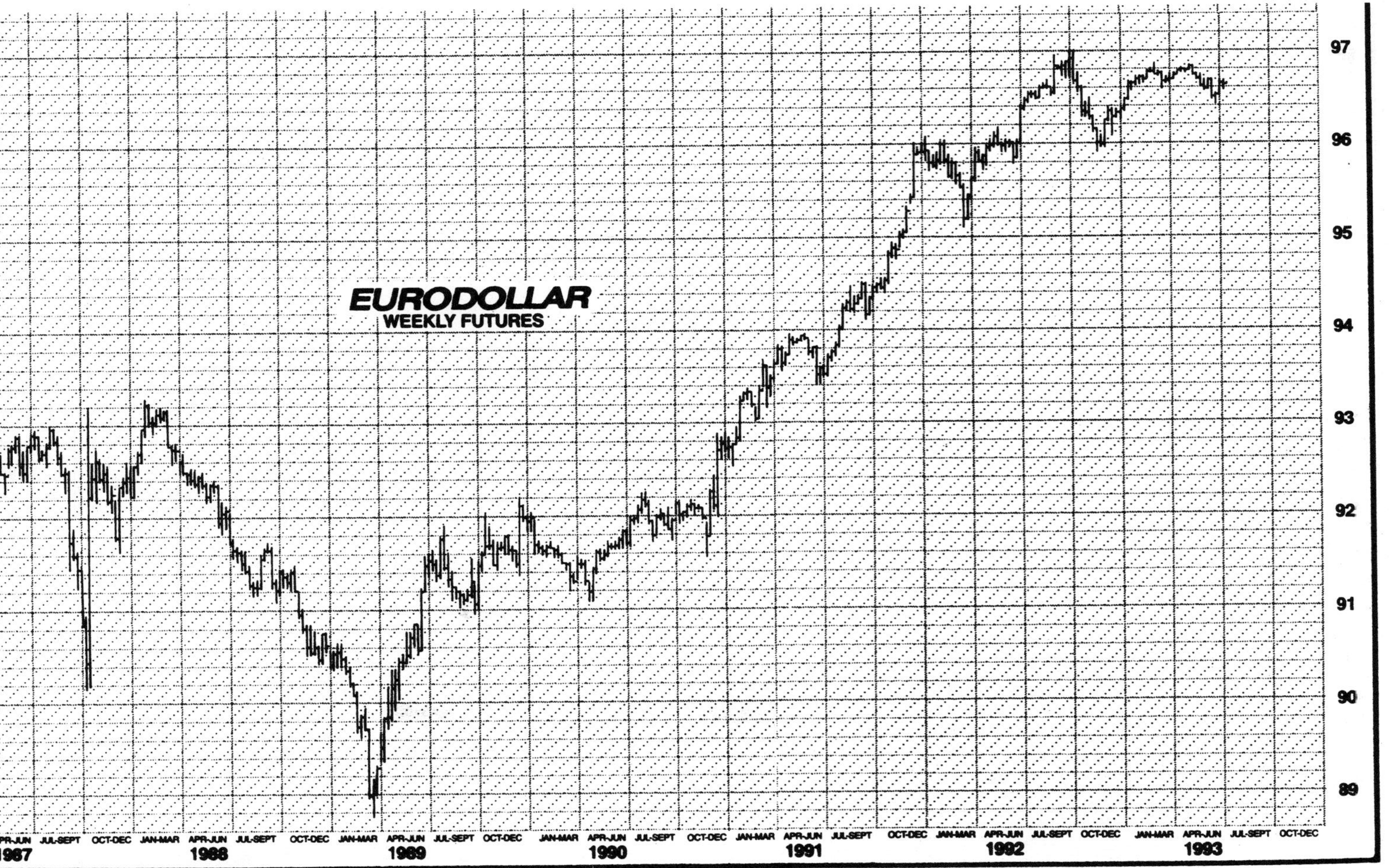

Source: Courtesy of Commodity Price Charts, 219 Parkade, Cedar Falls, Iowa 50613.

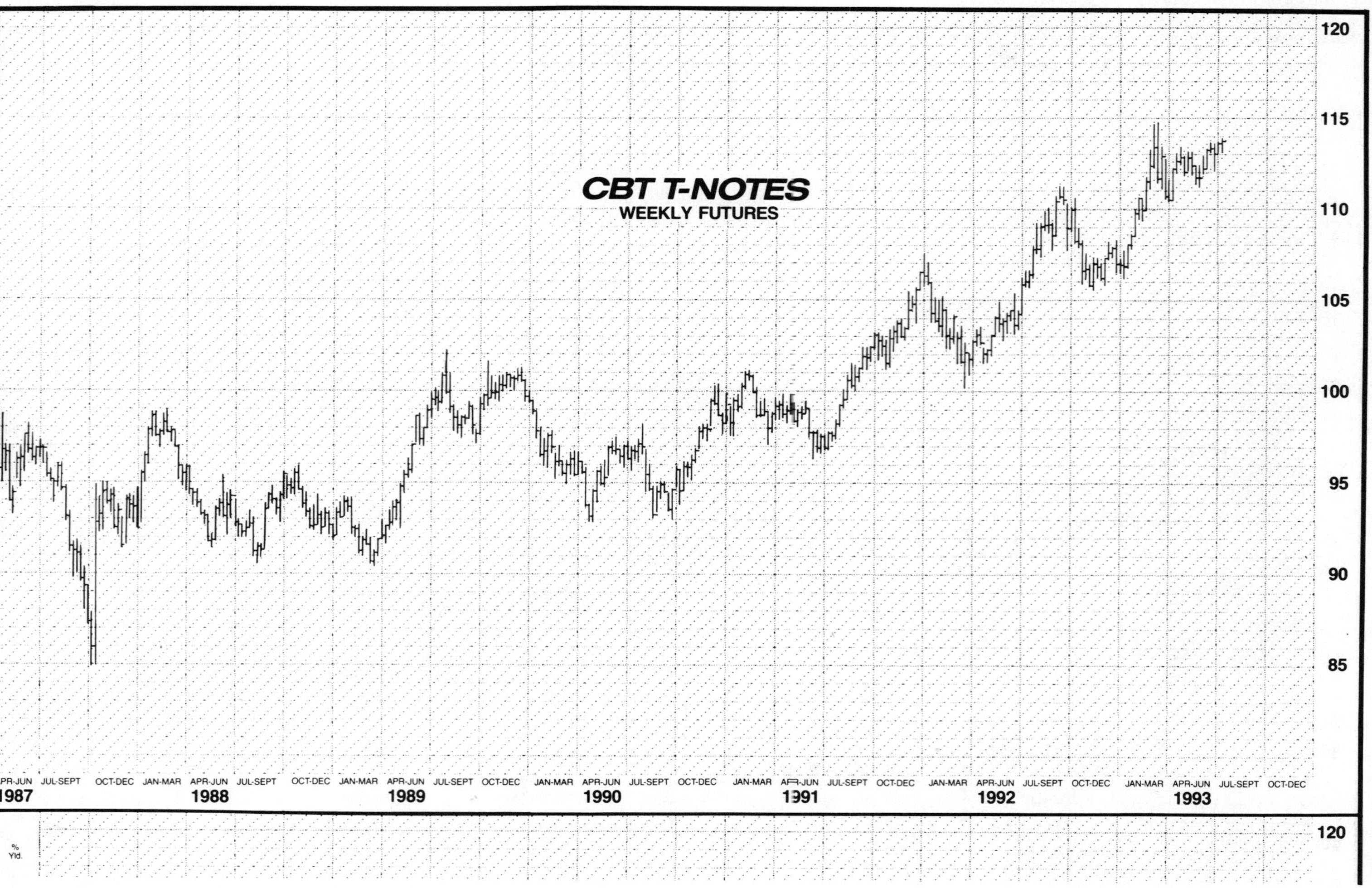
CBT T-NOTES
WEEKLY FUTURES
120
115
110
105
100
95
90
85
APR-JUN 1987
JUL-SEPT
OCT-DEC
JAN-MAR
APR-JUN 1988
JUL-SEPT
OCT-DEC
JAN-MAR
APR-JUN 1989
JUL-SEPT
OCT-DEC
JAN-MAR
APR-JUN 1990
JUL-SEPT
OCT-DEC
JAN-MAR
APR-JUN 1991
JUL-SEPT
OCT-DEC
JAN-MAR
APR-JUN 1992
JUL-SEPT
OCT-DEC
JAN-MAR
APR-JUN 1993
JUL-SEPT
OCT-DEC
% Yld.
120

Source: Courtesy of Commodity Price Charts, 219 Parkade, Cedar Falls, Iowa 50613.

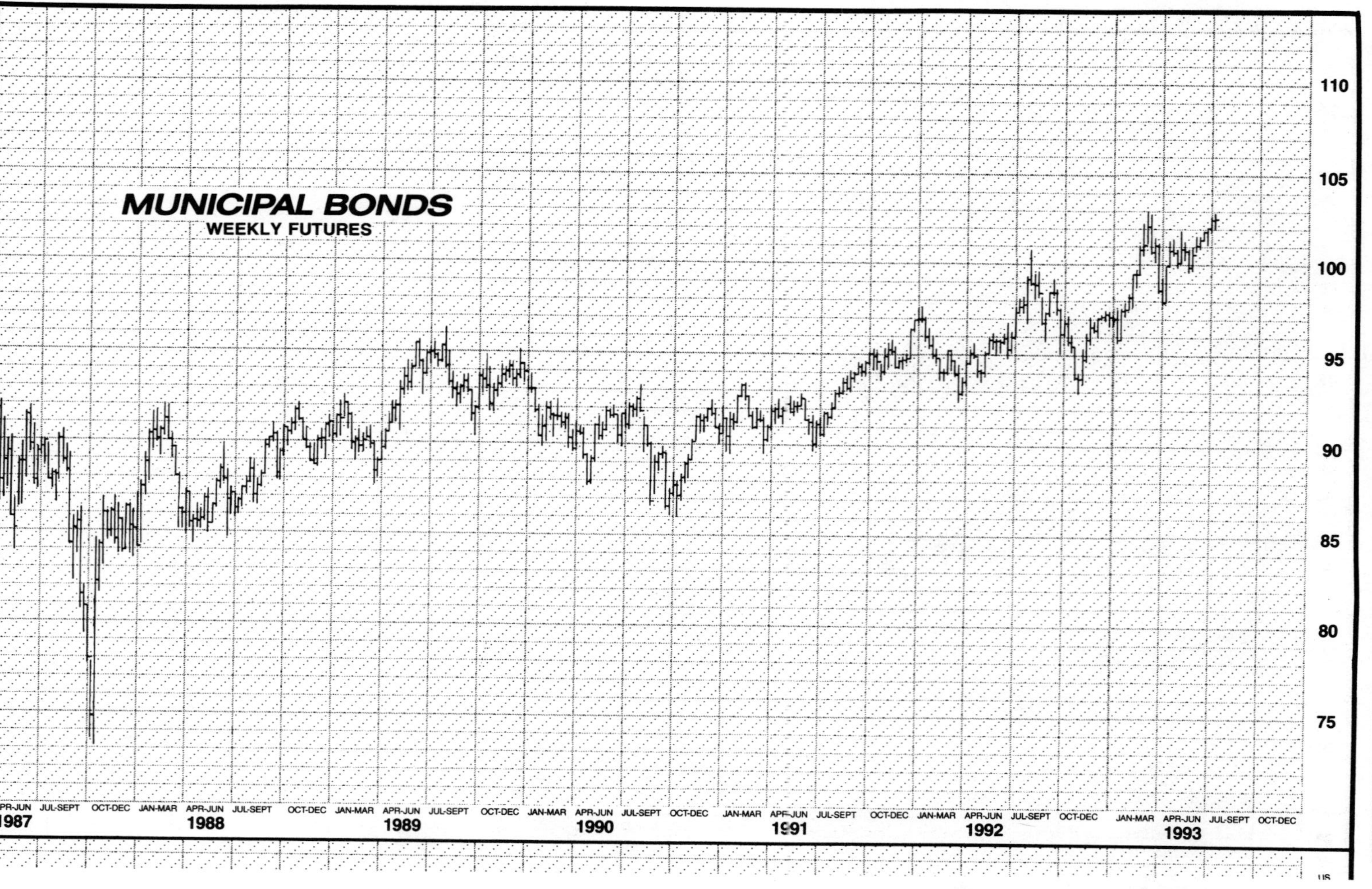
MUNICIPAL BONDS
WEEKLY FUTURES
110
105
100
95
90
85
80
75
APR-JUN JUL-SEPT OCT-DEC
1987
JAN-MAR APR-JUN JUL-SEPT OCT-DEC
1988
JAN-MAR APR-JUN JUL-SEPT OCT-DEC
1989
JAN-MAR APR-JUN JUL-SEPT OCT-DEC
1990
JAN-MAR APR-JUN JUL-SEPT OCT-DEC
1991
JAN-MAR APR-JUN JUL-SEPT OCT-DEC
1992
JAN-MAR APR-JUN JUL-SEPT OCT-DEC
1993

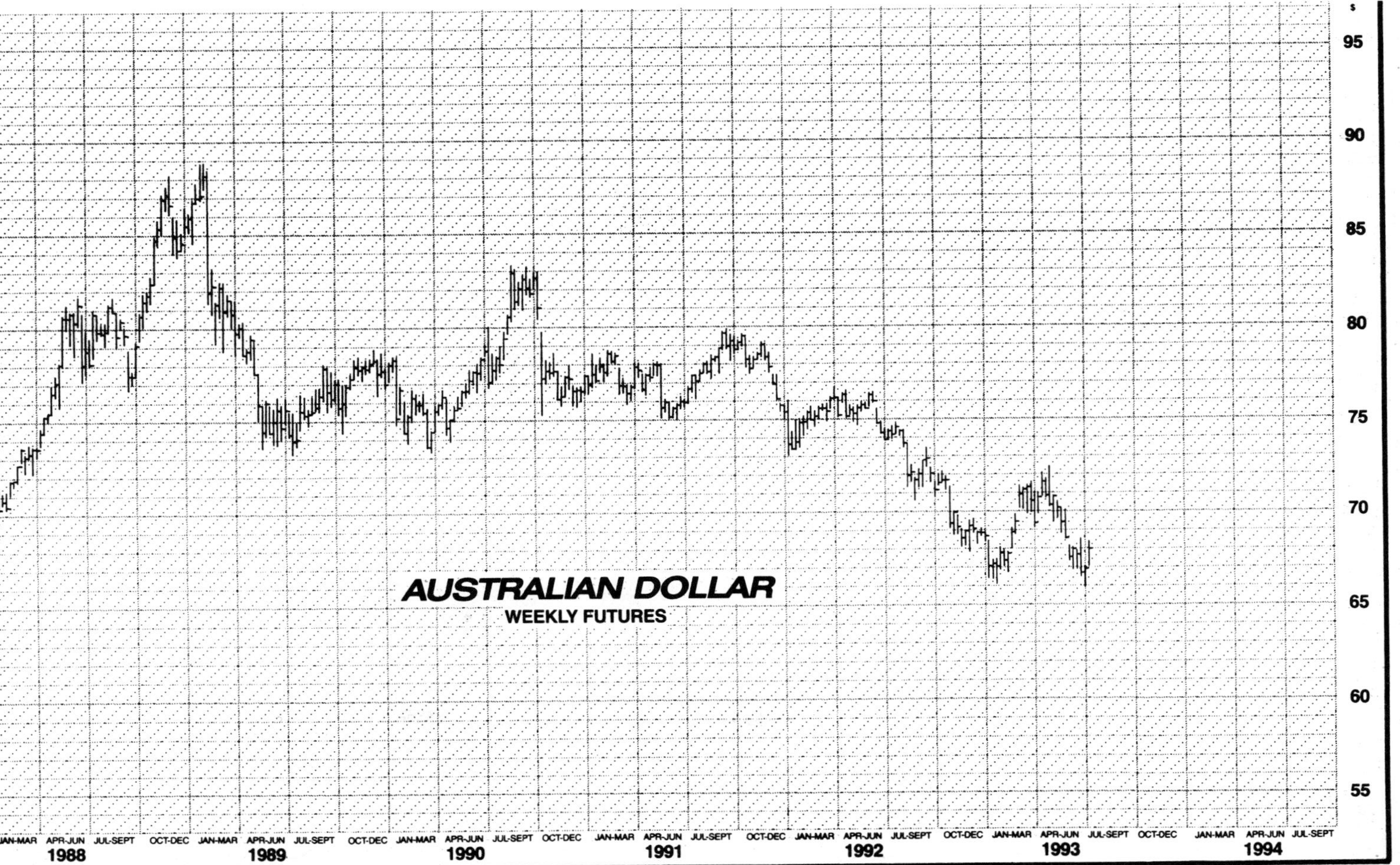

Source: Courtesy of Commodity Price Charts, 219 Parkade, Cedar Falls, Iowa 50613.

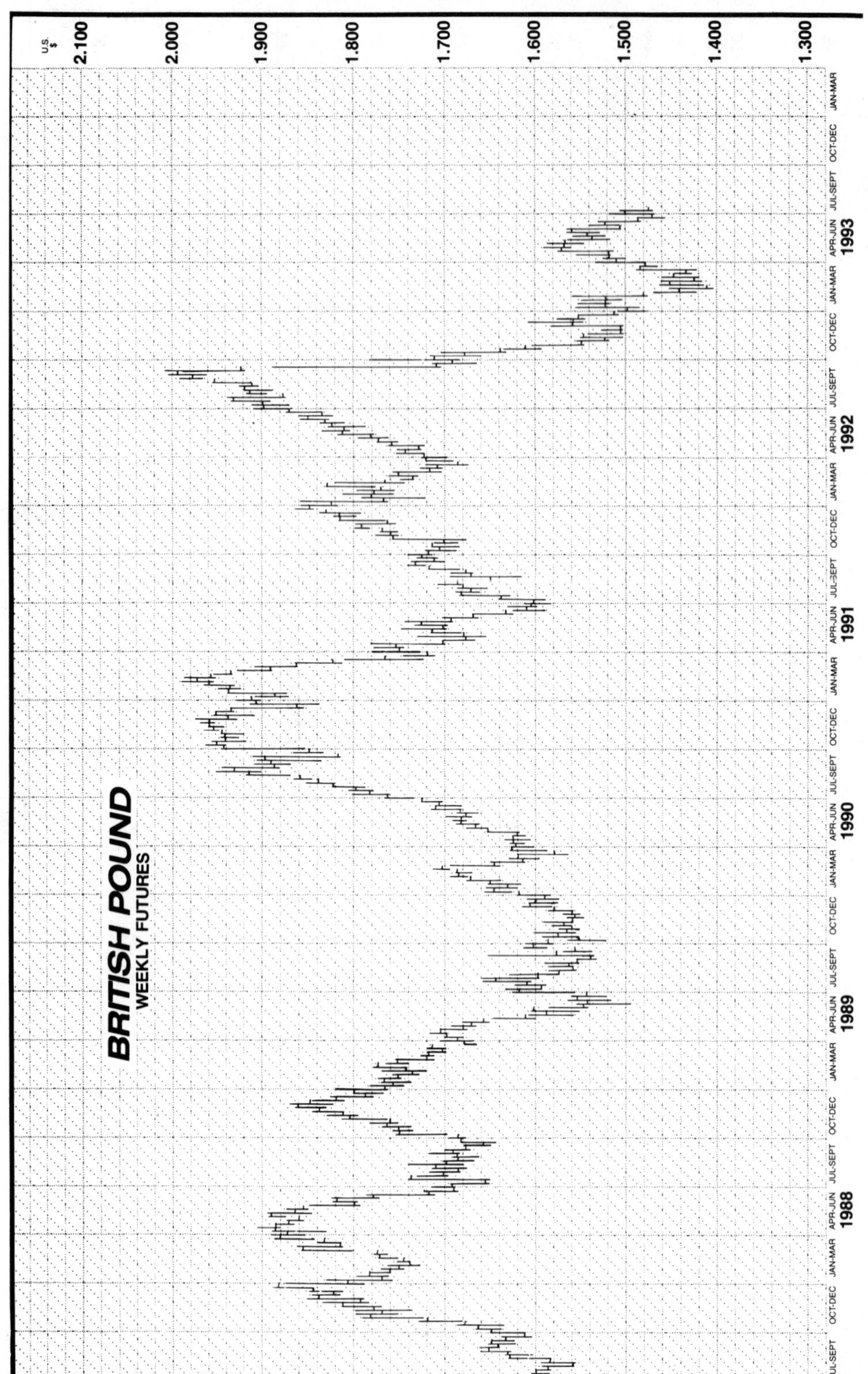
BRITISH POUND
WEEKLY FUTURES
U.S. $
2.100
2.000
1.900
1.800
1.700
1.600
1.500
1.400
1.300
JUL-SEPT
OCT-DEC
JAN-MAR
APR-JUN
1988
JUL-SEPT
OCT-DEC
JAN-MAR
APR-JUN
1989
JUL-SEPT
OCT-DEC
JAN-MAR
APR-JUN
1990
JUL-SEPT
OCT-DEC
JAN-MAR
APR-JUN
1991
JUL-SEPT
OCT-DEC
JAN-MAR
APR-JUN
1992
JUL-SEPT
OCT-DEC
JAN-MAR
APR-JUN
1993
JUL-SEPT
OCT-DEC
JAN-MAR

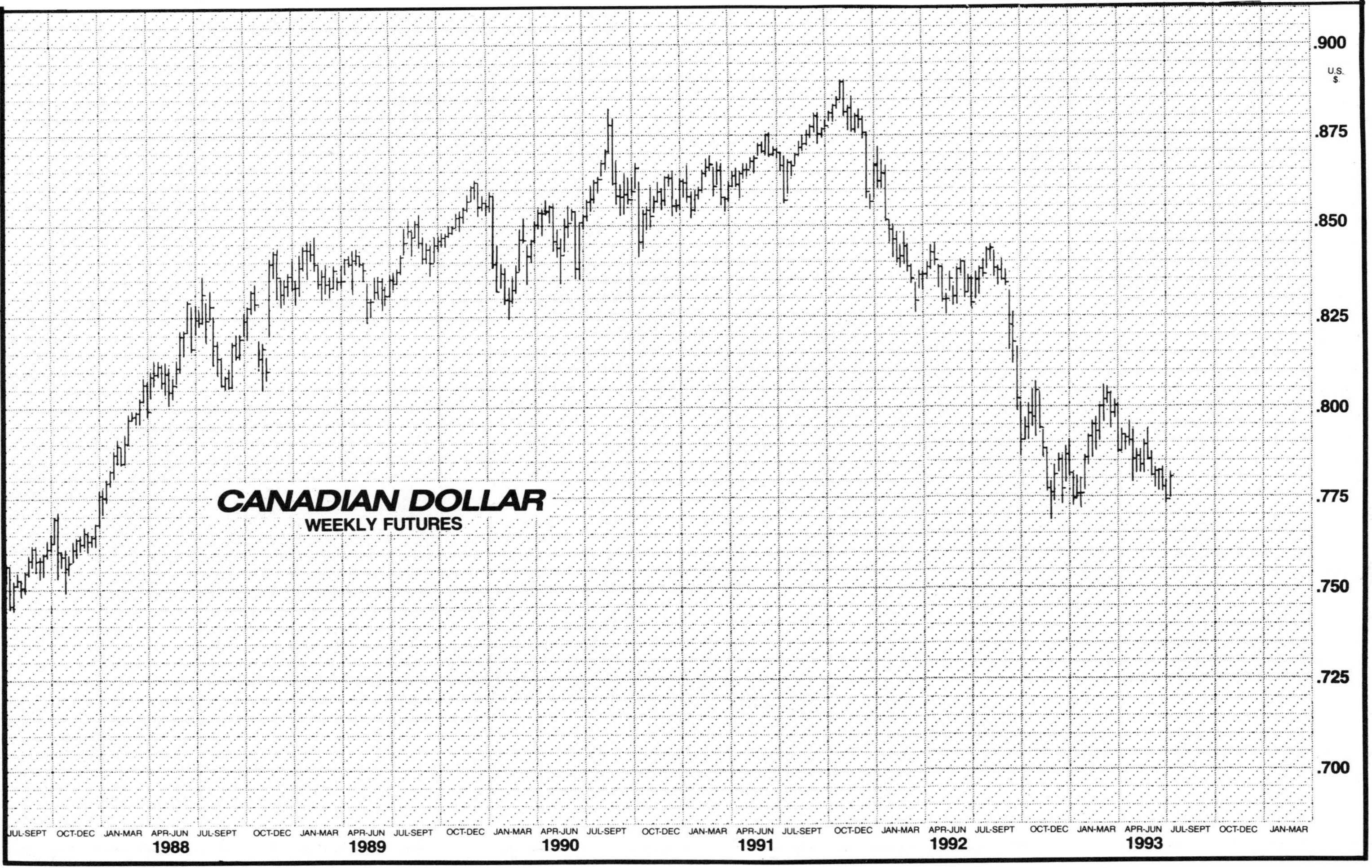

Source: Courtesy of Commodity Price Charts, 219 Parkade, Cedar Falls, Iowa 50613.

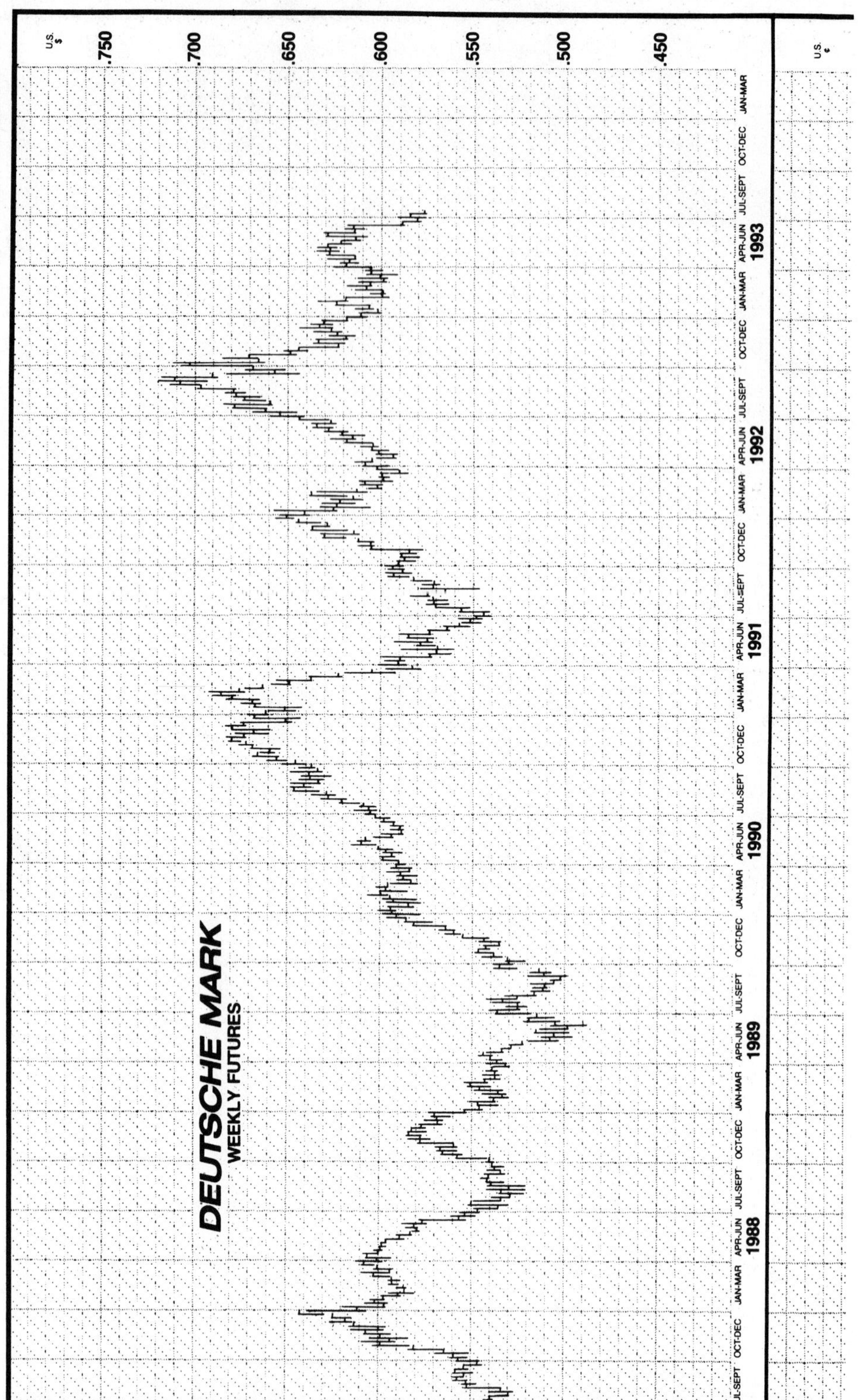
DEUTSCHE MARK
WEEKLY FUTURES
U.S. $
.750
.700
.650
.600
.550
.500
.450
U.S. ¢
JUL-SEPT OCT-DEC JAN-MAR APR-JUN JUL-SEPT OCT-DEC JAN-MAR APR-JUN JUL-SEPT OCT-DEC JAN-MAR APR-JUN JUL-SEPT OCT-DEC JAN-MAR APR-JUN JUL-SEPT OCT-DEC JAN-MAR APR-JUN JUL-SEPT OCT-DEC JAN-MAR APR-JUN JUL-SEPT OCT-DEC JAN-MAR
1988
1989
1990
1991
1992
1993

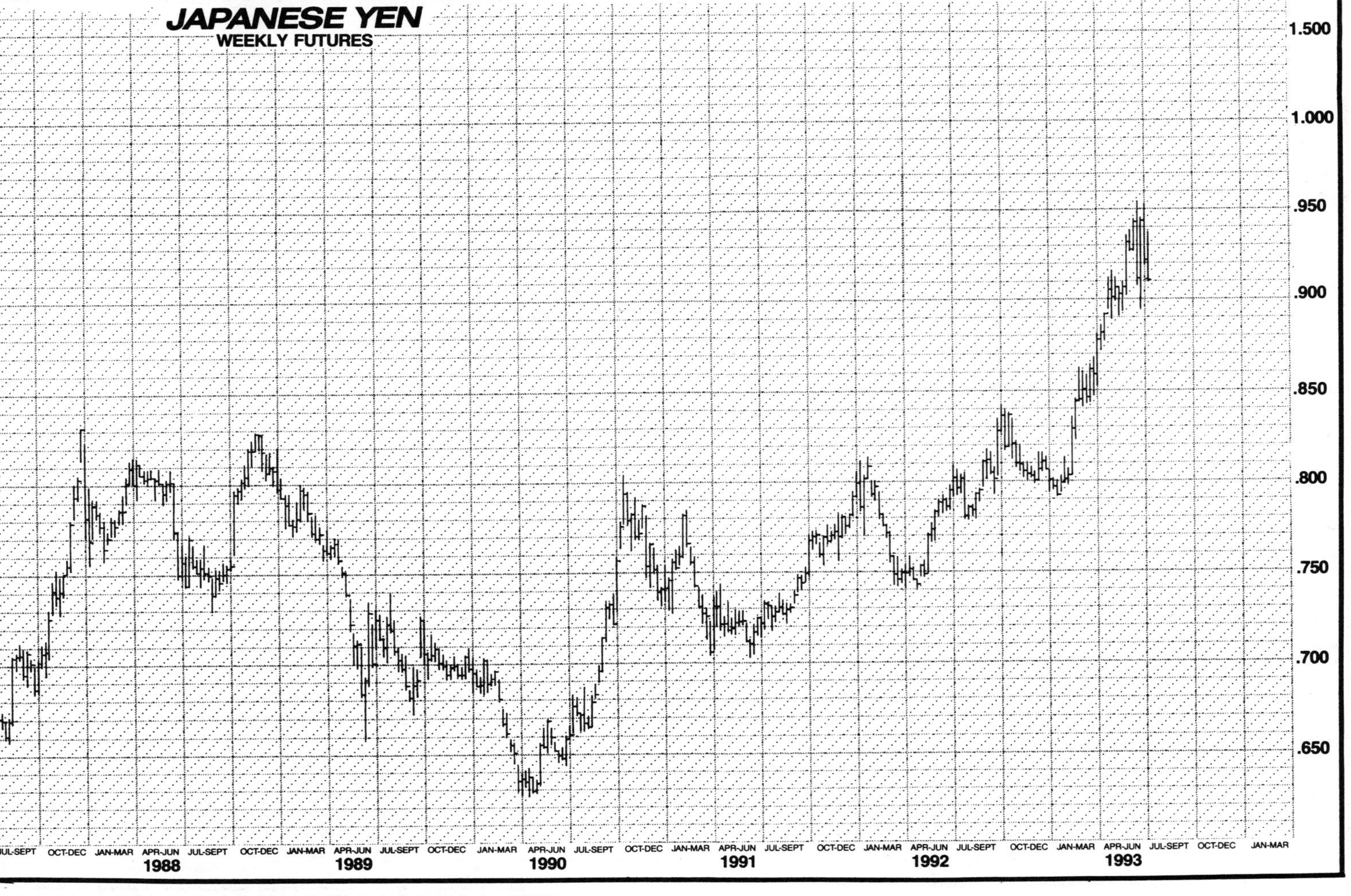

Source: Courtesy of Commodity Price Charts, 219 Parkade, Cedar Falls, Iowa 50613.

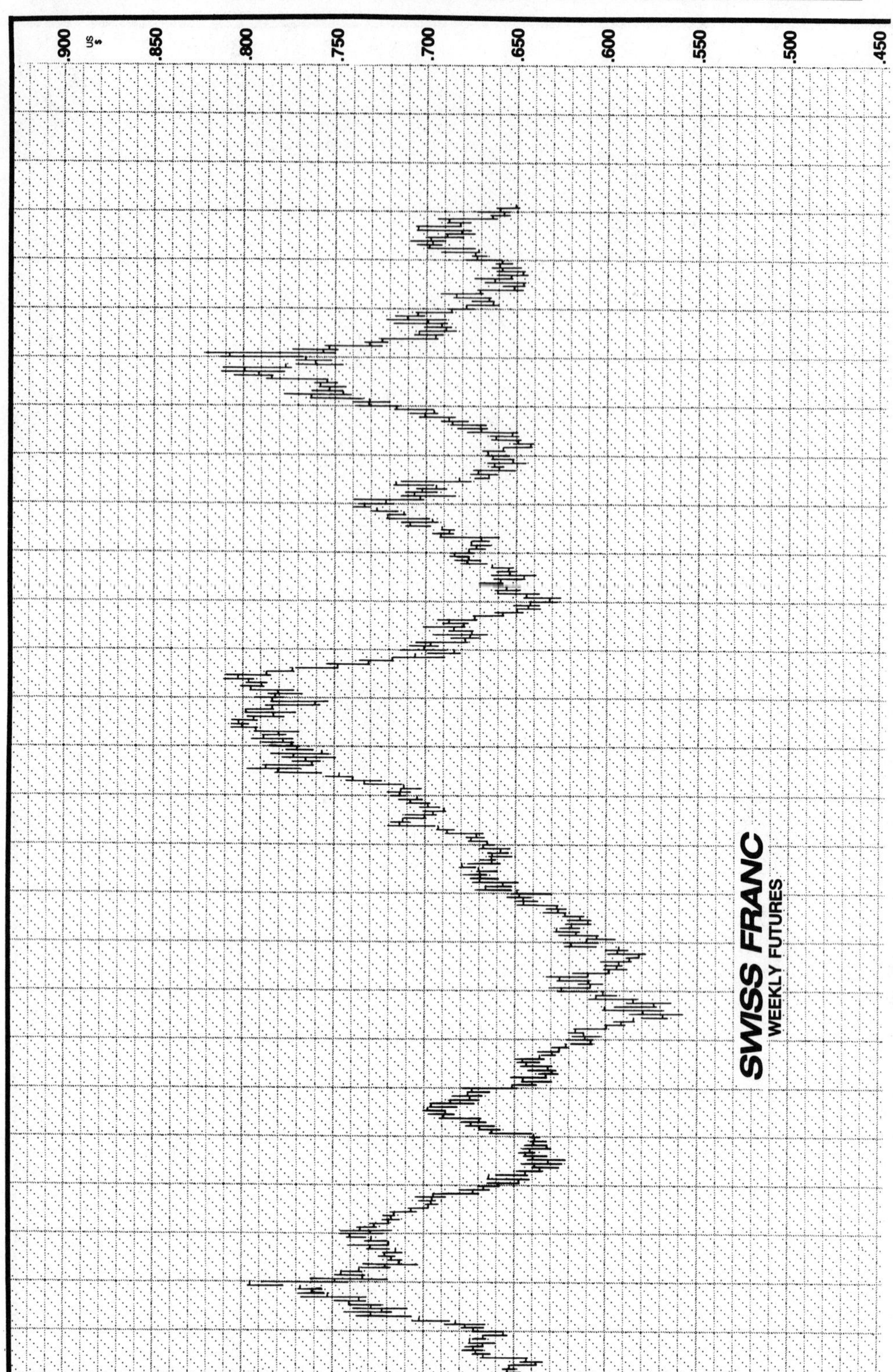
SWISS FRANC
WEEKLY FUTURES
US $
.900
.850
.800
.750
.700
.650
.600
.550
.500
.450

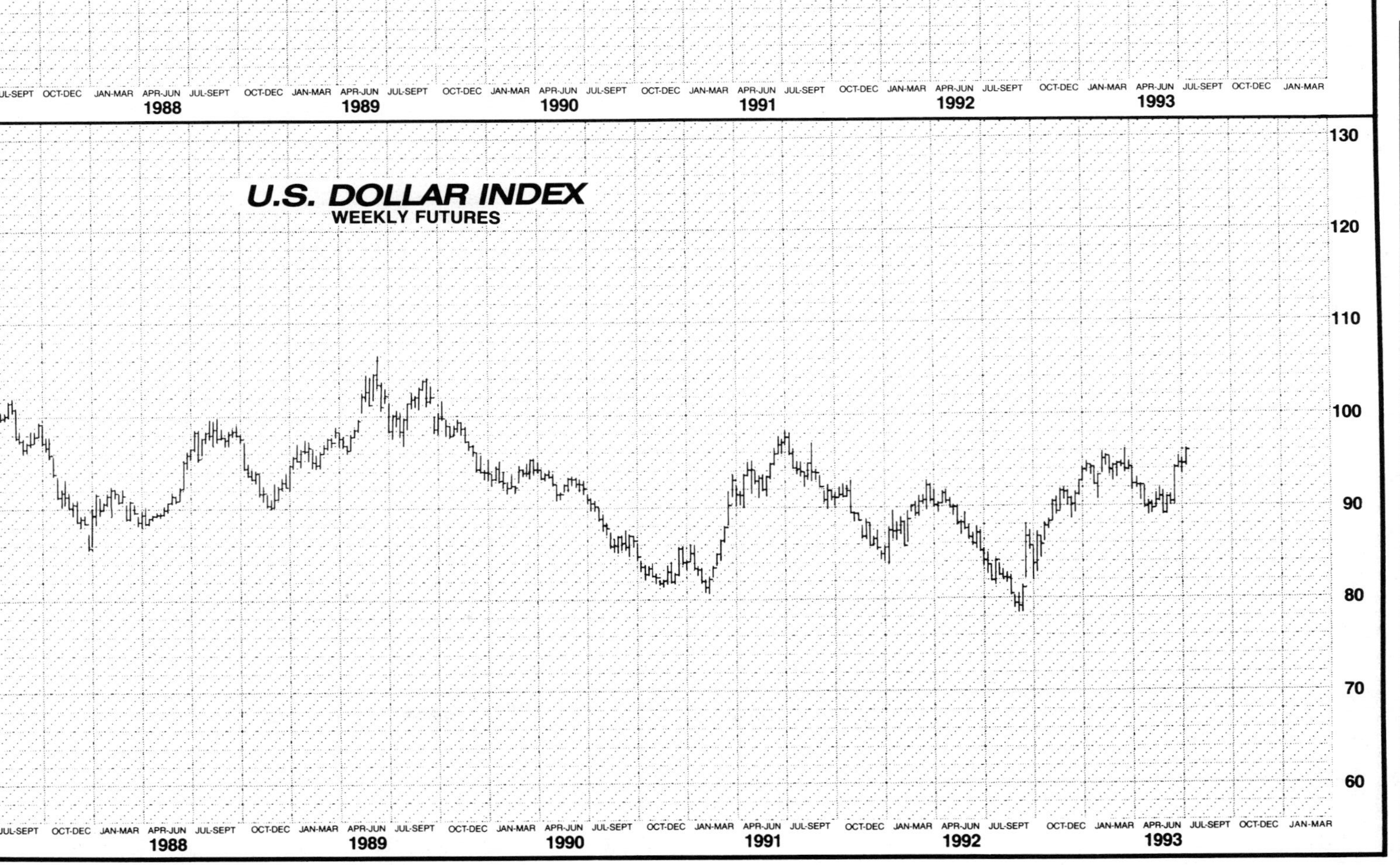

Source: Courtesy of Commodity Price Charts, 219 Parkade, Cedar Falls, Iowa 50613.

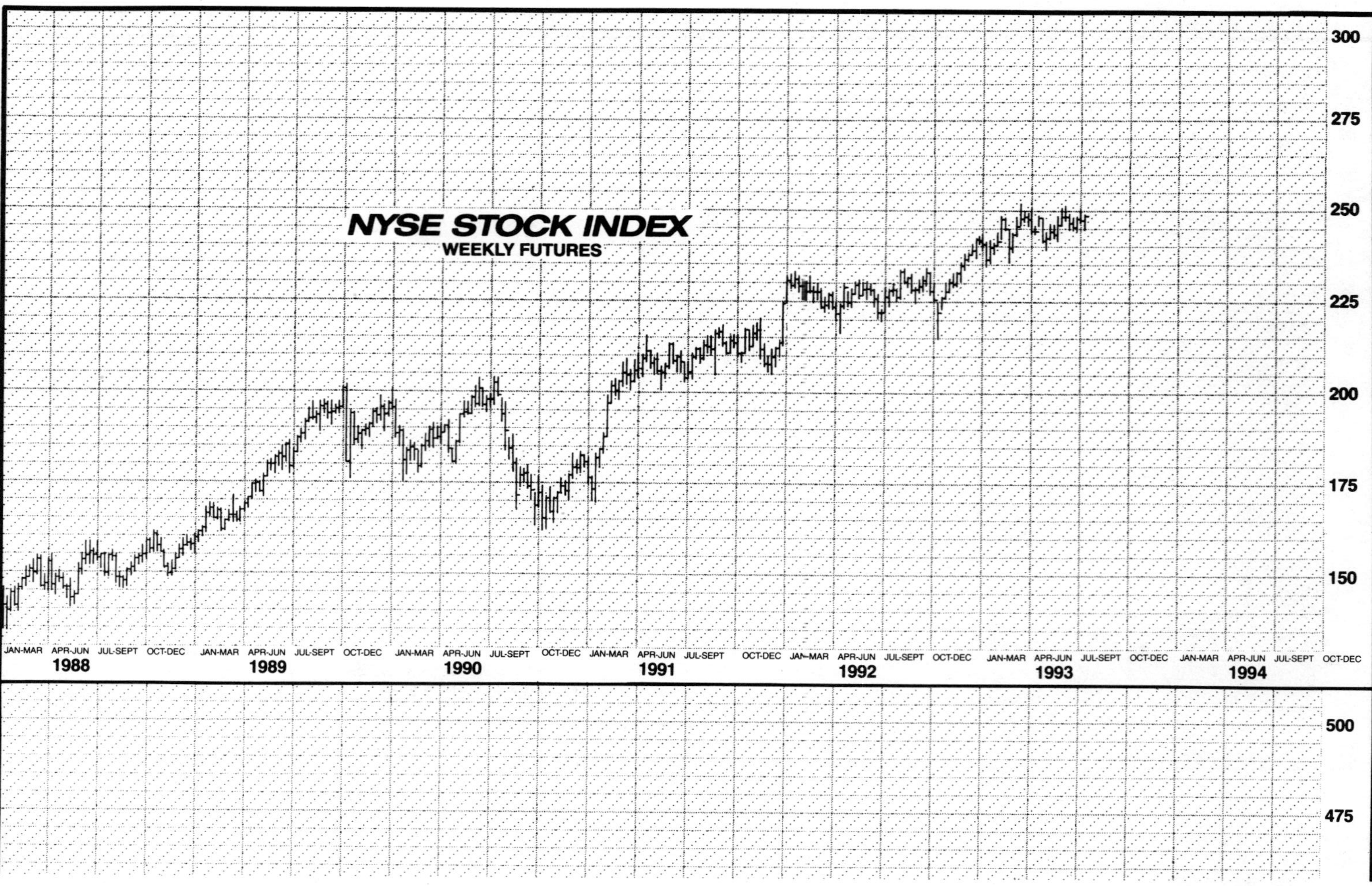
NYSE STOCK INDEX
WEEKLY FUTURES
300
275
250
225
200
175
150
500
475
JAN-MAR APR-JUN JUL-SEPT OCT-DEC
1988
1989
1990
1991
1992
1993
1994

Source: Courtesy of Commodity Price Charts, 219 Parkade, Cedar Falls, Iowa 50613.

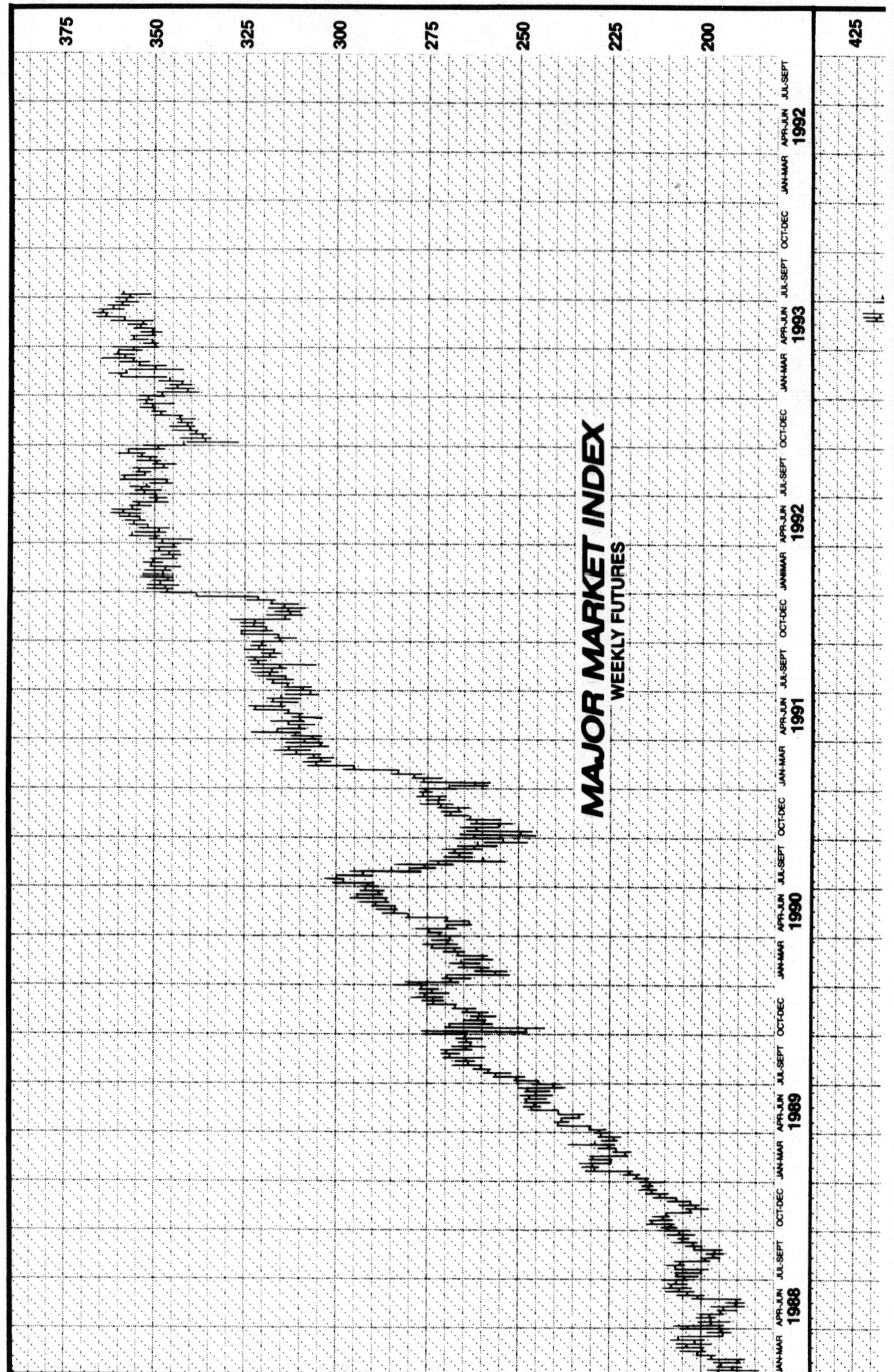
MAJOR MARKET INDEX
WEEKLY FUTURES
375
350
325
300
275
250
225
200
425
JAN-MAR APR-JUN JUL-SEPT OCT-DEC
1988
1989
1990
1991
1992
1993

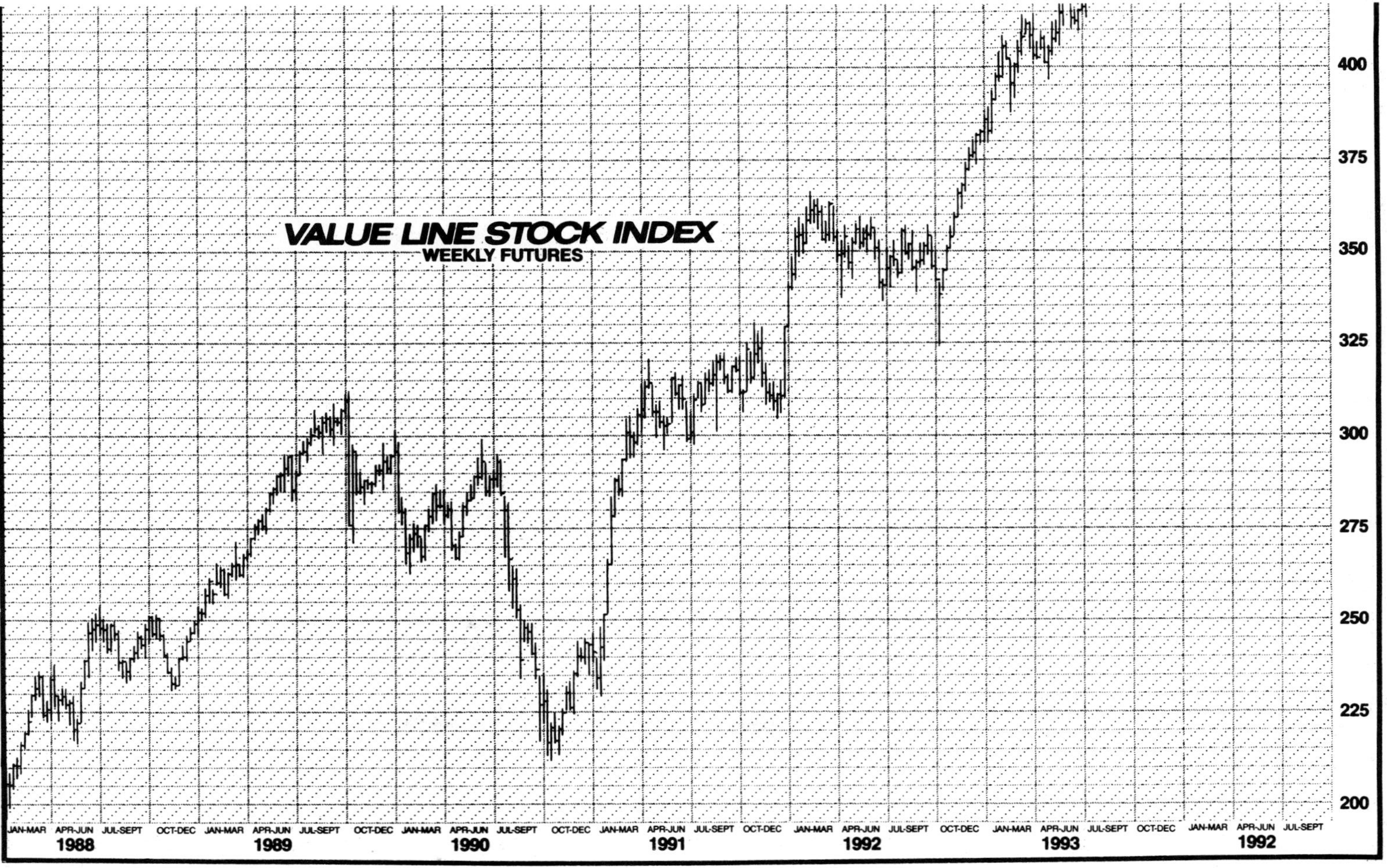

Source: Courtesy of Commodity Price Charts, 219 Parkade, Cedar Falls, Iowa 50613.

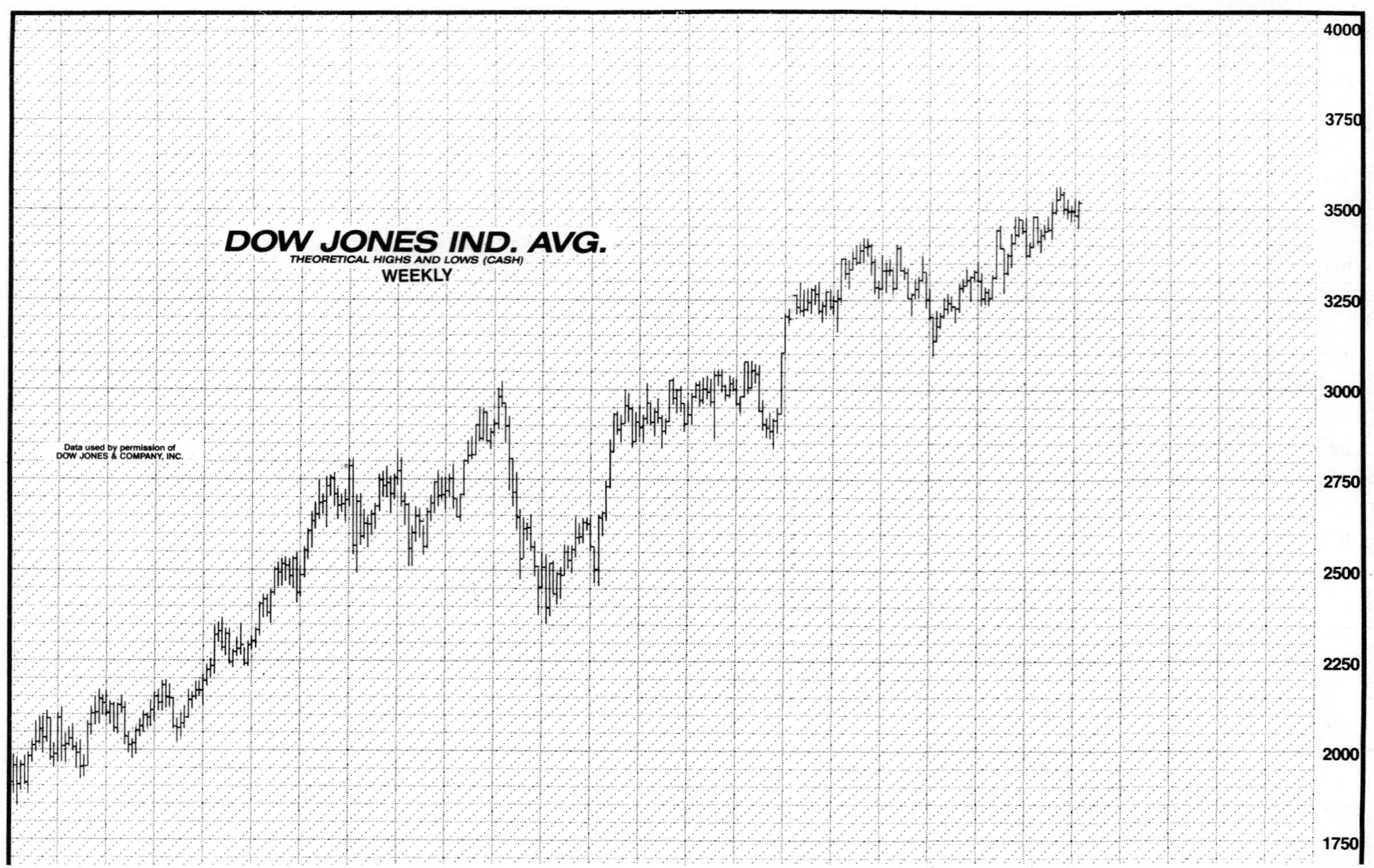

DOW JONES IND. AVG.
THEORETICAL HIGHS AND LOWS (CASH)
WEEKLY
Data used by permission of
DOW JONES & COMPANY, INC.
4000
3750
3500
3250
3000
2750
2500
2250
2000
1750

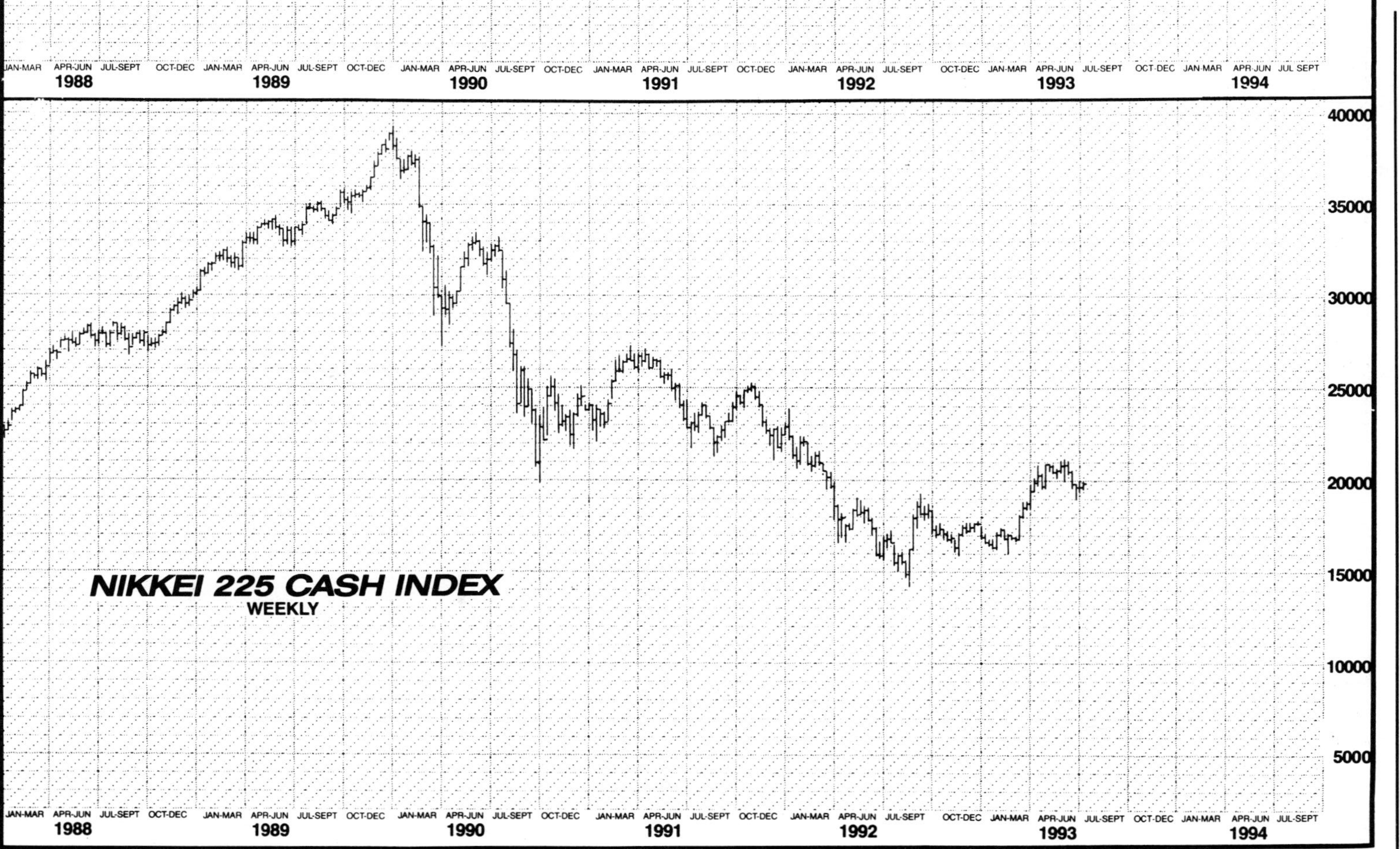

Source: Courtesy of Commodity Price Charts, 219 Parkade, Cedar Falls, Iowa 50613.

These weekly charts are plotted through July 9, 1993. Weekly charts are published on a quarterly schedule, and the next mailing in on October 8, 1993. Monthly charts are published semi-annually. The next mailing will be August 13, 1993.

Weekly High, Low & Close Charts of the Nearest Futures Contract: Long-term charts are plotted for the nearest futures contract on a weekly basis. During the week of change-over, the price action of both the expiring contract and the next one are included in the week's range.

Contract months used for plotting CPC weekly and monthly supplements.

Commodity	Contract months
Cattle	Feb., Apr., June, Aug., Oct., Dec.,
Hogs	Feb., Apr., June, July, Aug., Oct., Dec.,
Feeder Cattle	Jan., March, Apr., May, Aug., Sept., Oct., Nov.
Pork Bellies	Feb., March, May, July, Aug.
Corn	March, May, July, Sept., Dec.
Oats	March, May, July, Sept., Dec.
Soybeans	Jan., March, May, July, Aug., Sept., Nov.,
Soybean Meal	Jan., March, May, July, Aug., Sept., Oct., Dec.
Soybean Oil	Jan., March, May, July, Aug., Sept., Oct., Dec.
Chicago Wheat	March, May, July, Sept., Dec.
K.C. Wheat	March, May, July, Sept., Dec.
Mpls. Wheat	March, May, July, Sept., Dec.
Cotton	March, May, July, Oct., Dec.
Lumber	Jan., March, May, July, Sept., Nov.
Crude Oil	All contracts
Reg. Gas	All contracts
Heating Oil	All cor .racts
Currencies	March, June, Sept., Dec.
Int. Rates	March, June, Sept., Dec.
Stock Indices	March, June, Sept., Dec. (except MMI)
Major Market Index	All contracts
Cocoa	March, May, July, Sept., Dec.
Coffee	March, May, July, Sept., Dec.
Orange Juice	Jan., March, May, July, Sept., Nov.
Sugar	March, May, July, Oct.
Copper	March, May, July, Sept., Dec.
Silver	March, May, July, Sept., Dec.
Gold	Feb., June, Aug., Oct., Dec.
Palladium	March, June, Sept., Dec.
Platinum	Jan., Apr., July, Oct.

Source: Courtesy of Commodity Price Charts, 219 Parkade, Cedar Falls, Iowa 50613.

Computer Services and Educational Material for Business and Finance

Selected On-Line Business/ Financial Data Bases

On-line data bases are collections of computer stored data which are retrievable by remote terminals. The data bases are collected and organized by a so-called *producer*. The latter provides the data base to a *vendor* who distributes the data by means of a telecommunication network to the user. Often a vendor will offer a large number of different data bases. In some instances the producer and vendor are the same.

Using an on-line data base requires: (1) a *terminal* (a typewriter-like device usually equipped with a video display) to receive data and send commands to the vendor's computers, and (2) a *modem* for coupling the terminal to a telephone line. Printouts (hard copy) of the desired information can be obtained with the aid of electronic printers located at the user's terminal or, alternatively, ordered from the vendor.

The user accesses the data base by dialing a telephone number and then typing (on the terminal keyboard) a password provided by the vendor. Searching the data base is done with special commands and procedures peculiar to each base.

The contents of data bases vary. Some provide statistical data only—usually in the form of time series. Other bases provide bibliographic references and, in some instances, abstracts or the full text of articles.

Specifics concerning data base contents, instructions, and prices are available from vendors. Listed below are some major business data bases and vendors. More complete information concerning data bases is available from the sources given below.

ABI Inform
Provides references on all areas of business management with emphasis on "how-to" information.
Producer: Data Courier Inc. (Louisville, KY)
Vendors: BRS, DIALOG, SDC

Accountants Index
Contains reference information on accounting, auditing taxation, management and securities.
Producer: American Institute of Certified Public Accountants (New York, NY)
Vendors: SDC

American Profile
Provides statistical information on U.S. households including population, income, dependents, and also data on types of businesses in an area.
Producer: Donnelley Marketing (Stamford, CT)
Vendors: Business Information Service

Business Credit Service
Provides business credit and financial information.
Producer: TRW, Inc. (Orange, CA)
Vendors: TRW

Canadian Business and Current Affairs
English language business and popular periodicals
Producer: Micromedia Limited (Toronto, Ontario)
Vendor: DIALOG, CISTI

CIS Index
Contains references and abstracts from nearly every publication resulting from Senate and House Committee meetings since 1970.
Producer: Congressional Information Services, Inc. (Washington, DC)
Vendors: Dialog, SDC

Commodities
Contains over 41,000 times series of current commodity prices for the U.S., Canada, U.K., and France.
Producer: Wolff Research (London, U.K.)
Vendor: I. P. Sharp

Compendex (Computerized Engineering Index)
Contains over 1 million citations and abstracts to the world wide engineering literature.
Producer: Engineering Information Inc. (New York)
Vendor: BRS, D-STAR, DIALOG.

CompuServe, Inc.
Provides reference, statistical and full text retrieval of information of personal in-

terest including health, recipes, gardening, financial and investment data including the Compustat and Value Line data bases.

Producer: CompuServe, Inc. (Columbus, OH)

Vendor: CompuServe

Compustat

Provides very extensive financial data on companies.

Producer: Standard And Poor's Compustat Service, Inc. (Englewood, CO)

Vendors: ADP, Business Information Services, CompuServe, Data Resources, Chase Econometrics/Interactive Data Corp.

Disclosure II

Provides extracts of 10K and other reports filed with the Securities and Exchange Commission.

Producer: Disclosure Inc. (Bethesda, Maryland)

Vendors: Business Information Services (Control Data). Dialog, Dow Jones, New York Times Information Services, Mead Data Central.

Dow Jones News/Retrieval Service and Stock Quote Reporters

Contains text of articles appearing in major financial publications including the *Wall Street Journal* and *Barrons*. Quote Service provides quotes on stocks, bonds, mutual funds.

Producer: Dow Jones & Company (New York, NY)

Vendors: BRS, Dow Jones & Company

DRI Capsule/EEI Capsule

Provides over 3700 U.S. social and economic statistical time series such as population, income, money supply data, etc.

Producers: Data Resources, Inc. (Lexington, MA) and Evans Economics Inc. (Washington, DC)

Vendors: Business Information Services, United Telecom Group, I. P. Sharp

Federal Register Abstracts

Provides coverage of federal regulatory agencies as published in the Federal Register.

Producer: Capitol Services (Washington, DC)

Vendors: DIALOG, SDC

GTE Financial System One Quotation Service

Provides current U.S. and Canadian quotations and statistical data on stocks, bonds, options, commodities and other market data.

Producer: GTE Information Systems (Reston, VA)

Vendor: GTE Information Systems, Inc.

The Information Bank

Provides an extensive current affairs data source consisting of abstracts from numerous English language publications.

Producer: The New York Times Information Service

Vendor: The New York Times Information Service

LEXIS

Contains full text references to a wide range of legal information including court decisions, regulations, government statutes.

Producer: Mead Data Central (New York, NY)

Vendor: Mead Data Central

Media General Financial Services

Provides extensive historical fundamental and technical data and calculations on U.S. publicly owned companies. Also provides data on industries, the financial markets, mutual funds and corporate bonds.

Producer: Media General Financial Services (Richmond, VA)

Vendors: Dow Jones News Retrieval, Dialog, Thomson Financial Networks, Randall—Helms Fiduciary Consultants, Telescan, Lotus One Source (CDROM)

NEXIS

Provides full text business and general news including management, technology, finance, science, politics, religion.

Producer: Mead Data Central (New York, NY)

Vendor: Mead Data Central

PTS Marketing and Advertising Reference Service

Provides citations with abstracts & articles on the marketing and advertising of consumer goods and services.

Producer: Predicast, Inc. (Cleveland, OH)

Vendors: DIALOG, BRS, DATA-STAR

PTS Prompt

Covers world wide business news on new products, market data, etc.

Producer: Predicast, Inc. (Cleveland, OH)

Vendors: ADP, BRS, DIALOG

Quick Quote
Provides current quotations, volume, high-low data for securities of U.S. public corporations.
Producer: CompuServe Inc.
Vendor: CompuServe

Quotron 800
Provides up to the minute quotation and statistics on a broad range of securities such as stocks, bonds, options, commodities.
Producer: Quotron Systems Inc. (Los Angeles, CA)
Vendor: Quotron Systems Inc.

The Source (has been acquired by CompuServe)
Producer: Source Telecomputing (McLean, VA)
Vendor: Source Telecomputing Corp.

Trinet Company Data Base
Provides data on about 250,000 companies in the U.S.
Producer: Trinet, Inc. (Parsippany, NJ)
Vendors: DRI, DIALOG, Mead Data Central

For further information on data bases:

Computer Readable Data Bases, Gale Research (835 Penobscot Building, Detroit, MI 48226) A comprehensive data base and CD-ROM directory, revised annually.

Data Base Vendors

ADP Data Services, Inc.
175 Jackson Plaza
Ann Arbor, MI 48106
313-769-6800

BRS, Inc.
1200 Route 7
Latham, NY 12110
518-783-1161
800-235-1209

Chase Econometrics/Interactive Data Corporation
95 Hayden Avenue
Lexington, MA 02173
617-890-8100

CompuServe, Inc.
5000 Arlington Centre Boulevard
Columbus, OH 43220
614-457-8600
800-848-8990

Data Resources, Inc. (DRI)
1750 K Street NW
Washington, DC 20006
202-663-7720

DIALOG Information Services, Inc.
3460 Hillview Avenue
Palo Alto, CA 94304
415-858-3810
800-334-2564

Dow Jones & Company, Inc.
P.O. Box 300
Princeton, NJ 08540
609-452-2000
800-257-5114

General Electric Information Services Company
401 North Washington Street
Rockville, MD 20850
301-294-5405

GTE Education Services
8505 Freeport Parking
Irving, TX 75063
214-929-3000

Mead Data Central
P.O. Box 933
Dayton, OH 45401
800-227-4908

The New York Times Information Services, Inc.
229 West 43 Street
New York, NY 10036
800-543-6862

Quotron Systems, Inc.
12731 West Jefferson Boulevard
P.O. Box 66914
Los Angeles, CA 90066
213-827-4600

SDC Search Service/Orbit
8000 Westpark Drive
McLean, VA 22102
703-442-0900
800-456-7248

I. P. Sharp Associates
Exchange Tower
Toronto, Ontario, Canada M5X IE3
416-364-5361
800-387-1588

TRW Information Services Division
505 City Parkway West
Orange, CA 92668
714-385-7000

Noteworthy Software of Interest to Investors

The following provides a brief description of moderately priced software products of special interest to investors.

The EQUALIZER (Charles Schwab & Co., 101 Montgomery Street, San Francisco, CA 94104)

To use this software it is necessary to open an account with the discount brokerage firm of Charles Schwab & Co. The EQUALIZER includes the following features:

- access to financial information and data via Dow Jones News Retrieval and Standard and Poor's Marketscope
- price quotes on securities and mutual funds provided by Schwab, Dow Jones, or Warner Communications
- portfolio maintenance and record keeping
- trading capabilities (via Charles Schwab, of course)

This is excellent software for the active investor. The instruction manual which accompanies the software is first class.

QUICKEN (Intuit, 66 Willow Place, Menlo Park, CA 04025)

This is a leading program for maintaining records and managing personal finances. QUICKEN permits users to record deposits, monitor investments, keep track of saving, and print out checks as they become due. The software can also be used for small business and bookkeeping.

A 'help' program is provided which facilitates start up. The instruction manual accompanying QUICKEN is excellent. Also available at bookstores are other manuals.

WEALTHBUILDER (developed for *Money Magazine* by Reality Technologies, Inc., 3624 Market Street, Philadelphia, PA 19104) is a program intended to guide users on the development of investment strategies to meet their goals (home purchase, college education, retirement, etc.). Given the investor's financial goals, risk tolerance, net worth, and the like, the program provides an allocation of investments among equities, mutual funds, bonds, precious metals, and money market funds.

Information for allocating funds among each type of investment is available (for a price) on quarterly updated disks which contain data provided by Standard & Poor. CompuServe, the online data base, now provides a service for users of WEALTHBUILDERS.

The program is recommended for serious financial planning.

MANAGING YOUR MONEY (MECA Ventures, Inc., 355 Riverside Avenue, Westport, CT 06801) is a popular personal financial program providing the following features:

- budget and checkbook program
- a tax estimator
- an estate and insurance planner
- a financial calculator
- a portfolio manager

In addition to the above the program has a built in name filing capability and a word processor.

QUANT IX (Quant Software, 5900 North Port Washington Road, Milwaukee, WI 53217) is an excellent and relatively inexpensive portfolio managtock analyzer with record keeping capability. The software also provides for downloading data from CompuServe and Warner Communications. A unique feature is the availability of six different methods for evaluating stocks.

OPTIONS TOOLS DELUX (Richard Kedrow, 25 Illinois Avenue, Schaumburg, IL 60913). This helpful software provides option investors with the capability of calculating theoretical option values using the Black-Scholes and binomial models, hedge ratios, volatility, breakeven values, and covered call analysis.

BUSINESS PLAN GENERATOR (Essex Financial Group, 714 Market Street, Philadelphia, PA 19106) is a very useful computer program intended to help in the development of business plans. The underlying philosophy is that of Dynamic Planning which views planning as an ongoing procedure responding to changes in the business environment, and provides for feedback into the planning process. The program generates all of the expected planning projections; profit and loss statements, balance sheets, cash flows, and numerous financial ratios. The program also permits taking into account the effects of acquisitions. The *Business Plan Generator* requires the use of lotus 1-2-3 since it functions as an overlay of the latter.

DEALMAKER II (ValueSource, 1939 Grand Avenue, San Diego, CA 92109) is a sophisticated business evaluation program intended for buyers, sellers, and brokers. Other applications include evaluations of businesses for such purposes as marital dissolution, estate and gift taxes, employee stock options, and going public.

Twelve evaluation methods are provided, including book value, liquidation value, discounted earnings, the use of industry P/E ratios, and others.

The program also allows for consideration of projected post acquisition financial statements and for the effects on buyer and seller of different ways of financing the acquisition.

Screening Software

With thousands of companies listed on the exchanges, identifying promising investment opportunities is a daunting task. Fortunately this arduous chore can be greatly facilitated with the screening programs described below.

Investor's Alliance

Investor's Alliance provides a data base service to members comprising nearly 5000 companies traded over the counter and on the exchanges. The data are provided on diskettes which are updated quarterly. However, users can also update more frequently by going online. A screening capability is also included. Though the cost of this service is very modest the available data are surprisingly extensive.

Investor's Alliance, Inc.
219 Commercial Boulevard
Fort Lauderdale, FL 33308-4440
Telephone: 305-491-5100

MarketBase

MarketBase is an impressive software package providing key financial and market data on *all* companies traded in the NYSE, AMEX, and NASDAQ exchanges—over 5200 companies in all. The data spans a five year period. Updates are provided (depending on the subscription terms) on a weekly, monthly, or quarterly basis. Bi-Monthly and bi-Weekly updates are also available.

Over fifty financial and market criteria are included for screening. Companies may be screened by selecting a combination of criteria; for example, the PE ratio, revenues, earnings growth, market capitalization, SIC Code, and others. *MarketBase* also permits users to define their own selection criteria. Once screened, companies may be further explored by obtaining annual reports, 10-Q, press releases, and other materials by phoning the company. Although *MarketBase* software does not provide phone numbers, these may be obtained by calling the vendor. The software also lacks online communication capability.

MarketBase is an important resource for the serious investor. For further information contact:

MarketBase, Inc.
368 Hillside Avenue
P.O. Box 37
Needham Heights, MA 02194
Telephone: 800-735-0700

Value/Screen

Value/Screen provides access to about 1600 stocks composing the Value Line data base. Reportedly, these account for 90% of all trading on U.S. exchanges. Screening is carried out utilizing a wide variety of financial, market, and rating variables. Provisions are also available for user defined screening criteria. A rather elegant screening option displays particular screening criteria by means of a histogram.

Value/Screen is equipped with an online communications capability providing access to the Dow Jones News Retrieval Services.

Updates are available weekly, monthly, or quarterly. Data can also be down loaded online.

For complete details, contact:

Value Line Publishing, Inc.
711 Third Avenue
New York, NY 10017
Telephone: 800-654-0508

Home Study Course for Investors

Several very good self study courses of interest to investors are worthy of mention here.

CEI FUTURES AND OPTIONS HOME STUDY COURSE (Commodities Educational Institute, 219 Parkade, Cedar Falls, IA 50613) is intended to train professionals and consists of some 21 audio tapes and two binders of notes and supplemental materials. The emphasis of this course is on commodity futures though some attention is given to financial futures and options on futures. Topics covered include the economic function of the futures market, how the futures market works, technical analysis, hedging, rules and regulations, financial futures, stock indexes, options on futures.

Purchasers of this course can attend 5 day work shops held in various cities at reduced rates.

FUTURES TRADING COURSE (Futures Industry Association, 2001 Pennsylvania Avenue, N.W., Washington, D.C. 20006) is comprised of three volumes which cover much of the same ground as the CEI course described above. The Institute also runs seminars and workshops for those wishing to acquire professional qualifications.

HOME STUDY COURSE OF THE AMERICAN ASSOCIATION OF INDIVIDUAL INVESTORS (AAII), (AAII, 625 North Michigan Avenue, Chicago, IL 60611) is an excellent course which provides coverage of the entire field of investments; stocks, bonds, mutual funds, futures, options, real estate, and more. Purchasers of this course receive updated material from time to time. The association also holds comprehensive national investment seminars on topics of current interest which are also available on audio tape. A recent seminar occupied some 25 tapes and is accompanied by a substantial set of notes.

FORBES STOCK MARKET COURSE (Forbes, Inc., 60 Fifth Avenue, New York, NY 10011) is somewhat more elementary than the AAII described above and focuses almost exclusively on the stock market. A small section of the course is devoted to options and warrants. The course should appeal to investors who want a readable basic survey of the equities market.

Future Employment Opportunities

Every 2 years, the Bureau of Labor Statistics develops projections of the labor force, economic growth, industry output and employment, and occupational employment under three sets of alternative assumptions. These projections usually cover a 10- to 15-year period and provide a framework for the discussion of job outlook in each occupational statement in the *Handbook*. All of the approximately 250 statements in this edition of the *Handbook* identify the principal factors affecting job prospects and indicate how these factors are expected to affect the occupation in the future. This chapter uses the moderate alternative of each projection to provide a framework for the individual job outlook discussions.

Population Trends

Population trends affect employment opportunities in a number of ways. First of all, changes in the size and composition of the population influence the demand for goods and services—for example, the population aged 85 and over will grow more than three times as fast as the total population between 1990 and 2005, increasing the demand for health services. Equally important, population changes produce corresponding changes in the size and characteristics of the labor force.

The U.S. civilian noninstitutional population, aged 16 and over, is expected to grow more slowly over the next 15 years than it did during the previous 15-year period, increasing from about 188 million to 218 million. However, even slower population growth will increase the demand for goods and services, as well as the demand for workers in many occupations and industries.

The age structure will shift toward relatively fewer children and youth and a growing proportion of middle-aged and older people well into the 21st century. The decline in the proportion of children and youth reflects the lower birth rates that prevailed during the 1970's and 1980's; the impending large increase in the middle-aged population reflects the aging of the "baby boom" generation born after World War II; and the very rapid growth in the number of old people is attributable to high birth rates prior to the Great Depression of the 1930's, together with improvements in medical technology that have made it possible for most Americans to survive into old age.

Minorities and immigrants will constitute a larger share of the U.S. population in 2005 than they do today. Substantial increases in the number of Hispanics, Asians, and blacks are anticipated, reflecting net immigration, and higher birth rates among blacks and Hispanics. Substantial inflows of immigrants, both documented and undocumented, are expected to continue. The arrival of immigrants from every corner of the world has significant implications for the labor force, because immigrants tend to be of working age but of different educational and occupational backgrounds than the U.S. population as a whole.

Population growth varies greatly among geographic regions, affecting the demand for goods and services and, in turn, workers in various occupations and industries. Between 1980 and 1990, the population of the Midwest and the Northeast grew by only 1.4 percent and 3.4 percent, respectively, compared with 13.4 percent in the South and 22.2 percent in the West. These differences reflect the movement of people seeking new jobs or retiring, as well as higher birth rates in some areas than in others.

Projections by the Bureau of the Census indicate that the West will continue to be the fastest growing region, increasing about 19 percent between 1990 and 2005. In the South, the population is expected to increase about 15 percent. The number of people in the Northeast is projected to increase slightly, by about 4 percent, while the Midwest population is expected to remain about the same.

Geographic shifts in the population alter the demand for and the supply of workers in local job markets. Moreover, in areas dominated by one or two industries, local job markets may be extremely sensitive to the economic fortunes of those industries. For these and other reasons, local employment opportunities may differ substantially from the projections for the Nation as a whole presented in the *Handbook*.

Labor Force Trends

Population is the single most important factor governing the size and composition of

Source: *Occupational Outlook Handbook* 1992–1993, U.S. Department of Labor, Bureau of Labor Statistics.

the labor force, which includes people who are working, or looking for work. The civilian labor force totaled 125 million in 1990 and is expected to reach 151 million by 2005. This projected increase—21 percent—represents a slowdown in both the number added to the labor force and the rate of labor force growth, largely due to slower population growth (chart 1).

America's workers will be an increasingly diverse group as we approach the year 2005. White non-Hispanic men will make up a smaller share of the labor force, and women and minority group members will comprise a larger share than in 1990. White non-Hispanics have historically been the largest component of the labor force, but their share has been dropping and is expected to fall from 79 percent in 1990, to 73 percent by 2005. Whites are projected to grow more slowly than blacks, Asians, and others, but will experience the largest numerical increase. Hispanics will add about 7 million workers to the labor force from 1990 to 2005, increasing by 75 percent. Despite this dramatic growth, Hispanics' share of the labor force will only increase from 8 percent to 11 percent, as shown in chart 2. Blacks, Hispanics, and Asian and other racial groups will account for roughly 35 percent of all labor force entrants between 1990 and 2005.

Women will continue to join the labor force in growing numbers. The number of women in the labor force will increase faster than the total labor force, but more slowly than between 1975 and 1990. In the late 1980s, the labor force participation of women

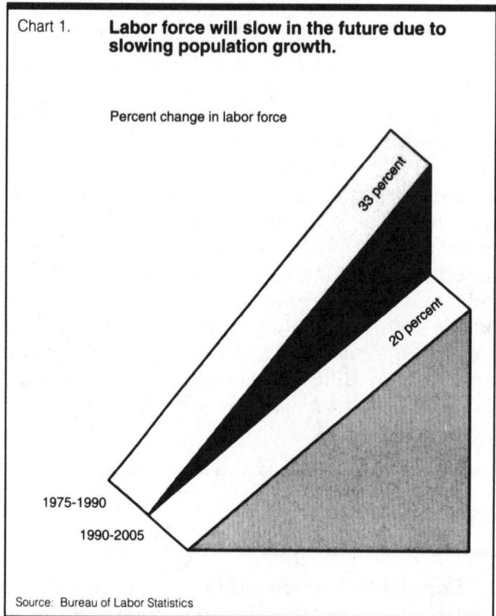
Chart 1. **Labor force will slow in the future due to slowing population growth.**

Source: Bureau of Labor Statistics

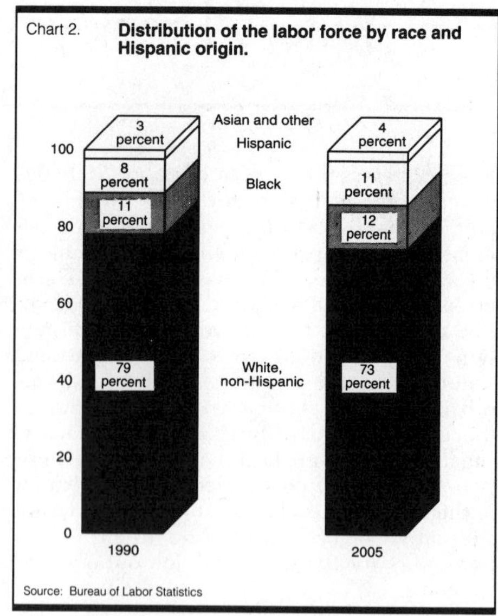
Chart 2. **Distribution of the labor force by race and Hispanic origin.**

Source: Bureau of Labor Statistics

under age 40 began to increase more slowly than in the past, in part because of the increases in births that have occurred in recent years. Nevertheless, women were only 40 percent of the labor force in 1975; by 2005, they are expected to constitute 47 percent.

The changing age structure of the population will directly affect tomorrow's labor force. As the proportion of young workers declines, the pool of experienced workers will increase (chart 3). In 1990, the median age of the labor force was 36.6 years; by 2005, it will be 40.6 years.

Between 1975 and 1990, the youth labor force (16 to 24 years of age) dropped by 1.4 million, a 6-percent decline. In contrast, the number of youths in the labor force will increase by 2.8 million over the 1990–2005 period, reflecting an increase of 13 percent, still growing more slowly than the total labor force. As a result, young people are expected to comprise a slightly smaller percentage of the labor force in 2005 than in 1990. Among youths, the teenage labor force (16 to 19 years of age) will increase by 18 percent over the 1990–2005 period, a numerical increase of 1.4 million. The labor force 20 to 24 years of age is projected to increase by 10 percent, also a numerical increase of 1.4 million. The total youth labor force accounted for 24 percent of the entire labor force in 1975, fell to 17 percent in 1990, and should decline further to 16 percent by 2005.

The scenario should be different for prime-age workers (25 to 54 years of age). The baby boom generation will continue to add members to the labor force, but their share of the labor force peaked in 1985. These workers

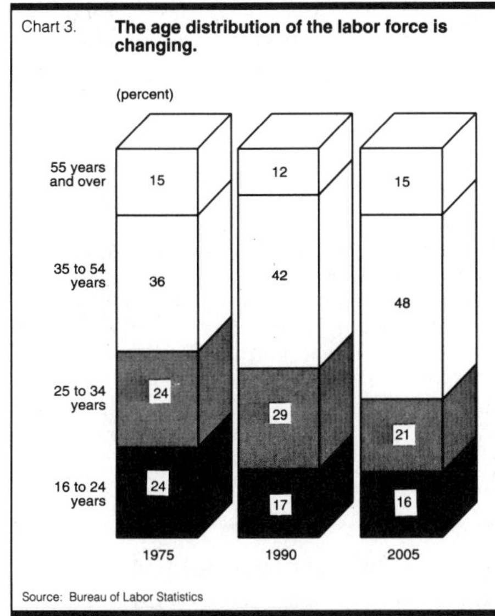

Chart 3. **The age distribution of the labor force is changing.**

Source: Bureau of Labor Statistics

accounted for 61 percent of the labor force in 1975, and rose significantly to 71 percent in 1990, but should decline slightly to 69 percent by 2005. The growing proportion of workers between the ages of 45 and 54 is particularly striking. These workers should account for 24 percent of the labor force by the year 2005, up from 16 percent in 1990. Because workers in their mid-forties to mid-fifties usually have substantial work experience and tend to be more stable than younger workers, this could result in improved productivity and a larger pool of experienced applicants from which employers may choose.

The number of older workers, aged 55 and above, is projected to grow about twice as fast as the total labor force between 1990 and 2005, and about five times as fast as the number of workers aged 55 and above grew between 1975 and 1990. As the baby boomers grow older, the number of workers aged 55 to 64 will increase; they exhibit higher labor force participation than their older counterparts. By 2005, workers aged 55 and over will comprise 15 percent of the labor force, up from 12 percent in 1990.

In recent years, the level of educational attainment of the labor force has risen dramatically. Between 1975 and 1990, the proportion of the labor force aged 25 to 64 with at least 1 year of college increased from 33 to 47 percent, while the proportion with 4 years of college or more increased from 18 to 26 percent (chart 4). Projected rates of employment growth are faster for occupations requiring higher levels of education or training than for those requiring less.

The emphasis on education will continue. Three out of the 4 fastest growing occupational groups will be executive, administrative, and managerial; professional specialty; and technicians and related support occupations. These occupations generally require the highest levels of education and skill, and will make up an increasing proportion of new jobs. Office and factory automation, changes in consumer demand, and substitution of imports for domestic products are expected to cause employment to stagnate or decline in many occupations that require little formal education—apparel workers and textile machinery operators, for example. Opportunities for high school dropouts will be increasingly limited, and workers who cannot read and follow directions may not even be considered for most jobs.

Employed high school dropouts are more likely to have low paying jobs with little advancement potential, while workers in occupations requiring higher levels of education have higher incomes. In addition, many of the occupations projected to grow most rapidly between 1990 and 2005 are among those with higher earnings.

Nevertheless, even slower growing occupations that have a large number of workers will provide many job openings resulting from the need to replace workers who leave the labor force or transfer to other occupations. Consequently, workers with all levels of education and training will continue to be in demand, although advancement opportunities will be best for those with the most education and training.

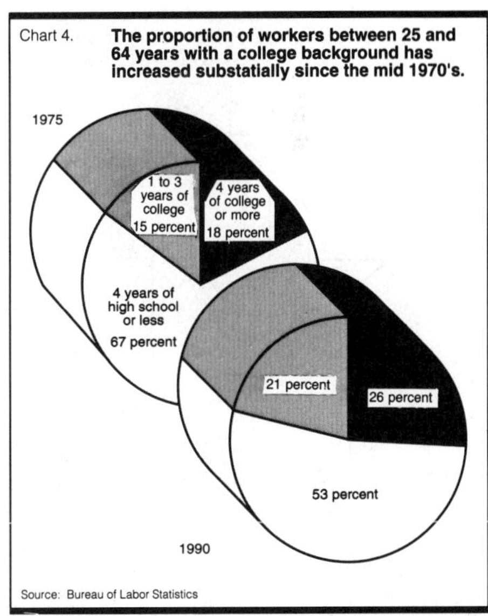

Chart 4. **The proportion of workers between 25 and 64 years with a college background has increased substatially since the mid 1970's.**

Source: Bureau of Labor Statistics

Employment Change

Total employment is expected to increase from 122.6 million in 1990 to 147.2 million in 2005, or by 20 percent. Reflecting a slowdown in labor force growth, this is only slightly more than half the rate of increase recorded during the previous 15-year period.

The 24.6 million jobs that will be added to the U.S. economy by 2005 will not be evenly distributed across major industrial and occupational groups—causing some restructuring of employment. Continued faster than average employment growth among occupations that require relatively high levels of education or training is expected. The following two sections examine projected employment change from both industrial and occupational perspectives. The industrial profile is discussed in terms of wage and salary employment, except for agriculture, forestry, and fishing, which includes self-employed and unpaid family workers. The occupational profile is viewed in terms of total employment (wage and salary, self-employed, and unpaid family workers).

Industrial Profile

The long-term shift from goods-producing to service-producing employment is expected to continue (chart 5). For example, service-producing industries—including transportation, communications, and utilities; retail and wholesale trade; services; government; and finance, insurance, and real estate—are expected to account for approximately 23 million of the 24.6 million new jobs created by the year 2005. In addition, the services division within this sector—which includes health, business, and educational services—contains 16 of the 20 fastest growing industries, and 12 of the 20 industries adding the most jobs. Expansion of service sector employment is linked to a number of factors, including changes in consumer tastes and preferences, legal and regulatory changes, advances in science and technology, and changes in the way businesses are organized and managed. Specific factors responsible for varying growth prospects in major industry divisions are discussed below.

Service-Producing Industries

Services. Services is both the largest and the fastest growing division within the service-producing sector (chart 6). This division provided 38 million jobs in 1990; employment is expected to rise 34.7 percent to 50.5 million by 2005, accounting for almost one-half of all new jobs. Jobs will be found in small firms and in large corporations, in state and local governments, and in industries as diverse as banking, hospitals, data processing, and management consulting. The two largest industry groups in this division, health services and business services, are projected to continue

Chart 5. **Industries providing services will account for about four out of five jobs by the year 2005.**

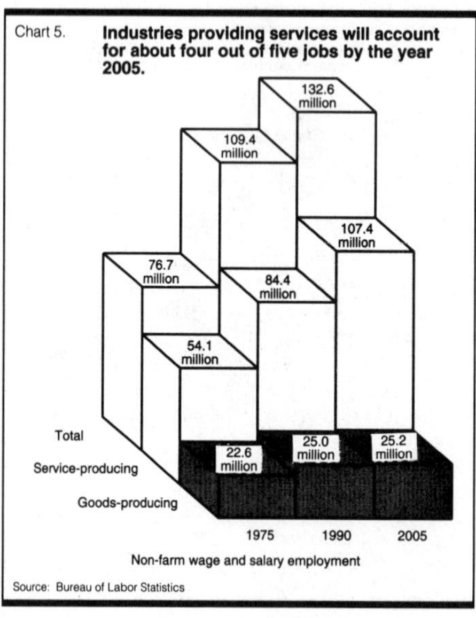

Source: Bureau of Labor Statistics

Chart 6. **Some industries will grow more rapidly than others.**

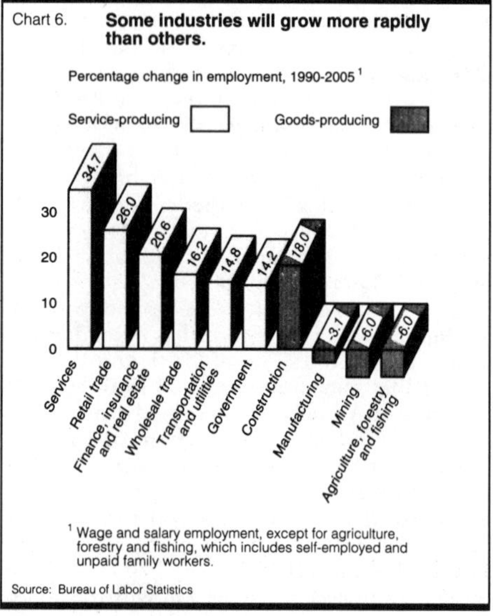

[1] Wage and salary employment, except for agriculture, forestry and fishing, which includes self-employed and unpaid family workers.

Source: Bureau of Labor Statistics

to grow very fast. In addition, social, legal, and engineering and management services industries further illustrate this division's strong growth.

Health care will continue to be one of the fastest growing industries in the economy. Employment in the health services industries is projected to grow from 8.9 to 12.8 million. Improvements in medical technology, and a growing and aging population will increase the demand for health services. Employment in home health care services—the fastest growing industry in the economy—nursing homes, and offices and clinics of physicians and other health practitioners is projected to increase the most rapidly throughout this period. However, not all health industries will grow at the same rapid rate. For example, hospitals, both public and private, will continue to be the largest, but slowest growing health care industry.

Business services industries also will generate many jobs. Employment is expected to grow from 5.2 million in 1990 to 7.6 million in 2005. Personnel supply services, made up primarily of temporary help agencies, is the largest sector in this group and will continue to add many jobs. However, due to the slowdown in labor force participation by young women, and the proliferation of personnel supply firms in recent years, this industry will grow more slowly than during the 1975–90 period, although still faster than the average for all industries. Business services also includes one of the fastest growing industries in the economy—computer and data processing services. This industry's rapid growth stems from advances in technology, world wide trends toward office and factory automation, and increases in demand from business firms, government agencies, and individuals.

Education, both private and public, is expected to add 2.3 million jobs to the 9.4 million in 1990. This increase reflects population growth and, in turn, rising enrollments projected for elementary, secondary, and post-secondary schools. The elementary school age population (ages 5–13) will rise by 3.8 million between 1990 and 2005, the secondary school age (14–17) by 3.2 million, and the traditional post-secondary school age (18–24) by 1.4 million. In addition, continued rising enrollments of older, foreign, and part-time students are expected to enhance employment in postsecondary education. Not all of the increase in employment in education, however, will be for teachers; teacher aides, counselors, and administrative staff also are projected to increase.

Employment in social services is expected to increase by 1.1 million, bringing the total to 2.9 million by 2005, reflecting the growing elderly population. For example, residential care institutions, which provide around-the-clock assistance to older persons and others who have limited ability for self-care, is projected to be one of the fastest growing industries in the U.S. economy. Other social services industries that are projected to grow rapidly include child daycare services and individual and miscellaneous social services, which includes elderly daycare and family social services.

Retail and wholesale trade. Employment in retail and wholesale trade is expected to rise by 26 and 16 percent, respectively; from 19.7 to 24.8 million in retail trade and from 6.2 to 7.2 million in wholesale trade. Guided by higher levels of personal income and continued increases in women's labor force participation, the fastest projected job growth in retail trade is in apparel and accessory stores and eating and drinking establishments, with the latter employing the most workers in this sector. Substantial numerical increases in retail employment are anticipated in food stores, automotive dealers and service stations, and general merchandise stores.

Finance, insurance, and real estate. Employment is expected to increase by 21 percent—adding 1.4 million jobs to the 1990 level of 6.7 million. The demand for financial products and services is expected to continue unabated, but bank mergers, consolidations, and closings—resulting from overexpansion and competition from nonbank corporations that offer bank-like services—are expected to limit job growth. The fastest growing industry within this sector is expected to be nondepository holding and investment offices, which includes businesses that compete with banks, such as finance companies and mortgage brokers.

Transportation, communications, and public utilities. Overall employment will increase by 15 percent. Employment in the transportation sector is expected to increase by 25 percent, from 3.6 to 4.4 million jobs. Truck transportation will account for 47 percent of all new jobs; air transportation will account for 32 percent. The projected gains in transportation jobs reflect the continued shift from rail to road freight transportation, rising personal incomes, and growth in foreign trade. In addition, deregulation in the transportation industry has increased personal and business travel options, spurring strong job growth in the passenger transportation arrangement industry, which includes travel agencies. Reflecting laborsaving technology and industry competition, employment in communications is projected to decline by 13 percent. Employment in utilities, however, is expected to grow about as fast as the average, adding 160,000 new jobs, highlighted by one of the fastest growing industries in the economy—water supply and sanitary services.

Government. Between 1990 and 2005, government employment, excluding public education and public hospitals, is expected to increase 14 percent, from 9.5 million to 10.8 million jobs. This growth will occur in state and local government; employment in the Federal Government is expected to decline by 31,000 jobs.

Goods-Producing Industries

Employment in this sector peaked in the late 1970's, and has not recovered from the recessionary period of the early 1980's and the trade imbalances that began in the mid-1980's. Although overall employment in goods-producing industries is expected to show little change, growth prospects within the sector vary considerably.

Construction. Construction, the only goods-producing industry projected to grow, is expected to add 923,000 jobs between 1990 and 2005. Construction employment is expected to increase by 18 percent, from 5.1 to 6.1 million. Increases in road and bridge construction will offset the slowdown in demand for new housing, reflecting the slowdown in population growth and the overexpansion of office building construction in recent years.

Manufacturing. Manufacturing employment is expected to decline by 3 percent from the 1990 level of 19.1 million. The projected loss of manufacturing jobs reflects productivity gains achieved from increased investment in manufacturing technologies as well as a winnowing out of less efficient operations.

The composition of manufacturing employment is expected to shift since most of the jobs that will disappear are production jobs. The number of professional, technical, and managerial positions in manufacturing firms will increase.

Mining. Mining employment is expected to decline from 712,000 to 669,000—a 6-percent decline. Underlying this projection is the assumption that domestic oil production will drop and oil imports will rise sharply, reducing employment in the crude petroleum industry. However, the expected rise in oil prices should spark exploration and, consequently, a slight increase in employment in the oil field services industry. In addition, employment in coal mining should continue to decline sharply due to the expanded use of laborsaving machinery.

Agriculture, forestry, and fishing. Overall employment in agriculture, forestry, and fishing has been declining for many decades and this trend is expected to continue—the number of jobs is projected to decline by 6 percent, from 3.3 million to 3.1 million.

The decline in agricultural, forestry, and fishing jobs reflects a decrease of 410,000 in the number of self-employed workers. Wage and salary positions are expected to increase by 214,000—with especially strong growth in the agricultural services industry, which includes landscape, horticultural, and farm management services.

Occupational Profile

Continued expansion of the service-producing sector conjures up an image of a work force dominated by cashiers, retail sales workers, and waiters. However, although service sector growth will generate millions of clerical, sales, and service jobs, it also will create jobs for financial managers, engineers, nurses, electrical and electronics technicians, and many other managerial, professional, and technical workers. In fact, the fastest growing occupations will be those that require the most formal education and training.

This section furnishes an overview of projected employment in 12 categories or "clusters" of occupations based on the Standard Occupational Classification (SOC). The SOC is used by all Federal agencies that collect occupational employment data, and is the organizational framework for grouping statements in the Handbook.

In the discussion that follows, projected employment change is described as growing faster, slower, or the same as the average for all occupations. (These phrases are explained on page 612.) While occupations that are growing fast generally offer good opportunities, the numerical change in employment also is important because large occupations, such as retail sales worker, may offer many more new jobs than a small, fast-growing occupation, such as paralegal (chart 7).

Technicians and related support occupations. Workers in this group provide technical assistance to engineers, scientists, and other professional workers, as well as operate and program technical equipment. Employment in this cluster is expected to increase by 37 percent, from 4.2 to 5.8 million, making it the fastest growing occupational cluster in the economy (chart 8). It also contains one of the fastest growing occupations—paralegals. Employment of paralegals is expected to increase much faster than average as utilization of these workers in the rapidly expanding legal services industry increases. Health technicians and technologists, such as radiologic and

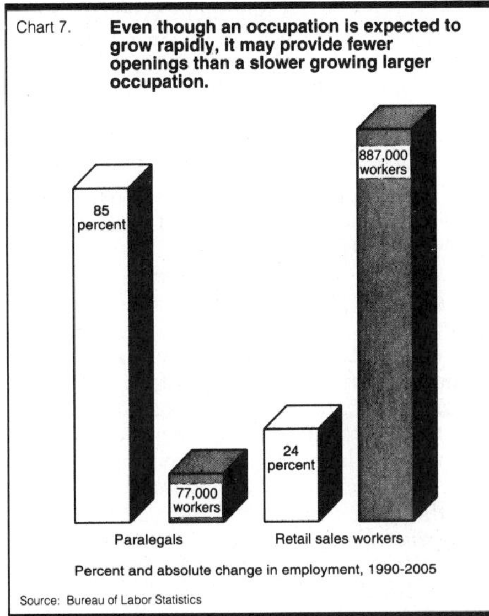

Chart 7. **Even though an occupation is expected to grow rapidly, it may provide fewer openings than a slower growing larger occupation.**

Source: Bureau of Labor Statistics

surgical technologists, and computer programmers will add large numbers of jobs. Growth in other occupations, such as broadcast technicians, will be limited by laborsaving technological advances.

Professional specialty occupations. Workers in these occupations perform a wide variety of duties, and are employed in almost every industry. Employment in this cluster is expected to grow by 32 percent, from 15.8 to 20.9 million jobs, continuing to grow faster than average, and significantly increasing its share of total employment by 2005. Much of this growth is a result of rising demand for computer specialists; social and recreation workers; lawyers; health diagnosing and treating occupations; and engineers.

Chart 8. **Employment change will vary widely by broad occupational group.**

Occupational group	Percent change in employment, 1990-2005
Total, all occupations	20
Technicians and related support occupations	37
Professional specialty occupations	32
Service occupations	29
Executive, administrative, and managerial occupations	27
Marketing and sales occupations	24
Transportation and material moving occupations	21
Construction trades and extractive occupations	20
Mechanics, installers, and repairers	16
Administrative support occupations, including clerical	13
Handlers, equipment cleaners, helpers, and laborers	8
Agriculture, forestry, fishing, and related occupations	5
Production occupations	-4

Source: Bureau of Labor Statistics

Service occupations. This group includes a wide range of workers in protective services, food and beverage preparation, health services, and cleaning and personal services. Employment in these occupations is expected to grow by 29 percent, faster than average, from 19.2 to 24.8 million. An expanding population and economy, combined with higher personal incomes and increased leisure time, will spur demand for many different types of services. For example, employment of flight attendants, homemaker-home health aides, and preschool workers should all grow much faster than average.

Executive, administrative, and managerial occupations. Workers in this cluster establish policies, make plans, determine staffing requirements, and direct the activities of businesses, government agencies, and other organizations. Those in management support occupations provide technical assistance to managers. Employment in this cluster is expected to increase by 27 percent, from 12.5 to 15.9 million, reflecting faster than average growth. Growth will be spurred by the increasing number and complexity of business operations and result in large employment gains, especially in the services industry division. However, many businesses will streamline operations, reducing administrative costs and employing fewer managers, thus offsetting increases in employment.

Employment in these occupations tends to be driven by industry growth. For example, employment of health services managers will grow much faster than average, while only average growth is expected for wholesale and retail buyers and merchandise managers.

Hiring requirements in many managerial and administrative jobs are becoming more stringent. Work experience, specialized training, or graduate study will be increasingly necessary. Familiarity with computers will continue to be important as a growing number of firms rely on computerized management information systems.

Marketing and sales occupations. Workers in this cluster sell goods and services, purchase commodities and property for resale, and stimulate consumer interest. Employment in this cluster is projected to increase by 24 percent, from 14.1 to 17.5 million jobs, about as fast as average. Demand for services sales representatives, travel agents, and securities and financial services sales workers is expected to grow much faster than average due to strong growth in the industries that employ them. Many part- and full-time job openings are expected for retail sales workers and cashiers due to the large size, high turnover, and faster than average employment growth in these occupations. Opportunities for higher paying sales jobs, however, will tend to be more competitive.

Transportation and material moving occupations. Workers in this cluster operate the equipment used to move people and equipment. Employment in this group is expected to increase by 21 percent, from 4.7 to 5.7 million jobs. Faster than average growth is expected for busdrivers, while average growth is expected for truckdrivers, reflecting rising school enrollments and growing demand for transportation services. Equipment improvements and automation should result in materials moving equipment operators increasing more slowly than the average. In addition, railroad transportation workers and water transportation workers are projected to show little change in employment as technological advances increase productivity.

Construction trades and extractive occupations. Workers in this group construct, alter, and maintain buildings and other structures, and operate drilling and mining equipment. Overall employment in this group is expected to rise from 4 to 4.8 million. Virtually all of the new jobs will be in construction. Spurred by new projects and alterations to existing structures, average employment growth is expected in construction. On the other hand, increased automation, continued stagnation in the oil and gas industries, and slow growth in demand for coal, metal, and other materials will result in little change in employment of extractive workers.

Mechanics, installers, and repairers. These workers adjust, maintain, and repair automobiles, industrial equipment, computers, and many other types of equipment. Overall employment in these occupations is expected to grow by 16 percent—from 4.9 to 5.7 million—due to increased use of mechanical and electronic equipment. One of the fastest growing occupations in this group is expected to be computer and office machine repairers, reflecting the increased use of these types of machines. Communications equipment mechanics, installers, and repairers, and telephone installers and repairers, in sharp contrast, are expected to record a decline in employment due to laborsaving advances.

Administrative support occupations, including clerical. Workers in this largest major occupational group perform the wide variety of administrative tasks necessary to keep organizations functioning smoothly. The group as a whole is expected to grow by 13 percent, from 22.0 to 24.8 million jobs, more slowly than average. Technological advances are projected to slow employment growth for stenographers and typists, word processors, and data entry keyers. Others, such as receptionists and information clerks, will grow much faster than average, spurred by rapidly expanding industries such as business services. Because of their large size and substantial turnover, clerical occupations will offer abundant opportunities for qualified jobseekers in the years ahead.

Handlers, equipment cleaners, helpers, and laborers. Workers in this group assist skilled workers and perform routine, unskilled tasks. Overall employment is expected to increase by only 8 percent, slower than average, from 4.9 to 5.3 million jobs as routine tasks are automated. Employment of construction laborers, however, is expected to increase about as fast as average, reflecting growth in the construction industry.

Agriculture, forestry, and fishing occupations. Workers in these occupations cultivate plants, breed and raise animals, and catch fish. Although demand for food, fiber, and wood is expected to increase as the world's population grows, the use of more productive farming and forestry methods and the consolidation of smaller farms are expected to result in only a 5-percent increase in employment, from 3.5 to 3.7 million jobs. Employment of farm operators and farm workers is expected to rapidly decline, reflecting greater productivity; the need for skilled farm managers, on the other hand, should result in average employment growth in that occupation.

Production occupations. Workers in these occupations set up, install, adjust, operate, and tend machinery and equipment and use handtools and hand-held power tools to fabricate and assemble products. Employment is expected to decline by 4 percent, from 12.8 to 12.3 million. Increases in imports, overseas production, and automation—including robotics and advanced computer techniques—will result in little change or slight declines in overall employment. Relative to other occupations, employment in many production occupations is more sensitive to fluctuations in the business cycle and competition from imports.

Replacement Needs

Most jobs through the year 2005 will become available as a result of replacement needs. Thus, even occupations with little or no employment growth or slower than average employment growth may still offer many job openings.

Replacement openings occur as people leave occupations. Some transfer to other oc-

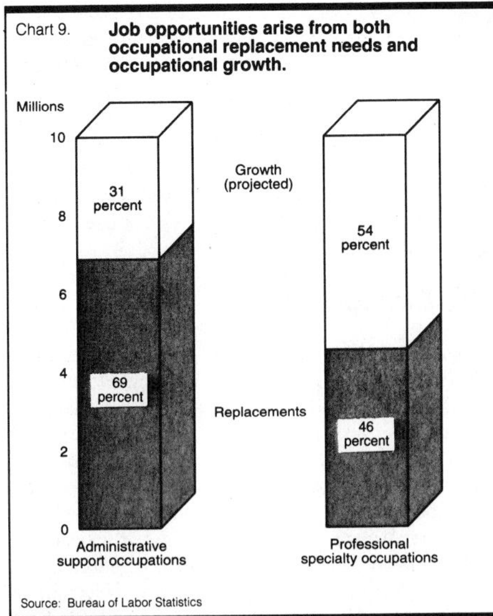

Chart 9. **Job opportunities arise from both occupational replacement needs and occupational growth.**

cupations as a step up the career ladder or to change careers. Others stop working in order to return to school, to assume household responsibilities, or to retire.

The number of replacement openings and the proportion of job openings made up by replacement needs varies by occupation. Occupations with the most replacement openings generally are large, with low pay and status, low training requirements, and a high proportion of young and part-time workers. The occupations with relatively few replacement openings, on the other hand, are those with high pay and status, lengthy training requirements, and a high proportion of prime working age, full-time workers. Workers in these occupations generally have spent several years acquiring education or training that often is not applicable to other occupations. For example, among professional specialty occupations, only 46 percent of total job opportunities result from replacement needs, as opposed to 69 percent among administrative support occupations (chart 9).

Interested in More Detail?

Readers interested in more information about projections and detail on the labor force, economic growth, industry and occupational employment, or methods and assumptions should consult the November 1991 *Monthly Labor Review* or *Outlook 1990–2005*, BLS Bulletin 2402. Information on the limitations inherent to economic projections also can be found in either of these two publications. For additional occupational data, as well as statistics on educational and training completions, see the 1992 edition of *Occupational Projections and Training Data*, BLS Bulletin 2401.

Key Phrases in the *Handbook*

Changing employment between 1990 and 2005

If the statement reads . . .	**Employment is projected to . . .**
Grow much faster than the average	Increase 35 percent or more
Grow faster than the average	Increase 25 to 34 percent
Grow about as fast as the average	Increase 14 to 24 percent
Grow more slowly than the average	Increase 5 to 13 percent
Show little change	Increase or decrease 4 percent or less
Decline	Decrease 5 percent or more

Opportunities and competition for jobs

If the statement reads . . .	**Job openings compared to jobseekers may be . . .**
Excellent opportunities	Much more numerous
Very good opportunities	More numerous
Good or favorable opportunities	About the same
May face competition	Fewer
May face keen competition	Much fewer

U.S. Demographics

Projected Population Trends

Population Size and Growth

Over the last 60 years the population of the United States grew by almost 130 million to 252 million in 1991. In the middle series, the population is projected to increase another 130 million over the next 60 years to 383 million, a 50 percent increase. The lowest and highest series project the population to be only 276 million or possibly as high as 507 million respectively by 2050.

The U.S. population is projected to reach 275 million in 2000, a growth of 25.4 million or 10.2 percent since 1990. During the 1980's the population grew 21.7 million or 9.5 percent. Only during the 1950's were more people added to the nation's population than are projected to be added during the 1990's.

The average annual rate of population growth would decrease in the middle series by over 50 percent, from 1.04 per 1,000 population between 1990 and 1995 to 0.49 between 2040 and 2050, though a short plateau between 2005 and 2015 temporarily slows this steady decline. Because the annual number of immigrants is assumed to remain constant, slowing natural increase is the primary force causing this decrease in the rate of change. The projected fall of the rate of natural increase is predominately due to a dramatic increase in the crude death rate. Even so, natural increase would not drop below zero during the projection period, and the population would not stop growing in the middle series. After 2020, the U.S. would grow more slowly than ever before.

The lowest series projects the population to grow slowly, peak in the year 2027 at 287 million, then gradually decline. The average annual percent change would decrease throughout the projected period. Conversely, the highest series projects the population to increase quite steadily over the next 60 years with most rapid growth between 1995 and 2020, over 1.2 average annual percent change. After 2020, this rate would begin to decline as the survivors of the baby boom reach the high mortality ages.

Age Distribution

Median Age. In all the projection series, the future U.S. population will be older than it is now. In the middle series, the median age of the population will steadily increase from 32.8 in 1991 to 35.7 in 2000, peak at 39.4 in 2035, then decrease slightly to 39.3 by 2050.

Baby Boom. This increasing median age is driven by the aging of a major part of the population born during the Baby Boom after World War II (1946 to 1964). About 30 percent of the population in 1992 were born during the Baby Boom. As this population ages, the median age will rise. People born during the Baby Boom will be between the ages of 36 and 54 at the turn of the century. In 2011, the first members of the baby boom will reach age 65 and the Baby-Boom population will have decreased to 25 percent of the total population (in the middle series). The last of the Baby Boom population will reach age 65 in the year 2029. By that time, the Baby-Boom population is projected to be only about 17 percent of the total population.

Dependency Ratio. The dependency ratio indicates how many children and elderly there would be for every 100 people of working age, between 18 and 64 years. The middle series projections indicate that the dependency ratio would decrease from 62.9 in 1992 to 60.0 in 2010. As people born during the Baby Boom begin to reach age 65, this ratio is projected to increase to 67.4 by 2020, 77.5 in 2030, and 78.0 in 2040.

Younger Ages. The age group under 18 will increase by about 5 million by the turn of the century, then grow another 18 million by 2050. However, during the projected period this age group's proportion of the total population may never be as large as it is today, declining from almost 26 percent of the total population in 1992 to 23 percent in 2050.

The elementary school-age population (5 to 13) would increase by over 4 million during the 1990's to over 36 million by 2000. After 2002, smaller cohorts born near the end of the twentieth century would cause this population to decline for 8 years. However, this population would start to increase again by 2011. By 2020, the elementary school popula-

Source: Excerpted from *Population Projections of the United States, by Age, Sex, and Race, and Hispanic Origin, 1988 to 2080* by Jennifer Cheeseman Day, U.S. Bureau of the Census, Current Population Reports, Series P25–1092.

tion would increase to over 38 million and to over 44 million by 2050.

The high school-age population (14 to 17) is projected to continue to grow from almost 14 million in 1992 to over 17 million in 2005. As the smaller cohort born near the end of the twentieth century enters high school, the high school population would start to decline by 2010. After 2015, the high school-age population would begin to increase again to almost 17 million by 2020 and almost 20 million by 2050.

The age group of 18 to 21—the primary group entering the labor force, college, and the military—is projected to soon begin to grow again for the first time since peaking at 17.4 million in 1980. This age group is projected to decline from 15.2 million in 1991 to 13.8 million in 1994, then increase to 15.7 million in 2000 and 17.8 million in 2010 (a new all-time high).

The population aged 25 to 44 would scarcely change size from 1991 to 2000, but the number of 35 to 44 year olds would grow 5.4 million while those aged 25 to 34 would decrease 5.5 million.

None of the total population growth of 23 million from 1991 to 2000 is projected to occur in the population under age 35.

The age group of 45 to 54 year olds is projected to increase the most (44 percent) from 1991 to 2000. It would grow from 25.7 million in 1991 to 37.1 million in 2000. This growth of 11.4 million represents one-half of the nation's expected total growth during this period.

The Elderly. The oldest age groups are projected to increase during the next 60 years, both in number and as a proportion of the population. In 1992, there are expected to be 32 million people aged 65 and over, about 12.6 percent of the population. By 2000, this group would grow to almost 35 million and 12.7 percent of the population, and by 2050, almost 79 million and represent 20.6 percent of the population.

However, during the next two decades the elderly population (aged 65 and older) is projected to grow more slowly than it has in many decades. From 1991 to 2010, it would grow only 1.2 percent a year, compared with its average annual growth of 2.4 percent from 1950 to 1990.

After 2010, when the survivors of the Baby Boom start to enter this age group, the proportion 65 and over would increase dramatically from 13.3 percent in 2010 to over 20 percent by 2030, from 39.7 million elderly persons to 69.8 million. The average annual rate of increase for this age group during those 20 years would be 2.8 percent.

The population aged 85 and over would be the fastest-growing broad age group, doubling in size from 1991 to the year 2020, and increasing fivefold by the year 2050. In 1992, 3.3 million people would be age 85 and over. By 2050, this figure would increase to over 17 million. Both increased life expectancy and the increased number of people entering these age groups contribute to the population explosion in these older ages.

The population 100 years and over, though numerically small, is also projected to grow substantially. In 1992, the population would be 45,000, growing to 77,000 by 2000, and to over 1 million by 2050.

In the future, the ratio of males to females in the elderly population may become more balanced. This results from the assumption that male life expectancy will continue to improve faster than that of females. Currently, women dominate the 65-and-over population with a 60-percent majority. By 2050, the female proportion of this age group is projected to decrease to slightly more than half (54 percent). Moreover, this changing sex ratio is also evident in the oldest age groups. The 85-and-over population would change from about 72-percent female in 1992 to 63-percent female in 2050. In the age group 100 and over, the change would also be noticeable, dropping from 80-percent female in 1992 to 75 percent in 2050.

Race and Hispanic Origin Distribution

The table on page 570 shows the future changes in race/ethnic composition of the population according to the middle series. The race and Hispanic origin distribution of the U.S. population is projected to become more diverse. As the Black, American Indian, Asian, and Hispanic populations increase their proportions of the total population, the White population proportion would decrease. This decrease is even more pronounced for non-Hispanic White.

By the turn of the century, the White proportion of the population is projected to decrease to less than 82 percent of the population. About 13 percent of the population would be Black, 4.5 percent of the population would be Asian and Pacific Islander, and the remaining 0.9 percent of the population would consist of American Indians, Eskimos, and Aleuts. People of Hispanic origin would constitute 11 percent of the total population. The White population who are not of Hispanic origin would be less than 72 percent of the total population.

By 2050, 71.8 percent of the population is projected to be White, 16.2 percent will be Black, 1.2 percent would be American Indian, Eskimo and Aleut, and 10.7 percent will be Asian and Pacific Islander. The Hispanic-origin population would increase to 21.1 percent, and the non-Hispanic White population would decline to 52.7 percent.

Similar distribution changes are projected to occur in both the highest and lowest series, though less so in the lowest series and more so in the highest series. However, compared to the middle series, the Black population would not have as large a share in either alternative series. In the lowest series, both the White population and the American Indian population would have a larger share of the total population than in the middle series, while all the other groups would have a smaller share. In the highest series, the Asian and Hispanic populations would have larger shares of the total population than in the middle series.

Trends and Population Growth. The White population is projected to be the slowest-growing race group during the next 60 years, increasing in the middle series only 29 percent by 2050. In fact, the non-Hispanic segment of the White population would stop growing by 2029, largely by virtue of the cessation of net increase, at a peak of 207.7 million and then slowly decrease. Yet by 2050, the total White population would contain about 62 million more people than in 1992. The increase by the total White population after 2029 would be due entirely to growth in the number of White Hispanics.

Non-Hispanic Whites are likely to contribute less and less to the total population growth in this country. Although non-Hispanic Whites make up almost 75 percent of the total population in 1992, they would contribute only 30 percent of the total population growth between 1992 and 2000. This percentage of growth would decrease to 21 percent between 2000 and 2010, and decrease to 13 percent from 2010 to 2030. The non-Hispanic White population would contribute nothing to population growth after 2030 because it would be declining in size.

With almost twice the White population's annual rate of change in 1992, the Black population would grow at a faster pace than the White population. The Black population would increase over 4 million by 2000, almost 9 million by 2010, and over 19 million by 2030. During the next 60 years, the Black population would grow by almost 100 percent to 62 million. Therefore, the Black share of the total U.S. population is expected to slowly increase from 12 percent in 1992 to 13 percent in 2000, 14 percent in 2010, 15 percent in 2030, and 16 percent in 2050.

The Asian and Pacific Islander population is projected to continue to be the fastest-growing race group with annual growth rates that may exceed 4 percent during the 1990's. By the turn of the century, the Asian population would expand to over 12 million, double its current size by 2009, triple by 2024, and quadruple by 2038. By the middle of the next century, this population group would have expanded to 5 times its current size, to 41 million.

In the middle series, the Asian population's share of the U.S. population is projected to increase from 3.3 percent in 1992 to 4.5 percent in 2000, 6 percent in 2010, 8 percent in 2030, and 11 percent in 2050. This population would account for 19.2 percent of the nation's growth from 1992 to 2000, 22 percent from 2000 to 2010, 25 percent from 2010 to 2030, and 32 percent from 2030 to 2050. Each year after 2002, the Asian and Pacific Islander population would add more people to the population of the United States than would the non-Hispanic White group.

Immigration is an integral part of this group's growth. Throughout the projection period Asian immigration would be higher than natural increase. In fact, the number of Asian immigrants is projected to exceed the number of Asian births for the next thirty years. In total, over 3 million surviving net Asian immigrants and their surviving descendants would be added to the U.S. population between 1991 and 2000, and 30 million post-1991 surviving Asian net immigrants and their surviving descendants would be added to the population by 2050.

In contrast to the growth trends of the Asian population, the American Indian, Eskimo, and Aleut population would experience nearly all of its growth by natural increase. The American Indian population is projected to grow steadily, from 2.2 million in 1992 to 2.4 million in 2000, 2.8 million in 2010, 3.6 million in 2030, and 4.6 million in 2050. The percent of the population that is American Indian, Eskimo, and Aleut would rise from 0.8 percent in 1992 to 1.0 percent around 2020 and 1.2 percent in 2050.

Growth of the Hispanic-origin population will probably be a major element of the total population growth. The Hispanic population would contribute 33 percent of the nation's population growth from 1992 to 2000, 37 percent from 2000 to 2010, 43 percent from 2010 to 2030, and 57 percent from 2030 to 2050. This growth of the Hispanic population over the next 60 years may be influenced more from natural increase than immigration.

By 2000, the Hispanic-origin population may increase to 31 million. By 2020, the Hispanic population is projected to double its current size to almost 49 million, and more than triple its current size to over 80 million by 2050. In fact, after 1995, the Hispanic population is projected to add more people to the United States every year than would the non-Hispanic White population (or any other group).

Age Structure. Hispanics were the youngest population group in 1990 with half the population younger than age 26. As the total U.S. population ages, the Hispanic population is projected to age quicker than both the American Indian and Black populations. The median age of the Hispanic population would be higher than the American Indian population's median age by 2010, and higher than the Black population's median age by 2045.

The White population is projected always to be the oldest segment of the population. In 1992, the non-Hispanic White median age would be 36, increasing to a peak of age 45 by 2040.

As specific age groups increase or decrease more rapidly than the entire population, they signal possible on-coming trends. For instance, due to lower birth and immigration rates, the non-Hispanic White population under age 20 would be less than 50 percent of the total population under age 20 by the year 2035.

Total Resident Population: 1990 to 2050

(Resident population. Numbers in thousands. As of July 1. Consistent with the 1990 Census, as enumerated)

Year	Lowest series	Middle series	Highest series
Estimate			
1990	(X)	249,415	(X)
Projections			
1995	260,715	262,754	264,685
2000	268,108	274,815	281,306
2005	273,605	286,324	298,773
2010	278,078	298,109	317,895
2020	285,200	322,602	360,123
2030	286,710	344,951	405,130
2040	282,286	364,349	453,687
2050	275,647	382,674	506,740

X Not applicable.

Sources: Tables 1 and 3 and Current Population Reports, Series P-25, No. 1086.

Percent Distribution of the Population, by Race and Hispanic Origin

(As of July 1. Resident population. Consistent with the 1990 Census, as enumerated)

		Race					Not of Hispanic origin, by race			
	Total	White	Black	American Indian[1]	Asian[2]	Hispanic origin[3]	White	Black	American Indian[1]	Asian[2]
MIDDLE SERIES										
Estimate										
1990	100.0	83.9	12.3	0.8	3.0	9.0	75.7	11.8	0.7	2.8
Projections										
1995	100.0	82.8	12.6	0.9	3.7	10.1	73.6	12.1	0.7	3.5
2000	100.0	81.7	12.9	0.9	4.5	11.1	71.6	12.3	0.8	4.2
2005	100.0	80.7	13.2	0.9	5.2	12.2	69.6	12.6	0.8	4.9
2010	100.0	79.6	13.6	0.9	5.9	13.2	67.6	12.8	0.8	5.5
2020	100.0	77.7	14.2	1.0	7.2	15.2	63.9	13.3	0.9	6.8
2030	100.0	75.8	14.8	1.0	8.4	17.2	60.2	13.8	0.9	7.9
2040	100.0	73.8	15.5	1.1	9.6	19.2	56.4	14.4	1.0	9.1
2050	100.0	71.8	16.2	1.2	10.7	21.1	52.7	15.0	1.1	10.1
LOWEST SERIES										
2050	100.0	74.3	15.1	1.3	9.3	18.4	57.4	14.1	1.1	8.9
HIGHEST SERIES										
2050	100.0	71.6	15.7	1.1	11.6	22.7	51.3	14.3	0.9	10.9

[1]American Indian represents American Indian, Eskimo, and Aleut.
[2]Asian represents Asian and Pacific Islander.
[3]Persons of Hispanic origin may be of any race.

Source: Tables 2 and 3 and 1990 CPH-L-74.

Population by Age: 1990 to 2050

(In thousands. As of July 1. Resident population. Consistent with the 1990 Census, as enumerated)

Year	Total	Under 5 years	5 to 13 years	14 to 17 years	18 to 24 years	25 to 34 years	35 to 44 years	45 to 64 years	65 years and over	85 years and over	100 years and over
ESTIMATE											
1990	249,415	18,874	32,000	13,312	26,829	43,136	37,765	46,277	31,224	3,050	[1]36
PROJECTIONS											
Lowest series											
1995	260,715	19,165	34,185	14,644	24,623	40,469	42,296	51,998	33,335	3,575	51
2000	268,108	17,438	35,247	15,454	25,438	36,310	43,995	60,258	33,968	4,055	66
2005	273,605	16,531	33,436	16,587	27,123	34,697	40,978	69,678	34,575	4,442	89
2010	278,078	16,356	31,203	15,835	28,742	36,028	36,782	76,439	36,694	4,852	103
2020	285,200	16,709	30,566	14,096	25,901	39,579	36,486	74,680	47,182	4,820	130
2030	286,710	15,735	30,494	14,367	24,724	35,587	39,946	67,830	58,027	5,569	152
2040	282,286	15,336	28,841	13,900	25,081	34,670	35,986	70,911	57,560	7,933	167
2050	275,647	15,153	28,464	13,299	23,706	34,732	35,055	70,080	55,157	9,228	250
Middle series											
1995	262,754	19,553	34,372	14,754	24,903	40,844	42,500	52,235	33,594	3,638	54
2000	274,815	18,908	36,051	15,734	26,117	37,416	44,662	61,042	34,886	4,289	77
2005	286,324	18,959	35,782	17,020	28,111	36,495	42,284	71,257	36,414	4,937	118
2010	298,109	19,730	35,425	16,908	30,007	38,367	38,853	79,115	39,705	5,702	160
2020	322,602	21,388	38,068	16,847	29,685	43,024	39,786	80,179	53,627	6,480	278
2030	344,951	21,961	40,368	18,449	31,275	42,629	44,364	76,069	69,839	8,381	435
2040	364,349	23,192	41,739	19,159	33,530	45,329	43,977	81,836	75,588	13,221	620
2050	382,674	24,411	44,223	19,999	34,482	48,020	46,626	86,038	78,876	17,652	1,170
Highest series											
1995	264,685	19,949	34,551	14,857	25,175	41,214	42,726	52,434	33,778	3,685	55
2000	281,306	20,448	36,846	15,999	26,773	38,524	45,461	61,722	35,534	4,484	82
2005	298,773	21,621	38,176	17,433	29,066	38,281	43,828	72,660	37,707	5,372	134
2010	317,895	23,640	39,904	17,971	31,231	40,655	41,191	81,513	41,790	6,473	196
2020	360,123	27,101	46,782	19,817	33,570	46,391	43,396	85,211	57,855	8,028	407
2030	405,130	30,104	52,439	23,206	38,690	49,906	49,228	83,826	77,731	11,083	746
2040	453,687	34,355	58,778	25,662	43,627	57,323	52,886	92,198	88,857	18,374	1,198
2050	506,740	38,645	66,797	29,009	48,381	63,826	60,428	101,728	97,926	26,160	2,491

[1]April 1, 1990

Source: Tables 2 and 3 and Current Population Reports, Series P25, *U.S. Population Estimates, by Age, Sex, Race, and Hispanic Origin: 1980 to 1991*, forthcoming, and 1990 CPH-L-74.

Percent Distribution of the Population by Age: 1990 to 2050

(In percent. As of July 1. Resident population. Consistent with the 1990 Census, as enumerated)

Year	Total	Under 5 years	5 to 13 years	14 to 17 years	18 to 24 years	25 to 34 years	35 to 44 years	45 to 64 years	65 years and over	85 years and over	100 years and over
ESTIMATE											
1990	100.0	7.6	12.8	5.3	10.8	17.3	15.1	18.6	12.5	1.2	0.0
PROJECTIONS											
Lowest Series											
1995	100.0	7.4	13.1	5.6	9.4	15.5	16.2	19.9	12.8	1.4	0.0
2000	100.0	6.5	13.1	5.8	9.5	13.5	16.4	22.5	12.7	1.5	0.0
2005	100.0	6.0	12.2	6.1	9.9	12.7	15.0	25.5	12.6	1.6	0.0
2010	100.0	5.9	11.2	5.7	10.3	13.0	13.2	27.5	13.2	1.7	0.0
2020	100.0	5.9	10.7	4.9	9.1	13.9	12.8	26.2	16.5	1.7	0.0
2030	100.0	5.5	10.6	5.0	8.6	12.4	13.9	23.7	20.2	1.9	0.1
2040	100.0	5.4	10.2	4.9	8.9	12.3	12.7	25.1	20.4	2.8	0.1
2050	100.0	5.5	10.3	4.8	8.6	12.6	12.7	25.4	20.0	3.3	0.1
Middle Series											
1995	100.0	7.4	13.1	5.6	9.5	15.5	16.2	19.9	12.8	1.4	0.0
2000	100.0	6.9	13.1	5.7	9.5	13.6	16.3	22.2	12.7	1.6	0.0
2005	100.0	6.6	12.5	5.9	9.8	12.7	14.8	24.9	12.7	1.7	0.0
2010	100.0	6.6	11.9	5.7	10.1	12.9	13.0	26.5	13.3	1.9	0.1
2020	100.0	6.6	11.8	5.2	9.2	13.3	12.3	24.9	16.6	2.0	0.1
2030	100.0	6.4	11.7	5.3	9.1	12.4	12.9	22.1	20.2	2.4	0.1
2040	100.0	6.4	11.5	5.3	9.2	12.4	12.1	22.5	20.7	3.6	0.2
2050	100.0	6.4	11.6	5.2	9.0	12.5	12.2	22.5	20.6	4.6	0.3
Highest Series											
1995	100.0	7.5	13.1	5.6	9.5	15.6	16.1	19.8	12.8	1.4	0.0
2000	100.0	7.3	13.1	5.7	9.5	13.7	16.2	21.9	12.6	1.6	0.0
2005	100.0	7.2	12.8	5.8	9.7	12.8	14.7	24.3	12.6	1.8	0.0
2010	100.0	7.4	12.6	5.7	9.8	12.8	13.0	25.6	13.1	2.0	0.1
2020	100.0	7.5	13.0	5.5	9.3	12.9	12.1	23.7	16.1	2.2	0.1
2030	100.0	7.4	12.9	5.7	9.6	12.3	12.2	20.7	19.2	2.7	0.2
2040	100.0	7.6	13.0	5.7	9.6	12.6	11.7	20.3	19.6	4.0	0.3
2050	100.0	7.6	13.2	5.7	9.5	12.6	11.9	20.1	19.3	5.2	0.5

Source: Derived from table on page 571.

Women in Business: Information Sources

Not only are women starting businesses at twice the rate of men but women owned businesses are also growing in diversity. If the present trend continues, almost 40% of small businesses will be owned by women by the year 2000. As the number of women entrepreneurs continues to increase so does the amount of business related information targeted to them. The following is a selected list of information sources that should prove helpful.

OFFICE OF WOMEN'S BUSINESS OWNERSHIP (OWBO)
Small Business Administration (SBA)
409 Third Street SE
Washington, DC 20416
OWBO Telephone: 202-205-6673
Fax: 202-205-7064

The Office of Women's Business Ownership (OWBO) offers both current and potential women business owners access to a variety of services and resources. These include prebusiness workshops, technical, financial and management information and training conferences on exporting, access to capital, and selling to the Federal Government.

Each SBA office has a women's representative who can explain the resources that are available and provide guidance on how to access them. The regional coordinator for your area will direct you to your local representative. The coordinator's telephone numbers are given below:

ME, VT, MA, NH, CT, RI	(617) 451-2040
NY, NJ, PR, VI	(212) 264-1450
PA, DE, MD, VA, DC, WV	(215) 962-3710
NC, SC, KY, TN, GA, AL, MS, FL	(404) 347-2797
MN, WI, MI, OH, IN, IL	(312) 353-0357
NM, TX, OK, AR, LA	(214) 767-7611
KS, MO, IA, NE	(816) 426-3316
MT, ND, SD, WY, UT, CO	(303) 294-7020
CA, NV, AZ, HI	(415) 744-6402
WA, OR, ID, AK	(206) 553-5676

ENTREPRENEURIAL ASSISTANCE CENTERS

There are 27 Demonstration Centers throughout the United States established by the SBA and private companies to assist women interested in either starting or expanding a small business. These Centers provide one to one, woman-to-woman counseling on all aspects of business and include for example, legal, marketing, accounting, and budgeting information. These non-profit Centers charge only a nominal charge for their services.

To locate the Demonstration Center nearest your area call the SBA Answer Desk at 800-827-5722.

AMERICAN WOMEN'S ECONOMIC DEVELOPMENT CORPORATION (AWED)
641 Lexington Avenue
New York, NY 10022
Telephone: 212-688-1900
Fax: 212-688-2718

The American Women's Economic Development Corporation (AWED) is a non-profit organization providing entrepreneurial women with management training and business counseling. Some of the courses offered by AWED are: Starting Your Own Business, Managing Your Own Business, Finance, as well as Chief Executive Roundtables and a Business Development Roundtable. Admission to AWED training programs is based on an application and a personal interview. Modest fees are charged for the above.

NATIONAL ASSOCIATION FOR FEMALE EXCECUTIVES, INC. (NAFE)
127 West 24th Street
New York, NY 10011
Telephone: 212-645-0770

The National Association for Female Executives, Inc. (NAFE) is the largest businesswomen's organization in the United States. It is a professional association dedicated to the advancement of women in the workplace through education, networking and public advocacy. NAFE functions to support women in business and to help them succeed in achieving their career goals and financial independence.

Among the benefits of membership are a venture capital fund to assist entrepreneurial members; regional conferences, seminar programs and special events to encourage education and networking; and low-interest loans and credit cards, low-cost insurance, resume service and "How-To" career guides.

WOMEN IN FRANCHISING (WIF)
175 West Jackson Avenue
Chicago, IL 60604
Telephone: 312-431-1467

Provides specialized franchise information and training services for minorities and women.

SERVICE CORPS OF RETIRED EXECUTIVES (SCORE)
409 Third Street SW
Washington, DC 20024

This organization of volunteers provides counseling to small business people. Volunteers include former or active accountants, business owners, corporation executives and lawyers. To obtain the name of the National SCORE Women's Business Ownership Coordinators nearest you call the National Volunteer Director at 410-266-8746.

STATE SPONSORED WOMEN ASSISTANCE PROGRAMS

Many states have specific programs geared for women-owned businesses. To locate the nearest office call your state's Department of Economic Development.

BUSINESS FINANCING SOURCES

OFFICE OF WOMEN'S BUSINESS OWNERSHIP (OWBO)
Small Business Administration (SBA)
409 Third Street SE
Washington, DC 20416
OWBO Telephone: 202-205-6673
SBA Answer Desk: 800-827-5722

NATIONAL FEDERATION OF BUSINESS AND PROFESSIONAL WOMEN'S CLUBS, INC. (BPW)
2012 Massachusetts Avenue, N.W.
Washington, DC 20036
Telephone: 202-293-1100

They offer an unsecured personal loan of up to $7,500 payable over 6 years or a home-equity loan of up to $100,000.

NATIONAL ASSOCIATION FOR FEMALE EXECUTIVES, INC. (NAFE)
127 West 24th Street
New York, NY 10011
Telephone: 212-645-0770

As a NAFE member, an individual can qualify for Loans-by-Mail, up to $35,000. When an individual qualifies, a signature is all that is needed. This is an immediate credit line. NAFE's Venture Capital Fund will provide from $5,000 to $50,000 in funding to NAFE members. Members must submit a business plan in writing to the review board and they make the selections.

For additional capital sources for startup companies and small businesses see page 217.

PUBLICATIONS:

A list of SBA publications and video tapes for starting and managing a small business is available from your local SBA office.

A recent SBA publication *Women Business Owners: Selling to the Federal Government* is designed to help women business owners by providing them with information about marketing their goods and services to the federal government. Available from your local U.S. Government Bookstore or by mail or telephone from the Superintendent of Documents in Washington, D.C. Telephone: 202-783-3238.

WOMEN'S BUREAU
U.S. Department of Labor
200 Constitution Avenue, NW
Washington, DC 20210
Telephone: 202-219-6611

The Women's Bureau publishes a variety of material for women business owners, including:

A Working Woman's Guide To Her Job Rights
Directory of Non Traditional Training and Employment Programs Serving Women
Alternative Work Patterns
State Maternity/Parental Leave Laws
Women Business Owners
Women in Labor Unions

Single copies of publications are available free of charge from the Department of Labor.

The *Encyclopedia of Women's Associations Worldwide*, edited by L. R. Greenfield, contains 6,000 organizations throughout the world concerning women and women's issues. Among the information included are the purpose of the organization, languages of correspondence, publications, conventions, and meetings. Entries are arranged by subject and organized alphabetically. Published by Gale Research Inc., P.O. Box 33477, Detroit, MI 48232-5477. Telephone: 800-977-GALE.

Fight Suppliers Who Won't Give You Credit is available from the Federal Trade Commission (FTC). Telephone: 202-326-2222.

Explains credit rights under the law, what to do if you feel credit has been unfairly denied, and gives information on how to establish credit.

Entrepreneurial Woman, published by *Entrepreneur Magazine*, contains information appropriate to its title. Address: 2392 Morse Avenue, Irvine, CA 92714-6234. Telephone: 714-261-2315.

Executive Female is published by the National Association of Female Executives (NAFE) and contains material of interest to women in the work force. Address: NAFE, 127 West 27th Street, New York, NY 10011. Membership in NAFE includes a subscription to the above publication.

Steps to Small Business Financing is available from the American Bankers Association, 1120 Connecticut Avenue NW, Washington, DC 20036. Telephone: 202-663-5456. A booklet that describes and explains the steps a firm should take to obtain financing.

The European Community (EC)

Where to Get Information[1]

Information on the European Community, copies of EC legislation, lists of reference standards and notified bodies, current status of legislation in progress, status of U.S.-EC MRA discussions:

Single Internal Market Information Service, Office of European Community Affairs, U.S. Department of Commerce, Room 3036, Washington, D.C. 20230, tel. (202) 482-5276, fax (202) 482-2155

The Department of Commerce also has a standards officer stationed in Brussels: Seymour Greenfield, Commercial Section, U.S. Mission to the EC, PSC 82, Box 002, APO AE 09724, tel. 32-2-513-4450

Information on European standards work in progress:

CEN/CENELEC Third Countries Unit, Rue de Stassart 36, B-1050 Brussels, tel. (32-2) 519-6811, fax (32-2)519-6819

American National Standards Institute, 11 West 42nd St., New York, N.Y. 10018, tel. (212) 642-4900, fax (212) 302-1286

National Center for Standards and Certification Information, National Institute of Standards and Technology, U.S. Department of Commerce, Administration Building 101, Room A629, Gaithersburg, Md. 20899, tel. (301) 975-4040, EC-92 Hotline: (301) 921-4164 (also has detailed information on foreign certification bodies and procedures)

Copies of European standards:

American National Standards Institute (see above)

Global Engineering Documents, 2805 McGaw Ave., P.O. Box 19539, Irvine, Calif. 92714, tel. (800) 854-7179, (714) 261-1455, (202) 429-2860, fax (714) 261-7892

[1] For more extensive information on the EC see the Business One Irwin *International Almanac: Business and Investment*, Business One Irwin, Homewood, IL.

Source: *Business America*, March 8, 1993.

Information on ISO 9000:

Single Internal Market Information Sevice, U.S. Department of Commerce (see above)

Office of Standards Code and Information, National Institute of Standards and Technology, U.S. Department of Commerce, tel. (301) 975-4031

American Society for Quality Control, 310 West Wisconsin Ave., Milwaukee, Wis. 52303, tel. (800) 248-1946, (414) 272-8575

U.S. Government Agency Contacts and Information Resources[1]

U.S. Trade Representative

Office of the Deputy U.S. Trade Representative
Tel: (202) 395-5114 Fax: (202) 395-3911

Office of Europe and the Mediterranean
Tel: (202) 395-4620 Fax: (202) 395-3911

Director, Non-Tariff Measures
Tel: (202) 395-3063 Fax: (202) 395-3911

Department of State

Bureau of European and Canadian Affairs
Office of EC/OECD Affairs
Tel: (202) 647-2395 Fax: (202) 647-9959

Bureau of Economic and Business Affairs
Office of Developed Country Trade
Tel: (202) 647-2742 Fax: (202) 647-0173

Office of the Legal Adviser
Tel: (202) 647-5242 Fax: (202) 647-1037

Office of Aviation Programs and Policy
Tel: (202) 647-7973 Fax: (202) 647-8628

Department of the Treasury

Office of Industrial nations and Global Analysis
Tel: (202) 566-2856 Fax: (202) 566-8066

Office of International Banking and Portfolio Investment
Tel: (202) 566-5628 Fax: (202) 566-8066

Office of International Investment
Tel: (202) 343-9150 Fax: (202) 566-8066

Office of International Trade
Tel: (202) 566-8108 Fax: (202) 566-8066

[1] Source: *Europe 1992: A Business Guide to U.S. Government Resources*, U.S. Government Interagency Task Force on EC 1992. Available from the Superintendent of Documents, Government Printing Office, Washington, DC 20402.

Department of Commerce
Single Internal Market:
1992 Information Service
Tel: (202) 482-5276 Fax: (202) 482-2155

Office of European Community Affairs
Tel: (202) 482-5276 Fax: (202) 482-2155

Office of Service Industries
Tel: (202) 482-3734 Fax: (202) 482-4775

Industry Sector Outreach Coordinator
Office of Industrial Trade
Tel: (202) 482-3703

Trade Development Industry Experts:

Textiles and Apparel:
Office of Textiles and Apparel
Tel: (202) 482-3587

Service Industries:
Office of Service Industries
Tel: (202) 482-1134

Information Technology, Instrumentation and Electronics:
Office of Telecommunications
Tel: (202) 482-4466

Chemicals, Construction Industry Products and Basic Industries:
Office of Basic Industries
Tel: (202) 482-0606

Autos:
Office of Automotive Affairs
Tel: (202) 482-0669

Consumer Goods
Office of Consumer Goods
Tel: (202) 482-5783

Construction Projects and Industrial Machinery:
Office of the DAS for Capital Goods and International Construction
Tel: (202) 482-2474

Aerospace:
Office of Aerospace Policy & Analysis
Tel: (202) 482-4222

Industrial Trade Staff Cross-Sectional Policy Analysis
Tel: (202) 482-3703

Department of Agriculture
Foreign Agricultural Service
International Trade Policy Division
Western Europe Group
Tel: (202) 382-9013 Fax: (202) 382-8069

Foreign Agricultural Service Information Division
Tel: (202) 447-7115 Fax: (202) 382-1727

Department of Defense
Office of International Economics and Energy Affairs
Tel: (202) 697-3248 Fax: (202) 693-2161

Environmental Protection Agency
Office of International Activities
Tel: (202) 382-4870 Fax: (202) 382-4470

Food and Drug Administration
Office of Health Affairs
Tel: (301) 443-6143 Fax: (301) 443-1309

United States Information Agency
Office of European Affairs
Tel: (202) 485-8570 Fax: (202) 485-8821

U.S. International Trade Commission
Office of Executive and International Liaison
Tel: (202) 252-1146 Fax: (202) 252-2139

Department of Justice
Antitrust Division
Foreign Commerce Section
Tel: (202) 633-2464 Fax: (202) 786-5868

Department of Labor
Bureau of International Labor Affairs
Office of International Economic Affairs
Tel: (202) 523-6096 Fax: (202) 523-4071

Securities and Exchange Commission
Office of Economic Analysis
Tel: (202) 272-7359 Fax: (202) 272-7050

Office of International Affairs
Tel: (202) 272-2306 Fax: (202) 272-3636 or 272-7050

Small Business Administration
Office of International Trade
Tel: (202) 653-7794 Fax: (202) 254-6429

Department of Transportation
Office of the Secretary
Office of Policy and International Affairs
Tel: (202) 366-9150 or 366-2431 Fax: (202) 426-7106

U.S. Diplomatic Missions to the EC Member Countries

U.S. Mission to the European Communities in Brussels
Tel: 32-2-513-4450; TELEX: 846-21336
Attn: Economic Section

Belgium
American Embassy Brussels
Tel: 32-2-513-3830; TELEX: 846-21336
Attn: Economic or Commercial Section

Denmark
American Embassy Copenhagen
Tel: 45-1-42-31-44; TELEX: 22216
Attn: Economic or Commercial Section

Federal Republic of Germany
American Embassy Bonn
Tel: 49-228-3391; TELEX: 885-452
Attn: Economic, Commercial, or Financial Section

France
American Embassy Paris
Tel: 33-1-42-96-12-02; TELEX: 650221
Attn: Economic, Commercial, or Financial Section

Greece
American Embassy Athens
Tel: 30-1-721-2951; TELEX: 21-5548
Attn: Economic or Commercial Section

Ireland
American Embassy Dublin
Tel: 353-1-688777; TELEX: 93684
Attn: Economic or Commercial Section

Italy
American Embassy Rome
Tel: 39-6-46741; TELEX: 625847 or 622322
Attn: Economic, Commercial, or Financial Section

Luxembourg
American Embassy Luxembourg
Tel: 352-460123; TELEX: 461401
Attn: Economic Section

Netherlands
American Embassy The Hague
Tel: 31-70-62-49-11; TELEX: 044-31016
Attn: Economic or Commercial Section

Portugal
American Embassy Lisbon
Tel: 351-1-726-6600; TELEX: 12528
Attn: Economic or Commercial Section

Spain
American Embassy Madrid
Tel: 34-1-276-3400/3600; TELEX: 27763
Attn: Economic or Commercial Section

United Kingdom
American Embassy London
Tel: 44-01-499-9000; TELEX: 266777
Attn: Economic, Commercial, or Financial Section

European Trade Development Offices[1]

These offices provide commercial information resources developed by the European governments themselves.

Embassy of Belgium
Economic Section
Belgian Foreign Trade Office Representative
3330 Garfield Street, NW
Washington, D.C. 20008
Tel: (202) 333-6900 Fax: (202) 333-3079

Royal Danish Embassy
Economic Section
3200 Whitehaven Street, NW
Washington, D.C. 20008
Tel: (202) 234-4000 Fax: (202) 378-1470

German-American Chamber of Commerce
New York Head Office
666 Fifth Avenue
New York, N.Y. 10103
Tel: (212) 974-8830 Fax: (212) 974-8867

French Industrial Development Agency
610 Fifth Avenue
New York, N.Y. 10020
Tel: (212) 757-9340 Fax: (212) 245-1568

Embassy of Greece
Economic Office
1636 Connecticut Avenue, NW
Washington, D.C. 20009
Tel: (202) 745-7100 Fax: (202) 265-4291

Industrial Development Authority of Ireland
Two Grand Central Towers
140 East 45th Street
New York, N.Y. 10017
Tel: (212) 972-1000 Fax: (212) 687-8739

Italian Trade Commission
499 Park Avenue
New York, N.Y. 10022
Tel: (212) 980-1500 Fax: (212) 758-1050

Board of Economic Development (Luxembourg)
801 Second Avenue
New York, N.Y. 10017
Tel: (212) 370-9870 Fax: (212) 697-5529

Netherlands Foreign Investment Agency
One Rockefeller Plaza
New York, N.Y. 10020
Tel: (212) 246-1434 Fax: (212) 246-9769

Portuguese Trade Commission
1900 L Street, NW
Washington, D.C. 20036
Tel: (202) 331-8222 Fax: (202) 331-8236

Embassy of Spain
Minister for Economic and Commercial Affairs
2558 Massachusetts Avenue, NW
Washington, D.C. 20008
Tel: (202) 265-8600 Fax: (202) 265-9478

[1] The U.S. Government relays these addresses for the benefit of the reader but cannot vouch for the information provided by each addressee.

British Trade Development Office
Inward Investment Bureau
845 Third Avenue
New York, N.Y. 10020
Tel: (212) 593-2258 Fax: (212) 326-0456

European Community Information: Publications

U.S. Government Publications

Department of State, Bureau of European and Canadian Affairs

The European Community's Program to Complete a Single Market by 1992 (July 1988)

Financial Services and the European Community's Single Market Program (January 1989)

Copies are available from the U.S. Department of State, EUR/RPE, 2201 C St., NW, Washington, DC 20520; Tel: (202) 647-2395

Department of State, Bureau of Public Affairs

The European Community's Program for a Single Market in 1992 (November 1988)

Copies are available from the Department of State, Bureau of Public Affairs, 2201 C St., NW, Washington, DC 20520; Tel: (202) 647-6575 or 6576

Office of the U.S. Trade Representative

Completion of the European Community Internal Market: An Initial Assessment of Certain Economic Policy Issues Raised by Aspects of the EC's Program (December 1988)

Available from USTR, 600 17th St., NW, Washington, DC 20506; Tel: (202) 395-3230.

Department of Commerce

EC 1992: A Commerce Department Analysis of European Community Directives, International Trade Administration

The Commerce Department's three-volume series analyzes each of the EC 1992 directives that could have an effect on U.S. business. Copies can be purchased from the U.S. Government Printing Office, Washington, DC 20402; Tel: (202) 783-3238.

Europe Now/A Report (Quarterly): Newsletter providing summaries of the latest developments of the EC's 1992 Program).

Available from Office of European Community Affairs, Room H3036, International Trade Administration, U.S. Department of Commerce, Washington, DC 20230 (202-482-5276)

EC 1992: Growth Markets: Provides information for U.S. firms interested in taking advantage of the expanding opportunities created by the EC's 1992 Internal Market Program. This is available from the Superintendent of Documents, U.S. Government Printing Office, Washington, DC 20402 (202-783-3238)

Congressional Research Service

The European Communities' 1992 Plan: An Overview of the Proposed Single Market (September 1988). Copies can be obtained by contacting your congressional representative.

Small Business Administration

Exporter's Guide to Federal Resources for Small Business. A specially designed guide for smaller firms interested in exporting, prepared by the Small Business Administration and AT&T. Available from the U.S. Government Printing Office, Washington, DC 20402.

National Institute of Standards and Technology

A Summary of the New European Community Approach to Standards Development, NSBIR 88-3793 (June 1988). An extensive summary of the EC initiatives on standards. Obtain this review and other related materials through the Office of Standards Code and Information, National Institute of Standards and Technology, Administration Building, Room A629, Gaithersburg, MD 20899; Tel: (301) 975-4040.

U.S. International Trade Commission

The Effects of Greater Economic Integration within the European Community on the United States (July 1989). The ITC has prepared a major analytical report on EC 1992 for Congress. Copies of this publication are available from the U.S. International Trade Commission, 500 E St., SW, Room 112A, Washington, DC 20436; Tel: (202) 252-1807 or 1809.

European Community Publications

The EC delegation in Washington can provide a wide variety of information about Community institutions and policies, including a number of useful publications. Some of the publications are free. They can be obtained from the Delegation of the European Communities, 2100 M Street, NW, 7th Floor, Washington, DC 20037; Tel: (202) 862-9500.

The following publications can be purchased from the European Communities' sales agent, UNIPUB, 4611F Assembly Drive, Lanham, MD 20706-4391; Tel: (800) 274-4888 or (301) 459-7666:

Completing the Internal Market, the EC's 1985 "White Paper," which outlines the monetary and financial integration aspects of the single market.

Official Journal, similar to the U.S. Federal Register, is the publication in which notifications of EC directives and regulations are first published. Subscriptions are available.

Other Publications

Michael Callingaert, *The 1992 Challenge from Europe: Development of the European Community's Internal Market,* National Planning Association.

Written by a former U.S. Foreign Service officer, this is the most comprehensive study of the 1992 initiative from the U.S. point of view, including analysis of the outlook for specific sectors of the U.S. economy. Copies can be obtained from the National Planning Association, 1616 P St., NW, Washington, DC 20036; Tel: (202) 265-7685.

Paolo Cecchini, et al., *The European Challenge—1992: The Benefits of a Single Market,* Gower Publishing (1988):

An executive summary of the Cecchini Report, *The Costs of Non-Europe,* prepared especially for the English-speaking business reader. For purchase from Gower Publishing, Old Post Road, Brookfield, VT 05036; Tel: (802) 276-3162.

Joint Economic Committee of the U.S. Congress, *Europe 1992: Long-Term Implications for the U.S. Economy* (April 1989)

This report has an extensive and very useful bibliography. Copies available from the Publications Clerk, Dirksen Senate Office Building, Room G-01, Washington, DC 20515; Tel: (202) 224-3582.

Private Sector Export-Support Network[1]

AT&T and several multinational corporations operate "The Export Hotline," a fax information retrieval system designed to help U.S. companies learn about worldwide markets. The database contains up-to-date information on 50 key industries of all major trading partners of the United States; it can be accessed from anywhere in the United States 24 hours a day. Companies can find out how to use the service by calling 1-800-USA-XPORT, toll-free. The only expense for users is the cost of the fax calls. The AT&T hotline complements the Trade Information Center (tel. 1-800-USA-TRADE), which offers one-on-one attention.

Several private sector organizations that focus on export and trade issues are listed below.

- U.S. Council for International Business, 1212 Avenue of the Americas, New York, N.Y. 10036; tel. (212) 354-4480.
- American Association of Exporters and Importers, 11 W. 42nd St., New York, N.Y. 10036; tel. (212) 944-2230.
- Federation of International Trade Associations, 1851 Alexander Bell Drive, Reston, Va. 22091; tel. (703) 391-6108.
- World Trade Centers Association, One World Trade Center, New York, N.Y. 10048; tel. (212) 313-4600.
- Foreign Credit Interchange Bureau/National Association of Credit Managers, 520 Eighth Ave., New York, N.Y. 10018; tel. (212) 947-5368.
- National Council on International Trade and Documentation, 350 Broadway, New York, N.Y. 10013; tel. (212) 925-1400.
- National Customs Brokers and Forwarders Association of America, One World Trade Center, New York, N.Y. 10048; tel. (212) 432-0050.
- Export Managers Association of California, 14549 Victory Boulevard, Van Nuys, Calif. 91411; tel. (213) 749-8698.

[1] Source: International Trade Administration, U.S. Department of Commerce.

Investing in Gold, Diamonds and Collectibles

Investing in Gold

Gold has been one of the more widely promoted investment vehicles over the last several years. Prices moved from about $140 per ounce in early 1977 to over $800 in early 1980. However, by August 1985 prices declined to $291 an ounce but climbed to over $380.00 by May 1993. Because of such large fluctuations, the metal has stimulated a great deal of speculative interest among many investors.

Investment in gold can be made in a variety of ways:

Gold bullion (bars and wafers) This can be purchased through many stock brokers, bullion currency dealers, and some investment (mutual fund) companies. The purity of gold is indicated by the fineness. Pure gold has a fineness of 1.000 and corresponds to 24 karats.* Each bar is stamped with the fineness as determined by an assay, the refiner's number, a bar identification number and the weight. A bar fineness of .995 or better is acceptable.

Individuals who accept delivery of gold bars and who subsequently wish to resell must have the bar reassayed prior to sale because of the possibility of adulteration with cheaper metals. Because of the latter possibility, individuals should always buy from reputable dealers, and the bar should bear the stamp of well recognized refiners or assayers. Individuals taking physical possession of the metal also have sales taxes, storage, and insurance costs.

The purchaser may arrange to have the dealer (or agent) retain physical possession of the bullion. In this case, evidence of ownership is provided by a *gold deposit certificate* (receipt) issued by the dealer. Since gold certificates are generally non-negotiable or assignable, there is no loss if it is stolen. The gold deposit certificate method of buying bullion eliminates sales taxes, storage risks (though the dealer will charge a modest storage fee) and the need for assay on resale. It is probably the most convenient way of purchasing gold.

* This "karats" is not to be confused with the "carats" that apply to diamonds.

Gold bullion coins Bullion coins are issued in large number by several governments which guarantee their gold content. They have no numismatic value. The best known gold bullion coins are the U.S. Gold One Ounce, South African Krugerrand, Canadian Maple Leaf, Austrian 100 Corona and the Gold Mexican 50 peso. The first three coins have a pure gold content of one ounce. The Austrian Corona has a gold content of .9802 ounce and the Mexican peso 1.2057 ounces. The premium (cost above the gold value) varies from dealer to dealer. For those who do not want to take physical possession, deposit certificates are available for the coins.

One of the largest bullion dealers is Deak International Gold Line (800-289-3325) headquartered in Santa Ana, California. Gold coins can also be purchased at banks where there is generally a very low premium over the gold content value.

Gold stocks The stocks of a number of Canadian and U.S. gold mining companies are traded on the New York (N), American (A) and Over-The-Counter (O) exchanges. Of course, with stocks, the investor is not just buying into gold, but also into the many special problems associated with running a company—production costs, quality of the ore, lifetime of the deposit, etc. However, many gold stocks pay dividends, whereas other gold investments do not pay any return during the holding period.

South African gold mines are traded on the Over-The-Counter Market by means of ADR (American Depository Receipt). ADR is a claim on foreign stocks (South African gold shares, in this case) held by the foreign branches of large U.S. banks. Holders of ADRs are entitled to dividends which, in the case of South African gold shares, may be substantial. The ADRs of these companies are listed in *The Wall Street Journal.*

Some major South African gold mining companies are:

Blyvooruitzicht
Buffelsfontein
Driefontein
Free Consolidated
Kloof

Orange Free State
President Brand
Randfontein
Western Deep Levels

Mutual funds specializing in gold and precious metals A number of mutual funds specializing in gold and precious metals stocks provide diversification among a number of issues thereby reducing risk associated with any particular stock.

Options on gold stocks Put and call options are available on Homestake Mining (Chicago Options Exchange) and on ASA Limited (American Options Exchange). These options may be used for leveraged speculation or for hedging existing gold holdings. Holders of call options gain if the gold shares increase, while holders of put options benefit if prices decline.

The Philadelphia Stock Exchange trades a gold/silver option based on an index of seven different stocks in the industry.

Options on gold bullion Put and call options on gold bullion arc traded on the International Options Market (IOM) of the Montreal Stock Exchange. IOM options are on 10 ounces of gold. Contract months are Feb/May/Aug/Nov.

Monex (Newport Beach, CA) provides put and call options on 32.15 ounces of gold. The Monex options are not tradeable but can be exercized during the option period. Expiration periods are 30, 60, 90, and 185 days.

Since options are paid in full, they are not subject to margin calls or forced liquidation as is the case with futures contracts. At this time, quotations on bullion options are not available in the daily press.

Gold futures contract Gold futures contracts are obligations to buy or sell 100 ounces of gold on or before a specified date at a specified price. Futures contracts must be exercised if held to maturity, while options contracts need not be exercised if held to maturity. Futures contracts are purchased on margin, and hence, are subject to margin call and possible forced liquidation. They are widely quoted in the financial press, and the market is highly organized.

As with options, futures contracts may be used for leveraged speculation or for hedging. Speculators will buy contracts if they anticipate a price increase or sell contracts in anticipation of a price decrease.

Gold futures are traded on the N.Y. Commodity Exchange, the International Monetary Market of the Chicago Mercantile Exchange, and other markets.

Options on Gold Futures Contracts Options on Gold Futures contracts (the right to buy and sell a gold futures contract rather than the metal) are actively traded on the New York Comex. The futures contract underlying the options is for 100 ounces of gold. Contract months are April/Aug./Dec. Gold futures options premiums are reported daily in the *Wall Street Journal.*

Investing in Diamonds

Diamond prices are very volatile. For example, they have appreciated on the average of about 12.6% over the ten-year period 1969–1979 (compared to a consumer price index of 6.1% during the same period of time). There have been periods (the recession of 1973—1974 and in 1981) when the price of investment quality diamonds slipped as much as 40%. A major factor stabilizing the market is DeBeers, a South African diamond company which handles as much as 80% of the world's diamonds. While the appreciation of diamonds has been impressive, potential buyers should be aware that prices are not quoted in the daily newspapers; therefore, selling the stones at a profit may be difficult. Quotes are available in the *Rappaport Diamond Report,* 15 West 47 Street, New York, NY 10036, (212) 354-0575. Another good source of information on the diamond industry is the Diamond Registry, 580 Fifth Avenue, New York, NY 10036, (212) 575-0444. The registry publishes a monthly newsletter which includes price ranges, trends, and forecasts as well as other pertinent material.

To locate reputable gem dealers check with the Diamond Registry (address above) or the

American Gem Society
5901 West 3rd Street
Los Angeles, CA 90036-2898
(213) 936-4367

American Diamond Industry Association

71 West 47 Street
New York, NY 10036
(212) 575-0525

Buyers should only deal with reputable firms, and the stones should be certified by an independent laboratory such as the Gemological Institute of America and International Gemological Institute with offices in New York City.

Diamonds are ranked in terms of the 4 C's—carat (one carat equals 1/142 ounces weight), color, clarity, and cut.

Carat For investment purposes the diamond should be more than .5 carat. However, diamonds of more than 2 carats may be difficult to sell.

Color There are six main categories, each with subdivisions:

D,E,F—Colorless
G,H,I,J—Near colorless
K,L,M—Faint yellow
N,O,P,Q,R—Very light yellow
S,T,U,V,W,X,Y,Z—Light yellow
Fancy yellow stone

Color should be in the range from D to H. However, Fancy Yellow Stones often command very high prices because of their scarcity.

Clarity Although bubbles, lines, and specks (inclusions) are natural to diamonds, they may interfere with the passage of light through the diamond. With a 10X magnification, a professional appraiser can grade the diamond according to the ten clarity grades:

FL—Flawless
IF—Internally flawless
VVS-1, VVS-2—Very, very slight inclusions
VS-1, VS-2—Very slight inclusions
SI-1, SI-2—Slight inclusions
I-1, I-2, I-3—Imperfect

Investment grade stones should be in the range FL to VS-2.

Cut There are several types of cuts—oval, marquise, pear shaped, round brilliant and emerald. Round brilliant stones are preferred for investment purposes. Proportions are important, and the preferred values are:

Depth % (total depth divided by girdle diameter): 57% to 63%.
Table (table diameter divided by girdle diameter): 57% to 66%.
Girdle thickness should be neither very thick nor very thin.

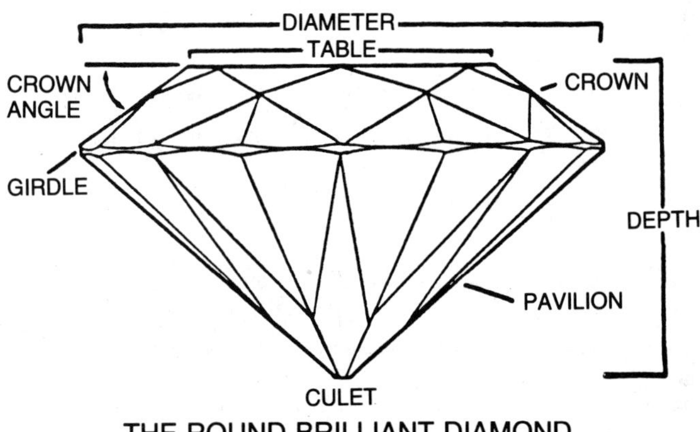

THE ROUND BRILLIANT DIAMOND

Investing in Collectibles

SOTHEBY'S ART INDEX—($ BASIS)

CATEGORY	1975	1976	1977	1978	1979	1980	1981	1982	1983	1984	1985	1986	1987	1988	1989	1990	1991	1992
Old Master Paintings	100	105	131	173	224	255	201	205	239	278	289	303	373	469	754	865	728	811
19th C. European Paintings	100	99	118	160	215	225	179	184	201	230	249	279	323	421	575	634	625	637
Impressionist Art	100	107	114	133	175	206	248	267	307	356	380	490	723	1255	1845	1471	913	913
Modern Paintings	100	105	108	132	178	204	249	245	282	336	364	512	757	1138	1684	1600	1018	1037
Contemporary Art	100	105	127	159	197	239	285	342	392	444	497	551	609	856	1627	1456	1165	1040
American Paintings	100	129	171	255	315	350	450	450	556	589	667	698	871	958	1371	1174	1142	1180
Continental Ceramics	100	121	154	213	261	336	293	266	284	284	284	290	331	467	505	572	796	863
Chinese Ceramics	100	159	181	241	353	462	445	436	459	486	486	526	581	815	875	997	1003	928
English Silver	100	89	95	124	165	205	175	189	219	261	306	343	381	388	420	453	439	461
Continental Silver	100	89	92	113	146	179	140	139	156	175	181	201	220	296	367	395	436	428
American Furniture	100	109	120	134	150	172	209	213	239	289	330	404	459	484	510	510	516	527
French & Continental Furniture	100	104	121	148	197	232	228	234	257	272	273	299	319	409	500	564	648	648
English Furniture	100	125	156	195	244	256	279	267	328	382	419	517	634	822	822	867	924	906
AGGREGATE	100	111	128	164	217	253	249	252	286	324	344	403	512	737	1038	983	787	793

Please Note: The Old Master Painting category was last updated in July 1992

1975 = 100($)

Sotheby's Art Index reflects subjective analyses and opinions of Sotheby's art experts, based on auction sales and other information deemed relevant. Nothing in Sotheby's Art Index is intended or should be relied upon as investment advice or as a prediction or guarantee of future performance or otherwise.

Notes Relating to the Art Index:

1) In each case, the figures are shown in absolute terms, without making any allowances for inflation.
2) All figures are expressed in terms of the U.S. dollar.
3) The basis for the series is September 1975 = 100.
4) Up to and including 1981, the figures were calculated yearly only, in September of each year. From 1982, the figures quoted are calculated in December of each year.
5) The Aggregate Index is a weighted figure.

Source:

MEDIAN SALES PRICE OF EXISTING SINGLE-FAMILY HOMES FOR METROPOLITAN AREAS* (not seasonally adjusted in thousands of dollars)

Metropolitan Area	1990	1991	1992	1992 I	1992 II	1992 III	1992 IV	1993 Ir
Akron, OH	$67.7	$71.8	$79.3	$75.5	$80.5	$78.3	$82.4	$77.4
Albany/Schenectady/Troy, NY	106.9	110.3	111.4	109.4	110.2	112.5	112.6	109.9
Albuquerque, NM	84.5	86.8	92.0	86.7	90.7	93.6	96.5	94.4
Amarillo, TX	N/A	57.5	58.1	57.6	58.7	58.0	58.0	59.7
Orange Cnty. (Anaheim/Santa Ana MSA), CA**	242.4	239.7	234.9	235.4	238.1	234.0	230.8	222.2
Appleton/Oshkosh/Neenah, WI	63.3	66.4	71.0	72.0	69.2	71.6	71.7	74.6
Atlanta, GA	86.4	89.3	N/A	N/A	N/A	N/A	N/A	87.5
Atlantic City, NJ	111.8	110.6	109.1	110.0	114.5	107.0	104.4	101.4
Aurora/Elgin, IL	107.2	114.4	118.8	118.9	119.5	117.6	119.0	116.5
Austin/San Marcos, TX	N/A	N/A	83.8	80.9	82.2	85.0	86.1	86.6
Baltimore, MD	105.9	110.1	113.4	111.5	113.3	114.8	113.8	113.2
Baton Rouge, LA	64.9	69.4	73.6	71.8	72.8	74.4	74.6	72.8
Beaumont/Port Arthur, TX	53.6	57.5	61.5	59.9	62.2	58.8	66.5	60.3
Biloxi/Gulfport, MS	57.6	58.2	62.4	56.6	62.0	64.7	64.3	60.8
Birmingham, AL	80.8	86.0	90.9	89.5	88.6	92.5	93.4	89.0
Boise City, ID	69.2	76.8	83.1	79.4	81.0	84.4	86.1	86.4
Boston, MA	174.1	170.1	171.1	168.2	173.3	175.1	165.2	160.5
Bradenton, FL	69.6	N/A	82.1	80.4	82.4	86.7	79.8	84.3
Buffalo/Niagara Falls, NY	77.2	79.7	81.7	79.7	79.9	83.4	84.3	84.2
Canton, OH	62.1	67.3	71.1	70.1	71.4	72.2	70.7	67.1
Cedar Rapids, IA	59.0	62.9	71.9	67.2	70.3	75.6	72.9	73.4
Champaign/Urbana/Rantoul, IL	66.8	65.9	66.6	64.2	67.5	68.4	64.9	68.7
Charleston, SC	76.2	79.4	82.3	82.0	80.6	81.9	84.8	86.2
Charleston, WV	62.0	65.7	70.3	68.4	69.1	70.9	71.8	75.4
Charlotte/Gastonia/Rock Hill, NC/SC	93.1	101.4	102.2	107.2	99.7	103.5	100.3	102.8
Chattanooga, TN/GA	68.0	70.8	73.0	72.7	73.8	71.6	73.7	69.8
Chicago, IL	116.8	131.1	136.8	132.8	138.0	138.5	136.9	131.2
Cincinnati, OH/KY/IN	79.8	84.9	88.6	87.5	89.1	89.6	87.7	85.6
Cleveland, OH	80.6	86.2	90.7	88.1	92.3	89.9	91.8	89.2
Colorado Springs, CO	N/A	N/A	86.9	84.6	85.0	89.3	87.6	88.5
Columbia, SC	77.1	80.5	84.7	85.1	85.2	83.4	85.2	82.3
Columbus, OH	81.6	85.2	91.0	90.3	90.7	92.5	90.2	88.0
Corpus Christi, TX	63.2	64.3	67.5	62.5	70.4	67.7	69.6	66.6

Source: NATIONAL ASSOCIATION OF REALTORS®, Research Division, 777 14th Street, NW, Washington, D.C. 20005.

(continued)

MEDIAN SALES PRICE OF EXISTING SINGLE-FAMILY HOMES FOR METROPOLITAN AREAS* (not seasonally adjusted in thousands of dollars) ***(continued)***

Metropolitan Area	1990	1991	1992	1992 I	1992 II	1992 III	1992 IV	1993 Ir
Dallas, TX	89.5	88.3	91.3	90.8	92.1	92.2	89.8	89.5
Davenport/Moline/Rock Island, IA,IL	N/A	N/A	54.8	51.4	55.5	55.9	54.9	54.5
Dayton/Springfield, OH	71.6	76.3	81.2	78.8	82.0	82.5	80.4	78.4
Daytona Beach, FL	64.1	66.3	66.2	65.1	66.7	66.9	65.6	67.6
Denver, CO	86.4	89.1	96.2	94.5	95.6	98.0	96.3	96.3
Des Moines, IA	60.5	68.2	73.0	71.2	72.0	74.1	74.5	71.6
Detroit, MI	76.7	80.6	81.3	77.5	79.5	81.4	87.4	92.2
El Paso, TX	63.6	66.0	67.5	65.9	66.7	69.3	67.8	67.9
Eugene/Springfield, OR	66.6	73.7	79.7	75.1	79.5	80.9	82.4	80.4
Fargo/Moorhead, ND/MN	64.0	67.2	70.7	72.0	68.5	70.1	72.6	67.3
Ft. Lauderdale/Hollywood/Pompano Beach, FL	92.6	96.2	99.1	94.1	100.2	99.7	101.0	99.5
Ft. Myers/Cape Coral, FL	69.3	71.3	71.1	69.3	70.1	73.2	72.0	76.4
Ft. Worth/Arlington, TX	76.7	77.6	80.2	80.7	79.8	80.9	79.5	79.7
Gainesville, FL	73.7	74.9	79.1	75.7	80.2	78.6	80.7	80.4
Gary/Hammond, IN	63.8	70.3	76.1	75.5	72.9	77.8	78.1	79.4
Grand Rapids, MI	68.3	70.7	73.1	73.0	72.9	73.7	72.6	73.9
Green Bay, WI	N/A	66.1	72.9	71.1	71.3	75.6	73.4	76.9
Greensboro/Winston-Salem/High Point, NC	87.1	86.1	88.4	85.3	88.1	89.9	90.2	89.3
Greenville/Spartanburg, SC	73.9	77.5	82.9	79.6	82.7	85.4	83.3	82.8
Hartford, CT	157.3	148.2	141.1	141.5	144.1	142.4	137.7	135.5
Honolulu, HI	352.0	340.0	349.0	342.0	339.5	350.0	352.0	347.0
Houston, TX	70.7	74.0	80.2	78.2	79.7	80.9	81.9	78.0
Indianapolis, IN	74.8	79.1	83.7	80.1	84.1	84.4	84.6	83.8
Jacksonville, FL	72.4	73.7	76.8	75.1	74.7	79.0	77.6	74.1
Kalamazoo, MI	60.4	64.9	69.6	69.0	69.9	71.4	68.0	66.0
Kansas City, MO/KS	74.1	76.6	79.5	76.1	79.7	81.9	79.4	79.1
Knoxville, TN	75.4	78.8	80.1	78.3	79.2	81.7	81.5	82.4
Lake County, IL	107.2	113.9	119.6	117.7	120.6	121.6	117.3	121.4
Lansing/East Lansing, MI	63.3	66.7	69.9	68.2	69.3	71.6	70.1	69.8
Las Vegas, NV	93.0	101.4	104.3	101.4	105.6	106.4	103.4	105.2
Lexington/Fayette, KY	75.0	75.6	78.7	78.3	78.2	78.8	79.3	76.9
Lincoln, NE	60.4	62.7	67.7	66.2	67.7	67.2	69.4	69.0
Los Angeles Area, CA**	212.1	218.9	213.2	217.0	216.6	211.1	208.1	199.7

Louisville, KY/IN	$60.8	$65.4	$69.5	$69.7	$68.5	$70.9	$69.1	$69.9
Madison, WI	82.3	87.7	94.9	89.4	92.9	96.9	98.6	97.7
Melbourne/Titusville/Palm Bay, FL	72.2	72.0	74.8	72.8	73.9	75.8	75.9	72.7
Memphis, TN/AR/MS	78.1	82.5	85.3	83.6	85.5	86.0	85.9	84.2
Miami/Hialeah, FL	89.3	93.7	97.1	96.6	96.3	92.9	103.7	98.0
Milwaukee, WI	84.4	90.0	97.0	96.1	95.7	99.3	97.2	98.4
Minneapolis/St. Paul, MN/WI	88.7	91.1	94.2	94.7	94.7	92.5	94.9	96.4
Mobile, AL	59.1	60.8	64.8	63.3	63.7	65.0	66.7	66.2
Montgomery, AL	69.3	76.2	79.7	79.6	78.4	79.2	81.3	79.1
Nashville, TN	81.8	86.9	88.8	89.0	89.2	89.2	87.9	87.0
New Haven/Meriden, CT	153.3	153.2	145.8	142.4	148.2	147.6	142.6	142.6
New Orleans, LA	67.8	71.8	73.6	70.2	73.7	75.5	74.5	73.0
New York/N. New Jersey/Long Island, NY/NJ/CT	174.9	173.5	172.7	168.8	175.4	175.3	170.3	168.0
Bergen/Passaic, NJ	187.7	187.1	187.6	179.8	188.2	192.3	187.1	182.8
Middlesex/Somerset/Hunterdon, NJ	161.7	158.4	168.9	163.7	168.9	173.3	167.1	158.5
Monmouth/Ocean, NJ	137.2	134.4	139.2	138.2	142.0	140.3	135.8	135.3
Nassau/Suffolk, NY	161.0	159.2	158.6	157.4	162.1	158.1	156.9	158.0
Newark, NJ	187.0	178.8	184.4	179.8	188.9	190.1	176.8	174.6
Norfolk/Virginia Bch/Newport News, VA	N/A	91.7	94.8	92.5	93.7	97.7	94.0	94.0
Oklahoma City, OK	53.2	57.0	61.6	59.8	60.0	63.2	62.7	61.1
Omaha, NE/IA	63.0	66.5	69.4	67.4	67.8	71.1	71.2	64.3
Orlando, FL	82.8	86.3	87.6	86.2	88.5	87.4	87.8	86.9
Peoria, IL	50.4	55.8	59.1	54.1	60.0	59.9	60.5	57.5
Philadelphia, PA/NJ	108.7	118.4	117.0	119.7	120.7	112.0	117.1	108.9
Phoenix, AZ	84.0	85.5	86.8	84.7	87.2	87.6	87.1	86.3
Pittsburgh, PA	70.1	74.2	78.6	74.8	80.0	79.5	78.3	75.9
Portland, OR	79.5	88.5	97.7	94.9	97.4	96.6	100.9	99.6
Providence, RI	127.9	124.3	118.5	118.4	119.3	118.6	117.7	112.5
Raleigh/Durham, NC	N/A	100.8	105.9	101.0	105.6	107.9	107.5	101.3
Reno, NV	109.7	115.1	117.9	116.3	119.5	118.3	117.1	118.2
Richland/Kennewick/Pasco, WA	61.6	70.3	84.2	77.4	82.2	85.0	92.5	96.4
Richmond/Petersburg, VA	87.5	92.5	93.9	96.7	93.1	97.0	90.4	89.4
Riverside/San Bernardino, CA**	132.1	137.6	136.2	137.5	136.2	135.9	135.6	135.4
Rochester, NY	79.8	81.5	84.7	83.8	83.8	86.3	84.3	83.3
Rockford, IL	68.9	71.2	75.7	72.4	77.6	75.5	77.3	75.1
Sacramento, CA**	137.5	137.7	132.0	135.0	135.5	134.4	132.2	130.4
Saginaw/Bay City/Midland, MI	48.1	51.5	N/A	N/A	61.5	60.2	56.5	56.4
Saint Louis, MO/IL	76.7	79.4	83.2	83.0	83.6	84.4	81.6	80.9
Salt Lake City/Ogden, UT	69.4	72.8	76.5	73.2	75.1	79.5	77.9	78.0

(continued)

MEDIAN SALES PRICE OF EXISTING SINGLE-FAMILY HOMES FOR METROPOLITAN AREAS* (not seasonally adjusted in thousands of dollars) *(concluded)*

Metropolitan Area	1990	1991	1992	1992				1993
				I	II	III	IV	Ir
San Antonio, TX	63.6	64.9	70.4	68.0	69.6	73.0	70.0	72.6
San Diego, CA**	183.2	187.5	183.8	182.5	185.2	185.6	181.1	175.5
San Francisco Bay Area, CA**	259.3	258.5	254.8	247.3	262.0	258.7	257.1	249.3
Sarasota, FL	89.8	89.0	93.2	93.5	90.8	93.5	94.5	88.9
Seattle, WA	142.0	143.1	145.7	141.3	145.9	147.5	147.2	145.0
Shreveport, LA	61.4	64.0	66.3	64.5	67.4	68.6	63.8	66.1
Sioux Falls, SD	57.8	63.6	69.0	66.6	69.0	69.5	70.4	70.7
South Bend/Mishawaka, IN	56.5	59.1	62.9	62.5	63.5	62.0	64.1	63.0
Spokane, WA	55.5	64.5	76.3	71.3	75.8	75.3	80.4	79.1
Springfield, IL	61.1	66.6	67.7	69.3	67.9	66.2	67.7	67.6
Springfield, MA	120.0	117.1	115.1	116.9	115.6	116.8	111.3	106.3
Springfield, MO	N/A	N/A	62.8	59.6	63.1	63.7	63.9	64.3
Syracuse, NY	80.7	77.7	80.4	77.4	79.4	82.4	80.7	85.6
Tacoma, WA	85.9	98.2	107.8	100.8	108.8	107.8	111.0	109.1
Tampa/St. Petersburg/Clearwater, FL	71.4	71.3	72.6	70.1	72.5	74.2	73.3	69.9
Toledo, OH	62.8	68.8	71.5	74.0	71.2	70.1	71.0	65.8
Topeka, KS	57.6	58.2	64.7	61.8	68.7	63.7	62.9	62.9
Trenton, NJ	145.1	147.5	138.1	128.4	137.5	141.7	145.9	132.9
Tucson, AZ	N/A	N/A	N/A	N/A	N/A	81.9	82.5	80.3
Tulsa, OK	63.9	65.4	68.3	68.5	67.8	68.6	68.2	68.2
Washington, DC/MD/VA	150.5	156.7	157.8	152.5	159.9	160.0	157.2	153.5
Waterloo/Cedar Falls, IA	41.3	45.4	47.2	41.7	46.2	49.9	49.4	44.3
W. Palm Beach/Boca Raton/Delray Beach, FL	108.0	116.3	114.1	110.7	115.1	118.4	111.7	108.6
Wichita, KS	62.4	65.9	68.6	67.8	67.7	69.9	69.0	69.3
Wilmington, DE/NJ/MD	109.8	116.5	117.2	113.5	118.9	118.3	120.6	115.7
Worcester, MA	136.8	N/A	128.0	127.9	128.6	128.9	125.6	122.4
Youngstown/Warren, OH	51.1	54.5	57.6	54.3	59.3	57.7	57.6	58.6

*All areas are metropolitan statistical areas (MSA) as defind by the US Office of Management and Budget as of 1992. They include the named central city and surrounding areas. **Provided by the California Association of REALTORS. N/A Not Available r Revised

Source: NATIONAL ASSOCIATION OF REALTORS®, Research Division, 777 14th Street, NW, Washington, D.C. 20005.

SALES AND MEDIAN SALES PRICE OF APARTMENT CONDOS AND CO-OPS

Year		U.S.	Northeast	Midwest	South	West	U.S.	Northeast	Midwest	South	West
		Seasonally Adjusted Annual Rates					Not Seasonally Adjusted				
1990		350,000	63,000	59,000	111,000	117,000	$83,600	$110,200	$69,000	$66,100	$95,500
1991		339,000	66,000	61,000	109,000	103,000	85,700	106,800	73,700	68,200	106,100
1992		366,000	78,000	67,000	115,000	106,000	84,900	103,200	75,800	69,600	107,100
1992	I	367,000	76,000	70,000	117,000	103,000	$84,000	$101,400	$74,300	$68,700	$114,100
	II	365,000	75,000	65,000	113,000	111,000	85,600	104,700	75,500	71,100	106,800
	III	342,000	77,000	63,000	104,000	98,000	85,100	104,400	75,400	69,300	110,200
	IV	389,000	82,000	71,000	125,000	111,000	84,800	101,400	78,000	69,000	102,500
1993	I r	388,000	84,000	76,000	123,000	105,000	$82,100	$96,800	$73,100	$68,500	$110,200

r Revised

Source: NATIONAL ASSOCIATION OF REALTORS®, Research Division, 777 14th Street, NW, Washington, D.C. 20005.

HOUSING AFFORDABILITY

Year		Existing Single-Family Home	Mortgage Rate*	Monthly P & I Payment	Payment as % Income	Median Family Income	Qualifying Income**	Affordability Indexes		
								Composite	Fixed	ARM
1990		$95,500	10.04%	$673	22.8%	$35,353	$32,286	109.5	106.5	118.3
1991		100,300	9.30	663	22.1	35,939	31,825	112.9	109.9	124.2
1992		103,700	8.11	615	20.0	36,837	29,523	124.8	120.2	145.1
1992	Apr	$103,500	8.55%	$640	21.2%	$36,239	$30,701	118.0	113.8	137.6
	May	103,100	8.48	633	20.9	36,314	30,385	119.5	115.1	138.7
	Jun	105,500	8.34	639	21.1	36,389	30,692	118.6	113.9	136.2
	Jul	102,800	8.05	606	20.0	36,464	29,103	125.3	120.6	146.8
	Aug	105,000	7.90	611	20.1	36,539	29,305	124.7	120.2	145.5
	Sep	103,500	7.70	590	19.4	36,614	28,336	129.2	124.6	148.5
	Oct	103,400	7.64	586	19.2	36,689	28,144	130.4	125.3	154.0
	Nov	102,700	7.77	590	19.3	36,763	28,308	129.9	124.4	153.0
	Dec	104,200	7.80	600	19.6	36,837	28,804	127.9	121.5	150.3
1993	Jan	$103,100	7.75%	$591	19.2%	$36,899	$28,363	130.1	123.9	150.4
	Feb	103,600	7.51	580	18.8	36,960	27,844	132.7	126.4	156.3
	Mar r	105,100	7.39	582	18.9	37,022	27,916	132.6	127.4	159.6
	Apr p	105,400	7.26	576	18.6	37,083	27,638	134.2	128.8	157.7
	Apr p							This month	Month Ago	Year Ago
	Northeast	$139,700	7.12%	$753	22.1%	$40,939	$36,132	113.3	111.7	113.3
	Midwest	85,700	7.13	462	14.5	38,151	22,175	172.0	170.9	172.0
	South	91,700	7.05	491	17.9	32,925	23,545	139.8	138.7	118.2
	West	142,700	7.04	763	24.0	38,167	36,618	104.2	101.8	87.1

*Effective rate on loans closed on existing homes - Federal Housing Finance Board. Regional interest rates from HSH Associates; Butler, NJ

**Based on current lending requirements of the Federal National Mortgage Association using a 20 percent down payment.

p Preliminary r Revised

Source: NATIONAL ASSOCIATION OF REALTORS®, Research Division, 777 14th Street, NW, Washington, D.C. 20005.

FIRST-TIME HOMEBUYER AFFORDABILITY

Year		Starter Home Price	10% Down Payment	Loan Amount	Effective Interest Rate*	Effective I Rate Plus PMI	Monthly Payment	Prime First-Time Median Income	Qualifying Income	Affordability Indexes: First-Time Buyer	Affordability Indexes: Composite
1990		$81,200	$8,120	$73,080	10.04%	10.29%	$657	$22,842	$31,538	72.4	109.5
1991		85,300	8,530	76,770	9.30	9.55	648	23,345	31,120	75.0	112.9
1992		88,100	8,810	79,290	8.11	8.36	602	23,625	28,887	81.8	124.9
1992	I	$87,700	$8,770	$78,930	8.36%	8.61%	$613	$23,415	$29,427	79.6	120.2
	II	88,400	8,840	79,560	8.46	8.71	624	23,485	29,934	78.5	118.9
	III	88,200	8,820	79,380	7.88	8.13	590	23,555	28,304	83.2	126.6
	IV	87,900	8,790	78,840	7.74	7.99	578	23,625	27,742	85.2	130.1
1993	Ir	$88,300	$8,830	$79,470	7.55%	7.80%	$572	$23,743	$27,460	86.5	132.1

*Effective rate on loans closed on existing homes - Federal Housing Finance Board. r Revised

Source: NATIONAL ASSOCIATION OF REALTORS®, Research Division, 777 14th Street, NW, Washington, D.C. 20005.

AVERAGE PER ACRE VALUE OF FARM REAL ESTATE, BY STATE, 1986–93[1]

State	As of February 1				As of January 1				Percent change
	1986	1987	1988	1989	1990	1991	1992	1993	1992-93
	Dollars								Percent
Northeast:	1,340	1,491	1,586	1,763	1,722	1,703	1,711	1,753	2
Maine	854	885	962	1,019	1,019	978	931	992	7
New Hampshire	1,682	1,847	2,112	2,237	2,237	2,148	2,045	2,178	7
Vermont	1,060	1,114	1,124	1,190	1,190	1,142	1,087	1,158	7
Massachusetts	2,761	3,012	3,553	3,763	3,763	3,612	3,439	3,662	6
Rhode Island	3,284	3,389	4,748	5,028	5,028	4,827	4,595	4,894	7
Connecticut	3,372	3,557	4,171	4,417	4,417	4,240	4,036	4,299	7
New York	843	960	993	1,024	974	1,031	1,051	1,119	6
New Jersey	2,997	3,729	3,969	4,543	4,634	4,912	4,774	4,536	-5
Pennsylvania	1,332	1,540	1,579	1,874	1,807	1,757	1,820	1,747	-4
Delaware	1,684	1,677	1,765	2,058	2,259	2,248	2,126	2,362	11
Maryland	2,023	2,009	2,261	2,462	2,420	2,196	2,255	2,521	12
Lake States:	797	707	788	819	841	906	916	950	4
Michigan	1,012	924	971	983	1,005	1,085	1,105	1,130	2
Wisconsin	836	777	826	846	803	853	870	932	7
Minnesota	694	587	700	745	805	873	873	896	3
Corn Belt:	972	900	1,003	1,100	1,096	1,129	1,158	1,193	3
Ohio	1,136	1,097	1,199	1,262	1,204	1,217	1,249	1,267	1
Indiana	1,167	1,061	1,158	1,244	1,244	1,275	1,303	1,366	5
Illinois	1,232	1,149	1,262	1,383	1,389	1,433	1,500	1,503	0
Iowa	873	786	947	1,101	1,102	1,157	1,178	1,245	6
Missouri	648	604	640	673	679	689	689	715	4
Northern Plains:	360	331	368	398	425	440	449	462	3
North Dakota	334	303	319	326	340	368	358	388	8
South Dakota	267	238	269	291	328	351	365	370	1
Nebraska	416	400	457	523	550	556	569	580	2
Kansas	415	373	413	435	462	467	484	494	2
Appalachia:	1,025	1,004	1,037	1,077	1,111	1,059	1,089	1,129	4
Virginia	1,179	1,154	1,198	1,333	1,516	1,295	1,363	1,295	-5
West Virginia	616	633	682	702	613	625	719	696	-3
North Carolina	1,254	1,259	1,263	1,317	1,263	1,243	1,264	1,319	4
Kentucky	941	878	896	911	981	962	993	1,084	9
Tennessee	935	936	1,001	1,002	996	988	985	1,049	6
Southeast:	1,038	1,055	1,130	1,194	1,253	1,254	1,212	1,235	2
South Carolina	870	792	871	939	909	948	931	871	-6
Georgia	853	889	920	998	1,012	995	902	964	7
Florida	1,537	1,605	1,790	1,887	2,085	2,133	2,062	2,074	1
Alabama	803	786	800	822	839	791	832	863	4
Delta States:	880	757	781	797	782	797	771	802	4
Mississippi	778	685	697	713	728	754	738	757	3
Arkansas	779	724	761	778	750	770	724	759	5
Louisiana	1,191	921	940	954	915	905	905	945	4
Southern Plains:	579	532	531	516	495	482	472	480	2
Oklahoma	520	475	480	521	497	486	494	512	4
Texas	594	546	544	515	495	481	466	471	1
Mountain:	267	257	257	260	267	286	288	295	2
Montana	233	200	205	209	238	243	252	270	7
Idaho	631	552	572	595	661	659	687	691	1
Wyoming	159	157	147	142	149	153	138	149	8
Colorado	360	368	369	367	358	410	367	383	4
New Mexico	161	156	180	191	196	230	239	225	-6
Arizona	271	299	279	274	263	285	302	305	1
Utah	476	451	425	421	389	403	425	464	9
Nevada	219	240	227	234	194	219	231	215	-7
Pacific:	1,201	1,084	1,089	1,129	1,163	1,206	1,198	1,190	-1
Washington	840	756	739	757	779	798	792	782	-1
Oregon	570	541	542	535	571	583	603	657	9
California	1,730	1,554	1,575	1,657	1,704	1,787	1,765	1,722	-2
48 States	640	599	632	661	668	681	684	700	2

1/ Value of farmland and buildings in nominal dollars.

Source: *Agricultural Resources: Agricultural Land Values,* Economics Research Service, U.S. Department of Agriculture.

Industrial Real Estate Market: Selected Cities*

Atlanta, Georgia: Industrial

Atlanta, Georgia

Market Data

Inventory (sf)	Central City	Suburban
Total	43,400,000	211,600,000
Vacant	9,050,000	33,150,000
Vacancy Rates	20.9%	15.7%
Under Construction	200,000	3,500,000
Net Absorption	450,000	9,250,000

Prime Source of Financing: Commercial Banks, Pension Funds, Owner Financing

Mortgage Money Supply: Tight

Sales Prices ($/sf)	Central City	Suburban
Less than 5,000 sf	25.00-30.00	35.00-45.00
5,000 to 19,999 sf	20.00-25.00	30.00-35.00
20,000 to 39,999 sf	16.00-20.00	18.00-25.00
40,000 to 59,999 sf	15.00-18.00	16.00-18.00
60,000 to 99,999 sf	12.00-15.00	14.00-16.00
More than 99,999 sf	10.00-14.00	12.00-15.00
High Tech/R&D	40.00-60.00	45.00-70.00

Construction Costs	
Less than 5,000 sf	40.00-50.00
5,000 to 19,999 sf	25.00-35.00
20,000 to 39,999 sf	20.00-25.00
40,000 to 59,999 sf	16.00-20.00
60,000 to 99,999 sf	14.50-16.00
More than 99,999 sf	13.00-15.00
High Tech/R&D	30.00-40.00

Gross Lease Prices	Central City	Suburban
Less than 5,000 sf	3.00-4.00	3.50-5.00
5,000 to 19,999 sf	2.50-3.50	3.00-4.50
20,000 to 39,999 sf	2.25-3.00	2.75-3.75
40,000 to 59,999 sf	2.00-2.50	2.50-3.00
60,000 to 99,999 sf	1.75-2.25	1.75-2.50
More than 99,999 sf	1.50-2.00	1.50-2.25
High Tech/R&D	6.00-7.00	5.00-7.00

Vacancy Indicators	
Less than 5,000 sf	Moderate Oversupply
5,000 to 19,999 sf	Moderate Oversupply
20,000 to 39,999 sf	Moderate Oversupply
40,000 to 59,999 sf	Moderate Oversupply
60,000 to 99,999 sf	Moderate Shortage
More than 99,999 sf	Substantial Shortage
High Tech/R&D	Moderate Oversupply

Site Prices ($/sf)	Central City	Suburban
Improved Sites		
Less than 2 acres	1.75-2.50	2.00-3.00
2 to 5 acres	1.75-2.50	1.75-3.00
5 to 10 acres	1.75-2.50	1.50-2.75
More than 10 acres	1.75-2.50	1.50-2.50
Unimproved Sites		
Less than 10 acres	0.50-1.00	1.00-2.00
10 to 100 acres	0.50-1.00	0.75-1.75
More than 100 acres	0.50-1.00	0.50-1.25

Composition of Absorption	
Warehouse/Distribution	85%
Manufacturing	5%
High Tech/R&D	10%
Composition of Inventory	
Warehouse/Distribution	90%
Manufacturing	0%
High Tech/R&D	10%
Dollar Volume - Sales	
Warehouse/Distribution	Up 11-15%
Manufacturing	Same
High Tech/R&D	Same
Dollar Volume - Leases	
Warehouse/Distribution	Up 11-15%
Manufacturing	Same
High Tech/R&D	Same

Rate of Construction	
Warehouse/Distribution	Down 6-10%
Manufacturing	Same
High Tech/R&D	Down 11-15%

Outlook

Sales Prices	
Warehouse/Distribution	Up 11-15%
Manufacturing	Same
High Tech/R&D	Up 1-5%
Lease Prices	
Warehouse/Distribution	Up 1-5%
Manufacturing	Same
High Tech/R&D	Same
Site Prices	Same
Absorption	
Warehouse/Distribution	Up 11-15%
Manufacturing	Same
High Tech/R&D	Same
Construction	
Warehouse/Distribution	Up 11-15%
Manufacturing	Same
High Tech/R&D	Same
Dollar Volume - Sales	Up 11-15%
Dollar Volume - Leases	Same

1992 Review

As Atlanta felt the effects of the national recession, construction slowed to half the level of a year ago. New construction was fueled by build-to-suits for large national companies. Atlanta's traditional role as the Southeast's distribution hub was affirmed, as warehouses accounted for 85 percent of total net absorption. Suburban industrial space, which already makes up 83 percent of total inventory, gained market share in both construction and occupancy. While overall vacancy dropped from 18.1 percent in 1991 to 16.5 percent this year, lease prices were steady in most sectors. The 1996 Olympics are already starting to stimulate the region's economy.

1993 Forecast

Build-to-suits and relocations are expected to continue being Atlanta's primary source of industrial demand. Firms are trying to lock in on today's lower interest rates for longer terms. SIOR's reporter expects there to be very little speculative space built in the next 12 months. However, some developers, propelled by perceived shortages of units of 60,000 sq. ft. or more, are considering construction of "spec" warehouse space.

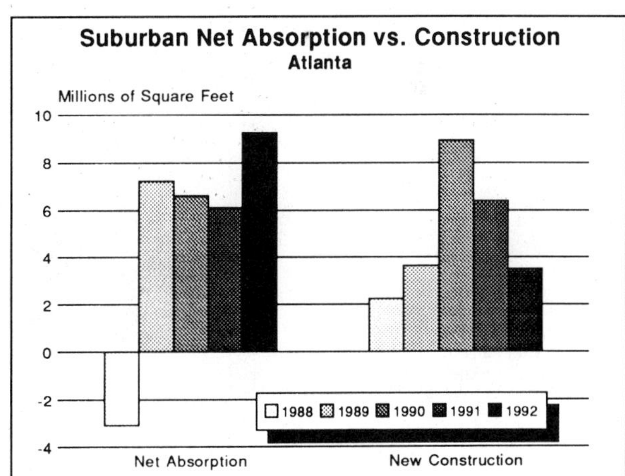

Source: Reprinted from *Comparative Statistics of Industrial and Office Real Estate Markets* (1993) with permission of the Society of Industrial and Office REALTORS®.

* See Glossary of Terms on page 622.

Chicago, Illinois: Industrial

Central City and Suburban-Chicago, Illinois

Market Data

Inventory (sf)	Central City	Suburban
Total	185,000,000	544,000,000
Vacant	21,000,000	53,400,000
Vacancy Rates	11.4%	9.8%
Under Construction	0	2,300,000
Net Absorption	2,000,000	-6,500,000

Prime Source of Financing: Commercial Banks, Owner Financing, Private Investors

Mortgage Money Supply: Tight

Sales Prices ($/sf)	Central City	Suburban
Less than 5,000 sf	40.00	45.00
5,000 to 19,999 sf	25.00	40.00
20,000 to 39,999 sf	20.00	37.00
40,000 to 59,999 sf	18.00	33.00
60,000 to 99,999 sf	18.00	27.00
More than 99,999 sf	15.00	24.00
High Tech/R&D	n/a	n/a

Construction Costs	
Less than 5,000 sf	40.00
5,000 to 19,999 sf	35.00
20,000 to 39,999 sf	30.00
40,000 to 59,999 sf	25.00
60,000 to 99,999 sf	22.00
More than 99,999 sf	20.00
High Tech/R&D	40.00-70.00

Net Lease Prices	Central City	Suburban
Less than 5,000 sf	4.00	5.25
5,000 to 19,999 sf	3.00	4.80
20,000 to 39,999 sf	2.75	4.00
40,000 to 59,999 sf	2.50	3.50
60,000 to 99,999 sf	2.50	3.50
More than 99,999 sf	2.25	3.00
High Tech/R&D	n/a	7.15

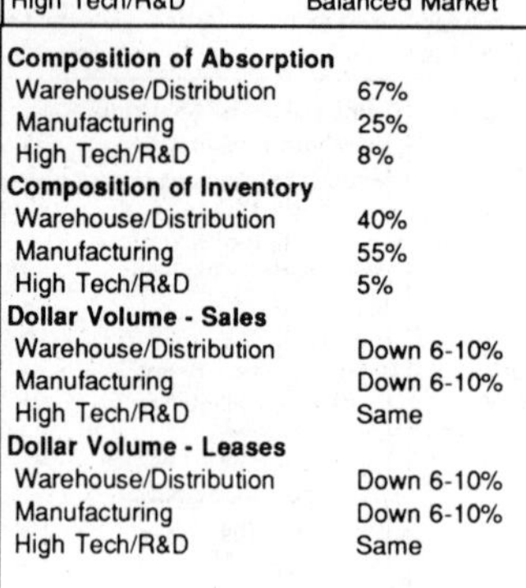

Vacancy Indicators	
Less than 5,000 sf	Balanced Market
5,000 to 19,999 sf	Balanced Market
20,000 to 39,999 sf	Moderate Oversupply
40,000 to 59,999 sf	Substantial Oversupply
60,000 to 99,999 sf	Substantial Oversupply
More than 99,999 sf	Balanced Market
High Tech/R&D	Balanced Market

Site Prices ($/sf)	Central City	Suburban
Improved Sites		
Less than 2 acres	1.50-6.00	4.00-4.50
2 to 5 acres	1.50-6.00	3.00-3.75
5 to 10 acres	1.50-4.00	2.50-3.50
More than 10 acres	1.00-4.00	1.75-2.50
Unimproved Sites		
Less than 10 acres	n/a	n/a
10 to 100 acres	n/a	1.00-1.50
More than 100 acres	n/a	0.50-1.00

Composition of Absorption	
Warehouse/Distribution	67%
Manufacturing	25%
High Tech/R&D	8%
Composition of Inventory	
Warehouse/Distribution	40%
Manufacturing	55%
High Tech/R&D	5%
Dollar Volume - Sales	
Warehouse/Distribution	Down 6-10%
Manufacturing	Down 6-10%
High Tech/R&D	Same
Dollar Volume - Leases	
Warehouse/Distribution	Down 6-10%
Manufacturing	Down 6-10%
High Tech/R&D	Same

Rate of Construction	
Warehouse/Distribution	Up 50%
Manufacturing	Up 50%
High Tech/R&D	Same

Outlook

Sales Prices	
Warehouse/Distribution	Same
Manufacturing	Same
High Tech/R&D	Same
Lease Prices	
Warehouse/Distribution	Same
Manufacturing	Same
High Tech/R&D	Same
Site Prices	Down 6-10%
Absorption	
Warehouse/Distribution	Up 6-10%
Manufacturing	Up 6-10%
High Tech/R&D	Up 1-5%
Construction	
Warehouse/Distribution	Down 1-5%
Manufacturing	Down 1-5%
High Tech/R&D	Same
Dollar Volume - Sales	Up 1-5%
Dollar Volume - Leases	Same

1992 Review

Chicago's industrial market encompasses approximately 730 million sq. ft. The size of this market implies that there are submarkets within the central city that would not necessarily track the same. The surprisingly strong showing for the total market can be attributed to Chicago's southern region where almost a dozen transactions in excess of 100,000 sq. ft. each were completed, lowering vacancy rates. By contrast, the north and central regions of the city softened in 1992. Demand came from a variety of users including steel, paper, and transportation equipment. Prices fell and many transactions were motivated by lower acquisition costs.

1993 Forecast

Pending transactions and the planned demolition of several large and obsolete facilities will further reduce vacancy in the central city. The southern region will be strong in 1993; the north and central regions will stabilize. There may be some spec development but most development in '93 will be build-to-suits. A new in-city business park will provide the first new industrial construction in several years. Sales and lease prices are expected to remain flat, however.

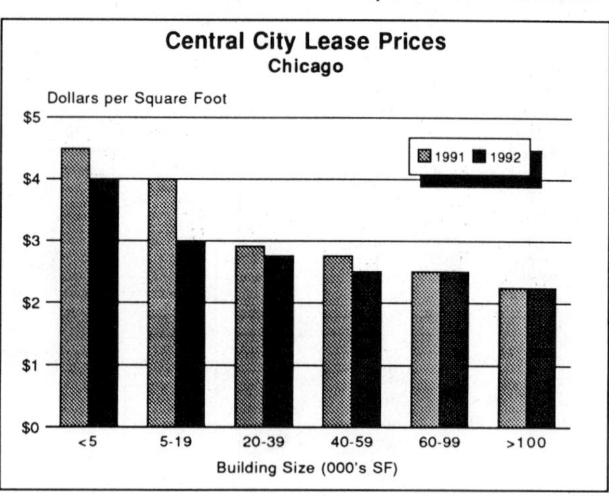

Houston, Texas: Industrial

Houston, Texas

Market Data

Inventory (sf)	Central City	Suburban
Total	70,000,000	200,000,000
Vacant	16,000,000	18,000,000
Vacancy Rates	22.9%	9.0%
Under Construction	0	350,000
Net Absorption	0	-2,000,000

Prime Source of Financing: Insurance Companies, Commercial Banks, Owner Financing

Mortgage Money Supply: Tight

Sales Prices ($/sf)	Central City	Suburban
Less than 5,000 sf	20.00-40.00	15.00-45.00
5,000 to 19,999 sf	20.00-35.00	15.00-35.00
20,000 to 39,999 sf	18.00-30.00	15.00-35.00
40,000 to 59,999 sf	15.00-30.00	15.00-30.00
60,000 to 99,999 sf	12.00-25.00	12.00-23.00
More than 99,999 sf	12.00-20.00	12.00-23.00
High Tech/R&D	15.00-50.00	15.00-50.00

Construction Costs	
Less than 5,000 sf	25.00-40.00
5,000 to 19,999 sf	20.00-35.00
20,000 to 39,999 sf	20.00-35.00
40,000 to 59,999 sf	18.00-30.00
60,000 to 99,999 sf	15.00-28.00
More than 99,999 sf	14.00-25.00
High Tech/R&D	25.00-50.00

Gross Lease Prices	Central City	Suburban
Less than 5,000 sf	2.50-4.00	2.50-4.00
5,000 to 19,999 sf	2.20-4.00	2.20-4.00
20,000 to 39,999 sf	2.00-3.25	2.00-3.25
40,000 to 59,999 sf	2.00-3.25	2.00-3.25
60,000 to 99,999 sf	1.80-3.00	1.80-3.00
More than 99,999 sf	1.80-2.80	1.80-2.80
High Tech/R&D	3.50-8.00	3.50-8.00

Vacancy Indicators	
Less than 5,000 sf	Moderate Shortage
5,000 to 19,999 sf	Balanced Market
20,000 to 39,999 sf	Balanced Market
40,000 to 59,999 sf	Moderate Shortage
60,000 to 99,999 sf	Substantial Shortage
More than 99,999 sf	Substantial Shortage
High Tech/R&D	Moderate Oversupply

Site Prices ($/sf)	Central City	Suburban
Improved Sites		
Less than 2 acres	1.50-6.00	0.70-5.00
2 to 5 acres	1.50-6.00	0.70-5.00
5 to 10 acres	1.50-5.00	0.70-4.00
More than 10 acres	1.00-5.00	0.50-4.00
Unimproved Sites		
Less than 10 acres	1.50-5.00	0.25-2.50
10 to 100 acres	1.00-3.00	0.20-2.00
More than 100 acres	n/a	0.10-1.00

Rate of Construction	
Warehouse/Distribution	Down 6-10%
Manufacturing	Same
High Tech/R&D	Down 1-5%

Composition of Absorption	
Warehouse/Distribution	50%
Manufacturing	30%
High Tech/R&D	20%
Composition of Inventory	
Warehouse/Distribution	51%
Manufacturing	36%
High Tech/R&D	13%
Dollar Volume - Sales	
Warehouse/Distribution	Down 1-5%
Manufacturing	Down 1-5%
High Tech/R&D	Down 1-5%
Dollar Volume - Leases	
Warehouse/Distribution	Down 1-5%
Manufacturing	Down 1-5%
High Tech/R&D	Down 1-5%

Outlook

Sales Prices	
Warehouse/Distribution	Up 1-5%
Manufacturing	Same
High Tech/R&D	Same
Lease Prices	
Warehouse/Distribution	Up 1-5%
Manufacturing	Up 1-5%
High Tech/R&D	Up 1-5%
Site Prices	Down 1-5%
Absorption	
Warehouse/Distribution	Same
Manufacturing	Same
High Tech/R&D	Same
Construction	
Warehouse/Distribution	Up 1-5%
Manufacturing	Same
High Tech/R&D	Same
Dollar Volume - Sales	Same
Dollar Volume - Leases	Same

1992 Review

In 1992, the Houston industrial market suffered from reduced demand due to the national recession and uncertainty about the future. Flat absorption in the central city and two million sq. ft. of negative absorption in the suburbs combined to increase overall industrial vacancy from 11.9 percent in 1991 to 12.6 percent in 1992. The only demand came from companies relocating operations from the east and west coasts and from local firms relocating and expanding. Companies looking for new facilities are almost always going into controlled industrial parks.

1993 Forecast

The local SIOR correspondent foresees modest improvement in occupancy with only slight changes in rental rates. Existing facilities will continue to be available at below replacement cost. However, since well-located, better-quality warehouse space is not readily available, build-to-suit construction will occur, primarily in planned office and industrial parks. The Houston industrial market is expected to benefit from the Free Trade Agreement with Mexico.

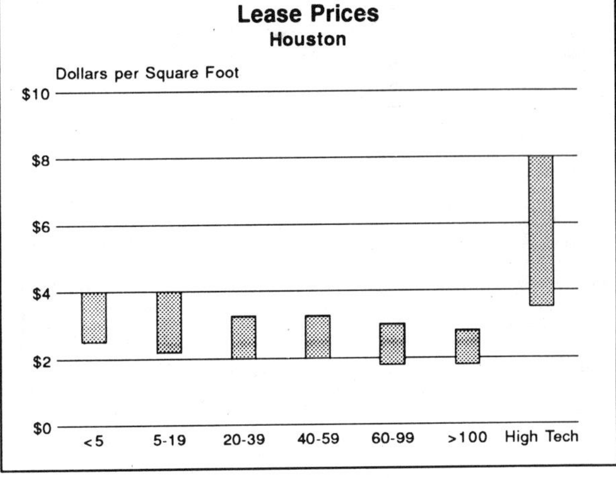

Los Angeles-Central, California: Industrial

Los Angeles-Central, California

Market Data

Inventory (sf)	Central City	Suburban
Total	322,000,000	-
Vacant	31,711,000	-
Vacancy Rates	9.8%	-
Under Construction	268,948	-
Net Absorption	n/a	-

Prime Source of Financing: Owner Financing, SBA thru Comm. Bank

Mortgage Money Supply: Tight

Sales Prices ($/sf)	Central City	Suburban
Less than 5,000 sf	70.00-100.00	-
5,000 to 19,999 sf	60.00-80.00	-
20,000 to 39,999 sf	50.00-60.00	-
40,000 to 59,999 sf	40.00-50.00	-
60,000 to 99,999 sf	40.00-50.00	-
More than 99,999 sf	35.00-40.00	-
High Tech/R&D	70.00-110.00	-

Construction Costs	
Less than 5,000 sf	n/a
5,000 to 19,999 sf	n/a
20,000 to 39,999 sf	n/a
40,000 to 59,999 sf	n/a
60,000 to 99,999 sf	n/a
More than 99,999 sf	n/a
High Tech/R&D	n/a

Net Lease Prices	Central City	Suburban
Less than 5,000 sf	6.00-7.40	-
5,000 to 19,999 sf	4.50-6.60	-
20,000 to 39,999 sf	4.20-5.40	-
40,000 to 59,999 sf	3.00-4.20	-
60,000 to 99,999 sf	3.00-3.60	-
More than 99,999 sf	2.52-3.60	-
High Tech/R&D	6.00-12.00	-

Vacancy Indicators	
Less than 5,000 sf	Moderate Oversupply
5,000 to 19,999 sf	Moderate Oversupply
20,000 to 39,999 sf	Balanced Market
40,000 to 59,999 sf	Balanced Market
60,000 to 99,999 sf	Moderate Oversupply
More than 99,999 sf	Substantial Oversupply
High Tech/R&D	Balanced Market

Site Prices ($/sf)	Central City	Suburban
Improved Sites		
Less than 2 acres	13.00-40.00	-
2 to 5 acres	13.00-25.00	-
5 to 10 acres	13.00-20.00	-
More than 10 acres	17.00	-
Unimproved Sites		
Less than 10 acres	15.00	-
10 to 100 acres	10.00	-
More than 100 acres	n/a	-

Rate of Construction	
Warehouse/Distribution	Down 1-5%
Manufacturing	Down 1-5%
High Tech/R&D	Down 1-5%

Composition of Absorption	
Warehouse/Distribution	80%
Manufacturing	20%
High Tech/R&D	0%
Composition of Inventory	
Warehouse/Distribution	75%
Manufacturing	25%
High Tech/R&D	0%
Dollar Volume - Sales	
Warehouse/Distribution	Down 6-10%
Manufacturing	Down 6-10%
High Tech/R&D	Down 6-10%
Dollar Volume - Leases	
Warehouse/Distribution	Down 1-5%
Manufacturing	Down 1-5%
High Tech/R&D	Down 1-5%

Outlook

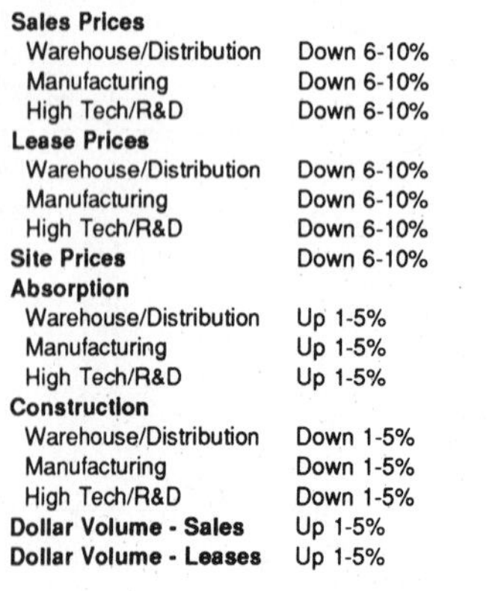

Sales Prices	
Warehouse/Distribution	Down 6-10%
Manufacturing	Down 6-10%
High Tech/R&D	Down 6-10%
Lease Prices	
Warehouse/Distribution	Down 6-10%
Manufacturing	Down 6-10%
High Tech/R&D	Down 6-10%
Site Prices	Down 6-10%
Absorption	
Warehouse/Distribution	Up 1-5%
Manufacturing	Up 1-5%
High Tech/R&D	Up 1-5%
Construction	
Warehouse/Distribution	Down 1-5%
Manufacturing	Down 1-5%
High Tech/R&D	Down 1-5%
Dollar Volume - Sales	Up 1-5%
Dollar Volume - Leases	Up 1-5%

1992 Review

The demand for Central Los Angeles industrial facilities was weak in 1992. L.A. had the dubious distinction of suffering the greatest employment decrease of any U.S. city in 1992. The most active segment of the local industrial market seems to be small- to medium-sized firms. Industrial users continue to prefer leasing facilities for short terms as opposed to purchasing. The most noticeable trend in the Central Los Angeles industrial market is the migration of manufacturing out of the state in search of lower operating costs, especially worker's compensation rates.

1993 Forecast

The weak Southern California economy, with continuing cutbacks in the aerospace/defense industries, will continue to produce conservative attitudes toward real estate decisions in 1993. As a result, there will be virtually no speculative development in the market in the coming year. Absorption will remain positive but weak with warehouse/distribution facilities leading the way. In an effort to attract interest, owners will be forced to lower prices by as much as 10 percent. A period of protracted economic restructuring may be in store for Central L.A.

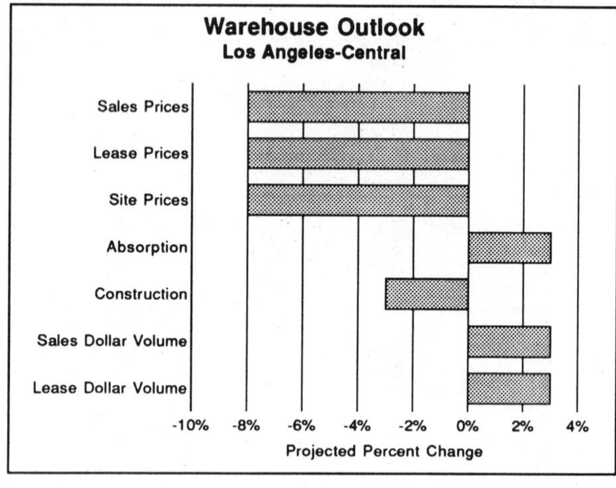

Los Angeles-East, California: Industrial

Buena Park, Cerritos, La Mirada, and Santa Fe Springs

Market Data

Inventory (sf)	Central City	Suburban
Total	74,000,000	-
Vacant	5,900,000	-
Vacancy Rates	8.0%	-
Under Construction	0	-
Net Absorption	-1,000,000	-

Prime Source of Financing: SBA

Mortgage Money Supply: Tight

Sales Prices ($/sf)	Central City	Suburban
Less than 5,000 sf	65.00	-
5,000 to 19,999 sf	60.00	-
20,000 to 39,999 sf	55.00	-
40,000 to 59,999 sf	50.00	-
60,000 to 99,999 sf	45.00	-
More than 99,999 sf	40.00	-
High Tech/R&D	45.00	-

Construction Costs	
Less than 5,000 sf	32.00
5,000 to 19,999 sf	28.00
20,000 to 39,999 sf	25.00
40,000 to 59,999 sf	23.00
60,000 to 99,999 sf	18.00
More than 99,999 sf	16.00
High Tech/R&D	43.00

Net Lease Prices	Central City	Suburban
Less than 5,000 sf	5.40	-
5,000 to 19,999 sf	4.80	-
20,000 to 39,999 sf	3.80	-
40,000 to 59,999 sf	3.60	-
60,000 to 99,999 sf	3.20	-
More than 99,999 sf	3.20	-
High Tech/R&D	4.50	-

Vacancy Indicators	
Less than 5,000 sf	Moderate Oversupply
5,000 to 19,999 sf	Moderate Oversupply
20,000 to 39,999 sf	Moderate Oversupply
40,000 to 59,999 sf	Moderate Oversupply
60,000 to 99,999 sf	Moderate Oversupply
More than 99,999 sf	Moderate Oversupply
High Tech/R&D	Moderate Oversupply

Site Prices ($/sf)	Central City	Suburban
Improved Sites		
Less than 2 acres	10.00	-
2 to 5 acres	9.00	-
5 to 10 acres	8.00	-
More than 10 acres	7.00	-
Unimproved Sites		
Less than 10 acres	6.00	-
10 to 100 acres	6.00	-
More than 100 acres	6.00	-

Rate of Construction	
Warehouse/Distribution	Down 20%
Manufacturing	Down 20%
High Tech/R&D	Down 20%

Composition of Absorption	
Warehouse/Distribution	70%
Manufacturing	25%
High Tech/R&D	5%
Composition of Inventory	
Warehouse/Distribution	60%
Manufacturing	35%
High Tech/R&D	5%
Dollar Volume - Sales	
Warehouse/Distribution	Down 20%
Manufacturing	Down 20%
High Tech/R&D	Down 20%
Dollar Volume - Leases	
Warehouse/Distribution	Down 40%
Manufacturing	Down 40%
High Tech/R&D	Down 40%

Outlook

Sales Prices	
Warehouse/Distribution	Down 6-10%
Manufacturing	Down 6-10%
High Tech/R&D	Down 6-10%
Lease Prices	
Warehouse/Distribution	Down 6-10%
Manufacturing	Down 6-10%
High Tech/R&D	Down 6-10%
Site Prices	Down 6-10%
Absorption	
Warehouse/Distribution	Same
Manufacturing	Same
High Tech/R&D	Same
Construction	
Warehouse/Distribution	Down 1-5%
Manufacturing	Down 1-5%
High Tech/R&D	Down 1-5%
Dollar Volume - Sales	Down 6-10%
Dollar Volume - Leases	Down 6-10%

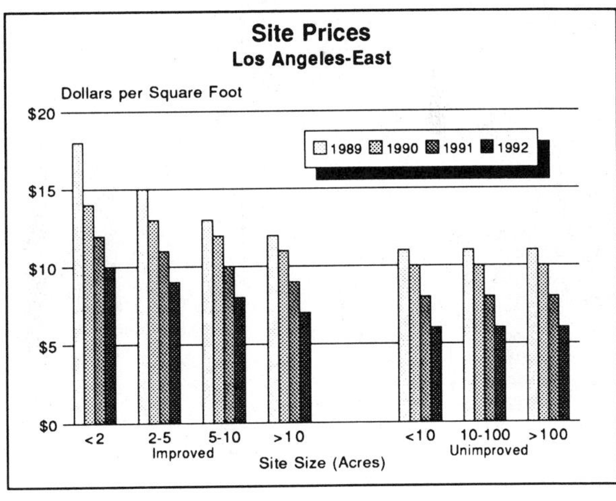

1992 Review

Demand for space in the East Los Angeles industrial market was slow in 1992. There were several signs of a contracting market including a halt in land sales, very slow building sales, and dropping lease prices. As the price structure in the market adjusts downward, the mix of users is shifting. While aerospace and defense industries are shrinking, Asian companies are growing in the area. Taiwanese importers of computer equipment are representative of this trend. At an eight percent vacancy rate, this submarket is one of the healthiest locations in the L.A. basin, and should expect to rebound early in the regional recovery.

1993 Forecast

The outlook for the East Los Angeles industrial market is for a continuation of the 1992 contraction. Site, sales, and lease prices are expected to fall by as much as 10 percent in 1993. The result will be no speculative development in the coming year. All developers are very cautious about the market. Absorption will continue to be dominated by warehouse/distribution users.

Los Angeles-Orange County, California: Industrial

Los Angeles-Orange County, California

Market Data

Inventory (sf)	Central City	Suburban
Total	-	183,365,536
Vacant	-	32,974,071
Vacancy Rates	-	18.0%
Under Construction	-	0
Net Absorption*	-	8,519,212

Prime Source of Financing: Insurance Companies, Owner Financing, SBA

Mortgage Money Supply: Tight

Sales Prices ($/sf)	Central City	Suburban
Less than 5,000 sf	-	65.00-85.00
5,000 to 19,999 sf	-	60.00-80.00
20,000 to 39,999 sf	-	55.00-72.00
40,000 to 59,999 sf	-	55.00-70.00
60,000 to 99,999 sf	-	48.00-65.00
More than 99,999 sf	-	41.00-55.00
High Tech/R&D	-	60.00-120.00

Construction Costs	
Less than 5,000 sf	28.00-31.00
5,000 to 19,999 sf	24.00-28.00
20,000 to 39,999 sf	22.00-24.00
40,000 to 59,999 sf	20.00-22.00
60,000 to 99,999 sf	17.00-20.00
More than 99,999 sf	15.00-17.50
High Tech/R&D	45.00-55.00

Net Lease Prices	Central City	Suburban
Less than 5,000 sf	-	5.40-8.50
5,000 to 19,999 sf	-	4.80-7.20
20,000 to 39,999 sf	-	4.20-5.60
40,000 to 59,999 sf	-	4.20-5.40
60,000 to 99,999 sf	-	3.95-4.60
More than 99,999 sf	-	3.89-4.20
High Tech/R&D	-	5.70-13.30

Vacancy Indicators	
Less than 5,000 sf	Moderate Oversupply
5,000 to 19,999 sf	Moderate Oversupply
20,000 to 39,999 sf	Moderate Oversupply
40,000 to 59,999 sf	Moderate Oversupply
60,000 to 99,999 sf	Moderate Oversupply
More than 99,999 sf	Moderate Oversupply
High Tech/R&D	Substantial Oversupply

Site Prices ($/sf)	Central City	Suburban
Improved Sites		
Less than 2 acres	-	9.75-20.00
2 to 5 acres	-	8.00-17.00
5 to 10 acres	-	7.00-15.00
More than 10 acres	-	7.00-15.00
Unimproved Sites		
Less than 10 acres	-	n/a
10 to 100 acres	-	n/a
More than 100 acres	-	n/a

Composition of Absorption	
Warehouse/Distribution	59%
Manufacturing	26%
High Tech/R&D	15%
Composition of Inventory	
Warehouse/Distribution	20%
Manufacturing	50%
High Tech/R&D	30%
Dollar Volume - Sales	
Warehouse/Distribution	Down 1-5%
Manufacturing	Down 1-5%
High Tech/R&D	Down 1-5%
Dollar Volume - Leases	
Warehouse/Distribution	Up 1-5%
Manufacturing	Up 1-5%
High Tech/R&D	Up 1-5%

Rate of Construction	
Warehouse/Distribution	Down 100%
Manufacturing	Down 100%
High Tech/R&D	Down 100%

Outlook

Sales Prices	
Warehouse/Distribution	Down 6-10%
Manufacturing	Down 6-10%
High Tech/R&D	Down 6-10%
Lease Prices	
Warehouse/Distribution	Down 1-5%
Manufacturing	Down 1-5%
High Tech/R&D	Down 6-10%
Site Prices	Down 1-5%
Absorption	
Warehouse/Distribution	Same
Manufacturing	Same
High Tech/R&D	Same
Construction	
Warehouse/Distribution	Same
Manufacturing	Same
High Tech/R&D	Same
Dollar Volume - Sales	Down 1-6%
Dollar Volume - Leases	Up 1-5%

1992 Review

Industrial real estate demand in Orange County was stifled by the regional downturn. Many properties took as long as 15 months to lease or sell. Owners must discount prices heavily to attract interest. In a recent survey, 25 percent of all manufacturing firms expressed interest in or have plans to leave the state. The local economy is suddenly forced to cope with employment weakness and slow consumer markets. The state is also suffering from difficult financial times and funding to counties has been cut.

1993 Forecast

The only construction to take place in the market in 1993 will be build-to-suits and construction related to land sales and subsequent user construction. The struggling economy and further defense industry layoffs will force further declines in sales and lease prices. What growth does occur will come from Los Angeles firms moving south or from local firms relocating or expanding. The 18 percent vacancy rate in the Orange County industrial market indicates unbalanced conditions that could persist at least through the mid-nineties.

* Figure is for gross absorption.

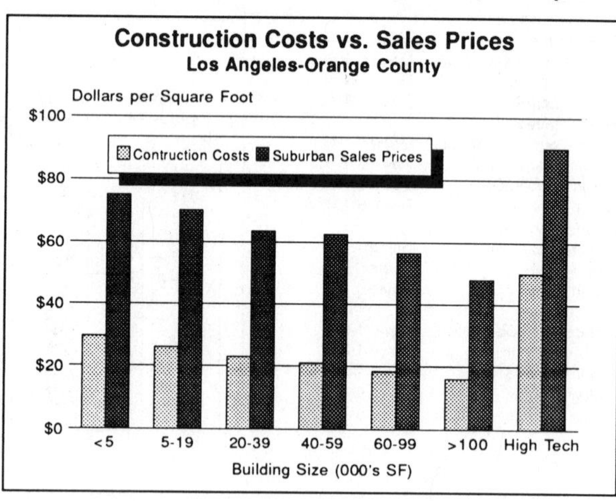

Los Angeles-San Bernardino County, California: Industrial

San Bernardino/Riverside Metropolitan Area

Market Data

Inventory (sf)	Central City	Suburban
Total	97,000,000	-
Vacant	18,000,000	-
Vacancy Rates	18.6%	-
Under Construction	1,000,000	-
Net Absorption	6,000,000	-

Prime Source of Financing: Owner Financing

Mortgage Money Supply: Tight

Sales Prices ($/sf)	Central City	Suburban
Less than 5,000 sf	50.00	-
5,000 to 19,999 sf	40.00	-
20,000 to 39,999 sf	35.00	-
40,000 to 59,999 sf	32.00	-
60,000 to 99,999 sf	28.00	-
More than 99,999 sf	26.00	-
High Tech/R&D	n/a	-

Construction Costs	
Less than 5,000 sf	25.00
5,000 to 19,999 sf	22.00
20,000 to 39,999 sf	20.00
40,000 to 59,999 sf	17.00
60,000 to 99,999 sf	14.00
More than 99,999 sf	12.50
High Tech/R&D	n/a

Net Lease Prices	Central City	Suburban
Less than 5,000 sf	4.56	-
5,000 to 19,999 sf	3.96	-
20,000 to 39,999 sf	3.72	-
40,000 to 59,999 sf	3.60	-
60,000 to 99,999 sf	3.12	-
More than 99,999 sf	2.52	-
High Tech/R&D	n/a	-

Vacancy Indicators	
Less than 5,000 sf	Moderate Oversupply
5,000 to 19,999 sf	Moderate Oversupply
20,000 to 39,999 sf	Balanced Market
40,000 to 59,999 sf	Balanced Market
60,000 to 99,999 sf	n/a
More than 99,999 sf	Moderate Oversupply
High Tech/R&D	Substantial Oversupply

Site Prices ($/sf)	Central City	Suburban
Improved Sites		
Less than 2 acres	5.00	-
2 to 5 acres	4.50	-
5 to 10 acres	4.00	-
More than 10 acres	3.75	-
Unimproved Sites		
Less than 10 acres	2.75	-
10 to 100 acres	2.00	-
More than 100 acres	1.00	-

Composition of Absorption	
Warehouse/Distribution	90%
Manufacturing	10%
High Tech/R&D	0%
Composition of Inventory	
Warehouse/Distribution	80%
Manufacturing	15%
High Tech/R&D	5%
Dollar Volume - Sales	
Warehouse/Distribution	Down 20%
Manufacturing	Down 20%
High Tech/R&D	Down 11-15%
Dollar Volume - Leases	
Warehouse/Distribution	Down 11-15%
Manufacturing	Down 11-15%
High Tech/R&D	Down 11-15%

Rate of Construction	
Warehouse/Distribution	Down
Manufacturing	Down
High Tech/R&D	Down

Outlook

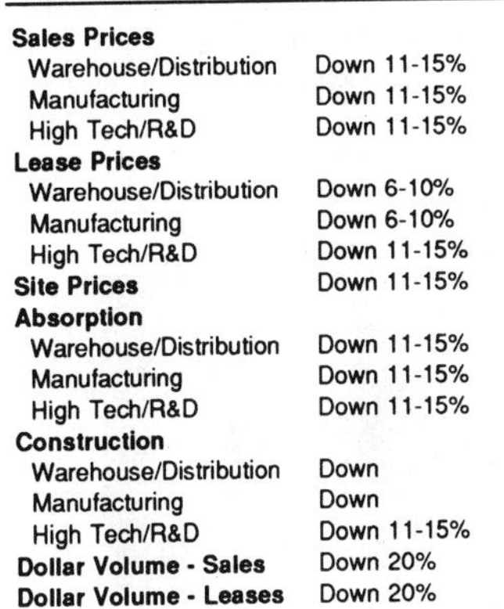

Sales Prices	
Warehouse/Distribution	Down 11-15%
Manufacturing	Down 11-15%
High Tech/R&D	Down 11-15%
Lease Prices	
Warehouse/Distribution	Down 6-10%
Manufacturing	Down 6-10%
High Tech/R&D	Down 11-15%
Site Prices	Down 11-15%
Absorption	
Warehouse/Distribution	Down 11-15%
Manufacturing	Down 11-15%
High Tech/R&D	Down 11-15%
Construction	
Warehouse/Distribution	Down
Manufacturing	Down
High Tech/R&D	Down 11-15%
Dollar Volume - Sales	Down 20%
Dollar Volume - Leases	Down 20%

1992 Review

San Bernardino's industrial properties outperformed most other Los Angeles markets in 1992. Massively overbuilt in the 80s, idle capacity is gradually being absorbed. With little new construction and six million sq. ft. of net absorption last year, the overall vacancy rate fell from 24 percent in 1991 to 18.6 percent in 1992. The market for mid-sized properties is now balanced while the remainder of the market is still oversupplied. Defense industry cutbacks, local policy constraints, and a financially weak state government, notwithstanding, this was a much improved market in the past 12 months.

1993 Forecast

Many national companies have found San Bernardino a cost efficient way to service all of Southern California. Soft land prices and comparatively cheap building prices will continue to attract industry to the area. New projects in the San Bernardino industrial market will lack the financing and market support to make them feasible. Despite recent gains, several years of inventory remain to be absorbed. SIOR's reporter sees significant downside risk in 1993, as Southern California battles its deep regional recession.

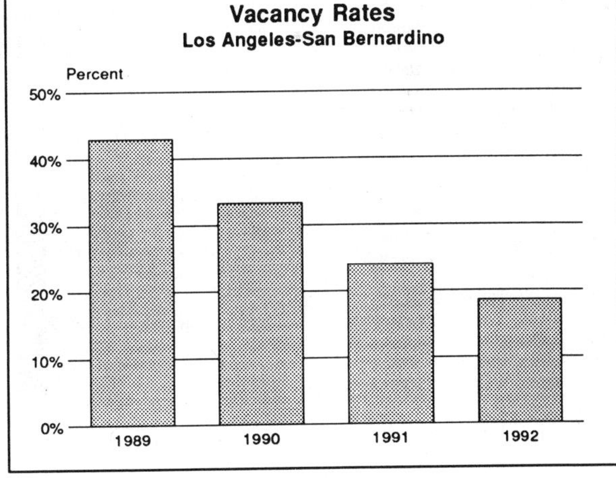

Los Angeles-San Fernando Valley, California: Industrial

Los Angeles-San Fernando Valley, California

Market Data

Inventory (sf)	Central City	Suburban
Total	139,100,000	37,339,699
Vacant	11,348,409	1,972,462
Vacancy Rates	8.2%	5.3%
Under Construction	0	50,000
Net Absorption	1,330,591	652,237

Sales Prices ($/sf)	Central City	Suburban
Less than 5,000 sf	n/a	n/a
5,000 to 19,999 sf	79.00	67.00
20,000 to 39,999 sf	61.00	55.00
40,000 to 59,999 sf	50.00	53.00
60,000 to 99,999 sf	49.00	51.00
More than 99,999 sf	48.00	49.00
High Tech/R&D	60.00	60.00

Net Lease Prices	Central City	Suburban
Less than 5,000 sf	n/a	n/a
5,000 to 19,999 sf	5.70	5.40
20,000 to 39,999 sf	5.00	4.48
40,000 to 59,999 sf	4.80	4.48
60,000 to 99,999 sf	4.50	4.28
More than 99,999 sf	4.20	4.20
High Tech/R&D	7.20	7.20

Site Prices ($/sf)	Central City	Suburban
Improved Sites		
Less than 2 acres	18.00	9.00
2 to 5 acres	15.00	8.00
5 to 10 acres	13.00	8.00
More than 10 acres	n/a	5.00
Unimproved Sites		
Less than 10 acres	n/a	4.00
10 to 100 acres	n/a	2.50
More than 100 acres	n/a	1.50

Rate of Construction	
Warehouse/Distribution	Down 80%
Manufacturing	Down 80%
High Tech/R&D	Down 100%

Prime Source of Financing: Insurance Companies

Mortgage Money Supply: Moderate

Construction Costs	
Less than 5,000 sf	30.00
5,000 to 19,999 sf	28.00
20,000 to 39,999 sf	23.00
40,000 to 59,999 sf	18.50
60,000 to 99,999 sf	17.00
More than 99,999 sf	15.00
High Tech/R&D	24.00

Vacancy Indicators	
Less than 5,000 sf	Moderate Oversupply
5,000 to 19,999 sf	Substantial Oversupply
20,000 to 39,999 sf	Substantial Oversupply
40,000 to 59,999 sf	Substantial Oversupply
60,000 to 99,999 sf	Substantial Oversupply
More than 99,999 sf	Substantial Oversupply
High Tech/R&D	Substantial Oversupply

Composition of Absorption	
Warehouse/Distribution	50%
Manufacturing	45%
High Tech/R&D	5%
Composition of Inventory	
Warehouse/Distribution	50%
Manufacturing	40%
High Tech/R&D	10%
Dollar Volume - Sales	
Warehouse/Distribution	Down 10%
Manufacturing	Down 10%
High Tech/R&D	Down 10%
Dollar Volume - Leases	
Warehouse/Distribution	Down 10%
Manufacturing	Down 10%
High Tech/R&D	Down 10%

Outlook

Sales Prices	
Warehouse/Distribution	Same
Manufacturing	Same
High Tech/R&D	Down 1-5%
Lease Prices	
Warehouse/Distribution	Same
Manufacturing	Same
High Tech/R&D	Down 6-10%
Site Prices	Down 11-15%
Absorption	
Warehouse/Distribution	Same
Manufacturing	Same
High Tech/R&D	Same
Construction	
Warehouse/Distribution	Same
Manufacturing	Same
High Tech/R&D	Same
Dollar Volume - Sales	Same
Dollar Volume - Leases	Same

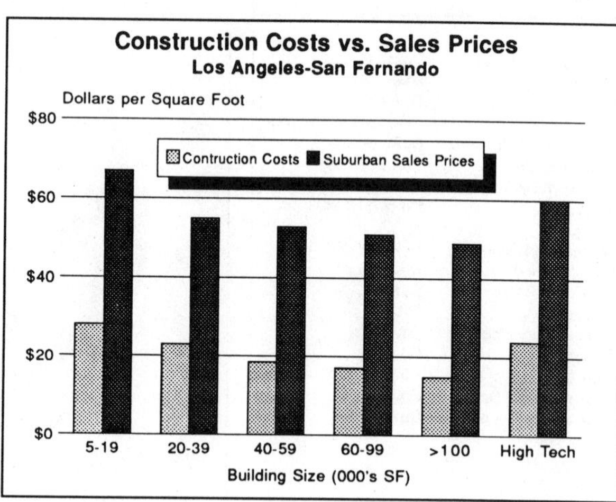

1992 Review

Leasing activity maintained a steady pace in the San Fernando Valley industrial market this year. In 1992 almost two million sq. ft. of positive absorption reduced overall vacancies by 0.9 percentage points. This was a hard-won achievement as increased defense cutbacks and generally weak economic conditions limited industrial growth in the region. Many local companies opted to renegotiate existing lease terms instead of upgrading facilities. Others are moving to cheaper locations to save on operating costs. The local SIOR reporter feels the market to be predominantly price-conscious and bottom-line driven.

1993 Forecast

While the mortgage money supply is reported to be moderate, no significant speculative development will take place due to the lack of demand. Rents will hold steady or decline as owners undercut one another to attract tenants. The marketwide vacancy rate of 7.5 percent indicates some fundamental strengths in the Valley. Price discounting may prove to be an effective strategy if continued positive absorption erodes the supply of available space.

Los Angeles-San Gabriel Valley, California: Industrial

San Gabriel Valley

Market Data

Inventory (sf)	Central City	Suburban
Total	-	50,000,000
Vacant	-	14,000,000
Vacancy Rates	-	28.0%
Under Construction	-	n/a
Net Absorption	-	2,000,000

Prime Source of Financing: Owner Financing

Mortgage Money Supply: Tight

Sales Prices ($/sf)	Central City	Suburban
Less than 5,000 sf	-	65.00
5,000 to 19,999 sf	-	60.00
20,000 to 39,999 sf	-	50.00
40,000 to 59,999 sf	-	45.00
60,000 to 99,999 sf	-	35.00
More than 99,999 sf	-	34.00
High Tech/R&D	-	n/a

Construction Costs	
Less than 5,000 sf	30.00
5,000 to 19,999 sf	22.00-25.00
20,000 to 39,999 sf	19.00
40,000 to 59,999 sf	15.00-17.00
60,000 to 99,999 sf	12.00
More than 99,999 sf	10.00
High Tech/R&D	n/a

Net Lease Prices	Central City	Suburban
Less than 5,000 sf	-	4.20
5,000 to 19,999 sf	-	3.00
20,000 to 39,999 sf	-	2.80-3.00
40,000 to 59,999 sf	-	2.70-2.80
60,000 to 99,999 sf	-	2.50-2.70
More than 99,999 sf	-	2.40
High Tech/R&D	-	n/a

Vacancy Indicators	
Less than 5,000 sf	Substantial Oversupply
5,000 to 19,999 sf	Substantial Oversupply
20,000 to 39,999 sf	Substantial Oversupply
40,000 to 59,999 sf	Substantial Oversupply
60,000 to 99,999 sf	Substantial Oversupply
More than 99,999 sf	Substantial Oversupply
High Tech/R&D	Substantial Oversupply

Site Prices ($/sf)	Central City	Suburban
Improved Sites		
Less than 2 acres	-	7.50
2 to 5 acres	-	7.00
5 to 10 acres	-	6.50
More than 10 acres	-	n/a
Unimproved Sites		
Less than 10 acres	-	n/a
10 to 100 acres	-	n/a
More than 100 acres	-	n/a

Composition of Absorption	
Warehouse/Distribution	80%
Manufacturing	20%
High Tech/R&D	0%
Composition of Inventory	
Warehouse/Distribution	80%
Manufacturing	20%
High Tech/R&D	0%
Dollar Volume - Sales	
Warehouse/Distribution	Down 90%
Manufacturing	Down 90%
High Tech/R&D	Same
Dollar Volume - Leases	
Warehouse/Distribution	Down 25%
Manufacturing	Down 25%
High Tech/R&D	Same

Rate of Construction	
Warehouse/Distribution	Down 75%
Manufacturing	Down 75%
High Tech/R&D	n/a

Outlook

Sales Prices	
Warehouse/Distribution	Down 25-30%
Manufacturing	Down 35%
High Tech/R&D	n/a
Lease Prices	
Warehouse/Distribution	Down 20%
Manufacturing	Down 35%
High Tech/R&D	n/a
Site Prices	Down 25-30%
Absorption	
Warehouse/Distribution	Down 25%
Manufacturing	Down 25%
High Tech/R&D	n/a
Construction	
Warehouse/Distribution	Down 75%
Manufacturing	Down 75%
High Tech/R&D	n/a
Dollar Volume - Sales	n/a
Dollar Volume - Leases	n/a

1992 Review

The San Gabriel Valley industrial market is dominated by warehouse/distribution operations. Like the rest of Southern California, this area has been feeling the effects of a financially weak state economy and the declining role of defense-related industries as a major employer. The result has been a shortage of demand for this area's warehouse space and a vacancy rate that was highest of all submarkets comprising the L.A. basin. The local SIOR reporter indicates a very soft market fostering lower sales and lease prices. The number of sale and lease offers have fallen by 25 percent from a year ago.

1993 Forecast

Tight mortgage money supply and a severe lack of demand will lead to virtually no speculative industrial construction in 1993. What construction does take place will come in the form of build-to-suits for very high credit firms. The massive supply of vacant space has contributed to a dismal outlook for 1993. Every market indicator is expected to fall dramatically in the coming year. The SIOR reporter anticipates market conditions to deteriorate through 1994.

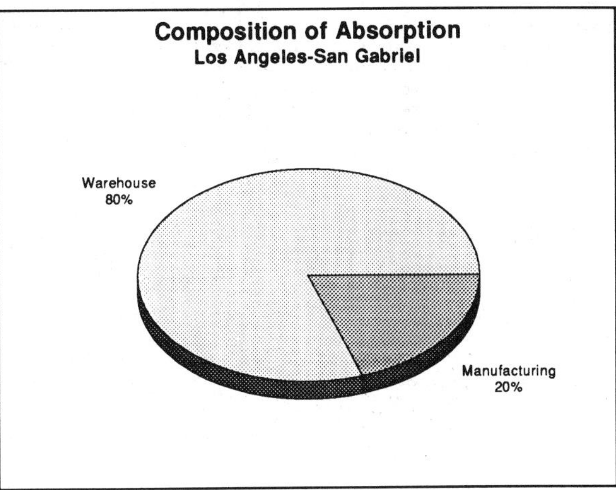

Los Angeles-South Bay, California: Industrial

Los Angeles-South Bay, California

Market Data

Inventory (sf)	Central City	Suburban
Total	-	175,000,000
Vacant	-	30,302,875
Vacancy Rates	-	17.3%
Under Construction	-	41,315
Net Absorption	-	642,125

Prime Source of Financing: Owner Financing, Credit Companies

Mortgage Money Supply: Tight

Sales Prices ($/sf)	Central City	Suburban
Less than 5,000 sf	-	80.00
5,000 to 19,999 sf	-	58.00
20,000 to 39,999 sf	-	55.00
40,000 to 59,999 sf	-	50.00
60,000 to 99,999 sf	-	45.00
More than 99,999 sf	-	40.00
High Tech/R&D	-	75.00

Construction Costs	
Less than 5,000 sf	32.20
5,000 to 19,999 sf	28.00
20,000 to 39,999 sf	22.20
40,000 to 59,999 sf	19.10
60,000 to 99,999 sf	16.45
More than 99,999 sf	15.25
High Tech/R&D	54.00

Net Lease Prices	Central City	Suburban
Less than 5,000 sf	-	6.00
5,000 to 19,999 sf	-	4.60
20,000 to 39,999 sf	-	4.20
40,000 to 59,999 sf	-	3.72
60,000 to 99,999 sf	-	3.40
More than 99,999 sf	-	3.00
High Tech/R&D	-	7.50

Vacancy Indicators	
Less than 5,000 sf	Substantial Oversupply
5,000 to 19,999 sf	Substantial Oversupply
20,000 to 39,999 sf	Substantial Oversupply
40,000 to 59,999 sf	Substantial Oversupply
60,000 to 99,999 sf	Substantial Oversupply
More than 99,999 sf	Substantial Oversupply
High Tech/R&D	Substantial Oversupply

Site Prices ($/sf)	Central City	Suburban
Improved Sites		
Less than 2 acres	-	15.00
2 to 5 acres	-	13.00
5 to 10 acres	-	10.00
More than 10 acres	-	n/a
Unimproved Sites		
Less than 10 acres	-	n/a
10 to 100 acres	-	n/a
More than 100 acres	-	n/a

Composition of Absorption	
Warehouse/Distribution	85%
Manufacturing	10%
High Tech/R&D	5%
Composition of Inventory	
Warehouse/Distribution	85%
Manufacturing	10%
High Tech/R&D	5%
Dollar Volume - Sales	
Warehouse/Distribution	Down 1-5%
Manufacturing	Down 6-10%
High Tech/R&D	Down 11-15%
Dollar Volume - Leases	
Warehouse/Distribution	Down 11-15%
Manufacturing	Down 11-15%
High Tech/R&D	Down 11-15%

Rate of Construction	
Warehouse/Distribution	Down 90%
Manufacturing	Down 90%
High Tech/R&D	Down 90%

Outlook

Sales Prices	
Warehouse/Distribution	Down 6-10%
Manufacturing	Down 6-10%
High Tech/R&D	Down 11-15%
Lease Prices	
Warehouse/Distribution	Down 1-5%
Manufacturing	Down 1-5%
High Tech/R&D	Down 1-5%
Site Prices	Down 11-15%
Absorption	
Warehouse/Distribution	Same
Manufacturing	Down 11-15%
High Tech/R&D	Down 11-15%
Construction	
Warehouse/Distribution	Down 6-10%
Manufacturing	Down 6-10%
High Tech/R&D	Down 6-10%
Dollar Volume - Sales	Same
Dollar Volume - Leases	Same

1992 Review

A rugged year of civil strife, bank mergers, and manufacturing contraction has tested the strength of the South Bay economy. Most industrial property owners suffered from falling rents and a lack of potential tenants. The rising cost of doing business has led several firms to leave the market in search of lower operating expenses and greater local political support. The result has been an increasing vacancy in every market segment.

1993 Forecast

The prospects facing the South Bay industrial market appear bleak for 1993. High costs are expected to force manufacturers to continue their mass exodus. The local SIOR reporter anticipates no speculative construction due to the lack of financing and demand and the high cost of land. The only bright spot in the area is port oriented activity. Los Angeles' role as a major import/export center is expected to improve as world economies continue to globalize.

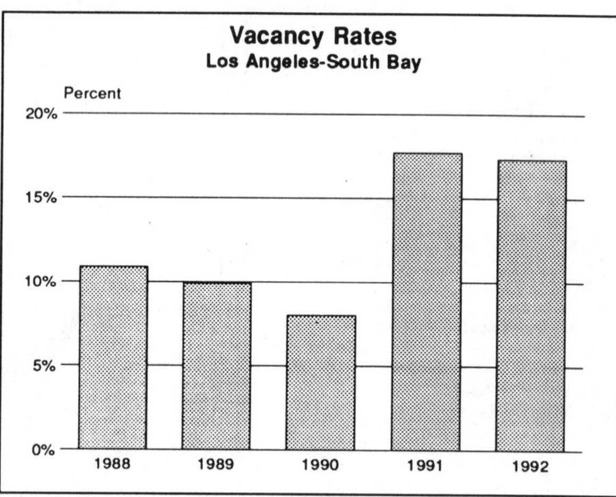

Los Angeles-West, California: Industrial

Los Angeles-West, California

Market Data

Inventory (sf)	Central City	Suburban
Total	n/a	-
Vacant	5,007,614	-
Vacancy Rates	n/a	-
Under Construction	0	-
Net Absorption	n/a	-

Prime Source of Financing: Insurance Companies

Mortgage Money Supply: Not Available

Sales Prices ($/sf)	Central City	Suburban
Less than 5,000 sf	60.00-110.00	-
5,000 to 19,999 sf	60.00-100.00	-
20,000 to 39,999 sf	50.00-90.00	-
40,000 to 59,999 sf	50.00-90.00	-
60,000 to 99,999 sf	50.00-90.00	-
More than 99,999 sf	50.00-90.00	-
High Tech/R&D	80.00-100.00	-

Construction Costs	
Less than 5,000 sf	40.00-50.00
5,000 to 19,999 sf	30.00-40.00
20,000 to 39,999 sf	30.00-40.00
40,000 to 59,999 sf	30.00-40.00
60,000 to 99,999 sf	20.00-40.00
More than 99,999 sf	20.00-40.00
High Tech/R&D	30.00-50.00

Net Lease Prices	Central City	Suburban
Less than 5,000 sf	4.80-14.00	-
5,000 to 19,999 sf	4.80-13.50	-
20,000 to 39,999 sf	4.80-13.00	-
40,000 to 59,999 sf	4.80-10.00	-
60,000 to 99,999 sf	4.80-9.00	-
More than 99,999 sf	4.80-8.00	-
High Tech/R&D	7.20-14.00	-

Vacancy Indicators	
Less than 5,000 sf	Moderate Oversupply
5,000 to 19,999 sf	Moderate Oversupply
20,000 to 39,999 sf	Moderate Oversupply
40,000 to 59,999 sf	Moderate Oversupply
60,000 to 99,999 sf	Moderate Oversupply
More than 99,999 sf	Moderate Oversupply
High Tech/R&D	Moderate Oversupply

Site Prices ($/sf)	Central City	Suburban
Improved Sites		
Less than 2 acres	15.00-50.00	-
2 to 5 acres	15.00-50.00	-
5 to 10 acres	15.00-50.00	-
More than 10 acres	15.00-50.00	-
Unimproved Sites		
Less than 10 acres	15.00-50.00	-
10 to 100 acres	15.00-50.00	-
More than 100 acres	n/a	-

Composition of Absorption	
Warehouse/Distribution	45%
Manufacturing	10%
High Tech/R&D	45%
Composition of Inventory	
Warehouse/Distribution	n/a
Manufacturing	n/a
High Tech/R&D	n/a
Dollar Volume - Sales	
Warehouse/Distribution	Down 60%
Manufacturing	Down 60%
High Tech/R&D	Down 60%
Dollar Volume - Leases	
Warehouse/Distribution	Down 11-15%
Manufacturing	Down 11-15%
High Tech/R&D	Down 11-15%

Rate of Construction	
Warehouse/Distribution	Down 80%
Manufacturing	Down 80%
High Tech/R&D	Down 80%

Outlook

Sales Prices	
Warehouse/Distribution	Down 20%
Manufacturing	Down 20%
High Tech/R&D	Down 20%
Lease Prices	
Warehouse/Distribution	Down 20%
Manufacturing	Down 20%
High Tech/R&D	Down 20%
Site Prices	Down 20%
Absorption	
Warehouse/Distribution	Down 11-15%
Manufacturing	Down 11-15%
High Tech/R&D	Down 11-15%
Construction	
Warehouse/Distribution	Down 80%
Manufacturing	Down 80%
High Tech/R&D	Down 80%
Dollar Volume - Sales	Down 70%
Dollar Volume - Leases	Down 20%

1992 Review

Industrial property owners in the West Los Angeles market had a difficult time leasing space in 1992. Demand slipped and the supply of vacant space on the market rose as layoffs continued in the electronics, aerospace, and defense industries. The local economy has been hard hit by the effects of plant relocations, job losses and falling real estate prices. In spite of an oversupply in every market segment, lease and sales prices fell only slightly. Aggregate transaction volumes were off sharply after beginning to slide in 1991.

1993 Forecast

The West Los Angeles market will experience virtually no development in 1993. Retrofits and remodeling will be the only form of construction in the coming year. While manufacturing firms continue to contract, warehouse, distribution, and service industries will produce some activity in the market. SIOR's observer reports market indicators point to another year of poor performance for West Los Angeles industrial property. Financing is nearly impossible to arrange, and even risk takers are concerned about the possibility of an extended free-fall in real estate values.

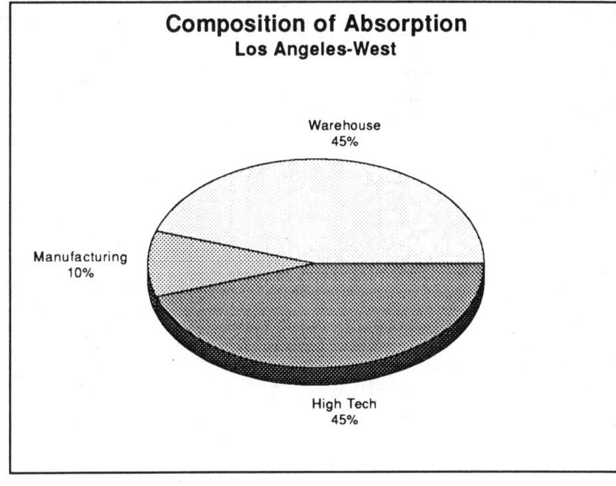

New York City, New York: Industrial

Manhattan, New York, New York (Generally represents loft buildings)

Market Data

Inventory (sf)	Central City	Suburban
Total	n/a	-
Vacant	n/a	-
Vacancy Rates	n/a	-
Under Construction	0	-
Net Absorption	n/a	-

Prime Source of Financing: Insurance Companies, Commercial Banks, Owner Financing

Mortgage Money Supply: Tight

Sales Prices ($/sf)	Central City	Suburban
Less than 5,000 sf	30.00-120.00	-
5,000 to 19,999 sf	30.00-120.00	-
20,000 to 39,999 sf	25.00-110.00	-
40,000 to 59,999 sf	25.00-110.00	-
60,000 to 99,999 sf	25.00-110.00	-
More than 99,999 sf	25.00-110.00	-
High Tech/R&D	n/a	-

Construction Costs	
Less than 5,000 sf	n/a
5,000 to 19,999 sf	n/a
20,000 to 39,999 sf	n/a
40,000 to 59,999 sf	n/a
60,000 to 99,999 sf	n/a
More than 99,999 sf	n/a
High Tech/R&D	n/a

Net Lease Prices	Central City	Suburban
Less than 5,000 sf	5.00-20.00	-
5,000 to 19,999 sf	5.00-20.00	-
20,000 to 39,999 sf	4.50-15.00	-
40,000 to 59,999 sf	4.50-15.00	-
60,000 to 99,999 sf	4.00-15.00	-
More than 99,999 sf	4.00-15.00	-
High Tech/R&D	n/a	-

Vacancy Indicators	
Less than 5,000 sf	Moderate Oversupply
5,000 to 19,999 sf	Moderate Oversupply
20,000 to 39,999 sf	Balanced Market
40,000 to 59,999 sf	Balanced Market
60,000 to 99,999 sf	Balanced Market
More than 99,999 sf	Moderate Shortage
High Tech/R&D	Substantial Shortage

Site Prices ($/sf)	Central City	Suburban
Improved Sites		
Less than 2 acres	n/a	-
2 to 5 acres	n/a	-
5 to 10 acres	n/a	-
More than 10 acres	n/a	-
Unimproved Sites		
Less than 10 acres	n/a	-
10 to 100 acres	n/a	-
More than 100 acres	n/a	-

Composition of Absorption	
Warehouse/Distribution	n/a
Manufacturing	n/a
High Tech/R&D	0%
Composition of Inventory	
Warehouse/Distribution	40%
Manufacturing	60%
High Tech/R&D	0%
Dollar Volume - Sales	
Warehouse/Distribution	Same
Manufacturing	Same
High Tech/R&D	Same
Dollar Volume - Leases	
Warehouse/Distribution	Down
Manufacturing	Down
High Tech/R&D	Down

Rate of Construction	
Warehouse/Distribution	Same
Manufacturing	Same
High Tech/R&D	Same

Outlook

Sales Prices	
Warehouse/Distribution	Same
Manufacturing	Same
High Tech/R&D	Same
Lease Prices	
Warehouse/Distribution	Down 1-5%
Manufacturing	Down 1-5%
High Tech/R&D	Same
Site Prices	Same
Absorption	
Warehouse/Distribution	Up 1-5%
Manufacturing	Up 1-5%
High Tech/R&D	Same
Construction	
Warehouse/Distribution	Same
Manufacturing	Same
High Tech/R&D	Same
Dollar Volume - Sales	Up 1-5%
Dollar Volume - Leases	Up 1-5%

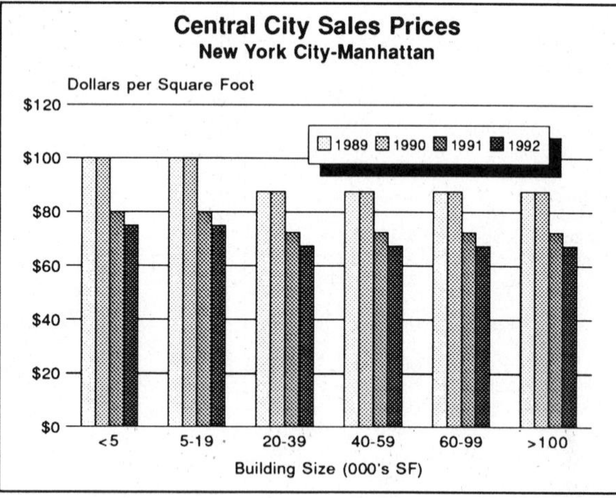

1992 Review

Manhattan's industrial inventory has evolved to two primary functions. The 2,500 to 10,000 sq. ft. single-story buildings are used as taxi fleet garages or auto repair and installation facilities. The larger multi-story loft buildings are used for light manufacturing, the printing trade, the garment industry, or warehouse/distribution functions. Due to a weak office market, loft buildings are no longer being converted to secondary or tertiary office use. Demand has declined slightly over the past year. Leasing is the only means of acquiring space due to the lack of inventory desirable to buyers.

1993 Forecast

New York City's industrial market will hold steady in 1993. Lease prices, which fell somewhat in 1992, will continue to drop moderately. Speculative development is not a factor in the market due to a lack of demand and available sites. The availability of off-shore investment capital has diminished. Relocations to the suburbs and to other New York City boroughs will continue moderately, as tenants take advantage of single-story buildings in these areas.

New York City-Bronx, New York: Industrial

New York City-Bronx, New York

Market Data

Inventory (sf)	Central City	Suburban
Total	30,000,000	-
Vacant	3,500,000	-
Vacancy Rates	11.7%	-
Under Construction	n/a	-
Net Absorption	-1,000,000	-

Prime Source of Financing: Commercial Banks, Owner Financing

Mortgage Money Supply: Not Available

Sales Prices ($/sf)	Central City	Suburban
Less than 5,000 sf	40.00	-
5,000 to 19,999 sf	35.00	-
20,000 to 39,999 sf	35.00	-
40,000 to 59,999 sf	35.00	-
60,000 to 99,999 sf	30.00	-
More than 99,999 sf	30.00	-
High Tech/R&D	n/a	-

Construction Costs	
Less than 5,000 sf	n/a
5,000 to 19,999 sf	n/a
20,000 to 39,999 sf	n/a
40,000 to 59,999 sf	n/a
60,000 to 99,999 sf	n/a
More than 99,999 sf	n/a
High Tech/R&D	n/a

Net Lease Prices	Central City	Suburban
Less than 5,000 sf	5.00	-
5,000 to 19,999 sf	4.50	-
20,000 to 39,999 sf	4.50	-
40,000 to 59,999 sf	4.50	-
60,000 to 99,999 sf	4.00	-
More than 99,999 sf	4.00	-
High Tech/R&D	3.50	-

Vacancy Indicators	
Less than 5,000 sf	Moderate Oversupply
5,000 to 19,999 sf	Moderate Oversupply
20,000 to 39,999 sf	Moderate Oversupply
40,000 to 59,999 sf	Moderate Oversupply
60,000 to 99,999 sf	Moderate Oversupply
More than 99,999 sf	Substantial Oversupply
High Tech/R&D	n/a

Site Prices ($/sf)	Central City	Suburban
Improved Sites		
Less than 2 acres	n/a	-
2 to 5 acres	n/a	-
5 to 10 acres	n/a	-
More than 10 acres	n/a	-
Unimproved Sites		
Less than 10 acres	n/a	-
10 to 100 acres	n/a	-
More than 100 acres	n/a	-

Composition of Absorption	
Warehouse/Distribution	70%
Manufacturing	25%
High Tech/R&D	5%
Composition of Inventory	
Warehouse/Distribution	70%
Manufacturing	25%
High Tech/R&D	5%
Dollar Volume - Sales	
Warehouse/Distribution	Down 25%
Manufacturing	Down 25%
High Tech/R&D	Down 25%
Dollar Volume - Leases	
Warehouse/Distribution	Down 25%
Manufacturing	Down 25%
High Tech/R&D	Down 25%

Rate of Construction	
Warehouse/Distribution	Down 11-15%
Manufacturing	Down 11-15%
High Tech/R&D	Down 11-15%

Outlook

Sales Prices	
Warehouse/Distribution	n/a
Manufacturing	n/a
High Tech/R&D	n/a
Lease Prices	
Warehouse/Distribution	n/a
Manufacturing	n/a
High Tech/R&D	n/a
Site Prices	n/a
Absorption	
Warehouse/Distribution	n/a
Manufacturing	n/a
High Tech/R&D	n/a
Construction	
Warehouse/Distribution	n/a
Manufacturing	n/a
High Tech/R&D	n/a
Dollar Volume - Sales	n/a
Dollar Volume - Leases	n/a

1992 Review

The Bronx industrial market is marked by an older inventory. The market is not growing but is holding steady. As one of New York City's five boroughs, the local facilities principally serve as distribution points for Manhattan. The Bronx also benefits from its supply of low-cost labor. The recession has taken its toll on the market, with falling prices and an oversupply in every market sector. Dollar volume of sales and leases continued its decline in 1992 with a 25 percent decrease in transaction volume.

1993 Forecast

The future of the Bronx industrial market is closely tied to the health of the New York economy. Even when New York does recover, there will be only a minor impact on the Bronx market due to its older generation space and a lack of available industrial sites. The lingering regional recession is expected to hold prices down. Loft buildings are especially hard to market. Local economic conditions and restrictive lending practices will make construction impossible in 1993.

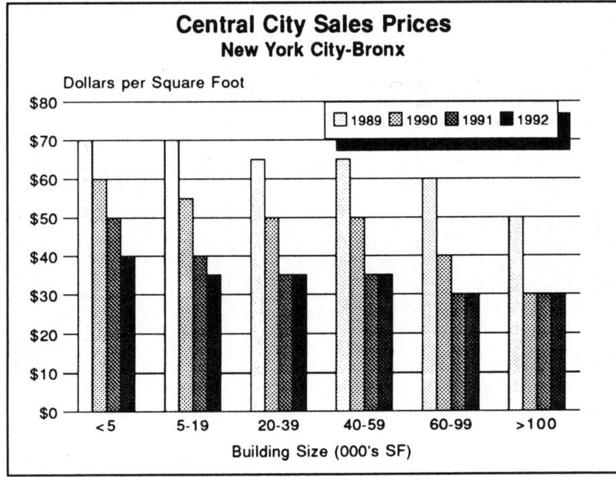

New York City-Brooklyn/Queens, New York: Industrial

New York City-Brooklyn/Queens, New York

Market Data

Inventory (sf)	Central City	Suburban
Total	330,000,000	-
Vacant	61,000,000	-
Vacancy Rates	18.5%	-
Under Construction	0	-
Net Absorption	-9,000,000	-

Prime Source of Financing: Owner Financing

Mortgage Money Supply: Tight

Sales Prices ($/sf)	Central City	Suburban
Less than 5,000 sf	25.00-35.00	-
5,000 to 19,999 sf	20.00-35.00	-
20,000 to 39,999 sf	20.00-35.00	-
40,000 to 59,999 sf	15.00-30.00	-
60,000 to 99,999 sf	10.00-30.00	-
More than 99,999 sf	10.00-25.00	-
High Tech/R&D	35.00-45.00	-

Construction Costs	
Less than 5,000 sf	45.00
5,000 to 19,999 sf	45.00
20,000 to 39,999 sf	40.00
40,000 to 59,999 sf	35.00
60,000 to 99,999 sf	35.00
More than 99,999 sf	35.00
High Tech/R&D	125.00

Gross Lease Prices	Central City	Suburban
Less than 5,000 sf	4.00-6.00	-
5,000 to 19,999 sf	3.50-5.00	-
20,000 to 39,999 sf	3.00-4.50	-
40,000 to 59,999 sf	2.75-4.00	-
60,000 to 99,999 sf	2.50-4.00	-
More than 99,999 sf	2.25-3.75	-
High Tech/R&D	4.00-5.00	-

Vacancy Indicators	
Less than 5,000 sf	Moderate Oversupply
5,000 to 19,999 sf	Substantial Oversupply
20,000 to 39,999 sf	Substantial Oversupply
40,000 to 59,999 sf	Substantial Oversupply
60,000 to 99,999 sf	Substantial Oversupply
More than 99,999 sf	Substantial Oversupply
High Tech/R&D	Moderate Oversupply

Site Prices ($/sf)	Central City	Suburban
Improved Sites		
Less than 2 acres	10.00-20.00	-
2 to 5 acres	10.00-15.00	-
5 to 10 acres	9.00-15.00	-
More than 10 acres	8.00-15.00	-
Unimproved Sites		
Less than 10 acres	n/a	-
10 to 100 acres	n/a	-
More than 100 acres	n/a	-

Rate of Construction	
Warehouse/Distribution	Down 90%
Manufacturing	Down 90%
High Tech/R&D	Down 100%

Composition of Absorption	
Warehouse/Distribution	80%
Manufacturing	18%
High Tech/R&D	2%
Composition of Inventory	
Warehouse/Distribution	65%
Manufacturing	30%
High Tech/R&D	5%
Dollar Volume - Sales	
Warehouse/Distribution	Down 35%
Manufacturing	Down 40%
High Tech/R&D	Down 25%
Dollar Volume - Leases	
Warehouse/Distribution	Down 30%
Manufacturing	Down 40%
High Tech/R&D	Down 30%

Outlook

Sales Prices	
Warehouse/Distribution	Down 11-15%
Manufacturing	Down 11-15%
High Tech/R&D	Down 20-25%
Lease Prices	
Warehouse/Distribution	Down 11-15%
Manufacturing	Down 20-25%
High Tech/R&D	Down 11-15%
Site Prices	Down 6-10%
Absorption	
Warehouse/Distribution	Down 6-10%
Manufacturing	Down 11-15%
High Tech/R&D	Down 11-15%
Construction	
Warehouse/Distribution	Down 90%
Manufacturing	Down 100%
High Tech/R&D	Down 100%
Dollar Volume - Sales	Down 20-25%
Dollar Volume - Leases	Down 20-25%

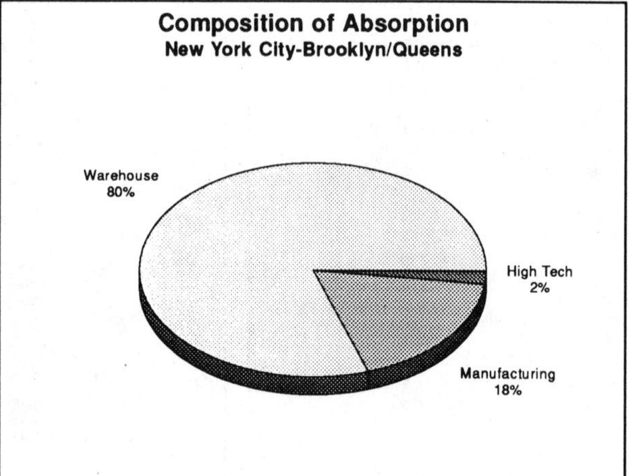

1992 Review

The demand for industrial space in Brooklyn and Queens continues to soften, marked by nine million sq. ft. of negative absorption in 1992. Only the most price-conscious transactions are taking place. Sales are more active than leasing with a majority of the financing being provided by the sellers. Most larger transactions are sales resulting from prices so reduced that carrying costs are equal to or less than rental charges for similar space. The majority of market activity is coming from lateral movement there are few exceptions.

1993 Forecast

The local and regional economy, which is service oriented and largely dependent on the financial markets, will trudge forward at a sluggish pace in 1993. Speculative development is nonexistent. If construction does take place in the market, it will be build-to-suit. The industrial market, which is driven primarily by warehouse users, will see a further decline in sales and lease prices in 1993. However, this is not expected to spark increased activity in the market.

New York-Nassau/Suffolk Counties, New York: Industrial

Nassau/Suffolk Counties, New York

Market Data

Inventory (sf)	Central City	Suburban
Total	-	233,000,000
Vacant	-	17,192,704
Vacancy Rates	-	7.4%
Under Construction	-	n/a
Net Absorption	-	-1,340,558

Prime Source of Financing: Commercial Banks, Pension Funds

Mortgage Money Supply: Ample

Sales Prices ($/sf)	Central City	Suburban
Less than 5,000 sf	-	50.00-60.00
5,000 to 19,999 sf	-	45.00-55.00
20,000 to 39,999 sf	-	40.00-50.00
40,000 to 59,999 sf	-	35.00-45.00
60,000 to 99,999 sf	-	33.00-43.00
More than 99,999 sf	-	25.00-35.00
High Tech/R&D	-	50.00

Construction Costs	
Less than 5,000 sf	n/a
5,000 to 19,999 sf	n/a
20,000 to 39,999 sf	n/a
40,000 to 59,999 sf	n/a
60,000 to 99,999 sf	n/a
More than 99,999 sf	n/a
High Tech/R&D	n/a

Net Lease Prices	Central City	Suburban
Less than 5,000 sf	-	4.75-6.25
5,000 to 19,999 sf	-	5.25-5.75
20,000 to 39,999 sf	-	4.75-5.50
40,000 to 59,999 sf	-	4.25-5.00
60,000 to 99,999 sf	-	4.00-4.50
More than 99,999 sf	-	3.75-4.25
High Tech/R&D	-	5.00-7.00

Vacancy Indicators	
Less than 5,000 sf	Moderate Oversupply
5,000 to 19,999 sf	Moderate Oversupply
20,000 to 39,999 sf	Moderate Oversupply
40,000 to 59,999 sf	Moderate Oversupply
60,000 to 99,999 sf	Moderate Oversupply
More than 99,999 sf	Moderate Oversupply
High Tech/R&D	Substantial Oversupply

Site Prices ($/sf)	Central City	Suburban
Improved Sites		
Less than 2 acres	-	n/a
2 to 5 acres	-	n/a
5 to 10 acres	-	n/a
More than 10 acres	-	n/a
Unimproved Sites		
Less than 10 acres	-	n/a
10 to 100 acres	-	n/a
More than 100 acres	-	n/a

Rate of Construction	
Warehouse/Distribution	Down
Manufacturing	Down
High Tech/R&D	Down

Composition of Absorption	
Warehouse/Distribution	70%
Manufacturing	20%
High Tech/R&D	10%
Composition of Inventory	
Warehouse/Distribution	50%
Manufacturing	30%
High Tech/R&D	20%
Dollar Volume - Sales	
Warehouse/Distribution	Up 11-15i%
Manufacturing	Up 6-10%
High Tech/R&D	Up 1-5%
Dollar Volume - Leases	
Warehouse/Distribution	Up 1-5%
Manufacturing	Up 1-5%
High Tech/R&D	Up 1-5%

Outlook

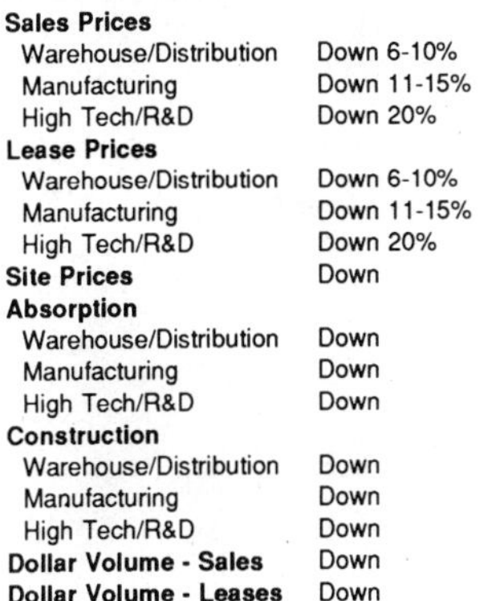

Sales Prices	
Warehouse/Distribution	Down 6-10%
Manufacturing	Down 11-15%
High Tech/R&D	Down 20%
Lease Prices	
Warehouse/Distribution	Down 6-10%
Manufacturing	Down 11-15%
High Tech/R&D	Down 20%
Site Prices	Down
Absorption	
Warehouse/Distribution	Down
Manufacturing	Down
High Tech/R&D	Down
Construction	
Warehouse/Distribution	Down
Manufacturing	Down
High Tech/R&D	Down
Dollar Volume - Sales	Down
Dollar Volume - Leases	Down

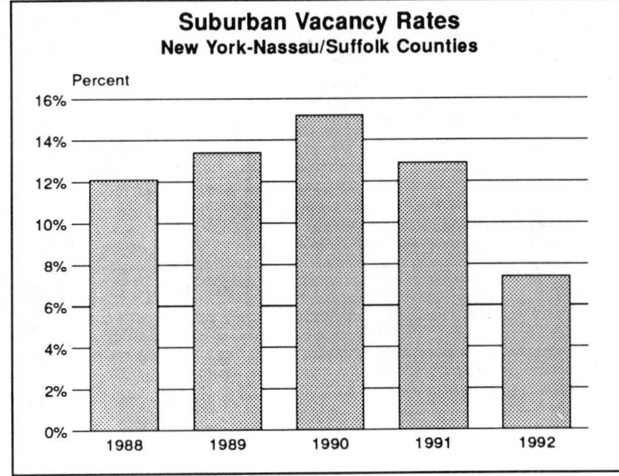

1992 Review

Activity in the Long Island industrial market improved in 1992. However, conditions are well below the very active market that was characteristic of the mid-1980s. Nassau and Suffolk counties continue to be saddled with an oversupply of quality high-tech buildings resulting from the decline of defense-related industry. The strongest demand is for warehouse buildings with high ceilings and multiple loading docks. Except in isolated situations, the sale of industrial sites has been totally stagnant.

1993 Forecast

The local defense economy will continue to struggle with layoffs. New construction will be limited to a few build-to-suits. An oversupply of vacant industrial buildings and lenders who are unwilling to supply funds to investor/landlords makes speculative industrial construction unlikely in 1993. Mortgage financing is available to only the most credit worthy space users. The outlook for the coming year is for a continued decline in sales and lease prices, especially in High Tech/R&D space.

New York-Rockland/Westchester Counties, New York: Industrial

New York-Rockland/Westchester Counties

Market Data

Inventory (sf)	Central City	Suburban
Total	-	35,000,000
Vacant	-	3,000,000
Vacancy Rates	-	8.6%
Under Construction	-	0
Net Absorption	-	0

Prime Source of Financing: Owner Financing

Mortgage Money Supply: Tight

Sales Prices ($/sf)	Central City	Suburban
Less than 5,000 sf	-	65.00
5,000 to 19,999 sf	-	55.00
20,000 to 39,999 sf	-	45.00
40,000 to 59,999 sf	-	40.00
60,000 to 99,999 sf	-	37.00
More than 99,999 sf	-	35.00
High Tech/R&D	-	80.00

Construction Costs	
Less than 5,000 sf	65.00
5,000 to 19,999 sf	55.00
20,000 to 39,999 sf	50.00
40,000 to 59,999 sf	45.00
60,000 to 99,999 sf	40.00
More than 99,999 sf	38.00
High Tech/R&D	80.00

Net Lease Prices	Central City	Suburban
Less than 5,000 sf	-	10.00
5,000 to 19,999 sf	-	8.50
20,000 to 39,999 sf	-	7.50
40,000 to 59,999 sf	-	7.00
60,000 to 99,999 sf	-	6.50
More than 99,999 sf	-	6.00
High Tech/R&D	-	12.00

Vacancy Indicators	
Less than 5,000 sf	Moderate Shortage
5,000 to 19,999 sf	Balanced Market
20,000 to 39,999 sf	Balanced Market
40,000 to 59,999 sf	Balanced Market
60,000 to 99,999 sf	Balanced Market
More than 99,999 sf	Balanced Market
High Tech/R&D	Balanced Market

Site Prices ($/sf)	Central City	Suburban
Improved Sites		
Less than 2 acres	-	n/a
2 to 5 acres	-	n/a
5 to 10 acres	-	n/a
More than 10 acres	-	n/a
Unimproved Sites		
Less than 10 acres	-	3.50-8.00
10 to 100 acres	-	3.00-8.00
More than 100 acres	-	n/a

Rate of Construction	
Warehouse/Distribution	Same
Manufacturing	Same
High Tech/R&D	Same

Composition of Absorption	
Warehouse/Distribution	80%
Manufacturing	10%
High Tech/R&D	10%
Composition of Inventory	
Warehouse/Distribution	75%
Manufacturing	15%
High Tech/R&D	10%
Dollar Volume - Sales	
Warehouse/Distribution	Same
Manufacturing	Same
High Tech/R&D	Same
Dollar Volume - Leases	
Warehouse/Distribution	Down 1-5%
Manufacturing	Down 1-5%
High Tech/R&D	Down 1-5%

Outlook

Sales Prices	
Warehouse/Distribution	Down 1-5%
Manufacturing	Down 1-5%
High Tech/R&D	Down 1-5%
Lease Prices	
Warehouse/Distribution	Down 1-5%
Manufacturing	Down 1-5%
High Tech/R&D	Down 1-5%
Site Prices	Down 1-5%
Absorption	
Warehouse/Distribution	Same
Manufacturing	Same
High Tech/R&D	Same
Construction	
Warehouse/Distribution	Same
Manufacturing	Same
High Tech/R&D	Same
Dollar Volume - Sales	Down 1-5%
Dollar Volume - Leases	Down 1-5%

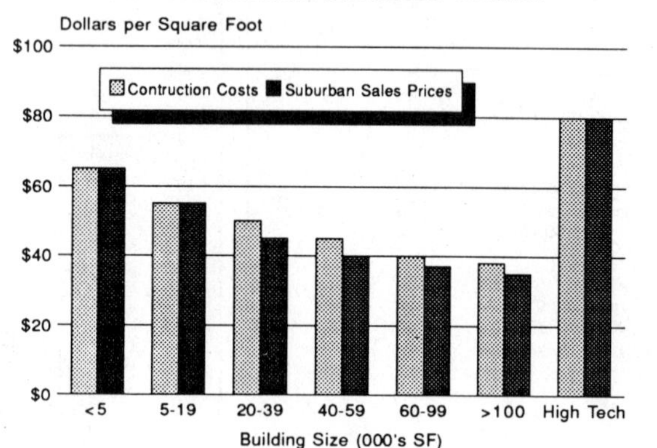

1992 Review

The local economy is still struggling through the recession. Lease and sales demand has not changed significantly from a year ago and vacancy remains stagnated at 8.6 percent. The local SIOR reporter foresees little evidence that the present state of the economy will improve soon, as layoffs by major employers, most notably IBM, continue. However, the modest volume of transactions has maintained a relatively well balanced market with a moderate shortage of lots of space smaller than 5,000 sq. ft.

1993 Forecast

Local market participants remain skeptical about the future of this industrial market. Indicators in 1993 point to less activity and declining prices. There is little chance of any speculative development getting underway in the coming year due to strict lending standards and cautious developers. Primary absorption will continue to come from warehouse/distribution users.

Office Real Estate Market: Selected Cities*

Atlanta, Georgia: Office

Atlanta, Georgia

Market Data

	Class A		Class B	
Inventory (sf)	**CBD**	**Outside CBD**	**CBD**	**Outside CBD**
Total	32,411,196	64,732,839	n/a	n/a
Vacant	5,404,891	9,075,613	n/a	n/a
Vacancy Rate	16.7%	14.0%	n/a	n/a
Vacant Sublease	394,137	1,539,000	n/a	n/a
Under Construction	0	335,000	n/a	n/a
Substantial Rehab	786,716	235,458	n/a	n/a
Net Absorption	1,334,997	1,535,610	n/a	n/a
Rental Rates ($/sf)				
Lowest	15.00	16.00	9.50	9.50
Highest	28.50	32.00	14.90	15.75
Weighted Average	22.51	21.53	12.76	12.91
Sales Prices ($/sf)				
Lowest	n/a	n/a	n/a	n/a
Highest	n/a	n/a	n/a	n/a
Weighted Average	n/a	n/a	n/a	n/a

Utility Rates: CBD $1.68 per sf; Outside CBD $1.68 per sf

Parking Ratio: CBD - 1 per 500 sf; Outside CBD - 1 per 250 sf

Standard Work Letter: n/a, typically based on dollars per square foot

Operating Cost Escalation: Base Year

Rate of Return: n/a

Cumulative Discount Rate: 20%

Landlord Concessions
- Rental Abatement
- Lease Assumptions
- Moving Allowance
- Interior Improvements
- Club Memberships

Leasing Activity Profile

Major Activity
- Fortune 500 Firms
- Legal/Accounting
- Insurance
- Finance/Banking
- Government

Minor Activity
- Business Services
- Sales

Mortgage Money Supply: Tight

Prime Source of Financing: Insurance Companies

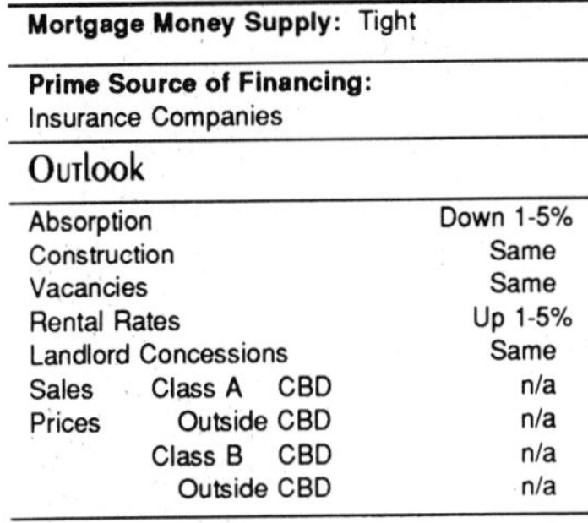

Outlook

Absorption		Down 1-5%
Construction		Same
Vacancies		Same
Rental Rates		Up 1-5%
Landlord Concessions		Same
Sales Prices	Class A CBD	n/a
	Outside CBD	n/a
	Class B CBD	n/a
	Outside CBD	n/a

1992 Review

Absorption of office space in Atlanta rose to nearly three million sq. ft. in 1992, nearly double the 1991 total. Leasing in the two towers completed downtown this year contributed to the net increase in occupied stock, as did a number of deals signed for sublease space. Highly reduced rental rates were largely responsible for the increased activity in the re-let market. Despite the increase in absorption, however, the vacancy rate in the CBD rose in 1992, as new construction outstripped demand by almost two to one. Atlanta's suburban office markets fared better; although just over one million sq. ft. of new space was added in 1992, the vacancy rate fell to an average of 14 percent.

1993 Forecast

Although absorption is projected to decline slightly in 1993, the virtual absence of new construction should allow the market to improve. Already, large blocks of contiguous space, especially in the Perimeter and Northwest areas, are hard to come by. Atlanta's economy is expected to pick up steam as the 1996 Olympics approach, increasing the number of area jobs that could contribute in an indirect way to added demand for office space. Landlord concessions, which currently reduce asking rents by an average of 20 percent, are not likely to diminish in 1993, but asking rents should rise by a range of one to five percent, in the judgement of SIOR's local researcher.

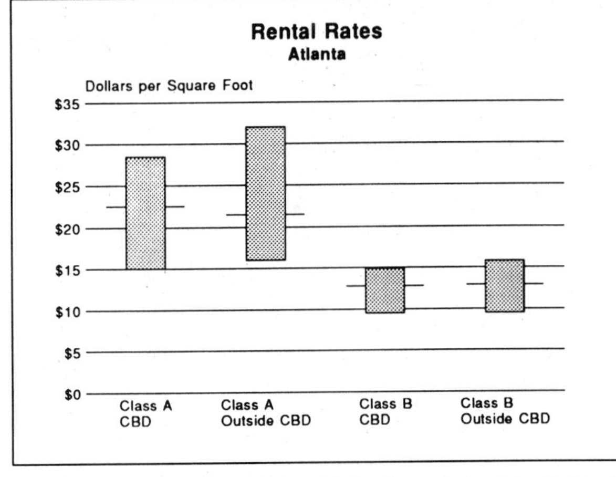

Source: Reprinted from *Comparative Statistics of Industrial and Office Real Estate Markets* (1993) with permission of the Society of Industrial and Office REALTORS®.

* See Glossary of Terms on page 622.

Chicago, Illinois: Office

Chicago, Illinois

Market Data

	Class A		Class B	
Inventory (sf)	**CBD**	**Outside CBD**	**CBD**	**Outside CBD**
Total	51,914,503	24,676,937	44,377,469	31,766,728
Vacant	12,749,314	4,536,479	10,125,084	6,983,698
Vacancy Rate	24.6%	18.4%	22.8%	22.0%
Vacant Sublease	1,420,429	644,292	1,450,252	434,545
Under Construction	0	0	0	70,000
Substantial Rehab	0	0	0	0
Net Absorption	-1,460,000	443,979	-1,700,808	-156,587
Rental Rates ($/sf)				
Lowest	22.65	18.50	14.00	10.00
Highest	47.00	33.69	24.00	23.00
Weighted Average	33.45	25.67	21.21	20.10
Sales Prices ($/sf)				
Lowest	n/a	35.00	n/a	25.00
Highest	n/a	75.00	n/a	50.00
Weighted Average	n/a	n/a	n/a	n/a

Utility Rates: CBD $1.40 per sf; Outside CBD $0.75 per sf; Separately Metered

Parking Ratio: CBD - n/a; Outside CBD - 1 per 250 sf

Standard Work Letter: $17.50 per sf, typically based on dollars per square foot

Operating Cost Escalation: Base Year - Varies, Net Lease w/Passthrough

Rate of Return: n/a

Cumulative Discount Rate: 10-50%

Landlord Concessions
- Parking
- Rental Abatement
- Lease Assumptions
- Moving Allowance
- Interior Improvements
- Architectural

Leasing Activity Profile

Major Activity
- Fortune 500 Firms
- Legal/Accounting
- Insurance

Minor Activity
- Business Services
- Sales
- Finance/Banking
- Engineering/Architecture
- Government

Mortgage Money Supply: Tight

Prime Source of Financing: Commercial Banks, Owner Financing

Outlook

Absorption		n/a
Construction		Same
Vacancies		Down 1-5%
Rental Rates		Same
Landlord Concessions		Same
Sales Prices	Class A CBD	Same
	Outside CBD	Same
	Class B CBD	Same
	Outside CBD	Same

1992 Review

The pool of vacant space continued to swell in metropolitan Chicago, rising to more than 34 million sq. ft. during 1992. Major relocations to the suburbs by Sears Roebuck & Company and Ameritech, as well as cutbacks at AT&T have had a tremendous impact on the CBD, returning large blocks of space to the market just as 4.6 million sq. ft. of new space came on line. The result was a downtown vacancy rate of more than 24 percent in the Class "A" market. Although leasing remained brisk, most of the activity involved renegotiations of existing leases or upgrades to higher quality space, resulting in few gains in occupied space. Rental rates, which ranged from $10.00 to $47.00 marketwide, were reduced by as much 50 percent once landlord concessions were taken into account.

1993 Forecast

Based on econometric forecasts, job growth in the Chicago MSA should gain momentum in 1993. Many of these new positions will be office-using, which should help to reduce some of the excess supply burdening most of the market. With the end of the latest building cycle, it is unlikely that downtown Chicago will see new development for at least three to five years, providing a welcome respite for property owners. Construction could resume in the suburbs, but nearly all activity to date has been in build-to-suits. During 1993, early renegotiations of leases should remain widespread as tenants attempt to capitalize on soft market conditions.

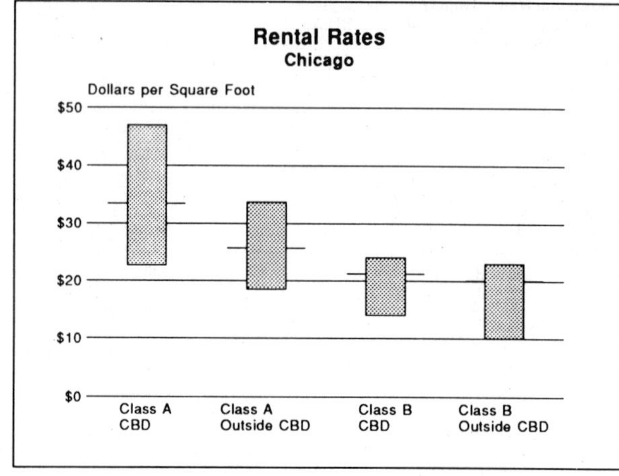

Houston, Texas: Office

Houston, Texas

Market Data

Inventory (sf)	Class A CBD	Class A Outside CBD	Class B CBD	Class B Outside CBD
Total	25,200,000	34,337,000	8,890,000	66,744,000
Vacant	3,518,000	4,210,000	2,901,000	18,522,000
Vacancy Rate	14.0%	12.3%	32.6%	27.8%
Vacant Sublease	600,000	1,450,000	200,000	1,700,000
Under Construction	0	1,533,000	0	0
Substantial Rehab	n/a	n/a	n/a	n/a
Net Absorption	-85,000	1,032,000	-367,000	1,660,000
Rental Rates ($/sf)				
Lowest	13.55	11.20	10.20	9.69
Highest	24.00	16.38	15.32	14.00
Weighted Average	16.64	13.38	12.26	11.69
Sales Prices ($/sf)				
Lowest	50.00	n/a	21.00	n/a
Highest	97.00	n/a	45.00	n/a
Weighted Average	77.00	n/a	35.00	n/a

Utility Rates: CBD n/a; Outside CBD n/a; Not Separately Metered

Parking Ratio: CBD - 1 per 1,500 sf; Outside CBD - 1 per 275 sf

Standard Work Letter: $11.00 per sf, typically based on dollars per square foot

Operating Cost Escalation: Base Year

Rate of Return: 10.00%

Cumulative Discount Rate: 5-15%

Landlord Concessions
- Parking
- Lease Assumptions
- Moving Allowance
- Interior Improvements
- Club Memberships

Leasing Activity Profile

Major Activity
- Legal/Accounting
- Insurance
- Business Services
- Engineering/Architecture
- Medical

Minor Activity
- Fortune 500 Firms
- Sales
- Government
- Energy

Mortgage Money Supply: Ample

Prime Source of Financing: Insurance Companies

Outlook

Absorption	Up 1-5%
Construction	Up 1-5%
Vacancies	Down 1-5%
Rental Rates	Up 1-5%
Landlord Concessions	Up 6-10%
Sales Prices Class A CBD	Same
Class A Outside CBD	Up 1-5%
Class B CBD	Same
Class B Outside CBD	Down 1-5%

1992 Review

Demand fell below anticipated levels in 1992 due to oil and gas cutbacks. Although Houston's economy is far more diversified than it was five years ago, energy still plays a significant role in the economy. Since local gas and oil companies are dependent on a healthy nation, gains in Houston's office market demand are tied to the U.S. recovery. After two years of modest improvement, lackluster demand caused rents to flatten in 1992, but concessions have dropped as well. Free rent has been virtually eliminated in Houston, with landlords preferring to offer a lower base rate rather than forego revenue in the early months or years of the lease.

1993 Forecast

With the acceleration of the national recovery in 1993, conditions in Houston's office market are also expected to improve. Steady expansion in the engineering industry, as well as growth in the more traditional office-using sectors of FIRE and services, should contribute. Following the completion of four new projects under construction in 1992, no new speculative development has been proposed. However, the declining availability of large blocks of contiguous Class "A" space has sparked interest in the build-to-suit market.

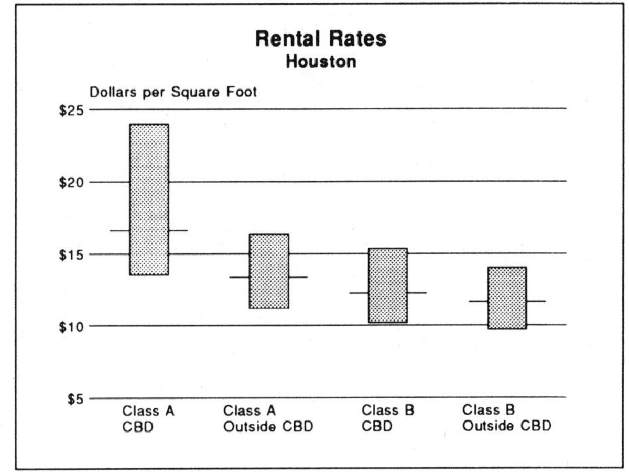

Los Angeles-Central, California: Office

Downtown Los Angeles, California

Market Data

Inventory (sf)	Class A CBD	Class A Outside CBD	Class B CBD	Class B Outside CBD
Total	24,975,218	-	6,224,949	-
Vacant	6,870,884	-	1,456,461	-
Vacancy Rate	27.5%	-	23.4%	-
Vacant Sublease	n/a	-	n/a	-
Under Construction	0	-	0	-
Substantial Rehab	n/a	-	n/a	-
Net Absorption	45,697	-	31,173	-
Rental Rates ($/sf)				
Lowest	18.99	-	12.00	-
Highest	40.00	-	20.00	-
Weighted Average	26.00	-	16.00	-
Sales Prices ($/sf)				
Lowest	n/a	-	n/a	-
Highest	n/a	-	n/a	-
Weighted Average	n/a	-	n/a	-

Utility Rates: CBD $2.30 per sf; Outside CBD n/a; Not Separately Metered

Parking Ratio: CBD - 1 per 1,000 sf; Outside CBD - n/a

Standard Work Letter: n/a, typically based on dollars per square foot

Operating Cost Escalation: Base Year

Rate of Return: n/a

Cumulative Discount Rate: 15-20%

Landlord Concessions
- Rental Abatement
- Lease Assumptions
- Interior Improvements

Leasing Activity Profile

Major Activity
- Insurance
- Government

Minor Activity
- Fortune 500 Firms
- Legal/Accounting
- Business Services
- Finance/Banking
- Engineering/Architecture

Mortgage Money Supply: Not Available

Prime Source of Financing:

Outlook

Absorption	Up 1-5%
Construction	n/a
Vacancies	Down 1-5%
Rental Rates	Up 1-5%
Landlord Concessions	Down 1-5%
Sales Prices Class A CBD	n/a
Outside CBD	n/a
Class B CBD	n/a
Outside CBD	n/a

1992 Review

With the completion of approximately 3.4 million sq. ft. in 1992, the building boom in downtown Los Angeles has finally come to an end. Over the last several years, more than 10 million sq. ft. of new offices have risen in downtown Los Angeles, changing the city's skyline and flooding the market with new supply. As of late 1992, an estimated 26 percent of the market was unoccupied, almost all of which was concentrated in Class "A" properties. Despite Los Angeles' crippled economy, net absorption remained positive in 1992, reaching 1.7 million sq. ft. According to SIOR's reporter, buildings completed within the last two to three years captured the majority of leasing activity last year.

1993 Forecast

Downtown Los Angeles enters 1993 a severely overbuilt office market. Moreover, as L.A. struggles through another troubled year, consolidations and business failures will return still more space to the market. But given the wide variety of new buildings and the steep decline in asking rents, many of Los Angeles' healthier firms are expected to sign leases this year, taking advantage of the tenants' market. Such gains are projected to offset downsizing elsewhere in the market, producing a slight increase in net absorption in 1993. Since no new construction is underway, this rise in demand should lower the vacancy rate somewhat over the next 12 months.

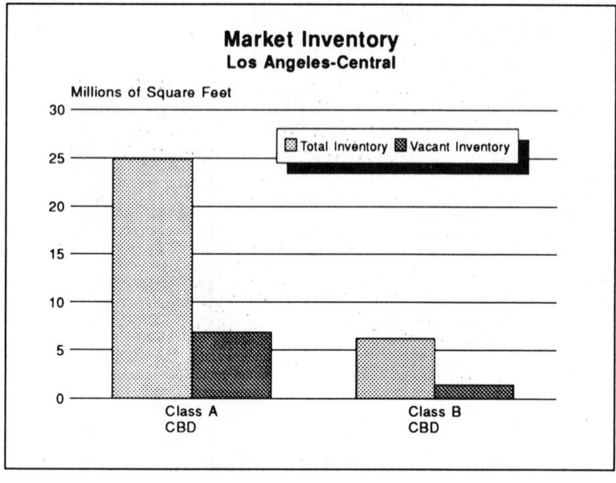

Los Angeles-Orange County, California: Office

Los Angeles-Orange County, California

Market Data

Inventory (sf)	Class A CBD	Class A Outside CBD	Class B CBD	Class B Outside CBD
Total	54,496,689	-	-	-
Vacant	11,524,937	-	-	-
Vacancy Rate	21.1%	-	-	-
Vacant Sublease	939,514	-	-	-
Under Construction	0	-	-	-
Substantial Rehab	n/a	-	-	-
Net Absorption	1,156,285	-	-	-
Rental Rates ($/sf)				
Lowest	19.25	15.00	16.25	15.00
Highest	33.40	20.50	24.50	18.50
Weighted Average	n/a	n/a	n/a	n/a
Sales Prices ($/sf)				
Lowest	72.00	66.70	51.90	50.00
Highest	110.00	88.60	100.00	90.00
Weighted Average	n/a	n/a	n/a	n/a

Utility Rates: CBD $1.65-1.75 per sf; Outside CBD n/a; Not Separately Metered

Parking Ratio: CBD - 1 per 250 sf; Outside CBD - 1 per 250 sf

Standard Work Letter: $26.00 per sf, typically based on dollars per squre foot

Operating Cost Escalation: Base Year

Rate of Return: 10.25%

Cumulative Discount Rate: 15%

Landlord Concessions
- Parking
- Lease Assumptions
- Moving Allowance
- Interior Improvements
- Lower Contract Rents

Leasing Activity Profile

Major Activity
- Legal/Accounting
- Insurance
- Government
- Energy

Minor Activity
- Fortune 500 Firms
- Business Services
- Sales
- Finance/Banking
- Engineering/Architecture

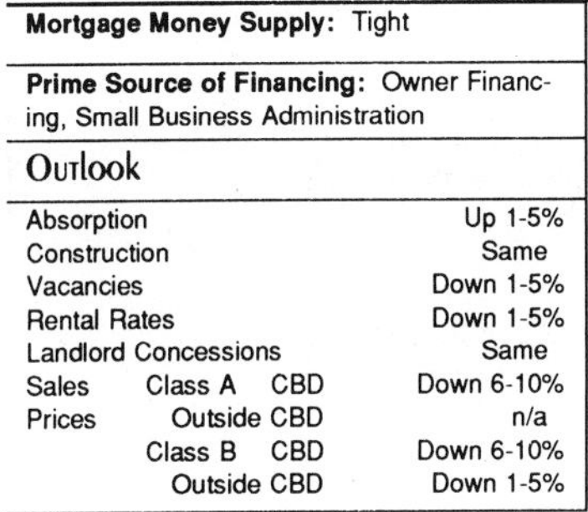

Mortgage Money Supply: Tight

Prime Source of Financing: Owner Financing, Small Business Administration

Outlook

Absorption		Up 1-5%
Construction		Same
Vacancies		Down 1-5%
Rental Rates		Down 1-5%
Landlord Concessions		Same
Sales Prices	Class A CBD	Down 6-10%
	Outside CBD	n/a
	Class B CBD	Down 6-10%
	Outside CBD	Down 1-5%

1992 Review

With more than 11 million sq. ft. of unoccupied space, representing a vacancy rate of 21.1 percent, Orange County's office market ended 1992 substantially overbuilt. After several years of heavy new construction, office properties faced stiff competition for tenants last year in a market that was also hounded by a troubled economy. SIOR's correspondents report that demand for office space was down in 1992 for a third consecutive year as a result of significant employment losses. Downsizing by insurance, communications, and financial firms limited net absorption to just over one million sq. ft. in 1992. Other firms, especially those involved in back-office operations, have left the county altogether, relocating to areas with lower wage, tax, and living costs.

1993 Forecast

The outlook for Orange County's office market in 1993 is clouded by ominous signals of long-term economic restructuring. With an estimated 20 percent of the workforce employed in manufacturing, much of it defense-related, the additional cutbacks proposed in federal spending do not bode well for the MSA's economic health. On the bright side, Orange County's high concentration of talented scientists and engineers makes it a prime location for high-tech firms with commercial applications. Office market conditions are not likely to change dramatically in 1993.

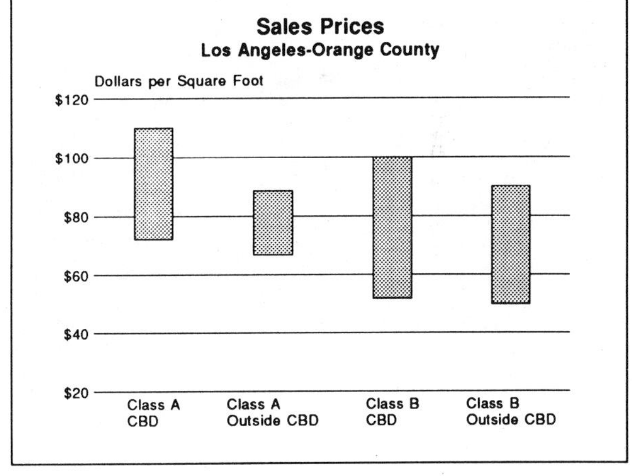

Los Angeles-San Bernardino County, California: Office

Ontario, Riverside, and San Bernardino (Inland Empire), California

Market Data

	Class A		Class B	
Inventory (sf)	**CBD**	**Outside CBD**	**CBD**	**Outside CBD**
Total	460,425	1,540,213	2,049,592	4,875,371
Vacant	145,700	387,541	265,438	1,267,256
Vacancy Rate	31.6%	25.2%	13.0%	26.0%
Vacant Sublease	n/a	n/a	n/a	n/a
Under Construction	0	71,069	0	0
Substantial Rehab	n/a	n/a	n/a	n/a
Net Absorption	68,170	226,797	109,465	251,050
Rental Rates ($/sf)				
Lowest	21.00	16.20	12.00	12.00
Highest	23.40	21.60	19.80	18.60
Weighted Average	22.32	17.64	16.56	15.60
Sales Prices ($/sf)				
Lowest	122.12	71.44	n/a	53.13
Highest	122.12	127.02	n/a	122.34
Weighted Average	122.12	80.38	n/a	81.93

Utility Rates: CBD $1.44 per sf; Outside CBD $1.51 per sf; Not Separately Metered

Parking Ratio: CBD - 1 per 250 sf; Outside CBD - 1 per 250 sf

Standard Work Letter: $20.00 per sf, typically based on dollars per square foot

Operating Cost Escalation: Base Year and Stop - $6.00

Rate of Return: 10.00%

Cumulative Discount Rate: 12.5%

Landlord Concessions
- Parking
- Rental Abatement
- Interior Improvements

Leasing Activity Profile

Major Activity
- Legal/Accounting
- Insurance

Minor Activity
- Fortune 500 Firms
- Business Services
- Sales
- Finance/Banking
- Engineering/Architecture
- Government
- Energy

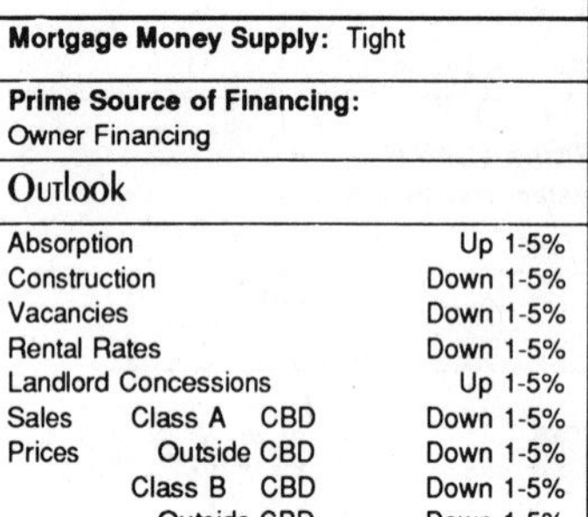

Mortgage Money Supply: Tight

Prime Source of Financing:
Owner Financing

Outlook

Absorption		Up 1-5%
Construction		Down 1-5%
Vacancies		Down 1-5%
Rental Rates		Down 1-5%
Landlord Concessions		Up 1-5%
Sales Prices	Class A CBD	Down 1-5%
	Outside CBD	Down 1-5%
	Class B CBD	Down 1-5%
	Outside CBD	Down 1-5%

1992 Review

Despite seemingly unending expansion in the 1980s, the San Bernardino-Riverside MSA joined California and the rest of the nation in the '90s recession. Benefiting from the high costs and congestion of the Los Angeles and Orange County markets, San Bernardino-Riverside's population increased by 82 percent during the last decade, fueling rapid growth in the construction, FIRE, trade, and services sectors. Still largely a bedroom community, however, San Bernardino's health is tied to the economies of Los Angeles and Anaheim, both of which were severely distressed in 1992. In response to slower job growth, net absorption dropped to 655,000 sq. ft. in 1992, roughly half the 1991 total.

1993 Forecast

For truly strong job growth to resume in the San Bernardino-Riverside MSA, the Southern California coastal economies must first return to health. Given the myriad problems debilitating these areas, recovery during 1993 does not seem likely. Still, with lower housing and labor costs than its neighbors to the west, San Bernardino will record modest gains in the coming year, enough to support a slight rise in the office market's occupancy rate. Steady leasing among insurance and legal firms should allow for a noticeable drop in vacant stock. Two new projects could go forward in 1993: a 72,000 sq. ft. building in the Tri-City market and a 60,000 sq. ft. property on Haven Avenue in Ontario.

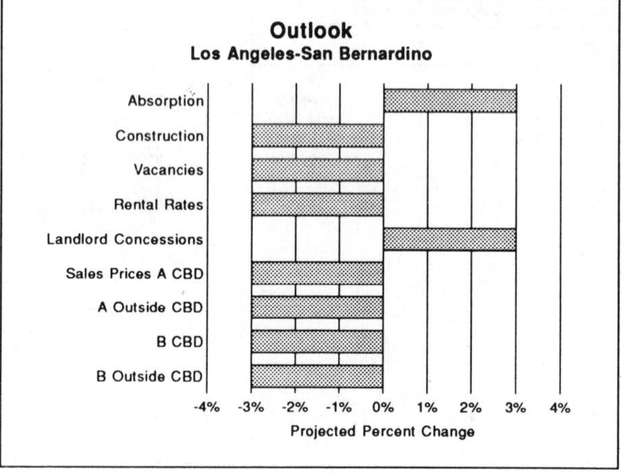

Los Angeles-San Fernando Valley, California: Office

Los Angeles-San Fernando Valley, California

Market Data

	Class A		Class B	
Inventory (sf)	**CBD**	**Outside CBD**	**CBD**	**Outside CBD**
Total	-	17,000,000	-	6,640,000
Vacant	-	2,750,000	-	840,000
Vacancy Rate	-	16.2%	-	12.7%
Vacant Sublease	-	n/a	-	n/a
Under Construction	-	n/a	-	n/a
Substantial Rehab	-	n/a	-	n/a
Net Absorption	-	544,000	-	539,000
Rental Rates ($/sf)				
Lowest	-	22.00	-	17.00
Highest	-	28.00	-	22.50
Weighted Average	-	25.00	-	20.00
Sales Prices ($/sf)				
Lowest	-	195.00	-	125.00
Highest	-	285.00	-	175.00
Weighted Average	-	250.00	-	150.00

Utility Rates: CBD n/a
Outside CBD $1.00 per sf
Not Separately Metered

Parking Ratio: CBD - n/a
Outside CBD - 1 per 250 sf

Standard Work Letter: $21.00 per sf, typically based on dollars per square foot

Operating Cost Escalation: Base Year

Rate of Return: 10.00%

Cumulative Discount Rate: 8%

Landlord Concessions
- Rental Abatement
- Interior Improvements

Leasing Activity Profile

Major Activity
- Aerospace

Minor Activity
- Fortune 500 Firms
- Legal/Accounting
- Insurance
- Government

Mortgage Money Supply: Tight

Prime Source of Financing: Vulture Funds

Outlook

Absorption	Up 1-5%
Construction	Up 1-5%
Vacancies	Up 11-15%
Rental Rates	Same
Landlord Concessions	Same
Sales Prices Class A CBD	n/a
Outside CBD	Same
Class B CBD	n/a
Outside CBD	Same

1992 Review

Despite the dizzying job losses in the Los Angeles economy, demand for San Fernando Valley office space was fairly strong in 1992, totaling just over one million sq. ft. While massive lay-offs by Los Angeles' aerospace manufacturers is wreaking havoc on the general economy, employment among the San Fernando Valley's office users remained fairly stable. Vacancy rates in the Class "A" market did increase over the year in response to new supply, but only marginally. In the Class "B" market, demand for lower-priced space helped to shore up occupancy levels, holding the vacancy rate steady despite some downsizing by back-office space users.

1993 Forecast

Although net absorption is projected to rise slightly in 1993, the overall vacancy rate in the San Fernando Valley is also likely to increase as the full force of Los Angeles' recession hits the market. While job losses in manufacturing dominated the declines in 1992, cutbacks in other sectors will continue in 1993, affecting demand for office space. According to SIOR's reporter, vacancy rates in the San Fernando Valley could rise significantly in 1993.

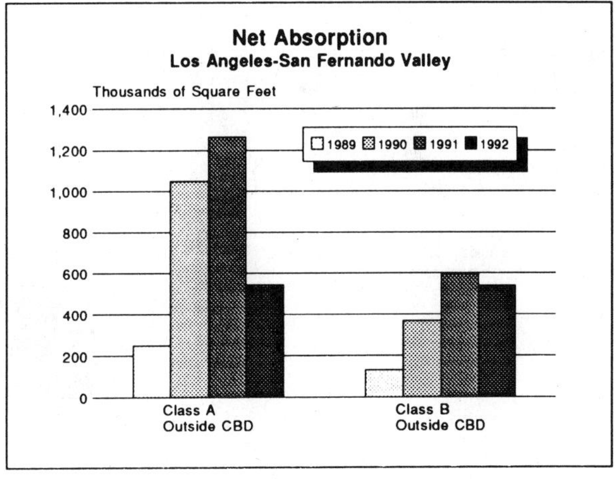

Los Angeles-San Gabriel Valley, California: Office

Los Angeles-San Gabriel Valley

Market Data

	Class A		Class B	
Inventory (sf)	**CBD**	**Outside CBD**	**CBD**	**Outside CBD**
Total	-	3,200,000	-	5,250,000
Vacant	-	325,000	-	1,451,250
Vacancy Rate	-	10.2%	-	27.6%
Vacant Sublease	-	35,000	-	45,000
Under Construction	-	0	-	0
Substantial Rehab	-	0	-	0
Net Absorption	-	355,000	-	-251,250
Rental Rates ($/sf)				
Lowest	-	18.60	-	15.00
Highest	-	21.60	-	18.00
Weighted Average	-	19.80	-	16.20
Sales Prices ($/sf)				
Lowest	-	95.00	-	55.00
Highest	-	125.00	-	95.00
Weighted Average	-	105.00	-	75.00

Utility Rates: CBD n/a
Outside CBD $2.25 per sf
Not Separately Metered

Parking Ratio: CBD - n/a
Outside CBD - 1 per 250 sf

Standard Work Letter: $23.00 per sf, typically based on dollars per square foot

Operating Cost Escalation: Base Year

Rate of Return: 11.25%

Cumulative Discount Rate: 12-15%

Landlord Concessions
- Parking
- Rental Abatement
- Interior Improvements

Leasing Activity Profile

Major Activity
- Insurance
- Sales
- Engineering/Architecture
- Government

Minor Activity
- Fortune 500 Firms
- Legal/Accounting
- Business Services
- Finance/Banking
- Energy

Mortgage Money Supply: Tight

Prime Source of Financing: n/a

Outlook

Absorption		Same
Construction		Same
Vacancies		Down 1-5%
Rental Rates		Same
Landlord Concessions		Same
Sales Prices	Class A CBD	n/a
	Outside CBD	Same
	Class B CBD	n/a
	Outside CBD	Same

1992 Review

San Gabriel Valley's 8.3 million sq. ft. office market treaded water in 1992, with just 150,000 sq. ft. added to the inventory and only 104,000 sq. ft. absorbed. The composite vacancy rate for Class "A" and "B" properties edged up to 21.0 percent, compared to 20.8 percent in 1991. While leasing activity had a limited net effect in the overall market, important shifts took place between older and newer properties. San Gabriel's three million sq. ft. Class "A" submarket tightened significantly in 1992, with the vacancy rate dropping seven percentage points to 10.2 percent. By contrast, negative net absorption of 250,000 sq. ft. in Class "B" properties pushed the vacancy rate up five percentage points to 27.6 percent.

1993 Forecast

Further retrenchment of the Los Angeles economy in 1993 will continue to depress San Gabriel Valley's office market. Cutbacks by area banks and insurance firms will limit the number of back-office jobs added in San Gabriel while the faltering aerospace industry will hurt its manufacturing sector. Aggressive environmental legislature is also having an impact on area producers, prompting many to leave the state. Given these setbacks, another stagnant year is forecasted for the office market. Essentially no change in absorption or rental rates is likely to occur in 1993, but the absence of new construction should allow for some reduction in the Class "A" vacancy rate.

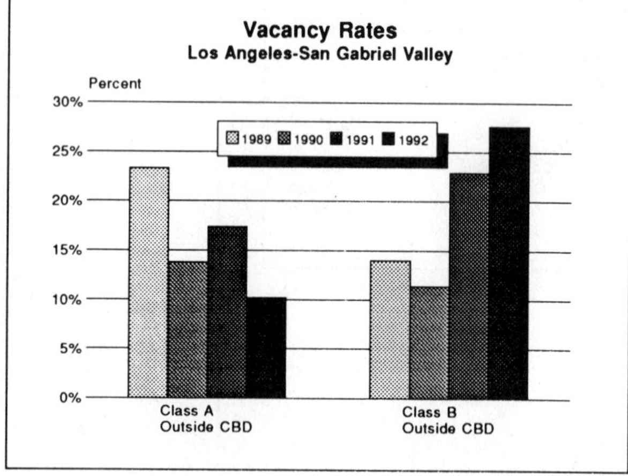

Los Angeles-South Bay, California: Office

Los Angeles - South Bay, California

Market Data

Inventory (sf)	Class A CBD	Class A Outside CBD	Class B CBD	Class B Outside CBD
Total	-	15,270,796	-	14,958,973
Vacant	-	3,324,495	-	3,375,160
Vacancy Rate	-	21.8%	-	22.6%
Vacant Sublease	-	644,044	-	346,377
Under Construction	-	206,500	-	0
Substantial Rehab	-	0	-	0
Net Absorption	-	194,941	-	-123,498
Rental Rates ($/sf)				
Lowest	-	12.00	-	10.44
Highest	-	36.00	-	25.20
Weighted Average	-	21.72	-	17.16
Sales Prices ($/sf)				
Lowest	-	60.00	-	50.00
Highest	-	100.00	-	60.00
Weighted Average	-	n/a	-	n/a

Utility Rates: CBD n/a; Outside CBD $1.80 per sf; Not Separately Metered

Parking Ratio: CBD - n/a; Outside CBD - 1 per 250 sf

Standard Work Letter: $30.00 per sf, typically based on dollars per square foot

Operating Cost Escalation: Base Year

Rate of Return: 11.00%

Cumulative Discount Rate: 20-30%

Landlord Concessions
- Parking
- Rental Abatement
- Lease Assumptions
- Moving Allowance
- Interior Improvements
- Signing Bonuses

Leasing Activity Profile

Major Activity
- Legal/Accounting
- Government
- Transportation

Minor Activity
- Fortune 500 Firms
- Insurance
- Business Services
- Energy

Mortgage Money Supply: Tight

Prime Source of Financing: Owner Financing

Outlook

Absorption		Same
Construction		Down 90%
Vacancies		Down 1-5%
Rental Rates		Same
Landlord Concessions		Same
Sales Prices	Class A CBD	n/a
	Outside CBD	Same
	Class B CBD	n/a
	Outside CBD	Same

1992 Review

During 1992, the University of California, Los Angeles, reported that the state was in its worst slump since the 1930s. Cutbacks in defense spending, falling real estate prices, natural disasters (earthquakes, droughts, wildfires), and the riots in Los Angeles combined to severely depress the state's economy. According to Dun & Bradstreet, California led the nation in business failures in 1992. Topping off the bad news, the state's inability to swiftly resolve its budget crisis prompted Wall Street to downgrade California's credit rating. Given this inauspicious backdrop, South Bay's office market lost comparatively little ground in 1992. In fact, the vacancy rate actually edged down from 23 to 22 percent. However, with absorption totaling just 71,000 sq. ft. for the year, and vacant stock reaching nearly seven million, the market was clearly in distress.

1993 Forecast

The late 1992 completion of 206,500 sq. ft. in El Segundo should cap speculative construction in the South Bay office market until some improvement in the economy is detected. During 1993, lay-offs are expected to continue at McDonnell Douglas and Hughes Aircraft and will ultimately result in the elimination of an estimated 10,000 aerospace jobs by early 1994. The full effect of these losses on the office market is difficult to forecast, but SIOR's correspondent expects another stagnant year, with most tenants waiting for the dust to settle before making a long-term commitment.

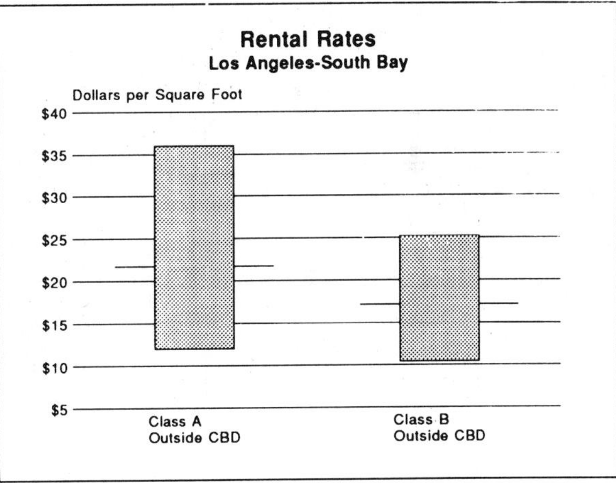

Los Angeles-West, California: Office

Los Angeles-West, California

Market Data

Inventory (sf)	Class A CBD	Class A Outside CBD	Class B CBD	Class B Outside CBD
Total	-	34,900,000	-	16,850,000
Vacant	-	6,950,000	-	4,800,000
Vacancy Rate	-	19.9%	-	28.5%
Vacant Sublease	-	1,650,000	-	950,000
Under Construction	-	400,000	-	0
Substantial Rehab	-	1,700,000	-	850,000
Net Absorption	-	1,600,000	-	-650,000
Rental Rates ($/sf)				
Lowest	-	18.00	-	13.80
Highest	-	45.00	-	23.40
Weighted Average	-	27.61	-	17.64
Sales Prices ($/sf)				
Lowest	-	131.00	-	90.00
Highest	-	283.00	-	186.00
Weighted Average	-	167.00	-	115.00

Utility Rates: CBD n/a
Outside CBD $1.80 per sf
Not Separately Metered

Parking Ratio: CBD - n/a
Outside CBD - 1 per 333 sf

Standard Work Letter: $39.00 per sf, typically based on dollars per square foot

Operating Cost Escalation: Base Year and Stop - $9.50

Rate of Return: 10.00%

Cumulative Discount Rate: 15-20%

Landlord Concessions
- Parking
- Rental Abatement
- Lease Assumptions
- Moving Allowance
- Interior Improvements
- Signing Bonuses

Leasing Activity Profile

Major Activity
- Legal/Accounting
- Insurance
- Finance/Banking
- Entertainment

Minor Activity
- Fortune 500 Firms
- Business Services
- Sales
- Engineering/Architecture
- Government

Mortgage Money Supply: Tight

Prime Source of Financing:
Commercial Banks, Owner Financing

Outlook

Absorption		Same
Construction		Down 75%
Vacancies		Same
Rental Rates		Same
Landlord Concessions		Same
Sales Prices	Class A CBD	n/a
	Outside CBD	Down 1-5%
	Class B CBD	n/a
	Outside CBD	Same

1992 Review

While devastating losses in the aerospace, banking, computer, and real estate industries buffeted the Los Angeles economy in 1992, the Los Angeles West office market actually recorded a modest gain in overall occupancy. Even though the recession has limited expansions by law, accounting, and other business services firms that tenant West Los Angeles office space, the primary user—the entertainment industry—has thus far been virtually unaffected. Vacancy rates in West L.A. declined slightly in 1992, dropping from 23.4 percent to 22.7 percent. All of the net gain in occupancy occurred in the Class "A" market.

1993 Forecast

Occupancy rates in the West Los Angeles office market are projected to hold steady in 1993 despite further deterioration of the county's economy. West Los Angeles' high vacancy rates—the product of a zoning variance that kicked off a building boom several years ago—continue to limit rent growth, making current rates highly attractive to firms with long-term plans. Motion picture and television production companies, as well as talent agencies that require a West Los Angeles address, should continue to sign leases in 1993, offsetting declines in other sectors. Given the current oversupply, the lack of financing, and the inability to achieve preleasing proformas, a number of proposed projects will remain shelved in 1993.

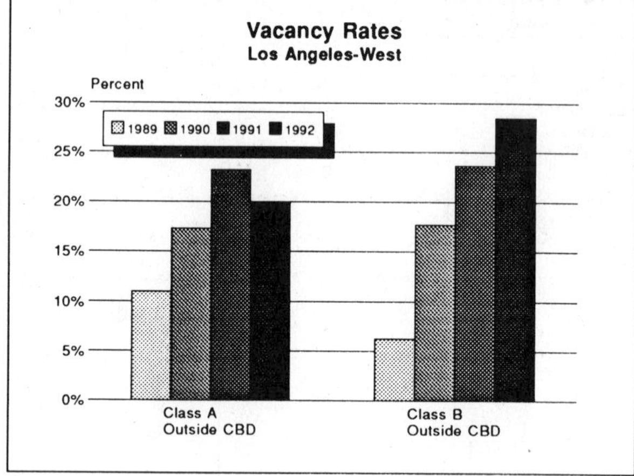

New York City, New York: Office

Manhattan, New York

Market Data

Inventory (sf)	Class A CBD	Class A Outside CBD	Class B CBD	Class B Outside CBD
Total	173,187,676	79,180,903	77,536,427	28,638,730
Vacant	28,402,778	14,569,286	15,274,676	7,142,248
Vacancy Rate	16.4%	18.4%	19.7%	24.9%
Vacant Sublease	6,927,507	1,979,522	1,318,119	544,990
Under Construction	323,811	n/a	n/a	n/a
Substantial Rehab	3,378,600	4,562,000	0	0
Net Absorption	1,914,056	-996,249	-891,287	-354,366
Rental Rates ($/sf)				
Lowest	33.60	23.25	18.20	14.51
Highest	52.80	38.25	36.20	28.90
Weighted Average	38.02	28.65	28.10	23.20
Sales Prices ($/sf)				
Lowest	n/a	n/a	n/a	n/a
Highest	n/a	n/a	n/a	n/a
Weighted Average	n/a	n/a	n/a	n/a

Utility Rates: CBD $2.35 per sf, Outside CBD n/a, Not Separately Metered

Parking Ratio: CBD - n/a, Outside CBD - n/a

Standard Work Letter: $40.00 per sf, typically based on dollars per square foot

Operating Cost Escalation: Base Year

Rate of Return: 12.00%

Cumulative Discount Rate: 20-25%

Landlord Concessions
- Rental Abatement
- Lease Assumptions
- Moving Allowance
- Interior Improvements

Leasing Activity Profile

Major Activity
- Legal/Accounting
- Business Services
- Finance/Banking
- Publishing/Media

Minor Activity
- Fortune 500 Firms
- Insurance
- Sales
- Engineering/Architecture
- Government

Mortgage Money Supply: Tight

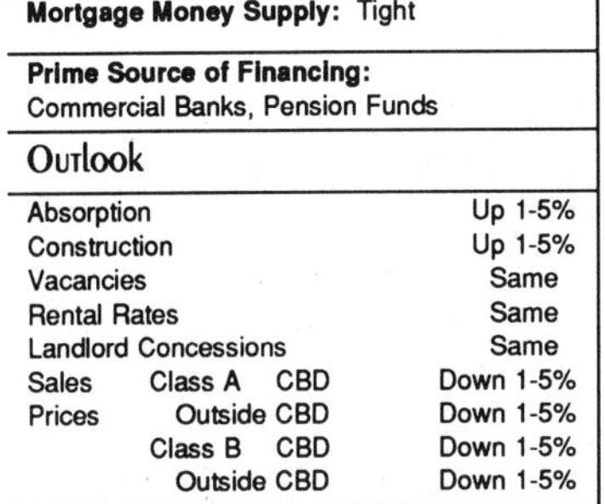

Prime Source of Financing:
Commercial Banks, Pension Funds

Outlook

Absorption			Up 1-5%
Construction			Up 1-5%
Vacancies			Same
Rental Rates			Same
Landlord Concessions			Same
Sales Prices	Class A	CBD	Down 1-5%
		Outside CBD	Down 1-5%
	Class B	CBD	Down 1-5%
		Outside CBD	Down 1-5%

1992 Review

It appears the worst is over for New York City. After 12 quarters of decline and losses of well over 100,000 jobs, the economy was expanding in late 1992, albeit modestly. Plagued by high wage and operating costs, manufacturing continued to shed jobs. But the good news for the office market was the slow improvement in the FIRE and Service sectors. While consolidations still hampered the banking industry, rising profits on Wall Street initiated cautious hiring among securities and commodities firms. These gains were too small and too late in the year to offer much support for occupancy rates in 1992. Manhattan's supply of vacant space increased slightly during the year, especially among older downtown buildings.

1993 Forecast

Speculative development in Manhattan is at a virtual standstill, with the exception of 565 Fifth Avenue, nearing completion. No new buildings are underway. With the soft real estate market, increased opportunities exist for some companies to reduce occupancy and create more efficient work spaces for employees. Relocations to neighboring cities have been curtailed due to an aggressive Manhattan market and the terms being offered by landlords for the city's most desirable office space.

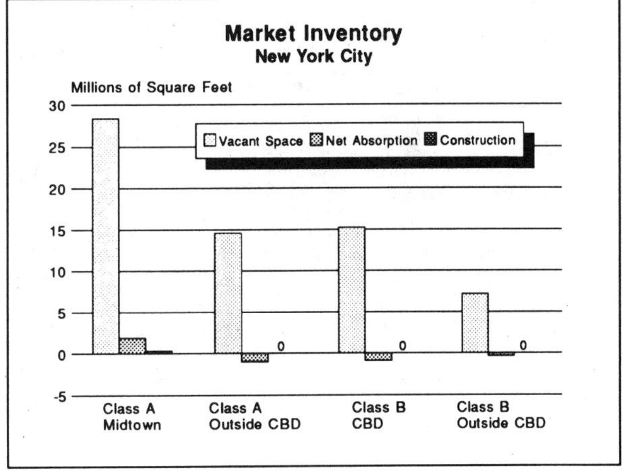

New York-Nassau / Suffolk Counties, New York: Office

Nassau and Suffolk Counties, New York

Market Data

	Class A		Class B	
Inventory (sf)	**CBD**	**Outside CBD**	**CBD**	**Outside CBD**
Total	-	22,365,000	-	13,419,000
Vacant	-	4,753,000	-	2,987,000
Vacancy Rate	-	21.3%	-	22.3%
Vacant Sublease	-	316,000	-	292,000
Under Construction	-	n/a	-	n/a
Substantial Rehab	-	n/a	-	n/a
Net Absorption	-	-262,000	-	-191,000
Rental Rates ($/sf)				
Lowest	-	15.00	-	11.00
Highest	-	32.00	-	21.00
Weighted Average	-	n/a	-	n/a
Sales Prices ($/sf)				
Lowest	-	n/a	-	n/a
Highest	-	n/a	-	n/a
Weighted Average	-	n/a	-	n/a

Utility Rates: CBD $2.00 per sf; Outside CBD $2.00 per sf; Not Separately Metered

Parking Ratio: CBD - 1 per 250 sf; Outside CBD - 1 per 200 sf

Standard Work Letter: $20.00 per sf, typically based on dollars per square foot

Operating Cost Escalation: Base Year

Rate of Return: 6.00%

Cumulative Discount Rate: 15-20%

Landlord Concessions
- Parking
- Rental Abatement
- Lease Assumptions
- Moving Allowance
- Interior Improvements

Leasing Activity Profile

Major Activity
- Legal/Accounting
- Insurance
- Finance/Banking

Minor Activity
- Fortune 500 Firms
- Sales
- Engineering/Architecture
- Government
- Energy

Mortgage Money Supply: Moderate

Prime Source of Financing: Commercial Banks

Outlook

Absorption		Same
Construction		Down 6-10%
Vacancies		Up 6-10%
Rental Rates		Down 6-10%
Landlord Concessions		Up 1-5%
Sales Prices	Class A CBD	Down 6-10%
	Outside CBD	Down 6-10%
	Class B CBD	Down 6-10%
	Outside CBD	Down 6-10%

1992 Review

The Nassau-Suffolk office market struggled through another difficult year in 1992. Continuing layoffs by defense and high-technology firms buffeted the economy, causing a severe shortage in tax revenues and contributing to declines in nearly every other employment sector. Occupancy levels dropped by a total of 453,000 sq. ft. This figure would have been higher had it not been for a slight increase in demand that occurred as a result of significantly lower rental rates. Properties foreclosed on and remarketed by mortgagees at substantially lower prices sparked some leasing activity in 1992, but obviously not enough to counteract the effects of space returning to the market.

1993 Forecast

Prospects for 1993 in the Nassau-Suffolk market are far from promising. Some of the highest personal and corporate expenses in the nation will continue to be a hinderance to new business formation and may drive a few more companies out. Both Nassau and Suffolk county governments are grappling with revenue shortages that may lead to cuts in services. Given these inauspicious omens, SIOR's correspondent forecasts another year of negative net absorption for the office market, accompanied by declining rental rates and a slight increase in landlord concessions.

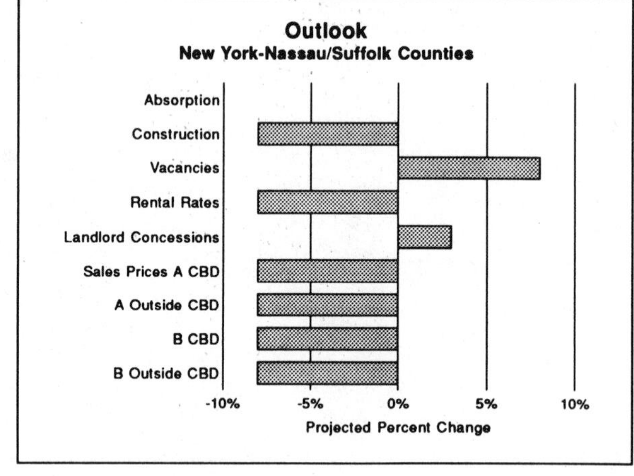

New York-Rockland / Westchester Counties, New York: Office

New York - Rockland / Westchester Counties

Market Data

	Class A		Class B	
Inventory (sf)	**CBD**	**Outside CBD**	**CBD**	**Outside CBD**
Total	2,200,000	7,200,000	3,700,000	12,400,000
Vacant	600,000	1,368,000	1,295,000	2,600,000
Vacancy Rate	27.3%	19.0%	35.0%	21.0%
Vacant Sublease	270,000	150,000	25,000	100,000
Under Construction	0	0	0	0
Substantial Rehab	0	0	0	36,000
Net Absorption	-254,000	-340,000	-65,000	140,000
Rental Rates ($/sf)				
Lowest	22.00	18.00	18.00	16.00
Highest	24.50	n/a	19.00	16.75
Weighted Average	22.75	n/a	18.75	16.50
Sales Prices ($/sf)				
Lowest	n/a	n/a	n/a	n/a
Highest	n/a	n/a	n/a	n/a
Weighted Average	n/a	n/a	n/a	n/a

Utility Rates: CBD $2.25 per sf; Outside CBD $2.00 per sf; Not Separately Metered

Parking Ratio: CBD - 1 per 500 sf; Outside CBD - 1 per 200 sf

Standard Work Letter: $18.00 per sf, typically based on dollars per square foot

Operating Cost Escalation: Base Year

Rate of Return: 0.00%

Cumulative Discount Rate: n/a

Landlord Concessions
- Rental Abatement
- Lease Assumptions
- Moving Allowance
- Interior Improvements

Leasing Activity Profile

Major Activity
- Business Services
- Government

Minor Activity
- Legal/Accounting
- Insurance
- Sales
- Finance/Banking
- Engineering/Architecture

Mortgage Money Supply: Not Available

Prime Source of Financing: n/a

Outlook

Absorption	Up 6-10%
Construction	Same
Vacancies	Up 6-10%
Rental Rates	Flat
Landlord Concessions	Up 6-10%
Sales Prices Class A CBD	n/a
Outside CBD	n/a
Class B CBD	n/a
Outside CBD	n/a

1992 Review

Located just north and west of New York City, the Rockland and Westchester County economies are closely linked to Manhattan. Since a large number of residents commute to jobs in the city, the trade and services industries, among others, in these two counties are dependent on healthy Manhattan employment gains if they are to grow. It is not surprising then that another year of losses in Manhattan last year coincided with a poor year for the Rockland and Westchester County office markets. During 1992 absorption in the two counties declined, falling to a negative 519,000 sq. ft. Rents also fell considerably. According to SIOR's correspondent, Class "A" space in 1992 was marketed at rents near what Class "B" space had cost five years before.

1993 Forecast

According to local economists, the worst of the recession is behind the New York area. As job growth picks up speed in New York in 1993, the Westchester and Rockland office markets should begin to see some improvement. Based on projections by SIOR's area researcher, however, the recovery will be slow. Although demand for space should increase in 1993, rental rates will remain flat. In addition, the value of concessions offered by landlords is expected to rise.

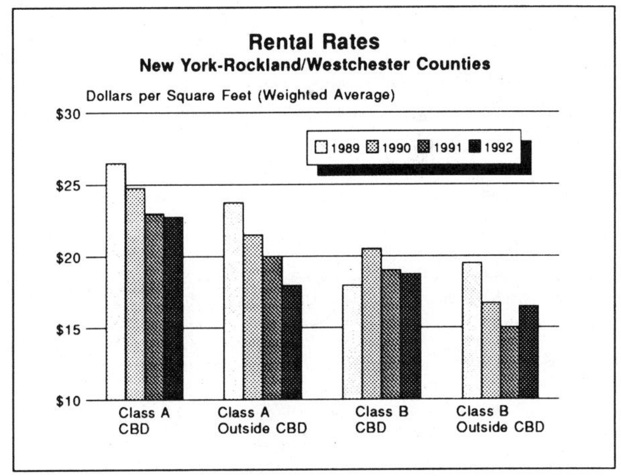

Glossary of Terms

DEMOGRAPHICS

Population. The 1992 population projection for the MSA. Figures are based on data from National Planning Data Corporation.

Population Growth Rate. The annual percentage change in populations between 1983 and 1992 for the MSA. Figures are based on data from National Planning Data Corporation.

Unemployment Rate. The percent of labor force unemployed in September 1992 as published by the Bureau of Labor Statistics in Employment and Earnings.

Median Household Income. The estimated median household income for 1992 as published by National Planning Data Corporation.

Cost of Living Index. Measures relative price levels for consumer goods and services in participating areas, as published by American Chamber of Commerce Researchers Association (ACCRA).

Demographic Rankings. This ranks local statistics against other U.S. Metropolitan markets.

INDUSTRIAL MARKETS

Prime Industrial Building. A prime industrial building is in the top 25 percent of the most desired industrial properties in a given market area. Such buildings are considered to be for general purpose uses such as industrial, research, warehouse and/or manufacturing.

Central City/Suburban. Since the definition of urban and suburban varies widely, it is the responsibility of the individual survey respondent to reflect his or her area's particular characteristics.

Total Inventory. Total square footage (sq. ft.) of rentable industrial space, vacant and occupied, ready for tenant finish. Includes owner occupied space.

Vacant Inventory. Total square footage of vacant rentable industrial space, including sublease.

Net Absorption. Net change in occupied space.

Under Construction. Industrial space in construction stages, ground has been broken. Does not include planned projects.

Construction Costs. Construction costs reflect only hard construction costs such as general contractor, overhead, and profit, but exclude architectural and engineering fees, financing fees, and mortgage/ brokerage fees for both construction and permanent financing.

Lease Prices. A gross lease is one in which the tenant's rent includes real estate taxes, fire and extended coverage insurance, as well as maintenance of the roof structure and outside walls. A net lease is one in which the tenant assumes the operating expenses of the leased premises.

Improved Sites. Improved sites are in the top 25 percent of overall desirability of the existing inventory. Such sites are in a "ready-to-build" condition and are essentially level and graded and serviced with all necessary utilities. Rail service may or may not be available.

Unimproved Sites. These sites are also in the top 25 percent of overall desirability of the existing inventory and zoned for industrial use. Streets and utilities may not yet be installed, but are reasonably close and available. Rail service may or may not be available.

Prime High-Technology Building. Generally, high-technology (high-tech) buildings are 50 percent or more office, fully air-conditioned, 12-18' clear height, have extensive landscaping and parking, and are architecturally impressive. In some areas of the country where high-tech industries are not prevalent, this building could be used as a showroom or as pure office. These properties are sometimes called "flex buildings."

OFFICE MARKETS

CBD. Central Business District space located near the historical urban core, commonly associated with traditional government and financial districts in most cities.

Outside CBD. Outside the CBD includes both suburban area and "urban clusters" with areas of high office space concentrations that often rival nearby CBDs.

Class "A." Excellent locations, high-quality tenants, high-quality finish, well-maintained, professionally managed, and usually new, or old buildings that are competitive with new buildings.

Class "B." Good location, professionally managed, fairly high-quality construction and tenancy. Class "B" buildings generally show very little functional obsolescence and deterioration.

Total Inventory. Total square footage (sq. ft.) of rentable space, vacant and occupied, ready for tenant finish. Includes owner occupied space.

Vacant Inventory. Total square footage of vacant rentable space, including sublease.

Current Construction. Total square footage presently under construction includes any space that will be available for occupancy before the end of 1992.

Substantial Rehabilitation. Repair/replacement of building interior finish and/or systems requiring temporary displacement of tenants.

Net Absorption. Net change in occupied stock.

Rental Rate. Minimum, maximum, and weighted average quoted gross rental rate for competitive office space in each class, in U.S. dollars per square foot ($/sq. ft.).

Gross Rental. Services included in the rental rate vary from market to market.

Sales Prices. Minimum, maximum, and weighted average sales prices for competitive office space in each class, in U.S. dollars per square foot ($/sq. ft.).

Weighted Average Rental Rate. Average quoted rental rate weighted by the vacant space available at the rental rate, in each class.

Average Utility Rates. Figures presented are dollars per square foot per year.

Standard Work Letter. Sometimes called a construction rider, this refers to the work that the landlord will do for the tenant, typically to finish out the interior of the space.

Typical Parking Ratio. The ratio refers to the availability of parking spaces per number of square feet leased by a tenant.

Operating Cost Escalation. Operating cost escalation refers to the procedure used to adjust rents over the term of a lease.

Cumulative Discount Rate. The rental rate discount factor is the cumulative effect of landlord lease concessions on gross rental rates. It is expressed as a percentage of base rent.

MISCELLANEOUS TERMS

Maquiladora. The twin plant operation that has grown up along the U.S./Mexico border, in which goods are shipped into Mexico for assembly and finishing work using lower cost labor, and then are distributed through the U.S. market. Import duties are payable only on the imputed value added in the assembly process.

FIRE Sector. An acronym standing for Finance, Insurance and Real Estate, one of the major industry groupings in the Standard Industrial Classification system established by the U.S. Department of Commerce.

Back-filling. A colloquialism referring to the re-leasing of space once occupied by a tenant that has relocated elsewhere.

Source: Reprinted from *Comparative Statistics of Industrial and Office Real Estate Markets* (1993) with permission of the Society of Industrial and Office REALTORS®.

Real Estate Investment Trusts (REITs)

WHAT IS A REIT?

A REIT is essentially a corporation or trust that combines the capital of many investors to acquire or provide financing for all forms of real estate. A REIT serves much like a mutual fund for real estate. Its shares are freely traded, often on a major stock exchange.

A corporation or trust that qualifies as a REIT generally does not pay corporate income tax to the Internal Revenue Service (IRS). This is a unique feature and one of the most attractive aspects of a REIT. Most states honor this federal exemption and do not require REITs to pay state income tax. This means that nearly all of a REITs income can be distributed to shareholders, and there is no double taxation of the income to the shareholder.

WHAT QUALIFIES A REIT?

In order for a corpotation or trust to qualify as a REIT it must comply with certain provisions within the Internal Revenue Code. As required by the Tax Code, a REIT must:

- be a corporation, business trust or similar association;
- be managed by a board of directors or trustees;
- have shares that are fully transferable;
- have a minimum of 100 shareholders;
- have no more than 50 percent of the shares held by five or fewer individuals during the last half of each taxable year;
- invest at least 75 percent of total assets in real estate assets;
- derive at least 75 percent of gross income from rents from real property, or interest on mortgages on real property;
- derive no more than 30 percent of gross income from the sale of real property held for less than four years, securities held for less than six months or certain prohibited transactions;
- pay dividends of at least 95 percent of REIT taxable income.

Source: Excerpted from *Real Estate Investment Trusts: Frequently Asked Questions About REITS*, National Association of Real Estate Investment Trusts, Inc., 1129 Twentieth Street, N.W., Washington, D.C. 20036.

ARE REITS LIMITED PARTNERSHIPS?

No. REITs are not partnerships. There are important organizational and operational differences between REITs and limited partnerships.

One of the major differences between REITs and limited partnerships is how annual tax information is reported to investors. An investor in a REIT receives IRS Form 1099 from the REIT, indicating the amount and type of income received during the year. An investor in a partnership receives a very complicated Internal Revenue Service Schedule K-1.

The oversight/corporate governance features of a REIT are believed to be far superior to the partnership.

Other important differences between REITs and limited partnerships are shown in the accompanying chart.

HOW MANY REITS ARE THERE?

There are over 200 REITs operating in the United States today. Their assets total $50 billion. About two-thirds of these trade on the national stock exchanges:

- New York Stock Exchange—61 REITs
- American Stock Exchange—61 REITs
- NASDAQ National Market System—19 REITs

WHAT TYPES OF REITS ARE THERE?

The REIT industry has a diverse profile, which offers many attractive opportunities to investors. REIT industry analysts often classify REITs in one of three investment approaches:

Equity REITs own real estate. Their revenue comes principally from rent. REIT industry investments in property ownership have increased steadily for 30 years.

Mortgage REITs loan money to real estate owners. Their revenue comes principally from interest earned on their mortgage loans.

Hybrid REITs combine the investment strategies of both equity REITs and mortgage REITs.

REITs can also be distinguished by . . .

Type of Property . . .

Some REITs invest in a variety of property types—office buildings, shopping centers, apartments, warehouses, etc. Other REITs specialize in one property type only, such as shopping centers. Health care REITs specialize in health care facilities: hospitals, including acute care, rehabilitation and psychiatric, medical office buildings, nursing homes, and congregate and assisted living centers.

Geographic Focus . . .

Some REITs invest throughout the country. Others specialize in one region only or even a single metropolitan area.

HOW DO I INVEST IN A REIT?

An individual may invest in a publicly traded REIT, which in most cases is listed on a major stock exchange, by purchasing shares through a stock broker. An investor can enlist the services of a broker, investment advisor or financial planner to help analyze his or her financial objectives. These individuals also may be able to recommend an appropriate REIT for the investor.

An investor can also contact a REIT directly for a copy of the company's annual report, prospectus and other financial information.

Potential investors can also contact the National Association of Real Estate Investment Trusts (NAREIT) for a free listing of all publicly traded REITs, with exchange symbols, and a list of educational publications available.

For more information, contact NAREIT, 1129 Twentieth Street, N.W., Suite 705, Washington, D.C., 20036 (202) 785-8717.

IMPORTANT DIFFERENCES: REITS VS. PARTNERSHIPS

	REITs	**Partnerships**
Liquidity	*Yes, most REITs are listed on stock exchanges*	*No, when liquidity exists, generally much less than REITs*
Minimum Investment Amount	*None*	*Typically $2,000-$5,000*
Reinvestment Plans	*Yes, including some at discounts*	*No*
Ability to Leverage Investments without Incurring UBIT for Tax-Exempt Accounts	*Yes, this makes REITs suitable for individual IRAs, KEOGH and other pension plans*	*No*
Investor Control	*Yes, investors re-elect directors and, in some cases, approve advisors annually*	*No, controlled by general partner who cannot be easily removed by limited partners*
Independent Directors	*Yes, state law typically requires majority to be independent of management*	*No*
Beneficial Ownership	*At least 100 shareholders required -- most REITs have thousands*	*Shared between any number of limited and general partners*
Ability to Grow by Additional Public Offerings of Stock	*Yes*	*No*

PUBLICLY TRADED REITS

AMERICAN STOCK EXCHANGE

ASR Investments Corp.	ASR
Angeles Mortgage Investment Trust	ANM
Angeles Participating Mortgage Trust	APT
Arizona Land Income Corporation	AZL
Banyan Hotel Investors Trust	VHT
Banyan Short Term Income Trust	VST
Boddie-Noell Restaurant Properties, Inc.	BNP
Bradley Real Estate Trust	BTR
CNL Realty Investors, Inc.	NNN
California Jockey Club	CJ
Capital Housing and Mortgage Partners	CAP
Columbia Real Estate Investments, Inc.	CIV
Copley Properties, Inc.	COP
EastGroup Properties	EGP
EquiVest, Inc.	EVI
HMG/Courtland Properties, Inc.	HMG
HealthVest	HVT
Income Opportunity Realty Trust	IOT
Koger Equities, Inc.	KE
Landsing Pacific Fund	LPF
Lincoln N.C. Realty Fund Incorporated	LRF
Linpro Specified Properties Trust	LPO
MIP Properties	MIP
MSA Realty Trust	SSS
Medical Properties, Inc.	MPP
Meridian Point Realty Trust IV	MPD
Meridian Point Realty Trust VI	MPF
Meridian Point Realty Trust VII	MPG
Meridian Point Realty Trust VII	MPH
Metropolitan Realty Corporation	MET
One Liberty Properties, Inc.	OLP
Pennsylvania Real Estate Investment Trust	PEI
Pittsburgh West Virginia Railroad	PW
Presidential Realty Corporation	PDL.A
Property Capital Trust	PCT
PS Business Parks, Inc.	PSB
Partners Preferred Yield, Inc.	PYA
Partners Preferred Yield II, Inc.	PYB
Partners Preferred Yield III, Inc.	PYC
Public Storage Properties VI, Inc.	PSF
Public Storage Properties VII, Inc.	PSH
Public Storage Properties VIII,Inc.	PSJ
Public Storage Properties IX, Inc.	PSK
Public Storage Properties X, Inc.	PSL
Public Storage Properties XI, Inc.	PSM
Public Storage Properties XII, Inc.	PSN
Public Storage Properties XIV, Inc.	PSP
Public Storage Properties XV, Inc.	PSQ
Public Storage Properties XVI, Inc.	PSU
Public Storage Properties XVII, Inc.	PSV
Public Storage Properties XVIII, Inc.	PSW
Public Storage Properties XIX, Inc.	PSY
Public Storage Properties XX, Inc.	PSZ
RYMAC Mortgage Investment Corporation	RM
Resort Income Investors, Inc.	RII
Southwerstern Property Trust	SWP
Storage Properties, Inc.	PSA
Vanguard Real Estate Fund I	VRO
Vanguard Real Estate Fund II	VRT
Washington Real Estate Investment Trust	WRE
Western Investment Real Estate Trust	WIR

NASDAQ NATIONAL MARKET SYSTEM

Allied Capital Commercial Corp.	ALCC
Banyan Strategic Land Fund II	VSLF
Banyan Strategic Land Trust	VLANS
The Chicago Dock and Canal Trust	DOCKS
CleveTrust Realty Investors	CTRIS
Continental Mortgage and Equity Trust	CMETS
Crocker Realty Investors	CRKR
Eastover Corporation	EASTS
INVG Mortgage Securities Corporation	INVG
Mellon Participating Mortgage Trust	MPMTS
Meridian Point Realty Trust '83	MPTBS
Monmouth Real Estate Investment Corp.	MNRTA
National Income Realty Trust	NIRTS
Nooney Realty Trust, Inc.	NRTI
Price REIT	PRET
Sierra Real Estate Equity Trust '84	SETC
Vinland Properties, Inc.	VIPTS
Wetterau Properties, Inc.	WTPR

NEW YORK STOCK EXCHANGE

Americana Hotels and Realty Corporation	AHR
American Health Properties, Inc.	AHE
Asset Investors Corporation	AIC
BRE Properties, Inc.	BRE
BRT Realty Trust	BRT
Banyan Mortgage Investment Fund	VMG
Berkshire Realty Company	BRI
Burnham Pacific Properties, Inc.	BPP
CRI Insured Mortgage Investments II, Inc.	CMM
CRI Liquidating REIT, Inc	CFR
CV REIT	CVI
California Real Estate Investment Trust	CT
Capstead Mortgage Corporation	CMO
Carr Realty Corporation	CRE
Countrywide Mortgage Investments, Inc.	CWM
Cousins Properties Incorporated	CUZ
Del-Val Financial Corporation	DVL
Developers Diversified Realty Corp.	DDR
Dial REIT, Inc.	DR
Duke Realty Investments, Inc.	DRE
EQK Realty Investors I	EKR
Federal Realty Investment Trust	FRT
First Union Real Estate Investments	FUR
HRE Properties	HRE
Health & Rehabilitation Properties Trust	HRP
Health Care Property Investors, Inc.	HCP
Health Care REIT, Inc.	HCN
Health Equity Properties, Inc.	EQP
Homeplex Mortgage Corporation	HPX
Hotel Investors Trust	HOT
ICM Property Investors Incorporated	ICM
IRT Property Company	IRT
Kimco Realty Corporation	KIM
Kranzco Realty Trust	KRT
LNH REIT, Inc.	LHC
LTC Properties, Inc.	LTC
Liberte Investors	LBI
MGI Properties	MGI
Manufactured Home Communities, Inc.	MHC
Meditrust	MT
Merry Land & Investment Company	MRY
Mortgage and Realty Trust	MRT
National Health Investors	NHI
Nationwide Health Properties, Inc.	NHP
New Plan Realty Trust	NPR
Omega Healthcare Investors, Inc.	OHI
Property Trust of America	PTR
Prudential Realty Corporation	PRT
RPS Realty Trust	RPS
REIT of California	RCT
Realty Refund Trust	RRF
Resource Mortgage Capital, Inc.	RMR
Rockefeller Center Properties, Inc.	RCP
Santa Anita Realty Enterprises, Inc.	SAR
Sizeler Property Investors, Inc.	SIZ
Storage Equities, Inc.	SEQ
TIS Mortgage Investment Company	TIS
Taubman Centers, Inc.	TCO
Trammell Crow Real Estate Investors	TCR
Transcontinental Realty Investors	TCI
United Dominion Realty Trust	UDR
Universal Health Realty Income Trust	UHT
Weingarten Realty Investors	WRI
Wellsford Residential Property Trust	WRP

OTHER OVER-THE-COUNTER

Arlington Realty Investors	RYNMS
Central Realty Investors	CMRT
Century Realty Trust	CRLTS
Commonwealth Equity Trust	CWLES
Fifty Associates	FFTY
First REIT of New Jersey	FRET
Harbor American Health Care Trust, Inc.	HAHC
Pacific Real Estate Investment Trust	PCIFS
Real Estate Fund Investment Trust	REFI

NASDAQ SUPPLEMENTAL LIST

Cedar Income Fund 1, Ltd.	CEDR
First Continental REIT	FCRES
Royale Investments, Inc.	RLIN
USP Real Estate Investment Trust	USPTS

Source: National Association of Real Estate Investment Trusts, Inc., 1129 20th Street, N.W., Washington, D.C. 20036.

Glossary of Real Estate and REIT Terms

This glossary of terminology used in conjunction with discussions of real estate investment trusts has been prepared by the Research Department of the National Association of Real Estate Investment Trusts. Credit should be given to Realty Income Trust, a NAREIT member, which produced a glossary of terms upon which NAREIT drew heavily.

Acceleration clause A condition in a loan contract or mortgage note which permits the lender to demand immediate repayment of the entire balance if the contract is breached or conditions for repayment occur, such as sale or demolition.

Accrued interest or rent An amount of interest or rent which has been earned but which may not have been received in the same period as earned. On many short-term first mortgages, accrued interest is not received in cash until permanent financing is obtained.

Acquisition loan See C&D loan.

Advisor A REIT's investment advisor (usually pursuant to a renewable one-year contract) provides analysis of proposed investments, servicing of the portfolio, and other advisory services. Fee limits for advisory services are prescribed by many state securities regulators. Also spelled "adviser."

Amortization The process of retiring debt or recovering a capital investment through scheduled, systematic repayments of principal; that portion of fixed mortgage payment applied to reduction of the principal amount owed.

Anchor tenant An important tenant, usually with an excellent credit rating (also known as a triple-A tenant), which takes a large amount of space in a shopping center or office building and is usually one of the first tenants to commit to lease. The anchor tenant usually is given lower rent because of the desirability of having that tenant at the property, both because of its credit rating and its ability to generate traffic.

Appraisal An opinion by an expert of the value of a property as of a specified date, supported by the presentation and analysis of relevant data. The appraisal may be arrived at by any or all of three methods: the cost approach (cost to reproduce), the market approach (comparison with other similar properties), or the income approach (capitalization of actual or projected income figures).

Assessed value The value of a property which is assigned to it by a taxing authority for purposes of assessing property taxes; often assessed value bears a fixed relationship by local statute to market value.

Asset swaps See swap program.

Assets Anything of value owned by the company. Assets are either financial, as cash or bonds; or physical, as real or personal property. For REIT tax purposes, more than 75% of the trust's assets must be property owned or securities backed by real estate.

Assumption of mortgage When the responsibility for repaying existing indebtedness secured by property is "assumed" by the second purchaser. In most jurisdictions, this relieves the first owner of the original obligations, at least to the extent that can be satisfied by sale of this asset after foreclosure.

Attribution More than 50% of a REIT's shares cannot be held by fewer than six people (otherwise it becomes a personal holding company for tax purposes). When someone has indirect control over someone else's shares (such as a trustee over shares held for the benefit of another) then "control" for personal holding company purposes may be "attributed." This complicated legal topic of "attribution" arises, however, only when the REIT's shares are held by a few.

Audit An examination of the financial status and operations of an enterprise, based mostly on the books of account, and undertaken to assure conformity to generally accepted accounting principles and to secure information for, or to check the accuracy of, the enterprise's balance sheet, income statement, and/or cash flow statement.

Balloon mortgage A mortgage loan which provides for periodic payments, which may include both interest and principal, but which leaves the loan less than fully amortized at maturity, requiring a final large payment which is the "balloon." Usually the term does not apply to an "interest only" loan whose full principal is due upon maturity or upon call during its life.

Bankrupt When liabilities exceed assets, Federal laws enable the entity to dissolve in an orderly fashion (Chapter VII), or permit a court officer to restructure the company into a survivor "going business" (Chapter X), or permit existing management to do the same under court supervision (Chapter XI), or to do so despite the preferred position of secured creditors if real property is the only asset of the business (Chapter XII).

Source: National Association of Real Estate Trusts, 1101 Seventeenth Street, N.W., Washington, D.C. 20036.

Beneficial owner The person who ultimately benefits from ownership of shares or other securities—in contrast to "nominees" (often pseudonyms for control of investment professionals so as to facilitate security transactions without having to track down beneficial owners to participate in each step of the procedures).

Blue sky laws State laws regulating conditions of sale of securities of companies (particularly those just starting out of the "clear blue sky") for the protection of the investing public. National stock exchange rules usually supercede state laws pursuant to a "blue chip" exemption contained in such state laws. The federal securities laws dovetail with state laws and pertain to publicly held companies, primarily as to accounting and disclosure practices.

Bond A debt certificate which (a) represents a loan to a trust, (b) bears interest, and (c) matures on a stated future date. Short term bonds (generally with a maturity of five years or less from the date of issuance) are often called notes. See debentures.

Book value per share Shareholder equity as adjusted to tangible net worth (assets minus liabilities plus paid-in capital) per share outstanding.

Borrower A person or entity who received something of value, ordinarily money, and is obligated to pay it back, as the debtor to the creditor, usually pursuant to a note or "IOU" containing terms and conditions.

Broker A person who is paid to act as an intermediary in connection with a transaction, in contrast to a dealer or principal who buys or sells for his own account. In the REIT world, the term "broker" usually refers to a real estate salesman, although the term is also used for "stockbrokers" too.

Building lien An encumbrance upon the property by the contractor or subcontractors. Also known as a "mechanic's" or "materialman's" lien.

Building permit Written permission by the local municipality (usually through the building inspector or other agent) allowing construction work on a piece of property in accordance with plans which were submitted and conforming to local building codes and regulations.

Business trust An unincorporated business in which assets are given to trustees for management to hold or to sell, as investments. The business trust form was first fully developed in Massachusetts, under common law, and the term "Massachusetts business trust" is sometimes used to describe entities formed in other states. It is a form of business through a trustee or trustees who hold legal title to the property of the business. Capital contributions are made to the trustees by the beneficiaries whose equitable title and interest in the property of the trust are evidenced by trust certificates, usually called shares of beneficial interest. The earnings of the trust are paid to them, as dividends are paid to stockholders. The beneficiaries generally enjoy limited liability, as the control and management of the trust rests solely with the trustees, but the trust form or organization can be distinguished from a corporation. Early REIT tax laws relied on this distinction to define eligible real estate operations.

Capital gain The amount by which the net proceeds from resale of a capital item exceed the adjusted cost (or "book value") of the asset. If a capital asset is held for more than twelve months before disposition it is taxed on a more favorable basis than a gain after a shorter period of time.

Capitalization rate The rate of return utilized to value a given cash flow, the sum of a Discount Rate and a Capital Recapture Rate. It is applied to any income stream with a finite term over which the invested principal is to be returned to the investor or lender.

Cash flow The revenue remaining after all cash expenses are paid, i.e., non-cash charges such as depreciation are not included in the calculation.

Cash flow per share. Cash flow divided by the common shares outstanding. Shareholders must make this computation themselves since the SEC has prohibited companies from stating this calculation.

Net cash flow. Generally determined by net income plus depreciation less principal payments on long-term mortgages.

Cash on cash return The "cash flow" from a property expressed as a percentage of the cash "equity" invested in a property.

Chapter X See bankrupt.

Collateral An item of value, such as real estate or securities, which a borrower pledges as security. A mortgage gives the creditor the right to seize the real estate collateral after non-performance of the debtor.

Commitment A promise to make an investment at some time in the future if certain specified conditions are met. A REIT may charge a fee to the borrower at the time of making the commitment. A REIT's level of commitments minus expected repayments can be regarded as an indication of future funding requirements.

"Take-out" commitment is one provided by the anticipated long-term lender, usually with complicated terms and conditions that must be met before the "take-out" becomes effective.

"Gap" commitment is an anticipated short-term loan to cover part of the final "take-out" that the long-term lender refuses to advance until certain conditions are met (like 90% rent-up of an apartment after construction is completed). The amount above the "floor" or basic part of the loan is the "gap," and the gap commitment is issued to enable the construction lender to make a construction loan commitment for the full amount of the take-out loan instead of only for the "floor" amount.

"Standby" commitment is one that the lender and borrower doubt will be used. It exists as reassurance to a short-term construction lender that if, after completion of a building, the borrower cannot find adequate long-term "take-out" financing, the construction lender will be repaid.

Compensating balances Money which is sometimes required by banks to be held in checking accounts by borrowers, as part of their loan agreement.

Condominium A form of fee ownership of whole units or separate portions of multi-unit buildings which facilitates the formal filing, recording and financing of a divided interest in real property. The condominium concept may be used for apartments, offices and other professional uses. See cooperatives.

Conduit tax treatment So long as most (if not all) earnings are passed along by an entity, then federal taxation is avoided at the entity's level. REITs, mutual funds, and certain kinds of holding companies are eligible for "conduit tax treatment" under certain conditions.

Constant The agreed-upon periodic (usually monthly) payment to pay the face interest rate, with any residual amount going to amortize the loan.

Construction and development loan (C&D) A short-term loan for the purpose of constructing a building, shopping center, or other improvement upon real estate, or developing a site in preparation for construction. A C&D loan is normally disbursed in increments (called *draws* or *draw-downs*) as building proceeds, rather than in a single disbursement, and is conditioned upon compliance with a variety of factors. It is usually repaid with the proceeds of the permanent loan. A land loan or purchase and development loan is sometimes made for the purpose of acquiring unimproved vacant land, usually as a future building site and for financing improvements to such land (street, sewers, etc.) as a prerequisite to construction of a building upon the site.

Contingent interest Interest on a loan that is payable only if certain conditions occur, in contrast to interest that becomes an accrued liability (whether or not paid) at a specific time.

Cooperative A form of ownership whereby a structure is owned by a corporation or trust with each individual owner holding stock in the corporation representative of the value of his apartment. Title to the apartment is evidenced by a proprietary lease which often does not qualify as adequate collateral for some lenders.

Cost-to-carry The concept specified by the accounting profession to be used by REITs in computing anticipated interest cost on debt needed to "carry" non-earning or partially-earning assets until they're restored to earning status or sold.

Current liabilities Money owed and due to be paid within one year.

Dealer Someone who buys property with the purpose of selling it at a profit rather than holding it as an investment. A dealer's profits are taxed at the ordinary income rate rather than the capital gains rate regardless of how long the property is held for resale (in contrast to the investor who sells a property after a year and pays at the capital gains rate). A REIT is not permitted to be a dealer unless it is willing to pay a 100% tax on gains from such sales in the year in which it is deemed to be a dealer; sales of foreclosed property do not fall within this definition. See principal.

Debenture An obligation which is secured only by the general credit of the issuing trust, as opposed to being secured by a direct lien on its assets, real estate or otherwise. A debenture is a form of a bond.

Declaration of trust Similar to articles of incorporation for a corporation, this document contains rules for operation of the trust, selection of its governing trustees, etc., and is the keystone of a REIT.

Deed A legal instrument which conveys title from one to another. It must be (a) made between competent parties (b) have legally sound subject matter (c) correctly state what is being conveyed (d) contain good and valuable consideration (e) be properly executed by the parties involved and (f) be delivered to be valid.

Deed in lieu of foreclosure The device by which title to property is conveyed from the mortgagor (borrower) to the mortgagee (lender) as an alternative to foreclosure. While this procedure can transfer effective control more quickly, many lenders eschew it because undiscovered prior liens (from a workman who was never paid but hadn't gotten around to filing his valid, but late, claim for example) remain enforceable in contrast to the more formal foreclosure procedures which wipe out prior claims after due notice.

Deferred maintenance The amount of repairs that should have been made to keep a property in good running condition, but which have been put off. The term contemplates the desirability of immediate expenditures, although it does not necessarily denote inadequate maintenance in the past.

Deficiency dividend The process of paying an "extra" dividend after the close of the fiscal year so as to comply with REIT tax requirements to pay out more than 90% of income. See dividend.

Depreciation The loss in value of a capital asset, due to wear and tear which cannot be compensated for by ordinary repairs, or an allowance made to allow for the fact that the asset may become obsolete before it wears out. The purpose of a depreciation charge is to write off the original cost of an asset by equitably distributing charges against its operation over its useful life, matching "cost" to the period in which it was used to generate earnings. Depreciation is an optional noncash expense recognizable for tax purposes. If the REIT pays out more than its taxable earnings, then it is distributing a "return of capital" or—as is commonly stated in the industry—"paying out depreciation."

Development loans See Construction and development loan.

Dilution The situation which results when an increase occurs in a company's outstanding securities without a corresponding increase in the company's assets and/or income.

Discount rate An interest rate used to convert a future system of payments into a single present value. See capitalization rate.

Dividend or distribution The distribution of cash or stock to shareholders of a company which is made periodically as a means of distributing all or a portion of net income or cash flow. Technically, a dividend can be paid only from net taxable income, so many REITs distribute cash and later characterize their distributions as capital gains or a tax-free return of capital if net taxable income is less than the cash paid out.

Dividend or distribution yield The annual dividend or distribution rate for a security expressed as a percent of its market price. For most REITs, the "annualized" rate is the previous quarter's distribution times four, regardless of how the distribution is characterized.

Draw A request from a borrower to obtain partial payment from the lender pursuant to a loan commitment. The lender reassures himself that the borrower has completed the required steps (such as putting in the concrete properly) before advancing money. Often, the borrower submits bills from subcontractors, which are then "paid" by the lender after inspecting the subcontractor's work. In such cases, the check is usually made out to the subcontractor but must be signed by the borrower, too, so that the lender ends up only with one borrower. See construction and development loan.

Effective borrowing costs The cost of borrowing after adjustment for compensating balances or fees in lieu of compensating balances, and selling expenses in the case of publicly sold debt.

Encumbrance A legal right or interest in real estate which diminishes its value. Encumbrances can take a number of forms, such as easements, zoning restrictions, mortgages, etc.

Entrepreneur An individual who is responsible for a commercial or real estate activity who takes a certain risk of loss in a transaction for the right to enjoy any profit which may result.

Equity The interest of the shareholders in a company as measured by their paid-in capital and undistributed income. The term is also used to describe (i) the difference between the current market value of a property and the liens or mortgages which encumber it or (ii) the cash which makes up the difference between the mortgage(s) and the construction or sale price.

Equity leveraging The process by which shares are sold at a premium above book value (in anticipation of greater earnings).

Equity participation Usually, the right of an investor to participate to some extent in the increased value of a project by receiving a percentage of the increased income from the project. If a REIT were to participate in a percentage of the net income of a venture (such as the shopping center's owner/lessor), then it could be deemed to be a partner in an active business. Thus, most REIT leases spell out the "equity participation" as a percentage of gross receipts or sales (which is a more stable measure of sales activity, anyway, and one readily identifiable from the lessor's federal income tax statement).

Escrow A deposit of "good faith" money which is entrusted to a third party (often a bank) until fulfillment of certain conditions and agreements, when the escrow may be released or applied as payment for the purchase of property or for services rendered.

Estoppel certificate An instrument used

when a mortgage or lease is assigned to another. The certificate sets forth the exact remaining balance of the lease or mortgage as of a certain date and verifies any promises to tenants that may have been made by the first owner for which the second owner may be held accountable.

Exculpatory clause A clause which relieves one of liability for injuries or damages to another. Exculpatory clauses are placed in REIT documents with the intention of eliminating personal liability of its trustees, shareholders and officers.

Expenses The costs which are charges against current operations or earnings of a building, company or other reporting entity. They may have been "paid out" in cash, or accrued to be paid later, or charged as a bookkeeping procedure to reflect the "using up" of assets (as in depreciation) utilized in the production of income during the period of current operations.

Face value The value which is shown on the face of an instrument such as a bond, debenture or stock certificate. The "face rate" of a debt instrument is often known as its "coupon rate."

Fair market value See Market value.

Fee or fee simple Title to a property which is absolute, good and marketable; ownership without condition.

Fiduciary A relationship of trust and confidence between a person charged with the duty of acting for the benefit of another and the person to whom such duty is owed, as in the case of guardian and ward, trustee and beneficiary, executor and heir.

First mortgage That mortgage which has a prior claim over all other liens against real estate. In some jurisdictions, real estate taxes, mechanics liens, court costs, and other involuntary liens may take priority over such a contractual lien: title companies "clear" properties so as to reassure first mortgage lenders (and owners) of their uncontested position and to guarantee them of that position under certain conditions.

Fiscal year The 12-month period selected as a basis for computing and accounting for a business. A fiscal year need not coincide with the calendar year, except for all REITs initially qualifying for special tax treatment after 1976.

Fixed assets Assets, such as land, buildings and machinery, which cannot be quickly converted into cash. For REITs, most "fixed assets" are real property although some (like furniture in an apartment lobby) may be personal property.

Fixed charges Those interest charges, insurance costs, taxes and other expenses which remain relatively constant regardless of revenue. See net lease.

Floating rate A variable interest rate charged for the use of borrowed money. It is determined by charging a specific percentage above a fluctuating base rate, usually the prime rate as announced by a major commercial bank.

Floor loan A portion or portions of a mortgage loan commitment which is less than the full amount of the commitment and which may be funded upon conditions less stringent than those required for funding the full amount, or the "ceiling" of the loan. For example, the floor loan, equal to perhaps 80% of the full amount of the loan, may be funded upon completion of construction without any occupancy requirements, but substantial occupancy of the building may be required for funding the full amount of the loan, which is referred to as the "ceiling." See commitment, gap.

Foreclosure The legal process of enforcing payment of a debt by taking the properties which secure the debt, once the terms of the obligation are not followed. Upon foreclosure, the entire debt might not be fully discharged by transfer and disposition of the property (as determined by the courts). If so, a "deficiency judgment" may be obtained, at which point the lender is like any other creditor in attempting to get the debtor to pay the deficiency. Collection of the deficiency judgment in major real estate transactions is rare, but it becomes a major factor in negotiations if the borrower decides to return to the real estate business in the future.

Fully diluted earnings The hypothetical earnings per share of a company, computed after giving effect to the number of shares which would be outstanding if all convertible debt and warrants were exercised, and also to any reduction in interest payments resulting from such exercise.

Gap commitment See commitment, gap. Also see floor loan.

General lien A lien against the property of an individual or other entity generally, rather than against specific items of realty or personal property.

Ground lease See sale-leaseback.

Holding company A corporation that owns or controls the operations of various other companies. Many REITs were sponsored by bank or insurance holding companies whose subsidiary companies advise and manage REITs, pursuant to contracts with the REIT's trustees.

Independent contractor A firm hired to actively manage property investments. A tax-qualified REIT must hire an independent contractor to manage and operate its property, so as to distinguish itself as an investor rather than an active manager.

Income property Developed real estate, such as office buildings, shopping centers, apartments, hotels and motels, warehouses and some kinds of agricultural or industrial property, which produce a flow of income—in contrast to non-income generating real estate like raw land which would be bought and held for a speculative profit upon resale or development.

Indenture The legal document prepared in connection with, for example, a bond issue, setting forth the terms of the issue, its specific security, remedies in case of default, etc. It may also be called the "deed of trust."

Indentured trustee A trustee, generally the trust department of a major bank, which represents the interest of bondholders under a publicly offered issue.

Insider A person close to a trust who has intimate knowledge of financial developments before they become public knowledge.

Interest rate The percentage rate which an individual pays for the use of borrowed money for a given period of time.

Intermediate-term loan A loan for a term of three to ten years which is usually not fully amortized at maturity. Often, developers will seek interim loans by which to pay off construction financing, in anticipation of obtaining long-term financing at a later date on more favorable terms, either because long-term rates decline generally or because the project can show an established, stable earnings history.

Interim loan A type of loan which is to be repaid out of the proceeds of another loan. Ordinarily, not self-liquidating (amortized), the lender evaluates the risk of obtaining refinancing as much as the period risk. See C&D loans.

Investment advisor See advisor.

Joint venture The entity which is created when two or more persons or corporate entities join together to carry out a specific business transaction of real estate development. A joint venture is usually of limited duration and usually for a specific property; it can be treated as a partnership for tax purposes. The parties have reciprocal and paralleling rights and obligations.

Junior mortgage loan Any mortgage loan in which the lien and the right of repayment is subordinate to that of another mortgage loan or loans. A "second mortgage" is a junior mortgage. "Third, fourth," etc. mortgages are always deemed to be secondary.

Land loan See Construction and development loan.

Land-purchase leaseback See sale-leaseback.

Late charge The charge which is levied against a borrower for a payment which was not made in a timely manner.

Lease A contract between the owner of property (lessor) and a tenant (lessee) setting forth the terms, conditions and consideration for the use of the property for a specified period of time at a specified rental. See sale-leaseback and net lease.

Leasehold improvements The cost of improvements or betterments to property leased for a period of years, often paid for by the tenant. Such improvements ordinarily become the property of the lessor (owner) on expiration of the lease; consequently their cost is normally amortized over the life of the lease if the lessor pays for them.

Leverage The process of borrowing upon one's capital base with the expectation of generating a profit above the cost of borrowing.

Liability management The aspect of the management of a company concerned with the planning and procurement of funds for investment through the sale of equity, public debt and bank borrowings. In the REIT industry, the phrase contrasts to "asset management" or the real estate side of the business.

Line of credit Usually, an agreement between a commercial bank and a borrower under which the bank agrees to provide unsecured credit to the borrower upon certain terms and conditions. Normally, the borrower may draw on all or any part of the credit from time to time.

Limited partnership A partnership which limits certain of the partners' (the limited partners) liability to the amount of their investment. At least one partner (the "general partner") is fully liable for the obligations of the partnership and its operations, usually with the limited partners participating as investors only.

Loan loss reserve A reserve set up to offset asset values in anticipation of losses that are reasonably expected. Initially, REITs had insufficient operating experience to anticipate losses in any one class of investments or for a portfolio as a whole, so tax authorities would not permit substantial contributions toward a reserve as an allowable period expense. When difficulties arose, the conversion of short-term loans to longer-term property holdings required some form of recognition of likely losses in the financial statements. A novel procedure for REITs was devised by requiring, for book purposes, computation of additions to the reserve based in part on the probable cost of sustaining the troubled assets over the longer period of time necessary to "cure" the problem. Also known as "allowance for losses."

Loan run-off The rate at which an existing mortgage portfolio will reduce (or "run-off") to zero if no new loans are added to the portfolio.

Loan swaps See asset swaps.

Long-term mortgage Any financing, whether in the form of a first or junior mortgage, the term of which is ten years or more. It is generally fully amortized.

Loss carry forwards The net operating loss (NOL) incurred in prior years, which may be applied for tax purposes against future earnings, thereby reducing taxable income. For REITs (which must pay out most of their taxable income), NOLs can be carried forward eight years; for non-REIT-taxed companies, NOL can be carried forward for only seven years.

Market value The highest price in terms of money which a property will bring in a competitive and open market under all conditions requisite to a fair sale—the buyer and the seller each acting prudently, knowledgeably, and at arm's length. See appraisal.

Moratorium A period in which payments of debts or other performance of a legal obligation is suspended temporarily, usually because of unforeseen circumstances which make timely payment or performance difficult or impossible. This forebearance can be whole or partial.

Mortgage A publicly recorded lien by which the property is pledged as security for the payment of a debt valid even beyond death ("mort" is death in French). In some states a mortgage is an actual conveyance of the property to the creditor until the terms of the mortgage are satisfied. While there is always a "note" secured by a mortgage document, both the note and mortgage instrument are commonly called "the mortgage." For types, see: first, junior, short-term, long-term, wrap-around and construction and development mortgage definitions.

Mortgage banker A non-depository lender who makes loans secured by real estate and then usually packages and sells those loans in large groups to institutional investors, pursuant to a "long-term commitment" he has negotiated with the life insurance company or other institutional investor. Mortgage bankers frequently arrange to service these mortgages for the out-of-town institutions, collecting regular payments, keeping the lender up to date on the progress of the loan, escrowing payments for taxes and insurance premiums, and, if necessary, administering foreclosure proceedings. Many REITs were sponsored by mortgage bankers.

Mortgage constant The total annual payments of principal and interest (annual debt service) on a mortgage with level-payment amortization schedule, expressed as a percentage of the initial principal amount of the loan.

Mortgagee in possession A lender or one who holds a mortgage who has taken possession of a property in order to protect an interest in the property. Usually, this is done with commercial properties as to which rents, management fees and other disbursements continue even if the mortgage is in default. The possession must be taken with the consent of the mortgagor (or a court, in cases of foreclosure) and the mortgagee must be careful to do only those things to the property that the mortgagor (or court) will agree to accept, should it resume its role as a creditworthy owner.

Net Income The dollar amount that remains after all expenses, including taxes, are deducted from gross income. For regular companies, it is also called after-tax profit, the "bottom line" figure of how a company has performed with its investors' money. For REITs, it is net taxable income which, if fully distributed, is not taxed.

Net lease A lease, sometimes called a net-net (insurance and taxes) or even a net-net-net lease (insurance, taxes, and maintenance) in which the tenant pays all costs, including insurance, taxes, repairs, upkeep and other expenses, and the rental payments are "net" of all these expenses. See lease and fixed charges.

Net worth The remaining asset value of a property company or other entity after deduction of all liabilities against it.

Non-accrual loans See non-earning investments.

Non-earning investments The category of loans or investments which are not earning the originally anticipated rate of return. Some may be characterized as "partially earning." When interest is recorded as earned rather than as received (accrued interest), "non-accrual investments" are those which management expects not to receive interest as originally contemplated. In the vernacular, nonearning investments are "problem loans" or "troubled properties."

Non-qualified REIT A REIT that was formerly qualified, or conducts its affairs as if it is qualified, but that has elected for the tax year in question to be treated like a normal business corporation for tax purposes. Thus, some restraints (primarily against active management and holding property for sale) are lifted, while REIT conduit tax treatment is lost.

Occupancy rate The amount of space or number of apartments or offices or hotel rooms which are rented as compared with the total amount or number available. The rate is usually expressed as a percentage.

Operating expenses Expenses arising out of or relating to business activity such as interest expense, professional fees, salaries, etc.

Operating income Income received directly from business activity in the normal course, as contrasted with capital gains income, or other extraordinary income.

Option A right to buy or lease property at a certain specified price for specified terms. Consideration is typically given for the option, which is exercisable over a limited time span. If the option is not exercised, the consideration is forfeited. A loan to a developer secured by his option to obtain real estate is considered a "qualified" REIT asset.

Origination The process by which a loan is created, including the search for (or receipt of) the initial plans, the analysis and structuring of the proposed financing, and the review and acceptance procedures by which the commitment to make the investment is finally issued.

Overage income Rental income above a guaranteed minimum depending on a particular level of profit or retail sales volume by the tenant, payable under the terms of a lease.

Participations A lender often "participates out" or sells a portion of his loan to another lender while retaining a portion and managing the investment. REITs buy real estate secured participations as well as originating them.

Par value The face value assigned to a security when it is issued. The stated par value of a security generally has nothing to do with its market or book value.

Passivity The state of owning investments but not actively managing them (as a property management firm does for the investor) or engaging in trading the securities (like a broker or dealer). This "passivity" test is implicit behind several of the REIT tax requirements.

Pension funds Money which is accumulated in trust to fund pensions for companies or unions and which is frequently invested in part in real estate. A co-mingled real estate pension fund account is managed, usually under contract to a financial institution, much like a REIT except that its shares are not publicly traded but instead sold to other pension funds.

Permanent financing See long-term loan.

Point An amount which represents 1% of the maximum principal amount of an investment. Used in connection with a discount from, or a share of, a principal amount deducted at the time funds are advanced, it represents additional compensation to the lender.

Portfolio The investments of a company, including investments in mortgages and/or ownership of real property. REIT portfolios usually consist of equity in property, short-term mortgages, long-term mortgages and/or subordinated land sale-lease-backs.

Portfolio turnover The average length of time from the funding of investments until they are paid off or sold.

Preferred shares Stocks which have prior claim on distributions (and/or assets in the event of dissolution) up to a certain definite amount before the shares of beneficial interest are entitled to anything. As a form of ownership, preferred shares stand behind senior subordinated and secured debtholders in dissolution, as well as other creditors.

Prepayment penalty The penalty which is imposed on the borrower for payment of the mortgage before it is due. Often a mortgage contains a clause specifying that there is to be no prepayment penalty, or limits the prepayment penalty to only the first few years of the mortgage term.

Price earning ratio A ratio which consists of the market price divided by current annualized earnings per share. Such a computation is now found in most daily stock listings. For REITs, annualization of quarterly earnings is computed by multiplying the most recent distribution by four, regardless of the distribution's later characterization as a dividend, return-of-capital, or capital gains.

Prime lending rate The rate at which commercial banks will lend money from time to time to their most credit-worthy customers, used as a base for most loans to financial intermediaries such as REITs.

Principal The buyer or seller in a real estate transaction as distinguished from an agent.

Principal The sum of money loaned. The amount of money to be repaid on a loan excluding interest charges.

Prior lien A lien or mortgage ranking ahead of some other lien. A prior lien need not itself be a first mortgage.

Pro forma Projected or hypothetical as opposed to actual as related, for example, to a balance sheet or income statement.

Problem investments See nonearning investments.

Prospectus A document describing an investment opportunity; the detailed description of new securities which must be supplied to prospective interstate purchasers under the Securities Act of 1933.

Provision for loan losses Periodic allocation of funds to loan loss reserves in recognition of a decline in the value of a loan or loans in a trust's portfolio due to a default on the part of the borrowers.

Proxy An authorization given by a registered security holder to vote stock at the annual meeting or at a special meeting of security holders.

Purchase and leaseback See sale-leaseback.

Pyramiding In stock market transactions, this term refers to the practice of borrowing against unrealized "paper" profits in securities to make additional purchases. In corporate finance, it refers to the practice of creating a speculative capital structure by a series of holding companies, whereby a relatively small amount of voting stock in the parent company controls a large corporate system. In real estate, it refers to the practice of financing 100% or more of the value of the property.

Qualified assets Assets which meet tax requirements for special REIT tax treatment, i.e. real property. In any tax year, 75% of a REIT's assets must be invested in real property, either through ownership or by securities secured by real estate. A "partially qualified" asset is one that qualifies under the 90% test of being a passive investment in a security, but not under the 75% real estate test.

Qualified income That portion of income which is classified as interest, rents, or other gain from real property, as spelled out in the REIT tax laws.

Raw land Land which has not been developed or improved.

RCA See revolving credit agreement.

Real estate investment trust (REIT, pronounced "reet") A trust established for the benefit of a group of investors which is managed by one or more trustees who hold title to the assets for the trust and control its acquisitions and investments, at least 75% of which are real estate related. A major advantage of a REIT is that no federal income tax need be paid by the trust if certain qualifications are met. Congress enacted these special tax provisions to encourage an assembly method, which is essentially designed to provide for investment in real estate what the mutual provided for investment in securities. The REIT provides the small investor with a means of combining his funds with those of others, and protects him from the double taxation that would be levied against an ordinary corporation or trust.

Revolving credit agreement (or "revolver") A formal credit agreement between a group of banks and a REIT, the terms of which are reviewed periodically when it is "rolled over" or "revolved" or refinanced by a similar agreement. For many trusts, "revolvers" have replaced informal lines of credit extended by individual banks to REITs, thereby providing a uniform (and usually restrictive) approach by all creditors, reassuring each bank that others in the RCA would not be paid off preferentially.

Registration statement The forms filed by a company with the Securities and Exchange Commission in connection with an offering of new securities or the listing of outstanding securities on a national exchange.

Reserves for loss See loan loss reserve.

Return of capital A distribution to shareholders in excess of the trust's earnings and profits, usually consisting of either depreciation or repayment of principal from properties or mortgages held by the trust. Each shareholder receiving such a distribution is required to reduce the tax basis of his shares by the amount of such distribution. For financial accounting purposes, what constitutes a return of capital may differ from that determined under Federal income tax requirements.

Return on equity A figure which consists of net income for the period divided by equity and which is normally expressed as a percentage.

Right of first refusal The right or option granted by a seller to a buyer, to have the first opportunity of acquiring a property.

Rights offering The privilege extended to a shareholder of subscribing to additional stock of the same or another class or to bonds, usually at a price below the market and in an amount proportional to the number of shares already held. Rights must be exercised within a time limit and often may be sold if the holder does not wish to purchase additional shares.

Sale-leaseback A common real estate transaction whereby the investor buys property from and simultaneously leases it back to, the seller. This enables the previous owner (often a developer) to "cash out" on an older property while retaining control.

Land sale-leaseback—this procedure,

made common by several REITs that specialize in the transaction, affects only the land under income—producing improvements (such as shopping centers, etc.)—leaving the depreciable improvements in the hands of those who might benefit from the tax consequences. Since the improvements were probably financed with the proceeds of a first mortgage which remains in effect, the rights of the new investor are made second, or junior, to those of the first mortgage holder. Hence the common phrase "subordinated land sale-leaseback." In return for accepting a less secure position, the new investor usually obtains an "overage" clause whereby additional rent is paid anytime gross income of the shopping center (or whatever) exceeds a pre-determined floor.

Seasoned issues Securities of large, established companies which have been known to the investment public for a period of years, covering good times and bad.

Second mortgages See junior mortage loan.

Secured mortgages See junior mortgage loan.

Secured debt For REITs, senior mortgage debt secured by specific properties. In case of default on "nonrecourse" debt, the lender may assume property ownership but may not pursue other assets of the lender.

Senior mortgage A mortgage which has first priority.

Senior unsecured debt Funds borrowed under open lines without security. Most bank lines to REITs were unsecured.

Shares of beneficial interest Tradable shares in a REIT. Analogous to common stock in a corporation.

Shareholders' equity Primarily money invested by shareholders through purchase of shares, plus the accumulation of that portion of net income that has been reinvested in the business since the commencement of operations.

Short-term mortgage A loan upon real estate for a term of three years or less, bearing interest payable periodically, with principal usually payable in full at maturity.

Sinking fund An arrangement under which a portion of a bond or preferred stock issue is retired periodically, in advance of its fixed maturity. The company may either purchase a stipulated quantity of the issue itself, or supply funds to a trustee or agent for that purpose. Retirement may be made by call at a fixed price, or by inviting tenders, or by purchase in the open market.

Sponsor The entity which initiated the formation of a REIT and usually acts (often via a subsidiary) as investment advisor to the trust thereafter. The sponsor puts the reputation of its institution on the line for the REIT and usually arranges lines of credit, provides support services and, occasionally, compensating balances.

Spread Difference between percentage return on an investment and cost of funds to support the investment.

Standby commitment See commitment, standby.

Standing loan Usually not amortized, the loan is secured by completed property that has not yet been refinanced with a "permanent" long-term mortgage.

Subordinated debt Debt which is junior to secured and unsecured senior debt, it may be convertible into shares of beneficial interest for REITs. Senior subordinated debt is senior to other subordinated debt.

Subordinated ground lease See sale-leaseback.

Swap program A procedure for reducing debt (by a troubled REIT) by trading an asset to the creditor in return for cancellation of part of a loan to the REIT. Often a cash premium payment is made in addition to reduction of the debt. The premium may then be distributed to the other creditors pro rata. The amount of the cash premium, or the ratio of cash-to-debt reduction to be applied against the value of the asset, is sometimes determined by a sealed-bid "auction" process as set forth in the "revolving credit agreement" between the creditors and the REIT. See RCA.

Syndicate A group of investors who transact business for a limited period of time and sometimes with a single purpose. It is a short-term partnership.

Take-out commitment See commitment.

Tax shelter The various aspects of an investment which offer relief from income taxes or opportunities to claim deductions from taxable income. Although tax shelters are an important facet of real estate investment, they do not have a direct influence on REIT investment choices because qualified trusts are exempt from income taxes.

Usury The charging of interest rates for the use of money higher than what's allowed by local law.

Warrants Stock purchase warrants or options give the holder rights to purchase shares of stock, generally running for a longer period of time than ordinary subscription rights given shareholders. Warrants are often attached to other securities, but they may be issued separately or detached after issuance.

Working capital Determined by subtracting current liabilities from current assets. It represents the amount available to carry on the day-to-day operation of the business.

Work-out When a borrower has problems, the process undertaken by the lender to help the borrower "work out" of the problems becomes known itself as a "work out." The presumption during a "work out" is that the borrower will eventually resume a more normal debtor's position once problems are solved within (presumably) a reasonably short time.

Wrap-around mortgage A type of junior mortgage used to refinance properties on which there is an existing first mortgage loan. The face amount of the wrap-around loan is equivalent to the unpaid balance on the existing mortgage plus cash advanced to the property owner upon funding. Such loans carry a higher interest rate than the existing mortgage. The wrap-around lender assumes the obligation to maintain payments of principal and interest on the existing mortgage so as to enhance his right to make claim from his secondary position.

Yield In the stock market, the rate of annual distribution or dividend expressed as a percentage of price. Current yield is found by dividing the market price into the distribution rate in dollars. In real estate, the term refers to the effective annual amount of income which is being accrued on an investment expressed as a percentage of its value.

Business Information Directory

General Reference Sources

The *United States Government Manual* is an annual publication. It describes the organization, purposes, and programs of most government agencies and lists top personnel. Available from the Superintendent of Documents, Government Printing Office, Washington, DC 20402.

Washington Information Directory is an annual publication listing, by topic, organizations and publications which provide information on a wide range of subjects. It also lists congressional committee assignments, regional federal offices, embassies, and state and local officials. Published by the Congressional Quarterly, Inc., 1414 22nd Street NW, Washington, DC 20037.

Statistical Abstract of the United States, published annually by the Bureau of the Census, is the standard summary on the social, political, and economic statistics of the United States. It includes data from both government and private sources. Appendix II gives a comprehensive list of sources. Available from the Superintendent of Documents, Government Printing Office, Washington, DC 20402.

Who Knows: A Guide to Washington Experts, Washington Researchers, 2612 P Street NW, Washington, DC 20007.

Population information on all aspects of national and world population is provided by the Population Reference Bureau, Inc., 777 14th Street NW, Washington, DC, or call 202–689–8040.

Washington Researchers Publishing provides reports and guidance to information on a fee basis. Write Washington Researchers, 2612 P Street NW, Washington, DC 20007, or call 202–333–3499.

FEDfind which explains how to get services and publications from the U.S. Government is published by ICUC Press, P.O. Box 1447-NR, Springfield, VA 22151.

Standard Rate and Data Service provides information on periodical circulation and advertising rates. Published by Standard Rates and Data Service, Inc., 5201 Old Orchard Road, Skokie, IL 60077–1021.

National Directory of Addresses and Telephone Numbers. A national business directory that lists all SEC registered companies, major accounting and law firms, banks, and financial institutions, associations, unions, etc. Included are 50,000 fax numbers. Published by General Information, Inc., 11715 North Creek Parkway South, Bothell, WA 98011.

Encyclopedia of Information Systems and Services. This edition offers comprehensive international coverage of computer-based information systems and services. Includes details on information providers, access services, sources of information, and support services. Listings are now arranged in a single volume covering about 5,000 information organizations, systems, and services located in the United States and 70 other countries. More than 30,000 organizations, services, and products are identified. Published by Gale Research Co. (address given below).

Encyclopedia of Business Information Sources edited by James Woy. A large range of information sources are listed under 1000 alphabetically arranged business subjects. Easy access to key line, print, and electronic sources of information. Also reflects subjects of current interest, new technologies, and new industries. Some 23,000 entries describe 39 types of business information sources arranged in five categories: National and International Organizations, Government Agencies and Programs, Facilities and Services, Research and Education, and Publications and Information Services. Available from Gale Research Co. (address given below).

Business Organizations, Agencies and Publications Directory, lists organizations, agencies and information services that promote, coordinate, and regulate commercial activity in the U.S. Gale Research Co., 835 Penobscot Building, Detroit, MI 48226.

Professional and trade organizations and publications are a major source of contacts and information. Key directories to these sources are listed below:

The World Guide to Trade Associations gives a comprehensive national and international listing of associations. Published by R. R. Bowker Co., 121 Chanlon Road, New Providence, NJ 07974.

Ulrich's International Periodical Directory covers both domestic and foreign periodicals. Published by R. R. Bowker Co., 121 Chanlon Road, New Providence, NJ 07974.

Standard Periodical Directory covers U.S. and Canadian periodicals. Published by Oxbridge Communications, Inc., 150 Fifth Avenue, New York, NY 10011.

The following four publications are available from Gale Research Co., 835 Penobscot Building, Detroit MI 48226.

Encyclopedia of Associations contains detailed entries on over 22,000 active organizations, clubs, and other non-profit organizations.

The Gale Directory of Publications and Broadcast Media, a guide to newspapers, magazines and other periodicals, as well as radio, television and cable companies.

Directories in Print, contains more than 10,000 detailed entries on directories published in the United States and Canada. Directories outside the U.S. and Canada are listed in *International Directories in Print* and city and state directories are listed in *City and State Directories in Print.*

Trade Directories of the World is published annually (with monthly updates) by Croner Publications, 34 Jericho Turnpike, Jericho, New York 11753.

National Trade and Professional Associations of the United States. A comprehensive listing of professional trade and labor associations, including addresses, membership size, publications by the associations, and convention schedules. An annual published by Columbia Books, 777 14th Street NW, Washington, DC 20005.

Encyclopedia of Banking and Finance, is a comprehensive source on subjects indicated in the title. Bankers Publishing Co., 210 South Street, Boston, MA.

Guide to American Directories, published by B. Klein Publications, Inc., P.O. Box 8503, Coral Springs, FL 33065.

Directory of Marketing Research Houses and Services is an annual available from the American Marketing Association, 310 Madison Avenue, New York, NY 10017.

The Data Informer directs decision makers to unusual sources of computerized and noncomputerized information on markets, companies, demographics, and technology. Included are little-known commercial databases and free professional bulletin boards, public documents at the federal, state and local governments, reports published by private and non-profit organizations, and free experts in both the public and private sector. Published monthly, and available from: *Information USA, Inc.,* P.O. Box 15700, Chevy Chase, MD 20815. 301-657-1200.

BUSINESS AND ECONOMICS INFORMATION

Government publications referred to below may be obtained from the Government Printing Office (GPO), Washington, DC, 20402, unless otherwise indicated.

Census Catalog and Guide is an annual one-step guide to Census Bureau resources. Includes explanations of the censuses and surveys of business, manufacturing, and population, names and phone numbers of over 1,600 sources of assistance—Census Bureau specialists, State and local agencies, and private companies.

Business and economic information is provided by the following key references.

Survey of Current Business is a major publication which is supplemented on a weekly basis with *Current Statistics.* The publication contains articles as well as comprehensive statistics on all aspects of the economy, including data on the GNP, employment, wages, prices, finance, foreign trade, and production by industrial sector. (GPO)

Economic Indicators is a monthly summary-type publication prepared by the Council of Economic Advisers. It contains charts and tables on natural output, income, spending, employment, unemployment, wages, industrial production, construction, prices, money, credit, federal finance, and international statistics. (GPO)

Federal Reserve Bulletin is a monthly issued by the Federal Reserve System, containing articles and very extensive tabulated data on all aspects of the monetary situation, credit, mortgage markets, interest rates, and stock and bond yields. Available from the Board of Governors, Federal Reserve System, Washington, DC 20551.

Monthly Labor Review. This monthly publication provides articles and statistics on employment, productivity, wages, earnings, prices, wage settlements, and work stoppages. (GPO)

U.S. Industrial Outlook is an annual providing evaluations and projections of all major industrial and commercial segments of the domestic economy. (GPO)

Quarterly Financial Report for Manufacturing, Mining, and Trade Corporations is issued by the Bureau of the Census of the U.S. Department of Commerce. It covers corporate financial statistics including sales, profits, assets, and financial ratios, classified by industry group and size. (GPO)

Current Industrial Reports are a series of over 100 monthly, quarterly, semiannual, and annual reports on major products manufactured in the United States. For subscription, contact the Bureau of the Census, U.S. Department of Commerce, Washington, DC 20233. (GPO)

Annual Survey of Manufacturers. General statistics of manufacturing activity for industry groups, individual industries, states, and geographical regions are provided. (GPO)

County Business Patterns is an annual publication on employment and payrolls, which include a separate paperbound report for each state. (GPO)

Foreign Trade is a Bureau of the Census publication giving monthly reports on U.S. foreign trade. (GPO)

Population: Current Report is a series of monthly and annual reports covering population changes and socioeconomic characteristics of the population. (GPO)

Retail Sales: Current Business Report is a weekly report which provides retail statistics. (GPO)

Wholesale Trade, Sales and Inventories: Current Business Report provides a monthly report on wholesale trade. (GPO)

The Economic Bulletin Board of the Department of Commerce includes same day postings of data provided by both the Bureau of Labor Statistics and the Bureau of Economic Analysis. There are updates from the Bureau of the Census on the principal indicators, monetary statistics and foreign trade. For information call (202) 482-1986.

CORPORATE INFORMATION

The major sources of information on publicly held corporations (as well as government and municipal issues) are: *Moody's Investor Services, Inc.*, owned by Dun & Bradstreet, 99 Church Street, New York, NY 10007, and *Standard & Poor's Corp.*, owned by McGraw-Hill, 25 Broadway, New York, NY 10004.

Standard & Poor's *Corporate Records* and Moody's *Manuals* are large multivolume works published annually and kept up to date with daily (for Standard & Poor's) or semiweekly (for Moody's) reports. The services provide extensive coverage of industrials, public utilities, transportation, banks, and financial companies. Also included are municipal and government issues.

In addition, the above corporations provide computerized data services and magnetic tapes. Compustat tapes, containing major corporate financial data, are available from Investor's Management Services, Inc., Denver, CO, a subsidiary of Standard & Poor's. Time-sharing access to Compustat and other financial data bases is available through Interactive Data Corporation, Waltham, MA.

Media General Financial Services, 301 East Grace Street, Richmond, VA, 23219, maintains a database of corporate and industry information on 5500 companies. It can be accessed via Dow Jones News Retrieval, Dialog, Thomson Financial Networks, Randall-Helms Fiduciary Consultants, Lotus One Source (CD-ROM). Media General Financial Services also provides data on the financial markets, mutual funds and corporate bonds.

The Media General Financial Services proprietary product line also includes direct sales of its data through magnetic tapes, diskettes, custom research applications, specialized screening and report services.

DISCLOSURE II, available from Disclosure, Inc., (5161 River Road, Bethesda, MD 20816) provides an on line data base of corporate information for some 10,000 companies. Disclosure II can be used via the Dow Jones Retrieval Service, New York Times Information Service, Lockheed's DIALOG Information Services, Inc., ADP, CompuServe, among others.

Also available from Disclosure is MICRO/SCAN: Disclosure II, a monthly diskette service which provides information on dividends per share, 4-year growth rate in earnings per share, price/book value, etc. For information call 800–638–8076.

The 10-K and other corporate reports are filed with the Securities and Exchange Commission and are available at local SEC offices, investor relations departments of publicly traded companies, as well as various private services, such as Disclosure Inc. which provides a complete microfiche service. *The SEC News Digest*, formerly published by the government, is now available from Disclosure, Inc. (address above). Included in the *Digest* is a daily listing of 8K reports, a daily Acquisitions of Securities Report, as well as information about what's happening inside the SEC.

Disclosure Inc. has two additional services helpful for researching a corporation. Through the *SEC Watch Service* any report filed by a company with the SEC can be retrieved while corporate information such as prospective supplements and tender offers can be retrieved through the *SEC Research Service.*

Betchel Information Service located at 1801 Research Boulevard, Rockville, MD 20850 is another SEC document retrieval service. The Index of financial documents is updated several times a day.

Major trade directories include the annual *Thomas Register of American Manufacturers* (published by Thomas Publishing Company, 1 Pennsylvania Plaza, New York, NY 10005) and Dun & Bradstreet's *Reference Book of Manufacturers.*

Thomas Register includes in two volumes an alphabetical listing of manufacturers, giving address, phone number, product, subsidiaries, plant location, and an indication of assets. Dun & Bradstreet's *Reference Book* covers similar information, including sales and credit. Dun & Bradstreet's *Million Dollar Directory* series provides data on U.S. companies whose net worth is $1,000,000 and up, including information on privately held corporations; also published is a companion volume the *Billion Dollar Directory* which tracks America's corporate families.

How to Find Information About Private

Companies includes strategies for private company investigation, sources for private company intelligence, and how to find information about private companies. Published by Washington Researchers, 2612 P Street NW, Washington, DC 20007.

The *Corporate Directory*, published by Cambridge Information Group, 7200 Wisconsin Avenue, Bethesda MD 20814 is a two volume compendium of over 9500 public companies. Included is such information as corporate officers, majority stockholders, SIC members, major subsidiaries, P/E ratio, etc.

Monitor Publishing, 104 Fifth Avenue, New York, NY 10011 publishes four directories that list, among other items, names, titles, and addresses of the managers of the listed companies in the U.S. and abroad. The volumes are: *The Corporate 1000* (a quarterly), *The Financial 1000, The Over-the-Counter 1000*, and *The International 1000*. Monitor also publishes the *Blue Book of Canadian Business*.

Directory of Investment Research, an annual published by Nelson Publishing, 1 Gateway Plaza, Port Chester, NY lists security analysts with a subject specialty, top corporate officers, and brokerage firms researching a given company.

Register of Corporations is published by Standard and Poor's Corp., 345 Hudson Street, New York, NY 10014.

Directory of Corporate Affiliations and International Directory of Corporate Affiliations are references to the structure of major domestic and international corporations. Published by National Register Publishing Company, 3004 Glen View Road, Wilmette, IL 60091.

How to Find Company Intelligence in State Documents provides information filed by companies with the state governments and also business related data collected by the states. Washington Researchers Publishing, 2612 P Street NW, Washington, DC 20007.

How to Find Information About Companies: The Corporate Intelligence Source Book provides information on sources helpful in researching either private or public companies. Available from Washington Researchers Publishing. (See above for the address.)

Ward's Business Directory of U.S. Private and Public Companies 1991. Company profiles on 85,000 private and public U.S. businesses—over 90% of which are privately held. Available from Gale Research, Inc., 835 Penobscot Building, Detroit, MI 48226.

Future earnings projections of listed companies based on surveys by securities analysts are provided by Lynch, Jones, and Ryan, 345 Hudson Street, New York, NY 10013 (212-243-3137).

Zacks Investment Research, Inc., 155 North Wacker Drive, Chicago, IL 60606 also provides future earnings projections.

The Corporate Finance Sourcebook, published by the National Register Publishing Company, Macmillan Directory Division, P.O. Box 609, Wilmette, IL 60091, provides information on sources of capital, financial intermediaries and specialized financial sources.

Information on foreign corporations is provided in *World Trade Data Reports*, distributed by the District Offices of the U.S. Department of Commerce.

TRACKING FEDERAL GOVERNMENT DEVELOPMENTS

Commerce Business Daily (*CB*). This daily provides information on contract awards and subcontract opportunities, Defense Department awards, and surplus sales. *CB* is available on-line from: United Communications Group, 8701 Georgia Avenue, Silver Springs, MD 20910; DIALOG Information Services, 3460 Hillview Avenue, Palo Alto, CA 94304; or Data Resources, Inc., 2400 Hartwell Avenue, Lexington, ME 02173. Available from the Superintendent of Documents, Government Printing Office, Washington, DC 20402.

Federal Register. This daily provides information on federal agency regulations and other legal documents. Available from the Superintendent of Documents, Government Printing Office, Washington, DC 20402.

CQ Weekly Report. This major service follows every important piece of legislation through both houses of Congress and reports on the political and lobbying pressures being applied. Available from the Congressional Quarterly Service, 1414 22nd Street, Washington, DC 20037.

Daily Report for Executives. A daily series of reports giving Washington developments that affect all aspects of business operations. Available from the Bureau of National Affairs, Inc., 1231 25th Street NW, Washington, DC 20037.

The *Bureau of National Affairs, Inc.* (address above) and the *Commerce Clearing House, Inc.* (4025 West Peterson Avenue, Chicago, IL 60646), publish a large number of valuable weekly loose-leaf reports covering developments in all aspects of law, government regulations, and taxation.

INDEX PUBLICATIONS

Indexes of a wide variety of articles appearing in periodicals, trade presses, and financial services dealing with corporations, industry, and finance are given in the following:

Business Periodicals Index published by

H. W. Wilson Co., 950 University Avenue, Bronx, NY.

Funk and Scott Index of Corporations and Industries, published by Predicast, Inc., 11001 Cedar Street, Cleveland, OH 44141.

Major newspaper indexes are:

Wall Street Journal Index published by Dow Jones & Co. Inc., 22 Cortlandt Street, New York, NY 10007 (monthly).

New York Times Index published by the New York Times Company, 229 W. 43rd Street, New York, NY 10036 (semimonthly, cumulates annually).

TRACKING ECONOMIC INDICATORS

Composite Index of Leading Economic Indicators: Each month the Bureau of Economic Analysis compiles this data from the 12 leading economic indicators. This material appears each month in the *Bureau's Survey of Current Business* available by subscription from:

Superintendent of Documents
Government Printing Office
Washington, DC 20402

Consumer Price Index (*CPI*) (changes in cost of goods to customers): For these monthly reports prepared by the Bureau of Labor Statistics write:

Bureau of Labor Statistics
Department of Labor
Postal Square Building
2 Massachusetts Avenue NE
Washington, DC 20212

CPI 24 hour hotline: 202-606-7828.

Producer Price Index (*PPI*) (measures changes in prices received in primary markets by producers). For monthly reports write:

Bureau of Labor Statistics
Department of Labor
Postal Square Building
2 Massachusetts Avenue NE
Washington, DC 20212

PPI 24 hour hotline: 202-606-7828.

Available from the Bureau of Labor Statistics (BLS) are press releases on *State and Metropolitan Area Unemployment* (issued monthly), the *Employment Cost Index* (issued quarterly, and the *Employment Situation Study* (released monthly). To subscribe write:

Bureau of Labor Statistics
Department of Labor
Postal Square Building
2 Massachusetts Avenue NE
Washington, DC 20212

Unemployment Insurance Claims Weekly may be obtained by calling or by writing:

Employment and Training Administration
Department of Labor
Postal Square Building
2 Massachusetts Avenue NE
Washington, DC 20212

Releases on the *Money Supply* (Report H-6, issued weekly) and on *Consumer Credit* (Report G-19, issued monthly) may be obtained from the

Publications Services
Federal Reserve Board
Washington, DC 20551
202-452-3244

Personal Consumption Expenditure Deflator is prepared monthly by the Bureau of Economic Analysis of the Department of Commerce. This information appears in a press release *Personal Income and Outlays* and can be obtained in writing from the

Public Information Office Order Desk
Bureau of Economic Analysis
Department of Commerce
Washington, DC 20230

For information call 202-523-0777.

Monthly Trade Report (index of retail sales and accounts receivable) is compiled by the Bureau of the Census and published in *Current Business Reports* as part of what is known as the BR series. Also available are *Current Business Reports Wholesale Trade* and *Current Business Reports Selected Services.* To subscribe contact the Superintendent of Documents (Address given below). For a sample copy call: 301-763-4100.

Value of New Construction Put in Place is a Census Bureau monthly report (part of the C-30 Series) which charts the dollar amount of new construction. It is available on an annual subscription basis from the Superintendent of Documents, Government Printing Office, Washington, DC 20402. For a sample copy call: 301-763-5717.

Joint Economic Committee of Congress Reports

Reports on the economic issues studied by the Joint Economic Committee are available free of charge from:

Joint Economic Committee of Congress
Dirksen Senate Office Building
Washington, DC 20510
202–224–5321

TRACKING CONGRESSIONAL ACTION

Congressional action information can be obtained from several sources. The Legis Office will provide information on whether legislation has been introduced, who sponsored it, and its current status. For House or Senate action, call 202–225–1772.

Cloakrooms of both houses will provide details on what is happening on the floor of the chamber. House cloakrooms: Democrat 202–225–7330; Republican 202–225–7350. Senate cloakrooms: Democrat 202–224–4691; Republican 202–224–6391.

ASSISTANCE FROM U.S. GOVERNMENT AGENCIES

The **Office of Business Liaison (OBL)** serves as the focal point for contact between the Department of Commerce and the business community. Through the *Business Assistance Program* individuals and firms are guided through the entire government complex. Other services include dissemination of information and reports such as *Outlook*. Write Office of Business Liaison, U.S. Department of Commerce, Washington, DC 20230. This office is also a focal point for handling inquiries for domestic business information.

OBL telephone numbers:

Office of the Director	(202) 482-3942
Outreach Program	1360
Office of Private Sector Initiatives	3717
Business Assistance Program	3176
TDD	5691

Industry experts in the International Trade Administration can provide specifics about an industry.

Country experts in the Department of State provide up to date economic and political information on countries throughout the world, as well as background reports on specific countries. For information contact:

Country Desk Officers
U.S. Department of State
2201 C Street NW
Washington, DC 20520
Telephone: 202–647–4000

Major Bureau of Labor Statistics Indicators are available daily from a recorded message at 202–606-7828.

Economic news and highlights of the day are provided by phone from the Department of Commerce. For economic news call 202–393–4100. For news highlights call 202–393–1847.

The Energy Information Center will provide free information on energy and related matters. Write National Energy Information Center, Forrestal Building, 1000 Independence Avenue SW, Washington, DC 20585. Call 202–586–8800.

Technical and scientific information are provided by the **National Technical Information Service** of the Department of Commerce, 5285 Port Royal, Springfield, VA 22161, which handles requests about government-sponsored research of all kinds. There is a basic charge to research a subject. For information call 703–487–4600.

The **Census Bureau** produces detailed statistical information for the U.S. Information is available on population, housing, agriculture, manufacturing, retail trade, service industries, wholesale trade, foreign trade, mining, transportation, construction, and the revenues and expenditures of state and local governments. The Bureau also produces statistical studies of many foreign countries.

Information Sources in the Bureau of the Census

Frequently called numbers

Census Customer Services
(Data product & ordering information for computer tapes, CD-ROM's, microfiche, & some publications) .... (301) 763-4100
FAX .... (301) 763-4794
TDD .... (301) 763-2811

Agriculture Information 1-800-523-3215
Business Information .... (301) 763-1792
Census Job Information (Recording) .... (301) 763-6064
Census Personnel Locator .... (301) 763-7662
Congressioanl Affairs .... (301) 763-2446
Foreign Trade Information 763-5140/7754
General Information .... (301) 763-4100
Library .... (301) 763-5042
Population Information .... 763-5002/5020 (TTY)
Public Information Office (Press) ...... (301) 763-4040

Government, Commerce and Civic Relations 763-2436

Regional Assistance (Information services and data product information)
Atlanta, Georgia .... (404) 730-3833
Boston, Massachusetts .... (617) 565-7078
Charlotte, North Carolina .... (704) 344-6144
Chicago, Illinois .... (312) 353-6098
Dallas, Texas .... (214) 767-7105
Denver, Colorado .... (303) 969-7750
Detroit, Michigan .... (313) 226-7742
Kansas City, Kansas .... (913) 236-3711
Los Angeles, California .... (818) 904-6339
New York, New York .... (212) 264-4730
Philadelphia, Pennsylvania .... (215) 597-8313
Seattle, Washington .... (206) 728-5314

For a detailed telephone contact list .... (301) 763-4100

Information Sources in the U.S. Department of Commerce: Quick Reference List

Aeronautical Chart Sales .... (301) 436-6990
Business Assistance .... (202) 482-3176
Commerce Speakers .... (202) 482-1360
Copyright Information* .... (202) 479-0700
Consumer Affairs .... (202) 482-5001
District Export Councils .... (202) 482-2975
Energy Related Inventions-Evaluation .... (301) 975-5500

EXPORT
Counseling .... (202) 482-3181
Export Trading Companies .... (202) 482-5131
License/Application (STELA) .... (202) 482-2752
Fish Exports/Imports .... (202) 673-5335
Fishery Management Plans .... (202) 673-5268
Foreign Trade Zones .... (202) 482-2862
Freight Rates** .... (202) 366-2271
Industry/Products Information .... (202) 482-1461
Joint Ventures (National) .... (202) 482-1093
Metric Information .... (202) 482-3036
Minority Owned Business .... (202) 482-2414
Nautical Chart Sales .... (301) 436-6990
NTIS Sales Desk .... (703) 487-4650
Overseas Customer Lists .... (202) 482-3181
Overseas Marketing .... (202) 482-3022
Patent Information .... (703) 557-5168
Productivity Enhancement Information .... (202) 482-0940

PROCUREMENT
Bidder's List .... (202) 482-3387
Federal Procurement Conferences .... (202) 482-3387
MBDA Profile System .... (202) 482-1958

Small Business .... (202) 482-1472
Women Owned Business .... (202) 482-3387

PUBLICATIONS
"Business America" Magazine ..... (202) 482-3251
Commerce Business Daily .... (202) 482-0632
NIST Reference Materials .... (301) 975-2012
Survey of Current Business .... (202) 523-0777
Quality Award .... (301) 975-2036
Sea Grant Research .... (301) 443-8923

SMALL BUSINESS
Assistance .... (202) 482-3176
Procurement/Set Asides .... (202) 482-3387
Technology .... (202) 482-8111
Standards & Codes for Products ..... (301) 975-4036

STATISTICS
Business Cycles .... (202) 523-0800
Capital Investment .... (202) 523-0791
Gross National Product .... (202) 482-0669
Foreign Travelers to U.S. .... (202) 482-4028
Housing Starts .... (301) 763-2880
Income Data .... (301) 763-5060
International Investment .... (202) 523-0659
International Trade Balance .... (202) 523-0620
Leading Economic Indicators ...... (202) 523-0777
Personal Income, Outlays and Savings .... (202) 523-0832
Personal Income by County .... (202) 523-0966
Population .... (301) 763-5002
Price Indexes .... (202) 523-0828
Regional Projections .... (202) 523-0946
Retail Trade Data .... (301) 763-5294
Trade Statistics .... (202) 482-2185

* Handled by the Library of Congress
** Handled by Maritime Commission

Source: *Business Services Directory,* U.S. Department of Commerce, Office of Business Liaison.

COMMODITIES: SOURCES OF GOVERNMENT INFORMATION

Information on various commodities may be obtained by calling the following:

Office of Industries
International Trade Commission
Telephone: 202–523–0146

Bureau of Mines
The Bureau uses three basic classifications:
Ferrous Metals
Telephone: 202–634–1010
Nonferrous Metals
Telephone: 202–634–1055
Industrial Minerals
Telephone: 202–634–1202

Crops Branch
Department of Agriculture
Telephone: 202–786–1840

Metals, Minerals and Commodities
Trade Development
Telephone: 202–482–0575

Minerals Industries
Bureau of the Census
Telephone: 202–763–5938 031

Industry and Commodity Classification
Bureau of the Census
Telephone: 202–763–1935

Federal Agricultural Service: Commodity and Marketing Divisions
Dairy, Livestock and Poultry . . . . (202) 477-8031
Grain and Feed Division . . . . (202) 477-6219
Horticulture and Tropical Products . . . . (202) 477-6590
Oilseed and Oilseed Products . . . . (202) 447-7037
Tobacco, Cotton and Seeds . . . . (202) 382-9516
Forest Products . . . . (202) 382-8138

Available through the Government Printing Office (202–783–3238) are the Bureau of the Census Publications, *U.S. Imports, U.S.A. Commodities by Country* and *U.S. Exports Schedule 13, Commodities by Country*.

DOING BUSINESS WITH THE FEDERAL GOVERNMENT

Publications

Doing Business with the Federal Government contains helpful material for marketing products or services to the Government, i.e., how to make products known, how and where to obtain the necessary forms and papers to get started, and how to bid on Government contracts. It also provides a geographical listing of Business Service Centers that have information about contract opportunities, as well as whom to contact and where to go for the information needed to sell to individual Government agencies. A list of Business Service Centers is given below.

The *Commerce Business Daily* tells, for example, what products and services the Government is buying, which agencies are buying, due dates for bids, how to get complete specifications. Each weekday, the *Commerce Business Daily* gives a complete listing of products and services wanted by the U.S. Government. Each listing includes product or service, along with a short description, name and address of agency, deadline for proposals or bids, phone number to request specifications, and solicitation numbers of product or service needed. Issued Monday through Friday.

The *Federal Acquisition Regulation* (FAR) is the primary source of procurement regulations used by all Federal agencies in their acquisition of supplies and services. It sets forth all the provisions and clauses that are used in Government contracting. Because the clauses in a specific solicitation for bids refer to a numbered provision of FAR rather than providing the full text, the FAR is necessary to understand the solicitation. Subscription service consists of a basic manual and supplementary material for an indeterminate period.

The *United States Government Purchasing and Sales Directory* contains an alphabetical listing of the products and services bought by all military departments and a separate listing for civilian agencies. It also includes an explanation of the ways in which the Small Business Administration can help a business obtain Government prime contracts and subcontracts, data on Government sales of surplus property, and comprehensive descriptions of the scope of the Government market for research and development.

The *Small Business Subcontracting Directory* is designed to aid small business professionals interested in subcontracting opportunities within the Department of Defense (DOD). The guide is arranged alphabetically by state and includes the name and address of each current DOD prime contractor as well as the product or service being provided to DOD. It also includes the name and telephone number for each DOD Small Business Liaison Officer who knows what the subcontracted products and services are, what the prime contracting firm has purchased in the past, what it is presently purchasing, and what it may be planning to purchase in the future.

The *Federal Register* provides the official version of public regulations issued by the Federal agencies. It also includes announcements of grants and other funding information, as well as data on the availability of Government contracts.

U.S. GENERAL SERVICES ADMINISTRATION: BUSINESS SERVICE CENTERS

The Business Service Centers are a one stop, one point of contact for information on General Services Administration and other Government contract programs. The primary function is to provide advice on doing business with the Federal Government. The Centers provide information, assistance, and counseling and sponsor business clinics, procurement conferences, and business opportunity meetings.

Business representatives interested in selling products and services to the Government should contact the nearest Business Service Center given below.

Mailing Address and Telephone	Area of Service
Business Service Center General Services Administration Tip O'Neill Federal Building 10 Causeway Street Boston, MA 02109 (617) 565–8100	Connecticut, Maine, Massachusetts, New Hampshire, Rhode Island, and Vermont
Business Service Center General Services Administration 26 Federal Plaza New York, NY 10007 (212) 264–1234	New Jersey, New York, Puerto Rico, and Virgin Islands
Business Service Center General Services Administration 7th and D Streets, SW., RM. 1050 Washington, DC 20407 (202) 472–1804	District of Columbia, nearby Maryland, Virginia
Business Service Center General Services Administration 9th and Market Streets Room 5151 Philadelphia, PA 19107 (215) 597–9613	Delaware, Pennsylvania, West Virginia, Maryland, Virginia
Business Service Center General Services Administration 401 West Peachtree Atlanta, GA 30303 (404) 221–5103	Alabama, Florida, Georgia, Kentucky, Mississippi, North Carolina, South Carolina, and Tennessee
Business Service Center General Services Administration 230 South Dearborn Street Chicago, IL 60604 (312) 353–5383	Illinois, Indiana, Ohio, Michigan, Minnesota, and Wisconsin
Business Service Center General Services Administration 1500 East Bannister Road Kansas City, MO 64131 (816) 926–7203	Iowa, Kansas, Missouri, and Nebraska
Business Service Center General Services Administration 819 Taylor Street Fort Worth, TX 76102 (817) 334–3284	Arkansas, Louisiana, New Mexico, Oklahoma, and Texas

Mailing Address and Telephone	Area of Service
Business Service Center General Services Administration Building 41, Denver Federal Center Denver, CO 80225 (303) 236–7408	Colorado, Montana, North Dakota, South Dakota, Utah, and Wyoming
Business Service Center General Services Administration 525 Market Street San Francisco, CA 94105 (415) 744–5050	California (northern), Hawaii, and Nevada (except Clark County)
Business Service Center General Services Administration 300 North Los Angeles Street Los Angeles, CA 90012 (213) 894–3210	Arizona, Los Angeles, California (southern), and Nevada (Clark County only)
Business Service Center General Services Administration 15th and C Streets, SW Auburn, WA 98001 (206) 931–7956	Alaska, Idaho, Oregon, and Washington

FEDERAL AND STATE GOVERNMENT ASSISTANCE AVAILABLE TO U.S. BUSINESSES: CENTER FOR THE UTILIZATION OF FEDERAL TECHNOLOGY

Government support of technical innovation is growing rapidly both at the Federal and State levels. A helpful source for information regarding the transfer of Federal technology to the U.S. economy is the **Center for the Utilization of Federal Technology (CUFT),** which is part of the National Technical Information Service (NTIS) of the U.S. Department of Commerce, (703) 487-4805. One of its major roles is to link U.S. businesses with federally developed technologies and resources having commercial or practical application. By working directly with U.S. Government agencies, CUFT has prepared a number of directories and catalogs to alert companies to these valuable Government resources.

Its most recent directory, *Directory of Federal and State Business Assistance–A Guide for New and Growing Companies,* presents full descriptions to financial, management, innovation, and information programs and services established to help both large and small firms in their day-to-day operations.

A companion directory, *Directory of Federal Laboratory and Technical Resources–A Guide to Services, Facilities, and Expertise,* provides detailed descriptions of technology-oriented Federal resources. Especially notable are the entries describing the technical information centers offering information assistance in focused technology areas.

Also available are the *Federal Technology Catalogs–Guides to New and Practical Technologies* which annually offer full descriptions to more than 1,200 new technologies and R&D developments. Another annual catalog series, *Catalog of Government Inventions Available for Licensing.* The *Catalog* contains information on licensing and marketing government-owned-inventions, frequently with the benefit of exclusive licensing and/or with the protection of foreign patent rights. To order write the National Technical Information Service, 5285 Port Royal Road, Springfield, VA 22161 or call 703-487-4650.

BUSINESS ASSISTANCE PROGRAM: COMMERCE DEPARTMENT

The Business Assistance program is designed to shorten the time it takes a businessperson to track down information within the labyrinth of government bureaus and agencies. Business Assistance Program staffers can provide information or direct inquiries to the proper authority on such subjects as regulatory changes, government programs, services, policies, and even relevant government publications for the business community. For information call 202–482–3176 or write: Business Assistance Program Business Liason Office, Rm 5898-C, Department of Commerce, Washington, DC 20230.

FEDERAL INFORMATION CENTER (FIC)

The FIC is a focal point for obtaining information about the federal government and often about state and local governments. A member of the center's staff can either provide information or direct inquiries to an expert who can.

Either call (301) 722-9098 or the phone number listed below for the area that is appropriate for you:

Eastern Time
Zone . . . . .800-347-1997 . . . 9:00 AM–5:00 PM
Central Time
Zone . . . . .800-366-2998 . . . 9:00 AM–5:30 PM
Mountain Time
Zone . . . . .800-357-3997 . . .10:30 AM–7:30 PM
Pacific Time
Zone . . . . .800-726-4995 . . .10:30 AM–7:30 PM
Alaska . . . . .800-729-8003 . . .12:30 AM–3:30 PM
Hawaii . . . . .800-733-5996 . . . 1:30 AM–10:30 PM

To write, mail your inquiry to the Federal Information Center, P.O. Box 600, Cumberland, MD 21502. Users of Telecommunications Devices for the Deaf (TDD/TTY) may call toll-free from any point in the United States by dialing (800) 326-2996.

State Information Guide

Regional Manufacturers Directories

Connecticut/Rhode Island Manufacturers Directory, Commerce Register®, 190 Godwin Avenue, Midland Park, NJ 07432

Directory of Central Atlantic States Manufacturers, George D. Hall Company, 50 Congress Street, Boston, MA 02109

Directory of New England Manufacturers, The, George D. Hall Company, 50 Congress Street, Boston, MA 02109

Maine/New Hampshire/Vermont Directory of Manufacturers, MacRAE's, 817 Broadway, New York, NY 10003

Maryland/DC/Delaware Manufacturers Directory, MacRAE's, 817 Broadway, New York, NY 10003

Massachusetts/Rhode Island Manufacturers Directory, MacRAE's, 817 Broadway, New York, NY 10003

New York Metro Directory of Manufacturers, Commerce Register®, 190 Godwin Avenue, Midland Park, NJ 07432

New England Manufacturers Directory, George D. Hall Company, 50 Congress Street, Boston, MA 02109

New York Upstate Directory of Manufacturers, Commerce Register®, 190 Godwin Avenue, Midland Park, NJ 07432

North/South Carolina/Virginia, MacRAE's, 817 Broadway, New York, NY 10003

Interstate Manufacturers' and Industrial Directory, Bell Directory Publishers, Inc., 1995 Broadway, New York, NY 10023

Midwest Manufacturers' and Industrial Directory, Industrial Directory Publishers, David Whitney Building, Detroit, MI 48226

State Sales Guides, Dun & Bradstreet, Inc., 99 Church Street, New York, NY 10007

Upstate New York Directory of Manufacturers, Commerce Register®, 190 Godwin Avenue, Midland Park, NJ 07432

State Business Assistance Publications

Directory of Incentives for Business Investment and Development in the U.S., The Urban Institute Press, available from United Press of America, 4720 Boston Way, Lanham, MD 20706. State by state guide to economic business incentives. Included are descriptions of state assistance and financial assistance programs.

Monthly Checklist of State Publications, Superintendent of Documents. Washington, DC 20402. A monthly list of documents and publications received from the States.

The National Directory of State Agencies, Cambridge Information Group, 7200 Wisconsin Avenue, Bethesda, MD 20814-9777. Names, titles, addresses and telephone numbers of state officials.

State Administrative Officials Classified by Function, Council of State Governments, Iron Works Pike, P.O. Box 1190, Lexington, KY 40578. Names, titles, telephone numbers and addresses of state officials and administrators.

Business Assistance Centers by State

Business/Industry Data Centers (BDIC's) offer assistance in business related matters. Such assistance includes information gathering, location of expert help, and guidance on new technologies. Most of these centers also are able to offer other types of assistance, such as market feasibility, or at least link businesses with appropriate contacts.

To find out where a center for a given state is located, contact the Department of Commerce for that state or call 301-763-1580.

State Data Center Program of the Bureau of the Census

Access to the many statistical products available from the Bureau of the Census is provided through the services of the joint federal-state cooperative State Data Center Program. Through the Program, the Bureau furnishes statistical products, training in the data access and use, technical assistance, and consultation to states which, in turn, disseminate the products and provide assistance in their use.

Additional information on the State Data Program and a list of the State Data Centers can be obtained by contacting the User Services staff in any of the Bureau's regional offices or by calling the Data User Services Division of the Bureau of the Census at 301-763-1580.

State Information Offices*

Alabama

STATE CAPITOL, MONTGOMERY, AL 36130
(205) 242-8000

INFORMATION OFFICES

Commerce/Economic Development
Alabama Development Office
401 Adams Avenue
Montgomery, AL 36130
Department of Economic & Community Affairs
401 Adams Avenue
Montgomery, AL 36130
Corporate
Secretary of State
P.O. Box 5616
Montgomery, AL 36103
Taxation
Department of Revenue
Gordon Persons Building
50 Ripley Street
Montgomery, AL 36130
State Chamber of Commerce
Business Council of Alabama
468 S. Perry Street
P.O. Box 76
Montgomery, AL 36101
International Commerce
Department of International Trade
Alabama Development Office
401 Adams Avenue
Montgomery, AL 36130
Banking
State Banking Department
101 S. Union Street
Montgomery, AL 36130
Securities
Alabama Securities Exchange Commission
770 Washington Street
Montgomery, AL 36130
Labor and Industrial Relations
Department of Industrial Relations
649 Monroe Street
Montgomery, AL 36130
Alabama Department of Labor
Administrative Building
1789 Congressman W. L. Dickinson Drive
National Guard Credit Union
Montgomery, AL 36130
Insurance
Department of Insurance
135 S. Union Street
Montgomery, AL 36130

* See page 217 for Small Business Administration Regional Office telephone numbers.

Uniform Industrial Code
Alabama Development Office
401 Adams Street
Montgomery, AL 36130

INDUSTRIAL AND BUSINESS DIRECTORIES

Alabama Directory of Mining and Manufacturing, Alabama Development Office, State Capitol, Montgomery, AL 36130
Alabama Manufacturers Register, Manufacturers' News, Inc., 1633 Central Street, Evanston, IL 60201
Alabama International Trade Directory, Alabama Development Office, State Capitol, Montgomery, AL 36130
Top Businesses in Alabama, State Capitol, Montgomery, AL 36130
Birmingham Industrial Directory, Birmingham Chamber of Commerce, 1914 6th Avenue, Birmingham, AL 35203

Alaska

STATE CAPITOL, JUNEAU, AK 99811
(907) 465-2111

INFORMATION OFFICES

Commerce/Economic Development
Department of Commerce & Economic Development
P.O. Box 110800
Juneau, AK 99811-0800
Corporate
Department of Commerce & Economic Development
Corporation Section
P.O. Box 110808
Juneau, AK 99811-0808
Taxation
Department of Revenue
P.O. Box 110420
Juneau, AK 99811-0420
State Chamber of Commerce
Alaska State Chamber of Commerce
310 2nd Street
Juneau, AK 99801
International Commerce
Office of International Trade
3601 C Street
Anchorage, AK 99503
Banking
Division of Banking, Securities and Corporations
Department of Commerce & Economic Development
P.O. Box 110808
Juneau, AK 99811-0808
Securities
Division of Banking, Securities and Corporations

Department of Commerce and Economic Development
P.O. Box 11808
Juneau, AK 99811-0808

Labor and Industrial Relations
Department of Labor
P.O. Box 21149
Juneau, AK 99802-1149

Insurance
Division of Insurance
Department of Commerce and Economic Development
P.O. Box 110805
Juneau, AK 99811-0805

Uniform Industrial Code
Uniform Commercial Code Office
Division of Management
Department of Natural Resources
P.O. Box 107005
Anchorage, AK 99510-7005

INDUSTRIAL AND BUSINESS DIRECTORIES

Alaska Petroleum and Industrial Directory, 409 W. Northern Lights Boulevard, Anchorage, AK 99603

Arizona

State Capitol, Phoenix, AZ 85007
(602) 542-4331

INFORMATION OFFICES

Commerce/Economic Development
Department of Commerce
3800 N. Central Avenue
Phoenix, AZ 85012

Corporate
Arizona Corporation Commission
1200 W. Washington Avenue
Phoenix, AZ 85007

Taxation
Department of Revenue
1600 W. Monroe
Phoenix, AZ 85007

State Chamber of Commerce
Arizona State Chamber of Commerce
1221 E. Osborn Road
Phoenix, AZ 85014

Banking
Banking Department
3225 N. Central
Phoenix, AZ 85012

Insurance
Insurance Department
3030 N. 3rd Street
Phoenix, AZ 85012

Securities
Arizona Corporation Commission
1200 W. Washington Avenue
Phoenix, AZ 85007

International Commerce
International Trade
Department of Commerce
3800 N. Central Avenue
Phoenix, AZ 85012

Labor and Industrial Relations
Industrial Commission
800 W. Washington Street
Phoenix, AZ 85005

INDUSTRIAL AND BUSINESS DIRECTORIES

Arizona Industrial Directory, Phoenix Chamber of Commerce, 34 W. Monroe, Phoenix, AZ 85003; Manufacturers' News, 1633 Central Street, Evanston, IL 60201

Arizona USA International Trade Directory, Arizona State Department of Commerce, 3800 N. Central Avenue, Phoenix, AZ 85012

Directory of Arizona Manufacturers, Phoenix Chamber of Commerce, 34 W. Monroe, Phoenix, AZ 85003

Arkansas

State Capitol, Little Rock, AR 72201
(501) 682-3000

INFORMATION OFFICES

Commerce/Economic Development
Arkansas Industrial Development Commission
Big Mac Building
One State Capitol Mall
Little Rock, AR 72201

Corporate
Secretary of State
Corporations Department
State Capitol
Little Rock, AR 72201

Taxation
State Revenue Office
Department of Finance and Administration
Joel Y. Ledbetter Building
7th and Wolfe Streets
Little Rock, AR 72201

State Chamber of Commerce
Arkansas State Chamber of Commerce
410 South Cross
Little Rock, AR 72201

International Commerce
Arkansas Industrial Development Commission
Big Mac Building
One State Capitol Mall
Little Rock, AR 72201

Banking
State Bank Department
323 Center Street
Tower Building
Little Rock, AR 72201

Securities
Arkansas Securities Department
Heritage West Building
201 East Markham
Little Rock, AR 72201

Labor and Industrial Relations
Arkansas Department of Labor
10421 West Markham
Little Rock, AR 72205

Insurance
Arkansas Insurance Department
400 University Tower Building
Little Rock, AR 72204

Ombudsman
State Claims Commission
State Capitol
Little Rock, AR 72201

INDUSTRIAL AND BUSINESS DIRECTORIES

Arkansas Directory of Manufacturers, Arkansas Industrial Development Commission, One State Capitol Mall, Little Rock, AR 72201; Manufacturers' News, 1633 Central Street, Evanston, IL 60201

Arkansas State and County Economic Data (annual), Research and Public Service, Division of Regional Economic Analysis, 2801 South University, Little Rock, AR 72204

California

State Capitol, Sacramento, CA 95814
(916) 332-9900

INFORMATION OFFICES

Commerce/Economic Development
Trade and Commerce Agency
801 K Street
Sacramento, CA 95814

Corporate
Secretary of State
1230 "J" Street
Sacramento, CA 95814

Taxation
Board of Equalization
450 N Street
Sacramento, CA 95814

State Chamber of Commerce
California Chamber of Commerce
1027 10th Street
P.O. Box 1736
Sacramento, CA 95814

International Commerce
California State World Trade Commission
801 K Street
Sacramento, CA 95814

Banking
State Banking Department
11 Pine Street
San Francisco, CA 94111-5613

Securities
Department of Corporations
1107 9th Street
Sacramento, CA 95814

Labor and Industrial Relations
Department of Industrial Relations
455 Golden Gate Avenue
P.O. Box 420603
San Francisco, CA 94842
or
2422 Arden Way
Sacramento, CA 95825

Insurance
Department of Insurance
600 S. Commonwealth Avenue
Los Angeles, CA 90005
or
770 "L" Street
Sacramento, CA 93814

INDUSTRIAL AND BUSINESS DIRECTORIES

California Handbook, California Institute of Public Affairs, P.O. Box 49040, Sacramento, CA 95818

California International Trade Register, Database Publishing Company, P.O. Box 7440, Newport Beach, CA 92658; Manufacturers' News, Inc., 1633 Central Street, Evanston, IL 60201

California Manufacturers Register, Database Publishing Company, P.O. Box 7440, Newport Beach, CA 92658; Manufacturers' News, Inc., 1633 Central Street, Evanston, IL 60201

California Manufacturers Register, Database Publishing Company, P.O. Box 7440, Newport Beach, CA 92658; Manufacturers' News, Inc., 1633 Central Street, Evanston, IL 60201

California Services Register, Database Publishing Company, P.O. Box 7440, Newport Beach, CA 92658; Manufacturers' News, Inc., 1633 Central Street, Evanston, IL 60201

San Francisco County Commerce and Industry Directory, Database Publishing Company, P.O. Box 7440, Newport Beach, CA 92658; Manufacturers' News, Inc., 1633 Central Street, Evanston, IL 60201

Southern California Business Directory and Buyers Guide, Database Publishing Company, P.O. Box 7440, Newport Beach, CA 92658; Manufacturers' News, Inc., 1633 Central Street, Evanston, IL 60201

Colorado

State Capitol, Denver, CO 80203
(303) 866-5000

INFORMATION OFFICES

Commerce/Economic Development
Office of Business Development
World Trade Center
1625 Broadway
Denver, CO 80202

Corporate
Secretary of State
Civic Center Plaza
1560 Broadway
Denver, CO 80202

Taxation
Colorado Department of Revenue
Department of Revenue
1375 Sherman Street
Denver, CO 80203

State Chamber of Commerce
Colorado Association of Commerce and Industry
1776 Lincoln Street
Denver, CO 80203

International Commerce
Office of Business Development
International Trade Office
1625 Broadway
Denver, CO 80202

Banking
Division of Banking
1560 Broadway
Denver, CO 80202

Securities
Division of Securities
Department of Regulatory Agencies
1580 Lincoln Street
Denver, CO 80203

Labor and Industrial Relations
Division of Labor
1120 Lincoln Street
Denver, CO 80203-2140

Insurance
Division of Insurance
1560 Broadway
Denver, CO 80202

Uniform Commercial Code
Commercial Recordings Division
1560 Broadway
Denver, CO 80202

INDUSTRIAL AND BUSINESS DIRECTORIES

Directory of Colorado Manufacturers, Business Research Division, Graduate School of Business Administration, Campus Box 420, University of Colorado, Boulder, CO 80309; Manufacturers' News, Inc., 1633 Central Street, Evanston, IL 60201

Connecticut

STATE CAPITOL, HARTFORD, CT 06106
(203) 566-4200

INFORMATION OFFICES

Commerce/Economic Development
Department of Economic Development
865 Brook Street
Rocky Hill, CT 06067

Corporate
Secretary of State
Corporations Division
30 Trinity Street
Hartford, CT 06106

Taxation
Department of Revenue Services
92 Farmington Avenue
Hartford, CT 06105

State Chamber of Commerce
Connecticut Business and Industry Association
370 Asylum Street
Hartford, CT 06103

International Commerce
Department of Economic Development
865 Brook Street
Rocky Hill, CT 06067

Banking
Department of Banking
44 Capitol Avenue
Hartford, CT 06106

Securities
Divisions of Securities & Business Investments
Department of Banking
44 Capitol Avenue
Hartford, CT 06106

Labor and Industrial Relations
Department of Labor
200 Folly Brook Boulevard
Wethersfield, CT 06109

Insurance
Department of Insurance
165 Capitol Avenue
Hartford, CT 06106

Uniform Industrial Code
Department of Economic Development
865 Brook Street
Rocky Hill, CT 06107

Business Ombudsman
Department of Economic Development
865 Brook Street
Rocky Hill, CT 06067

INDUSTRIAL AND BUSINESS DIRECTORIES

Classified Business Directory—State of Connecticut, Connecticut Directory Co., Inc., 322 Main Street, Stamford, CT 06901

Connecticut Classified Business Directory, Connecticut Directory Co., Inc., 322 Main Street, Stamford, CT 06901

Connecticut Service Directory, George D. Hall Co., 50 Congress Street, Boston, MA 02109

Directory of Connecticut Manufacturers, George D. Hall Co., 50 Congress Street, Boston, MA 02109

Directory of Connecticut Manufacturing Establishments, Connecticut Department of Labor, 200 Folly Brook Boulevard, Wethersfield, CT 06109

MacRAE's State Industrial Directory Connecticut/Rhode Island, MacRAE's Industrial Directories, 817 Broadway, New York, NY 10003

Delaware

Legislative Hall, Dover, DE 19901
(302) 739-4101

INFORMATION OFFICES

Commerce/Economic Development
Delaware Development Office
99 Kings Highway
P.O. Box 1401
Dover, DE 19903

Corporate
Secretary of State
Corporations Department
Townsend Building
P.O. Box 898
Dover, DE 19903

Taxation
Department of Finance
Division of Revenue
Carvel State Office Building
820 N. French Street
Wilmington, DE 19801

International Commerce
Delaware Development Office
99 Kings Highway
P.O. Box 1401
Dover, DE 19903

State Chamber of Commerce
Delaware State Chamber of Commerce, Inc.
One Commerce Center
Wilmington, DE 19801

Banking
State Bank Commission
Department of State
Thomas Collins Building
P.O. Box 1401
Dover, DE 19903

Labor and Industrial Relations
Division of Industrial Affairs
Department of Labor
Carvel State Office Building
820 N. French Street
Wilmington, DE 19801

Insurance
State Insurance Commission
841 Silver Lake Boulevard
Rodney Building
Dover, DE 19901

INDUSTRIAL AND BUSINESS DIRECTORIES

Delaware Directory of Commerce and Industry, Delaware State Chamber of Commerce, One Commerce Center, Wilmington, DE 19801; Manufacturers' News, Inc., 1633 Central Street, Evanston, IL 60201

MacRAE's State Industrial Directory Maryland/DC/Delaware, MacRAE's Industrial Directories, 817 Broadway, New York, NY 10003

Florida

State Capitol, Tallahassee, FL 32399
(904) 488-1234

INFORMATION OFFICES

Commerce/Economic Development
Department of Commerce
Collins Building
107 W. Gaines Street
Tallahassee, FL 32399-2000

Division of Economic Development
Department of Commerce
Collins Building
Tallahassee, FL 32399-2000

Corporate
Secretary of State
Division of Corporations
409 E. Gaines Street
Tallahassee, FL 32301

Taxation
Department of Revenue
Carlton Building
Tallahassee, FL 32399-0100

State Chamber of Commerce
Florida Chamber of Commerce
P.O. Box 11309
Tallahassee, FL 32302-3309

International Commerce
Florida Department of Commerce
Division of International Trade and Development
Collins Building
107 W. Gaines Street
Tallahassee, FL 32399-2000

Banking
Florida Department of Banking & Finance
The Capitol
Tallahassee, FL 32399-0350

Securities
Florida Department of Banking & Finance
Division of Securities
The Capitol
Tallahassee, FL 32399-0350

Labor and Industrial Relations
Florida Department of Labor and Employment Security
Atkins Building

1320 Executive Center Drive, East
Tallahassee, FL 32399-2152

Insurance
Florida Department of Insurance
The Capitol
Tallahassee, FL 32399-0300

Commercial Information Services
Florida Department of State
Bureau of Information Services
407 E. Gaines Street
Tallahassee, FL 32301

Business Ombudsman
Florida Department of Commerce
Bureau of Business Assistance
Collins Building
107 W. Gaines Street
Tallahassee, FL 32399

INDUSTRIAL AND BUSINESS DIRECTORIES

Florida Manufacturers Register, Manufacturers' News, Inc., 1633 Central Street, Evanston, IL 60201

South Florida International Trade and Services Directory 1990, World Trade Center Miami, One World Trade Plaza, 80 SW 8th St., Suite 1800, Miami, FL 33130

Directory of International Manufacturing and Commercial Operations In Florida, Florida Department of Commerce, Division of International Trade and Development, Collins Building, Tallahassee, FL 32399-2000

Directory of Florida Industries, Florida Chamber of Commerce, Trend Book Division, P.O. Box 611, St Petersburg, FL 33731

Georgia

State Capitol, Atlanta, GA 30334
(404) 656-2000

INFORMATION OFFICES

Commerce/Economic Development
Department of Industry, Trade, and Tourism
P.O. Box 1776
285 Peachtree Center Avenue, N.E.
Atlanta, GA 30301-1776

Corporate
Business Services and Regulations Division
Secretary of State
2 Martin Luther King Jr. Drive, S.E.
Atlanta, GA 30334

Taxation
Department of Revenue
270 Washington Street, S.W.
Atlanta, GA 30334

State Chamber of Commerce
Business Council of Georgia
233 Peachtree Street
Atlanta, GA 30303-2705

International Commerce
Department of Industry and Trade
P.O. Box 1776
285 Peachtree Center Avenue
Atlanta, GA 30303-1776

Banking
Department of Banking and Finance
2990 Brandywine Road
Atlanta, GA 30341

Securities
Business Services and Regulations Division
Secretary of State
2 Martin Luther King Jr. Drive, S.E.
Atlanta, GA 30334

Labor and Industrial Relations
Department of Labor
148 International Boulevard
Atlanta, GA 30303

Insurance
Office of Commissioner of Insurance
2 Martin Luther King Jr. Drive, S.E.
Atlanta, GA 30334

INDUSTRIAL AND BUSINESS DIRECTORIES

Georgia Manufacturers Register, Manufacturers' News, Inc., 1633 Central Street, Evanston, IL 60201

Georgia Manufacturing Directory, Department of Industry, Trade, and Tourism, P.O. Box 1776, 285 Peachtree Center Avenue, Atlanta, GA 30301-1776

Georgia World Trade Directory, Business Council of Georgia, 233 Peachtree Street, Atlanta, GA 30303

Industrial Sites in Georgia, Georgia Power Company, Box 4545, Atlanta, GA 30303

Georgia International Trade Directory, Department of Industry, Trade, and Tourism, P.O. Box 1776, 285 Peachtree Center Avenue, Atlanta, GA 30301-1776

Georgia Directory of International Services, World Congress Institute, 1 Park Place S, Fulton Federal Building, Atlanta, GA 30303

International Companies with Facilities in Georgia. Department of Industry, Trade, and Tourism, P.O. Box 1776, 285 Peachtree Center Avenue, Atlanta, GA 30301-1776

Hawaii

State Capitol, Honolulu, HI 96813
(808) 548-6222

INFORMATION OFFICES

Commerce/Economic Development

Department of Business, Economic Development & Tourism
737 Bishop Street
Honolulu, HI 96813

Department of Commerce and Consumer Affairs
1010 Richards Street
Honolulu, HI 96813

Corporate

Department of Commerce and Consumer Affairs
Business Registration Division
P.O. Box 40
Honolulu, HI 96810

Taxation

Department of Taxation
830 Punchbowl Street
Honolulu, HI 96813

State Chamber of Commerce

Chamber of Commerce of Hawaii
735 Bishop Street
Honolulu, HI 96813

International Commerce

International Business Center of Hawaii
201 Merchant Street
Honolulu, HI 96813

Hawaii Foreign-Trade Zone No. 9
Pier 2
Honolulu, HI 96813

Banking

Financial Institutions Division
Department of Commerce and Consumer Affairs
1010 Richards Street
Honolulu, HI 96813

Securities

Financial Institutions Division
Department of Commerce and Consumer Affairs
1010 Richards Street
Honolulu, HI 96813

Labor and Industrial Relations

Department of Labor and Industrial Relations
830 Punchbowl Street
Honolulu, HI 96813

Insurance

Insurance Division
Department of Commerce and Consumer Affairs
1010 Richards Street
Honolulu, HI 96813

Business Ombudsman

Office of the Ombudsman
465 S. King Street
Honolulu, HI 96813

INDUSTRIAL AND BUSINESS DIRECTORIES

Directory of Manufacturers, State of Hawaii, Chamber of Commerce of Hawaii, Dillingham Building, 735 Bishop Street, Honolulu, HI 96813

Hawaii Business Directory, Hawaii Business Directory, Inc., 1164 Bishop Street, Honolulu, HI 96813

Idaho

State Capitol, Boise, ID 83720
(208) 334-2411

INFORMATION OFFICES

Mailing address for all state offices is:
Statehouse
Boise, ID 83720

Commerce/Economic Development

Department of Commerce
700 W. State Street
Boise, ID 83720

Corporate

Secretary of State
State Capitol
Boise, ID 83720

Taxation

Department of Revenue and Taxation
700 W. State Street
Boise, ID 83720

State Chamber of Commerce

Idaho Association of Commerce and Industry
805 West Idaho
Boise, ID 83702

International Commerce

Department of Commerce
700 W. State Street
Boise, ID 83720

Banking

Department of Finance
700 W. State Street
Boise, ID 83720

Securities

Department of Finance
700 W. State Street
Boise, ID 83720

Labor and Industrial Relations

Department of Labor and Industrial Services
277 N. 6th Street
Boise, ID 83720

Insurance

Department of Insurance
700 W. State Street
Boise, ID 83720

Uniform Industrial Code

Department of Labor and Industrial Services

277 N. 6th Street
Boise, ID 83720

Business Ombudsman
Department of Commerce
700 W. State Street
Boise, ID 83720

INDUSTRIAL AND BUSINESS DIRECTORIES

Idaho Manufacturing Directory, Center for Business and Research, University of Idaho, Moscow, ID 83843; Manufacturers' News, Inc., 1633 Central Street, Evanston, IL 60201

Idaho Opportunities, Department of Commerce, 700 W. State Street, Boise, ID 83720

Illinois

State House, Springfield, IL 62706
(217) 782-2000

INFORMATION OFFICES

Commerce/Economic Development
Department of Commerce and Community Affairs
620 E. Adams Street
Springfield, IL 62701

Corporate
Secretary of State
Business Services
Michael Howlett Building
Springfield, IL 62756

Taxation
Department of Revenue
101 W. Jefferson Street
Springfield, IL 62708

State Chamber of Commerce
Illinois State Chamber of Commerce
20 N. Wacker Drive
Chicago, IL 60606

International Commerce
Department of Commerce & Community Affairs
100 W. Randolph Street
Chicago, IL 60601

Banking
Department of Financial Institutions
100 W. Randolph Street
Chicago, IL 60601

Securities
Secretary of State
840 S. Spring Street
Springfield, IL 62704

Labor and Industrial Relations
Department of Labor
100 N. 1st, Alzina Building
Springfield, IL 62706

Department of Commerce & Community Affairs
620 E. Adams Street
Springfield, IL 62701

Insurance
Department of Insurance
320 W. Washington Street
Springfield, IL 62767

Uniform Industrial Code
Secretary of State
Uniform Commercial Code
Michael Howlett Building
Springfield, IL 62756

Business Ombudsman
Attorney General
500 South Second Street
Springfield, IL 62706

INDUSTRIAL AND BUSINESS DIRECTORIES

Chicago Buyers' Guide, Chicago Association of Commerce and Industry, 130 S. Michigan Avenue, Chicago, IL 60603

Chicago Cook County and Illinois Industrial Directory, Manufacturers' News, Inc., 1633 Central Street, Evanston, IL 60201

Chicago Geographic Edition, Manufacturers' News, Inc., 1633 Central Street, Evanston, IL 60201

Illinois Industrial Directory, Manufacturers' News, Inc., 1633 Central Street, Evanston, IL 60201

Illinois Manufacturers Directory, Manufacturers' News, Inc., 1633 Central Street, Evanston, IL 60201

Illinois Services Directory, Manufacturers' News, Inc., 1633 Central Street, Evanston, IL 60201

Development Finance Programs, Department of Commerce and Community Affairs, 620 E. Adams, Springfield, IL 62701

Indiana

State House, Indianapolis, IN 46204
(317) 232-3140

INFORMATION OFFICES

Commerce/Economic Development
Department of Commerce
1 N. Capitol Avenue
Indianapolis, IN 46204

Corporate
Secretary of State
Corporation Section
Indiana Government Center South
Indianapolis, IN 46204

Taxation
Department of Revenue
100 N. Senate Avenue
Indianapolis, IN 46204

State Board of Tax Commissioners
150 W. Market Street
Indianapolis, IN 46204

State Chamber of Commerce
Indiana Chamber of Commerce
1 N. Capitol Avenue
Indianapolis, IN 46204

International Commerce
International Trade Division
Indiana Department of Commerce
1 N. Capitol Avenue
Indianapolis, IN 46204

Banking
Department of Financial Institutions
Indiana Government Center South
Indianapolis, IN 46204

Securities
Secretary of State
Securities Commission
1 N. Capitol Avenue
Indianapolis, IN 46204

Labor and Industrial Relations
Indiana Department of Labor
Indiana Government Center South
Indianapolis, IN 46204

Insurance
Indiana Department of Insurance
311 W. Washington Street
Indianapolis, IN 46204

Uniform Industrial Code
Secretary of State
Uniform Commercial Code Division
Indiana Government Center South
Indianapolis, IN 46204

Business Ombudsman
Business Ombudsman Office
Department of Commerce
1 N. Capitol Avenue
Indianapolis, IN 46204

INDUSTRIAL AND BUSINESS DIRECTORIES

Indiana Manufacturers Directory, Manufacturers' News, Inc., 1633 Central Street, Evanston, IL 60201

Iowa

State Capitol, Des Moines, IA 50319
(515) 281-5011

INFORMATION OFFICES

Commerce/Economic Development
Department of Economic Development
200 E. Grand Avenue
Des Moines, IA 50309

Corporate
Secretary of State
Corporation Division
Hoover Building
Des Moines, IA 50319

Taxation
Department of Revenue and Finance
Hoover Building
Des Moines, IA 50319

International Commerce
Department of Economic Development
200 E. Grand Avenue
Des Moines, IA 50309

Banking
Department of Commerce
Banking Division
200 E. Grand Avenue
Des Moines, IA 50309

Iowa Housing Finance Authority
200 E. Grand Avenue
Des Moines, IA 50309

Securities
Department of Commerce
Insurance Division
Securities Bureau
Lucas Building
Des Moines, IA 50319

Labor
Department of Employment Service
Division of Industrial Services
1000 E. Grand Avenue
Des Moines, IA 50319

Bureau of Labor
1000 E. Grand Avenue
Des Moines, IA 50319

Insurance
Department of Commerce
Insurance Division
Lucas Building
Des Moines, IA 50319

INDUSTRIAL AND BUSINESS DIRECTORIES

Iowa Manufacturers Register, Iowa Department of Economic Development, 200 E. Grand Avenue, Des Moines, IA 50309; Manufacturers' News, Inc., 1633 Central Street, Evanston, IL 60201

Doing Business in Iowa, Iowa Department of Economic Development, 200 E. Grand Avenue, Des Moines, IA 50309

Kansas

State House, Topeka, KS 66612
(913) 296-0111

INFORMATION OFFICES

Commerce/Economic Development
Department of Commerce
400 S.W. 8th Street
Topeka, KS 66603-3957

Corporate
Secretary of State
State House
Corporation Department
Topeka, KS 66612

Taxation
Department of Revenue
Docking State Office Building

915 Harrison Street
Topeka, KS 66612-1588

State Chamber of Commerce
Kansas Chamber of Commerce and Industry
500 Bank IV Tower
One Townsite Plaza
Topeka, KS 66603-3460

International Commerce
Department of Commerce
400 S.W. 8th Street
Topeka, KS 66603-3959

Banking
Banking Department
700 Jackson Street
Topeka, KS 66603-3714

Securities
Securities Commissioner of Kansas
618 S. Kansas
Topeka, KS 66603-3804

Labor and Industrial Relations
Department of Human Resources
401 Topeka
Topeka, KS 66603-3182

Insurance
Insurance Department
420 S.W. 9th Street
Topeka, KS 66612-1678

Business Ombudsman
Department of Commerce
400 S.W. 8th Street
Topeka, KS 66603-3957

INDUSTRIAL AND BUSINESS DIRECTORIES

Directory of Kansas Manufacturers and Products, Kansas Department of Commerce, 400 W. 8th Street, Topeka, KS 66603-3957; Manufacturers' News, Inc., 1633 Central Street, Evanston, IL 60201

Kansas Association Directory, Kansas Department of Commerce, 400 S.W. 8th Street, Topeka, KS 66603-3957

Kansas Aerospace Directory, Kansas Department of Commerce, 400 S.W. 8th Street, Topeka, KS 66603-3957

Kansas Agribusiness Directory, Kansas Department of Commerce, 400 S.W. 8th Street, Topeka, KS 66603-3957

Kansas International Trade Resource Directory, Kansas Department of Commerce, 400 S.W. 8th Street, Topeka, KS 66603-3957

Kansas Job Shop Directory, Kansas Department of Commerce, 400 S.W. 8th Street, Topeka, KS 66603-3957

Kentucky

State Capitol, Frankfort, KY 40601
(502) 564-3130

INFORMATION OFFICES

Commerce/Economic Development
Kentucky Economic Development Cabinet
Capital Plaza Office Tower
Frankfort, KY 40601

Corporate
Office of Secretary of State
Corporation Division
Capitol Building
Frankfort, KY 40601

Taxation
Kentucky Revenue Cabinet
Capitol Annex
Frankfort, KY 40601

State Chamber of Commerce
Kentucky Chamber of Commerce
Versailles Road
P.O. Box 817
Frankfort, KY 40602

International Commerce
Kentucky Economic Development Cabinet
Office of International Marketing
Capitol Plaza Tower
Frankfort, KY 40601

Banking
Kentucky Department of Financial Institutions
Division of Banking and Thrift Institutions
911 Leawood Drive
Frankfort, KY 40601-3392

Securities
Kentucky Department of Financial Institutions
Division of Securities
911 Leawood Drive
Frankfort, KY 40601-3392

Labor Industrial Relations
Kentucky Labor Cabinet
The 127 Building
Frankfort, KY 40601

Insurance
Kentucky Department of Insurance
229 West Main Street
P.O. Box 517
Frankfort, KY 40602

Uniform Industrial Code
Kentucky Department of Housing, Buildings, and Construction
The 127 Building
Frankfort, KY 40601

Business Ombudsman
Kentucky Department of Existing Business and Industry
Capitol Plaza Tower
Frankfort, KY 40601

INDUSTRIAL AND BUSINESS DIRECTORIES

Kentucky International Trade Directory, Kentucky Economic Development Cabinet, Capitol Plaza Tower, Frankfort, KY 40601

Kentucky Directory of Manufacturers, Kentucky Economic Development Cabinet, Capitol Plaza Tower, Frankfort, KY 40601
Kentucky Manufacturers Register, Manufacturers' News, Inc., 1633 Central Street, Evanston, IL 60201; Harris Publishing Co., 2057 Aurora Road, Twinsburg, OH 44087-1999

Louisiana

State Capitol, Baton Rouge, LA 70804
(504) 342-7015

INFORMATION OFFICES

Commerce/Economic Development
Department of Economic Development
P.O. Box 94185
Baton Rouge, LA 70804-9185
Corporate
Secretary of State
Division of Corporation
P.O. Box 94125
Baton Rouge, LA 70804-9125
Taxation
Department of Revenue and Taxation
P.O. Box 3440
Baton Rouge, LA 70823
State Chamber of Commerce
Louisiana Association of Business and Industry
P.O. Box 80258
Baton Rouge, LA 70898
International Commerce
Department of Economic Development
Office of International Trade, Finance and Development
P.O. Box 94185
Baton Rouge, LA 70804-9185
Banking
Department of Economic Development
Office of Financial Institutions
P.O. Box 94095
Baton Rouge, LA 70804
Securities
Louisiana Securities Commission
315 Louisiana State Office Building
325 Loyola Avenue
New Orleans, LA 70112
Labor and Industrial Relations
Department of Employment and Training
P.O. Box 94094
Baton Rouge, LA 70804-9094
Insurance
Office of Insurance Rating Commission
P.O. Box 94157
Baton Rouge, LA 70804
Uniform Industrial Code
Department of Economic Development
P.O. Box 94185
Baton Rouge, LA 70804-9185
Department of Employment Security and Training
Department of Employment and Training
P.O. Box 94094
Baton Rouge, LA 70804-9094
Business Ombudsman
Department of Economic Development
P.O. Box 94185
Baton Rouge, LA 70804-9185

INDUSTRIAL AND BUSINESS DIRECTORIES

Louisiana Manufacturers Register, Manufacturers' News, Inc., 1633 Central Street, Evanston, IL 60201
Louisiana Directory of Manufacturers, Department of Economic Development, 101 France Street, Baton Rouge, LA 70802
Louisiana International Trade Directory, World Trade Center, 2 Canal Street, New Orleans, LA 70130

Maine

State House, Augusta, ME 04333
(207) 289-1110

INFORMATION OFFICES

Commerce/Economic Development
Department of Economic and Community Development
193 State Street
State House Station #59
Augusta, ME 04333
Corporate
Department of State
Division of Corporations
Statehouse Station #101
Augusta, ME 04333
Private Development Associations
Maine Development Foundation
1 Memorial Circle
Augusta, ME 04330
Taxation
Bureau of Taxation
Department of Finance
State House Station #24
Augusta, ME 04333
State Chamber of Commerce
Maine State Chamber of Commerce and Industry
126 Sewall Street
Augusta, ME 04330
International Commerce
Department of Economic and Community Development
193 State Street
State House Station #59
Augusta, ME 04333

Banking
Bureau of Banking
Hallowell Annex
Correspondence to:
State House Station #36
Hallowell, ME 04347

Securities
Bureau of Banking
Securities Division
State House Station #121
Augusta, ME 04333

Labor and Industrial Relations
Department of Labor
20 Union Street
P.O. Box 309
Augusta, ME 04330

Insurance
Bureau of Insurance
Hallowell Annex
Hallowell, ME 04347
Correspondence to:
State House #34
Augusta, ME 04333

INDUSTRIAL AND BUSINESS DIRECTORIES

Maine Marketing Directory, Department of Economic and Community Development, State House Station #59, Augusta, ME 04333

MacRAE's State Industrial Directory Maine/New Hampshire/Vermont, MacRAE's Industrial Directories, 817 Broadway, New York, NY 10003

Maine Manufacturing Directory, Tower Publishing Company, 34 Diamond Street, Portland, ME 04101; Manufacturers' News, Inc., 1633 Central Street, Evanston, IL 60201

Maryland

State House, Annapolis, MD 21401
(410) 974-3901

INFORMATION OFFICES

Commerce/Economic Development
Department of Economic and Employment Development
217 E. Redwood Street
Baltimore, MD 21202

Corporate
State Department of Assessments and Taxation
301 W. Preston Street
Baltimore, MD 21201

Taxation
Comptroller of the Treasury
Louis L. Goldstein Treasury Building
P.O. Box 466
Annapolis, MD 21404

State Chamber of Commerce
Maryland Chamber of Commerce
275 West Street
Annapolis, MD 21401

International Commerce
Department of Economic and Employment Development
Maryland International Division
World Trade Center
401 East Pratt Street
Baltimore, MD 21202

Maryland Port Administrator
Office of Port Administration
World Trade Center
401 E. Pratt Street
Baltimore, MD 21202

Banking
State Banking Commission
Department of Licensing and Regulation
34 Market Place
Baltimore, MD 21202

Securities
Division of Securities
Office of the Attorney General
200 St. Paul Place
Baltimore, MD 21202

Labor and Industrial Relations
Division of Labor and Industry
Department of Licensing and Regulation
501 St. Paul Place
Baltimore, MD 21202

Insurance
State Insurance Division
Department of Licensing and Regulation
501 St. Paul Place
Baltimore, MD 21202

Business Ombudsman
Department of Economic and Employment Development
Maryland Business Assistance Center
217 East Redwood Street
Baltimore, MD 21202

INDUSTRIAL AND BUSINESS DIRECTORIES

Maryland Industry Directory, Harris Publishing Company, 2057 Aurora Road, Twinsburg, OH 44087

Maryland Manufacturers Directory, Manufacturers' News, Inc., 1633 Central Street, Evanston, IL 60201

Maryland High-Tech Directory, Corporate Technology Info. Services Inc., Suite 200, 12 Alfred Street, Woburn, MA 01801

Massachusetts

State House, Boston, MA 02133
General Information: (617) 727-2121

INFORMATION OFFICES

Commerce/Economic Development

Executive Office of Economic Affairs
2101 McCormack Building
1 Ashburton Place
Boston, MA 02108

Massachusetts Department of Commerce and Development
Division of Economic Development
100 Cambridge Street
Boston, MA 02202

Department of Commerce and Development
Leverett Saltonstall Building
100 Cambridge Street
Boston, MA 02202

Corporate

Secretary of State
1 Ashburton Place
Boston, MA 02108

Taxation

Accounting Bureau/Department of Revenue
Leverett Saltonstall Building
100 Cambridge Street
Boston, MA 02202

International Commerce

Office of International Trade and Investment
100 Cambridge Street
Boston, MA 02202

Banking

Division of Banks and Loan Agencies
100 Cambridge Street
Boston, MA 02202

Securities

Secretary of State
Securities Division
1 Ashburton Place
Boston, MA 02108

Labor and Industrial Relations

Executive Office of Labor
1 Ashburton Place
Boston, MA 02108

Department of Labor and Industries
Executive Office of Economic Affairs
100 Cambridge Street
Boston, MA 02202

Insurance

Division of Insurance
100 Cambridge Street
Boston, MA 02202

INDUSTRIAL AND BUSINESS DIRECTORIES

Directory of Directors in the City of Boston and Vicinity, Bankers Service Co., 14 Beacon Street, Boston, MA 02108

Directory of Massachusetts Manufacturers, George D. Hall Co., 50 Congress Street, Boston, MA 02109

MacRAE's State Industrial Directory Massachusetts/Rhode Island, MacRAE's Industrial Directories, 817 Broadway, New York, NY 10003

Massachusetts Service Directory, George D. Hall Co., 50 Congress Street, Boston, MA 02109

Massachusetts State Industrial Directory, State Industrial Directories Corp., 2 Penn Plaza, New York, NY 10001

Michigan

State Capitol, Lansing, MI 48913
(517) 373-1837

INFORMATION OFFICES

Commerce/Economic Development

Department of Commerce
525 W. Ottawa Street
P.O. Box 30004
Lansing, MI 48909

Corporate

Corporation and Securities Bureau
6546 Mercantile Way
Lansing, MI 48909

Taxation

Bureau of Collection
Department of Treasury
Treasury Building
P.O. Box 30199
Lansing, MI 48909

State Chamber of Commerce

Michigan State Chamber of Commerce
600 S. Walnut
Lansing, MI 48933

International Commerce

Michigan International Office
Department of Commerce
525 W. Ottawa Street
P.O. Box 30225
Lansing, MI 48909

Banking

Financial Institutions Bureau
Department of Commerce
Grand Plaza
206 E. Michigan
P.O. Box 30224
Lansing, MI 48909

Securities

Corporation and Securities Bureau
Department of Commerce
6546 Mercantile Way
P.O. Box 30199
Lansing, MI 48909

Labor and Industrial Relations

Bureau of Employment Relations
Department of Labor
State of Michigan Plaza Building
1200 Sixth Street
Detroit, MI 48226

Department of Labor
Victor Office Center
201 North Washington
P.O. Box 30015
Lansing, MI 48909
Insurance
Ottawa Building
P.O. Box 30220
Lansing, MI 48909

INDUSTRIAL AND BUSINESS DIRECTORIES

Harris Michigan Marketers Industrial Directory, Harris Publishing Company, 2057 Aurora Road, Twinsburg, OH 44139

Michigan Manufacturers Directory, Manufacturers' News, Inc., 1633 Central Street, Evanston, IL 60201

Minnesota

State Capitol, St. Paul, MN 55155
(612) 296-6013

INFORMATION OFFICES

Commerce/Economic Development
Department of Trade and Economic Development
500 Metro Square
121-7th Place East
St. Paul, MN 55101-2146

Minnesota Department of Commerce
Commerce Building
133 E. 7th Street
St. Paul, MN 55101
Corporate
Secretary of State
Domestic or Foreign Corporations
180 State Office Building
St. Paul, MN 55155
Taxation
Department of Revenue
10 River Park Plaza
St. Paul, MN 55146
State Chamber of Commerce
Minnesota Chamber of Commerce
480 Cedar Street
St. Paul, MN 55101
International Commerce
Minnesota Trade Office
1000 World Trade Center
St. Paul, MN 55101
Banking
Minnesota Department of Commerce
Banking Division
Commerce Building
133 E. 7th Street
St. Paul, MN 55101
Securities
Minnesota Department of Commerce
Registration Unit
Commerce Building
133 E. 7th Street
St. Paul, MN 55101
Labor and Industrial Relations
Minnesota Department of Labor and Industry
443 Lafayette Road
St. Paul, MN 55155
Insurance
Minnesota Department of Commerce
Policy Analysis Division
Commerce Building
133 E. 7th Street
St. Paul, MN 55101
Business Ombudsman
Department of Trade and Economic Development
Small Business Assistance Office
500 Metro Square
121-7th Place East
St. Paul, MN 55101-2146

INDUSTRIAL AND BUSINESS DIRECTORIES

Minnesota Directory of Manufacturers, Manufacturers' News, Inc., 1633 Central Street, Evanston, IL 60201; State Industrial Directories Corp., 2 Penn Plaza, New York, NY 10001

Minnesota Manufacturer's Register, Manufacturers' News, Inc., 1633 Central Street, Evanston, IL 60201

Mississippi

Office of the Governor, Jackson, MS 39205
(601) 359-3100

INFORMATION OFFICES

Commerce/Economic Development
Mississippi Department of Economic and Community Development
P.O. Box 849
Jackson, MS 39205
Division of International Development
P.O. Box 849
Jackson, MS 39205
Corporate
Secretary of State
P.O. Box 136
Jackson, MS 39205
Taxation
Tax Commission
102 Woolfolk Building
Jackson, MS 39201
State Chamber of Commerce
P.O. Box 1849
Jackson, MS 39205-1849

Banking
Department of Banking and Consumer Finance
1206 Woolfolk State Office Building
Jackson, MS 39205

International Commerce
Department of Economic and Community Development
P.O. Box 849
Jackson, MS 39205

Securities
Secretary of State's Office
Securities Division
P.O. Box 136
Jackson, MS 39205

Labor and Industrial Relations
Employment Security Commission
1520 W. Capitol Street
Jackson, MS 39205

Insurance
Department of Insurance
1804 Sillers Building
Jackson, MS 39205

INDUSTRIAL AND BUSINESS DIRECTORIES

Mississippi Manufacturers' Directory, Research Division, Department of Economic and Community Development, P.O. Box 849, Jackson, MS 39205; Manufacturers' News, Inc., 1633 Central Street, Evanston, IL 60201

Missouri

STATE INFORMATION, JEFFERSON CITY, MO 65101
(314) 751-2000

INFORMATION OFFICES

Commerce/Economic Development
Department of Economic Development
Economic Development Programs
P.O. Box 118
Jefferson City, MO 65102

Corporate
Secretary of State
Corporations Division
600 West Main Street
P.O. Box 778
Jefferson City, MO 65102

Taxation
Department of Revenue
Division of Taxation and Collections
Truman State Office Building
P.O. Box 629
Jefferson City, MO 65105

State Chamber of Commerce
Missouri Chamber of Commerce
428 East Capitol Avenue
P.O. Box 149
Jefferson City, MO 65102

International Commerce
International Business Development
Economic Development Program
Truman State Office Building
P.O. Box 118
Jefferson City, MO 65102

Banking
Missouri Division of Finance
Truman State Office Building
P.O. Box 716
Jefferson City, MO 65102

Securities
Office of the Secretary of State
Securities Division
600 West Main Street
P.O. Box 778
Jefferson City, MO 65102

Labor and Industrial Relations
Missouri Dept. of Labor & Industrial Relations
3315 West Truman Boulevard
Jefferson City, MO 65109

Insurance
Missouri Division of Insurance
Truman State Office Building
P.O. Box 690
Jefferson City, MO 65102

Uniform Industrial Code
Missouri Division of Labor Standards
P.O. Box 449
Jefferson City, MO 65102

INDUSTRIAL AND BUSINESS DIRECTORY

Contacts Influential: Commerce and Industrial Directory (for Kansas City Area), Contacts Influential, Inc., 2405 Grand Avenue, Kansas City, MO 64108

Missouri Manufacturers' Register, Manufacturers' News, Inc., 1633 Central Street, Evanston, IL 60201

Montana

STATE CAPITOL, HELENA, MT 59620
(406) 444-3111

INFORMATION OFFICES

Commerce/Economic Development
Department of Commerce
1424 9th Avenue
Helena, MT 59620-0501

Census and Economic Information Center
Department of Commerce
1429 9th Avenue
Helena, MT 59620-0501

Corporate
Secretary of State
Business Services Bureau
State Capitol Building
Helena, MT 59620-2801

State Chamber of Commerce
Montana Chamber of Commerce
P.O. Box 1730
Helena, MT 59624
International Commerce
International Trade Office
Montana Department of Commerce
1424 9th Avenue
Helena, MT 59620-0501
Banking
Commissioner of Financial Institutions
Montana Department of Commerce
1520 East 6th Avenue
Helena, MT 59620-0543
Securities
Securities Division
State Auditor's Office
Sam Mitchell Building
Helena, MT 59620-0301
Labor & Industrial Relations
Commissioner's Office
Montana Department of Labor & Industry
Lockey and Roberts
Helena, MT 59620-1501
Insurance
Insurance Department
State Auditor's Office
Sam Mitchell Building
Helena, MT 59620-0301
Uniform Commercial Code
Secretary of State
Uniform Commercial Code Bureau
State Capitol Building
Helena, MT 59620-2801
Business Ombudsman
Small Business Advocate
Montana Department of Commerce
1424 9th Avenue
Helena, MT 59620-0501

INDUSTRIAL AND BUSINESS DIRECTORIES

Montana Manufacturers and Products Directory, Department of Commerce, 1424 9th Avenue, Helena, MT 59620; Manufacturers' News, Inc., 1633 Central Street, Evanston, IL 60201

Montana Business & Industrial Location Guide, Department of Commerce, 1424 9th Avenue, Helena, MT 59620

Nebraska

State Capitol, Lincoln, NE 68509
(402) 471-2311

INFORMATION OFFICES

Commerce/Economic Development
Department of Economic Development
301 Centennial Mall South
P.O. Box 94666
Lincoln, NE 68509-4666
Corporate
Secretary of State
Corporation Division
P.O. Box 94608
Lincoln, NE 68509-4608
Taxation
Department of Revenue
301 Centennial Mall South
P.O. Box 94818
Lincoln, NE 68509-4818
State Chamber of Commerce
Nebraska Chamber of Commerce and Industry
1320 Lincoln Mall
P.O. Box 95128
Lincoln, NE 68509
International Commerce
Nebraska Department of Economic Development
Business Recruitment Division
P.O. Box 94666
Lincoln, NE 68509-4666
Banking
Department of Banking and Finance
301 Centennial Mall South
P.O. Box 95006
Lincoln, NE 68509-5006
Securities
Department of Banking and Finance
The Atrium
1200 N Street
P.O. Box 95006
Lincoln, NE 68509-5006
Labor and Industrial Relations
Nebraska Department of Labor
550 South 16th Street
P.O. Box 94600
Lincoln, NE 68509-4600
Insurance
Department of Insurance
The Terminal Building
941 O Street
Lincoln, NE 68508
Uniform Industrial Code
Uniform Commercial Code Division
301 Centennial Mall South
P.O. Box 95104
Lincoln, NE 68509-5104
Business Ombudsman
One-Stop Center
Department of Economic Development
P.O. Box 94666
Lincoln, NE 68509-4666

INDUSTRIAL AND BUSINESS DIRECTORIES

A Directory of Lincoln, Nebraska Manufacturers, Lincoln Chamber of Commerce, 1221 N. Street, Lincoln, NE 68508

Nebraska Manufacturers Register, Manufacturers' News, Inc., 1633 Central Street, Evanston, IL 60201

Directory of Nebraska Manufacturers and Their Products, Nebraska State Department of Economic Development, P.O. Box 94666, Lincoln, NE 68509-4666

Directory of Manufacturers for the Omaha Metropolitan Area, Omaha Economic Development Council, 1301 Harney, Omaha, NE 68102.

Directory of Major Employers for the Omaha Area, Omaha Economic Development Council, 1301 Harney, Omaha, NE 68102

Nevada

State Capitol, Carson City, NV 89710
(702) 687-5670

INFORMATION OFFICES

Commerce/Economic Development
Department of Commerce
1665 Hot Springs Road
Carson City, NV 89710

Commission on Economic Development
5151 S. Carson Street
Carson City, NV 89710

Corporate
Secretary of State
Capitol Complex
Carson City, NV 89710

Taxation
Department of Taxation
1340 S. Curry Street
Carson City, NV 89710

State Chamber of Commerce
Nevada Chamber of Commerce Association
P.O. Box 3499
Reno, NV 89505

International Commerce
Commission on Economic Development
International Office
3770 Howard Hughes Parkway #295
Las Vegas, NV 89158

Banking
Financial Institutions Division
406 E. Second Street
Carson City, NV 89710

Securities
Secretary of State
Capitol Complex
Carson City, NV 89710

Labor and Industrial Relations
Labor Commission
1445 Hot Springs Road
Carson City, NV 89710

Department of Industrial Relations
1390 S. Curry Street
Carson City, NV 89710

Insurance
Insurance Department
1665 Hot Springs Road
Carson City, NV 89710

INDUSTRIAL AND BUSINESS DIRECTORIES

Directory of Nevada Mine Operations, Division of Mine Inspection Department of Industrial Relations, 1380 S. Curry Street, Carson City, NV 89710

Nevada Industrial Directory, Gold Hill Publishings Co., Inc., P.O. Drawer F, Virginia City, NV 89440; Manufacturers' News, Inc., 1633 Central Street, Evanston, IL 60201

New Hampshire

State House, Concord, NH 03301
(603) 271-1110

INFORMATION OFFICES

Commerce/Economic Development
Department of Resources and Economic Development
Division of Economic Development
172 Pembroke Road
Concord, NH 03302

Corporate
Secretary of State
Corporations Division
State House Annex
Concord, NH 03301

Taxation
Board of Taxation
61 S. Spring Street
Concord, NH 03301

Department of Revenue Administration
61 S. Spring Street
Concord, NH 03301

State Chamber of Commerce
Business and Industry Association of New Hampshire
122 N. Main Street
Concord, NH 03301

International Commerce
Department of Resources & Economic Development
Division of Economic Development
172 Pembroke Road
Prescott Park—Concord, NH 03302

Banking
Banking Department
State of New Hampshire
169 Manchester Street
Concord, NH 03301

New Hampshire Banking Association
125 N. Main Street
Concord, NH 03301

Securities
Insurance Department, Securities Division
State of New Hampshire
State House
Concord, NH 03301

Labor and Industrial Relations
Department of Employment Security
State of New Hampshire
32 S. Main Street
Concord, NH 03301

Department of Labor
95 Pleasant Street
Concord, NH 03301

Insurance
Insurance Department
State of New Hampshire
169 Manchester Street
Concord, NH 03301

Standard Industrial Code
Department of Employment Security
State of New Hampshire
32 S. Main Street
Concord, NH 03301

INDUSTRIAL AND BUSINESS DIRECTORIES

Made in New Hampshire, New Hampshire Office of Industrial Development, Department of Resources, Concord, NH 03301

MacRAE's State Industrial Directory Maine/New Hampshire/Vermont, MacRAE's Industrial Directories, 817 Broadway, New York, NY 10003

New Hampshire Manufacturing Directory, Tower Publishing Company, 34 Diamond Street, Portland, ME 04111

New Jersey

State House, Trenton, NJ 08625
(609) 777-2500

INFORMATION OFFICES

Commerce/Economic Development
Department of Commerce and Economic Development
20 W. State Street, CN 820
Trenton, NJ 08625

Division of Travel and Tourism
20 W. State Street, CN 826
Trenton, NJ 08625

Economic Development Authority
Capitol Place One, CN 990
200 S. Warren Street
Trenton, NJ 08625

Corporate
Secretary of State
Division of Commercial Recording
820 Bear Tavern Road, CN 308
W. Trenton, NJ 08625

Taxation
Department of Treasury
Division of Taxation
50 Barrack Street, CN 240
Trenton, NJ 08625

State Chamber of Commerce
New Jersey State Chamber of Commerce
1 State Street Square
50 W. State Street
Trenton, NJ 08608

International Commerce
Division of International Trade
P.O. Box 47024
153 Halsey Street
Newark, NJ 07102

Banking
Department of Banking
20 W. State Street, CN 040
Trenton, NJ 08625

Securities
Bureau of Securities
2 Gateway Center
Newark, NJ 07102

Labor and Labor Relations
Department of Labor and Industry
John Fitch Plaza, CN 110
Trenton, NJ 08625

Insurance
Department of Insurance
20 W. State Street, CN 325
Trenton, NJ 08625

Business Ombudsman
Department of Public Advocate
CN 850, Justice Complex
25 Market Street
Trenton, NJ 08625

INDUSTRIAL AND BUSINESS DIRECTORIES

New Jersey Manufacturers Directory, George D. Hall Co., 50 Congress Street, Boston, MA 02109; Manufacturers' News, Inc., 1633 Central Street, Evanston, IL 60201

MacRAE's New Jersey State Industrial Directory, MacRAE's Industrial Directories, 817 Broadway, New York, NY 10003

The New Jersey Directory of Manufacturers, Commerce Register®, Inc., 190 Godwin Avenue, Midland Park, NJ 07432

New Mexico

State Capitol, Santa Fe, NM 87503
(505) 827-3000

INFORMATION OFFICES

Commerce/Economic Development
Economic Development Department
Joseph M. Montoya Building

1100 St. Francis Drive
Santa Fe, NM 87503

Corporate
State Corporation Commission
P.O. Drawer 1269
Santa Fe, NM 87501

Taxation
Taxation and Revenue Department
P.O. Box 630
Manuel Lujan Sr. Building
Santa Fe, NM 87509-0630

State Chamber of Commerce
Association of Commerce and Industry of New Mexico
4001 Indian School NE
Albuquerque, NM 87110

International Commerce
Trade Division
Economic Development Department
Joseph M. Montoya Building
1100 St. Francis Drive
Santa Fe, NM 87503

Banking
Financial Institutions Division
Regulation and Licensing Department
P.O. Box 25101
Santa Fe, NM 87504

Securities
Securities Division
Financial Institutions Division
Regulation and Licensing Department
P.O. Box 25101
Santa Fe, NM 87503

Labor and Industrial
1896 Pacheso Street
Aspen Plaza Building
Santa Fe, NM 87501

Insurance
State Corporation Commission
P.O. Drawer 1269
Santa Fe, NM 87501

INDUSTRIAL AND BUSINESS DIRECTORIES

New Mexico Manufacturing Directory, Manufacturers' News, Inc., 1633 Central Street, Evanston, IL 60201

New Mexico Directory of Manufacturers, Economic Development Division, New Mexico Economic Development, Joseph M. Montoya Building, 1100 St. Francis Drive, Santa Fe, NM 87503

New York

State Capitol, Albany, NY 12224
(518) 474-2121

INFORMATION OFFICES

[illegible]nomic Development
[illegible]mic Development
Albany, NY 12245
Division of Regional Economic Development
One Commerce Plaza
Albany, NY 12245

Corporate
Secretary of State
162 Washington Avenue
Albany, NY 12231

Taxation
Department of Taxation and Finance
State Campus Building #9
Albany, NY 12227

State Chamber of Commerce
Business Council of New York State
152 Washington Avenue
Albany, NY 12210

Small Business Advisory Board
Division for Small Business
1515 Broadway
New York, NY 10036

International Commerce
Department of Economic Development
1515 Broadway
New York, NY 10036

Banking
Department of Banking
194 Washington Avenue
New York, NY 12210

Labor and Industrial Relations
Department of Labor
State Campus
Albany, NY 12240

Insurance
Department of Insurance
Empire State Plaza
Agency Building #1
Albany, NY 12257

Business Ombudsman
Department of Economic Development
Division for Small Business
1515 Broadway
New York, NY 10036

INDUSTRIAL AND BUSINESS DIRECTORIES

New York Manufacturers' Directory, George D. Hall Co., 50 Congress Street, Boston, MA 02109; Manufacturers' News, 1633 Central Street, Evanston, IL 60201

MacRAE's New York State Industrial Directory, MacRAE's Industrial Directories, 817 Broadway, New York, NY 10003

The New York State Directory, Cambridge Information Group, 7200 Wisconsin Avenue, Bethesda, MD 20814–9777

North Carolina

General Assembly
State Legislative Building,

RALEIGH, NC 27601-1096
(919) 733-1110 (government information)
733-7928 (legislators)

INFORMATION OFFICES

Commerce/Economic Development
Department of Commerce
430 N. Salisbury Street
Raleigh, NC 27603-5900
Corporate
Secretary of State
Corporation Division
300 N. Salisbury Street
Raleigh, NC 27603-5909
Taxation
Department of Revenue
501 N. Salisbury Street
Raleigh, NC 27634
State Chamber of Commerce
North Carolina Citizens for Business and Industry
P.O. Box 2508
Raleigh, NC 27602
International Commerce
International Development
Department of Commerce
430 N. Salisbury Street
Raleigh, NC 27603-5900
Banking
Banking Commission
Department of Commerce
430 N. Salisbury Street
Raleigh, NC 27603-5900
Securities
Secretary of State
Securities Division
300 N. Salisbury Street
Raleigh, NC 27603-5909
Labor and Industrial Relations
Department of Labor
4 W. Edenton Street
Raleigh, NC 27601-1092
Insurance
Department of Insurance
430 N. Salisbury Street
Raleigh, NC 27603-5908
Business Ombudsman
Business Assistance
Department of Commerce
430 N. Salisbury Street
Raleigh, NC 27603-5900

INDUSTRIAL AND BUSINESS DIRECTORIES

Directory of North Carolina Manufacturing Firms, North Carolina Department of Commerce, Raleigh, NC 27603; Manufacturers' News, Inc., 1633 Central Street, Evanston, IL 60201

MacRAE's State Industrial Directory North/South Carolina/Virginia, MacRAE's Industrial Directories, 817 Broadway, New York, NY 10003

North Carolina Manufacturers Directory, George D. Hall Co., 50 Congress Street, Boston, MA 02109

North Dakota

STATE CAPITOL, BISMARCK, ND 58505
(701) 224-2000

INFORMATION OFFICES

Commerce/Economic Development
Economic Development & Finance
1833 East Bismarck Expressway
Bismarck, ND 58504
Corporate
Corporation Department
Office of the Secretary of State
600 East Boulevard Avenue
Bismarck, ND 58505-0500
Taxation
Tax Department
600 East Boulevard Avenue
Bismarck, ND 58505-0599
State Chamber of Commerce
Greater North Dakota Association—State Chamber of Commerce
P.O. Box 2467
Fargo, ND 58102
International Commerce
North Dakota World Trade
Economic Development & Finance
1833 East Bismarck Expressway
Bismarck, ND 58504
Banking
State Banking Commission
600 East Boulevard Avenue
Bismarck, ND 58505-0510
Securities
Securities Commissioner
600 East Boulevard
Bismarck, ND 58505
Labor and Industrial Relations
State Commissioner of Labor
600 East Boulevard
Bismarck, ND 58505
Insurance
Insurance Commissioner
600 East Boulevard Avenue
Bismarck, ND 58505-0320
Uniform Industrial Code
Secretary of State
600 East Boulevard Avenue
Bismarck, ND 58505-0500
Business Ombudsman
Economic Development & Finance
1833 East Bismarck Expressway
Bismarck, ND 58504

INDUSTRIAL AND BUSINESS DIRECTORIES

North Dakota Directory of Manufacturers, Economic Development & Finance, 1833 East Bismarck Expressway, Bismarck, ND 58504; Manufacturers' News, Inc., 1633 Central Street, Evanston, IL 60201

Strictly Business, Frontier Directory Co., Inc., 515 E. Main Street, Bismarck, ND 58501

Ohio

STATE HOUSE, COLUMBUS, OH 43215
(614) 466-3455
State Operator: (614) 466-2000

INFORMATION OFFICES

Commerce/Economic Development
Ohio Department of Development
77 S. High Street
P.O. Box 1001
Columbus, OH 43266-0101

Corporate
Secretary of State
Corporation Section
30 E. Broad Street
Columbus, OH 43266-0418

Taxation
Department of Taxation
30 E. Broad Street
Columbus, OH 43266-0420

State Chamber of Commerce
Ohio Chamber of Commerce
35 E. Gay Street
Columbus, OH 43215-1192

International Commerce
Ohio Department of Development
International Trade Division
77 S. High Street
P.O. Box 1001
Columbus, OH 43266-0101

Banking
Ohio Department of Commerce
Division of Banks
77 S. High Street
Columbus, OH 43266-0544

Securities
Ohio Department of Commerce
Division of Securities
77 S. High Street
Columbus, OH 43266-0544

Labor and Industrial Relations
Ohio Department of Industrial Relations
2323 W. Fifth Avenue
P.O. Box 825
Columbus, OH 43266-0567

[illegible]
[illegible]t of Insurance

Uniform Industrial Code
Industrial Commission of Ohio
Division of Safety and Hygiene
246 N. High Street
Columbus, OH 43266-0589

Business Ombudsman
Ohio Department of Development
Small and Developing Business Division
Minority Business Development Division
77 S. High Street
P.O. Box 1001
Columbus, OH 43266-0101

INDUSTRIAL AND BUSINESS DIRECTORIES

Akron, Ohio Membership Directory and Buyers Guide, Akron Regional Development Board, 1 Cascade Plaza, Akron, OH 44308-1192

The Chamber Directory, Toledo Area Chamber of Commerce, 218 Huron Street, Toledo, OH 43604

Manufacturers Directory, Columbus Regional Information Service, 37 North High Street, Columbus, OH 43215-3181

Harris Ohio Industrial Directory, Harris Publishing Company, 2057 Aurora Road, Twinsburg, OH 44087-9988

Ohio Manufacturers Directory, Manufacturers' News, Inc., 1633 Central Street, Evanston, IL 60201

Oklahoma

STATE CAPITOL, OKLAHOMA CITY, OK 73105
(405) 521-1601

INFORMATION OFFICES

Commerce/Economic Development
Department of Commerce
6601 Broadway Extension
Oklahoma City, OK 73116

Corporate
Secretary of State
State Capitol
Oklahoma City, OK 73105

Taxation
Tax Commission
M. C. Connors Building
2501 N. Lincoln Boulevard
Oklahoma City, OK 73105

State Chamber of Commerce
Oklahoma State Chamber of Commerce & Industry
4020 N. Lincoln Boulevard
Oklahoma City, OK 73105

International Commerce
International Trade Division
Department of Commerce
6601 Broadway Extension
Oklahoma City, OK 73116

Banking
Oklahoma Banking Department
4100 N. Lincoln Boulevard
Oklahoma City, OK 73105
Securities
Oklahoma Securities Commission
Will Rogers Building
2401 N. Lincoln Boulevard
Oklahoma City, OK 73105
Labor and Industrial Relations
Oklahoma Labor Department
4001 N. Lincoln Boulevard
Oklahoma City, OK 73105
Insurance
Insurance Commission
1901 N. Walnut Street
P.O. Box 53408
Oklahoma City, OK 73152
Uniform Industrial Code
Universal Commercial Code Division
County Clerk's Office
County Court House
Oklahoma City, OK 73102

INDUSTRIAL AND BUSINESS DIRECTORIES

Oklahoma Directory of Manufacturers and Products, Media/Marketing & Advertising, Department of Commerce, 6601 Broadway Extension, Oklahoma City, OK 73116
Oklahoma Manufacturers Register, Manufacturers' News, Inc., 1633 Central Street, Evanston, IL 60201

Oregon

STATE CAPITOL, SALEM, OR 97310
(503) 378-3131

INFORMATION OFFICES

Commerce/Economic Development
Economic Development Department
775 Summer Street N.E.
Salem, OR 97310
Corporate
Corporation Division
Office of Secretary of State
Commerce Building
158 12th Street N.E.
Salem, OR 97310
Taxation
Department of Revenue
Revenue Building
955 Center Street
Salem, OR 97310
International Commerce
International Trade Division
Economic Development Department
One World Trade Center
121 S.W. Salmon
Portland, OR 97204
Banking
Finance Section
Division of Finance and Corporate Securities
Department of Insurance and Finance
21 Labor and Industries Building
Salem, OR 97310
Securities
Corporate Securities Section
Division of Finance and Corporate Securities
Department of Insurance and Finance
21 Labor and Industries Building
Salem, OR 97310
Labor and Industry
Bureau of Labor and Industries
800 N.E. Oregon Street
Portland, OR 97232
Insurance
Insurance Division
Department of Insurance and Finance
Labor and Industries Building
Salem, OR 97310
Uniform Industrial Code
Building Codes Agency
1535 Edgewater N.W.
Salem, OR 97310

INDUSTRIAL AND BUSINESS DIRECTORIES

Directory of Oregon Manufacturers, International Trade Directory, and *Directory of Oregon Wood Products Manufacturers*, Economic Development Department, 775 Summer Street N.E., Salem, OR 97310; Manufacturers' News, Inc., 1633 Central Street, Evanston, IL 60201
Oregon Business Directory, American Directory Publishing Co., Inc., 5711 S. 86th Circle, P.O. Box 27347, Omaha, NE 68127

Pennsylvania

MAIN CAPITOL BUILDING, HARRISBURG, PA 17120
(717) 787-2121

INFORMATION OFFICES

Department of Commerce
Department of Commerce
Office of the Secretary
Forum Building
Harrisburg, PA 17120

Office of International Development
Department of Commerce
Forum Building
Harrisburg, PA 17120

Office of Program Management
Department of Commerce

Forum Building
Harrisburg, PA 17120

Business Resource Network
Department of Commerce
Forum Building
Harrisburg, PA 17120

Office of Technology Development
Department of Commerce
Forum Building
Harrisburg, PA 17120

International Commerce
Department of Commerce
Office of International Development
Forum Building
Harrisburg, PA 17120

Corporate
Department of State
Bureau of Corporations
308 North Office Building
Harrisburg, PA 17120

Taxation
Department of Revenue
P.O. Box 8903
Harrisburg, PA 17105

State Chamber of Commerce
Pennsylvania Chamber of Business and Industry
417 Walnut Street
Harrisburg, PA 17101-1596

Banking
Department of Banking
333 Market Street
Harristown II
Harrisburg, PA 17101-2290

Securities
Securities Commission
East Gate Office Building
1010 N. 7th Street
Harrisburg, PA 17102

Labor and Industrial Relations
Department of Labor & Industry
Labor & Industry Building
7th & Forester Streets
Harrisburg, PA 17120

Insurance
Department of Insurance
1321 Strawberry Square
Harrisburg, PA 17120

INDUSTRIAL AND BUSINESS DIRECTORIES

Harris Pennsylvania Industrial Directory of Pennsylvania, Department of Commerce, Harris Publishing Company, 2057-2 Aurora Road, Twinsburg, OH 44087

MacRAE's State Industrial Directory Pennsylvania, MacRAE's Industrial Directories, 817 Broadway, New York, NY 10003

Pennsylvania Manufacturers Register, Manufacturers' News, Inc., 1633 Central Street, Evanston, IL 60201

Rhode Island

State House, Providence, RI 02903
(401) 277-2000

INFORMATION OFFICES

Commerce/Economic Development
Department of Economic Development
7 Jackson Walkway
Providence, RI 02903

Taxation
Division of Taxation
Department of Administration
One Capitol Hill
Providence, RI 02908

Corporate
Secretary of State
Corporation Department
100 N. Main Street
Providence, RI 02903

State Chamber of Commerce
Rhode Island Chamber of Commerce
30 Exchange Terrace
Providence, RI 02903

International Commerce
Rhode Island Department of Economic Development
7 Jackson Walkway
Providence, RI

Banking
Department of Business Regulation
Banking Division
233 Richmond Street
Providence, RI 02903

Securities
Department of Business Regulation
Banking Division
233 Richmond Street
Providence, RI 02903

Labor and Industrial Relations
Department of Labor
220 Elmwood Avenue
Providence, RI 02907

Insurance
Department of Business Regulation
Insurance Division
233 Richmond Street
Providence, RI 02903

Business Ombudsman
Business Development Division
Department of Economic Development
7 Jackson Walkway
Providence, RI 02903

INDUSTRIAL AND BUSINESS DIRECTORIES

MacRAE's State Industrial Directory Massachusetts/Rhode Island, MacRAE's Industrial Directories, 817 Broadway, New York, NY 10003

Rhode Island Directory of Manufacturers, Department of Economic Development, 7 Jackson Walkway, Providence, RI 02903; Manufacturers' News, Inc., 1633 Central Street, Evanston, IL 60201

South Carolina

STATE HOUSE, COLUMBIA, SC 29211
(803) 734-9818

INFORMATION OFFICES

Commerce/Economic Development
South Carolina State Development Board
P.O. Box 927
1201 Main Street
Columbia, SC 29202

Taxation
Tax Commission
P.O. Box 125
Columbia Mill Building
Columbia, SC 29201

Corporate
Secretary of State
P.O. Box 11350
Columbia, SC 29211

State Chamber of Commerce
South Carolina Chamber of Commerce
1201 Main Street
Columbia, SC 29202

International Commerce
South Carolina State Development Board
1201 Main Street
P.O. Box 927
Columbia, SC 29202

Labor and Industrial Relations
South Carolina Labor Department
Landmark Center, 3600 Forest Drive
P.O. Box 11329
Columbia, SC 29211-1329

Insurance
South Carolina Department of Insurance
1612 Marion Street
P.O. Box 100105
Columbia, SC 29202-3105

Banking
State Treasurer's Office
Wade Hampton Building
Banking Operations
P.O. Drawer 11778
Columbia, SC 29211

Securities
Secretary of State
Securities Division
P.O. Box 11350
1205 Pendleton Street
Columbia, SC 29201

Business Ombudsman
SC Department of Consumer Affairs
P.O. Box 5757
2801 Devine Street
Columbia, SC 29250-5757

INDUSTRIAL AND BUSINESS DIRECTORIES

Industrial Directory of South Carolina, South Carolina State Development Board, P.O. Box 927, 1201 Main Street, Columbia, SC 29202; Manufacturers' News, Inc., 1633 Central Street, Evanston, IL 60201

MacRAE's State Industrial Directory North Carolina/South Carolina/Virginia, MacRAE's Industrial Directories, 817 Broadway, New York, NY 10003

South Dakota

STATE CAPITOL, PIERRE, SD 57501-5070
(605) 773-3011

INFORMATION OFFICES

Commerce/Economic Development
Governor's Office of Economic Development
711 Wells Avenue
Pierre, SD 57501

Department of Commerce and Regulation
910 E. Sioux
Pierre, SD 57501

Corporate
Secretary of State
Corporation Division
Capitol Building
Pierre, SD 57501

Taxation
Department of Revenue
Kneip Building
Pierre, SD 57501

State Chamber of Commerce
Industry & Commerce Association of South Dakota
P.O. Box 190
Pierre, SD 57501

International Commerce
Governor's Office of Economic Development
711 Wells Avenue
Pierre, SD 57501

Banking
Department of Commerce and Regulation
Division of Banking
105 S. Euclid
Pierre, SD 57501

Securities
Department of Commerce and Regulation
Division of Securities
910 E. Sioux
Pierre, SD 57501

Labor and Industrial Relations
Department of Labor
Division of Labor and Management
Kneip Building
Pierre, SD 57501

Insurance
Department of Commerce and Regulation
Division of Insurance
910 E. Sioux
Pierre, SD 57501

INDUSTRIAL AND BUSINESS DIRECTORIES

South Dakota Manufacturers and Processors Directory, Governor's Office of Economic Development, 711 Wells Avenue, Pierre, SD 57501; Manufacturers' News, Inc., 1633 Central Street, Evanston, IL 60201

South Dakota Export Directory, Governor's Office of Economic Development, 711 Wells Avenue, Pierre, SD 57501

Tennessee

State Capitol, Nashville, TN 37243-001
(615) 741-2001

INFORMATION OFFICES

Commerce/Economic Development
Department of Economic and Community Development
Rachel Jackson Building
320 6th Avenue North
Nashville, TN 37243-0405

Corporate
Secretary of State
Records Division
James K. Polk Building
Nashville, TN 37243-0306

Taxation
Department of Revenue
1200 Andrew Jackson Building
500 Deaderick Street
Nashville, TN 37242-1099

International Commerce
Department of Economic & Community Development
International Sales & Marketing
Rachel Jackson Building
320 6th Avenue North
Nashville, TN 37243-0405

Banking
Department of Financial Institutions
John Sevier Building
500 Charlotte Avenue
Nashville, TN 37243-0705

Securities
Department of Commerce & Insurance
Securities Division
500 James Robertson Parkway
Nashville, TN 37243

Labor and Industrial Relations
Department of Labor
501 Union Building
Nashville, TN 37243-0655

Insurance
Department of Commerce & Insurance
Insurance Division
500 James Robertson Parkway
Nashville, TN 37243

Business Ombudsman
Department of Economic & Community Development
Business & Industry Services Division
Rachel Jackson Building
320 6th Avenue North
Nashville, TN 37243

INDUSTRIAL AND BUSINESS DIRECTORIES

Directory of Tennessee Manufacturers, M. Lee Smith Publishers, 162 Fourth Avenue, P.O. Box 198867, Nashville, TN 37219; Manufacturers' News, Inc., 1633 Central Street, Evanston, IL 60201

Texas

State Capitol, Austin, TX 78701
State Information: (512) 463-4630

INFORMATION OFFICES

Commerce/Economic Development
Office of Economic Development and International Relations
P.O. Box 12428
Austin, TX 78711

Corporate
Secretary of State
P.O. Box 12697
1019 Brazos
Austin, TX 78711

Taxation
Comptroller of Public Accounts
104 LBJ State Office Building
Austin, TX 78774

State Chamber of Commerce
Texas State Chamber of Commerce
300 West 15th Street
Austin, TX 78752

Tourism Department
P.O. Box 12008
Austin, TX 78711

Lower Rio Grand Valley Chamber of Commerce
P.O. Box 1499
Weslaco, TX 78596

International Commerce
Office of Economic Development and International Relations
P.O. Box 12428, Capitol Station
Austin, TX 78711

Banking
Texas Department of Banking
2601 North Lamar
Austin, TX 78705-4294

Securities
State Securities Board
P.O. Box 13167, Capitol Station
1800 San Jacinto St.
Austin, TX 78711-3167

Labor and Industrial Relations
Texas Department of Labor and Standards
P.O. Box 13193, Capitol Station
Austin, TX 78711-3193

Insurance
Texas State Board of Insurance
State Insurance Building
1110 San Jacinto
Austin, TX 78701-1998

Uniform Industrial Code
Uniform Commercial Code Section
Secretary of State's Office
P.O. Box 12887, Capitol Station
Austin, TX 78711

Business Ombudsman
Ombudsman Division
P.O. Box 12728
Austin, TX 78711

INDUSTRIAL AND BUSINESS DIRECTORIES

Dallas Business Guide, Dallas Chamber of Commerce, Fidelity Tower, Dallas, TX 75201

Directory of Texas Manufacturers, Bureau of Business Research, University of Texas, Austin, TX 78712; State Industrial Directories Corp., 2 Penn Plaza, New York, NY 10001

Fort Worth Directory of Manufacturers, Fort Worth Area Chamber of Commerce, 700 Throckmorton Street, Fort Worth, TX 76102

Texas Exporter-Importer Directory, Gulf International Trades, Box 52717, Houston, TX 77052

Texas Manufacturers Register, Manufacturers' News, Inc., 1633 Central Street, Evanston, IL 60201

Utah

State Capitol, Salt Lake City, UT 8414 (801) 538-3000

INFORMATION OFFICES

Commerce/Economic Development
Department of Commerce
160 East 300 South
Salt Lake City, UT 84145

Department of Business and Economic Development
324 South State
Salt Lake City, UT 84111

Office of Planning & Budget
Data Resources Section
116 Capitol Building
Salt Lake City, UT 84114

Corporate
Division of Corporations
Heber M. Wells Building
160 E. 300 South
Salt Lake City, UT 84145

Taxation
Department of State Tax Commission
Heber M. Wells Building
160 E. 300 South
Salt Lake City, UT 84134

International Commerce
International Business Development
Division of Business & Economic Development
324 South State
Salt Lake City, UT 84111

Banking
Financial Institutions
324 S. State
P.O. Box 89
Salt Lake City, UT 84110-0089

Securities
Division of Securities
Heber M. Wells Building
160 E. 300 South
P.O. Box 45802
Salt Lake City, UT 84145-0802

Labor and Industrial Relations
Industrial Commission of Utah
Heber M. Wells Building
160 E. 300 South
Salt Lake City, UT 84111

Insurance
Department of Insurance
3110 State Office Building
Salt Lake City, UT 84114

Licensing
Division of Occupational and Professional Licensing
160 East 300 South
P.O. Box 45802
Salt Lake City, UT 84145-0802

Uniform Industrial Code
Employment Security/Job Service
174 Social Hall Avenue
Salt Lake City, UT 84147

INDUSTRIAL AND BUSINESS DIRECTORIES

Utah Directory of Business and Industry, Utah Division of Business and Economic Development, 324 South State, Salt Lake City, UT 84111; Manufacturers' News, Inc., 1633 Central Street, Evanston, IL 60201

Vermont

State House, Montpelier, VT 05602
(802) 828-3333

INFORMATION OFFICES

Commerce/Economic Development
Agency of Development and Community Affairs
Department of Economic Development
109 State Street
Montpelier, VT 05602
Corporate
Secretary of State
Corporation Department
26 Terrace Street
Montpelier, VT 05602
Taxation
Department of Taxes
Agency of Administration
109 State Street
Montpelier, VT 05602
International Commerce
Agency of Development and Community Affairs
Pavillion Office Bldg
109 State Street
Montpelier, VT 05609
State Chamber of Commerce
Vermont State Chamber of Commerce
P.O. Box 37
Montpelier, VT 05602
Insurance
Department of Banking and Insurance
120 State Street
Montpelier, VT 05602
Banking
Department of Banking and Insurance
89 Main Street
Montpelier, VT 05602
Securities
Department of Banking and Insurance
89 Main Street
Montpelier, VT 05602
Labor and Industrial Relations
Department of Labor and Industry
National Life Building
Montpelier, VT 05602
Uniform Commercial Code
Department of Banking and Insurance
89 Main Street
Montpelier, VT 05602
Business Ombudsman
Agency Development and Community Affair
Department of Economic Development
109 State Street
Montpelier, VT 05602

INDUSTRIAL AND BUSINESS DIRECTORIES

MacRAE's State Industrial Directory Maine/New Hampshire/Vermont, MacRAE's Industrial Directories, 817 Broadway, New York, NY 10003

Vermont Manufacturing Directory, Tower Publishing, 34 Diamond Street, Portland, ME 04112; Manufacturers' News, Inc., 1633 Central Street, Evanston, IL 60201

Vermont Directory of Manufacturers, Vermont Agency of Development and Community Affairs, Montpelier, VT 05602

Vermont Yearbook, The National Survey, Chester, VT 05143

Virginia

State Capitol, Richmond, VA 23219
(800) 422-2319

INFORMATION OFFICES

Commerce/Economic Development
Department of Economic Development
P.O. Box 798
1021 East Cary Street
Richmond, VA 23206-0798
Corporate
State Corporation Commission
Tyler Building
1300 East Main Street
Richmond, VA 23219
Taxation
Department of Taxation
2200 W. Broad Street
P.O. Box 1880
Richmond, VA 23282-1880
State Chamber of Commerce
Virginia Chamber of Commerce
9 South Fifth Street
Richmond, VA 23219
International Commerce
Department of Economic Development
P.O. Box 798
1021 East Cary Street
Richmond, VA 23206-0798
Banking
State Corporation Commission
Bureau of Financial Institutions
Tyler Building
1300 East Main Street
Richmond, VA 23219
Securities
State Corporation Commission
Division of Securities and Retail Franchising
Tyler Building
1300 East Main Street
Richmond, VA 23219

Labor and Industrial Relations
Department of Labor and Industry
Powers-Taylor Building
13 S. 13th Street
Richmond, VA 23219

Insurance
State Corporation Commission
Bureau of Insurance
Tyler Building
1300 East Main Street
Richmond, VA 23219

Employment and Unemployment Information
Virginia Employment Commission
Economic Information Services Division
703 E. Main Street
Richmond, VA 23219

Consumer Ombudsman
Department of Agriculture and Consumer Services
Division of Consumer Affairs
P.O. Box 1163
Richmond, VA 23209

INDUSTRIAL AND BUSINESS DIRECTORIES

Virginia Industrial Directory, Chamber of Commerce, 9 South Fifth Street, Richmond, VA 23219

Virginia Manufacturers Directory, Manufacturers' News, Inc., 1633 Central Street, Evanston, IL 60201

MacRAE's State Industrial Directory North Carolina/South Carolina/Virginia, MacRAE's Industrial Directories, 817 Broadway, New York, NY 10003

Washington

101 General Administration Building,
Olympia, WA 98504
(206) 753-5630

INFORMATION OFFICES

Commerce/Economic Development
Department of Trade and Economic Development
101 General Administration Building
Olympia, WA 98504

Corporate
Secretary of State
Corporate Division
505 E. Union
Olympia, WA 98504

Taxation
Department of Revenue
412 General Administration Building
Olympia, WA 98504

State Chamber of Commerce
Association of Washington Business
1414 S. Cherry Street
Olympia, WA 98501

International Commerce
Department of Trade & Economic Development
Domestic & International Trade Division
2600 Westin Building
2001 Sixth Avenue
Seattle, WA 98121

Banking
General Administration Building
Banking & Consumer Finance
219 General Administration Building
Olympia, WA 98504

Securities
Department of Licensing Building
Att: Securities Division
7240 Martin Way
Olympia, WA 98506

Labor and Industrial Relations
Department of Labor & Industries
Employment Standards—Apprenticeship
Crime Victims Division
406 Legion Way SE
Olympia, WA 98504

Insurance
Insurance Commissioner's Office
Insurance Building
Olympia, WA 98504

Uniform Commercial Code
Department of Licensing
Business License Services
405 Black Lake Boulevard
Olympia, WA 98504

Business Ombudsman
Department of Trade & Economic Development
Business Assistance Center
919 Lakeridge Way, S.W.
Olympia, WA 98504

INDUSTRIAL AND BUSINESS DIRECTORIES

Directory of Advanced Technology Industries in Washington State, Economic Development Partnership for Washington State, 18000 Pacific Highway South, Seattle, WA 98188

Business Assistance in Washington State, Washington State International Trade Directory, Department of Trade and Economic Development, 101 General Administration Building, Olympia, WA 98504

Minority Women Business Enterprises, Office of Minority Women Business Enterprises, 406 S. Water Street, Olympia, WA 98504

Washington Manufacturers Register, Times Mirror Press, P.O. Box 7440, Newport Beach, CA 92658

Washington Forest Industry Mill Directory (1984), Department of Natural Resources, 1065 S. Capitol Way, Olympia, WA 98504

Directory of Washington Mining Operations, Department of Natural Resources, Division of Geology, Olympia, WA 98504

Washington Manufacturers Register, Database Publishing, 523 Superior Avenue, Newport Beach, CA 92663; Manufacturers' News, Inc., 1633 Central Street, Evanston, IL 60201

West Virginia

STATE CAPITOL, CHARLESTON, WV 25305
(304) 558-3456

INFORMATION OFFICES

Commerce/Economic Development
West Virginia Development Office
State Capitol
Charleston, WV 25305

Corporate
Secretary of State
Corporate Division
Building 1
1900 Washington Street East
Charleston, WV 25305

Taxation
Department of Tax and Revenue
Building 1
1900 Washington Street East
Charleston, WV 25305

State Chamber of Commerce
P.O. Box 2789
1101 Kanawha Valley Building
Charleston, WV 25330-2789

International Commerce
West Virginia Development Office
1900 Washington Street East
Building 6
Charleston, WV 25305

Banking
Division of Banking
1900 Washington Street East
Charleston, WV 25305

Securities
Auditor's Office
Building 1
Charleston, WV 25305

Labor & Industrial Relations
Division of Labor
1900 Washington Street East
Building 1
Charleston, WV 25305

Insurance
Insurance Commission
2019 Washington Street East
Charleston, WV 25305

Uniform Industrial Code
Secretary of State
1900 Washington Street East
Building 1
Charleston, WV 25305

Business Ombudsman
West Virginia Development Office
Building 6
Charleston, WV 25305

INDUSTRIAL AND BUSINESS DIRECTORIES

West Virginia Manufacturers Register, Manufacturers' News, Inc., 1633 Central Street, Evanston, IL 60201, Harris Publishing, 2057 Aurora Road, Twinsburg, OH 44087

Wisconsin

STATE CAPITOL, MADISON, WI 53702
(608) 266-2211

INFORMATION OFFICES

Commerce/Economic Development
Department of Development
123 W. Washington Avenue
Box 7970
Madison, WI 53707-7970

Corporate
Secretary of State
Corporate Division
30 W. Miffin Street
Box 7848
Madison, WI 53707-7848

Taxation
Department of Revenue
125 S. Webster Avenue
P.O. Box 8933
Madison, WI 53708-8933

State Chamber of Commerce
Wisconsin Association of Manufacturers and Commerce
501 E. Washington Avenue
Box 352
Madison, WI 53701

International Commerce
International Business Services
Department of Development
Box 7970
123 W. Washington Avenue
Madison, WI 53707-7970

Banking
Banking, Office of the Commissioner
131 W. Wilson Avenue
P.O. Box 7876
Madison, WI 53707-7876

Securities
Securities—Office of the Commissioner
111 W. Wilson Avenue
Box 1768
Madison, WI 53701-1768

Labor and Industrial Relations
Department of Industry, Labor, and Human Relations
201 E. Washington Avenue

P.O. Box 7946
Madison, WI 53707-7946

Insurance
Office of the Commissioner of Insurance
121 E. Wilson Street
Box 7873
Madison, WI 53707-7873

Uniform Industrial Code
Department of Industry, Labor and Human Relations
201 E. Washington Avenue
Box 7969
Madison, WI 53707

Business Ombudsman
Small Business Ombudsman
Department of Development
123 W. Washington Avenue
Box 7970
Madison, WI 53707

INDUSTRIAL AND BUSINESS DIRECTORIES

Classified Directory of Wisconsin Manufacturers, Wisconsin Association of Manufacturers and Commerce, 501 E. Washington Avenue, Box 352, Madison, WI 53701; State Industrial Directories Corp., 2 Penn Plaza, New York, NY 10001

Wisconsin Exporters Directory, Wisconsin Department of Development, 123 W. Washington Avenue, Box 7920, Madison, WI 53707

Wisconsin Manufacturers Register, Manufacturers' News, Inc., 1633 Central Street, Evanston, IL 60201

Wisconsin Local Development Organizations (annual), Wisconsin Department of Development, 123 W. Washington Avenue, Box 7970, Madison, WI 53707

Wisconsin Services Directory, Wisconsin Association of Manufacturers and Commerce, 501 E. Washington Avenue, Box 352, Madison, WI 53701

Wyoming

State Capitol, Cheyenne, WY 82002
(307) 777-7011

INFORMATION OFFICES

Commerce/Economic Development
Economic Development and Stabilization Board
Herschler Building
Cheyenne, WY 82002

Wyoming Small Business Development Center
130 N. Ash
Casper, WY 82601

Corporate
Secretary of State
Corporate Division
State Capitol
Cheyenne, WY 82002

Taxation
Department of Revenue and Taxation
Herschler Building
Cheyenne, WY 82002

International Commerce
International Trade Office
Herschler Building
Cheyenne, WY 82002

Banking
State Examiner
Herschler Building
Cheyenne, WY 82002

Securities
Secretary of State
Securities Division
State Capitol
Cheyenne, WY 82002

Labor and Industrial Relations
Department of Labor and Statistics
Herschler Building
Cheyenne, WY 82002

Insurance
Insurance Commission
Herschler Building
Cheyenne, WY 82002

Uniform Industrial Code
Industrial Siting Administration
Herschler Building
2301 Central
Cheyenne, WY 82002

Industrial Development Division
Economic Planning Development and Stabilization Board
Herschler Building
Cheyenne, WY 82002

INDUSTRIAL AND BUSINESS DIRECTORIES

Wyoming Directory of Manufacturing and Mining, Manufacturers' News, Inc., 1633 Central Street, Evanston, IL 60201; Economic Development and Stabilization Board, Herschler Building, Cheyenne, WY 82002

Puerto Rico

Capitol, San Juan, PR 00901
(809) 724-6040 (House of Representatives)
(809) 724-2030 (Senate)

INFORMATION OFFICES

Commerce/Economic Development
Puerto Rico Department of Commerce
P.O. Box S 4275
San Juan, PR 00905

Puerto Rico Economic Development Administration
G.P.O. Box 2350
San Juan, PR 00936

Puerto Rico Planning Board
P.O. Box 41119
San Juan, PR 00940

Government Development Bank
P.O. Box 42001
Minillas Station
Santurce, PR 00940

Economic Development Bank
P.O. Box 5009
Hato Rey, PR 00929-5009

Taxation

Puerto Rico Department of Treasury
P.O. Box S-4515
San Juan, PR 00901

Office of Industrial Tax Exemption
P.O. Box 2121
Hato Rey, PR 00918-2121

International Commerce

Foreign Export
GPO Box 362350
San Juan, PR 00936

Chamber of Commerce

Chamber of Commerce of Puerto Rico
P.O. Box 3789
San Juan, PR 00904

Puerto Rico Manufacturers Association

P.O. Box 2410
Hato Rey, PR 00919

Securities

Office of the Commissioner of Financial Institutions
P.O. Box 70324
San Juan, PR 00936

Labor and Industrial Relations

Puerto Rico Labor Relations Board
P.O. Box 4048
San Juan, PR 00905

National Labor Relations Board
Federal Building
Charlos E. Chardon Street
Hato Rey, PR 00918

Insurance

Office of the Insurance Commissioner
P.O. Box 8330, Fdez Juncos Station
Santurce, PR 00910

Puerto Rico Insurance Companies Association, Inc.
P.O. Box 3395
San Juan, PR 00936

Uniform Industrial Code

Department of Labor and Human Resources
505 Muñoz Rivera Avenue
Prudencio Rivera Martínez Building
Hato Rey, PR 00918

Business Ombudsman

Ombudsman Office
1205 Ponce de León Avenue
Banco de San Juan
Santurce, PR 00907-3995

International Commerce

Puerto Rico Department of Commerce
External Trade Promotion Program
P.O. Box S 4275
San Juan, PR 00905

US Department of Commerce
International Trade Administration
Charlos E. Chardon Street
Federal Building
Hato Rey, PR 00918

Puerto Rico Chamber of Commerce
International Trade Division
P.O. Box 3789
San Juan, PR 00904

Banking

Puerto Rico Bankers Association
Banco Popular Center
Hato Rey, PR 00918

INDUSTRIAL AND BUSINESS DIRECTORIES

Puerto Rico Official Industrial and Trade Directory, Witcom Group, Inc., P.O. Box 2310, San Juan, PR 00902

The Businessman's Guide to Puerto Rico, Puerto Rico Almanacs, Inc., P.O. Box 9582, Santurce, Puerto Rico 00908

Government Budget, Receipts, and Deficits: Historical Data[1]

Overview of the Budget Process

Executive Budget Formulation Process

During budget formulation, the President establishes general budget and fiscal policy guidelines. Under a multi-year planning system, policy guidance and planning ceilings are given to agencies for both the upcoming budget year and for the four following years and provide the initial guidelines for preparation of agency budget requests.

The budget formulation process begins not later than the spring of each year, at least nine months before the budget is transmitted. Executive branch agencies prepare their budget requests based on the guidelines provided by the President through the Office of Management and Budget (OMB) and the detailed instructions on preparation of budget estimates provided in this Circular. Executive branch departments and agencies are required to submit initial budget materials to OMB beginning in September, in accordance with the schedule in section 10.3. Other materials are submitted throughout the fall and winter on a schedule supplied by OMB. Budget data are required for the past, current, and upcoming budget year, as well as for the four years following the budget year.

Following submission of initial materials, hearings or less formal discussions with agencies are scheduled by OMB representatives. These hearings and discussions provide OMB an opportunity to obtain a better understanding of agency policies and programs, efforts to improve agency management (including highrisk areas) and program delivery, and to discuss specific problems. They also enable agencies to justify budget requests orally and provide additional information in response to specific questions.

After review of budget submissions, OMB staff prepare issue papers and recommendations on major issues for discussion with the Director.

After the review process is completed, decisions on budget requests are passed back to the agencies. If an agency disagrees with some aspect of the passback and considers it sufficiently important to pursue, it may submit an appeal to OMB. If OMB and the agency cannot reach agreement, appeals may be made to the President. Upon receipt of final decisions for the current and budget year, agencies revise their budget requests promptly to bring them into accord with these decisions. These final estimates are transmitted to Congress in the President's budget. In accordance with current law, the budget must be transmitted to Congress not later than the first Monday in February.

During the budget formulation process, management issues are reviewed, and proposals for improvements in agency management and program delivery are reflected in final budget decisions.

After transmittal of the budget, allowance letters are sent to agency heads formally advising them of decisions on budget and multi-year planning estimates; employment ceilings; goals for management improvements; and significant policy, program, and administrative matters. The multi-year planning estimates then become the starting point in planning for the budget to be transmitted to Congress the following year.

Executive and Congressional Budget Processes

The executive budget formulation process described above is prescribed by OMB, in accordance with the Budget and Accounting Act of 1921, as amended. The following timetable highlights significant dates culminating in transmittal of the President's budget and subsequent updates of the budget. It also reflects the congressional budget procedures established by the Congressional Budget Act of 1974 (2 U.S.C. 621), as amended, and by the Budget Enforcement Act of 1990 (BEA), Public Law 101–508, which amended the Gramm-Rudman-Hollings (G-R-H) law (Public Law 99–177, as amended by Public Law 100–119).

Source: Office of Management and Budget, Circular No. A-11.

[1] See page 708 for notes to Exhibits on pages 688–707.

THE BUDGET PROCESS

ACTION TO BE COMPLETED

The Executive Budget Process	Timing	The Congressional Budget Process
Agencies subject to executive branch review submit initial budget request materials.	September 1	
Fiscal year begins.	October 1	Fiscal year begins.
Agencies not subject to executive branch review submit budget request materials.	October 15	
	10 days after end of session	CBO issues its final sequester report.
OMB issues its final sequestration report;[1] President issues sequestration order, if necessary.	15 days after end of session	
	30 days later	Comptroller General issues compliance report.
Legislative branch and the judiciary submit budget request materials.	November–December	
	5 days before President's budget transmittal	CBO issues its sequestration preview report
President transmits the budget to Congress, including OMB sequestration preview report.	Not later than the first Monday in February	
OMB sends allowance letters to agencies.	February–March	
	February 15	Congressional Budget Office reports to the Budget Committees on the President's budget.
	Within 6 weeks of President's budget transmittal	Committees submit views and estimates to Budget Committees.

	April 1	Senate Budget Committee reports concurrent resolution on the budget.
	April 15	Congress completes action on concurrent resolution.
	May 15	House may consider appropriations bills in the absence of a concurrent resolution on the budget.
	June 10	House Appropriations Committee reports last appropriations bill.
	June 15	Congress completes action on reconciliation legislation.
	June 30	House completes action on annual appropriations bills.
	After completion of action on discretionary, direct spending, or receipts legislation.	CBO provides estimate of the impact of legislation as soon as practicable.
President transmits the Mid-Session Review, updating the budget estimates.	July 15	
OMB provides agencies with policy guidance for the upcoming budget.	July–August	
	August 15	CBO issues its sequestration update report.
OMB issues its sequestration update report	August 20	

[1] A "within session" sequestration is triggered within 15 days after enactment of appropriations that are enacted after the end of a session for the budget year and before July 1, if they breach the category spending limit for that fiscal year. A "lookback" reduction to a category limit is applied for appropriations enacted after June 30th for the fiscal year in progress that breach a category limit for that fiscal year and is applied to the next fiscal year.

Note.—OMB also reports to Congress on the impact of enacted legislation and provides an explanation of any differences between OMB and CBO estimates, within 5 calendar days of enactment of legislation.

Glossary of Budget Terms[1]

BALANCES OF BUDGET AUTHORITY—These are amounts of budget authority provided in previous years that have not been outlayed. Obligated balances are amounts that have been obligated but not yet outlayed. Unobligated balances are amounts that have not been obligated and that remain available for obligation under law.

BREACH—A breach is the amount by which new budget authority or outlays within a category of discretionary appropriations for a fiscal year is above the cap on new budget authority or outlays for that category for that year.

BUDGET—The *Budget of the United States Government* (this document) sets forth the President's comprehensive financial plan and indicates the President's priorities for the Federal Government.

BUDGET AUTHORITY (BA)—Budget authority is the authority provided by Federal law to incur financial obligations that will result in outlays. Specific forms of budget authority include:

- provisions of law that make funds available for obligation and expenditure (other than borrowing authority), including the authority to obligate and expend offsetting receipts and collections;
- borrowing authority, which is authority granted to a Federal entity to borrow (e.g., through the issuance of promissory notes or monetary credits) and to obligate and expend the borrowed funds;
- contract authority, which is the making of funds available for obligation but not for expenditure; and
- offsetting receipts and collections as negative budget authority.

BUDGETARY RESOURCES—Budgetary resources comprise new budget authority, unobligated balances of budget authority, direct spending authority, and obligation limitations.

BUDGET TOTALS—The budget includes totals for budget authority, outlays, and receipts. Some presentations in the budget distinguish on-budget totals from off-budget totals. On-budget totals reflect the transactions of all Federal Government entities except those excluded from the budget totals by law. Off-budget totals reflect the transactions of Government entities that are excluded from the on-budget totals by law. Currently excluded are the social security trust funds (Federal Old-Age and Survivors Insurance and Federal Disability Insurance Trust Funds) and the Postal Service. The on- and off-budget totals are combined to derive a total for Federal activity.

CAP—This is the term commonly used to refer to legal limits on the budget authority and outlays for each fiscal year for each of the discretionary appropriations categories. A sequester is required if an appropriation for a category causes a breach in the cap.

CATEGORIES OF DISCRETIONARY APPROPRIATIONS—Through 1993, discretionary appropriations are categorized as defense, international, or domestic. Separate spending limits (caps) are applied to each category. The appropriations in each of the categories are determined by lists of existing appropriations in a 1990 congressional report[2] or, in the case of new appropriations, in consultation among the Office of Management and Budget and the congressional Committees on Appropriations and the Budget. For 1994 and 1995, all discretionary appropriations constitute a single category.

COST—The term cost, when used in connection with Federal credit programs, means the estimated long-term cost to the Government of a direct loan or loan guarantee, calculated on a net present value basis. The term excludes administrative costs and any incidental effects on governmental receipts or outlays. Present value is a standard financial concept that allows for the time value of money, that is, for the fact that a given sum of money is worth more at present than in the future because interest can be earned on it. The cost of direct loans and loan guarantees is a net present value because collections are offset against disbursements.

CREDIT PROGRAM ACCOUNT—A credit program account receives an appropriation for the cost of a direct loan or loan guarantee program, from which such cost is disbursed to a financing account for the program.

DEFICIT—A deficit is the amount by which outlays exceed Governmental receipts.

DIRECT LOAN—A direct loan is a disbursement of funds by the Government to a non-Federal borrower under a contract that requires the repayment of such funds with or without interest. The term includes the purchase of, or participation in, a loan made by another lender. The term does not include the acquisition

[1] These basic terms and other budget terms, concepts, and procedures are described more fully in *The Budget System and Concepts of the United States Government,* a pamphlet available from the Government Printing Office. References to requirements in law generally refer to the Balanced Budget and Emergency Deficit Control Act of 1985 (also known as the Gramm-Rudman-Hollings Act), as amended. The Act was most recently amended by the Budget Enforcement Act of 1990 (Title XIII of Public Law 101–508). These requirements are discussed in various parts of the *Budget.*

[2] The joint statement of the managers accompanying the conference report on the Omnibus Budget Reconciliation Act of 1990 (Public Law 101–508).

of a federally guaranteed loan in satisfaction of default claims or the price support loans of the Commodity Credit Corporation. (*Cf.* LOAN GUARANTEE.)

DIRECT SPENDING—Direct spending, which sometimes is called mandatory spending, is a category of outlays from budget authority provided in law other than appropriations acts, entitlement authority, and the budget authority for the food stamp program. (*Cf.* DISCRETIONARY APPROPRIATIONS.)

DISCRETIONARY APPROPRIATIONS—Discretionary appropriations is a category of budget authority that comprises budgetary resources (except those provided to fund direct-spending programs) provided in appropriations acts. (*Cf.* DIRECT SPENDING.)

EMERGENCY APPROPRIATION—An emergency appropriation is an appropriation in a discretionary category that the President and the Congress have designated as an emergency requirement. Such appropriations result in an adjustment to the cap for the category.

FEDERAL FUNDS—Federal funds are the moneys collected and spent by the Government other than those designated as trust funds. Federal funds include general, special, public enterprise, and intragovernmental funds. (*Cf.* TRUST FUNDS.)

FINANCING ACCOUNT—A financing account receives the cost payments from a credit program account and includes other cash flows to and from the Government resulting from direct loan obligations or loan guarantee commitments made on or after October 1, 1991. At least one financing account is associated with each credit program account. For programs with direct and guaranteed loans, there are separate financing accounts for direct loans and guaranteed loans. The transactions of the financing accounts are not included in the budget totals. (*Cf.* LIQUIDATING ACCOUNT)

FISCAL YEAR—The fiscal year is the Government's accounting period. It begins on October 1st and ends on September 30th, and is designated by the calendar year in which it ends.

GENERAL FUND—The general fund consists of accounts for receipts not earmarked by law for a specific purpose, the proceeds of general borrowing, and the expenditure of these moneys.

LIQUIDATING ACCOUNT—A liquidating account includes all cash flows to and from the Government resulting from direct loan obligations and loan guarantee commitments prior to October 1, 1991. (*Cf.* FINANCING ACCOUNT.)

LOAN GUARANTEE—A loan guarantee is any guarantee, insurance, or other pledge with respect to the payment of all or a part of the principal or interest on any debt obligation of a non-Federal borrower to a non-Federal lender. The term does not include the insurance of deposits, shares, or other withdrawable accounts in financial institutions. (*Cf.* DIRECT LOAN.)

MANDATORY SPENDING—See DIRECT SPENDING.

MAXIMUM DEFICIT AMOUNTS—These are amounts specified in and subject to certain adjustments under law. If the deficit for the year in question is estimated to exceed the adjusted maximum deficit amount for that year by more than a specified margin, a sequester of the excess deficit is required.

INTRAGOVERNMENTAL FUNDS—Intragovernmental funds are accounts for business-type or market-oriented activities conducted primarily within and between Government agencies and financed by offsetting collections that are credited directly to the fund.

OBLIGATIONS—Obligations are binding agreements that will result in outlays, immediately or in the future. Budgetary resources must be available before obligations can be incurred legally.

OFF-BUDGET—See BUDGET TOTALS.

OFFSETTING COLLECTIONS—Offsetting collections are collections from the public that result from business-type or market-oriented activities and collections from other Government accounts. These collections are deducted from gross disbursements in calculating outlays, rather than counted in Governmental receipt totals. Some are credited directly to appropriation or fund accounts; others, called offsetting receipts, are credited to receipt accounts. The authority to spend offsetting collections is a form of budget authority. (*Cf.* RECEIPTS, GOVERNMENTAL.)

ON-BUDGET—See BUDGET TOTALS.

OUTLAYS—Outlays are the measure of Government spending. They are payments to liquidate obligations (other than the repayment of debt), net of refunds and offsetting collections. Outlays generally are recorded on a cash basis, but also include many cash-equivalent transactions, the subsidy cost of direct loans and loan guarantees, and interest accrued on public issues of the public debt.

PAY-AS-YOU-GO—This term refers to requirements in law that result in a sequester if the estimated combined result of legislation affecting direct spending or receipts is an increase in the deficit for a fiscal year.

PUBLIC ENTERPRISE FUNDS—Public enterprise funds are accounts for business or market-oriented activities conducted primarily with the public and financed by offsetting collections that are credited directly to the fund.

RECEIPTS, GOVERNMENTAL—Governmental receipts are collections that result primarily from the Government's exercise of its sovereign power to tax or otherwise compel payment. They are compared to outlays in calculating a surplus or deficit. (*Cf.* OFFSETTING COLLECTIONS.)

SEQUESTER—A sequester is the cancellation of budgetary resources provided by discretionary appropriations or direct spending legislation, following various procedures prescribed in law. A sequester may occur in response to a discretionary appropriation that causes a breach, in response to increases in the deficit resulting from the combined result of legislation affecting direct spending or receipts (referred to as a "pay-as-you-go" sequester), or in response to a deficit estimated to be in excess of the maximum deficit amounts.

SPECIAL FUNDS—Special funds are Federal fund accounts for receipts earmarked for specific purposes and the associated expenditure of those receipts. (*Cf.* TRUST FUNDS.)

SUBSIDY—This term means the same as cost when it is used in connection with Federal credit programs.

SURPLUS—A surplus is the amount by which receipts exceed outlays.

SUPPLEMENTAL APPROPRIATION—A supplemental appropriation is one enacted subsequent to a regular annual appropriations act when the need for funds is too urgent to be postponed until the next regular annual appropriations act.

TRUST FUNDS—Trust funds are accounts, designated by law as trust funds, for receipts earmarked for specific purposes and the associated expenditure of those receipts. (*Cf.* SPECIAL FUNDS.)

Source: *Budget of the United States Government, Fiscal 1994,* Executive Office of the President, Office of Management and Budget.

THE FEDERAL GOVERNMENT DOLLAR
FISCAL YEAR 1994
ESTIMATE

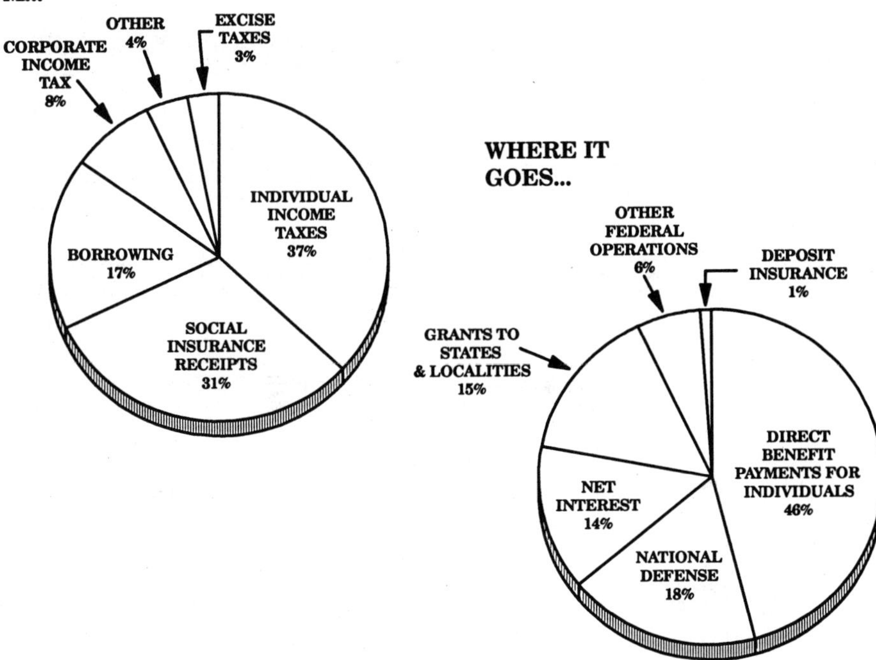

Source: *Budget of the United States Government,* Fiscal year 1994. Executive Office of the President, Office of Management and Budget.

RECEIPTS BY SOURCE AS PERCENTAGES OF GDP: 1934–1993

Fiscal Year	Individual Income Taxes	Corporation Income Taxes	Social Insurance Taxes and Contributions			Excise Taxes	Other	Total Receipts		
			Total	(On-Budget)	(Off-Budget)			Total	(On-Budget)	(Off-Budget)
1934	0.7	0.6	*	(*)	......	2.2	1.3	4.9	(4.9)	......
1935	0.8	0.8	*	(*)	......	2.1	1.6	5.3	(5.3)	......
1936	0.9	0.9	0.1	(0.1)	......	2.1	1.1	5.1	(5.1)	......
1937	1.3	1.2	0.7	(0.4)	(0.3)	2.2	0.9	6.2	(5.9)	(0.3)
1938	1.5	1.5	1.8	(1.3)	(0.4)	2.1	0.9	7.7	(7.2)	(0.4)
1939	1.2	1.3	1.8	(1.2)	(0.6)	2.1	0.8	7.2	(6.6)	(0.6)
1940	0.9	1.3	1.9	(1.3)	(0.6)	2.1	0.7	6.9	(6.3)	(0.6)
1941	1.2	1.9	1.7	(1.1)	(0.6)	2.3	0.7	7.7	(7.1)	(0.6)
1942	2.3	3.3	1.7	(1.1)	(0.6)	2.4	0.6	10.3	(9.7)	(0.6)
1943	3.7	5.4	1.7	(1.1)	(0.6)	2.3	0.5	13.7	(13.0)	(0.6)
1944	9.8	7.4	1.7	(1.1)	(0.6)	2.4	0.5	21.7	(21.0)	(0.6)
1945	8.7	7.5	1.6	(1.0)	(0.6)	3.0	0.5	21.3	(20.7)	(0.6)
1946	7.6	5.6	1.5	(0.9)	(0.6)	3.3	0.6	18.5	(17.9)	(0.6)
1947	8.0	3.9	1.5	(0.9)	(0.7)	3.2	0.6	17.3	(16.6)	(0.7)
1948	7.8	3.9	1.5	(0.9)	(0.7)	3.0	0.6	16.8	(16.2)	(0.7)
1949	5.9	4.3	1.4	(0.8)	(0.6)	2.9	0.5	15.0	(14.4)	(0.6)
1950	5.9	3.9	1.6	(0.8)	(0.8)	2.8	0.5	14.8	(14.0)	(0.8)
1951	6.9	4.5	1.8	(0.8)	(1.0)	2.8	0.5	16.5	(15.5)	(1.0)
1952	8.2	6.2	1.9	(0.8)	(1.1)	2.6	0.5	19.4	(18.4)	(1.1)
1953	8.2	5.8	1.9	(0.7)	(1.1)	2.7	0.5	19.1	(18.0)	(1.1)
1954	8.0	5.7	2.0	(0.7)	(1.2)	2.7	0.5	18.9	(17.7)	(1.2)
1955	7.5	4.6	2.0	(0.7)	(1.3)	2.4	0.5	17.0	(15.7)	(1.3)
1956	7.7	5.0	2.2	(0.7)	(1.5)	2.4	0.5	17.9	(16.4)	(1.5)
1957	8.1	4.8	2.3	(0.7)	(1.5)	2.4	0.6	18.3	(16.7)	(1.5)
1958	7.7	4.5	2.5	(0.7)	(1.8)	2.4	0.7	17.8	(16.0)	(1.8)
1959	7.6	3.6	2.4	(0.7)	(1.7)	2.2	0.6	16.5	(14.8)	(1.7)
1960	8.1	4.3	2.9	(0.8)	(2.1)	2.3	0.8	18.3	(16.2)	(2.1)
1961	8.0	4.1	3.2	(0.8)	(2.3)	2.3	0.7	18.3	(15.9)	(2.3)

1962	8.2	3.7	3.1	(0.9)	(2.2)	2.3	0.7	18.0	(15.7)	(2.2)
1963	8.1	3.7	3.4	(1.0)	(2.4)	2.3	0.8	18.2	(15.8)	(2.4)
1964	7.8	3.8	3.5	(0.9)	(2.6)	2.2	0.8	18.0	(15.4)	(2.6)
1965	7.3	3.8	3.3	(0.8)	(2.5)	2.2	0.9	17.4	(14.9)	(2.5)
1966	7.5	4.1	3.5	(0.9)	(2.6)	1.8	0.9	17.8	(15.2)	(2.6)
1967	7.8	4.3	4.1	(1.0)	(3.1)	1.7	0.9	18.8	(15.7)	(3.1)
1968	8.1	3.4	4.0	(1.1)	(2.9)	1.7	0.9	18.1	(15.1)	(2.9)
1969	9.4	4.0	4.2	(1.1)	(3.1)	1.6	0.9	20.2	(17.1)	(3.1)
1970	9.2	3.3	4.5	(1.1)	(3.4)	1.6	1.0	19.6	(16.2)	(3.4)
1971	8.2	2.5	4.5	(1.1)	(3.4)	1.6	1.0	17.8	(14.4)	(3.4)
1972	8.3	2.8	4.6	(1.1)	(3.5)	1.3	1.1	18.1	(14.6)	(3.5)
1973	8.1	2.8	5.0	(1.3)	(3.6)	1.3	0.9	18.1	(14.5)	(3.6)
1974	8.5	2.8	5.3	(1.5)	(3.8)	1.2	1.0	18.8	(14.9)	(3.8)
1975	8.1	2.7	5.6	(1.5)	(4.1)	1.1	1.0	18.5	(14.3)	(4.1)
1976	7.8	2.5	5.4	(1.4)	(3.9)	1.0	1.0	17.7	(13.8)	(3.9)
TQ	8.7	1.9	5.7	(1.6)	(4.0)	1.0	1.0	18.3	(14.2)	(4.0)
1977	8.2	2.9	5.6	(1.5)	(4.0)	0.9	1.0	18.5	(14.5)	(4.0)
1978	8.4	2.8	5.6	(1.7)	(4.0)	0.9	0.9	18.5	(14.6)	(4.0)
1979	9.0	2.7	5.7	(1.7)	(4.0)	0.8	0.9	19.1	(15.0)	(4.0)
1980	9.2	2.4	6.0	(1.7)	(4.3)	0.9	1.0	19.6	(15.3)	(4.3)
1981	9.6	2.1	6.2	(1.8)	(4.4)	1.4	1.0	20.2	(15.8)	(4.4)
1982	9.5	1.6	6.5	(1.9)	(4.6)	1.2	1.1	19.8	(15.2)	(4.6)
1983	8.7	1.1	6.3	(1.9)	(4.4)	1.1	0.9	18.1	(13.7)	(4.4)
1984	8.1	1.5	6.5	(2.0)	(4.5)	1.0	0.9	18.0	(13.5)	(4.5)
1985	8.4	1.5	6.7	(2.0)	(4.7)	0.9	0.9	18.5	(13.8)	(4.7)
1986	8.3	1.5	6.7	(2.0)	(4.7)	0.8	1.0	18.2	(13.5)	(4.7)
1987	8.8	1.9	6.8	(2.0)	(4.8)	0.7	0.9	19.2	(14.4)	(4.8)
1988	8.3	2.0	7.0	(1.9)	(5.0)	0.7	0.9	18.9	(13.9)	(5.0)
1989	8.6	2.0	6.9	(1.9)	(5.1)	0.7	0.9	19.2	(14.1)	(5.1)
1990	8.5	1.7	7.0	(1.8)	(5.2)	0.6	1.0	18.9	(13.7)	(5.2)
1991	8.3	1.7	7.0	(1.8)	(5.2)	0.8	0.9	18.7	(13.5)	(5.2)
1992	8.1	1.7	7.0	(1.9)	(5.2)	0.8	0.9	18.6	(13.4)	(5.2)
1993 estimate	8.3	1.7	7.1	(1.9)	(5.2)	0.8	0.8	18.6	(13.4)	(5.2)

* 0.05 percent or less.

Source: *Budget Baselines, Historical Data, And Alternatives For The Future*, 1993, Executive Office of the President, Office of Management and Budget.

PERCENTAGE COMPOSITION OF RECEIPTS BY SOURCE: 1934–1993

Fiscal Year	Individual Income Taxes	Corporation Income Taxes	Social Insurance Taxes and Contributions			Excise Taxes	Other	Total Receipts		
			Total	(On-Budget)	(Off-Budget)			Total	(On-Budget)	(Off-Budget)
1934	14.2	12.3	1.0	(1.0)	....	45.8	26.7	100.0	(100.0)	....
1935	14.6	14.7	0.9	(0.9)	....	39.9	30.0	100.0	(100.0)	....
1936	17.2	18.3	1.3	(1.3)	....	41.6	21.6	100.0	(100.0)	....
1937	20.3	19.3	10.8	(5.9)	(4.9)	34.8	14.9	100.0	(95.1)	(4.9)
1938	19.1	19.1	22.8	(17.1)	(5.7)	27.6	11.5	100.0	(94.3)	(5.7)
1939	16.3	17.9	25.3	(17.3)	(8.0)	29.7	10.7	100.0	(92.0)	(8.0)
1940	13.6	18.3	27.3	(18.9)	(8.4)	30.2	10.7	100.0	(91.6)	(8.4)
1941	15.1	24.4	22.3	(14.4)	(7.9)	29.3	9.0	100.0	(92.1)	(7.9)
1942	22.3	32.2	16.8	(10.6)	(6.1)	23.2	5.5	100.0	(93.9)	(6.1)
1943	27.1	39.8	12.7	(8.0)	(4.7)	17.1	3.3	100.0	(95.3)	(4.7)
1944	45.0	33.9	7.9	(5.0)	(3.0)	10.9	2.2	100.0	(97.0)	(3.0)
1945	40.7	35.4	7.6	(4.7)	(2.9)	13.9	2.4	100.0	(97.1)	(2.9)
1946	41.0	30.2	7.9	(4.8)	(3.2)	17.8	3.1	100.0	(96.8)	(3.2)
1947	46.6	22.4	8.9	(5.1)	(3.8)	18.7	3.5	100.0	(96.2)	(3.8)
1948	46.5	23.3	9.0	(5.1)	(3.9)	17.7	3.5	100.0	(96.1)	(3.9)
1949	39.5	28.4	9.6	(5.3)	(4.3)	19.0	3.5	100.0	(95.7)	(4.3)
1950	39.9	26.5	11.0	(5.7)	(5.3)	19.1	3.4	100.0	(94.7)	(5.3)
1951	41.9	27.3	11.0	(4.9)	(6.0)	16.8	3.1	100.0	(94.0)	(6.0)
1952	42.2	32.1	9.7	(4.3)	(5.4)	13.4	2.6	100.0	(94.6)	(5.4)
1953	42.8	30.5	9.8	(3.9)	(5.9)	14.2	2.7	100.0	(94.1)	(5.9)
1954	42.4	30.3	10.3	(3.8)	(6.6)	14.3	2.7	100.0	(93.4)	(6.6)
1955	43.9	27.3	12.0	(4.2)	(7.8)	14.0	2.8	100.0	(92.2)	(7.8)
1956	43.2	28.0	12.5	(3.9)	(8.6)	13.3	3.0	100.0	(91.4)	(8.6)
1957	44.5	26.5	12.5	(4.0)	(8.5)	13.2	3.3	100.0	(91.5)	(8.5)
1958	43.6	25.2	14.1	(4.0)	(10.1)	13.4	3.7	100.0	(89.9)	(10.1)
1959	46.3	21.8	14.8	(4.3)	(10.5)	13.3	3.7	100.0	(89.5)	(10.5)
1960	44.0	23.2	15.9	(4.4)	(11.5)	12.6	4.2	100.0	(88.5)	(11.5)
1961	43.8	22.2	17.4	(4.6)	(12.8)	12.6	4.0	100.0	(87.2)	(12.8)

1962	45.7	20.6	17.1	(4.8)	(12.3)	12.6	4.0	100.0	(87.7)	(12.3)
1963	44.7	20.3	18.6	(5.3)	(13.3)	12.4	4.1	100.0	(86.7)	(13.3)
1964	43.2	20.9	19.5	(5.0)	(14.5)	12.2	4.2	100.0	(85.5)	(14.5)
1965	41.8	21.8	19.0	(4.7)	(14.3)	12.5	4.9	100.0	(85.7)	(14.3)
1966	42.4	23.0	19.5	(4.9)	(14.6)	10.0	5.1	100.0	(85.4)	(14.6)
1967	41.3	22.8	21.9	(5.5)	(16.4)	9.2	4.7	100.0	(83.6)	(16.4)
1968	44.9	18.7	22.2	(5.9)	(16.3)	9.2	5.0	100.0	(83.7)	(16.3)
1969	46.7	19.6	20.9	(5.4)	(15.5)	8.1	4.7	100.0	(84.5)	(15.5)
1970	46.9	17.0	23.0	(5.7)	(17.4)	8.1	4.9	100.0	(82.6)	(17.4)
1971	46.1	14.3	25.3	(6.1)	(19.2)	8.9	5.4	100.0	(80.8)	(19.2)
1972	45.7	15.5	25.4	(6.1)	(19.2)	7.5	6.0	100.0	(80.7)	(19.2)
1973	44.7	15.7	27.3	(7.4)	(20.0)	7.0	5.2	100.0	(80.0)	(20.0)
1974	45.2	14.7	28.5	(8.0)	(20.5)	6.4	5.2	100.0	(79.5)	(20.5)
1975	43.9	14.6	30.3	(7.9)	(22.4)	5.9	5.4	100.0	(77.6)	(22.4)
1976	44.2	13.9	30.5	(8.2)	(22.3)	5.7	5.8	100.0	(77.7)	(22.3)
TQ	47.8	10.4	31.0	(8.9)	(22.2)	5.5	5.3	100.0	(77.8)	(22.2)
1977	44.3	15.4	29.9	(8.3)	(21.6)	4.9	5.3	100.0	(78.4)	(21.6)
1978	45.3	15.0	30.3	(8.9)	(21.4)	4.6	4.8	100.0	(78.6)	(21.4)
1979	47.0	14.2	30.0	(8.8)	(21.2)	4.0	4.8	100.0	(78.8)	(21.2)
1980	47.2	12.5	30.5	(8.6)	(21.9)	4.7	5.1	100.0	(78.1)	(21.9)
1981	47.7	10.2	30.5	(8.8)	(21.7)	6.8	4.8	100.0	(78.3)	(21.7)
1982	48.2	8.0	32.6	(9.4)	(23.2)	5.9	5.3	100.0	(76.8)	(23.2)
1983	48.1	6.2	34.8	(10.3)	(24.5)	5.9	5.0	100.0	(75.5)	(24.5)
1984	44.8	8.5	35.9	(11.0)	(24.9)	5.6	5.2	100.0	(75.1)	(24.9)
1985	45.6	8.4	36.1	(10.8)	(25.4)	4.9	5.0	100.0	(74.6)	(25.4)
1986	45.4	8.2	36.9	(10.9)	(26.0)	4.3	5.2	100.0	(74.0)	(26.0)
1987	46.0	9.8	35.5	(10.5)	(25.0)	3.8	4.9	100.0	(75.0)	(25.0)
1988	44.1	10.4	36.8	(10.2)	(26.6)	3.9	4.8	100.0	(73.4)	(26.6)
1989	45.0	10.4	36.3	(9.7)	(26.6)	3.5	4.8	100.0	(73.4)	(26.6)
1990	**45.3**	9.1	**36.9**	**(9.5)**	**(27.3)**	3.4	5.4	**100.0**	**(72.7)**	**(27.3)**
1991	**44.4**	9.3	**37.6**	**(9.7)**	**(27.9)**	4.0	4.7	**100.0**	**(72.1)**	**(27.9)**
1992	**43.6**	9.2	**37.9**	(10.2)	**(27.7)**	4.2	5.1	**100.0**	**(72.3)**	**(27.7)**
1993 estimate	**44.5**	**9.2**	**38.0**	(10.1)	**(27.8)**	4.1	4.2	**100.0**	**(72.2)**	**(27.8)**

Source: *Budget Baselines, Historical Data, And Alternatives For The Future*, 1993, Executive Office of the President, Office of Management and Budget.

COMPOSITION OF OUTLAYS IN CURRENT AND IN CONSTANT (FY 1987) DOLLARS: 1977–1993

Category	TQ	1977	1978	1979	1980	1981	1982	1983	1984
In millions of current dollars									
Total outlays	95,975	409,218	458,746	503,485	590,947	678,249	745,755	808,380	851,846
National defense [1]	22,269	97,241	104,495	116,342	133,995	157,513	185,309	209,903	227,413
Nondefense:									
Payments for individuals	45,534	196,978	211,761	233,837	278,530	324,658	357,924	396,523	401,209
Direct payments [2]	(40,449)	(174,268)	(186,967)	(206,276)	(245,879)	(286,807)	(319,123)	(353,951)	(355,856)
Grants to State and local governments	(5,085)	(22,710)	(24,795)	(27,561)	(32,652)	(37,851)	(38,800)	(42,572)	(45,353)
All other grants	10,819	45,609	53,035	55,204	58,707	56,836	49,327	49,837	52,129
Net Interest [2]	6,949	29,901	35,458	42,636	52,538	68,774	85,044	89,828	111,123
All other [2]	14,611	54,369	69,716	72,942	87,118	98,509	94,251	96,265	91,929
Undistributed offsetting receipts [2]	−4,206	−14,879	−15,720	−17,476	−19,942	−28,041	−26,099	−33,976	−31,957
Total nondefense	73,707	311,977	354,251	387,143	456,951	520,736	560,446	598,478	624,433
In billions of constant (FY 1987) dollars									
Total outlays	181.5	740.9	773.9	781.7	832.1	867.7	891.1	921.1	933.5
National defense [1]	42.4	176.8	177.2	180.4	187.1	198.2	214.3	230.4	241.7
Nondefense:									
Payments for individuals	86.3	357.6	358.9	365.7	394.9	420.5	435.6	459.8	446.5
Direct payments [2]	(76.7)	(316.3)	(316.9)	(322.6)	(348.6)	(371.5)	(388.4)	(410.5)	(396.0)
Grants to State and local governments	(9.6)	(41.2)	(42.0)	(43.1)	(46.3)	(49.0)	(47.2)	(49.4)	(50.5)
All other grants	20.5	82.9	89.3	84.9	81.2	72.4	59.2	57.5	57.8
Net Interest [2]	13.1	54.0	59.5	65.9	74.4	88.4	101.8	103.2	122.3
All other [2]	27.0	95.8	114.8	111.8	122.9	123.2	111.1	108.6	100.0
Undistributed offsetting receipts [2]	−7.8	−26.2	−25.9	−26.9	−28.5	−35.1	−30.9	−38.4	−34.8
Total nondefense	139.2	564.2	596.7	601.2	645.0	669.5	676.8	690.8	691.7

As percentages of GDP

Total outlays	21.6	21.3	21.3	20.7	22.3	22.9	23.9	24.4	23.1
National defense [1]	5.0	5.1	4.8	4.8	5.1	5.3	5.9	6.3	6.2
Nondefense:									
Payments for individuals	10.2	10.3	9.8	9.6	10.5	11.0	11.5	12.0	10.9
Direct payments [2]	(9.1)	(9.1)	(8.7)	(8.5)	(9.3)	(9.7)	(10.2)	(10.7)	(9.6)
Grants to State and local governments	(1.1)	(1.2)	(1.2)	(1.1)	(1.2)	(1.3)	(1.2)	(1.3)	(1.2)
All other grants	2.4	2.4	2.5	2.3	2.2	1.9	1.6	1.5	1.4
Net Interest [2]	1.6	1.6	1.6	1.8	2.0	2.3	2.7	2.7	3.0
All other [2]	3.3	2.8	3.2	3.0	3.3	3.3	3.0	2.9	2.5
Undistributed offsetting receipts [2]	−0.9	−0.8	−0.7	−0.7	−0.8	−0.9	−0.8	−1.0	−0.9
Total nondefense	16.6	16.3	16.4	15.9	17.3	17.6	18.0	18.0	16.9
Addendum: GDP ($ billions)	445.0	1,917.2	2,155.0	2,429.5	2,644.1	2,964.4	3,122.2	3,316.5	3,695.0

As percentages of outlays

Total outlays	100.0	100.0	100.0	100.0	100.0	100.0	100.0	100.0	100.0
National defense [1]	23.2	23.8	22.8	23.1	22.7	23.2	24.8	26.0	26.7
Nondefense:									
Payments for individuals	47.4	48.1	46.2	46.4	47.1	47.9	48.0	49.1	47.1
Direct payments [2]	(42.1)	(42.6)	(40.8)	(41.0)	(41.6)	(42.3)	(42.8)	(43.8)	(41.8)
Grants to State and local governments	(5.3)	(5.5)	(5.4)	(5.5)	(5.5)	(5.6)	(5.2)	(5.3)	(5.3)
All other grants	11.3	11.1	11.6	11.0	9.9	8.4	6.6	6.2	6.1
Net Interest [2]	7.2	7.3	7.7	8.5	8.9	10.1	11.4	11.1	13.0
All other [2]	15.2	13.3	15.2	14.5	14.7	14.5	12.6	11.9	10.8
Undistributed offsetting receipts [2]	−4.4	−3.6	−3.4	−3.5	−3.4	−4.1	−3.5	−4.2	−3.8
Total nondefense	76.8	76.2	77.2	76.9	77.3	76.8	75.2	74.0	73.3

See footnotes at end of table.

(continued)

COMPOSITION OF OUTLAYS IN CURRENT AND IN CONSTANT (FY 1987) DOLLARS: 1977–1993—*(Concluded)*

Category	1985	1986	1987	1988	1989	1990	1991	1992	1993 estimate
In millions of current dollars									
Total outlays	946,391	990,336	1,003,911	1,064,140	1,143,172	1,252,691	1,323,785	1,381,791	1,474,935
National defense [1]	252,748	273,375	281,999	290,361	303,559	299,331	273,292	298,361	289,299
Nondefense:									
Payments for individuals	427,302	451,261	471,277	500,656	536,030	584,090	650,318	728,985	789,249
Direct payments [2]	(377,950)	(397,036)	(413,522)	(438,222)	(468,677)	(506,958)	(557,821)	(616,782)	(660,023)
Grants to State and local governments	(49,352)	(54,225)	(57,755)	(62,434)	(67,353)	(77,132)	(92,497)	(112,204)	(129,226)
All other grants	56,388	57,978	50,498	52,760	54,370	58,004	61,889	65,793	74,062
Net Interest [2]	129,504	136,047	138,652	151,838	169,266	184,221	194,541	199,429	202,771
All other [2]	113,147	104,682	97,941	105,492	117,158	163,661	183,102	128,503	156,767
Undistributed offsetting receipts [2]	−32,698	−33,007	−36,455	−36,967	−37,212	−36,615	−39,356	−39,280	−37,213
Total nondefense	693,643	716,961	721,912	773,780	839,613	953,360	1,050,493	1,083,431	1,185,636
In billions of constant (FY 1987) dollars									
Total outlays	1,001.3	1,017.3	1,003.9	1,027.1	1,057.2	1,110.1	1,122.0	1,138.4	1,180.0
National defense [1]	261.2	276.4	282.0	283.3	285.9	272.3	240.1	253.6	239.5
Nondefense:									
Payments for individuals	458.6	467.5	471.3	480.0	490.4	509.5	540.4	589.3	618.9
Direct payments [2]	(405.6)	(411.4)	(413.5)	(420.2)	(428.8)	(442.2)	(463.5)	(498.5)	(517.4)
Grants to State and local governments	(53.0)	(56.2)	(57.8)	(59.9)	(61.6)	(67.3)	(77.0)	(90.8)	(101.5)
All other grants	59.8	59.6	50.5	50.8	50.3	52.0	53.7	56.0	61.2
Net Interest [2]	137.3	140.1	138.7	146.5	156.3	163.2	165.2	164.6	163.1
All other [2]	118.7	107.6	97.9	102.4	108.6	145.5	155.7	107.1	127.1
Undistributed offsetting receipts [2]	−34.3	−34.0	−36.5	−35.8	−34.4	−32.4	−33.2	−32.2	−29.7
Total nondefense	740.1	740.8	721.9	743.8	771.3	837.8	882.0	884.8	940.6

As percentages of GDP

Total outlays	23.9	23.5	22.5	22.1	22.1	22.9	23.5	23.5	23.9
National defense[1]	6.4	6.5	6.3	6.0	5.9	5.5	4.9	5.1	4.7
Nondefense:									
Payments for individuals	10.8	10.7	10.6	10.4	10.4	10.7	11.5	12.4	12.8
Direct payments[2]	(9.5)	(9.4)	(9.3)	(9.1)	(9.1)	(9.3)	(9.9)	(10.5)	(10.7)
Grants to State and local governments	(1.2)	(1.3)	(1.3)	(1.3)	(1.3)	(1.4)	(1.6)	(1.9)	(2.1)
All other grants	1.4	1.4	1.1	1.1	1.1	1.1	1.1	1.1	1.2
Net Interest[2]	3.3	3.2	3.1	3.2	3.3	3.4	3.5	3.4	3.3
All other[2]	2.9	2.5	2.2	2.2	2.3	3.0	3.3	2.2	2.5
Undistributed offsetting receipts[2]	−0.8	−0.8	−0.8	−0.8	−0.7	−0.7	−0.7	−0.7	−0.6
Total nondefense	17.5	17.0	16.2	16.1	16.2	17.4	18.7	18.5	19.2
Addendum: GDP ($ billions)	3,967.7	4,219.0	4,452.4	4,808.4	5,173.3	5,467.1	5,632.6	5,868.6	6,164.4

As percentages of outlays

Total outlays	100.0	100.0	100.0	100.0	100.0	100.0	100.0	100.0	100.0
National defense[1]	26.7	27.6	28.1	27.3	26.6	23.9	20.6	21.6	19.6
Nondefense:									
Payments for individuals	45.2	45.6	46.9	47.0	46.9	46.6	49.1	52.8	53.5
Direct payments[2]	(39.9)	(40.1)	(41.2)	(41.2)	(41.0)	(40.5)	(42.1)	(44.6)	(44.7)
Grants to State and local governments	(5.2)	(5.5)	(5.8)	(5.9)	(5.9)	(6.2)	(7.0)	(8.1)	(8.8)
All other grants	6.0	5.9	5.0	5.0	4.8	4.6	4.7	4.8	5.0
Net Interest[2]	13.7	13.7	13.8	14.3	14.8	14.7	14.7	14.4	13.7
All other[2]	12.0	10.6	9.8	9.9	10.2	13.1	13.8	9.3	10.6
Undistributed offsetting receipts[2]	−3.5	−3.3	−3.6	−3.5	−3.3	−2.9	−3.0	−2.8	−2.5
Total nondefense	73.3	72.4	71.9	72.7	73.4	76.1	79.4	78.4	80.4

[1] Includes a small amount of grants to State and local governments and direct payments for individuals.
[2] Includes some off-budget amounts; most of the off-budget amounts are direct payments for individuals (social security benefits).

Source: *Budget Baselines, Historical Data, And Alternatives For The Future*, 1993, Executive Office of the President, Office of Management and Budget.

TOTAL GOVERNMENT EXPENDITURES AS PERCENTAGES OF GDP: 1947–1992

Fiscal Year	Total Government Expenditures	Federal Government Outlays			Addendum: Federal Grants	State and Local Government Expenditures From Own Sources (NIPA Basis)
		Total	On-Budget	Off-Budget		
1947	20.4	15.5	15.3	0.1	(0.7)	4.9
1948	17.7	12.1	11.9	0.1	(0.7)	5.6
1949	21.0	14.8	14.6	0.2	(0.8)	6.2
1950	23.1	16.0	15.8	0.2	(0.9)	7.1
1951	21.0	14.5	14.1	0.4	(0.8)	6.4
1952	26.3	19.9	19.4	0.5	(0.7)	6.4
1953	27.2	20.9	20.3	0.6	(0.8)	6.3
1954	26.0	19.3	18.5	0.8	(0.8)	6.8
1955	25.1	17.8	16.8	1.0	(0.8)	7.3
1956	24.2	17.0	15.8	1.2	(0.8)	7.2
1957	25.0	17.5	16.1	1.4	(0.8)	7.5
1958	26.4	18.4	16.7	1.7	(1.0)	8.0
1959	27.2	19.2	17.3	1.9	(1.3)	8.0
1960	26.1	18.3	16.1	2.2	(1.4)	7.8
1961	27.3	18.9	16.6	2.3	(1.3)	8.4
1962	27.7	19.2	16.8	2.4	(1.4)	8.4
1963	27.6	19.0	16.5	2.6	(1.4)	8.5
1964	27.5	19.0	16.4	2.5	(1.6)	8.6
1965	26.2	17.6	15.2	2.5	(1.6)	8.6
1966	27.0	18.3	15.6	2.7	(1.7)	8.7

1967	28.8	19.8	17.3	2.6	(1.9)	9.0
1968	30.3	21.0	18.4	2.6	(2.1)	9.3
1969	29.5	19.8	17.1	2.7	(2.1)	9.6
1970	29.7	19.9	17.1	2.8	(2.3)	9.8
1971	30.4	20.0	16.9	3.1	(2.5)	10.4
1972	30.3	20.1	16.9	3.2	(2.8)	10.2
1973	29.0	19.3	15.7	3.6	(3.2)	9.7
1974	29.1	19.2	15.5	3.7	(3.0)	10.0
1975	32.4	22.0	18.0	4.0	(3.2)	10.4
1976	32.4	22.1	17.9	4.1	(3.4)	10.4
TQ	32.1	21.6	17.2	4.4	(3.5)	10.5
1977	31.0	21.3	17.1	4.2	(3.5)	9.7
1978	30.4	21.3	17.1	4.2	(3.5)	9.1
1979	29.7	20.7	16.6	4.1	(3.3)	9.0
1980	31.5	22.3	18.0	4.3	(3.3)	9.2
1981	31.9	22.9	18.3	4.6	(3.0)	9.0
1982	33.3	23.9	19.0	4.8	(2.7)	9.4
1983	33.8	24.4	19.9	4.4	(2.6)	9.4
1984	32.1	23.1	18.6	4.5	(2.5)	9.0
1985	33.0	23.9	19.4	4.5	(2.5)	9.2
1986	32.9	23.5	19.1	4.3	(2.6)	9.4
1987	32.5	22.5	18.2	4.4	(2.3)	9.9
1988	32.0	22.1	17.9	4.2	(2.3)	9.9
1989	31.9	22.1	18.0	4.1	(2.2)	9.8
1990	33.0	22.9	18.8	4.1	(2.3)	10.1
1991	34.1	23.5	19.2	4.3	(2.6)	10.6
1992	34.4	23.5	19.2	4.3	(2.9)	10.9

Source: *Budget Baselines, Historical Data, And Alternatives For The Future*, 1993, Executive Office of the President, Office of Management and Budget.

TOTAL GOVERNMENT EXPENDITURES BY MAJOR CATEGORY OF EXPENDITURE AS PERCENTAGES OF GDP: 1947–1992

Fiscal Year	Total Government	Defense and International	Net Interest	Federal Payments For Individuals		Other Federal	State and Local From Own Sources (Except Net Interest)
				Social Security and Medicare	Other		
1947	20.4	8.3	1.9	0.2	3.9	1.2	4.8
1948	17.7	5.5	1.8	0.2	3.5	1.1	5.6
1949	21.0	7.3	1.8	0.2	3.6	1.9	6.1
1950	23.1	6.9	1.8	0.3	4.9	2.1	7.0
1951	21.0	8.7	1.5	0.5	2.8	1.1	6.4
1952	26.3	14.3	1.4	0.6	2.6	1.0	6.4
1953	27.2	15.1	1.4	0.7	2.3	1.4	6.3
1954	26.0	13.8	1.3	0.9	2.5	0.7	6.8
1955	25.1	11.7	1.3	1.1	2.6	1.1	7.3
1956	24.2	10.8	1.2	1.3	2.4	1.3	7.2
1957	25.0	11.1	1.2	1.5	2.4	1.3	7.5
1958	26.4	11.2	1.3	1.8	2.9	1.3	8.0
1959	27.2	10.9	1.2	2.0	2.8	2.4	8.0
1960	26.1	10.1	1.4	2.3	2.5	2.0	7.8
1961	27.3	10.2	1.3	2.4	3.0	2.1	8.4
1962	27.7	10.4	1.3	2.5	2.7	2.3	8.4
1963	27.6	10.0	1.3	2.6	2.7	2.4	8.5
1964	27.5	9.5	1.3	2.6	2.6	2.9	8.6
1965	26.2	8.3	1.2	2.5	2.4	3.1	8.6
1966	27.0	8.7	1.2	2.8	2.3	3.3	8.7

1967	28.8	9.7	1.2	3.1	2.4	3.4	9.1
1968	30.3	10.3	1.2	3.4	2.5	3.5	9.4
1969	29.5	9.4	1.3	3.6	2.6	2.9	9.7
1970	29.7	8.7	1.3	3.7	2.9	3.1	10.0
1971	30.4	7.9	1.3	4.1	3.6	3.0	10.5
1972	30.3	7.3	1.2	4.2	3.9	3.3	10.3
1973	29.0	6.3	1.2	4.5	3.7	3.4	9.9
1974	29.1	6.1	1.3	4.7	3.9	3.0	10.2
1975	32.4	6.2	1.2	5.1	5.0	4.1	10.7
1976	32.4	5.7	1.3	5.3	5.4	4.1	10.6
TQ	32.1	5.6	1.3	5.4	4.8	4.2	10.7
1977	31.0	5.4	1.3	5.4	4.8	4.1	9.9
1978	30.4	5.2	1.3	5.4	4.4	4.6	9.5
1979	29.7	5.1	1.3	5.4	4.2	4.2	9.5
1980	31.5	5.5	1.3	5.7	4.8	4.3	9.9
1981	31.9	5.8	1.6	6.0	4.9	3.9	9.8
1982	33.3	6.3	1.8	6.5	5.0	3.4	10.3
1983	33.8	6.7	1.8	6.8	5.2	3.0	10.3
1984	32.1	6.6	2.1	6.4	4.4	2.6	9.9
1985	33.0	6.8	2.3	6.5	4.3	3.0	10.1
1986	32.9	6.8	2.3	6.4	4.3	2.7	10.4
1987	32.5	6.6	2.2	6.4	4.2	2.3	10.8
1988	32.0	6.3	2.3	6.3	4.1	2.3	10.8
1989	31.9	6.1	2.3	6.3	4.1	2.4	10.8
1990	33.0	5.7	2.4	6.5	4.2	3.1	11.1
1991	34.1	5.1	2.6	6.8	4.8	3.4	11.5
1992	34.4	5.4	2.6	7.1	5.4	2.4	11.6

Source: *Budget Baselines, Historical Data, And Alternatives For The Future*, 1993, Executive Office of the President, Office of Management and Budget.

TOTAL GOVERNMENT EXPENDITURES BY MAJOR CATEGORY OF EXPENDITURE: 1947–1992

(in billions of dollars)

Fiscal Year	Total Government	Defense and International	Net Interest	Federal Payments For Individuals		Other Federal	State and Local From Own Sources (Except Net Interest)
				Social Security and Medicare	Other		
1947	45.4	18.6	4.3	0.4	8.6	2.6	10.8
1948	43.6	13.7	4.4	0.5	8.5	2.7	13.8
1949	55.0	19.2	4.6	0.6	9.5	5.0	16.1
1950	61.3	18.4	4.9	0.7	12.9	5.7	18.7
1951	65.7	27.2	4.7	1.5	8.8	3.4	20.1
1952	89.4	48.8	4.7	2.0	8.9	3.4	21.7
1953	98.9	54.9	5.2	2.6	8.3	5.1	22.8
1954	95.9	50.9	4.8	3.3	9.3	2.6	25.0
1955	96.5	45.0	4.9	4.3	10.0	4.3	27.9
1956	100.8	44.9	5.2	5.4	9.8	5.4	30.0
1957	109.6	48.6	5.4	6.5	10.5	5.6	32.9
1958	118.4	50.2	5.7	8.0	12.9	5.7	35.9
1959	130.6	52.2	5.9	9.5	13.2	11.4	38.4
1960	131.8	51.1	7.1	11.4	12.8	10.0	39.5
1961	141.3	52.8	6.8	12.2	15.3	10.7	43.5
1962	153.7	58.0	7.0	14.0	14.9	13.0	46.7
1963	161.1	58.7	7.9	15.5	15.5	13.9	49.6
1964	172.2	59.7	8.2	16.2	16.0	18.4	53.7
1965	176.0	55.9	8.4	17.1	16.0	20.6	58.0
1966	198.4	63.7	9.0	20.3	16.8	24.4	64.3

1967	228.7	77.0	9.5	24.5	18.7	27.0	72.0
1968	256.9	87.2	10.1	28.4	21.4	30.0	79.7
1969	272.7	87.1	11.7	33.0	24.2	26.6	90.1
1970	292.2	86.0	12.8	36.4	28.4	30.4	98.1
1971	319.2	83.0	13.2	42.6	38.0	31.7	110.6
1972	347.4	84.0	14.2	47.7	45.3	38.2	118.1
1973	369.1	80.8	15.3	57.2	47.5	42.8	125.5
1974	409.1	85.1	17.8	65.7	54.7	42.4	143.5
1975	489.6	93.6	18.7	77.7	76.2	61.6	161.9
1976	546.4	96.1	22.5	89.6	91.0	68.4	178.9
TQ	142.7	24.7	6.0	24.0	21.5	18.8	47.7
1977	594.7	103.6	25.6	104.5	92.5	78.7	189.8
1978	655.6	112.0	28.4	116.7	95.0	99.5	203.9
1979	721.8	123.8	30.8	130.8	103.1	103.2	230.1
1980	834.2	146.7	34.6	151.0	127.5	113.2	261.1
1981	945.1	170.6	46.3	179.1	145.5	114.2	289.4
1982	1,038.9	197.6	57.3	203.1	154.8	105.2	320.9
1983	1,120.2	221.8	59.3	224.0	172.5	100.3	342.4
1984	1,185.6	243.3	78.1	237.0	164.2	96.2	366.8
1985	1,311.0	268.9	91.9	256.1	171.2	120.7	402.2
1986	1,387.3	287.5	95.7	270.7	180.5	115.5	437.2
1987	1,445.6	293.6	97.8	285.0	186.3	100.3	482.6
1988	1,538.5	300.8	108.7	302.5	198.1	110.8	517.5
1989	1,651.5	313.1	118.9	324.4	211.6	124.7	558.7
1990	1,806.3	313.1	131.1	353.8	230.3	171.3	606.8
1991	1,922.2	289.1	145.1	380.7	269.6	189.8	647.9
1992	2,020.3	314.5	154.6	414.3	314.7	138.9	683.4

Source: *Budget Baselines, Historical Data, And Alternatives For The Future,* 1993, Executive Office of the President, Office of Management and Budget.

TOTAL GOVERNMENT SURPLUSES OR DEFICITS (−) IN ABSOLUTE AMOUNTS AND AS PERCENTAGES OF GDP: 1947–1992

Fiscal Year	In Billions of Current Dollars					As Percentages of GDP		
	Total Government	Federal Government			State and Local (NIPA Basis)	Total Government	Total Federal	State and Local
		Total	On-Budget	Off-Budget				
1947	5.6	4.0	2.9	1.2	1.6	2.5	1.8	0.7
1948	12.4	11.8	10.5	1.2	0.6	5.0	4.8	0.2
1949	0.4	0.6	−0.7	1.3	−0.2	0.2	0.2	−0.1
1950	−4.4	−3.1	−4.7	1.6	−1.3	−1.7	−1.2	−0.5
1951	5.6	6.1	4.3	1.8	−0.6	1.8	1.9	−0.2
1952	−2.0	−1.5	−3.4	1.9	−0.4	−0.6	−0.4	−0.1
1953	−6.2	−6.5	−8.3	1.8	0.3	−1.7	−1.8	0.1
1954	−1.4	−1.2	−2.8	1.7	−0.3	−0.4	−0.3	−0.1
1955	−4.6	−3.0	−4.1	1.1	−1.6	−1.2	−0.8	−0.4
1956	3.2	3.9	2.5	1.5	−0.8	0.8	0.9	−0.2
1957	2.5	3.4	2.6	0.8	−0.9	0.6	0.8	−0.2
1958	−4.8	−2.8	−3.3	0.5	−2.0	−1.1	−0.6	−0.5
1959	−14.6	−12.8	−12.1	−0.7	−1.8	−3.0	−2.7	−0.4
1960	0.7	0.3	0.5	−0.2	0.4	0.1	0.1	0.1
1961	−3.6	−3.3	−3.8	0.4	−0.2	−0.7	−0.6	−*
1962	−7.1	−7.1	−5.9	−1.3	*	−1.3	−1.3	*
1963	−4.5	−4.8	−4.0	−0.8	0.3	−0.8	−0.8	*
1964	−5.3	−5.9	−6.5	0.6	0.6	−0.8	−0.9	0.1
1965	−0.7	−1.4	−1.6	0.2	0.7	−0.1	−0.2	0.1
1966	−3.1	−3.7	−3.1	−0.6	0.6	−0.4	−0.5	0.1

1967	−10.2	−8.6	−12.6	4.0	−1.6	−1.3	−1.1	−0.2
1968	−24.7	−25.2	−27.7	2.6	0.5	−2.9	−3.0	0.1
1969	2.8	3.2	−0.5	3.7	−0.4	0.3	0.4	−*
1970	0.8	−2.8	−8.7	5.9	3.7	0.1	−0.3	0.4
1971	−23.6	−23.0	−26.1	3.0	−0.5	−2.2	−2.2	−0.1
1972	−15.2	−23.4	−26.4	3.1	8.2	−1.3	−2.0	0.7
1973	−0.1	−14.9	−15.4	0.5	14.8	−*	−1.2	1.2
1974	4.4	−6.1	−8.0	1.8	10.5	0.3	−0.4	0.8
1975	−47.4	−53.2	−55.3	2.0	5.9	−3.1	−3.5	0.4
1976	−66.7	−73.7	−70.5	−3.2	7.0	−4.0	−4.4	0.4
TQ	−16.5	−14.7	−13.3	−1.4	−1.8	−3.7	−3.3	−0.4
1977	−30.8	−53.7	−49.8	−3.9	22.9	−1.6	−2.8	1.2
1978	−26.3	−59.2	−54.9	−4.3	32.9	−1.2	−2.7	1.5
1979	−14.8	−40.2	−38.2	−2.0	25.3	−0.6	−1.7	1.0
1980	−50.5	−73.8	−72.7	−1.1	23.3	−1.9	−2.8	0.9
1981	−51.1	−79.0	−74.0	−5.0	27.9	−1.7	−2.7	0.9
1982	−101.0	−128.0	−120.1	−7.9	27.0	−3.2	−4.1	0.9
1983	−172.7	−207.8	−208.0	0.2	35.1	−5.2	−6.3	1.1
1984	−130.0	−185.4	−185.7	0.3	55.4	−3.5	−5.0	1.5
1985	−157.9	−212.3	−221.7	9.4	54.4	−4.0	−5.4	1.4
1986	−165.5	−221.2	−238.0	16.7	55.8	−3.9	−5.2	1.3
1987	−106.0	−149.8	−169.3	19.6	43.8	−2.4	−3.4	1.0
1988	−115.6	−155.2	−194.0	38.8	39.6	−2.4	−3.2	0.8
1989	−106.7	−152.5	−205.2	52.8	45.8	−2.1	−2.9	0.9
1990	−189.0	−221.4	−278.0	56.6	32.4	−3.5	−4.0	0.6
1991	−252.9	−269.5	−321.7	52.2	16.7	−4.5	−4.8	0.3
1992	−273.8	−290.2	−340.3	50.1	16.4	−4.7	−4.9	0.3

*If dollars, $50 million or less. If percent, 0.05 percent or less.

Source: *Budget Baselines, Historical Data, And Alternatives For The Future*, 1993, Executive Office of the President, Office of Management and Budget.

SUMMARY OF RECEIPTS, OUTLAYS, AND SURPLUSES OR DEFICITS(–) IN CURRENT DOLLARS, CONSTANT (FY 1987) DOLLARS, AND AS PERCENTAGES OF GDP: 1940–1993

(dollar amounts in billions)

Fiscal Year	In Current Dollars			In Constant (FY 1987 Dollars)			Addendum: Composite Deflator	As Percentages of GDP		
	Receipts	Outlays	Surplus or Deficit(–)	Receipts	Outlays	Surplus or Deficit(–)		Receipts	Outlays	Surplus or Deficit(–)
1940	6.5	9.5	–2.9	67.0	96.8	–29.9	0.0978	6.9	9.9	–3.1
1941	8.7	13.7	–4.9	86.3	135.3	–49.0	0.1009	7.7	12.1	–4.4
1942	14.6	35.1	–20.5	131.2	315.1	–183.9	0.1115	10.3	24.8	–14.5
1943	24.0	78.6	–54.6	200.2	655.2	–455.0	0.1199	13.7	44.8	–31.1
1944	43.7	91.3	–47.6	377.1	787.1	–410.0	0.1160	21.7	45.3	–23.6
1945	45.2	92.7	–47.6	395.8	812.6	–416.8	0.1141	21.3	43.7	–22.4
1946	39.3	55.2	–15.9	329.4	463.0	–133.6	0.1193	18.5	26.0	–7.5
1947	38.5	34.5	4.0	257.4	230.6	26.9	0.1496	17.3	15.5	1.8
1948	41.6	29.8	11.8	269.3	192.9	76.4	0.1543	16.8	12.1	4.8
1949	39.4	38.8	0.6	249.1	245.5	3.7	0.1582	15.0	14.8	0.2
1950	39.4	42.6	–3.1	241.4	260.5	–19.1	0.1634	14.8	16.0	–1.2
1951	51.6	45.5	6.1	324.2	285.9	38.3	0.1592	16.5	14.5	1.9
1952	66.2	67.7	–1.5	406.7	416.0	–9.3	0.1627	19.4	19.9	–0.4
1953	69.6	76.1	–6.5	406.6	444.5	–37.9	0.1712	19.1	20.9	–1.8
1954	69.7	70.9	–1.2	394.9	401.4	–6.5	0.1765	18.9	19.3	–0.3
1955	65.5	68.4	–3.0	363.4	380.0	–16.6	0.1801	17.0	17.8	–0.8
1956	74.6	70.6	3.9	391.1	370.4	20.7	0.1907	17.9	17.0	0.9
1957	80.0	76.6	3.4	396.6	379.7	16.9	0.2017	18.3	17.5	0.8
1958	79.6	82.4	–2.8	374.9	388.0	–13.0	0.2124	17.8	18.4	–0.6
1959	79.2	92.1	–12.8	352.4	409.5	–57.1	0.2249	16.5	19.2	–2.7
1960	92.5	92.2	0.3	393.4	392.1	1.3	0.2351	18.3	18.3	0.1
1961	94.4	97.7	–3.3	392.1	406.0	–13.9	0.2407	18.3	18.9	–0.6
1962	99.7	106.8	–7.1	406.8	436.0	–29.2	0.2450	18.0	19.2	–1.3
1963	106.6	111.3	–4.8	418.9	437.6	–18.7	0.2544	18.2	19.0	–0.8
1964	112.6	118.5	–5.9	433.8	456.6	–22.8	0.2596	18.0	19.0	–0.9

1965	116.8	118.2	−1.4	440.8	446.1	−5.3	0.2650	17.4	17.6	−0.2
1966	130.8	134.5	−3.7	478.9	492.4	−13.5	0.2732	17.8	18.3	−0.5
1967	148.8	157.5	−8.6	529.2	560.0	−30.7	0.2812	18.8	19.8	−1.1
1968	153.0	178.1	−25.2	522.6	608.6	−86.0	0.2927	18.1	21.0	−3.0
1969	186.9	183.6	3.2	604.4	593.9	10.5	0.3092	20.2	19.8	0.4
1970	192.8	195.6	−2.8	587.5	596.1	−8.7	0.3282	19.6	19.9	−0.3
1971	187.1	210.2	−23.0	533.5	599.1	−65.7	0.3508	17.8	20.0	−2.2
1972	207.3	230.7	−23.4	554.9	617.5	−62.6	0.3736	18.1	20.1	−2.0
1973	230.8	245.7	−14.9	582.7	620.3	−37.6	0.3961	18.1	19.3	−1.2
1974	263.2	269.4	−6.1	611.2	625.4	−14.2	0.4307	18.8	19.2	−0.4
1975	279.1	332.3	−53.2	586.6	698.5	−111.9	0.4758	18.5	22.0	−3.5
1976	298.1	371.8	−73.7	584.7	729.3	−144.6	0.5098	17.7	22.1	−4.4
TQ	81.2	96.0	−14.7	153.6	181.5	−27.9	0.5287	18.3	21.6	−3.3
1977	355.6	409.2	−53.7	643.8	740.9	−97.2	0.5523	18.5	21.3	−2.8
1978	399.6	458.7	−59.2	674.0	773.9	−99.8	0.5928	18.5	21.3	−2.7
1979	463.3	503.5	−40.2	719.3	781.7	−62.4	0.6441	19.1	20.7	−1.7
1980	517.1	590.9	−73.8	728.1	832.1	−104.0	0.7102	19.6	22.3	−2.8
1981	599.3	678.2	−79.0	766.6	867.7	−101.0	0.7817	20.2	22.9	−2.7
1982	617.8	745.8	−128.0	738.2	891.1	−152.9	0.8369	19.8	23.9	−4.1
1983	600.6	808.4	−207.8	684.3	921.1	−236.8	0.8776	18.1	24.4	−6.3
1984	666.5	851.8	−185.4	730.4	933.5	−203.2	0.9125	18.0	23.1	−5.0
1985	734.1	946.4	−212.3	776.6	1,001.3	−224.6	0.9452	18.5	23.9	−5.4
1986	769.1	990.3	−221.2	790.0	1,017.3	−227.3	0.9735	18.2	23.5	−5.2
1987	854.1	1,003.9	−149.8	854.1	1,003.9	−149.8	1.0000	19.2	22.5	−3.4
1988	909.0	1,064.1	−155.2	877.3	1,027.1	−149.8	1.0361	18.9	22.1	−3.2
1989	990.7	1,143.2	−152.5	916.2	1,057.2	−141.0	1.0813	19.2	22.1	−2.9
1990	1,031.3	1,252.7	−221.4	914.0	1,110.1	−196.2	1.1284	18.9	22.9	−4.0
1991	1,054.3	1,323.8	−269.5	893.6	1,122.0	−228.4	1.1798	18.7	23.5	−4.8
1992	1,091.6	1,381.8	−290.2	899.4	1,138.4	−239.1	1.2138	18.6	23.5	−4.9
1993 estimate	1,147.6	1,474.9	−327.3	918.1	1,180.0	−261.9	1.2499	18.6	23.9	−5.3

Source: *Budget Baselines, Historical Data, And Alternatives For The Future*, 1993, Executive Office of the President, Office of Management and Budget.

SUMMARY OF RECEIPTS, OUTLAYS, AND SURPLUSES OR DEFICITS(–) AS PERCENTAGES OF GDP: 1934–1993

Year	GDP (in billions of dollars)	Total			On-Budget			Off-Budget		
		Receipts	Outlays	Surplus or Deficit(–)	Receipts	Outlays	Surplus or Deficit(–)	Receipts	Outlays	Surplus or Deficit(–)
1934	60.4	4.9	10.8	–5.9	4.9	10.8	–5.9	....	....	....
1935	68.7	5.3	9.3	–4.1	5.3	9.3	–4.1	....	....	....
1936	77.5	5.1	10.6	–5.6	5.1	10.6	–5.6	....	....	....
1937	86.8	6.2	8.7	–2.5	5.9	8.7	–2.8	0.3	–*	0.3
1938	87.8	7.7	7.8	–0.1	7.2	7.8	–0.6	0.4	–*	0.5
1939	87.8	7.2	10.4	–3.2	6.6	10.4	–3.8	0.6	–*	0.6
1940	95.4	6.9	9.9	–3.1	6.3	9.9	–3.7	0.6	–*	0.6
1941	112.5	7.7	12.1	–4.4	7.1	12.1	–5.0	0.6	*	0.6
1942	141.8	10.3	24.8	–14.5	9.7	24.7	–15.0	0.6	*	0.6
1943	175.4	13.7	44.8	–31.1	13.0	44.7	–31.7	0.6	0.1	0.6
1944	201.7	21.7	45.3	–23.6	21.0	45.2	–24.2	0.6	0.1	0.6
1945	212.0	21.3	43.7	–22.4	20.7	43.7	–23.0	0.6	0.1	0.6
1946	212.5	18.5	26.0	–7.5	17.9	25.9	–8.0	0.6	0.1	0.5
1947	222.9	17.3	15.5	1.8	16.6	15.3	1.3	0.7	0.1	0.5
1948	246.7	16.8	12.1	4.8	16.2	11.9	4.3	0.7	0.1	0.5
1949	262.7	15.0	14.8	0.2	14.4	14.6	–0.3	0.6	0.2	0.5
1950	265.8	14.8	16.0	–1.2	14.0	15.8	–1.8	0.8	0.2	0.6
1951	313.5	16.5	14.5	1.9	15.5	14.1	1.4	1.0	0.4	0.6
1952	340.5	19.4	19.9	–0.4	18.4	19.4	–1.0	1.1	0.5	0.5
1953	363.8	19.1	20.9	–1.8	18.0	20.3	–2.3	1.1	0.6	0.5
1954	368.0	18.9	19.3	–0.3	17.7	18.5	–0.8	1.2	0.8	0.5
1955	384.7	17.0	17.8	–0.8	15.7	16.8	–1.1	1.3	1.0	0.3
1956	416.3	17.9	17.0	0.9	16.4	15.8	0.6	1.5	1.2	0.3
1957	438.3	18.3	17.5	0.8	16.7	16.1	0.6	1.5	1.4	0.2
1958	448.1	17.8	18.4	–0.6	16.0	16.7	–0.7	1.8	1.7	0.1
1959	480.2	16.5	19.2	–2.7	14.8	17.3	–2.5	1.7	1.9	–0.1
1960	504.6	18.3	18.3	0.1	16.2	16.1	0.1	2.1	2.2	–*
1961	517.0	18.3	18.9	–0.6	15.9	16.6	–0.7	2.3	2.3	0.1
1962	555.2	18.0	19.2	–1.3	15.7	16.8	–1.1	2.2	2.4	–0.2

1963	584.5	18.2	19.0	−0.8	15.8	16.5	−0.7	2.4	2.6	−0.1
1964	625.3	18.0	19.0	−0.9	15.4	16.4	−1.0	2.6	2.5	0.1
1965	671.0	17.4	17.6	−0.2	14.9	15.2	−0.2	2.5	2.5	*
1966	735.4	17.8	18.3	−0.5	15.2	15.6	−0.4	2.6	2.7	−0.1
1967	793.3	18.8	19.8	−1.1	15.7	17.3	−1.6	3.1	2.6	0.5
1968	847.2	18.1	21.0	−3.0	15.1	18.4	−3.3	2.9	2.6	0.3
1969	925.7	20.2	19.8	0.4	17.1	17.1	−0.1	3.1	2.7	0.4
1970	985.4	19.6	19.9	−0.3	16.2	17.1	−0.9	3.4	2.8	0.6
1971	1,050.9	17.8	20.0	−2.2	14.4	16.9	−2.5	3.4	3.1	0.3
1972	1,147.8	18.1	20.1	−2.0	14.6	16.9	−2.3	3.5	3.2	0.3
1973	1,274.0	18.1	19.3	−1.2	14.5	15.7	−1.2	3.6	3.6	*
1974	1,403.6	18.8	19.2	−0.4	14.9	15.5	−0.6	3.8	3.7	0.1
1975	1,509.8	18.5	22.0	−3.5	14.3	18.0	−3.7	4.1	4.0	0.1
1976	1,684.2	17.7	22.1	−4.4	13.8	17.9	−4.2	3.9	4.1	−0.2
TQ	445.0	18.3	21.6	−3.3	14.2	17.2	−3.0	4.0	4.4	−0.3
1977	1,917.2	18.5	21.3	−2.8	14.5	17.1	−2.6	4.0	4.2	−0.2
1978	2,155.0	18.5	21.3	−2.7	14.6	17.1	−2.5	4.0	4.2	−0.2
1979	2,429.5	19.1	20.7	−1.7	15.0	16.6	−1.6	4.0	4.1	−0.1
1980	2,644.1	19.6	22.3	−2.8	15.3	18.0	−2.8	4.3	4.3	−*
1981	2,964.4	20.2	22.9	−2.7	15.8	18.3	−2.5	4.4	4.6	−0.2
1982	3,122.2	19.8	23.9	−4.1	15.2	19.0	−3.8	4.6	4.8	−0.3
1983	3,316.5	18.1	24.4	−6.3	13.7	19.9	−6.3	4.4	4.4	*
1984	3,695.0	18.0	23.1	−5.0	13.5	18.6	−5.0	4.5	4.5	*
1985	3,967.7	18.5	23.9	−5.4	13.8	19.4	−5.6	4.7	4.5	0.2
1986	4,219.0	18.2	23.5	−5.2	13.5	19.1	−5.6	4.7	4.3	0.4
1987	4,452.4	19.2	22.5	−3.4	14.4	18.2	−3.8	4.8	4.4	0.4
1988	4,808.4	18.9	22.1	−3.2	13.9	17.9	−4.0	5.0	4.2	0.8
1989	5,173.3	19.2	22.1	−2.9	14.1	18.0	−4.0	5.1	4.1	1.0
1990	5,467.1	18.9	22.9	−4.0	13.7	18.8	−5.1	5.2	4.1	1.0
1991	5,632.6	18.7	23.5	−4.8	13.5	19.2	−5.7	5.2	4.3	0.9
1992	5,868.6	18.6	23.5	−4.9	13.4	19.2	−5.8	5.2	4.3	0.9
1993 estimate	6,164.4	18.6	23.9	−5.3	13.4	19.6	−6.2	5.2	4.3	0.9

* 0.05 percent or less.

Source: *Budget Baselines, Historical Data, And Alternatives For The Future*, 1993, Executive Office of the President, Office of Management and Budget.

NOTES TO HISTORICAL TABLES

Because of the numerous changes in the way budget data have been presented over time, there are inevitable difficulties in trying to produce comparable data to cover so many years. The general rule underlying all of these tables is to provide data in as meaningful and comparable a fashion as possible. To the extent feasible, the data are presented on a basis consistent with current budget concepts. When a structural change is made, insofar as possible the data are adjusted for all years.

In November 1990, the President signed the Omnibus Budget Reconciliation Act of 1990. Part of this legislation was the Budget Enforcement Act, which not only provided new enforcement mechanisms, but also included significant changes in budget concepts. The major conceptual change is in the measurement of Federal credit activity in the budget. Under current law, only the subsidy cost (the cost to the Government, including the cost associated with loan defaults) of direct loans or loan guarantees be recorded as budget authority and outlays. The remaining financial transactions are recorded as means of financing the deficit. This concept applies only to direct loan obligations and loan guarantee commitments made in 1992 and later years. Unfortunately, the historical data prior to 1992 could not be converted to this new measurement basis. Thus, data prior to 1992 are on a cash flow or pre-credit reform basis. Data for 1992 and beyond are on a cash flow basis for direct loans and loan guarantees made in earlier years, but reflect the subsidy cost or post-credit reform concepts for the forty or so budget program accounts providing direct loans or loan guarantees.

Coverage

The Federal Government has used the unified or consolidated budget concept as the foundation for its budgetary analysis and presentation since the 1969 budget. The basic guidelines for the unified budget were presented in the *Report of the President's Commission on Budget Concepts* (October 1967). The Commission recommended the budget include all Federal fiscal activities unless there were exceptionally persuasive reasons for exclusion. Nevertheless, from the very beginning some programs were perceived as warranting special treatment. Indeed, the Commission itself recommended a bifurcated presentation: a "unified budget" composed of an "expenditure account" and a "loan account." The distinction between the expenditure account and the loan account proved to be confusing and caused considerable complication in the budget for little benefit. As a result, this distinction was eliminated starting with the 1974 budget. However, even prior to the 1974 budget, the Export-Import Bank had been excluded by law from the budget totals, and other exclusions followed. The structure of the budget was gradually revised to show the off-budget transactions in many locations along with the on-budget transactions, and the off-budget amounts were added to the on-budget amounts in order to show total Federal spending.

The Balanced Budget and Emergency Deficit Control Act of 1985 (Public Law 99–177) repealed the off-budget status of all then existing off-budget entities, but it included a provision immediately moving the Federal old-age, survivors, and disability insurance funds (collectively known as social security) off-budget. To provide a consistent time series, the budget historical data show social security off-budget for all years since its inception, and show all formerly off-budget entities on-budget for all years. Subsequent law (OBRA 1989) moved the Postal Service fund off-budget, starting in fiscal year 1989. Prior to that year, the Postal Service fund is shown on-budget.

Though social security and the Postal Service are now off-budget, they continue to be Federal programs. Indeed, social security currently accounts for around one-third of all Federal receipts and one-quarter of all Federal spending. Hence, the budget documents include these funds and focus on the Federal totals that combine the on-budget and off-budget amounts. Various budget tables and charts show total Federal receipts, outlays, and surpluses and deficits, and divide these totals between the portions that are off-budget and the remainder of Federal transactions, all of which are on-budget.

Changes in Historical Outlays and Deficit

The outlay and deficit totals for 1991 published in the 1993 budget have increased from $1,323.0 billion and $268.7 billion to 1,323.8 billion and $269.5 billion, respectively. These increases correct errors in recording certain TVA purchases and sales of Treasury debt securities. Purchases and sales had been classified as outlays and offsets to outlays, respectively, instead of nonexpenditure transactions; increases and decreases in holdings of Treasury debt by Government accounts had not been recorded. The corrections do not affect total Federal debt. The increases in debt held by Government accounts are offset by equal deductions in debt held by the public. Similar corrections were made to the outlay and deficit totals for 1989 and 1990.

NOTE ON THE FISCAL YEAR

The Federal fiscal year begins on October 1 and ends on the subsequent September 30. It is designated by the year in which it ends; for example, fiscal year 1990 began October 1, 1989 and ended on September 30, 1990. Prior to fiscal year 1977 the Federal fiscal years began on July 1 and ended on June 30. In calendar year 1976 the July–September period was a separate accounting period (known as the transition quarter or TQ) to bridge the period required to shift to the new fiscal years.

Concepts Relevant to the Historical Tables

Budget (or "on-budget") receipts constitute the income side of the budget; they are composed almost entirely of taxes or other compulsory payments to the Government. Any income from business-type activities (e.g., interest income or sale of electric power), and any income by Government accounts arising from payments by other Government accounts is offset in computing *budget outlays* (spending). This method of accounting permits users to easily identify the size and trends in Federal taxes and other compulsory income, and in Federal spending financed from taxes, other compulsory income, or borrowing. *Budget surplus* refers to any excess of budget receipts over budget outlays, while *budget deficit* refers to any excess of budget outlays over budget receipts.

The terms *off-budget receipts, off-budget outlays, off-budget surpluses,* and *off-budget deficits* refer to similar categories for off-budget activities. The sum of the on-budget and off-budget transactions constitute the consolidated or total Federal Government transactions.

The budget is divided between two fund groups, federal funds and trust funds. The Federal funds grouping includes all receipts and outlays not specified by law as being trust funds. All Federal funds are on-budget (except for the Postal Service fund starting with fiscal year 1989). Most trust funds are on-budget, but as explained in the general notes above, the two social security retirement trust funds are shown off-budget for all years.

The term *trust fund* as used in Federal budget accounting is frequently misunderstood. In the private sector, "trust" refers to funds of one party held by a second party (the trustee) in a fiduciary capacity. In the Federal budget, the term "trust fund" means only the law requires that the funds must be accounted for separately and used only for specified purposes and that the account in which the funds are deposited is designated as being a "trust fund." A change in law may change the future receipts and the terms under which the fund's resources are spent. The determining factor as to whether a particular fund is designated as a "Federal" fund or "trust" fund is the law governing the fund.

The largest trust funds are for retirement and social insurance (e.g., civil service and military retirement, social security, medicare, and unemployment benefits), financed largely by social insurance taxes and contributions and payments from the general fund (the main component of Federal funds). However, there are also major trust funds for transportation (highway and airport and airways) and for other programs that are financed in whole or in part by *user charges.*

The budget documents do not separately show user charges, but frequently there is confusion between the concept of user charges and the concept of offsetting collections. User charges are charges for services rendered. Such charges may take the form of taxes (budget receipts), such as highway excise taxes used to finance the highway trust fund. They may also take the form of business-type charges, in which case they are offsetting collections—offset against budget outlays rather than being recorded as budget receipts. Examples of such charges are the proceeds from the sale of electric power by the Tennessee Valley Authority and voluntary medical insurance premiums paid to the supplementary medical insurance trust fund. User charges may go to the general fund of the Treasury or they may be "earmarked." If the funds are earmarked, it means the collections are separately identified and used for a specified purpose—they are not commingled (in an accounting sense) with any other money. This does not mean the money is actually kept in a separate bank account (all money in the Treasury is merged for efficient cash management), but any earmarked funds are accounted for in such a way that the balances are always identifiable and available for the stipulated purposes.

U.S. BUDGET RECEIPTS AND OUTLAYS (millions of dollars)[1]

Source or type	Fiscal year 1991	Fiscal year 1992	Calendar year 1991 H1	Calendar year 1991 H2	Calendar year 1992 H1[r]	Calendar year 1992 H2	Calendar year 1993 Feb.	Calendar year 1993 Mar.	Calendar year 1993 Apr.
RECEIPTS									
1 **All sources**	**1,054,265**	**1,090,513[r]**	**540,504**	**519,181[r]**	**560,350**	**540,506[r]**	**66,138[r]**	**83,453**	**132,122**
2 Individual income taxes, net	467,827	476,122	232,389	234,939	236,646	246,961	23,947	27,935	56,137
3 Withheld	404,152	408,352	193,440	210,552	198,868	215,591	33,652	40,006	32,691
4 Presidential Election Campaign Fund	32	30	31	1	20	10	4	6	6
5 Nonwithheld	142,693	149,342	109,405	33,296	110,997	39,371	967	5,253	44,755
6 Refunds	79,050	81,691	70,487	8,910	73,237	8,011	10,677	17,330	21,315
Corporation income taxes									
7 Gross receipts	113,599	117,951	58,903	54,016	61,681	58,022	2,510	14,644	19,272
8 Refunds	15,513	17,680	7,904	8,649	9,402	7,219	1,719	1,920	1,477
9 Social insurance taxes and contributions, net	396,011	413,689	214,303	186,839	224,569	192,599	34,251	33,652	49,176
10 Employment taxes and contributions[2]	370,526	385,491	199,727	175,802	208,110	180,758	31,623	32,980	45,164
11 Self-employment taxes and contributions[3]	25,457	24,421	22,150	3,306	20,433	3,988	1,487	873	12,183
12 Unemployment insurance	20,922	23,410	12,296	8,721	14,070	9,397	2,259	240	3,581
13 Other net receipts[4]	4,563	4,788	2,279	2,317	2,389	2,445	369	432	431
14 Excise taxes	42,430	45,570	20,703	24,429	22,389	23,456	3,342	4,514	4,168
15 Customs deposits	15,921	17,359	7,488	8,694	8,146	9,497	1,347	1,598	1,544
16 Estate and gift taxes	11,138	11,143	5,631	5,507	5,701	5,733	822	977	1,898
17 Miscellaneous receipts[5]	22,852	26,522[r]	8,991	13,406[r]	10,695	11,472[r]	1,639[r]	2,051	1,404
OUTLAYS									
18 **All types**	**1,323,757**	**1,380,657[r]**	**632,153**	**694,364[r]**	**704,288**	**723,367[r]**	**113,732[r]**	**128,030[r]**	**124,034**
19 National defense	272,514	298,361	122,089	147,669	147,076	155,501	22,903	25,511	27,192
20 International affairs	16,167	16,106	7,592	7,691	8,542	9,911	1,253	1,181	536
21 General science, space, and technology	15,946	16,409	7,496	8,472	7,951	8,521	1,325	1,103	1,444
22 Energy	2,511	4,509	1,235	1,698	1,442	3,109	399	560	431
23 Natural resources and environment	18,708	20,017	8,324	11,130	8,606	11,617	1,282	1,549	1,709
24 Agriculture	14,864	14,997	7,684	7,418	7,526	8,881	1,145	4,244	2,666
25 Commerce and housing credit	75,639	9,753	17,992	36,534	15,620	−7,843	−3,532	−1,368	−3,961
26 Transportation	31,531	33,759	14,748	17,093	15,676	18,477	2,093	3,383	2,591
27 Community and regional development	7,432	7,923	3,552	3,783	3,903	4,540	690	760	987
28 Education, training, employment, and social services	41,479	45,248	21,234	21,114	23,635	20,922	4,068	4,607	3,695
29 Health	71,183	89,570	35,608	41,459	44,107	47,223	8,053	8,379	8,883
30 Social security and medicare	373,495	406,569	190,247	193,098	205,500	232,109	35,005	37,235	37,236
31 Income security	171,618	197,867	88,778	87,693	104,457	98,693	21,259	21,056	20,408
32 Veterans benefits and services	31,344	34,133	14,326	17,425	15,597	18,561	2,649	4,090	4,332
33 Administration of justice	12,295	14,450	6,187	6,574	7,435	7,283	1,060	1,270	1,581
34 General government	11,358	12,939	5,212	6,794	5,050	8,138	994	1,040	655
35 Net interest[6]	195,012	199,429	98,556	99,149	100,394	98,549	15,893	16,415	16,585
36 Undistributed offsetting receipts[7]	−39,356	−39,280	−18,702	−20,436	−18,229	−20,914	−2,809	−2,987	−2,935

1. Functional details do not sum to total outlays for calendar year data because revisions to monthly totals have not been distributed among functions. Fiscal year total for outlays does not correspond to calendar year data because revisions from the *Budget* have not been fully distributed across months.
2. Old-age, disability, and hospital insurance, and railroad retirement accounts.
3. Old-age, disability, and hospital insurance.
4. Federal employee retirement contributions and civil service retirement and disability fund.
5. Deposits of earnings by Federal Reserve Banks and other miscellaneous receipts.
6. Includes interest received by trust funds.
7. Consists of rents and royalties for the outer continental shelf and U.S. government contributions for employee retirement.

SOURCES. U.S. Department of the Treasury, *Monthly Treasury Statement of Receipts and Outlays of the U.S. Government*, and the U.S. Office of Management and Budget, *Budget of the U.S. Government, Fiscal Year 1994*.

Source: *Federal Reserve Bulletin*, Board of Governors of the Federal Reserve System.

FEDERAL DEBT SUBJECT TO STATUTORY LIMITATION

Billions of dollars, end of month

Item	1991				1992				1993
	Mar. 31	June 30	Sept. 30	Dec. 31	Mar. 31	June 30	Sept. 30	Dec. 31	Mar. 31
1 **Federal debt outstanding**	**3,492**	**3,563**	**3,683**	**3,820**	**3,897**	**4,001**	**4,083**	**4,196**	n.a.
2 Public debt securities	3,465	3,538	3,665	3,802	3,881	3,985	4,065	4,177	4,231
3 Held by public	2,598	2,643	2,746	2,833	2,918	2,977	3,048	3,129	n.a.
4 Held by agencies	867	895	920	969	964	1,008	1,016	1,048	n.a.
5 Agency securities	27	25	18	19	16	16	18	19	n.a.
6 Held by public	26	25	18	19	16	16	18	19	n.a.
7 Held by agencies	0	0	0	0	0	0	0	0	n.a.
8 **Debt subject to statutory limit**	**3,377**	**3,450**	**3,569**	**3,707**	**3,784**	**3,891**	**3,973**	**4,086**	**4,140**
9 Public debt securities	3,377	3,450	3,569	3,706	3,783	3,890	3,972	4,085	4,139
10 Other debt[1]	0	0	0	0	0	0	0	0	0
MEMO									
11 Statutory debt limit	4,145	4,145	4,145	4,145	4,145	4,145	4,145	4,145	4,145

1. Consists of guaranteed debt of Treasury and other federal agencies, specified participation certificates, notes to international lending organizations, and District of Columbia stadium bonds.

SOURCES. U.S. Treasury Department, *Monthly Statement of the Public Debt of the United States* and *Treasury Bulletin*.

Source: *Federal Reserve Bulletin*, Board of Governors of the Federal Reserve System.

Omnibus Budget Reconciliation Act of 1993

KPMG Peat Marwick

Introduction

"We are seizing control of our economic destiny. This is just the beginning, just the first step in our attempts to assert control over our financial affairs, to invest in our future, and to grow our economy." President Bill Clinton, after the Senate gave final approval to his deficit reduction package.

"Again, does it raise taxes? Obviously, it is the biggest tax increase in the history of the world according to my colleague, the Senator from New York [Senate Finance Committee Chairman] ***Moynihan. It was not my statement; it was his. We are willing to accept it."*** Senator Bob Dole (R-KS), discussing the now-enacted tax bill

On August 10, 1993, President Clinton signed the Omnibus Budget Reconciliation Act of 1993 (the "Act").* Although a few of Clinton's original high-priority proposals — such as the investment tax credit and the broad-based Btu energy tax — ended up on the cutting-room floor, the broad outlines of his original plan remained intact: estimated deficit reduction of close to $500 billion over five years; some tax incentives and investment spending; cuts in defense and Medicare spending; an energy tax; and most of the additional tax burden falling on higher-income individuals.

Is this the ground-breaking, biggest-ever plan as claimed by supporters, or is it *deja vu* all over again? Apart from media commentary, during the debate on this package there was little reference to the Omnibus Budget Reconciliation Act of 1990, which also was designed to slice close to $500 billion from the deficit. As Clinton claims to deliver on his promise for deficit reduction, it may be less clear from this legislation that he is delivering on his promise for change. The likeness to the 1990 Act is perhaps too close for comfort: raising income tax rates, adding almost a nickel a gallon to the gasoline tax, cutting defense and Medicare spending; and reducing the deficit (only three percent more in 1993 than in 1990). And, as in 1990, spending cuts are heavily backloaded, with about 80 percent of the total cuts coming in 1997 and 1998.

Will this plan reduce the deficit?

Much more important than the size of the package is whether it will actually reduce the deficit and spur long-term economic growth. We know this plan will not come close to balancing the budget in the next five years. It is better explained, and was designed, as a stopgap that will prevent the deficit from rising. But it could suffer the same fate as the 1990 legislation. The deficit reduction could be overwhelmed by small, random economic forecasting errors and other unanticipated factors that could cause the deficit to soar, even though Clinton, like the supporters of the 1990 deal, can honestly claim that the deficit is smaller than it would have been otherwise. On the other hand, a bit of good luck — an unexpected small spurt in economic growth, a small slowdown in the growth rate of health costs — could make the plan look like a tremendous success.

Inside

*The date of signature is the date of enactment, which is important for some effective dates.

Who pays the new taxes?

In choosing a target of $250 billion in additional taxes over five years, Clinton faced a daunting task in deciding whose taxes should be increased, particularly after promising a middle-class tax cut and business incentives. But the politics were easier for him than for President Bush in 1990 with his ill-fated "no new taxes" pledge. Clinton believed higher-income individuals were not paying their "fair share" and therefore relied on a principle of "fairness" to raise their taxes. But he couldn't get it all by "soaking the rich." And even adding the higher tax rate on large corporations didn't achieve his target. He then found he could not leave the middle class unscathed, let alone give them the promised tax cut.

Rather than increasing middle-class income taxes, he chose to tax them indirectly through a broad-based Btu energy tax, which was eventually dropped for a modest (4.3 cents a gallon) gasoline tax. To offset partially the regressivity of the gas tax and to further Clinton's social policy goals, the earned income tax credit was expanded substantially (the gas tax raises $24 billion, the earned income tax credit expansion costs $22 billion).

A few of Clinton's investment incentives survived, including: research and other credits, incentives for small business, empowerment zones, passive loss relief for real estate developers, and alternative minimum tax (AMT) depreciation relief. Congress resisted, or was unwilling to pay for, further new spending through tax incentives.

The tax portion of the package strikes a blow at two key principles of the Tax Reform Act of 1986: exchanging lower tax rates for a broadened tax base and eliminating tax incentives. The 1993 top individual tax rate is now more than 40 percent above the 1986 Act level (an increase from 28 percent to 39.6 percent). In 1986, the theory was that the economy would operate more efficiently if businesses could compete on an equal basis without being influenced by various incentives in the tax code. The new theory is that government intervention through the tax code will redirect investment to more productive uses.

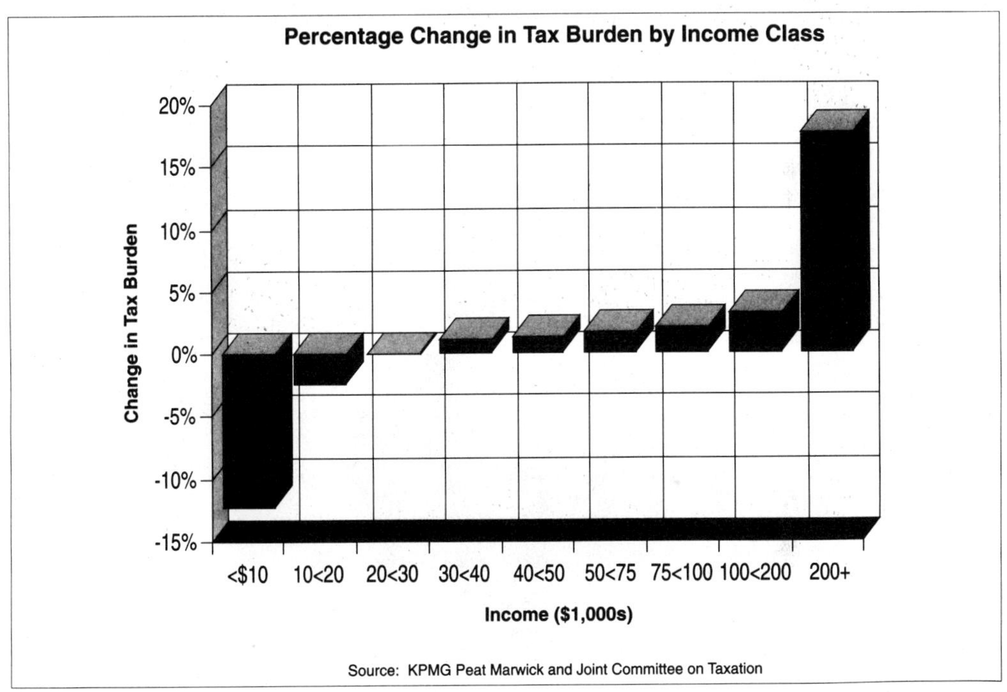

What lies ahead?

Several smaller tax initiatives are waiting in the wings, including technical corrections to previous tax legislation and simplification proposals. There is also a pent-up demand for an opportunity to use the tax system to accomplish members' social and fiscal policy goals. Although a second tax bill in 1993 is unlikely, one is possible in 1994.

Many economists believe there will be no real progress toward truly balancing the budget without significant entitlement restraint and some middle-class tax increases. Yet one result of any significant health and welfare reform could be an *expansion* of entitlements. And further tax increases will be extremely difficult. This plan taxes upper-income individuals about as much as is feasible, leaving only the middle class to tax. That appears to be a political non-starter, at least in the short term.

We've seen that even a package which demanded relatively little sacrifice on the part of the vast majority of the American people was extraordinarily difficult to move through Congress. This package's spending cuts and tax increases are equal to about 1-1/2 percent of the personal income expected over the period. Two more packages of this size would be required to cure the annual deficit problem by the rest of this decade, assuming no expansion of government spending. Clearly, the deficit will be with us for a long time to come. It could delay and constrain the scope of health and welfare reform. Unless the economy improves, the deficit shows every sign of limiting Clinton's choices during the remainder of his presidency.

"Our fiscal problems do not exist because wealthy Americans aren't paying enough taxes. Our fiscal problems exist because of rapid, uncontrolled growth in programs that primarily benefit the middle class."

"Shared sacrifice, Mr. President: It is our highest ideal and the only way we will build the moral consensus needed to end this nightmare of borrowing from our children."
Senator Bob Kerrey (D-NE), announcing his decision to vote for the deficit reduction package

*****

This letter highlights the tax provisions of the Act and provides planning ideas. Many of the provisions are complex and far-reaching, and they may require your immediate action. The information in this letter is general in nature and is not intended to cover all the provisions as they may apply to your business, your investments, or you. Therefore, we encourage you to contact us to discuss your particular circumstances.

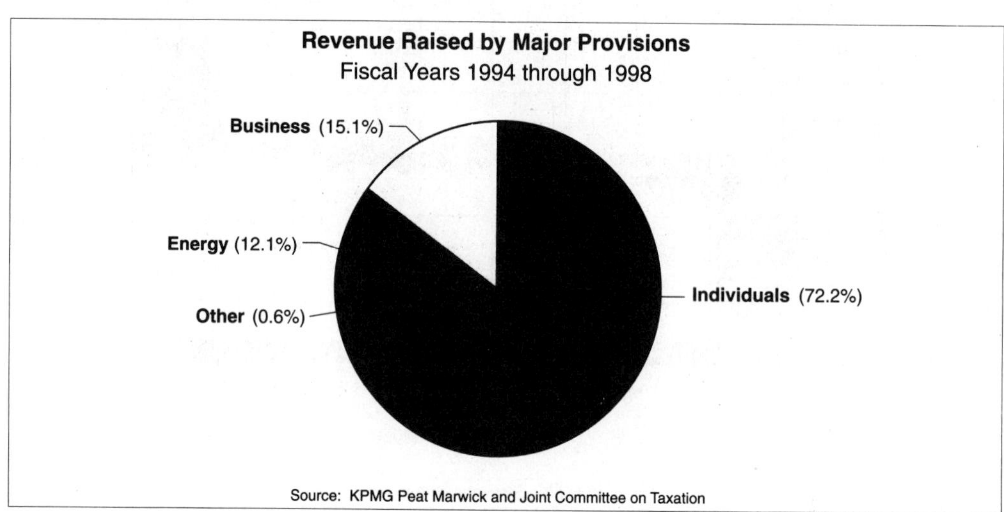

Provisions Affecting Individuals Generally

Individual Tax Rates

Beginning in 1993, a new 36-percent tax rate applies to taxable income of more than $140,000 for a married couple filing a joint return ($115,000 for an unmarried individual). The existing 15-, 28-, and 31-percent tax brackets continue to apply as under prior law.

A fifth tax bracket of 39.6 percent, referred to as a "surtax," applies to taxpayers with taxable income of more than $250,000, whatever their filing status (however, married individuals filing separately will pay the surtax beginning at $125,000 of taxable income).

As under prior law, capital gains are taxed at a maximum 28-percent rate (*i.e.*, the surtax does not apply to capital gains).

The thresholds for the new 36-percent and 39.6-percent tax brackets will not be indexed for inflation until January 1, 1995. Thus, for the 1994 tax year, the thresholds for imposition of the 28-percent and 31-percent tax rates will be adjusted for inflation from their 1993 levels, but the higher-rate thresholds will not be adjusted. All of the rate bracket thresholds will be indexed for inflation after 1994.

The current-law phaseout of personal exemptions and disallowance of a portion of itemized deductions are both made permanent.

OBSERVATION: Taxpayers subject to the surtax (except married individuals filing separate returns) will face a marginal tax rate of at least 39.6 percent. A taxpayer will effectively face an additional 0.74 percent marginal rate for each personal exemption, to the extent exemptions are still being phased out above the surtax level of taxable income, and an additional 1.2 percent marginal rate if the scaleback of itemized deductions still applies when taxable income is above the surtax level. For example, a taxpayer with four exemptions would face a marginal income tax rate of up to 43.76 percent.

Also effective for 1993, the individual alternative minimum tax (AMT) rate is increased. The AMT rate is currently 24 percent on all alternative minimum taxable income (AMTI) in excess of an exemption of up to $40,000 on a joint return ($30,000 for a single individual). The rate is increased to 26 percent, with a second 28-percent bracket starting at $175,000 of AMTI in excess of the exemption. The maximum exemption is raised to $45,000 on a joint return ($33,750 for an unmarried person). There is no surtax on AMT liability.

OBSERVATION: The increase in the top individual tax rates also increases the so-called marriage penalty/bonus (the difference in total tax liability of a couple filing as single taxpayers versus filing married on a joint return). Consider this example:

Joe is a single father with two children; Jane is a single mother of one. Each earns $100,000, has $20,000 of itemized deductions, and files as a head of household.

Under present law, their combined separate tax liabilities if both were to file as single taxpayers would be $33,814; if they marry and file a joint return, their liability would increase to $40,430, resulting in a marriage penalty of $6,616. Under the new law, their combined separate tax liabilities remain the same, but their married filing jointly liability would rise to $41,156, increasing their marriage penalty by $726 to $7,342.

The marriage penalty under the new law can also affect more severely workers at low income levels because of the expansion of the earned income tax credit, which is reduced when family earned income exceeds a certain amount that is the same for both married and single taxpayers.

Individuals who realize a marriage bonus under present law will in many cases increase that bonus under the new law.

Revised tax withholding tables are not planned for the remainder of 1993, and the Act waives 1993 estimated tax penalties resulting from the tax rate changes. Thus, individuals may compute their September 15, 1993, and January 18, 1994, estimated tax payments as if old-law rates were in effect but will need to make a catch-up payment by April 15, 1994, the due date for 1993 individual tax returns.

However, because of the potential burden from imposing the higher tax rates retroactively, individuals can elect to pay the portion of their increased 1993 income tax liability arising from the new 36- and 39.6-percent rates in three installments, due April 15, 1994, 1995, and 1996. The deferral election does not apply to increased liability due to the new AMT rates. Interest and penalties will not be charged on the deferred tax payments, but all unpaid tax will become due if an installment payment is missed. The election must be made on the 1993 tax return.

OBSERVATION: Some states' income tax rates may also be retroactively increased as a result of the January 1, 1993, effective date for federal individual rate increases.

Change in 1993 Income Tax Liability Attributable to Rate Increases

AGI	Current Law	New Law	Increase in Tax	Increase as % of AGI	Percentage Increase in Tax
$60,000	$5,675	$5,675	-0-	-0-	-0-
$100,000	$14,411	$14,411	-0-	-0-	-0-
$140,000	$23,760	$23,760	-0-	-0-	-0-
$180,000	$34,088	$34,088	-0-	-0-	-0-
$260,000	$56,165	$59,429	$3,264	1.26%	5.81%
$340,000	$76,894	$84,298	$7,404	2.18%	9.63%
$420,000	$96,982	$109,959	$12,977	3.09%	13.38%
$500,000	$117,070	$135,620	$18,550	3.71%	15.85%

These calculations are for a family of four filing a joint return with itemized deductions equal to 22 percent of AGI and no capital gains.

STRATEGIES:

- If you expect to be subject to the new 36- and 39.6-percent marginal tax rates, consider investing more of your savings in municipal bonds. Municipal bonds generally are not subject to federal income tax, and certain municipal bonds are not subject to state income tax. We can advise you which municipal bonds are exempt from both federal and state taxes.

  The chart below shows the rate of return that taxable bonds must yield before federal tax to equal various tax-exempt bond yields.

- You should maximize the amount of income you deposit in tax-deferred retirement programs. If your employer sponsors a section 401(k) plan, you should consider making the maximum contribution permitted (for 1993, the maximum amount you can defer is $8,994).
- If you have funds you can invest for an extended period of time, you might also consider investing in tax-deferred annuities and life insurance investment products. The cash values of tax-deferred annuities accumulate tax free until you receive payments. The increase in the cash surrender value of life insurance is not subject to income tax unless you sell or surrender the policy.
- Because the maximum tax rate on capital gains remains 28 percent, you should seek out investments that generate capital gains. By exchanging ordinary income for capital gains, you can increase your after-tax rate of return by 19 percent.

  Incentive stock options (ISOs) provide an excellent means for converting otherwise ordinary compensation income into capital gains. If you expect to be given stock options in the future, you should consider requesting that the option arrangement be structured as ISOs.

- Although you will not be subject to penalties resulting from an underpayment of 1993 estimated taxes attributable to an increase in rates, you should consider

When tax-exempt bond yield is:

	3%	4%	5%	6%	7%	8%
Tax Rates	**Taxable yields necessary to generate the same amount after tax are:**					
15%	3.53	4.71	5.88	7.06	8.24	9.41
28%	4.17	5.56	6.94	8.33	9.72	11.11
31%	4.35	5.80	7.25	8.70	10.14	11.59
36%	4.69	6.25	7.81	9.38	10.94	12.50
39.6%	4.97	6.62	8.28	9.93	11.59	13.25

putting aside the extra taxes that will be due on April 15, 1994, to avoid unpleasant surprises.

Although the election to pay in installments any additional 1993 tax liability resulting from the new rates allows you to postpone the payment of a portion of your tax, you should *not* accelerate additional *unearned* income into 1993 to take advantage of this deferral. The installments apply only to the portion of tax in excess of 31 percent. By accelerating income into 1993, you would actually accelerate the payment of most of the tax (*i.e.*, 31 percent of the additional 1993 income). The opportunity cost of this acceleration will more than offset any benefit obtained from deferring that portion of the tax imposed at 36 percent or 39.6 percent over the next two years. However, see the discussion below under Expanded FICA Taxes.

- With the increase in the top individual tax rate, shareholders in profitable S corporations that retain most of their income on an annual basis should consider whether it is advantageous to retain their S corporation status.
- KPMG Peat Marwick can help you determine the tax effect of various strategies. The interplay of the tax rate increases, the phaseout of exemptions, the reduced itemized deductions, and the increased AMT rate make actual calculations extremely important.

Estate and Trust Income Tax Rates

The income tax rates applicable to estates and trusts are greatly increased, compared to current law:

Estate and Trust Taxable Income Brackets

	Old Law	New Brackets
15%	0 - $3,750	$0 - $1,500
28%	$3,750 - $11,250	$1,500 - $3,500
31%	Over $11,250	$3,500 - $5,500
36%	—	$5,500 - $7,500
39.6%	—	Over $7,500

As with the individual income tax rate changes, these new rates and brackets are effective for taxable years beginning after 1992. The election to pay any increased 1993 income tax over three years is *not* available to trusts and estates.

Estimated Tax Payments

In taxable years beginning after 1993, individuals with adjusted gross income (AGI) of more than $150,000 in the preceding taxable year can as a safe harbor base their estimated tax payments on 110 percent of their preceding year's tax liability. Individuals with a preceding-year AGI of $150,000 or less can use a safe harbor of 100 percent. The current "special" estimated tax rules that prevent some taxpayers with AGI of more than $75,000 from using a safe harbor based on their preceding year's tax are repealed. As under present law, individuals can instead make payments based on 90 percent of the current year's liability, using actual or annualized tax liability.

OBSERVATION: First quarter 1994 estimated tax payments, the first to be computed under the new rules, are due April 15, 1994, the same deadline for paying any additional 1993 tax liability attributable to the higher tax rates and other changes made by the Act. The first quarter 1994 estimated payment will need to take the new higher tax rates into account. If the 1994 first quarter payment is to be based on the preceding year's tax, an individual with 1993 AGI of more than $150,000 will need to pay in an amount equal to 27.5 percent of the full amount of tax liability shown on the 1993 return (even if the election is made to pay the 1993 tax in installments).

For estates and trusts, AGI is defined to include deductions for various administrative expenses, the personal exemption deduction, amounts that are required to be distributed currently, and any other amounts properly paid or credited for the tax year.

Estate and Gift Tax Rate

The 53-percent and 55-percent top estate and gift tax rates on taxable transfers over $2.5 million and $3 million, respectively, which expired at the end of 1992, are reinstated retroactively. The higher rates are effective for gifts made and individuals dying on or after January 1, 1993. The graduated rates and unified credit phase out for taxable estates of between $10 million and $21.04 million. The 55-percent rate also applies for generation-skipping tax purposes.

Taxation of Social Security Benefits

Beginning in 1994, some taxpayers receiving Social Security benefits will be taxed on up to 85 percent of those benefits, while others will continue, as under current law, to be taxed on up to 50 percent of the benefits. The higher percentage applies to taxpayers whose gross income, plus 50 percent of their benefits, exceeds $44,000 on a joint return ($34,000 for an unmarried person). These taxpayers must include in gross income the *lesser of*:

- 85 percent of the total benefits received, *or*

- 85 percent of the amount by which adjusted gross income plus one-half of the Social Security benefits exceeds the $44,000 or $34,000 threshold, *plus* the *smaller of*:
  - the amount included under current law, or
  - $6,000 (joint return) or $4,500 (unmarried taxpayer).

Example: A married couple filing a joint return has $10,000 of Social Security benefits and $40,000 of other income. Under current law, $5,000 of those benefits would be included in gross income. In 1994, they would include in income $5,850: the *lesser of* $8,500 (85 percent of $10,000) *or* $5,850 (the sum of $850 [85 percent of ($40,000 plus [50 percent of $10,000] minus $44,000)] *plus* the *smaller of* [$5,000 or $6,000]).

Revenues from the increased taxation of Social Security benefits will be transferred to the Medicare Hospital Insurance (HI) Trust Fund.

OBSERVATION: Taxing 85 percent of Social Security benefits is intended to approximate the portion of private qualified pension benefits taxed. According to the Administration, about 13 percent of Social Security recipients will be subject to the 85 percent inclusion.

Earned Income Credit

In taxable years beginning after December 31, 1993, the earned income credit will be increased and modified by making a full credit available at a lower amount of earned income than under current law and by phasing the credit out over a higher amount of earned income. The credit will be simplified by eliminating the two "supplementary" credits for workers with young children and workers who purchase medical insurance coverage.

For the first time, a credit will be allowed to workers without children, limited to workers age 25 through 64 who cannot be claimed as a dependent on another taxpayer's return. This credit will amount to an offset of the Social Security tax on the first $4,000 of wages (*i.e.*, a credit of $306), completely phased out when income reaches $9,000.

The IRS is required to notify taxpayers who have qualifying children and who receive tax refunds on account of the credit that they may be eligible to receive the credit currently in their paychecks. Advance payments of the credit will be limited, however, to 60 percent of the maximum credit allowable to a worker with one child ($1,223 in 1994). The IRS is also directed to study ways to improve the notice program and to ensure that homeless individuals are aware of the credit.

Moving Expenses

Effective for expenses incurred after 1993, the deduction for expenses incurred in connection with moving to a new location for employment-related reasons is limited to the costs of moving household goods and personal effects to the new residence and travel and lodging costs during the move. No deduction will be allowed for:

- meal expenses,
- expenses incurred while searching for a new home after obtaining employment,

Earned Income Credit

	Credit %	Maximum Earned Income	Maximum Credit	Phaseout Begins	Phaseout %	Phaseout Ends
One-Child Family:						
1994	26.3	$7,750	$2,038	$11,000	15.98	$23,760
1995 and thereafter	34.0	6,170	2,098	11,310	15.98	24,440
Two or More Children:						
1994	30.0	$8,425	$2,527	$11,000	17.68	$25,300
1995	36.0	8,660	3,118	11,310	20.22	26,728
1996 and thereafter	40.0	8,900	3,560	11,630	21.06	28,533

The maximum earned income amounts, and the level at which the phaseout begins, will be adjusted for inflation, beginning in 1995. The numbers above assume inflation of about 2.8 percent annually.

- the costs of selling the old residence (or settling a lease) or purchasing (or acquiring a lease on) a new home, or
- temporary lodging after obtaining employment.

Also, the new work location must be at least 50 miles (rather than the current-law 35 miles) further away from the old residence than was the old location. However, reimbursed moving expenses will be excluded from income (unless the taxpayer previously deducted them), and unreimbursed moving expenses will be a deduction in computing adjusted gross income rather than an itemized deduction.

OBSERVATION: A Senate proposal to limit the total moving expense deduction to $10,000 was dropped in conference.

Limit Pension Compensation Cap to $150,000

Under current law, compensation in excess of $200,000 annually (indexed for inflation; the 1993 limit is $235,840) cannot be considered when calculating the level of retirement benefit that may be paid to an employee or the level of contribution that may be made to an employee's retirement plan. The limit is reduced to $150,000 for plan years beginning after 1993. Previously accrued benefits are not affected.

The $150,000 limit will be indexed for inflation in years after 1994 but only when the indexed limit reaches an increment of $10,000 in excess of $150,000. Transition rules are provided for certain participants in retirement plans of state and local governments, and for certain collectively bargained plans.

OBSERVATION: The $150,000 limit can affect those earning far less than $150,000 when salary is projected for funding defined benefit plans. This reduction will also make it more difficult to comply with certain qualified plan nondiscrimination rules and, consequently, may lead to a reduction in the amount highly compensated employees can contribute to 401(k) plans.

Expanded FICA Taxes

The cap on wages or self-employment income subject to the 1.45 percent (2.9 percent for self-employment income) Medicare Hospital Insurance (HI) portion of the Social Security (FICA) tax will not apply after December 31, 1993. In 1993, the cap is $135,000. Thus, employees and employers will be subject in 1994 to the 1.45 percent tax on all wages; self-employed individuals will be subject to the 2.9 percent tax on all self-employment income (and will be allowed a deduction for half of these taxes in computing taxable income).

STRATEGY: You should consider accelerating *earned* income into 1993 to avoid the higher HI tax.

OBSERVATIONS:

- Deferred compensation generally is not subject to Social Security tax until the time any substantial risk of forfeiture on its receipt is lifted. Thus, repeal of the wage cap means that employers and employees may have a larger liability for Social Security tax on deferred compensation several years after the compensation was earned.
- The taxation of high-income workers through payroll taxes to fund Medicare and Medicaid benefits may be revisited when Congress reviews the Administration's health care proposals.

Self-Employed Health Insurance Deduction

The deduction allowed to self-employed individuals for 25 percent of the amount paid during the taxable year for health insurance for themselves and their families is extended through December 31, 1993, retroactive to July 1, 1992. Whether an individual is disqualified for the deduction because of coverage under an employer's plan is determined on a month-by-month basis, beginning in 1993.

OBSERVATIONS:

- You may want to file an amended 1992 return to claim a larger deduction.
- The self-employed health insurance deduction is also likely to be revisited during consideration of health care reform.

Tax Relief for Disaster Damage to a Home

Under the Act, insurance proceeds received for a principal residence or any of its contents destroyed in a Presidentially declared disaster area on or after September 1, 1991, will be generally tax free, under more lenient rules than usually apply to exclude gains from involuntary conversions. At the taxpayer's election, proceeds are taxable only to the extent that they are received for a qualifying principal residence (or any of its "scheduled" contents) and are not reinvested within four years to acquire similar property.

OBSERVATIONS:

- The effective date makes this relief available to residences damaged by Hurricane Bob in 1991, Hurricanes Andrew and Iniki and Typhoon Omar in 1992, the flooding in the Midwest, as well as other recent natural disasters.
- You may need to file amended returns to claim the benefits.

Provisions Affecting Corporations Generally

Tax Rates

A new 35-percent tax rate is applied to corporate taxable income in excess of $10 million, effective January 1, 1993. Corporate income of less than $10 million will continue to be taxed at 34 percent, with lower rates on the first $75,000 (the "benefit" of the lower rates is recaptured when taxable income exceeds $100,000). When taxable income exceeds $15 million, an additional tax (three percent of taxable income over $15 million, but not more than $100,000) will be imposed to recapture the benefit of the 34-percent rate on the first $10 million of income. Corporations will pay a flat 35-percent tax rate on all income when their taxable income exceeds $18,333,333.

Under the new rate structure, the maximum corporate capital gains tax rate is also increased to 35 percent. However, the corporate AMT rate remains 20 percent.

The Act waives 1993 estimated tax penalties resulting from the tax rate change.

Because of the January 1, 1993, effective date, fiscal-year corporations are subject to a blended tax rate for their tax year that includes January 1, 1993. Corporations that have already filed a tax return for this fiscal year may need to make an additional payment. If, however, the corporation has extended the due date for a fiscal-year return, the conference report states that Congress intends the extension be deemed valid even though the tax paid with the extension request was computed under prior law.

OBSERVATION: Under FAS Statement No. 109, the effects of the higher corporate tax rate — and other changes made by the Act — are recognized in determining financial statement income and deferred tax assets and liabilities in the period that includes the date of enactment.

Accumulated Earnings Tax and Personal Holding Company Tax

With the increase in the highest individual income tax rate, the Act increases the tax rate on corporate accumulated earnings and undistributed personal holding company income commensurately to 39.6 percent, for taxable years beginning after 1992.

Estimated Tax Payments

In taxable years beginning after 1993, corporations are required to make estimated tax payments based on 100 percent of their current-year tax liability, using either annualized or actual liability, unless they are eligible to base their payments on 100 percent of the preceding year's tax. The rule allowing a first quarter payment equal to 25 percent of the preceding year's liability is retained.

Corporations that annualize their taxable income to compute their estimated tax payments will be required to elect, at the time of their first quarter payments, which months' incomes will be used in the computation. They will be allowed the following choices:

Corporate Estimated Tax Payments

Payment for	General Rule	Alternative A	Alternative B
1st quarter	3 months	2 months	3 months
2nd quarter	3 months	4 months	5 months
3rd quarter	6 months	7 months	8 months
4th quarter	9 months	10 months	11 months

OBSERVATION: Corporations that make annualization method estimated tax payments should review their business's earnings cycle and determine which of the three alternatives will permit them to make the lowest payments during the year. A corporation that traditionally has a strong fourth quarter and elects the general rule can defer paying tax on fourth quarter earnings until the due date of the tax return. A new option can be elected each year.

Limitations on Executive Compensation Deductions

Generally, no deduction will be allowed to any corporation required to register its stock with the SEC for compensation in excess of $1 million paid to the chief executive officer or the four other highest paid officers. However, the disallowance will not apply to any performance-based compensation — such as stock options or stock appreciation rights — paid after the executive achieves goals previously set by a directors' compensation committee and approved by the shareholders in a separate vote. It will also not apply to commissions based on income generated directly by the employee, to qualified retirement plan contributions (including salary reductions), or to nontaxable benefits.

This disallowance will apply to amounts deductible in taxable years beginning after 1993, with an exception for remuneration paid under a written contract binding in effect on February 17, 1993, and unchanged thereafter.

OBSERVATION: Due to the recent SEC disclosure rules on executive compensation, board of director compensation committees have been taking a more active role in setting executive compensation. This tax law change will increase that activism. The expanded SEC-required disclosures will give shareholders more information on which to base their votes required for deductibility of compensation of more than $1 million. KPMG Peat Marwick has experience in assisting clients in developing objective performance-based criteria for setting executive compensation.

Stock-for-Debt Exception to the Cancellation of Indebtedness Income Rules

The Act repeals the rule allowing a bankrupt or insolvent corporation to exchange its debt for stock in the corporation without recognizing COD income or reducing its tax attributes. This change is effective for stock transferred for debt on or after January 1, 1995, except in bankruptcy or insolvency proceedings initiated before January 1, 1994.

OBSERVATION: The stock-for-debt exception has enabled many troubled corporations to reorganize and find new investors without diminishing the corporation's value; repeal of the exception, largely for revenue purposes, could make it difficult for some companies to survive bankruptcy.

Provisions Affecting Businesses and Investments Generally

Investment Incentives

Expensing Trade or Business Property

Effective for taxable years beginning after 1992, up to $17,500 a year of tangible property (section 1245 property) that is used in a trade or business can be expensed, rather than depreciated. This is an increase from the current-law limit of $10,000. The $17,500 limit is reduced, dollar-for-dollar, as the taxpayer's total amount of eligible property placed in service for the year exceeds $200,000.

STRATEGY: Taxpayers should review their 1993 capital expenditures and should consider adjusting their investment for the remainder of the year to maximize the amount that can be expensed.

Alternative Minimum Tax Depreciation

For property placed in service after December 31, 1993, the depreciation component of the corporate alternative minimum tax (AMT) adjusted current earnings (ACE) adjustment is eliminated. The other AMT depreciation rules are unchanged.

OBSERVATIONS:

- For property placed in service before 1994, an ACE depreciation adjustment will continue, and records of ACE adjusted basis must be maintained. In many cases, this will benefit taxpayers by creating negative ACE depreciation adjustments in future years.
- Corporations have argued that the alternative minimum tax has impeded capital growth and added unwarranted complexity to computing tax liability. Repeal of the ACE adjustment removes one of the adjustments that can push corporations into paying AMT and eliminates one major element of AMT complexity.

R&E Credit

The research and experimentation credit, which expired after June 30, 1992, is retroactively reinstated and extended for costs paid or incurred through June 30, 1995. As under current law, the credit is 20 percent of the amount of qualified research expenses for the taxable year over a base amount of expenses calculated on the taxpayer's experience. In taxable years beginning after 1993, companies that did not have gross receipts in at least three years during the period 1984-1988 generally can compute their base amount with a formula that is more generous than current law.

OBSERVATION: Taxpayers may want to amend returns to claim the credit for costs paid or incurred after June 30, 1992.

Capital Gains Exclusion for Individuals

Individuals who invest in stock in "small" corporations after the date of enactment and hold such stock for at least five years will have an opportunity to exclude up to 50 percent of any gain when the stock is sold. Only investments by individuals (directly or through a partnership, S corporation, mutual fund, or common trust fund) in original issues of stock qualify. The stockholder must pay cash or property (other than stock) or receive the stock as compensation for services (other than as an underwriter). A small company is one that (on a controlled-group basis) has gross assets of no more than $50 million, including the amount paid for the stock, from January 1, 1993, through the date the stock is acquired. The company must engage in the active conduct of a trade or business for substantially all of the taxpayer's holding period for the exclusion to be allowed. The gain eligible for the exclusion for stock in any company may not exceed ten times the taxpayer's original basis in the stock of such corporation (or, if greater, $10 million). Fifty percent of the excluded gain will be an alternative minimum tax preference item.

Stock will not be qualified if the corporation purchases other shares of its stock from the taxpayer within two years before or two years after the taxpayer's purchase, or if the corporation redeemed or redeems more than five percent of its stock within one year before or one year after the taxpayer's purchase. Also, stock would not satisfy the five-year holding period if the taxpayer holds an offsetting short position with respect to the stock during that period.

Investments in S corporations, DISCs, former DISCs, section 936 corporations, RICs, REITs, REMICs, and cooperatives will not qualify. Additionally, the exclusion is not available for investments in corporations engaged in personal or professional services, banking, insurance, financing, leasing, investing, farming, mineral extraction, or hospitality activities, or those whose gross assets consist more than 10 percent (in value) of investment real estate. The exclusion also will be denied for stock in corporations that have investments in nonsubsidiary corporations of more than 10 percent (in value) of their net assets. The assets of a corporation and its 50-percent or greater subsidiaries will be aggregated to determine if the corporation's stock qualifies.

Targeted Jobs Credit

The targeted jobs credit, which expired after June 30, 1992, is retroactively reinstated but will not apply to wages paid to individuals who begin work after December 31, 1994.

OBSERVATION: Amended returns may be required to claim the credit for wages paid to employees hired after June 30, 1992. Unfortunately, as was the case in 1986 (when the credit lapsed and was retroactively reinstated), the Act does not provide any means of satisfying the eligibility certification requirements for employees who began work while the credit had lapsed if the employer failed to make a timely written request for certification. The IRS responded to this issue in 1986 by taking the position that no credit is available in this situation.

Educational Assistance

The income exclusion for educational assistance provided under an employer plan, which expired July 1, 1992, is retroactively reinstated, but only for payments or expenses incurred after June 30, 1992, and before January 1, 1995. The Act clarifies that other amounts provided by an employer for education or training are nontaxable to the employee only if they qualify as a working condition fringe benefit, after December 31, 1988.

OBSERVATION: Amended returns and Forms W-2 may be required to ensure that assistance provided in 1992 is properly reported. The conference report states that Congress expects the IRS to use its existing authority to alleviate administrative problems and facilitate refunds arising from the lapse in the exclusion.

Tax-Exempt Bonds

- The authority for state and local governments to issue "small-issue" tax-exempt bonds for private manufacturing and agricultural facilities is extended retroactively to July 1, 1992, and made permanent. The one-year "placed in service" rule is suspended so that the one-year period will not expire before January 1, 1994, to enable tax-exempt financing to be secured for projects placed in service shortly before or during the period authorization lapsed.
- State and local governments are authorized to issue tax-exempt private activity bonds to finance government-owned high-speed rail facilities without regard to the state annual private activity bond volume limitations, beginning in 1994.

Orphan Drug Credit

The credit for clinical testing expenses of drugs to treat rare diseases or conditions, which expired after June 30, 1992, is retroactively reinstated and extended through December 31, 1994.

Real Estate Provisions

Passive Activity Relief for Real Estate Professionals

Effective for taxable years beginning after 1993, passive activity loss relief is provided for persons who perform more than half of their personal services, and at least 750 hours of such services, for real property trades or businesses in which they materially participate. On a joint return, at least one spouse must separately satisfy this requirement for either spouse to be eligible. For qualifying taxpayers, income or loss from their rental real estate activities will not automatically be characterized as passive income or loss and will be nonpassive if the taxpayer materially participates in that activity for the year. Services performed as an employee will count in the determination only if the employee owns five percent or more of the employer for whom the services are performed. A closely held C corporation will be eligible if it derives more than half of its gross receipts from real property trades or businesses in which the corporation materially participates.

If you are a real estate professional who is engaged in more than one real property trade or business, both the "more than one-half of personal services" test and the "more than 750 hours of services" test can be satisfied by aggregating all the services that you perform for any real property trade or business in which you materially participate.

OBSERVATION: For purposes of the employee services rule, a partner is not considered an employee of a partnership.

STRATEGIES:

- If you own more than five percent of the stock of a real estate corporation of which you are also an employee and are thinking about reducing your stock ownership below five percent, consider the potential adverse effects of doing so.
- If you have a suspended passive activity loss in 1993 from a real estate activity that, under the new rules, will not be treated as a passive activity after 1993, your suspended loss will be deductible against any post-1993 income or gain generated by that activity. Existing law permits unused losses of a former passive activity to be deducted against income from that activity even after it ceases to be a passive activity.

Real Property Indebtedness

Effective for discharges of indebtedness on or after January 1, 1993, individuals and S corporations can elect to exclude from gross income certain cancellation of debt (COD) income from debt secured by real property that is used in the taxpayer's trade or business. The exclusion does not apply to qualified farm indebtedness. The amount excluded cannot exceed — and will reduce — the basis of the taxpayer's depreciable real property. The amount excluded also cannot exceed the principal amount of debt (before the discharge) in excess of the fair market value of the property securing the debt. For partnerships, the qualified debt is determined at the entity level, and the election is made at the partner level. A debt incurred or assumed after 1992 will qualify for the exclusion only if it was incurred or assumed to acquire, construct, reconstruct, or substantially improve the property (or to refinance pre-1993 qualifying real property business debt).

Depreciation of Nonresidential Real Property

The recovery period for depreciating nonresidential real property placed in service on or after May 13, 1993, is increased from 31.5 years to 39 years for regular tax purposes. Property acquired under a contract that was binding before May 13, 1993, or for which construction had begun by that date, is exempt from the longer recovery period if placed in service before January 1, 1994.

STRATEGIES:

- It may be possible to depreciate parts of a building over 31.5 years if those parts are placed in service before 1994, even if the rest of the building is not.
- Given that the AMT depreciation period for this property is 40 years, if the tax cost would be minimal, taxpayers may wish to elect to use the longer AMT recovery period to avoid the need to keep two sets of depreciation records.

Low-Income Housing Credit

The low-income housing tax credit is made permanent, retroactive to July 1, 1992, with several modifications to the credit that are generally effective upon enactment.

Mortgage Revenue Bonds and Mortgage Credit Certificates

The authority for state and local governments to issue tax-free mortgage revenue bonds and mortgage credit certificates is extended retroactively to July 1, 1992, and made permanent, with several technical changes.

Exempt Organizations' Real Estate and Other Investments

Beginning in 1994, the rules are liberalized concerning unrelated business taxable income (UBTI) exemptions for debt-financed rental income received by qualified pension and retirement plan trusts and other "qualified organizations." The current prohibitions on sale-leaseback transactions and on seller-financing will be relaxed. In addition, the prohibitions against contingent purchase prices and participating mortgages will be relaxed when the real property is acquired from a financial institution that is in conservatorship or receivership. Virtually *all* tax-exempt organizations will be permitted to buy and sell property, including mortgages, from failed financial institutions without generating UBTI but only if the organization spends less than 20 percent of the selling price on improvements. An exempt organization's share of income from a publicly traded partnership will no longer be deemed to be unrelated business income without regard to the source of the income at the partnership level.

The Act also liberalizes the current exclusion for exempt organizations' options activities in securities and expands the exclusion to include real estate options and deposits. Title-holding companies will not lose their tax-exempt status on account of receiving small amounts of unrelated income that is incidental to holding real property (*e.g.*, parking lot income).

Pension trusts will now be able to invest freely in real estate investment trusts (REITs) because they will no longer be viewed as individuals for purposes of the REIT five-or-fewer test, which provides that five or fewer individuals cannot own more than 50 percent of a REIT's stock. REIT dividends, however, will be UBTI to a pension trust that owns more than 10 percent of a pension-held REIT, in proportion to the UBTI of the REIT to total REIT income.

Provisions to Prevent Conversion of Ordinary Income to Capital Gain

The Act includes several provisions that are intended to forestall various investment strategies that might become more attractive with the increased differential between the top marginal tax rate on ordinary income and the maximum 28-percent rate on capital gains.

- Effective for taxable years beginning after 1992, net capital gain generally will not be considered investment income for purposes of computing the investment interest limitation, except to the extent the taxpayer elects to forego the 28-percent maximum rate on the gain.

  STRATEGIES:

  - Taxpayers in the upper-income tax brackets who have both net capital gain and excess investment interest expense generally will be better off foregoing the lower capital gain tax rate and deducting the additional investment interest expense.
  - In certain situations, advance planning may enable investment interest expense to be converted into fully deductible trade or business interest expense. This could avoid the need to have any capital gains taxed at ordinary rates. For example, if a partner in a partnership or an S corporation shareholder has excess investment interest expense, the loan giving rise to such interest could be restructured by having the partnership or S corporation borrow money that is then distributed to the partner or shareholder to pay off the original debt; the interest paid by the partnership or S corporation can then flow through to the partner or shareholder as deductible trade or business interest expense.
  - This new limitation on the deduction of investment interest expense should be considered in evaluating the after-tax cost of investment borrowing.

- Amounts received by a partner in liquidation of a partnership interest that are attributable to substantially appreciated inventory will be treated as ordinary income even if the fair market value of the inventory received is less than 10 percent of the value of all partnership property other than money. This provision is effective for sales, exchanges, and distributions after April 30, 1993.
- The Act subjects all market discount bonds purchased after April 30, 1993, even those issued before July 18, 1984, to the market discount rules. In general, these rules recharacterize a portion of the gain on disposition of market discount bonds as ordinary income and require the deferral of interest incurred to purchase or carry the bonds under certain circumstances.
- Market discount on tax-exempt obligations purchased after April 30, 1993, is subject to the general rule that recharacterizes a portion of any gain as ordinary income upon disposition. Any gain treated as ordinary, as under current law, is not treated as tax-exempt income.
- A purchaser of preferred stock after April 30, 1993, that is stripped of dividend rights is required to recognize the stock's stated redemption price in excess of the purchase price as ordinary income (not as a dividend or interest) under rules similar to those that apply to bonds with original issue discount.

  OBSERVATION: The Act does not address treatment of the holder of the dividend rights with respect to the availability of the dividends-received deduction. Further, the legislation implies that, contrary to the position taken by the IRS, tax ownership of dividend income can be divorced from tax ownership of the underlying stock.

- The Act recharacterizes as ordinary income a portion of what would otherwise be capital gain on the disposition of property in certain covered "conversion transactions" entered into after April 30, 1993, that are structured to produce a return based on the time value of the net investment, including certain straddles, transactions marketed and sold as producing capital gains, and other transactions specified by the IRS. This will not apply to most transactions of options dealers or commodities traders in the ordinary course of their business.

OBSERVATION: These special rules are directed at sophisticated financial transactions. Many standard tax-planning investment strategies will remain effective to convert ordinary income into capital gains.

Financial Institutions and Products

Mark-to-Market Accounting for "Securities Dealers"

The Act requires that securities that are inventory in the hands of a dealer be inventoried at fair market value. Securities that are held by a dealer that are not inventory must be marked to market at year end or such earlier time as the IRS may prescribe. Accordingly, the cost method and lower of cost or market method are no longer available for these dealers. Any gain or loss on securities subject to mark-to-market accounting generally will be treated as ordinary income or loss.

For purposes of these rules, "securities" and a "dealer" are defined more broadly than under current law. "Securities" include stock, partnership interests, evidences of indebtedness (including loans originated), interest rate, currency, or equity notional principal contracts (but not other notional principal contracts, for example, those based on the price of commodities, oil, or wheat), and interests in derivative financial products. The term securities also includes other positions that are hedges of securities described above.

A "dealer" is any person that either regularly purchases securities from, or sells securities to, customers in the ordinary course of a trade or business, or regularly offers to enter into, assume, offset, assign, or otherwise terminate positions in securities with customers in the ordinary course of a trade or business.

Securities properly identified as held for investment, and hedges of securities so identified, are not subject to the mark-to-market rules. Also, the mark-to-market rules do not apply to hedges of any position, right to income, or liability that is not a security in the hands of the taxpayer, and is identified as such. The conference report states that accounting systems that track "global hedging" risk management strategies are generally considered to satisfy the identification requirements.

The committee reports state that financial accounting rules are not dispositive of whether securities or evidences of indebtedness are treated as held for investment under these rules.

This provision is effective for taxable years ending on or after December 31, 1993; the cumulative income effect of switching to this new accounting method is to be recognized ratably over five taxable years, beginning with the first year ending on or after December 31, 1993. Accordingly, calendar-year taxpayers must include in 1993 income one-fifth of the December 31, 1992, mark-to-market adjustment, either negative or positive.

A special rule for certain floor specialists and market makers that used the LIFO inventory method for at least five years to account for "qualified securities" allows them to spread the income effect related to those securities over as long as 15 years.

Federal Savings and Loan Insurance Corporation (FSLIC) Assistance

A recipient of tax-free FSLIC assistance that was credited on or after March 4, 1991, in connection with the disposition of "covered" assets is required to treat that assistance as compensation for any losses claimed on dispositions or charge-offs of those assets, effectively denying them any tax loss (or loss carryforward) for those assets. Net operating losses carried to taxable years ending on or after March 4, 1991, must be reduced to the extent of tax-free FSLIC assistance received with respect to assets disposed of and charge-offs made in taxable years ending before March 4, 1991.

OBSERVATION: Amended returns will be necessary in some cases.

Amortization of Intangible Assets

Effective for purchases after the date of enactment, taxpayers are required to amortize most intangibles (including goodwill, going concern value, and covenants not to compete) used in a trade or business or income-producing activity over a 15-year period on a straight-line method. Exceptions apply for:

- Interests in land, existing leases, debt, stock and partnership interests, sport franchises, most intangibles created by the taxpayer, and other items.
- Most commercially available computer software, and software that is not acquired as part of the purchase of a trade or business. Such software will instead be amortized using the straight-line method over 36 months.
- Mortgage servicing rights that are purchased, but not as part of an acquisition of a trade or business. These rights

will instead be amortized on a straight-line basis over 108 months.

A taxpayer can elect to apply the 15-year amortization rule to intangibles acquired after July 25, 1991. If this election is made, it applies to any and all intangibles acquired during the period after July 25, 1991, through the date of enactment. It would also apply to any and all acquisitions during that period by any taxpayer that is under common control with the taxpayer at any time after August 2, 1993, and on or before the date the election is made. The Act also allows a taxpayer to elect out of the 15-year amortization requirement for property acquired under a written binding contract in effect on the date of enactment. These two elections are mutually exclusive. The IRS is expected to require a taxpayer making either of these elections to do so on its tax return for the period including the date of enactment.

OBSERVATIONS:

- Congress considered, but did not adopt, a provision that would have provided more generous amortization rules for acquisitions of businesses that have made certain software expenditures.
- The only simplification measure to be included from the tax bills vetoed by President Bush in 1992 is the tax treatment of acquired intangible assets. Taxpayers (and the IRS) are no longer required to distinguish intangible assets that have a determinable value and life, and therefore are amortizable, from nonamortizable goodwill and going concern value.
- The U.S. Supreme Court's decision in *Newark Morning Ledger* earlier this year gave taxpayers authority to amortize various purchased intangible assets that have some resemblance to goodwill but that had a determinable value and useful life (such as customer lists). There are thousands of open IRS examinations involving such issues for years before the elective effective date of the new intangibles provision. In the conference report, Congress urges the IRS to expedite the settlement of these old cases and to take into account the principles of the new amortization rules to produce consistent results for similarly situated taxpayers.

Other Provisions

AMT Treatment of Appreciated Charitable Contribution Property

The alternative minimum tax (AMT) preference item for the appreciated value of charitable contributions of *tangible* personal property is repealed, effective for contributions made after June 30, 1992. The AMT preference item for the appreciated value of charitable contributions of other property is repealed, effective for contributions made after December 31, 1992. Thus, beginning in 1993, the full fair market value of charitable contributions of any property, including stock, is fully deductible for AMT purposes. The relief does not apply to any deduction carryover from a contribution made prior to the effective date.

OBSERVATION: Taxpayers may want to file amended 1992 returns.

The Act also clarifies that no adjustment related to the earnings and profits effects of any charitable contribution is to be made in computing adjusted current earnings for corporate AMT purposes.

Donee Acknowledgements

Beginning in 1994, charitable contribution deductions of $250 or more will be denied when the taxpayer has not received a contemporaneous written acknowledgement from the charity.

The acknowledgement from the charity must include a "good faith estimate" of the value of any goods or services received by the taxpayer from the charity in connection with the contribution. The donee is not required to value any property or services contributed that the taxpayer claims to have a value of $250 or more, but must still provide a receipt. The value of any intangible religious benefit received that is generally unavailable outside the donative context does not need to be valued, but the benefit must be acknowledged.

A written disclosure must also be provided to a taxpayer who makes a donation of more than $75, with a similar good faith estimate of value, if the charity gives the taxpayer goods or services of more than de minimis value in return for the donation. The statement must inform the donor that a deduction is allowed only for the value of the donation in excess of the value of the goods or services received from the organization. A $10 penalty will be imposed on a donee organization for each failure to disclose such information (capped at $5,000 per event or mailing).

Study of Advance Valuations of Charitable Contributions

Under the Act, Congress directs Treasury to prepare a report on the development of advance valuation procedures for charitable gifts of tangible personal property, to be submitted within a year after enactment.

OBSERVATION: The purpose of the Treasury study is to determine whether procedures can be adopted that would enable taxpayers to obtain agreement from the IRS as to the value of a charitable gift of tangible personal property (for example, art works) before the gift is made. Congress believes that such a procedure would reduce uncertainty and disputes that arise between taxpayers and the IRS over deductions claimed on tax returns for charitable contributions of property.

Meal and Entertainment Expense Deduction

Effective in taxable years beginning after 1993, the current 20-percent disallowance for business meal and entertainment expenses is increased to a 50-percent disallowance.

Club Dues

No deduction is allowed for amounts paid or incurred as club dues after 1993 (including business, social, athletic, luncheon, sporting, airline, and hotel clubs). The disallowance will not apply to amounts paid for specific services (such as meals) provided by the club, if such amounts are otherwise deductible.

OBSERVATION: This provision does *not* apply to any capitalized pre-1994 club membership costs (such as initiation fees) that would otherwise be deductible as a loss on the termination of a club membership.

Lobbying Expenses

No deduction is allowed for lobbying expenses paid or incurred after 1993. Lobbying expenses are defined as expenditures incurred in connection with attempts to influence federal or state legislation through communication with a member or employee of a federal or state legislative body, or with any other government official or employee involved in the formulation of legislation. Costs of directly communicating with senior executive branch officials to influence their official actions or positions are also nondeductible. As under present law, expenses for grassroots lobbying and participation in political campaigns will not be deductible. The disallowance extends to expenses incurred for research, preparation, planning, or coordination of lobbying activities. Merely monitoring legislation, without attempting to influence it, is not a lobbying activity. A de minimis rule exempts from the disallowance a taxpayer's direct expenditures to influence legislation or senior executive branch officials that do not exceed $2,000 a year. Also, communications compelled by subpoena or otherwise by federal or state law are not intended to be subject to the disallowance rule.

The provision does not apply to expenditures related to influencing legislation in local governing bodies, such as city councils. In addition, those in the trade or business of lobbying can deduct expenses paid or incurred in lobbying on behalf of others.

The disallowance will apply to the portion of dues paid to an organization (*e.g.*, a trade association or labor union) that are attributable to lobbying. For this purpose, an organization's lobbying expenses will be treated as coming only from its dues income. Organizations must report the amount of lobbying expenses (if more than de minimis) and nondeductible dues payments to the IRS, and must notify dues-paying members of the nondeductible portion, but are not required to report each nondeductible dues payment to the IRS. If the organization fails to provide notices, it will be subject to a tax equal to the underreported amount multiplied by the highest corporate tax rate, though the IRS can waive the tax if the organization agrees to correct the failure. As an alternative to the disclosure requirements, an organization may elect to pay a proxy tax, equal to the highest corporate rate. In this case, no portion of the members' dues will be deemed nondeductible.

Furthermore, a portion of a donor's contributions to charities and similar organizations will be nondeductible if the organization engages in lobbying activities of direct interest to the donor and a principal purpose of the donation was to secure a deduction for the lobbying activity expense.

Business Travel Expense

Beginning in 1994, a business travel deduction will be denied for the expenses of a taxpayer's spouse, dependent, or companion, unless those expenses would be deductible without regard to the taxpayer.

Expanded FICA Tax on Employers

The elimination of the $135,000 cap on the hospital insurance portion of the Social Security tax also extends to the employer portion (1.45 percent) of the 2.9 percent tax on wages above that level, beginning in 1994.

Luxury Taxes

The 10-percent luxury excise tax on purchases of certain boats, aircraft, furs, and jewelry is repealed, retroactively to January 1, 1993. The luxury excise tax on automobiles is retained, but the $30,000 threshold will be indexed annually for inflation (rounded to the next lowest $2,000 increment), for automobiles sold on or after the date of enactment (the indexed 1993 limitation will be $32,000). Exemptions from the tax are provided for automobile equipment required to make a vehicle suitable for use by a disabled person (effective January 1, 1991), and for a dealer's use of an automobile purchased as a demonstrator vehicle (effective January 1, 1993). The Act gives taxpayers who paid tax on equipment in a vehicle for a disabled person at least one year from the date of enactment to claim a refund, even if the statute of limitations would otherwise expire.

Taxpayers who have previously paid luxury tax on purchases now not subject to the tax are entitled to a refund. The refund must be requested from the seller of the taxed item, who will then obtain a refund from the IRS. Retailers must satisfy certain documentation requirements for customer refunds to obtain their own refund from the IRS.

Attribute Reduction from Discharge of Indebtedness Rules

Beginning in 1994, a taxpayer that is eligible to reduce certain tax attributes rather than recognize income from the cancellation of indebtedness (COD) will be required to reduce its suspended passive activity losses and credit carryovers and its alternative minimum tax credits along with other attributes.

Partner Liquidation Payments

For partners withdrawing, retiring, or dying on or after January 5, 1993, liquidating payments from the partnership are treated as made in exchange for the partner's interest in partnership property, generally treated as capital gain. The provision will not apply if there was a written binding contract in effect on January 4, 1993 — specifying the amount and timing of any payments — to purchase the partner's interest upon later retirement or withdrawal. General partners in service partnerships can continue to treat such payments as a distributive share or guaranteed payment — generally treated as ordinary income to the withdrawing or retiring partner and deductible by the partnership — as under current law.

Vaccine Excise Tax

The excise tax on sales or uses of certain vaccines, which expired January 1, 1993, is reinstated, effective for sales and uses after the date of enactment. A floor stocks tax is imposed on supplies of vaccine that have not previously been taxed that are held on the date of enactment. The floor stocks tax is due at the end of the sixth month after the month of enactment (*i.e.*, February 28, 1994). The Vaccine Compensation Trust Fund, which is funded by the excise tax, is also made permanent.

Prohibition on Changes in Pediatric Vaccines

Any group health plan that provided coverage for pediatric vaccines on May 1, 1993, will be subject to the same excise tax penalty levied on COBRA health plan coverage violations if the group health plan reduces that coverage after May 1, 1993. The tax applies in plan years beginning after the date of enactment.

OBSERVATION: This is the first "mandated" health care benefit imposed by the federal government. The tax laws, ERISA, and other legislation have imposed myriad requirements on employers, insurance companies, and other plan sponsors that decide to provide a certain benefit, but never before has a reduction of a specific welfare benefit been penalized by ERISA or the tax laws.

Special Rule for Inpatient Hospital Services in New York State

In lieu of a waiver of ERISA requirements for health care plans in New York, the Act contains a provision designed to prohibit ERISA-pre-empted health plans from avoiding the New York state tax on hospital services.

Provisions Affecting International Operations and Foreign Taxpayers

Limitation on Section 936 Possessions Tax Credit

For taxable years beginning after 1993, the Act imposes a limitation on the tax credit allowed to a U.S. corporation for U.S. tax on income earned in Puerto Rico or a U.S. possession.

The portion of the credit for U.S. tax on possession business income — as computed under current law — will be subject to one of two limits, to be chosen by the taxpayer:

- A fixed percentage of the amount allowed under current law: 60 percent in 1994, phased in ratably to 40 percent in 1998; or
- The sum of:
  - 60 percent of qualified possessions compensation paid (generally defined as 85 percent of the Social Security tax wage limit for each possessions employee plus certain fringe benefit expense),

- A portion of the depreciation deductions on possessions business property (ranging from 15 to 65 percent, depending on the property's recovery period), and
- Possessions income taxes paid, subject to other limitations (unless the company has elected the profit-split method for allocating income from intangible property).

An election to take a credit for a fixed percentage of the current-law credit can be made only in the first taxable year beginning after 1993 in which the corporation is a possessions corporation and remains in effect until revoked. A corporation that has elected the profit-split method can deduct a portion of its possessions income taxes.

There is no change to the computation of the portion of the credit for U.S. tax on qualified possession source investment income (QPSII).

Affiliated possessions corporations are granted an election to compute the possession tax credit on a consolidated basis.

For purposes of computing the alternative minimum tax foreign tax credit, a separate income basket will be required for certain dividends from a possessions corporation.

The current-law limitation on the "cover over" of rum excise taxes to Puerto Rico and the Virgin Islands is temporarily increased, effective October 1, 1993.

OBSERVATION: This provision is intended to reduce the benefit of the possession tax credit to U.S. corporations that establish capital-intensive businesses in Puerto Rico that generate substantial income without significant job creation there.

Earnings Stripping

The original effective date of the earnings stripping rules is modified to eliminate the exemption for interest on a fixed-term obligation issued on or before July 10, 1989, effective in taxable years beginning after 1993. Also, the rules are expanded to apply to interest paid to unrelated persons on indebtedness subject to a "disqualified guarantee" — generally, a guarantee by a related foreign person — unless a gross basis (withholding) tax is imposed on the interest. A guarantee is broadly defined, for this purpose, to include *any* arrangement under which a person (directly or indirectly) assures the payment of another person's obligation under any indebtedness. As under current law, if the statutory 30 percent withholding tax is reduced to zero by a treaty, none of the interest is subject to a gross basis tax. If the statutory rate is reduced to an intermediate rate, a portion of the interest subject to a disqualified guarantee will be treated as subject to a gross basis tax.

Transfer Pricing Valuation Misstatement Penalties

In taxable years beginning after 1993, the threshold amount of a net section 482 transfer price adjustment for imposition of a penalty for a transfer pricing valuation misstatement is reduced from $10 million to the lesser of $5 million or 10 percent of gross receipts for the 20-percent penalty, and to the lesser of $20 million or 20 percent of gross receipts for the 40-percent penalty. Significant statutory changes are made to the reasonable cause and good faith exception. To have any part of the section 482 adjustment disregarded for purposes of the substantial penalty computation, generally a taxpayer must properly document the reasonableness of its transfer pricing methodology and provide such documentation to the IRS within 30 days of the government's request.

Portfolio Interest

For debt obligations issued after April 7, 1993, the portfolio interest exemption from U.S. tax is modified to exempt certain interest whose rate is contingent on the income, cash flow, or fair market value of property of the debtor or a related party. This rule does not override existing treaty withholding rates and will be effective for interest received after 1993.

STRATEGY: If a debt instrument has a minimum noncontingent interest rate, only the portion of the contingent interest that is in excess of such minimum will be disqualified from portfolio interest treatment. Therefore, a minimum noncontingent interest rate (*e.g.*, 6 percent of the principal) generally should be provided to assure that at least a portion of the interest qualifies for the portfolio interest exemption.

Conduit Arrangements

The Act grants Treasury broad authority to prescribe regulations to recharacterize any multiple-party financing transaction as one directly between two or more parties to prevent avoidance of tax. Future IRS regulations may apply to back-to-back loan transactions and transactions involving debt guarantees or equity investments.

Anti-Deferral Regime

A new anti-deferral regime is established that requires U.S. shareholders of controlled foreign corporations (CFCs) to recognize currently a deemed dividend amount equal to the lesser of certain earnings or the excess passive assets of their CFCs. The provision applies only for earnings accumulated or earned in taxable years beginning after September 30, 1993. Passive assets are defined generally under the current passive foreign investment company (PFIC) rules, though valued by reference to their adjusted basis, with special rules for valuing leased property and certain intangible assets. Passive assets will be excessive for a taxable year if their average value (computed at the end of each quarter of that year) exceeds 25 percent of the average value of all assets. Previously taxed amounts will be exempt when distributed.

A special rule is provided to treat CFCs within the same chain (connected through a top-tier CFC) as a single corporation, and then to apportion the aggregate excess passive assets of the group to the CFCs based on each member's share of the total earnings of the group.

STRATEGY: Taxpayers that may be affected by this special rule should consider reorganizing the ownership structure of their CFCs.

Passive Foreign Investment Company (PFIC) and Subpart F Rules

A number of changes are made to the PFIC and subpart F rules in addition to other rules relating to investments in foreign corporations, including:

- The test to determine PFIC status of a controlled foreign corporation is revised, beginning after September 30, 1993, to base asset valuation on adjusted basis rather than fair market value. This change is likely to qualify more foreign corporations with certain low-basis business intangibles (*e.g.*, goodwill) as PFICs.

  Foreign corporations other than CFCs may continue to value their assets, for purposes of the PFIC test, using the fair market value of their assets. Such corporations, however, may make an irrevocable election to base their asset valuation using the adjusted basis of the assets. Also, the PFIC rules are amended to treat certain deemed income from a CFC — from an increase in investment of earnings in U.S. property under section 956 or under the new anti-deferral rule — as distributions from the PFIC. This amendment eliminates the existing tax planning idea of affirmatively using section 956 prior to a distribution by a PFIC to eliminate the deferred tax and interest charge on the distribution.

  Passive income for the PFIC test does not include any income derived in the active conduct of a securities business by certain CFCs.

  The Act also makes adjustments to the PFIC asset test. Any tangible personal property leased to a foreign corporation under a lease with a term of at least 12 months will be treated as actually owned by the corporation. The adjusted basis of leased property will be deemed to be the unamortized portion of the present value of the lease payments.

  The adjusted basis of the total assets of a CFC will be increased by certain net R&E expenditures paid or incurred during the current year and the two preceding taxable years.

  The adjusted basis of the total assets of a CFC will be increased by 300 percent of the royalties and other payments made for the use of certain intangible property.

  OBSERVATION: These adjustments should make it easier for certain foreign corporations to avoid PFIC status.

- The mechanism of determining a U.S shareholder's income from an increase of investment of CFC earnings in U.S. property is changed to require the calculation of investment in U.S. property as the average of amounts held at the end of each quarter of the year.

- The application of the subpart F same-country exception is limited in the case of certain dividends received by CFCs. Amounts distributed with respect to stock owned by the CFC will not qualify for the same-country exception to the extent that the distributed earnings and profits were accumulated by the distributing corporation during periods when the CFC did not hold the stock, directly or indirectly. This provision codifies a similar rule in the regulations.

These new subpart F and PFIC rules apply for tax years of CFCs beginning after September 30, 1993, and to the tax years of U.S. shareholders in which, or with which, those CFC tax years end.

Allocation of Research and Experimental Expenditures

For one year, a multinational corporation's research and experimental (R&E) expenditures generally will be allocated 50 percent to the place of performance and 50 percent based on source of gross sales or gross income. Treasury is authorized to prescribe regulations to make adjustments for cost-sharing arrangements and "contract research." This statutory rule generally will apply for the first taxable year beginning on or before August 1, 1994, following expiration of Revenue Procedure 92-56, which generally allocates 64 percent of the expenditure based on place of performance and the remainder based on sales income or gross income. Revenue Procedure 92-56 applies during the last six months of a taxpayer's first taxable year beginning after August 1, 1991, and during the succeeding taxable year. Thus, for a calendar year taxpayer, the new rule generally will apply for 1994.

OBSERVATION: This one-year statutory allocation of R&E expenditures is the latest in a string of temporary legislative and administrative overrides (dating back to 1981) to regulations that were issued in 1977.

STRATEGY: Taxpayers should consider accelerating into 1993 expenditures for research and development to be performed in the United States to take advantage of the expiring 64-percent place-of-performance percentage. This action can be important if the taxpayer is in an excess foreign tax credit position.

Working Capital Exception for Foreign Oil and Gas and Shipping Income

The foreign tax credit rules are amended to prevent the cross-crediting of foreign taxes on foreign oil and gas extraction income (FOGEI), foreign oil-related income (FORI), and subpart F shipping income by placing investment income related to these types of income in the passive category for foreign tax credit limitation purposes. In addition, passive income related to foreign oil and gas extraction is excluded from the computation of the FOGEI and FORI foreign tax credit limitations. This amendment applies in tax years beginning after 1992.

Dispositions of U.S. Real Property Interests

The minimum U.S. tax rate on net gains from U.S. real property gains by nonresident alien individuals is increased from 21 percent to 26 percent (28 percent to the extent the net gain exceeds $175,000), in taxable years beginning after 1992.

Exports of Unprocessed Timber

Several tax provisions applying to exporters of unprocessed timber (such as logs and cants) that are softwood are amended, effective for transactions after the date of enactment, to discourage such exports:

- Such timber will not be "export property" for purposes of the DISC and FSC rules.
- Income from the sale of any such timber cut from an area in the United States will be domestic-source income under the source rules for inventory income.
- Generally, income of a CFC from sales or milling such timber will be subpart F income.

OBSERVATION: The Administration endorsed these tax provisions as part of a broader plan to restrict timber harvesting in the Northwest.

Compliance Provisions

Information Reporting of Discharges of Indebtedness

Banks, thrift institutions, credit unions, the FDIC, RTC, NCUA, and other federal agencies are required to issue Forms 1099 on discharges of indebtedness of $600 or more. The requirement is generally effective for discharges (in whole or in part) on or after January 1, 1994; federal agencies will need to report discharges that occur after enactment.

OBSERVATION: Congress has directed the IRS to issue guidance coordinating this new reporting requirement with reporting already required on foreclosures and abandonments.

Substantial Understatement Penalty Modification

For tax returns with original due dates after 1993, a taxpayer's ability to avoid a penalty for a substantial understatement of income tax by disclosing the position giving rise to the understatement will be limited by requiring the disclosed position to have at least a "reasonable basis," and not just be "nonfrivolous." Because the negligence penalty does not apply, under current law, if the taxpayer has a reasonable basis for the tax return position, the disclosure exception to the negligence penalty will no longer be relevant. A disclosure exception will still apply, however, to avoid a penalty for disregarding rules or regulations.

Interest on IRS Refunds

An interest-free period of up to 45 days will be imposed on a refund arising from any type of original tax return if the overpayment is refunded within 45 days after the later of the original due date of the return or the date the return was filed. A similar rule will apply to deny interest on amended returns and claims for refunds (but only for the period from the date the amended return or claim is filed) when the IRS pays the refund within 45 days. Also, the interest paid on tax adjustments initiated by the IRS will be eliminated for 45 days of the overpayment period. Extension of the 45-day rule to refunds of taxes other than income taxes will apply to returns with original due dates after 1993; extension of the

45-day rule to amended returns and claims for refund will apply to returns and claims filed after 1994 (regardless of the tax period involved); and denial of interest on IRS adjustments will apply to refunds paid after 1994.

Withholding on Bonuses

The income tax withholding rate is increased from 20 percent to 28 percent on bonuses and similar supplemental wage payments after 1993.

Employer Tax Credit for FICA Taxes Paid on Tip Income

Food or beverage establishments that pay FICA tax on employee tip income are allowed each year to elect a nonrefundable income tax credit (rather than a deduction) for their portion of the FICA tax attributable to tips in excess of those treated as wages for purposes of satisfying the minimum wage laws. The credit is available for taxes paid after 1993 but may not be carried back to taxable years ending before date of enactment.

OBSERVATION: This credit was provided to offset partially the cutback of the deduction for meal and entertainment expenses from 80 percent to 50 percent, discussed above.

Reporting Service Payments to Corporations

Congress considered, *but did not adopt*, a provision requiring payment for services performed by corporations to be reported to the IRS on a Form 1099. However, the conference report notes that Congress understands that the effectiveness of information reporting will be improved, and the reporting burden on businesses lessened, if a comprehensive taxpayer identification number (TIN) matching system is implemented. In the conference report, Congress encourages the IRS to establish such a program as soon as practicable.

Energy Taxes

Transportation Fuels Tax

A permanent 4.3 cents-per-gallon transportation fuels excise tax is imposed, beginning October 1, 1993, in addition to existing federal excise taxes on motor fuels (gasoline, diesel fuel, and special motor fuels) used for highway transportation or in motorboats; gasoline and jet fuel used in commercial and noncommercial aviation (with a delayed effective date for commercial aviation); gasoline used in off-highway nonbusiness uses (for example, small engines and recreational trail uses); diesel fuel used in trains; fuels used in inland waterways transportation; and compressed natural gas used in highway motor vehicles or motorboats.

The proceeds of the new 4.3 cents-per-gallon transportation fuels tax are to be deposited in the Treasury's General Fund, rather than in any of the trust funds for highways, airports, mass transit, inland waterways, or other dedicated purposes in which most of the existing excise taxes are deposited.

In addition, the Act extends until October 1, 1999, the 2.5 cents-per-gallon tax on gasoline, diesel fuel, and special motor fuels, scheduled to expire on October 1, 1995. However, only 1.25 cents per gallon of this extended tax will apply to railroad diesel fuel. Revenue from the 2.5 cents-per-gallon extended tax derived from highway fuels will be deposited in the Highway Trust Fund. Other revenue, including that from railroad diesel fuel, will continue to be deposited in the Treasury's General Fund.

Exempted from the new tax are: home heating oil; gasoline and diesel fuel used on farms for farming purposes; off-highway business uses of fuel; fuels used by state and local governments and by nonprofit educational organizations; exported fuels; fuel for military ships and aircraft; and fuel used in transporting exported goods.

The collection of the new tax will piggyback on the collection mechanisms in place for the existing excise taxes. The excise tax on compressed natural gas will be collected on the fuel's retail sale or use, under the provisions currently in place for collecting the special motor fuels tax.

Also, beginning January 1, 1994, the tax on highway diesel fuel is extended to fuel used in motorboats, with an exemption for most business use of a boat other than providing recreation. The revenues from this tax will be deposited in the Treasury's General Fund.

A floor stocks tax equal to the 4.3 cents a gallon transportation fuels tax increase will apply to supplies of gasoline and diesel fuel to which title is held on October 1, 1993. Fuels held for exempt uses are not subject to the floor stocks tax, and a general de minimis exemption is provided each person for up to 4,000 gallons of gasoline and 2,000 gallons of diesel or aviation fuel that would otherwise be taxable (this exemption applies on a controlled group basis). The

Tax Rates
(expressed in cents per gallon)

	Current Law	New Rate
Gasoline/Special Motors Fuels:		
Highway Use	14.1	18.4
Noncommercial Aviation	15.1	19.4
Commercial Aviation	0.1	4.4*
Diesel:		
Highway Use	20.1	24.4
Railroad Use	2.6	6.9
Nongasoline Aviation Fuel:		
Noncommercial	17.6	21.9
Commercial	0.1	4.4*
Inland Waterways Fuel	17.1	21.4**

Compressed natural gas used as fuel in highway vehicles or motorboats: 48.54 cents per thousand cubic feet, with an exception for school buses and intercity passenger buses.

*****

* The tax increase on commercial aviation fuel will not apply until October 1, 1995.

** The inland waterways fuel tax is scheduled to increase an additional 2 cents per gallon on January 1, 1994, and 3 cents per gallon on January 1, 1995, under legislation enacted in 1988.

floor stocks tax will need to be paid by November 30, 1993. A floor stocks tax will also be imposed on commercial aviation fuel, on October 1, 1995.

OBSERVATION: The size and shape of additional taxes on energy was one of the most contentious issues throughout the legislative process. Clinton proposed a broad-based tax based on the Btu content of most fuels, to be imposed generally at the producer level. Clinton argued that this tax would promote environmental and conservation concerns, as well as raise substantial revenue (approximately $73 billion over five years) to support investment incentives and deficit reduction. This tax would have resulted in roughly a 7.6 cents-per-gallon tax increase on gasoline and would have applied to energy produced from coal, natural gas, and electricity. The House accepted the Btu tax but made major changes, including movement of the collection point generally to the retail level and the addition of several exemptions. The Senate dropped the Btu tax and adopted a transportation fuels tax almost identical to that included in the Act (which raises approximately $23 billion over five years).

Federal taxation of transportation fuels will continue to be a pressing issue before Congress in the next few years. The current 0.1 cents-per-gallon Leaking Underground Storage Tank tax and 17.5 cents per gallon of the tax on noncommercial aviation fuel are scheduled to expire at the end of 1995. Although the new 4.3 cents-per-gallon transportation tax is permanent, the other taxes on highway and motorboat fuels expire after September 30, 1999. Even with the new tax, the U.S. tax rates on highway fuels are very low compared to those in other industrial countries.

Diesel Fuel Tax Collections

The collection point for the diesel excise tax is moved to the terminal rack (as it is for the gasoline excise tax) from, generally, the wholesale distribution point. Generally, the tax-free or reduced-tax purchases of diesel fuel that can be made under current law continue to be allowed. Diesel fuel that is purchased for tax-exempt or reduced-tax use must be dyed and marked (as required by the IRS) when it leaves the terminal rack. A penalty will be imposed for misuse of dyed fuels equal to $10 a gallon of the fuel involved (with a minimum penalty of $1,000).

The change to the collection point is effective January 1, 1994, with a floor stocks tax imposed on any untaxed fuel held on that date that would have been previously taxed had the new collection scheme been in effect, to be paid by July 31, 1994.

Finally, the Act strengthens the authority of the IRS to enter and inspect fuel production and storage facilities to determine compliance with the fuel excise taxes.

Empowerment Zones and Other Community Development Initiatives

The initial focal point of the $20 billion tax bill vetoed by President Bush in November 1992 was federal assistance to economically distressed urban areas, spurred on by the vicious riots in Los Angeles in April 1992. Although the vetoed bill also contained a vast array of tax changes, it would have provided a substantial set of incentives for business and investment located in 50 federally designated enterprise zones. The enterprise zone concept had been proposed numerous times during the 1980s.

The Act includes a modest set of incentives based on the enterprise zone concept, including about $2.5 billion of tax provisions and $1 billion in block grants for various social programs. The Democratic leadership is referring to some of these limited incentives as pilot projects. Whether these limited targeted provisions will lead to further and bigger incentives in the future will depend in large part on how well the deficit is dealt with in later years.

Empowerment Zones and Enterprise Communities

Up to nine "empowerment zones" and 95 "enterprise communities" may be designated in 1994 and 1995 by the Secretaries of Housing and Urban Development (HUD) and Agriculture as geographic areas in which certain activities qualify for special federal tax incentives. About two-thirds of these are to be in urban areas and the remainder in rural areas.

The zones and communities are to be selected from areas nominated by state and local governments. To be eligible, an urban area must have a general poverty rate of at least 20 percent and poverty rates of 25 or 35 percent in prescribed percentages of its census tracts, a maximum population of 200,000, and an area of no more than 20 square miles. Rural areas must meet the poverty rate criteria and have a population of no more than 30,000 and an area of no more than 1,000 square miles.

Also, nominating state and local governments will need to present a strategic plan for the area, stating specific steps for economic development that involve local residents, institutions, and organizations as partners; committing state, local, and private resources to the area; and identifying ways to measure the success of the plan, including the extent to which local residents will be empowered to become economically self-sufficient. The plan must generally refrain from assisting establishments from relocating into the area. Zone designations will generally last ten years.

A 20-percent credit will be allowed to an employer (instead of a deduction) for the first $15,000 of wages and training expenses for an employee who lives and works in a zone (the credit is to be phased out over the period 2002 through 2004). The credit will not be allowed to employees of golf courses, country clubs, massage parlors, liquor stores, gambling facilities, farms with assets of more than $500,000, and other statutory "ineligible" trades or businesses. This credit can offset up to 25 percent of the employer's tentative minimum tax but cannot be carried back to a taxable year ending before 1994.

For a "zone business," there will be an increased limit on expensing depreciable business property (which the Act generally raises from $10,000 to $17,500) to $37,500 for zone business property (including buildings and certain renovations). For qualified zone property, the $37,500 limit is reduced when total investment exceeds $200,000 a year, but at only half the rate for other property. A "zone business" is one that derives at least 80 percent of gross income from an active qualified business in a zone, uses substantially all of its business assets and employee services in the zone, and has a workforce at least 35 percent of whom are zone residents. Every trade or business of a corporation or partnership must be conducted in a zone for any of them to qualify as a zone business. The statutory "ineligible" trades or businesses mentioned above will not qualify. Real estate rental will qualify as a zone business only if the rentals are of business (*i.e.*, nonresidential) real property and at least half the gross rental income is from zone businesses; rentals of tangible personal property will qualify only if substantially all the rentals are to zone businesses or residents.

A new class of tax-exempt bonds is authorized to finance facilities (including land and existing property) in zones or communities that are to be used principally by a zone or community business, limited to $3 million per business in any single zone or community and $20 million per business in all zones and communities. These bonds, however, will be subject to the current state volume caps.

Low-Income Housing Credit for HOME Block Grant Funded Housing

Builders using HOME block grant funds for building affordable housing will be eligible for the more generous 70-percent present value low-income housing tax credit after the date of enactment if at least 40 percent of the residents of the property have income 50 percent or below the area median income. In high-cost housing areas, only 25 percent or more of the residents must meet the 50-percent area median income test.

Investment in Specialized Small Business Investment Companies

Two tax incentives are provided for investment in a corporation or partnership licensed as a "Specialized Small Business Investment Company" (SSBIC) by the Small Business Administration:

- An investment in a SSBIC whose stock would otherwise qualify for the 50-percent capital gains exclusion will not be disqualified if it is not engaged in an active trade or business.
- C corporations and individuals can defer taxation of gains from dispositions of publicly traded stock on or after the date of enactment to the extent the proceeds are reinvested in stock of (or a partnership interest in) a SSBIC. The gain eligible for deferral is capped at $50,000 a year (up to $500,000 in the aggregate) for an individual and at $250,000 a year ($1 million in the aggregate) for a corporation.

Community Development Corporations

HUD is authorized to designate, no later than June 30, 1994, up to 20 tax-exempt charitable organizations as Community Development Corporations (CDCs) that will promote employment and business opportunities for low-income individuals residing in the CDC's locale (not necessarily in an empowerment zone or enterprise community); eight of the CDCs must be in rural areas. A tax credit of 50 percent, for regular tax purposes, spread ratably over ten years, will be allowed for cash contributions to a CDC, limited to an aggregate of $2 million of credit-eligible contributions to each CDC. Contributions to CDCs will also be deductible to the extent allowed under current law.

Incentives for Businesses on Indian Reservations

An accelerated depreciation schedule is provided for property placed in service after 1993 whose initial and continued use is in an active trade or business on an Indian reservation (including real estate rental but excluding gambling establishments), for both regular tax and alternative minimum tax, as shown in the table.

Accelerated depreciation is also available for property outside a reservation that connects to infrastructure (*e.g.*, roads, power lines, water systems, communications facilities) on the reservation.

Depreciation Schedule for Indian Reservations

ACRS Recovery Class	Zone Depreciation Period
3-year property	2 years
5-year property	3 years
7-year property	4 years
10-year property	6 years
15-year property	9 years
20-year property	12 years
Nonresidential real property	22 years

These businesses are also allowed a 20-percent nonrefundable tax credit, beginning in 1994, for up to $20,000 a year of wages and health insurance costs of tribe members who work on and live on or near a reservation. The credit is allowed only for employees with wages of $30,000 or less (indexed in later years) and only to the extent the qualified portion of the employer's payroll for eligible employees on the reservation increases from 1993. No deduction will be allowed for the credit amount. The credit is to be recaptured if the employee is fired less than one year after beginning work. The credit cannot reduce alternative minimum tax and cannot be carried back to a year ending before the date of enactment.

If you have any questions regarding the provisions of the Omnibus Budget Reconciliation Act of 1993, please contact the KPMG Peat Marwick office nearest you.

Index

D

H

I

J